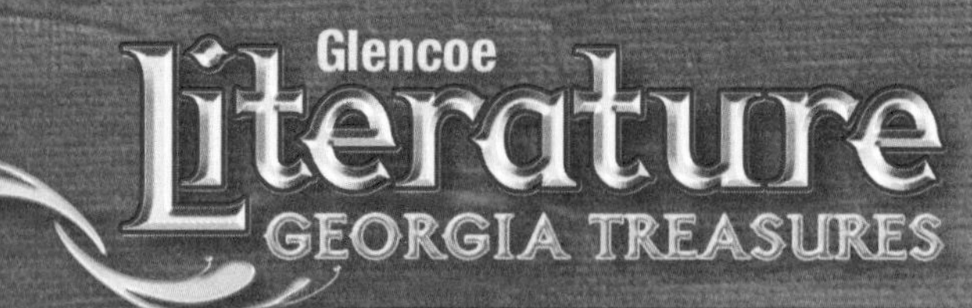

Textbook Internet resources are just a click away!

STEP 1 Go to glencoe.com

STEP 2 Connect to resources by entering QuickPass™ codes.

LOG ON Literature Online

GL17527u1 — Enter this code with appropriate unit numbers.

STEP 3 Access your Online Student Edition, handheld downloads, games, and more:

Literature and Reading Resources

- Author Search
- Literature Classics
- Big Question Web Quests
- Literary and Text Elements eFlashcards and Games
- Interactive Reading Practice

Selection Resources

- Audio Summaries
- Selection Quizzes
- Selection Vocabulary eFlashcards and Games
- Reading-Writing Connection Activities

Vocabulary and Spelling Resources

- Academic and Selection Vocabulary eFlashcards and Games
- Multi-Language Glossaries
- Spelling Games

Writing, Grammar, and Research Resources

- Interactive Writing Models
- Writing and Research Handbook
- Graphic Organizers
- Sentence-Combining Activities
- Publishing Options

Media Literacy, Speaking, Listening, and Viewing Resources

- Media Analysis Guides
- Project Ideas and Templates
- Presentation Tips and Strategies

Assessment Resources

- End-of-Unit Assessment
- Test-Taking Tips and Strategies

On the Cover:

Newcomb, John (20th C./American)

Chrystal Lake, 1998.

Acrylic on Canvas.

Program Consultants

Jeffrey D. Wilhelm, Ph.D.
Douglas Fisher, Ph.D.
Kathleen A. Hinchman, Ph.D.
David G. O'Brien, Ph.D.
Taffy Raphael, Ph.D.
Cynthia Hynd Shanahan, Ed.D.

Acknowledgments

Grateful acknowledgment is given authors, publishers, photographers, museums, and agents for permission to reprint the following copyrighted material. Every effort has been made to determine copyright owners. In case of any omissions, the Publisher will be pleased to make suitable acknowledgments in future editions.

Acknowledgments continued on page R72.

Image Credits:

COVER John Newcomb/SuperStock, (bkgd)Farinaz Taghavi/Getty Images; **GA13** Photodisc Collection/Getty Images; **GA22** John Van Hasselt/Corbis Sygma/CORBIS; **GA23** (cw from top) David Muench/CORBIS, Joseph Sohm/Visions of America/CORBIS, James Randklev/Getty Images, (bkgd)W. Cody/CORBIS; **GA24** (t)Joe McDonald/CORBIS; (cr)S3672/CORBIS; (cl)Courtesy American Antiquarian Society; (b)Carsten Reisinger/Shutterstock; **GA25** (t)CORBIS, (c)Ibo mask from the Mmwo Society, Nigeria, 19th-20th century (polychrome wood), African/Musee des Arts d'Afrique et d'Oceanie, Paris Giraudon/Bridgeman Art Library, (bl)Cheryl Casey/Shutterstock, (br)Jupiter Unlimited; **GA26** (t)Courtesy of State Archives of Florida, (c)Image Source/CORBIS, (b)Jupiter Unlimited; **GA27** (cw from top)Flip Schulke/CORBIS, AP Images, Courtesy United States Government, kwest/Shutterstock; **GA28–GA29** Photodisc/Getty Images; **GA28** (t)Bettmann/CORBIS, (b)EVERETT COLLECTION; **GA29** EVERETT COLLECTION; **GA32** Jung Im Jang/SuperStock; **GA33** Images.com/CORBIS; **GA34** (t)Steve Vidler/SuperStock, (b)Rick Rickman; **GA37** Steve Vidler/SuperStock; **GA38** Affordable Illustration Source/Images.com/CORBIS; **GA41** Scot Frei/CORBIS; **GA42** image 100/SuperStock; **GA43** Reuters/CORBIS; **GA44** Lou Wall/CORBIS; **GA45** Private Collection/Bridgeman Art Library; **GA49** Farm Security Administration, Office of War Information Photograph Collection/Library of Congress; **GA52** David Brooks/CORBIS; **GA58** Dinah Mite Activities; **GA59** Creatas/PunchStock.

The McGraw·Hill Companies

Send all inquiries to:
Glencoe/McGraw-Hill
8787 Orion Place
Columbus, OH 43240-4027

ISBN: 978-0-07-880752-7
MHID: 0-07-880752-2

Printed in the United States of America.

2 3 4 5 6 7 8 9 058/055 13 12 11 10 09

Program Consultants

Senior Program Consultants

Jeffrey D. Wilhelm, Ph.D. Jeffrey Wilhelm is Professor of English Education at Boise State University and Director of the Boise State Writing Project. He specializes in reading and adolescent literacy and does research on ways to engage readers and writers. A middle and high school teacher for thirteen years, Wilhelm is author or coauthor of eleven books, including the award-winning works *You Gotta BE the Book* and *Reading Don't Fix No Chevys.*

Douglas Fisher, Ph.D. Douglas Fisher is Professor of Language and Literacy Education at San Diego State University. He is also Director of the award-winning City Heights Educational Pilot, a project for improving urban adolescent literacy. Fisher has published many articles on reading and literacy and has coauthored *Improving Adolescent Literacy: Strategies That Work.*

Program Consultants

Kathleen A. Hinchman, Ph.D. Kathleen Hinchman is Professor and Chair, Reading and Language Arts Center, School of Education, Syracuse University. A former middle school English and reading teacher, Hinchman researches social perspectives toward literacy. She is coauthor of three books on reading and literacy, including *Principled Practices for a Literate America: A Framework for Literacy and Learning in the Upper Grades.*

David G. O'Brien, Ph.D. David O'Brien is Professor of Literacy Education at the University of Minnesota and a former classroom teacher. O'Brien's research explores reading in content areas as well as ways to motivate learners to engage in school-based literacy tasks. He is conducting studies on the use of technology-based literacy, using computers and related technology.

Taffy Raphael, Ph.D. Taffy Raphael is Professor of Literacy Education at the University of Illinois at Chicago (UIC). She does literacy research on upper elementary and middle school students and has coauthored several books, including *Book Club: A Literature-Based Curriculum* and *Book Club for Middle School.* She has received the International Reading Association (IRA) Outstanding Educator Award and is in the IRA Hall of Fame.

Cynthia Hynd Shanahan, Ed.D. Cynthia Hynd Shanahan is Professor in the Reading, Writing, and Literacy program at the University of Illinois at Chicago (UIC). She is also a consultant with the Center for Literacy at UIC. Hynd Shanahan has been a classroom teacher and has taught reading instruction to elementary-level through college-level teachers. She has authored a chapter in the book *Engaged Reading,* edited by John T. Guthrie and Donna Alverman.

Advisory Board

Special Consultants

Donald R. Bear, Ph.D.
Donald R. Bear is Professor, Department of Curriculum and Instruction Director, E. L. Cord Foundation Center for Learning and Literacy at the University of Nevada, Reno. He is the author of *Words Their Way* and *Words Their Way with English Learners.*

Jana Echevarria, Ph.D.
Jana Echevarria is Professor, Educational Psychology, California State University, Long Beach, and Principal Researcher, National Research and Development Center of English Language Learners. She is the author of *Making Content Comprehensible for English Learners: The SIOP Model.*

Dinah Zike, M.Ed.
Dinah Zike was a classroom teacher and a consultant for many years before she began to develop Foldables®—a variety of easily created graphic organizers. Zike has written and developed more than 150 supplemental books and materials used in classrooms worldwide. Her *Big Book of Books and Activities* won the Teacher's Choice Award.

The Writers' Express
Immediate Impact. Lasting Transformation. wex.org

Glencoe National Reading and Language Arts Advisory Council

Wanda J. Blanchett, Ph.D.
Associate Dean for Academic Affairs and Associate Professor of Exceptional Education, School of Education
University of Wisconsin-Milwaukee
Milwaukee, Wisconsin

William G. Brozo, Ph.D.
Professor of Literacy
Graduate School of Education, College of Education and Human Development
George Mason University
Fairfax, Virginia

Nancy Drew, Ed.D.
LaPointe Educational Consultants
Corpus Christi, Texas

Susan Florio-Ruane, Ed.D.
Professor, College of Education
Michigan State University
East Lansing, Michigan

Nancy Frey, Ph.D.
Associate Professor of Literacy in Teacher Education
School of Teacher Education
San Diego State University
San Diego, California

Victoria Ridgeway Gillis, Ph.D.
Associate Professor
Reading Education
Clemson University
Clemson, South Carolina

Kimberly Lawless, Ph.D.
Associate Professor
Curriculum, Instruction and Evaluation
College of Education
University of Illinois at Chicago
Chicago, Illinois

Sharon Fontenot O'Neal, Ph.D.
Associate Professor
Texas State University
San Marcos, Texas

William Ray, M.A.
Lincoln-Sudbury Regional High School
Sudbury, Massachusetts

Janet Saito-Furukawa, M.Ed.
English Language Arts Specialist
District 4
Los Angeles, California

Bonnie Valdes, M.Ed.
Independent Reading Consultant
CRISS Master Trainer
Largo, Florida

Georgia Teacher Advisory Board

Jane Anthony
Muscogee County
Midland Middle School
Midland, GA

Judy Bauer
Thomas County
Thomas County Middle School
Thomasville, GA

Dawn Bolles
Muscogee County
Midland Middle School
Midland, GA

Madeleine Bowers
Richmond County
East Augusta Middle School
Augusta, GA

Dr. Wayne Campbell
Atlanta Public Schools
S. E. Coan Middle School
Atlanta, GA

Robin Cartright
Thomas County
Thomas County Middle School
Thomasville, GA

Debbie Frost
Dublin City Schools
Dublin Middle School
Dublin, GA

Claudia Henderson
Polk County Schools
Cedartown Middle School
Cedartown, GA

Sharon Hood
Baldwin County
Oak Hill Middle School
Milledgeville, GA

Trista Hooten-Young
Newton County
Cousins Middle School
Covington, GA

Clementine "Tina" Johnson
Muscogee County
Marshall Middle School
Columbus, GA

Pamela Smith-Ross
Atlanta Public Schools
Model Reading Teacher

April Swain
Rockdale County
Edwards Middle School
Conyers, GA

Susan Tolbert
Oconee County
Malcolm Bridge Middle School
Bogart, GA

Georgia Performance Standards

Reading and Literature

STANDARDS

ELA6R1 The student demonstrates comprehension and shows evidence of a warranted and responsible explanation of a variety of literary and informational texts.

For literary texts, the student identifies the characteristics of various genres and produces evidence of reading that:

a. Identifies and analyzes sensory details and figurative language.

b. Identifies and analyzes the author's use of dialogue and description.

c. Relates a literary work to historical events of the period.

d. Applies knowledge of the concept that theme refers to the message about life and the world that the author wants us to understand whether implied or stated.

e. Identifies and analyzes the elements of setting, characterization, plot, and the resolution of the conflict of a story or play:

i. internal/external conflicts

ii. character conflicts, characters vs. nature, characters vs. society

iii. antagonist/protagonist.

f. Identifies the speaker and recognizes the difference between first- and third-person narration.

g. Defines and explains how tone is conveyed in literature through word choice, sentence structure, punctuation, rhythm, repetition, and rhyme.

h. Responds to and explains the effects of sound, figurative language, and graphics in order to uncover meaning in literature:

i. Sound (e.g., alliteration, onomatopoeia, rhyme scheme)

ii. Figurative language (i.e., simile, metaphor, hyperbole, personification)

iii. Graphics (i.e., capital letters, line length, bold face print, italics).

i. Compares traditional literature and mythology from different cultures.

j. Identifies and analyzes similarities and differences in mythologies from different cultures.

For informational texts, the student reads and comprehends in order to develop understanding and expertise and produces evidence of reading that:

a. Applies knowledge of common textual features (e.g., paragraphs, topic sentences, concluding sentences, glossary, index).

b. Applies knowledge of common graphic features (i.e., graphic organizers, diagrams, captions, illustrations, charts, tables, graphs).

c. Applies knowledge of common organizational structures and patterns (e.g., transitions, logical order, cause and effect, classification schemes).

d. Identifies and analyzes main ideas, supporting ideas, and supporting details.

e. Follows multi-step instructions to complete or create a simple product.

ELA6R2 The student understands and acquires new vocabulary and uses it correctly in reading and writing.

The student

a. Determines the meaning of unfamiliar words by using word, sentence, and paragraph clues.

b. Uses knowledge of Greek and Latin affixes to understand unfamiliar vocabulary.

c. Identifies and interprets words with multiple meanings.

d. Uses reference skills to determine pronunciations, meanings, alternate word choices, and parts of speech of words.

ELA6R3 The student reads aloud, accurately (in the range of 95%), familiar material in a variety of genres, in a way that makes meaning clear to listeners.

The student

a. Uses letter-sound knowledge to decode written English and uses a range of cueing systems (e.g., phonics and context clues) to determine pronunciation and meaning.

b. Uses self-correction when subsequent reading indicates an earlier miscue (self-monitoring and self-correcting strategies).

c. Reads with a rhythm, flow, and meter that sounds like everyday speech (prosody).

Reading Across the Curriculum

ELA6RC1 The student reads a minimum of 25 grade-level appropriate books or book equivalents (approximately 1,000,000 words) per year from a variety of subject disciplines. The student reads both informational and fictional texts in a variety of genres and modes of discourse, including technical texts related to various subject areas.

ELA6RC2 The student participates in discussions related to curricular learning in all subject areas.

The student

a. Identifies messages and themes from books in all subject areas.

b. Responds to a variety of texts in multiple modes of discourse.

c. Relates messages and themes from one subject area to those in another area.

d. Evaluates the merits of texts in every subject discipline.

e. Examines the author's purpose in writing.

f. Recognizes and uses the features of disciplinary texts (e.g., charts, graphs, photos, maps, highlighted vocabulary).

ELA6RC3 The student acquires new vocabulary in each content area and uses it correctly.

The student

a. Demonstrates an understanding of contextual vocabulary in various subjects.

b. Uses content vocabulary in writing and speaking.

c. Explores understanding of new words found in subject area texts.

ELA6RC4 The student establishes a context for information acquired by reading across subject areas.

The student

a. Explores life experiences related to subject area content.

b. Discusses in both writing and speaking how certain words and concepts relate to multiple subjects.

c. Determines strategies for finding content and contextual meaning for unfamiliar words or concepts.

Writing

ELA6W1 The student produces writing that establishes an appropriate organizational structure, sets a context and engages the reader, maintains a coherent focus throughout, and provides a satisfying closure.

The student

a. Selects a focus, an organizational structure, and a point of view based on purpose, genre expectations, audience, length, and format requirements.

b. Writes texts of a length appropriate to address the topic or tell the story.

c. Uses traditional structures for conveying information (e.g., chronological order, cause and effect, similarity and difference, and posing and answering a question).

d. Uses appropriate structures to ensure coherence (e.g., transition elements).

ELA6W2 The student demonstrates competence in a variety of genres.

The student produces a narrative (fictional, personal) that:

a. Engages readers by establishing and developing a plot, setting, and point of view that are appropriate to the story (e.g., varied beginnings, standard plot line, cohesive devices).

b. Creates an organizing structure appropriate to purpose, audience, and context.

c. Includes sensory details and concrete language to develop plot, setting, and character (e.g., vivid verbs, descriptive adjectives, and varied sentence structures).

d. Uses a range of strategies (e.g., suspense, figurative language, dialogue, expanded vocabulary, movement, gestures, expressions).

e. Excludes extraneous details and inconsistencies.

f. Provides a sense of closure appropriate to the writing.

The student produces writing (multi-paragraph expository composition such as description, explanation, comparison and contrast, or problem and solution) that:

a. Engages the reader by establishing a context, creating a speaker's voice, and otherwise developing reader interest.

b. Establishes a statement as the main idea or topic sentence.

c. Develops a controlling idea that conveys a perspective on the subject.

d. Creates an organizing structure appropriate to purpose, audience, and context.

- **e.** Develops the topic with supporting details.
- **f.** Excludes extraneous and inappropriate information.
- **g.** Follows an organizational pattern appropriate to the type of composition.
- **h.** Concludes with a detailed summary linked to the purpose of the composition.

The student produces technical writing (friendly letters, thank-you notes, formula poems, instructions) that:

- **a.** Creates or follows an organizing structure appropriate to purpose, audience, and context.
- **b.** Excludes extraneous and inappropriate information.
- **c.** Follows an organizational pattern appropriate to the type of composition.
- **d.** Applies rules of Standard English.

The student produces a response to literature that:

- **a.** Engages the reader by establishing a context, creating a speaker's voice, and otherwise developing reader interest.
- **b.** Demonstrates an understanding of the literary work.
- **c.** Advances a judgment that is interpretive, analytic, evaluative, or reflective.
- **d.** Organizes an interpretation around several clear ideas, premises, or images.
- **e.** Supports a judgment through references to the text.
- **f.** Provides a sense of closure to the writing.

The student produces a multi-paragraph persuasive essay that:

- **a.** Engages the reader by establishing a context, creating a speaker's voice, and otherwise developing reader interest.
- **b.** States a clear position of a proposition or proposal.
- **c.** Supports the position with organized and relevant evidence.
- **d.** Excludes information and arguments that are irrelevant.
- **e.** Creates an organizing structure appropriate to a specific purpose, audience, and context.
- **f.** Anticipates and addresses readers' concerns and counter-arguments.
- **g.** Provides a sense of closure to the writing.

ELA6W3 The student uses research and technology to support writing.

The student

- **a.** Uses organizational features of electronic text (e.g., bulletin boards, databases, keyword searches, e-mail addresses) to locate relevant information.
- **b.** Includes researched information in different types of products (e.g., compositions, multimedia presentations, graphic organizers, projects, etc.).
- **c.** Cites references.

ELA6W4 The student consistently uses the writing process to develop, revise, and evaluate writing.

The student

- **a.** Plans and drafts independently and resourcefully.
- **b.** Revises manuscripts to improve the organization and consistency of ideas within and between paragraphs.
- **c.** Edits to correct errors in spelling, punctuation, etc.

Conventions

ELA6C1 The student demonstrates understanding and control of the rules of the English language, realizing that usage involves the appropriate application of conventions and grammar in both written and spoken formats.

The student

- **a.** Identifies and uses the eight basic parts of speech and demonstrates that words can be different parts of speech within a sentence.
    - **i.** Identifies and uses nouns—abstract, common, collective, plural, and possessive.
    - **ii.** Identifies and uses pronouns—personal, possessive, interrogative, demonstrative, reflexive, and indefinite.
    - **iii.** Identifies and uses adjectives—common, proper, and demonstrative.
    - **iv.** Identifies and uses verbs—action (transitive/intransitive), linking, and state-of-being.
    - **v.** Identifies and uses verb phrases—main verbs and helping verbs.
    - **vi.** Identifies and uses adverbs.
    - **vii.** Identifies and uses prepositional phrases (preposition, object of the preposition, and any of its modifiers).
    - **viii.** Identifies and uses conjunctions—coordinating, correlative, and common subordinating.
    - **ix.** Identifies and uses interjections.
- **b.** Recognizes basic parts of a sentence (subject, verb, direct object, indirect object, predicate noun, predicate adjective).
- **c.** Identifies and writes simple, compound, complex, and compound-complex sentences, avoiding fragments and run-ons.
- **d.** Demonstrates appropriate comma and semicolon usage (compound and complex sentences, appositives, words in direct address).
- **e.** Uses common spelling rules, applies common spelling patterns, and develops and masters words that are commonly misspelled.
- **f.** Produces final drafts that demonstrate accurate spelling and the correct use of punctuation and capitalization.

Listening/Speaking/Viewing

ELA6LSV1 The student participates in student-to-teacher, student-to-student, and group verbal interactions.

The student

- **a.** Initiates new topics in addition to responding to adult-initiated topics.
- **b.** Asks relevant questions.
- **c.** Responds to questions with appropriate information.
- **d.** Confirms understanding by paraphrasing the adult's directions or suggestions.
- **e.** Displays appropriate turn-taking behaviors.
- **f.** Actively solicits another person's comments or opinions.
- **g.** Offers own opinion forcefully without being domineering.
- **h.** Responds appropriately to comments and questions.
- **i.** Volunteers contributions and responds when directly solicited by teacher or discussion leader.
- **j.** Gives reasons in support of opinions expressed.
- **k.** Clarifies, illustrates, or expands on a response when asked to do so.
- **l.** Employs a group decision-making technique such as brainstorming or a problem-solving sequence (e.g., recognizes problem, defines problem, identifies possible solutions, selects optimal solution, implements solution, evaluates solution).
- **m.** Writes a response to/reflection of interactions with others.

ELA6LSV2 The student listens to and views various forms of text and media in order to gather and share information, persuade others, and express and understand ideas. The student will select and critically analyze messages using rubrics as assessment tools.

When responding to visual and oral texts and media (e.g., television, radio, film productions, and electronic media), the student:

- **a.** Identifies persuasive and propaganda techniques used in media and identifies false and misleading information.
- **b.** Identifies the tone, mood, and emotion conveyed in the oral communication.

When delivering or responding to presentations, the student:

- **a.** Gives oral presentations or dramatic interpretations for various purposes.
- **b.** Shows appropriate changes in delivery (e.g., gestures, vocabulary, pace, visuals).
- **c.** Uses language for dramatic effect.
- **d.** Uses rubrics as assessment tools.
- **e.** Uses electronic media for presentations.

What Are the Georgia CRCT Grade 6 Tests?

The Georgia Criterion-Referenced Competency Tests (CRCT) measure how well students have met the Georgia Performance Standards (GPS) in five content areas: Reading, English/Language Arts, Mathematics, Science, and Social Studies. The skills and strategies you will learn in *Glencoe Literature* can help you get ready for the Georgia CRCT Reading and English/Language Arts Tests.

How Can I Prepare for the Test?

Pages GA12–GA21 of this textbook include a section called Countdown to the CRCT Reading and English/Language Arts Tests. The Reading and English/Language Arts Tests contain passages and questions that are similar to the multiple-choice questions on the Grade 6 CRCT Reading and English/Language Arts Tests.

How Does *Glencoe Literature* Help Me Prepare for the Test?

Your textbook contains several opportunities to help you prepare for the tests every day. Take advantage of these so you don't need to cram before the test.

- The **Countdown to CRCT** section gives you practice with the kinds of questions you will find on the CRCT Reading and English/Language Arts Tests.
- The **After You Read** pages following many of the reading selections contain multiple-choice questions that allow you to practice evaluating, interpreting, and using other critical thinking skills and reading strategies. These pages also include vocabulary and grammar features.
- The **Assessment** at the end of every unit helps you prepare for the multiple-choice format of the tests.

Test-Taking Tips

Before a game, professional athletes get ready by developing a positive attitude. They clear their minds, pump-up their confidence, and picture themselves performing well. You can apply similar strategies to prepare for the CRCT tests. Here are some tips to help you succeed:

- Go to bed early the night before the test. Eat a good breakfast in the morning.
- Read all test directions carefully. Listen carefully if test directions are read aloud. Ask questions about directions that you don't understand.
- Relax. Most people get nervous when taking a test. It's natural. Just do your best.
- Compare the numbers for test items with the numbers on your answer sheet. Be sure your answers are in the right place.

Multiple-Choice Items

A multiple-choice item on the CRCT Reading and English/Language Arts Tests usually includes an incomplete sentence or a question with four responses. You then choose the response that best completes the sentence or answers the question. Use this checklist to help you answer multiple-choice items.

- ☑ Read each question carefully and think of your own answer before you choose one of the printed answer choices.
- ☑ Read all of the answer choices for a question before you mark an answer. You might find a better choice if you keep reading.
- ☑ Eliminate any responses that are clearly wrong. Then focus your attention on the responses that may be correct.
- ☑ Answer questions you are sure about first. If you do not know the answer, skip it and go back to that question later.

Test Practice Workbook

A *Georgia State Assessment and Practice Workbook* is available to help you prepare for the grade 6 CRCT tests. The workbook explains how the Reading and English/Language Arts Tests are scored, provides test-taking strategies, and includes a practice test with passages and questions similar to those on the test.

Surf's Up

Surfing became a common pastime in Polynesia as long ago as 2000 B.C. When Polynesians arrived in Hawaii around A.D. 400, they brought the sport of surfing with them. Early surfboards were very long and heavy, made from Hawaiian trees, and polished with coral. These 100- to 200-pound surfboards were so heavy that the rider had to be towed out to the wave by a five-man canoe! When surfing became more widely popular in the 1900s, the boards were still heavy and dense. Surfers had difficulty moving these unwieldy boards through the waves; they simply aimed their surfboards for shore and hoped for the best.

An American surfer named Tom Blake created a much lighter board in the 1920s. Blake's board was made from plywood and crossbeams, so it was partly hollow and weighed thirty or forty pounds less than the older-style boards. In 1935 Blake attached a fin to the bottom of the board, which made the board much more stable and easier to steer. Throughout the twentieth century, lighter boards were constructed from balsa wood and new materials such as fiberglass and polyurethane. These boards give surfers more control of the speed and direction. Today's surfers use lighter, stronger, and faster surfboards than the surfers of long ago, but surfers' love of catching big waves has remained the same throughout the centuries.

ELA6R1.d

1. What is the main idea of this passage?
   - A. Surfing was a common pastime in Polynesia.
   - B. Tom Blake created a lighter board in the 1920s.
   - C. Improvements have been made to surfboards over the years.
   - D. Balsa wood is used in making surfboards.

ELA6RC2.e

2. What is the purpose of this passage?
   - A. to analyze the reasons why people go surfing
   - B. to persuade the reader to go surfing
   - C. to inform readers about the history of the surfboard
   - D. to entertain readers with funny anecdotes

ELA6C1.e

1. Which underlined word below has a spelling error?

   A. Was she able to utilize the materials?

   B. Did you recieve the letter on time?

   C. Was the professor at school?

   D. When did Jonathan go swimming?

ELA6C1.f

2. In the sentence below, what change should be made to correct the capitalization error?

> My family took a car trip to Portland, maine.

   A. Use a capital *F* in *family*.

   B. Use a capital *T* in *trip*.

   C. Use a small letter *p* in *Portland*.

   D. Use a capital *M* in *Maine*.

ELA6C1.a/iv

3. Which word or words correctly fill the blank in the sentence below?

> Marco _____ his mother yesterday by painting the living room.

   A. helped

   B. helps

   C. helping

   D. has helped

ELA6C1.c

Use the paragraph below to answer question 4.

> [1] Eliza wanted to work on an interesting science project. [2] She thought about it for a while she wanted to win a contest. [3] She decided to find out if certain kinds of music can help plants grow. [4] In her experiment, she used many kinds of music, such as hip-hop, classical, and jazz.

4. Which sentence below is a run-on sentence?

   A. sentence 1

   B. sentence 2

   C. sentence 3

   D. sentence 4

ELA6W4.c

5. Which change should be made to the sentence below?

> Were learning how to dance for the party in fall.

   A. Change *Were* to *We're*.

   B. Change *learning* to *learn*.

   C. Change the word *for* to *four*.

   D. Change *fall* to *Fall*.

How to Put Together Your New Ant Town

This kit comes complete with base, front and back windows, lid, soil, and a tube of ants to start your colony. Please follow instructions carefully.

1. Place the large window labeled FRONT into the front slot of the base. Place the large window labeled BACK into the rear slot of the base.
2. Fill the Ant Town with the soil provided. The soil should come up to the line marked on the back window. Gently shake the Ant Town until the soil is level.
3. Snap the lid hinges on the sides into place.
4. Adhere or attach the lid to the lid hinges, and secure it by tightening the enclosed screws. Place the ants into the Ant Town and quickly close the lid.

ELA6R1.d

1. Which one of the following do you MOST likely need to put together the Ant Town?

   A. water

   B. some string

   C. a hammer

   D. a screwdriver

ELA6R1.c

2. What is the last step before closing the lid on the Ant Town?

   A. Attach the lid to the hinges.

   B. Fill the Ant Town with soil.

   C. Place the ants into the Ant Town.

   D. Shake the Ant Town until the soil is level.

ELA6R2.a

3. What is another word for *adhere* as it is used in this passage?

   A. join

   B. snap

   C. close

   D. shake

ELA6R1.d

4. Which generalization is supported by this passage?

   A. Ants are insects that require much food and attention.

   B. The kit includes everything you need to build an ant habitat.

   C. Queen ants are the most important members of ant colonies.

   D. You should ask an adult to help you put the kit together.

GA Countdown to the CRCT English/Language Arts Test 

WEEK 4

ELA6C1.a/vii

1. Which word in the sentence below is a preposition?

The squirrel found a nut and ran up the tree.

A. squirrel
B. took
C. up
D. tree

ELA6C1.b

2. What is the complete subject of the sentence below?

Henry Ford is the father of the assembly line.

A. Henry Ford
B. is the father
C. the father
D. of the assembly line

ELA6C1.d

3. How should the punctuation be corrected in the sentences below?

Machines, which are tools, are used to make work easier. A lever a shovel, and a wedge are types of simple machines.

A. Remove the comma after *Machines*.
B. Add a comma after *work*.
C. Add a comma after *lever*.
D. Remove the comma after *shovel*.

ELA6W2.e

4. Which sentence BEST develops the topic sentence with supporting details?

On Saturday, we watched a parade on Main Street.

A. The restaurants on the street were crowded.
B. The floats in the parade were decorated with flowers.
C. That night my father and I watched a movie.
D. On Sunday, my brother and I went swimming.

ELA6W2.f

5. Which sentence should be removed from the paragraph below?

My friend and I follow a routine when we go to the movies. We buy our tickets. Then he stands on line for popcorn. I go to find good seats. I like movies that are funny.

A. We buy our tickets.
B. Then he stands on line for popcorn.
C. I go to find good seats
D. I like movies that are funny.

A Man, His Son, and a Donkey

A man and his son were once going with their donkey to market. As the two were walking along by the donkey's side, a countryman passed them and said: "You fools, what is a donkey for but to ride on?"

So the man put his son on the donkey, and they went on their way. But soon they passed a group of men, one of whom said: "See that lazy youngster, he lets his father walk while he rides."

So the man ordered his son to get off the donkey and got on himself. But they hadn't gone far when they passed two women, one of whom said to the other: "Shame on that lazy lout to let his poor little son trudge along."

Well, the man didn't know what to do. At last he pulled his son up before him on the donkey. By this time they had come to the town, and the passersby began to jeer and point at them. The man stopped and asked what they were scoffing at. The men said: "Aren't you ashamed of yourself for overloading that poor donkey of yours?"

The man and his son got off and tried to think what to do. They thought and they thought, till at last they cut down a pole, tied the donkey's feet to it, and raised the pole and the donkey to their shoulders. They went along amid the laughter of all who met them until they came to Market Bridge, when the donkey wiggled one of his feet loose, kicked out, and caused the boy to drop his end of the pole. In the struggle the donkey fell over the bridge with a huge splash, into the water.

"That will teach you," said an old man who had followed them: "Please all, and you will please none."

ELA6R1.d

1. What is the meaning of the word *lout* as it is used in this passage?

   A. a silly, awkward person

   B. a happy, contented person

   C. a mean, callous person

   D. a thieving, mischievous person

ELA6R1.e

2. The climax of the story occurs when the

   A. donkey falls into the water.

   B. boy rides the donkey.

   C. man and the boy carry the donkey.

   D. old man follows the man and the boy.

ELA6C1.a/iii

1. In the sentence below, the underlined word *enormous* is what part of speech?

> We saw an enormous pumpkin at the country fair.

A. noun
B. adjective
C. adverb
D. verb

ELA6C1.b

2. What is the complete subject of the sentence below?

> The happy campers blazed a trail through the woods.

A. The happy campers
B. campers
C. blazed a trail through the woods
D. through the woods

ELA6W2c

3. Which of the following sentences contains vivid verbs?

A. I made a salad and ate it.
B. I chopped and diced tomatoes.
C. I put the tomatoes in a salad bowl.
D. I gave the salad to my mother.

Use the outline below to answer question 4.

> I. Plant Life
>   A. Seaweed
>   B. Coral
>   C. Rockweed
>
> II. Animal Life
>   A. Jellyfish
>   B. Crab
>   C.

ELA6W2.e

4. Which of the following entries fits at subheading C, under "Animal Life"?

A. Sea grass
B. Sand
C. Sea turtle
D. Atlantic Ocean

ELA6C1.a/viii

5. Which sentence below contains a coordinating conjunction?

A. Maria and I have band practice today.
B. Neither Jake nor John can find a pen.
C. Although I like orange juice, I don't like oranges.
D. I have not seen her since she moved.

"A Bird Came Down the Walk" by Emily Dickinson

A bird came down the walk:
He did not know I saw:
He bit an angle-worm in halves
And ate the fellow, raw.

And then he drank a dew
From a convenient grass,
And then hopped sidewise to the wall
To let a beetle pass.

He glanced with rapid eyes
That hurried all abroad, —
They looked like frightened beads,
I thought;
He stirred his velvet head

Like one in danger; cautious,
I offered him a crumb,
And he unrolled his feathers
And rowed him softer home

Than oars divide the ocean,
Too silver for a seam,
Or butterflies, off banks of noon,
Leap, splashless, as they swim.

ELA6R1.h/ii

1. The speaker compares the bird's eyes to
   A. oars.
   B. convenient grass.
   C. frightened beads.
   D. unrolled feathers.

ELA6R1.h/ii

2. The poet uses which of the following kind of figurative language to compare the bird's wings to oars?
   A. simile
   B. metaphor
   C. hyperbole
   D. personification

ELA6R1.g

3. Which of the following statements BEST describes the speaker's attitude toward the subject of the poem?
   A. The author is annoyed with nature.
   B. The author has great appreciation for nature.
   C. The author believes that the life of a bird is grim.
   D. The author is unmoved by the animals she writes about.

ELA6C1.a/iv

1. In the sentence below, the underlined word *appears* is what part of speech?

> Ricardo appears happy about his test score.

A. verb

B. preposition

C. conjunction

D. adverb

Use the paragraph below to answer question 2.

> My Aunt Barbara lived in Japan for several years. During that time, she taught English to middle school students. She took piano lessons while she was in Japan and now she plays piano for customers in local cafes. When she isn't teaching English or playing piano, Aunt Barbara renovates her home. She has put in a new floor and has built a new deck in her backyard.

ELA6W2.b

2. What of the following sentences BEST states the main idea of the paragraph?

A. Aunt Barbara is a teacher.

B. Aunt Barbara lived in several parts of the world.

C. Aunt Barbara enjoys playing music.

D. Aunt Barbara is a person who has many talents.

ELA6C1.a/ii

3. In the sentence below, the underlined word mine is what kind of pronoun?

> The book with the red cover is mine.

A. interrogative pronoun

B. possessive pronoun

C. indefinite pronoun

D. personal pronoun

ELA6C1.e

4. Which correction should be made to the sentence below?

> I asked a question and Carlos replyed promptly.

A. Change *asked* to *asking*.

B. Change *Carlos* to *carlos*.

C. Change *replyed* to *replied*.

D. Change *promptly* to *prompt*.

ELA6C1.b

5. In the sentence below, which word is the direct object?

> Pasqual jumped rope at school.

A. Pasqual

B. jumped

C. rope

D. school

Georgia Authors

Many well-known American writers were born in Georgia or lived there. Georgia writers have written about the state's landscapes. They have written about major events in its history, from frontier life to the civil rights movement. Myths, legends, and folktales have also been an important part of Georgia literature. As you read, take notes about the myths and tales you find and about how Georgia's literature shows a sense of time and place.

Looking Ahead

The following selections appear in your textbook. These writers are either from Georgia or have important ties to the state.

Historical Overview

- The spoken myths and folktales of the Native Americans of the Southeast were the first literature in what is now the state of Georgia.
- The first writings were the letters and journals of explorers and settlers.
- In the 1800s, Georgia literature included humorous stories, lyric poetry, and retellings of African American folktales.
- In the mid-20th century, Georgia authors often wrote about social problems such as poverty.
- Georgia authors today come from many different ethnic groups.

LITERARY GEORGIA

Toccoa Falls

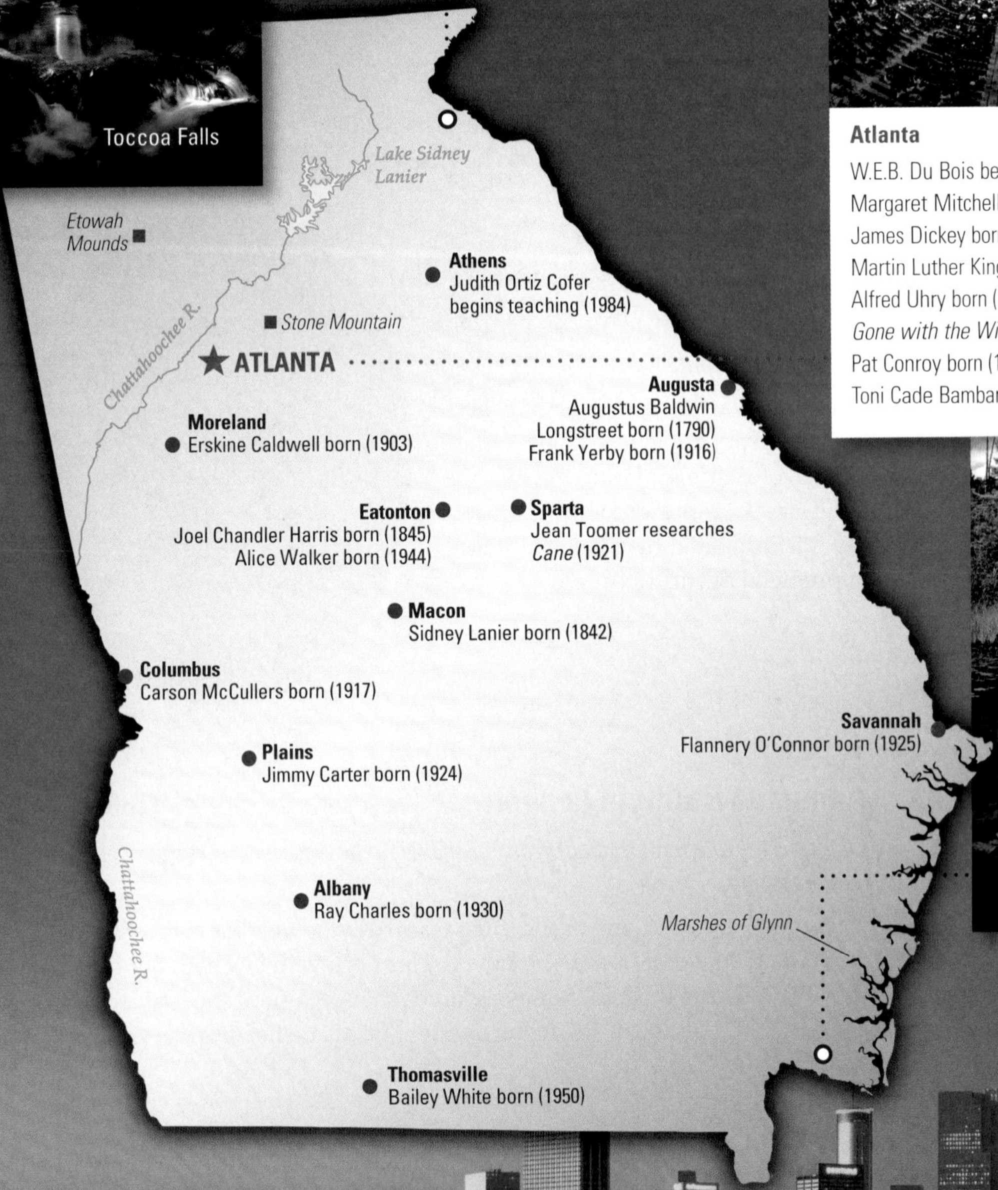

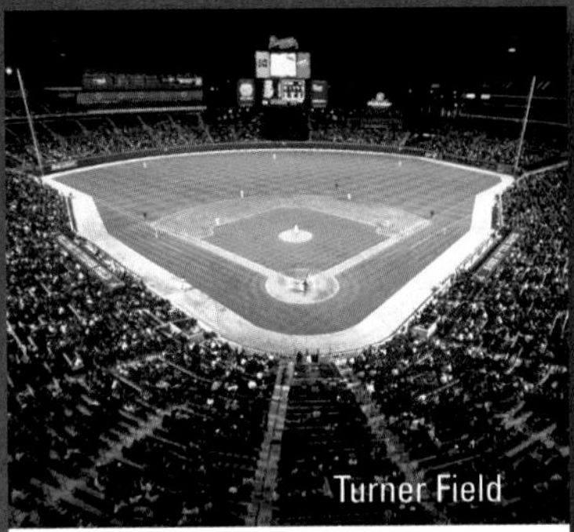

Turner Field

Atlanta

W.E.B. Du Bois begins teaching (1897)
Margaret Mitchell born (1900)
James Dickey born (1923)
Martin Luther King Jr. born (1929)
Alfred Uhry born (1936)
Gone with the Wind premieres (1939)
Pat Conroy born (1945)
Toni Cade Bambara teaches (1978)

Lake Sidney Lanier
Etowah Mounds
Athens Judith Ortiz Cofer begins teaching (1984)
Stone Mountain
Chattahoochee R.
ATLANTA
Augusta Augustus Baldwin Longstreet born (1790) Frank Yerby born (1916)
Moreland Erskine Caldwell born (1903)
Eatonton Joel Chandler Harris born (1845) Alice Walker born (1944)
Sparta Jean Toomer researches *Cane* (1921)
Macon Sidney Lanier born (1842)
Columbus Carson McCullers born (1917)
Savannah Flannery O'Connor born (1925)
Plains Jimmy Carter born (1924)
Okefenokee swamp
Albany Ray Charles born (1930)
Marshes of Glynn
Chattahoochee R.
Thomasville Bailey White born (1950)

TRY IT

Find the places on the map associated with the Georgia authors listed in Looking Ahead on GA22.

In Their Own Words

Cherokee Oral Tradition | "How the World Was Made"

Cherokee people lived in the mountains of northern Georgia.

"At first the world was very soft and wet. The Great Buzzard, the father of all the buzzards we see now, flew all over the earth, low down near the ground, and it was still soft. When he reached the Cherokee country, he was very tired and his wings began to flap and strike the ground, and wherever they struck the earth there was a valley, and where they turned up again there was a mountain. The Cherokee country remains full of mountains to this day."

William Bartram | *Travels* (1791)

Bartram explored the wilderness of the Southeast. He tells a legend of a paradise in the middle of the vast Okefenokee swamp.

"The river St. Mary has its source from a vast lake, or marsh, called [Okefenokee], which . . . . in the wet season, appears as a lake, and contains some large islands or knolls, of rich high land; one of which the present generation of the Creeks represent to be a most blissful spot of the earth: they say it is inhabited by a [special] race of Indians, whose women are [supremely] beautiful."

Augustus Baldwin Longstreet | *Georgia Scenes* (1835)

Longstreet wrote humor about frontier life. Here he describes a young woman's awful singing.

"She now . . . raised one of the most unearthly howls that ever issued from the throat of a human being. . . . Her neck vein swelled, her chin flew up, her face flushed, her eye glared; she screamed, she howled, she yelled. . . . 'Good Lord,' said a bystander, 'if this be her *singing*, what must her *crying* be!'"

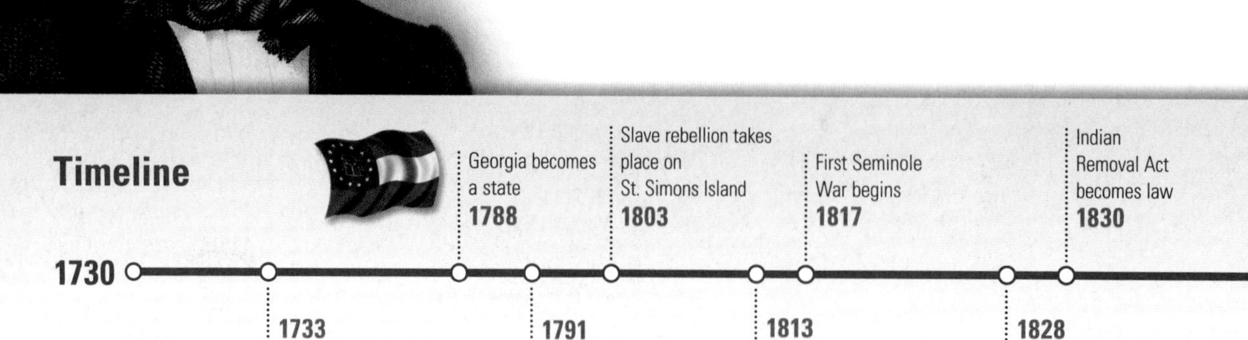

Timeline

1730

1733 James Oglethorpe founds Georgia colony

Georgia becomes a state **1788**

1791 William Bartram's *Travels* is published; includes descriptions of Georgia

Slave rebellion takes place on St. Simons Island **1803**

1813 Creek War breaks out

First Seminole War begins **1817**

1828 Elias Boudinot begins publishing the *Cherokee Phoenix* newspaper

Indian Removal Act becomes law **1830**

Joel Chandler Harris | "The Moon in the Mill-Pond" (1883)

Harris retold African American folktales. He created a character named Uncle Remus who tells tales to a young friend.

"One night when the little boy made his usual visit to Uncle Remus, he found the old man sitting up in his chair fast asleep. The child said nothing. He was prepared to exercise a good deal of patience upon occasion, and the occasion was when he wanted to hear a story."

African American Folklore | "The Magic Hoe"

African American folklore often has its roots in Africa.

"I have heard about a magic hoe that folks put in the garden. They speak certain words to it; then the hoe goes ahead and cultivates the garden without anyone touching it. They just tell it to do the work and it does it."

Respond and Think Critically

1. Which of the tales presented on pages GA24–25 did you find the most appealing? Why?
2. A myth often explains a fact of nature. Which of the tales on pages GA24–25 is a myth? Why?
3. Why do you think enslaved Africans in America preserved the tradition of the magic hoe?

1835 Augustus Baldwin Longstreet's *Georgia Scenes* is published

1861 Civil War begins; Georgia secedes from the Union

1864 Union forces capture Atlanta; March to the Sea follows

1868 Atlanta becomes state capital

1877 Sidney Lanier writes "Song of the Chattahoochee"

1880 Joel Chandler Harris's *Uncle Remus: His Songs and His Sayings* is published

1903 W.E.B Du Bois's *The Souls of Black Folk* is published

1917 United States enters World War I

1923 Jean Toomer's *Cane* is published

1930

Spotlight: Tall Tales

A popular kind of folk tale is the tall tale, a story that uses exaggeration to create humor. Tall tales are often told in frontier or wilderness areas. Storyteller Lem Griffis lived on the edge of Georgia's Okefenokee swamp. Here he tells a tall tale about Georgia rattlesnakes so poisonous that their venom causes even a walking stick to swell up.

Lem Griffis | "The Snakebit Walking Cane" (1966)

"We have some o' the most deadly poison snakes here 'an most anyplace in the world, I reckon. Uncle Paul, he come down to see us one time. An' he walked with a walkin' cane; went t' carry one after he was ninety-six. An' he was walkin' aroun' though the woods out here; one of them poisonous snakes struck at his leg an' hit that walkin' cane. He walked a little fu'ther, noticed that walkin' cane begin t' get heavy, an' he looked at it an' it 'as all swollen up. He couldn' carry it but a little ways fu'ther, before it got s' big an' heavy he jus' had t' leave it.

He thought lots of 'is walkin' cane, so nex' mornin' 'e went down t' see about it. By that time it 'as swollen up 'til it was just an enormous-size log. He notified feller t' have a sawmill t' come get that log an' saw it up inta lumber. But by that time it 'as swollen so large it couldn' be moved; so 'e moved his sawmill to it, an' 'e sawed enough crossties outta that swollen-up walkin' cane to build ten miles of railroad. After 'e got his railroad built there come up a awful heavy rain, washed all the poison outta them crossties; so he gathered them up an' sold 'em for toothpicks!"

TRY IT

Take an experience of your own or a story you have heard and use exaggeration to turn it into a tall tale.

Timeline

1930

1936 Margaret Mitchell's *Gone with the Wind* is published; wins Pulitzer Prize

1939 Film of *Gone with the Wind* premieres in Atlanta

1940 Carson McCullers's first novel is published

1941 United States enters World War II

1955 Flannery O'Connor's first collection of short stories is published

1963 Martin Luther King Jr. delivers "I Have a Dream" speech

1964 Martin Luther King Jr. receives the Nobel Peace Prize

Martin Luther King Jr. | "I Have a Dream" (1963)

In his most famous speech, Dr. King referred to a Georgia landmark.

Let freedom ring from Stone Mountain of Georgia.

Let freedom ring from Lookout Mountain of Tennessee.

Let freedom ring from every hill and molehill of Mississippi.

From every mountainside, let freedom ring.

Bailey White | "Buzzard" (1993)

Driving down the road, White encounters what she thinks is a buzzard.

"The buzzard turned his head and looked at me. He stood up on his big yellow legs. His head was snow white. His eyes were gold. He wasn't a buzzard. He was a bald eagle.

Then, not until after I had brought the car to a full stop, he spread his wings and with a slow swoop lifted himself into the air. He turned his head and gave me a long look through the car wind-shield with his level yellow eyes. Then he slowly wheeled up into the sky until he was just a black dot against the blue.

I turned the car off. I thought about that glare he had given me: What are you doing here? it had said. When I got started again, I drove slower and felt smaller. I think it does us all good to get looked at like that now and then by a wild animal."

1972 Pat Conroy's *The Water Is Wide* is published

1976 Jimmy Carter is elected U.S. president

1979 Ray Charles performs "Georgia on My Mind" for legislature; later adopted as state song

1983 Alice Walker wins Pulitzer Prize for fiction

1987 Alfred Uhry's play *Driving Miss Daisy* is produced; wins Pulitzer Prize

1993 Bailey White's *Mama Makes Up Her Mind* is published

2000 Georgia Writers Hall of Fame opens

2002 Jimmy Carter receives the Nobel Peace Prize

2010

Literature on Film: *The Member of the Wedding*

Carson McCullers's novel *The Member of the Wedding* was published in 1946. The main character is a 12-year-old girl, Frankie Addams. The novel is set in Georgia in the "green and crazy summer" of 1944: "This was the summer when for a long time she had not been a member. She belonged to no club and was a member of nothing in the world. Frankie had become an unjoined person who hung around in doorways, and she was afraid."

Meet Carson McCullers

Growing up in Columbus, Georgia, the young Carson McCullers liked both piano and writing. She finished high school at sixteen and went to New York City to study music. But on her second day in the city she lost her tuition money on the subway. She turned to writing, supporting herself with part-time jobs. Her first novel, *The Heart Is a Lonely Hunter*, was published in 1940, when she was twenty-two. Troubled with severe health problems throughout her life, McCullers died in 1967 at the age of 50. She remains a highly regarded American author.

The Novel

During her first months in New York City, McCullers spent much of her free time by the waterfront. She dreamed of journeys to other places. Her character Frankie is a dreamer too. She is troubled by the problems of growing up. Looking in a mirror, she doesn't like what she sees: "This summer she had grown so tall that she was almost a big freak, and her shoulders were narrow, her legs too long."

(Left to right) Ethel Waters as Berenice, Brandon De Wilde as John Henry, and Julie Harris as Frankie from the 1952 feature film

Frankie is also confused by the effect of World War II on her Georgia town: "It was the year when Frankie thought about the world. And she did not see it as a round school globe, with the colors neat and different-colored. She thought of the world as huge and cracked and loose and turning a thousand miles an hour. The geography book at school was out of date; the countries of the world had changed. Frankie read the war news in the paper, but there were so many foreign places, and the war was happening so fast, that sometimes she did not understand."

Frankie's only friends are her family's African American cook, Berenice, and a six-year-old cousin, John Henry. When her soldier brother comes home to be married, Frankie is invited to be a member of the wedding. Hoping to escape from the life she knows, Frankie tells herself that her brother and his wife will take her along on their honeymoon.

(Left to right) Anna Paquin and Alfre Woodard from the 1997 television production

Film and Television Versions

McCullers herself adapted *The Member of the Wedding* for the stage. The play opened on Broadway in January 1950. It was a hit, running for over 500 performances. The leads included Julie Harris (as Frankie), Ethel Waters (as Berenice), and Brandon De Wilde (as John Henry). Harris, Waters, and De Wilde all re-created their roles in a successful 1952 film version. In her film debut, Julie Harris was nominated for an Academy Award for Best Actress. In 1997, Atlanta native Fielder Cook directed a television production of *The Member of the Wedding*, starring Anna Paquin as Frankie and Alfre Woodard as Berenice.

Respond and Think Critically

1. What did you find most interesting about the career of Carson McCullers?
2. How was McCullers like the heroine of her novel, Frankie Addams?
3. What do the images from the two different films tell you about the relation between Frankie and Berenice?

Book Overview

UNIT FOUR

UNIT FIVE

UNIT SIX

Reference Section

UNIT ONE

WHAT Makes a Hero?

BQ Explore the BIG Question

Part 1 Helping Others

Part 2 Clever Solutions

Unit Challenge

UNIT TWO

WHY Read?

BQ Explore the **BIG** Question

Part 1 *Learning About the World*

Part 2 *Exploring Traditions*

UNIT THREE

WHAT Makes You Who You Are?

BQ Explore the BIG Question

Part 1 Family and Friends

Part 2 *Dreams and Goals*

Part 3 *Character Traits*

Part 2 *Freedom and Equality*

UNIT FIVE

WHAT Brings Out the Best in You?

BQ Explore the BIG Question

Part 1 Using Inner Strength

Part 2 Putting Others First

UNIT SIX

WHAT Are Worthwhile Goals?

Part 1 *Loyalty and Understanding*

Part 2 *Knowledge and Wisdom*

Reference Section

Selections by Genre

Fiction

Poetry

Drama

Folktales and Myths

Graphic Stories

Nonfiction

Essays and Speeches

Biography, Autobiography, Memoirs, Letters

Informational Texts

Functional Documents

Features

Perspectives

Award-winning nonfiction book excerpts and primary source documents

TIME

High-interest, informative magazine articles

Comparing Literature

UNIT ONE

UNIT TWO

UNIT THREE

UNIT FOUR

UNIT FIVE

UNIT SIX

Genre Focus

Independent Reading

Assessment

Skills Workshops

Writing Workshops

Speaking, Listening, and Viewing Workshops

Grammar Workshops

Vocabulary Workshops

Media Workshops

Unit Challenge

UNIT ONE

UNIT TWO

UNIT THREE

UNIT FOUR

UNIT FIVE

UNIT SIX

How to Use *Glencoe Literature*

Consultant's Note

People read for enjoyment, to help themselves think, to solve problems, and to get work done. Their reading is often organized around "inquiry" questions. These questions help them explore how what they learn can help make a difference in the real world.

—Jeffrey Wilhelm

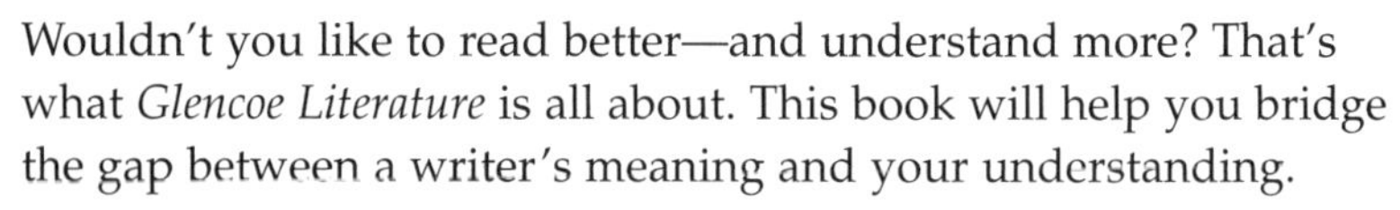

Wouldn't you like to read better—and understand more? That's what *Glencoe Literature* is all about. This book will help you bridge the gap between a writer's meaning and your understanding.

The next few pages will show you some of the ways *Glencoe Literature* can help you read, think, and write better.

What's in it for you?

Every unit in *Glencoe Literature* is built around a **Big Question,** a question that you will want to think about, talk about, maybe even argue about, and finally answer. The unit's reading selections will help you come up with your answers.

Organization

Units contain:

- A **Unit Opener** that introduces and helps you explore the unit's Big Question. A short reading selection uses the themes of the unit's **Parts** to guide you through ways of approaching the Big Question.
- **Literature selections** such as short stories, poems, plays, and biographies.
- **Informational texts** such as nonfiction; newspaper, online, and magazine articles; textbook lessons; and interviews.
- A **Genre Focus** that guides you through the features of a main genre from the unit.
- **Functional documents** such as signs, schedules, letters, and instructions.
- A **Comparing Literature** feature that gives you a chance to compare and contrast pieces of writing.
- A **Writing Workshop** to help you express your ideas about the Big Question through a specific form of writing.
- A **Speaking, Listening, and Viewing Workshop** to help you make oral presentations and become a better listener.
- A **Unit Challenge** in which you'll answer the Big Question.

Reading and Thinking

As an active reader, you'll use *Glencoe Literature* to develop your reading and thinking skills.

BEFORE YOU READ sets the stage for the selection and previews the skills and strategies that will guide your reading.

MEET THE AUTHOR introduces you to the real-life story of the writer whose work you will read and write about.

The **LITERARY ELEMENT** and the **READING SKILL** or **STRATEGY** give you the basic tools you will use to read and analyze the selection.

As you read the **LITERATURE SELECTIONS**, you will see that parts of the text are highlighted in different colors. On the side of the page are color-coded questions that help you think about and understand the selection.

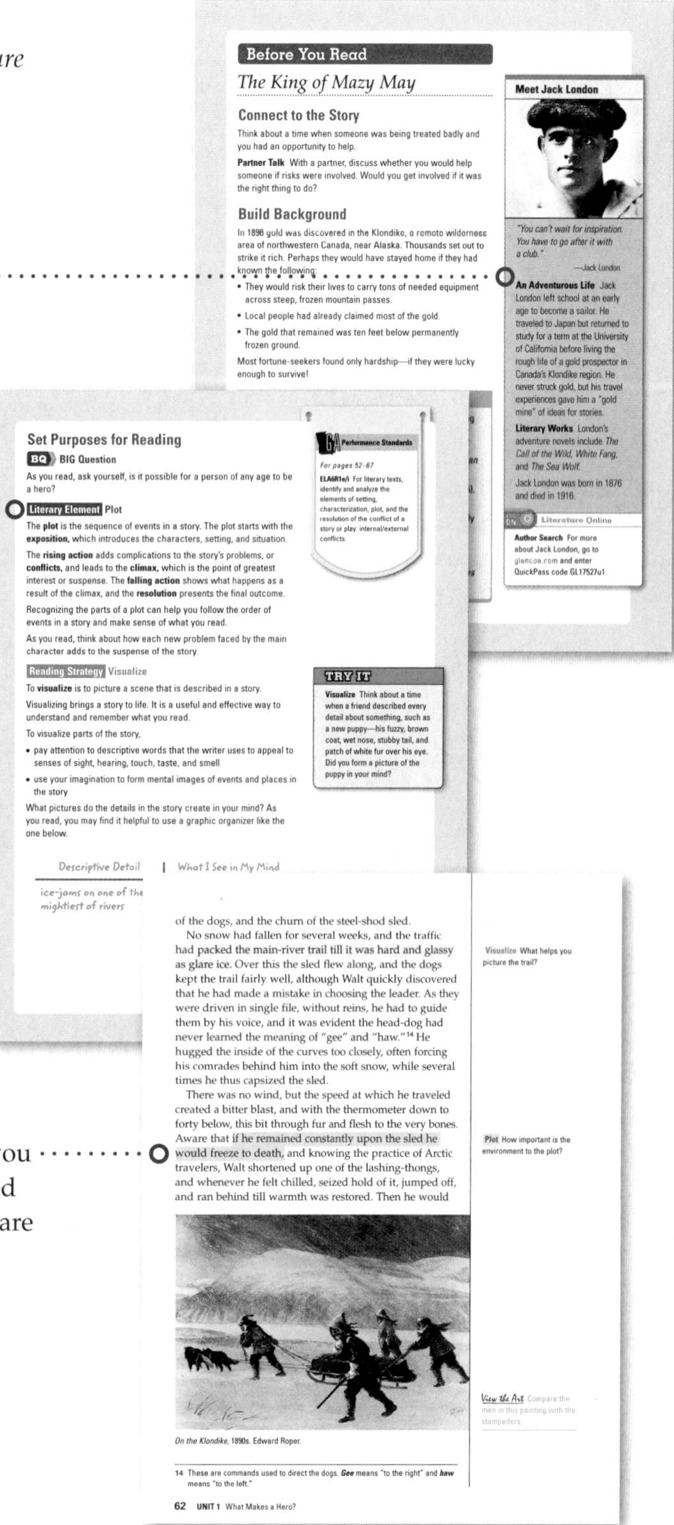

VOCABULARY A new vocabulary word is in **bold** type when it first appears in the reading selection.

VOCABULARY The word and its pronunciation, part of speech, and definition appear at the bottom of the same page.

Walt has walked all the fourteen years of his life in sun-tanned, moose-hide **moccasins,** and he can go to the Indian camps and "talk big" with the men, and trade calico[2] and beads with them for their precious furs. He can make bread without baking-powder, yeast or hops, shoot a moose at three hundred yards, and drive the wild wolf-dogs fifty miles a day on the packed trail.

Last of all, he has a good heart, and is not afraid of the darkness and loneliness, of man or beast or thing. His father is a good man, strong and brave, and Walt is growing up like him.

Walt was born a thousand miles or so down the Yukon, in a trading-post below the Ramparts. After his mother died, his father and he came on up the river, step by step, from camp to camp, till now they are settled down on the Mazy May Creek in the Klondike[3] country. Last year they and several others had spent much toil and time on the Mazy May, and **endured** great hardships; the creek, in turn, was just beginning to show up its richness and to reward them for their heavy labor. But with the news of their discoveries, strange men began to come and go through the short days and long nights, and many unjust things they did to the men who had worked so long upon the creek.

Si Hartman had gone away on a moose-hunt, to return and find new stakes driven and his claim jumped.[4] George Lukens and his brother had lost their claims in a like manner, having delayed too long on the way to Dawson to record them. In short, it was an old story, and

Visual Vocabulary

Moccasins are shoes with a sole and no heel, usually made from one piece of leather.

Plot What are your first impressions of Walt?

Plot What sets the newcomers apart from the men who live on the Mazy May?

2 ***Calico*** is a type of cotton cloth with a pattern on it. The word comes from Calicut, the town in India where the cloth was first made.

3 The Yukon River flows from Canada's Yukon Territory through Alaska to the Bering Sea. It was a major route to the Klondike during the gold rush of 1897–1898. The ***Klondike*** is the name of both a river and a gold-mining region in the Yukon Territory of Canada near the Alaskan border.

4 A ***claim*** was a piece of land that a prospector claimed to be his or her own. The prospector drove wooden ***stakes*** into the ground to mark its boundaries, and then recorded the claim with the gold commissioner in the city of ***Dawson***. Someone who ***jumped a claim*** took over and recorded a claim for land that had been staked out, but not yet recorded, by someone else.

Vocabulary

endured (en doord ʹ) *v.* underwent hardship without giving up; put up with

The King of Mazy May 55

VISUAL VOCABULARY Some vocabulary words are explained with the help of a picture.

FOOTNOTES Selection footnotes explain words or phrases that you may not know to help you understand the story.

Klondike Gold Rush, 1904. Artist Unknown.

But Walt only yelled the harder at the dogs, and dashed round the bend with a couple of revolver bullets singing after him. At the next bend they had drawn up closer still, and the bullets struck uncomfortably near to him; but at this point the Mazy May straightened out and ran for half a mile as the crow flies. Here the dogs stretched out in their long wolf-swing, and the stampeders, quickly winded, slowed down and waited for their own sled to come up.

Looking over his shoulder, Walt reasoned that they had not given up the chase for good, and that they would soon be after him again. So he wrapped the fur robe about him to shut out the stinging air, and lay flat on the empty sled, encouraging the dogs, as he well knew how.

At last, twisting abruptly between two river islands, he came upon the mighty Yukon sweeping grandly to the north. He could not see from bank to bank, and in the quick-falling twilight it loomed[13] a great white sea of frozen stillness. There was not a sound, save the breathing

BQ BIG Question What does Walt's reasoning reveal about him?

Visualize What image helps you picture the Yukon?

13 Something that ***loomed*** came into view in a way that seemed large and threatening.

The King of Mazy May 61

BIG QUESTION These side notes help keep you focused on the unit's Big Question as you read.

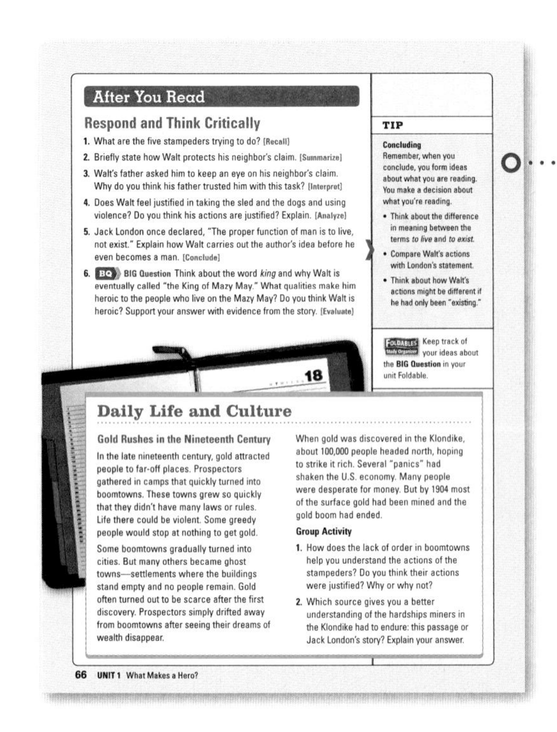

After You Read

Respond and Think Critically

1. What are the five stampeders trying to do? [Recall]
2. Briefly state how Walt protects his neighbor's claim. [Summarize]
3. Walt's father asked him to keep an eye on his neighbor's claim. Why do you think his father trusted him with this task? [Interpret]
4. Does Walt feel justified in taking the sled and the dogs and using violence? Do you think his actions are justified? Explain. [Analyze]
5. Jack London once declared, "The proper function of man is to live, not exist." Explain how Walt carries out the author's idea before he even becomes a man. [Conclude]
6. BQ BIG Question Think about the word *king* and why Walt is eventually called "the King of Mazy May." What qualities make him heroic to the people who live on the Mazy May? Do you think Walt is heroic? Support your answer with evidence from the story. [Evaluate]

TIP

Concluding

Remember, when you conclude, you form ideas about what you are reading. You make a decision about what you're reading.

- Think about the difference in meaning between the terms *to live* and *to exist*.
- Compare Walt's actions with London's statement.
- Think about how Walt's actions might be different if he had only been "existing."

FOLDABLES Study Organizer Keep track of your ideas about the BIG Question in your unit Foldable.

Daily Life and Culture

Gold Rushes in the Nineteenth Century

In the late nineteenth century, gold attracted people to far-off places. Prospectors gathered in camps that quickly turned into boomtowns. These towns grew so quickly that they didn't have many laws or rules. Life there could be violent. Some greedy people would stop at nothing to get gold.

Some boomtowns gradually turned into cities. But many others became ghost towns—settlements where the buildings stand empty and no people remain. Gold often turned out to be scarce after the first discovery. Prospectors simply drifted away from boomtowns after seeing their dreams of wealth disappear.

When gold was discovered in the Klondike, about 100,000 people headed north, hoping to strike it rich. Several "panics" had shaken the U.S. economy. Many people were desperate for money. But by 1904 most of the surface gold had been mined and the gold boom had ended.

Group Activity

1. How does the lack of order in boomtowns help you understand the actions of the stampeders? Do you think their actions were justified? Why or why not?
2. Which source gives you a better understanding of the hardships miners in the Klondike had to endure: this passage or Jack London's story? Explain your answer.

66 UNIT 1 What Makes a Hero?

Wrap up the selection with **AFTER YOU READ.** Explore what you have learned through a wide range of reading, thinking, vocabulary, and writing activities.

Vocabulary

VOCABULARY WORDS may be new to you or seem difficult, but they are important words. Vocabulary words from each selection are introduced on the **BEFORE YOU READ** page. Each word is accompanied by its pronunciation, its part of speech, its definition, and the page number on which it first appears. The vocabulary word is also used in a sample sentence. The first appearance of each vocabulary word is highlighted in the Literature selection.

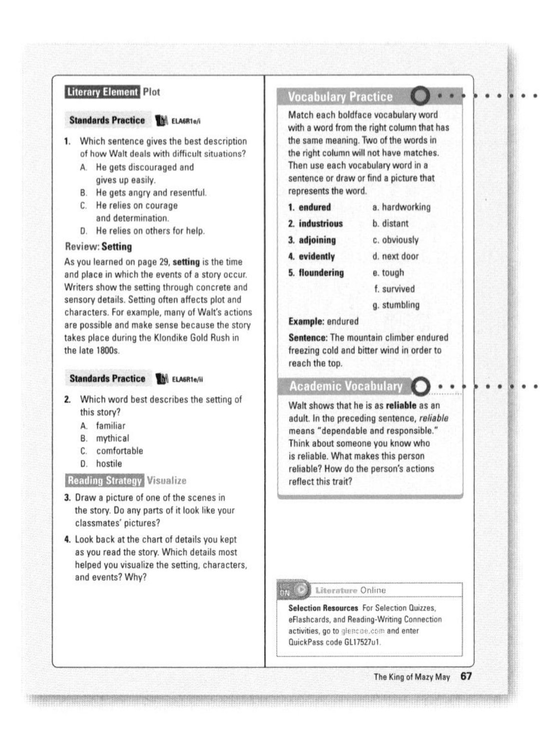

Literary Element Plot

Standards Practice ELA6R1e/i

1. Which sentence gives the best description of how Walt deals with difficult situations?
   A. He gets discouraged and gives up easily.
   B. He gets angry and resentful.
   C. He relies on courage and determination.
   D. He relies on others for help.

Review: Setting

As you learned on page 29, **setting** is the time and place in which the events of a story occur. Writers show the setting through concrete and sensory details. Setting often affects plot and characters. For example, many of Walt's actions are possible and make sense because the story takes place during the Klondike Gold Rush in the late 1800s.

Standards Practice ELA6R1e/ii

2. Which word best describes the setting of this story?
   A. familiar
   B. mythical
   C. comfortable
   D. hostile

Reading Strategy Visualize

3. Draw a picture of one of the scenes in the story. Do any parts of it look like your classmates' pictures?
4. Look back at the chart of details you kept as you read the story. Which details most helped you visualize the setting, characters, and events? Why?

Vocabulary Practice

Match each boldface vocabulary word with a word from the right column that has the same meaning. Two of the words in the right column will not have matches. Then use each vocabulary word in a sentence or draw or find a picture that represents the word.

1. **endured** a. hardworking
2. **industrious** b. distant
3. **adjoining** c. obviously
4. **evidently** d. next door
5. **floundering** e. tough
f. survived
g. stumbling

Example: endured

Sentence: The mountain climber endured freezing cold and bitter wind in order to reach the top.

Academic Vocabulary

Walt shows that he is as **reliable** as an adult. In the preceding sentence, *reliable* means "dependable and responsible." Think about someone you know who is reliable. What makes this person reliable? How do the person's actions reflect this trait?

Literature Online

Selection Resources For Selection Quizzes, eFlashcards, and Reading-Writing Connection activities, go to glencoe.com and enter QuickPass code GL17527u1.

The King of Mazy May 67

VOCABULARY PRACTICE On the **AFTER YOU READ** pages, you will be able to practice using the vocabulary words in an exercise. This exercise will show you how to use a vocabulary strategy to understand new or difficult words.

ACADEMIC VOCABULARY Many of the **AFTER YOU READ** pages also introduce you to examples of academic vocabulary. These are words that you come across in your schoolwork. You will be asked to use these words to answer questions.

Organizing Information

FOLDABLES For every unit, you'll be shown how to make a ***Foldable*** that will help you keep track of your thoughts about the Big Question. See page R8 for more about Foldables.

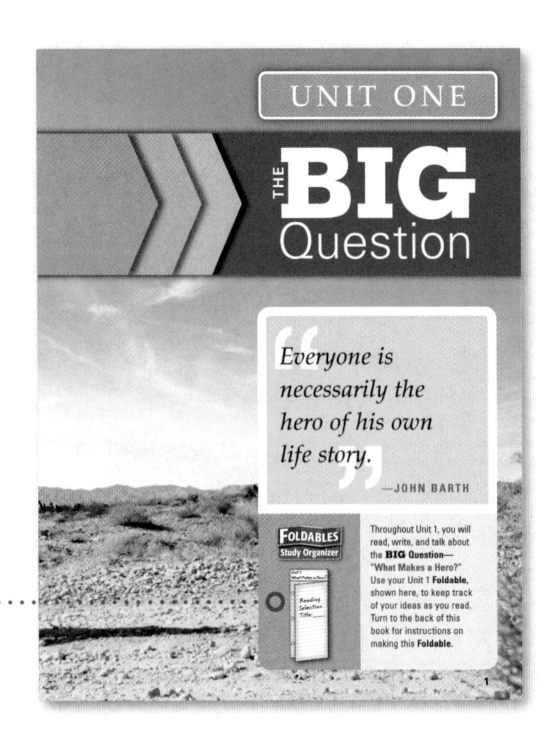

UNIT ONE

THE BIG Question

"*Everyone is necessarily the hero of his own life story.*"

—JOHN BARTH

FOLDABLES Study Organizer

Throughout Unit 1, you will read, write, and talk about the **BIG Question**—"What Makes a Hero?" Use your Unit 1 **Foldable**, shown here, to keep track of your ideas as you read. Turn to the back of this book for instructions on making this **Foldable.**

1

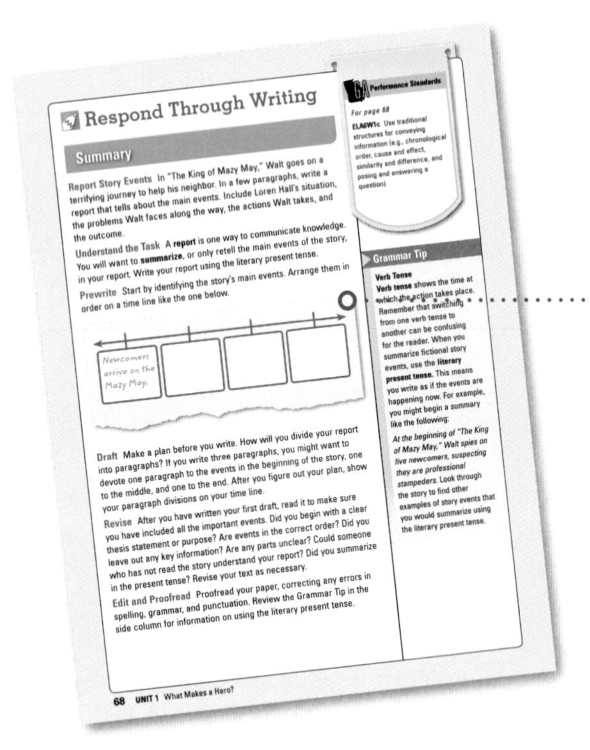

Respond Through Writing

Summary

Report Story Events In "The King of Mazy May," Walt goes on a terrifying journey to help his neighbor. In a few paragraphs, write a report that tells about the main events. Include Loren Hall's situation, the problems Walt faces along the way, the actions Walt takes, and the outcome.

Understand the Task A **report** is one way to communicate knowledge. You will want to **summarize**, or only retell the main events of the story, in your report. Write your report using the literary present tense.

Prewrite Start by identifying the story's main events. Arrange them in order on a time line like the one below.

Newcomers arrive on the Mazy May.

Draft Make a plan before you write. How will you divide your report into paragraphs? If you write three paragraphs, you might want to devote one paragraph to the events in the beginning of the story, one to the middle, and one to the end. After you figure out your plan, show your paragraph divisions on your time line.

Revise After you have written your first draft, read it to make sure you have included all the important events. Did you begin with a clear thesis statement or purpose? Are events in the correct order? Did you leave out any key information? Are any parts unclear? Could someone who has not read the story understand your report? Did you summarize in the present tense? Revise your text as necessary.

Edit and Proofread Proofread your paper, correcting any errors in spelling, grammar, and punctuation. Review the Grammar Tip in the side column for information on using the literary present tense.

GA Performance Standards

For page 68

ELA6W1c Use traditional structures for conveying information (e.g., chronological order, cause and effect, similarity and difference, and posing and answering a question).

Grammar Tip

Verb Tense

Verb tense shows the time at which the action takes place. Remember that switching from one verb tense to another can be confusing for the reader. When you summarize fictional story events, use the **literary present tense.** This means you write as if the events are happening now. For example, you might begin a summary like the following:

At the beginning of "The King of Mazy May," Walt spies on five newcomers, suspecting they are professional stampeders. Look through the story to find other examples of story events that you would summarize using the literary present tense.

68 UNIT 1 What Makes a Hero?

GRAPHIC ORGANIZERS In *Glencoe Literature*, you will use different kinds of graphic organizers to help you arrange information. These graphic organizers include, among others, Venn diagrams, compare-and-contrast charts, cluster diagrams, and chain-of-events charts.

Writing Workshops

Each unit in *Glencoe Literature* includes a Writing Workshop. The workshop walks you through the writing process as you work on an extended piece of writing related to the unit.

- You will use helpful strategies to meet writing goals.
- You will learn tips and polish your critical thinking skills as you analyze workshop models.
- You will focus on mastering specific aspects of writing, including organization, grammar, and vocabulary.
- You will use a writing plan to evaluate your own writing.

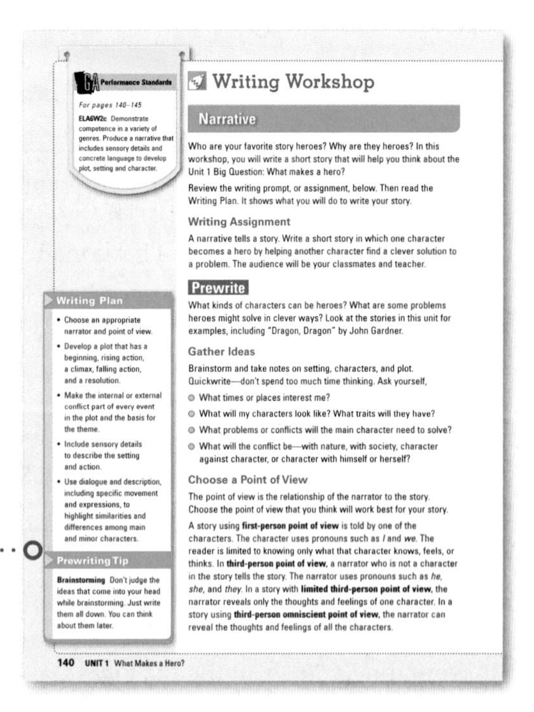

GA Performance Standards

For pages 140–145

ELA6W2c Demonstrate competence in a variety of genres. Produce a narrative that includes sensory details and concrete language to develop plot, setting and character.

Writing Workshop

Narrative

Who are your favorite story heroes? Why are they heroes? In this workshop, you will write a short story that will help you think about the Unit 1 Big Question: What makes a hero?

Review the writing prompt, or assignment, below. Then read the Writing Plan. It shows what you will do to write your story.

Writing Assignment

A narrative tells a story. Write a short story in which one character becomes a hero by helping another character find a clever solution to a problem. The audience will be your classmates and teacher.

Writing Plan

- Choose an appropriate narrator and point of view.
- Develop a plot that has a beginning, rising action, a climax, falling action, and a resolution.
- Make the internal or external conflict part of every event in the plot and the basis for the theme.
- Include sensory details to describe the setting and action.
- Use dialogue and description, including specific movement and expressions, to highlight similarities and differences among main and minor characters.

Prewrite

What kinds of characters can be heroes? What are some problems heroes might solve in clever ways? Look at the stories in this unit for examples, including "Dragon, Dragon" by John Gardner.

Gather Ideas

Brainstorm and take notes on setting, characters, and plot. Quickwrite—don't spend too much time thinking. Ask yourself,

- What times or places interest me?
- What will my characters look like? What traits will they have?
- What problems or conflicts will the main character need to solve?
- What will the conflict be—with nature, with society, character against character, or character with himself or herself?

Choose a Point of View

The point of view is the relationship of the narrator to the story. Choose the point of view that you think will work best for your story.

A story using **first-person point of view** is told by one of the characters. The character uses pronouns such as *I* and *we*. The reader is limited to knowing only what that character knows, feels, or thinks. In **third-person point of view**, a narrator who is not a character in the story tells the story. The narrator uses pronouns such as *he*, *she*, and *they*. In a story with **limited third-person point of view**, the narrator reveals only the thoughts and feelings of one character. In a story using **third-person omniscient point of view**, the narrator can reveal the thoughts and feelings of all the characters.

Prewriting Tip

Brainstorming Don't judge the ideas that come into your head while brainstorming. Just write them all down. You can think about them later.

140 UNIT 1 What Makes a Hero?

Assessment

Following each unit, you will be tested on the literature, reading, and vocabulary skills you learned. This test will give you the practice you need to succeed while providing an assessment of your understanding of the unit objectives.

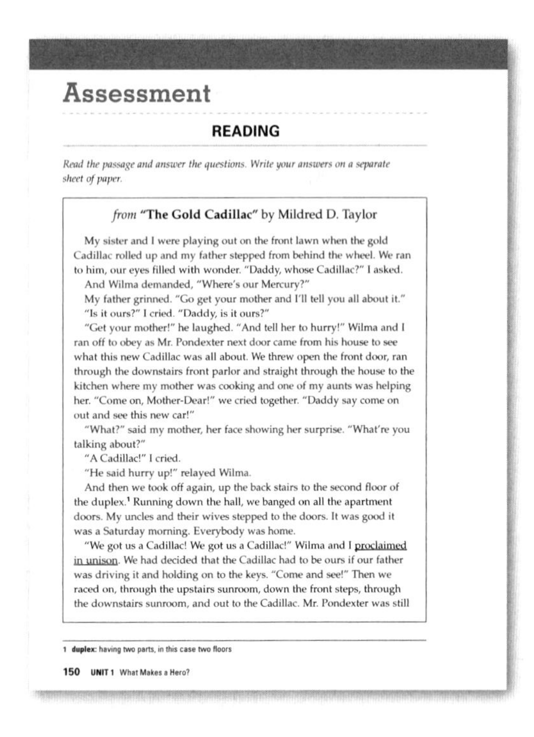

Assessment

READING

Read the passage and answer the questions. Write your answers on a separate sheet of paper.

from **"The Gold Cadillac"** by Mildred D. Taylor

My sister and I were playing out on the front lawn when the gold Cadillac rolled up and my father stepped from behind the wheel. We ran to him, our eyes filled with wonder. "Daddy, whose Cadillac?" I asked.

And Wilma demanded, "Where's our Mercury?"

My father grinned. "Go get your mother and I'll tell you all about it."

"Is it ours?" I cried. "Daddy, is it ours?"

"Get your mother!" he laughed. "And tell her to hurry!" Wilma and I ran off to obey as Mr. Pondexter next door came from his house to see what this new Cadillac was all about. We threw open the front door, ran through the downstairs front parlor and straight through the house to the kitchen where my mother was cooking and one of my aunts was helping her. "Come on, Mother-Dear!" we cried together. "Daddy say come on out and see this new car!"

"What?" said my mother, her face showing her surprise. "What're you talking about?"

"A Cadillac!" I cried.

"He said hurry up!" relayed Wilma.

And then we took off again, up the back stairs to the second floor of the duplex.[1] Running down the hall, we banged on all the apartment doors. My uncles and their wives stepped to the doors. It was good it was a Saturday morning. Everybody was home.

"We got us a Cadillac! We got us a Cadillac!" Wilma and I proclaimed in unison. We had decided that the Cadillac had to be ours if our father was driving it and holding on to the keys. "Come and see!" Then we raced on, through the upstairs sunroom, down the front steps, through the downstairs sunroom, and out to the Cadillac. Mr. Pondexter was still

1 **duplex:** having two parts, in this case two floors

150 UNIT 1 What Makes a Hero?

Reading and Thinking with Foldables®

by Dinah Zike, M.Ed., Creator of Foldables®

Foldables® are three-dimensional interactive graphic organizers for taking notes and organizing your ideas. They're also fun! You will fold paper, cut tabs, write, and manipulate what you have made in order to organize information; review skills, concepts, and strategies; and assess your learning.

Using Dinah Zike's Foldables in Reading and Literature Classes

Use Foldables before, during, and after reading selections in *Glencoe Literature.*

- Before you read: Your unit Foldable will help you focus on your purpose for reading by reminding you about the Big Question.
- During reading: Your unit Foldable will help you stay focused and engaged. It will also help you track key ideas and your thoughts about each selection to help you answer the Big Question. Using the Foldable will also encourage you to use higher level thinking skills in approaching text.
- After reading: Your Foldable will help you review your thoughts from your reading and analyze, interpret, and evaluate various aspects of the Big Question. Your Foldable notes will also help you with your unit challenge. These notes can stimulate rich group discussions and inquiry as well.

As you read, you'll make notes about the Big Question. Later, you'll use these notes to complete the Unit Challenge. See pages R8–R9 for help with making Foldable 1. This diagram shows how it should look.

Become an active reader. Track and reorganize information so that you can better understand the selection.

1. Make one page for each selection. At the end of the unit, you'll staple the pages together into one Foldable.
2. Label the front of the fold-over page with the selection title.
3. Open the fold-over page. On the right side, write the label My Purpose for Reading.
4. Open the Foldable all the way. At the top center, write the label The Big Question.

Selection title here

Practice reading and following step-by-step directions.

Use the illustrations that make the directions easier to follow.

Be Computer Safe and Smart

Cyber Safety

As you explore the *Glencoe Literature* program, you will have many opportunities to go online. When you use the Internet at school or at home, you enter a kind of community—the cyber world. In this online world, you need to follow safety rules and to protect yourself. Here are some tips to keep in mind:

- Be a responsible cyber citizen. Use the Internet to share knowledge that makes people's lives better. Respect other people's feelings and do not break any laws.
- Beware of cyber bullying. People can be hurt and embarrassed by comments that have been made public. You should immediately tell your teacher or counselor if you feel threatened by another student's computer postings.
- Do not give out personal information, such as your address and telephone number, without your parents' or guardians' permission.
- Tell your teacher, parent, or guardian right away if you find or read any information that makes you feel uneasy or afraid.
- Do not e-mail your picture to anyone.
- Do not open e-mail or text messages from strangers.
- Do not tell anyone your Internet password.
- Do not make illegal copies of computer games and programs or CD-ROMs.

Words To Know

cyber world the world of computers and high-tech communications

cyber safety actions that protect Internet users from harm

cyber ethics responsible code of conduct for using the Internet

cyber bully a person who uses technology to frighten, bother, or harm someone else

cyber citizen a person who uses the Internet to communicate

LOG ON **Literature** Online

For more about Internet safety and responsibility, go to glencoe.com.

The What, Why, and How of Reading

You'll need to use the skills and strategies in the following chart to respond to questions and prompts in the selections. As you begin a new lesson, look carefully at the **Reading Skill** or **Strategy** on the **Before You Read** pages. Then find those skills or strategies in this chart and read about what they are, how to use them, and why they're important. The more you refer to the chart, the more these active reading skills or strategies will become a natural part of the way you read.

What is it?	Why is it important?	How to do it
Preview Previewing is looking over a selection before you read.	Previewing lets you begin to see what you already know and what you'll need to know. It helps you set a purpose for reading.	Look at the title, illustrations, headings, captions, and graphics Look at how ideas are organized. Ask questions about the text.
Skim Skimming is looking over an entire selection quickly to get a general idea of what the piece is about.	Skimming will tell you what a selection is about. If the selection you skim isn't what you're looking for, you won't need to read the entire piece.	Read the title of the selection and quickly look over the entire piece. Read headings and captions and maybe part of the first paragraph to get a general idea of the selection's content.
Scan Scanning is glancing quickly over a selection in order to find specific information.	Scanning helps you pinpoint information quickly. It saves you time when you have a number of selections to look at.	As you move your eyes quickly over the lines of text, look for key words or phrases that will help you locate the information you're looking for.
Predict Predicting is taking an educated guess about what will happen in a selection.	Predicting gives you a reason to read. You want to find out if your prediction and the selection events match, don't you? As you read, adjust or change your prediction if it doesn't fit what you learn.	Combine what you already know about an author or subject with what you learned in your preview to guess what will be included in the text.
Set a Purpose Setting a purpose for reading is deciding why you are reading.	Setting a purpose for reading helps you decide on the reading strategies you use with a text.	Ask yourself if you are reading to understand new information, to find specific information, or to be entertained.

What is it?	Why is it important?	How to do it
Clarify Clarifying is looking at difficult sections of text in order to clear up what is confusing.	Authors often build ideas one on another. If you don't clear up a confusing passage, you may not understand main ideas or information that comes later.	Go back and reread a confusing section more slowly. Look up words you don't know. Ask questions about what you don't understand. Sometimes you may want to read on to see if further information helps you.
Question Questioning is asking yourself whether information in a selection is important. Questioning is also regularly asking yourself whether you've understood what you've read.	When you ask questions as you read, you're reading strategically. As you answer your questions, you're making sure that you'll get the gist of a text.	Have a running conversation with yourself as you read. Keep asking: Is this idea important? Why? Do I understand what this is about? Might this information be on a test later?
Visualize Visualizing is picturing a writer's ideas or descriptions in your mind's eye.	Visualizing is one of the best ways to understand and remember information in fiction, nonfiction, and informational text.	Carefully read how a writer describes a person, place, or thing. Then ask yourself: What would this look like? Can I see how the steps in this process would work?
Monitor Comprehension Monitoring your comprehension means thinking about whether you're understanding what you're reading.	The whole point of reading is to understand a piece of text. When you don't understand a selection, you're not really reading it.	Keep asking yourself questions about main ideas, characters, and events. When you can't answer a question, review, read more slowly, or ask someone to help you.
Identify Sequence Identifying sequence is finding the logical order of ideas or events.	In a work of fiction, events are usually presented in chronological (time) order. With nonfiction, understanding the logical sequence of ideas in a piece helps you follow a writer's train of thought. You'll remember ideas better when you know the logical order a writer uses.	Ask yourself what the author is trying to do: Tell a story? Explain how something works? Present information? Look for clues or signal words that might point to time order, steps in a process, or order of importance.
Connect Connecting means linking what you read to events in your own life or to other selections you've read.	You'll "get into" your reading and recall information and ideas better by connecting events, emotions, and characters to your own life.	Ask yourself: Do I know someone like this? Have I ever felt this way? What else have I read that is like this selection?

What is it?	Why is it important?	How to do it
Summarize Summarizing is stating the main ideas of a selection in your own words and in a logical sequence.	Summarizing shows whether you've understood something. It teaches you to rethink what you've read and to separate main ideas from supporting information.	Ask yourself: What is this selection about? Answer who, what, where, when, why, and how? Put that information in a logical order.
Determine Main Idea Determining an author's main idea is finding the most important thought in a paragraph or in a selection.	Finding main ideas gets you ready to summarize. You also discover an author's purpose for writing when you find the main ideas in a selection.	Think about what you know about the author and the topic. Look for how the author organizes ideas. Then look for the one idea that all of the sentences in a paragraph or all the paragraphs in a selection are about.
Respond Responding is telling what you like, dislike, or find surprising or interesting in a selection.	When you react in a personal way to what you read, you'll enjoy a selection more and remember it better.	As you read, think about how you feel about story elements or ideas in a selection. What's your reaction to the characters in a story? What grabs your attention as you read?
Review Reviewing is going back over what you've read to remember what's important and to organize ideas so you'll recall them later.	Reviewing is especially important when you have new ideas and a lot of information to remember.	Filling in a graphic organizer, such as a chart or diagram, as you read helps you organize information. These study aids will help you review later.
Interpret Interpreting is when you use your own understanding of the world to decide what the events or ideas in a selection mean. It's more than just understanding and remembering the facts.	Every reader constructs meaning on the basis of what he or she understands about the world. Finding meaning as you read is all about you interacting with the text.	Think about what you already know about yourself and the world. Ask yourself: What is the author really trying to say here? What larger idea might these events be about?
Infer Inferring is when you use your reason and experience to guess what an author does not come right out and say.	Making inferences is a large part of finding meaning in a selection. Inferring helps you look more deeply at characters and points you toward the theme or message in a selection.	Look for clues the author provides. Notice descriptions, dialogue, events, and relationships that might tell you something the author wants you to know.

What is it?	Why is it important?	How to do it
Draw Conclusions Drawing a conclusion is using a number of pieces of information to make a general statement about people, places, events, and ideas.	Drawing conclusions helps you find connections between ideas and events. It's another tool to help you see the larger picture.	Notice specific details about characters, ideas, and events as you read. Can you make a general statement on the basis of these details? For example, do a character's actions lead you to conclude that he or she is kind?
Analyze Analyzing is looking at separate parts of a selection in order to understand the entire selection.	Analyzing helps you look critically at a piece of writing. When you analyze a selection, you'll discover its theme or message, and you'll learn the author's purpose for writing.	To analyze a story, think about what the author is saying through the characters, the setting, and the plot. To analyze nonfiction, look at how the writer has organized main ideas. What do those ideas suggest?
Synthesize Synthesizing is combining ideas in order to reach a new understanding.	Synthesizing helps you move to a higher level of thinking. Creating something new of your own goes beyond remembering what you learned from someone else.	Think about the ideas or information you've learned in a selection. Ask yourself: Do I understand something more than the main ideas here? Can I create something else from what I now know?
Evaluate Evaluating is making a judgment or forming an opinion about something you have read. You can evaluate a character, an author's purpose, or the reliability of information in an article or text.	Evaluating can help you become a wise, sensible reader. Many selections—especially text you read online—require careful judgments about an author's qualifications and about the reliability of information presented.	As you read, ask yourself: Is this character realistic and believable? Is this author qualified to write on this subject? Is this author biased? Does this author present opinions as facts?

WHAT Makes a Hero?

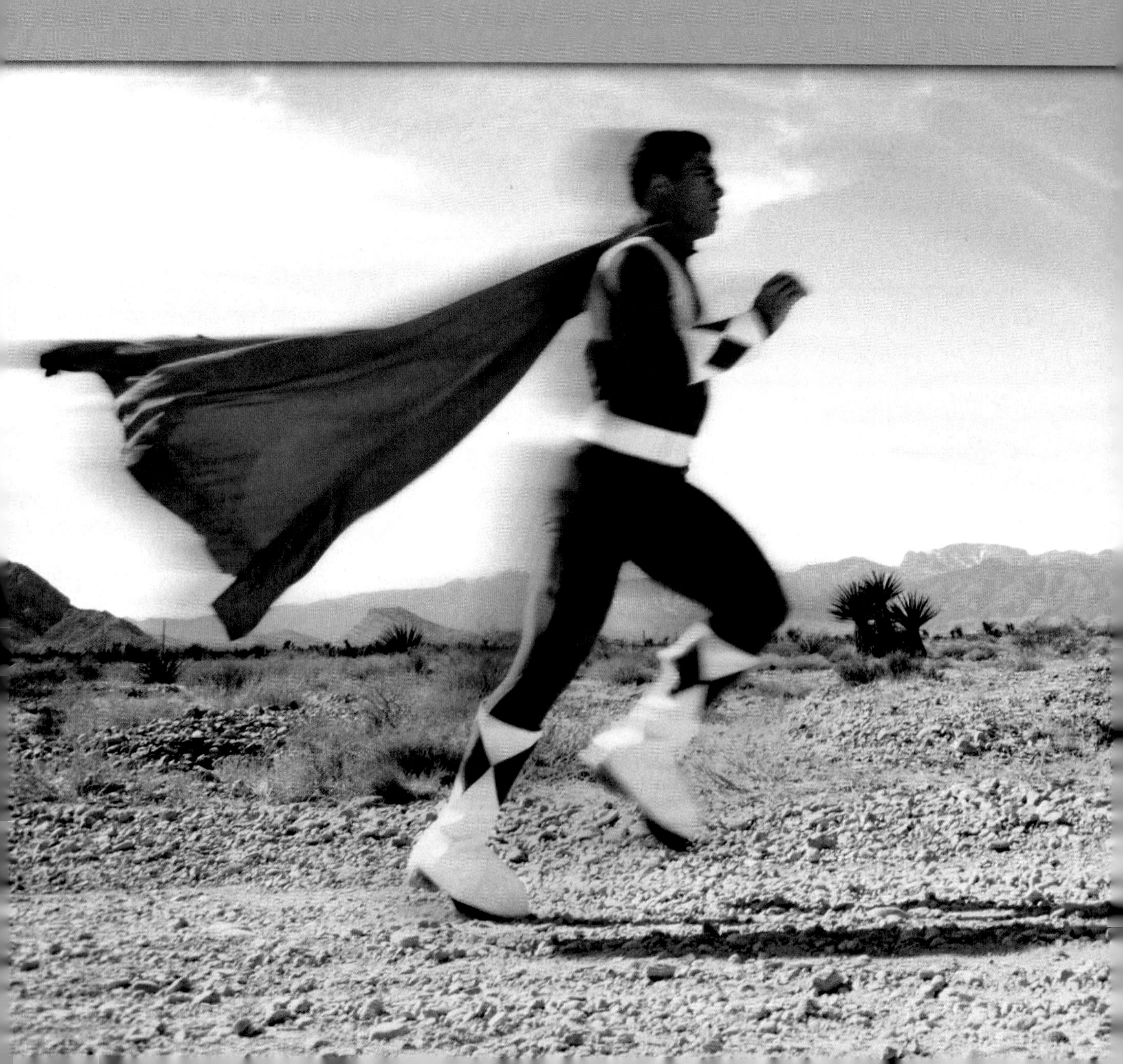

UNIT ONE

THE BIG Question

"Everyone is necessarily the hero of his own life story."

—JOHN BARTH

Throughout Unit 1, you will read, write, and talk about the **BIG Question—"What Makes a Hero?"** Use your Unit 1 **Foldable,** shown here, to keep track of your ideas as you read. Turn to the back of this book for instructions on making this **Foldable.**

Explore the BIG Question

WHAT Makes a Hero?

Superhero costumes are a popular choice for parties. Why do people admire heroes? Have you read about heroes in stories? In real life? Who are *your* heroes? Explore the qualities and achievements that make you look up to someone.

Think about two ways a person can become a hero:

- Helping Others
- Clever Solutions

What You'll Read

Reading about many different kinds of heroes can help you explore the idea for yourself. In this unit, reading **short fiction**—writing that is about people and situations the author invents—is a great way to meet heroic characters. The short fiction you will read includes short stories, folktales, tall tales, and fairy tales. You will also read essays, informational articles, and other texts that can lead you to discover answers to the Big Question.

What You'll Write

As you explore the Big Question, you'll write notes in your Unit 1 **Foldable.** Later, you'll use these notes to complete two writing assignments related to the Big Question.

1. **Write a Short Story**
2. **Choose a Unit Challenge**
   - **On Your Own Activity: A Hero for Today**
   - **Group Activity: Local Heroes Who Inspire**

What You'll Learn

Literary Elements

narrator and point of view

setting

text structure

plot

theme

character

dialogue

characterization

tone

Reading Skills and Strategies

connect to personal experience

identify cause-and-effect relationships

determine main idea and supporting details

visualize

make predictions about plot

compare and contrast characters

interpret graphic stories

analyze plot

analyze story elements

The Fly

Mai Vo-Dinh

Everyone in the village knew the usurer,[1] a rich and smart man. Having accumulated a fortune over the years, he settled down to a life of leisure in his big house surrounded by an immense garden and guarded by a pack of ferocious dogs.

But still unsatisfied with what he had acquired, the man went on making money by lending it to people all over the county at exorbitant[2] rates. The usurer reigned supreme in the area, for numerous were those who were in debt to him.

One day, the rich man set out for the house of one of his peasants. Despite repeated reminders, the poor laborer just could not manage to pay off his long-standing debt. Working himself to a shadow, the peasant barely succeeded in making ends meet. The moneylender was therefore determined that if he could not get his money back this time, he would proceed to confiscate[3] some of his debtor's most valuable belongings. But the rich man found no one at the peasant's house but a small boy of eight or nine playing alone in the dirt yard.

"Child, are your parents home?" the rich man asked.

"No, sir," the boy replied, then went on playing with his sticks and stones, paying no attention whatever to the man.

Set a Purpose for Reading

Read this folktale to discover how even a young boy can outsmart a more powerful opponent.

1 A ***usurer*** (ū′ zhər ər) is someone who lends money, especially at a high interest rate.

2 ***Exorbitant*** means "beyond what is proper, reasonable, or usual."

3 If you ***confiscate*** something, you take it away by authority.

View the Art In what ways might this scene be similar to the village in the folktale?

"Then, where are they?" the rich man asked, somewhat irritated, but the little boy went on playing and did not answer.

When the rich man repeated his query, the boy looked up and answered, with deliberate slowness, "Well, sir, my father has gone to cut living trees and plant dead ones and my mother is at the market place selling the wind and buying the moon."

"What? What in heaven are you talking about?" the rich man commanded. "Quick, tell me where they are, or you will see what this stick can do to you!" The bamboo walking stick in the big man's hand looked indeed menacing.

After repeated questioning, however, the boy only gave the same reply. Exasperated,[4] the rich man told him, "All right, little devil, listen to me! I came here today to take the money your parents owe me. But if you tell me where they really are and what they are doing, I will forget all about the debt. Is that clear to you?"

BQ BIG Question
How is this courageous?

4 An ***exasperated*** person is greatly irritated.

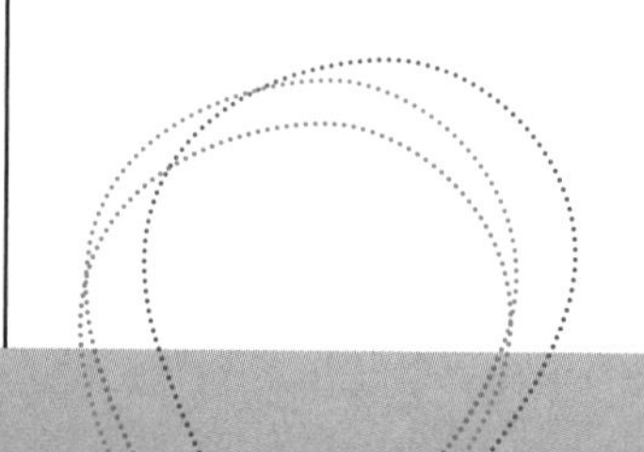

"Oh, sir, why are you joking with a poor little boy? Do you expect me to believe what you are saying?" For the first time the boy looked interested.

"Well, there is heaven and there is earth to witness my promise," the rich man said, pointing up to the sky and down to the ground.

But the boy only laughed. "Sir, heaven and earth cannot talk and therefore cannot testify. I want some living thing to be our witness."

Catching sight of a fly alighting[5] on a bamboo pole nearby, and laughing inside because he was fooling the boy, the rich man proposed, "There is a fly. He can be our witness. Now, hurry and tell me what you mean when you say that your father is out cutting living trees and planting dead ones, while your mother is at the market selling the wind and buying the moon."

Looking at the fly on the pole, the boy said, "A fly is a good enough witness for me. Well, here it is, sir. My father has simply gone to cut down bamboos and make a fence with them for a man near the river. And my mother . . . oh, sir, you'll keep your promise, won't you? You will free my parents of all their debts? You really mean it?"

"Yes, yes, I do solemnly swear in front of this fly here." The rich man urged the boy to go on.

"Well, my mother, she has gone to the market to sell fans so she can buy oil for our lamps. Isn't that what you would call selling the wind to buy the moon?"

Shaking his head, the rich man had to admit inwardly that the boy was a clever one. However, he thought, the little genius still had much to learn, believing as he did that a fly could be a witness for anybody. Bidding the boy good-by, the man told him that he would soon return to make good his promise.

A few days had passed when the moneylender returned. This time he found the poor peasant couple at home, for it was late in the evening. A nasty scene

5 ***Alighting*** means "landing on."

BQ BIG Question

What opportunity does the boy see?

BQ BIG Question

How can you tell the boy is honest?

Shadow. Pham Duc Cuong. Private Collection.

ensued,[6] the rich man claiming his money and the poor peasant apologizing and begging for another delay. Their argument awakened the little boy who ran to his father and told him, "Father, father, you don't have to pay your debt. This gentleman here has promised me that he would forget all about the money you owe him."

"Nonsense," the rich man shook his walking stick at both father and son. "Nonsense, are you going to stand there and listen to a child's inventions? I never spoke a word to this boy. Now, tell me, are you going to pay or are you not?"

The whole affair ended by being brought before the mandarin[7] who governed the county. Not knowing what to believe, all the poor peasant and his wife could do was to bring their son with them when they went to court. The little boy's insistence[8] about the rich man's promise was their only encouragement.

---

6 If something ***ensued,*** it followed or came afterward.

7 When emperors ruled China, a high public official was called a ***mandarin.***

8 ***Insistence*** means "persisting in a course of action."

The mandarin began by asking the boy to relate exactly what had happened between himself and the moneylender. Happily, the boy hastened to tell about the explanations he gave the rich man in exchange for the debt.

"Well," the mandarin said to the boy, "if this man here has indeed made such a promise, we have only your word for it. How do we know that you have not invented the whole story yourself? In a case such as this, you need a witness to confirm it, and you have none." The boy remained calm and declared that naturally there was a witness to their conversation.

"Who is that, child?" the mandarin asked.

"A fly, Your Honor."

"A fly? What do you mean, a fly? Watch out, young man, fantasies are not to be tolerated in this place!" The mandarin's benevolent[9] face suddenly became stern.

"Yes, Your Honor, a fly. A fly which was alighting on this gentleman's nose!" The boy leapt from his seat.

"Insolent[10] little devil, that's a pack of lies!" The rich man roared indignantly,[11] his face like a ripe tomato. "The fly was *not* on my nose; *he was on the housepole . . .*" But he stopped dead. It was, however, too late.

The majestic[12] mandarin himself could not help bursting out laughing. Then the audience burst out laughing. The boy's parents too, although timidly, laughed. And the boy, and the rich man himself, also laughed. With one hand on his stomach, the mandarin waved the other hand toward the rich man:

"Now, now, that's all settled. You have indeed made your promises, dear sir, to the child. *Housepole or no housepole, your conversation did happen after all!* The court says you must keep your promise."

And still chuckling, he dismissed all parties.

BQ BIG Question

Why is the boy so eager to tell his story?

BQ BIG Question

How did the boy outsmart the rich man?

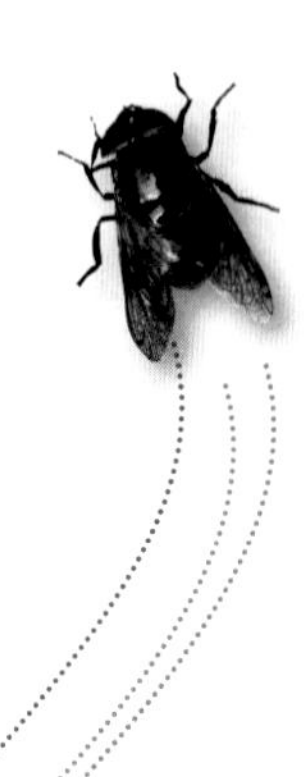

9 ***Benevolent*** means "kindly and generous."

10 An ***insolent*** person is offensively rude.

11 When someone speaks ***indignantly,*** that person is angry in response to meanness or injustice.

12 ***Majestic*** means "with impressive or awesome dignity."

After You Read

Respond and Think Critically

1. Use your own words to retell how the boy found a clever solution to his parents' problem. **[Summarize]**
2. What does the mandarin mean when he says, "fantasies are not to be tolerated in this place"? **[Interpret]**
3. Why do you think the boy tells a riddle rather than explaining where his parents are? **[Infer]**
4. What lesson does the story teach? How worthwhile is the lesson? Support your answer. **[Evaluate]**

Writing

Write a Personal Response What makes the boy in the story a hero? Write a brief but detailed response that explains *what* the boy does that makes him a hero and *why* he does it. Discuss what qualities the boy shows throughout the story and how those qualities affect the plot and the resolution of the conflict. Organize your interpretation around specific examples from the text. You may want to begin your paragraph with this sentence:

"The boy is a hero because __________."

For page 8

ELA6W2a Demonstrate competence in a variety of genres. Produce a response to literature that engages the reader by establishing a context, creating a speaker's voice, and otherwise developing reader interest.

Literature Online

Unit Resources For additional skills practice, go to glencoe.com and enter QuickPass code GL17527u1.

Part 1

Helping Others

The Operation, 1948. Barbara Hepworth. Pencil and oil on paper. Private Collection, ©Agnew's, London.

BQ BIG Question What Makes a Hero?

In the picture *The Operation,* how is the medical team working together to help another person? What workers who devote their lives to helping others do you admire?

Before You Read

The Scribe

Connect to the Story

Think about a time when you helped another person. Recall how you felt about it.

QuickWrite Freewrite for a few minutes about what you did and how it made you feel. What do your actions say about you?

Build Background

"The Scribe" describes a neighborhood in which few people use bank accounts. Instead, they rely on check-cashing services. A check-cashing service is a business where people can cash a check for a fee. Customers can also use the service to get a cash advance—that is, they can borrow money to be repaid later. However, they must pay a fee to borrow the money. Other services may be offered as well, such as paying utility bills. Some people prefer to use a check-cashing service rather than open an account at a bank.

Vocabulary

minimum (min′ ə məm) *adj.* least possible; lowest; smallest (p. 13).
The minimum passing grade in this class is 70 percent.

veteran (vet′ ər ən) *n.* one who has served in the armed forces (p. 14).
My uncle is a veteran who served in the Gulf War.

criticized (krit′ ə sīzd′) *v.* found fault with (p. 16).
During the basketball game, the coach criticized the player for dropping the ball.

disability (dis′ ə bil′ ə tē) *n.* something that causes a loss or lack of ability (p. 17).
A person with a disability may require wheelchair access to a building.

muster (mus′ tər) *v.* to find and gather together; collect or summon (p. 18).
She had to muster her strength to make it to the finish line.

Meet Kristin Hunter

Every one of us is a wonder. Every one of us has a story.
—Kristin Hunter

An Early Start Kristin Hunter began writing a newspaper column for the *Pittsburgh Courier* when she was only fourteen. As an adult, she wrote her first novel in her spare time while working for an advertising agency. Many of her novels for young adults describe the challenges and joys of growing up in an African American neighborhood.

Literary Works Kristin Hunter is the author of many novels for adults and young people, including *The Soul Brothers and Sister Lou.* "The Scribe" was published in 1973.

Kristin Hunter was born in 1931.

Literature Online

Author Search For more about Kristin Hunter, go to glencoe.com and enter QuickPass code GL17527u1.

Set Purposes for Reading

BQ BIG Question

As you read, ask yourself, what obstacles get in the narrator's way, and how does the narrator find another way to help others?

Literary Element Narrator and Point of View

The **narrator** is the person who tells a story. In fiction, the narrator may be a character in the story. **Point of view** is the relationship of the narrator to the story. A story told by a character who is referred to as "I" uses **first-person point of view.** A story in which the narrator is outside the story and and reveals the thoughts and actions of at least one character uses **third-person point of view.**

Identifying the narrator and point of view can help you understand how a character thinks, feels, or sees the world.

As you read, ask yourself, how does James feel about what takes place inside the Silver Dollar Check Cashing Service?

Reading Strategy Connect to Personal Experience

When you **connect to personal experience,** you link something to your own life. For example, you might think about how a situation in a story is like one that you experienced.

Connecting to personal experience as you read can help you better appreciate and understand a story. Making connections between your own experiences and the events in a story can help you understand why characters behave the way they do.

To connect to personal experience as you read, ask yourself,

- Have I had an experience like this?
- Have I felt or acted like this character?
- What would I do in this situation?

Finding connections can help deepen your understanding of the story. As you read, you may find it helpful to use a graphic organizer like the one below.

Detail	My Connection
James sees a woman being treated rudely.	Like James, I felt angry when I saw someone being treated badly.

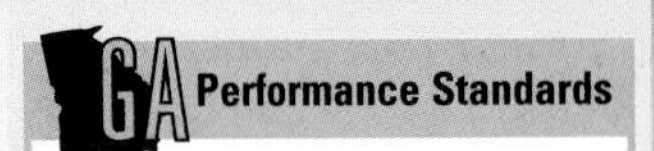

GA Performance Standards

For pages 10–22

ELA6R1f For literary texts, identify the speaker and recognize the difference between first- and third-person narration.

TRY IT

Connect to Personal Experience You notice a new student on the first day of school. You remember a time when you were a new student and didn't know anyone. What do you do next?

Thinking, 1984. Carlton Murrel. Oil on board. Private Collection.

THE SCRIBE

Kristin Hunter

We been living in the apartment over the Silver Dollar Check Cashing Service five years. But I never had any reason to go in there till two days ago, when Mom had to go to the Wash-a-Mat and asked me to get some change.

And man! Are those people who come in there in some bad shape.

Old man Silver and old man Dollar, who own the place, have signs tacked up everywhere:

NO LOUNGING, NO LOITERING[1]
THIS IS NOT A WAITING ROOM
and
MINIMUM CHECK CASHING FEE, 50¢
and
LETTERS ADDRESSED, 50¢
and
LETTERS READ, 75¢
and
LETTERS WRITTEN, ONE DOLLAR

Connect to Personal Experience How do these signs remind you of signs you have seen?

And everybody who comes in there to cash a check gets their picture taken like they're some kind of criminal.

After I got my change, I stood around for a while digging the action. First comes an old lady with some kind of long form to fill out. The mean old man behind the counter points to the "One Dollar" sign. She nods. So he starts to fill it out for her.

"Name?"

"Muskogee Marie Lawson."

"SPELL it!" he hollers.

"M, m, u, s—well, I don't exactly know, sir."

"I'll put down 'Marie,' then. Age?"

"Sixty-three my last birthday."

"Date of birth?"

"March twenty-third"—a pause—"I think, 1900."

"Look, Marie," he says, which makes me mad, hearing him first-name a dignified old gray-haired lady like that, "if you'd been born in 1900, you'd be seventy-two. Either I put that down, or I put 1910."

Narrator and Point of View What does the narrator reveal about himself here?

"Whatever you think best, sir," she says timidly.

He sighs, rolls his eyes to the ceiling, and bangs his fist on the form angrily. Then he fills out the rest.

---

1 ***Loitering*** (loi′ tər ing) is lingering about a place without a purpose.

Vocabulary

minimum (min′ ə məm) *adj.* least possible; lowest; smallest

"One dollar," he says when he's finished. She pays like she's grateful to him for taking the trouble.

Next is a man with a cane, a **veteran** who has to let the government know he moved. He wants old man Silver to do this for him, but he doesn't want him to know he can't do it himself.

Connect to Personal Experience How do you act when you are in a similar situation?

"My eyes are kind of bad, sir. Will you fill this thing out for me? Tell them I moved from 121 South 15th Street to 203 North Decatur Street."

Old man Silver doesn't blink an eye. Just fills out the form, and charges the crippled man a dollar.

And it goes on like that. People who can't read or write or count their change. People who don't know how to pay their gas bills, don't know how to fill out forms, don't know how to address envelopes. And old man Silver and old man Dollar cleaning up on all of them. It's pitiful. It's disgusting. Makes me so mad I want to yell.

And I do, but mostly at Mom. "Mom, did you know there are hundreds of people in this city who can't read and write?"

Mom isn't upset. She's a wise woman. "Of course, James," she says. "A lot of the older people around here haven't had your advantages. They came from down South, and they had to quit school very young to go to work.

"In the old days, nobody cared whether our people got an education. They were only interested in getting the crops in." She sighed. "Sometimes I think they *still* don't care. If we hadn't gotten you into that good school, you might not be able to read so well either. A lot of boys and girls your age can't, you know."

"But that's awful!" I say. "How do they expect us to make it in a big city? You can't even cross the streets if you can't read the 'Walk' and 'Don't Walk' signs."

Narrator and Point of View How does the author's use of point of view influence how you react to the information given so far?

"It's hard," Mom says, "but the important thing to remember is it's no disgrace. There was a time in history when nobody could read or write except a special class of people."

Vocabulary

veteran (vet′ ər ən) *n.* one who has served in the armed forces

Harlem Street Scene, 1942. Jacob Lawrence. Gouache on paper, 21 × 20 3/4 in. Private Collection. © ARS, NY.

View the Art How does this painting help you picture the neighborhood in which the Silver Dollar Check Cashing Service is located?

And Mom takes down her Bible. She has three Bible study certificates and is always giving me lessons from Bible history. I don't exactly go for all the stuff she believes in, but sometimes it *is* interesting.

"In ancient times," she says, "no one could read or write except a special class of people known as scribes.[2] It was their job to write down the laws given by the rabbis and the judges.[3] No one else could do it.

2 ***Scribes*** were educated people who served as copyists, editors, and teachers.

3 ***The rabbis and the judges*** were the teachers and rulers of the ancient Hebrews.

"Jesus **criticized** the scribes," she goes on, "because they were so proud of themselves. But he needed them to write down his teachings."

"Man," I said when she finished, "that's something."

My mind was working double time. I'm the best reader and writer in our class. Also it was summertime. I had nothing much to do except go to the park or hang around the library and read till my eyeballs were ready to fall out, and I was tired of doing both.

Narrator and Point of View Using what you know about the narrator so far, what do you think he will do next?

So the next morning, after my parents went to work, I took Mom's card table and a folding chair down to the sidewalk. I lettered a sign with a Magic Marker, and I was in business. My sign said:

PUBLIC SCRIBE—ALL SERVICES FREE

The Arab Scribe, Cairo, 1852. John Frederick Lewis. 18 1/4 x 24 in. Private Collection.

Vocabulary

criticized (krit′ ə sīzd) *v.* found fault with

I set my table up in front of the Silver Dollar and waited for business. Only one thing bothered me. If the people couldn't read, how would they know what I was there for?

But five minutes had hardly passed when an old lady stopped and asked me to read her grandson's letter. She explained that she had just broken her glasses. I knew she was fibbing, but I kept quiet.

I read the grandson's letter. It said he was having a fine time in California but was a little short. He would send her some money as soon as he made another payday. I handed the letter back to her.

"Thank you, son," she said, and gave me a quarter.

I handed that back to her too.

Connect to Personal Experience If you had been in this situation, how would you have responded?

The word got around. By noontime I had a whole crowd of customers around my table. I was kept busy writing letters, addressing envelopes, filling out forms, and explaining official-looking letters that scared people half to death.

I didn't blame them. The language in some of those letters—"Establish whether your **disability** is one-fourth, one-third, one-half, or total, and substantiate[4] in paragraph 3 (b) below"—would upset anybody. I mean, why can't the government write English like everybody else?

Most of my customers were old, but there were a few young ones too. Like the girl who had gotten a letter about her baby from the Health Service and didn't know what "immunization"[5] meant.

At noontime one old lady brought me some iced tea and a peach, and another gave me some fried chicken wings. I was really having a good time when the shade of all the people standing around me suddenly vanished. The sun hit me like a ton of hot bricks.

Only one long shadow fell across my table. The shadow of a tall, heavy, blue-eyed cop. In our neighborhood, when they see a cop, people scatter. That was why the back of my neck was burning.

---

4 When you ***substantiate*** something, you give evidence to prove a claim.

5 An ***immunization*** is medicine given to protect against disease.

Vocabulary

disability (dis′ ə bil′ ə tē) *n.* something that causes a loss or lack of ability

"What are you trying to do here, sonny?" the cop asks.

"Help people out," I tell him calmly, though my knees are knocking together under the table.

"Well, you know," he says, "Mr. Silver and Mr. Dollar have been in business a long time on this corner. They are very respected men in this neighborhood. Are you trying to run them out of business?"

"I'm not charging anybody," I pointed out.

"That," the cop says, "is exactly what they don't like. Mr. Silver says he is glad to have some help with the letter writing. Mr. Dollar says it's only a nuisance[6] to them anyway and takes up too much time. But if you don't charge for your services, it's unfair competition."

Well, why not? I thought. After all, I could use a little profit.

"All right," I tell him. "I'll charge a quarter."

"Then it is my duty to warn you," the cop says, "that it's against the law to conduct a business without a license. The first time you accept a fee, I'll close you up and run you off this corner."

He really had me there. What did I know about licenses? I'm only thirteen, after all. Suddenly I didn't feel like the big black businessman anymore. I felt like a little kid who wanted to holler for his mother. But she was at work, and so was Daddy.

"I'll leave," I said, and did, with all the cool I could **muster.** But inside I was burning up, and not from the sun.

One little old lady hollered "You big bully!" and shook her umbrella at the cop. But the rest of those people were so beaten down they didn't say anything. Just shuffled back on inside to give Mr. Silver and Mr. Dollar their hard-earned money like they always did.

I was so mad I didn't know what to do with myself that afternoon. I couldn't watch TV. It was all soap operas anyway, and they seemed dumber than ever. The library

BQ BIG Question

Part of being a hero is showing courage. Does James show courage here? Why or why not?

Connect to Personal Experience When have you felt the same way James does here?

---

6 A ***nuisance*** is something that is annoying or unpleasant.

Vocabulary

muster (mus′ tər) *v.* to find and gather together; collect or summon didn't appeal to me either. It's not air-conditioned, and the day was hot and muggy.

Finally I went to the park and threw stones at the swans in the lake. I was careful not to hit them, but they made good targets because they were so fat and white. Then after a while the sun got lower. I kind of cooled off and came to my senses. They were just big, dumb, beautiful birds and not my enemies. I threw them some crumbs from my sandwich and went home.

Narrator and Point of View
What does the narrator's reaction reveal about him?

"Daddy," I asked that night, "how come you and Mom never cash checks downstairs in the Silver Dollar?"

"Because," he said, "we have an account at the bank, where they cash our checks free."

"Well, why doesn't everybody do that?" I wanted to know.

"Because some people want all their money right away," he said. "The bank insists that you leave them a minimum balance."

"How much?" I asked him.

"Only five dollars."

"But that five dollars still belongs to you after you leave it there?"

"Sure," he says. "And if it's in a savings account, it earns interest."

"So why can't people see they lose money when they pay to have their checks cashed?"

"A lot of *our* people," Mom said, "are scared of banks, period. Some of them remember the Depression,[7] when all the banks closed and the people couldn't get their money out. And others think banks are only for white people. They think they'll be insulted, or maybe even arrested, if they go in there."

Wow. The more I learned, the more pitiful it was. "Are there any black people working at our bank?"

"There didn't used to be," Mom said, "but now they have Mr. Lovejoy and Mrs. Adams. You know Mrs. Adams, she's nice. She has a daughter your age."

"Hmmm," I said, and shut up before my folks started

---

7 The ***Depression***, or Great Depression, was a period of high unemployment from 1929 through the 1930s.

to wonder why I was asking all those questions.

The next morning, when the Silver Dollar opened, I was right there. I hung around near the door, pretending to read a copy of *Jet* magazine.

"Psst," I said to each person who came in. "I know where you can cash checks *free*."

It wasn't easy convincing them. A man blinked his red eyes at me like he didn't believe he had heard right. A carpenter with tools hanging all around his belt said he was on his lunch hour and didn't have time. And a big fat lady with two shopping bags pushed past me and almost knocked me down, she was in such a hurry to give Mr. Silver and Mr. Dollar her money.

Connect to Personal Experience What types of situations make you feel as strongly as James does about helping others?

But finally I had a little group who were interested. It wasn't much. Just three people. Two men—one young, one old—and the little old lady who'd asked me to read her the letter from California. Seemed the grandson had made his payday and sent her a money order.

"How far is this place?" asked the young man.

"Not far. Just six blocks," I told him.

"Aw shoot. I ain't walking all that way just to save fifty cents."

So then I only had two. I was careful not to tell them where we were going. When we finally got to the Establishment Trust National Bank, I said, "This is the place."

"I ain't goin' in there," said the old man. "No sir. Not me. You ain't gettin' me in *there*." And he walked away quickly, going back in the direction where we had come.

To tell the truth, the bank did look kind of scary. It was a big building with tall white marble **pillars**. A lot of Brink's armored trucks and Cadillacs were parked out front. Uniformed guards walked back and forth inside with guns. It might as well have a "Colored Keep Out" sign.

Visual Vocabulary

Pillars are freestanding, upright structures, usually of stone, wood, or metal, that serve as a support for a building.

Narrator and Point of View How does the narrator's description of the building reflect his own mood at the moment?

Whereas the Silver Dollar is small and dark and funky and dirty. It has trash on the floors and tape across the broken windows.

I looked at the little old lady. She smiled back bravely. "Well, we've come this far, son," she said. "Let's not turn back now."

So I took her inside. Fortunately Mrs. Adams's window was near the front.

"Hi, James," she said.

"I've brought you a customer," I told her.

Mrs. Adams took the old lady to a desk to fill out some forms. They were gone a long time, but finally they came back.

"Now, when you have more business with the bank, Mrs. Franklin, just bring it to me," Mrs. Adams said.

"I'll do that," the old lady said. She held out her shiny new bankbook. "Son, do me a favor and read that to me."

"Mrs. Minnie Franklin," I read aloud. "July 9, 1972. Thirty-seven dollars."

"That sounds real nice," Mrs. Franklin said. "I guess now I have a bankbook, I'll have to get me some glasses."

Mrs. Adams winked at me over the old lady's head, and I winked back.

"Do you want me to walk you home?" I asked Mrs. Franklin.

"No thank you, son," she said. "I can cross streets by myself all right. I know red from green."

And then she winked at both of us, letting us know she knew what was happening.

"Son," she went on, "don't ever be afraid to try a thing just because you've never done it before. I took a bus up here from Alabama by myself forty-four years ago. I ain't thought once about going back. But I've stayed too long in one neighborhood since I've been in this city. Now I think I'll go out and take a look at *this* part of town."

Then she was gone. But she had really started me thinking. If an old lady like that wasn't afraid to go in a bank and open an account for the first time in her life, why should I be afraid to go up to City Hall and apply for a license?

Wonder how much they charge you to be a scribe?

BQ BIG Question

How do both James and Mrs. Franklin show the qualities of a hero?

After You Read

Respond and Think Critically

1. How do Mr. Silver and Mr. Dollar treat their customers? Find details from the selection to support your answer. **[Recall]**
2. What does the narrator mean when he says, "And old man Silver and old man Dollar cleaning up on all of them"? **[Interpret]**
3. Compare the Silver Dollar Check Cashing Service with the Establishment Trust National Bank. **[Compare]**
4. **Literary Element** **Narrator and Point of View** How does the first-person point of view in "The Scribe" shape the way readers feel about the customers at the Silver Dollar Check Cashing Service? **[Analyze]**
5. **Reading Strategy** **Connect to Personal Experience** How do the personal connections in your graphic organizer help you better understand the characters and events in the story? **[Analyze]**
6. **BQ** **BIG Question** How do James and Mrs. Franklin help each other? Is either character a hero? Explain. **[Conclude]**

Vocabulary Practice

Choose the sentence that uses the vocabulary word correctly.

1. **A.** The **minimum** age for admittance to the play is twelve.
   B. The highest, or **minimum,** deposit in an account is $1,000.
2. **A.** The **veteran** hoped to serve in the armed forces one day.
   B. My grandfather is a **veteran** of World War II.
3. **A.** The reviewer liked the play so much that he **criticized** it.
   B. In the past, some people **criticized** women in politics.
4. **A.** Sidewalks in our town were designed to help people with a physical **disability** cross the street more easily.
   B. Many people were amazed at Mozart's **disability** to play classical piano at a very young age.
5. **A.** Ana had to **muster** her way into the long line.
   B. It was difficult to **muster** the energy to take the test.

Writing

Write a Journal Entry Think about a time when you helped someone or someone helped you. Write a journal entry about your experience and any unexpected benefits that resulted from it.

TIP

Interpreting
To answer question 2, recall details about how Mr. Silver and Mr. Dollar interact with customers. Compare these details with how you would like to be treated.

- Reread the signs in the Silver Dollar Check Cashing Service. What does the first sign tell you about the owners?
- Why might the owners photograph each customer who cashes a check? What does this tell you about the owners?
- Reread how the owners treat Muskogee Marie Lawson and the veteran.
- Notice what the narrator says and how he feels when he witnesses these interactions.

Keep track of your ideas about the **BIG Question** in your unit Foldable.

Literature Online

Selection Resources
For Selection Quizzes, eFlashcards, and Reading-Writing Connection activities, go to glencoe.com and enter QuickPass code GL17527u1.

Vocabulary Workshop

Word Parts

Connection to Literature

"And old man Silver and old man Dollar cleaning up on all of them. It's pitiful. It's disgusting."

—Kristin Hunter, "The Scribe"

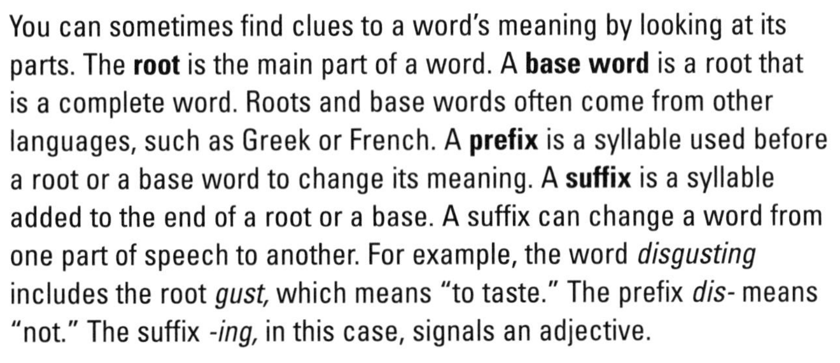

You can sometimes find clues to a word's meaning by looking at its parts. The **root** is the main part of a word. A **base word** is a root that is a complete word. Roots and base words often come from other languages, such as Greek or French. A **prefix** is a syllable used before a root or a base word to change its meaning. A **suffix** is a syllable added to the end of a root or a base. A suffix can change a word from one part of speech to another. For example, the word *disgusting* includes the root *gust,* which means "to taste." The prefix *dis-* means "not." The suffix *-ing,* in this case, signals an adjective.

Here are some other word parts from "The Scribe."

Word Part	Meaning or Effect	Examples
root/base		
fin	end	finished, finally
gust	taste	disgusting, gusto
scrib, script	write	scribes, describe
prefix		
dis-	not, opposite of	disgrace, disability
un-	not	unfair
suffix		
-ful	full of	pitiful
-ment	forms a noun	government, establishment

TRY IT: Use the chart above to help you answer each question. Pay attention to how the pronunciation of a root can change when a prefix or suffix is added.

1. What does the root in *scribble* mean?
2. From its word parts, what does *disability* mean?
3. How would you change *accomplish* from a verb to a noun? Use the word in a sentence.

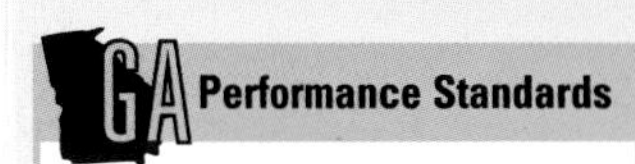

Performance Standards

For page 23

ELA6R2b Understand and acquire new vocabulary. Use knowledge of Greek and Latin affixes to understand unfamiliar vocabulary.

Tip

Vocabulary Terms The **root** is the main part of a word and tells what the word is about. **Prefixes** and **suffixes** change the meaning or part of speech of a word.

Test-Taking Tip Use word parts to help you understand the meaning of a word from another language, such as the French word *brunette.* The base word *brun* means "dark-haired." The suffix *-ette* indicates that the subject is small and female.

Literature Online

Vocabulary For more vocabulary practice, go to glencoe.com and enter QuickPass code GL17527u1.

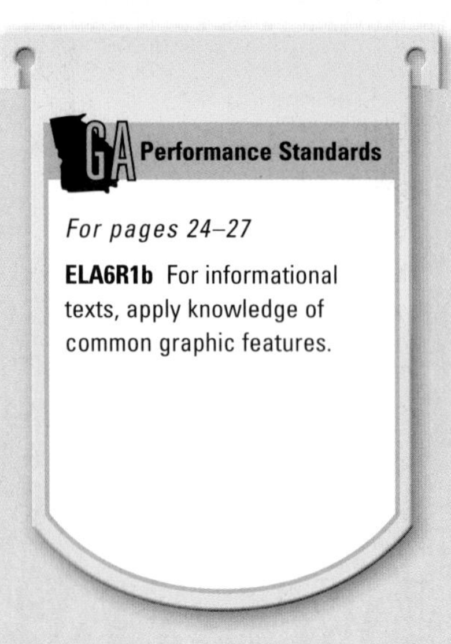

GA Performance Standards
For pages 24–27
ELA6R1b For informational texts, apply knowledge of common graphic features.

Set a Purpose for Reading

Read to learn how a storm brought out the best in people.

Preview the Article

1. What does the **title** suggest the article is about?
2. What clues about the main text do you get from the **section headings** and **subheadings**?

Reading Strategy

Activate Prior Knowledge

When you activate prior knowledge, you use what you already know to understand a new text. Think about what you already know about hurricanes.

What I Know

1. Violent ocean storms
2. High winds, flooding

TIME

Hurricane HEROES

As storms slammed the South in 2004, some brave folks risked their lives to help others.

By THOMAS FIELDS-MEYER, STEVE HELLING, and LORI ROZSA

Charley, Frances, Ivan, Jeanne: four hurricanes in six weeks; more than 150 deaths and $44 billion in damage. Faced with wrecked bridges, shattered condos, floods, and mudslides, millions of people in Florida, Georgia, and Alabama had to decide when to flee, what to save, or whom to help. Meet three people who made it through and helped many others along the way.

A Medical Marathon[1]

Ron Wegner treated wounds—some invisible

Wegner, 57, commander of Florida's 35-member Disaster Medical Assistance Team, spent several weeks living in Charley's and Ivan's disaster zones. He put in 20-hour shifts and helped treat everything from broken bones to heart attacks. Still, he says his most memorable patient was an 83-year-old woman. She

1 Originally, a ***marathon*** was a 26-mile foot race. Now the word is also used to refer to anything that lasts a long time and is difficult to bear.

came into the makeshift[2] emergency unit in the parking lot of a damaged Pensacola hospital where Wegner was stationed after Ivan. She showed him a bruise on her hand. "She admitted she hadn't really been injured, but her house was destroyed and she was alone, and she wanted to talk to somebody. So for 25 minutes I held her hand and we talked," he says. "Really, her problem was just as important as a chain-saw accident."

Wegner is an anesthetist[3] who lives in Tampa. Like all of the disaster volunteers, Wegner was paid by the federal government what he would usually have earned in his regular job. Wegner is the nerve center of the medical team. "He's the ringmaster of the circus," says Butch Kinerney, a spokesperson[4] for the Federal Emergency Management Agency.[5] In the first three days after Ivan, Wegner's team treated 460 people. Though he misses his girlfriend and 25-year-old daughter, there were no complaints from Wegner. "We've got our comfortable lives to go back to," he says. "A lot of these people have nothing."

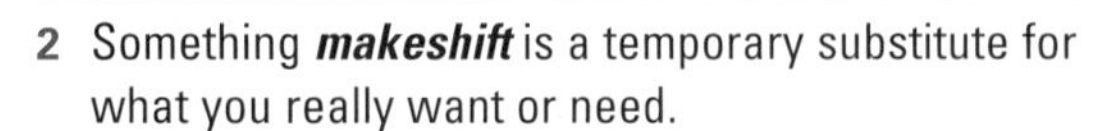

2 Something ***makeshift*** is a temporary substitute for what you really want or need.

3 An ***anesthetist*** is the person who gives drugs to put a patient to sleep before surgery.

4 A ***spokesperson*** is someone who speaks on behalf of others.

5 The ***Federal Emergency Management Agency*** responds to natural and manmade disasters. It's often referred to by its initials, FEMA (fē′ mə).

Karena Cawthorn/Silver Image

"You see so many people just wandering about, stunned," says Ron Wegner (in Gulf Breeze, Florida).

He Came, He Saw, He Sawed

Jim Williams went out on many limbs

Driving to work the morning after Hurricane Charley ripped through Sanford, Florida, mail carrier Williams was so stunned by the number of fallen trees he saw that he had to pull over. The area "was just devastated," says Williams, 45, who grew up in the quiet community 25 miles north of Orlando. "I sat in my truck and cried."

Then he took action. Returning home, Williams grabbed his chain saw and headed to the home of a friend's parents, where two huge oak trees had fallen. He sawed the rest of the day to clear the couple's driveway. Every day for the next three weeks, Williams delivered the mail through the cleanup from Charley and Frances. But he also spent hours after work using his chain saw wherever he could help—particularly outside the homes of retired people along his 18-mile mail route.

Williams spent nearly five hours clearing a 40-foot oak from atop the home of Ginny Taffer, 79, and husband Gene, 83. "He was my angel," says Ginny. What motivates Williams? He says that when his son James, 10 (with wife Gail, 47; he also has a daughter Leah, 16), was ill with lymphoma[6] at 6, he made a pledge to help people. Besides, he adds, "I was raised right and taught to do the right thing."

Trapped in a Collapsing Hotel

Melissa Baldwin fought her fears and saved her guests

On August 13, 2004, the fierce winds of Charley ripped the roof off of a wing of the Best Western Waterfront in Punta Gorda, Florida. Fearing for her life, Melissa Baldwin, assistant manager of the motel, phoned her fiancé, Ted Barkenquast, from the front lobby. "Tell Mom and Dad I love them," she yelled as windows shattered around her. Then the phone went dead. Recalls Barkenquast: "All I could do was think the worst."

But the storm brought out the best in Baldwin, 33, who suffers from epileptic seizures[7] that can be brought on by stress. "I figured if I was going to go down, I'd go down saving lives," she

6 ***Lymphoma*** is a type of cancer.

7 Epilepsy is a nervous-system disorder that causes attacks called ***seizures.*** An epileptic seizure may include loss of consciousness and violent shaking of the body.

"I did what I could to help," says Jim Williams, who refused payment but did accept one offering: a pecan pie.

Ben Baker/Redux

Ben Baker/Redux

"I didn't have time to be scared," says Melissa Baldwin (at the hurricane-devastated Best Western).

says. She raced upstairs to the fifth floor. Then working her way down, she moved 56 guests and employees to a windowless second-floor hall. Baldwin also ran outside and gathered people from a building next door. "It sounded like a freight train was going through the building. The wind was screaming, and people were screaming," she recalls. "I honestly thought, *So this is how I'm going to die."*

Unable to move an elderly man in room 112, she helped him into a bathtub and cushioned his body with pillows. When one woman resisted, "I said, 'I'm not overreacting. Just trust me,'" says Balwin. The hurricane pounded the hotel so hard that walls collapsed and air-conditioning units were ripped away from the building. When the winds died down after midnight, Baldwin handed a list of the 56 guests—all breathing and unharmed—to a rescue worker. The worker marveled, "I can't believe you're all alive."

Says Baldwin's coworker Lee Phillips, "Melissa was so comforting to the guests. If there were 15 of me, I don't think I could have been as comforting. She didn't crack." Baldwin is just happy everyone scraped through. "I don't know if I'll ever get over it," she says. "But the hurricane helped show me how strong I really am."

Respond and Think Critically

1. Write a brief summary of the main ideas of the article. For help on writing a summary, see page 170. **[Summarize]**
2. **Text to Self** What would you have done if you were in Melissa Baldwin's position? **[Connect]**
3. Why might the illness of Jim Williams's son have inspired Williams to help others? **[Infer]**
4. Ron Wegner says the problem of his 83-year-old patient "was just as important as a chain-saw accident." Why might the two problems be similar? **[Compare]**
5. **Reading Strategy** **Activate Prior Knowledge** Look at your graphic organizer again. Of the things you already knew about hurricanes before reading the selection, which was most useful to you in understanding the selection? Explain why.
6. **BQ** **BIG Question** What do you think is the article's main message about heroes in times of disaster? Do you agree? Explain.

Before You Read

The Dog of Pompeii

Connect to the Story

Have you ever responded to a weather emergency, such as a warning about a flood, tornado, or hurricane?

Partner Talk With a partner, talk about how you prepared (or would prepare) for an emergency.

Build Background

"The Dog of Pompeii" is a work of historical fiction—a story that contains characters invented by the author and is based on historical facts or events.

- In A.D. 79, Pompeii was a city of about 20,000 people.
- Wealthy Romans liked Pompeii's closeness to the Mediterranean Sea.
- Mount Vesuvius, the volcano that overlooked the city, had not erupted in several hundred years.

Vocabulary

ambitious (am bish′ əs) *adj.* full of a strong desire to succeed or to achieve something; eager (p. 33). *The ambitious politician was determined to become president.*

pondering (pon′ dər ing) *v.* weighing something in the mind; considering or thinking carefully (p. 35). *A traveler stood at the crossroads, pondering which way to go.*

dislodging (dis loj′ ing) *v.* moving or forcing out of a place or position (p. 37). *Dislodging the huge boulder that blocked the mouth of the tunnel was a job that called for dynamite.*

heed (hēd) *v.* pay careful attention to (p. 39). *It is helpful to heed the advice of people who have more experience than we do.*

excavators (eks′ kə vā′ tərz) *n.* people who uncover something by digging (p. 40). *Excavators burrowed through the ruins of the ancient palace in search of the lost treasure.*

Meet Louis Untermeyer

"At ten I fancied myself a storyteller. My brother was a rewarding listener."
—Louis Untermeyer

A Storyteller As a boy, Louis Untermeyer made up exciting adventure stories to tell his brother as they fell asleep at night. About school, Untermeyer recalled, "I excelled in nothing." But he did like to read and write. In high school, he began to compose his own poems. As an adult, Untermeyer first earned his living as a jeweler. Later he became a full-time writer and editor.

Literary Works Louis Untermeyer wrote, edited, or translated more than 100 books for young people and adults.

Louis Untermeyer was born in 1885 and died in 1977.

LOG ON  **Literature** Online

Author Search For more about Louis Untermeyer, go to glencoe.com and enter QuickPass code GL17527u1.

Set Purposes for Reading

BQ BIG Question

As you read, notice the ways in which the dog, Bimbo, helps his friend, Tito, during an emergency in Pompeii.

Literary Element Setting

Setting includes the time and the place in which events in a story occur. Writers show the setting through details they provide about characters and places in the story. They use **concrete details,** or specific information, and **sensory details,** or information that appeals to the reader's five senses and brings the story to life. For example, "life in Pompeii" is a concrete detail because it tells the reader only where the story takes place. But "the open-air theaters rocked with laughing crowds" is a sensory detail because it helps the reader see, hear, and feel what is going on.

Knowing a story's setting helps you understand the story. Details about the setting help you picture the time and place of the story.

As you read, ask yourself, how does the setting contribute to the problem in the story and its resolution?

Reading Skill Identify Cause-and-Effect Relationships

Identifying **cause** and **effect** means figuring out what happened (the effect) and the reason it happened (the cause).

Identifying cause-and-effect relationships in a story helps you understand events and how they affect the development of the plot.

As you read, use these tips to look for cause-and-effect relationships:

- Look for signal words such as *because, so,* and *since.*
- Ask yourself what action or event is happening.
- Think about the possible results, or effects, of the action or event.

Record causes and effects as you read. You may find it helpful to use a graphic organizer like the one below.

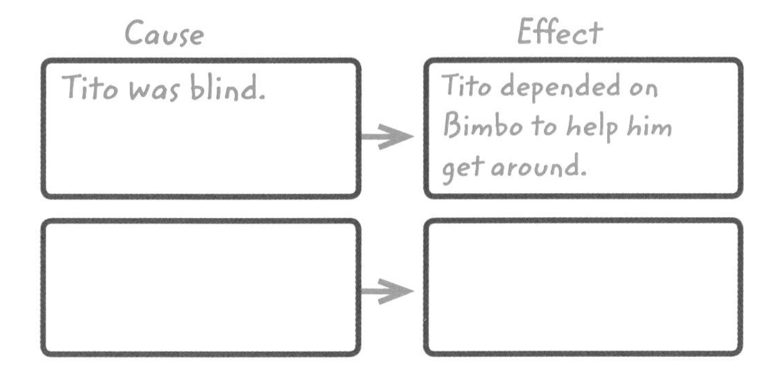

For pages 28–42

ELA6R1a For literary texts, identify and analyze sensory details and figurative language.

TRY IT

Identify Cause-and-Effect Relationships Your friend Steve almost failed his last science test. He is worried about his science grade, so he studies hard for the next quiz. What causes him to study? What will probably be the effect of his work?

THE DOG OF POMPEII

Louis Untermeyer

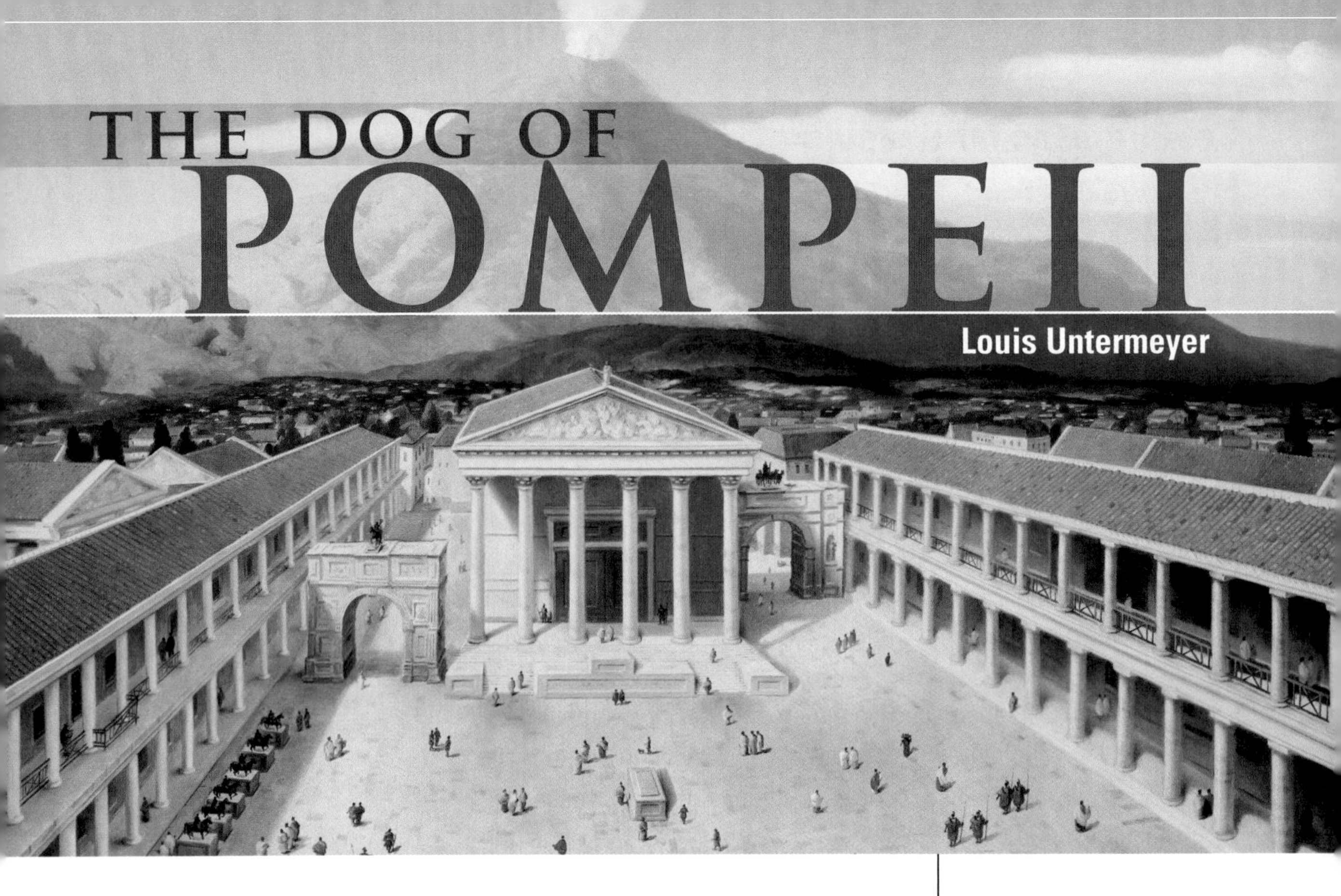

Tito and his dog Bimbo lived (if you could call it living) under the wall where it joined the inner gate. They really didn't live there; they just slept there. They lived anywhere. Pompeii was one of the gayest of the old Latin towns, but although Tito was never an unhappy boy, he was not exactly a merry one.

The streets were always lively with shining chariots and bright red trappings;[1] the open-air theaters rocked with laughing crowds; sham-battles[2] and athletic sports were free for the asking in the great stadium. Once a year the Caesar visited the pleasure-city and the fire-works lasted for days; the sacrifices in the Forum were better than a show. But Tito saw none of these things. He was blind—had been blind from birth. He was known to every one in the poorer quarters. But no one could say how old he was, no one remembered his parents, no one could tell where he came from. Bimbo was another mystery. As long as

Setting What image of Pompeii do the sensory details in this paragraph create in your mind?

1 ***Trappings*** are pieces of decorated cloth that are spread over the harnesses or saddles of horses.

2 ***Sham-battles*** are imitation battles.

people could remember seeing Tito—about twelve or thirteen years—they had seen Bimbo. Bimbo had never left his side. He was not only dog, but nurse, pillow, playmate, mother and father to Tito.

Identify Cause-and-Effect Relationships Why do you think Bimbo does so much for Tito?

Did I say Bimbo never left his master? (Perhaps I had better say comrade, for if any one was the master, it was Bimbo.) I was wrong. Bimbo did trust Tito alone exactly three times a day. It was a fixed routine, a custom understood between boy and dog since the beginning of their friendship, and the way it worked was this: Early in the morning, shortly after dawn, while Tito was still dreaming, Bimbo would disappear. When Tito awoke, Bimbo would be sitting quietly at his side, his ears cocked, his stump of a tail tapping the ground, and a fresh-baked bread—more like a large round roll—at his feet. Tito would stretch himself; Bimbo would yawn; then they would breakfast. At noon, no matter where they happened to be, Bimbo would put his paw on Tito's knee and the two of them would return to the inner gate. Tito would curl up in the corner (almost like a dog) and go to sleep, while Bimbo, looking quite important (almost like a boy) would disappear again. In half an hour he'd be back with their lunch. Sometimes it would be a piece of fruit or a scrap of meat, often it was nothing but a dry crust. But sometimes there would be one of those flat rich cakes, sprinkled with raisins and sugar, that Tito liked so much. At supper-time the same thing happened, although there was a little less of everything, for things were hard to snatch in the evening with the streets full of people. Besides, Bimbo didn't approve of too much food before going to sleep. A heavy supper made boys too restless and dogs too stodgy[3]—and it was the business of a dog to sleep lightly with one ear open and muscles ready for action.

BQ BIG Question

What are some of Bimbo's heroic traits?

But, whether there was much or little, hot or cold, fresh or dry, food was always there. Tito never asked where it came from and Bimbo never told him. There was plenty of rain-water in the hollows of soft stones; the old egg-woman at the corner sometimes gave him a cupful of

3 If an animal or a person is ***stodgy***, the animal or person is heavy and slow in movement or dull and lacking in interest.

strong goat's milk; in the grape-season the fat wine-maker let him have drippings of the mild juice. So there was no danger of going hungry or thirsty. There was plenty of everything in Pompeii—if you knew where to find it—and if you had a dog like Bimbo.

Identify Cause-and-Effect Relationships Why do some of the people of Pompeii share things with Bimbo?

As I said before, Tito was not the merriest boy in Pompeii. He could not romp with the other youngsters and play Hare-and-Hounds and I-spy and Follow-your-Master and Ball-against-the-Building and Jack-stones and Kings-and-Robbers with them. But that did not make him sorry for himself. If he could not see the sights that delighted the lads of Pompeii he could hear and smell things they never noticed. He could really see more with his ears and nose than they could with their eyes. When he and Bimbo went out walking he knew just where they were going and exactly what was happening.

Identify Cause-and-Effect Relationships Why are Tito's senses of hearing and smell so sharp?

"Ah," he'd sniff and say, as they passed a handsome villa,[4] "Glaucus Pansa is giving a grand dinner tonight. They're going to have three kinds of bread, and roast pigling, and stuffed goose, and a great stew—I think bear-stew—and a fig-pie." And Bimbo would note that this would be a good place to visit tomorrow.

Or, "H'm," Tito would murmur, half through his lips, half through his nostrils. "The wife of Marcus Lucretius is expecting her mother. She's shaking out every piece of goods in the house; she's going to use the best clothes—the ones she's been keeping in pine-needles and camphor[5]—and there's an extra girl in the kitchen. Come, Bimbo, let's get out of the dust!"

Street Musicians, before A.D. 79. Dioscurides of Samos. Mosaic from the Villa of Cicero, Pompeii. Musea Archeologico Nazionale, Naples, Italy.

Or, as they passed a small but elegant dwelling opposite the public-baths, "Too bad! The tragic poet is ill again. It must be a bad fever this time, for they're trying smoke-fumes instead of medicine. Whew! I'm glad I'm not a tragic poet!"

Or, as they neared the Forum, "Mm-m! What good things they have in the Macellum today!" (It really was a sort of butcher-grocer-market-place, but Tito didn't know

4 A ***villa*** is a house, especially one in the country or at the seashore.

5 ***Pine-needles*** and ***camphor*** are used to keep moths out of clothes.

any better. He called it the Macellum.) "Dates from Africa, and salt oysters from sea-caves, and cuttlefish, and new honey, and sweet onions, and—ugh!—water-buffalo steaks. Come, let's see what's what in the Forum." And Bimbo, just as curious as his comrade, hurried on. Being a dog, he trusted his ears and nose (like Tito) more than his eyes. And so the two of them entered the center of Pompeii.

Setting What would you expect to smell as you walked near the Forum?

The Forum was the part of the town to which everybody came at least once during each day. It was the Central Square and everything happened here. There were no private houses; all was public—the chief temples, the gold and red bazaars,[6] the silk-shops, the town-hall, the booths belonging to the weavers and jewel-merchants, the wealthy woolen market, the shrine of the household gods. Everything glittered here. The buildings looked as if they were new—which, in a sense, they were. The earthquake of twelve years ago had brought down all the old structures and, since the citizens of Pompeii were **ambitious** to rival Naples and even Rome, they had seized the opportunity to rebuild the whole town. And they had done it all within a dozen years. There was scarcely a building that was older than Tito.

Identify Cause-and-Effect Relationships Why has the city of Pompeii been rebuilt so quickly?

Tito had heard a great deal about the earthquake, though being about a year old at the time, he could scarcely remember it. This particular quake had been a light one—as earthquakes go. The weaker houses had been shaken down, parts of the out-worn wall had been wrecked; but there was little loss of life, and the brilliant new Pompeii had taken the place of the old. No one knew what caused these earthquakes. Records showed they had happened in the neighborhood since the beginning of time. Sailors said that it was to teach the lazy city-folk a lesson and make them appreciate those who risked the dangers of the sea to bring them luxuries and protect their town from invaders. The priests said that the gods took

6 ***Bazaars*** are marketplaces in which a variety of goods is sold.

Vocabulary

ambitious (am bish′ əs) *adj.* full of a strong desire to succeed or to achieve something; eager this way of showing their anger to those who refused to worship properly and who failed to bring enough sacrifices to the altars and (though they didn't say it in so many words) presents to the priests. The tradesmen said that the foreign merchants had corrupted[7] the ground and it was no longer safe to traffic in[8] imported goods that came from strange places and carried a curse with them. Every one had a different explanation—and every one's explanation was louder and sillier than his neighbor's.

Identify Cause-and-Effect Relationships What do various groups think is the cause of the earthquakes? Why does each group have a different opinion?

They were talking about it this afternoon as Tito and Bimbo came out of the side-street into the public square. The Forum was the favorite promenade[9] for rich and poor. What with the priests arguing with the politicians, servants doing the day's shopping, tradesmen crying their wares, women displaying the latest fashions from Greece and Egypt, children playing hide-and-seek among the marble columns, knots of soldiers, sailors, peasants from the provinces—to say nothing of those who merely came to lounge and look on—the square was crowded to its last inch. His ears even more than his nose guided Tito to the place where the talk was loudest. It was in front of the Shrine of the Household Gods that, naturally enough, the householders were arguing.

"I tell you," rumbled a voice which Tito recognized as bathmaster Rufus's, "there won't be another earthquake in my lifetime or yours. There may be a tremble or two, but earthquakes, like lightnings, never strike twice in the same place."

"Do they not?" asked a thin voice Tito had never heard. It had a high, sharp ring to it and Tito knew it as the accent of a stranger. "How about the two towns of Sicily that have been ruined three times within fifteen years by the eruptions of Mount Etna? And were they not warned? And does that column of smoke above Vesuvius mean nothing?"

---

7 Something that is ***corrupted*** has been changed from good to bad.

8 The expression ***traffic in*** means "buy or sell."

9 A ***promenade*** is a public place or area for leisurely walking either for pleasure or display.

"That?" Tito could hear the grunt with which one question answered another. "That's always there. We use it for our weather-guide. When the smoke stands up straight we know we'll have fair weather; when it flattens out it's sure to be foggy; when it drifts to the east—"

"Yes, yes," cut in the edged voice. "I've heard about your mountain barometer.[10] But the column of smoke seems hundreds of feet higher than usual and it's thickening and spreading like a shadowy tree. They say in Naples—"

"Oh, Naples!" Tito knew this voice by the little squeak that went with it. It was Attilio, the **cameo**-cutter. "*They* talk while we suffer. Little help we got from them last time. Naples commits the crimes and Pompeii pays the price. It's become a proverb with us. Let them mind their own business."

"Yes," grumbled Rufus, "and others, too."

"Very well, my confident friends," responded the thin voice which now sounded curiously flat. "We also have a proverb—and it is this: Those who will not listen to men must be taught by the gods. I say no more. But I leave a last warning. Remember the holy ones. Look to your temples. And when the smoke-tree above Vesuvius grows to the shape of an umbrella-pine, look to your lives."

Tito could hear the air whistle as the speaker drew his **toga** about him and the quick shuffle of feet told him the stranger had gone.

"Now what," said the cameo-cutter, "did he mean by that?"

"I wonder," grunted Rufus, "I wonder."

Tito wondered, too. And Bimbo, his head at a thoughtful angle, looked as if he had been doing a heavy piece of **pondering**. By nightfall the argument had been forgotten. If the smoke had increased no one saw it in the dark.

10 A ***barometer*** is something that indicates change. The people of Pompeii used the mountain's smoke to predict the weather. Today, weather forecasters use an instrument called a barometer to measure changes in atmospheric pressure.

Vocabulary

pondering (pon′ dər ing) *v.* weighing something in the mind; considering or thinking carefully

Visual Vocabulary

A **cameo** is a piece of jewelry made from a precious or semiprecious stone or a shell that consists of different colored layers. The darker layer serves as a background for a figure, usually the head of a woman in profile that is carved in relief from the lighter layer.

Setting Setting includes not only time and place but also people's attitudes, beliefs, and values. What are some of the attitudes of the people of Pompeii?

Visual Vocabulary

The **toga** (tō′ gə) was the loose outer garment worn by men of the Roman Empire. It was a long cloth that was draped over the entire body, often covering the left arm and leaving the right arm exposed. The color and design of a man's toga indicated his social position.

Besides, it was Caesar's birthday and the town was in a holiday mood. Tito and Bimbo were among the merry-makers, dodging the charioteers who shouted at them. A dozen times they almost upset baskets of sweets and jars of Vesuvian wine, said to be as fiery as the streams inside the volcano, and a dozen times they were cursed and cuffed. But Tito never missed his footing. He was thankful for his keen[11] ears and quick instinct—most thankful of all for Bimbo.

They visited the uncovered theater and, though Tito could not see the faces of the actors, he could follow the play better than most of the audience, for their attention wandered—they were distracted by the scenery, the costumes, the by-play,[12] even by themselves—while Tito's whole attention was centered in what he heard. Then to the city-walls, where the people of Pompeii watched a mock naval-battle in which the city was attacked by the sea and saved after thousands of flaming arrows had been exchanged and countless colored torches had been burned. Though the thrill of flaring ships and lighted skies was lost to Tito, the shouts and cheers excited him as much as any and he cried out with the loudest of them.

The next morning there were *two* of the beloved raisin and sugar cakes for his breakfast. Bimbo was unusually active and thumped his bit of a tail until Tito was afraid he would wear it out. The boy could not imagine whether Bimbo was urging him to some sort of game or was trying to tell something. After a while, he ceased to notice Bimbo. He felt drowsy. Last night's late hours had tired him. Besides, there was a heavy mist in the air—no, a thick fog rather than a mist—a fog that got into his throat and scraped it and made him cough. He walked as far as the marine gate to get a breath of the sea. But the blanket of haze had spread all over the bay and even the salt air seemed smoky.

BQ BIG Question

What might account for Bimbo's unusual behavior?

---

11 ***Keen*** ears are highly sensitive.

12 ***By-play*** refers to actions or conversations that take place apart from the main action or conversation, especially in a theatrical production.

He went to bed before dusk and slept. But he did not sleep well. He had too many dreams—dreams of ships lurching[13] in the Forum, of losing his way in a screaming crowd, of armies marching across his chest, of being pulled over every rough pavement of Pompeii.

Identify Cause-and-Effect Relationships What may be the cause of Tito's strange dreams?

He woke early. Or, rather, he was pulled awake. Bimbo was doing the pulling. The dog had dragged Tito to his feet and was urging the boy along. Somewhere. Where, Tito did not know. His feet stumbled uncertainly; he was still half asleep. For a while he noticed nothing except the fact that it was hard to breathe. The air was hot. And heavy. So heavy that he could taste it. The air, it seemed, had turned to powder, a warm powder that stung his nostrils and burned his sightless eyes.

Then he began to hear sounds. Peculiar sounds. Like animals under the earth. Hissings and groanings and muffled cries that a dying creature might make **dislodging** the stones of his underground cave. There was no doubt of it now. The noises came from underneath. He not only heard them—he could feel them. The earth twitched; the twitching changed to an uneven shrugging of the soil. Then, as Bimbo half-pulled, half-coaxed him across, the ground jerked away from his feet and he was thrown against a stone-fountain.

Setting How has the city that Bimbo and Tito know so well changed since the previous day?

The water—hot water—splashing in his face revived him. He got to his feet, Bimbo steadying him, helping him on again. The noises grew louder; they came closer. The cries were even more animal-like than before, but now they came from human throats. A few people, quicker of foot and more hurried by fear, began to rush by. A family or two—then a section—then, it seemed, an army broken out of bounds. Tito, bewildered though he was, could recognize Rufus as he bellowed past him, like a water-buffalo gone mad. Time was lost in a nightmare.

Identify Cause-and-Effect Relationships Why are people rushing?

It was then the crashing began. First a sharp crackling,

13 ***Lurching*** ships move suddenly in an uneven manner or plunge forward or to the side.

Vocabulary

dislodging (dis loj′ ing) *v.* moving or forcing out of a place or position like a monstrous snapping of twigs; then a roar like the fall of a whole forest of trees; then an explosion that tore earth and sky. The heavens, though Tito could not see them, were shot through with continual flickerings of fire. Lightnings above were answered by thunders beneath. A house fell. Then another. By a miracle the two companions had escaped the dangerous side-streets and were in a more open space. It was the Forum. They rested here a while—how long he did not know.

Tito had no idea of the time of day. He could *feel* it was black—an unnatural blackness. Something inside—perhaps the lack of breakfast and lunch—told him it was past noon. But it didn't matter. Nothing seemed to matter. He was getting drowsy, too drowsy to walk. But walk he must. He knew it. And Bimbo knew it; the sharp tugs told him so. Nor was it a moment too soon. The sacred ground of the Forum was safe no longer. It was beginning to rock, then to pitch, then to split. As they stumbled out of the square, the earth wriggled like a caught snake and all the columns of the temple of Jupiter came down. It was the end of the world—or so it seemed. To walk was not enough now. They must run. Tito was too frightened to know what to do or where to go. He had lost all sense of direction. He started to go back to the inner gate; but Bimbo, straining his back to the last inch, almost pulled his clothes from him. What did the creature want? Had the dog gone mad?

Identify Cause-and-Effect Relationships What is making Tito feel so sleepy?

Then, suddenly, he understood. Bimbo was telling him the way out—urging him there. The sea-gate of course. The sea-gate—and then the sea. Far from falling buildings, heaving ground. He turned, Bimbo guiding him across open pits and dangerous pools of bubbling mud, away from buildings that had caught fire and were dropping their burning beams. Tito could no longer tell whether the noises were made by the shrieking sky or the agonized[14] people. He and Bimbo ran on—the only silent beings in a howling world.

Baker's stall offering fresh bread and cakes (detail). Wallpainting from the Casa del Panettiere, Pompeii.

14 People who are ***agonized*** are in great pain.

New dangers threatened. All Pompeii seemed to be thronging toward the marine-gate and, squeezing among the crowds, there was the chance of being trampled to death. But the chance had to be taken. It was growing harder and harder to breathe. What air there was choked him. It was all dust now—dust and pebbles, pebbles as large as beans. They fell on his head, his hands—pumice-stones[15] from the black heart of Vesuvius. The mountain was turning itself inside out. Tito remembered a phrase that the stranger had said in the Forum two days ago: "Those who will not listen to men must be taught by the gods." The people of Pompeii had refused to **heed** the warnings; they were being taught now—if it was not too late.

Setting What is going on in the city as the mountain erupts?

Suddenly it seemed too late for Tito. The red hot ashes blistered his skin, the stinging vapors tore his throat. He could not go on. He staggered toward a small tree at the side of the road and fell. In a moment Bimbo was beside him. He coaxed. But there was no answer. He licked Tito's hands, his feet, his face. The boy did not stir. Then Bimbo did the last thing he could—the last thing he wanted to do. He bit his comrade, bit him deep in the arm. With a cry of pain, Tito jumped to his feet, Bimbo after him. Tito was in despair, but Bimbo was determined. He drove the boy on, snapping at his heels, worrying his way through the crowd; barking, baring his teeth, heedless of kicks or falling stones. Sick with hunger, half-dead with fear and sulphur-fumes, Tito pounded on, pursued by Bimbo. How long he never knew. At last he staggered through the marine-gate and felt soft sand under him. Then Tito fainted. . . .

BQ BIG Question

Why do you think the dog who is such a devoted friend bites his companion?

Some one was dashing sea-water over him. Some one was carrying him toward a boat.

"Bimbo," he called. And then louder, "Bimbo!" But Bimbo had disappeared.

15 ***Pumice-stones*** are rocks formed by volcanic activity. They are light in weight and full of small openings.

Vocabulary

heed (hēd) *v.* pay careful attention to

Voices jarred against each other. "Hurry—hurry!" "To the boats!" "Can't you see the child's frightened and starving!" "He keeps calling for some one!" "Poor boy, he's out of his mind." "Here, child—take this!"

They tucked him in among them. The oar-locks creaked; the oars splashed; the boat rode over toppling waves. Tito was safe. But he wept continually.

"Bimbo!" he wailed. "Bimbo! Bimbo!"

He could not be comforted.

Eighteen hundred years passed. Scientists were restoring the ancient city; **excavators** were working their way through the stones and trash that had buried the entire town. Much had already been brought to light—statues, bronze instruments, bright **mosaics**, household articles; even delicate paintings had been preserved by the fall of ashes that had taken over two thousand lives. Columns were dug up and the Forum was beginning to emerge.

It was at a place where the ruins lay deepest that the Director paused.

"Come here," he called to his assistant. "I think we've discovered the remains of a building in good shape. Here are four huge millstones that were most likely turned by slaves or mules—and here is a whole wall standing with shelves inside it. Why! It must have been a bakery. And here's a curious thing. What do you think I found under this heap where the ashes were thickest? The skeleton of a dog!"

"Amazing!" gasped his assistant. "You'd think a dog would have had sense enough to run away at the time. And what is that flat thing he's holding between his teeth? It can't be a stone."

"No. It must have come from this bakery. You know it looks to me like some sort of cake hardened with the years. And, bless me, if those little black pebbles aren't raisins. A raisin-cake almost two thousand years old! I wonder what made him want it at such a moment?"

"I wonder," murmured the assistant.

Vocabulary

excavators (eks′ kə vā′ tərz) *n.* people who uncover something by digging

Visual Vocabulary

Mosaics (mō za′iks) are designs made of variously colored bits of glass or stone set in a surface such as plaster.

Identify Cause-and-Effect Relationships Why are the excavators surprised to find a dog's skeleton in the ruins of the bakery?

BQ BIG Question

Why might the dog have come to the bakery to get a raisin-cake in the middle of a disaster?

After You Read

Respond and Think Critically

1. In Pompeii, where does Tito live and with whom? Why? **[Recall]**
2. Summarize what you learned about life in Pompeii before the eruption of Mount Vesuvius. **[Summarize]**
3. In your own words, repeat the warning that the stranger with the thin voice gives to the people of Pompeii. **[Paraphrase]**
4. Reread the descriptions of Tito's walks and theater visits with Bimbo. What can you infer about Tito's character from these descriptions? **[Infer]**
5. Did you find the story's ending effective? Why or why not? **[Evaluate]**
6. **BQ BIG Question** What do Bimbo's actions throughout the story suggest about him? Judging by his actions and the character traits they suggest, do you think that Bimbo is a hero? Explain. **[Conclude]**

TIP

Inferring

Here are some tips to help you answer question 4. Remember that an inference is a logical guess made by using evidence in the story and what you know from experience.

- What does Tito notice as he and Bimbo walk through Pompeii?
- What does Tito notice at the theater?
- What traits must someone have to notice everything that Tito notices?

Keep track of your ideas about the **BIG Question** in your unit Foldable.

Connect to Social Studies

Ancient Rome

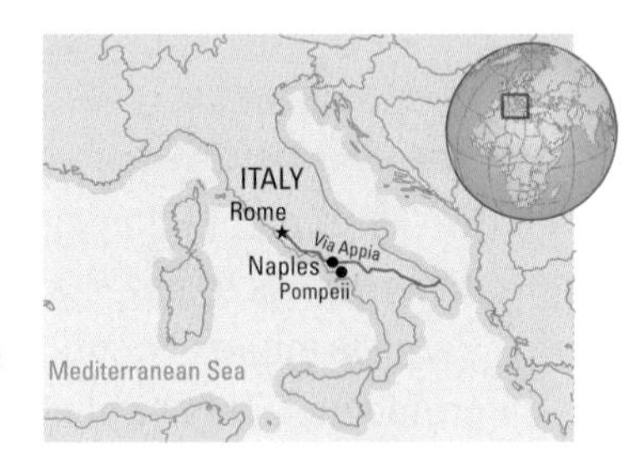

At the time Pompeii was destroyed by Mount Vesuvius, it was part of the Roman Empire. The vast empire stretched from Britain and Spain to northern Africa and parts of the Middle East. Rome was at its center.

The Roman Empire is known for its achievements in many areas, including architecture, transportation, engineering, military matters, and language. It is especially well-known for its systems of government.

As a young city, Rome had a government similar to a democracy—government by the people. Roman citizens met in large groups called assemblies to make decisions. Later, as Roman rule spread, the style of government changed. Rome became an empire, or a union of countries ruled by an emperor. At the time of Pompeii's destruction, Titus was the emperor of Rome.

Group Activity Discuss the following questions with your classmates.

1. How might the destruction of Pompeii have affected the Roman Empire?
2. How was life in Pompeii probably similar to life in Rome?

Literary Element Setting

1. Where and when does this story take place?
2. The author of this story describes Pompeii in great detail. How do you think he learned about Pompeii?
3. Name two concrete details the author provides about Pompeii. Name two sensory details the author provides about Pompeii.

Review: Narrator and Point of View

As you learned on page 11, the **narrator** is the person who tells a story. The relationship of the narrator to the story is called **point of view.**

If **first-person point of view** is used, the narrator is a character in the story and is referrred to as *I*. The reader sees everything through that character's eyes.

If **third-person point of view** is used, the narrator is outside the story. In **limited third-person point of view,** the narrator reveals the thoughts of only one character. In **omniscient third-person point of view,** the narrator reveals the thoughts of many or all of the characters and provides background information important to the story.

4. Who is the narrator of "The Dog of Pompeii"?
5. From what point of view is the story told?
6. Why might the author have decided to tell the story from this point of view?

Reading Skill Identify Cause-and-Effect Relationships

Standards Practice  ELA6R1e/ii

7. At the end of the story, Bimbo goes back to the bakery for a raisin-cake. What is the effect of his choice?
   A. He saves Tito.
   B. He dies in the bakery.
   C. He becomes lost in Pompeii.
   D. He wants to bring Tito some food.

Vocabulary Practice

On a separate sheet of paper, write the vocabulary word that correctly completes each sentence. If none of the words fits the sentence, write *none.*

ambitious **pondering**
dislodging **heed** **excavators**

1. Park rangers spent the morning ________ the hungry mother bear and her cubs from our well-stocked camper.
2. The ________ student studied every day hoping to get the highest score.
3. My little brothers are always ________ each other of cheating at cards.
4. Before the tennis match, the champion sat nervously ________ the strategy she would use to win.
5. The ________ weather caused traffic to move at a snail's pace.
6. The young fisherman did not ________ his mother's advice; he spent his whole allowance on minnows.
7. Excited archaeologists worked alongside ________ to uncover the bones of a rare dinosaur.

Academic Vocabulary

In "The Dog of Pompeii," Bimbo **persists** in his efforts to get Tito to the sea-gate. *Persists* means "continues despite problems." Think about a time when you continued to do something even though it was difficult. What did you do and what was the result of your hard work?

LOG ON **Literature** Online

Selection Resources For Selection Quizzes, eFlashcards, and Reading-Writing Connection activities, go to glencoe.com and enter QuickPass code GL17527u1.

Respond Through Writing

Research Report

Investigate Volcanoes In "The Dog of Pompeii," the eruption of Mount Vesuvius destroys the city of Pompeii. In a research report, investigate how volcanoes form, why they erupt, and what happens when they erupt.

Understand the Task A research report focuses on **facts,** rather than on your own **opinions** or ideas. You will need to gather facts that answer three important questions: *How do volcanoes form? Why do they erupt? What can happen during an eruption?* Decide on a thesis statement, or your main point.

Prewrite To start, focus on finding credible sources. A credible source, such as an encyclopedia, provides accurate information. Gather facts, details, examples, and explanations from these sources. Use a chart like the one below to organize your findings.

How do volcanoes form?	Why do volcanoes erupt?	What happens when volcanoes erupt?

Draft Before you begin writing, make an outline of your report. You may want to write an introduction, a paragraph about each question in your chart, and then a conclusion.

Revise After you have written your first draft, read it aloud. Is your writing clear? Does each sentence give important information about volcanoes? Does each paragraph flow easily into the next? At the end of your paper, list all the sources of information that you used in preparing your report on a bibliography page. See the Writing Handbook at the back of this book for more guidelines on writing a research report and preparing a bibliography.

Edit and Proofread Proofread your paper, correcting any errors in spelling, grammar, and punctuation. See the Word Bank in the side column for a list of words that you can use in your writing.

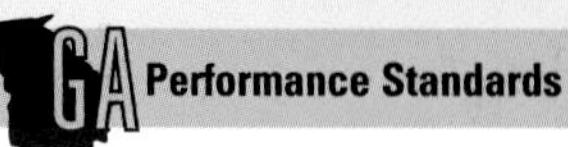

Performance Standards

For page 43

ELA6W3b Use research and technology to support writing. Include research information in different types of products.

Word Bank

The following words may be useful in your research report:

consequence

detect

dramatic

factor

precede

trigger

For pages 44–45

ELA6R1e/iii For literary texts, identify and analyze the elements of setting, characterization, plot, and the resolution of the conflict of a story or play: antagonist/protagonist.

Genre Focus: Short Fiction

Fiction is writing that is about people and situations the author invents. **Short fiction** usually tells about one major event and has only a few characters. You can usually read a **short story** in a single sitting. A short story has the same elements as a novel: setting, characters, plot, point of view, and theme.

Short fiction includes stories about realistic events, as well as folktales, fairy tales, legends, myths, fables, and tall tales.

Literary Elements

Setting **Setting** is the time and place of the action in a literary work. Setting can also include customs, values, and beliefs of a place or a time. Authors describe the setting by using details. **Concrete details** provide information; **sensory details** bring the setting to life by appealing to the five senses.

Characters **Characters** are the actors in a story. They can be people, animals, robots, or whatever the author chooses. The main character is called the **protagonist.** The methods an author uses to develop the personality of a character are called **characterization.** In **direct characterization,** the story's narrator tells you about a character. In **indirect characterization,** the author reveals a character's personality through the character's words and actions and what other characters think and say about that character.

Plot The **plot** is the basic structure of a piece of fiction. The plot begins with the **exposition,** which introduces the setting, characters, and situation. The **rising action** adds complications to the story's **conflicts,** or problems, leading to the story's **climax,** or point of greatest interest or suspense. The **falling action** is the result of the climax, and the **resolution** is the final outcome.

Point of View **Point of view** is the perspective from which a piece of fiction is told. The person telling the story is the **narrator**. In **first-person point of view,** the narrator is a character in the story. In a story with a **limited third-person point of view,** the narrator is outside the story and reveals the thoughts of only one character. In **omniscient point of view,** the narrator is also outside the story but can reveal the thoughts of several characters.

Theme The **theme** is the message about life the reader takes from a piece of fiction. A theme may be stated directly or it may be **implied**—suggested by what the characters learn or by what their experiences reveal.

TRY IT

Use one of the graphic organizers on the next page to examine the literary elements of a piece of short fiction in this unit.

Characteristics of the Genre

To better understand the literary elements in short fiction and how authors use literary elements to create effects and achieve their purposes, look at the examples in the characterization chart and plot diagram below.

Characterization Chart for Mr. Silver from "The Scribe"

Detail from the Story	Personality Trait It Reveals	Direct or Indirect Characterization
The narrator calls Mr. Silver "the mean old man."	meanness	direct (narrator's statement)
Mr. Silver hollers "SPELL it!" at a customer.	lack of respect	indirect (character's words)
Mr. Silver sighs, rolls his eyes, and bangs on a form.	impatience	indirect (character's actions)

Plot Diagram for "The Dog of Pompeii"

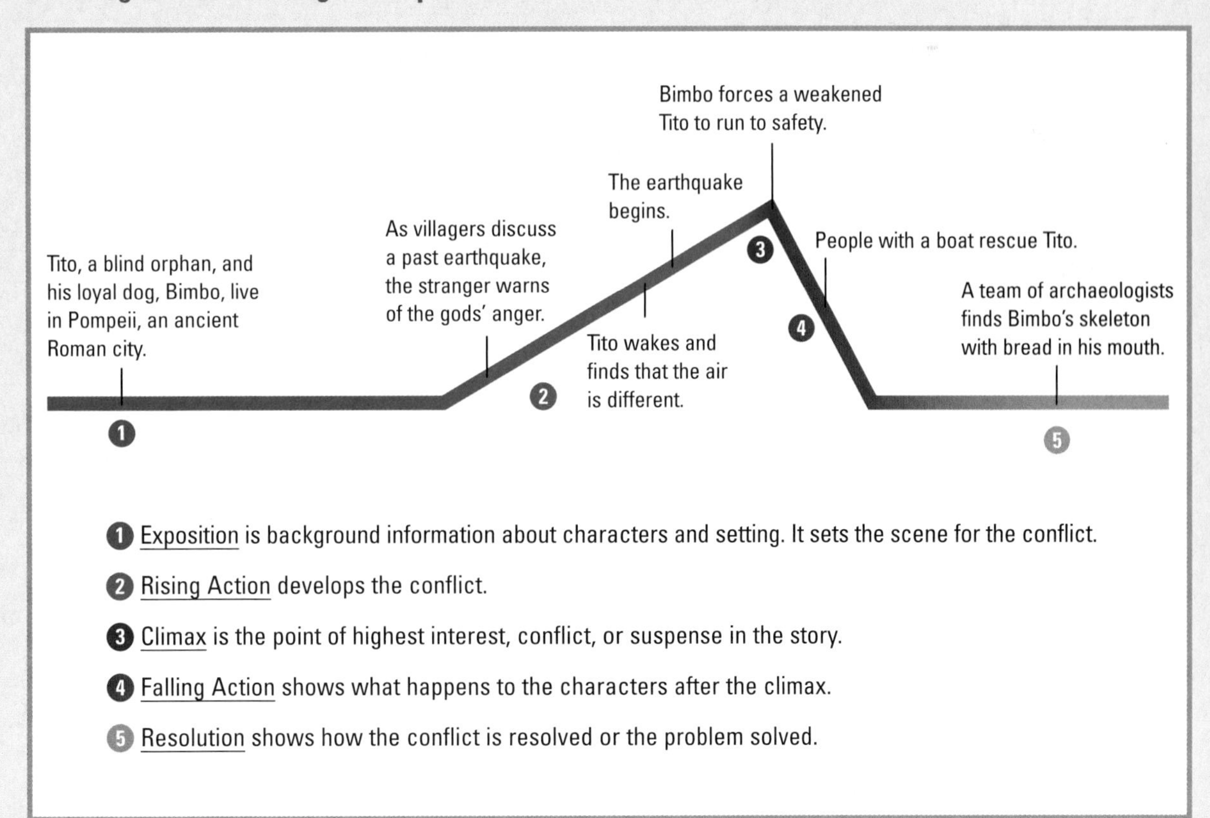

Bimbo forces a weakened Tito to run to safety.
The earthquake begins.
As villagers discuss a past earthquake, the stranger warns of the gods' anger.
People with a boat rescue Tito.
Tito, a blind orphan, and his loyal dog, Bimbo, live in Pompeii, an ancient Roman city.
A team of archaeologists finds Bimbo's skeleton with bread in his mouth.
Tito wakes and finds that the air is different.
1
2
3
4
5

1. Exposition is background information about characters and setting. It sets the scene for the conflict.
2. Rising Action develops the conflict.
3. Climax is the point of highest interest, conflict, or suspense in the story.
4. Falling Action shows what happens to the characters after the climax.
5. Resolution shows how the conflict is resolved or the problem solved.

Before You Read

What Exactly Is a Hero?

Connect to the Essay

Think about someone you would call a hero.

Partner Talk With a partner, talk about why the person is a hero. Discuss qualities or actions that you think make someone heroic.

Build Background

In this essay, T. A. Barron talks about some real-life heroes from the past and present with whom you may be unfamiliar.

- Winston Churchill was the prime minister of the United Kingdom during World War II. Joining forces with the United States and the Soviet Union, Churchill led the fight against Nazi Germany.
- Jane Goodall is a researcher who has spent her life studying chimpanzees in Africa. She has fought to protect chimpanzees in the wild.

Vocabulary

essential (i sen′ shəl) *adj.* basic; fundamental (p. 49). *Protein is an essential part of a healthful diet.*

prominent (prom′ ə nənt) *adj.* well-known or important; notable (p. 49). *The police chief and mayor are prominent people in our town.*

economic (ek′ ə nom′ ik) *adj.* relating to money matters (p. 49). *The large inheritance ended the family's economic problems.*

prevail (pri vāl′) *v.* to be victorious; triumph (p. 50). *The coach told the track star that she would prevail at the 100-yard dash.*

conscious (kon′ shəs) *adj.* deliberate; intentional (p. 50). *He made a conscious effort to be friendly to the new neighbor.*

Meet T. A. Barron

"A life—whether seamstress or poet, farmer or king—is measured not by its length, but by the worth of its deeds, and the power of its dreams."

—T. A. Barron

Businessman Turned Writer T. A. Barron was a businessman in New York before he moved back to his home state of Colorado to become a writer and an environmentalist. He believes that everyone has the potential to become a hero by serving others and protecting the planet. Barron even created a national award for children who perform extraordinary public service.

Literary Works Barron's award-winning books include *The Great Tree of Avalon* trilogy and *The Lost Years of Merlin* series.

T. A. Barron was born in 1952.

LOG ON **Literature** Online

Author Search For more about T. A. Barron, go to glencoe.com and enter QuickPass code GL17527u1.

Set Purposes for Reading

BQ BIG Question

As you read this essay, ask yourself, what does the author say a hero is—and is not?

Literary Element Text Structure

Text structure is the particular order or pattern a writer uses to present ideas. **Comparing and contrasting** is one way a writer can structure text. Comparing and contrasting means telling the ways that people, things, or ideas are alike and different.

Writers can use signal words and phrases, such as *similarly, like,* and *also* to show how two things are alike or *in contrast, but,* and *however* to point out differences.

As you read, ask yourself, how does the author use text structure to present his views about what makes a person a hero?

Reading Skill Determine Main Idea and Supporting Details

The **main idea** is the most important idea in a paragraph or passage. The ideas that support or tell more about the main idea are called **supporting details.** Sometimes an author clearly states the main idea in a topic sentence. Other times an author will suggest the main idea by providing a variety of clues.

Determining the main idea and supporting details helps you understand the most important idea in a paragraph or passage.

To determine main idea and supporting details, ask yourself,

- What is each sentence about?
- Are any sentences more important than others?
- What main idea do the supporting details point out?

As you read, note the main idea and details. You may find it helpful to use a graphic organizer like the one below.

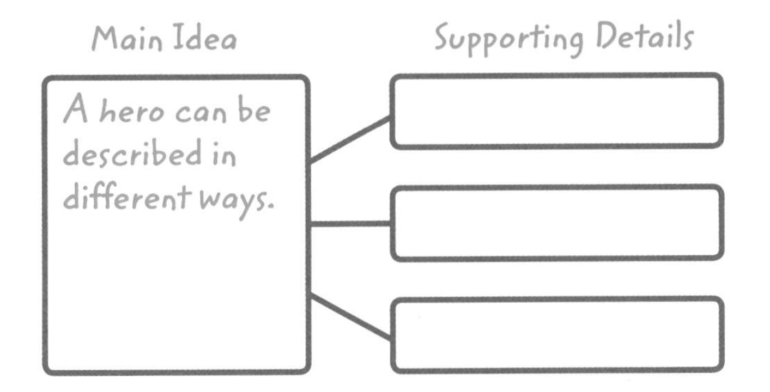

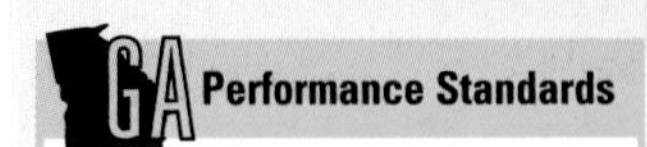

GA Performance Standards

For pages 46–51

ELA6R1c For informational texts, apply knowledge of common organizational structures and patterns.

TRY IT

Determine Main Idea and Supporting Details Think about a story most of your classmates would know, such as a common fairy tale, legend, or myth. Discuss the main idea. What supporting details point out or tell more about the main idea? Share ideas with your classmates.

What Exactly Is a Hero?

T. A. Barron

Just like life, a hike is a journey—full of ups and downs, long climbs, deep doubts, painful losses, real triumphs, and plenty of surprises. We may make some good friends on the way, but much of the time we walk alone. And as with our own lives, we can't see very far down the trail. We can only keep walking, and do our best to prepare ourselves for whatever twists and turns lie ahead.

Now, to survive that sort of journey, maybe even with grace, we need some **essential** qualities. Courage, for one. Perseverance. And wisdom. The very same qualities it takes to be a hero.

What exactly is a hero? What does the word really mean?

Determine Main Idea and Supporting Details How can you tell this is the essay's main idea?

Let's start with what a hero does *not* mean: a celebrity. In our society, we often confuse the two, but they are really very different. As different as the two kinds of sage—the person who has grown immensely wise over time, and the sweet but short-lived herb that decorates the prairies.

A hero is someone who, faced with a tough challenge, reaches down inside and finds the courage, strength, and wisdom to triumph. That person could be a girl or a boy; a **prominent** leader or the person next door; a member of any race, culture, or **economic** group. But in every case, it's someone whose special qualities of character make a real difference.

A celebrity, by contrast, is just someone who has won our attention—whether for fifteen seconds or fifteen years. The celebrity's fame could have come from entertaining us, serving us . . . or even harming us. Now, don't get me wrong. Sometimes heroes can become so well known that they also become celebrities. Abraham Lincoln was, in his day, both at once. So was Winston Churchill over fifty years ago. And so is Jane Goodall today. But the two ideas are still quite different. For a hero, what counts is character. For a celebrity, what counts is fame.

Text Structure How would you explain the differences the author points out? How does the parallel structure of the sentences help show the contrast?

Vocabulary

essential (i sen′ shəl) *adj.* basic; fundamental

prominent (prom′ ə nənt) *adj.* well-known or important; notable

economic (ek′ ə nom′ ik) *adj.* relating to money matters

Here's another way to think about it: A hero does something truly important, regardless of whether anyone ever notices. But a celebrity is all about being noticed—being a famous face or name or number on a **jersey.** One of them, you could say, is a real meal cooking on the campfire. The other is a flash in the pan.

Heroism, then, is about *character*. The qualities a person carries down inside. Or, to put this in hiking terms: The most important piece of equipment that any hiker brings on the trail isn't a backpack, a sleeping bag, or even a map. No, it's the hiker himself or herself! That person's head, heart, and soul. In just the same way, heroes **prevail** not because of the tools or weapons they carry outside—but because of what they carry *inside.*

Lao-tzu, the Chinese philosopher, pointed out long ago that even the greatest journey begins with a single step. That is true, and well worth remembering. But frankly, I would have said it differently: Every journey begins with a single *person*. A hiker—and whatever inner qualities he or she brings to the trail.

Just how are those inner qualities revealed? Through our choices. For every choice matters, whether it's big or small, **conscious** or unconscious, repeated or rare. And every choice is an expression of who we are.

Our choices, then, are like footsteps. Each one takes us farther down the trail, affecting the route we take, the pace we set, and the deeds we do along the way. And each one is shaped by two primary forces: our own inner selves and the trail itself—the landscape of life. So our inner qualities shape our choices, our choices become our footsteps, and our footsteps become our journey.

Visual Vocabulary

A **jersey** is a knitted shirt an athlete wears as part of a uniform.

Text Structure How are the author's words different from Lao-tzu's famous saying?

BQ BIG Question

How does this ending connect to the author's main idea about what makes a hero?

Vocabulary

prevail (pri vāl′) *v.* to be victorious; triumph

conscious (kon′shəs) *adj.* deliberate; intentional

After You Read

Respond and Think Critically

1. Why do people sometimes confuse celebrities with heroes? **[Summarize]**
2. In your own words, briefly state what the author says a hero is. **[Paraphrase]**
3. What does the author mean by saying a hero is like "a real meal cooking on the campfire"? **[Interpret]**
4. **Literary Element** **Text Structure** Does the author effectively use comparison and contrast to explore what a hero is? Give examples to support your answer. **[Analyze]**
5. **Reading Skill** **Determine Main Idea and Supporting Details** Look at the graphic organizer you made about the main idea and supporting details. Which details are most important to understanding the main idea? **[Analyze]**
6. **BQ** **BIG Question** What have you learned from this essay about what a hero really is? **[Evaluate]**

Writing

Write a Letter Write the author a letter and tell him why you agree or disagree with his ideas about heroes. Remember to be persuasive and to support your opinions with facts, examples, or other evidence.

Vocabulary Practice

Match each boldface vocabulary word with a word from the right that has the same meaning. Two of the words to the right will not have matches. Then write a sentence using each vocabulary word or draw or find a picture that represents the word.

1. **essential**	a. financial	f. significant
2. **prominent**	b. triumph	g. deliberate
3. **economic**	c. lovely	
4. **prevail**	d. basic	
5. **conscious**	e. pressure	

Example:
prominent

Sentence: The woman who owns the construction company is a prominent member of the community.

TIP

Paraphrasing
When you paraphrase, you restate someone else's ideas in your own words. Here are some tips to help you paraphrase. Use these tips to answer question 2.

- Locate sentences in the essay that define a hero.
- Note the key points about a hero.
- Restate important ideas that would apply to the entire essay.

Keep track of your ideas about the **BIG Question** in your unit Foldable.

Literature Online

Selection Resources
For Selection Quizzes, eFlashcards, and Reading-Writing Connection activities, go to glencoe.com and enter QuickPass code GL17527u1.

Before You Read

The King of Mazy May

Connect to the Story

Think about a time when someone was being treated badly and you had an opportunity to help.

Partner Talk With a partner, discuss whether you would help someone if risks were involved. Would you get involved if it was the right thing to do?

Build Background

In 1896 gold was discovered in the Klondike, a remote wilderness area of northwestern Canada, near Alaska. Thousands set out to strike it rich. Perhaps they would have stayed home if they had known the following:

- They would risk their lives to carry tons of needed equipment across steep, frozen mountain passes.
- Local people had already claimed most of the gold.
- The gold that remained was ten feet below permanently frozen ground.

Most fortune-seekers found only hardship—if they were lucky enough to survive!

Vocabulary

endured (en doord′) *v.* underwent hardship without giving up; put up with (p. 55). *To finish the marathon, Maria endured heat, aching muscles, and exhaustion.*

industrious (in dus′ trē əs) *adj.* hardworking (p. 56). *Erin, an industrious student, had the highest score on the test.*

adjoining (ə joi′ ning) *adj.* located next to; adjacent (p. 56). *We heard voices coming from the adjoining room.*

evidently (ev′ ə dənt lē) *adv.* clearly, apparently, obviously (p. 57). *Jon was evidently excited because he couldn't stop fidgeting.*

floundering (floun′ dər ing) *v.* to move with stumbling motions; struggle awkwardly or clumsily (p. 63). *The horses were floundering in the deep mud.*

Meet Jack London

"You can't wait for inspiration. You have to go after it with a club."

—Jack London

An Adventurous Life Jack London left school at an early age to become a sailor. He traveled to Japan but returned to study for a term at the University of California before living the rough life of a gold prospector in Canada's Klondike region. He never struck gold, but his travel experiences gave him a "gold mine" of ideas for stories.

Literary Works London's adventure novels include *The Call of the Wild, White Fang,* and *The Sea Wolf.*

Jack London was born in 1876 and died in 1916.

LOG ON  Literature Online

Author Search For more about Jack London, go to glencoe.com and enter QuickPass code GL17527u1.

Set Purposes for Reading

BQ BIG Question

As you read, ask yourself, is it possible for a person of any age to be a hero?

Literary Element Plot

The **plot** is the sequence of events in a story. The plot starts with the **exposition,** which introduces the characters, setting, and situation.

The **rising action** adds complications to the story's problems, or **conflicts,** and leads to the **climax,** which is the point of greatest interest or suspense. The **falling action** shows what happens as a result of the climax, and the **resolution** presents the final outcome.

Recognizing the parts of a plot can help you follow the order of events in a story and make sense of what you read.

As you read, think about how each new problem faced by the main character adds to the suspense of the story.

Reading Strategy Visualize

To **visualize** is to picture a scene that is described in a story.

Visualizing brings a story to life. It is a useful and effective way to understand and remember what you read.

To visualize parts of the story,

- pay attention to descriptive words that the writer uses to appeal to senses of sight, hearing, touch, taste, and smell
- use your imagination to form mental images of events and places in the story

What pictures do the details in the story create in your mind? As you read, you may find it helpful to use a graphic organizer like the one below.

Descriptive Detail	What I See in My Mind
ice-jams on one of the mightiest of rivers	thick blocks of ice over rushing water

GA Performance Standards

For pages 52–67

ELA6R1e/i For literary texts, identify and analyze the elements of setting, characterization, plot, and the resolution of the conflict of a story or play: internal/external conflicts.

TRY IT

Visualize Think about a time when a friend described every detail about something, such as a new puppy—his fuzzy, brown coat, wet nose, stubby tail, and patch of white fur over his eye. Did you form a picture of the puppy in your mind?

Shooting the white-horse rapids en route to the Klondike gold fields, 1898. Hand-colored halftone.

The King of Mazy May

Jack London

Walt Masters is not a very large boy, but there is manliness in his make-up, and he himself, although he does not know a great deal that most boys know, knows much that other boys do not know.

He has never seen a train of cars or an elevator in his life, and for that matter, he has never once looked upon a cornfield, a plow, a cow, or even a chicken. He has never had a pair of shoes on his feet, or gone to a picnic or a party, or talked to a girl. But he has seen the sun at midnight, watched the ice-jams on one of the mightiest of rivers, and played beneath the northern lights,[1] the one white child in thousands of square miles of frozen wilderness.

Visualize How does this description help you imagine the setting of the story?

1 The ***northern lights*** are streams and arches of moving colored light. They are seen at times in the night sky over northern regions of Earth. The light comes from atoms speeding through Earth's magnetic field. When such lights appear in the southern hemisphere, they are called the "southern lights."

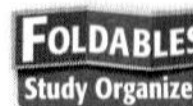

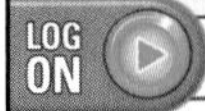

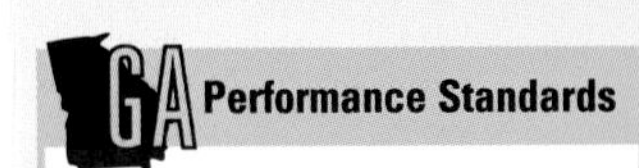

Walt has walked all the fourteen years of his life in sun-tanned, moose-hide **moccasins,** and he can go to the Indian camps and "talk big" with the men, and trade calico[2] and beads with them for their precious furs. He can make bread without baking-powder, yeast or hops, shoot a moose at three hundred yards, and drive the wild wolf-dogs fifty miles a day on the packed trail.

Last of all, he has a good heart, and is not afraid of the darkness and loneliness, of man or beast or thing. His father is a good man, strong and brave, and Walt is growing up like him.

Walt was born a thousand miles or so down the Yukon, in a trading-post below the Ramparts. After his mother died, his father and he came on up the river, step by step, from camp to camp, till now they are settled down on the Mazy May Creek in the Klondike[3] country. Last year they and several others had spent much toil and time on the Mazy May, and **endured** great hardships; the creek, in turn, was just beginning to show up its richness and to reward them for their heavy labor. But with the news of their discoveries, strange men began to come and go through the short days and long nights, and many unjust things they did to the men who had worked so long upon the creek.

Si Hartman had gone away on a moose-hunt, to return and find new stakes driven and his claim jumped.[4] George Lukens and his brother had lost their claims in a like manner, having delayed too long on the way to Dawson to record them. In short, it was an old story, and

Visual Vocabulary

Moccasins are shoes with a sole and no heel, usually made from one piece of leather.

Plot What are your first impressions of Walt?

Plot What sets the newcomers apart from the men who live on the Mazy May?

2 ***Calico*** is a type of cotton cloth with a pattern on it. The word comes from Calicut, the town in India where the cloth was first made.

3 The Yukon River flows from Canada's Yukon Territory through Alaska to the Bering Sea. It was a major route to the Klondike during the gold rush of 1897–1898. The ***Klondike*** is the name of both a river and a gold-mining region in the Yukon Territory of Canada near the Alaskan border.

4 A ***claim*** was a piece of land that a prospector claimed to be his or her own. The prospector drove wooden ***stakes*** into the ground to mark its boundaries, and then recorded the claim with the gold commissioner in the city of ***Dawson***. Someone who ***jumped a claim*** took over and recorded a claim for land that had been staked out, but not yet recorded, by someone else.

Vocabulary

endured (en doord′) *v.* underwent hardship without giving up; put up with quite a number of the earnest, **industrious** prospectors[5] had suffered similar losses.

But Walt Masters's father had recorded his claim at the start, so Walt had nothing to fear, now that his father had gone on a short trip up the White River prospecting for quartz. Walt was well able to stay by himself in the cabin, cook his three meals a day, and look after things. Not only did he look after his father's claim, but he had agreed to keep an eye on the **adjoining** one of Loren Hall, who had started for Dawson to record it.

Loren Hall was an old man, and he had no dogs, so he had to travel very slowly. After he had been gone some time, word came up the river that he had broken through the ice at Rosebud Creek, and frozen his feet so badly that he would not be able to travel for a couple of weeks. Then Walt Masters received the news that old Loren was nearly all right again, and about to move on afoot for Dawson, as fast as a weakened man could.

Visualize What do you see in your mind when you imagine Loren Hall's accident?

Walt was worried, however; the claim was liable to be jumped at any moment because of this delay, and a fresh stampede[6] had started in on the Mazy May. He did not like the looks of the newcomers, and one day, when five of them came by with crack[7] dog-teams and the lightest of camping outfits, he could see that they were prepared to make speed, and resolved to keep an eye on them. So he locked up the cabin and followed them, being at the same time careful to remain hidden.

Plot What is the new complication to the plot?

He had not watched them long before he was sure that they were professional stampeders, bent[8] on jumping all the claims in sight. Walt crept along the snow at the rim of the creek and saw them change many stakes, destroy old ones, and set up new ones.

---

5 ***Prospectors*** are people who explore an area for mineral or oil deposits.

6 Usually a ***stampede*** is a sudden rush of animals. In this story, the word refers to the rush of people searching for gold in the Klondike.

7 Here, ***crack*** means "excellent, first-rate."

8 Here, ***bent*** means "determined" or "intending."

Vocabulary

industrious (in dus′ trē əs) *adj.* hardworking

adjoining (ə joi′ ning) *adj.* located next to; adjacent

In the afternoon, with Walt always trailing on their heels, they came back down the creek, unharnessed their dogs, and went into camp within two claims of his cabin. When he saw them make preparations to cook, he hurried home to get something to eat himself, and then hurried back. He crept so close that he could hear them talking quite plainly, and by pushing the underbrush aside he could catch occasional glimpses of them. They had finished eating and were smoking around the fire.

Plot How might this fact change the plot?

"The creek is all right, boys," a large, black-bearded man, evidently the leader said, "and I think the best thing we can do is to pull out tonight. The dogs can follow the trail; besides, it's going to be moonlight. What say you?"

"But it's going to be beastly cold," objected one of the party. "It's forty below zero now."

"An'sure, can't ye keep warm by jumpin' off the sleds an' runnin' after the dogs?" cried an Irishman. "An' who wouldn't? The creek as rich as a United States mint! Faith, it's an ilegant chanst[9] to be gettin' a run fer yer money! An' if ye don't run, it's mebbe you'll not get the money at all, at all."

"That's it," said the leader. "If we can get to Dawson and record, we're rich men; and there is no telling who's been sneaking along in our tracks, watching us, and perhaps now off to give the alarm. The thing for us to do is to rest the dogs a bit, and then hit the trail as hard as we can. What do you say?"

Evidently the men had agreed with their leader, for Walt Masters could hear nothing but the rattle of the tin dishes which were being washed. Peering out cautiously, he could see the leader studying a piece of paper. Walt knew what it was at a glance—a list of all the unrecorded claims on Mazy May. Any man could get these lists by applying to the gold commissioner at Dawson.

Visualize To which sense does this image appeal?

9 ***Ilegant chanst*** is the character's way of saying "elegant chance," meaning "excellent opportunity."

Vocabulary

evidently (ev′ ə dənt lē) *adv.* clearly, apparently, obviously

"Thirty-two," the leader said, lifting his face to the men.

"Thirty-two isn't recorded, and this is thirty-three. Come on; let's take a look at it. I saw somebody had been working on it when we came up this morning."

Three of the men went with him, leaving one man to remain in camp. Walt crept carefully after them till they came to Loren Hall's shaft. One of the men went down and built a fire on the bottom to thaw out the frozen gravel, while the others built another fire on the dump and melted water in a couple of gold-pans. This they poured into a piece of canvas stretched between two logs, used by Loren Hall in which to wash his gold.

View the Art What do you think the man is weighing? How important is the measurement?

Miners in Dawson City Bank, 1898. S. Begg. Hand-colored halftone.

In a short time a couple of buckets of dirt were sent up by the man in the shaft, and Walt could see the others grouped anxiously about their leader as he proceeded to wash it. When this was finished, they stared at the broad streak of black sand and yellow gold-grains on the bottom of the pan, and one of them called excitedly for the man who had remained in camp to come. Loren Hall had struck it rich, and his claim was not yet recorded. It was plain that they were going to jump it.

Visualize Can you picture what the claim-jumpers are looking at?

Walt lay in the snow, thinking rapidly. He was only a boy, but in the face of the threatened injustice against old lame Loren Hall he felt that he must do something. He waited and watched, with his mind made up, till he saw the men begin to square up new stakes. Then he crawled away till out of hearing, and broke into a run for the camp of the stampeders. Walt's father had taken their own dogs with him prospecting, and the boy knew how impossible it was for him to undertake the seventy miles to Dawson without the aid of dogs.

BQ BIG Question

What heroic qualities does Walt have?

Gaining the camp, he picked out, with an experienced eye, the easiest running sled and started to harness up the stampeders' dogs. There were three teams of six each, and from these he chose ten of the best. Realizing how necessary it was to have a good head-dog, he strove to discover a leader amongst them; but he had little time in which to do it, for he could hear the voices of the returning men. By the time the team was in shape and everything ready, the claim-jumpers came into sight in an open place not more than a hundred yards from the trail, which ran down the bed of the creek. They cried out to him, but he gave no heed, grabbing up one of their fur sleeping-robes which lay loosely in the snow, and leaping upon the sled.

Plot How does this increase the tension of the plot?

"Mush! Hi! Mush on!"[10] he cried to the animals, snapping the keen-lashed whip among them.

---

10 Dog-sled drivers say "Mush!" to order their dogs to begin pulling or to move faster. Early French fur traders in Canada used the command "Marchons!" (meaning "March! Go!"), but English and American dogsledders mispronounced it, saying **"Mush on!"**

The dogs sprang against the yoke-straps,[11] and the sled jerked under way so suddenly as to almost throw him off. Then it curved into the creek, poising perilously[12] on one runner. He was almost breathless with suspense, when it finally righted with a bound and sprang ahead again. The creek bank was high and he could not see, although he could hear the cries of the men and knew they were running to cut him off. He did not dare to think what would happen if they caught him; he only clung to the sled, his heart beating wildly, and watched the snow-rim of the bank above him.

Suddenly, over this snow-rim came the flying body of the Irishman, who had leaped straight for the sled in a desperate attempt to capture it; but he was an instant too late. Striking on the very rear of it, he was thrown from his feet, backward, into the snow. Yet, with the quickness of a cat, he had clutched the end of the sled with one hand, turned over, and was dragging behind on his breast, swearing at the boy and threatening all kinds of terrible things if he did not stop the dogs; but Walt cracked him sharply across the knuckles with the butt of the dog-whip till he let go.

Plot What does this tell you about the claim-jumpers and their determination?

It was eight miles from Walt's claim to the Yukon—eight very crooked miles, for the creek wound back and forth like a snake, "tying knots in itself," as George Lukens said. And because it was so crooked, the dogs could not get up their best speed, while the sled ground heavily on its side against the curves, now to the right, now to the left.

Travelers who had come up and down the Mazy May on foot, with packs on their backs, had declined to go around all the bends, and instead had made short cuts across the narrow necks of creek bottom. Two of his pursuers had gone back to harness the remaining dogs, but the others took advantage of these short cuts, running on foot, and before he knew it they had almost overtaken him.

"Halt!" they cried after him. "Stop, or we'll shoot!"

---

11 ***Yoke-straps*** are part of the dog's harness.

12 ***Perilously*** means "dangerously; at risk of injury."

Klondike Gold Rush, 1904. Artist Unknown.

But Walt only yelled the harder at the dogs, and dashed round the bend with a couple of revolver bullets singing after him. At the next bend they had drawn up closer still, and the bullets struck uncomfortably near to him; but at this point the Mazy May straightened out and ran for half a mile as the crow flies. Here the dogs stretched out in their long wolf-swing, and the stampeders, quickly winded, slowed down and waited for their own sled to come up.

Looking over his shoulder, Walt reasoned that they had not given up the chase for good, and that they would soon be after him again. So he wrapped the fur robe about him to shut out the stinging air, and lay flat on the empty sled, encouraging the dogs, as he well knew how.

BQ BIG Question
What does Walt's reasoning reveal about him?

At last, twisting abruptly between two river islands, he came upon the mighty Yukon sweeping grandly to the north. He could not see from bank to bank, and in the quick-falling twilight it loomed[13] a great white sea of frozen stillness. There was not a sound, save the breathing

Visualize What image helps you picture the Yukon?

13 Something that ***loomed*** came into view in a way that seemed large and threatening.

of the dogs, and the churn of the steel-shod sled.

No snow had fallen for several weeks, and the traffic had packed the main-river trail till it was hard and glassy as glare ice. Over this the sled flew along, and the dogs kept the trail fairly well, although Walt quickly discovered that he had made a mistake in choosing the leader. As they were driven in single file, without reins, he had to guide them by his voice, and it was evident the head-dog had never learned the meaning of "gee" and "haw."[14] He hugged the inside of the curves too closely, often forcing his comrades behind him into the soft snow, while several times he thus capsized the sled.

Visualize What helps you picture the trail?

There was no wind, but the speed at which he traveled created a bitter blast, and with the thermometer down to forty below, this bit through fur and flesh to the very bones. Aware that if he remained constantly upon the sled he would freeze to death, and knowing the practice of Arctic travelers, Walt shortened up one of the lashing-thongs, and whenever he felt chilled, seized hold of it, jumped off, and ran behind till warmth was restored. Then he would

Plot How important is the environment to the plot?

On the Klondike, 1890s. Edward Roper.

View the Art Compare the men in this painting with the stampeders.

14 These are commands used to direct the dogs. ***Gee*** means "to the right" and ***haw*** means "to the left."

climb on and rest till the process had to be repeated.

Looking back he could see the sled of his pursuers, drawn by eight dogs, rising and falling over the ice hummocks[15] like a boat in a seaway. The Irishman and the black-bearded leader were with it, taking turns in running and riding.

Night fell, and in the blackness of the first hour or so, Walt toiled desperately with his dogs. On account of the poor lead-dog, they were constantly **floundering** off the beaten track into the soft snow, and the sled was as often riding on its side or top as it was in the proper way. This work and strain tried his strength sorely. Had he not been in such haste he could have avoided much of it, but he feared the stampeders would creep up in the darkness and overtake him. However, he could hear them occasionally yelling to their dogs, and knew from the sounds that they were coming up very slowly.

Plot What effect might this have on Walt?

When the moon rose he was off Sixty Mile, and Dawson was only fifty miles away. He was almost exhausted, and breathed a sigh of relief as he climbed on the sled again. Looking back, he saw his enemies had crawled up within four hundred yards. At this space they remained, a black speck of motion on the white river-breast. Strive as they would, they could not shorten this distance, and strive as he would he could not increase it.

Visualize Why does London describe the men as "a black speck of motion"?

He had now discovered the proper lead-dog, and he knew he could easily run away from them if he could only change the bad leader for the good one. But this was impossible, for a moment's delay, at the speed they were running, would bring the men behind upon him.

When he got off the mouth of Rosebud Creek, just as he was topping a rise, the ping of a bullet on the ice beside him, and the report[16] of a gun, told him that they were this time shooting at him with a rifle. And from then on, as he

---

15 ***Hummocks*** are ridges or hills on ice.

16 A gun's ***report*** is the sound it makes when fired.

Vocabulary

floundering (floun′ dər ing) *v.* to move with stumbling motions; struggle awkwardly or clumsily

Klondike Gold Rush, 1898. Edward Roper.

cleared the summit of each ice-jam, he stretched flat on the leaping sled till the rifle-shot from the rear warned him that he was safe till the next ice-jam.

Now it is very hard to lie on a moving sled, jumping and plunging and yawing[17] like a boat before the wind, and to shoot through the deceiving moonlight at an object four hundred yards away on another moving sled performing equally wild antics.[18] So it is not to be wondered at that the black-bearded leader did not hit him.

Plot Why do the shots miss Walt?

After several hours of this, during which, perhaps, a score[19] of bullets had struck about him, their ammunition began to give out and their fire slackened. They took greater care, and only whipped a shot at him at the most favorable opportunities. He was also beginning to leave them behind, the distance slowly increasing to six hundred yards.

Lifting clear on the crest of a great jam off Indian River, Walt Masters met his first accident. A bullet sang past his ears, and struck the bad lead-dog.

The poor brute plunged in a heap, with the rest of the team on top of him.

17 When a sled is ***yawing,*** it is turning accidentally from a straight course.

18 ***Antics*** are odd, silly, or comical actions.

19 A ***score*** is twenty.

Like a flash, Walt was by the leader. Cutting the traces with his hunting knife, he dragged the dying animal to one side and straightened out the team.

He glanced back. The other sled was coming up like an express-train. With half the dogs still over their traces, he cried, "Mush on!" and leaped upon the sled just as the pursuing team dashed abreast of him.

The Irishman was just preparing to spring for him,—they were so sure they had him that they did not shoot,—when Walt turned fiercely upon them with his whip.

He struck at their faces, and men must save their faces with their hands. So there was no shooting just then. Before they could recover from the hot rain of blows, Walt reached out from his sled, catching their wheel-dog[20] by the fore legs in mid-spring, and throwing him heavily. This brought the whole team into a snarl, capsizing the sled and tangling his enemies up beautifully.

Away Walt flew, the runners of his sled fairly screaming as they bounded over the frozen surface. And what had seemed an accident proved to be a blessing in disguise. The proper lead-dog was now to the fore, and he stretched low to the trail and whined with joy as he jerked his comrades along.

Visualize What picture do the words "runners of his sled fairly screaming" help you create in your mind?

By the time he reached Ainslie's Creek, seventeen miles from Dawson, Walt had left his pursuers, a tiny speck, far behind. At Monte Cristo Island he could no longer see them. And at Swede Creek, just as daylight was silvering the pines, he ran plump into the camp of old Loren Hall.

Plot How would you characterize the action at this point compared to what has come before?

Almost as quick as it takes to tell it, Loren had his sleeping furs rolled up, and had joined Walt on the sled. They permitted the dogs to travel more slowly, as there was no sign of the chase in the rear, and just as they pulled up at the gold commissioner's office in Dawson, Walt, who had kept his eyes open to the last, fell asleep.

And because of what Walt Masters did on this night, the men of the Yukon have become very proud of him, and always speak of him now as the King of Mazy May.

BQ BIG Question

How has Walt, a young boy, become a hero to the men who live on the Mazy May?

20 The ***wheel-dog*** is the dog nearest the front end of the sled. Dogsledders borrowed the term from horse teams, in which the wheel horse is the horse nearest the front wheels of a wagon or carriage.

After You Read

Respond and Think Critically

1. What are the five stampeders trying to do? **[Recall]**
2. Briefly state how Walt protects his neighbor's claim. **[Summarize]**
3. Walt's father asked him to keep an eye on his neighbor's claim. Why do you think his father trusted him with this task? **[Interpret]**
4. Does Walt feel justified in taking the sled and the dogs and using violence? Do you think his actions are justified? Explain. **[Analyze]**
5. Jack London once declared, "The proper function of man is to live, not exist." Explain how Walt carries out the author's idea before he even becomes a man. **[Conclude]**
6. **BQ** **BIG Question** Think about the word *king* and why Walt is eventually called "the King of Mazy May." What qualities make him heroic to the people who live on the Mazy May? Do you think Walt is heroic? Support your answer with evidence from the story. **[Evaluate]**

TIP

Concluding
Remember, when you conclude, you form ideas about what you are reading. You make a decision about what you're reading.

- Think about the difference in meaning between the terms *to live* and *to exist.*
- Compare Walt's actions with London's statement.
- Think about how Walt's actions might be different if he had only been "existing."

Keep track of your ideas about the **BIG Question** in your unit Foldable.

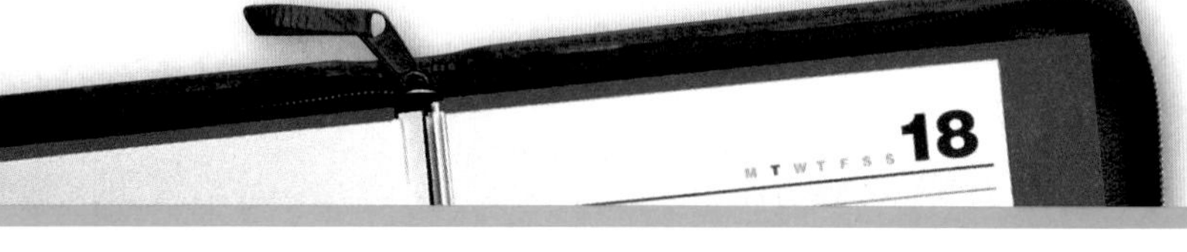

Daily Life and Culture

Gold Rushes in the Nineteenth Century

In the late nineteenth century, gold attracted people to far-off places. Prospectors gathered in camps that quickly turned into boomtowns. These towns grew so quickly that they didn't have many laws or rules. Life there could be violent. Some greedy people would stop at nothing to get gold.

Some boomtowns gradually turned into cities. But many others became ghost towns—settlements where the buildings stand empty and no people remain. Gold often turned out to be scarce after the first discovery. Prospectors simply drifted away from boomtowns after seeing their dreams of wealth disappear.

When gold was discovered in the Klondike, about 100,000 people headed north, hoping to strike it rich. Several "panics" had shaken the U.S. economy. Many people were desperate for money. But by 1904 most of the surface gold had been mined and the gold boom had ended.

Group Activity

1. How does the lack of order in boomtowns help you understand the actions of the stampeders? Do you think their actions were justified? Why or why not?
2. Which source gives you a better understanding of the hardships miners in the Klondike had to endure: this passage or Jack London's story? Explain your answer.

Literary Element Plot

Standards Practice  ELA6R1e/i

1. Which sentence gives the best description of how Walt deals with difficult situations?
   A. He gets discouraged and gives up easily.
   B. He gets angry and resentful.
   C. He relies on courage and determination.
   D. He relies on others for help.

Review: Setting

As you learned on page 29, **setting** is the time and place in which the events of a story occur. Writers show the setting through concrete and sensory details. Setting often affects plot and characters. For example, many of Walt's actions are possible and make sense because the story takes place during the Klondike Gold Rush in the late 1800s.

Standards Practice  ELA6R1e/ii

2. Which word best describes the setting of this story?
   A. familiar
   B. mythical
   C. comfortable
   D. hostile

Reading Strategy Visualize

3. Draw a picture of one of the scenes in the story. Do any parts of it look like your classmates' pictures?
4. Look back at the chart of details you kept as you read the story. Which details most helped you visualize the setting, characters, and events? Why?

Vocabulary Practice

Match each boldface vocabulary word with a word from the right column that has the same meaning. Two of the words in the right column will not have matches. Then use each vocabulary word in a sentence or draw or find a picture that represents the word.

1. **endured**	a. hardworking
2. **industrious**	b. distant
3. **adjoining**	c. obviously
4. **evidently**	d. next door
5. **floundering**	e. tough
	f. survived
	g. stumbling

Example: endured

Sentence: The mountain climber endured freezing cold and bitter wind in order to reach the top.

Academic Vocabulary

Walt shows that he is as **reliable** as an adult. In the preceding sentence, *reliable* means "dependable and responsible." Think about someone you know who is reliable. What makes this person reliable? How do the person's actions reflect this trait?

Literature Online

Selection Resources For Selection Quizzes, eFlashcards, and Reading-Writing Connection activities, go to glencoe.com and enter QuickPass code GL17527u1.

 Respond Through Writing

Summary

Report Story Events In "The King of Mazy May," Walt goes on a terrifying journey to help his neighbor. In a few paragraphs, write a report that tells about the main events. Include Loren Hall's situation, the problems Walt faces along the way, the actions Walt takes, and the outcome.

Understand the Task A **report** is one way to communicate knowledge. You will want to **summarize,** or only retell the main events of the story, in your report. Write your report using the literary present tense.

Prewrite Start by identifying the story's main events. Arrange them in order on a time line like the one below.

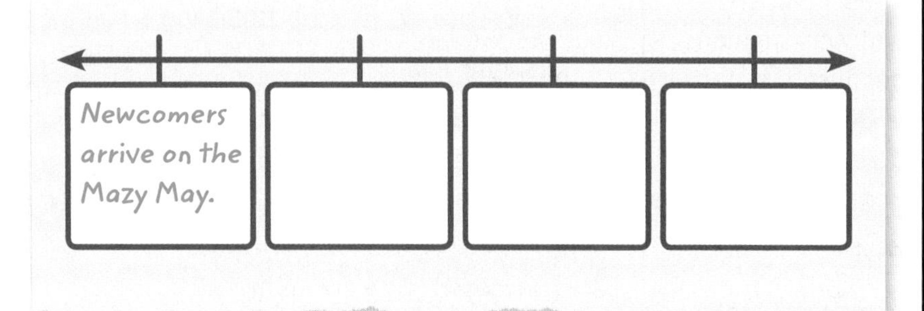

Draft Make a plan before you write. How will you divide your report into paragraphs? If you write three paragraphs, you might want to devote one paragraph to the events in the beginning of the story, one to the middle, and one to the end. After you figure out your plan, show your paragraph divisions on your time line.

Revise After you have written your first draft, read it to make sure you have included all the important events. Did you begin with a clear thesis statement or purpose? Are events in the correct order? Did you leave out any key information? Are any parts unclear? Could someone who has not read the story understand your report? Did you summarize in the present tense? Revise your text as necessary.

Edit and Proofread Proofread your paper, correcting any errors in spelling, grammar, and punctuation. Review the Grammar Tip in the side column for information on using the literary present tense.

Performance Standards

For page 68

ELA6W1c Use traditional structures for conveying information (e.g., chronological order, cause and effect, similarity and difference, and posing and answering a question).

Grammar Tip

Verb Tense

Verb tense shows the time at which the action takes place. Remember that switching from one verb tense to another can be confusing for the reader. When you summarize fictional story events, use the **literary present tense.** This means you write as if the events are happening now. For example, you might begin a summary like the following:

At the beginning of "The King of Mazy May," Walt spies on five newcomers, suspecting they are professional stampeders. Look through the story to find other examples of story events that you would summarize using the literary present tense.

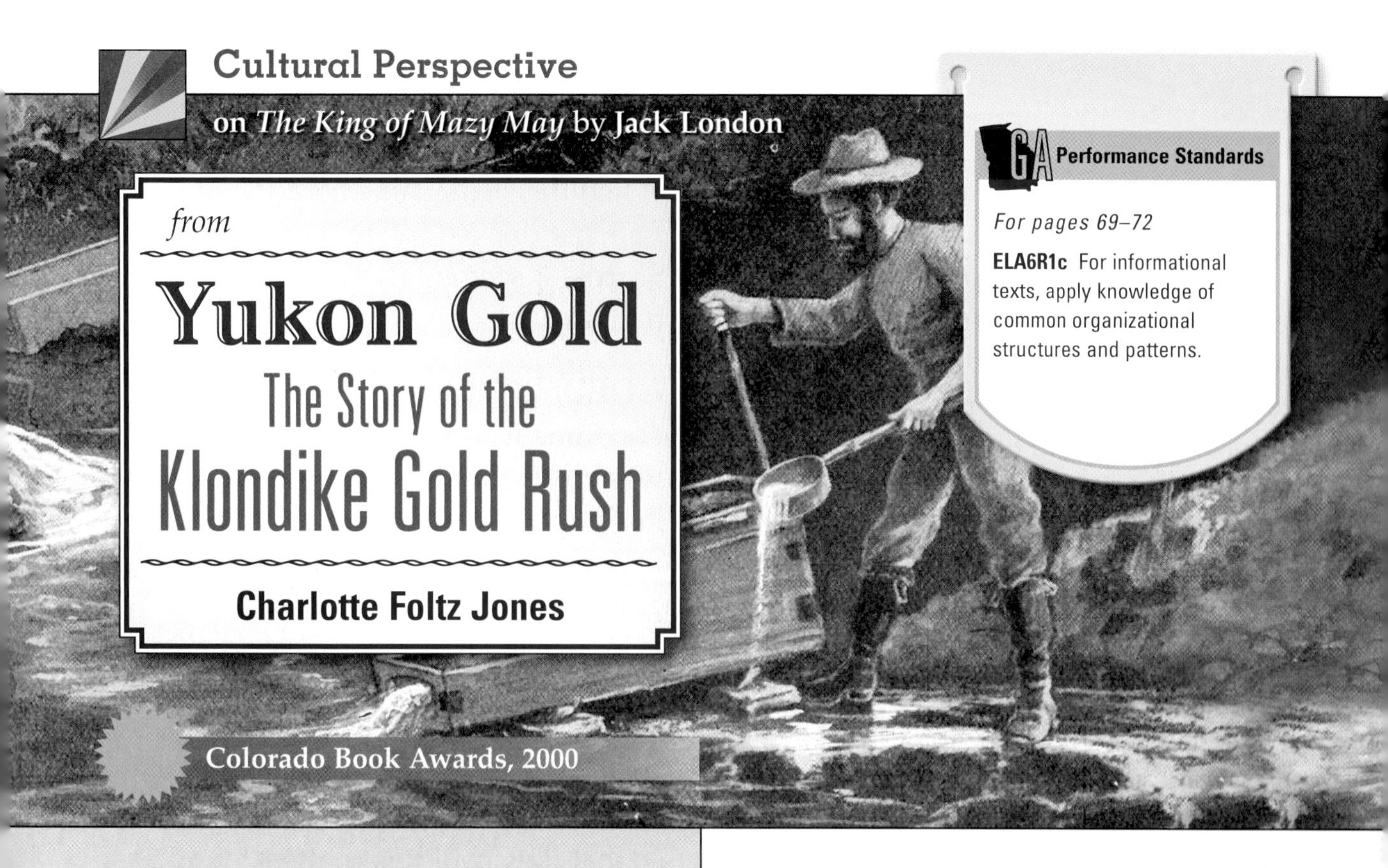

Set a Purpose for Reading

Read to learn what effect the discovery of gold had on people during the Klondike Gold Rush.

Build Background

During a depression in 1893, thousands of people in the United States were without jobs or money. Dreams of finding gold lured people to the Yukon. Most of them knew nothing about the risks.

Reading Skill Analyze Text Structure

Text structure includes the order in which an author presents ideas. An author may tell a story in chronological order, or the order in which events happen. As you read from *Yukon Gold: The Story of the Klondike Gold Rush,* use a time line like the one below to show events in the order in which they occur.

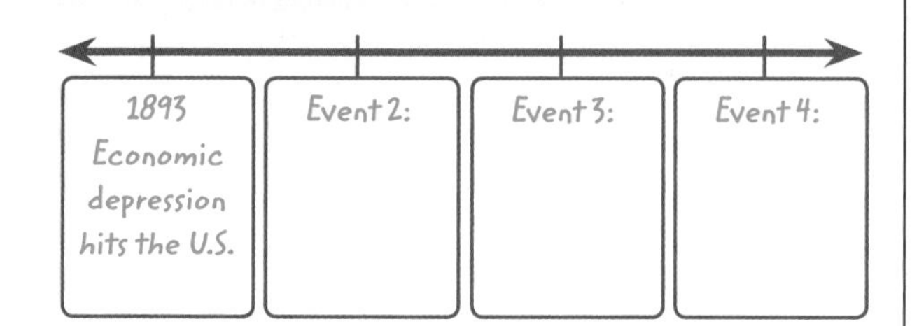

AMERICA NEEDED A MIRACLE

Gold!

The word is electrifying. Even in a world where most of us see gold only in jewelry or as a decoration on our mother's dishes, *gold* still stirs excitement and visions of great wealth.

But a century ago, gold was magical. It could turn a poor person into a millionaire, and there were many poor people.

The economy of the United States fell into a depression in 1893. In this "Panic of 1893," 156 railroads claimed bankruptcy, 15,000 businesses failed, and 642 banks closed, wiping out the savings of thousands of people. One quarter of the country's industries stopped production. Four million people out of a population of 65 million could not get jobs.

A man felt lucky if he could get work for a day or two.

Today there are welfare programs for unemployed people, but one hundred years ago there was no help. There were few jobs and thousands of people had no money to buy food or pay the rent. Stores closed because customers could not afford to buy their goods.

People lost hope. Some people starved to death. Many committed suicide. Others went crazy.

With so much hardship, people dreamed of instant wealth and would do anything to get rich in a hurry. The vision of thousands of dollars in gold was captivating.

When people can't find jobs, they get restless. They believe there is opportunity "somewhere else" and all they have to do is get "there." So when stories of gold spread, it was easy for people to catch "gold fever."

How to reach the

KLONDIKE.

COLUMBIA NAVIGATION AND TRADING COMPANY.

S. S. City of Columbia (1900 tons) will depart from the Old Dominion Line Pier 26, North River,

Wednesday, Dec. 1st, for

ST. MICHAEL,

connecting with Company's river steamers for

DAWSON CITY.

Fare to Dawson City, including 1000 pounds of baggage, $680.00 up, according to accommodation. Passengers desiring to meet the ship at San Francisco or Seattle will be provided with transportation by rail to either point at same rate.

For passage tickets and further information apply to the agents,

RAYMOND & WHITCOMB,
31 East Fourteenth Street, New York.
296 Washington St., Boston, Mass.
1005 Chestnut St., Philadelphia, Pa.
95 Adams St., Chicago, Ill.

The people who joined the rush for gold had been waiting for a miracle. When the steamships *Excelsior* and *Portland* docked in San Francisco and Seattle, it seemed that their miracle had arrived.

GOLD FEVER

For some it was greed. For some it was adventure. For many it was their last hope.

People of all professions had gold fever.

In Seattle there were so many people in the streets that the streetcars couldn't get through. They would not have gotten through anyway: Half of the streetcar motormen had quit their jobs so that they could go to the Klondike.

Catholic nuns went. University football players went. The prizefighter Montana Kid went. So did farmers, clerks, cowboys, bakers, bankers, doctors, seamen, students, preachers, entertainers, lawyers, dentists, businessmen, and members of the Salvation Army.

Twelve of Seattle's police officers resigned within four days. Most of Tacoma's fire department resigned. Stores closed since their clerks had walked out—heading for the goldfields. Jurors in San Francisco threatened to quit if a trial was too long. They, too, wanted to leave for the goldfields!

The day after the *Portland's* arrival, the steamer *Al-ki* left Seattle. It is amazing that it was underway less than twenty-four hours after the gold rush began.

A prospector pans for gold in Northern California. Hand-tinted photograph, circa 1890.

By July 27, fifteen hundred people had left Seattle for the Klondike. Nine more ships were in the harbor, loaded and ready to sail.

During the middle week of August alone, 2,800 people sailed from Seattle for the Klondike. By the first of September, 9,000 people and 36,000 tons of equipment and supplies had left from Seattle.

Newspapers ran articles of advice, information, and news of good fortune. But there were also warnings coming out of the North. Too many people were pouring in and there would not be enough food during the coming winter.

People in Dawson began to panic. Six steamboats carrying supplies were headed for Dawson, but they got stranded on sandbars when the river became too shallow to navigate. Captain John J. Healy felt certain *his* ship would arrive with food and supplies. He was partly right. His vessel came into port in Dawson before the freeze-up. But when it was unloaded, it was carrying only whiskey! Someone downriver had decided there was not enough profit in food and sent whiskey instead.

The residents of Dawson were warned they must leave. Many tried to get downriver, but the river froze and trapped the steamers in the ice before they could get to St. Michael. Some residents went through the mountains, but most of them lost fingers and toes to frostbite. Meanwhile, people from all over Canada, the United States, and the world were rushing to get to the Yukon for their share of the gold.

During the winter of 1897–98, a million people made plans to go to the Klondike. Approximately 100,000 stampeders actually started out. Forty thousand reached the Yukon goldfields by the summer of 1898. The rest either got a short distance and returned home or reached Seattle and discovered they could not afford to outfit themselves and pay for ship passage.

Most of the stampeders were men, but women also went to the Klondike. Many went with their husbands, but others went for the adventure. Some wives set out while their husbands stayed home. Some women went to support their families. Some caught gold fever and went strictly for the riches. Some went as newspaper reporters.

Most of the people who set out for the Klondike had led sedentary lives and were not in condition for the difficult trip that lay ahead of them. They were not in physical shape to get a ton of supplies two thousand miles north. They knew little about packing, pack animals, tenting, wilderness survival, enduring arctic weather, building boats, or navigation.

Most hardly knew where the Yukon or the Klondike was.

Some trusted experts to give them advice, but often those "experts" were giving advice strictly for their own profit.

The majority of the men who headed for the Klondike had only a vague idea of the hardships they were about to face. They believed they would pick gold nuggets out of a stream with little effort, and some even took sacks along in which to carry home the gold. Each was convinced he would return a wealthy man.

Respond and Think Critically

1. Write a brief summary of the main events in this excerpt before you answer the following questions. For help with writing a summary, see page 68. **[Summarize]**
2. Who left to search for gold in the Klondike? Why do you think so many people in various professions left? **[Recall and Interpret]**
3. Do you think so many people would have participated in the Klondike Gold Rush if the economy had been better at home? Explain why or why not. **[Infer]**
4. **Text to Text** The excerpt explains gold fever in this way: "For some it was greed. For some it was adventure. For many it was their last hope." Which reason best reflects the motivation of the stampeders in "The King of Mazy May"? Explain your answer. **[Connect]**
5. **Reading Skill** **Analyze Text Structure** Find some examples of time-order words, dates, and months in the excerpt. How can these words help you understand the sequence of events?
6. **BQ** **BIG Question** Do you think the people who joined the rush for gold had heroic qualities? Why or why not?

Part 2

Clever Solutions

'Raleigh unclasped the rich cloak from his shoulders and laid it over the damp earth,' illustration from 'Heroes & Heroines of English History.' Alice S. Hoffman Browne, Gordon Frederick Browne. Color lithograph. Private Collection.

BQ BIG Question What Makes a Hero?

Soldier, explorer, nobleman, and poet—Sir Walter Raleigh was one of the most colorful heroes in English history. The picture shows a famous story in which Sir Walter Raleigh cleverly solves a problem. How does he help Queen Elizabeth walk across a puddle without getting her royal feet wet? What clever solutions to problems have you observed?

Before You Read

All Stories Are Anansi's

Connect to the Folktale

Think of a time when you played a trick on someone, or when someone played a trick on you.

Quickwrite Freewrite for a few minutes about the trick. What happened? How did it feel to trick someone or to be tricked?

Build Background

Heroes in myths are often brave and strong and may even have supernatural powers. However, many cultures have folktales about a different kind of hero—a trickster. A trickster may be physically weak, but is able to use humor and cunning to get what he or she wants.

Anansi is a favorite character of many African and Caribbean folktales. He is usually a spider or a spiderlike man. Anansi is a trickster who tries to make everything turn out well—for himself. His tricks are surprising, clever, and fun to read.

Tricksters have common characteristics across cultures:

- The trickster is usually a smaller, weaker character who must use intelligence to outsmart a more powerful opponent.
- Clever tricksters get themselves out of trouble, but in many stories they get right back into it.

Vocabulary

yearned (yurnd) *v.* felt a strong and deep desire (p. 76). *I yearned for a cold drink on a particularly hot summer day.*

dispute (dis pūt′) *n.* difference of opinion; argument or debate (p. 77). *My sister and I flipped a coin to settle our dispute over which movie to watch.*

accustomed (ə kus′ təmd) *adj.* being in the habit or custom (p. 78). *The campers are accustomed to sleeping in tents.*

acknowledge (ak nol′ ij) *v.* to recognize the authority, validity, or claims of (p. 79). *Kit and Kim acknowledge that their mother was protecting them when she had them wear helmets to ride their bicycles.*

Meet Harold Courlander

"Folktales have no special meaning for me unless they convey human values."

—Harold Courlander

A World Traveler Like all folktales, this story was passed around by word of mouth long before it was written. This version is a retelling by Harold Courlander. Courlander spent his life collecting folktales, especially from Africa. He was most interested in tales that showed the values of the groups from whom the stories came.

Literary Works Harold Courlander published collections of folktales and also wrote books about the tales he collected and the people who told them. "All Stories Are Anansi's" was published in 1957.

Harold Courlander was born in 1908 and died in 1996.

Literature Online

Author Search For more about Harold Courlander, go to glencoe.com and enter QuickPass code GL17527u1.

Set Purposes for Reading

BQ BIG Question

As you read, ask yourself, does Anansi have the qualities of a real-life hero? How does he use his brains to outsmart his opponents?

Literary Element Theme

A story's **theme** is the message about life the author wants to share. Many works have a theme that is not stated but is gradually revealed through plot, character, setting, or point of view. Folktales from different cultures often have similar themes, or **universal themes.** To gather clues about the theme, notice the events of the plot and pay attention to what the characters do, say, or learn.

As you read, think about what the theme may be. Ask yourself, what is the author's message about trickery and trickster heroes?

Reading Strategy Make Predictions About Plot

When you **make predictions,** you make educated guesses about story events and outcomes.

Making predictions before and during your reading can increase your understanding of the story. Knowing the structure of a trickster tale can help you make predictions. A trickster tale usually has a weaker character who wants something, uses trickery to get it, and is rewarded or punished for his trickery in the end. As you read, gather new information, determine if your prediction is correct, and adjust it as needed.

To make predictions about plot, pay attention to

- what you already know about trickster tales
- the story's events and what the characters do and say
- how earlier predictions may or may not change

You may find it helpful to use a graphic organizer like the one below. As you read, complete a similar graphic organizer for each major part in the story—beginning, middle, and right before the end.

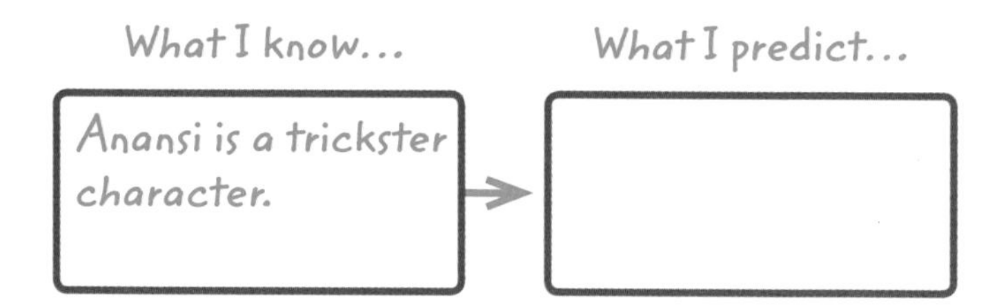

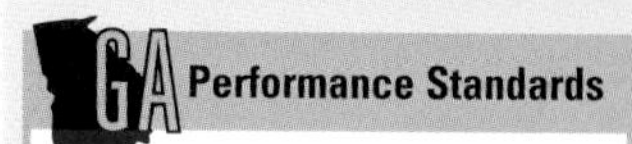

Performance Standards

For pages 74–80

ELA6R1d For literary texts, apply knowledge of the concept that theme refers to the message about life and the world that the author wants us to understand whether implied or stated.

TRY IT

Make Predictions Make up the first part of a story and ask a partner to predict the outcome. For example, *Roger came in soaking wet, so. . . . Last year our soccer team lost every game, so. . . . My dad is happy with my report card, so. . . .* Then switch roles. Remember that more than one prediction might make sense.

All Stories Are Anansi's

Harold Courlander

In the beginning, all tales and stories belonged to Nyame,[1] the Sky God. But Kwaku Anansi, the spider, **yearned** to be the owner of all the stories known in the world, and he went to Nyame and offered to buy them.

The Sky God said: "I am willing to sell the stories, but the price is high. Many people have come to me offering to buy, but the price was too high for them. Rich and powerful families have not been able to pay. Do you think you can do it?"

Anansi replied to the Sky God: "I can do it. What is the price?"

"My price is three things," the Sky God said. "I must first have Mmoboro, the hornets. I must then have Onini, the great python. I must then have Osebo, the leopard. For these things I will sell you the right to tell all stories."

Anansi said: "I will bring them."

He went home and made his plans. He first cut a gourd from a vine and made a small hole in it. He took a large

Mask (Okorashi Oma), wood & pigment 10 1/2 × 6 3/4 × 4 in. Harn Museum of Art Collection, University of Florida, gift of Rod McGalliard, 1990.13.103.

Make Predictions About Plot What could the price be, if not money or influence?

1 ***Nyame*** is pronounced (en yä′ mā).

Vocabulary

yearned (yurnd) *v.* felt a strong and deep desire

calabash and filled it with water. He went to the tree where the hornets lived. He poured some of the water over himself, so that he was dripping. He threw some water over the hornets, so that they too were dripping. Then he put the calabash on his head, as though to protect himself from a storm, and called out to the hornets: "Are you foolish people? Why do you stay in the rain that is falling?"

The hornets answered: "Where shall we go?"

"Go here, in this dry gourd," Anansi told them.

The hornets thanked him and flew into the gourd through the small hole. When the last of them had entered, Anansi plugged the hole with a ball of grass, saying: "Oh, yes, but you are really foolish people!"

He took his gourd full of hornets to Nyame, the Sky God. The Sky God accepted them. He said: "There are two more things."

Anansi returned to the forest and cut a long bamboo pole and some strong vines. Then he walked toward the house of Onini, the python, talking to himself. He said: "My wife is stupid. I say he is longer and stronger. My wife says he is shorter and weaker. I give him more respect. She gives him less respect. Is she right or am I right? I am right, he is longer. I am right, he is stronger."

When Onini, the python, heard Anansi talking to himself, he said: "Why are you arguing this way with yourself?"

The spider replied: "Ah, I have had a **dispute** with my wife. She says you are shorter and weaker than this bamboo pole. I say you are longer and stronger."

Onini said: "It's useless and silly to argue when you can find out the truth. Bring the pole and we will measure."

So Anansi laid the pole on the ground, and the python came and stretched himself out beside it.

"You seem a little short," Anansi said.

The python stretched further.

"A little more," Anansi said.

"I can stretch no more," Onini said.

"When you stretch at one end, you get shorter at the

Vocabulary

dispute (dis pūt′) *n.* difference of opinion; argument or debate

Visual Vocabulary

A **calabash** (kal′ ə bash′) is a gourd, or a dried fruit of a tropical plant.

Theme What does Anansi do that makes the hornets seem foolish?

Make Predictions About Plot How might Anansi use the pole to trick Onini?

other end," Anansi said. "Let me tie you at the front so you don't slip."

He tied Onini's head to the pole. Then he went to the other end and tied the tail to the pole. He wrapped the vine all around Onini, until the python couldn't move.

"Onini," Anansi said, "it turns out that my wife was right and I was wrong. You are shorter than the pole and weaker. My opinion wasn't as good as my wife's. But you were even more foolish than I, and you are now my prisoner."

Anansi carried the python to Nyame, the Sky God, who said: "There is one thing more."

Osebo, the leopard, was next. Anansi went into the forest and dug a deep pit where the leopard was **accustomed** to walk. He covered it with small branches and leaves and put dust on it, so that it was impossible to tell where the pit was. Anansi went away and hid. When Osebo came prowling in the black of night, he stepped into the trap Anansi had prepared and fell to the bottom. Anansi heard the sound of the leopard falling, and he said: "Ah, Osebo, you are half-foolish!" When morning came, Anansi went to the pit and saw the leopard there.

"Osebo," he asked, "what are you doing in this hole?"

"I have fallen into a trap," Osebo said. "Help me out."

"I would gladly help you," Anansi said. "But I'm sure that if I bring you out, I will have no thanks for it. You will get hungry, and later on you will be wanting to eat me and my children."

"I swear it won't happen!" Osebo said.

"Very well. Since you swear it, I will take you out," Anansi said.

He bent a tall green tree toward the ground, so that its top was over the pit, and he tied it that way. Then he tied a rope to the top of the tree and dropped the other end of it into the pit.

"Tie this to your tail," he said.

Osebo tied the rope to his tail.

Make Predictions About Plot How do you know Anansi is not done with his trick? How might Anansi complete his trick on Osebo?

Theme Why does Anansi tell Osebo this? How will it benefit Anansi?

Vocabulary

accustomed (ə kus′ təmd) *adj.* being in the habit or custom

"Is it well tied?" Anansi asked.

"Yes, it is well tied," the leopard said.

"In that case," Anansi said, "you are not merely half-foolish, you are all-foolish."

And he took his knife and cut the other rope, the one that held the tree bowed to the ground. The tree straightened up with a snap, pulling Osebo out of the hole. He hung in the air head downward, twisting and turning. And while he hung this way, Anansi killed him with his weapons.

Then he took the body of the leopard and carried it to Nyame, the Sky God, saying: "Here is the third thing. Now I have paid the price."

Nyame said to him: "Kwaku Anansi, great warriors and chiefs have tried, but they have been unable to do it. You have done it. Therefore, I will give you the stories. From this day onward, all stories belong to you. Whenever a man tells a story, he must **acknowledge** that it is Anansi's tale."

In this way Anansi, the spider, became the owner of all stories that are told. To Anansi all these tales belong.

Theme How is Anansi successful when others more powerful have failed?

BQ BIG Question

How does Anansi use clever solutions to outsmart his opponents?

Vocabulary

acknowledge (ak nol′ ij) *v.* to recognize the authority, validity, or claims of

View the Art This stool was intended for a king. Why might a leopard stool be appropriate for a king?

Cameroon beaded stool with leopard design. The Field Museum, Chicago, IL.

After You Read

Respond and Think Critically

1. How does Anansi get the python to agree to be tied to the pole? [Recall]
2. Summarize the three things Anansi had to do to pay for all the stories in the world. [Summarize]
3. Why is it important to Anansi to own the stories? [Infer]
4. **Literary Element** **Theme** What message about life is the author trying to get across to the reader? How do the plot and characters help reveal it? [Evaluate]
5. **Reading Strategy** **Make Predictions About Plot** Look back at the graphic organizer you completed as you read. Which of your predictions were correct? Which did you need to adjust? Explain how making predictions helped you understand or enjoy the story. [Analyze]
6. **BQ** **BIG Question** Why might some people consider Anansi a hero who deserves to be rewarded? [Conclude]

TIP

Inferring
Here are some tips to help you answer question 3. Remember that when you infer, you make a guess using clues from the story.

- Recall what you know about all the stories in the world. Who has them? What does this say about the owner?
- Recall what you know about Anansi. Why might he want the stories?
- Think about what everyone else must do when Anansi owns the stories. What does this mean for Anansi?

Vocabulary Practice

On a separate sheet of paper, write the vocabulary word that correctly completes each sentence.

yearned
dispute
accustomed
acknowledge

1. I ______ to bring the adorable puppy home, but we already own three cats.
2. A bike rider must ______ a pedestrian's right of way.
3. The two friends made up soon after their ______.
4. Tim wasn't ______ to the snow, having lived in a tropical climate all his life.

Keep track of your ideas about the **BIG Question** in your unit Foldable

Writing

Write a Scene Scan the story. Review Anansi's tricks and what happens to him at the end. Then write your own brief scene for Anansi that has a different outcome for the trickster. Be sure to include a clearly described setting, a conflict or obstacle for Anansi to overcome, and clear, lively descriptions of the action.

LOG ON Literature Online

Selection Resources
For Selection Quizzes, eFlashcards, and Reading-Writing Connection activities, go to glencoe.com and enter QuickPass code GL17527u1.

Before You Read

Dragon, Dragon

Connect to the Fairy Tale

What do you think it would be like to live in a fairy-tale world of castles, wizards, and dragons?

Partner Talk With a partner, talk about what life might be like in a fairy tale, where anything is possible.

Build Background

"Dragon, Dragon" is a modern fairy tale. It was written in the style of tales that have been handed down for hundreds of years. The story seems to be a typical fairy tale at first. A dragon terrorizes a kingdom. A brave hero goes on a quest to slay the dragon and win the fair maiden's hand. But you'll notice one difference—humor. Look for humor in

- the ways the dragon troubles the kingdom
- what the queen is turned into and how she's taken care of
- the advice the cobbler gives his sons

Read carefully to find all the ways the author has fun with the typical elements of fairy tales.

Vocabulary

plagued (plāgd) *v.* troubled or annoyed (p. 84). *Even though we kept the food in closed containers, ants plagued our picnic.*

ravaged (rav′ ijd) *v.* laid waste to; destroyed (p. 84). *Rabbits ravaged Jon's vegetable garden, so he built a fence around it.*

tyrant (tī′ rənt) *n.* one who uses power or authority in a cruel and unjust manner (p. 85). *Our school's soccer coach is strict, but she isn't a tyrant.*

quest (kwest) *n.* search or pursuit made in order to get an object or accomplish a goal (p. 87). *The boy was on a quest to find his misplaced homework.*

meekly (mēk′ lē) *adv.* patiently and mildly; gently (p. 87). *Despite students' excitement on the last day of school, the teacher meekly tried to get their attention.*

Meet John Gardner

"Life follows art. If we celebrate bad values in our arts, we're going to have a bad society."

—John Gardner

A True Artist John Gardner grew up around books. As an adult, he wrote novels, short stories, books on writing, and more. When he wasn't writing, he was teaching and studying classic literature. Gardner wanted his books to deliver a moral message. "True art is moral," he said. "It seeks to improve life." He is best known for his novel *Grendel,* the retelling of an ancient legend about the warrior Beowulf, who slays monsters and a dragon.

Literary Works Gardner wrote novels, poetry, essays, and short stories.

John Gardner was born in 1933 and died in 1982.

LOG ON  **Literature** Online

Author Search For more about John Gardner, go to glencoe.com and enter QuickPass code GL17527u1.

Set Purposes for Reading

BQ BIG Question

As you read, ask yourself, what makes the hero of this tale different from other heroes?

GA Performance Standards

For pages 81–94

ELA6R1e/ii For literary texts, identify and analyze the elements of setting, characterization, plot, and the resolution of the conflict of a story or play: character conflicts, characters vs. nature, characters vs. society.

Literary Element Character

A **character** is a person or creature in a literary work. A character who shows varied traits is a **round character.** A character who reveals only one trait is a **flat character.** Characters central to a story and typically fully developed are the **main characters. Minor characters** display few personality traits and are used to help develop the story.

Recognizing the types of characters in a story is important. The sequence of events, or the plot, usually revolves around a conflict involving the main character and the actions he or she takes to resolve that conflict.

As you read, try to identify each character's traits.

Reading Skill Compare and Contrast Characters

To **compare and contrast characters,** look for similarities and differences in the way characters think, look, and act.

Comparing and contrasting characters can help you understand why characters act the way they do and what effect they have on the plot, the conflict, and the resolution.

To **compare and contrast characters,** pay attention to

- what each character says, thinks, and does
- ways at least two characters are the same
- ways at least two characters are different

As you read, you may find it helpful to use a graphic organizer like the one on the right. Write ways characters are the same in the area where the circles overlap.

TRY IT

Compare and Contrast You want your new friend, Tina, to meet two of your best friends. Tina asks you to describe your friends so she knows what to expect when she meets them. How will you tell her ways they are alike and different?

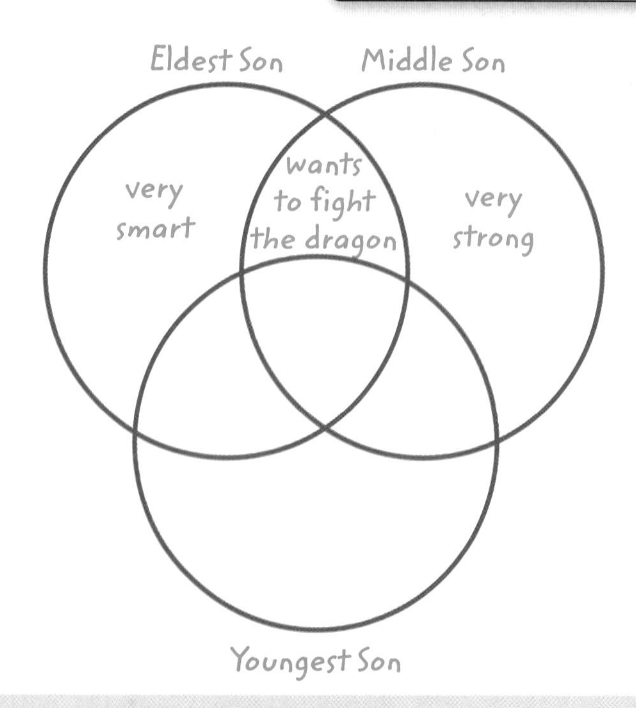

Buff earthenware tile, depicting a fantastic dragon, c.1882–1888. William de Morgan. Merton Abbey. Fitzwilliam Museum, University of Cambridge.

Dragon, Dragon

John Gardner

There was once a king whose kingdom was **plagued** by a dragon. The king did not know which way to turn. The king's knights were all cowards who hid under their beds whenever the dragon came in sight, so they were of no use to the king at all. And the king's wizard[1] could not help either because, being old, he had forgotten his magic spells. Nor could the wizard look up the spells that had slipped his mind, for he had unfortunately misplaced his wizard's book many years before. The king was at his wit's end.

Every time there was a full moon the dragon came out of his lair and **ravaged** the countryside. He frightened maidens and stopped up chimneys and broke store windows and set people's clocks back and made dogs bark until no one could hear himself think.

Compare and Contrast Characters How are these characters different from typical characters in a fairy tale?

He tipped over fences and robbed graves and put frogs in people's drinking water and tore the last chapters out of novels and changed house numbers around so that people crawled into bed with their neighbors' wives.

He stole spark plugs out of people's cars and put firecrackers in people's cigars and stole the clappers from all the church bells and sprung every bear trap for miles around so the bears could wander wherever they pleased.

And to top it all off, he changed around all the roads in the kingdom so that people could not get anywhere except by starting out in the wrong direction.

Character Do you think the dragon will be a main character or a minor character in this story? Explain your reasoning.

"That," said the king in a fury, "is enough!" And he called a meeting of everyone in the kingdom.

Now it happened that there lived in the kingdom a wise old cobbler[2] who had a wife and three sons. The cobbler and his family came to the king's meeting and stood way in back by the door, for the cobbler had a feeling that since he was nobody important there had probably been some

---

1 A ***wizard*** is a magician or sorcerer.

2 A ***cobbler*** is a person who makes or mends shoes.

Vocabulary

plagued (plāgd) *v.* troubled or annoyed

ravaged (rav′ ijd) *v.* laid waste to; destroyed

mistake, and no doubt the king had intended the meeting for everyone in the kingdom except his family and him.

"Ladies and gentlemen," said the king when everyone was present. "I've put up with that dragon as long as I can. He has got to be stopped."

All the people whispered amongst themselves, and the king smiled, pleased with the impression he had made.

But the wise cobbler said gloomily, "It's all very well to talk about it—but how are you going to do it?"

And now all the people smiled and winked as if to say, "Well, King, he's got you there!"

The king frowned.

"It's not that His Majesty hasn't tried," the queen spoke up loyally.

"Yes," said the king, "I've told my knights again and again that they ought to slay that dragon. But I can't *force* them to go. I'm not a **tyrant.**"

"Why doesn't the wizard say a magic spell?" asked the cobbler.

"He's done the best he can," said the king.

The wizard blushed and everyone looked embarrassed. "I used to do all sorts of spells and chants when I was younger," the wizard explained. "But I've lost my spell book, and I begin to fear I'm losing my memory too. For instance, I've been trying for days to recall one spell I used to do. I forget, just now, what the deuce[3] it was for. It went something like—

Bimble
Wimble
Cha, Cha
CHOOMPF!

Suddenly, to everyone's surprise, the queen turned into a rosebush.

"Oh dear," said the wizard. "Now you've done it," groaned the king. "Poor Mother," said the princess.

Compare and Contrast Characters How are the king and the cobbler different?

BQ BIG Question
What traits will the hero of this story need?

---

3 ***What the deuce*** is an expression of surprise or doubt, similar to "what on Earth."

Vocabulary

tyrant (tī′ rənt) *n.* one who uses power or authority in a cruel and unjust manner

"I don't know what can have happened," the wizard said nervously, "but don't worry, I'll have her changed back in a jiffy." He shut his eyes and racked his brain for a spell that would change her back.

But the king said quickly, "You'd better leave well enough alone. If you change her into a rattlesnake we'll have to chop off her head."

Meanwhile the cobbler stood with his hands in his pockets, sighing at the waste of time. "About the dragon . . ." he began.

Character How would you describe the cobbler's role in the story? Is he a main character or a minor character?

"Oh yes," said the king. "I'll tell you what I'll do. I'll give the princess' hand in marriage to anyone who can make the dragon stop."

"It's not enough," said the cobbler. "She's a nice enough girl, you understand. But how would an ordinary person support her? Also, what about those of us that are already married?"

"In that case," said the king, "I'll offer the princess' hand or half the kingdom or both—whichever is most convenient."

The cobbler scratched his chin and considered it. "It's not enough," he said at last. "It's a good enough kingdom, you understand, but it's too much responsibility."

"Take it or leave it," the king said.

"I'll leave it," said the cobbler. And he shrugged and went home.

But the cobbler's eldest son thought the bargain was a good one, for the princess was very beautiful and he liked the idea of having half the kingdom to run as he pleased. So he said to the king, "I'll accept those terms, Your Majesty. By tomorrow morning the dragon will be slain."

Compare and Contrast Characters How are the cobbler and his eldest son different?

"Bless you!" cried the king.

"Hooray, hooray, hooray!" cried all the people, throwing their hats in the air.

The cobbler's eldest son beamed with pride, and the second eldest son looked at him enviously. The youngest son said timidly, "Excuse me, Your Majesty, but don't you think the queen looks a little unwell? If I were you I think I'd water her."

"Good heavens," cried the king, glancing at the queen who had been changed into a rosebush, "I'm glad you mentioned it!"

Now the cobbler's eldest son was very clever and was known far and wide for how quickly he could multiply fractions in his head. He was perfectly sure he could slay the dragon by somehow or other playing a trick on him, and he didn't feel that he needed his wise old father's advice. But he thought it was only polite to ask, and so he went to his father, who was working as usual at his cobbler's bench, and said, "Well, Father, I'm off to slay the dragon. Have you any advice to give me?"

Character Is the eldest son a flat or round character? How do you know?

The cobbler thought a moment and replied, "When and if you come to the dragon's lair, recite the following poem.

Dragon, dragon, how do you do?
I've come from the king to murder you.

Say it very loudly and firmly and the dragon will fall, God willing, at your feet."

"How curious!" said the eldest son. And he thought to himself, "The old man is not as wise as I thought. If I say something like that to the dragon, he will eat me up in an instant. The way to kill a dragon is to outfox[4] him." And keeping his opinion to himself, the eldest son set forth on his **quest.**

When he came at last to the dragon's lair, which was a cave, the eldest son slyly disguised himself as a peddler and knocked on the door and called out, "Hello there!"

BQ BIG Question
Do you think the eldest son will slay the dragon and become a hero? Why or why not?

"There's nobody home!" roared a voice.

The voice was as loud as an earthquake, and the eldest son's knees knocked together in terror.

"I don't come to trouble you," the eldest son said **meekly.** "I merely thought you might be interested in looking at some of our brushes. Or if you'd prefer," he

4 To ***outfox*** is to outsmart.

Vocabulary

quest (kwest) *n.* search or pursuit made in order to get an object or accomplish a goal

meekly (mēk′ lē) *adv.* patiently and mildly; gently

St. George and the Dragon, 1456. Paolo Uccello. Oil on canvas, 57 x 73 in. National Gallery, London.

added quickly, "I could leave our catalog with you and I could drop by again, say, early next week."

"I don't want any brushes," the voice roared, "and I especially don't want any brushes next week."

"Oh," said the eldest son. By now his knees were knocking together so badly that he had to sit down.

Suddenly a great shadow fell over him, and the eldest son looked up. It was the dragon. The eldest son drew his sword, but the dragon lunged and swallowed him in a single gulp, sword and all, and the eldest son found himself in the dark of the dragon's belly. "What a fool I was not to listen to my wise old father!" thought the eldest son. And he began to weep bitterly.

"Well," sighed the king the next morning, "I see the dragon has not been slain yet."

"I'm just as glad, personally," said the princess, sprinkling the queen. "I would have had to marry that eldest son, and he had warts."

Compare and Contrast Characters How does the princess compare with other fairy-tale princesses you're familiar with?

Now the cobbler's middle son decided it was his turn to try. The middle son was very strong and was known far and wide for being able to lift up the corner of a church. He felt perfectly sure he could slay the dragon by simply laying into him, but he thought it would be only polite to ask his father's advice. So he went to his father and said to him, "Well, Father, I'm off to slay the dragon. Have you any advice for me?"

The cobbler told the middle son exactly what he'd told the eldest.

"When and if you come to the dragon's lair, recite the following poem.

Dragon, dragon, how do you do?
I've come from the king to murder you.

Say it very loudly and firmly, and the dragon will fall, God willing, at your feet."

"What an odd thing to say," thought the middle son. "The old man is not as wise as I thought. You have to take these dragons by surprise." But he kept his opinion to himself and set forth.

When he came in sight of the dragon's lair, the middle son spurred his horse to a gallop and thundered into the entrance swinging his sword with all his might.

BQ BIG Question
How is the middle son like heroes you have read or heard about?

But the dragon had seen him while he was still a long way off, and being very clever, the dragon had crawled up on top of the door so that when the son came charging in he went under the dragon and on to the back of the cave and slammed into the wall. Then the dragon chuckled and got down off the door, taking his time, and strolled back to where the man and the horse lay unconscious from the terrific blow. Opening his mouth as if for a yawn, the dragon swallowed the middle son in a single gulp and put the horse in the freezer to eat another day.

"What a fool I was not to listen to my wise old father," thought the middle son when he came to in the dragon's belly. And he too began to weep bitterly.

That night there was a full moon, and the dragon ravaged the countryside so terribly that several families moved to another kingdom.

Character Are these families main or minor characters? How do you know?

"Well," sighed the king in the morning, "still no luck in this dragon business, I see."

"I'm just as glad, myself," said the princess, moving her mother, pot and all, to the window where the sun could get at her. "The cobbler's middle son was a kind of humpback."

Now the cobbler's youngest son saw that his turn had come. He was very upset and nervous, and he wished he had never been born. He was not clever, like his eldest brother, and he was not strong, like his second-eldest brother. He was a decent, honest boy who always minded his elders.

He borrowed a **suit of armor** from a friend of his who was a knight, and when the youngest son put the armor on it was so heavy he could hardly walk. From another knight he borrowed a sword, and that was so heavy that the only way the youngest son could get it to the dragon's lair was to drag it along behind his horse like a plow.

When everything was in readiness, the youngest son went for a last conversation with his father.

"Father, have you any advice to give me?" he asked.

"Only this," said the cobbler. "When and if you come to the dragon's lair, recite the following poem.

Dragon, dragon, how do you do?
I've come from the king to murder you.

Say it very loudly and firmly, and the dragon will fall, God willing, at your feet."

"Are you certain?" asked the youngest son uneasily.

"As certain as one can ever be in these matters," said the wise old cobbler.

And so the youngest son set forth on his quest. He traveled over hill and dale and at last came to the dragon's cave. The dragon, who had seen the cobbler's youngest son while he was still a long way off, was seated up above the door, inside the cave, waiting and smiling to himself. But minutes passed and no one came thundering in. The dragon frowned, puzzled, and was tempted to peek out. However, reflecting that patience seldom goes unrewarded, the dragon kept his head up out of sight and went on waiting. At last, when he could stand it no longer, the dragon craned his neck and looked. There at the entrance of the cave stood a trembling young man in a suit of armor twice his size, struggling with a sword so heavy he could lift only one end of it at a time.

At sight of the dragon, the cobbler's youngest son began to tremble so violently that his armor rattled like a house

Compare and Contrast Characters Because the youngest son is different from his brothers, what do you think will happen to him?

Visual Vocabulary

A **suit of armor** is a protective covering for the body, often made of metal. Knights wore suits of armor to protect themselves during combat.

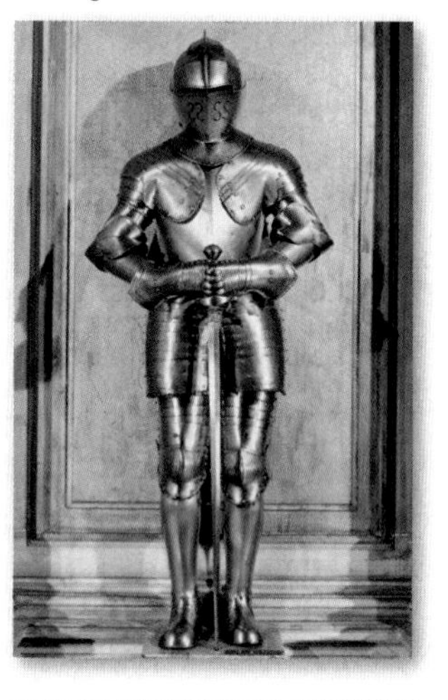

Character What clues tell you the dragon is a round character?

caving in. He heaved[5] with all his might at the sword and got the handle up level with his chest, but even now the point was down in the dirt. As loudly and firmly as he could manage, the youngest son cried—

Dragon, dragon, how do you do?
I've come from the king to murder you.

"What?" cried the dragon, flabbergasted.[6] "You? *You?* Murder *Me???*" All at once he began to laugh, pointing at the little cobbler's son. *"He he he ho ha!"* he roared, shaking all over, and tears filled his eyes. *"He he he ho ho ho ha ha!"* laughed the dragon. He was laughing so hard he had to hang onto his sides, and he fell off the door and landed on his back, still laughing, kicking his legs helplessly, rolling from side to side, laughing and laughing and laughing.

BQ BIG Question
How might the youngest son's poem lead to the dragon's defeat?

The cobbler's son was annoyed. "I *do* come from the king to murder you," he said. "A person doesn't like to be laughed at for a thing like that."

"He he he!" wailed the dragon, almost sobbing, gasping for breath. "Of course not, poor dear boy! But really, *he he,* the *idea* of it, *ha ha ha!* And that simply ri*dic*ulous *poem!"* Tears streamed from the dragon's eyes and he lay on his back perfectly helpless with laughter.

"It's a good poem," said the cobbler's youngest son loyally. "My father made it up." And growing angrier he shouted, "I want you to stop that laughing, or I'll—I'll—" But the dragon could not stop for the life of him. And suddenly, in a terrific rage, the cobbler's son began flopping the sword end over end in the direction of the dragon. Sweat ran off the youngest son's forehead, but he labored on, blistering mad, and at last, with one supreme heave, he had the sword standing on its handle a foot from the dragon's throat. Of its own weight the sword fell, slicing the dragon's head off. *"He he ho huk,"* went the dragon—and then he lay dead.

Compare and Contrast Characters How is the youngest son different from the hero in a typical fairy tale?

The two older brothers crawled out and thanked their younger brother for saving their lives. "We have learned our lesson," they said.

---

5 Here, ***heaved*** means "lifted an object with force."

6 To be ***flabbergasted*** is to be astonished.

Mt. St. Michel, 15th century. Limbourg Brothers. From Tres Riches Heures du Duc de Berry. MS 65/1284. Fol. 195r. France 15th c. Musée Condé, Chantilly, France.

Then the three brothers gathered all the treasures from the dragon's cave and tied them to the back end of the youngest brother's horse, and tied the dragon's head on behind the treasures, and started home.

"I'm glad I listened to my father," the youngest son thought. "Now I'll be the richest man in the kingdom."

There were hand-carved picture frames and silver spoons and boxes of jewels and chests of money and silver compasses and maps telling where there were more treasures buried when these ran out. There was also a curious old book with a picture of an owl on the cover, and inside, poems and odd sentences and recipes that seemed to make no sense.

When they reached the king's castle the people all leaped for joy to see that the dragon was dead, and the princess ran out and kissed the youngest brother on the forehead, for secretly she had hoped it would be him.

"Well," said the king, "which half of the kingdom do you want?"

"My wizard's book!" exclaimed the wizard. "He's found my wizard's book!" He opened the book and ran his finger under the words and then said in a loud voice, "Glmuzk, shkzmlp, blam!"

Instantly the queen stood before them in her natural shape, except she was soaking wet from being sprinkled too often. She glared at the king.

"Oh dear," said the king, hurrying toward the door.

BQ BIG Question

Do you think the youngest son is the hero of the story? Why or why not?

Character Is the queen a flat or round character? How do you know?

After You Read

Respond and Think Critically

1. Why is the king frustrated with his knights and wizard? **[Recall]**
2. Briefly describe the damage the dragon has caused throughout the kingdom. **[Summarize]**
3. Notice that the author repeatedly refers to the cobbler as the "wise old cobbler." Does this affect how you think of the character? Explain. **[Interpret]**
4. The wizard's book contains "poems and odd sentences and recipes that seemed to make no sense." What do you think the author is implying with this description? **[Infer]**
5. Which problems in the kingdom are ones that you would expect to find in a typical fairy tale? **[Compare]**
6. **BQ** **BIG Question** What ideas does this tale offer about what makes a hero—or does *not* make a hero? Explain your answer, using information from the story and from your graphic organizer. **[Evaluate]**

Vocabulary Practice

Choose the sentence that correctly uses the vocabulary word.

1. **A.** The farmer was **plagued** with a good harvest.

   B. Harsh winds and hail **plagued** the countryside.
2. **A.** Termites **ravaged** the woodwork throughout the old mansion.

   B. I **ravaged** the house to get it ready for company.
3. **A.** The **tyrant**'s actions were so cruel that the people rebelled.

   B. King Henry was a kind and gentle ruler; he was a true **tyrant.**
4. **A.** The **quest** from my home to my school takes only three minutes.

   B. We roamed the neighborhood on a **quest** for adventure.
5. **A.** Mira **meekly** apologized for making so much noise.

   B. The bold knight **meekly** brandished his sword.

Academic Vocabulary

In "Dragon, Dragon," each of the cobbler's sons has a different **strategy** for slaying the dragon.

In the preceding sentence, *strategy* means "a plan used to achieve a goal." What strategy does each brother use? Which strategy is successful?

TIP

Summarizing

Here are some tips to help you answer question 2. Remember that when you summarize, you retell the main ideas or events.

- Skim the selection to identify what the dragon has done.
- Retell the dragon's actions in your own words.
- Remember that a summary should be much shorter than the original.

Keep track of your ideas about the **BIG Question** in your unit Foldable.

Literature Online

Selection Resources
For Selection Quizzes, eFlashcards, and Reading-Writing Connection activities, go to glencoe.com and enter QuickPass code GL17527u1.

Literary Element Character

1. What purpose do the minor characters serve in the story?
2. Who is an example of a round character in the story? What traits does this character have?
3. Do you agree that round characters are usually more interesting than flat characters? Provide examples from the story to support your opinion.

Review: Theme

As you learned on page 75, a **theme** is a message about life the author wants to share. In this modern fairy tale, the author gives the traditional fairy tale hero a twist. This raises the question "What makes a hero?"

Standards Practice  ELA6R1d

4. What is one theme of this modern fairy tale?
   - A. A hero always has to trust in his or her own strength.
   - B. A hero must be strong, smart, and brave.
   - C. A hero can be the most unlikely person.
   - D. A hero always does what he or she is told.

Reading Skill Compare and Contrast Characters

Standards Practice  ELA6R1e

5. What is one way the wizard and the king are similar?
   - A. Both dislike the wise old cobbler.
   - B. Both talk more than they act.
   - C. Both have a beautiful daughter.
   - D. Both can do magic.

Grammar Link

Main and Helping Verbs A **verb** is a word that shows action or a state of being. A **helping verb** is a verb that helps the main verb tell about an action or make a statement.

In these sentences, the main verb is in boldface type, and the helping verb or verbs are underlined.

The kingdom <u>was</u> **plagued** by a dragon.

The wizard <u>had been</u> **looking** for his book of spells.

The cobbler <u>will</u> **give** advice to the king.

The eldest brother <u>could have</u> **followed** his father's advice.

A **verb phrase** is one or more helping verbs followed by a main verb. In each sentence above, the underlined and boldface words form a verb phrase.

Practice Look for two or three sentences in "Dragon, Dragon" that contain verb phrases. Think about how each helping verb contributes to the meaning of the verb. Write the sentences on a sheet of paper. Then circle the main verb and underline the helping verb or verbs.

Speaking and Listening

Performance With a small group, write and perform a skit based on "Dragon, Dragon." Decide whether you will use only a narrator or have the actors speak their lines. Use simple props for the settings and simple costumes for the characters.

Before You Read

Three Queens of Egypt

Connect to the Web Article

Have you ever been a leader? Perhaps you helped lead your friends in a project or your sports team in a game.

Partner Talk With a partner, talk about what it takes to be a leader. What qualities does a good leader have? How should a leader act?

Build Background

Cleopatra (klē ə pat′ rə), Hatshepsut (hat shep′ so͞ot), and Nefertiti (nef′ ər tē′ tē) were queens in ancient Egypt. They ruled Egypt more than 2,000 years ago, when most women had few rights.

Egypt is a country in northeastern Africa. The Nile is a river that travels more than 4,000 miles through East Africa to the Mediterranean Sea. Most cultural and historical sites of ancient Egypt can be found along the banks of the Nile. Egypt is famous for its grand pyramids, which were built long ago as burial places for pharaohs. *Pharoah* (fär′ ō) is the title used for kings of ancient Egypt.

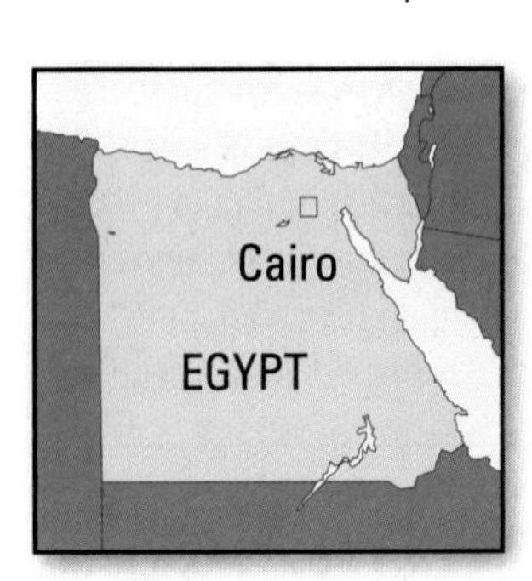

Vocabulary

inherit (in her′ it) *v.* to receive something, such as property or a title, from the former owner at his or her death (p. 97). *Anya will inherit her mother's handmade quilts.*

reign (rān) *n.* period of rule of a king or queen (p. 97). *The queen's reign lasted for many decades.*

political (pə lit′ i kəl) *adj.* relating to government (p. 98). *The city's political leaders are planning to improve the parks.*

intrigued (in trēgd′) *v.* fascinated; made curious (p. 98). *Intrigued by the painting, Jason researched it thoroughly.*

waged (wājd) *v.* carried on or engaged in, such as a war, a battle, or a contest (p. 99). *One country waged war against a neighboring country to gain more land.*

Meet Vicki León

"That's my real goal: to reveal our whole human history and to give us a balanced look at our shared past."

—Vicki León

Many Interests Vicki León is the author of numerous travel and nature books, but she is proudest of her series of books about real-life women of long ago. León says, "I've become a historical detective, following clues about female achievers until I've unearthed enough to write about them."

Literary Works León is the author of many books, including her *Uppity Women* series, which covers women from ancient times through the 1870s.

Literature Online

Author Search For more about Vicki León, go to glencoe.com and enter QuickPass code GL17527u1.

Set Purposes for Reading

BQ BIG Question

As you read, ask yourself, how did these queens use their abilities to solve problems and rule successfully?

Literary Element Anecdote

An **anecdote** is a short written or oral account of an interesting or amusing event from a person's life. An anecdote may be only a few sentences long. "Three Queens of Egypt" contains several anecdotes about the lives of three female rulers.

Writers often use anecdotes to support their opinions, reveal the personality of a person, grab the reader's attention, or entertain.

As you read, ask yourself, how does the author's use of anecdotes help me understand why these women are important historical figures?

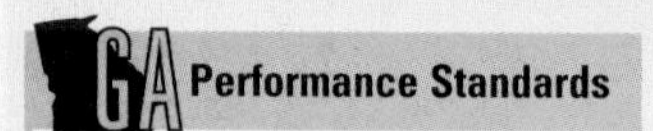

GA Performance Standards

For pages 95–101

ELA6RC2d Evaluate the merits of texts in every subject discipline.

ELA6RC2e Examine the author's purpose in writing.

Reading Strategy Monitor Comprehension

To *monitor* is to keep track of something. *Comprehension* is understanding. When you **monitor comprehension,** you think about whether you understand what you are reading.

Monitoring comprehension helps you make sure you understand important ideas as you read. One way to improve your comprehension is by rereading or slowing down when the material is difficult.

To monitor comprehension, follow these tips to improve your understanding of a passage:

- Reread the passage slowly and carefully.
- Ask yourself questions about ideas, characters, and events.
- Look at context clues and footnotes for help with words you don't understand.
- Read on to see if later information helps.

Use these strategies to understand important information about the three queens in this selection. You may find it helpful to use a chart like the one below.

Questions I have	Clues or possible answers
Why did Cleopatra crush a pearl earring?	

TRY IT

Monitor Comprehension You read a science lesson on volcanoes. When you finish, you realize that you didn't understand the explanation of how magma forms beneath Earth's surface. What do you do?

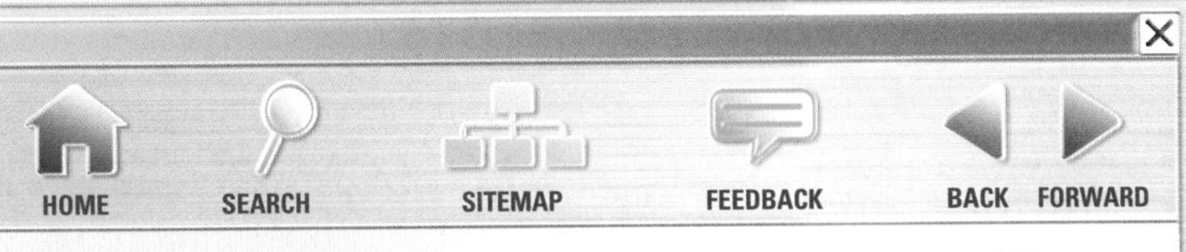

INFORMATIONAL TEXT

WEB SITE

kids.nationalgeographic.com

Three Queens of Egypt

Vicki León

Girls of ancient Egypt had it a lot better than most. By age 12, they could wear makeup. They walked their pet geese and played ball for fun. As women, they had rights not accepted elsewhere. They could buy and sell property, **inherit** stuff—even sue someone!

Still, men were usually in charge. But that didn't stop some women from defying tradition[1] and taking over. Cleopatra, Hatshepsut, and Nefertiti were three outrageous queens who showed the ancient world what girl power was all about.

Monitor Comprehension Monitor your comprehension by explaining the rights women and girls had in ancient Egypt. If necessary, reread.

Cleopatra: Political Party Girl (**Reign**: 51 B.C. to 30 B.C.)

Marc Antony was fuming. The ruler of half the Roman empire waited impatiently for the queen of Egypt to arrive. She was late—on purpose. And when she finally glittered up the Cydnus River on a ship with silver oars, Cleopatra had the nerve to make him board her ship. How dare she?

Anecdote What does this anecdote tell you about Cleopatra's personality?

1 By ***defying tradition***, the women were acting against accepted beliefs or customs.

Vocabulary

inherit (in her′ it) *v.* to receive something, such as property or a title, from the former owner at his or her death

reign (rān) *n.* period of rule of a king or queen

Antony shouldn't have been surprised at the queen's bold behavior. Cleo had star power with the brains to match. Queen by 18, she had her hands full: bad harvests, a forced marriage to her brother, plots to overthrow her. (To fight back, she even ordered hits[2] on some of her relatives!) Forced to flee her capital of Alexandria, she convinced powerful Roman leader Julius Caesar to help her regain control. But four years later Caesar was assassinated. Cleo was back to square one.[3]

Enter Marc Antony. She needed his **political** support. He needed money. Rich party girl Cleo tempted him with excess[4] by betting that she could blow a fortune on dinner. **Intrigued**, Antony watched as Cleo crushed a pearl earring into her now-priceless drink. That's all it took for the charmed yet greedy Antony to become hopelessly devoted to the queen. With his help, Cleopatra battled to keep Egypt out of the hands of her enemies. She lost. But instead of surrendering, she took her life—probably with the help of a poisonous snake.

Cleopatra left few words. But Egyptologists[5] think they may have found an order signed by the queen. On it, the busy ruler had scribbled: "Make it so."

Monitor Comprehension
Monitor your comprehension by explaining Cleopatra's action. If necessary, reread.

2 When Cleopatra ***ordered hits,*** she commanded others to kill certain people.

3 ***Assassinated*** means "murdered, especially a public figure." ***Back to square one*** means that Cleopatra had to start over with her plan to regain control of Egypt.

4 Here, ***excess*** means "action or behavior that goes beyond what is usual, proper, just, or necessary."

5 ***Egyptologists*** are people who study ancient Egypt.

Vocabulary

political (pə lit′i kəl) *adj.* relating to government

intrigued (in trēgd′) *v.* fascinated; made curious

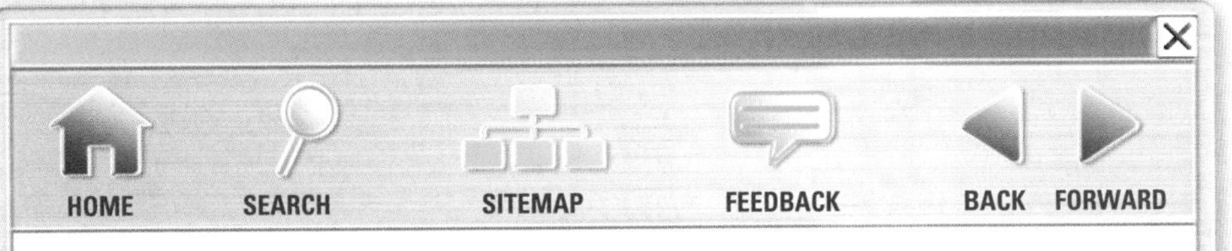

Hatshepsut: Built to Last (Reign: 1479 B.C. to 1458 B.C.) Wearing the royal headdress, with a pharaoh's traditional fake beard on her chin, Hatshepsut was officially the "female king" of Egypt. Not bad for a girl who was forced to wed her 8-year-old half-brother at 13.

Now for action! Hatshepsut **waged** successful warfare against fierce invaders. She created a magnificent temple to the sun god, Amun. Organizing a five-ship expedition to faraway lands, she brought ivory, ebony, gold, and trees to Egypt. Trees? Egypt needed them to grow fragrant incense,[6] burned by the ton in the temple's ceremonies.

To celebrate her 15th year of rule, Hat had two 100-foot **obelisks** erected. (They looked a lot like the tall, narrow Washington Monument.) Getting the granite for the structures down the Nile River took a long barge, 27 boats, and 850 rowers!

Hat was an excellent ruler—so good that she kept the pharaoh-to-be on the sidelines until she died. But she lives on in spirit. In modern Egypt, Hatshepsut's wonders, from an obelisk to an incense tree, are still standing after nearly 3,500 years.

Visual Vocabulary

Obelisks (ob′ə lisks) are tall, narrow, four-sided stone pillars. Ancient obelisks were made of a single piece of stone.

Anecdote What does this anecdote tell you about Hatshepsut and the way she ruled?

Monitor Comprehension How does Hatshepsut continue to live on after her death? Reread, if necessary, to find the answer.

6 ***Incense*** is a substance that is burned to create a pleasant smell.

Vocabulary

waged (wājd) *v.* carried on or engaged in, such as a war, a battle, or a contest

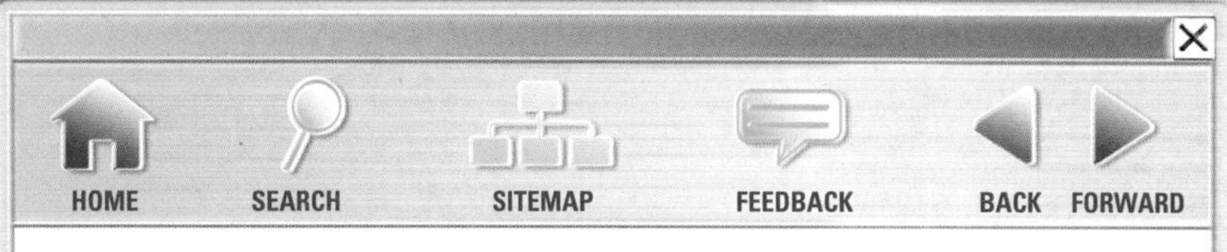

Nefertiti: Rebel with a Cause

(Reign: 1336 B.C. to 1334 B.C.)

Although Nefertiti translates as "the beautiful one has come," Egyptologists hotly debate what she really looked like. But this queen was more than just a face.

Nefertiti co-ruled with her pharaoh-husband, and they had big changes in mind. One day they made a shocking proclamation[7] that Egyptians would now worship only one god. To honor the religion, the royal couple built a new capital city called Akhetaten that was filled with exciting new art and architecture.

Their world didn't last. When Tutankhamun (King Tut to us) became pharaoh, the new capital was abandoned. Though some of the art was rescued, gone was the one-god religion from the ancient world. In the modern world, though, Nefertiti remains a name—and a face—that won't soon be forgotten. ❧

Anecdote How does this anecdote help you understand what Nefertiti and her husband valued?

BQ BIG Question

Why will Nefertiti and the other queens be remembered?

7 A ***proclamation*** is an official public announcement.

After You Read

Respond and Think Critically

1. How did Cleopatra convince Marc Antony to help her? **[Recall]**
2. Using your own words, describe some of the bold actions taken by Hatshepsut during her reign. **[Paraphrase]**
3. In what ways was Nefertiti "more than just a face"? **[Interpret]**
4. **Literary Element** **Anecdote** Which anecdote from this selection do you think is the most memorable? Why? How do you think the author decided which anecdotes to include? **[Evaluate]**
5. **Reading Strategy** **Monitor Comprehension** Which monitoring strategies did you use as you read this article? How did the strategies help you understand the text? **[Analyze]**
6. **BQ** **BIG Question** How did each of these queens use clever solutions to solve problems? What makes each of their lives so memorable? **[Conclude]**

Vocabulary Practice

On a separate sheet of paper, write the following sentences with the vocabulary word that correctly completes each sentence. If none of the words fits the sentence, write *none.*

inherit **reign** **political** **intrigued** **waged**

1. Voting is a _______ right of people who are eighteen years and older.
2. The king's _______ lasted thirty years.
3. Five-year-old Sam _______ the boring TV show.
4. The pharaoh _______ war against his enemies.
5. We were _______ by the clown's juggling act.
6. The boy decided to _______ money for the poor.
7. Molly will _______ an antique clock from her grandparents.

Writing

Write a Scene Imagine that you witnessed one of the events described in anecdotes in this selection. Write a scene of one or two paragraphs in which you describe the queen's actions for future generations to read. Make sure all the plot elements are clear and engaging. Use expressive language and descriptive words to enhance the tone.

TIP

Interpreting

Here are some tips to help you answer question 3. Remember that when you interpret, you use your own understanding to figure out what something means.

- Skim the section about Nefertiti.
- Look for references to Nefertiti's appearance. What is meant by the phrase "more than just a face"?
- What were some of the actions taken by Nefertiti?
- Do her actions relate to her appearance? Explain.

Keep track of your ideas about the **BIG Question** in your unit Foldable.

Literature Online

Selection Resources
For Selection Quizzes, eFlashcards, and Reading-Writing Connection activities, go to glencoe.com and enter QuickPass code GL17527u1.

Before You Read

Street Magic

Connect to the Graphic Story

Think of a time when you felt unsure about what might happen next.

Quickwrite Freewrite for a few minutes about your experience. What were your emotions? What did you learn from the experience?

Build Background

This selection is from Will Eisner's graphic novel *Minor Miracles.*

- Eisner was one of the first people to use the term *graphic novel* for a long story told through dialogue and drawings. The story he had written was serious, and he didn't want to call it a comic book.
- *Minor Miracles* and many of Eisner's other graphic novels tell about the tough situations some young people deal with every day in their neighborhoods.

Vocabulary

immigrant (im′ ə grənt) *adj.* coming into a country or region of which one is not a native in order to live there (p. 104). *After living in a new country, members of an immigrant group may learn that country's native language.*

outrages (out′ rāj əz) *n.* violent or cruel acts (p. 104). *The principal said the messages spray-painted on school property were outrages.*

authority (ə thôr′ ə tē) *n.* a good source of information or advice (p. 104). *The food critic was an authority on local restaurants.*

application (ap′ lə kā′ shən) *n.* a putting to use (p. 104). *Mia was proud of her application of survival skills in the woods.*

Meet Will Eisner

"My interest is not the superhero, but the little man who struggles to survive in the city."

—Will Eisner

Comic Book Artist Will Eisner grew up in New York City. Many of his stories come from his own experiences growing up in an immigrant neighborhood. Eisner tells his stories with words and pictures in comics and graphic novels.

Literary Works In the 1940s Eisner created a popular comic strip about a masked detective, "The Spirit." In 1978 he published *A Contract with God,* considered by many to be the first graphic novel. "Street Magic" was published in 2000.

Will Eisner was born in 1917 and died in 2005.

Literature Online

Author Search For more about Will Eisner, go to glencoe.com and enter QuickPass code GL17527u1.

Set Purposes for Reading

BQ BIG Question

As you read, ask yourself, how do the cousins avoid trouble with the other young men in their neighborhood?

Literary Element Dialogue

Dialogue is conversation between characters in a story. Most of the writing in a graphic novel is dialogue. The dialogue appears in balloons above or beside the characters' heads.

Be sure to read all dialogue carefully. Writers use dialogue to move a story's plot forward. Dialogue can also reveal a character's personality.

As you read, ask yourself what each character's words tell you about him or her. Is the character funny, threatening, smart?

Reading Strategy Interpret Graphic Stories

Graphic stories include words and pictures. When you **interpret graphic stories,** you figure out what the stories are about. The introduction, dialogue, and illustrations give you clues about the plot, characters, and setting.

Details in the pictures, such as the expression on a character's face, are important because they show emotion and personality. How the words are written can show the emotions, speed, and sound level of dialogue. For example, boldface type means that a word is being stressed.

To interpret graphic stories, pay attention to

- visual clues about the setting
- the characters' body language, which includes the expressions on their faces and the movements of their hands
- dialogue that moves the plot along and reveals what the characters are like
- how the words look on the page

Use these details to help you understand the story. You may find it helpful to use a graphic organizer like the one below.

Details About Setting	Details About Plot	Details About Characters
Clothing—story may take place in past		

GA Performance Standards

For pages 102–112

ELA6R1b For literary texts, identify and analyze the author's use of dialogue and description.

TRY IT

Interpret Graphic Stories
Find a familiar comic strip in a newspaper or online. Look at the pictures but don't read the words. What details about the setting, plot, and characters can you figure out just from the pictures?

Street Magic

Will Eisner

Immigrant *families on our block believed they were in hostile territory. Survival skills were brought from the old country. They were kept as magic spells the family used when dealing with the predictable* ***outrages*** *of neighborhood life. They were not formally taught. They were learned by emulating*[1] *older and more experienced family members.*

Cousin Mersh, for instance, was an ***authority*** *on the* ***application*** *of street magic.*

Interpret Graphic Stories
What can you tell about Mersh and his cousin based on the illustration?

1 To learn survival skills by ***emulating*** others is to try to equal what others know and can do by imitating them.

Vocabulary

immigrant (im′ ə grənt) *adj.* coming into a country or region of which one is not a native in order to live there

outrages (out′ rāj əz) *n.* violent or cruel acts

authority (ə thôr′ ə tē) *n.* a good source of information or advice

application (ap′ lə kā′ shən) *n.* a putting to use

Dialogue What plot background does this dialogue provide?

Interpret Graphic Stories By looking at the pictures, what can you tell about the setting?

Interpret Graphic Stories In a short story, phrases such as *he said* let you know who is talking. In this graphic story, how can you tell who is speaking?

Dialogue How does the dialogue on this page move the plot forward?

Dialogue What do you learn about the bully from the way the words of his dialogue are written?

Interpret Graphic Stories Look at the drawing. What do you think the bullies are trying to do? How do you know?

Interpret Graphic Stories
Contrast the look on Mersh's face with the look on his cousin's face.

Interpret Graphic Stories
How do the bullies feel? How do you know?

BQ BIG Question

If you were Mersh and had to come up with a clever solution at this point, what would it be?

Interpret Graphic Stories What does Mersh's action tell you about his personality?

Dialogue How can you tell from his answer how the bully holding the hat feels now?

BQ BIG Question

How does Mersh outsmart the bullies?

Dialogue What does their conversation tell you about the relationship between the two cousins?

After You Read

Respond and Think Critically

1. In what kind of neighborhood do Mersh and his young cousin live? **[Recall]**
2. Briefly summarize the plan that one of the bullies makes to beat Mersh up "fair and square." **[Summarize]**
3. Why does the author call the immigrants' survival skills "magic spells" and "street magic"? **[Interpret]**
4. **Literary Element** **Dialogue** What does the dialogue among the bullies reveal about their personalities? **[Infer]**
5. **Reading Strategy** **Interpret Graphic Stories** Review the notes from the chart you made. Which details were most important in conveying the story—words, pictures, or both? Explain. **[Evaluate]**
6. **BQ** **BIG Question** In what ways do you think Mersh is a hero? **[Conclude]**

TIP

Concluding
To answer question 6, try this strategy:

- Ask yourself, what qualities does a hero have?
- Look for evidence in the story that shows whether Mersh has some of these qualities.

Keep track of your ideas about the **BIG Question** in your unit Foldable.

Vocabulary Practice

Match each boldface vocabulary word with a word from the right column that has the same meaning. Two of the words in the right column will not have matches. Then use each vocabulary word in a sentence or draw or find a picture that represents the word.

1. **immigrant**	a. use
2. **outrages**	b. ignorant
3. **authority**	c. foreign
4. **application**	d. expert
	e. general
	f. offenses

Example: immigrant
Sentence: Immigrant children often pick up a new language quickly.

Writing

Write a Scene Think of a time when you or someone you know came up with a clever solution to a problem. Create a scene from a graphic story that shows the solution. Remember that graphic stories use the same basic elements as text narratives. These elements include plot, characters and characterization, setting, and dialogue.

Literature Online

Selection Resources
For Selection Quizzes, eFlashcards, and Reading-Writing Connection activities, go to glencoe.com and enter QuickPass code GL17527u1.

Before You Read

Stray

Connect to the Story

Think about a time when you deeply wanted something, even though there were plenty of good reasons for you not to have it.

Partner Talk With a partner, talk about what you wanted so much. Did you get it? Why or why not? What was your reaction?

Build Background

"Stray" is a short story about a family that takes in a stray dog.

- Although animal shelters—often called pounds—try to find new homes for many animals, some cats and dogs cannot be adopted. They may be too sick or have behavior problems. Sometimes there are not enough people willing to adopt the animals.
- Animal shelters take in 6 to 8 million dogs and cats each year in the United States. About half of that number of animals go unadopted because not enough homes are found for them. That means about 3 to 4 million dogs and cats are euthanized, or killed in a merciful manner.

Vocabulary

eaves (ēvz) *n.* lower edge of a sloping roof projecting beyond the sides of a building (p. 115).
Mr. Chavez hung the holiday lights from the eaves of the house.

grudgingly (gruj′ing lē) *adv.* angrily; resentfully (p. 116).
Danica grudgingly shared her piece of cake with her younger brother.

lain (lān) *v.* placed one's body in a flat position on the ground or other surface (p. 117).
We heard that the campers had lain in their sleeping bags until almost noon.

starvation (star vā′ shən) *n.* act or instance of suffering or dying of hunger (p. 118).
Eliminating starvation is a critical issue in some developing countries.

Meet Cynthia Rylant

"I love being a writer because I want to leave something here on Earth to make it better, prettier, stronger."

—Cynthia Rylant

Appalachian Childhood When Cynthia Rylant was four years old, she went to live with her grandparents in West Virginia. Her experiences from that time are an important part of the stories she tells. Rylant writes to make the world a better place, saying, "Every person is able to add beauty."

Literary Works Rylant has written more than 60 books and won the Newbery Medal in 1993.

Cynthia Rylant was born in 1954.

Literature Online

Author Search For more about Cynthia Rylant, go to glencoe.com and enter QuickPass code GL17527u1.

Set Purposes for Reading

BIG Question

As you read, ask yourself, why is it sometimes difficult to act heroically?

Literary Element Characterization

Characterization is the way a writer develops a character's personality. In **direct characterization,** the story's narrator makes direct statements about a character's personality. In **indirect characterization,** the writer reveals a character's personality through the character's words and actions and through what other characters think and say about that character.

Understanding characterization helps you determine the effects the characters have on the plot and resolution of the conflict.

As you read, ask yourself, what are the personalities of Doris and her parents, and what happens when they take in a stray puppy?

Reading Skill Analyze Plot

When you **analyze plot,** or the story's events, you pay attention to the five stages of the plot—exposition, rising action, climax, falling action, and resolution.

Analyzing plot helps you understand what you read.

To analyze plot, pay attention to

- the exposition, which introduces the characters, setting, and conflict
- the rising action, or how the conflict develops
- the climax, which is the point of greatest interest or suspense
- the falling action, or what happens after the climax
- the resolution, or final outcome

You may find it helpful to use a graphic organizer like the one below. Identify the stages in the plot of "Stray" as you read.

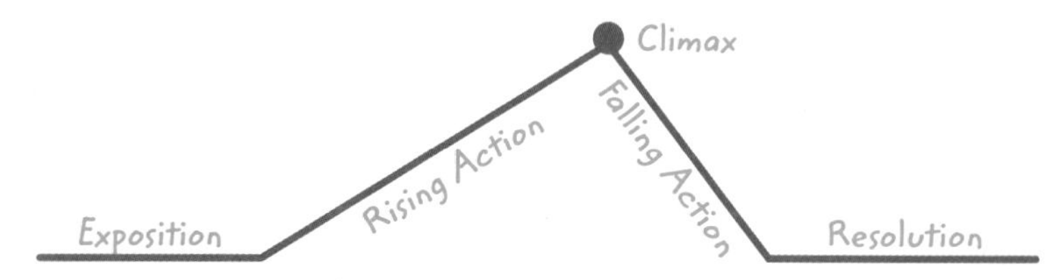

Characters: Doris, Mr. Lacey, Mrs. Lacey
Setting:
Conflict:

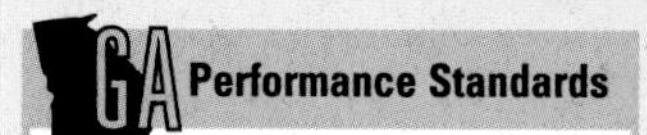

Performance Standards

For pages 113–119

ELA6R1e/ii For literary texts, identify and analyze the elements of setting, characterization, plot, and the resolution of the conflict of a story or play.

TRY IT

Analyze Plot You and a friend are watching a confusing movie. It is hard to understand some parts of the plot. What can you and your friend discuss to help you understand the plot?

Stray

Cynthia Rylant

In January, a puppy wandered onto the property of Mr. Amos Lacey and his wife, Maggie, and their daughter, Doris. Icicles hung three feet or more from the **eaves** of houses, snowdrifts swallowed up automobiles, and the birds were so fluffed up they looked comic.

The puppy had been abandoned,[1] and it made its way down the road toward the Laceys' small house, its tail between its legs, shivering.

Doris, whose school had been called off because of the snow, was out shoveling the cinder-block front steps when she spotted the pup on the road. She set down the shovel.

"Hey! Come on!" she called.

The puppy stopped in the road, wagging its tail timidly,[2] trembling with shyness and cold.

Doris trudged through the yard, went up the shoveled drive and met the dog.

Analyze Plot What do you think has happened to the puppy?

1 An ***abandoned*** puppy has been given up or left behind.

2 If a puppy behaves ***timidly,*** it acts fearfully and without courage.

Vocabulary

eaves (ēvz) *n.* lower edge of a sloping roof projecting beyond the sides of a building

Sleeping Blue Dog.
Jung Im Jang.

View the Art How would you describe the feeling you get when you look at this painting? What elements of the painting add to the feeling?

"Come on, pooch."

"Where did *that* come from?" Mrs. Lacey asked as soon as Doris put the dog down in the kitchen.

Mr. Lacey was at the table, cleaning his fingernails with his pocketknife. The snow was keeping him home from his job at the warehouse.

"I don't know where it came from," he said mildly, "but I know for sure where it's going."

Characterization What can you tell about Mr. Lacey based on his words?

Doris hugged the puppy hard against her. She said nothing.

Because the roads would be too bad for travel for many days, Mr. Lacey couldn't get out to take the puppy to the pound in the city right away. He agreed to let it sleep in the basement, while Mrs. Lacey **grudgingly** let Doris feed it table scraps. The woman was sensitive about throwing out food.

By the looks of it, Doris figured the puppy was about six months old and on its way to being a big dog. She thought it might have some shepherd in it.

Four days passed and the puppy did not complain. It never cried in the night or howled at the wind. It didn't tear up everything in the basement. It wouldn't even follow Doris up the basement steps unless it was invited.

It was a good dog.

Several times Doris had opened the door in the kitchen that led to the basement, and the puppy had been there, all stretched out, on the top step. Doris knew it had

Vocabulary

grudgingly (gruj′ ing lē) *adv.* angrily; resentfully

wanted some company and that it had **lain** against the door, listening to the talk in the kitchen, smelling the food, being a part of things. It always wagged its tail, eyes all sleepy, when she found it there.

Even after a week had gone by, Doris didn't name the dog. She knew her parents wouldn't let her keep it, that her father made so little money any pets were out of the question, and that the pup would definitely go to the pound when the weather cleared.

Still, she tried talking to them about the dog at dinner one night.

"She's a good dog, isn't she?" Doris said, hoping one of them would agree with her.

Her parents glanced at each other and went on eating.

"She's not much trouble," Doris added. "I like her." She smiled at them, but they continued to ignore her.

"I figure she's real smart," Doris said to her mother. "I could teach her things."

Mrs. Lacey just shook her head and stuffed a forkful of sweet potato in her mouth. Doris fell silent, praying the weather would never clear.

But on Saturday, nine days after the dog had arrived, the sun was shining and the roads were plowed. Mr. Lacey opened up the trunk of his car and came into the house.

Doris was sitting alone in the living room, hugging a pillow and rocking back and forth on the edge of a chair. She was trying not to cry but she was not strong enough. Her face was wet and red, her eyes full of distress.[3]

Mrs. Lacey looked into the room from the doorway.

"Mama," Doris said in a small voice. "Please."

Mrs. Lacy shook her head.

"You know we can't afford a dog, Doris. You try to act more grown-up about this."

Doris pressed her face into the pillow.

Outside, she heard the trunk of the car slam shut, one of the doors open and close, the old engine cough and choke and finally start up.

Analyze Plot How is the author introducing rising tension?

Characterization How does Mrs. Lacey's attitude here compare with her attitude earlier?

---

3 Someone in ***distress*** is suffering in body or mind.

Vocabulary

lain (lān) *v.* placed one's body in a flat position on the ground or other surface

"Daddy," she whispered. "Please."

She heard the car travel down the road, and though it was early afternoon, she could do nothing but go to her bed. She cried herself to sleep, and her dreams were full of searching and searching for things lost.

It was nearly night when she finally woke up. Lying there, like stone, still exhausted, she wondered if she would ever in her life have anything. She stared at the wall for a while.

But she started feeling hungry, and she knew she'd have to make herself get out of bed and eat some dinner. She wanted not to go into the kitchen, past the basement door. She wanted not to face her parents.

But she rose up heavily.

Her parents were sitting at the table, dinner over, drinking coffee. They looked at her when she came in, but she kept her head down. No one spoke.

Doris made herself a glass of powdered milk and drank it all down. Then she picked up a cold biscuit and started out of the room.

"You'd better feed that mutt before it dies of **starvation**," Mr. Lacey said.

Doris turned around.

"What?"

"I said, you'd better feed your dog. I figure it's looking for you."

Doris put her hand to her mouth.

"You didn't take her?" she asked.

"Oh, I took her all right," her father answered. "Worst-looking place I've ever seen. Ten dogs to a cage. Smell was enough to knock you down. And they give an animal six days to live. Then they kill it with some kind of a shot."

Doris stared at her father.

"I wouldn't leave an *ant* in that place," he said. "So I brought the dog back."

Mrs. Lacey was smiling at him and shaking her head as if she would never, ever, understand him.

Mr. Lacey sipped his coffee.

"Well," he said, "are you going to feed it or not?"

Analyze Plot How would you describe the level of suspense at this point in the story?

BQ BIG Question

What is heroic about Mr. Lacey's bringing the dog back?

Vocabulary

starvation (star vā′ shən) *n.* act or instance of suffering or dying of hunger

After You Read

Respond and Think Critically

1. Why do Doris's parents let the dog stay at first? [Recall]
2. Even though Doris knows her parents won't let her keep the dog, she tries talking with them about it at dinner. What would you have said to get them to change their minds? [Connect]
3. Doris never names the dog. How would you explain that? [Infer]
4. **Literary Element** **Characterization** How would you describe the relationship between Doris and her parents? [Evaluate]
5. **Reading Skill** **Analyze Plot** Look back at the graphic organizer you completed as you read. What events make up this story's falling action? [Analyze]
6. **BQ** **BIG Question** How are Doris's actions heroic? [Conclude]

Vocabulary Practice

Choose the sentence that uses the vocabulary word correctly.

1. **A.** Water dripped from the **eaves** onto the front lawn.
   B. Karen took the **eaves** down to the basement.
2. **A.** The birds had **lain** quickly through the air to escape the coming storm.
   B. The dog had **lain** close to the fire to stay warm during the cold night.
3. **A.** Catherine was very happy as she **grudgingly** ate the delicious meal.
   B. Raymond **grudgingly** gave up his good seat at the concert.
4. **A.** Because of a famine, many people were suffering from **starvation.**
   B. Because of their **starvation,** the actors were filled with energy and excitement.

Writing

Write a Letter Write a persuasive letter from Doris's point of view that argues for keeping the stray puppy. Be sure to support the argument with organized and relevant reasons. Anticipate counterarguments her parents might make and address those concerns in the letter. Proofread your letter for errors in spelling, punctuation, and grammar.

TIP

Connecting
Here are some tips to help you answer question 2. Remember that when you make a connection, you examine how a situation is similar to something in your own life.

- Recall the reasons Doris's parents give for rejecting the idea of keeping the stray dog.
- Skim to remind yourself how Doris tries to get her parents to change their minds.
- Put yourself in Doris's position and add what you would say in the same circumstance.

Keep track of your ideas about the **BIG Question** in your unit Foldable.

Literature Online

Selection Resources
For Selection Quizzes, eFlashcards, and Reading-Writing Connection activities, go to glencoe.com and enter QuickPass code GL17527u1.

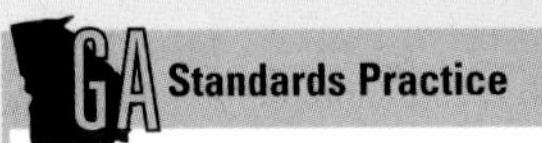

For pages 120–121

ELA6C1c Identify and write simple, compound, and complex, and compound-complex sentences, avoiding fragments and run-ons.

Grammar Workshop

Sentence Combining

Too many short sentences can make writing sound choppy or boring. In "Stray," Cynthia Rylant combines sentences in a variety of ways to make her writing lively and clear. She includes simple, compound, complex, and compound-complex sentence structures.

Simple Sentences

A simple sentence has only one main clause—also called an independent clause—and no dependent, or subordinate, clauses. Main clauses have a subject and a predicate and can stand alone as a sentence. Look at this simple sentence from the story:

> *"She set down the shovel."*

Compound Sentences

When you have written a few simple sentences that are closely related in meaning, try combining them to form compound sentences. A compound sentence contains two or more simple sentences. You can combine two or more related simple sentences into a compound sentence by using conjunctions such as *and, but,* or *or.* Look at this sentence from the story:

> *"She cried herself to sleep, and her dreams were full of searching and searching for things lost."*

Rylant uses the coordinating conjunction *and* to join the two closely related main clauses. Other coordinating conjunctions include *but, so, or, nor, for,* and *yet.*

Watch Out!

When you use a coordinating conjunction to combine two main clauses, remember to add a comma before the conjunction.

Complex Sentences

A dependent clause, also called a subordinate clause, has a subject and a predicate, but it makes sense only when attached to a main clause. Look at this sentence from the story:

> *"Because the roads would be too bad for travel for many days, Mr. Lacey couldn't get out to take the puppy to the pound in the city right away."*

The first clause is dependent—it does not make sense on its own. Subordinating conjunctions, words such as *after, as, when, where,* or *because,* often begin dependent clauses. If a dependent clause begins the sentence, put a comma after the clause.

Helpful Hint

Recognizing common subordinating conjunctions can help you to identify subordinate clauses: *after, although, as, as if, as though, because, before, if, since, so, that, though, till, unless, until, when, where, whereas, while.*

Compound-Complex Sentences

Look at the following sentence from the story:

> *"They looked at her when she came in, but she kept her head down."*

Look at each clause in the sentence and identify it as a main clause (independent) or as a subordinate clause (dependent).

> *They looked at her* (main clause)
>
> *when she came in,* (subordinate clause)
>
> *but she kept her head down.* (main clause)

A compound-complex sentence contains two or more main clauses and one or more subordinate clauses. Notice that the main clauses in the sentence from the story express complete thoughts. The subordinate clause depends on the rest of the sentence to make sense and contains the subordinating conjunction *when.*

TRY IT: Sentence Combining

Combine the sentences in each numbered item into one new sentence, using the sentence types and conjunctions given.

1. compound sentence

- **a.** Four days passed.
- **b.** The puppy did not complain.

coordinating conjunction: *and*

2. complex sentence

- **a.** He agreed to let it sleep in the basement.
- **b.** Mrs. Lacey grudgingly let Doris feed it table scraps.

subordinating conjunction: *while*

3. compound-complex sentence

- **a.** Mr. Lacey seemed stern.
- **b.** He was kind.
- **c.** He didn't want the puppy to be harmed.

subordinating conjunction: *although*

coordinating conjunction: *and*

Watch Out!

A dependent clause may appear at the beginning, in the middle, or at the end of a sentence. Put a comma after a dependent clause when it begins a sentence. Put a comma before and after the dependent clause when it appears in the middle of a sentence.

Helpful Hint

Sometimes a short sentence is more effective than a long one. Include a variety of sentence structures to ensure your writing expresses your ideas in an interesting way.

Grammar For more grammar practice, go to glencoe.com and enter QuickPass code GL17527u1.

Before You Read

Pecos Bill

Connect to the Tall Tale

What does it mean to be "larger than life"? Who do you think is a modern-day, larger-than-life hero?

Quickwrite Write down the names of people you consider to be larger-than-life heroes. What makes them special or different from other kinds of heroes?

Build Background

Some tall-tale heroes are based on real people, such as Casey Jones, a train engineer on the Illinois Central Railroad who died heroically holding his brake during a crash. On the other hand, the Paul Bunyan stories were probably made up by loggers.

Pecos Bill had a different kind of beginning. He was not a real person, and he wasn't made up by a group. In 1923 Edward O'Reilly wrote a magazine story with a cowboy hero named Pecos Bill. Other writers used the character and wrote more fantastic adventures featuring him.

Vocabulary

desolate (des′ ə lit) *adj.* empty of people; deserted (p. 124). *No life could be seen in the desolate landscape.*

coincidence (kō in′ si dəns) *n.* the occurrence of unrelated events that appear to be connected (p. 125). *It is a coincidence that Claire and her best friend have the same birthday.*

parched (pärcht) *adj.* dried out or shriveled, usually from heat (p. 129). *The ground was parched and cracked after many weeks without rain.*

cyclone (sī′ klōn) *n.* a violent windstorm in which winds move in a circle, such as in a tornado, and which commonly brings heavy rain (p. 129).
Our neighbor's roof blew off during the cyclone.

barren (bar′ ən) *adj.* containing little or no plant life; bare (p. 130). *Animals must look hard to find food in the barren desert.*

Meet Mary Pope Osborne

"Reading and writing are about the magic of the imagination."
—Mary Pope Osborne

Armchair Adventurer To Mary Pope Osborne, writing stories is like going on an adventure without ever leaving home. As a writer, she has traveled on the back of a moonhorse, visited the imaginary world of the ancient Greek gods, and worked as a detective. In real life, she has lived in a cave in Greece, traveled through Asia, and written more than fifty books.

Literary Works Osborne is probably best known for her *Magic Treehouse* series. She has also written nonfiction, picture books, and novels for young adults.

Mary Pope Osborne was born in 1949.

Literature Online

Author Search For more about Mary Pope Osborne, go to glencoe.com and enter QuickPass code GL17527u1.

Set Purposes for Reading

BQ BIG Question

As you read, ask yourself how Pecos Bill is different from other cowboys you've read about. What qualities make him a tall-tale hero?

Literary Element Tone

The **tone** of a work is the author's attitude toward a subject. For example, the tone may be threatening, serious, or light. The tone of a tall tale is usually light, humorous, or boastful. One way the author creates tone is through word choice. In "Pecos Bill," the author uses slang, exaggeration, and funny expressions to create humor.

Recognizing the author's choice of words and details that create the tone helps you understand the story.

As you read, ask yourself, what word choices help me understand the author's attitude toward Pecos Bill?

Reading Skill Analyze Story Elements

Tall tales are imaginative stories of adventures or amazing feats of folk heroes. Like other stories, tall tales contain **story elements** such as **plot, characters, setting,** and **theme.** In a tall tale, the descriptions of the characters and events in the plot are exaggerated, but the settings are realistic. These elements work together to convey the theme.

Analyzing the story elements in a tall tale helps you to realize that the author's purpose is to entertain you by making the characters and events more amazing than they could possibly be in real life.

To **analyze story elements** in a tall tale, pay attention to

- the exaggerated qualities of characters
- the humorous and impossible deeds in the plot
- the realistic setting
- the main point of the story

As you read, look for characteristics of tall tales: larger-than-life hero, exaggeration, and humor. You may find it helpful to use a graphic organizer like the one below.

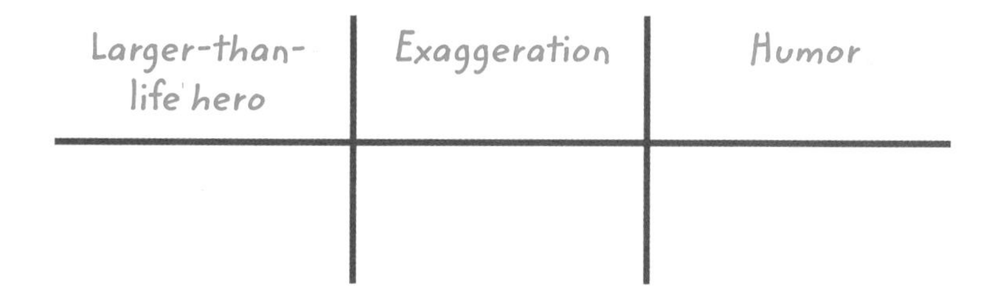

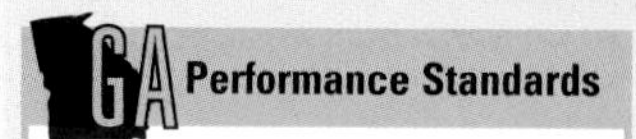

GA Performance Standards

For pages 122–134

ELA6R1g For literary texts, define and explain how tone is conveyed in literature through word choice, sentence structure, punctuation, rhythm, repetition, and rhyme.

TRY IT

Analyze Story Elements Think about tall-tale heroes you have read or heard about such as Paul Bunyan, Johnny Appleseed, or Davy Crockett. How are parts of the stories the same? How are they different?

Pecos Bill

Mary Pope Osborne

Ask any coyote near the Pecos River in western Texas who was the best cowboy who ever lived, and he'll throw back his head and howl, "Ah-hooo!" If you didn't know already, that's coyote language for *Pecos Bill.*

When Pecos Bill was a little baby, he was as tough as a pine knot. He teethed on horseshoes instead of teething rings and played with grizzly bears instead of teddy bears. He could have grown up just fine in the untamed land of eastern Texas. But one day his pappy[1] ran in from the fields, hollering, "Pack up, Ma! Neighbors movin' in fifty miles away! It's gettin' too crowded!"

Analyze Story Elements
How does Pecos Bill fit the description of a tall-tale hero?

Before sundown Bill's folks loaded their fifteen kids and all their belongings into their covered wagon and started west.

As they clattered across the **desolate** land of western Texas, the crushing heat nearly drove them all crazy. Baby Bill got so hot and cross that he began to wallop his big

1 ***Pappy*** is a changed form of *papa*, so here it refers to Pecos Bill's father.

Vocabulary

desolate (des′ ə lit) *adj.* empty of people; deserted

brothers. Pretty soon all fifteen kids were going at one another tooth and nail. Before they turned each other into catfish bait, Bill fell out of the wagon and landed *kerplop* on the sun-scorched desert.

The others were so busy fighting that they didn't even notice the baby was missing until it was too late to do anything about it.

Well, tough little Bill just sat there in the dirt, watching his family rattle off in a cloud of dust, until an old coyote walked over and sniffed him.

"Goo-goo!" Bill said.

Now it's an amazing **coincidence**, but "Goo-goo" happens to mean something similar to "Glad to meet you" in coyote language. Naturally the old coyote figured he'd come across one of his own kind. He gave Bill a big lick and picked him up by the scruff of the neck and carried him home to his den.

Tone How does the author want you to feel when you read this sentence?

Bill soon discovered the coyote's kinfolk[2] were about the wildest, roughest bunch you could imagine. Before he knew it, he was roaming the prairies with the pack. He howled at the moon, sniffed the brush, and chased lizards across the sand. He was having such a good time, scuttling about naked and dirty on all fours, that he completely forgot what it was like to be a human.

Pecos Bill's coyote days came to an end about seventeen years later. One evening as he was sniffing the sagebrush, a cowpoke[3] came loping by on a big horse. "Hey, you!" he shouted. "What in the world are you?"

2 ***Kinfolk*** is another word for relatives.

3 ***Cowpoke*** is slang for *cowboy*.

Vocabulary

coincidence (kō in′ si dəns) *n.* the occurrence of unrelated events that appear to be connected

Bill sat on his haunches[4] and stared at the feller.[5]

"What *are* you?" asked the cowpoke again.

"Varmint,"[6] said Bill hoarsely, for he hadn't used his human voice in seventeen years.

"No, you ain't!"

"Yeah, I am. I got fleas, don't I?"

"Well, that don't mean nothing. A lot of Texans got fleas. The thing varmints got that you ain't got is a tail."

Tone How does this create a humorous tone?

"Oh, yes, I do have a tail," said Pecos Bill.

"Lemme see it then," said the cowpoke.

Bill turned around to look at his rear end, and for the first time in his life he realized he didn't have a tail.

"Dang," he said. "But if I'm not a varmint, what am I?"

"You're a cowboy! So start acting like one!"

Bill just growled at the feller like any coyote worth his salt would. But deep down in his heart of hearts he knew the cowpoke was right. For the last seventeen years he'd had a sneaking suspicion that he was different from that pack of coyotes. For one thing, none of them seemed to smell quite as bad as he did.

So with a heavy heart he said good-bye to his four-legged friends and took off with the cowpoke for the nearest ranch.

Analyze Story Elements How does the plot shift at this point?

Acting like a human wasn't all that easy for Pecos Bill. Even though he soon started dressing right, he never bothered to shave or comb his hair. He'd just throw some water on his face in the morning and go around the rest of the day looking like a wet dog. Ignorant cowpokes claimed Bill wasn't too smart. Some of the meaner ones liked to joke that he wore a ten-dollar hat on a five-cent head.

The truth was Pecos Bill would soon prove to be one of the greatest cowboys who ever lived. He just needed to find the kind of folks who'd appreciate him. One night when he was licking his dinner plate, his ears perked up. A couple of ranch hands were going on about a gang of wild cowboys.

"Yep. Those fellas are more animal than human," one ranch hand was saying.

---

4 To sit on your ***haunches*** is to squat.

5 A ***feller*** is a boy or a man.

6 A ***varmint*** is a pesky, annoying animal or person.

"Yep. Them's the toughest bunch I ever come across. Heck, they're so tough, they can kick fire out of flint rock with their bare toes!"

Tone How does this affect your impression of the gang?

"Yep. 'N' they like to bite nails in half for fun!"

"Who are these fellers?" asked Bill.

"The Hell's Gate Gang," said the ranch hand. "The mangiest,[7] meanest, most low-down bunch of low-life varmints that ever grew hair."

"Sounds like my kind of folks," said Bill, and before anyone could holler whoa, he jumped on his horse and took off for Hell's Gate Canyon.

Bill hadn't gone far when disaster struck. His horse stepped in a hole and broke its ankle.

"Dang!" said Bill as he stumbled up from the spill. He draped the lame critter around his neck and hurried on.

Analyze Story Elements Why does this plot detail belong in a tall tale?

After he'd walked about a hundred more miles, Bill heard some mean rattling. Then a fifty-foot rattlesnake reared up its ugly head and stuck out its long, forked tongue, ready to fight.

"Knock it off, you scaly-hided fool. I'm in a hurry," Bill said.

The snake didn't give a spit for Bill's plans. He just rattled on.

---

7 The word ***mangiest*** comes from ***mange***, a skin disease of animals that causes loss of hair in spots. So *mangiest* means "the most shabby or worn out in appearance."

Before the cussed[8] varmint could strike, Bill had no choice but to knock him cross-eyed."Hey, feller," he said, holding up the dazed snake. "I like your spunk.[9] Come go with us." Then he wrapped the rattler around his arm and continued on his way.

After Bill had hiked another hundred miles with his horse around his neck and his snake around his arm, he heard a terrible growl. A huge mountain lion was crouching on a cliff, getting ready to leap on top of him.

"Don't jump, you mangy bobtailed fleabag!" Bill said.

Well, call any mountain lion a mangy bobtailed fleabag, and he'll jump on your back for sure. After this one leaped onto Bill, so much fur began to fly that it darkened the sky. Bill wrestled that mountain lion into a headlock, then squeezed him so tight that the big cat had to cry uncle.

BQ BIG Question
What qualities make Bill larger than life?

When the embarrassed old critter started to slink off, Bill felt sorry for him. "Aw, c'mon, you big silly," he said. "You're more like me than most humans I meet."

He saddled up the cat, jumped on his back, and the four of them headed for the canyon, with the mountain lion screeching, the horse neighing, the rattler rattling, and Pecos Bill hollering a wild war whoop.

When the Hell's Gate Gang heard those noises coming from the prairie, they nearly fainted. They dropped their dinner plates, and their faces turned as white as bleached desert bones. Their knees knocked and their six-guns shook.

Tone What is the tone of the gang's response to Bill?

"Hey, there!" Bill said as he sidled up to their campfire, grinning. "Who's the boss around here?"

A nine-foot feller with ten pistols at his sides stepped forward and in a shaky voice said, "Stranger, I was. But from now on, it'll be you."

"Well, thanky, pardner," said Bill. "Get on with your dinner, boys. Don't let me interrupt."

Once Bill settled down with the Hell's Gate Gang, his true genius revealed itself. With his gang's help, he put together the biggest ranch in the southwest. He used New Mexico as a corral and Arizona as a pasture.

---

8 Here, the word ***cussed*** means "stubborn and difficult to deal with."

9 ***Spunk*** means "courage and spirit."

He invented **tarantulas** and scorpions as practical jokes. He also invented roping. Some say his rope was exactly as long as the equator; others argue it was two feet shorter.

Things were going fine for Bill until Texas began to suffer the worst drought[10] in its history. It was so dry that all the rivers turned as powdery as biscuit flour. The **parched** grass was catching fire everywhere. For a while Bill and his gang managed to lasso water from the Rio Grande.[11] When that river dried up, they lassoed water from the Gulf of Mexico.

No matter what he did, though, Bill couldn't get enough water to stay ahead of the drought. All his horses and cows were starting to dry up and blow away like balls of tumbleweed. It was horrible.

Just when the end seemed near, the sky turned a deep shade of purple. From the distant mountains came a terrible roar. The cattle began to stampede, and a huge black funnel of a **cyclone** appeared, heading straight for Bill's ranch.

The rest of the Hell's Gate Gang shouted, "Help!" and ran.

But Pecos Bill wasn't scared in the least. "Yahoo!" he hollered, and he swung his lariat and lassoed that cyclone around its neck.

Bill held on tight as he got sucked up into the middle of the swirling cloud. He grabbed the cyclone by the ears and pulled himself onto her back. Then he let out a whoop and headed that twister across Texas.

The mighty cyclone bucked, arched, and screamed like a wild bronco. But Pecos Bill just held on with his legs and used his strong hands to wring the rain out of her wind. He wrung out rain that flooded Texas, New Mexico, and

10 A ***drought*** is a long period of very dry weather.

11 The ***Rio Grande*** is a large river that forms part of the border between Texas and Mexico. The words mean "large river" in Spanish.

Vocabulary

parched (pärcht) *adj.* dried out or shriveled, usually from heat

cyclone (sī′ klōn) *n.* a violent windstorm in which winds move in a circle, such as in a tornado, and which commonly brings heavy rain

Visual Vocabulary

Tarantulas are large, hairy spiders. Their bite can be painful, but it is not usually dangerous to humans.

Analyze Story Elements
How is this event typical of a tall tale?

Arizona, until finally he slid off the shriveled-up funnel and fell into California. The earth sank about two hundred feet below sea level in the spot where Bill landed, creating the area known today as Death Valley.

Analyze Story Elements
Why is a place such as Death Valley in the story?

"There. That little waterin' should hold things for a while," he said, brushing himself off.

After his cyclone ride, no horse was too wild for Pecos Bill. He soon found a young colt that was as tough as a tiger and as crazy as a streak of lightning. He named the colt Widow Maker and raised him on barbed wire[12] and dynamite. Whenever the two rode together, they back-flipped and somersaulted all over Texas, loving every minute of it.

One day when Bill and Widow Maker were bouncing around the Pecos River, they came across an awesome sight: a wild-looking, red-haired woman riding on the back of the biggest catfish Bill had ever seen. The woman looked like she was having a ball, screeching, "Ride 'em, cowgirl!" as the catfish whipped her around in the air.

Analyze Story Elements
How is the characterization of the woman typical of a tall tale?

"What's your name?" Bill shouted.

"Slue-foot Sue! What's it to you?" she said. Then she war-whooped away over the windy water.

Thereafter all Pecos Bill could think of was Slue-foot Sue. He spent more and more time away from the Hell's Gate Gang as he wandered the **barren** cattle-lands, looking for her. When he finally found her lonely little cabin, he was so love-struck he reverted[13] to some of his old coyote ways. He sat on his haunches in the moonlight and began a-howling and ah-hooing.

Well, the good news was that Sue had a bit of coyote in her too, so she completely understood Bill's language. She stuck her head out her window and ah-hooed back to him that she loved him, too. Consequently Bill and Sue decided to get married.

---

12 ***Barbed wire*** has sharp points. On the plains, ranchers made fences from barbed wire to keep cattle in and cattle thieves out.

13 Here, the word ***reverted*** means "returned to an earlier behavior."

Vocabulary

barren (bar′ ən) *adj.* containing little or no plant life; bare

Visual Vocabulary

A **bustle** is a pad or frame that used to be worn by women at the back of a skirt just below the waist. The bustle look was fashionable for much of the 1800s.

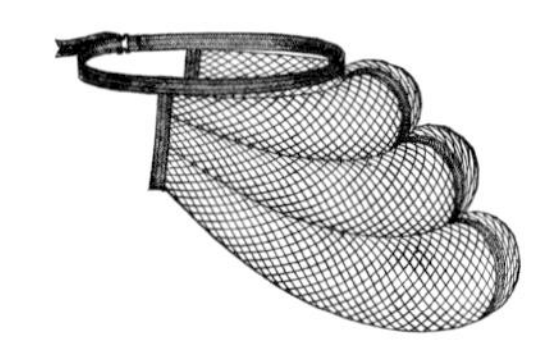

On the day of the wedding Sue wore a beautiful white dress with a steel-spring **bustle**, and Bill appeared in an elegant buckskin suit.

But after a lovely ceremony, a terrible catastrophe occurred. Slue-foot Sue got it into her head that she just had to have a ride on Bill's wild bronco, Widow Maker.

"You can't do that, honey," Bill said. "He won't let any human toss a leg over him but me."

"Don't worry," said Sue. "You know I can ride anything on four legs, not to mention what flies or swims."

Tone How does the use of the word *honey* help you understand the author's attitude toward Bill?

Bill tried his best to talk Sue out of it, but she wouldn't listen. She was dying to buck on the back of that bronco. Wearing her white wedding dress with the bustle, she jumped on Widow Maker and kicked him with her spurs.

Well, that bronco didn't need any thorns in his side to start bucking to beat the band. He bounded up in the air with such amazing force that suddenly Sue was flying high into the Texas sky. She flew over plains and mesas, over canyons, deserts, and prairies. She flew so high that she looped over the new moon and fell back to earth.

But when Sue landed on her steel-spring bustle, she rebounded right back into the heavens! As she bounced back and forth between heaven and earth, Bill whirled his lariat above his head, then lassoed her. But instead of bringing Sue back down to earth, he got yanked into the night sky alongside her!

BQ BIG Question
How does Bill's behavior show his heroic qualities?

Together Pecos Bill and Slue-foot Sue bounced off the earth and went flying to the moon. And at that point Bill must have gotten some sort of foothold in a moon crater—because neither he nor Sue returned to earth. Not ever.

Folks figure those two must have dug their boot heels into some moon cheese and raised a pack of wild coyotes just like themselves. Texans'll tell you that every time you hear thunder rolling over the desolate land near the Pecos River, it's just Bill's family having a good laugh upstairs. When you hear a strange ah-hooing in the dark night, don't be fooled—that's the sound of Bill howling *on* the moon instead of *at* it. And when lights flash across the midnight sky, you can bet it's Bill and Sue riding the backs of some white-hot shooting stars.

Analyze Story Elements
What makes this a good ending for a tall tale?

After You Read

Respond and Think Critically

1. Who raised Bill and why? **[Recall]**
2. What amazing feats has Bill already accomplished by the time he meets the Hell's Gate Gang? **[Summarize]**
3. What does exaggeration add to this story? Think about a time when you exaggerated. What did exaggeration add to your story? **[Connect]**
4. Where do Bill and Sue live after their wedding? Do you think this is a good ending to the story? Explain your answer. **[Interpret]**
5. What personality traits of Pecos Bill do you admire? Are there also traits that you dislike? Explain your answer. **[Evaluate]**
6. **BQ** **BIG Question** Why might someone be interested in tall tales about Pecos Bill? Give reasons to support your answer. **[Conclude]**

TIP

Concluding

Here are some tips to help you answer question 6. Remember, when you draw a conclusion, you form ideas about what you are reading.

To conclude, group related facts together and make a decision about what they mean.

- Recall the characters and the setting in the story.
- Compare Pecos Bill with a real-life cowboy.
- Think about reasons someone might admire a hero such as Pecos Bill.

Vocabulary Practice

Identify whether each pair of words has the same or the opposite meaning. Then write a sentence using each vocabulary word or draw or find a picture that represents the word.

cyclone and twister

parched and dry

barren and fruitful

desolate and empty

coincidence and plan

Example:

cyclone and twister = same meaning

Sentence: Officials turned on the tornado sirens when someone saw a cyclone near town.

Keep track of your ideas about the **BIG Question** in your unit Foldable.

Academic Vocabulary

The **consequence** of lassoing Sue as she bounced back and forth between earth and sky was that Bill got yanked into the sky too.

In the preceding sentence, *consequence* means "the result from an earlier action." Think about a time when you took some kind of action. What was the consequence of the action?

Literature Online

Selection Resources

For Selection Quizzes, eFlashcards, and Reading-Writing Connection activities, go to glencoe.com and enter QuickPass code GL17527u1.

Literary Element Tone

1. If you were reading about cowboys and the American West in a history textbook, would the tone be the same as in the story? Why or why not?
2. How would you summarize the tone in "Pecos Bill"?

Review: Plot

As you learned on page 53, **plot** is the sequence of events in a story. The plot starts with an introduction to the characters, setting, and situation. The **rising action** adds complications to the story's problems, or **conflicts.** The **climax** occurs at the most dramatic or emotional moment. The **falling action** leads to the **resolution,** or final outcome of the story.

Standards Practice  ELA6R1e/iii

3. Which words best describe Bill in the story?
   A. sad and weak
   B. shy and curious
   C. brave and strong
   D. polite and hopeful

Reading Skill Analyze Story Elements

Standards Practice  ELA6R1e/iii

4. Which of the following phrases best describes the character development of Bill?
   A. wild child to cowboy hero
   B. timid boy to bold man
   C. civilized human to animal
   D. criminal to law-abiding citizen

Grammar Link

Present Perfect Tense The **tense** of a verb expresses time. To form the **present perfect tense,** use the helping verb *have* or *has* and the past participle of the main verb. (For most verbs, the past participle is the same as the past tense.)

Use the present perfect tense to talk about an action or a condition that occurred at some indefinite time in the past. For example:

> We learn in the story that Pecos Bill **has invented** tarantulas and scorpions as practical jokes.

Also use this tense to talk about something that happened and is still happening now. For example:

> I **have** always **imagined** the Hell's Gate Gang as a tough-looking bunch of cowboys.

Practice Think about Pecos Bill and what happens to him in the story. Then write your own sentences about the story using present perfect tense. Make sure your sentences are consistently in the past tense or consistently about something that is happening now.

Write with Style

Apply Tone Think about an interesting person you know. What does this person look like? Does he or she have special characteristics or abilities? How would you describe his or her personality traits? Write a character sketch. How could you exaggerate this person's traits to make the person into a larger-than-life hero? Describe what your hero looks like and the amazing things this hero can do. Choose words and details that create a humorous tone.

Comparing Literature

The Courage That My Mother Had and *My Father Is a Simple Man*

Performance Standards

For pages 135–139

ELA6R1d For literary texts, apply knowledge of the concept that theme refers to the message about life and the world that the author wants us to understand whether implied or stated.

BQ BIG Question

As you read these paired poems, ask yourself, why do the speakers consider their parents to be heroes?

Literary Element Theme

The **theme** is the lesson about life that the author of a story or poem wants to share with readers. It is not the same as the subject. For example, the subject of a story might be a football game, but its theme might be that it is dangerous to care only about winning. Some selections have a stated theme, which the author puts directly into words. Most have an implied theme, at which the author only hints. You can figure out the themes of these poems by noticing their titles and the details the authors use.

Reading Skill Compare and Contrast Theme

Every day you compare and contrast things. To compare them, you look at their similarities. To contrast them, you look at their differences. For example, to decide which of two routes to take to the library on a bicycle, you compare and contrast them: Both are a mile long, but one is paved and the other is rough.

You can deepen your understanding of literature if you compare and contrast literary elements, such as theme. To compare and contrast the themes of "The Courage That My Mother Had" and "My Father Is a Simple Man," use a chart like the one below. Below each title, fill in details like subject, tone, and speaker.

Title	The Courage That My Mother Had	My Father Is a Simple Man
Subject		

Literature Online

Author Search For more about Edna St. Vincent Millay and Luis Omar Salinas, go to at glencoe.com and enter QuickPass code GL17527u1.

Meet the Authors

Edna St. Vincent Millay

Millay wrote poetry, dramatic works, and even texts for operas. She was born in Maine in 1892 and died in 1950.

Luis Omar Salinas

Salinas writes about experiences of Mexican Americans. He was born in Texas in 1937.

The Way It Is (detail). GG Kopilak. Private Collection.

The Courage That My Mother Had

Edna St. Vincent Millay

The courage that my mother had
Went with her, and is with her still:
Rock from New England quarried;°
Now granite in a granite hill.

The golden brooch my mother wore
She left behind for me to wear;
I have no thing I treasure more:
Yet, it is something I could spare.

Oh, if instead she'd left to me
The thing she took into the grave!—
That courage like a rock, which she
Has no more need of, and I have.

3 ***Quarried*** means "cut or blasted from the earth, usually for use in construction."

5 A ***brooch*** is an ornamental pin that is fastened with a clasp and usually worn at the neck on clothing.

Comparing Literature How does the speaker feel about the brooch the mother left? How does the speaker feel she compares with the mother?

My Father Is a Simple Man

Luis Omar Salinas

I walk to town with my father
to buy a newspaper. He walks slower
than I do so I must slow up.
The street is filled with children.
We argue about the price
of pomegranates,° I convince

Comparing Literature
Based on first line of the poem, what do you think it will be about?

---

6 ***Pomegranates*** are pulpy, golden-red fruits with many seeds.

him it is the fruit of scholars.°
He has taken me on this journey
and it's been lifelong.
He's sure I'll be healthy
so long as I eat more oranges,
and tells me the orange
has seeds and so is perpetual;°
and we too will come back
like the orange trees.
I ask him what he thinks
about death and he says
he will gladly face it when
it comes but won't jump
out in front of a car.
I'd gladly give my life
for this man with a sixth
grade education, whose kindness
and patience are true . . .
The truth of it is, he's the scholar,
and when the bitter-hard reality
comes at me like a punishing
evil stranger, I can always
remember that here was a man
who was a worker and provider,
who learned the simple facts
in life and lived by them,
who held no pretense.°
And when he leaves without
benefit of fanfare° or applause
I shall have learned what little
there is about greatness.

Comparing Literature
What do you learn about what the speaker's father believes?

---

7 ***Scholars*** are people who have a great deal of knowledge.

13 ***Perpetual*** means "continuing forever."

33 ***Held no pretense*** means that the father did not act or speak in a way meant to impress others.

35 ***Fanfare*** is noise, excitement, fuss, or activity meant to attract attraction.

Comparing Literature

BQ BIG Question

Now use the unit Big Question to help you compare and contrast "The Courage That My Mother Had" and "My Father Is a Simple Man." With a group of classmates, discuss questions such as

- What does each speaker admire about his or her parent?
- What do you think is each speaker's idea of what makes a person a hero? In what ways are the speakers' ideas similar? Different?
- What do you think makes a person a hero?
- In what ways is your idea of a hero similar to or different from the ideas of the speakers?

Support each answer with evidence from the readings.

Literary Element Theme

Use the details you wrote in your comparison chart for "The Courage That My Mother Had" and "My Father Is a Simple Man" to help you decide what the theme of each poem is. Then, with a partner, answer the following questions.

1. What are the themes of the poems?
2. What do the themes have in common? Focus on the similarities between the subjects of the poems, the personal qualities the speakers admire, and the speakers' feelings about their parents.
3. In what ways do the themes of these poems differ? Discuss what is different about the subjects, the admired personal qualities, and the speakers' feelings about their parents.

Write to Compare

In one or two paragraphs, compare and contrast the feelings of the speakers in "The Courage That My Mother Had" and "My Father Is a Simple Man." Focus on their desire and on their ability to possess the admired personal qualities of their parents. Use these ideas as you write.

- State the personal qualities the speaker in each poem admires.
- Tell whether each speaker desires to possess the parent's admired personal quality.
- Tell whether each speaker feels he or she will be able to possess the parent's admired personal qualities.
- Include lines from the poems that support your statements about the speakers' feelings.

Writing Tip

Citing Poetry When you are quoting lines from a poem in your paragraphs, use slashes to indicate line breaks. Example: "and we too will come back / like the orange trees."

Literature Online

Selection Resources For Selection Quizzes, eFlashcards, and Reading-Writing Connection activities, go to glencoe.com and enter QuickPass code GL17527u1.

Performance Standards

For pages 140–145

ELA6W2c Produce a narrative that includes sensory details and concrete language to develop plot, setting and character.

Writing Workshop

Narrative

Who are your favorite story heroes? Why are they heroes? In this workshop, you will write a short story that will help you think about the Unit 1 Big Question: What makes a hero?

Review the writing prompt, or assignment, below. Then read the Writing Plan. It shows what you will do to write your story.

Writing Assignment

A narrative tells a story. Write a short story in which one character becomes a hero by helping another character find a clever solution to a problem. The audience will be your classmates and teacher.

Writing Plan

- Choose an appropriate narrator and point of view.
- Develop a plot that has a beginning, rising action, a climax, falling action, and a resolution.
- Make the internal or external conflict part of every event in the plot and the basis for the theme.
- Include sensory details to describe the setting and action.
- Use dialogue and description, including specific movement and expressions, to highlight similarities and differences among main and minor characters.

Prewriting Tip

Brainstorming Don't judge the ideas that come into your head while brainstorming. Just write them all down. You can think about them later.

Prewrite

What kinds of characters can be heroes? What are some problems heroes might solve in clever ways? Look at the stories in this unit for examples, including "Dragon, Dragon" by John Gardner.

Gather Ideas

Brainstorm and take notes on setting, characters, and plot. Quickwrite—don't spend too much time thinking. Ask yourself,

- What times or places interest me?
- What will my characters look like? What traits will they have?
- What problems or conflicts will the main character need to solve?
- What will the conflict be—with nature, with society, character against character, or character with himself or herself?

Choose a Point of View

The point of view is the relationship of the narrator to the story. Choose the point of view that you think will work best for your story.

A story using **first-person point of view** is told by one of the characters. The character uses pronouns such as *I* and *we.* The reader is limited to knowing only what that character knows, feels, or thinks. In **third-person point of view,** a narrator who is not a character in the story tells the story. The narrator uses pronouns such as *he, she,* and *they.* In a story with **limited third-person point of view,** the narrator reveals only the thoughts and feelings of one character. In a story using **third-person omniscient point of view,** the narrator can reveal the thoughts and feelings of all the characters.

Get Organized

Use your notes to make a story plan that includes a characterization chart and a plot diagram.

CHARACTERIZATION CHART

Detail from Story	Personality Trait It Reveals	Direct or Indirect Characterization
Mark Johnson says Billy is "in for it."	anger	direct (narrator's statement)

PLOT DIAGRAM

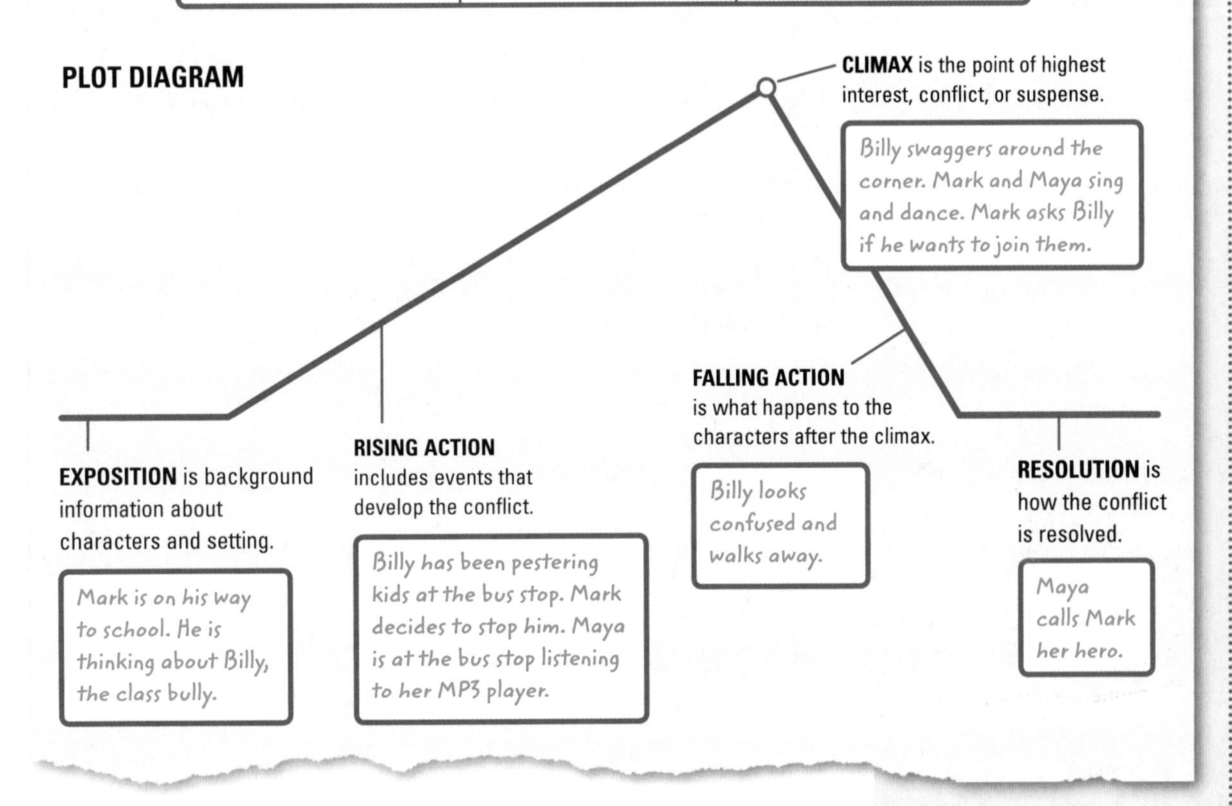

CLIMAX is the point of highest interest, conflict, or suspense.
Billy swaggers around the corner. Mark and Maya sing and dance. Mark asks Billy if he wants to join them.
EXPOSITION is background information about characters and setting.
Mark is on his way to school. He is thinking about Billy, the class bully.
RISING ACTION includes events that develop the conflict.
Billy has been pestering kids at the bus stop. Mark decides to stop him. Maya is at the bus stop listening to her MP3 player.
FALLING ACTION is what happens to the characters after the climax.
Billy looks confused and walks away.
RESOLUTION is how the conflict is resolved.
Maya calls Mark her hero.

Draft

Get It on Paper

- Review your story plan and notes on character, setting, and conflict.
- Open your story with a surprising statement, a striking setting, a conversation, or an exciting action sequence.
- Continue by telling the events in your story plan in the order in which they occur. For each event, freewrite what happens.
- Don't worry about paragraphs, spelling, grammar, or punctuation.
- When fifteen minutes are up, read what you have written.

Drafting Tip

Signal Words Use words such as *before, then, next, while, after,* and *later* to make the order of events clear.

Develop Your Draft

1. Write from the **point of view** of the **narrator** you chose for your story. Use the correct pronouns.

> "Billy is really in for it now!" Mark Johnson said to himself as he angrily grabbed his books. . . .

2. Determine details for each stage of your **plot**.

> Exposition—Ever since school started in the fall, "Billy the Bully" had been pestering kids waiting for the school bus.

3. Make every action in the plot add to the **conflict** of your story.

> "Uh-oh," Mark muttered. "I'd better warn her before Billy gets here and pulls one of his tricks."

4. Add **sensory details** to describe the setting and action clearly.

> Suddenly the air was charged with electricity, as it is before a thunderstorm.

5. Use description and dialogue to develop the **main and minor characters.**

> Billy just stood there staring at them with his mouth open. Mark smiled at him and invited calmly, "Want to join us?"

Apply Good Writing Traits: Organization

Read the sentence below from "Dragon, Dragon." Which word helps you understand the order of events?

As you draft your story, decide which words will clearly show the order of events. After you finish, read your draft and ask yourself if any events are missing or seem out of place.

> Now the cobbler's middle son decided it was his turn to try.

Analyze a Student Model

"Billy is really in for it now!" Mark Johnson said to himself as he angrily grabbed his books on his way to Manzanita Middle School. Ever since school started in the fall, "Billy the Bully" had been pestering kids waiting for the school bus. Yesterday was the last straw for Mark when Billy took Maya's science book and threw it in a mud puddle. Mark really cared about his friends and hated to see them hurt.

As Mark walked to the bus stop a few minutes later, he thought about all the bad things Billy had done to him and his friends. He needed to find a way to give that bully a taste of his own medicine. But how? Mark was still thinking hard as he arrived at the bus stop. There was no sign of Billy, but Maya was standing there plugged into her MP3 player. Her eyes were closed, and she looked like she was on another planet. "Uh-oh," Mark muttered. "I'd better warn her before Billy gets here and pulls one of his tricks."

Before Mark even finished his thought, Billy swaggered around the corner, wearing a bright red cap, whistling loudly, and kicking stones out of his way. Suddenly the air was charged with electricity, as it is before a thunderstorm. Mark's eyes lit up and he sprang into action.

He strode over to Maya and pointed to her ear. As she removed her earphone, he began waving his hands like an orchestra conductor and singing along with the music. Maya joined in. Then they began to dance. Billy just stood there staring at them with his mouth open. Mark smiled at him and invited calmly, "Want to join us?" Billy looked confused, and his face got red. He hung his head, walked by the bus stop, and kept on walking. Maya watched Billy go and turned to Mark. "That's showing him, Mark," she cooed. "You're my hero."

Point of View and Narrator

This is third-person point of view because the narrator is outside of the story.

Plot

Notice the background information about Billy in the exposition.

Conflict

Include external conflict (the conflict between Mark and Billy) and internal conflict (Mark's conflict within himself), such as the last sentence in the first paragraph.

Sensory Details

Give specific details that help readers see and feel the setting and action.

Dialogue

Have characters speak in a way that tells readers about their personalities.

Revise

Now it's time to revise your draft so your ideas really shine. Revising is what makes good writing great, and great writing takes work!

Peer Review Trade drafts with a partner. Use the chart below to review your partner's draft by answering the questions in the *What to do* column. Talk about your peer review after you have glanced at each other's drafts and have written the answers to the questions. Next, follow the suggestions in the *How to do it* column to revise your draft.

Revising Plan

What to do	How to do it	Example
Can the reader easily identify the narrator and the point of view?	Use the pronouns *I* and *me* for the first-person point of view and *he, she, him, her,* and *they* for the third-person point of view.	"Billy is really in for it now!" ^Mark Johnson I said to ^himself ~~myself~~ as ^he ~~I~~ angrily grabbed ^his ~~my~~ books.
Did you include all stages of the plot?	Write about events in the order they happen. Use expressions such as *before* and *an hour later* to make the order clear. Add any events that are missing.	As Mark walked to the bus stop ^a few minutes later, he thought about all the bad things Billy had done to him and his friends.
Is the conflict part of every event and the basis for the theme?	Include events that help develop the conflict and theme. Get rid of details that don't belong.	Mark was still thinking hard as he arrived at the bus stop. ~~He suddenly remembered that he had a social studies test that afternoon.~~
Have you used sensory details to describe the setting and action?	Choose specific, concrete words that help readers see, hear, smell, taste, or touch.	As she removed her earphone, he ~~was moving around~~ ^began waving his hands like an orchestra conductor and singing along with the music.
Does the reader know the characters better through your careful use of dialogue and description?	Write dialogue that reflects a character's personality and shows how he or she thinks or feels.	~~"Thank you," she said.~~ ^"That's showing him, Mark," she cooed. "You're my hero."

Edit and Proofread

For your final draft, read your narrative one sentence at a time. An editing and proofreading checklist may help you spot errors. Use the proofreading symbols in the chart inside the back cover of this book to mark needed changes. Then make corrections.

Grammar Focus: Punctuation of Dialogue

Readers can learn a lot about characters from their conversations with other characters. Be sure to use quotation marks for dialogue and apply other punctuation rules. Below are examples of problems with punctuation of dialogue from the Workshop Model and their solutions.

Problem: It is unclear which words are spoken.

Billy is really in for it now! Mark Johnson said to himself.

Solution: Put quotation marks before and after spoken words.

"Billy is really in for it now!" Mark Johnson said to himself.

Problem: Punctuation is used incorrectly within the quotation.

"That's showing him, Mark she cooed."

Solution A: Put a comma and a quotation mark at the end of the spoken words. Then add the speaker tag and a period.

"That's showing him, Mark," she cooed.

Solution B: Begin with the speaker tag followed by a comma. Then enclose the spoken words and end punctuation in quotation marks.

She cooed, "That's showing him, Mark."

Present

It's almost time to share your writing with others. Write your narrative neatly in print or cursive on a separate sheet of paper. If you have access to a computer, type your narrative on the computer and check the spelling. Save your document to a disk and print it out.

Grammar Tip

Question Marks and Exclamation Points When dialogue ends with a question mark or an exclamation point, put the end quotation marks after the punctuation. "Did you see that?" Kelly asked. "What a race!" Tina shouted.

Revising Tip

Speaker Tags Use precise words that give clues about a character's tone of voice. Occasionally replace *said* with words such as *admitted, explained, whispered,* or *cooed.*

Presenting Tip

Classroom Anthology Work with your teacher or a small group to organize and copy each narrative onto a single disk to store as a classroom anthology.

LOG ON **Literature** Online

Writing and Research For editing and publishing tools, go to glencoe.com and enter QuickPass code GL17527u1.

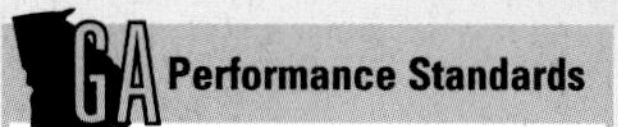

Performance Standards

For page 146

ELA6LSV2a When delivering or responding to presentations, give oral presentations or dramatic interpretations for various purposes.

Speaking, Listening, and Viewing Workshop

Narrative Presentation

Activity

Connect to Your Writing Deliver an oral presentation of a narrative to your classmates. You might want to adapt the narrative you wrote for the Writing Workshop on pages 140–145. Remember that you focused on the Unit 1 Big Question: What makes a hero?

Plan Your Presentation

Reread your story and highlight the sections you want to include in your presentation. Just like your written narrative, your narrative presentation should have a plot with a beginning, a middle, and an end, and it should describe a specific setting. Make sure to include dialogue and descriptive details.

Rehearse Your Presentation

Practice your presentation several times. Try rehearsing in front of a mirror where you can watch your movements and facial expressions. You may use note cards to remind you of the story's important events, but practice your narrative enough times that you won't lose eye contact with your audience.

Deliver Your Presentation

- Speak clearly and precisely.
- Adjust your speaking style and gestures to fit individual characters.
- Change the pace of your speaking to help emphasize important moments throughout your story.
- Change the tone or volume of your voice to communicate emotions or build suspense.

Listening to Appreciate

As you listen, take notes on what you like about the story and its delivery. Use the following types of statement frames to share your appreciation with the storyteller.

- I liked the gesture/voice _______ that you used for the character _______ because _______.
- The general mood of this story seems like _______ to me. You cleverly created that mood by _______.

Presentation Checklist

Answer the following questions to evaluate your presentation.

- ❑ Did you speak clearly and precisely—and in a style that fit your characters?
- ❑ Did you change the pace of your speaking to fit the story's action?
- ❑ Did you vary the tone or volume of your voice to add interest to the story?
- ❑ Did you make eye contact with your audience?

Literature Online

Speaking, Listening, and Viewing For project ideas, templates, and presentation tips, go to glencoe.com and enter QuickPass code GL17527u1.

Unit Challenge

Answer the Big Question

In Unit 1, you explored the Big Question through reading, writing, speaking, and listening. Now it's time for you to complete one of the Unit Challenges below with your answer to the Big Question.

WHAT Makes a Hero?

Use the notes you took in your Unit 1 **Foldable** to complete the Unit Challenge of your choice.

Before you present your Unit Challenge, be sure it meets the requirements below. Use this first plan if you choose to write a story about what kind of hero the world needs today.

On Your Own Activity: A Hero for Today

- ❑ Choose a personal hero you know or have heard about. Decide what problem your hero will solve. List the skills or the traits your hero will need to solve the problem.
- ❑ Use the ideas on your list to write a story about your hero's adventures. How does your hero solve the problem? Be sure to include concrete details to describe the hero's skills, the plot development, and the setting.
- ❑ Tell your classmates about the adventures. Use expressive body language and the appropriate tone of voice for different parts of the story.

Use this second plan if you choose to tell about local heroes.

Group Activity: Local Heroes Who Inspire

- ❑ Write four questions to ask classmates about their heroes.
- ❑ Ask questions slowly and give people time to answer them fully. Listen carefully and write down their answers.
- ❑ Using your classmates' responses, write a paragraph describing each hero and attach a picture if you have one.
- ❑ Read your paragraphs aloud using eye contact, appropriate body language, and vocal inflections.

For page 147

ELA6W2c Demonstrate competence in a variety of genres. Produce a narrative that includes sensory details and concrete language to develop plot, setting, and character.

Independent Reading

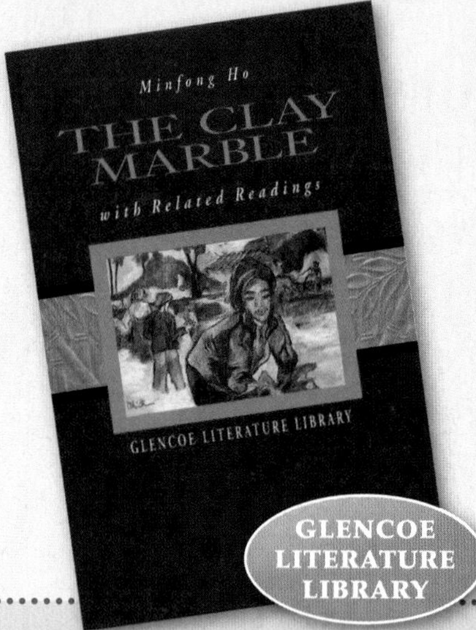

Fiction

To read more about the BIG Question, choose one of these books from your school or local library.

The Clay Marble

by Minfong Ho

During the 1970s, twelve-year-old Dara and her family struggle to survive in war-torn Cambodia. Read to find out how a new friend helps Dara find a way to be reunited with her family after their refugee camp is bombed.

Anansi the Spider: A Tale from the Ashanti

by Gerald McDermott

Anansi the Spider, the wise and mischievous hero of traditional folktales of Ghana, gets into all sorts of trouble but is saved by his six sons. Read to find out how Anansi decides which son to reward with a very special gift.

The Call of the Wild
GLENCOE LITERATURE LIBRARY

The Call of the Wild

by Jack London

This classic book relates the adventures of a dog named Buck. When Buck is kidnapped from his comfortable California home and forced to work as a sled dog in the Yukon gold rush of the late 1800s, he doesn't know what lies ahead. Follow Buck as he fights to survive in the big, wide world.

Where the Red Fern Grows

by Wilson Rawls

A boy and his dogs roam the Ozarks, searching for raccoons. Victory over a mountain lion turns to tragedy, but the boy learns about loyalty and determination—and that all things are possible if you focus on the task.

Nonfiction

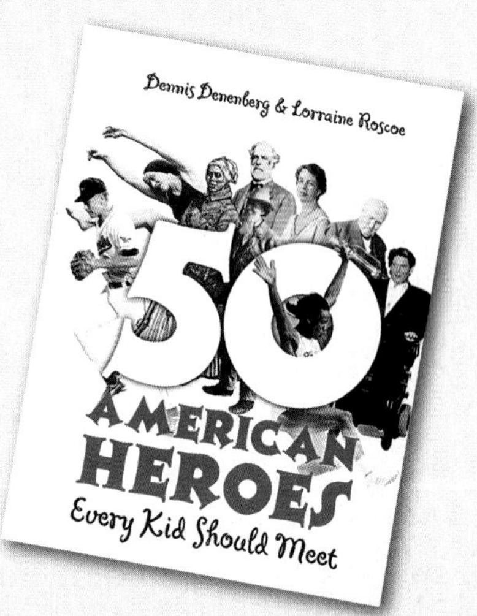

50 American Heroes Every Kid Should Meet

by Dennis Denenberg and Lorraine Roscoe

This book contains short biographies of famous people from various eras and fields of accomplishment. Read to learn more about such heroes as Cesar Chavez, Susan B. Anthony, Frederick Douglass, Dolores Huerta, John Glenn, and Harriet Tubman.

First in the Field: Baseball Hero Jackie Robinson

by Derek T. Dingle

This photobiography focuses on the childhood and early adulthood of the man who was the first African American player in the major leagues. The book includes a time line of African American milestones in sports history.

The Endless Steppe: Growing Up in Siberia

by Esther Hautzig

This autobiography tells how the author and her family were taken from their remote Siberian village in 1941 and sent to a labor camp. Young Esther, her mother, and her grandmother must try to stay together and make a new life in extremely difficult conditions.

Write a Review

Write a review for your classmates of the book you read. Evaluate the author's craft as you explain what you found interesting, unusual, exciting, or even annoying in the book. Explain why you would or would not recommend the book. Include specific examples and descriptive details to support your ideas.

Assessment

READING

Read the passage and answer the questions. Write your answers on a separate sheet of paper.

from **"The Gold Cadillac"** by Mildred D. Taylor

My sister and I were playing out on the front lawn when the gold Cadillac rolled up and my father stepped from behind the wheel. We ran to him, our eyes filled with wonder. "Daddy, whose Cadillac?" I asked.

And Wilma demanded, "Where's our Mercury?"

My father grinned. "Go get your mother and I'll tell you all about it."

"Is it ours?" I cried. "Daddy, is it ours?"

"Get your mother!" he laughed. "And tell her to hurry!" Wilma and I ran off to obey as Mr. Pondexter next door came from his house to see what this new Cadillac was all about. We threw open the front door, ran through the downstairs front parlor and straight through the house to the kitchen where my mother was cooking and one of my aunts was helping her. "Come on, Mother-Dear!" we cried together. "Daddy say come on out and see this new car!"

"What?" said my mother, her face showing her surprise. "What're you talking about?"

"A Cadillac!" I cried.

"He said hurry up!" relayed Wilma.

And then we took off again, up the back stairs to the second floor of the duplex.[1] Running down the hall, we banged on all the apartment doors. My uncles and their wives stepped to the doors. It was good it was a Saturday morning. Everybody was home.

"We got us a Cadillac! We got us a Cadillac!" Wilma and I <u>proclaimed in unison</u>. We had decided that the Cadillac had to be ours if our father was driving it and holding on to the keys. "Come and see!" Then we raced on, through the upstairs sunroom, down the front steps, through the downstairs sunroom, and out to the Cadillac. Mr. Pondexter was still

---

1 **duplex:** having two parts, in this case two floors

there. Mr. LeRoy and Mr. Courtland from down the street were there too and all were admiring the Cadillac as my father stood proudly by, pointing out the various features.

"Brand-new 1950 Coupe de Ville!" I heard one of the men saying.

"Just off the showroom floor!" my father said. "I just couldn't resist it."

My sister and I eased up to the car and peeked in. It was all gold inside. Gold leather seats. Gold carpeting. Gold dashboard. It was like no car we had owned before. It looked like a car for rich folks.

"Daddy, are we rich?" I asked. My father laughed.

"Daddy, it's ours, isn't it?" asked Wilma, who was older and more practical than I. She didn't intend to give her heart too quickly to something that wasn't hers.

"You like it?"

"Oh, Daddy, yes!"

He looked at me. "What 'bout you, 'lois?"

"Yes, sir!"

My father laughed again. "Then I expect I can't much disappoint my girls, can I? It's ours all right!"

Wilma and I hugged our father with our joy. My uncles came from the house and my aunts, carrying their babies, came out too. Everybody surrounded the car and owwed and ahhed. Nobody could believe it.

Then my mother came out.

Everybody stood back grinning as she approached the car. There was no smile on her face. We all waited for her to speak. She stared at the car, then looked at my father, standing there as proud as he could be. Finally she said,

"You didn't buy this car, did you, Wilbert?"

"Gotta admit I did. Couldn't resist it."

"But . . . but what about our Mercury? It was perfectly good."

"Don't you like the Cadillac, Dee?"

"That Mercury wasn't even a year old!"

My father nodded. "And I'm sure whoever buys it is going to get themselves a good car. But we've got ourselves a better one. Now stop frowning, honey, and let's take ourselves a ride in our brand-new Cadillac!"

My mother shook her head. "I've got food on the stove," she said and turning away walked back to the house.

There was an awkward silence and then my father said, "You know Dee never did much like surprises. Guess this here Cadillac was a bit too much for her. I best go smooth things out with her."

Everybody watched as he went after my mother. But when he came back, he was alone.

1. The narrator of this passage is
   A. a father.
   B. a mother.
   C. a neighbor of the family.
   D. one of the family's daughters.

2. Which phrase BEST identifies the setting of this passage?
   A. a new car showroom
   B. a sidewalk and front lawn
   C. inside and outside the narrator's house
   D. the first and second floors of a family home

3. The reader learns about the father's character mainly through
   A. his wife's behavior.
   B. his own words and actions.
   C. what other characters say about him.
   D. the author's description of his thoughts.

4. What technique does the author use to inform the reader that the father has purchased the car?
   A. dialogue
   B. description
   C. characterization
   D. supporting details

5. The sensory details in this passage appeal mostly to the sense of
   A. touch.
   B. hearing.
   C. smell.
   D. sight.

6. During the course of this passage, the father's mood changes from
   A. fear to irritation.
   B. calmness to anger.
   C. sadness to happiness.
   D. confidence to concern.

7. What is the meaning of the phrase *proclaimed in unison* in this passage?
   A. announced the news publicly and together
   B. spoke politely and in a normal tone of voice
   C. thought the words but did not actually say them
   D. took turns telling their relatives about the new car

8. What is the meaning of the word *practical* in this passage?
   A. curious
   B. sensible
   C. educated
   D. emotional

9. Into which period of American history does the setting of this passage fit?
   A. the depression after the Civil War
   B. the Roaring Twenties after World War I
   C. the post-World War II prosperity
   D. the economic boom of the Computer Age

10. In this passage, the major conflict between the mother and father has to do with their attitudes about
    A. their children.
    B. spending money.
    C. the neighborhood.
    D. politeness and manners.

11. What main idea does the author support by describing how the neighbors gather around the car?
    A. The car was not as good as it looked.
    B. Buying a Cadillac was a special thing to do.
    C. The mother was unhappy with her husband.
    D. This purchase made the father a neighborhood joke.

12. What does the story suggest is the reason that the mother walks back into the house?
    A. Everyone around the car has fallen silent.
    B. She is eager to prepare a meal.
    C. She has no interest in seeing the car.
    D. She is upset with her husband's purchase.

 **Literature** Online

Standards Practice For more standards practice, go to glencoe.com and enter QuickPass code GL17527u1.

ENGLISH/LANGUAGE ARTS

Choose the best answer for each question. Write your answers on a separate sheet of paper.

1. Which verb forms should be used to complete the sentence below?

   > After we ____________ in Italy for two years, we ____________ to return to the United States.

   A. lived, deciding
   B. had lived, decided
   C. are living, will decide
   D. lived, decide

2. Which pronoun should be used to complete the sentence below?

   > The girls feared that they had lost ____________ way on the trail.

   A. her
   B. she
   C. their
   D. them

3. Which sentence below is NOT a complete sentence?

   A. How did you get here?
   B. By taking a bus, then a subway.
   C. A good movie is showing at Marketplace Theater.
   D. We can have lunch before we go to the movie.

4. Which sentence BEST combines the three sentences below?

   > My father is very pleased.
   > He is pleased with his new job.
   > His new job is at Carson's Motorworks.

   A. My father is very pleased with his new job at Carson's Motorworks.
   B. The job of the pleased father is a job that is at Carson's Motorworks.
   C. The father is very pleased with his job, and the job is at Carson's Motorworks.
   D. The pleased father is of the Carson's Motorworks new job.

5. Which sentence below contains a plural possessive noun?

   A. I accidentally stepped on my cat's tail.
   B. It was easy to see the horses' excitement.
   C. We thought the porch was our best work.
   D. What do you know about your family's history?

WRITING

Read your assigned topic in the box below. Use one piece of paper to jot down ideas and organize your thoughts. Then neatly write your essay on another sheet of paper.

Expository Writing Topic

Writing Situation

It is your turn to present a program to your Speaker's Club. You have been asked to explain a process in a humorous way. Think of a process you understand well enough to explain to others—for example, how to bathe a dog or clean out a closet.

Directions for Writing

Write an essay to read at the program explaining the process to your fellow club members. Include specific details and amusing examples to show each step clearly.

Writing Checklist

- ☐ Focus on a single topic.
- ☐ Organize your main points in a clear, logical order.
- ☐ Support your ideas or viewpoints with details and examples.
- ☐ Use precise, vivid words.
- ☐ Vary the length and structure of your sentences.
- ☐ Use clear transition words to connect ideas.
- ☐ Correct any errors in spelling, capitalization, punctuation, and usage.

WHY Read?

UNIT TWO

THE BIG Question

Once you've learned to read, you'll be forever set free.

—FREDERICK DOUGLASS

FOLDABLES® Study Organizer

Throughout Unit 2, you will read, write, and talk about the **BIG Question—"Why Read?"** Use your Unit 2 **Foldable,** shown here, to keep track of your ideas as you read. Turn to the back of this book for instructions on making this **Foldable.**

Explore the BIG Question

WHY Read?

How do you find out what is happening in the world, what route a city bus takes, where a movie is showing, or what's on the menu at a restaurant? You find out by reading. Explore how reading can help you get the information you need.

Think about how reading can help you meet these goals:

- Learning About the World
- Exploring Traditions

What You'll Read

Reading different types of works can help you explore the world. In this unit, **informational texts**—nonfiction that conveys facts and information without giving personal opinions—are excellent sources of information. You will also read short stories, folktales, poetry, and other texts that can lead you to discover answers to the Big Question.

What You'll Write

As you explore the Big Question, you'll write notes in your Unit 2 **Foldable.** Later you'll use these notes to complete two writing assignments related to the Big Question.

1. **Write a Functional Document**
2. **Choose a Unit Challenge**
    - **On Your Own Activity: Conduct Interviews**
    - **Group Activity: Comic Strip**

What You'll Learn

Literary Elements

author's purpose
flashback
imagery
description
text features
oral tradition
folktale
haiku
conflict
text structure

Reading Skills and Strategies

question
skim and scan
connect to today
recognize author's purpose
analyze text structure
determine main idea and supporting details
make inferences about character
identify cause-and-effect relationships

To Young Readers

Gwendolyn Brooks

The Library, 1960. Jacob Lawrence. Tempera on fiberboard, 60.9 x 75.8 cm. National Museum of American Art, Washington, DC. © ARS, NY.

Good books are
bandages
and voyages
and linkages° to Light;

are keys and hammers,
ripe redeemers,°
dials and bells and
healing hallelujah.

Good books are good nutrition.
A reader is a Guest
nourished, by riches of the Feast,
to lift, to launch, and to applaud the world.

4 ***Linkages*** is another way of saying *links,* or connections.
6 ***Redeemers*** are rescuers or saviors.

Set a Purpose for Reading

Read this poem to discover the many things that reading can do for you.

BQ BIG Question

How might a book be a key or a hammer?

After You Read

Respond and Think Critically

1. Use your own words to retell what the poem says about good books. **[Summarize]**
2. What is the tone of this poem? **[Identify]**
3. What does the poet mean when she says that good books are "ripe redeemers"? **[Interpret]**
4. Do you agree with the poet about the power of reading? Why or why not? **[Evaluate]**

Writing

Reader Response Notice the many comparisons in this poem, which are meant to suggest to readers the purposes that good books can serve. These include *bandage, voyage, linkage, key, hammer, bell,* and *nutrition*. Pick your favorite comparison and write a paragraph about what it means in the poem and why you like it. Use evidence and examples from the text to support your interpretation and ideas. You may want to begin your paragraph with this topic sentence:

This poem says that a good book can be a __________.
This means __________.

La Lectura (Reading). Arturo Gordon Vargas. Private collection.

GA Performance Standards

For page 160

ELA6W2d Demonstrate competence in a variety of genres. Produce a response to literature that organizes an interpretation around several clear ideas, premises, or images.

LOG ON Literature Online

Selection Resources For Selection Quizzes, eFlashcards, and Reading-Writing Connection activities, go to glencoe.com and enter QuickPass code GL17527u2.

Part 1

Learning About the World

Line School, 1986. Ditz. Private Collection.

BQ BIG Question Why Read?

How is the student in the picture showing that she is curious about the world around her? What have you learned through reading that has made you wonder about the world?

Before You Read

Tracking Trash

Connect to the Article

What are some common items that you might expect to see washed up on a beach? Have you ever found an interesting or unusual item on the shore?

List List common and uncommon items you might find on a beach. Make a guess about where each item came from.

Build Background

Oceanographers are scientists who study oceans. "Tracking Trash" focuses on how these scientists learn about ocean currents.

- The oceans of the world are huge and cover about 70% of Earth's surface. Three major oceans, the Pacific, the Atlantic, and the Indian, surround Earth's land masses. North of the arctic circle, the Atlantic Ocean is often referred to as the Arctic Ocean. The region surrounding Antarctica is known as the Antarctic Ocean.
- The routes of ocean currents are difficult to trace because forces such as gravity, wind, and temperature affect them.

Earth's Oceans

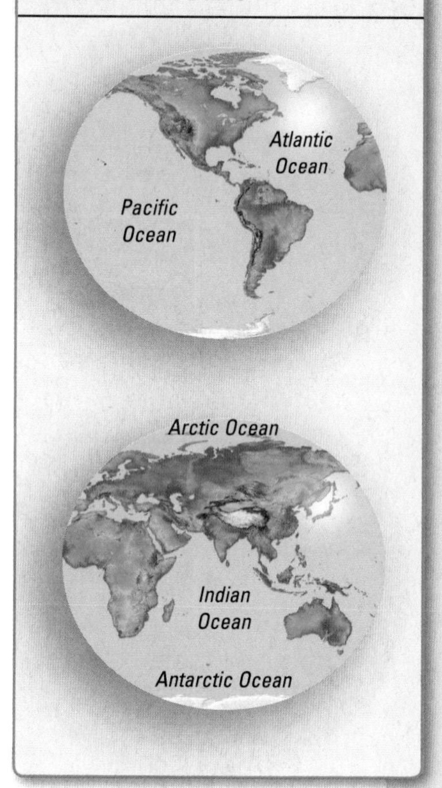

Vocabulary

soggy (sog′ ē) *adj.* filled with water to the point that no more can be absorbed (p. 164). *Hungry ducks dove for the soggy crackers we had tossed into the water.*

predict (pri dikt′) *v.* to say or guess ahead of time what is going to happen, using observation, experience, or reason (p. 165). *Scientists can predict when a volcano will erupt.*

seasonal (sē′ zə nəl) *adj.* affected by the seasons; happening at a certain season (p. 165). *Jim prefers to prepare dishes that feature seasonal vegetables.*

abandoned (ə ban′ dənd) *adj.* deserted, left behind (p. 167). *The storm-tossed ship, abandoned by its crew, sank beneath the waves.*

theory (thē′ ər ē) *n.* a guess based on evidence (p. 167). *Kareem has a theory that cats are smarter than dogs.*

Set Purposes for Reading

BQ BIG Question

As you read, ask yourself, what am I learning about the world by reading "Tracking Trash"?

Literary Element Author's Purpose

The **author's purpose** is what the author tries to do by writing a particular work—to **entertain**, to **inform**, to **persuade**, or to **express emotion**. Sometimes the author has more than one purpose. In an informational article, such as "Tracking Trash," the author's main purpose is to inform readers about a topic.

Knowing the author's purpose helps you understand why you are reading. You will be ready to watch for examples that tell you what the author wants to communicate. You will notice the author's choice of words that carry special meanings.

Reading Strategy Question

When you **question** as you read, you have a conversation with yourself by asking and trying to answer questions about the text. Questioning is a way of checking how well you understand what the author is telling you.

It is useful to question as you read informational texts. Looking for answers to your questions helps you stay focused and involved. As an active reader, you gain a better understanding of what you read.

To question as you read, ask yourself,

- Why does the author include this detail, this example, or these words?
- Do I understand what the author means here or should I reread it?
- What surprises me about this detail?
- What am I curious about?

You may find it helpful to use a graphic organizer like the one below. Use your graphic organizer to take logical notes that will help you track your questions and answers and help you clarify your understanding of the text.

Detail, Example, or Words	My Question
Junk falls off cargo ships.	Why does it fall off?

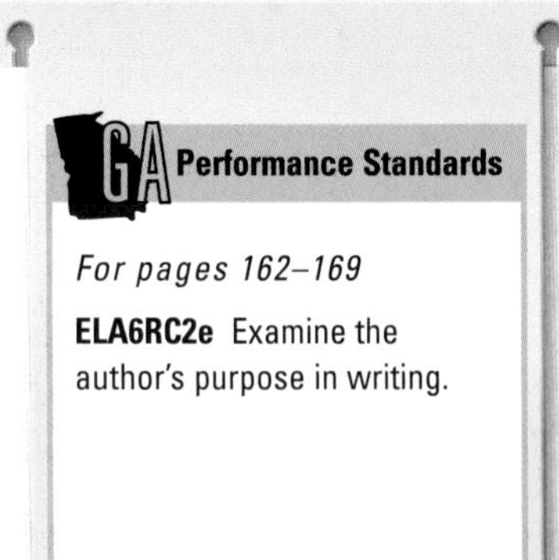

GA Performance Standards
For pages 162–169
ELA6RC2e Examine the author's purpose in writing.

TRY IT

Question You are on a beach on a warm day. You see someone wearing a winter coat and building a sand castle around a huge pile of shoes. What questions would you be asking yourself at this moment?

Tracking Trash

Rachel Young

Scientist Curtis Ebbesmeyer studies the trash that washes ashore on beaches—from bathtub toys to hockey gloves—to learn about the movement of ocean currents.

Oceanographer Curtis Ebbesmeyer studied currents for many years without giving a thought to the junk, known as **flotsam,** that falls off cargo ships and drifts through the world's oceans. Then, in 1991, his mother showed him a newspaper article about beachcombers[1] in his home state of Washington who had come across brand-new Nike sneakers that had washed ashore. The shoes, some of the 80,000 that fell off a ship called the *Hansa Carrier* on May 28, 1990, traveled the seas for months before currents dumped them on Washington beaches. Other shoes landed at other Pacific Ocean beaches—one even made its way to Hawaii.

Lucky beachcombers traded with one another to get a matched pair of **soggy** yet still wearable shoes. But Ebbesmeyer realized that the Nikes were good for more than just playing basketball. The shoes, which had ridden ashore on ocean currents, might be used to track those mysterious rivers of water that move through the sea.

Question What question could you ask about the trip the shoes made?

Visual Vocabulary

Flotsam is the floating wreckage of a ship or of cargo swept overboard from a ship.

1 ***Beachcombers*** are people who search for things along a shore.

Vocabulary

soggy (sog′ ē) *adj.* filled with water to the point that no more can be absorbed

An understanding of how fast currents move and where they flow can help scientists **predict** such things as hurricanes and the **seasonal** journeys of certain fish. But currents are difficult to study. "The only way you can see them is if you watch something drifting along," says Ebbesmeyer. Early oceanographers dropped bottles into the ocean to see where they'd wash up. According to Ebbesmeyer, flotsam can be as useful as those drift bottles—maybe even more useful, because there's just so much of it.

Every day giant boats called container ships carry goods from the countries where they're made to the rest of the world. These ships transport a whopping 100 million containers a year. Of those, a few thousand fall overboard during storms, and some of those containers open, spilling their contents into the ocean. Each container is the size of the trailer on a semitruck, so each open container equals a lot of flotsam—10 thousand sneakers or 5 million plastic shopping bags in just one. "You get to study the ocean with huge numbers of free drifters," Ebbesmeyer says.

Question What conversation might you have with yourself to help you understand Ebbesmeyer's statement?

Author's Purpose Why does the author mention this?

Vocabulary

predict (pri dikt′) *v.* to say or guess ahead of time what is going to happen, using observation, experience, or reason

seasonal (sē′ zə nəl) *adj.* affected by the seasons; happening at a certain season

Beachcombers found dozens of new Nike sneakers on Washington shores. The sneakers were soggy but wearable—as long as you could find a matching pair.

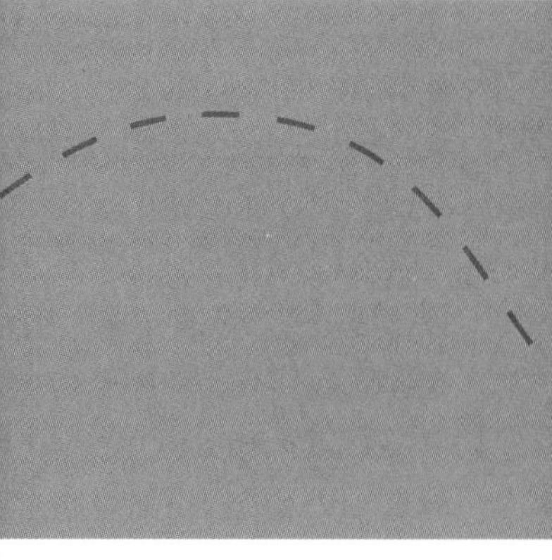

Because Ebbesmeyer learned the exact date and place where the shipment of Nikes fell overboard, and then the date and place where more than a thousand of the shoes washed ashore, he could trace their paths through the ocean, then match them to models scientists created to predict how currents move. Ebbesmeyer and other scientists also used computer models to predict where more shoes might end up next.

Word got out that a scientist was interested in the odd things found on the beach, and Ebbesmeyer began getting tips from beachcombers all over the world. In November 1993 he learned that hundreds of children's bathtub toys—red beavers, blue frogs, green turtles, and yellow ducks—had been found along the shore in Sitka, Alaska. For a scientist trying to understand how flotsam floats along the currents, what could be better than a fleet of plastic ducks—toys that are made to float!

The ducks had been found, but to trace their paths through the ocean, Ebbesmeyer had to know where they'd been lost. After a year of detective work, he ended up on board a ship docked in Tacoma, Washington. The logbook entry for January 10, 1992, noted that a container filled with 29,000 bathtub toys fell overboard about half-way between China and Seattle.

Author's Purpose What is the author trying to point out here?

For the next 10 years, the sturdy toys sailed across the Pacific Ocean. The ducks moved even faster than the current, Ebbesmeyer found, because the top of each toy, which floated above water, worked like the sail of a ship blown by the wind. Most of the toys probably circled the North Pacific, a journey of three years and thousands of miles, but others got trapped in the huge still spaces at the center of circling currents. Computer models predicted some toys might float south toward Hawaii, while others would spin north through the Bering Strait that divides Alaska and Russia, then make their way through the Arctic Ocean and south to the Atlantic.

Ebbesmeyer predicted that the ducks would begin arriving in New England in 2001, and the company that made the toys offered $100 for any of its ducks found on Atlantic beaches. No one has won the reward yet—though

Question What might you wonder about this company's offer?

This map shows just a few of the many possible paths taken by the bathtub toys.

many people have sent in ducks made by other companies, perhaps **abandoned** at the beach by a forgetful toddler. (The $100 ducks will be stamped with the company's name, The First Years, and their color will have faded from bright yellow to white.)

Fifteen years after the ducks began their journey, Ebbesmeyer is hopeful that some will be found on a beach in England or Florida or Maine, proving his **theory** that some ducks traveled from the Pacific Ocean to the Atlantic. Either way, he'll keep using the forgotten junk that fills the seas to figure out all he can about currents. As he puts it, "You can learn a lot from a duck on the beach."

Vocabulary

abandoned (ə ban′ dənd) *adj.* deserted, left behind

theory (thē′ ər ē) *n.* a guess based on evidence

BQ BIG Question

In what ways has reading this informational article given you a better understanding of ocean currents?

After You Read

Respond and Think Critically

1. How did Curtis Ebbesmeyer become interested in tracking trash? **[Recall]**
2. What two important things can understanding the speed and the paths of currents help scientists predict? **[Identify]**
3. How does Ebbesmeyer use flotsam to track currents? Are his successes due more to luck or more to hard work? Support your answer with details from the article. **[Analyze]**
4. Does this article make you want to go and look for flotsam that has washed up on a beach? Why or why not? **[Connect]**
5. Considering the details provided in this article, how likely do you think it is that most of the lost plastic bath toys will be found? Explain. **[Infer]**
6. **BQ** **BIG Question** Give two reasons why someone might want to read this article. Did you find the article interesting? Explain. **[Evaluate]**

TIP

Analyzing
To answer question 3, think about the techniques that Ebbesmeyer uses and the importance of luck in his work.

- Review the methods Ebbesmeyer uses to track trash.
- Which conditions need to be right for him to find flotsam?
- How many of these conditions can he control?

Keep track of your ideas about the **BIG Question** in your unit Foldable.

Connect to Science

"Tracking Trash" focuses on flotsam that washes up on shore. Some flotsam, however, remains in the ocean for years and years. This is because it gets trapped in a gyre—a circular ocean current.

Wind patterns usually cause a gyre. Wind stirs up the water on the ocean's surface and causes it to move in a circle, much like a giant whirlpool. Although a gyre starts with wind on the ocean's surface, the water below often circulates as far down as 1,000 meters. Sometimes a gyre extends all the way to the seafloor.

Group Activity Discuss the following questions with your classmates:

1. How could gyres complicate the work of oceanographers?
2. What do you think eventually happens to trash that is trapped in gyres?

Literary Element Author's Purpose

Standards Practice  ELA6RC2e

1. All of the following are purposes of the author in "Tracking Trash" EXCEPT
   A. to inform the reader about the behavior of currents.
   B. to tell the reader how to find ducks on the beach.
   C. to explain to the reader what flotsam is.
   D. to describe how oceanographers work.

Review: Text Structure

As you learned on page 47, **text structure** is the order in which ideas are presented in a text. The text structure of this article is **chronological order**. Most of the events are narrated in the order in which they occurred, and the author uses phrases such as *in 1991*, *in November 1993*, and *for the next 10 years* to make this order clear.

You may find it helpful to use a graphic organizer like the one below to put events in the article in order. Add as many boxes as you need.

First Event: Nike shoes fell off cargo ship. Signal Words: May 28, 1990

Second Event: Ebbesmeyer read article about shoes. Signal Words:

Reading Strategy Question

Standards Practice  ELA6R1d

2. Which of the following questions might help you better understand the article?
   A. Does Ebbesmeyer have a middle name?
   B. Why are the plastic bathtub-toy beavers red?
   C. Why don't beachcombers find something better to do?
   D. How do computer models predict currents?

Vocabulary Practice

For each set of words, decide whether the words have the same or opposite meanings. Then create a sentence for each vocabulary word or draw or find a picture that represents the word.

abandoned and protected
seasonal and unchanging
predict and forecast
soggy and crisp
theory and guess

Example:

abandoned and protected = opposite meanings

Sentence: We spied an abandoned house near the edge of the forest.

Academic Vocabulary

Curtis Ebbesmeyer checked a **document** from the shipping company to see whether any cargo had been lost. In this sentence, *document* is used as a noun and means "a written record." *Document* can also be used as a verb. For example: Ebbesmeyer was careful to document the date and place that the shoes fell into the ocean. What does *document* mean in this sentence? How do the two uses of *document* differ?

Literature Online

Selection Resources For Selection Quizzes, eFlashcards, and Reading-Writing Connection activities, go to glencoe.com and enter QuickPass code GL17527u2.

Respond Through Writing

Summary

Report Main Ideas and Events In two or three paragraphs, write a summary of "Tracking Trash" in which you report its main ideas and events.

Understand the Task When you **summarize,** you retell an article in your own words. You do not need to repeat all the information. Pick out the most important ideas and events. Then retell them simply and clearly.

Prewrite Skim the article to remind yourself of the main points and important details. Then jot down each main point, followed by any essential details. Keep track of these ideas in a graphic organizer like the one below.

Main Points	Essential Details
Ebbesmeyer studies currents.	Flotsam falls off ships and drifts through oceans.

Draft Before you begin writing, plan your summary. Decide how many paragraphs you will write and which points you will cover in each one. Think about how you will begin each paragraph. Write a topic sentence that makes it clear what each paragraph will be about.

Revise After you write your draft, read it over and think about ways you could improve it. Trade papers with one or two of your classmates and evaluate each other's drafts. Do the paragraphs follow a logical order? Does the summary cover all the main points and avoid unnecessary details? Rewrite any sections of your summary that you think you could improve.

Edit and Proofread When you have finished revising, proofread your summary to correct errors in spelling, grammar, and punctuation. Review the Grammar Tip in the side column for information on using commas in a series.

Performance Standards

For page 170

ELA6W2h Demonstrate competence in a variety of genres. Produce writing that concludes with a detailed summary linked to the purpose of the composition.

Grammar Tip

Commas in a Series

Use **commas** to separate three or more items in a series. For example:

Ebbesmeyer found shoes, bath toys, and shopping bags washed up on the beach.

Notice the comma before the word *and.* It is called a **serial comma.** Remember to use this comma before the word *and* or the word *or* when you list three or more items. Never use a comma before those words when you list only two items.

Before You Read

Functional Documents

Connect to the Functional Documents

Think about a time when you needed practical information to solve a problem or complete a task in everyday life.

Partner Talk With a partner, talk about forms or applications you have completed or instructions you have read. What kind of information did the documents contain? How did they help you?

Build Background

Functional documents have a practical purpose. The information they contain allows people to perform everyday tasks more easily or quickly.

- You read and fill out an **order form** when you send away for something, such as a magazine subscription. You may need to fill in the requested information by writing on the form's lines. Information on the form may be given in words, charts, or pictures. An **online form** works the same way but is in electronic form.
- When you want to open a bank account or apply for a job, you fill out an **application.** An application often includes questions and requires you to provide specific personal information.
- Documents that give **instructions** often explain a process in sequence, or step-by-step order. Technical instructions usually tell how to do something on a computer.

Set a Purpose for Reading

Reading Strategy Skim and Scan

Good readers adapt their reading to their purpose. When you preview a document, you should **skim,** or read it quickly for key ideas. When you need to find specific information, you **scan,** or search for the particular information you want.

- When you skim, pay attention to text features such as titles, headings, subheads, and words set in special type. Notice the text structure, or logical plan, in which information is presented.
- When you scan, quickly run your eyes over the material and look for key words and phrases important to your search.

GA Performance Standards

For pages 171–177

ELA6R1b For informational texts, apply knowledge of common graphic features.

ELA6RC2f Recognize and use the features of texts.

Understand Mail-Order Forms

What kind of functional document is this? Explain when someone might use it.

Want help with your new pet? Need the perfect gift?

Pet Care Magazine

FOR THE BEST IN PET CARE

for ages 10 to 14

☐ **24 issues for only $35.00**
Save up to $60 off the cover price!
That's like getting more than a *whole year FREE!*

☐ **12 issues for $17.97**
Save $29 off the cover price!

Name (please print)

Address Apt.

City/State/ZIP

Parent's e-mail address (**optional:**[1] to receive our pet care newsletter and offers that may be of interest)

☐ Payment is enclosed (check or money order).

☐ Bill me later

Please allow 6–8 weeks for delivery

If subscription[2] is a gift, fill out information below.

Name of gift recipient[3]

Address Apt.

City/State/ZIP

Gift message

Return your order form to

Pet Care Magazine
634 Westover Hills Dr.
Glenview, IL 12345

FREE **50 Great Tips for Responsible Dog Owners** booklet with your paid order

Skim Preview the mail-order form. What do you notice about the way information is shown on this page?

Scan Scan the document. What information must you provide if you want to send the magazine as a gift?

1 Something that is ***optional*** is not required.

2 When you buy a ***subscription*** to a magazine, you get the magazine for a certain period of time, such as one or two years, in return for a specified payment.

3 The ***recipient*** of a gift is the person who receives it.

Understand Applications

The title of the document identifies the form as a savings account application. What are the specific parts of the form?

VALLEY VIEW STATE BANK AND TRUST

Custodial[4] Savings Account

Date ______________

APPLICANT[5]

Print Name ______________________________

Address ______________________________

____

Date of Birth ______________________________

Social Security Number ______________________________

Mother's Maiden Name[6] ______________________________

Home Phone ______________________________

School/Employer ______________________________

APPLICANT TAXPAYER CERTIFICATION

(check all that apply)

__1) I am a U.S. citizen or resident alien. The taxpayer identification number (Social Security #) above is correct.

__2) I am exempt from reporting taxpayer information.

__3) I am a foreign nonresident alien.[7]

__4) I have applied for a taxpayer I.D. number. One has not yet been issued to me.

Skim Skim the bottom section of the document. What is the purpose of this section? How can you tell?

4 A ***custodial*** savings account is an account held in a minor's name. The adult, or **custodian,** controls the account, but the funds belong to the minor.

5 An ***applicant*** is a person who asks or applies for something.

6 A woman's ***maiden name*** was her last name before she took a married name.

7 A ***nonresident alien*** is a person who is not a U.S. citizen and lives in another country. A resident alien is a person who is not a U.S. citizen but lives in the United States.

VALLEY VIEW STATE BANK AND TRUST

Custodial Savings Account

CUSTODIAN INFORMATION The signature of the adult custodian is requred for all withdrawals from this account.

Scan When is a signature of the adult custodian required?

Print Name ____________________

Address ____________________

____

Date of Birth ____________________

Social Security # ____________________

Driver's License # ____________________

Issue Date ____________________

Employer ____________________

SIGNATURES

Applicant Signature ____________________

By signing above, I certify that the information herein[8] is to the best of my knowledge correct and complete.

Custodian Signature ____________________

By signing above, I understand that I am custodian for these assets[9] owned by the minor[10] signed here.

For Office Use Only

New Account Number ____________ Primary Officer ____________

Open Date ____________ Banking Officer ____________

Deposit Amount ____________ Interest Rate ____________

8 ***Herein*** is a legal term meaning "in this place." Here, it means "in this document."

9 ***Assets*** are things a person owns that are valuable or useful.

10 A ***minor*** is a person who is under the legal age of adulthood.

Understand Technical Instructions

How do the illustrated computer screens make the information easier to understand?

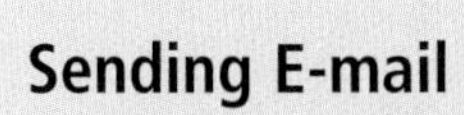

Sending E-mail

With the click of a button, e-mail, or electronic mail, lets you send messages to anyone with access to a computer. In addition to your message, you can also attach computer files or pictures.

To send e-mail, you need an e-mail address with four parts.

- The first part is the user name. This is the name you have chosen for yourself or that is assigned to you by your Internet service provider.
- The second part is the @ symbol, which stands for "at." This symbol separates the user name from the rest of the e-mail address.
- The third part is the domain name, which is the name of the service that hosts your e-mail account.
- The last part of an e-mail address is the suffix. The suffix indicates the type of organization that provides your e-mail service. Common suffixes are .com, .org, .edu, .gov, and .net.

Scan Scan the bulleted list. What are some common suffixes in an e-mail address?

To send an e-mail, follow these instructions.

1. After you start your computer, click on the icon that opens your e-mail feature. It should look something like this:
2. Guide the arrow to **New Mail** and click.
3. On the **To** line, type the e-mail address(es) of the person (or persons) you're writing to. Run all the letters together. Use the **Cc** line to send a copy of your message to another e-mail user.
4. Use the **Subject** line to let the person you're writing to know what your message is about. Be as brief as you can.
5. Type your **message** in the large text box. Keep messages short and to the point.

Skim Skim the document. How is the information organized?

6 Click **Tools** and then click **Spelling**. Then follow the spell-check directions.

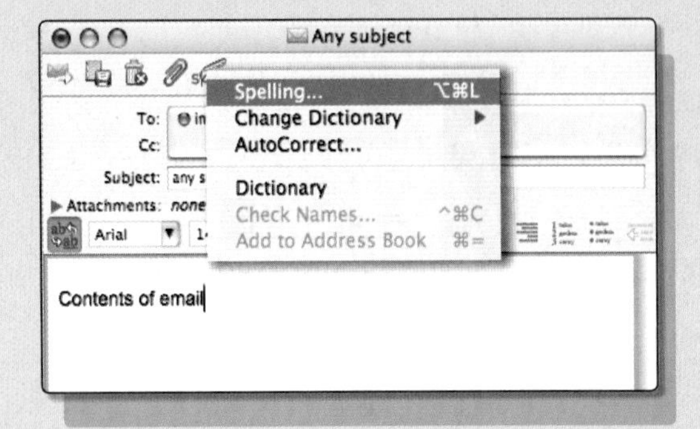

7 To **send** a file with your message, click the attachment feature (often indicated with a paper-clip icon) and follow the instructions.

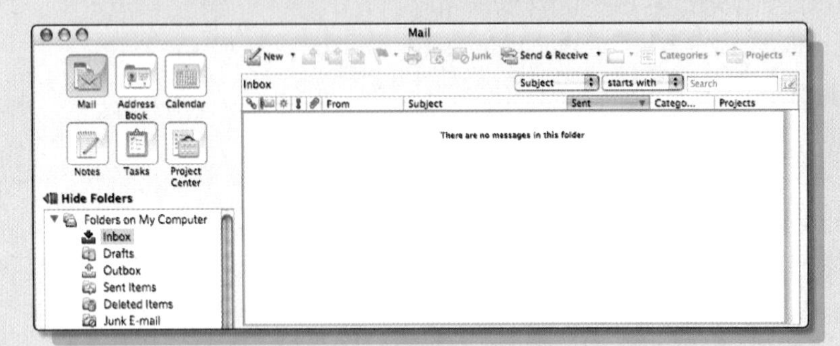

8 Click **Send** after you have checked that your message is friendly, polite, and correct.

Scan Scan this page for a keyword that tells you where to find information on sending files.

After You Read

Respond and Think Critically

Read the questions about the forms and instructions on pages 172–176 and select the best answer.

Standards Practice 

1. What is the main reason for the bulleted list in the e-mail instructions?
   A. to allow people to subscribe to the magazine
   B. to tell about the parts of an e-mail address
   C. to show how to attach a file to a message
   D. to describe the difficulty of sending e-mail

2. Why do two of the three functional documents include write-on lines?
   A. to show step-by-step order
   B. to help you get a job at a bank
   C. to call attention to chronological order
   D. to acquire customer information

3. The documents contain words in boldface (dark) type to
   A. divide the documents into major sections.
   B. provide a step-by-step guide.
   C. call attention to important information.
   D. call attention to charts or illustrations.

4. Which text features of the mail-order form let you know that you have some decisions to make?

5. What action would a person take to attach a file to an e-mail message? Which part of the document explains this?

Writing

Create a Form Think of a school or community club, team, or organization someone might want to join. Create an application.

- Make a list of the information and questions you would need to include on the application.
- Decide on a logical plan to help an applicant find, follow, and understand information.
- Use appropriate text features such as a title, heads, subheads, boldface text, write-on lines, boxes, or bulleted or numbered lists to organize your application.

Literature Online

Selection Resources For Selection Quizzes, eFlashcards, and Reading-Writing Connection activities, go to glencoe.com and enter QuickPass code GL17527u2.

Before You Read

The Sand Castle

Connect to the Story

Imagine spending your entire life indoors—without sun, wind, rain, birds, or trees. What would you miss most?

QuickWrite Write a paragraph about how your life would be different if you had to live indoors all of the time. How would you feel if you could never see sunlight again?

Build Background

"The Sand Castle" is fiction, but it has some basis in fact. Human activities are damaging the ozone, a thin layer of gas in Earth's atmosphere that protects us from the sun.

Ozone blocks many of the sun's harmful ultraviolet rays. Overexposure to these rays may lead to health problems. Unfortunately, the use of human-made chemicals has caused a large hole to form in the ozone layer.

Pollution traps the sun's heat in Earth's atmosphere. The trapped heat makes weather warmer, which may cause floods and storms. This temperature change is often referred to as global warming.

Vocabulary

vehicles (vē′ ə kəlz) *n.* devices designed or used for transporting persons or goods, such as an automobile, a sled, or a carriage (p. 182). *We saw a number of emergency vehicles parked near the accident site.*

interior (in tēr′ ē ər) *n.* inner side, surface, or part (p. 182). *The day was hot, so the family stayed in the cool interior of the house.*

hostile (host′ əl) *adj.* not offering a pleasant or sustaining environment (p. 183). *Scientists are developing crops that can survive in hostile conditions.*

forlorn (fôr lôrn′) *adj.* dejected; hopeless; wretched (p. 183). *Jorge felt forlorn when his best friend moved away.*

Meet Alma Luz Villanueva

"Poetry for me is the source, the mother tongue, the sun, moon, and stars."

—Alma Luz Villanueva

Native American Heritage Alma Luz Villanueva is a poet and novelist. She grew up in San Francisco and lived for many years with her grandmother, a Mexican Yaqui Indian. Villanueva uses themes from her heritage in her writing, such as the Native American sense of oneness with nature. She says that "when we touch the most personal, the most hidden within ourselves, we touch the universal."

Literary Works Villanueva has published short stories, novels, and many books of poetry.

Alma Luz Villanueva was born in 1944.

LOG ON **Literature** Online

Author Search For more about Alma Luz Villanueva, go to glencoe.com and enter QuickPass code GL17527u2.

Set Purposes for Reading

BQ BIG Question

As you read, ask yourself, how can reading a story about the future provide useful information about life today?

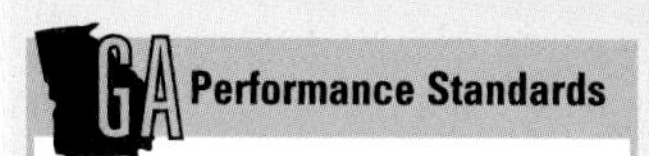

Literary Element Flashback

A **flashback** is an interruption in the normal time order of a story to show an event that happened earlier. A flashback gives readers information that may help explain, clarify, or add emphasis to the main events of the story.

In some stories, the author uses flashbacks to show events from a character's childhood that help explain how that character feels and behaves as an adult.

As you read, watch for flashbacks and think about the contrast between the world of Mrs. Pavloff's childhood and that of her adulthood. How do the flashbacks help the author meet her purpose?

Reading Strategy Connect to Today

When you **connect to today,** you link what you read to events and issues in today's world.

Connecting to today helps you understand the main ideas and the author's message. When reading a story that has an unusual or unfamiliar setting, it is important to consider how the events in the story relate to real issues in the world today.

To connect to today,

- identify the main issues in the story
- link events and issues in the story to those in today's world
- look for a message or lesson that the author might be trying to convey

As you read, think about ways that the events in the characters' lives can be linked to issues in the news today. You may find it helpful to use a graphic organizer like the one below.

Issue in the story	Issue in today's world
sun is dangerous	

GA Performance Standards

For pages 178–187

ELA6R1b For literary texts, identify and analyze the author's use of dialogue and description.

TRY IT

Connect to Today Imagine you read a story written in 1960 in which robots save humans from danger. How do you think the author felt about the effects of technology on people's lives?

The Sand Castle

Alma Luz Villanueva

"Have you dressed yet?" their grandmother called. "Once a month in the sun and they must almost be forced," she muttered. "Well, poor things, they've forgotten the warmth of the sun on their little bodies, what it is to play in the sea, yes. . . ." Mrs. Pavloff reached for her protective sun **goggles** that covered most of her face.

It screened all ultraviolet light[1] from the once life-giving sun; now, it, the sun, scorched the Earth, killing whatever it touched. The sea, the continents, had changed. The weather, as they'd called it in the last century, was entirely predictable now: warming.

Mrs. Pavloff slipped on the thick, metallic gloves, listening to her grandchildren squabble and she heard her mother's voice calling her, "Masha, put your bathing suit

Visual Vocabulary

Goggles are large, close-fitting glasses that protect the eyes. The goggles shown here protect a swimmer's eyes from chlorine. The ones in the story protect the characters' eyes from the sun's radiation.

Flashback What clues in the text help you know that a flashback is coming?

1 The sun's ***ultraviolet light*** is invisible, and it can be harmful.

under your clothes. It's so much easier that way without having to go to the bathhouse first. Hurry! Father's waiting!" She remembered the ride to the sea, the silence when the first shimmers of water became visible. Her father had always been first into the chilly water. "Good for the health!" he'd yell as he dove into it, swimming as far as he could, then back. Then he'd lie exhausted on the sand, stretched to the sun. Such happiness to be warmed by the sun.

Flashback How do Mrs. Pavloff's happy memories of the beach compare with her grandchildren's feelings about it?

Then the picnic. She could hear her mother's voice, "Stay to your knees, Masha! Only to your knees!" To herself: "She'd be a mermaid if I didn't watch," and she'd laugh. Masha would lie belly down, facing the sea and let the last of the waves roll over her. She hadn't even been aware of the sun, only that she'd been warm or, if a cloud covered it, cold. It was always there, the sun: its light, its warmth. But the sea—they traveled to it. So, she'd given all of her attention to the beautiful sea.

Connect to Today What issue in today's world does this passage make you think of?

She saw her father kneeling next to her, building the sand castle they always built when they went to the sea. Her job was to find seashells, bird feathers, and strips of seaweed to decorate it. How proud she'd felt as she placed her seashells where she chose, where they seemed most beautiful. Only then was the sand castle complete. She heard her father's voice, "The Princess's castle is ready, now, for her Prince! Come and look, Anna! What do you think?" She saw herself beaming with pride, and she heard her mother's laugh. "Fit for a queen, I'd say! Can I live in your castle, too, Masha? Please, Princess Masha?"

Radiance. Simon Cook. Acrylic on canvas. Private Collection.

"Of course, Mother! You can live with me always. . . . " She remembered her mother's laughing face, her auburn hair lit up by the sun, making her look bright and beautiful.

The sun, the sun, the sun. The scientists were saying that

with the remedies they were employing now and the remedies begun twenty years ago—they'd stopped all nuclear testing and all manufacturing of ozone-depleting chemicals[2] was banned[3] worldwide—the scientists were saying that the sun, the global problem, would begin to get better. Perhaps for her grandchildren's children. Perhaps they would feel the sun on their unprotected bodies. Perhaps they would feel the delicious warmth of the sun.

Connect to Today What message do you think the author might be trying to convey about global warming?

All **vehicles** were solar powered. The populations took buses when they needed transportation and people emerged mainly at night. So, most human activity was conducted after the sun was gone from the sky. Those who emerged during the day wore protective clothing. Everything was built to screen the sun's light. Sometimes she missed the natural light of her childhood streaming through the windows so intensely the urge to just run outside would overtake her. She missed the birds, the wild birds.

Flashback Compare conditions in Mrs. Pavloff's childhood memory with those in the main setting of the story. Have things gotten better or worse? Explain.

But today they were going out, outside in the daytime, when the sun was still in the sky. Masha knew they were squabbling because they hated to dress up to go outside. The clothing, the gloves, the goggles, were uncomfortable and cumbersome.[4] She sighed, tears coming to her eyes. Well, they're coming, Masha decided. They can remove their goggles and gloves on the bus.

The sea was closer now and the bus ride was comfortable within the temperature controlled **interior.** Those with memories of the sea signed up, bringing grandchildren,

---

2 ***Ozone-depleting chemicals*** reduce (deplete) the ozone layer. This upper layer of the atmosphere protects life on Earth by blocking certain types of harmful radiation.

3 ***Banned*** means "forbidden" or "outlawed."

4 Something that is ***cumbersome*** is hard to handle or carry because of its size or weight.

Vocabulary

vehicles (vē′ ə kəlz) *n.* devices designed or used for transporting persons or goods, such as an automobile, a sled, or a carriage

interior (in tēr′ ē ər) *n.* inner side, surface, or part children, friends, or just went alone. Masha had taken her grandchildren before, but they'd sat on the sand, listlessly,[5] sifting it through their gloved hands with bored little faces. She'd tried to interest them in the sea with stories of her father swimming in it as far as he could. But they couldn't touch it, so it, the sea, didn't seem real to them. What was it: a mass of undrinkable, **hostile** water. Hostile like the sun. They'd taken no delight, no pleasure, in their journey to the sea.

Beach Scene. Charles-Garabeol Atamian. Oil on canvas. Gavin Graham Gallery, Private Collection.

But today, yes, today we will build a sand castle. Masha smiled at her secret. She'd packed everything late last night to surprise them at the sea.

Why haven't I thought of it before? Masha asked herself, and then she remembered the dream, months ago, of building a sand castle with her father at the sea. It made her want to weep because she'd forgotten. She'd actually forgotten one of the most joyful times of her girlhood. When the sea was still alive with life.

Today we will build a sand castle.

Connect to Today How do these joyful memories add to the author's message about important issues in today's world?

They trudged[6] on the thick, dense sand toward the hiss of pale blue. Only the older people picked up their step, excited by the smell of salt in the air. Masha's grandchildren knew they'd be here for two hours and then trudge all the way back to the bus. The darkened goggles made the sunlight bearable. They hated this **forlorn** place where the sun had obviously drained the life out of everything. They were too young to express it, but they

5 ***Listlessly*** means "with little energy, interest, or concern."

6 ***Trudged*** means "walked steadily but with great effort."

Vocabulary

hostile (host′ əl) *adj.* not offering a pleasant or sustaining environment

forlorn (fôr lôrn′) *adj.* dejected; hopeless; wretched

felt it as they walked, with bored effort, beside their grandmother.

"We're going to build a sand castle today—what do you think of that?" Masha beamed, squinting to see their faces.

"What's a sand castle?" the boy mumbled.

"You'll see, I'll show you. . . ."

"Is it fun, Grandmama?" the girl smiled, taking her grandmother's hand.

"Yes, it's so much fun. I've brought different sized containers to mold the sand, and, oh, you'll see!"

The boy gave an awkward skip and nearly shouted, "Show us, Grandmama, show us what you mean!"

Masha laughed, sounding almost like a girl. "We're almost there, yes, we're almost there!"

The first circle of sandy shapes was complete, and the children were so excited by what they were building they forgot about their protective gloves.

"Now, we'll put a pile of wet sand in the middle and build it up with our hands and then we'll do another circle, yes, children?"

The children rushed back and forth from the tide line carrying the dark, wet sand. They only had an hour left. Their eyes, beneath the goggles, darted with excitement.

"Just don't get your gloves in the water, a little wet sand won't hurt, don't worry, children. When I was a girl there were so many birds at the sea we'd scare them off because they'd try to steal our food. Seagulls, they were, big white birds that liked to scream at the sea, they sounded like eagles to me. . . ."

"You used to eat at the sea, Grandmama?" the girl asked incredulously.[7]

"We used to call them picnics. . . ."

"What are eagles, Grandmama?" the boy wanted to know, shaping the dark sand with his gloved hands.

"They used to be one of the largest, most beautiful wild birds in the world. My grandfather pointed them out to me once. . . ." Until that moment, she'd forgotten that memory of nearly sixty years ago. They'd gone on a train,

BQ BIG Question What are you learning about the world of Mrs. Pavloff's grandchildren as you read this story?

Connect to Today What issue in the news today does this passage raise?

Flashback How does this sentence signal that another flashback is coming?

---

7 ***Incredulously*** means "having a hard time believing."

At the Beach. Edward Henry Potthast. Oil on canvas, 24 × 30 in. Private collection.

then a bus, to the village where he'd been born. She remembered her grandfather looking up toward a shrill, piercing cry that seemed to come from the sky. She'd seen the tears in her grandfather's eyes and on his cheeks. He'd pointed up to a large, dark flying-thing in the summer blue sky: "That's an eagle, my girl, the spirit of the people."

Sadness overtook Masha, but she refused to acknowledge its presence. The sand castle, Masha told herself sternly—the sand castle is what is important now. "I've brought a wonderful surprise, something to decorate the sand castle with when we're through building it."

"Show us, Grandmama, please?"

"Yes, please, please show us now!"

Masha sighed with a terrible, sudden happiness as she brought out the plastic bag. Quickly, she removed each precious shell from its protective cotton: eight perfect shells from all over the world.

"But Grandmama, these are your special shells! You said the sea doesn't make them anymore. . . ."

"It will, Anna, it will." Masha hugged her granddaughter and made her voice brighten with laughter. "Today we will decorate our sand castle with the most beautiful shells in the world, yes!"

Connect to Today What would happen if all ocean life died?

After You Read

Respond and Think Critically

1. What causes the sun in the story to be so dangerous? **[Recall]**
2. Summarize Mrs. Pavloff's memories of the day she spent at the beach with her parents. **[Summarize]**
3. Why is the memory of the eagle important to Mrs. Pavloff? What does it mean to her? **[Interpret]**
4. Do you think the children's attitudes change about the type of outing described in the story? Why or why not? **[Infer]**
5. Do the scientific ideas in this story help make it more believable? Why or why not? **[Evaluate]**
6. **BQ BIG Question** If you lived in the time of the story, what would you miss most about the world you live in now? Explain. **[Connect]**

TIP

Summarizing
Here are some tips to help you answer question 2. When you summarize, you retell the main ideas or events.

- Skim the section where Mrs. Pavloff remembers her day at the beach.
- Determine which memories are most important to her.
- Use only the most important details in your summary.

Keep track of your ideas about the **BIG Question** in your unit Foldable.

Connect to Art

Building a sand castle is a fun way to spend time at the beach. However, for some people, a sand castle is art. Some artists call themselves sand sculptors.

Sand sculptors like the idea of creating something that is a part of the natural landscape. They like knowing that sand sculptures are environmentally friendly. Many sand castles are almost as elaborate as real castles. (Some works can involve up to twenty tons of sand!) Of course, not all sand sculptures are castles. They can be giant faces, seashells, monkeys, trees—all created from nothing more than sand and water.

Over time, a sand sculpture crumbles. Wind and water erode the shape. Eventually the sand becomes part of the beach again.

Group Activity Discuss the following questions with your classmates.

1. If you created a sand sculpture, what would it be? What tools do you think you would need? How long would it take?
2. What do you think it means that sand sculptures are environmentally friendly?
3. Most sculptures are permanent. How do you think you would feel about creating a sculpture if you knew it might last only a few days or weeks?

Literary Element Flashback

1. How many flashbacks are there in the story? Where in the story do they occur?
2. What episodes from her childhood does Mrs. Pavloff recall in the flashbacks?
3. How do the episodes described in the flashbacks help develop the characters in the story? How do they help you understand the theme?

Review: Author's Purpose

As you learned on page 163, the **author's purpose** is the author's reason for writing. Most fiction writers want to entertain readers. Other purposes are to inform, to persuade, or to express emotion.

4. Do you think the only purpose of "The Sand Castle" is to entertain? Why or why not?
5. What are some words, phrases, and details that help you determine the author's purpose for writing this story?

Reading Strategy Connect to Today

6. Do you think the author's message in this story is important for today's readers? Why or why not?
7. What action do you think Villanueva would want readers to take today to prevent the conditions depicted in the story from happening in the future?

Vocabulary Practice

On a separate sheet of paper, write the following sentences with the vocabulary word that best completes each sentence. If none of the words fits the sentence, write *none.*

interior

hostile

vehicles

forlorn

1. The building's windows were covered, so we could see nothing of its ______.
2. After playing with his cousins all day, Ed felt ______ when they went home.
3. My uncle's old computer was the ______ of my science project.
4. The conditions on Mars are ______ to human life.
5. Many of the ______ in the parking lot are new.
6. The weather is looking ______, with not a cloud in the sky.

Academic Vocabulary

The setting and plot of "The Sand Castle" vividly **illustrate** possible future consequences of today's human activities.

In the preceding sentence, *illustrate* means "show or explain." Think about something you strongly believe. How could you illustrate this belief for someone else?

Literature Online

Selection Resources For Selection Quizzes, eFlashcards, and Reading-Writing Connection activities, go to glencoe.com and enter QuickPass code GL17527u2.

Respond Through Writing

Expository Essay

Interpret Theme Think about the theme of "The Sand Castle." Write a short expository essay in which you explain the theme.

Understand the Task A **theme** is a message or idea the author wishes to communicate to the reader. Sometimes a writer states the theme directly. More often, however, readers must figure out the theme from the story's details. In this essay, you will explain the theme of "The Sand Castle," using details and examples from the story.

Prewrite Your essay should have an **introduction**, a **body**, and a **conclusion**. In the introduction (the first paragraph), you state the purpose of your essay and explain what you think the theme of the story is. In the body (usually two or three paragraphs), you use examples from the story to support your idea about the theme. In the conclusion, you sum up your interpretation and evidence.

Draft Every paragraph should have a topic sentence. The topic sentence of the introduction, called a **thesis statement**, is also the topic sentence of the essay. Make a concept map of the story's main ideas, like the one below. Then write your draft based on these ideas.

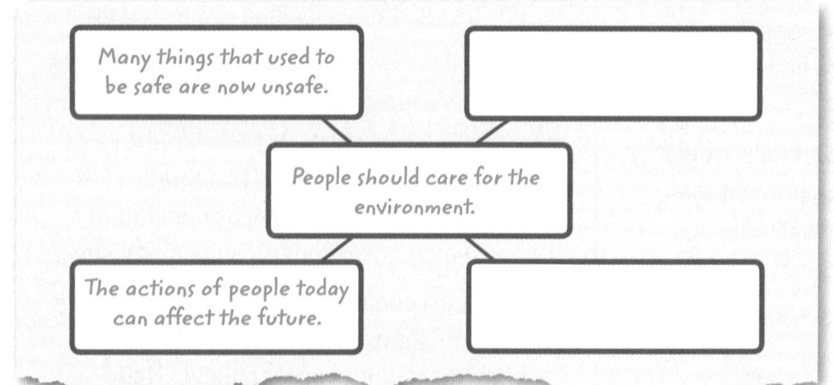

Many things that used to be safe are now unsafe.
People should care for the environment.
The actions of people today can affect the future.

Revise Read your draft several times. Do you have an introduction, a body, and a conclusion? You can use your concept map as a checklist to make sure you have included all the main ideas and essential details to back up your interpretation of the theme. Revise your draft to make sure ideas flow logically from one paragraph to the next.

Edit and Proofread Proofread your paper. Correct any errors in spelling, grammar, and punctuation. Try reading your essay aloud to make sure the writing flows. Make sure you have used quotation marks correctly. See the Word Bank in the side column for words you might use in your expository essay.

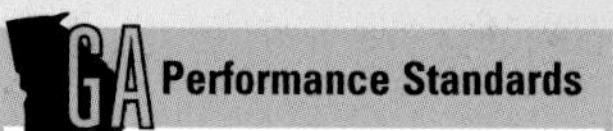

Performance Standards

For page 188

ELA6W2g Demonstrate competence in a variety of genres. Produce writing that follows an organizational pattern appropriate to the composition.

Word Bank

The following list contains some useful words you might want to include in your essay. Check their meanings in a dictionary first to make sure you use them correctly.

conservation
pollute
reduce
species
influence
potential

Grammar Workshop

Sentence Fragments

A sentence fragment is a group of words that is used as a complete sentence. It is not complete, however, because it lacks a subject, a predicate, or both.

Identifying Sentence Fragments

Look at these sentences from "The Sand Castle."

> *Then he'd lie exhausted on the sand, stretched to the sun. Such happiness to be warmed by the sun.*
>
> *Then the picnic.*

A complete sentence has a subject and a predicate and expresses a complete thought. The first sentence has a subject *(he)* and a predicate *(would lie)* and is a complete thought. The second and third sentences are fragments. The writer uses them to produce a special effect. The narrator is remembering her past, and the short, clipped sentences represent her faded memories. In this case, the incomplete thoughts are an intentional part of an experienced writer's storytelling style.

Ordinarily, you would add a subject and a predicate to the second sentence to fix the fragment, such as "He felt such happiness to be warmed by the sun." You would add a predicate to the third sentence, such as "Then the picnic began."

Often, the best way to fix a fragment is to combine it with a related sentence or another fragment to make a compound, complex, or compound-complex sentence, or to simply delete the fragment. For help with combining sentences and proper coordination and subordination, see pages 120–121.

TRY IT: Sentence Fragments

Rewrite these fragments as complete sentences by adding a subject, a predicate, or both to express a complete thought.

1. At most beaches.
2. The sun.
3. Build a sand castle.
4. Her grandchildren.
5. When the sea made shells.

GA Performance Standards

For page 189

ELA6C1c Identify and write simple, compound, and complex, and compound-complex sentences, avoiding fragments and run-ons.

Watch Out!

You may use fragments when talking informally with friends or writing personal letters. Use complete sentences, however, for school or business writing.

Helpful Hint

Fragments sometimes result from carelessness or thinking faster than you can write. Carefully formulate a sentence in your mind before you write it. Reread each sentence to ensure that you have avoided fragments.

Literature Online

Grammar For more grammar practice, go to glencoe.com and enter QuickPass code GL17527u2.

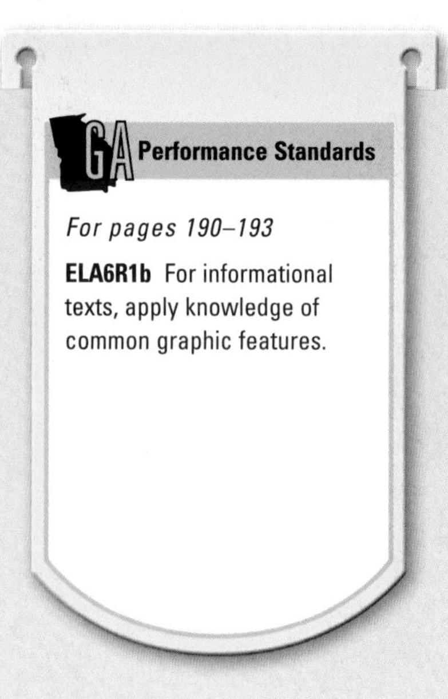

GA Performance Standards
For pages 190–193
ELA6R1b For informational texts, apply knowledge of common graphic features.

Set a Purpose for Reading

As you read, focus on what you can learn from reading accounts about professional athletes' reactions to their mistakes.

Preview the Article

1. What does the **title,** also called a headline, suggest the article is about?
2. Scan the **illustrations.** What do they add to the article?

Reading Strategy

Connect to Personal Experience
When you **connect to personal experience,** you relate the information you read to your own life. As you read, think about a mistake you've made and what you learned from it. Record your thoughts in a chart like the one below.

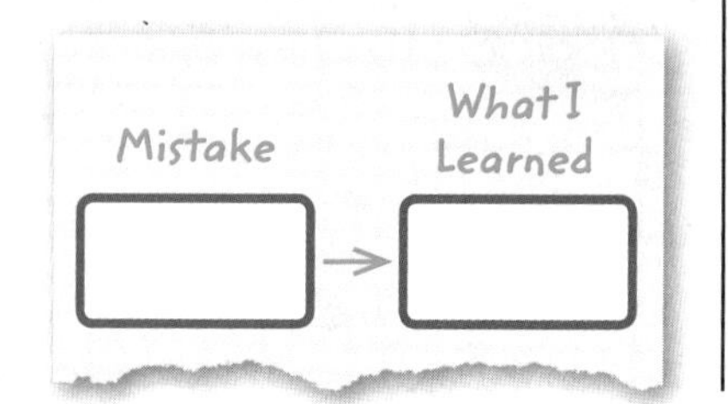

TIME

Nobody's PERFECT

Making a mistake is not the end of the world. It can be pretty funny!

DAVID FISCHER

Everyone makes mistakes, even great athletes. In sports, mistakes are called bloopers. The best way to get over a mistake is to figure out what you did wrong, correct it, and then laugh about it. Here are some of our favorite bloopers.

It's Not Over?

Suzy Favor Hamilton is one of the best distance runners in the United States, but in 1994 she lost a race because she lost count.

Suzy was competing in the mile event at a track meet in Fairfax, Virginia. The runners had to complete eight laps. Near the end of lap 7, Suzy sprinted into the lead. As soon as she crossed the finish line, she stopped running. Suzy thought that the race was over and that she had won! As she watched the other racers run past, she realized her mistake.

"I wanted to tell everybody to stop so that I could jump back in the race," says Hamilton.

Suzy Hamilton stopped running one lap before the race was over.

Keith Locke

Somebody Get Brett!

Quarterback Brett Favre[1] of the Green Bay Packers is cool under pressure. He proved how cool he can be when he led the Packers to victory in Super Bowl XXXI in 1997. But Brett wasn't always so calm.

In 1992, Brett was the Packers' second-string[2] quarterback. In the third game of the season, he went into action against the Cincinnati Bengals. In the fourth quarter, Green Bay trailed Cincinnati by 13 points. But in the last eight minutes of the game, Brett led Green Bay to two touchdowns.

After the second touchdown, he ran off the field. He started jumping and screaming. Brett was so busy celebrating that he forgot an important part of his job. To win the game, Green Bay needed to kick the extra point. Brett was supposed to be on the field, holding the ball for the kick!

Green Bay kicker Chris Jacke ran to the sideline and dragged Brett back onto the field. Chris then kicked the extra point, and the Packers won the game, 24–23.

1 ***Favre*** (färv)

2 A ***second-string*** player substitutes for a starting player.

Hey, Brett: Get in the game!

Keith Locke

Where's My Jersey?

Basketball forward Kevin Garnett of the Minnesota Timberwolves joined the NBA in 1995. He was 19 years old and straight out of high school.

During a game in the early days of his career, Kevin found that he had left something important behind in the locker room. Near the end of the first quarter, Minnesota's coach told Kevin to enter the game. Kevin ran to the scorer's table and pulled off his warm-up top. Then he looked down. Surprise! He was wearing only a T-shirt from practice. Kevin had to race back to the locker room to get the official game jersey that was part of his uniform.

Even though he's older now, Kevin sometimes still acts like a kid.

Look Out Below!

Midori Ito[3] of Japan is one of the best jumpers in figure skating. But during the 1991 World Championships, Midori jumped right out of the skating rink!

During the short program of the women's singles event, Midori was performing a jump. She started the jump too close to the edge of the rink. She flew over a 12-inch wooden barrier[4] at the edge of the ice and landed on a cameraman!

Midori got up, hopped back over the barrier, and completed her routine. She finished in fourth place.

3 ***Midori Ito*** (mə do͞or′ē ē′tō)

4 A ***barrier*** is something that blocks the way or holds two things apart.

Which Way Do I Go?

Jim Marshall was a star defensive end for the Minnesota Vikings from 1960 to 1979. He is best remembered for getting lost on the football field.

It happened in a 1964 game when the Vikings were playing the San Francisco 49ers. In the third quarter, a 49er running back fumbled[5] the football. Jim scooped up the loose ball and ran 66 yards to the end zone.

Jim was pumped.[6] He thought he had scored a touchdown. "A 49ers player ran up and gave me a hug," says Jim. "That's when I knew something was wrong." He had run to the wrong end zone!

The referee[7] ruled that Jim had scored a safety (2 points) for San Francisco. Even so, the Vikings won the game, 27–22. "I still feel embarrassed about that play," says Jim. "But I don't see any reason to hide. I know I was hustling. If people want to laugh, I'll go along with it."

Out By a Foot

Third baseman Dani Tyler of the United States women's softball team learned a lesson at the 1996 Summer Olympics: Always watch your step.

In the fifth inning of a scoreless game against Australia, Dani hit a

5 ***Fumbled*** means "lost one's grasp on something."

6 ***Pumped*** is a shortened slang expression for *pumped up,* which means "filled with excitement, strength, and energy."

7 A ***referee*** is a sports official who enforces the game rules.

Dani danced over the plate.

Keith Locke

home run. When she reached home plate, she leaped to high-five a teammate and jumped right over the plate! The umpire called her out because she never touched home. The United States lost the game in extra innings. It was the U.S. team's second international loss in 10 years.

After the game, Dani said, "From now on, I'm going to paint a big X on home plate and step on it with both feet." The United States went on to win the gold medal.

Wrong Target

At the 2004 Summer Olympic Games in Athens, Greece, Matthew Emmons of the United States was in first place before his final shot in the 50-meter rifle three-position[8] competition.

Matthew was one easy shot away from his second gold medal of the Olympics. All he needed to do was hit the target. So how did Matthew end up in eighth place? He shot at an Austrian competitor's target in the next lane. This Austrian competitor ended up winning the bronze medal.[9]

8 A ***three-position competition*** includes firing from a standing position, a kneeling position, and a prone (lying on the stomach) position.

9 A ***bronze medal*** is awarded to an athlete for winning third place.

Respond and Think Critically

1. Write a brief summary of the main events in this article. For help on writing a summary, see page 170. **[Summarize]**
2. What does Dani Tyler's quotation tell you about her? **[Infer]**
3. How do the title and the subheads convey the tone of the article? **[Analyze]**
4. Does the writer of the article prove his point that mistakes can be funny? Explain your answer. **[Evaluate]**
5. **Reading Strategy** **Connect to Personal Experience** What are some things you have done to get over a mistake?
6. **BQ** **BIG Question** Do you think it is helpful to read about mistakes successful people have made? Why or why not?

Before You Read

who knows if the moon's

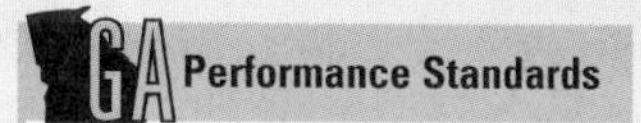

Performance Standards

For pages 194–197

ELA6R1a For literary texts, identify and analyze sensory details and figurative language.

Connect to the Poem

In your mind, picture a full moon.

QuickWrite Freewrite for a few minutes about the image in your mind. How does the moon look? What familiar objects does it look like? What does it make you think about or feel?

Build Background

People have been fascinated by the moon since ancient times. Its mystery and beauty have inspired interesting beliefs. In past cultures, some people thought of the moon as a god. Old legends tell about the power of the full moon turning people into animals or driving them insane. The word *lunatic,* which means "insane," comes from *luna,* the Latin word for "moon."

In the 1960s and 1970s, Apollo astronauts photographed the moon as they orbited it. We now know that the moon is a rocky body with many craters made by the impact of space objects. Lava has filled some of the craters, creating light and dark areas. Seen from Earth, these areas form what some people call "the man in the moon."

Set Purposes for Reading

BQ BIG Question

As you read, ask yourself, how does the poet feel about the moon?

Literary Element Imagery

Imagery is language that appeals to the five senses. It describes how something looks, sounds, feels, smells, or tastes.

Paying attention to imagery helps you visualize settings and characters in a text. It helps you almost see, hear, smell, taste, or feel what is being described. If you try to imagine what is described as you read, you are more likely to understand the text.

As you read the poem, try to picture what the imagery suggests.

LOG ON Literature Online

Author Search For more about E. E. Cummings, go to glencoe.com and enter QuickPass code GL17527u2.

Meet E. E. Cummings

Experimental Poet Edward Estlin Cummings is famous for his experiments with poetry. He wrote about common things such as love, spring, and sunsets. His poems constantly break the rules of grammar and capitalization. Lines don't begin with capital letters. Adjectives are used as nouns. Punctuation is left out or put in an unusual place. Cummings felt that breaking the rules helped him express his ideas in a more original way.

Literary Works Cummings published more than ten books of poetry.

E. E. Cummings was born in 1894 and died in 1962.

who knows if the moon's

E. E. Cummings

The Balloon, 1878. Pal Szinyei Merse. Oil on canvas, 41.5 x 39 cm. Magyar Nemzeti Galeria, Budapest, Hungary.

who knows if the moon's
a balloon,coming out of a keen° city
in the sky—filled with pretty people?
(and if you and i should

get into it,if they
should take me and take you into their balloon,
why then
we'd go up higher with all the pretty people

than houses and steeples and clouds:
go sailing
away and away sailing into a keen
city which nobody's ever visited,where

always
 it's
  Spring)and everyone's
in love and flowers pick themselves

Imagery In the speaker's imagination, what is the moon?

BQ BIG Question

To what kind of world does the speaker imagine being taken?

2 Here, ***keen*** means "wonderful" or "excellent."

After You Read

Respond and Think Critically

1. To whom is the speaker of the poem talking? **[Identify]**
2. Summarize what takes place in the poem. **[Summarize]**
3. What feelings does looking at the moon cause the speaker to express? **[Infer]**
4. What words or phrases appear more than once in the poem? Why do you think the poet repeats them? **[Analyze]**
5. How do the lack of capitalization and the unusual punctuation affect the poem? **[Evaluate]**
6. **BQ BIG Question** Would you like to live in the kind of world that the speaker imagines? Why or why not? **[Conclude]**

Academic Vocabulary

The speaker sees **similarities** between the moon and a balloon. In the preceding sentence, *similarities* means "likenesses." To become more familiar with the word *similarities*, complete a graphic organizer like the one below.

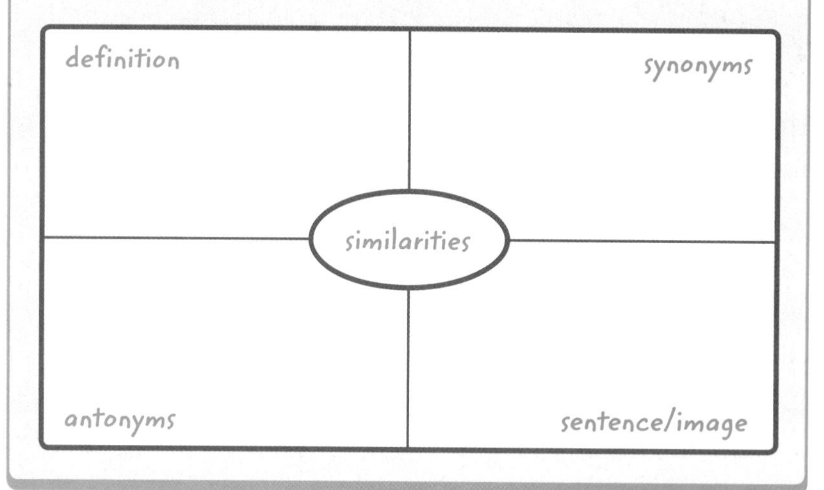

TIP

Analyzing
Here are some tips to help you answer question 4. Remember, a writer uses repetition to draw readers' attention to important details.

- Skim the poem to identify words or phrases used more than once.
- Think about the images that these words bring to mind.
- Think about the poem's main idea.
- How do the repeated words help the poet express his main idea?

Keep track of your ideas about the **BIG Question** in your unit Foldable.

LOG ON Literature Online

Selection Resources
For Selection Quizzes, eFlashcards, and Reading-Writing Connection activities, go to glencoe.com and enter QuickPass code GL17527u2.

Literary Element **Imagery**

1. What images give you the idea that the "balloon" would be going to an ideal place?
2. Describe a place where it is always spring. How would it look, sound, smell, and feel?

Review: Tone

As you learned on page 123, the **tone** of a piece of writing expresses its author's feelings and attitude toward a subject. The imagery an author uses in a poem helps create its tone. Pleasant images suggest a happy or amused tone. Dreary images convey a sad or angry tone.

Line length also helps create tone. Shorter lines can be read quickly, so they can create a light, upbeat tone. Long lines, which tend to be read more slowly, create a more thoughtful tone.

3. How would you describe the tone of the poem?
4. In a the graphic organizer like the one below, list two examples of images the poet uses and how each image helps create the tone of the poem.

Image	What tone is suggested?

Grammar Link

Past Perfect Tense To talk about something that happened (or didn't happen) before something else, you can use the **past perfect tense**. To form it, use the helping verb *had* and the past particle of the main verb.

The poet **had written** a poem about the moon before he ate breakfast.

The poet **had** never **written** a poem about the moon until he read one by someone else.

Don't use this tense to talk about only one event. Use it only if you're talking about something that happened before something else.

Wrong: This morning, the poet **had written** a poem.

Right: Before his wife got up, the poet **had written** a poem.

Practice Think about how the tense of verbs contributes to the meaning of sentences. Then write two sentences based on the poem that use the past perfect tense. Be sure that there are two events in each sentence.

Write with Style

Apply Imagery Think of an object that you find interesting or mysterious. Make a list of words or phrases you could use to describe the object. Try to include words that appeal to the five senses—sight, sound, touch, smell, and taste. Then use your imagery in a short poem about the object.

Before You Read

The Emperor's Silent Army: Terracotta Warriors of Ancient China

Connect to the Article

Think about a mystery. It could be a made-up story or it could be a real event from everyday life, history, or science.

Partner Talk With a partner, talk about something that is mysterious or unexplained. What makes it mysterious? Why aren't there explanations for some things?

Build Background

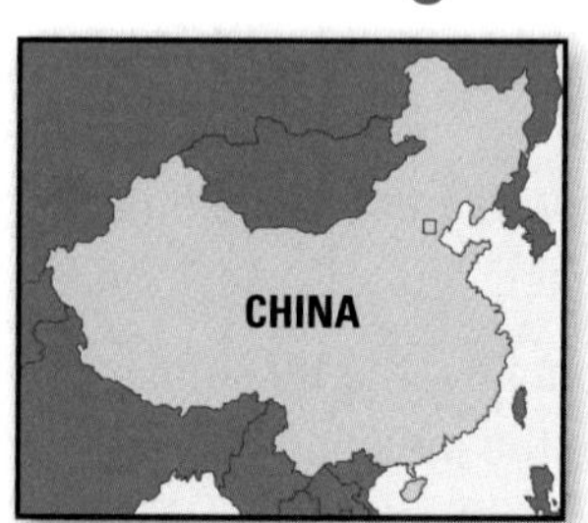

Today China is the third-largest country in the world. It is also the country with the largest population. Long ago, China was divided into many different kingdoms. Qin Shihuang (chin′ shir hwäng′) was the first emperor to rule over one united China.

The title of the article refers to terracotta warriors. *Terracotta* is an Italian word that means "baked earth." Terracotta is a kind of clay used for making bricks, pottery, and figurines, or statues.

Vocabulary

historian (his tôr′ ē ən) *n.* one who writes a history or about history (p. 204). *The historian wrote a book about the Civil War.*

civilized (siv′ ə līzed) *adj.* advanced beyond that which is primitive or savage (p. 204). *A civilized society has laws.*

eternal (i turn′ əl) *adj.* existing throughout all time (p. 205). *The Spanish explorer Juan Ponce de León searched for a "fountain of youth" in hopes of gaining eternal youth.*

precede (pri sēd′) *v.* to go or come before or ahead of (p. 205). *A meal of spaghetti and salad will precede the dessert.*

automatically (ô tə mat′ ik lē) *adv.* self-regulating; mechanically (p. 206). *The lights were set to turn off automatically at 9:00 P.M.*

Meet Jane O'Connor

"I loved books as a child and wrote books as a child."

—Jane O'Connor

A Lifelong Writer Jane O'Connor has worked as an editor and a publisher and has written more than thirty books. Sometimes she writes her books with her husband or her older son or with another author. O'Connor did a great deal of research before writing "The Emperor's Silent Army: Terracotta Warriors of Ancient China."

Literary Works Jane O'Connor has received awards for both fiction and nonfiction.

Jane O'Connor was born in 1947.

Literature Online

Author Search For more about Jane O'Connor, go to glencoe.com and enter QuickPass code GL17527u2.

Set Purposes for Reading

BQ BIG Question

As you read, ask yourself, what am I learning about the first emperor of China and how he viewed himself?

Literary Element Description

Description is writing that creates an impression of a setting, a person, an animal, an object, or an event by appealing to one or more of the five senses. Authors may use literary devices such as metaphors, similes, imagery, and symbolism to make their descriptions come alive.

Descriptive writing helps readers use their imagination to see the world in new ways. Descriptive details help readers see, hear, smell, taste, or feel the subject of the description.

As you read, ask yourself, how do vivid descriptions help readers visualize and understand the details in the article?

Reading Skill Recognize Author's Purpose

When you **recognize author's purpose,** you figure out the author's intention. The purpose may be to entertain, to inform, to persuade or to express emotion. An author may have more than one purpose.

Recognizing an author's purpose can help you get more out of your reading.

To **recognize author's purpose,** pay attention to

- the author's choice of words
- the organization of the writing
- important elements such as the title and headings
- facts, details, and descriptions

Then use these clues to think about the author's reason for writing. As you read, you may find it helpful to use a graphic organizer like the one below.

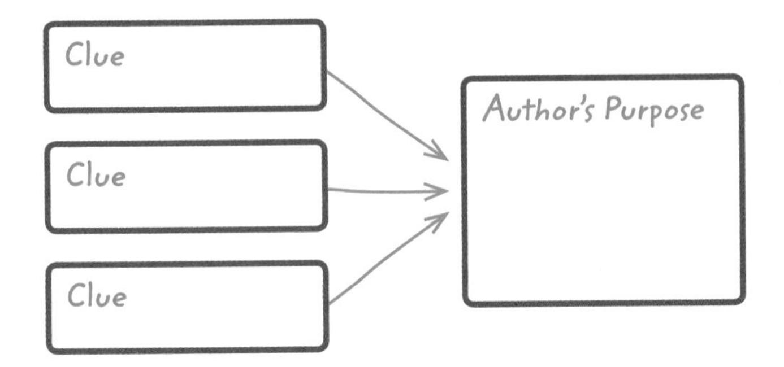

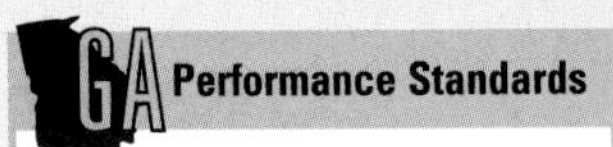

For pages 198–209

ELA6RC2d Evaluate the merits of texts in every subject discipline.

ELA6RC2e Examine the author's purpose in writing.

TRY IT

Recognize Author's Purpose
You wake up one Saturday morning to find a note from your mother. It reads, "If your friends are coming over today, they might be horrified by your messy room." What is the purpose of this note?

The Emperor's Silent Army

TERRACOTTA WARRIORS OF ANCIENT CHINA

Jane O'Connor

A Strange Discovery

Lintong County, People's Republic of China, March 1974

It's just an ordinary day in early spring, or so three farmers think as they trudge across a field in northern China. They are looking for a good place to dig a well. There has been a drought, and they must find water or risk losing their crops later in the year.

The farmers choose a spot near a grove of persimmon trees. Down they dig, five feet, ten feet. Still no water. They decide to keep on digging a little deeper. All of a sudden, one of the farmers feels his shovel strike against something hard. Is it a rock? It's difficult to see at the bottom of the dark hole, so the farmer kneels down for a closer look. No, it isn't a rock. It seems to be clay, and not raw clay but clay that has been baked and made into something. But what?

Recognize Author's Purpose What purpose does the question serve?

Now, more carefully, the men dig around the something. Perhaps it is a pot or a vase. However, what slowly reveals itself is the pottery head of a man who stares back at them, open-eyed and amazingly real looking. The farmers have never seen anything like it before. But they do remember stories that some of the old people in their village have told, stories of a "pottery man" found many years ago not far from where they are now. The villagers had been scared that the pottery man would bring bad luck so they broke it to bits, which were then reburied and forgotten.

Description What makes the pottery head lifelike?

The three well-diggers are not so superstitious.[1] They report their discovery to a local official. Soon a group of archaeologists[2] arrives to search the area more closely. Maybe they will find pieces of a clay body to go with the clay head.

In fact, they find much more.

During the weeks and months that follow, the archaeologists dig out more pottery men, which now are called by a more dignified term—terracotta figurines. The

1 People who are ***superstitious*** have unreasonable beliefs that are not based on scientific facts.

2 ***Archaeologists*** are scientists who study the past by examining the buildings, objects, and other remains of places where people once lived.

View the Photograph In what ways do the terracotta soldiers in the photograph match the description in the text?

figurines are soldiers. That much is clear. But they come from a time long ago, when Chinese warriors wore knee-length robes, armor made from small iron "fish scales," and elaborate topknot hairdos. All of the soldiers are life-size or a little bigger and weigh as much as four hundred pounds. They stand at attention as if waiting for the command to charge into battle. The only thing missing is their weapons. And those are found too—hundreds of real bronze swords, daggers, and battle-axes as well as thousands of scattered arrowheads—all so perfectly made that, after cleaning, their ancient tips are still sharp enough to split a hair!

Today, after years of work, terracotta soldiers are still being uncovered and restored. What the well-diggers stumbled upon, purely by accident, has turned out to be among the largest and most incredible archaeological discoveries of modern times. Along with the Great Pyramids in Egypt, the buried army is now considered one of the true wonders of the ancient world. Spread out

Recognize Author's Purpose Why is this important to know?

over several acres near the city of Xian, the soldiers number not in tens or hundreds but in the thousands! Probably 7,500 total. Until 1974, nobody knew that right below the people of northern China an enormous underground army has been standing guard, silently and watchfully, for more than 2,200 years. Who put them there?

One man.

Known as the fierce tiger of Qin, the divine[3] Son of Heaven, he was the first emperor of China.

Qin Shihuangdi, 259–210 B.C., First Emperor of China, 221–210 B.C., during Warring States period, from Album of portraits of 86 Chinese emperors, with Chinese historical notes, 18th century. The British Library, London.

3 ***Divine*** means "coming from God."

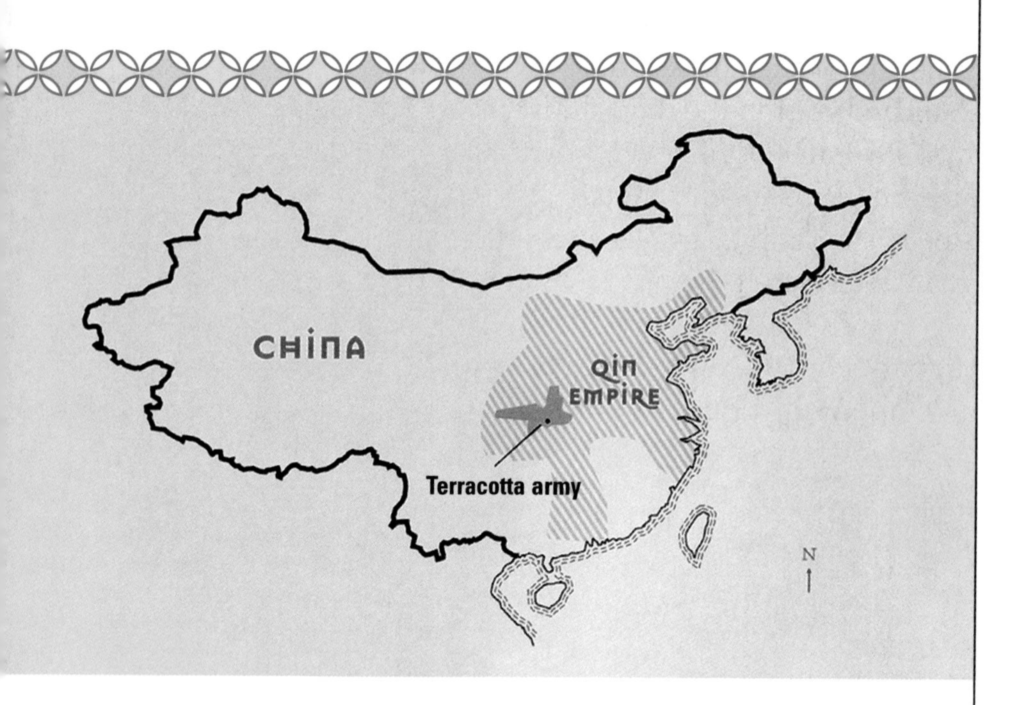

The Quest for Immortality

Before the time of Qin Shihuang, who lived from 259 to 210 B.C., there was no China. Instead, there were seven separate kingdoms, each with its own language, currency,[4] and ruler. For hundreds of years they had been fighting one another. The kingdom of Qin was the fiercest; soldiers received their pay only after they had presented their generals with the cut-off heads of enemy warriors. By 221 B.C. the ruler of the Qin kingdom had "eaten up his neighbors like a silkworm devouring a leaf," according to an ancient **historian.** The name China comes from Qin.

Recognize Author's Purpose In what order is the author organizing the information?

Description What two things does the simile in the quotation compare?

The king of Qin now ruled over an immense empire—around one million square miles that stretched north and west to the Gobi desert, south to present-day Vietnam, and east to the Yellow Sea. To the people of the time, this was the entire **civilized** world. Not for another hundred years would the Chinese know that empires existed beyond their boundaries. To the ruler of Qin, being called king

4 ***Currency*** is the medium of exchange, or money.

Vocabulary

historian (his tôr′ ē ən) *n.* one who writes a history or about history

civilized (siv′ ə līzed) *adj.* advanced beyond that which is primitive or savage was no longer grand enough. He wanted a title that no one else had ever had before. What he chose was Qin Shihuang. This means "first emperor, God in Heaven, and Almighty of the Universe" all rolled into one.

But no title, however superhuman it sounded, could protect him from what he feared most—dying. More than anything, the emperor wanted to live forever. According to legend, a magic elixir[5] had granted **eternal** life to the people of the mythical Eastern Islands. Over the years, the emperor sent expeditions out to sea in search of the islands and the magic potion. But each time they came back empty-handed.

If he couldn't live forever, then Qin Shihuang was determined to live as long as possible. He ate powdered jade and drank mercury[6] in the belief that they would prolong his life. In fact, these "medicines" were poison and may have caused the emperor to fall sick and die while on a tour of the easternmost outposts of his empire. He was forty-nine years old.

Recognize Author's Purpose Why has the author placed the word *medicines* in quotation marks?

If word of Qin Shihuang's death got out while he was away from the capital there might be a revolt.[7] So his ministers kept the news a secret. With the emperor's body inside his chariot, the entire party traveled back to the capital city. Meals were brought into the emperor's chariot; daily reports on affairs of state were delivered as usual—all to keep up the appearance that the emperor was alive and well. However, it was summer, and a terrible smell began to come from the chariot. But the clever ministers found a way to account for the stench. A cart was loaded with smelly salted fish and made to **precede** the chariot,

---

5 Today the word ***elixir*** usually refers to a drinkable substance that contains medicine. Long ago, some people believed that certain elixirs had the ability to extend life forever.

6 ***Jade*** is a green gemstone often used for making jewelry. ***Mercury*** is a silver-colored metal.

7 A ***revolt*** is a violent rebellion against those in charge.

Vocabulary

eternal (i turn′ əl) *adj.* existing throughout all time

precede (pri sēd′) *v.* to go or come before or ahead of overpowering and masking any foul odors coming from the dead emperor. And so Qin Shihuang returned to the capital for burial.

Description To what sense is this appealing? How do you know?

The tomb[8] of Qin Shihuang had been under construction for more than thirty years. It was begun when he was a young boy of thirteen and was still not finished when he died. Even incomplete, the emperor's tomb was enormous, larger than his largest palace. According to legend, it had a domed ceiling inlaid with clusters of pearls to represent the sun, moon, and stars. Below was a gigantic relief map[9] of the world, made from bronze. Bronze hills and mountains rose up from the floor, with rivers of mercury flowing into a mercury sea. Along the banks of the rivers were models of the emperor's palaces and cities, all exact replicas[10] of the real ones.

In ancient times, the Chinese believed that life after death was not so very different from life on earth. The soul of a dead person could continue to enjoy all the pleasures of everyday life. So people who were rich enough constructed elaborate underground tombs filled with silk robes, jewelry with precious stones, furniture, games, boats, chariots—everything the dead person could possibly need or want.

Recognize Author's Purpose How does this explain the emperor's tomb?

Qin Shihuang knew that grave robbers would try their best to loot the treasures in his tomb. So he had machines put inside the tomb that produced the rumble of thunder to scare off intruders, and mechanical crossbows at the entrance were set to fire arrows **automatically** should anyone dare trespass.[11] The emperor also made certain that the workers who carried his coffin in to its final resting place never revealed its exact whereabouts. As the men worked their way back through the tunnels to the tomb's entrance, a stone door came crashing down, and they were

8 A ***tomb*** is a room where a dead body is placed for burial.

9 A ***relief map*** shows the physical features of an area of land.

10 ***Replicas*** are copies.

11 ***Trespass*** means "to enter without permission."

Vocabulary

automatically (ô tə mat′ ik lē) *adv.* self-regulating; mechanically

left to die, sealed inside the tomb along with the body of the emperor.

Even all these measures, however, were not enough to satisfy the emperor. And so, less than a mile from the tomb, in underground trenches,[12] the terracotta warriors were stationed. Just as flesh-and-blood troops had protected him during his lifetime, the terracotta troops were there to protect their ruler against any enemy for all eternity.

BQ BIG Question
What does this tell you about the emperor?

Inside the Emperor's Tomb

What exactly is the terracotta army guarding so steadfastly?[13] What, besides the body of the dead emperor, is inside the tomb? The answer is that nobody knows. And the government of China has no plans at present to excavate[14] and find out.

In ancient China it was the custom to build a natural-looking hill on top of a person's tomb. The more important a person was, the bigger the hill. Thousands of years of

The body of the emperor, which has never been uncovered, may wear a jade funeral suit like this one found in the tomb of a Chinese princess from the late second century.

12 Here, ***trenches*** are long, narrow ditches used to protect soldiers during a battle.

13 ***Steadfastly*** means "faithfully."

14 ***Excavate*** means "to remove by digging."

harsh weather have worn down the emperor's mound; originally it was four hundred feet high, almost as high as the biggest of the three Great Pyramids in Egypt.

Like the ancient Egyptians, the ancient Chinese believed that the body of a dead person should be preserved as a "home" for the soul. However, the Chinese did not make a person's body into a **mummy.** They believed that jade had magic powers, among them the ability to keep a dead body from decaying. In Chinese tombs from the first century B.C., bodies of noblemen and princesses have been found wearing entire suits of jade. It is believed that Qin Shihuang is buried in just such a suit, the thousands of small tiles all beautifully carved and sewn together with gold thread. And over this jade burial outfit, his body is supposedly covered in a blanket of pearls.

As for all the things placed with the emperor, certainly they must be grand beyond imagining—silk robes embroidered with dragons, gem-encrusted crowns and jewelry, musical instruments, hand-carved furniture, lamps, beautiful dishes, cooking pots, and golden utensils. Like the pharaohs of ancient Egypt, the first emperor would have made certain that he had everything he might possibly want in the afterlife. But unless his tomb is excavated, what these treasures look like will remain a mystery.

Description How does the comparison help you picture the mound?

Visual Vocabulary

A **mummy** is a dead body that has been preserved and prepared for burial. The ancient Egyptians often wrapped mummies in bandages.

Recognize Author's Purpose What does the author want the reader to feel?

After You Read

Respond and Think Critically

1. In your own words, explain the extravagant measures Qin Shihuang took to protect himself after death. **[Paraphrase]**
2. Why are the terracotta soldiers a significant discovery? **[Interpret]**
3. What might be some reasons that the Chinese government has no plans to excavate Qin Shihuang's tomb? **[Infer]**
4. **Literary Element Description** Which descriptions are most valuable to understanding the text? **[Evaluate]**
5. **Reading Skill Recognize Author's Purpose** What do you think was the author's purpose for writing this article? Explain your answer. **[Analyze]**
6. **BQ BIG Question** From what you have learned about Qin Shihuang, would he approve of having his tomb excavated? **[Conclude]**

Vocabulary Practice

Respond to these questions.

1. If you needed factual information about World War I, would you read a book written by a **historian** or a fiction writer?
2. Which meal usually **precedes** lunch—breakfast or dinner?
3. Which runs **automatically**—a handheld spoon or a blender?
4. Which word describes a **civilized** country—lawless or lawful?
5. Which word describes **eternal** life—everlasting or short?

Writing

Write a Letter Imagine that you were one of the people who discovered the terracotta soldiers. Write a letter to a government official to inform the official about what you found. Use a formal tone for your letter and include only the most important details. Start with an introduction to explain why you are writing. Develop your main points in the body of the letter. End with a conclusion. Be sure to follow the form for a business letter, which includes a heading, an inside address, a salutation followed by a colon, a body, and a signature. See the Writing Handbook at the back of this book for guidelines on writing a business letter. Whether you type or handwrite your letter, it should have a neat appearance.

TIP

Paraphrasing
Here are some tips to help you paraphrase. Remember that when you paraphrase, you retell what you read in your own words.

- Skim the section called "The Quest for Immortality."
- Find specific details and reread them carefully.
- Look away from the book and retell the main ideas in your own words.

Keep track of your ideas about the **BIG Question** in your unit Foldable.

Literature Online

Selection Resources
For Selection Quizzes, eFlashcards, and Reading-Writing Connection activities, go to glencoe.com and enter QuickPass code GL17527u2.

Before You Read

Climate

Connect to the Textbook Lesson

Have you ever wondered why the weather is different from place to place? How would you describe the weather where you live? Is it the same all year, or does it change with the seasons?

QuickWrite Freewrite for a few minutes about the type of climate in which you would like to live. What would the weather be like? Why would you want to live there?

Build Background

Earth's rotation creates a climate that changes from place to place.

- The equator is an imaginary line that divides Earth halfway between the North and South poles.
- The closer you live to the equator, the warmer the climate will be.
- The amount of solar energy an area receives affects its climate.

Vocabulary

humidity (hū mid′ə tē) *n.* moisture or dampness, especially of the atmosphere (p. 212). *The laundry hanging on the clothesline felt damp from the humidity.*

factor (fak′tər) *n.* one of several things that brings about a result (p. 213). *The heavy rain was a factor in canceling the game.*

absorbs (ab sôrbz′) *v.* takes in and retains energy (p. 214). *A healthy plant absorbs sunlight.*

axis (ak′sis) *n.* a straight line passing through an object or a body around which the object or body rotates or seems to rotate (p. 214). *One complete rotation of Earth on its axis takes 24 hours.*

Set Purposes for Reading

BQ BIG Question

As you read, ask yourself, what can I learn about the world by reading a textbook lesson?

Literary Element Text Features

When you see a page of informational text, you first notice its **text features**, or special ways of presenting information. Text features include titles, heads, subheads, and graphics. **Titles** usually appear in large type and tell you what the text will be about. **Heads** emphasize the main points, and **subheads** often break down the information further. **Graphics**, including photos, drawings, maps, charts, and graphs, present information visually.

Text features break up large blocks of text into sections that are easier to read. You can use the features to help you find information quickly.

As you read, ask yourself, how do text features make the information in this science lesson easier to understand?

Reading Skill Analyze Text Structure

Writers organize their ideas in a way that fits their purpose. That pattern of organization is called **text structure.** One kind of text structure is **order of importance.** The writer arranges ideas from most important to least important—or the other way around. For example, a typical news article has a structure that goes from most important to least important.

Analyzing text structure involves recognizing the pattern or organization the author uses. This can help you locate and recall key information.

To **analyze order-of-importance text structure,** pay attention to

- the first few paragraphs, which often include the main idea
- the sequence in which events or ideas are presented
- signal words and phrases, such as *principal, central,* and *important*

You may find it helpful to use a graphic organizer like the one below. List important information in the order in which it appears in the text.

Climate

I. What Is Climate?

  A. What Causes Different Climates?

    1.

    2.

  B. Local Effects on Climate

    1.

    2.

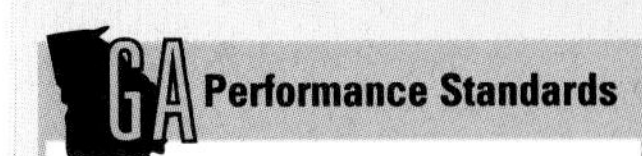

Performance Standards

For pages 210–217

ELA6R1b For informational texts, apply knowledge of common graphic features.

ELA6RC2d Evaluate the merits of texts in every subject discipline.

TRY IT

Analyze Text Structure Read the first few paragraphs of a magazine article and try to determine the main idea. Then read the remainder of the article. If the text supports the idea in the first few paragraphs, the article uses order-of-importance text structure.

Climate

What Is Climate?

You've probably noticed that the weather in other parts of the country is different from where you live. If you could see a map of the world's weather, you'd see even greater differences. Some parts of the world always seem rainy. Others are cold every winter. Figure 18-15 shows different patterns of climate (klī′ mit). Climate is the pattern of weather that occurs in a particular area over many years. To determine the climate of a region, scientists figure out the average weather conditions over a period of 30 years or more. They look at the average temperature, precipitation, air pressure,[1] **humidity**, and the number of days of sunshine in each area.

1 ***Precipitation*** is any form of water that falls to Earth, such as rain, snow, and hail. ***Air pressure*** is caused by gravity. It is the weight of the air around Earth pressing down on Earth's surface.

Vocabulary

humidity (hū mid′ ə tē) *n.* moisture or dampness, especially of the atmosphere

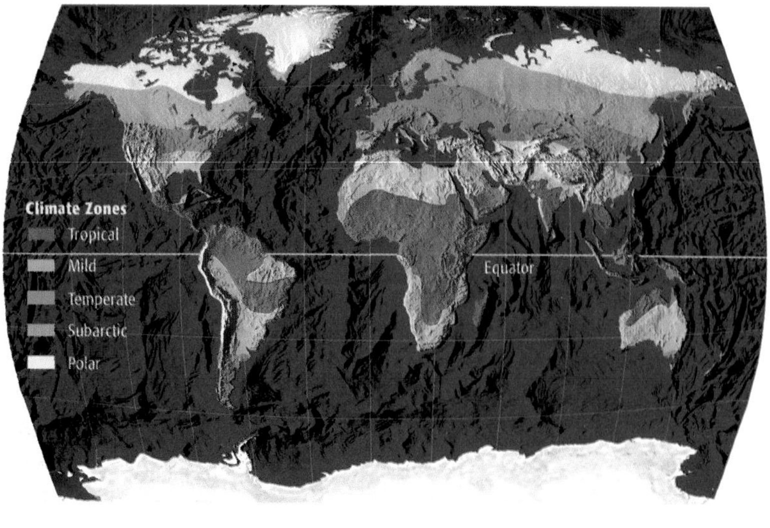

Text Features What do you think this section will explain? How do you predict other headers will help you find information?

BQ BIG Question

Look at Figure 18-15. What type of climate does your area have? What do you learn about the world by studying this type of information?

Figure 18-15
There are five main types of climate: polar, subarctic, temperate, mild, and tropical. *What type of climate does your area have?*

What Causes Different Climates?

Different parts of Earth receive different amounts of sunlight. The areas nearest the equator receive the most sunlight. They have a tropical climate with warm to hot temperatures year-round. Polar climates are found near the poles, where sunlight strikes Earth at a low angle. These places can get very cold. Some are always covered in ice. Subarctic, temperate (tem′ pər it), and mild climates lie between the tropics and the poles. Temperatures in these areas vary, but on average, they are not as hot as tropical climates and not as cold as polar climates. Is location the only **factor** that affects climate? No. Oceans, mountains, wind patterns, and even large cities can affect local climate.

Local Effects on Climate

Imagine you're at the beach on a summer day. You take a moment to enjoy the cool, refreshing breeze that blows in from the ocean. Ocean winds and ocean currents[2] affect the climate along the coasts. These areas are often cooler in the summer and warmer in the winter than areas located just a short distance inland.

As Figure 18-16 shows, mountains also affect local climate. On the side of the mountain that faces the wind, the climate is generally cool and wet. That's because air

Text Features Look at Figure 18-16. What is the purpose of the arrow? How does this graphic help you understand the way mountains affect local climate?

2 ***Currents*** are the flow of water in a certain direction.

Vocabulary

factor (fak′ tər) *n.* one of several things that brings about a result

Figure 18-16
The climate on the side of the mountain that faces away from the wind is generally dry and hot. *Why?*

cools as it moves up the mountain. As it cools, it drops its moisture as rain or snow. By the time the air reaches the top of the mountain, it is dry. The dry air continues over the mountain, heating up as it goes down the side of the mountain that faces away from the wind.

Cities can affect climate, too, especially in the summer. If you've ever walked barefoot on a hot street, you know that the street **absorbs** heat. So do parking lots and buildings. Some of the heat they absorb is sent back into the surrounding air. That makes the air in a city hotter.

Location, oceans, mountains, cities—now you know the things that cause different climates. Do climates of regions ever change? They have in the past. Some people think they might change again in the future.

Climate Changes

Look at Figure 18-17. About 20,000 years ago huge sheets of ice called glaciers covered much of Canada and parts of the United States. What caused this type of climate change? Scientists are not sure. Some think that the tilt of Earth's **axis** or the path of Earth's orbit may change over a long period of time. Others think that a huge

Text Features
How does the photograph help you understand what a glacier is?

Vocabulary

absorbs (ab sôrbz′) *v.* takes in and retains energy

axis (ak′ sis) *n.* a straight line passing through an object or a body and around which the object or body rotates or seems to rotate

Figure 18-17
This glacier in Argentina is similar to the ones that once covered large parts of North America.

Figure 18-18
Cutting down rain forests may increase the amount of carbon dioxide in the atmosphere. This, in turn, may lead to global warming.

volcanic eruption or a meteorite collision with Earth may have caused the climate change.

Some people think we're headed for another big climate change. But this time, the change will be caused by people, not by volcanoes or meteorites.

BQ BIG Question

Why might people read an informational article about climate? Who do you think would need to know about climate and why?

Will Earth's Climate Change Again?

Look at Figure 18-18. Some human activities, such as burning fossil fuels[3] to produce electricity and cutting down rain forests for farmland, increase the amount of carbon dioxide in the atmosphere. Carbon dioxide traps heat in the atmosphere. When there's more carbon dioxide, more heat is trapped, so temperature increases around the world. An increase in temperatures all over the world is called global warming.

Effects of Global Warming

Scientists are not sure what the effects of global warming will be. Some think rising temperatures might cause ice caps to melt. This, in turn, could cause a sudden rise in sea level and flooding along coastal areas. Other scientists aren't convinced that global warming is a problem. All scientists, though, warn against tampering with Earth's climate. We can help protect Earth from harmful climate change by using less electricity and recycling products to reduce our use of fossil fuels.

Analyze Text Structure

Sometimes text that uses order-of-importance text structure also organizes information from general to specific. Does this lesson present information in this way? Why do you think this is so?

3 ***Fossil fuels*** are fuels formed by animal or plant remains over millions of years.

After You Read

Respond and Think Critically

1. List the five main types of climate. **[Identify]**
2. Why does one side of a mountain usually get more precipitation than the other side? **[Recall]**
3. What causes different climates? **[Summarize]**
4. How do humans affect climate? Support your answer with reasons and examples from the text. **[Analyze]**
5. Scientists have mixed opinions about the effects of global warming. How might global warming affect the region where you live? **[Evaluate]**
6. **BQ** **BIG Question** Why are textbooks and other informational books important? **[Conclude]**

TIP

Analyzing
To answer question 4, try the following tips:

- Scan the text for key words and phrases that tell which factors affect climate. Ask yourself, which of these factors do humans control?
- Look at the title, heads, and graphics.What do they reveal about the effect humans have on climate?

Keep track of your ideas about the **BIG Question** in your unit Foldable.

Vocabulary Practice

Choose the sentence that uses the vocabulary word correctly.

1. **A.** Lack of experience was a **factor,** but it was not the only reason that Tom lost the election.
   B. Tom lost the election because the voters didn't like his **factor.**
2. **A.** When I looked outside and saw a **humidity,** I knew it would be a hot day.
   B. As soon as I stepped outside, I could feel the heat and **humidity.**
3. **A.** The globe is tilted to show Earth on its **axis.**
   B. The globe shows an **axis** running around the edge of the world.
4. **A.** The pavement is hot because it **absorbs** the sun's heat.
   B. Rain **absorbs** the sidewalk during a storm.

Academic Vocabulary

An increase in temperatures all over the world is called **global** warming. Using context clues, try to figure out the meaning of the word *global* in the preceding sentence. Check your answer in a dictionary or textbook.

Literature Online

Selection Resources
For Selection Quizzes, eFlashcards, and Reading-Writing Connection activities, go to glencoe.com and enter QuickPass code GL17527u2.

Literary Element **Text Features**

1. How do the heads help organize the information in the text? What information do you find under each subhead?
2. Choose one of the graphics and explain how it affects your understanding of the text.

Review: **Author's Purpose**

As you learned on page 163, an **author's purpose** is the author's intention in a particular work. Authors have many different reasons for writing: to entertain, to inform, to persuade, to express emotions. To understand the author's purpose, ask yourself the following questions:

- What is the genre, or type of literary work? This can give you a hint about the author's purpose. For example, editorials are often written to persuade.
- Who is the intended audience? Authors usually tailor their purpose to their readers.

3. Identify the textbook writer's purpose. How well do you think the writer succeeds in accomplishing that purpose? Explain your answer.

Reading Skill **Analyze Text Structure**

4. What is the most important factor that causes different climates? Where is this information located in the text?
5. Why did the writer place the section entitled "Effects of Global Warming" at the end of the lesson? What do you think would be the focus of the lesson if the writer had placed this section at the beginning?

Grammar Link

Future Tense There are two ways to show that an action will happen in the future. First, you can use the word *will* as a helping verb with the present tense of the main verb.

I **will read** more about climate to see how my actions affect it.

Second, you can use *going to* with *am, is,* or *are* along with the present tense of the main verb.

I **am going to read** more about climate to see how my actions affect it.

You also can use *not* or *never* with either of these phrases.

I **will** never **read** more about climate to see how my actions affect it.

I **am** never **going to read** more about climate to see how my actions affect it.

Practice Look back at the selection you read about climate. Find five verb phrases in the text. On a separate sheet of paper, rewrite them using the future tense.

Research and Report

Internet Connection Use the Internet to find an article about global warming. Use a reliable site such as an educational or a government site. These Web addresses will end in *.edu* or *.gov.* Take notes on what each paragraph says about global warming and its effects. Organize your notes into a graphic organizer like the one below.

Effects of Global Warming

1. ____________________
2. ____________________
3. ____________________
4. ____________________

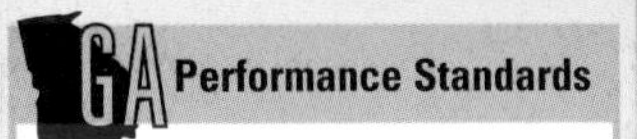

For pages 218–219

ELA6R1c For informational texts, apply knowledge of common organizational structures and patterns.

Genre Focus: Informational Text

Informational text is nonfiction writing that presents facts and information. Writers use informational text when they want to explain or inform. Reading informational text can help you get news, learn how to make something, or find facts for a report.

Magazine, newspaper, and online articles are forms of informational text, as are flyers, product descriptions, and textbooks.

Literary Elements

Text Structure The organization of a piece of writing is its text structure. Most informational text is presented in a logical way to help readers understand it easily. Writers of informational text choose the kind of structure that best presents the information.

One common text structure is **sequence,** the order in which thoughts are arranged. Three common forms of sequence are **chronological order,** the order in which events take place; **spatial order,** the order in which to look at objects; and **order of importance,** going from the most important to the least important or the other way around.

Another kind of text structure is **cause and effect.** It explores events or actions and the reasons for them. **Problem-and-solution** structure states a problem and suggests how to solve it. **Comparison-and-contrast** structure shows the similarities and differences between people, things, and ideas.

Text Features In informational text, certain features can help readers understand the content and the author's purpose. **Titles,** also called **headlines,** appear in large type and tell the topic of the selection. **Heads** and **subheads** organize related groups of paragraphs.

Informational texts may include **boldface terms,** or words printed in dark type so they stand out. **Footnotes** may appear at the bottom of a page to explain terms or phrases in the main text.

Graphics, which include photographs, diagrams, graphs, charts, maps, and illustrations, present information visually. A **caption** provides information about a graphic.

TRY IT

Using one of the graphic organizers on the next page, examine the organization of an informational text in this unit.

Characteristics of the Genre

To better understand literary elements in informational text and how writers use literary elements to create effects and achieve their purposes, look at the examples in the graphic organizers below.

Outline: "Nobody's Perfect"

I. It's Not Over?
- **A.** Suzy Favor Hamilton, distance runner
- **B.** Track meet in Virginia
- **C.** Stopped before race was over

II. Somebody Get Brett!
- **A.** Brett Favre, Green Bay Packers
- **B.** 1992 game against Cincinnati
- **C.** Ran off the field before final kick

Venn Diagram: "Climate"

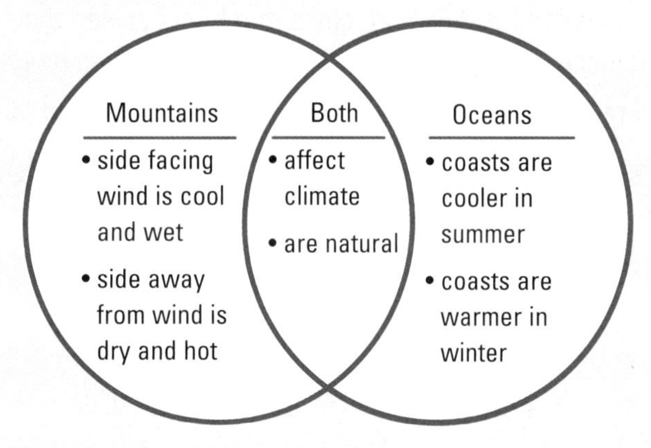

• side facing wind is cool and wet
• side away from wind is dry and hot

• coasts are cooler in summer
• coasts are warmer in winter

Cause-and-Effect Diagram: "Tracking Trash"

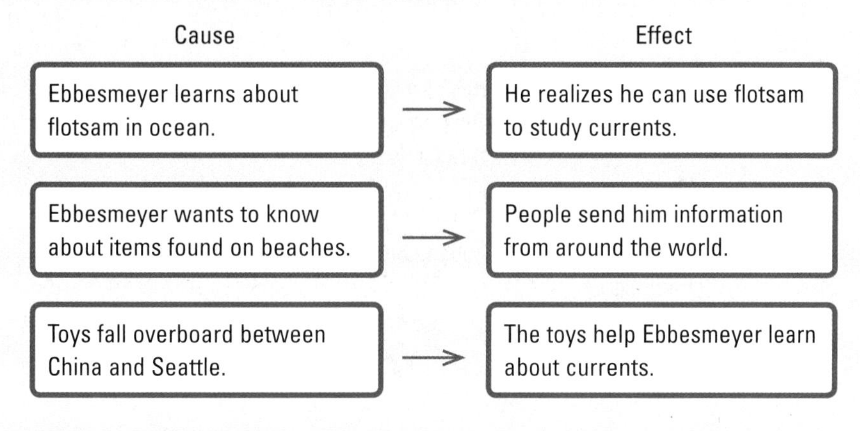

Cause
Effect
Ebbesmeyer learns about flotsam in ocean.
He realizes he can use flotsam to study currents.
Ebbesmeyer wants to know about items found on beaches.
People send him information from around the world.
Toys fall overboard between China and Seattle.
The toys help Ebbesmeyer learn about currents.

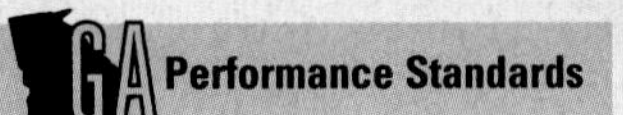

Performance Standards

For pages 220

ELA6R2a Acquire vocabulary. Determine the meaning of unfamiliar words by using word, sentence, and paragraph clues.

Vocabulary Workshop

Context Clues

Connection to Literature

"Imagine you're at the beach on a summer day. You take a moment to enjoy the cool, refreshing breeze."

—"Climate"

Context is the sentence or passage in which a word appears. Context often provides clues as to what an unfamiliar word means. Some **context clues** also can help you figure out shades of meaning between words. Compare the sentences above with this sentence: *At the shore, the bracing autumn breeze makes you feel alive.* The words *summer* and *autumn* are clues that help you see the shades of meaning between *refreshing* (cool) and *bracing* (cold).

Here are context clues for some other words from "Climate."

Word	Context Clue	How the Clue Helps
factors	*Oceans and wind patterns* are two factors that affect climate.	provides examples
glaciers	*Huge sheets of ice* called glaciers covered much of Canada.	provides a definition
moisture	Some areas have a lot of moisture in the air, but *other areas are very dry.*	provides a contrast
polar	Polar climates can get very cold. *Near the poles,* some places are always covered in ice.	restates the idea

TRY IT: Use context clues to define the underlined words below.

1. Cities can feel hot because concrete absorbs, or soaks up, heat from the sun.
2. Never extremely hot or cold, the coast had a temperate climate.
3. Scientists study hurricanes, lightning strikes, droughts, and other weather phenomena.

Tip

Test-Taking Tip To find context clues, look before and after an unfamiliar word for a definition, a synonym, an example, a contrast, or a restatement.

Vocabulary Terms When you read on your own, you can often figure out the meaning of a new word by looking at its context, the words and sentences that surround it.

Literature Online

Vocabulary For more vocabulary practice, go to glencoe.com and enter QuickPass code GL17527u2.

Part 2

Exploring Traditions

Pinata Making in Chicago. Franklin McMahon.

BQ BIG Question **Why Read?**

The people pictured in the painting are creating piñatas—colorful containers often filled with candy, toys, or gifts. This tradition is common in Mexico and in many Latin American countries. How does the painting show the value of this activity? What activities would you like to explore that relate to the traditions of your family or culture?

Before You Read

The End of the World

Connect to the Myth

Think of something that you wonder about or don't really understand.

Quickwrite Freewrite for a few minutes about your topic. Why is it important to you? Why do you want to understand it?

Build Background

Different categories of fiction have unique characteristics. Folktales, including **myths,** are traditional stories with unknown origins. Myths were passed down orally long before paper, pencils, or books were invented. A myth tells of extraordinary events from earlier times. It may explain some aspect of the natural world, human nature, or the beliefs and practices of a people. Some myths include gods, heroes, and supernatural events.

This myth is an **origin tale.** It explains something the earliest people saw, wondered about, or didn't understand. An origin tale may answer questions about how things began or how they came to be. It passes along a group's values and shows how things fit together in the group's view of life.

Set Purposes for Reading

BQ BIG Question

As you read, ask yourself, do I understand why the Sioux tell this story?

Literary Element Oral Tradition

Oral tradition refers to stories, knowledge, customs, and beliefs that are passed on by word of mouth from one generation to the next. Many traditional stories within various cultures have been passed on in this manner.

Oral literature was a way of recording the past, glorifying leaders, and teaching morals and traditions to young people. Oral tradition has kept alive stories from the past that otherwise might have been forgotten.

As you read, ask yourself, why is this story important to the Sioux?

Performance Standards

For pages 222–226

ELA6R1i For literary texts, compare traditional literature and mythology from different cultures.

Meet Jenny Leading Cloud

"The End of the World" is a tale that a Sioux woman named Jenny Leading Cloud told to authors and editors Richard Erdoes and Alfonso Ortiz. Their book, *American Indian Myths and Legends,* contains many tales Erdoes heard while he traveled as an artist to several reservations in the 1960s. Over a 25-year period, these two men collected dozens of tales from many different groups of Native Americans. The story told by Jenny Leading Cloud was published in 1984.

LOG ON **Literature** Online

Author Search For more about Jenny Leading Cloud, go to glencoe.com and enter QuickPass code GL17527u2.

The End of the World

Jenny Leading Cloud

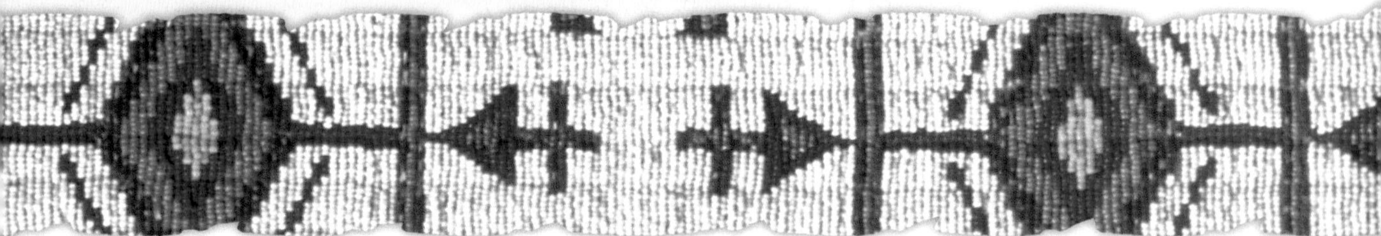

Somewhere, at a place where the prairie and the Mako Sica, the badlands,[1] meet, there is a hidden cave. Not for many generations has anyone been able to find it. Even now, with so many cars and highways and tourists, no one has found this cave.

In the cave lives an old woman. She is so old that her face looks like a shriveled-up walnut. She is dressed in **rawhide,** the way people used to go around before the white people came to this country. She is sitting there—has been sitting there for a thousand years or more—working on a blanket strip for her buffalo robe. She is making that blanket strip out of dyed porcupine quills, the way our ancestors did before white traders brought glass beads to this turtle continent. Resting beside her, licking his paws, watching her all the time, is a Shunka Sapa, a huge black dog. His eyes never wander from the old woman whose teeth are worn flat, worn down to little stumps from using them to flatten numberless porcupine quills.

A few steps from where the old woman sits working on her blanket strip, a big fire is kept going. She lit this fire a thousand or more years ago and has kept it alive ever since. Over the fire hangs a big earthenware pot, the kind some Indian people used to make before the white man came with his kettles of iron. Inside the big pot, wojapi is

Visual Vocabulary

Rawhide is the untanned skin of cattle or other animals.

Oral Tradition

How do you know the story was passed on?

1 A ***badland*** is a dry region that has numerous ridges and peaks cut by erosion, but little plant life; the ***Badlands*** is a region of South Dakota.

boiling and bubbling. Wojapi is berry soup. It is good and sweet and red. That wojapi has been boiling in that pot for a long time, ever since the fire was lit.

Every now and then the old woman gets up to stir the wojapi in the huge earthenware pot. She is so old and feeble[2] that it takes her a while to get up and hobble over to the fire. The moment the old woman's back is turned, the huge, black dog starts pulling out the porcupine quills from her blanket strip. This way, she never makes any progress, and her quillwork remains forever half finished. The Sioux people used to say that if the woman ever finished her blanket strip, in the very moment that she would thread the last porcupine quill to complete her design, the world would come to an end.

Oral Tradition What Sioux belief might the unfinished quillwork express?

BQ BIG Question

What can readers learn from this myth?

Watching the Pot Boil, A Cottage Interior. John Frederick Lewis. Victoria and Albert Museum, London.

2 A ***feeble*** person lacks physical strength or is weak.

After You Read

Respond and Think Critically

1. What prevents the old woman from finishing her work? **[Recall]**
2. Use your own words to retell the story. **[Summarize]**
3. Think about what prevents the old woman from completing her work. Has someone or something ever prevented you from finishing a task? What effect did it have? Explain your answer. **[Connect]**
4. Why do you think the storyteller presents the old woman doing ordinary tasks? **[Infer]**
5. The tone of a story shows an author's attitude toward the subject. Does the tone of this story match what the story is about? Support your answer. **[Conclude]**
6. **BQ** **BIG Question** What important lessons or values do you think the story tries to pass along? How important are these ideas? Explain your answer. **[Evaluate]**

Academic Vocabulary

In "The End of the World," the old woman has been **sustaining** the big fire for more than a thousand years.

In the preceding sentence, *sustaining* means "keeping up" or "keeping something going." To become more familiar with the word *sustaining,* complete a graphic organizer like the one below.

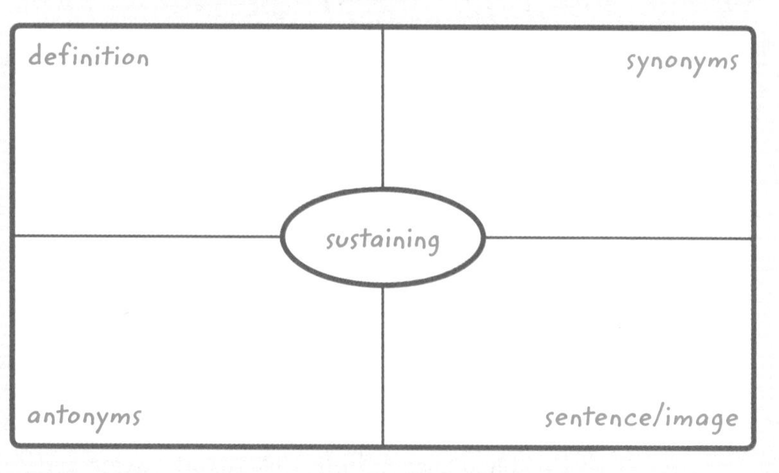

TIP

Inferring
Here are some tips to help you to infer. Remember that authors may not always directly state what they want you to understand in a story. To infer, use reasoning and your experience to come up with an idea that is based on the clues and details given in the story.

- Skim the story to find the woman's ordinary tasks.
- Think about why these tasks are important to the storyteller.
- What might they represent to the Sioux?

FOLDABLES Study Organizer Keep track of your ideas about the **BIG Question** in your unit Foldable.

LOG ON Literature Online

Selection Resources
For Selection Quizzes, eFlashcards, and Reading-Writing Connection activities, go to glencoe.com and enter QuickPass code GL17527u2.

Literary Element **Oral Tradition**

1. What values does "The End of the World" teach?
2. What vivid images describe the old woman? Why do you suppose she is described this way?
3. How does the story pass on information about the Sioux?

Review: Theme

As you learned on page 75, a **theme** is a message about life an author wants to share. The earliest people must have looked at the world around them and wondered, "How did this world come to be?" They made up stories that explained what they saw but didn't understand. Origin tales are folktales that answer questions about how things began or how they came to be. Often, these stories pass along a group's values and a key message.

4. What is this story explaining?
5. What beliefs, values, or practices are important to the theme?
6. What idea about life does the old woman best represent?
7. What idea about life does the dog best represent?

Grammar Link

Irregular Verbs All verbs have principal parts that are used to form the various tenses. Most verbs are **regular.** For example:

The old woman **lives** in a cave. (base word)

She **lived** there long ago. (past)

In fact, she **has lived** there for more than a thousand years. (past participle)

The past and past participle of **irregular verbs** are not formed by simply adding *-ed* to the base form. For example:

Every now and then the old woman **gets** up to stir the wojapi in the huge earthenware pot. (base word)

She **got** up to stir the pot at an earlier time. (past)

She **has gotten** up to stir the pot for more than a thousand years. (past participle)

Practice Look for examples of irregular verbs in the story. Then write your own sentences using the verbs.

Speaking and Listening

Oral Report Think about other myths that you have read. Choose one that you remember well, do research about the culture it comes from, and give an informative oral report. Your report should tell about the characters, setting, and plot. Be sure to include enough details to suggest the theme of the myth. Your report should also tell what the culture valued and what the myth explains. Make a draft. Rehearse your presentation, matching your words, pitch, and tone to your posture, gestures, and eye contact. Effectively incorporate pictures, slides, or visual technology as appropriate.

Before You Read

How the Snake Got Poison

Connect to the Folktale

If you could have any special talent or ability, what would you want it to be?

Partner Talk With a partner, talk about the benefits of the talent or ability. Discuss why it would make your life easier or better.

Build Background

A rattlesnake uses its fangs to inject venom, a poisonous substance, into its prey. The venom often stuns small animals, such as rodents, birds, or lizards, which the snake then swallows whole.

A rattlesnake is born with the first segment of a future rattle on the tip of its tail. Each time the snake grows and sheds its skin, a new segment develops and adds to the rattle. When a rattlesnake feels threatened, it coils its body and vibrates its tail. The segments click together and make a buzzing sound.

Set Purposes for Reading

BQ BIG Question

As you read, ask yourself, who is telling this story, and why is the person telling it?

Literary Element Folktale

A **folktale** is a traditional story that is orally passed down long before being written. The author is usually anonymous. Folktales include animal stories, trickster tales, fairy tales, myths, legends, and tall tales.

Folktales often explain something about nature or teach a moral lesson. They help us understand the culture of the people who told the stories and tell us what was important to that culture.

As you read, think about the benefits of keeping a folktale alive by telling it over and over again and passing it from generation to generation.

GA Performance Standards

For pages 227–231

ELA6RC4a Explore life experiences related to subject area content.

Meet Zora Neale Hurston

Florida Writer Zora Neale Hurston grew up in a close-knit African American town in rural Florida. She drew on her childhood memories to write novels and short stories. She also collected and published folktales told to her by African Americans in the South.

Literary Works Hurston is best known for her novel *Their Eyes Were Watching God.*

Zora Neale Hurston was born in 1891 and died in 1960.

LOG ON **Literature** Online

Author Search For more about Zora Neale Hurston, go to glencoe.com and enter QuickPass code GL17527u2.

Well, when God made de snake he put him in de bushes to ornament[1] de ground. But things didn't suit de snake so one day he got on de ladder and went up to see God.

"Good mawnin', God."

"How do you do, Snake?"

"Ah ain't so many, God, you put me down there on my belly in de dust and everything trods upon me and kills off my generations. Ah ain't got no kind of protection at all."

God looked off towards immensity[2] and thought about de subject for awhile, then he said, "Ah didn't mean for nothin' to be stompin' you snakes lak dat. You got to have some kind of a protection. Here, take dis poison and put it in yo' mouf and when they tromps on you, protect yo' self."

Folktale What can you tell about the people who passed on this folktale?

Folktale What characteristic of a folktale do you find in this passage?

1 To ***ornament*** something is to decorate it.

2 ***Immensity*** is hugeness or vastness. Here, when God looks toward immensity, he looks to the sky.

So de snake took de poison in his mouf and went on back.

So after awhile all de other varmints[3] went up to God.

"Good evenin', God."

"How you makin' it, varmints?"

"God, please do somethin' 'bout that snake. He' layin' in de bushes there wid poisin in his mouf and he's strikin' everything dat shakes de bush. He's killin' up our generations. Wese skeered to walk de earth."

So God sent for de snake and tole him:

"Snake, when Ah give you dat poison, Ah didn't mean for you to be hittin' and killin' everything dat shake de bush. I give you dat poison and tole you to protect yo' self when they tromples on you. But you killin' everything dat moves. Ah didn't mean for you to do dat."

De snake say, "Lawd, you know Ah'm down here in de dust. Ah ain't got no claws to fight wid, and Ah ain't got no feets to git me out de way. All Ah kin see is feets comin' to tromple me. Ah can't tell who my enemy is and who is my friend. You gimme dis protection in my mouf and Ah uses it."

God thought it over for a while then he says:

"Well, snake, I don't want yo' generations all stomped out and I don't want you killin' everything else dat moves. Here take dis bell and tie it to yo' tail. When you hear feets comin' you ring yo' bell and if it's yo' friend, he'll be keerful. If it's yo' enemy, it's you and him."

So dat's how de snake got his poison and dat's how come he got **rattles.**

Biddy, biddy, bend my story is end.

Turn loose de rooster and hold de hen.

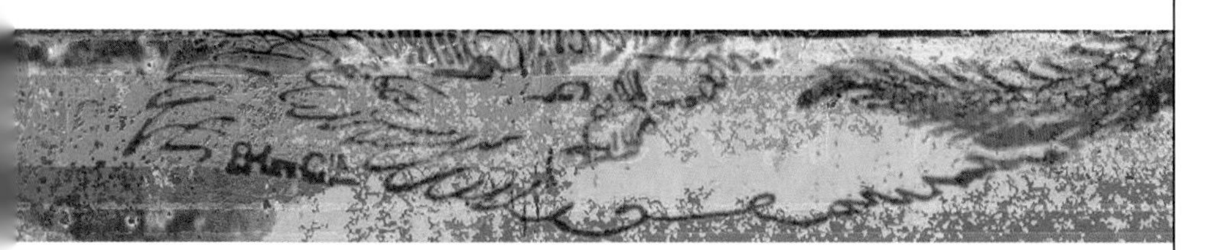

3 ***Varmints*** are troublesome animals.

Visual Vocabulary

Rattles are a series of connected, hollow segments of skin at the end of a rattlesnake's tail.

BQ BIG Question

Why would a culture want to pass this story along?

After You Read

Respond and Think Critically

1. In the folktale, why does God give the snake poison and a rattle? **[Recall]**
2. How do you feel when you think of snakes? Does this story affect your feelings about them in any way? Explain your answer. **[Connect]**
3. How would you compare the snake's concerns with the other animals' concerns? **[Compare]**
4. Why do you think the author uses words such as *ain't* and *gimme*? **[Infer]**
5. What is the moral, or lesson, of the story? **[Analyze]**
6. **BQ BIG Question** What can you tell about the storytellers and the reasons they would want to pass down this story from generation to generation? **[Conclude]**

Academic Vocabulary

After explaining his problems, the snake **obtained** two new features from God: poison and a rattle.

To become more familiar with the word *obtained,* fill out a graphic organizer like the one below.

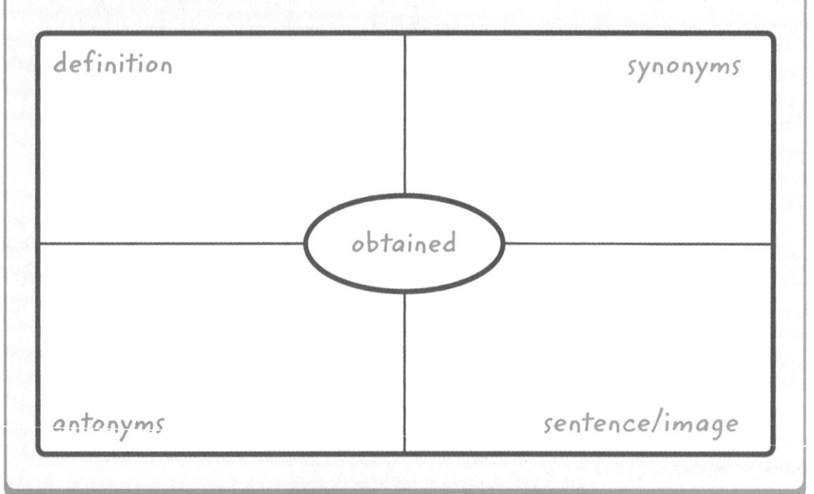

TIP

Comparing
Here are some tips to help you compare. Remember that when you compare, you point out the way two or more things are alike.

- Skim the folktale and reread any parts that tell what the snake is worried about.
- Be sure you understand what you read.
- Then skim the folktale to find any parts that tell what the other animals are worried about.
- Look for similarities between the two parts.

Keep track of your ideas about the **BIG Question** in your unit Foldable.

Literature Online

Selection Resources
For Selection Quizzes, eFlashcards, and Reading-Writing Connection activities, go to glencoe.com and enter QuickPass code GL17527u2.

Literary Element **Folktale**

1. What does this folktale explain?
2. How can you tell this is a traditional story that was passed down orally?

Review: **Dialogue**

As you learned on page 103, **dialogue** is a conversation between characters in a literary work. Dialogue is usually set off with quotation marks and dialogue tags, or markers that tell the reader who said what. Dialogue is important for many reasons. It helps bring characters to life by revealing their personalities. It moves the story's plot forward.

3. What does the dialogue suggest about the snake's personality?
4. How does the dialogue help advance the plot?
5. What does the dialogue suggest to you about the culture from which this folktale comes?

Partner Activity Work with a partner to record at least two examples of dialogue from the story. For each one, identify the speakers and think about the purpose of the dialogue. That is, tell whether the dialogue contributes to characterization, advances the plot, or serves some other purpose.

Dialogue	Speakers	Purpose

Grammar Link

Nouns

A **noun** names a person, a place, a thing, or an idea. There are two kinds of nouns: common nouns and proper nouns.

A **common noun** names *any* person, place, thing, or idea. For example:

So the snake took the poison in his mouth and went on back.

A **proper noun** names a particular person, place, thing, or idea. Proper nouns always begin with a capital letter. For example:

"Good mawnin', God."

"How do you do, Snake?"

Practice Draw two columns on a sheet of paper and add the headings *Common Noun* and *Proper Noun.* Look for examples of nouns in "How the Snake Got Poison" and write them in the appropriate column. Then find a recent essay or paragraph you have written and edit it for correct use of common and proper nouns.

Listening and Speaking

Performance Prepare a group performance of this folktale. Use the dialogue in the story to write your script. As you say your lines, use tone of voice, facial expressions, and body language to bring the characters to life. Rehearse your performance, working with group members to practice effective rate, volume, and pitch to maintain audience interest and attention. When you finish rehearsing, perform the folktale for your class.

Literary Perspective

on *How the Snake Got Poison* by Zora Neale Hurston

from DUST TRACKS ON A ROAD

by Zora Neale Hurston

GA Performance Standards

For pages 232–235

ELA6R1c For literary texts, relate a literary work to historical events of the period.

ELA6RC2d Evaluate the merits of texts.

Set a Purpose for Reading

Read to learn how Zora Neale Hurston's childhood experiences inspired the imaginative writings she created as an adult.

Build Background

Eatonville, Florida, the town where Zora Neale Hurston grew up, immersed her in African American folklife and shaped her as an author. Hurston spent much of her childhood on the porch of Joe Clarke's store. The stories she heard, the storytellers themselves, and the language they used influenced her future writing.

Reading Strategy Visualize

Visualizing is picturing an author's ideas or descriptions in your mind. As you read, choose details to sketch. Use a chart like the one below to help you visualize.

Story Detail	What I Picture in My Mind

No matter whether my probings[1] made me happier or sadder, I kept on probing to know. For instance, I had a stifled[2] longing. I used to climb to the top of one of the huge chinaberry trees which guarded our front gate, and look out over the world. The most interesting thing that I saw was the horizon. Every way I turned, it was there, and the same distance away. Our house then, was in the center of the world. It grew upon me that I ought to walk out to the horizon and see what the end of the world was like. The daring of the thing held me back for a while, but the thing became so urgent that I showed it to

1 Here, ***probings*** means "thorough examinations or investigations."

2 ***Stifled*** means "held back." A stifled longing is a desire that is not fulfilled because something prevents it.

my friend, Carrie Roberts, and asked her to go with me. She agreed. We sat up in the trees and disputed about what the end of the world would be like when we got there—whether it was sort of tucked under like the hem of a dress, or just was a sharp drop off into nothingness. So we planned to slip off from our folks bright and soon next morning and go see.

I could hardly sleep that night from the excitement of the thing. I had been yearning for so many months to find out about the end of things. I had no doubts about the beginnings. They were somewhere in the five acres that was home to me. Most likely in Mama's room. Now, I was going to see the end, and then I would be satisfied.

Sisy. Diana Ong.

As soon as breakfast was over, I sneaked off to the meeting place in the scrub palmettoes,[3] a short way from our house and waited. Carrie didn't come right away. I was on my way to her house by a round-about way when I met her. She was coming to tell me that she couldn't go. It looked so far that maybe we wouldn't get back by sundown, and then we would both get a whipping. When we got big enough to wear long dresses, we could go and stay as long as we wanted to. Nobody couldn't whip us then. No matter how hard I begged, she wouldn't go. The thing was too bold and brazen[4] to her thinking. We had a fight, then. I had to hit Carrie to keep my heart from stifling me. Then I was sorry I had struck my friend, and went on home and hid under the house with my

3 ***Scrub palmettoes*** are hardy palms, often found in the southern United States.

4 Someone who is ***brazen*** is shameless or defiant.

Lord Clermont's thoroughbred "Johnny" in a wooded landscape. John Best. Private Collection.

heartbreak. But I did not give up the idea of my journey. I was merely lonesome for someone brave enough to undertake it with me. I wanted it to be Carrie. She was a lot of fun, and always did what I told her. Well, most of the time, she did. This time it was too much for even her loyalty to surmount.[5] She even tried to talk me out of my trip. I couldn't give up. It meant too much to me. I decided to put it off until I had something to ride on, then I could go by myself.

So for weeks I saw myself sitting astride of a fine horse. My shoes had sky-blue bottoms to them, and I was riding off to look at the belly-band of the world.

It was summer time, and the mockingbirds sang all night long in the orange trees. Alligators trumpeted from their stronghold in Lake Belle. So fall passed and then it was Christmas time.

5 If you ***surmount*** something, you overcome it.

Papa did something different a few days before Christmas. He sort of shoved back from the table after dinner and asked us all what we wanted Santa Claus to bring us. My big brothers wanted a baseball outfit. Ben and Joel wanted air rifles. My sister wanted patent leather pumps and a belt. Then it was my turn. Suddenly a beautiful vision came before me. Two things could work together. My Christmas present could take me to the end of the world.

"I want a fine black riding horse with white leather saddle and bridles," I told Papa happily.

"You, what?" Papa gasped. "What was dat you said?"

"I said, I want a black saddle horse with . . ."

"A saddle horse!" Papa exploded. "It's a sin and a shame! Lemme tell you something right now, my young lady; you ain't white. Riding horse! Always trying to wear de big hat! I don't know how you got in this family nohow. You ain't like none of de rest of my young 'uns."

"If I can't have no riding horse, I don't want nothing at all," I said stubbornly with my mouth, but inside I was sucking sorrow. My longed-for journey looked impossible.

"I'll riding-horse you, Madam!" Papa shouted and jumped to his feet. But being down at the end of the table big enough for all ten members of the family together, I was near the kitchen door, and I beat Papa to it by a safe margin. He chased me as far as the side gate and turned back. So I did not get my horse to ride off to the edge of the world. I got a doll for Christmas.

Since Papa would not buy me a saddle horse, I made me one up. No one around me knew how often I rode my prancing horse, nor the things I saw in far places. Jake, my puppy, always went along and we made great admiration together over the things we saw and ate. We both agreed that it was nice to be always eating things.

Respond and Think Critically

1. Write a brief summary of the main ideas in this excerpt. For help on writing a summary, see page 170. **[Summarize]**
2. **Text to Text** What parts of young Zora's personality might explain her later interest in preserving folktales such as "How the Snake Got Poison"? **[Connect]**
3. What does Papa mean when he says to Zora, "Always trying to wear de big hat!"? **[Infer]**
4. How would you compare Papa's views with Zora's? **[Compare]**
5. **Reading Strategy** **Visualize** Form a picture in your mind of what the author saw from the chinaberry tree. In your own words, describe what she saw in as much detail as you can.
6. **BQ** **BIG Question** Zora Neale Hurston's style is influenced by the African American oral tradition. How is the narration in this selection like the narration in "How the Snake Got Poison"?

Before You Read

Four Haiku: Seasons

Connect to the Poems

Think about the four seasons. Try to picture each season in your mind.

List List three words or images that come to mind when you think about each season.

Build Background

These four poems are written in an unrhymed form of poetry called **haiku.** Haiku is a traditional Japanese form of poetry that has three lines and seventeen syllables.

These poems have been translated from Japanese into English. Because they are translations, the number of syllables is not the same as it is in Japanese. However, the translations do capture the meaning and feeling of the original poems.

Set Purposes for Reading

BQ BIG Question

As you read, ask yourself, what purpose and effect does each poem have?

Literary Element Haiku

In **haiku,** the first and third lines have five syllables each. The second line has seven syllables. The purpose of traditional haiku is to capture a flash of insight that occurs during an observation of nature.

Notice the images the poet chooses in each poem. In a few well-chosen words, the poet captures the feeling of a brief moment.

As you read, ask yourself, what emotion does each poem capture? What image does the poet use to create the emotion?

LOG ON Literature Online

Author Search For more about Yosa Buson, Naitō Jōsō, Kawabata Bōsha, and Yuzuru Miura, go to glencoe.com and enter Quickpass code GL17527u2.

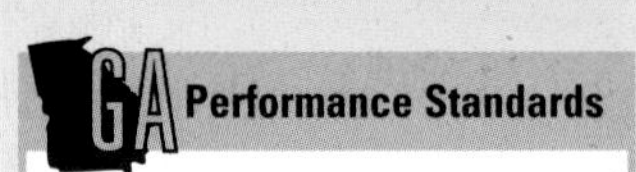

GA Performance Standards

For pages 236–239

ELA6R1h/iii For literary texts, respond to and explain the effects of graphics.

Meet the Authors

Yosa Buson

Yosa Buson is one of Japan's best-known writers of haiku. He was born in 1716 and learned his craft at a university in Tokyo. He was also a landscape painter and practiced an art that combined haiku with illustrations. Yosa Buson died in 1784.

Kawabata Bōsha

Kawabata Bōsha is an honored haiku poet in Japan. He was born in 1897 and died in 1941.

Yuzuru Miura

Yuzuru Miura is a modern poet. He has edited haiku anthologies and recently taught English literature at Chukyo University in Japan.

Naitō Jōsō

Naitō Jōsō was born in 1662. He was a samurai at one time and later became a priest. A sincere and faithful follower of haiku master Bashō, Jōsō mourned Bashō's death for three years.

Spring

Yosa Buson

Grasses are misty,
The waters silent—
A tranquil evening.

Haiku What feeling does the image of silent waters create?

Summer

Kawabata Bōsha

Firefly lights
Link up as a chain of beads
Along the water's edge.

Haiku How does the length of each line of the poem help capture a single moment?

Autumn

Yuzuru Miura

Red dragonflies
Flowing like a ripple
Toward the crimson sky.

Haiku How does the color of the sky affect how you picture the dragonflies?

Naitō Jōsō

The sleet falls
As if coming through the bottom
Of loneliness.

These poems reflect the importance of seasons in traditional haiku. How do the details in the poems reflect what is important in Japanese tradition?

Season's Quadrant, 1999. John Bunker. Watercolor on paper. Private collection.

After You Read

Respond and Think Critically

1. In "Spring," which image appeals to the sense of sound? **[Identify]**
2. In "Summer," what are the fireflies doing? **[Recall]**
3. In "Autumn," what do the words "flowing like a ripple" suggest? **[Interpret]**
4. In "Winter," what two things are being compared? Tell why you think the poet uses this comparison. **[Compare]**
5. **Literary Element Haiku** Count the syllables in each of the three lines of each poem. Which poem is closest to the standard syllable counts for haiku? Explain why. **[Analyze]**
6. **BQ BIG Question** Based on these poems—and the haiku form in general—what can you conclude about the role of nature in traditional Japanese culture? **[Conclude]**

Spelling Link

Patterns in Words with Two or More Syllables These words can often be confusing because many sounds can be spelled in more than one way. Think of the word *ripple* in "Autumn." How do you know that it should have two *p*'s instead of just one? The following spelling rule will help you recognize when to double consonants.

Rule: If an accented syllable ends in a single vowel followed by a single consonant, the consonant should be doubled before adding the next syllable. **Examples:** *bottom, worry, fuzzy, puffy*

There are exceptions to this rule. Here are a few of the most common ones. **Exceptions:** *super, cater, dozen, meter*

Practice On a sheet of paper, correct each of the following misspelled words. Then use each word in a sentence.

goly, hapen, peny, flufy

Writing

Write a Journal Entry Which season do you find most inspiring or interesting? In your journal, write a paragraph or several paragraphs that express your thoughts about the season. Include the feelings and the images you associate with that time of year. Now write a haiku based on the reflections in your journal entry. Remember, a haiku has five syllables in lines one and three and seven syllables in line two.

TIP

Comparing

To answer question 4, try this strategy:

- Look for a word or phrase that signals a comparison, such as *like* or *as*. In this poem, the phrase is *as if*.
- Identify the two things being joined by the comparing word or phrase.
- Think about what these two things have in common or why they make a good comparison.

Keep track of your ideas about the **BIG Question** in your unit Foldable.

Literature Online

Selection Resources
For Selection Quizzes, eFlashcards, and Reading-Writing Connection activities, go to glencoe.com and enter QuickPass code GL17527u2.

Before You Read

Ballpark Food

Connect to the Web Article

Have you ever felt that you paid too much for something? Did you wonder why the price was so high?

Partner Talk With a partner, talk about a time when you bought something from a vendor at a ballpark or other public place. Did you think the prices were fair? How much would the same items cost in a store?

Build Background

A group of 36 students, who call themselves the Snack Squad, decided to gather information about foods sold at baseball parks. The Snack Squad wanted to know if it was cheaper and more healthful for people to bring their own food to the ballpark rather than to eat the food sold there. They also wanted to know whether the advertisements in the ballparks had any effect on food sales. They put all the information into the quiz you are about to read.

Vocabulary

squad (skwod) *n.* a small group working for a common purpose (p. 242). *Ron is the police officer in charge of his squad.*

salary (sal′ ə rē) *n.* fixed sum of money regularly paid to a person for a job (p. 243). *Sarah earns a good salary at her engineering job.*

stadium (stā′dē əm) *n.* a large, usually roofless building surrounding an open area used for sporting events and equipped with many rows of seats (p. 243). *The stadium was packed with baseball fans.*

wages (wāj′əz) *n.* money paid to a person for work or services, especially on an hourly or a daily basis (p. 244). *The workers wanted an increase in their hourly wages.*

vendors (ven′dərz) *n.* people who sell goods (p. 244). *At the craft fair, vendors sold handmade pillows and wooden candlesticks.*

Author Search For more about the Snack Squad, go to glencoe.com and enter QuickPass code GL17527u2.

Set Purposes for Reading

BQ BIG Question

As you read, ask yourself, where does my money go at the ballpark, and how can I save some of it?

Literary Element Text Features

Readers can use newspapers, magazines, and Web pages to find information. **Text features** are special ways of presenting information and include titles, graphics, captions, and headings. In "Ballpark Food," the text is set as questions and answers. Numbers, questions, answer-choice letters, and answers are set in boldface type.

It is easier to find, follow, and understand information you need if you recognize and use text features. For example, boldface letters under each question let you know that these are the answer choices.

As you read, ask yourself, how do the text features help me understand the results of the Snack Squad's research?

Reading Skill Determine Main Idea and Supporting Details

The **main idea** is the most important idea in a paragraph or an article. Often, a topic sentence states the main idea. The other sentences add **supporting details**, or examples and reasons that explain the main idea.

When you determine main idea and supporting details, you remember key ideas and form your own opinions about them.

To **determine main idea and supporting details,** ask yourself,

- What is the main point of this article?
- What details support that point?
- Is the main idea stated directly, or do I need to identify it from the details in the text?

It is a good idea to record the main idea (or ideas) and supporting details as you read. You may find it helpful to use a graphic organizer like the one below.

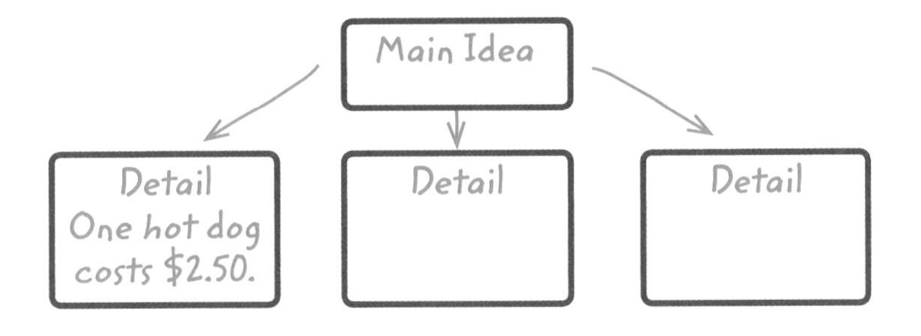

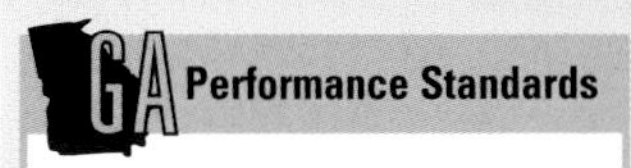

GA Performance Standards

For pages 240–246

ELA6R1b For informational texts, apply knowledge of common graphic features.

TRY IT

Determine Main Idea and Supporting Details "I don't think I can go to the movies tonight," your friend writes in an e-mail. "I have a ton of homework, and I'm supposed to watch my little brother. Plus, my mom can't drive me." What is the main idea of your friend's message? What details support it?

INFORMATIONAL TEXT
WEB SITE
zillions.org
Consumer Reports 4 Kids

BALLPARK

Do you have major-league complaints about the high price of ballpark food?

Take this quiz to see if you can guess what our 36-kid Snack **Squad** discovered when they visited baseball parks to buy and test their food.

1. **How did the price of hot dogs, soda, and peanuts at the ballpark compare to their price at a food store?**
   A. The food cost twice as much at the ballpark.
   B. It cost three to seven times more at the ballpark.
   C. Ballpark and food store prices were the same.

2. **Say you paid $2.50 for this hot dog at a ballpark. How much of that covers the cost of the hot dog and bun?**
   A. 10¢ **B.** 50¢ **C.** $1
   D. $1.50 **E.** $2

3. **Will most baseball parks let you bring in your own food?**
   A. Yes **B.** No

4. **How many ads do you think our Snack Squad spotted in the ballparks they visited?**
   A. None **B.** Just a few **C.** Dozens

Text Features
How can you tell this is a quiz?

Vocabulary

squad (skwod) *n.* a small group working for a common purpose

ANSWERS

1. B! Hot dogs, soda, and peanuts cost three to seven times more at the ballpark than at a store!

You almost need a major-league **salary** to afford ballpark food! The hot dogs, soda, and peanuts our Snack Squad bought cost three to seven times more than their local food stores charged. In Ohio, for example, $7.50 bought a hot dog, 24-ounce soda, and bag of about 90 peanuts at the Cincinnati Reds **stadium**. But that same $7.50 would buy five hot dogs, 190 ounces of soda, and about 380 peanuts at a grocery store!

Text Features What does this heading tell you about the items numbered 1–4 that follow?

Determine Main Idea and Supporting Details What main idea do these details support?

Vocabulary

salary (sal′ ə rē) *n.* fixed sum of money regularly paid to a person for a job

stadium (stā′ dē əm) *n.* a large, usually roofless building surrounding an open area used for sporting events and equipped with many rows of seats

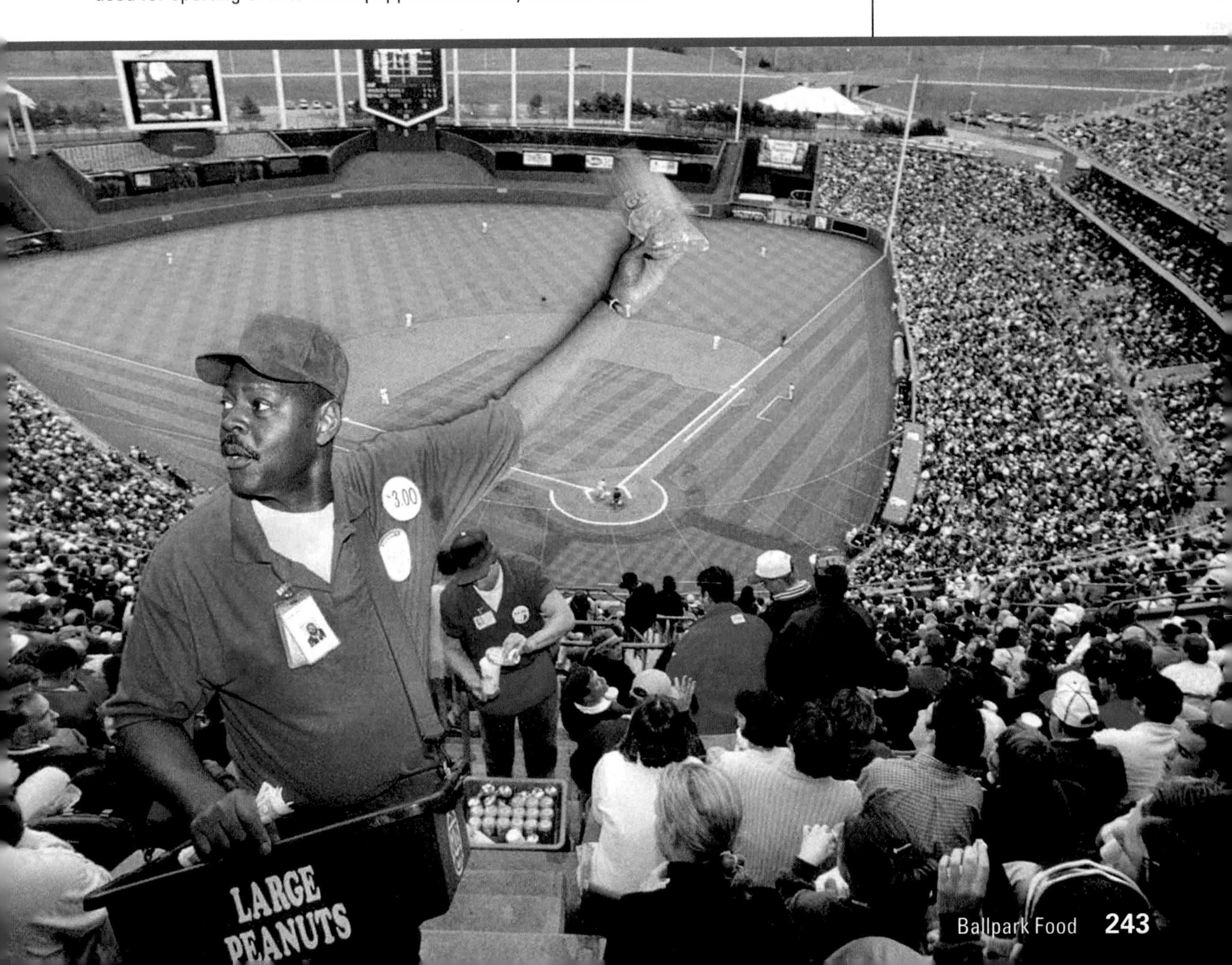

View the Art Complete this sentence to summarize what you learn from the Food-Price Scorecard: The next time I go to the ballpark, I'll be sure to ______.

2. B! Of the $2.50 you pay for a hot dog at a ballpark, only 50¢ goes for the cost of the hot dog and bun!

If the hot dog and bun and all the fixings only cost the concession companies (food-sellers) 50¢, where does the other $2 go? **Wages** for **vendors** who sell the hot dogs come to 50¢. The concession company takes 25¢ as a profit, and 25¢ covers cleaning, phones, and other costs. The biggest chunk of that hog-dog price ($1.00) goes to the baseball team and stadium owners!

BQ BIG Question

Where does your money go at the ballpark?

Vocabulary

wages (wāj′ əz) *n.* money paid to a person for work or services, especially on an hourly or a daily basis

vendors (ven′ dərz) *n.* people who sell goods

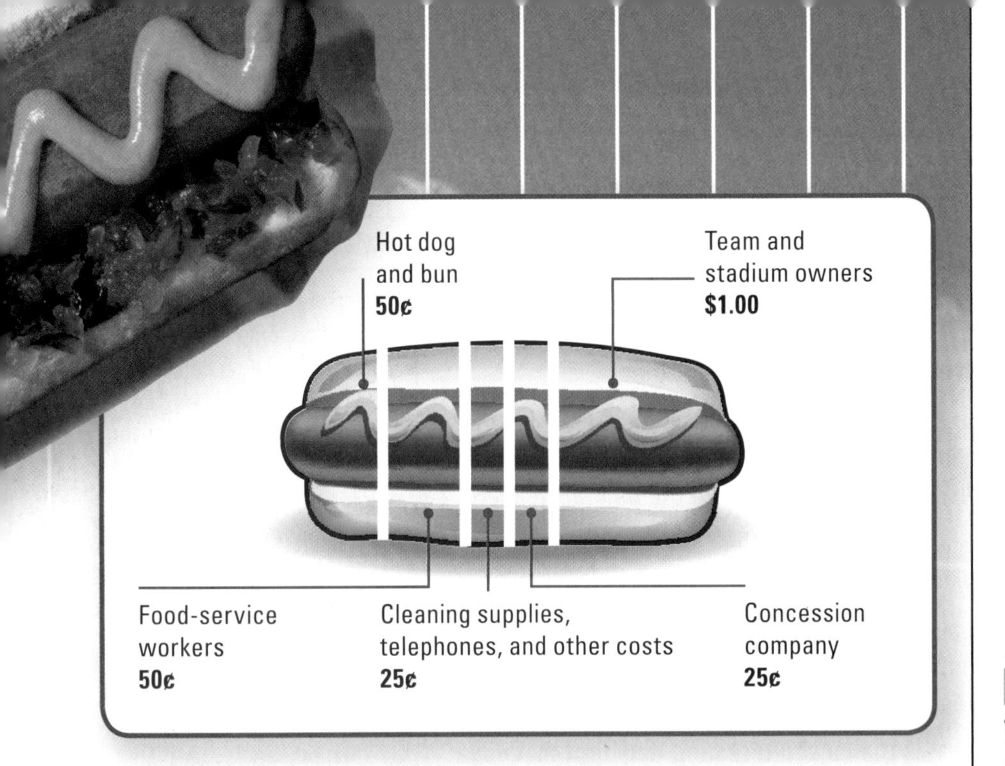

View the Art Who gets the greatest amount of the money you spend on a hot dog at the ballpark? How much do they get for each hot dog?

Visual Vocabulary

Turnstiles are posts with movable arms attached that allow only one person at a time to pass through an entrance on foot.

3. A! Yes, most ballparks will let you bring in your own food.

Nearly all major-league stadiums say they'll let fans bring food from home. When our Snack Squad brought their own food, some were stopped at the **turnstiles** and asked to open their packs. "They were just looking for cans," reported Peter, 11. Ushers have the right to inspect bags and take away glass bottles, cans, thermoses, and other items that could be thrown onto the field. Juice boxes and plastic bottles are usually okay. In the end, *none* of our testers had their food taken away.

Determine Main Idea and Supporting Details
What main idea does this detail support?

4. C! Snack Squad kids spotted dozens of ads in the ballparks they visited.

Kids spotted ads on their scorecards, ticket stubs, and seatbacks. They saw ads on lighting towers and at the concession stands. According to Tess, the sneakiest ads at the Oakland Coliseum were on the big-screen TV. "Right after replays, when everyone's attention was on the big screen, they showed commercials," she said.

After You Read

Respond and Think Critically

1. What problem with ballpark food does the writer mention in the paragraph under Answer 1? **[Identify]**
2. Why does food cost so much more at a ballpark than at a store? **[Recall]**
3. Besides reasons given in the text, what other reasons might owners have for banning bottles, cans, or thermoses in the ballpark? **[Infer]**
4. **Literary Element** **Text Features** Why do you think the writers chose to begin the article by having readers take a quiz? **[Infer]**
5. **Reading Skill** **Determine Main Idea and Supporting Details** Review the graphic organizer you made. How did you use information from the quiz to find the main idea and supporting details? **[Analyze]**
6. **BQ** **BIG Question** What is the most interesting new fact that you learned from reading this article? Explain whether this information changes what you might do at the ballpark. **[Conclude]**

TIP

Inferring
Here are some tips to help you answer question 3. Remember that when you **infer,** you combine what you read with what you know to figure out a meaning that is not directly stated.

- What do you already know about the price of food at a ballpark?
- What can you assume about the price of drinks at the ballpark?
- Who would profit most from the sale of drinks at the ballpark?

Vocabulary Practice

Identify whether each set of paired words has the same or opposite meaning. Then write a sentence using each vocabulary word in a sentence, or draw or find a picture that represents the word.

stadium and arena
squad and team
vendors and customers
wages and earnings
salary and cost

Example: stadium and arena = same meaning

Sentence: I like going to the baseball stadium in the city, but the local arena is just as comfortable.

FOLDABLES Study Organizer Keep track of your ideas about the **BIG Question** in your unit Foldable.

Writing

Write a Summary On page 170, you learned how to write a summary. Now think back over the article's main ideas and important details. Write a one-paragraph summary of the article, retelling the important points in your own words.

LOG ON Literature Online

Selection Resources
For Selection Quizzes, eFlashcards, and Reading-Writing Connection activities, go to glencoe.com and enter QuickPass code GL17527u2.

Media Workshop

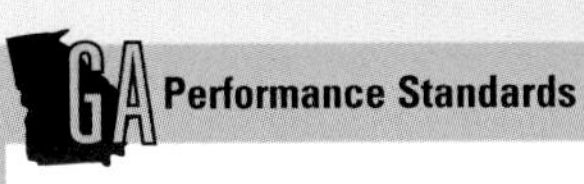

For page 247

ELA6RC2e Examine the author's purpose in writing.

ELA6RC2f Recognize and use the features of texts.

Media Elements

Media refers to radio, television, newspapers, magazines, the Internet, and other means of mass communication. **Media elements**—what you read, see, hear, and experience in the media—help you understand the information in articles and may point the way to more information. Different types of media may use different media elements. As you look at the examples below, think about each media element. What effect does it have on the article? How does each element help the article meet its purpose?

Magazine Article

It's Not Over?

Suzy Favor Hamilton is one of the best distance runners in the United States.

Hamilton stopped running before the race was over.

Online Article

It's Not Over?

Suzy Favor Hamilton is one of the best distance runners in the United States.

Read full article. Read more about Hamilton. Click for video clip.

Element	Explanation	Example
Text and Content	**Text** is all the words that you read and hear. All the text together makes up the **content,** or the information the article provides.	"Suzy Favor Hamilton is one of the best distance runners in the United States, but in 1994 she lost a race because she lost count."
Graphics and Color	**Graphics** are visuals, such as pictures or charts. Graphics in media can have lots of color.	A cartoon shows Suzy Hamilton standing still while other women are running.
Motion and Sound	**Motion** is movement you see. **Sound** is what you hear.	The online version of this article links to a video clip.
Structure	**Structure** is the way an article is set up. Print articles usually have sections with subheadings. Online articles might link text across Web pages.	The print article is divided into sections with headings such as "It's Not Over?" The online article includes links to the rest of the article and to more information on the topic.

TRY IT

Analyze Media Elements

Choose a newspaper or magazine article and find the same article on the newspaper or magazine's Web site. Use the two versions to answer these questions:

1. What is the article about?
2. What is the author's purpose?
3. Which media elements does the print article use to meet its purpose?
4. Which media elements does the online article use to meet its purpose?
5. Which version of the article do you think is more effective? Why?

Before You Read

Ta-Na-E-Ka

Connect to the Story

What do you usually do on a birthday? Do you sing a birthday song or blow out candles on a cake? Think about the different ways people celebrate growing up.

List List typical things you do to celebrate a birthday.

Build Background

"Ta-Na-E-Ka" is a short story about a tradition of the Kaw, or Kansa, Indians. Both *Kaw* and *Kansa* mean "people of the south wind." Originally the Kaw lived along the Kansas River, where they hunted buffalo and farmed. In 1873 the United States government moved the Kaw to Indian Territory, which is present-day Oklahoma.

Vocabulary

shrewdest (shrōōd′ ist) *adj.* the most clever in practical matters (p. 252).
The shrewdest player won the chess tournament.

ordeals (ôr dēlz′) *n.* experiences that are painful or difficult to endure (p. 253).
The storm and the flood that occurred afterward were terrible ordeals for the townspeople.

dejectedly (di jek′tid lē) *adv.* in a disheartened or depressed way (p. 255).
The losing team walked dejectedly to the locker room.

hospitality (hos′ pə tal′ə tē) *n.* the act of being welcoming to guests (p. 257).
Before leaving, the guests thanked the family for their hospitality.

Meet Mary Whitebird

A Mysterious Author Mary Whitebird is the pen name of a male writer who likes to keep his identity a secret. He has long had an interest in Native Americans and their culture.

Literary Works "Ta-Na-E-Ka" was published in 1973.

Literature Online

Author Search For more about Mary Whitebird, go to glencoe.com and enter QuickPass code GL17527u2.

Set Purposes for Reading

BQ BIG Question

As you read, ask yourself, what choices does Mary make and how do her actions affect the story?

Literary Element Conflict

Conflict is the central struggle between opposing forces in a story. An **external conflict** is the struggle of a character against an outside force, such as nature, society, fate, or another character. An **internal conflict** takes place within a character's mind. For example, the character might have to make a difficult choice.

Conflict is the gas that keeps the engine of a story running. It makes the story interesting because you wonder who or what will win.

As you read, ask yourself what conflicts the main characters face. What do you learn about the characters by the way they react to the conflicts?

Reading Strategy Make Inferences About Characters

When you **make inferences,** you make educated guesses using clues from a text. To **make inferences about characters**, pay attention to what they say and do. Combine this information with your own experience and knowledge to figure out things about the characters that the writer doesn't directly tell you.

When you make inferences about characters, you assess their qualities and analyze how they affect the plot and resolution, or outcome, of the conflict.

To **make inferences about a character,** pay attention to

- the character's thoughts, words, and actions
- your own background and knowledge
- what other characters say about the character

Record details about each main character. You may find it helpful to use a graphic organizer like the one below.

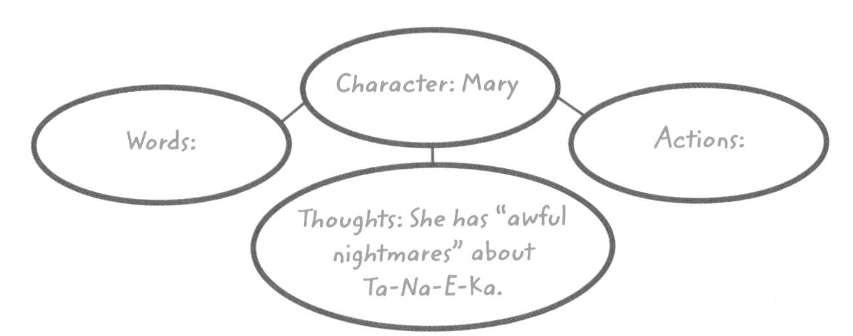

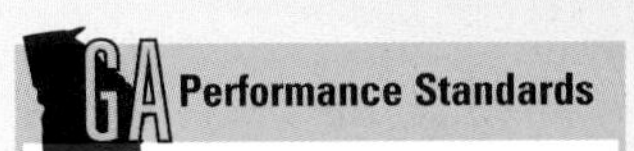

GA Performance Standards

For pages 248–261

ELA6R1e/i For literary texts, identify and analyze the elements of setting, characterization, plot, and the resolution of the conflict of a story or play: internal/external conflicts.

TRY IT

Make Inferences You come home after school and your house smells like pizza. Your dad comes out of the kitchen with flour on his hands and tomato-sauce stains on his shirt. What do you infer about your dad?

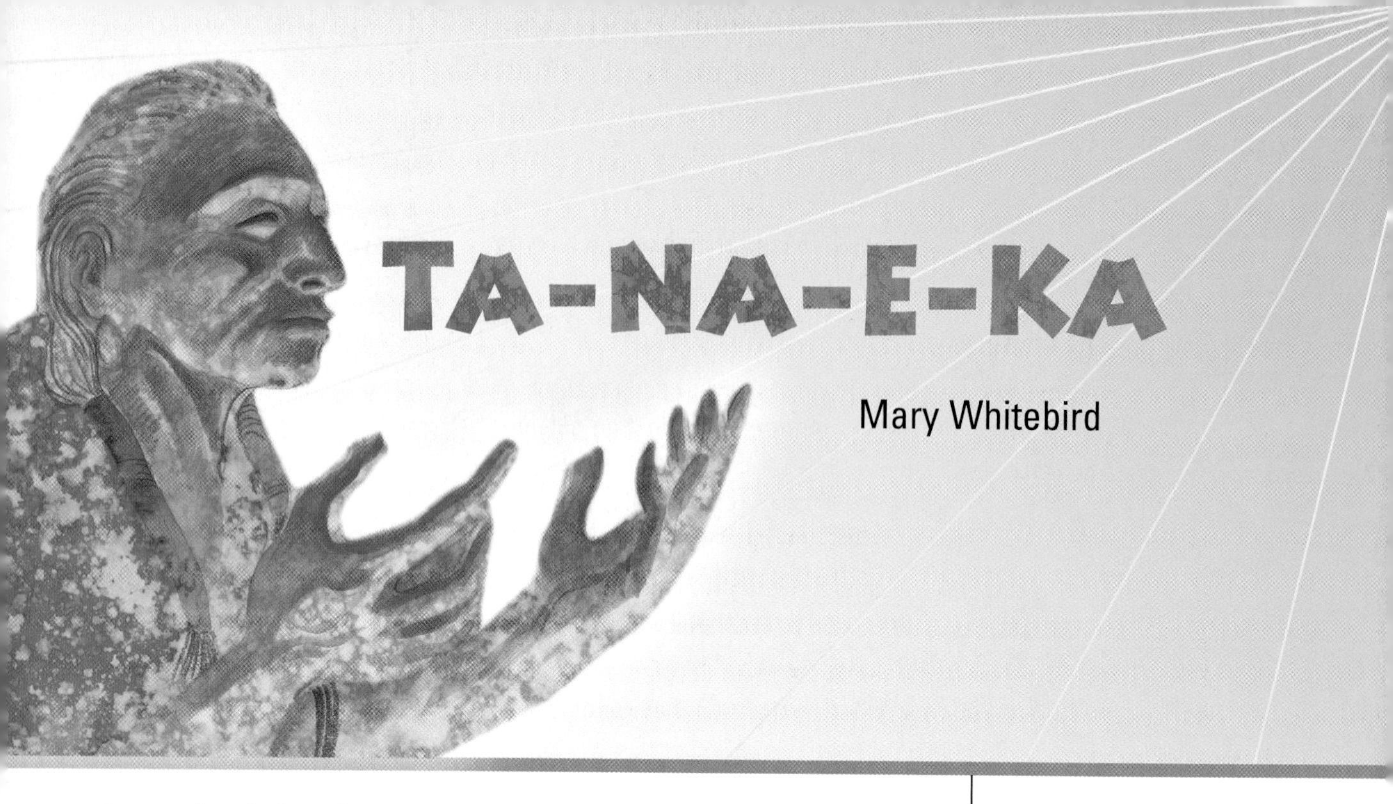

TA-NA-E-KA

Mary Whitebird

As my birthday drew closer, I had awful nightmares about it. I was reaching the age at which all Kaw Indians had to participate in Ta-Na-E-Ka.

Well, not all Kaws. Many of the younger families on the reservation were beginning to give up the old customs. But my grandfather, Amos Deer Leg, was devoted to tradition. He still wore handmade beaded moccasins instead of shoes and kept his iron-gray hair in tight braids. He could speak English, but he spoke it only with white men. With his family he used a Sioux dialect.[1]

Grandfather was one of the last living Indians (he died in 1953, when he was eighty-one) who actually fought against the U.S. Cavalry. Not only did he fight, he was wounded in a skirmish at Rose Creek—a famous encounter in which the celebrated Kaw chief Flat Nose lost his life. At the time, my grandfather was only eleven years old.

Make Inferences About Characters How might Grandfather's boyhood experience have affected him?

Eleven was a magic word among the Kaws. It was the time of Ta-Na-E-Ka, the "flowering of adulthood." It was the age, my grandfather informed us hundreds of times, "when a boy could prove himself to be a warrior and a girl took the first steps to womanhood."

---

1 ***Sioux*** is a language spoken by some Native Americans of the Great Plains. A ***dialect*** is a regional variety of a language.

"I don't want to be a warrior," my cousin Roger Deer Leg confided to me. "I'm going to become an accountant."

"None of the other tribes make girls go through the endurance ritual," I complained to my mother.

"It won't be as bad as you think, Mary," my mother said, ignoring my protests. "Once you've gone through it, you'll certainly never forget it. You'll be proud."

I even complained to my teacher, Mrs. Richardson, feeling that, as a white woman, she would side with me.

She didn't. "All of us have rituals of one kind or another," Mrs. Richardson said. "And look at it this way: How many girls have the opportunity to compete on equal terms with boys? Don't look down on your heritage."

Heritage, indeed! I had no intention of living on a reservation for the rest of my life. I was a good student. I loved school. My fantasies were about knights in armor and fair ladies in flowing gowns, being saved from dragons. It never once occurred to me that being an Indian was exciting.

Conflict What is the conflict?

But I've always thought that the Kaw were the originators of the women's liberation movement. No other Indian tribe—and I've spent half a lifetime researching the subject—treated women more "equally" than the Kaw. Unlike most of the sub-tribes of the Sioux Nation, the Kaw allowed men and women to eat together. And hundreds of years before we were "acculturated,"[2] a Kaw woman had the right to refuse a prospective husband even if her father arranged the match.

Make Inferences About Characters How might this have influenced the kind of person Mary has become?

The wisest women (generally wisdom was equated with age) often sat in tribal councils. Furthermore, most Kaw legends revolve around "Good Woman," a kind of supersquaw, a Joan of Arc[3] of the high plains. Good Woman led Kaw warriors into battle after battle, from which they always seemed to emerge victorious.

And girls as well as boys were required to undergo Ta-Na-E-Ka. The actual ceremony varied from tribe to

---

2 A group that is ***acculturated*** is forced to adopt another people's culture, in this case the culture of the European Americans.

3 ***Joan of Arc*** was a French heroine in the early 1400s.

tribe, but since the Indians' life on the plains was dedicated to survival, Ta-Na-E-Ka was a test of survival.

"Endurance is the loftiest virtue[4] of the Indian," my grandfather explained. "To survive, we must endure. When I was a boy, Ta-Na-E-Ka was more than the mere symbol it is now. We were painted white with the juice of a sacred herb and sent naked into the wilderness without so much as a knife. We couldn't return until the white had worn off. It wouldn't wash off. It took almost 18 days, and during that time we had to stay alive, trapping food, eating insects and roots and berries, and watching out for enemies. And we did have enemies—both the white soldiers and the Omaha warriors, who were always trying to capture Kaw boys and girls undergoing their endurance test. It was an exciting time."

"What happened if you couldn't make it?" Roger asked. He was born only three days after I was, and we were being trained for Ta-Na-E-Ka together. I was happy to know he was frightened, too.

"Many didn't return," Grandfather said. "Only the strongest and **shrewdest**. Mothers were not allowed to weep over those who didn't return. If a Kaw couldn't survive, he or she wasn't worth weeping over. It was our way."

"What a lot of hooey," Roger whispered. "I'd give anything to get out of it."

Conflict How does this express the main conflict between the young characters and Grandfather?

"I don't see how we have any choice," I replied.

Roger gave my arm a little squeeze. "Well, it's only five days."

Five days! Maybe it was better than being painted white and sent out naked for eighteen days. But not much better.

We were to be sent, barefoot and in bathing suits, into the woods. Even our very traditional parents put their foot down when Grandfather suggested we go naked. For five days we'd have to live off the land, keeping warm as best we could, getting food where we could. It was May, but on

4 The ***loftiest virtue*** is the most noble quality.

Vocabulary

shrewdest (shrōōd′ ist) *adj.* the most clever in practical matters the northernmost reaches of the Missouri River the days were still chilly and the nights were fiercely cold.

Conflict Is the cold weather an internal conflict or an external conflict?

Grandfather was in charge of the month's training for Ta-Na-E-Ka. One day he caught a grasshopper and demonstrated how to pull its legs and wings off in one flick of the fingers and how to swallow it.

I felt sick, and Roger turned green. "It's a darn good thing it's 1947," I told Roger teasingly. "You'd make a terrible warrior." Roger just grimaced.

I knew one thing. This particular Kaw Indian girl wasn't going to swallow a grasshopper no matter how hungry she got. And then I had an idea. Why hadn't I thought of it before? It would have saved nights of bad dreams about squooshy grasshoppers.

Make Inferences About Characters How might Mary's insistence affect the plot or conflict?

I headed straight for my teacher's house. "Mrs. Richardson," I said, "would you lend me five dollars?"

"Five dollars!" she exclaimed. "What for?"

"You remember the ceremony I talked about?"

"Ta-Na-E-Ka. Of course. Your parents have written me and asked me to excuse you from school so you can participate in it."

"Well, I need some things for the ceremony," I replied, in a half-truth. "I don't want to ask my parents for the money."

"It's not a crime to borrow money, Mary. But how can you pay it back?"

"I'll baby-sit for you ten times."

"That's more than fair," she said, going to her purse and handing me a crisp, new five-dollar bill. I'd never had that much money at once.

"I'm happy to know the money's going to be put to a good use," Mrs. Richardson said.

A few days later the ritual began with a long speech from my grandfather about how we had reached the age of decision, how we now had to fend for ourselves and prove that we could survive the most horrendous of **ordeals**. All the friends and relatives who had gathered at

Vocabulary

ordeals (ôr dēlz′) *n.* experiences that are painful or difficult to endure our house for dinner made jokes about their own Ta-Na-E-Ka experiences. They all advised us to fill up now, since for the next five days we'd be gorging[5] ourselves on crickets. Neither Roger nor I was very hungry.

"I'll probably laugh about this when I'm an accountant," Roger said, trembling.

"Are you trembling?" I asked.

"What do you think?"

"I'm happy to know boys tremble, too," I said.

At six the next morning, we kissed our parents and went off to the woods. "Which side do you want?" Roger asked. According to the rules, Roger and I would stake out "territories" in separate areas of the woods, and we weren't to communicate during the entire ordeal. "I'll go toward the river, if it's okay with you," I said.

"Sure," Roger answered. "What difference does it make?"

To me, it made a lot of difference. There was a marina a few miles up the river, and there were boats moored there. At least, I hoped so. I figured that a boat was a better place to sleep than under a pile of leaves.

BQ BIG Question

What problem is Mary hoping her choice will resolve?

"Why do you keep holding your head?" Roger asked.

"Oh, nothing. Just nervous," I told him. Actually, I was afraid I'd lose the five-dollar bill, which I had tucked into my hair with a bobby pin. As we came to a fork in the trail, Roger shook my hand. "Good luck, Mary."

"*N'ko-n'ta,*" I said. It was the Kaw word for "courage."

The sun was shining and it was warm, but my bare feet began to hurt immediately. I spied one of the berry bushes Grandfather had told us about. "You're lucky," he had

5 If you are ***gorging*** yourself, you are stuffing yourself with food.

said. "The berries are ripe in the spring, and they are delicious and nourishing." They were orange and fat, and I popped one into my mouth.

Argh! I spat it out. It was awful and bitter, and even grasshoppers were probably better tasting, although I never intended to find out.

I sat down to rest my feet. A rabbit hopped out from under the berry bush. He nuzzled the berry I'd spat out and ate it. He picked another one and ate that, too. He liked them. He looked at me, twitching his nose. I watched a red-headed woodpecker bore into an elm tree, and I caught a glimpse of a **civet cat** waddling through some twigs. All of a sudden I realized I was no longer frightened. Ta-Na-E-Ka might be more fun than I'd anticipated. I got up and headed toward the marina.

"Not one boat," I said to myself **dejectedly**. But the restaurant on the shore, "Ernie's Riverside," was open. I walked in, feeling silly in my bathing suit. The man at the counter was big and tough-looking. He wore a sweatshirt with the words "Fort Sheridan, 1944," and he had only three fingers on one of his hands. He asked me what I wanted.

"A hamburger and a milkshake," I said, holding the five-dollar bill in my hand so he'd know I had money.

"That's a pretty heavy breakfast, honey," he murmured.

"That's what I always have for breakfast," I lied.

"Forty-five cents," he said, bringing me the food. (Back in 1947, hamburgers were twenty-five cents and milkshakes were twenty cents.) "Delicious," I thought. "Better'n grasshoppers—and Grandfather never once mentioned that I couldn't eat hamburgers."

While I was eating, I had a grand idea. Why not sleep in the restaurant? I went to the ladies' room and made sure the window was unlocked. Then I went back outside and played along the riverbank, watching the water birds and trying to identify each one. I planned to look for a beaver dam the next day.

Visual Vocabulary

A **civet cat** is a catlike animal, native to Africa, Europe, and Asia. It has a narrow head, a pointed muzzle, and a slender body. In this story, the name is used for a spotted skunk.

BQ BIG Question

How are Mary's choices breaking the rules of Ta-Na-E-Ka?

Vocabulary

dejectedly (di jek′ tid lē) *adv.* in a disheartened or depressed way

The restaurant closed at sunset, and I watched the three-fingered man drive away. Then I climbed in the unlocked window. There was a night light on, so I didn't turn on any lights. But there was a radio on the counter. I turned it on to a music program. It was warm in the restaurant, and I was hungry. I helped myself to a glass of milk and a piece of pie, intending to keep a list of what I'd eaten so I could leave money. I also planned to get up early, sneak out through the window, and head for the woods before the three-fingered man returned. I turned off the radio, wrapped myself in the man's apron, and in spite of the hardness of the floor, fell asleep.

Make Inferences About Characters How might Mary's honesty affect the plot?

"What the heck are you doing here, kid?"

It was the man's voice.

It was morning. I'd overslept. I was scared.

"Hold it, kid. I just wanna know what you're doing here. You lost? You must be from the reservation. Your folks must be worried sick about you. Do they have a phone?"

"Yes, yes," I answered. "But don't call them."

I was shivering. The man, who told me his name was Ernie, made me a cup of hot chocolate while I explained about Ta-Na-E-Ka.

"Darnedest thing I ever heard," he said, when I was through. "Lived next to the reservation all my life and this is the first I've heard of Ta-Na whatever-you-call-it." He

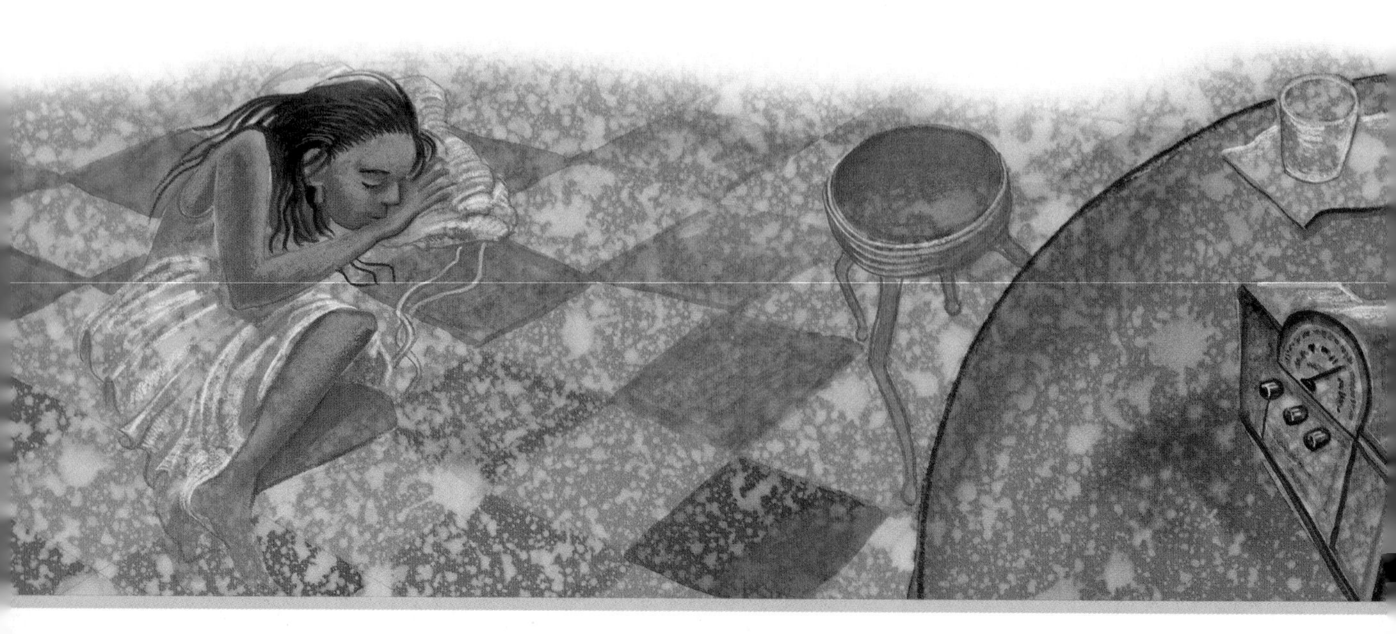

looked at me, all goose bumps in my bathing suit. "Pretty silly thing to do to a kid," he muttered.

That was just what I'd been thinking for months, but when Ernie said it, I became angry. "No, it isn't silly. It's a custom of the Kaw. We've been doing this for hundreds of years. My mother and my grandfather and everybody in my family went through this ceremony. It's why the Kaw are great warriors."

Conflict What causes the change in Mary's thinking?

"Okay, great warrior," Ernie chuckled, "suit yourself. And, if you want to stick around, it's okay with me." Ernie went to the broom closet and tossed me a bundle. "That's the lost-and-found closet," he said. "Stuff people left on boats. Maybe there's something to keep you warm."

The sweater fitted loosely, but it felt good. I felt good. And I'd found a new friend. Most important, I was surviving Ta-Na-E-Ka.

My grandfather had said the experience would be filled with adventure, and I was having my fill. And Grandfather had never said we couldn't accept **hospitality**.

I stayed at Ernie's Riverside for the entire period. In the mornings I went into the woods and watched the animals and picked flowers for each of the tables in Ernie's. I had never felt better. I was up early enough to watch the sun rise on the Missouri, and I went to bed after it set. I ate everything I wanted—insisting that Ernie take all my money for the food. "I'll keep this in trust for you, Mary," Ernie promised, "in case you are ever desperate for five dollars." (He did, too, but that's another story.)

Make Inferences About Characters What kind of man is Ernie?

I was sorry when the five days were over. I'd enjoyed every minute with Ernie. He taught me how to make Western omelets and to make Chili Ernie Style (still one of my favorite dishes). And I told Ernie all about the legends of the Kaw. I hadn't realized I knew so much about my people.

But Ta-Na-E-Ka was over, and as I approached my house, at about nine-thirty in the evening, I became nervous all over again. What if Grandfather asked me

Vocabulary

hospitality (hos′ pə tal′ ə tē) *n.* the act of being welcoming to guests about the berries and the grasshoppers? And my feet were hardly cut. I hadn't lost a pound and my hair was combed.

"They'll be so happy to see me," I told myself hopefully, "that they won't ask too many questions."

Conflict Why is Mary worried?

I opened the door. My grandfather was in the front room. He was wearing the ceremonial beaded deerskin shirt which had belonged to *his* grandfather. *"N'g'da'ma,"* he said. "Welcome back."

I embraced my parents warmly, letting go only when I saw my cousin Roger sprawled on the couch. His eyes were red and swollen. He'd lost weight. His feet were an unsightly mass of blood and blisters, and he was moaning: "I made it, see. I made it. I'm a warrior. A warrior."

My grandfather looked at me strangely. I was clean, obviously well-fed, and radiantly healthy. My parents got the message. My uncle and aunt gazed at me with hostility.

Finally my grandfather asked, "What did you eat to keep you so well?"

I sucked in my breath and blurted out the truth: "Hamburgers and milkshakes."

"Hamburgers!" my grandfather growled.

"Milkshakes!" Roger moaned.

"You didn't say we had to eat grasshoppers," I said sheepishly.

"Tell us all about your Ta-Na-E-Ka," my grandfather commanded.

I told them everything, from borrowing the five dollars, to Ernie's kindness, to observing the beaver.

"That's not what I trained you for," my grandfather said sadly.

I stood up. "Grandfather, I learned that Ta-Na-E-Ka is important. I didn't think so during training. I was scared stiff of it. I handled it my way. And I learned I had nothing to be afraid of. There's no reason in 1947 to eat grasshoppers when you can eat a hamburger."

BQ BIG Question
How have Mary's choices throughout the story led her to a greater understanding?

I was inwardly shocked at my own audacity.[6] But I liked it. "Grandfather, I'll bet you never ate one of those rotten berries yourself."

---

6 ***Audacity*** is boldness or daring.

Grandfather laughed! He laughed aloud! My mother and father and aunt and uncle were all dumbfounded. Grandfather never laughed. Never.

"Those berries—they are terrible," Grandfather admitted. "I could never swallow them. I found a dead deer on the first day of my Ta-Na-E-Ka—shot by a soldier, probably—and he kept my belly full for the entire period of the test!"

Grandfather stopped laughing. "We should send you out again," he said.

I looked at Roger. "You're pretty smart, Mary," Roger groaned. "I'd never have thought of what you did."

"Accountants just have to be good at arithmetic," I said comfortingly. "I'm terrible at arithmetic."

Roger tried to smile but couldn't. My grandfather called me to him. "You should have done what your cousin did. But I think you are more alert to what is happening to our people today than we are. I think you would have passed the test under any circumstances, in any time. Somehow, you know how to exist in a world that wasn't made for Indians. I don't think you're going to have any trouble surviving."

Grandfather wasn't entirely right. But I'll tell about that another time.

View the Art What kind of relationship between Mary and her grandfather does this painting show? Do you think it matches their relationship in the story? Why or why not?

After You Read

Respond and Think Critically

1. What is Mrs. Richardson's attitude toward Ta-Na-E-Ka? **[Recall]**
2. Identify why Mary thinks the Kaw were the originators of the women's liberation movement. **[Identify]**
3. In your own words, explain why endurance is so important to the Kaw. **[Paraphrase]**
4. How does Mary persuade Grandfather that she has truly passed her survival test? **[Analyze]**
5. In your opinion, does Mary complete Ta-Na-E-Ka fairly? Explain your answer. **[Evaluate]**
6. **BQ** **BIG Question** What did you learn about the tradition of Ta-Na-E-Ka from this story? **[Conclude]**

Vocabulary Practice

1. Which activities would most likely be **ordeals**—sleeping late every day for a week or shoveling snow every day for a week?
2. If your sister sighed **dejectedly,** how would you think she was feeling—satisfied or disappointed?
3. Which would you consider a sign of **hospitality**—a tray of holiday cookies or a locked door with a guard dog?
4. What would you expect from the **shrewdest** detective in a story—a clever solution or a careless mistake?

Academic Vocabulary

In "Ta-Na-E-Ka," the narrator describes how Grandfather "caught a grasshopper and **demonstrated** how to pull its legs and wings off in one flick of the fingers and how to swallow it." Using context clues, try to figure out the meaning of the word *demonstrated* in the previous sentence. Check your answer in a dictionary.

TIP

Analyzing

To answer question 4, think about what Mary says to her grandfather and why.

- Does she tell the truth or make up a story?
- What does she point out about Ta-Na-E-Ka?
- What abilities or insights do her words show?

Keep track of your ideas about the **BIG Question** in your unit Foldable.

Literature Online

Selection Resources

For Selection Quizzes, eFlashcards, and Reading-Writing Connection activities, go to glencoe.com and enter QuickPass code GL17527u2.

Literary Element Conflict

Standards Practice  ELA6R1e/ii

1. Which sentence best describes how Mary and her grandfather deal with difficulty?
   A. Both are easily distracted.
   B. Each is open to new and creative ideas.
   C. Both lack confidence in themselves.
   D. Each avoids conflicts.

Review: Plot

As you learned on page 53, **plot** is the sequence of events in a story. The **exposition** introduces the characters, setting, and situation. The **rising action** adds complications. The **climax** is the point of greatest interest or suspense in the story. The **falling action** is the result of the climax, and the **resolution** is the final outcome.

Refer to the plot diagram below as you determine how the events of the story fit into the plot.

2. What are two complications that are part of the rising action?
3. Identify the climax of the story.
4. Explain the story's falling action and resolution.

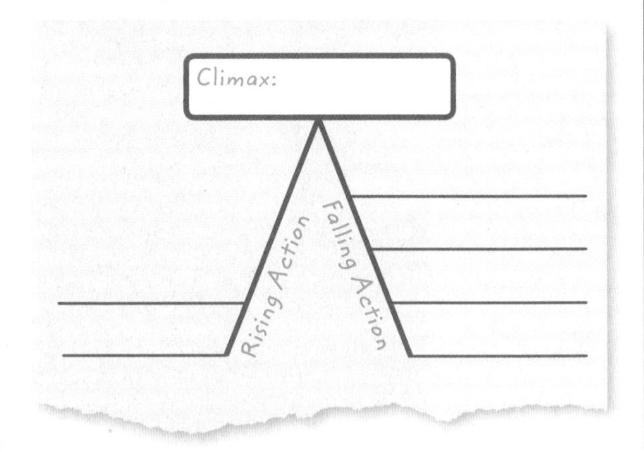

Reading Strategy

Make Inferences About Characters

Review your graphic organizers.

5. What can you infer about Grandfather from his reaction to Mary?
6. How might Mary's relationship with Grandfather change in the future?

Grammar Link

Pronoun Antecedents The noun or group of words that a pronoun refers to is called its **antecedent.** For example:

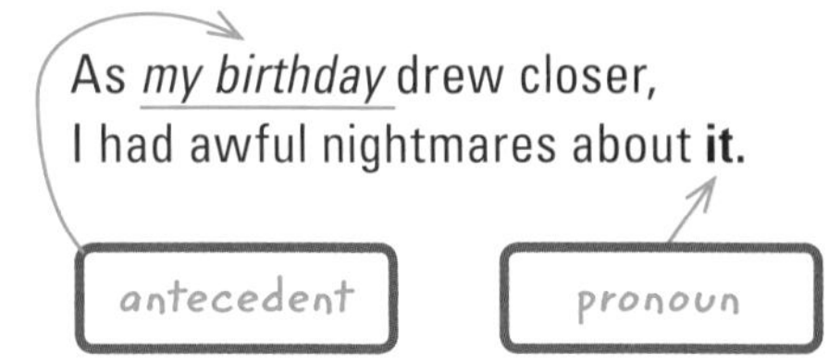

As my birthday drew closer,
I had awful nightmares about it.
antecedent
pronoun

When you use a pronoun, be sure that it clearly refers to its antecedent. Read the following sentences.

> *Mary complained to Mrs. Richardson about the ritual.* ***She*** *spoke about her heritage.*

The second sentence is not clear because the word *she* could refer to either Mary or Mrs. Richardson.

Clear pronoun antecedents make sure readers know to whom or what each pronoun refers.

Practice Look for two examples of clear pronoun antecedents in "Ta-Na-E-Ka." Copy the sentences on a sheet of paper and underline each pronoun and its antecedent. Then correct the following sentence so that the pronoun antecedent is clear.

> Grandfather and Roger are coming to the ceremony, but ***he*** doesn't want to take part.

Speaking and Listening

Literature Groups With a small group, discuss the conflicts between generations in the story. What do younger and older characters value? Support your opinions with evidence or pictures from the text. As you listen, compare other group members' opinions with your own.

Before You Read

These Walls Can Talk

Connect to the Article

Imagine that you are exploring a cave. You discover a cave drawing that is more than 20,000 years old. What do you do?

Partner Talk With a partner, discuss what actions you would take after this discovery.

Build Background

Scientists have found hundreds of caves and rocks decorated with art from prehistoric times. Cave art provides information about early humans, such as the clothing they wore, the animals they hunted, and the tools and weapons they used. This information helps scientists determine how humans lived before people began writing. Some experts believe that early humans used cave art to try to explain their world.

Vocabulary

artifacts (är′ tə fakts′) *n.* human-made objects used in the daily life of an ancient civilization (p. 265). *The history museum displays many artifacts from early cultures.*

probing (prōb′ ing) *v.* carrying out a thorough investigation or examination (p. 265). *The submarine was probing the ocean floor in search of new forms of life.*

intricately (in′tri kit lē) *adv.* in a complex way; in an elaborate manner (p. 265). *The intricately designed vase had overlapping patterns.*

plateau (pla tō′) *n.* elevated, fairly flat land area (p. 268). *The ruins of the ancient Aztec city are on a plateau overlooking the countryside.*

inhabitants (in hab′ət əntz) *n.* persons or animals that live permanently in a place (p. 268). *The inhabitants of the village fled when the volcano began to erupt.*

Set Purposes for Reading

BQ BIG Question

As you read, ask yourself, why is it important to preserve ancient art?

Literary Element Text Structure

Text structure is the way a piece of writing is organized. When writers use **problem-and-solution** structure, they state a problem and suggest a solution. Sometimes they suggest many solutions. Of course, it's up to you to decide whether they are right.

Writers of nonfiction articles often use a problem-and-solution structure. For example, the article "These Walls Can Talk" presents the problem that ancient rock art is being destroyed. The article then offers solutions to this problem.

As you read, ask yourself, what specific problems and solutions does this article mention?

Reading Skill Identify Cause-and-Effect Relationships

A **cause** is an event that makes something happen. What happens as a result of the cause is an **effect.** For example, if you don't study for a test (cause), you might get a failing grade (result).

Identifying cause-and-effect relationships in nonfiction articles will help you understand why certain events happen. For example, the following article discusses what is happening to ancient art (effects) and why (causes).

As you read, use these tips to identify cause-and-effect relationships:

- Ask yourself, what happened because of an event?
- Think about other causes and effects the event led to.
- Look for signal words and phrases such as *because, since,* and *as a result.*

Record causes and effects as you read. You may find it helpful to use a graphic organizer like the one below.

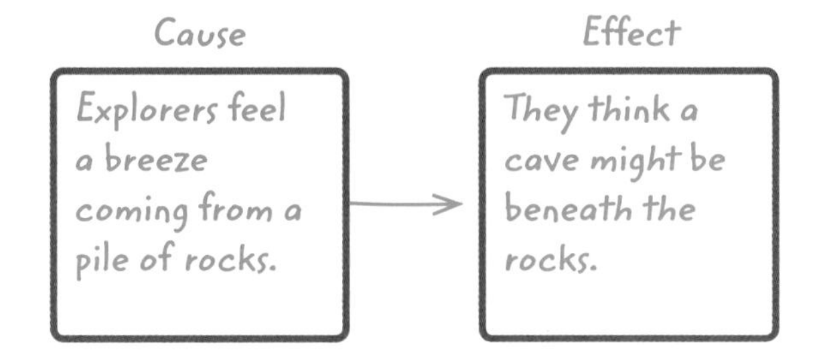

Cause
Explorers feel a breeze coming from a pile of rocks.
Effect
They think a cave might be beneath the rocks.

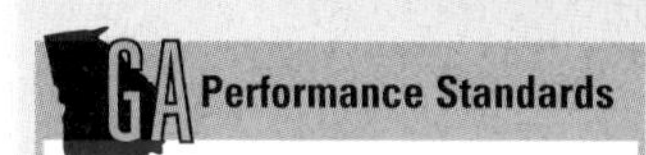

GA Performance Standards

For pages 262–270

ELA6R1c For informational texts, apply knowledge of common organizational structures and patterns.

TRY IT

Identify Cause-and-Effect Relationships You forget to return a library book. Then you get a note that says you must pay a fine. What is the cause of the fine? What will be the effect if you don't return the book soon?

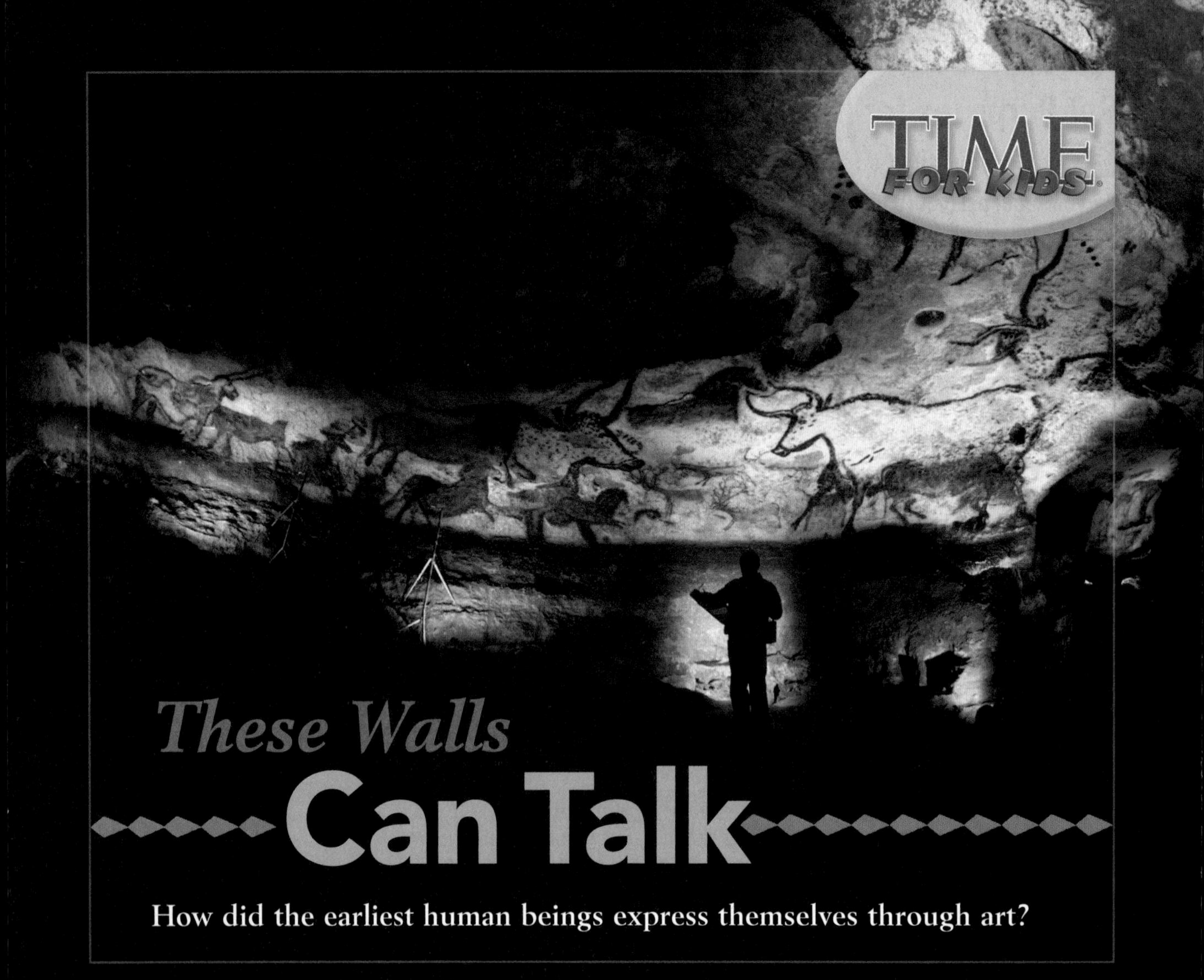

These Walls Can Talk

How did the earliest human beings express themselves through art?

If you're looking for archaeological finds that really rock, you can travel to Europe, Africa, and Australia to find some of the earliest examples of the human creative spirit.

Exploring Europe's Caves

In 1994, three people exploring a cliff in southeastern France felt a breeze wafting[1] from a pile of rock and debris. "That was a sign that there was a cave beneath it," recalls Jean-Marie Chauvet. With his companions, Chauvet cleared away an opening, then wriggled through a tunnel into a complex of large caves.

Identify Cause-and-Effect Relationships What caused the explorers to go into the tunnel?

1 ***Wafting*** means "floating or conveyed, such as on the wind."

Then, in the pale glow of their headlamps, the explorers noticed two red lines on a cavern wall. Chauvet recognized the markings as "characteristic of the Stone Age." They had discovered an immense archaeological trove[2] and, presumably, a clear window on prehistoric life.

Six days later they returned with portable lighting and plastic sheets that they spread about to avoid disturbing **artifacts** on the cavern floors. **Probing** deeper into the cavern system, they began coming upon exquisite, **intricately** detailed wall paintings and engravings of animals, as well as numerous images of human hands, some in red, others in black pigment.[3] "I thought I was dreaming," says Chauvet.

The art was in pristine[4] condition, apparently undisturbed for up to 20,000 years. The walls show images of lions, bison, deer, bears, horses, and some 50 woolly rhinos.

For now, tourists are not allowed in this amazing cave. The French Culture Ministry has put the Chauvet cave off-limits to all but a handful of anthropologists[5] and other experts. The French learned a lesson from a cave at Altamira in Spain, another site where amazing rock art has been discovered. Early unrestricted access to this Spanish cave obliterated[6] archaeological clues and led to the rapid deterioration of artwork. At another well-known site of cave art in France—the Lascaux caves—the caves have also been sealed. Visitors tour a carefully created replica instead.

BQ BIG Question

What can scientists learn about the traditions of ancient peoples from their paintings?

Text Structure What problem has been identified?

2 A ***trove*** is a collection of valuable objects.

3 A ***pigment*** is a substance used for coloring.

4 Something that is ***pristine*** is pure and unspoiled.

5 ***Anthropologists*** are scientists who study the physical, cultural, and behavioral development of humans.

6 ***Obliterated*** means "destroyed completely; removed all traces of."

Vocabulary

artifacts (är′ tə fakts′) *n.* human-made objects used in the daily life of an ancient civilization

probing (prōb′ ing) *v.* carrying out a thorough investigation or examination

intricately (in′ tri kit lē) *adv.* in a complex way; in an elaborate manner

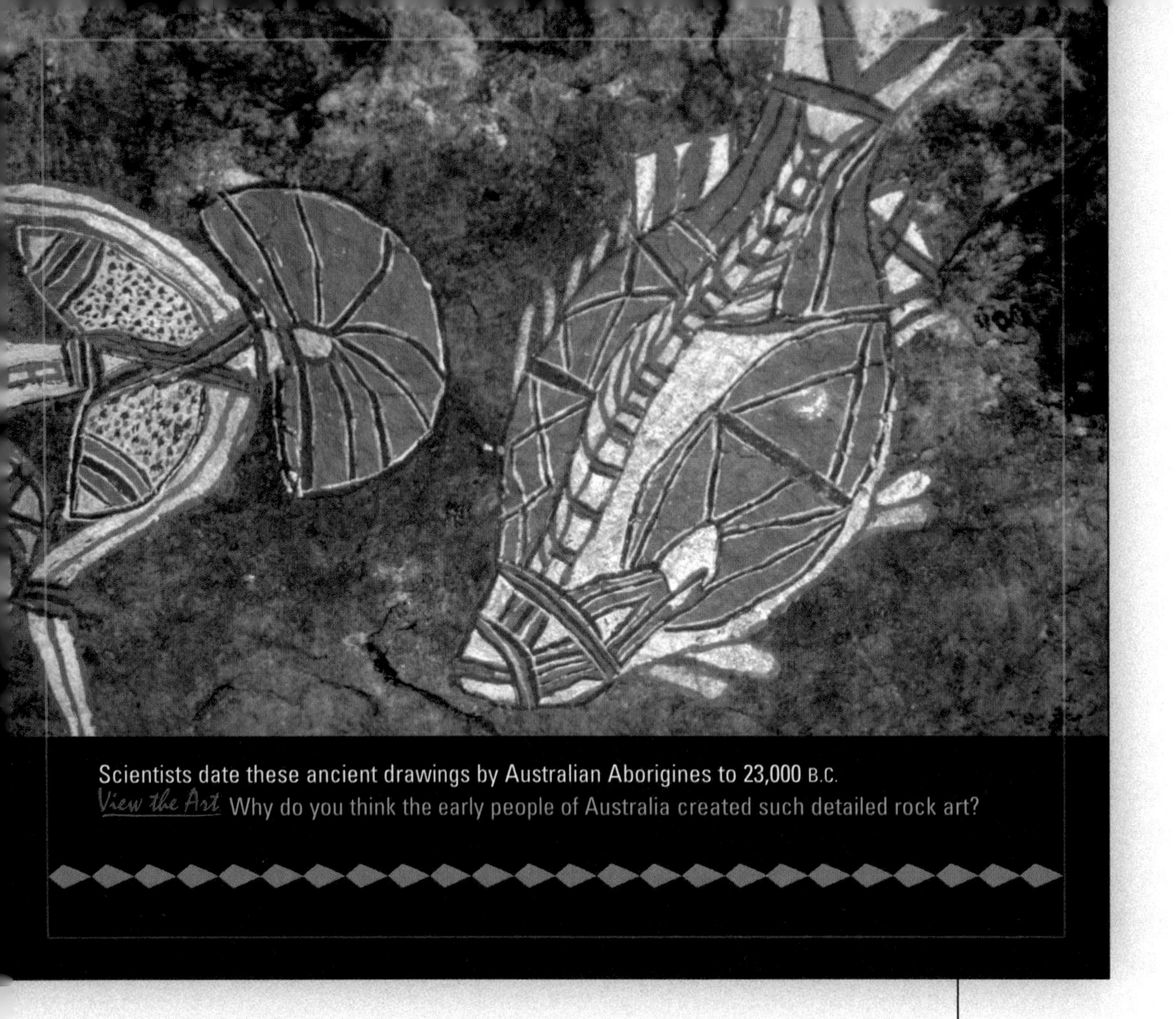

Scientists date these ancient drawings by Australian Aborigines to 23,000 B.C.

View the Art Why do you think the early people of Australia created such detailed rock art?

Saving the Rock Art of Africa

Equally beautiful works can be found in great abundance[7] on rock shelters, walls, and overhangs throughout the African continent. Unfortunately, these ancient masterpieces are deteriorating at an alarming rate, and they may disappear entirely unless something is done to save them.

Identify Cause-and-Effect Relationships What may happen if we don't save the ancient artwork?

In an effort to record Africa's vanishing trove of rock art, David Coulson, a Nairobi-based photographer, and Alexander Campbell, former director of Botswana's National Museum and Art Gallery, began crisscrossing the continent. They visited known sites and stumbled across new ones, photographing as much of the art as they could. Campbell is convinced that if examples of Africa's rock art were counted, they would total many hundreds of thousands of individual images.

Text Structure What is Coulson and Campbell's solution to the problem of vanishing rock art?

7 ***Abundance*** means "plentiful or overflowing supply."

Ancient paintings in a cave in Libya (northern Africa) show giraffes and other large wild animals.

Everywhere Coulson and Campbell went, they found images dulled by sunlight, wind, and water, and damaged by chemical seepage from mining operations, tourism, and outright vandalism. An unthinking tourist, unaware of the art's significance and value, can be much more than just a nuisance. Amateur photographers have been known to throw water and cola drinks on the art to enhance its contrast and make the colors more vivid.

Identify Cause-and-Effect Relationships What causes of art damage and deterioration are given in this paragraph?

How Old is the Rock Art of Australia?

The Australian continent abounds in Aboriginal[8] rock art, both paintings and engravings. Much of it lies in a 1,500-mile-long, **boomerang**-shaped area along the country's north coast.

Archaeologist Darrell Lewis of the Australian National University estimates that there are at least 10,000 rock-art sites on the Arnhem Land **plateau** alone, in the Northern Territory. "Each of these sites," he says, "can have several hundred paintings." But unlike early **inhabitants** of Europe, who often decorated caves over a short period and then abandoned them, the Australian Aborigines would return over and over to the same sites. This is a practice that still goes on today. Unraveling the history of a single site can thus be extremely complicated.

How old is Australia's art? It is clear that artists were at work in Australia at roughly the same time as their European cousins. Anthropologist Alan Thorne of the Australian National University claims that a small piece of red ochre (a kind of clay), dated to 50,000 years ago, was worn down on one side—like a piece of chalk—by humans. "Whether it was ground to paint a shelter or a person or part of a wall, I don't think anyone would disagree that it is evidence of art," says Thorne.

These ancient masterpieces found around the world offer windows into the rich lives of our prehistoric ancestors. But if nothing is done to save and preserve the rock art, some of these windows could close forever.

Visual Vocabulary

A **boomerang** is a flat, curved piece of wood that can be thrown so as to return to the thrower.

Text Structure Why does the writer end the essay this way? What idea does the writer want readers to take away?

8 ***Aboriginal*** rock art was created by the earliest people who lived in Australia.

Vocabulary

plateau (pla tō′) *n.* elevated, fairly flat land area

inhabitants (in hab′ət əntz) *n.* persons or animals that live permanently in a place

Visitors inspect cave art at Lascaux II, a replica of two of the Lascaux cave halls that was opened in 1983.

After You Read

Respond and Think Critically

1. What led to the discovery of the Chauvet cave in France? **[Recall]**
2. Why have David Coulson and Alexander Campbell taken the time to photograph rock art around the world? **[Infer]**
3. What difference between European and Australian traditions of creating art in caves does the article describe? **[Contrast]**
4. **Literary Element** **Text Structure** What main problem is discussed in this selection, and what solutions are described? **[Summarize]**
5. **Reading Skill** **Identify Cause-and-Effect Relationships** Name six causes of damage to ancient artwork. Which of these causes are natural? Which are human-made? **[Analyze]**
6. **BQ** **BIG Question** If you were given the task of preserving a single work of art made in the present day, what might you do? Explain. **[Evaluate]**

TIP

Contrasting
Here are some tips to help you contrast. Remember that when you contrast, you look for ways in which two or more things are different.

- Reread how early Europeans used caves.
- Reread how Australian Aborigines used caves.
- Think about what the two groups did differently.

Keep track of your ideas about the **BIG Question** in your unit Foldable.

Vocabulary Practice

Respond to these questions on a separate sheet of paper.

1. Where can you see **artifacts**—in the night sky or in a museum of ancient cultures?
2. What is an example of **intricately** designed art—a simple stick figure or an elaborate oil painting?
3. Which of these places might have a **plateau**—a mountainous area or a frozen lake?
4. Which of these has human **inhabitants**—the planet Earth or the Moon?
5. When is a detective **probing** for answers—during an investigation into a crime or after the crime has been solved?

Writing

Write a Letter Imagine that you are a world traveler who photographs ancient art. You want to write a letter to a newspaper to convince people to preserve this art. Think about why ancient art is important. Present the problem that ancient rock art is being destroyed and call for action to save and preserve it. Include appropriate supporting arguments and detailed evidence.

LOG ON **Literature** Online

Selection Resources
For Selection Quizzes, eFlashcards, and Reading-Writing Connection activities, go to glencoe.com and enter QuickPass code GL17527u2.

Comparing Literature

He Lion, Bruh Bear, and Bruh Rabbit and *The Toad and the Donkey*

BQ BIG Question

As you read these folktales, think about the life lessons you can learn from the lion in "He Lion, Bruh Bear, and Bruh Rabbit" and the donkey in "The Toad and the Donkey."

Literary Element Characters

You've learned that a **character** is a person or a creature in a literary work. Folktales sometimes have characters called tricksters. A **trickster** is usually smaller and weaker than the opponent but has the advantage of cleverness. As you read these folktales, look for tricksters who outwit their opponents.

Reading Skill Compare and Contrast

You compare and contrast in your daily life whenever you look for similarities and differences. When you meet new people, you look for ways that you are alike and ways that you are different.

You can deepen your understanding of a story by **comparing and contrasting** characters. On the following pages, you'll compare and contrast the characters in "He Lion, Bruh Bear, and Bruh Rabbit" with the characters in "The Toad and the Donkey." Use a chart like the one below to record details about the similarities and differences among the characters.

Character	Words that describe personality	Words that describe appearance	Is the character a trickster?
he Lion			
Bruh Bear			
Bruh Rabbit			
Toad			
Donkey			

Performance Standards

For pages 271–279

ELA6R1e/ii For literary texts, identify and analyze the elements of setting, characterization, plot, and the resolution of the conflict of a story or play: character conflicts, characters vs. nature, characters vs. society.

Meet the Authors

Virginia Hamilton

Virginia Hamilton's grandfather's story of his escape from slavery made her interested in stories as a way of preserving heritage.

Toni Cade Bambara

Toni Cade Bambara was a professor, writer, and activist. She took the name *Bambara* after she found the name on a sketchbook.

LOG ON Literature Online

Author Search For more about Virginia Hamilton and Toni Cade Bambara, go to glencoe.com and enter QuickPass code GL17527u2.

He Lion, Bruh Bear, and Bruh Rabbit

Virginia Hamilton

Emma's Lion, 1994. Christian Pierre. Acrylic on canvas. Private Collection.

Say that he Lion would get up each and every mornin. Stretch and walk around. He'd roar, "ME AND MYSELF. ME AND MYSELF," like that. Scare all the little animals so they were afraid to come outside in the sunshine. Afraid to go huntin or fishin or whatever the little animals wanted to do.

"What we gone do about it?" they asked one another. Squirrel leapin from branch to branch, just scared. **Possum** playin dead, couldn't hardly move him.

He Lion just went on, stickin out his chest and roarin, "ME AND MYSELF. ME AND MYSELF."

The little animals held a sit-down talk, and one by one and two by two and all by all, they decide to go see Bruh Bear and Bruh Rabbit. For they know that Bruh Bear been around. And Bruh Rabbit say he has, too.

So they went to Bruh Bear and Bruh Rabbit. Said, "We have some trouble. Old he Lion, him scarin everybody, roarin every mornin and all day, 'ME AND MYSELF. ME AND MYSELF,' like that."

"Why he Lion want to do that?" Bruh Bear said.

"Is that all he Lion have to say?" Bruh Rabbit asked.

"We don't know why, but that's all he Lion can tell us and we didn't ask him to tell us that," said the little animals. "And him scarin the children with it. And we wish him to stop it."

"Well, I'll go see him, talk to him. I've known he Lion a long kind of time," Bruh Bear said.

"I'll go with you," said Bruh Rabbit. "I've known he Lion most long as you."

That bear and that rabbit went off through the forest. They kept hearin somethin. Mumble, mumble. Couldn't make it out. They got farther in the forest. They heard it plain now. "ME AND MYSELF. ME AND MYSELF."

"Well, well, well," said Bruh Bear. He wasn't scared. He'd been around the whole forest, seen a lot.

"My, my, my," said Bruh Rabbit. He'd seen enough to know not to be afraid of an old he lion. Now old he lions could be dangerous, but you had to know how to handle them.

Visual Vocabulary

Possum is the informal form of *opossum.* An opossum is a small mammal native to North, Central, and South America. It has a white, pointed snout, a hairless, ratlike tail, and long, coarse, usually gray-and-white fur. When frightened, the opossum lies motionless, as if it were dead.

Comparing Literature One way to learn about a character's personality is through other characters' reactions to that character. What do you learn about he Lion from the little animals? List the details about he Lion on your comparison chart.

Comparing Literature Why isn't Bruh Bear or Bruh Rabbit afraid of he Lion?

The bear and the rabbit climbed up and up the cliff where he Lion had his lair.[1] They found him. Kept their distance. He watchin them and they watchin him. Everybody actin cordial.[2]

"Hear tell you are scarin everybody, all the little animals, with your roarin all the time," Bruh Rabbit said.

"I roars when I pleases," he Lion said.

"Well, might could you leave off the noise first thing in the mornin, so the little animals can get what they want to eat and drink?" asked Bruh Bear.

"Listen," said he Lion, and then he roared: "ME AND MYSELF. ME AND MYSELF. Nobody tell me what not to do," he said. "I'm the king of the forest, *me and myself*."

Comparing Literature What does he Lion's answer reveal about him?

"Better had let me tell you somethin," Bruh Rabbit said, "for I've seen Man, and I know him the real king of the forest."

He Lion was quiet awhile. He looked straight through that scrawny lil Rabbit like he was nothin atall. He looked at Bruh Bear and figured he'd talk to him.

"You, Bear, you been around," he Lion said.

"That's true," said old Bruh Bear. "I been about everywhere. I've been around the whole forest."

"Then you must know somethin," he Lion said.

"I know lots," said Bruh Bear, slow and quiet-like.

"Tell me what you know about Man," he Lion said. "He think him the king of the forest?"

"Well, now, I'll tell you," said Bruh Bear, "I been around, but I haven't ever come across Man that I know of. Couldn't tell you nothin about him."

So he Lion had to turn back to Bruh Rabbit. He didn't want to but he had to. "So what?" he said to that lil scrawny hare.

Comparing Literature Why does he Lion look down on Bruh Rabbit but respect Bruh Bear? What does he Lion's attitude say about him?

"Well, you got to come down from there if you want to see Man," Bruh Rabbit said. "Come down from there and I'll show you him."

He Lion thought a minute, an hour, and a whole day. Then, the next day, he came on down.

---

1 A ***lair*** is the home or resting place of a wild animal.

2 When people are ***acting cordial***, they are being polite and friendly.

He roared just once, "ME AND MYSELF. ME AND MYSELF. Now," he said, "come show me Man."

So they set out. He Lion, Bruh Bear, and Bruh Rabbit. They go along and they go along, rangin the forest. Pretty soon, they come to a clearin. And playin in it is a little fellow about nine years old.

"Is that there Man?" asked he Lion.

"Why no, that one is called Will Be, but it sure is not Man," said Bruh Rabbit.

So they went along and they went along. Pretty soon, they come upon a shade tree. And sleepin under it is an old, olden fellow, about ninety years olden.

"There must lie Man," spoke he Lion. "I knew him wasn't gone be much."

"That's not Man," said Bruh Rabbit. "That fellow is Was Once. You'll know it when you see Man."

So they went on along. He Lion is gettin tired of strollin. So he roars, "ME AND MYSELF. ME AND MYSELF." Upsets Bear so that Bear doubles over and runs and climbs a tree.

"Come down from there," Bruh Rabbit tellin him. So after a while Bear comes down. He keepin his distance from he Lion, anyhow. And they set out some more. Goin along quiet and slow.

In a little while they come to a road. And comin on way down the road, Bruh Rabbit sees Man comin. Man about twenty-one years old. Big and strong, with a big gun over his shoulder.

"There!" Bruh Rabbit says. "See there, he Lion? There's Man. You better go meet him."

"I will," says he Lion. And he sticks out his chest and he roars, "ME AND MYSELF. ME AND MYSELF." All the way to Man he's roarin proud, "ME AND MYSELF,

The Nightowls, 1994. Christian Pierre. Acrylic on canvas. Private Collection.

View the Art Which scene in the story does this painting remind you of? Why?

Comparing Literature What do you learn about Bruh Rabbit and Bruh Bear from their words and actions?

ME AND MYSELF!"

"Come on, Bruh Bear, let's go!" Bruh Rabbit says.

"What for?" Bruh Bear wants to know.

"You better come on!" And Bruh Rabbit takes ahold of Bruh Bear and half drags him to a thicket. And there he makin the Bear hide with him.

For here comes Man. He sees old he Lion real good now. He drops to one knee and he takes aim with his big gun.

Old he Lion is roarin his head off: "ME AND MYSELF! ME AND MYSELF!"

The big gun goes off: PA-LOOOM!

He Lion falls back hard on his tail.

The gun goes off again. PA-LOOOM!

He Lion is flyin through the air. He lands in the thicket.

"Well, did you see Man?" asked Bruh Bear.

"I seen him," said he Lion. "Man spoken to me unkind, and got a great long stick him keepin on his shoulder. Then Man taken that stick down and him speakin real mean. Thunderin at me and lightnin comin from that stick, awful bad. Made me sick. I had to turn around. And Man pointin that stick again and thunderin at me some more. So I come in here, cause it seem like him throwed some stickers at me each time it thunder, too."

"So you've met Man, and you know zactly what that kind of him is," says Bruh Rabbit.

"I surely do know that," he Lion said back.

Awhile after he Lion met Man, things were some better in the forest. Bruh Bear knew what Man looked like so he could keep out of his way. That rabbit always did know to keep out of Man's way. The little animals could go out in the mornin because he Lion was more peaceable. He didn't walk around roarin at the top of his voice all the time. And when he Lion did lift that voice of his, it was like, "Me and Myself and Man. Me and Myself and Man." Like that.

Wasn't too loud atall.

Comparing Literature How does he Lion's personality change after his encounter with Man?

The Toad and the Donkey

Toni Cade Bambara

One day Brother Spider didn't have nothing better to do so he asked ole Toad and ole Donkey to have a race across the island.

The donkey said, "What? You want me, the fastest dude around here, to race that little old hop frog. I've got a reputation, you know."

And the toad said, "Never mind all that, Big Mouth—let's race."

The donkey thought to himself, this is ridiculous. But since Brother Spider always had good prizes (Brother Spider was a terrific thief), he agreed.

"O.K.," said Spider. "The only rule is that Brother Donkey has to howl every mile so we can know where you all are."

Comparing Literature What does Donkey think of himself? What does he think of Toad?

Toad says, "Fine with me. Let's set the race for Saturday."

"Oh no," says Donkey, for he suspected something trickified. "Tomorrow morning."

So Toad went home for dinner and put it to the family like so: "Listen here, we spread out along the path in the bushes, then at every milepost when Mr. Donkey howls out, one of you steps out and howls too." So they each packed a little breakfast of gungo peas and sweet potato bread and bakes all wrapped up in tanya leaves and took up their positions along the road.

So the race began. And Spider lit a cigar and lay back.

Brother Donkey took off at a light trot, his tail stuck up in the air to match his nose, stopping every now and then to stick his face through somebody's fence to munch on some grass. And when he got to the first **milepost,** he sang out, "La, la, la. Here I am. Where are you? Ha, ha."

And way in front of him Uncle Julius Toad sang back, "Up here. La, la, la," and licked his fingers.

Which really surprised Donkey. So he cut out the grass eating and got a move on. But then he passed a well and decided he had time for a drink, for how much hopping can a toad do. And at the next post he sang out, "Tra, la, la. Here I am. Where are you?"

And way up ahead Aunt Minnie Toad sang back, "Up here. Ha, ha."

By the fifth post, Donkey started getting a little worried so he slashed himself with his tail like a horsewhip and started galloping. But Cousins Emery, Walter and Cecil Toad were on the case. And it's the same story each time. "Tra la la, I'm up the road ahead of you, Donkey."

And Donkey began to get sad in his mind when he realized he was not going to beat Toad. And he decided before he even got to the finish line that he would never race again. And donkeys have been kind of stubborn about running ever since.

Visual Vocabulary

A **milepost** is an upright piece of wood or other solid material set up, as on a highway, to mark the distance in miles to or from a certain place.

Comparing Literature How does Donkey react when he hears a toad's voice? What do you learn about Toad from the way Donkey reacts?

Comparing Literature Why do you think Donkey decides never to race again? What does his decision reveal about him?

Comparing Literature

BQ BIG Question

Now use the unit Big Question to compare and contrast "He Lion, Bruh Bear, and Bruh Rabbit" with "The Toad and the Donkey." With a group of classmates, discuss questions such as,

- What life lesson does each of these folktales teach?
- Which story did you like better? Why?
- How do these stories reflect the cultures from which they come?

Support each answer with evidence from the readings.

Literary Element Characters

Use the details you wrote in your comparison chart to think about the characters in "He Lion, Bruh Bear, and Bruh Rabbit" and "The Toad and the Donkey." With a partner, answer the following questions.

1. What do the main characters in these folktales have in common? Discuss some similarities in the characters' appearances, personalities, or the roles they play in the plot.
2. In what ways do the main characters in these folktales differ? You might discuss how the main characters change and whether the change is positive or negative. You might also discuss whether any of the characters are tricksters.

Write to Compare

In one or two paragraphs, compare and contrast the main characters in "He Lion, Bruh Bear, and Bruh Rabbit" and the "The Toad and the Donkey." Tell what lessons you have learned from them. You might focus on these ideas as you write.

- Describe the personality traits of each of the main characters and how they are revealed.
- Explain whether the main character in each story changes, and if so, whether the change is positive or negative.
- Discuss some lessons that can be learned from the characters in each story.

Be sure to start with a topic sentence that sums up what you learned from your comparison and to cite specific examples from the two folktales in your comparison. Place these examples near each other in your text to add emphasis to the comparisons and contrasts.

Writing Tip

Spelling One of the most important parts of editing is making sure that all words are spelled correctly. Even if you use a spellchecker on your computer, use a dictionary to look up words you're not sure about.

Literature Online

Selection Resources
For Selection Quizzes, eFlashcards, and Reading-Writing Connection activities, go to glencoe.com and enter QuickPass code GL17527u2.

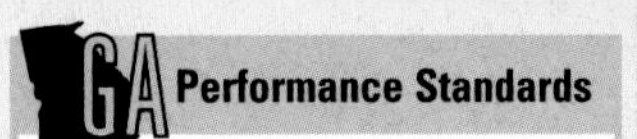

Performance Standards

For pages 280–285

ELA6W2a Demonstrate competence in a variety of genres. Produce technical writing that creates or follows an organizing structure appropriate to purpose, audience, and context.

Writing Workshop

Functional Document

Is there a cultural attraction, such as a fair, a park, a museum, a historic site, or a well-known landmark that you've read about and want to visit? Would you like to go there with some friends? In this workshop, you will write a travel document that will help you think about the Unit 2 Big Question: Why read?

Review the writing prompt, or assignment, below. Then read the Writing Plan. It will tell you what you will do to write your travel document.

Writing Assignment

A functional document gives readers useful facts, instructions, and other types of information for a specific purpose. Write an invitation to some friends to join you on your first trip to a specific cultural attraction. Include a map with travel directions. Your audience, those reading your document, will be the friends you are inviting on the trip.

Writing Plan

- Make the purpose of the document clear to the audience.
- Present information in logical and effective organizational patterns.
- Include supporting details to clarify information and interest the reader.
- Use visual aids to clarify and add to the information.
- Use text features to highlight and organize information.

Prewriting Tip

Sources Be sure to write down complete information on each source you use for your notes as you research. You may need to go back and check facts later.

Prewrite

Which cultural attractions would you like to visit? Review the selections in this unit. Some of the places and traditions in the selections might relate to a cultural attraction. If you have an e-mail account, send an e-mail to your friends (following the directions in Sending E-mail on pages 175–176) to find out where they would like to visit.

Gather Ideas

Make a list of places or attractions that you would like to visit with friends. Write down anything you know about the places or attractions.

Then use the Internet, resource books, or travel guides to research one or two of the most interesting places. Take notes about an airport, a train station, or a major highway where you would start your trip, the route you would take, and the landmarks you would see along the way.

Choose a Place

Review your notes and the information you have gathered. Then choose the place that you would most like to visit. Write a sentence that briefly summarizes why you have chosen this place.

I want to visit ____________________, because ______________.

Get Organized

Use your notes to make two charts: an invitation chart and a directions and map chart. Use the charts below to help you.

Invitation Chart (5*W*s and *H*)	
Who	the people being invited
What	a trip to the chosen cultural attraction
Where	the general location of the attraction
When	the dates of the trip
Why	the purpose of the trip
How	the mode of transportation

The directions and map chart should give your friends complete directions for the trip. Get specific details from your research.

Directions and Map Chart	
Details of Trip	
Starting Point	Merced, CA
Ending Point	Sequoia National Park, CA
Distance	
Cardinal/Ordinal Direction	

Draft

Now begin writing. Organize your ideas and add details.

Get It on Paper

- Review your notes and look at your charts.
- Your invitation should be only one paragraph. Open with a statement to interest your audience in the cultural attraction. Follow with the 5*W*s and *H*. End with a summary.
- Below the invitation, write your directions in order.
- As you write the directions, draw the same information on a sketch of a map.
- Don't worry about spelling, grammar, or punctuation right now.
- When you're finished, look over what you have written and drawn. Include more information if you need to.

Writing and Research
For prewriting, drafting, and revising tools, go to glencoe.com and enter QuickPass code GL17527u2.

Develop Your Draft

1. Keep the **purpose** and **audience** of your invitation in mind as you write. Begin with a statement that will excite your friends and catch their interest.

> *Would you like to visit a Land of Giants with me?*

2. Use a logical **organization** for each part of your travel document: invitation—order of importance; directions—chronological order; and map—spatial order.

> *Directions:*
> *1. Starting in Merced, CA, take Highway 99.*
> *2. Head SE on Highway 99 toward Fresno.*

3. Include **supporting details** that give your audience all the important facts and hold their interest.

> *In this magical forest, we'll see the world's largest trees, explore deep canyons and caves, and hike challenging mountain trails.*

4. Make sure your **visual aids** help your audience understand the document. Match the map exactly with the directions and mark it clearly.

> *Go east (left) at Highway 180.*

5. Use **text features** to make information clear. Add headings and map symbols such as a direction compass and distance scale.

Apply Good Writing Traits: Conventions

Conventions are the rules of language—grammar, usage, spelling, punctuation, capitalization, and paragraphing.

Following the rules of language makes your writing easier for others to read. As you draft your travel document, pay attention to the rules of language. After you finish, read your draft and ask yourself, "Did I use conventions to make my ideas easy to understand?"

Drafting Tip

Map Cut out each direction sentence and place it on the route it refers to on the map. Check to see that each step is covered by a direction line and that the directions and map match.

TRY IT

Analyzing Cartoons

In this cartoon, *fundamentals* means "the most important skills." With a partner, decide what Clint's problem is. How are the fundamentals in a sport like the conventions in writing?

Analyze a Student Model

YOU'RE INVITED!

Would you like to visit a Land of Giants with me? In this magical forest, we'll see the world's largest trees, explore deep canyons and caves, and hike challenging mountain trails. If we're lucky, we might even see some wild animals. It will be a fun, exciting trip. Will you join me?

Purpose and Audience
Be clear about your purpose and audience at the beginning.

Who: Alan, Carlos, Juma, Brianna, and Marie
What: a trip to Sequoia National Park
Where: 140 miles from Merced
When: Saturday, April 19
Why: to hike and see the giant sequoias and other natural wonders
How: Alan's dad will drive his van.

Organizational Pattern
Organize the invitation by order of importance.

How to Get There

1. Start in Merced, CA, and take Highway 99.
2. Head SE on Highway 99 toward Fresno. In about 20 miles, you'll come to the town of Chowchilla. After another 40 miles, you'll see the signs for Fresno.
3. Go east (left) on Highway 180. Squaw Valley is about 30 miles farther east. Stay on Highway 180 for about 50 more miles. It will lead right into the entrance to the park.

So, join me for a fun-filled trip to Sequoia National Park on April 19th. It'll be a great adventure!

Supporting Details
Be specific. Exact locations and ordinal directions help your audience follow directions.

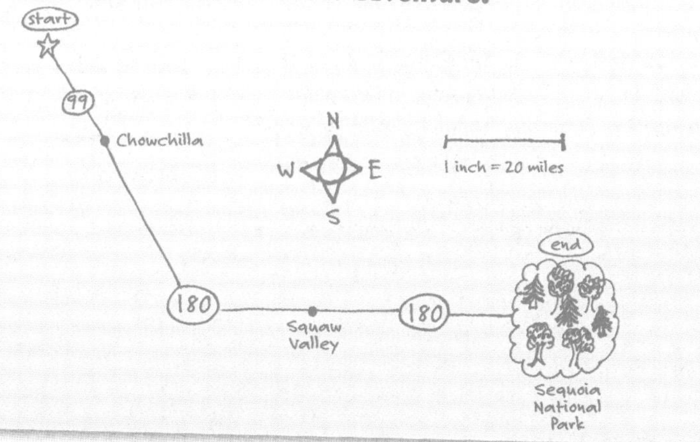

Visual Aids
Make sure the map and written directions match.

Text Features
Use map symbols, such as a compass rose, to help your audience read the map.

Revise

Now it's time to revise your draft so your ideas really shine. Revising is what makes good writing great, and great writing takes work!

Peer Review Trade drafts with a partner. Use the chart below to review your partner's draft by answering the questions in the *What to do* column. Talk about your peer review after you have glanced at each other's drafts and have written the answers to the questions. Next, follow the suggestions in the *How to do it* column to revise your draft.

Revising Tip

Technology You can use the design features of word-processing software to create graphics, adjust your margins, or experiment with various typefaces (fonts) for headings.

Revising Plan

What to do	How to do it	Example
Are the purpose and audience of your document clear?	Include the 5 *W*s and *H* in your invitation.	Who: ~~My friends~~ ^ Alan, Carlos, Juma, Brianna, and Marie
Is the invitation organized by order of importance? The directions by sequential order? The map by spatial order?	Present each type of information in the most logical order.	Why: to hike and see the giant sequoias and other natural wonders What: a trip to Sequoia National Park Where: 140 miles from Merced When: Saturday, April 19
Are there enough details to clarify information and interest your audience?	Think about what your audience needs to know. Use precise words to describe it.	~~Then come~~ ^ After another 40 miles, you'll see the signs for Fresno.
Does your visual aid agree with your written directions?	Read your written directions while following your map.	Squaw Valley is about 30 miles farther ~~south.~~ ^ east.
Have you included helpful text features?	Separate the parts of your document with headings. Add symbols to make your map easy to read.	^ How to Get There 1. Start in Merced, CA, and take Highway 99.

Edit and Proofread

For your final draft, read your travel document one sentence at a time. An editing and proofreading checklist may help you spot errors. Use the proofreading symbols in the chart inside the back cover of this book to mark needed changes. Then make corrections.

Grammar Focus: Capitalization

Capitalize a proper noun, which is the name of a particular person, place, thing, or idea. Words that are names of particular sections of the country are proper nouns and should be capitalized. However, words that simply indicate direction are not proper nouns. Below are examples of problems with capitalization from the Workshop Model and their solutions.

Problem: A proper noun is not capitalized.

You can park just inside the entrance to sequoia national park.

Solution: Capitalize the name of a particular place.

You can park just inside the entrance to Sequoia National Park.

Problem: A cardinal direction is capitalized.

Go East (left) at Highway 180.

Solution: Use a lowercase letter for a direction.

Go east (left) at Highway 180.

Problem: A particular geographic area is not capitalized.

We drove for three hours but never left the west.

Solution: Capitalize a section of the country.

We drove for three hours but never left the West.

Present

It's almost time to share your writing with others. Write your travel document neatly in print or cursive on a separate sheet of paper. If you have access to a computer, type your invitation and directions on the computer and check spelling. Save your document to a disk and print it out. Finally, add your map and pass your document around the class.

Grammar Tip

Proper Nouns Double-check proper nouns to make sure you have correctly spelled the names of people and places.

Presenting Tip

Invitation Put copies of your travel documents into envelopes and give an envelope to each invited friend as if it were a real invitation.

Literature Online

Writing and Research For editing and publishing tools, go to glencoe.com and enter QuickPass code GL17527u2.

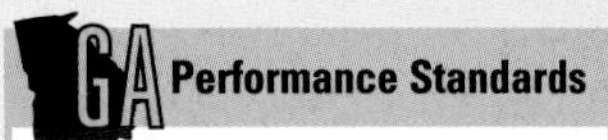

Performance Standards

For page 286

ELA6LSV2b When delivering or responding to presentations, show appropriate changes in delivery.

Speaking, Listening, and Viewing Workshop

Informative Presentation

Activity

Connect to Your Writing Deliver an informative presentation to your classmates. You might want to adapt the travel document you wrote for the Writing Workshop on pages 280–285. Remember that you focused on the Unit 2 Big Question: Why read?

Plan Your Presentation

Reread your travel document and highlight the sections you want to include in your presentation. Just like your invitation and directions, your informative presentation should include clear, well-researched facts and details about the 5 *W*s and *H* and each part of the trip.

Rehearse Your Presentation

Practice your informative presentation several times. Try rehearsing in front of a mirror where you can watch your movements and facial expressions. Practice enough times that you won't lose eye contact with your audience. Post an enlarged version of your map to refer to as you deliver your directions.

Deliver Your Presentation

- Speak clearly and precisely.
- Use visual aids to clarify your information.
- Change the tone or volume of your voice to communicate emotions or add emphasis. Also use appropriate gestures to help relay information.
- Change the pace of your speaking, slowing down to help clarify potentially confusing parts of the trip.

Listening to Learn

Take notes as you listen to make sure you understand the presentation. Use the following question frames to learn more about the information from the presenter:

- I was confused about one part. Can you please review _________?
- I was interested in ______________. Can you tell me more about it?
- I think the purpose of this trip is ________________. Is that correct?

Presentation Checklist

Answer the following questions to evaluate your presentation.

- ❑ Did you speak clearly and precisely?
- ❑ Did you use gestures and visual aids to help clarify information?
- ❑ Did you vary the tone and volume of your voice and the pace of your speaking to add interest to and clarify points in the presentation?
- ❑ Did you make eye contact with your audience?

Literature Online

Speaking, Listening, and Viewing For project ideas, templates, and presentation tips, go to glencoe.com and enter QuickPass code GL17527u2.

Unit Challenge

Answer the Big Question

In Unit 2, you explored the Big Question through reading, writing, speaking, and listening. Now it's time for you to complete one of the Unit Challenges below with your answer to the Big Question.

WHY Read?

Use the notes in your Unit 2 **Foldable** to complete the Unit Challenge of your choice.

Before you present your Unit Challenge, be sure it meets the requirements below. Use this first plan if you choose to interview friends and family to find out what they read and why.

On Your Own Activity: Conduct Interviews

- ❑ Prepare a list of interview questions, including "What have you read lately?" and "Why did you choose to read this?"
- ❑ Use your questions to interview three people you know.
- ❑ Summarize what you learn from each interview in a paragraph. Get permission before you use someone's name.
- ❑ Add a concluding paragraph that tells what you've learned from your interviews about why people read.

Use this second plan if you choose to create a comic strip about a superhero who fights illiteracy, which is the inability to read and write.

Group Activity: Comic Strip

- ❑ Brainstorm with your group to come up with a list of answers to the Big Question.
- ❑ Use your list to brainstorm with your group a storyline for your comic strip.
- ❑ Draw a rough draft of your comic strip, called a storyboard, with your group.
- ❑ Create your comic strip on clean paper. Color the drawings and check the text for spelling and grammar errors.
- ❑ Present your comic strip to the class.

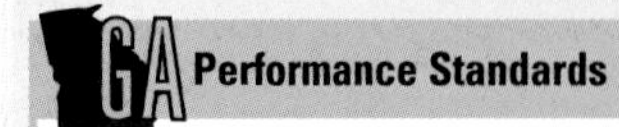

Performance Standards

For page 287

ELA6W2a Demonstrate competence in a variety of genres. Produce writing that engages the reader by establishing a context, creating a speaker's voice, and otherwise developing reader interest.

Independent Reading

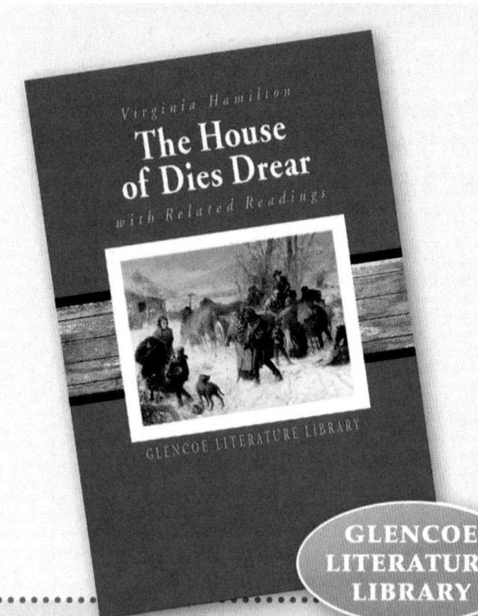

Fiction

To read more about the Big Question, choose one of these books from your school or local library.

The House of Dies Drear

by Virginia Hamilton

When Thomas moves into a house from the Civil War era, he decides to do some sleuthing. Soon he discovers that his new home was once a stop on the Underground Railroad. Exploring the dark passageways in and under the building, Thomas moves closer to the truth about his new home . . . and into harm's way.

The Firebringer and Other Great Stories

by Louis Untermeyer

This anthology is packed with tales retold from cultures near and far. Read one or two or ten of the legends in Untermeyer's book—but make sure you're ready to travel. Like all great story collections, *The Firebringer* will transport you to places you've never been.

I, Juan de Pareja

by Elizabeth Borton de Treviño

Young Juan is a slave of the great painter Diego Velázquez. He is also an artist himself. However, Spain's laws in the 1500s prohibit slaves from making art. What will happen to Juan when his secret is revealed?

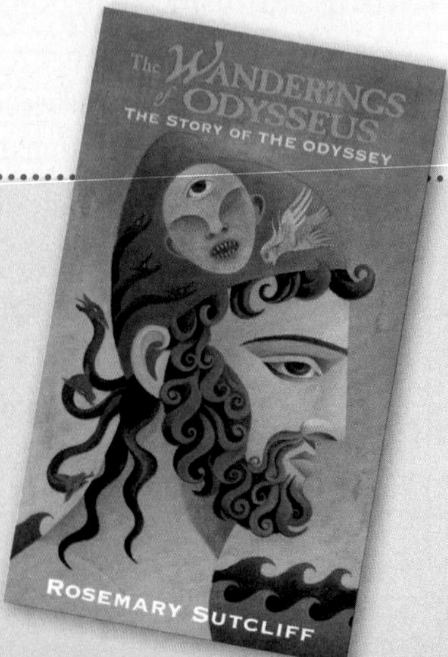

The Wanderings of Odysseus: The Story of the Odyssey

by Rosemary Sutcliff

This prose retelling of the Greek classic is a thrilling tale of adventure on the high seas and beyond. Odysseus, who struggles for ten years to reach his home, survives by courage and resourcefulness.

Nonfiction

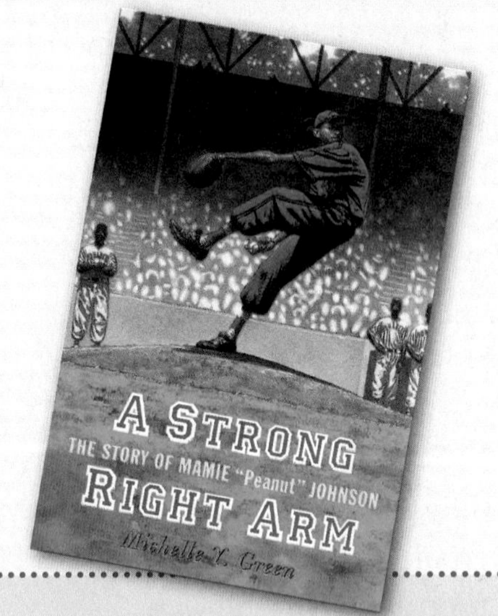

A Strong Right Arm: The Story of Mamie "Peanut" Johnson

by Michelle Y. Green

One of the first women to play professional baseball, Mamie Johnson (nicknamed Peanut) was a pitcher with the Negro League's Indianapolis Clowns in the 1950s. This biography details the struggles and triumphs that defined her as a ball player and as a person.

Top Secret: A Handbook of Codes, Ciphers, and Secret Writing

by Paul B. Janeczko

Want to learn how to write in code or how to write a note in invisible ink? Do you like puzzles and secrets? If so, this guide to the mysteries of cryptography—the study and use of secret messages—is a must-read for you.

Shipwreck at the Bottom of the World: The Extraordinary True Story of Shackleton and the *Endurance*

by Jennifer Armstrong

Shipwrecked in Antarctica, Sir Ernest Shackleton and his crew of 27 survived a brutal winter and walked more than 600 miles to a deserted island. Leaving 22 men behind and sailing 800 miles in a tiny open boat, Shackleton and five others made it to civilization. Then they led a rescue party to find those left behind.

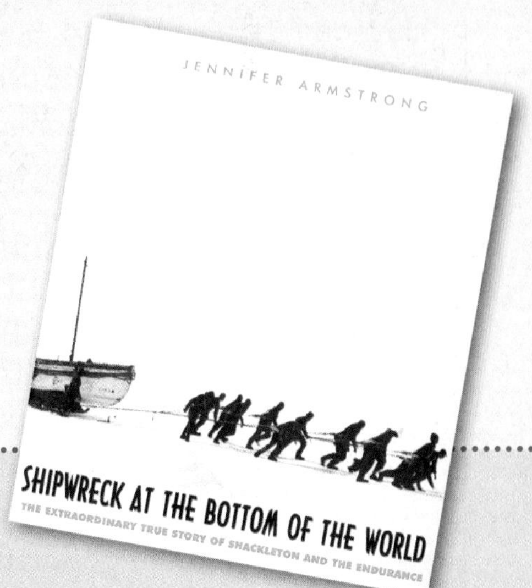

Write an Interview

Write an interview directing questions to the author of the book you read. Use what you know about the author and the book to think of questions and answers that can be supported by your reading. Include questions about important ideas, people, or events in the book. With a partner, present your interview to the class.

Assessment

READING

Read the passage and answer the questions. Write your answers on a separate sheet of paper.

The Everglades Forever?

Graceful white ibis soar through the sky. In the swamp below, lazy alligators lie still as logs. A tiny frog hops to a lily pad and lets out a big croak. It's just another day in Florida's Everglades—a unique <u>ecosystem</u> found only in the U.S.

The Everglades is about 4,000 square miles of freshwater marsh, rivers, and swamp. . . . The region, nicknamed the "river of grass," is home to more than 850 animal species, including 250 species of birds and 900 kinds of plants. Palms, pines, and oak trees as well as wildcats and panthers live in harmony in this wetland. Sounds like a natural paradise, right? It used to be. But after years of pollution and other abuse, the Everglades is dying.

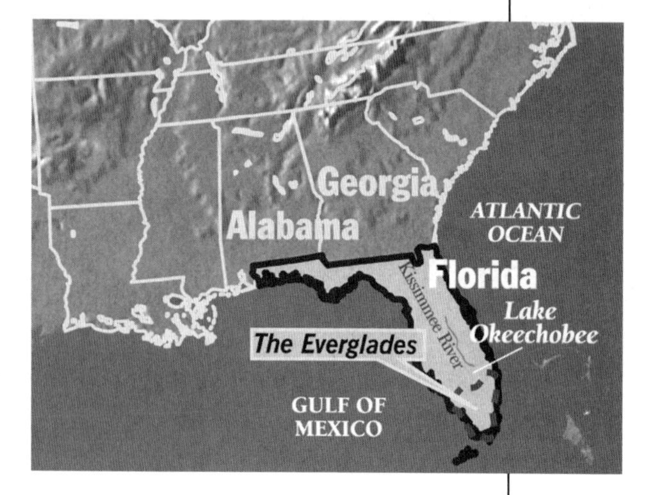

Humans Make Their Mark

More than 100 years ago, people began to settle nearby. The Everglades seemed worthless to them. They couldn't build homes or plant sugar cane, a profitable crop, on the marshy ground. So they dried out some of it.

In the 1920s, U.S. government engineers made bigger changes. . . . Without its natural water supply, the Everglades began to shrink. So did its plant and animal populations. . . .

Part of the swampland where thousands of animals once thrived is packed with houses and factories. . . . The wading-bird population is a tenth of what it was in the early 1900s. Alarming numbers of alligators and sparrows have vanished. Can the Everglades be saved?

1. Which statement below expresses the main idea of this passage?
   A. Alarming numbers of alligators and sparrows have vanished.
   B. After years of pollution and other abuse, the Everglades is dying.
   C. In the swamp below, alligators lie still as logs.
   D. The Florida Everglades is a unique ecosystem found only in the U.S.

2. What is the main reason the writer includes the first two sentences in the first paragraph?
   A. to describe the Everglades by using sensory details
   B. to explain his or her purpose for writing
   C. to establish an organizational pattern of cause and effect
   D. to persuade readers that the Everglades is worth saving

3. Which phrase below would make the BEST subhead for the first two paragraphs of the passage?
   A. The River of Grass
   B. Palms, Pines, and Oak Trees
   C. A Day in the Everglades
   D. A Natural Paradise

4. How is the text under the subhead "Humans Make Their Mark" organized?
   A. spatial order
   B. chronological order
   C. order of importance
   D. comparison-and-contrast

5. Which fact below can the reader learn ONLY from the graphic in this passage?
   A. The Everglades is in Florida.
   B. Human activity is affecting the Everglades.
   C. Lake Okeechobee lies to the north of the Everglades.
   D. The Everglades consists of about 4,000 square miles of wetlands.

6. In the context of this passage, the meaning of the word *ecosystem* is MOST likely
   A. a swampland in which many plants and animals live.
   B. a set of plants, animals, and land that interact to live.
   C. a region that contains mostly grass, trees, and birds.
   D. a natural area that is threatened by pollution.

Literature Online

Standards Practice For more standards practice, go to glencoe.com and enter QuickPass code GL17527u2.

from **"La Bamba"** by Gary Soto

Manuel was the fourth of seven children and looked like a lot of kids in his neighborhood: black hair, brown face, and skinny legs scuffed from summer play. But summer was giving way to fall: the trees were turning red, the lawns brown, and the pomegranate trees were heavy with fruit. Manuel walked to school in the frosty morning, kicking leaves and thinking of tomorrow's talent show. He was still amazed that he had volunteered. He was going to pretend to sing Ritchie Valens's "La Bamba" before the entire school.

Why did I raise my hand? he asked himself, but in his heart he knew the answer. He yearned for the limelight. He wanted applause as loud as a thunderstorm and to hear his friends say, "Man, that was bad!" And he wanted to impress the girls, especially Petra Lopez, the second-prettiest girl in his class. The prettiest was already taken by his friend Ernie. Manuel knew he should be reasonable, since he himself was not great-looking, just average.

Manuel kicked through the fresh-fallen leaves. When he got to school he realized he had forgotten his math workbook. If his teacher found out, he would have to stay after school and miss practice for the talent show. But fortunately for him, they did drills that morning.

During lunch Manuel hung around with Benny, who was also in the talent show. Benny was going to play the trumpet in spite of the fat lip he had gotten playing football.

"How do I look?" Manuel asked. He cleared his throat and started moving his lips in pantomime. No words came out, just a hiss that sounded like a snake. Manuel tried to look emotional, flailing his arms on the high notes and opening his eyes and mouth as wide as he could when he came to *"Para bailar la baaaaammmba."*

After Manuel finished, Benny said it looked all right, but suggested Manuel dance while he sang. Manuel thought for a moment and decided it was a good idea.

"Yeah, just think you're like Michael Jackson or someone like that," Benny suggested. "But don't get carried away."

7. Which pair of words BEST describes the mood of this passage?
   A. joy and wonder
   B. mystery and suspense
   C. unhappiness and dread
   D. excitement and nervousness

8. The descriptive details in the first paragraph provide evidence that
   A. soon it will be snowing.
   B. it is early in the school year.
   C. Manuel has acted foolishly.
   D. Manuel is shaking like a leaf.

9. Based on the way that Manuel and Benny behave toward each other, which of the following is a reasonable conclusion to draw?
   A. Manuel and Benny trust each other.
   B. Manuel and Benny are jealous of each other.
   C. Manuel and Benny are hiding their true feelings.
   D. Manuel and Benny have known each other for only a short time.

10. Based on this passage, you can infer that Manuel is
    A. extremely shy.
    B. a bit of a showoff.
    C. an excellent student.
    D. quite sure of himself.

11. Which quotation from the passage is an example of imagery?
    A. "'Man, that was bad!'"
    B. ". . . they did drills that morning."
    C. ". . . the second-prettiest girl in the class."
    D. ". . . just a hiss that sounded like a snake."

12. What conflict does the author begin to develop in this part of the story?
    A. an external conflict between Manuel and Benny
    B. an external conflict between Manuel and his teachers
    C. an internal conflict between Manuel's uncertainty and his desire to perform
    D. an internal conflict between Manuel's desire to impress the girls and his wish to be on stage

ENGLISH/LANGUAGE ARTS

Choose the best answer for each question. Write your answers on a separate sheet of paper.

1. Which word in the sentence below is an interjection?

Whoa, watch out for that pothole!

A. Whoa

B. out

C. for

D. pothole

2. What is the pattern of the sentence below?

My riding teacher is kind but firm.

A. subject--action verb--direct object

B. subject--linking verb--predicate noun

C. subject--action verb--adjective

D. subject--linking verb--predicate adjective

3. Which sentence below is written correctly?

A. Julia and Javier, they practice soccer together after school.

B. They have fun while they hone their skills.

C. Me and you should ask if we can join them.

D. I would like to play for a team; but I am rusty.

4. How should the punctuation be corrected in the sentence below?

Mr. Minnich, our school principal chooses the Student of the Week on Monday.

A. Add a semicolon after *chooses.*

B. Add a comma after *principal.*

C. Add a comma after *Week.*

D. Add a semicolon after *principal.*

5. In the sentence below, what change should be made to correct the capitalization error?

Mark asked, "Did general Sherman fight for the Union or the Confederacy?"

A. Use a capital *G* in *general.*

B. Use a small letter *d* in *Did.*

C. Use a small letter *u* in *Union* and a small letter *c* in *Confederacy.*

D. Use a capital *F* in *fight.*

WRITING

Read your assigned topic in the box below. Use one piece of paper to jot down ideas and organize your thoughts. Then neatly write your essay on another sheet of paper.

Persuasive Writing Topic

Writing Situation

You have been authorized to start a new club, organization, or sports team at your school. Now you have to get other students to join.

Directions for Writing

Write an essay describing the group you want to start and its purpose. Provide ideas and reasons that will persuade other students to join the group.

Writing Checklist

- ☐ Focus on a single topic.
- ☐ Organize your main points in a clear, logical order.
- ☐ Support your ideas or viewpoints with details and examples.
- ☐ Use precise, vivid words.
- ☐ Vary the length and structure of your sentences.
- ☐ Use clear transition words to connect ideas.
- ☐ Correct any errors in spelling, capitalization, punctuation, and usage.

WHAT Makes You Who You Are?

UNIT THREE

THE BIG Question

> *Learn to be quiet enough to hear the genuine within yourself so that you can hear it in others.*
>
> —MARIAN WRIGHT EDELMAN

FOLDABLES® Study Organizer

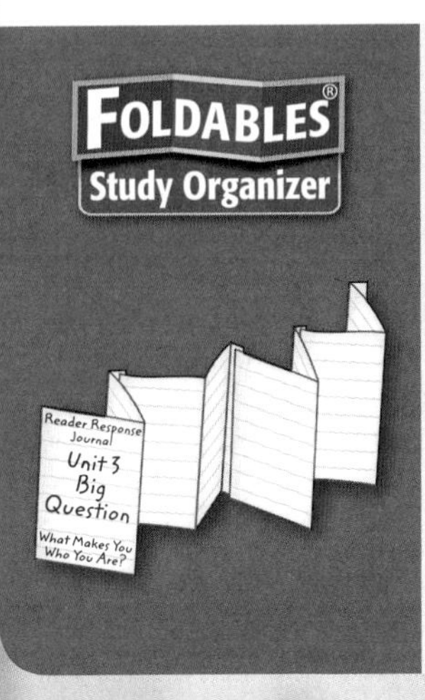

Reader Response Journal
Unit 3
Big Question
What Makes You Who You Are?

Throughout Unit 3, you will read, write, and talk about **the BIG Question—"What Makes You Who You Are?"** Use your Unit 3 **Foldable,** shown here, to keep track of your ideas as you read. Turn to the back of this book for instructions on making this **Foldable**.

Explore the BIG Question

WHAT Makes You Who You Are?

What do you see when you look in the mirror? There are many factors that make each person unique. For example, how do you interact with others? What are your special interests? What are your personality traits, or the qualities that make you *you?*

Explore what makes you who you are:

- Family and Friends
- Dreams and Goals
- Character Traits

What You'll Read

Reading about the ways other people define themselves can help you explore the idea for yourself. In this unit, **poetry**—a form of literature written in **verse,** or lines, instead of running text—can provide clues to help you understand what makes people who they are. You will also read an interview, short stories, and other texts that can lead you to discover answers to the Big Question.

What You'll Write

As you explore the Big Question, you'll write notes in your Unit 3 **Foldable.** Later, you'll use these notes to complete two writing assignments related to the Big Question.

1. **Write a Response to Literature**
2. **Choose a Unit Challenge**
   - **On Your Own Activity: Self-Portrait Collage**
   - **Group Activity: Play a Game: Who Am I?**

What You'll Learn

Literary Elements

line and stanza

alliteration and assonance

description

symbol

rhyme

characterization

metaphor and simile

foreshadowing

personification

rhythm and meter

diction

tone

myth

Reading Skills and Strategies

analyze cultural context

make inferences about characters

make predictions about plot

evaluate characterization

make generalizations about plot

Explore the BIG Question

Carmela Betagna, c.1880. John Singer Sargent. Oil on canvas, 23 1/2 × 19 1/2 in. Columbus Museum of Art. Bequest of Frederick W. Schumacher.

Eleven

Sandra Cisneros

What they don't understand about birthdays and what they never tell you is that when you're eleven, you're also ten, and nine, and eight, and seven, and six, and five, and four, and three, and two, and one. And when you wake up on your eleventh birthday you expect to feel eleven, but you don't. You open your eyes and everything's just like yesterday, only it's today. And you don't feel eleven at all. You feel like you're still ten. And you are—underneath the year that makes you eleven.

Like some days you might say something stupid, and that's the part of you that's still ten. Or maybe some days you might need to sit on your mama's lap because you're scared, and that's the part of you that's five. And maybe one day when you're all grown up maybe you will need to cry like if you're three, and that's okay. That's what I tell Mama when she's sad and needs to cry. Maybe she's feeling three.

Set a Purpose for Reading

Read this short story to learn what makes Rachel who she is at age eleven.

BQ BIG Question

Summarize what the narrator is saying about people's age in relation to who they are.

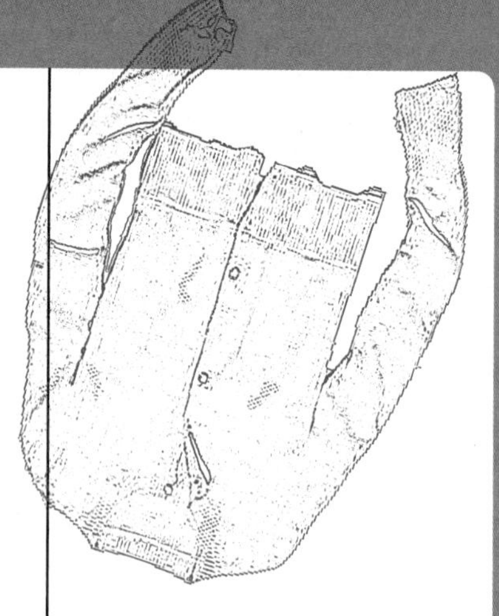

Because the way you grow old is kind of like an onion or like the rings inside a tree trunk[1] or like my little wooden dolls that fit one inside the other, each year inside the next one. That's how being eleven years old is.

You don't feel eleven. Not right away. It takes a few days, weeks even, sometimes even months before you say Eleven when they ask you. And you don't feel smart eleven, not until you're almost twelve. That's the way it is.

Only today I wish I didn't have only eleven years rattling inside me like pennies in a tin Band-Aid box. Today I wish I was one hundred and two instead of eleven because if I was one hundred and two I'd have known what to say when Mrs. Price put the red sweater on my desk. I would've known how to tell her it wasn't mine instead of just sitting there with that look on my face and nothing coming out of my mouth.

"Whose is this?" Mrs. Price says, and she holds the red sweater up in the air for all the class to see. "Whose? It's been sitting in the coatroom for a month."

"Not mine," says everybody. "Not me."

"It has to belong to somebody," Mrs. Price keeps saying, but nobody can remember. It's an ugly sweater with red plastic buttons and a collar and sleeves all stretched out like you could use it for a jump rope. It's maybe a thousand years old and even if it belonged to me I wouldn't say so.

Maybe because I'm skinny, maybe because she doesn't like me, that stupid Sylvia Saldívar[2] says, "I think it belongs to Rachel." An ugly sweater like that, all raggedy and old, but Mrs. Price believes her. Mrs. Price takes the sweater and puts it right on my desk, but when I open my mouth nothing comes out.

"That's not, I don't, you're not . . . Not mine," I finally say in a little voice that was maybe me when I was four.

BQ BIG Question

What do you think the sweater reveals about its owner?

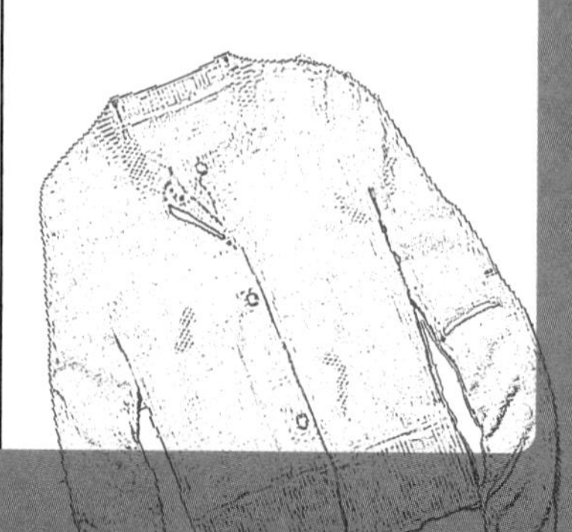

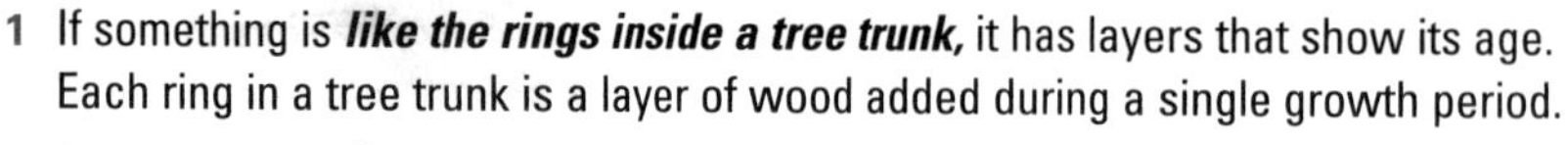

1 If something is ***like the rings inside a tree trunk,*** it has layers that show its age. Each ring in a tree trunk is a layer of wood added during a single growth period.

2 Saldívar (säl de′ vär)

"Of course it's yours," Mrs. Price says. "I remember you wearing it once." Because she's older and the teacher, she's right and I'm not.

Not mine, not mine, not mine, but Mrs. Price is already turning to page thirty-two, and math problem number four. I don't know why but all of a sudden I'm feeling sick inside, like the part of me that's three wants to come out of my eyes, only I squeeze them shut tight and bite down on my teeth real hard and try to remember today I am eleven, eleven. Mama is making a cake for me for tonight, and when Papa comes home everybody will sing Happy birthday, happy birthday to you.

But when the sick feeling goes away and I open my eyes, the red sweater's still sitting there like a big red

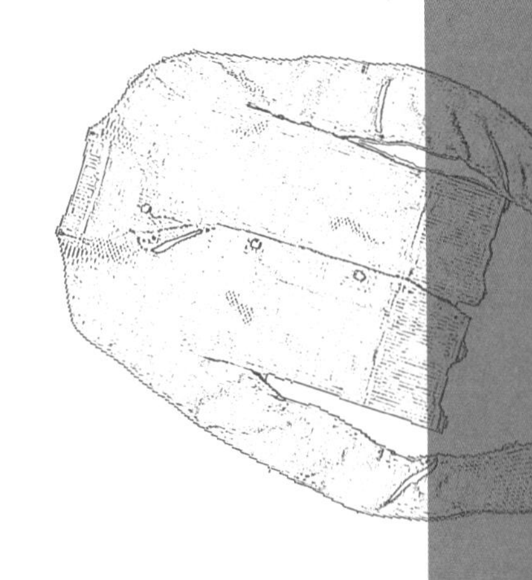

BQ BIG Question

Why does Rachel keep reminding herself that it's her birthday?

Girl Sitting in Classroom. Alberto Ruggieri.

mountain. I move the red sweater to the corner of my desk with my ruler. I move my pencil and books and eraser as far from it as possible. I even move my chair a little to the right. Not mine, not mine, not mine.

In my head I'm thinking how long till lunchtime, how long till I can take the red sweater and throw it over the school yard fence, or leave it hanging on a parking meter, or bunch it up into a little ball and toss it in the alley. Except when math period ends Mrs. Price says loud and in front of everybody, "Now, Rachel, that's enough," because she sees I've shoved the red sweater to the tippy-tip corner of my desk and it's hanging all over the edge like a waterfall, but I don't care.

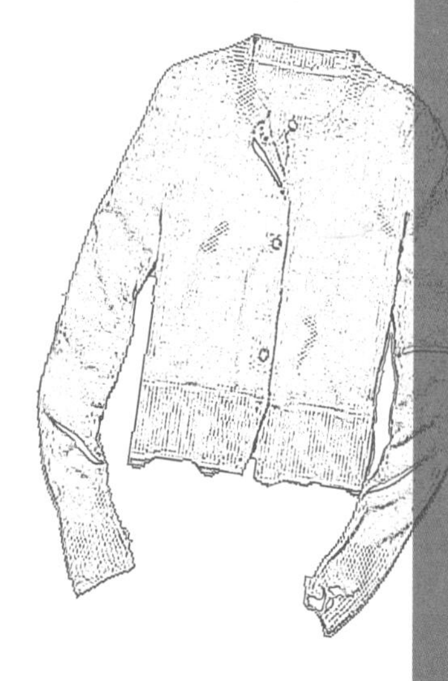

"Rachel," Mrs. Price says. She says it like she's getting mad. "You put that sweater on right now and no more nonsense."

"But it's not—"

"Now!" Mrs. Price says.

This is when I wish I wasn't eleven, because all the years inside of me—ten, nine, eight, seven, six, five, four, three, two, and one—are pushing at the back of my eyes when I put one arm through one sleeve of the sweater that smells like cottage cheese, and then the other arm through the other and stand there with my arms apart like if the sweater hurts me and it does, all itchy and full of germs that aren't even mine.

That's when everything I've been holding in since this morning, since when Mrs. Price put the sweater on my desk, finally lets go, and all of a sudden I'm crying in front of everybody. I wish I was invisible but I'm not. I'm eleven and it's my birthday today and I'm crying like I'm three in front of everybody. I put my head down on the desk and bury my face in my stupid clown-sweater arms. My face all hot and spit coming out of my mouth because I can't stop the little animal noises from coming out of me, until there aren't any more tears left in my eyes, and it's just my body

BQ BIG Question

What do you learn about Rachel and how she handles conflict?

shaking like when you have the hiccups, and my whole head hurts like when you drink milk too fast.

I wish I was invisible but I'm not.

But the worst part is right before the bell rings for lunch. That stupid Phyllis Lopez, who is even dumber than Sylvia Saldívar, says she remembers the red sweater is hers! I take it off right away and give it to her, only Mrs. Price pretends like everything's okay.

Today I'm eleven. There's a cake Mama's making for tonight, and when Papa comes home from work we'll eat it. There'll be candles and presents and everybody will sing Happy birthday, happy birthday to you, Rachel, only it's too late.

I'm eleven today. I'm eleven, ten, nine, eight, seven, six, five, four, three, two, and one, but I wish I was one hundred and two. I wish I was anything but eleven, because I want today to be far away already, far away like a runaway balloon, like a tiny *o* in the sky, so tiny-tiny you have to close your eyes to see it. ❧

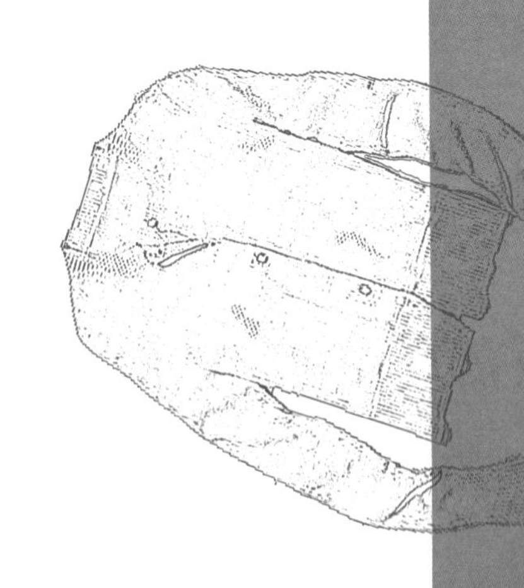

BQ BIG Question

What makes Rachel who she is on her eleventh birthday?

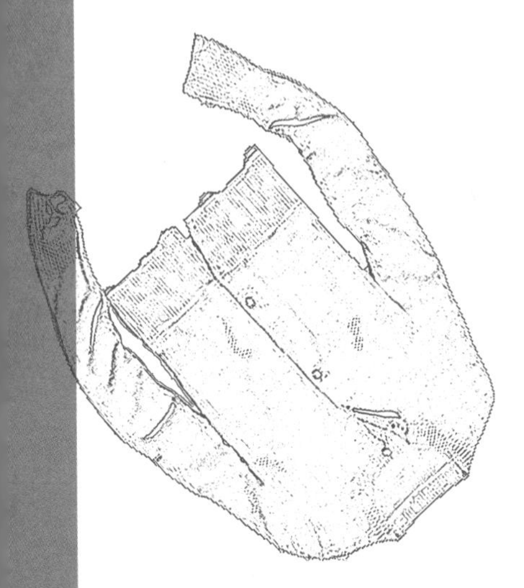

After You Read

Respond and Think Critically

1. Use your own words to retell what happens on Rachel's birthday. **[Summarize]**
2. One of the themes of the story is expressed when Rachel says "the way you grow old is kind of like an onion or like the rings inside a tree trunk." What does she mean? **[Interpret]**
3. At the end of the story, Mrs. Price "pretends like everything's okay." What can you infer about what Rachel wants Mrs. Price to do? **[Infer]**
4. Does Rachel "act her age" on her birthday? Explain. **[Evaluate]**

Write a Personal Response What makes Rachel want to be far away, "like a tiny *o* in the sky"? Write a one-paragraph response that explains *what* happens to Rachel and *why* she feels like she does. Discuss the personality traits that she reveals throughout the story. You may want to begin your paragraph with this sentence:

On her eleventh birthday, Rachel wants to be far away because ______.

For page 304

ELA6W2c Demonstrate competence in a variety of genres. Produce a response to literature that advances a judgment that is interpretive, analytic, evaluative, or reflective.

Literature Online

Unit Resources For additional skills practice, go to glencoe.com and enter QuickPass code GL17527u3.

Part 1

Family and Friends

Thanksgiving. Malcah Zeldis. Private Collection. ©ARS, NY.

BQ BIG Question What Makes You Who You Are?

What does this picture of a holiday dinner show about the group of people gathered at the table? How does sharing an experience with family members or friends affect the kind of person you are?

Before You Read

My Parents

Connect to the Poem

Think about a time when you wanted to belong to a group of people.

Quickwrite Freewrite for a few minutes about what you did to try to earn their respect or approval.

Build Background

A bully is a person who tries to hurt or control someone in a harmful way. Has someone ever told you, "Sticks and stones may break your bones, but names will never hurt you"? Often, we think of bullies as kids who hit or push other kids, but there are many ways to bully a person, and they all hurt. Using mean words, making someone feel unsafe, leaving someone out, and teasing are all ways people bully others.

- Bullying is a behavior that people learn.
- A bully bullies others to feel powerful.
- Bullies who don't get help often have trouble as adults.

Set Purposes for Reading

BQ BIG Question

As you read, ask yourself, how does the speaker deal with bullies?

Literary Element Line and Stanza

A **line** is a row of words in a poem. A **stanza** is a group of lines that forms a unit in a poem. Stanzas are, in effect, the paragraphs of a poem. They are usually set off by blank lines.

Lines and stanzas are important because they give a poem its shape on the page and help create the poem's meaning. Each stanza contains a single idea or helps develop the poem's main idea. Poets often use stanzas to organize the ideas and feelings in a poem. Line length also helps convey the poem's tone. For example, short lines can convey abrupt thoughts, while long lines can express a more rambling chain of ideas.

As you read, think about how each line and stanza adds to the meaning of the poem.

GA Performance Standards

For pages 306–308

ELA6R1h/iii For literary texts, respond to and explain the effects of graphics.

Meet Stephen Spender

An English Writer Sir Stephen Spender was born in London. He was a poet, a critic, and an editor. His early poetry was inspired by political and social unrest.

Sir Stephen Spender was born in 1909 and died in 1995.

LOG ON **Literature** Online

Author Search For more about Stephen Spender, go to glencoe.com and enter QuickPass code GL17527u3.

My Parents

Stephen Spender

Patrick Garland and Alexandra Bastedo, 1998. Stephen Finer. Oil on canvas. Private Collection.

View the Art What similarities do you find between the people in this painting and the children in the poem?

My parents kept me from children who were rough
Who threw words like stones and wore torn clothes
Their thighs showed through rags they ran in
 the street
And climbed cliffs and stripped by the country streams.

I feared more than tigers their muscles like iron
Their jerking hands and their knees tight on my arms
I feared the salt coarse° pointing of those boys
Who copied my lisp° behind me on the road.

They were lithe° they sprang out behind hedges
Like dogs to bark at my world. They threw mud
While I looked the other way, pretending to smile.
I longed to forgive them but they never smiled.

Line and Stanza How do the poet's word choices help create vivid images?

BQ BIG Question

How does the speaker deal with the bullies?

---

7 Something that is coarse is very rough. A ***coarse*** person has bad manners.

8 A ***lisp*** is a speech problem that affects making *s* and *z* sounds.

9 A ***lithe*** person moves easily and is very flexible.

After You Read

Respond and Think Critically

1. Use your own words to tell different ways the boys bully the speaker. **[Summarize]**
2. The speaker says that he feels the knees of the other boys "tight on my arms." What are the boys doing when he feels this? **[Infer]**
3. To what animals does the speaker compare the boys? What other comparisons does he make? **[Compare]**
4. Why do you think the speaker wants to forgive the boys for their cruel actions toward him? **[Interpret]**
5. **Literary Element** **Line and Stanza** Describe the key ideas in each stanza. **[Analyze]**
6. **BQ** **BIG Question** Why do you think Spender chose to call the poem "My Parents"? **[Conclude]**

TIP

Comparing
To answer question 3, remember that a simile is a figure of speech that uses *like* or *as* to compare two unlike things.

- Scan the poem for the words *like* or *as.*
- Identify the words that are linked by *like* or *as.*
- Think about what the comparisons mean.

Keep track of your ideas about the **BIG Question** in your unit Foldable.

Spelling Link

Patterns Based on Meaning The word *child* means "a young person, between infancy and youth." Think about the word *children* in "My Parents." Words that have related meanings often have related spellings. Notice that the word *child* appears in *children.* Can you think of more words related in meaning and spelling to *child?* For example, other related words are *childish, childhood,* and *childlike.*

Rule: Words related in meaning often have similar spelling patterns.

Examples: cloth, clothe, clothes, clothing

Practice On a sheet of paper, write the word *nation.* Then write other words that have a related meaning and spelling. Next to each word, write what you think it means. Then use a dictionary to check your spellings and definitions.

Writing

Write a Journal Entry Imagine that you and the speaker of the poem are friends. What would you say or do to help him? Would you say anything to the bullies? Observe your own surroundings to see how people handle bullies. Also ask a parent or a teacher for information on how to deal with bullies. Using your responses and observations, explain your thoughts in a journal entry.

Literature Online

Selection Resources
For Selection Quizzes, eFlashcards, and Reading-Writing Connection activities, go to glencoe.com and enter QuickPass code GL17527u3.

Before You Read

Same Song and *Maestro*

Connect to the Poems

Do you worry about your appearance, or are you happy with the way you look?

Partner Talk With a partner, talk about which is more important: who you are on the inside or who you appear to be. Why do you think people focus so much on appearances?

Build Background

Pat Mora often writes poems that celebrate her Mexican American heritage and the joy of accepting the things that make people different.

- She says that a big reason for writing poetry "is to help people feel less lonely."
- She recognizes that Mexican Americans are well aware of the borders in their lives. She likes to write about borders as places to bridge differences.
- A maestro is the master of an art. The word usually refers to a well-known and respected conductor, composer, or teacher of music.

Set Purposes for Reading

BQ BIG Question

As you read, ask yourself, how do our family and friends help make us who we are?

Literary Element Alliteration and Assonance

Alliteration is the repetition of consonant sounds at the beginnings of words. Assonance is the repetition of vowel sounds, especially within a line of poetry. The tongue twister "Peter Piper picked a peck of pickled peppers" contains both alliteration and assonance.

Poets often use alliteration and assonance to call attention to certain words, to add interest to the sound of a poem, or to create a certain tone or mood.

As you read, look for examples of alliteration and assonance.

GA Performance Standards

For pages 309–314

ELA6R1h/i For literary texts, respond to and explain the effects of sound.

Meet Pat Mora

"Poetry is words woven together to create a musical surprise."

—Pat Mora

Preserving Her Heritage Pat Mora grew up in Texas near Mexico and spoke mainly Spanish at home. She preserves her Hispanic heritage by using Spanish phrases and Mexican cultural references in her books.

Literary Works Mora writes poetry, stories, and novels.

Pat Mora was born in 1942.

LOG ON Literature Online

Author Search For more about Pat Mora, go to glencoe.com and enter QuickPass code GL17527u3.

Nancy's Sink, 2003. Pam Ingalls.

Same Song

Pat Mora

While my sixteen-year-old son sleeps,
my twelve-year-old daughter
stumbles into the bathroom at six a.m.
plugs in the curling iron
squeezes into faded jeans
curls her hair carefully
strokes Aztec Blue° shadow on her eyelids
smooths Frosted Mauve blusher° on her cheeks
outlines her mouth in Neon Pink°
peers into the mirror, mirror on the wall
frowns at her face, her eyes, her skin,
not fair.

At night this daughter
stumbles off to bed at nine
eyes half-shut while my son
jogs a mile in the cold dark
then lifts weights in the garage
curls and bench presses°
expanding biceps, triceps, pectorals,°
one-handed push-ups, one hundred sit-ups
peers into that mirror, mirror and frowns too.

Alliteration and Assonance
How does the emphasis created by the alliteration in these lines add to the mood of the poem?

BQ BIG Question
What do the son and daughter have in common?

---

7 ***Aztec Blue*** is a fancy name for a shade of blue.

8 ***Frosted Mauve*** is a silvery, pale purplish or rose color. ***Blusher*** is a kind of makeup used to add color to the cheeks.

9 ***Neon*** is an element used in some lights that can make them have very bright colors. Therefore, ***Neon Pink*** is a bright pink lipstick.

18 ***Curls and bench presses*** are two weight-lifting exercises for building muscles.

19 ***Biceps***, ***triceps***, and ***pectorals*** are muscles in the arms and chest. The ***biceps*** is the large muscle in the front of the upper arm. The ***triceps*** is the large muscle at the back of the upper arm. ***Pectorals*** are muscles that connect the chest walls to the bones of the upper arm and shoulder.

Maestro

Pat Mora

The Violinist, 1942. Raoul Dufy. Oil on panel. 22.5 x 14.5 cm. Private Collection. © ARS, NY.

He hears her
when he bows.
Rows of hands clap
again and again he bows
to stage lights and upturned faces
but he hears only his mother's voice

years ago in their small home
singing Mexican songs
one phrase at a time
while his father strummed the guitar
or picked the melody with quick fingertips.
Both cast their music in the air
for him to snare with his strings,
songs of *lunas* and *amor*°
learned bit by bit.
She'd nod, smile, as his bow slid
note to note, then the trio
voz, guitarra, violín°
would blend again and again
to the last pure note
sweet on the tongue.

Alliteration and Assonance
What assonance is in this line, and what sound does it mimic?

BQ BIG Question
Who or what has influenced the maestro to become who he is?

---

14 ***Lunas*** (lo͞o′ näs) and ***amor*** (a mōr′) mean "moons" and "love" in Spanish.

18 The phrase ***voz, guitarra, violín*** (vōs, gē tä′ rrä, vē ō lēn′) means "voice, guitar, violin" in Spanish.

After You Read

Respond and Think Critically

1. What steps does the daughter in "Same Song" take to get ready in the morning? **[Recall]**
2. In "Same Song," which part of the daughter's and son's appearance is most important to each? **[Identify]**
3. Why do you think the author repeats the phrase "mirror, mirror" in the two stanzas of "Same Song"? Explain the importance of the mirror. **[Analyze]**
4. Why does the maestro hear "only his mother's voice" as he bows on stage after a performance? **[Analyze]**
5. In line 17 of "Maestro," who are the people in the trio, and what musical role does each person have? **[Interpret]**
6. **BQ BIG Question** What does each poem say about what makes people who they are? How well does each poem get across its message? Use examples from the poems to support your ideas. **[Evaluate]**

Academic Vocabulary

When you **interpret** a poem or another piece of literature, you reveal or explain its meaning. For example, after reading about a character in a poem, you might *interpret* his or her actions to be heroic. To become more familiar with the word *interpret,* fill out a graphic organizer like the one below.

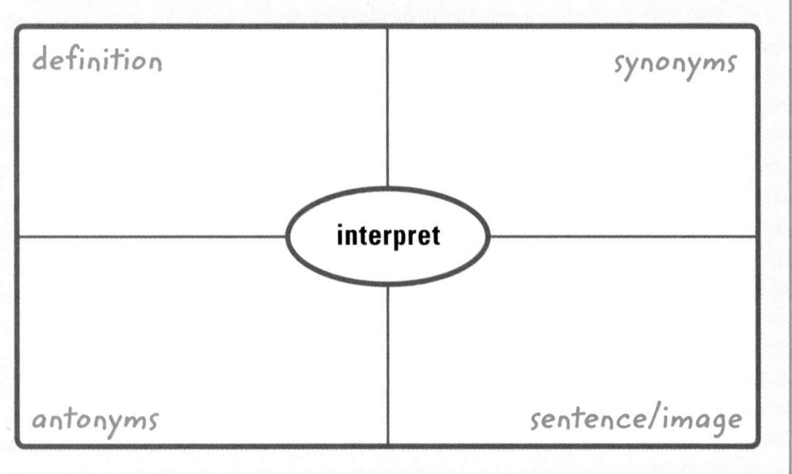

TIP

Analyzing
When you analyze, you look at separate parts of a piece of writing to understand the whole piece. Here are some tips to help you answer question 4.

- Look for details about the maestro's mother. How does she interact with her son?
- Which lines in the poem hint at how the maestro feels about his parents and their music?
- Recall how the audience responds to the maestro. How might he feel about music and his mother?

Keep track of your ideas about the **BIG Question** in your unit Foldable.

Literature Online

Selection Resources
For Selection Quizzes, eFlashcards, and Reading-Writing Connection activities, go to glencoe.com and enter QuickPass code GL17527u3.

Literary Element **Alliteration and Assonance**

1. Is the title of "Same Song" an example of assonance or alliteration? Explain your answer.
2. Both poems contain alliteration in their first lines. Why is this an effective way to begin a poem?
3. The titles of both poems concern music. What is the *song* in "Same Song"?

Review: Imagery

As you learned on page 194, **imagery** is language that helps readers see, hear, feel, smell, and taste the things authors describe in their works. Poets have another reason for carefully choosing their images. Carefully chosen images help poets get across the meaning of their poems.

4. In "Same Song," which images does the poet use to describe the daughter and son? What do these images tell you about each person?
5. Identify four images from "Maestro" that appeal to sight, sound, touch, and taste. Use a graphic organizer like the one below.

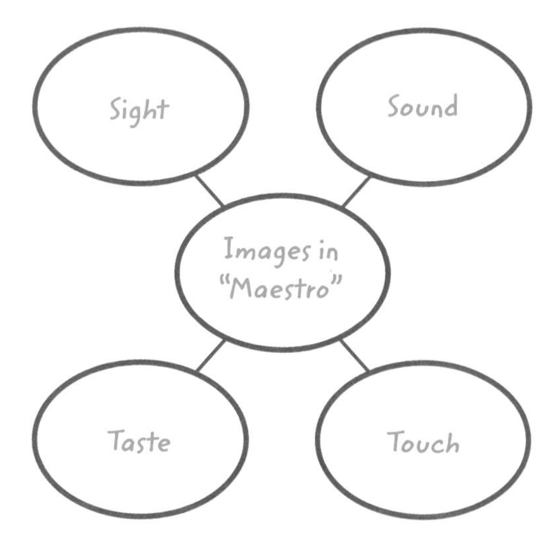

Grammar Link

Indefinite Pronouns An indefinite pronoun is a pronoun that does not refer to a particular person, place, or thing.

Many worry about appearance.

Most indefinite pronouns are either singular or plural. A few depend on how they are used in a sentence.

Singular: another, anybody, anyone, anything, each, either, everybody, everything, much, neither, nobody, no one, nothing, one, somebody, someone, something

Plural: both, few, many, others, several

Singular or plural: all, any, most, none, some

Often, an indefinite pronoun will be the subject of a sentence. The verb must agree with the pronoun in number.

- **Everyone** applauds the maestro. (singular)
- **Both** look into the mirror and frown. (plural)
- **All** of the maestro's performance was magnificent. (singular to agree with *performance*)
- **Some** of the songs were about love. (plural to agree with *songs*)

Practice Choose one indefinite pronoun from each of the three groups listed above. Use each pronoun to write a sentence about one of the poems. Make sure that the verbs agree with the pronouns in number.

Write with Style

Apply Sound Devices How do your family and friends help shape who you are? Write a poem of one or two stanzas. Express how your family or your friends have influenced you. Use alliteration and assonance in your poem.

Before You Read

The All-American Slurp

Connect to the Story

Think about a time when you felt awkward in a social setting because you didn't know what to do.

Quickwrite Freewrite for a few minutes about the situation and how you felt. Did you get any clues about how to act by observing others?

Build Background

Many thousands of people immigrate to the United States every year. During one year in the 1990s, about 54,000 people moved from China to the United States. More than 111,400 people came from Mexico; 14,700 from Cuba; and 41,300 from Vietnam.

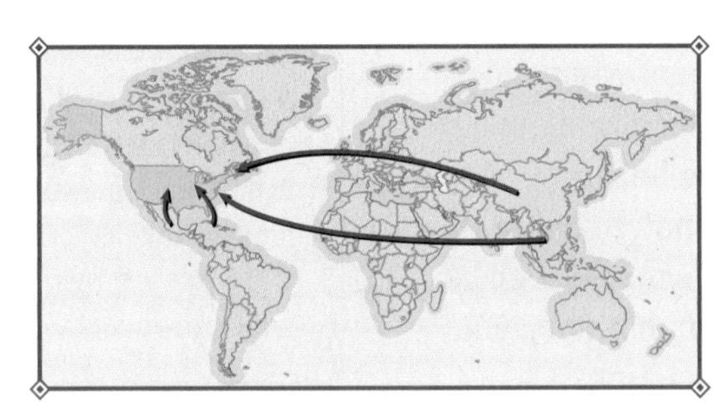

Vocabulary

lavishly (lav′ ish lē) *adv.* in a way that provides much more than is needed (p. 319). *The bed was lavishly covered with pillows.*

acquainted (ə kwān′ tid) *adj.* knowing someone, or each other, but not closely (p. 320). *I became acquainted with other athletes when I joined the soccer team.*

blouse (blous) *n.* a woman's or girl's shirt (p. 321). *Angela wore a matching blue blouse and skirt.*

boost (bo͞ost) *n.* something that aids or advances a person or thing (p. 322). *Earning a good score on the exam was a boost to Jorge's spirits.*

coping (kō′ ping) *v.* successfully dealing with something difficult (p. 328). *Since Marla's accident, she's been coping with a broken leg.*

Meet Lensey Namioka

"As a child, my greatest pleasure was reading. My aim is to write books that will give the same pleasure to young people today."

—Lensey Namioka

Inspired by Her Heritage Lensey Namioka was born in China. Her family moved to the United States when she was nine years old. Namioka's Chinese cultural heritage and her husband's Japanese heritage have inspired many of her books. She often writes with humor about misunderstandings between different cultures.

Literary Works Lensey Namioka is the author of many books, including *April and the Dragon Lady* and the *Yang Family* series.

Lensey Namioka was born in 1929.

Literature Online

Author Search For more about Lensey Namioka, go to glencoe.com and enter QuickPass code GL17527u3.

Set Purposes for Reading

BQ BIG Question

As you read, ask yourself, how important is it to be just like everyone else?

Literary Element Description

A **description** is a detailed explanation of a person, a place, a thing, or an event. Good descriptive writing brings experiences and events to life. It helps readers see, hear, smell, taste, and feel the story's details.

Descriptions help you gain a clearer picture of events in the story and may indirectly illustrate themes. For example, when the author says that her family packed themselves into a sofa, you can imagine four people jammed together on a sofa that barely holds them.

As you read "The All-American Slurp," ask yourself, how do the descriptions add to the humorous tone of the story?

Reading Skill Analyze Cultural Context

Analyzing, or looking at separate parts of a piece of writing to understand the whole piece, is a way to think critically about a story. **Cultural context** is the shared qualities and beliefs of people living in a particular place and time. When you **analyze cultural context,** you think about the time and place of a work, as well as the values of the people in that time and place. In this story, you will analyze both Chinese culture and American culture.

Sometimes people of cultures different from your own may speak or act in ways that seem strange to you. Analyzing cultural context will help you better understand the characters.

To **analyze cultural context,** pay attention to

- the time and place of the story
- the values of the characters, as shown through details and dialogue
- the characters' customs, especially those related to eating and drinking

As you read, you may find it helpful to use a graphic organizer like the one below.

Detail	What It Reveals
The family pulls strings out of the celery.	They aren't used to eating raw celery.

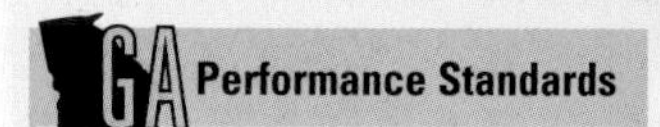

GA Performance Standards

For pages 315–330

ELA6R1a For literary texts, identify and analyze sensory details and figurative language.

TRY IT

Analyze Cultural Context You notice two boys whose culture is different from yours playing a game you don't recognize. It looks like fun. How can you find out more about the game?

The All-American Slurp

Lensey Namioka

Soup on Tabletop, 1999. Linda Montgomery.

The first time our family was invited out to dinner in America, we disgraced[1] ourselves while eating celery. We had emigrated[2] to this country from China, and during our early days here, we had a hard time with American table manners.

In China we never ate celery raw, or any other kind of vegetable raw. We always had to disinfect[3] the vegetables in boiling water first. When we were presented with our first relish tray, the raw celery caught us unprepared.

---

1 A person who has ***disgraced*** himself has brought shame upon himself.

2 A family who has ***emigrated*** has moved from one place or country to settle in another place.

3 When you ***disinfect*** something, you clean it to kill the germs on it.

We had been invited to dinner by our neighbors, the Gleasons. After arriving at the house, we shook hands with our hosts and packed ourselves into a sofa. As our family of four sat stiffly in a row, my younger brother and I stole glances at our parents for a clue as to what to do next.

Description What does this description reveal about how the narrator and her family are feeling?

Mrs. Gleason offered the relish tray to Mother. The tray looked pretty, with its tiny red radishes, curly sticks of carrots, and long, slender stalks of pale green celery. "Do try some of the celery, Mrs. Lin," she said. "It's from a local farmer, and it's sweet."

Mother picked up one of the green stalks, and Father followed suit. Then I picked up a stalk, and my brother did too. So there we sat, each with a stalk of celery in our right hand.

Mrs. Gleason kept smiling. "Would you like to try some of the dip, Mrs. Lin? It's my own recipe: sour cream and onion flakes, with a dash of Tabasco sauce."

Most Chinese don't care for dairy products, and in those days I wasn't even ready to drink fresh milk. Sour cream sounded perfectly revolting. Our family shook our heads in unison.[4]

Mrs. Gleason went off with the relish tray to the other guests, and we carefully watched to see what they did. Everyone seemed to eat the raw vegetables quite happily.

Mother took a bite of her celery. *Crunch.* "It's not bad!" she whispered.

Father took a bite of his celery. *Crunch.* "Yes, it *is* good," he said, looking surprised.

Analyze Cultural Context What does this tell you about the narrator's family?

I took a bite, and then my brother. *Crunch, crunch.* It was more than good; it was delicious. Raw celery has a slight sparkle, a zingy taste that you don't get in cooked celery. When Mrs. Gleason came around with the relish tray, we each took another stalk of celery, except my brother. He took two.

There was only one problem: long strings ran through the length of the stalk, and they got caught in my teeth.

---

4 When people speak or act in ***unison***, they say or do the same thing at the same moment.

When I help my mother in the kitchen, I always pull the strings out before slicing celery.

I pulled the strings out of my stalk.

Z-z-zip, z-z-zip. My brother followed suit. *Z-z-zip, z-z-zip, z-z-zip.* To my left, my parents were taking care of their own stalks. *Z-z-zip, z-z-zip, z-z-zip.*

Suddenly I realized that there was dead silence except for our zipping. Looking up, I saw that the eyes of everyone in the room were on our family. Mr. and Mrs. Gleason, their daughter Meg, who was my friend, and their neighbors the Badels—they were all staring at us as we busily pulled the strings of our celery.

Analyze Cultural Context Why is everyone staring at the Lins?

That wasn't the end of it. Mrs. Gleason announced that dinner was served and invited us to the dining table. It was **lavishly** covered with platters of food, but we couldn't see any chairs around the table. So we helpfully carried over some dining chairs and sat down. All the other guests just stood there.

Mrs. Gleason bent down and whispered to us, "This is a buffet dinner. You help yourselves to some food and eat it in the living room."

Our family beat a retreat back to the sofa as if chased by enemy soldiers. For the rest of the evening, too mortified to go back to the dining table, I nursed[5] a bit of potato salad on my plate.

Description What does this description suggest about how the Lins feel at this moment?

Next day Meg and I got on the school bus together. I wasn't sure how she would feel about me after the spectacle our family made at the party. But she was just the same as usual, and the only reference she made to the party was, "Hope you and your folks got enough to eat last night. You certainly didn't take very much. Mom never tries to figure out how much food to prepare. She just puts everything on the table and hopes for the best."

I began to relax. The Gleasons' dinner party wasn't so different from a Chinese meal after all. My mother also puts everything on the table and hopes for the best.

---

5 A person who ***nursed*** food or drink ate or drank it very slowly.

Vocabulary

lavishly (lav′ish lē) *adv.* in a way that provides much more than is needed

Meg was the first friend I had made after we came to America. I eventually got **acquainted** with a few other kids in school, but Meg was still the only real friend I had.

My brother didn't have any problems making friends. He spent all his time with some boys who were teaching him baseball, and in no time he could speak English much faster than I could—not better, but faster.

I worried more about making mistakes, and I spoke carefully, making sure I could say everything right before opening my mouth. At least I had a better accent than my parents, who never really got rid of their Chinese accent, even years later. My parents had both studied English in school before coming to America, but what they had studied was mostly written English, not spoken.

Father's approach to English was a scientific one. Since Chinese verbs have no tense, he was fascinated by the way English verbs changed form according to whether they were in the present, past imperfect, perfect, pluperfect, future, or future perfect tense. He was always making diagrams of verbs and their inflections,[6] and he looked for opportunities to show off his mastery of the pluperfect and future perfect tenses, his two favorites. "I shall have finished my project by Monday," he would say smugly.

Analyze Cultural Context
How might this cultural difference affect a Chinese person's ability to learn English?

Mother's approach was to memorize lists of polite phrases that would cover all possible social situations. She was constantly muttering things like "I'm fine, thank you. And you?" Once she accidentally stepped on someone's foot, and hurriedly blurted, "Oh, that's quite all right!" Embarrassed by her slip, she resolved to do better next time. So when someone stepped on *her* foot, she cried, "You're welcome!"

In our own different ways, we made progress in learning English. But I had another worry, and that was my appearance. My brother didn't have to worry, since Mother bought him blue jeans for school, and he dressed

---

6 ***Inflections*** are the forms and tenses of a word, which change depending on how the word is used in a sentence.

Vocabulary

acquainted (ə kwān′ tid) *adj.* knowing someone, or each other, but not closely like all the other boys. But she insisted that girls had to wear skirts. By the time she saw that Meg and the other girls were wearing jeans, it was too late. My school clothes were bought already, and we didn't have money left to buy new outfits for me. We had too many other things to buy first, like furniture, pots, and pans.

Analyze Cultural Context
Why do you think Mrs. Lin insists that girls wear skirts?

The first time I visited Meg's house, she took me upstairs to her room, and I wound up trying on her clothes. We were pretty much the same size, since Meg was shorter and thinner than average. Maybe that's how we became friends in the first place. Wearing Meg's jeans and T-shirt, I looked at myself in the mirror. I could almost pass for an American—from the back, anyway. At least the kids in school wouldn't stop and stare at me in the hallways, which was what they did when they saw me in my white **blouse** and navy blue skirt that went a couple of inches below the knees.

BQ BIG Question
Why does the narrator want to pass for an American?

When Meg came to my house, I invited her to try on my Chinese dresses, the ones with a high collar and slits up the sides. Meg's eyes were bright as she looked at herself in the mirror. She struck several sultry poses,[7] and we nearly fell over laughing.

The dinner party at the Gleasons' didn't stop my growing friendship with Meg. Things were getting better for me in other ways too. Mother finally bought me some jeans at the end of the month, when Father got his paycheck. She wasn't in any hurry about buying them at first, until I worked on her. This is what I did. Since we didn't have a car in those days, I often ran down to the neighborhood store to pick up things for her. The groceries cost less at a big supermarket, but the closest one was many blocks away. One day, when she ran out of flour, I offered to borrow a bike from our neighbor's son and buy a ten-pound bag of flour at the big supermarket. I mounted the boy's bike and waved to Mother. "I'll be back in five minutes!"

7 When Meg strikes ***sultry poses***, she is trying out different looks that she thinks are seductive or flirty.

Vocabulary

blouse (blous) *n.* a woman's or girl's shirt

Before I started pedaling, I heard her voice behind me. "You can't go out in public like that! People can see all the way up to your thighs!"

"I'm sorry," I said innocently. "I thought you were in a hurry to get the flour." For dinner we were going to have pot-stickers (fried Chinese dumplings), and we needed a lot of flour.

"Couldn't you borrow a girl's bicycle?" complained Mother. "That way your skirt won't be pushed up."

"There aren't too many of those around," I said. "Almost all the girls wear jeans while riding a bike, so they don't see any point buying a girl's bike."

We didn't eat pot-stickers that evening, and Mother was thoughtful. Next day we took the bus downtown and she bought me a pair of jeans. In the same week, my brother made the baseball team of his junior high school, Father started taking driving lessons, and Mother discovered rummage sales. We soon got all the furniture we needed, plus a dart board and a 1,000-piece jigsaw puzzle (fourteen hours later, we discovered that it was a 999-piece jigsaw puzzle). There was hope that the Lins might become a normal American family after all.

Then came our dinner at the Lakeview restaurant.

The Lakeview was an expensive restaurant, one of those places where a headwaiter dressed in **tails** conducted you to your seat, and the only light came from candles and flaming desserts. In one corner of the room a lady harpist played tinkling melodies.

Father wanted to celebrate, because he had just been promoted. He worked for an electronics company, and after his English started improving, his superiors[8] decided to appoint him to a position more suited to his training. The promotion not only brought a higher salary but was also a tremendous **boost** to his pride.

8 At work, Father's ***superiors*** are his managers or bosses.

Vocabulary

boost (bo͞ost) *n.* something that aids or advances a person or thing

Visual Vocabulary

The headwaiter is wearing a formal suit with a jacket that has long panels in the back. This kind of jacket is called **tails,** which is a nickname for "tailcoat."

Analyze Cultural Context
What is the narrator's picture of a normal American family? Why is it important to her that her family become one?

Description What details help readers picture the restaurant?

Saturday in Soho. Dale Kennington. Oil on canvas.

Up to then we had eaten only in Chinese restaurants. Although my brother and I were becoming fond of hamburgers, my parents didn't care much for western food, other than chow mein.[9]

But this was a special occasion, and Father asked his coworkers to recommend a really elegant restaurant. So there we were at the Lakeview, stumbling after the head-waiter in the murky dining room.

At our table we were handed our menus, and they were so big that to read mine I almost had to stand up again. But why bother? It was mostly in French, anyway.

Father, being an engineer, was always systematic. He took out a pocket French dictionary. "They told me that most of the items would be in French, so I came prepared." He even had a pocket flashlight, the size of a marking pen. While Mother held the flashlight over the menu, he looked up the items that were in French.

View the Art As you visualized the Lakeview restaurant, did it look like this painting? Explain.

Description How does this description capture what the narrator and her family are feeling?

9 ***Chow mein*** is a Chinese American dish made of shredded fish or meat and vegetables, served with fried noodles.

Italian Waiter.
Dale Kennington.
Oil on canvas.

"Pâté en croûte,"[10] he muttered. "Let's see . . . *pâté* is paste . . . *croûte* is crust . . . hmm . . . a paste in crust."

The waiter stood looking patient. I squirmed and died at least fifty times.

Description How does the description reveal what the narrator is feeling?

At long last Father gave up. "Why don't we just order four complete dinners at random?" he suggested.

"Isn't that risky?" asked Mother. "The French eat some rather peculiar things, I've heard."

"A Chinese can eat anything a Frenchman can eat," Father declared.

The soup arrived in a plate. How do you get soup up from a plate? I glanced at the other diners, but the ones at the nearby tables were not on their soup course, while the more distant ones were invisible in the darkness.

10 ***Pâté en croûte*** (pä tā ən kro͞ot′) is finely ground meat baked in a small pie shell.

Fortunately my parents had studied books on western etiquette[11] before they came to America. "Tilt your plate," whispered my mother. "It's easier to spoon the soup up that way."

She was right. Tilting the plate did the trick. But the etiquette book didn't say anything about what you did after the soup reached your lips. As any respectable Chinese knows, the correct way to eat your soup is to slurp. This helps to cool the liquid and prevent you from burning your lips. It also shows your appreciation.

Analyze Cultural Context Why might Americans fail to understand why the Chinese slurp their soup?

We showed our appreciation. *Shloop,* went my father. *Shloop,* went my mother. *Shloop, shloop,* went my brother, who was the hungriest.

The lady harpist stopped playing to take a rest. And in the silence, our family's consumption of soup suddenly seemed unnaturally loud. You know how it sounds on a rocky beach when the tide goes out and the water drains from all those little pools? They go *shloop, shloop, shloop.* That was the Lin family, eating soup.

Description Why does the narrator use the image of a rocky beach to describe eating soup?

At the next table a waiter was pouring wine. When a large *shloop* reached him, he froze. The bottle continued to pour, and red wine flooded the tabletop and into the lap of a customer. Even the customer didn't notice anything at first, being also hypnotized by the *shloop, shloop, shloop.*

It was too much. "I need to go to the toilet," I mumbled, jumping to my feet. A waiter, sensing my urgency, quickly directed me to the ladies' room.

I splashed cold water on my burning face, and as I dried myself with a paper towel, I stared into the mirror. In this perfumed ladies' room, with its pink-and-silver wallpaper and marbled sinks, I looked completely out of place. What was I doing here? What was our family doing in the Lakeview restaurant? In America?

The door to the ladies' room opened. A woman came in and glanced curiously at me. I retreated into one of the toilet cubicles and latched the door.

Time passed—maybe half an hour, maybe an hour. Then

11 ***Etiquette*** means the rules for manners or polite behavior, which vary in different places and cultures.

I heard the door open again, and my mother's voice. "Are you in there? You're not sick, are you?"

There was real concern in her voice. A girl can't leave her family just because they slurp their soup. Besides, the toilet cubicle had a few drawbacks as a permanent residence. "I'm all right," I said, undoing the latch.

Mother didn't tell me how the rest of the dinner went, and I didn't want to know. In the weeks following, I managed to push the whole thing into the back of my mind, where it jumped out at me only a few times a day. Even now, I turn hot all over when I think of the Lakeview restaurant.

But by the time we had been in this country for three months, our family was definitely making progress toward becoming Americanized. I remember my parents' first PTA[12] meeting. Father wore a neat suit and tie, and Mother put on her first pair of high heels. She stumbled only once. They met my homeroom teacher and beamed as she told them that I would make honor roll soon at the rate I was going. Of course Chinese etiquette forced Father to say that I was a very stupid girl and Mother to protest that the teacher was showing favoritism toward me. But I could tell they were both very proud.

Analyze Cultural Context
How are the Lins becoming more Americanized?

BQ BIG Question
How is the narrator affected by her parents' opinion of her?

The day came when my parents announced that they wanted to give a dinner party. We had invited Chinese friends to eat with us before, but this dinner was going to be different. In addition to a Chinese-American family, we were going to invite the Gleasons.

"Gee, I can hardly wait to have dinner at your house," Meg said to me. "I just *love* Chinese food."

That was a relief. Mother was a good cook, but I wasn't sure if people who ate sour cream would also eat chicken gizzards stewed in soy sauce.

Mother decided not to take a chance with chicken gizzards. Since we had western guests, she set the table with large dinner plates, which we never used in Chinese meals. In fact we didn't use individual plates at all, but picked up food from the platters in the middle of the table and brought it directly to our rice bowls. Following the

12 ***PTA*** stands for Parent-Teacher Association.

The Seto Kids. Pamela Chin Lee. Oil on canvas.

practice of Chinese-American restaurants, Mother also placed large serving spoons on the platters.

The dinner started well. Mrs. Gleason exclaimed at the beautifully arranged dishes of food: the colorful candied fruit in the sweet-and-sour pork dish, the noodle-thin shreds of chicken meat stir-fried with tiny peas, and the glistening pink **prawns** in a ginger sauce.

At first I was too busy enjoying my food to notice how the guests were doing. But soon I remembered my duties. Sometimes guests were too polite to help themselves and you had to serve them with more food.

I glanced at Meg, to see if she needed more food, and my eyes nearly popped out at the sight of her plate. It was piled with food: the sweet-and-sour meat pushed right against the chicken shreds, and the chicken sauce ran into the prawns. She had been taking food from a second dish before she finished eating her helping from the first!

Horrified, I turned to look at Mrs. Gleason. She was dumping rice out of her bowl and putting it on her dinner

Visual Vocabulary

Prawns are large shrimp.

plate. Then she ladled prawns and gravy on top of the rice and mixed everything together, the way you mix sand, gravel, and cement to make concrete.

I couldn't bear to look any longer, and I turned to Mr. Gleason. He was chasing a pea around his plate. Several times he got it to the edge, but when he tried to pick it up with his chopsticks, it rolled back toward the center of the plate again. Finally he put down his chopsticks and picked up the pea with his fingers. He really did! A grown man!

All of us, our family and the Chinese guests, stopped eating to watch the activities of the Gleasons. I wanted to giggle. Then I caught my mother's eyes on me. She frowned and shook her head slightly, and I understood the message: the Gleasons were not used to Chinese ways, and they were just **coping** the best they could. For some reason I thought of celery strings.

When the main courses were finished, Mother brought out a platter of fruit. "I hope you weren't expecting a sweet dessert," she said. "Since the Chinese don't eat dessert, I didn't think to prepare any."

"Oh, I couldn't possibly eat dessert!" cried Mrs. Gleason. "I'm simply stuffed!"

Meg had different ideas. When the table was cleared, she announced that she and I were going for a walk. "I don't know about you, but I feel like dessert," she told me, when we were outside. "Come on, there's a Dairy Queen down the street. I could use a big chocolate milkshake!"

Although I didn't really want anything more to eat, I insisted on paying for the milkshakes. After all, I was still hostess.

Meg got her large chocolate milkshake and I had a small one. Even so, she was finishing hers while I was only half done. Toward the end she pulled hard on her straws and went *shloop, shloop.*

"Do you always slurp when you eat a milkshake?" I asked, before I could stop myself.

Meg grinned. "Sure. All Americans slurp."

Analyze Cultural Context Why is the narrator horrified?

Description Why is this description humorous?

BQ BIG Question Why is the narrator surprised to hear Meg slurp? What does the narrator discover about herself and Meg?

Vocabulary

coping (kō′ ping) *v.* successfully dealing with something difficult

After You Read

Respond and Think Critically

1. What "mistakes" does the Lin family make at the Gleasons' dinner party? **[Recall]**
2. Why is it important to the narrator to get a pair of jeans? **[Interpret]**
3. Why does the narrator run and hide in the elegant restaurant? Give details from the story to support your answer. **[Infer]**
4. By the end of the story, how have the Lins changed? **[Compare]**
5. The narrator constantly tries to fit into American society. Do you think that fitting in is important? Why or why not? **[Evaluate]**
6. **BQ BIG Question** After reading "The All-American Slurp," what are your thoughts about what makes us who we are? How do our family, friends, and culture play a part in shaping who we are? **[Conclude]**

TIP

Inferring
When you infer, you use clues in the story and your own knowledge to figure something out. Here are some tips to help you infer why the narrator runs and hides:

- Review what happens in the restaurant.
- Think about how the narrator feels and what she does.
- Draw upon your own experiences to imagine how you would feel in that situation.

Keep track of your ideas about the **BIG Question** in your unit Foldable.

Vocabulary Practice

On a separate sheet of paper, write the vocabulary word that correctly completes each sentence. If none of the words fits the sentence, write *none.*

coping	**lavishly**	**boost**
blouse	**acquainted**	

1. The diners ________ praised the wonderful meal.
2. Ryan is ________ with a bad headache.
3. When the rain started, we ran ________ to the shed.
4. Jon became ________ with his classmates in the new school.
5. I felt a ________ to my pride when I received the award.
6. The cat ________ for the water bowl in its new home.
7. Liz bought a ________ to go with her blue skirt.

Academic Vocabulary

The narrator describes her family's **consumption** of soup as "unnaturally loud." In the preceding sentence, *consumption* is the act of eating. A **consumer** is someone who eats or drinks. A consumer can also be someone who buys an item or uses a service. In what ways are you a consumer?

Literature Online

Selection Resources
For Selection Quizzes, eFlashcards, and Reading-Writing Connection activities, go to glencoe.com and enter QuickPass code GL17527u3.

Literary Element **Description**

1. Three different dinners are described in the story. Use the chart below to list details that appeal to the five senses from each of the dinners.

Gleasons' house	French restaurant	Lins' house

2. Choose a scene from the story that does not involve food. List the details from the story that help you vividly picture the scene.

Review: Dialogue

As you learned on page 103, **dialogue** is conversation between characters in a story. Writers use dialogue to move a story's plot forward. Dialogue also reveals what the characters think and feel. Dialogue is usually set off with quotation marks and dialogue tags, or markers that tell the reader who said what.

3. Recall the dialogue that occurs between the narrator and her mother about the boy's bike. What does the dialogue show about the characters' thoughts and feelings? Use examples to explain your answer.
4. The narrator's mother and father try to improve their English skills. Give some examples of dialogue that show them trying to learn English.

Reading Skill **Analyze Cultural Context**

5. How do the Lin and Gleason families show that they are accepting of other cultures? Give examples to support your answer.
6. What customs, attitudes, and beliefs shape your culture? How is your culture similar to or different from that of the narrator?

Grammar Link

Adjectives and Adverbs Words that describe nouns or pronouns are **adjectives.** For example, the adjectives below are in bold type. The nouns they describe are underlined.

- I could use a **big chocolate** milkshake!
- I squirmed and died at least **fifty** times.
- The **celery** was delicious.

Adverbs describe verbs by giving information that answers *how, when, where,* or *to what extent* questions. They also describe adjectives and other adverbs. The adverbs below are in bold type. The words they describe are underlined.

- Our family sat **stiffly** in a row.
- I **soon** met other students.
- My two dogs played **outdoors.**
- She slurped her milkshake **rather loudly**.

Practice Look back at "The All-American Slurp" and find three sentences that contain adjectives, adverbs, or both. Write the sentences on a separate sheet of paper. Underline the adjectives and circle the adverbs.

Speaking and Listening

Literature Groups With a small group, discuss how a person's outlook can determine whether something is funny or sad. In a chart, list three events from the story in which the narrator uses humor to describe situations that are embarrassing for her and her family. How might each situation have turned out differently? Next to each event, list other possible outcomes. What helps the narrator and her family overcome these embarrassments?

Before You Read

Mad

Connect to the Poem

Think about where you like to go when you want to be alone.

List Make a list of the places you have in mind. Then add a few words that describe or tell why you've chosen each place.

Build Background

Poets carefully and selectively use words to get across an idea or feeling. Their word choices can reveal the tone of a poem or help you understand its theme. A poet may use language that appeals to your senses to help you form pictures in your mind as you read. Although a poem may tell about something that happens in real life, it can still contain fantastic images.

Set Purposes for Reading

As you read, ask yourself, how do the speaker's feelings about her mother change throughout the poem?

Literary Element Symbol

A **symbol** is something concrete, such as an object, a person, a place, or an experience, that stands for more than just itself. Symbols usually represent something abstract, such as an idea or a thought. For example, a flag often stands for freedom, and a heart can stand for love.

Identifying symbols can help you unlock the meaning of a poem and understand ideas or concepts the poet wants to emphasize.

As you read, ask yourself, which words or phrases are symbols for something else?

GA Performance Standards

For pages 331–333

ELA6R1d For literary texts, apply knowledge of the concept that theme refers to the message about life and the world that the author wants us to understand.

Meet Naomi Shihab Nye

Naomi Shihab Nye began writing poems when she was only six. Her first poems were about trees, friends, animals, and her funny grandmother. As an adult, her poetry often draws inspiration from her experiences as an Arab American. Nye has written essays, many books of poetry, picture books, and a novel.

Naomi Shihab Nye was born in 1952.

Literature Online

Author Search For more about Naomi Shihab Nye, go to glencoe.com and enter QuickPass code GL17527u3.

Untitled, 1948. Jacqueline Lamba. Oil on canvas, 102 x 77 cm. Private Collection. © ARS, NY.

MAD

Naomi Shihab Nye

I got mad at my mother
so I flew to the moon.
I could still see our house
so little in the distance
with its pointed roof.
My mother stood in the front yard
like a pin dot
searching for me.
She looked left and right for me.
She looked deep and far.
Then I whistled and she tipped her head.
It gets cold at night on the moon.
My mother sent up a silver thread
for me to slide down on.
She knows me so well.
She knows I like silver.

Symbol What does the moon represent?

Symbol What do you think the silver thread stands for?

After You Read

Respond and Think Critically

1. From the moon, how does the house look to the speaker? **[Recall]**
2. Think about how the speaker reacts when she gets angry. Is it similar to or different from the way you usually react? Explain your answer. **[Connect]**
3. Why does the speaker describe her mother as "a pin dot"? **[Infer]**
4. Which lines tell you that the speaker and her mother are trying to make up with each other? **[Interpret]**
5. **Literary Element Symbol** How does the poet's choice of the moon as a symbol give deeper meaning to the poem? Why do you think so? **[Analyze]**
6. **BQ BIG Question** How would you describe the speaker's overall feelings about her mother? Support your answer. **[Conclude]**

TIP

Connecting
Here are some tips to help you make a connection to the poem. Remember, when you make a connection, you combine your experience and prior knowledge with the words on the page.

- Ask yourself what you know about the topic.
- Ask yourself whether you have read lines in the poem that describe how the speaker is acting or feeling.
- Ask yourself what experiences you have had that compare or contrast with what you have read.

Keep track of your ideas about the **BIG Question** in your unit Foldable.

Spelling Link

Rule for *ie* and *ei* Words with the letters *ie* and *ei* can cause spelling problems. In some cases, such as *yield,* the *i* comes first. In other cases, such as *weigh,* the *e* comes first. The following spelling rule is a rhyme that helps you remember which spelling to use.

Rule:	Examples:
Put *i* before *e* →	retrieve, grieve
except after *c* →	deceive, receive
or when sounded like *a* → as in *neighbor* and *weigh.*	eighty, veil

Exceptions: *species, weird, either, neither, seize, leisure*

Practice On a sheet of paper, list these words: *relieve, freight, receive, retrieve, achieve.* Next to each word, write the rule that explains why it is spelled with *ei* or *ie.*

Writing

Write a Blurb How would you tell someone else about this poem? Write a blurb—a short, informal description—about the poem that you could post on a poetry Web site. Briefly explain what the poem is about and your opinion of it. Be sure to include your purpose for writing and an appropriate closing, including your name.

Literature Online

Selection Resources
For Selection Quizzes, eFlashcards, and Reading-Writing Connection activities, go to glencoe.com and enter QuickPass code GL17527u3.

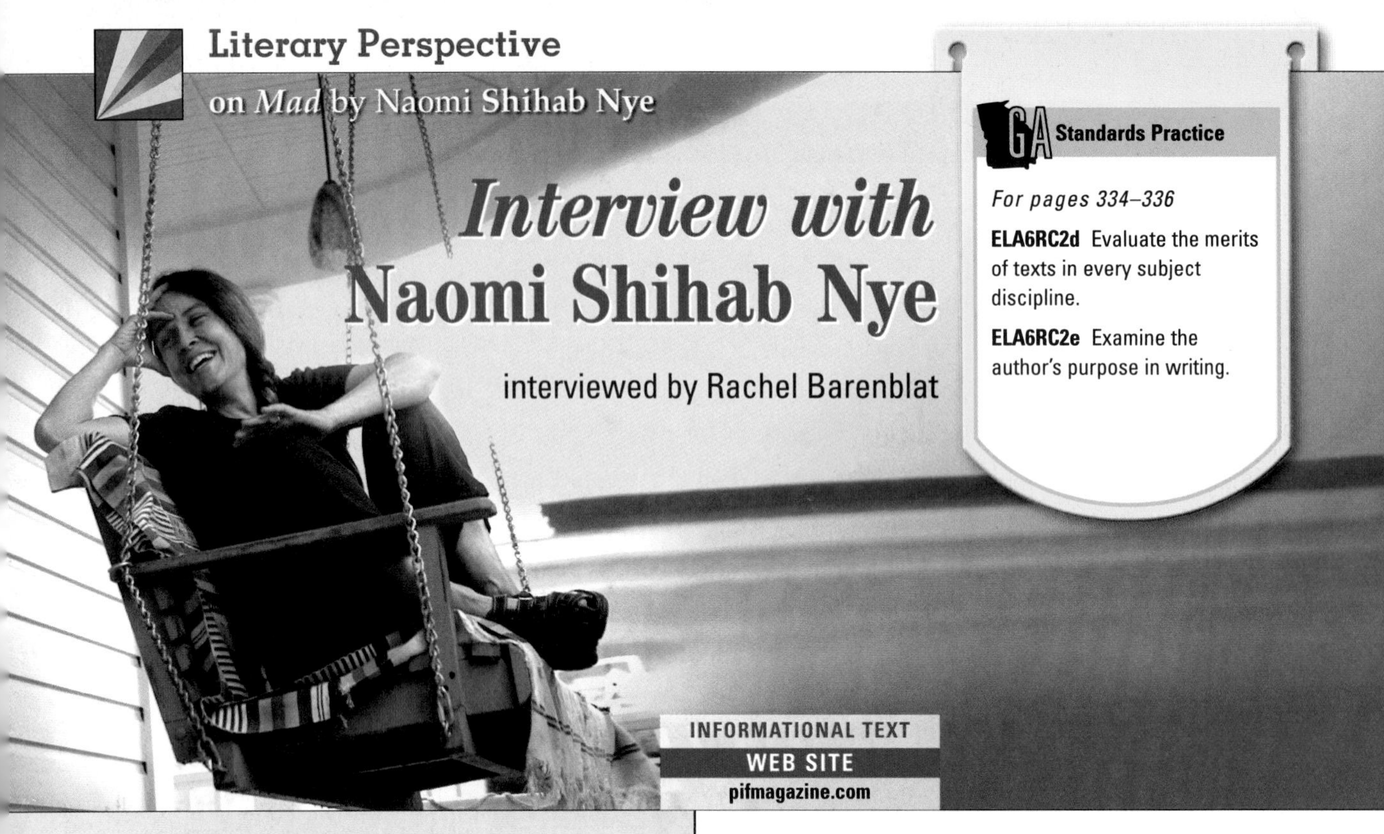

Interview with Naomi Shihab Nye

interviewed by Rachel Barenblat

Standards Practice

For pages 334–336

ELA6RC2d Evaluate the merits of texts in every subject discipline.

ELA6RC2e Examine the author's purpose in writing.

INFORMATIONAL TEXT
WEB SITE
pifmagazine.com

Set a Purpose for Reading

Read to learn Naomi Shihab Nye's beliefs about travel, home, reading, and writing.

Build Background

In this interview, Nye mentions living in many places with different cultures. However, her poem "Mad" has a theme that is common to all cultures—a girl who is angry with her mother.

Reading Skill Draw Conclusions About Author's Purpose

When you **draw conclusions about author's purpose,** you use details in a text to make a general statement about the author's goal. In this selection, the author (interviewer) wants to learn about Naomi Shihab Nye. As you read, use a two-column chart like the one below. Note the interviewer's questions and draw a conclusion about her purpose for asking each question.

Question	Purpose of Question

Rachel Barenblat: When did you start writing? Were you writing poems from the start?

Naomi Shihab Nye: I started writing when I was 6, immediately after learning HOW to write. Yes, I was writing poems from the start. Somehow—from hearing my mother read to me? from looking at books? from watching Carl Sandburg[1] on 1950s black-and-white TV?—I knew what a poem was. I liked the portable, comfortable shape of poems. I liked the space around them and the way you could hold your words at arm's length and look at them. And especially the way they took you to a deeper, quieter place, almost immediately.

1 ***Carl Sandburg*** (1878–1967) was one of America's most popular and successful poets. He frequently traveled throughout the United States, lecturing and reading his poems aloud. He also appeared on several television programs in the 1950s and 1960s.

"My heart will probably always belong to the Middle East..."

RB: What did you write about, in the beginning? What provided your first inspiration?

NSN: I wrote about all the little stuff a kid would write about: amazement over things, cats, wounded squirrels found in the street, my friend who moved away, trees, teachers, my funny grandma. At that time I wrote about my German grandma—I wouldn't meet my Palestinian grandma till I was 14.

RB: Place plays an important role in your writing, especially the places you have lived and the places that hold your roots. Tell me about the places that have been important to you.

NSN: The three main places I have lived—St. Louis, Jerusalem, San Antonio—are each deeply precious to me indeed, and I often find them weaving in and out of my writing. Each place has such distinctive neighborhoods and flavors. Gravity interests me—where we feel it, how we feel it.

RB: What about travel? How is writing about travel different from writing about home?

NSN: Sometimes while traveling in Mexico or India or any elsewhere, I feel that luminous[2] sense of being invisible as a traveler, having no long, historical ties, simply being a drifting eye—but after awhile, I grow tired of that feeling and want to be somewhere where the trees are my personal friends again.

RB: Where is your favorite place to travel?

NSN: My heart will probably always belong to the Middle East, travel-wise, but I have never been anywhere I disliked.

RB: Do you consider yourself a storyteller?

NSN: No, I don't consider myself a storyteller, per se.[3] I think of storytellers as being those fabulous people sitting on bales of hay at folk festivals. Truth is, I guess, we are all storytellers in different ways.

RB: Where do you usually write? Do you have a desk, an office, a favorite chair, a favorite tree?

NSN: I have a long wooden table where I write. Not a desk, really, as it doesn't have drawers. I wish it had drawers. I can write anywhere. Outside, of course, is always great. I am one of the few people I know who LOVES being in airports. Good thing. I can write and read well in them.

RB: What is your advice to writers, especially young writers who are just starting out?

NSN: Number one: Read, read, and then read some more. Always read. Find the voices that speak most to YOU. This is your pleasure and blessing, as well as responsibility!

---

2 ***Luminous*** means "full of light." Here, Nye is referring to a sense of clarity and wonder.

3 **Per se** is a Latin phrase that means "by or in itself." Nye is saying that she doesn't consider herself a storyteller by nature.

Respond and Think Critically

1. Summarize Nye's reasons for liking to write poems when she was young. For help on writing a summary, see page 170. **[Summarize]**
2. What does Nye mean when she says that after traveling she wants "to be somewhere where the trees are my personal friends again"? **[Interpret]**
3. Nye says that she is not a storyteller, because storytellers are "those fabulous people sitting on bales of hay at folk festivals." From this description, how do you think she sees herself and her poetry? **[Infer]**
4. **Text to Text** How is Nye's experience with traveling similar to that of the speaker in the poem "Mad"? **[Compare]**
5. **Reading Skill** **Draw Conclusions About Author's Purpose** What do you think is Barenblat's main purpose for interviewing Nye? Use the notes in your graphic organizer to help you answer this question.
6. **BQ** **BIG Question** Nye has lived, traveled, and written in different places. How do these experiences make her who she is?

Part 2

Dreams and Goals

Day Dreams, 1859. Thomas Couture. Oil on canvas. ©Walters Art Museum, Baltimore, MD.

BQ BIG Question **What Makes You Who You Are?**

Why does the boy in the painting *Day Dreams* look so thoughtful? How do your dreams and goals create an image of who you are?

Before You Read

I Dream a World and *Life Doesn't Frighten Me*

Connect to the Poems

Think about something that once frightened you but no longer does. What helped you overcome your fear? What would a perfect world be like?

Partner Talk With a partner, discuss some things that you would change if you could create an ideal world.

Build Background

During the early 1900s, large numbers of African Americans left the rural South and moved to northern cities. New York City's Harlem neighborhood became the center of a cultural movement known as the Harlem Renaissance. Langston Hughes was one of the movement's best-known writers.

Maya Angelou has named Langston Hughes as one of her favorite poets, along with Paul Laurence Dunbar, Countee Cullen, Georgia Douglas Johnson, Edgar Allan Poe, and William Shakespeare.

Set Purposes for Reading

BQ BIG Question

As you read the poems, ask yourself, what are the dreams and goals of each speaker?

Literary Element Rhyme

Rhyme is the repetition of identical or similar sounds of words that appear close to one another, such as *sing* and *ring* or *money* and *honey*. Rhyme that occurs at the ends of lines in a poem is called **end rhyme.** The pattern of rhyme formed by the end rhymes in a poem is called the **rhyme scheme.** To figure out the rhyme scheme, give each new end rhyme a different letter of the alphabet. For example, if the first four lines of a poem end with the words *star, far, high,* and *sky,* the rhyme scheme is *aabb.*

Rhyme adds to the musical quality of a poem and gives it a distinct character. It also makes the words easier to remember.

As you read the poems, ask yourself, how do the rhymes and rhyme scheme add to each poem's impact on the reader?

Performance Standards

For pages 337–343

ELA6R1h/i For literary texts, respond to and explain the effects of sound.

Meet the Authors

Langston Hughes

Langston Hughes is famous for his colorful portrayal of people and life in Harlem. He was born in 1902 and died in 1967.

Maya Angelou

Maya Angelou is a poet, educator, historian, playwright, actress, director, and civil rights activist. She was born in 1928.

Literature Online

Author Search For more about Langston Hughes and Maya Angelou, go to glencoe.com and enter QuickPass code GL17527u3.

I Dream a World

Langston Hughes

I dream a world where man
No other man will scorn,
Where love will bless the earth
And peace its paths adorn.
I dream a world where all
Will know sweet freedom's way,
Where greed no longer saps the soul
Nor avarice blights° our day.
A world I dream where black or white,
Whatever race you be,
Will share the bounties° of the earth
And every man is free,
Where wretchedness° will hang its head
And joy, like a pearl,
Attends the needs of all mankind —
Of such I dream, my world!

Rhyme What is the rhyme scheme of the first four lines?

BQ BIG Question

What might the poet have experienced to make him write this poem?

---

8 ***Avarice*** means "great desire for wealth or possessions; greed." **Blights** means "spoils or ruins."

11 **Bounties** are generous gifts.

13 ***Wretchedness*** is great unhappiness or discomfort.

Life Doesn't Frighten Me

Maya Angelou

Shadows on the wall
Noises down the hall
Life doesn't frighten me at all
Bad dogs barking loud
Big ghosts in a cloud
Life doesn't frighten me at all.

Mean old Mother Goose°
Lions on the loose
They don't frighten me at all
Dragons breathing flame
On my counterpane°
That doesn't frighten me at all

I go boo
Make them shoo
I make fun
Way they run
I won't cry
So they fly
I just smile
They go wild
Life doesn't frighten me at all.

Tough guys in a fight
All alone at night
Life doesn't frighten me at all.

Panthers in the park
Strangers in the dark
No, they don't frighten me at all.

Rhyme What is the rhyme scheme of the first stanza?

Rhyme How does the poem's rhyme scheme change in this stanza?

7 ***Mother Goose*** is said to be the author of many English nursery rhymes, although people are not sure where the name comes from.

11 A ***counterpane*** is a bedspread or quilt.

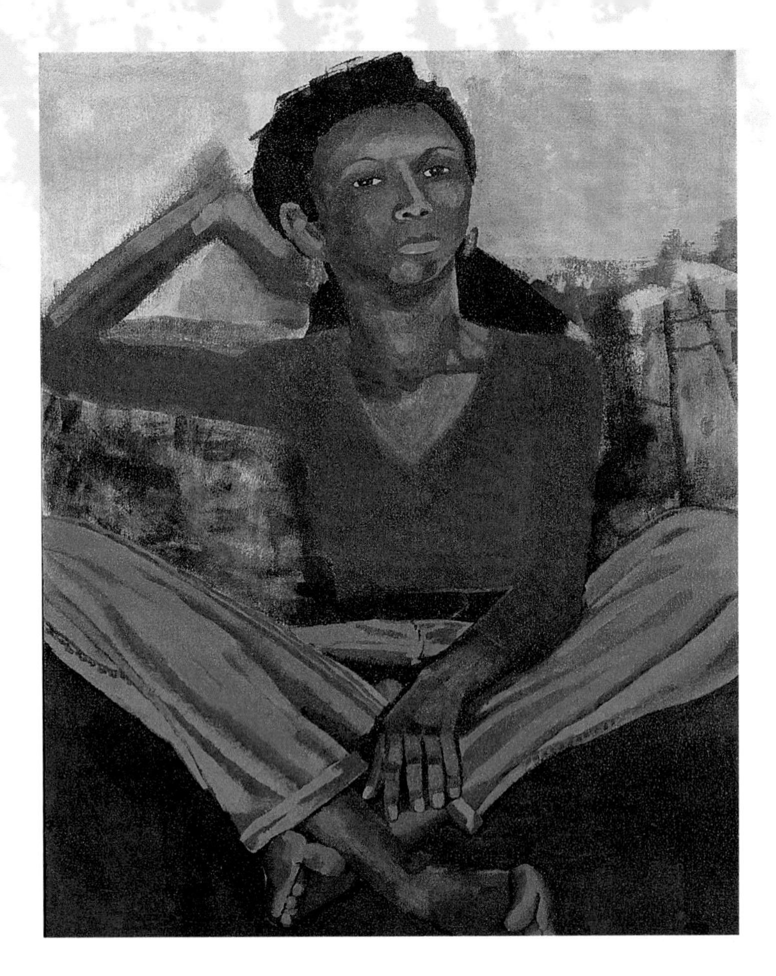

Fatima, 1994. Elizabeth Barakah Hodges. Acrylic, 12 x 20 in. Private Collection.

View the Art How would you describe this woman's expression and mood? Compare and contrast them with the personal qualities expressed by the speaker of the poem.

That new classroom where
Boys all pull my hair
(Kissy little girls
With their hair in curls)
They don't frighten me at all.

Don't show me frogs and snakes
And listen for my scream,
If I'm afraid at all
It's only in my dreams.

I've got a magic charm
That I keep up my sleeve,
I can walk the ocean floor
And never have to breathe.

Life doesn't frighten me at all
Not at all
Not at all.
Life doesn't frighten me at all.

Rhyme How do rhyme and rhyme scheme add to the mood of the poem?

BQ BIG Question

How does the speaker want to appear to others?

After You Read

Respond and Think Critically

1. What are three characteristics of the world the speaker dreams about in "I Dream a World"? **[Identify]**
2. According to the speaker in "Life Doesn't Frighten Me," when is the only time she is afraid? **[Recall]**
3. From the details the speaker mentions in "I Dream a World," how would you say that his real world differs from his dream? **[Infer]**
4. Give examples of realistic fears and imagined fears expressed in "Life Doesn't Frighten Me." Which worries do you think are worse, the realistic ones or the imagined ones? Explain. **[Compare]**
5. A refrain is a phrase or a line that is repeated throughout a poem. What is the refrain in "Life Doesn't Frighten Me"? Why do you think the poet chose to make this a refrain? **[Analyze]**
6. **BQ** **BIG Question** How does the way you respond to difficult or frightening situations help make you who you are? **[Conclude]**

Academic Vocabulary

In "I Dream a World," Langston Hughes is **contrasting** the way the world is with the way he wishes it could be.

To become more familiar with the word *contrasting,* fill out a graphic organizer like the one below.

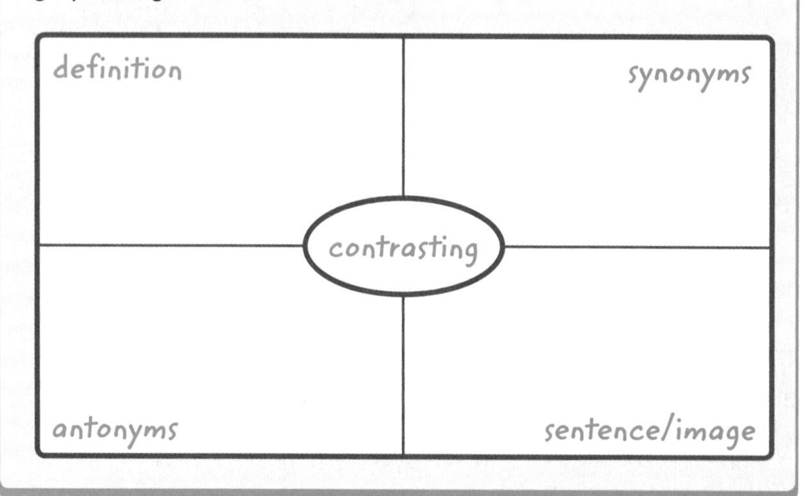

TIP

Inferring
When you infer, you figure out information that the author doesn't directly state by using clues in the text and your own knowledge and experience. Here are some tips to help you answer question 3.

- Look over the poem to find what the speaker says his dream world would be like.
- Compare the speaker's dream world with the world you know.
- How are these two worlds different?

Keep track of your ideas about the **BIG Question** in your unit Foldable.

LOG ON **Literature** Online

Selection Resources
For Selection Quizzes, eFlashcards, and Reading-Writing Connection activities, go to glencoe.com and enter QuickPass code GL17527u3.

Literary Element **Rhyme**

1. Which of the two poems has a more regular, or predictable, rhyme scheme? Support your answer with examples from the poems.
2. In "Life Doesn't Frighten Me," how does the poet's use of rhyme add to your understanding and enjoyment of the poem?

Review: **Alliteration and Assonance**

As you learned on page 309, **alliteration** is the repetition of consonant sounds, most often at the beginning of words and syllables. **Assonance** is the repetition of vowel sounds, especially in a line of poetry.

3. What are two examples of alliteration in "Life Doesn't Frighten Me"?
4. Find two examples of alliteration in "I Dream a World."
5. Find an example of assonance in stanza 6 of "Life Doesn't Frighten Me."

Grammar Link

Comparative and Superlative The **comparative** form of an adjective compares two things.

For one-syllable adjectives, form the comparative by adding the suffix *-er.* Add the word *more* or *less* before most adjectives with more than one syllable.

> The speaker of "Life Doesn't Frighten Me" is **braver** than I am.
>
> The real world is **less pleasant** than the world described in "I Dream a World."

The **superlative** form of an adjective compares more than two things.

For one-syllable adjectives, form the superlative by adding the suffix *-est.* Use the word *most* or *least* before most adjectives with more than one syllable.

> What is the **scariest** image in the poem "Life Doesn't Frighten Me"?
>
> Langston Hughes is the **most idealistic** poet I've read.

Practice Write two sentences about the poems you have just read. Use the comparative form of an adjective in one sentence and the superlative form of an adjective in the other.

Research and Report

Visual/Media Presentation Find some examples of pictures and music that relate to the theme of one of the poems you read. Present your examples to the class. If you have access to a computer, use it to help you display your examples. Otherwise, create your own display. Explain how the examples connect to the theme. Make sure to emphasize the most important points. Give credit to the creators of any material you use, and list the sources from which you drew your examples.

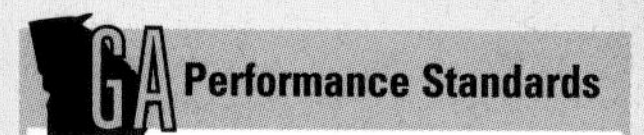

For pages 344–345

ELA6R1h/i/ii For literary texts, respond to and explain the effects of sound and figurative language.

Genre Focus: Poetry

A **poem** is a form of literature written in verse, or lines. Reading **poetry** is different from reading prose. A poet carefully chooses words not only for their meanings but for how the words look on the page, the way they sound, and how they relate to one another. Poets choose words that will appeal to readers' emotions, senses, and imaginations. Then they use these words to create effects of **sound** and **imagery.**

Haiku, free verse, sonnets, and odes are some forms of poetry.

Elements of Poetry

Structure Poetry is usually arranged in **lines.** A group of lines is called a **stanza.** Poems may have a regular **rhyme,** which is the repetition of similar sounds at the ends of lines. A **rhyme scheme** is the pattern formed by end rhymes. **Meter,** a regular pattern of stressed and unstressed syllables, gives a line of poetry a predictable **rhythm**, or pattern of beats.

Sound Poets may use sound devices to make a poem more vivid or to create a tone or mood. **Alliteration** is the repetition of consonant sounds at the beginnings of words. **Onomatopoeia** uses words that imitate or suggest the sound of what they describe, such as *hiss* or *thud.* Repeating consonant sounds in stressed syllables—such as *brick* and *clock*—is called **consonance**, and repeating vowel sounds is called **assonance.**

Imagery Poets use **imagery,** or "word pictures," to help readers visualize what they read. **Figurative language** communicates ideas beyond the literal meanings of words. For example, a **simile** uses *like* or *as* to compare seemingly unlike things. A **metaphor** implies the comparison instead of directly stating it. Poets use **personification** to write about an idea, an object, or an animal as if it were human. An **idiom** is an expression whose meaning cannot be understood by simply joining the meanings of the words, such as *I caught a cold.*

TRY IT

Using a web like the one on the next page, identify the elements of one poem in this unit.

Characteristics of the Genre

To better understand literary elements in poetry and how authors use literary elements to create effects and achieve their purposes, look at the examples in the web below.

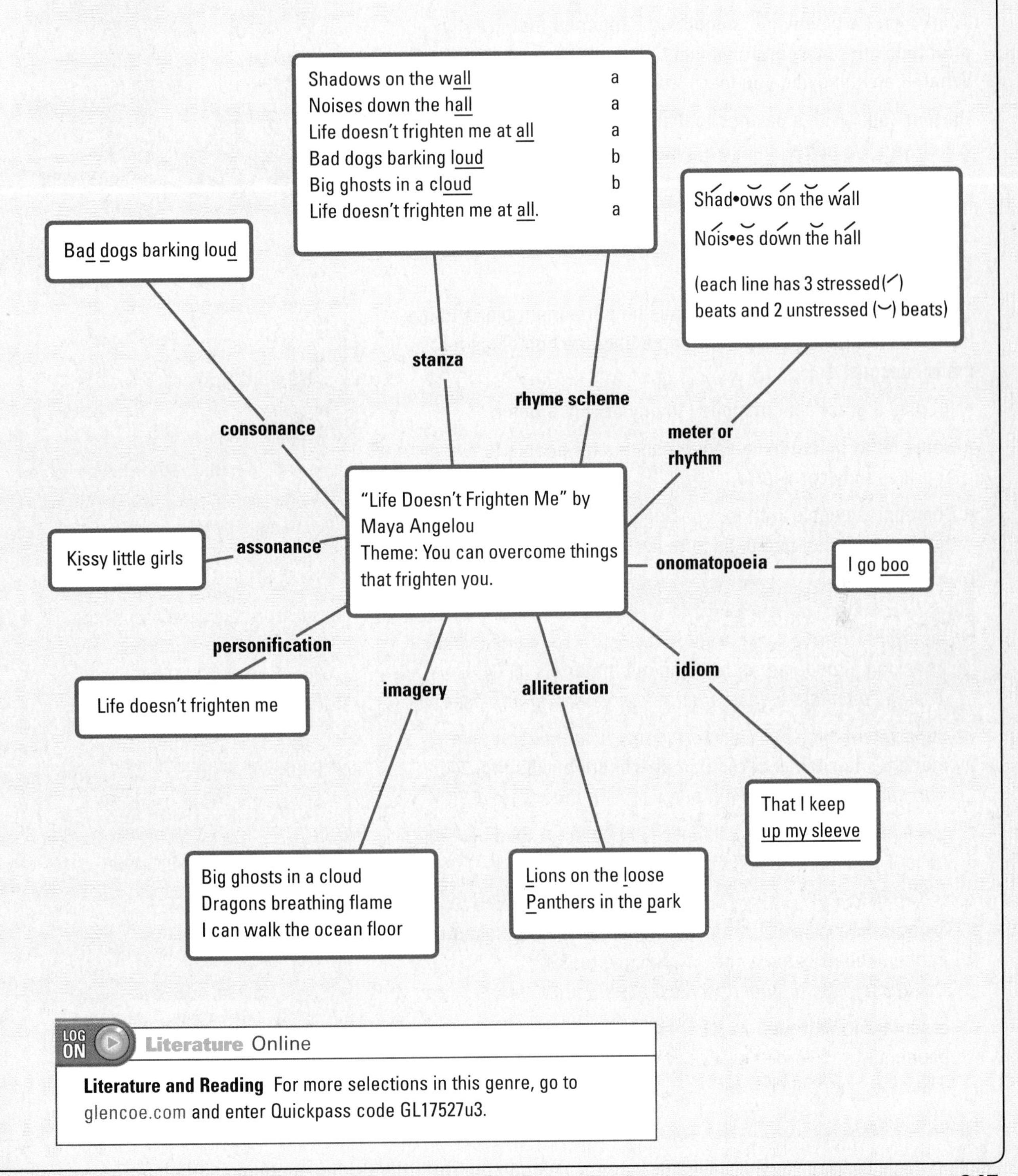

Shadows on the wall a
Noises down the hall a
Life doesn't frighten me at all a
Bad dogs barking loud b
Big ghosts in a cloud b
Life doesn't frighten me at all. a
Bad dogs barking loud
Shad•ows on the wall
Nois•es down the hall
(each line has 3 stressed beats and 2 unstressed beats)
stanza
rhyme scheme
consonance
meter or rhythm
"Life Doesn't Frighten Me" by Maya Angelou
Theme: You can overcome things that frighten you.
Kissy little girls
assonance
onomatopoeia
I go boo
personification
idiom
Life doesn't frighten me
imagery
alliteration
That I keep up my sleeve
Big ghosts in a cloud
Dragons breathing flame
I can walk the ocean floor
Lions on the loose
Panthers in the park

LOG ON Literature Online

Literature and Reading For more selections in this genre, go to glencoe.com and enter Quickpass code GL17527u3.

Before You Read

Geraldine Moore the Poet

Connect to the Story

Think about a time when something happened that greatly affected your family or community. How did you react at the time? What, if anything, did you learn from the experience?

Partner Talk With a partner, talk about how the community in which you live helps make you who you are. You might discuss some ways that your friends, neighbors, teachers, or family members have affected you.

Build Background

The number of Americans who have no permanent place to live has risen in the last 25 years. People become homeless for many reasons.

- It costs a great deal of money to buy or rent a home.
- Some cities do not have enough homes for people to buy or rent at prices they can afford.
- Sometimes people with low-paying jobs, or people who lose their jobs, cannot find a place to live.

Vocabulary

monitors (mon′ ə tərz) *n.* students with a special duty, such as taking attendance or handing out materials (p. 349).
The hall monitors helped other students find their classes.

superintendent (so͞o′ prin ten′ dənt) *n.* the person who manages and takes care of an apartment building (p. 349).
The superintendent did not allow pets in the building.

cylinders (sil′ ən dərz) *n.* long, round objects, solid or hollow, with flat ends, such as soup cans (p. 350).
Common cylinders include soda cans, pencils, and candles.

formula (fôr′ myə lə) *n.* a combination of symbols used in mathematics to state a rule or principle (p. 350).
David used the formula to solve the math problems.

manufacturing (man′ yə fak′ chər ing) *v.* making products, especially on a large scale or with machinery (p. 351).
The new company in town is manufacturing car parts.

Meet Toni Cade Bambara

"I work to tell the truth about people's lives. I work to celebrate struggle."
—Toni Cade Bambara

A Social Activist Toni Cade Bambara grew up in and near New York City. She was an author, a college professor, and a civil rights activist who worked to help her community. Many characters in Toni Cade Bambara's stories are women who get strength by seeking justice and telling their stories. Toni Cade added "Bambara" to her name after she found the name on a sketchbook in her great-grandmother's trunk.

Literary Works Bambara wrote screenplays, novels, and short stories, including "Raymond's Run."

Toni Cade Bambara was born in 1939 and died in 1995.

Literature Online

Author Search For more about Toni Cade Bambara, go to glencoe.com and enter QuickPass code GL17527u3.

Set Purposes for Reading

BQ BIG Question

As you read, ask yourself, how do Geraldine's experiences help make her who she is?

Literary Element Characterization

Characterization is the way a writer develops the personality of a character. A writer brings a character to life

- through the character's words, actions, thoughts, and feelings
- through what other characters think or say about the character
- by directly stating what the character is like

Characterization helps you understand characters and their actions. When you feel you know the characters, you can appreciate how they react to situations and feel a deeper connection to the story.

As you read, think about how the characters' traits influence their choices and the plot, conflict, and resolution of the story.

Reading Strategy Make Inferences About Characters

Sometimes people don't say what they are thinking. The same can be true of characters in a story. When you **make inferences,** you use clues to figure out something the author does not directly tell you. When you **make inferences about characters,** you make guesses about what characters think and feel.

Making inferences helps you understand characters. You many need to infer to determine the characters' deepest feelings and desires, which can be an important part of the story.

To **make inferences about a character,** think about

- what the character says and does
- how other characters react to the character
- what you know about people in general

Then think about *why* a character says or does something. You may find it helpful to use a graphic organizer like the one below.

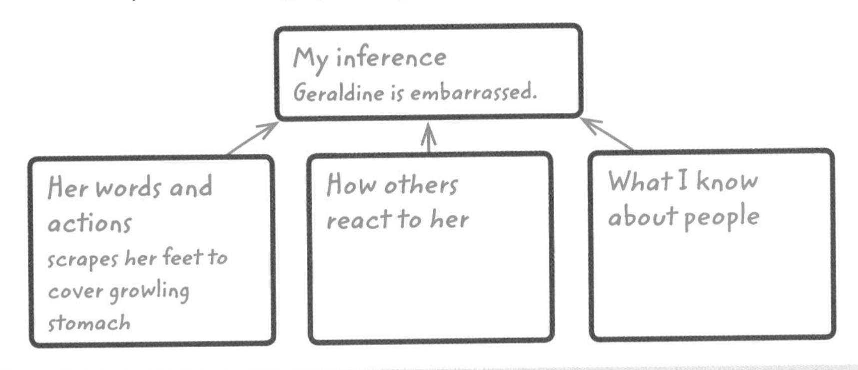

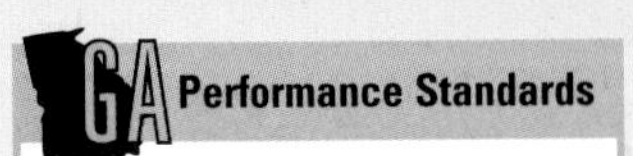

For pages 346–355

ELA6R1b For literary texts, identify and analyze the author's use of dialogue and description.

TRY IT

Make Inferences About Characters Your friends are getting ready for a guest's visit. The guest can't stand animals, so your friends must give their cat to a neighbor for the week. The guest won't eat anything they have in the kitchen, and she asks them to move the furniture. What can you **infer** about the guest?

Geraldine Moore the Poet

Toni Cade Bambara

The Reader #1, 1999. Diana Ong.

Geraldine paused at the corner to pull up her knee socks. The rubber bands she was using to hold them up made her legs itch. She dropped her books on the sidewalk while she gave a good scratch. But when she pulled the socks up again, two fingers poked right through the top of her left one.

Characterization What impression does this description give you of Geraldine?

"That stupid dog," she muttered to herself, grabbing at her books and crossing against traffic. "First he chews up my gym suit and gets me into trouble, and now my socks."

Geraldine shifted her books to the other hand and kept muttering angrily to herself about Mrs. Watson's dog, which she minded two days a week for a dollar. She passed the hot-dog man on the corner and waved. He shrugged as if to say business was very bad.

Must be, she thought to herself. *Three guys before you had to pack up and forget it. Nobody's got hot-dog money around here.*

Geraldine turned down her street, wondering what her sister Anita would have for her lunch. She was glad she didn't have to eat the free lunches in high school any more. She was sick of the funny-looking tomato soup and the dried-out cheese sandwiches and those oranges that were more green than orange.

When Geraldine's mother first took sick and went away, Geraldine had been on her own except when Miss Gladys next door came in on Thursdays and cleaned the apartment and made a meat loaf so Geraldine could have dinner. But in those days Geraldine never quite managed to get breakfast for herself. So she'd sit through social studies class, scraping her feet to cover up the noise of her stomach growling.

Make Inferences About Characters Why do you think Geraldine tries to hide the growling of her stomach?

Now Anita, Geraldine's older sister, was living at home waiting for her husband to get out of the Army. She usually had something good for lunch—chicken and dumplings if she managed to get up in time, or baked ham from the night before and sweet-potato bread. But even if there was only a hot dog and some baked beans—sometimes just a TV dinner if those soap operas[1] kept Anita glued to the TV set—anything was better than the noisy school lunchroom where **monitors** kept pushing you into a straight line or rushing you to the tables. Anything was better than that.

Visual Vocabulary

A **stoop** is a porch, a stairway entrance, or a small platform at the door of a house or an apartment building.

Geraldine was almost home when she stopped dead. Right outside her building was a pile of furniture and some boxes. That wasn't anything new. She had seen people get put out in the street before, but this time the ironing board looked familiar. And she recognized the big, ugly sofa standing on its arm, its under-belly showing the hole where Mrs. Watson's dog had gotten to it.

Miss Gladys was sitting on the **stoop**, and she looked up and took off her glasses. "Well, Gerry," she said slowly, wiping her glasses on the hem of her dress, "looks like you'll be staying with me for a while." She looked at the men carrying out a big box with an old doll sticking up over the edge. "Anita's upstairs. Go on up and get your lunch."

Characterization What does this reaction tell you about Miss Gladys?

Geraldine stepped past the old woman and almost bumped into the **superintendent**. He took off his cap to wipe away the sweat.

"Darn shame," he said to no one in particular. "Poor people sure got a hard row to hoe."

---

1 ***Soap operas*** are continuing stories on daytime television. They usually involve very dramatic situations.

Vocabulary

monitors (mon′ ə tərz) *n.* students with a special duty, such as taking attendance or handing out materials

superintendent (so͞o′ prin ten′ dənt) *n.* the person who manages and takes care of an apartment building

"That's the truth," said Miss Gladys, standing up with her hands on her hips to watch the men set things on the sidewalk.

Upstairs, Geraldine went into the apartment and found Anita in the kitchen.

"I dunno, Gerry," Anita said. "I just don't know what we're going to do. But everything's going to be all right soon as Ma gets well." Anita's voice cracked as she set a bowl of soup before Geraldine.

Make Inferences About Characters How do you think Anita feels about the responsibilities she has while her mother is gone?

"What's this?" Geraldine said.

"It's tomato soup, Gerry."

Geraldine was about to say something. But when she looked up at her big sister, she saw how Anita's face was getting all twisted as she began to cry.

That afternoon, Mr. Stern, the geometry teacher, started drawing cubes and **cylinders** on the board. Geraldine sat at her desk adding up a column of figures in her notebook—the rent, the light and gas bills, a new gym suit, some socks. Maybe they would move somewhere else, and she could have her own room. Geraldine turned the squares and triangles into little houses in the country.

"For your homework," Mr. Stern was saying with his back to the class, "set up your problems this way." He wrote GIVEN: in large letters, and then gave the **formula** for the first problem. Then he wrote TO FIND: and listed three items they were to include in their answers.

Geraldine started to raise her hand to ask what all these squares and angles had to do with solving real problems, like the ones she had. Better not, she warned herself, and sat on her hands. *Your big mouth got you in trouble last term.*

BQ BIG Question

What do you think makes Geraldine so outspoken?

In hygiene class,[2] Mrs. Potter kept saying that the body was a wonderful machine. Every time Geraldine looked up

2 A ***hygiene class*** is the same as a health class. Students learn how to get healthy and stay healthy.

Vocabulary

cylinders (sil′ən dərz) *n.* long, round objects, solid or hollow, with flat ends, such as soup cans

formula (fôr′myə lə) *n.* a combination of symbols used in mathematics to state a rule or principle

Chicago, Illinois: Public Art, 1978. Franklin McMahon. Polymer painting.

from her notebook, she would hear the same thing. "Right now your body is **manufacturing** all the proteins and tissues and energy you will need to get through tomorrow."

And Geraldine kept wondering, *How? How does my body know what it will need, when I don't even know what I'll need to get through tomorrow?*

As she headed down the hall to her next class, Geraldine remembered that she hadn't done the homework for English. Mrs. Scott had said to write a poem, and Geraldine had meant to do it at lunchtime. After all, there was nothing to it—a flower here, a raindrop there, moon, June, rose, nose. But the men carrying off the furniture had made her forget.

"And now put away your books," Mrs. Scott was saying as Geraldine tried to scribble a poem quickly. "Today we can give King Arthur's knights a rest. Let's talk about poetry."

Mrs. Scott moved up and down the aisles, talking about her favorite poems and reciting a line now and then. She got very excited whenever she passed a desk and could pick up the homework from a student who had remembered to do the assignment.

View the Art What feeling do you get when you look at this painting? Is it similar to the feeling you get from reading this story?

Characterization How does the author reveal Geraldine's view of writing poetry?

Vocabulary

manufacturing (man′ yə fak′ chər ing) *v.* making products, especially on a large scale or with machinery

"A poem is your own special way of saying what you feel and what you see," Mrs. Scott went on, her lips moist. It was her favorite subject.

"Some poets write about the light that . . . that . . . makes the world sunny," she said, passing Geraldine's desk. "Sometimes an idea takes the form of a picture—an image."

For almost half an hour, Mrs. Scott stood at the front of the room, reading poems and talking about the lives of the great poets. Geraldine drew more houses, and designs for curtains.

"So for those who haven't done their homework, try it now," Mrs. Scott said. "Try expressing what it is like to be . . . to be alive in this . . . this glorious world."

Characterization What might this say about Mrs. Scott's outlook on life? How is it different from Geraldine's?

"Oh, brother," Geraldine muttered to herself as Mrs. Scott moved up and down the aisles again, waving her hands and leaning over the students' shoulders and saying, "That's nice," or "Keep trying." Finally she came to Geraldine's desk and stopped, looking down at her.

"I can't write a poem," Geraldine said flatly, before she even realized she was going to speak at all. She said it very loudly, and the whole class looked up.

"And why not?" Mrs. Scott asked, looking hurt.

"I can't write a poem, Mrs. Scott, because nothing lovely's been happening in my life. I haven't seen a flower since Mother's Day, and the sun don't even shine on my side of the street. No robins come sing on my window sill."

Geraldine swallowed hard. She thought about saying that her father doesn't even come to visit any more, but changed her mind. "Just the rain comes," she went on, "and the bills come, and the men to move out our furniture. I'm sorry, but I can't write no pretty poem."

BQ BIG Question
What about Geraldine's life makes her feel like she can't write a pretty poem?

Teddy Johnson leaned over and was about to giggle and crack the whole class up, but Mrs. Scott looked so serious that he changed his mind.

"You have just said the most . . . the most poetic thing, Geraldine Moore," said Mrs. Scott. Her hands flew up to touch the silk scarf around her neck. "'Nothing lovely's been happening in my life.'" She repeated it so quietly that everyone had to lean forward to hear.

Portrait in Orange, Diana Ong.

"Class," Mrs. Scott said very sadly, clearing her throat, "you have just heard the best poem you will ever hear." She went to the board and stood there for a long time staring at the chalk in her hand.

"I'd like you to copy it down," she said. She wrote it just as Geraldine had said it, bad grammar and all.

Nothing lovely's been happening in my life.
I haven't seen a flower since Mother's Day,
And the sun don't even shine on my side of the street.
No robins come sing on my window sill.
Just the rain comes, and the bills come,
And the men to move out our furniture.
I'm sorry, but I can't write no pretty poem.

Mrs. Scott stopped writing, but she kept her back to the class for a long time—long after Geraldine had closed her notebook.

And even when the bell rang, and everyone came over to smile at Geraldine or to tap her on the shoulder or to kid her about being the school poet, Geraldine waited for Mrs. Scott to put the chalk down and turn around. Finally Geraldine stacked up her books and started to leave. Then she thought she heard a whimper—the way Mrs. Watson's dog whimpered sometimes—and she saw Mrs. Scott's shoulders shake a little. ❧

Make Inferences About Characters How does Mrs. Scott feel? What details help you infer this?

After You Read

Respond and Think Critically

1. Who is taking care of Geraldine? **[Recall]**
2. What happens when Geraldine goes home for lunch? **[Summarize]**
3. Geraldine says she "can't write no pretty poem." Why does Mrs. Scott say Geraldine's statements are poetic? **[Analyze]**
4. By telling Geraldine's story, what might the author be saying about people and problems in general? **[Interpret]**
5. Geraldine is sometimes angry about her life. Does she have a right to be angry? Explain your answer. **[Evaluate]**
6. **BQ** **BIG Question** Describe one experience in Geraldine's life and how it helped make her the person she is. Why do you think the experience affected her this way? **[Conclude]**

TIP

Summarizing
To help you answer question 2, remember that **summarizing** means restating the key points in your own words. Ask yourself,

- What is most important about Geraldine's lunchtime visit home?
- What other events happen in the story?
- What causes these events?

Keep track of your ideas about the **BIG Question** in your unit Foldable.

You're the Critic

What Is Most Important in Bambara's Stories?

Read these two excerpts of literary criticism. Together, these comments will give you more insight into "Geraldine Moore the Poet."

"Bambara's children arguably have essential lessons to teach their elders, if they listen well."

—Elizabeth Muther

Bambara's "insertion of themes related to the desires of Black women and girls disrupts . . . the stories' primary focus on classic realism."

—Elliott Butler-Evans

Group Activity Discuss the following questions with your classmates. Refer to the excerpts and give examples from "Geraldine Moore the Poet" to support your answers.

1. Do you agree with Muther that in this story Geraldine has essential lessons to teach adults? Explain.
2. What does Butler-Evans think Bambara's stories are mainly about? Do you agree with his opinion? Explain, giving examples from the story.
3. Which element of "Geraldine Moore the Poet" did you find more memorable—the characters or the realistic details? Why?

Literary Element Characterization

Standards Practice  ELA6R1b

1. Which words best describe Mrs. Scott?
   A. critical and discouraging
   B. confused and unclear
   C. thoughtless and uncaring
   D. open-minded and encouraging

Review: Conflict

As you learned on page 249, **conflict** is the struggle between two forces in a story. **External conflict** is when a character struggles against an outside force, such as another person, nature, or fate. **Internal conflict** occurs within the mind of a character. The character might be torn between two different feelings or goals.

Standards Practice  ELA6R1e/i

2. Which sentence gives the best description of how Geraldine handles external conflicts?
   A. She is easily distracted.
   B. She tries to be positive but doesn't always succeed.
   C. She criticizes those around her.
   D. She is unaware of the conflicts she faces.

Reading Strategy
Make Inferences About Characters

3. Looking over what Geraldine and Anita say and do, which sister do you think has better survival skills? Why do you think so? Use a graphic organizer like the one on page 347 to help make your inference and then support it.
4. What can you infer about Geraldine's family life from what she says about her mother and father?
5. Think about how Mrs. Scott acts in the classroom and the way she reacts to Geraldine's reasons for not writing a poem. What can you infer about her life?

Vocabulary Practice

Respond to these questions.

1. Which action is an example of **manufacturing**—making bottles or planting trees?
2. Which task might be performed by **monitors**—selling hot dogs or setting up desks in a classroom?
3. What might a **superintendent** do at work—drive a bus or fix a leaky faucet?
4. When would a **formula** be helpful—when doing a math assignment or when reading for pleasure?
5. Which objects resemble **cylinders**—apples or pieces of chalk?

Academic Vocabulary

Mr. Stern is the math **instructor** at Geraldine's school.

Instructor means the same thing as *teacher*.

Fill in the blanks in the sentence below based on the story.

_________ is the English instructor at Geraldine's school, and she teaches the students about _________.

Literature Online

Selection Resources For Selection Quizzes, eFlashcards, and Reading-Writing Connection activities, go to glencoe.com and enter QuickPass code GL17527u3.

Respond Through Writing

Short Story

Apply Characterization In "Geraldine Moore the Poet," Toni Cade Bambara creates memorable characters. Now it is your turn to write a short story, using **characterization** to bring the people in your story to life.

Understand the Task You have learned that writers bring **characters** to life by describing them and by letting them speak for themselves. Include vivid **sensory details** and **dialogue** in your story to show your characters' personalities and experiences. Your story should also have a **plot**. Remember that **conflict** is the most important part of the plot. Plot and conflict often grow from characters. If a character wants something but cannot have it, you have the beginning of a plot.

Prewrite First, decide what your story will be about. Imagine the characters. Think about what makes each one unique. Use a chart like the one below to keep track of them.

Character	Traits
Molly	short brown hair, likes basketball

Draft Before you begin writing, plan your story. Outline the main events of the plot. Pay attention to how you will begin and end your story. Think about the setting. Does the story happen in one place, or does it move from one setting to another?

Revise Read over your first draft. Think about anything you want to change. Does your story make sense? Are the characters developed? Ask a classmate to review your draft and provide feedback. Make changes as necessary.

Edit and Proofread Proofread your story, correcting errors in spelling, grammar, and punctuation. Review the Grammar Tip in the side column for information on quotation marks.

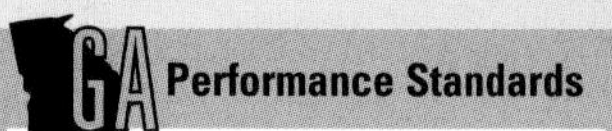

Performance Standards

For page 356

ELA6W2c Demonstrate competence in a variety of genres. Produce a narrative that includes sensory details and concrete language to develop plot, setting, and character.

Grammar Tip

Quotation Marks

When an author provides the exact words of a speaker, the author is using a **quotation.** Quotations are easy to spot, because **quotation marks** appear at the beginning and the end of the speaker's statement.

The following tips will help you write quotations.

- Use quotation marks before and after the speaker's exact words. Example: "I feel fine," said Joshua.
- When the quotation is a complete sentence, always capitalize the first letter of the first word. Example: "**H**e's my friend," she said.
- If a quotation is interrupted to identify the speaker, do *not* capitalize the first word of the second part of the sentence. Example: "She was," explained Kate, "**a** great teacher."

Before You Read

What I can do—I will— and *Fame is a bee*

For pages 357–359

ELA6R1h/ii For literary texts, respond to and explain the effects of figurative language.

Connect to the Poems

Think about something in nature that reminds you of something about yourself.

Partner Talk With a partner, talk about something in nature that reflects who you are. Discuss how it represents you.

Build Background

These two Emily Dickinson poems focus on images or ideas from nature.

- Dickinson frequently uses a punctuation mark that looks like a long dash. It signals the reader to take a long pause before continuing, which affects the rhythm of the poem and adds weight to the ideas.
- The poems are written in Dickinson's customary four-line stanzas. Both have end rhyme, or rhyme that occurs at the end of each line.

Set Purposes for Reading

BQ BIG Question

As you read, ask yourself, how do these poems reflect the way the world around Emily Dickinson shaped her life?

Literary Element Metaphor and Simile

Poets often use **figurative language** to express ideas beyond the literal meanings of words. Figurative language includes figures of speech, or expressions in which words are used in a different way than usual, to add beauty or force. A **metaphor** is a figure of speech that implies a comparison between seemingly unlike things, such as "My love *is* a rose." A **simile** uses *like* or *as* to compare seemingly unlike things. An example is "My love is *like* a rose."

It is important to pay attention to **metaphors** and **similes,** because they often express a poet's key ideas.

As you read, ask yourself, what is being compared in each poem?

Meet Emily Dickinson

Emily Dickinson is considered one of the great American poets, yet she published only a few poems during her lifetime. After Dickinson's death, her sister found more than 1,700 of Dickinson's poems hidden in a drawer and had them published.

Emily Dickinson was born in 1830 and died in 1886.

LOG ON Literature Online

Author Search For more about Emily Dickinson, go to glencoe.com and enter QuickPass code GL17527u3.

What I can do — I will —

Emily Dickinson

What I can do — I will —
Though it be little as a Daffodil —
That I cannot — must be
Unknown to possibility —

BQ BIG Question
What does the poet seem to be saying about goals?

Tropaioleum Speciosum, c. 1900. Katherine Cameron. Watercolor on paper. Private Collection.

Fame is a bee

Emily Dickinson

Fame is a bee.
  It has a song —
It has a sting —
  Ah, too, it has a wing.

Metaphor and Simile Why does the speaker compare fame to a bee?

After You Read

Respond and Think Critically

1. In the two poems, what objects in nature does the poet use to make comparisons? **[Identify]**
2. Paraphrase the last two lines of "What I can do — I will —." **[Paraphrase]**
3. What does the poet mean when she says that fame has a song, a sting, and a wing? **[Interpret]**
4. Why do you think the poet compares her effort to a daffodil instead of something else? **[Infer]**
5. **Literary Element** **Metaphor and Simile** How do metaphors and similes affect the meaning of each poem? Would the poems be as effective without them? Explain your answer. **[Evaluate]**
6. **BQ** **BIG Question** What does the poet seem to be saying about dreams and goals in these poems? **[Conclude]**

TIP

Interpreting

To answer question 3, ask yourself these questions:

- How does a bee's song sound?
- How does a bee's sting feel?
- What does having wings allow a bee to do?

Keep track of your ideas about the **BIG Question** in your unit Foldable.

Spelling Link

Suffixes and the Final *e* or the Final *y* Many words in English end in a silent *e*. Keep the *e* when adding a suffix that begins with a consonant: *time* + *ly* = *timely*. Drop the silent *e* when adding a suffix that begins with a vowel or *y*: *hide* + *ing* = *hiding*, *noise* + *y* = *noisy*. For a word ending in *le*, drop the *le* before adding the suffix *-ly*: *gentle* + *ly* = *gently*.

When you add a suffix to a word that ends in a final *y*, keep the *y*: *enjoy* + *ment* = *enjoyment*. For a word ending with a consonant + *y*, change the *y* to *i* unless the suffix begins with *i*. Keep the *y* to avoid having two *i's* together: *happy* + *ness* = *happiness*, *carry* + *ing* = *carrying*.

Practice On a sheet of paper, write the new word that is formed after the suffix is added:

simple + **ly** =

hurry + **ing** =

bake + **ing** =

silly + **ness** =

Writing

Write a Stanza If you could share one idea in a poem about pursuing your dreams, what would it be? Write a stanza of poetry that includes a metaphor or simile to express a key idea. If you create a simile, remember to use *like* or *as*.

Literature Online

Selection Resources
For Selection Quizzes, eFlashcards, and Reading-Writing Connection activities, go to glencoe.com and enter QuickPass code GL17527u3.

Before You Read

Wings

Connect to the Myth

Think about a time when you had to depend on your own resourcefulness to address a challenge.

Partner Talk With a partner, talk about how you coped with a new or difficult situation in a capable or skillful way.

Build Background

"Wings" tells the story of Daedalus (ded′əl əs). His name means "skillfully made." When the Greeks did not know who had built a structure, they gave the credit to Daedalus. The story begins in ancient Greece and then moves to Crete and Sicily. Recent archaeological excavations suggest that Daedalus was a real person. The story, though, is a myth, which is a traditional tale that may include gods, goddesses, heroes, and supernatural events. Myths often reflect a cultural group's beliefs and values.

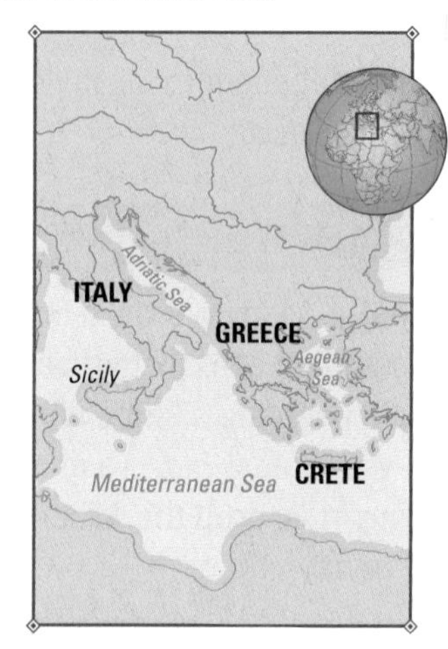

Vocabulary

exile (eg′ zīl) *n.* a person who is forced to leave his or her country or home (p. 364).
After war destroyed his homeland, Ivo lived as an exile.

devised (di vīzd′) *v.* thought out; invented; planned (p. 364).
Maria devised a clever way for the basketball team to raise money.

meager (mē′ gər) *adj.* scarcely enough; insufficient (p. 368).
With my meager allowance, I can't afford to go to the movies every week.

realm (relm) *n.* kingdom (p. 370).
The king promised justice to all who lived in his realm.

enraged (en rājd′) *adj.* greatly angered (p. 371).
An enraged bull charged the cowboy.

Meet Jane Yolen

"I think the worst thing in the world is the child who grows up without any connection to folk tradition. This is our connection with our history, and with human mystery too. These are the stories that carry the morality of generations."

—Jane Yolen

Inspired by Folk Culture Jane Yolen enjoys telling old stories that highlight modern problems. She heads Jane Yolen Books, which publishes science fiction and fantasy for young people.

Literary Works Jane Yolen has written more than one hundred books, including nonfiction and poetry, but she is especially known for her original fairy tales.

Jane Yolen was born in 1939.

Literature Online

Author Search For more about Jane Yolen, go to glencoe.com and enter QuickPass code GL17527u3.

Set Purposes for Reading

BQ BIG Question

As you read, ask yourself, what traits help Daedalus obtain his goals and dreams? Which traits get in his way?

Literary Element Foreshadowing

Foreshadowing is an author's use of hints or clues to prepare readers for events that will happen later in a story. For example, if a character in a story is warned by a friend not to climb in a rocky area alone but ignores the advice and has an accident, the warning foreshadows the accident.

Recognizing foreshadowing helps you predict what might happen. It builds suspense and keeps you engaged in the story.

As you read, look for details that may foreshadow a later event. Think about how the foreshadowing could affect the plot.

Reading Strategy Make Predictions About Plot

When you **make predictions about plot,** you make educated guesses about story events and outcomes. You base these predictions on information you have gathered in the text and your own knowledge.

Making predictions keeps you thinking while you read and can lead to a greater understanding of the story.

To make predictions about plot,

- use your prior knowledge to predict something that might happen next
- adjust your prediction as you read
- verify your prediction

As you read, you may find it helpful to use a graphic organizer like the one below.

Story details + What I know	Prediction	What actually happens
Daedalus designs a maze.	Theseus will get lost.	

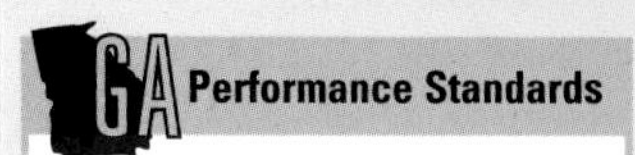

GA Performance Standards

For pages 360–373

ELA6R1j For literary texts, identify and analyze similarities and differences in mythologies from different cultures.

TRY IT

Make Predictions About Plot
Josh is the star football player at school and likes everyone to know it. A new student joins the team, and he outperforms Josh in their first practice. What do you think will happen next?

Wings

Jane Yolen

Ocean Birds, Gerrit Greve.

Once in ancient Greece, when the gods dwelt[1] on a high mountain overseeing the world, there lived a man named Daedalus who was known for the things he made.

He invented the axe, the bevel, and the awl.[2] He built statues that were so lifelike they seemed ready to move. He designed a maze[3] whose winding passages opened one into another as if without beginning, as if without end.

But Daedalus never understood the **labyrinth** *of his own heart. He was clever but he was not always kind. He was full of pride but he did not give others praise. He was a maker—but he was a taker, too.*

The gods always punish such a man.

Visual Vocabulary

A **labyrinth** (lab′ə rinth′) is a maze—a set of winding, interconnected passages in which it is easy to get lost.

Foreshadowing What does the warning foretell?

Athens[4] was the queen of cities and she had her princes.

---

1 ***Dwelt*** means "lived or resided."

2 A ***bevel*** is a tool for measuring and marking angles. An ***awl*** is a pointed tool used to make small holes or designs in materials.

3 A ***maze*** is an intricate, confusing network of paths or passageways, through which it is difficult to find one's way.

4 ***Athens*** is a city in Greece. In ancient times it was the cultural center of the Mediterranean region.

Daedalus was one. He was a prince and he was an artist, and he was proud of being both.

The very elements[5] were his friends, and the people of Athens praised him.

"The gods will love you forever, Daedalus," they cried out to him as he walked through the city streets.

The gods listened and did not like to be told what to do.

A man who hears only praise becomes deaf. A man who sees no rival to his art becomes blind. Though he grew rich and he grew famous in the city, Daedalus also grew lazy and careless. And one day, without thought for the consequences, he caused the death of his young nephew, Prince Talos, who fell from a tall temple.

BQ BIG Question
How has success had a negative impact on who Daedalus has become?

Even a prince cannot kill a prince. The king of Athens punished Daedalus by sending him away, away from all he loved: away from the colorful pillars of the temples, away from the noisy, winding streets, away from the bustling shops and stalls, away from his smithy,[6] away from the sound of the dark sea. He would never be allowed to return.

And the gods watched the exile from on high.

Many days and nights Daedalus fled from his past. He crossed strange lands. He crossed strange seas. All he carried with him was a goatskin flask,[7] the clothes on his back, and the knowledge in his hands. All he carried with him was grief that he had caused a child's death and grief that Athens was now dead to him.

He traveled a year and a day until he came at last to the island of Crete, where the powerful King Minos[8] ruled.

The sands of Crete were different from his beloved Athens, the trees in the meadow were different, the flowers and the houses and the little, dark-eyed people were different. Only the birds seemed the same to Daedalus, and the sky—the vast, open, empty road of the sky.

Foreshadowing What might Daedalus's familiarity with the birds and sky foreshadow?

---

5 To the ancient Greeks, the ***elements*** were air, water, fire, and earth.

6 A ***smithy*** is a workshop where someone (usually called a smith) crafts things out of metal.

7 A ***goatskin flask*** is a leather bottle to carry water or wine.

8 ***Minos*** (mī′ nəs)

But the gods found nothing below them strange.

Daedalus knew nothing of Crete but Crete knew much of Daedalus, for his reputation had flown on wings before him. King Minos did not care that Daedalus was an **exile** or that he had been judged guilty of a terrible crime.

"You are the world's greatest builder, Daedalus," King Minos said. "Build me a labyrinth in which to hide a beast."

"A cage would be simpler," said Daedalus.

"This is no ordinary beast," said the king. "This is a monster. This is a prince. His name is Minotaur[9] and he is my wife's own son. He has a bull's head but a man's body. He eats human flesh. I cannot kill the queen's child. Even a king cannot kill a prince. And I cannot put him in a cage. But in a maze such as you might build, I could keep him hidden forever."

Daedalus bowed his head, but he smiled at the king's praise. He built a labyrinth for the king with countless corridors and winding ways. He **devised** such cunning passages that only he knew the secret pathway to its heart—he, and the Minotaur who lived there.

Make Predictions About Plot What do you predict will happen to the Minotaur?

Yet the gods marked the secret way as well.

For many years Daedalus lived on the island of Crete, delighting in the praise he received from king and court. He made hundreds of new things for them. He made dolls with moving parts and a dancing floor inlaid with wood and stone for the princess Ariadne.[10] He made iron gates for the king and queen wrought[11] with cunning designs. He grew fond of the little dark-eyed islanders, and he married a Cretan wife. A son was born to them whom Daedalus named Icarus.[12] The boy was small like his mother but he had his father's quick, bright ways.

Foreshadowing What might happen to someone who has the same "quick, bright ways" as Daedalus?

9 ***Minotaur*** (min′ ə tôr)

10 ***Ariadne*** (ar′ ē ad′ nē)

11 ***Wrought*** means "made or formed." In reference to metal, it describes something that has been carefully shaped by hammering,

12 ***Icarus*** (ik′ ər əs)

Vocabulary

exile (eg′ zīl) *n.* a person who is forced to leave his or her country or home

devised (di vīzd′) *v.* thought out; invented; planned

The Minotaur, 1885. George Fredric Watts. Tate Gallery, London.

View the Art How does this painting make you feel about the Minotaur's situation?

Daedalus taught Icarus many things, yet the one Daedalus valued most was the language of his lost Athens. Though he had a grand house and servants to do his bidding, though he had a wife he loved and a son he adored, Daedalus was not entirely happy. His heart still lay in Athens, the land of his youth, and the words he spoke with his son helped keep the memory of Athens alive.

One night a handsome young man came to Daedalus' house, led by a lovesick Princess Ariadne. The young man spoke with Daedalus in that Athenian tongue.[13]

"I am Theseus,[14] a prince of Athens, where your name is still remembered with praise. It is said that Daedalus was

13 Here, ***tongue*** means "language."

14 ***Theseus*** (thē′ sē əs)

more than a prince, that he had the gods in his hands. Surely such a man has not forgotten Athens."

Daedalus shook his head. "I thought Athens had forgotten me."

"Athens remembers and Athens needs your help, O prince," said Theseus.

Make Predictions About Plot Do you think Daedalus will help the stranger? What clues help you make the prediction?

"Help? What help can I give Athens, when I am so far from home?"

"Then you do not know . . . ," Theseus began.

"Know what?"

"That every seven years Athens must send a tribute[15] of boys and girls to King Minos. He puts them into the labyrinth you devised and the monster Minotaur devours them there."

Horrified, Daedalus thought of the bright-eyed boys and girls he had known in Athens. He thought of his own dark-eyed son asleep in his cot. He remembered his nephew, Talos, whose eyes had been closed by death. "How can I help?"

"Only you know the way through the maze," said Theseus. "Show me the way that I may slay the monster."

"I will show you," said Daedalus thoughtfully, "but Princes Ariadne must go as well. The Minotaur is her half-brother. He will not hurt her. She will be able to lead you to him, right into the heart of the maze."

The gods listened to the plan and nodded gravely.

Foreshadowing What details hint that something bad will happen?

Daedalus drew them a map and gave Princess Ariadne a thread to tie at her waist, that she might unwind it as they went and so find the way back out of the twisting corridors.

Hand in hand, Theseus and Ariadne left and Daedalus went into his son's room. He looked down at the sleeping boy.

"I am a prince of Athens," he whispered. "I did what must be done."

If Icarus heard his father's voice, he did not stir. He was dreaming still as Ariadne and Theseus threaded their way to the very center of the maze. And before he awakened,

15 ***Tribute*** is a payment from one nation to another to ensure peace or protection. Here, it also refers to payment given under force.

they had killed the Minotaur and fled from Crete, taking the boys and girls of Athens with them. They took all hope of Daedalus' safety as well.

Then the gods looked thoughtful and they did not smile.

When King Minos heard that the Minotaur had been slain and Ariadne taken, he guessed that Daedalus had betrayed him, for no one else knew the secret of the maze. He ordered Daedalus thrown into a high prison tower.

"Thus do kings reward traitors!" cried Minos. Then he added, "See that you care for your own son better than you cared for my wife's unfortunate child." He threw Icarus into the tower, too, and slammed the great iron gate shut with his own hand.

Foreshadowing How do the king's words build suspense? What do they suggest will happen?

The tiny tower room, with its single window overlooking the sea, was Daedalus' home now. Gone was Athens where he had been a prince, gone was Crete where he had been a rich man. All he had left was one small room, with a wooden bench and straw pallets[16] on the floor.

Day after day young Icarus stood on the bench and watched through the window as the seabirds dipped and soared over the waves.

"Father!" Icarus called each day. "Come and watch the birds."

But Daedalus would not. Day after day, he leaned against the wall or lay on a pallet bemoaning[17] his fate and cursing the gods who had done this thing to him.

The gods heard his curses and they grew angry.

One bright day Icarus took his father by the hand, leading him to the window.

"Look, Father," he said, pointing to the birds. "See how beautiful their wings are. See how easily they fly."

Just to please the boy, Daedalus looked. Then he clapped his hands to his eyes. "What a fool I have been," he whispered. "What a fool. Minos may have forbidden me sea and land, but he has left me the air. Oh, my son, though the king is ever so great and powerful, he does not

Make Predictions About Plot What do you think Daedalus has in mind?

16 ***Pallets*** are small, thin straw mattresses.

17 ***Bemoaning*** means "grieving over" or "lamenting."

rule the sky. It is the gods' own road and I am a favorite of the gods. To think a child has shown me the way!"

Every day after that, Daedalus and Icarus coaxed the birds to their window with bread crumbs saved from their **meager** meals. And every day gulls, gannets, and petrels, cormorants and pelicans, shearwaters and grebes,[18] came to the sill. Daedalus stroked the feeding birds with his clever hands and harvested handfuls of feathers. And Icarus, as if playing a game, grouped the feathers on the floor in order of size, just as his father instructed.

Make Predictions About Plot What do you predict Daedalus is going to do?

But it was no game. Soon the small piles of feathers became big piles, the big piles, great heaps. Then clever Daedalus, using a needle he had shaped from a bit of bone left over from dinner and thread pulled out of his own shirt, sewed together small feathers, overlapping them with the larger, gently curving them in great arcs. He fastened the ends with molded candle wax and made straps with the leather from their sandals.

At last Icarus understood. "Wings, Father!" he cried, clapping his hands together in delight. "Wings!"

Daedalus or the Engineer. Andrea Pisano. Marble relief from the campanile. Museo dell'Opera del Duomo, Florence.

18 ***Gulls, gannets, and petrels, cormorants and pelicans, shearwaters and grebes*** are water birds.

Vocabulary

meager (mē′ gər) *adj.* scarcely enough; insufficient

At that the gods laughed, and it was thunder over water.

They made four wings in all, a pair for each of them. Icarus had the smaller pair, for he was still a boy. They practiced for days in the tower, slipping their arms through the straps, raising and lowering the wings, until their arms had grown strong and used to the weight. They hid the wings beneath their pallets whenever the guards came by.

At last they were ready. Daedalus kneeled before his son.

"Your arms are strong now, Icarus," he said, "but do not forget my warning."

The boy nodded solemnly, his dark eyes wide. "I must not fly too low or the water will soak the feathers. I must not fly too high or the sun will melt the wax."

Foreshadowing What might Daedalus's warning foreshadow?

"Remember," his father said. "Remember."

The gods trembled, causing birds to fall through the bright air.

Daedalus climbed onto the sill. The wings made him clumsy but he did not fall. He helped Icarus up.

First the child, then the man, leaped out into the air. They pumped once and then twice with their arms. The wind caught the feathers of the wings and pushed them upward into the Cretan sky.

Wingtip to wingtip they flew, writing the lines of their escape on the air. Some watchers below took them for eagles. Most took them for gods.

As they flew, Daedalus concentrated on long, steady strokes. He remembered earlier days, when the elements had been his friends: fire and water and air. Now, it seemed, they were his friends once more.

But young Icarus had no such memories to steady his wings. He beat them with abandon,[19] glorying in his freedom. He slipped away from his father's careful pattern along a wild stream of wind.

Make Predictions About Plot What do you predict will happen next?

"Icarus, my son—remember!" Daedalus cried out.

But Icarus spiraled[20] higher and higher and higher still. He did not hear his father's voice. He heard only the music of the wind; he heard only the sighing of the gods.

---

19 ***With abandon*** means "with complete surrender to one's impulses; free from constraint."

20 ***Spiraled*** means "moved along a winding or spiral-shaped course."

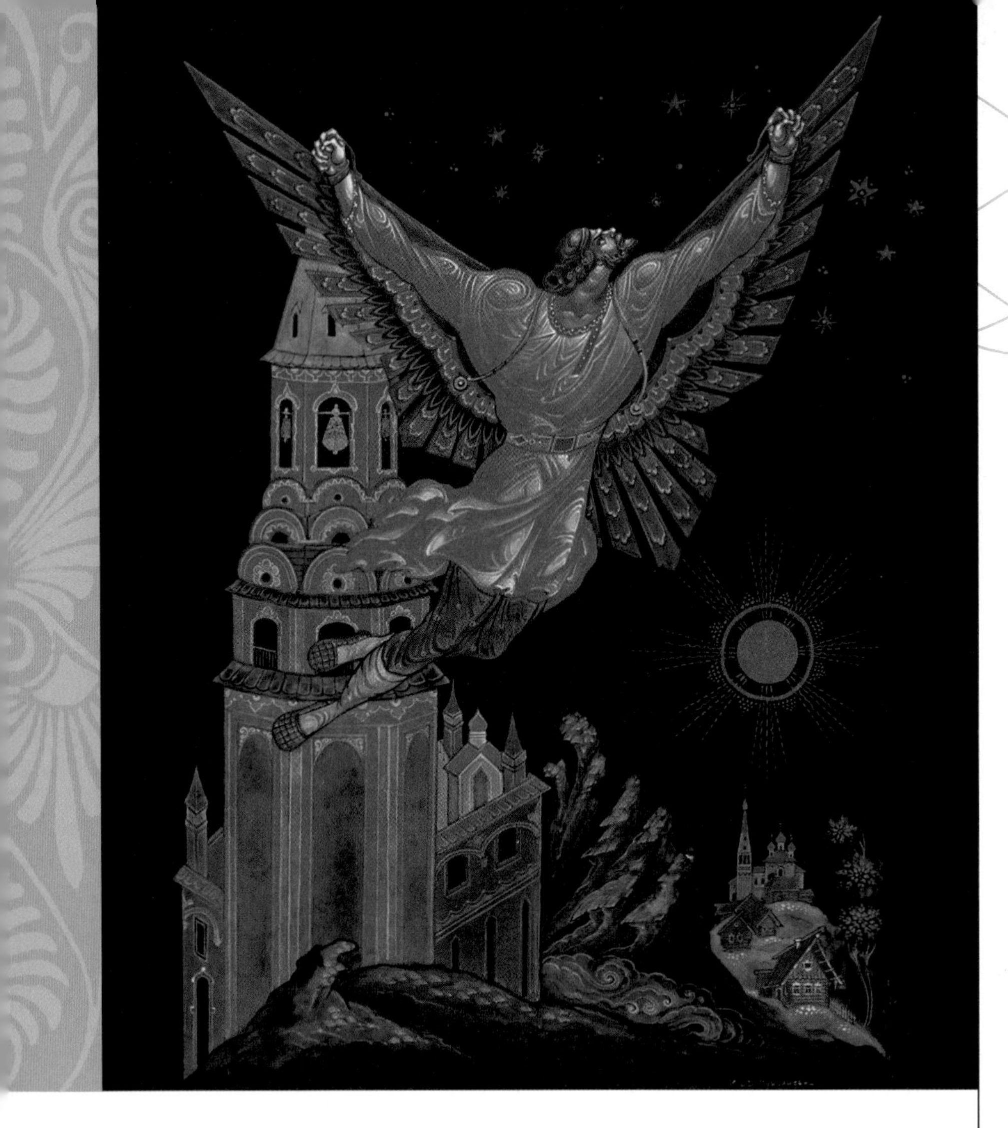

The Flight of Icarus, 1981. Boris and Kaleria Kukuliev. Color lithograph. Private Collection, Archives Charmet.

He passed the birds. He passed the clouds. He passed into the **realm** of the sun. Too late he felt the wax run down his arms; too late he smelled the singe[21] of feathers. Surprised, he hung solid in the air. Then, like a star in nova,[22] he tumbled from the sky, down, down, down into the waiting sea.

And the gods wept bitterly for the child.

"Where are you, my son?" Daedalus called. He circled the water, looking desperately for some sign. All he saw were

21 A ***singe*** is a light burn or scorch.

22 ***Nova*** is a stage of a star's life in which the star rapidly increases in brightness and then fades.

Vocabulary

realm (relm) *n.* kingdom

seven feathers afloat on the sea, spinning into different patterns with each passing wave.

Weeping, he flew away over the dark sea to the isle of Sicily. There he built a temple to the god Apollo,[23] for Apollo stood for life and light and never grew old but remained a beautiful boy forever. On the temple walls Daedalus hung up his beautiful wings as an offering to the bitter wisdom of the gods.

So Daedalus' story ended—and yet it did not. For in Sicily he was received kindly by King Cocalus,[24] who was well pleased with his skills.

Meanwhile, back in Crete, ***enraged*** *at his prisoners' escape, King Minos was determined to find and punish them. He proclaimed a great reward for anyone skilled enough to pass a silken thread through the closed spiral of a seashell. He knew that if Daedalus was alive, he could not resist the lure of such a game.*

Daedalus was sure he could easily solve the puzzle. He bored a small hole in one end of a shell, moistened it with a bit of honey, then closed up the hole. Fastening a thread to an ant, he put the insect into the shell. The ant scurried through the twisting labyrinth toward the sweet smell, running as easily as Princess Ariadne had run through the maze with the thread unwinding at her waist. When the ant emerged from the other end, it had pulled the silken thread through the spirals of the shell.

Though he used a false name to claim the prize, Daedalus did not fool King Minos. Minos knew the winner was his old enemy. So, with a mighty army, Minos sailed to Sicily to bring Daedalus back.

But King Cocalus would not give up Daedalus to the foreign invaders, and a great battle was fought. With Daedalus' help, King Cocalus was victorious and King Minos was killed. Minos was clever but he was not kind. He had a heart scabbed over with old remembered wounds.

The gods always punish such a man.

BQ BIG Question
How has this experience changed Daedalus?

Make Predictions About Plot Do you predict that Daedalus will take the challenge? Why or why not?

BQ BIG Question
In this story, when do the gods get in the way of a character's goals or dreams?

---

23 ***Apollo*** (ə pol′ ō)

24 ***Cocalus*** (kō′ kə ləs)

Vocabulary

enraged (en rājd′) *adj.* greatly angered

After You Read

Respond and Think Critically

1. What does Daedalus do that makes King Minos angry? How does King Minos respond? **[Recall]**
2. How does Daedalus's relationship with the Athenians change over the course of the story? **[Summarize]**
3. After Ariadne and Theseus kill the Minotaur, "the gods looked thoughtful and they did not smile." What does this mean? **[Infer]**
4. How is Daedalus's heart like a labyrinth? Does he ever come to understand it? Explain. **[Interpret]**
5. Do you think the story of Daedalus teaches an important lesson? Explain. **[Evaluate]**
6. **BQ** **BIG Question** Which of Daedalus's personality traits help him realize his dreams and goals? Which traits prevent him from obtaining them? **[Conclude]**

TIP

Interpreting
Here are some tips to help you answer question 4. To interpret, look at the details of the story and think about their greater meaning.

- Look at repeated images, words, or details that seem significant.
- Think about what the images and details might represent.

Keep track of your ideas about the **BIG Question** in your unit Foldable.

Vocabulary Practice

Respond to these questions.

1. Who is more likely to be an **exile**—someone who disagrees with the government or someone who supports the government?
2. If you **devised** clever party games, did you plan them or sell them?
3. Would a **realm** be ruled by a referee or by a king?
4. If you have a **meager** allowance, is it barely enough or more than you need?
5. If you are **enraged** about something, do you feel joy or anger?

Academic Vocabulary

In "Wings," the reactions of the gods are **parallel** to events in the plot. In the preceding sentence, *parallel* means "similar" or "corresponding in development." *Parallel* also has other meanings. For example: The bicycle path runs **parallel** to the street. What do you think *parallel* means in the preceding sentence? What is the difference between the two meanings?

LOG ON **Literature** Online

Selection Resources
For Selection Quizzes, eFlashcards, and Reading-Writing Connection activities, go to glencoe.com and enter QuickPass code GL17527u3.

Literary Element **Foreshadowing**

1. How do the gods' reactions foreshadow what will happen to Daedalus?
2. What details foreshadow Icarus's fate?

Review: Characterization

As you learned on page 114, **characterization** is the way a writer develops the personality of a character. One way a writer reveals character is through the character's words, thoughts, and actions.

Standards Practice  ELA6RC2e

3. Which words best describe Daedalus?
   A. angry and vengeful
   B. sorrowful and slow
   C. inventive but proud
   D. clever but jealous

Reading Strategy
Make Predictions About Plot

4. Review your chart of predictions. How did making predictions lead to a greater understanding of the story?
5. What clues might help the reader predict the outcome of the story?

Grammar Link

End Punctuation Different types of sentences have different purposes. The end punctuation must match the purpose of the sentence.

A **declarative** sentence makes a statement. It always ends with a period.

She saw the bus go by.

An **interrogative** sentence asks a question. It always ends with a question mark.

Are you ready to go**?**

An **exclamatory** sentence expresses a strong feeling. It ends with an exclamation point.

I can't believe it**!**

An **imperative** sentence gives a command. It may end with a period or, if the command is forceful, an exclamation point.

Please hand me a glass. Don't drop it**!**

Practice
Look for different types of sentences in "Wings." Then add correct end punctuation to each of the following sentences and identify its purpose.

1. That makes me furious
2. We went to visit friends
3. Can you design a labyrinth
4. Daedalus is very clever
5. Close the window

Speaking and Listening

Literature Groups With a small group, discuss the role of the gods in the myth of Daedalus. Why do you think they do not intervene to save Icarus? Why do they punish someone who is "clever but not always kind"? Support your ideas with details from the story. Listen to other group members to help clarify and elaborate.

Historical Perspective

on *Wings* by Jane Yolen

KING MINOS AND ART ON THE PALACE WALLS

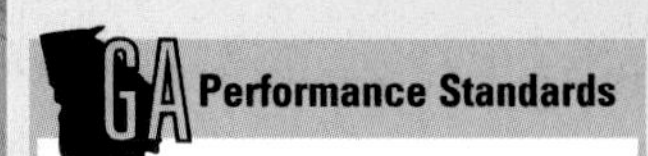

Performance Standards

For pages 374–376

ELA6R1d For informational texts, identify and analyze main ideas, supporting ideas, and supporting details.

Set a Purpose for Reading

Read this informational article about ancient Crete, which is the setting for a part of the myth told in "Wings."

Build Background

Although King Minos is a mythical character, Crete's Minoan civilization really existed and prospered. It was an influential civilization with extensive trade routes. Because the Minoans spoke a language we don't understand, everything we know about their culture is learned from archaeologists who study Crete's ruins, its art, and its tool artifacts.

Reading Skill Synthesize

To **synthesize**, combine information from this article and "Wings" to evaluate related topics. Take notes in an organizer like the one below.

Crete, an island in the Mediterranean and Aegean seas, was home to a thriving culture from around 3000 B.C. to 1200 B.C. This culture is called the Minoan civilization, after the legendary King Minos. After about 1400 B.C., it steadily declined. Fires—perhaps set by plundering invaders[1]—left many Minoan settlements in ruins. These lay buried and all but forgotten until the 1900s, when scholars began unearthing palaces decorated with delicate, lively frescoes—paintings made on plaster walls.

1 ***Plundering invaders*** are foreigners who attack a place and take or destroy things that are valuable there.

Many Minoan frescoes show scenes of animals or plants framed by geometrical patterns.[2] Some are filled with leaping fish, octopuses, and other sea life. On others, a lion walks regally[3] and monkeys chase each other through reeds. Paintings of human figures commonly show them from the

2 Something that is framed by ***geometrical patterns*** is surrounded by circles, triangles, squares, rectangles, or other pure shapes. These shapes form a border around the picture.

3 ***Regally*** means "in the manner of a king or queen." A lion that walks ***regally*** moves in a dignified way. The lion may be shown walking slowly with its head up, as if wearing a crown.

View the Photograph The Palace at Knossos, also known as the Palace of Minos, was excavated in the early 1900s. Much of the palace has been rebuilt from the ruins. What can people learn from visiting a site such as the one shown here?

side—men in brown and women in white. Red was a popular background color.

A number of frescoes featured bulls, recalling the legend of the Minotaur. Bulls probably held religious meaning for the people of ancient Crete. One fresco shows the sport of bull-leaping. In this sport, young acrobats vaulted[4] over the backs of charging bulls.

4 ***Acrobats*** are people with great balance and flexibility, who can move, turn, and twist their bodies in unusual ways. When acrobats ***vaulted*** over the back of a charging bull, they put their hands down on the back of the bull and jumped over it. They may have done a handstand, twisted or turned in the air, or done another kind of fancy movement as they jumped.

Respond and Think Critically

1. Write a brief summary of the main ideas in this article. For help on writing a summary, see page 170. **[Summarize]**
2. What are frescoes? Why are they important in helping us learn about ancient Crete? **[Recall and Interpret]**
3. Based on the fresco art of ancient Crete, how might sea life have been important to the culture? Explain. **[Infer]**
4. **Text to Text** In the story "Wings," Daedalus makes many beautiful art objects while he lives in Crete. What evidence from this article shows that the people of ancient Crete placed a high value on art? **[Connect]**
5. **Reading Skill** **Synthesize** In "Wings," there is a bloodthirsty monster called the Minotaur, which is half human and half bull. The article about ancient Crete reports that leaping over bulls was a sport there. Put these ideas together. How could you synthesize the information?
6. **BQ** **BIG Question** The culture of a people helps them define who they are. How does your culture help you define yourself?

Before You Read

Daydreamers

GA Performance Standards
For pages 377–381)
ELA6R1h/ii For literary texts, respond to and explain the effects of figurative language.

Connect to the Poem

Recall a time when you found yourself daydreaming. Think about where you were, what else was happening, and how your daydream made you feel.

Quickwrite Freewrite for a few minutes about a daydream you remember well. What was it about? Why is it so memorable?

Build Background

The poem you will read is about daydreaming.

- By daydreaming, people sometimes find solutions to problems or get ideas about how to do something. Daydreams can also be a way of dealing with fears of the unknown. Some artists and writers are daydreamers who turn their visions into art.
- In the poem, daydreams *hopscotch* and *doubledutch*. These are games many children play. In hopscotch, players hop on squares drawn on the ground while trying to pick up an object, such as a pebble, that they have thrown into one of the squares. Double Dutch is a fast-paced jump-rope game in which two ropes are swung in opposite directions at the same time.

Set Purposes for Reading

BQ BIG Question

As you read "Daydreamers," ask yourself, how does the poet connect daydreaming and becoming who you are?

Literary Element Personification

Personification is a figure of speech in which a writer gives human form or characteristics to an animal, an object, a force of nature, or an idea. Consider the sentence *The sun kissed my face.* The writer uses personification to describe how the sun's rays feel. However, the description is not literally true.

Personification can help you more vividly see and feel the author's point and establish a tone and a deeper meaning. It can also help you see something familiar in a different way. As you read, look for examples where the poet describes an idea or an object doing things only a human can do.

Meet Eloise Greenfield

Eloise Greenfield grew up in Washington, D.C., in a family with a strong sense of community. Her children's books often show how strong, loving communities can help make people who they are.

Greenfield has written poetry, picture books, and biographies, including *Rosa Parks* and *For the Love of the Game: Michael Jordan and Me.*

Eloise Greenfield was born in 1929.

Literature Online

Author Search For more about Eloise Greenfield, go to glencoe.com and enter QuickPass code GL17527u3.

Daydreamers

Eloise Greenfield

Lilith, 1996. Diane Griffiths. Watercolor and crayon.

View the Art Which lines from the poem would make a good caption for this painting? Explain why.

Personification What qualities of human behavior do the dreams take on?

Daydreamers . . .

holding their bodies still
for a time
letting the world turn around them

while their dreams hopscotch,
doubledutch, dance,

thoughts rollerskate,
crisscross,
bump into hopes and wishes.

Dreamers
thinking up new ways,
looking toward new days,

planning new tries,
asking new whys.
Before long,
hands will start to move again,
eyes turn outward,
bodies shift for action,
but for this moment they are still,

they are
the daydreamers,
letting the world dizzy itself
without them.

Scenes passing through their minds
make no sound
glide from hiding places
promenade° and return
silently

the children watch their memories
with spirit-eyes
seeing more than they saw before

feeling more
or maybe less
than they felt the time before
reaching with spirit-hands
to touch the dreams
drawn from their yesterdays
They will not be the same
after this growing time,
this dreaming.
In their stillness they have moved
forward

toward womanhood
toward manhood.
This dreaming has made them
new.

Personification Why does Greenfield describe the world as making itself dizzy?

BQ BIG Question
What is the poet saying about daydreaming and the role it plays in making people who they are?

27 To ***promenade*** is to walk in a slow, relaxed manner.

After You Read

Respond and Think Critically

1. What are the daydreamers doing while dreams go through their minds? **[Recall]**
2. How old do you think the daydreamers in the poem are? Use details from the poem to support your answer. **[Infer]**
3. How can daydreaming help people move forward? **[Interpret]**
4. Why is daydreaming important? Find reasons in the poem to support your answer. **[Analyze]**
5. If daydreaming is a good thing, as Greenfield implies, why do people sometimes discourage others from daydreaming too much? **[Evaluate]**
6. **BQ BIG Question** How do you think Eloise Greenfield would answer the question, "What makes people who they are?" Give evidence from the poem to support your answer. **[Conclude]**

Academic Vocabulary

Daydreamers, like the young people in the poem, are not usually physically active as they daydream. However, a lot of activity is going on in their minds. Such activity is called **mental** activity. To become more familiar with the word *mental,* fill out a graphic organizer like the one below.

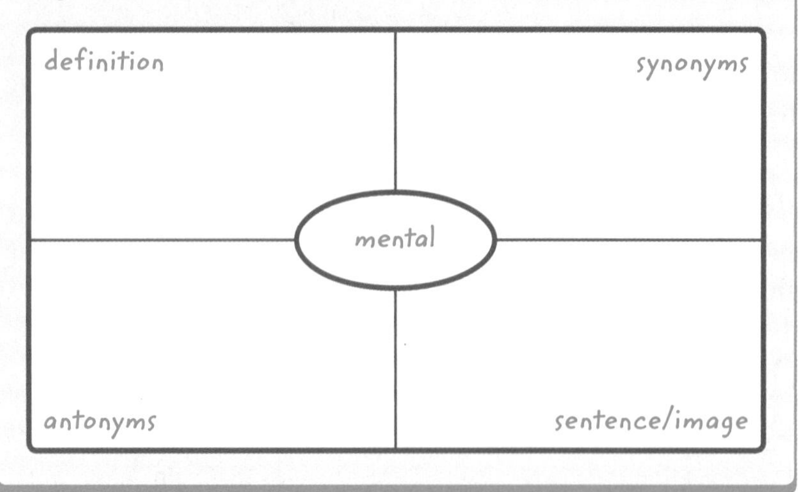

TIP

Analyzing
When you analyze, you look at separate parts of something to understand the whole piece. To answer question 4, follow these tips:

- Ask yourself, in what ways can daydreams be helpful?
- Skim the poem to look for words that show positive effects of daydreaming.
- Look for words near the end of the poem that sum up the poet's attitude toward daydreamers.

Keep track of your ideas about the **BIG Question** in your unit Foldable.

LOG ON **Literature** Online

Selection Resources
For Selection Quizzes, eFlashcards, and Reading-Writing Connection activities, go to glencoe.com and enter QuickPass code GL17527u3.

Literary Element **Personification**

1. Why is the image of daydreams promenading an example of personification?
2. What meaning does the image of the daydreamers letting the world dizzy itself (lines 21–22) convey?
3. Which example of personification in this poem did you enjoy the most? Explain why you enjoyed it.

Review: Line and Stanza

As you learned on page 306, a **stanza** is a group of lines forming a unit of a poem. The stanzas are the paragraphs of a poem. "Daydreamers" is divided into many stanzas. A line of space separates each stanza.

Use a chart like the one below to help you analyze the stanzas of the poem.

Number of lines in the poem	46
Number of stanzas	
Number of lines per stanza	
Number of complete sentences	

4. How many stanzas does this poem have? Does each stanza have the same number of lines? Are the lines in each stanza similar in length, or does the line length vary? Is each stanza a complete sentence?
5. Some of the lines in the poem have only one word. Why do you think the poet put only one word on lines 1 and 10?

Grammar Link

Subjects and Predicates Every sentence is made up of two parts: a subject and a predicate. The **subject** is the part that is doing or being something. The **predicate** is the part that tells what the subject is doing or being.

The **complete subject** contains all the words in the subject. The **complete predicate** contains all the words in the predicate. For example:

The process of daydreaming (**complete subject**) has helped writers create great works (**complete predicate**).

The **simple subject** is *only* the noun or pronoun that answers the question "who or what?" about the verb. The **simple predicate** is *only* the verb or verbs in the predicate.

In the following sentence, the simple subject is underlined once. The simple predicate is underlined twice.

Many people enjoy daydreaming.

Practice Reread the last nine lines of "Daydreamers." On a separate sheet of paper, write the three sentences that form these lines. For each sentence, underline the simple subject once and the simple predicate twice.

Write with Style

Apply Figurative Language Think about the daydreams and thoughts that help define you. Write these in a list. Choose two or three dreams or thoughts and picture them behaving the way a person does. Write a poem about one of the dreams or thoughts you selected. Include two or more examples of personification in your poem. Use a dictionary or a thesaurus to help you make vivid and descriptive word choices.

Performance Standards

For page 382

ELA6R2c Understand and acquire new vocabulary. Identify and interpret words with multiple meanings.

Vocabulary Workshop

Multiple-Meaning Words

Connection to Literature

"The three main places I have lived . . . are each deeply precious to me. . . . Gravity interests me—where we feel it, how we feel it."

—Naomi Shihab Nye

The word *gravity* is a **multiple-meaning word**—a word that has more than one definition. It can mean "the force that pulls things toward the center of Earth." It can also mean "seriousness or importance." For example, *She understood the gravity of the situation.* These dictionary definitions are called **denotations.** Words can also have **connotations**—implied meanings that suggest certain feelings. Nye uses *gravity* to mean "a strong emotional pull to a certain place."

Here are some other multiple-meaning words from "Interview with Naomi Shihab Nye."

Word	Meanings	Examples
long	a great deal of time	Great Britain has *long,* historical ties to India.
	of great length	I write at a *long* wooden table.
	to desire	Nye *longs* for home.
sense	a feeling	I have a *sense* of being invisible as a traveler.
	sight, hearing, smell, taste, or touch	Nye uses her *sense* of sight when traveling.

TRY IT: Using the chart above, write the correct meaning of the underlined word.

1. I long to taste tomatoes like the ones back home.
2. It didn't take Nye long to begin writing poetry.
3. Bill had the sense that he had forgotten something.

Tip

Test-Taking Tip You might come across a word that you think you know but that doesn't make sense in the sentence you're reading. That's a clue that it may have another meaning.

Vocabulary Terms Multiple-meaning words are words that have more than one definition. The definitions often are closely related, but sometimes they are quite different from one another.

Literature Online

Vocabulary For more vocabulary practice, go to glencoe.com and enter QuickPass code GL17527u3.

Part 3

Character Traits

Three Girls at Lunch. Hyacinth Manning. Acrylic on canvas.

BQ BIG Question What Makes You Who You Are?

In the painting *Three Girls at Lunch,* one young woman leans her head on her friend's shoulder. Another cups her head in her hand. What do these actions tell you about the girls' personalities? How do your friends reveal their character traits through behavior and actions?

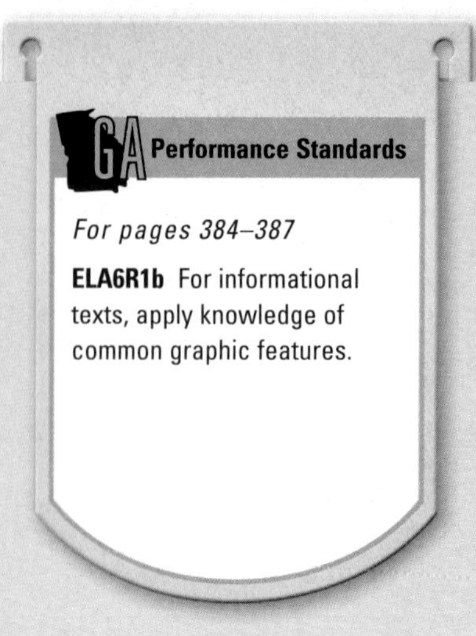

For pages 384–387

ELA6R1b For informational texts, apply knowledge of common graphic features.

Set a Purpose for Reading

Read to find out how genes shape who you are. As you read, think about the traits that make you unique.

Preview the Article

1. Based on the **title,** also called the headline, predict what you think the article is about.
2. Look at the article's **text features,** such as the heads, the quiz, the bulleted list, and the poem. How are these useful in a magazine article?

Reading Strategy

Connect to Today

Connecting an article to issues in today's world can help you understand what you read. As you read this article, recall news stories or movies you have seen about genetics.

Detail in Article	Where I've Heard of It
a chemical called DNA	movie about clones

TIME

The Gene SCENE

What makes you you?

By JORDAN BROWN

Genetics is the study of how special features, such as eye color, are passed on from one generation to another.

To find out more about special features, called traits, find a friend and grab some paper and a pencil. Ask each other these questions. Then write your answers on the paper.

1. Can you curl your tongue?

You:	❑ YES	❑ NO
Your Friend:	❑ YES	❑ NO

2. Can you wiggle your ears?

You:	❑ YES	❑ NO
Your Friend:	❑ YES	❑ NO

3. Can you raise just one of your eyebrows?

You:	❑ YES	❑ NO
Your Friend:	❑ YES	❑ NO

4. Do you have a "hitchhiker's thumb"?[1]

You:	❑ YES	❑ NO
Your Friend:	❑ YES	❑ NO

1 A ***hitchhiker's thumb*** is a rare trait in humans where the end joint of the thumb can be bent backward at an angle of at least 45 degrees.

Denis Finnin/American Museum of Natural History (4)

Congratulations!

You just did a genetics investigation.

Traits are a person's special features. Some traits are more common than others. Many people can curl their tongues. But eyebrow raisers, ear-wigglers, and people with a hitchhiker's thumb are harder to find.

Traits, such as the ability to roll your tongue, are passed on through genes. You get your genes from your parents. Genes are inside every living cell. They are made of a chemical called DNA.[2] Genes are tiny, but they carry tons of information.

2 ***DNA*** is a substance in the genes of cells that stores unique patterns of traits. It passes on all hereditary information from parent to child.

Here are some amazing things scientists have discovered so far:

- All living things have DNA. So you have something in common with zebras, trees, mushrooms, and even bacteria.
- There are about 30,000 genes in every cell of your body.
- Unless you are an identical twin, there is no one exactly like you. You are genetically unique.

Scientists are discovering many new secrets about life, such as what role genes play in determining what makes you you, whether people are healthy or sick, and how you grow. What they learn will greatly affect our future, from the medicine we take to the food we eat.

What Makes YOU YOU?
What Makes ME ME?

Genetics is fun!
So much to learn!
Oooh! But I have one concern.
I've searched and searched.
Where ARE my genes?
You've got to help me!
Spill the beans!

What makes you you?
What makes me me?
A lot is due to heredity.[3]
Your genes control
What makes you you,
From the color of your hair
To the size of your shoe.

Dogs and frogs are made of cells.
Bananas have them, too!
These teeny-tiny building blocks
Even make up YOU!

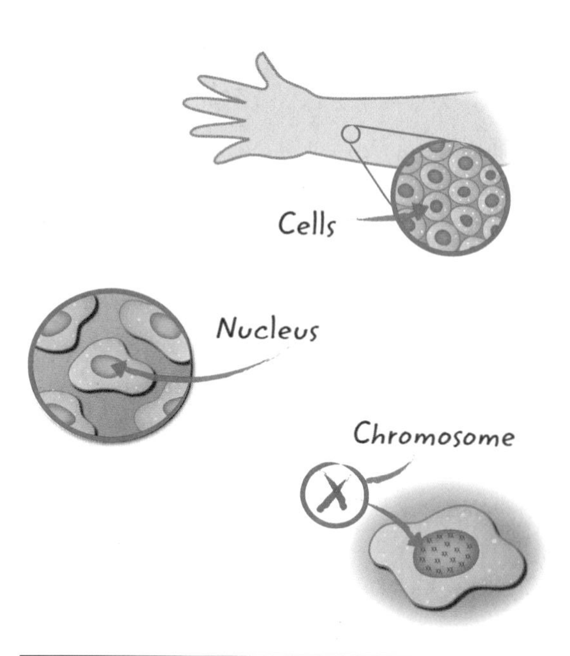

This thing here's the nucleus.[4]
It's small, but even so:
It tells the cell just what to do,
It really runs the show.

Then, there are your chromosomes,[5]
They're 46 in all!
Half from mom, and half from dad,
They're really, really small.

Your chromosomes are shaped
like coils.
They always come in pairs.
They're made of stuff called DNA,
That's shaped like spiral stairs.

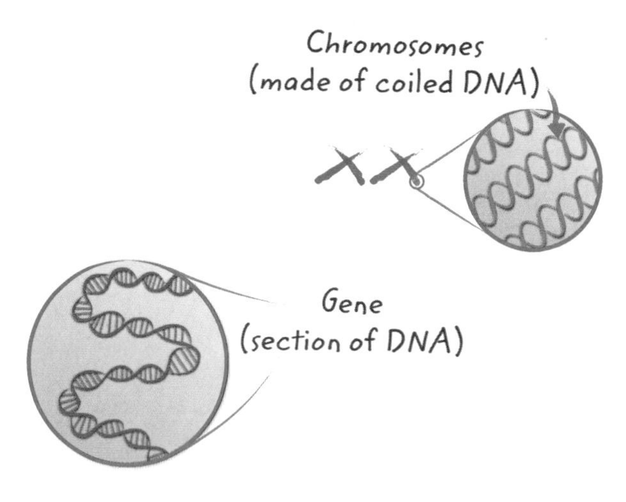

Genes are the sections of DNA,
Where many traits are placed.
Learning what each gene controls
Is the puzzle experts face.

3 ***Heredity*** is the process by which an animal or a plant genetically passes characteristics to its offspring.

4 A cell's ***nucleus*** is a small, central part of the cell that contains most of the cell's genetic material. The nucleus is essential to growth, reproduction, metabolism, and other important activities.

5 ***Chromosomes*** are tiny structures in the nuclei of plant and animal cells, made up chiefly of proteins and DNA. Chromosomes carry the genetic material that determines sex, size, color, and many other characteristics.

DNA is made of four bases
We call them G, C, A, and T.
These bases are in every plant
And animal you see!

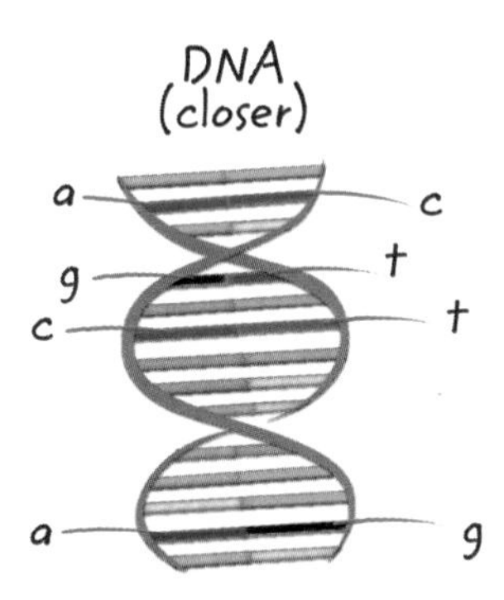

I GET IT NOW!
WHAT MAKES YOU YOU,
WHAT MAKES ME ME,
SHAPES EVERY LIVING THING
YOU SEE.
WE'RE ALL RELATED IN A WAY
BECAUSE WE ALL HAVE DNA!

Time & Life Pictures/Getty Images

Gregor Mendel, a scientist who lived in the 1800s, discovered the rules of genetics. By experimenting with pea plants, Mendel figured out how traits are passed from one generation to the next.

Thousands of different traits make you who you are. Some traits, such as eye color, are determined mostly or entirely by genes. These kind of traits are decided by nature.

Most traits, however, are due to a combination of nature (your genes) and nurture (everything in your life—where you live, the people you know, everything you experience). Scientists agree that both nature and nurture play important roles in making you who you are.

Respond and Think Critically

1. Use the heads to help you organize and write a brief summary of the article's main ideas. For help on writing a summary, see page 170. **[Summarize]**
2. **Text to Self** Which of the genetic traits that the article mentions can you observe in yourself or in people you know? **[Connect]**
3. Why might scientists' study of genes affect the food we eat? **[Infer]**
4. Think about some traits of people you know, such as hair color, height, athletic ability, and sense of humor. Which traits do you think are genetic? Which are not genetic? **[Compare]**
5. **Reading Strategy** **Connect to Today** Police can sometimes use DNA evidence to prove that a person was at a crime scene. What information in the article tells you why DNA would be a good tool for proving this?
6. **BQ** **BIG Question** What aspects about you are probably hereditary? What other factors have shaped who you are? Explain.

Before You Read

Whatif and *Jimmy Jet and His TV Set*

Performance Standards

For pages 388–393

ELA6R1g For literary texts, define and explain how tone is conveyed in literature through word choice, sentence structure, punctuation, rhythm, repetition, and rhyme.

Connect to the Poems

What is a worrywart? What does a worrywart worry about? What is a couch potato? What does a couch potato do?

List Make a list of worries that a worrywart might have. Then make a list of things a couch potato does and does not do. Share your lists with a partner.

Build Background

During the 1950s, Shel Silverstein served in the U.S. Army and worked for the armed forces newspaper *Stars and Stripes* as a cartoonist. Later he created cartoons, songs, humorous poetry for adults, and children's stories. His books of humorous poetry for young people continue to be very popular.

Set Purposes for Reading

As you read each poem, ask yourself, what traits does the main character have?

Literary Element **Rhythm and Meter**

Rhythm is the pattern of beats made by syllables that are meant to be stressed (spoken with greater force) and syllables that are meant to be softer. **Meter** is a regular, predictable rhythm.

Rhythm and **meter** create a musical quality that makes poetry fun to read. In the lines below, the stressed syllables are underlined. Read them aloud and listen for the rhythm and meter.

I'll <u>tell</u> you the <u>sto</u>ry of <u>Jim</u>my <u>Jet</u>—
And you <u>know</u> what I <u>tell</u> you is <u>true</u>.
He <u>loved</u> to <u>watch</u> his <u>T</u>V <u>set</u>
Al<u>most</u> as <u>much</u> as <u>you</u>.

As you read, listen for the pattern of stressed and unstressed syllables. Ask yourself, to what words or ideas do the stressed words call attention?

Meet Shel Silverstein

"When I was a kid . . . I couldn't play ball, I couldn't dance . . . so I began to write and draw instead."

—Shel Silverstein

Shel Silverstein was born in Chicago, Illinois. He is best known for his poetry and illustrations. Silverstein's most well-known works are *The Giving Tree* and *Where the Sidewalk Ends.*

Shel Silverstein was born in1930 and died in 1999.

LOG ON  Literature Online

Author Search For more about Shel Silverstein, go to glencoe.com and enter QuickPass code GL17527u3.

Whatif

Shel Silverstein

Last night, while I lay thinking here,
Some Whatifs crawled inside my ear
And pranced and partied all night long
And sang their same old Whatif song:
Whatif I'm dumb in school?
Whatif they've closed the swimming pool?
Whatif I get beat up?
Whatif there's poison in my cup?
Whatif I start to cry?
Whatif I get sick and die?
Whatif I flunk that test?
Whatif green hair grows on my chest?
Whatif nobody likes me?
Whatif a bolt of lightning strikes me?
Whatif I don't grow taller?
Whatif my head starts getting smaller?
Whatif the fish won't bite?
Whatif the wind tears up my kite?
Whatif they start a war?
Whatif my parents get divorced?
Whatif the bus is late?
Whatif my teeth don't grow in straight?
Whatif I tear my pants?
Whatif I never learn to dance?
Everything seems swell, and then
The nighttime Whatifs strike again!

Rhythm and Meter Read this line aloud. Which syllables do you stress?

BQ BIG Question

What does this poem reveal about the character traits of the speaker?

Jimmy Jet
and His TV Set

Shel Silverstein

I'll tell you the story of Jimmy Jet—
And you know what I tell you is true.
He loved to watch his TV set
Almost as much as you.

He watched all day, he watched all night
Till he grew pale and lean,
From "The Early Show" to "The Late Late Show"
And all the shows between.

Rhythm and Meter How do the stressed syllables draw attention to Jimmy Jet's problem?

He watched till his eyes were frozen wide,
And his bottom grew into his chair.

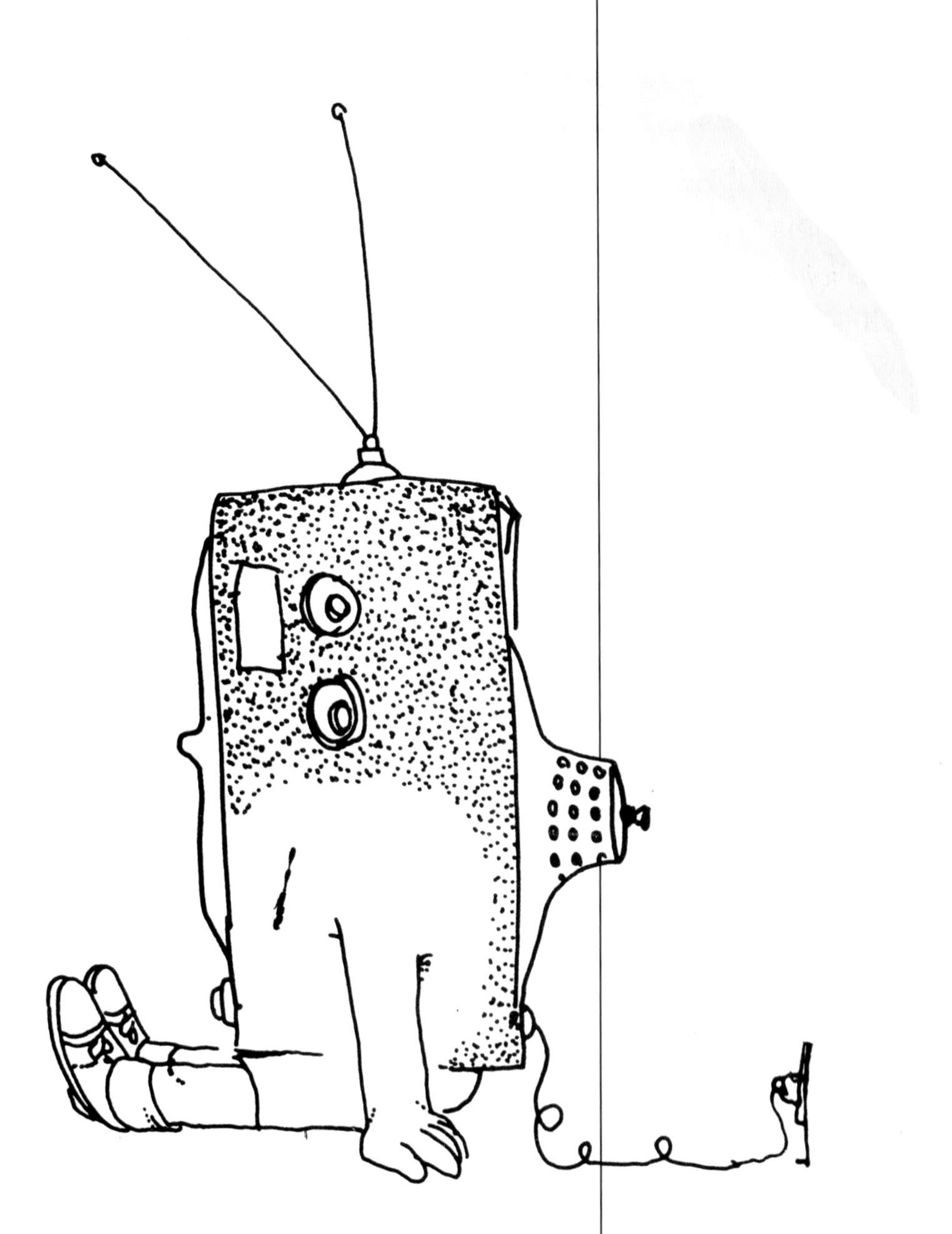

And his chin turned into a tuning dial,
And antennae grew out of his hair.

And his brains turned into TV tubes.
And his face to a TV screen.
And two knobs saying "VERT." and "HORIZ."
Grew where his ears had been.

And he grew a plug that looked like a tail
So we plugged in little Jim.
And now instead of him watching TV
We all sit around and watch him.

BQ BIG Question

How has watching TV affected Jimmy's personality?

After You Read

Respond and Think Critically

1. Where do the Whatifs sing their song? **[Recall]**
2. In your own words, explain what happens to Jimmy Jet. **[Paraphrase]**
3. About how old is the speaker of "Whatif"? What clues help you to infer this? **[Infer]**
4. Compare the speaker of "Whatif" with Jimmy Jet. How are they similar? **[Compare]**
5. What lessons can you learn from "Whatif" and "Jimmy Jet and His TV Set"? Are these lessons valuable? Why or why not? **[Evaluate]**
6. **BQ BIG Question** Which character is more like you—the speaker of "Whatif" or Jimmy Jet? Explain. **[Conclude]**

Academic Vocabulary

In "Jimmy Jet and His TV Set," Shel Silverstein raises a **significant** issue: What are the results of watching too much television? To become more familiar with the word *significant,* fill out a graphic organizer like the one below.

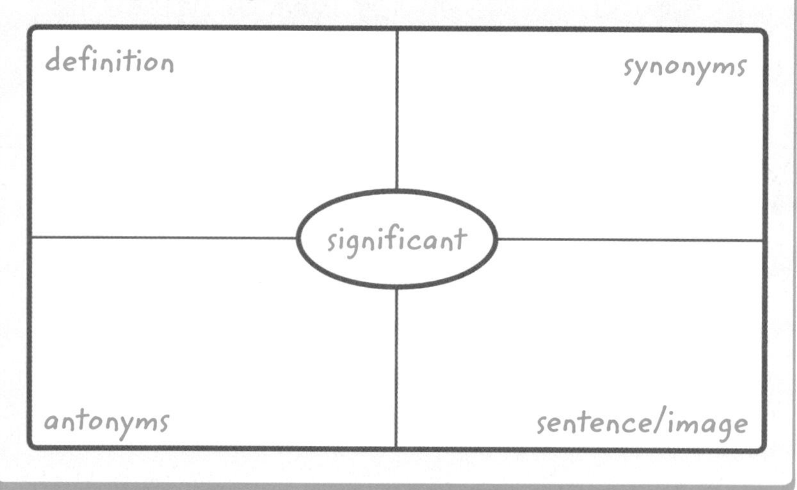

TIP

Comparing
Here are some tips to help you answer question 4. Remember, when you compare, you find similarities between two things.

- Identify each character's problem or struggle.
- Identify what happens to each character.
- What similarities do you notice?

Keep track of your ideas about the **BIG Question** in your unit Foldable.

Literature Online

Selection Resources
For Selection Quizzes, eFlashcards, and Reading-Writing Connection activities, go to glencoe.com and enter QuickPass code GL17527u3.

Literary Element **Rhythm and Meter**

1. A poem's rhythm can be regular (having a predictable pattern or meter) or irregular. Is the rhythm of "Jimmy Jet and His TV Set" regular or irregular? How can you tell?
2. How do the meter and rhythm in "Jimmy Jet and His TV Set" affect the poem's tone?

Review: Rhyme

As you learned on page 338, a **rhyme** is made of words whose sounds match, such as *jet* and *set* or *here* and *ear*. In poetry, rhymes can occur at the ends of lines or within a line.

A **rhyme scheme** is the pattern formed by the end rhymes in a poem. To identify the rhyme scheme, assign each new end rhyme in a poem a letter of the alphabet.

3. Where do the rhyming words occur in "Whatif"?
4. What is the rhyme scheme of "Whatif"?

Grammar Link

Compound Subjects and Predicates As you know, every complete sentence has a subject (*who* or *what*) and a predicate (what the subject *is* or *does*). You also know that complete subjects and predicates consist of more than one word.

- A **compound subject** has two or more simple subjects that have the same predicate. The subjects are most often joined by the word *and* or *or.*

  His family and friends watch Jimmy Jet.

- A **compound predicate** has two or more simple predicates, or verbs, that have the same subject. The predicates are most often connected by *and* or *or.*

  What if I flunk the test and cry?

- A sentence can have both a compound subject and a compound predicate.

  Jimmy and Johnny just sat and stared at the TV.

Practice In one of the poems, find a sentence that has a compound predicate. Then write your own sentence with a compound subject, a compound predicate, or both.

Write with Style

Apply Sound Devices Think of a person with a special or unusual trait. The person might be a worrywart, a brilliant thinker, or unusually strong. Write a poem about this person using rhythm, meter, and rhyme. Then read your poem aloud and have a partner tap along as you read. Does your poem have a smooth rhythm? Are there parts that sound awkward? Does your poem follow a rhyme scheme? Have your partner make suggestions for revising.

Before You Read

Flowers and Freckle Cream

Connect to the Story

Everyone makes mistakes. Think about a time when you learned something valuable from a mistake you made.

Quickwrite Freewrite for a few minutes and describe how learning from a mistake helped you become who you are.

Build Background

"Flowers and Freckle Cream" is about a young girl's struggle to recognize and appreciate her own special qualities. It is also about being able to learn from experiences and laugh about them later.

- The story is set in the1950s in the Appalachian region where the author grew up.
- Freckles are specks or spots on the skin that darken when exposed to the sun.

Vocabulary

flawless (flô′ lis) *adj.* having no mistakes; perfect (p. 396).
The flawless diamond was very expensive.

complexion (kəm plek′shən) *n.* color, texture, and appearance of the skin (p. 396).
The baby has a rosy complexion.

precisely (pri sīs′ lē) *adv.* exactly (p. 397).
The carpenter took care to cut the boards precisely.

veins (vānz) *n.* vessels that carry blood to the heart from other parts of the body (p. 398).
Most veins appear bluish in color because they carry blood with low levels of oxygen.

inadequate (in ad′ə kwit) *adj.* not good enough (p. 399).
The company's equipment is inadequate for this job.

Meet Elizabeth Ellis

"My favorite story is always the one I am just getting ready to tell next!"

—Elizabeth Ellis

Traveling Storyteller
Elizabeth Ellis learned to tell stories from her grandfather, who entertained her with ghost stories, legends, and folktales while she was growing up in the Appalachian Mountains. As an adult, Ellis travels all over the country telling her stories to children and adults. Ellis says she loves making a living this way because she has so much fun.

Literary Works "Flowers and Freckle Cream" appeared in *Best-Loved Stories Told at the National Storytelling Festival,* published in 1991.

Elizabeth Ellis was born in 1943.

LOG ON  Literature Online

Author Search For more about Elizabeth Ellis, go to glencoe.com and enter QuickPass code GL17527u3.

Set Purposes for Reading

BQ BIG Question

As you read, ask yourself, what lesson does Elizabeth learn from her experience with the freckle cream?

Literary Element Diction

Diction is an author's choice of words. Skilled authors carefully choose their words to convey a particular meaning or feeling. Sometimes authors use **idioms.** An idiom is an expression whose meaning is different from its literal (actual and ordinary) meaning. For example, if something is very easy, we may use the idiom "a piece of cake" to describe it.

It is important to pay attention to diction so you understand the author's real meaning, or overall message, and recognize his or her unique way of telling the story.

As you read, think about how the idioms and other word choices set the tone and advance the theme of the story.

Reading Strategy Evaluate Characterization

When you **evaluate,** you make a judgment or form an opinion. When you **evaluate characterization,** you form an opinion regarding the way the author has developed the personality of a character.

Evaluating characterization helps you decide how characters affect the overall plot and the resolution of the conflict.

To **evaluate characterization** as you read, ask yourself,

- How does the author use the character's words, thoughts, and actions to reveal his or her personality?
- What is stated directly about the character?
- What do other characters in the story say about that character?

Use these questions to evaluate characterization as you read. You may find it helpful to list the reasons for your evaluation in a graphic organizer like the one below.

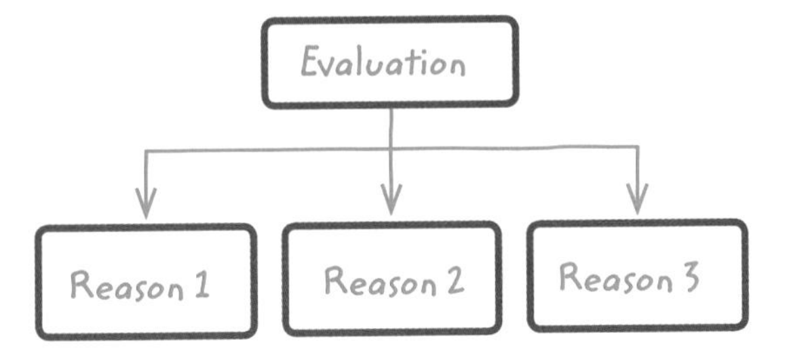

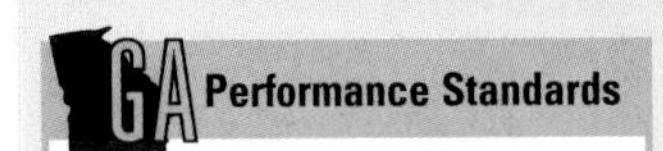

GA Performance Standards

For pages 394–400

ELA6R1h/ii For literary texts, respond to and explain the effects of figurative language.

TRY IT

Evaluate Characterization You are attending a play in order to review it for the school newspaper. In your review, you will evaluate the playwright's and actors' abilities to make the characters seem real. What elements should you pay attention to while watching the play?

Flowers and Freckle Cream

Elizabeth Ellis

When I was a kid about twelve years old, I was already as tall as I am now, and I had a lot of freckles. I had reached the age when I had begun to really look at myself in the mirror, and I was underwhelmed.[1] Apparently my mother was too, because sometimes she'd look at me and shake her head and say, "You can't make a silk purse out of a sow's ear."[2]

I had a cousin whose name was Janette Elizabeth, and Janette Elizabeth looked exactly like her name sounds. She had a waist so small that men could put their hands around it . . . and they did. She had waist-length naturally curly blond hair too, but to me her unforgivable sin was that she had a **flawless** peaches-and-cream **complexion**. I couldn't help comparing myself with her and thinking that my life would be a lot different if I had beautiful skin too—skin that was all one color.

Evaluate Characterization
How does the author bring Janette Elizabeth to life for the reader?

And then, in the back pages of Janette Elizabeth's *True Confessions* magazine, I found the answer: an advertisement for freckle-remover cream. I knew that I could afford it if I saved my money, and I did. The ad assured me that the product would arrive in a "plain

1 ***Underwhelmed*** is a word jokingly used to mean the opposite of *overwhelmed*, so it means "not at all impressed."

2 The phrase ***you can't make a silk purse out of a sow's ear*** is an idiom that means "you cannot make something beautiful out of something ugly."

Vocabulary

flawless (flô′ lis) *adj.* having no mistakes; perfect

complexion (kəm plek′ shən) *n.* color, texture, and appearance of the skin

A Rural Scene (detail), 1990.
Konstantin Rodko.
Oil on canvas.

brown wrapper."[3] Plain brown freckle color. For three weeks I went to the mailbox every day **precisely** at the time the mail was delivered.

I knew that if someone else in my family got the mail, I would never hear the end of it. There was no way that they would let me open the box in private. Finally, after three weeks of scheduling my entire day around the mail truck's arrival, my package came.

Diction What do you think the idiom "never hear the end of it" means?

I went to my room with it, sat on the edge of my bed, and opened it. I was sure that I was looking at a miracle. But I had gotten so worked up about the magical package that I couldn't bring myself to put the cream on. What if it didn't work? What would I do then?

Evaluate Characterization Do you think this is a believable reaction, considering what you know about Elizabeth so far?

I fell asleep that night without even trying the stuff. And

3 People ask for things to be delivered in a **plain brown wrapper** when they don't want anyone to know what the contents are.

Vocabulary

precisely (pri sīs′ lē) *adv.* accurately; exactly

when I got up the next morning and looked at my freckles in the mirror, I said, "Elizabeth, this is silly. You have to do it now!" I smeared the cream all over my body. There wasn't as much of it as I had thought there would be, and I could see that I was going to need a part-time job to keep me in freckle remover.

Later that day I took my **hoe** and went with my brother and cousins to the head of the holler[4] to hoe tobacco, as we did nearly every day in the summer. Of course, when you stay out hoeing tobacco all day, you're not working in the shade. And there was something important I hadn't realized about freckle remover: if you wear it in the sun, it seems to have a reverse effect. Instead of developing a peaches-and-cream complexion, you just get more and darker freckles.

By the end of the day I looked as though I had leopard blood in my **veins**, although I didn't realize it yet. When I came back to the house, my family, knowing nothing about the freckle-remover cream, began to say things like, "I've never seen you with that many freckles before." When I saw myself in the mirror, I dissolved into tears and hid in the bathroom.

My mother called me to the dinner table, but I ignored her. When she came to the bathroom door and demanded that I come out and eat, I burst out the door and ran by her, crying. I ran out to the well house[5] and threw myself down, and I was still sobbing when my grandfather came out to see what was wrong with me. I told him about how I'd sent for the freckle remover, and he didn't laugh—though he did suggest that one might get equally good results from burying a dead black cat when the moon was full.[6]

Visual Vocabulary

A **hoe** is a tool with a thin, flat blade set at an angle to a long handle, used for weeding and loosening soil.

Diction Does Elizabeth really dissolve? What does this mean?

---

4 The ***head of the holler*** is a phrase in Appalachian dialect. It refers to the opening of a small valley.

5 A ***well house*** is a shed that covers the deep hole where people used to get their fresh drinking water.

6 ***Burying a dead black cat when the moon was full*** refers to a superstitious practice. The grandfather suggests that using freckle cream has about as much chance of working as a superstitious practice.

Vocabulary

veins (vānz) *n.* vessels that carry blood to the heart from other parts of the body

It was clear that Grandpa didn't understand, so I tried to explain why I didn't want to have freckles and why I felt so **inadequate** when I compared my appearance with Janette Elizabeth's. He looked at me in stunned surprise, shook his head, and said, "But child, there are all kinds of flowers, and they are all beautiful." I said, "I've never seen a flower with freckles!" and ran back to my room, slamming the door.

When my mother came and knocked, I told her to go away. She started to say the kinds of things that parents say at times like that, but my grandfather said, "Nancy, leave the child alone." She was a grown-up, but he was her father. So she left me alone.

I don't know where Grandpa found it. It isn't at all common in the mountains where we lived then. But I know he put it in my room because my mother told me later. I had cried myself to sleep that night, and when I opened my swollen, sticky eyes the next morning, the first thing I saw, lying on the pillow next to my head, was a tiger lily.

BQ BIG Question

What does the tiger lily mean to Elizabeth? How do you think it makes her feel about who she is?

Tiger Lily, 1815.
Mrs. Frederick Hill.
Private Collection.

Vocabulary

inadequate (in ad′ ə kwit) *adj.* not good enough

After You Read

Respond and Think Critically

1. How does the author describe her appearance at the age of twelve? **[Recall]**
2. What qualities does Elizabeth's cousin have that make Elizabeth feel bad about herself? **[Summarize]**
3. Compare the way Elizabeth's mother treats her to the way Elizabeth's grandfather treats her. **[Compare]**
4. **Literary Element** **Diction** How does the author's use of idioms and Appalachian dialect, such as "the head of the holler," help readers understand Elizabeth? **[Analyze]**
5. **Reading Strategy** **Evaluate Characterization** Look back at your graphic organizer to evaluate characterization. Do you think the author thoroughly develops the character of Elizabeth? Explain. **[Evaluate]**
6. **BQ** **BIG Question** How do Elizabeth's freckles help make her who she is? **[Conclude]**

TIP

Comparing

Here are some tips to help you answer question 3.

- List details from the story that show the relationship between Elizabeth and her mother.
- List details from the story that show how Grandpa treats Elizabeth.
- Do you see any similarities or only differences? Summarize your findings.

Keep track of your ideas about the **BIG Question** in your unit Foldable.

Vocabulary Practice

On a separate sheet of paper, write the vocabulary word that best completes each sentence. If none of the words fits the sentence, write *none.*

flawless **complexion** **precisely** **veins** **inadequate**

1. The air was crisp and ________ this morning.
2. We learned in science class that the ________ carry blood to your heart.
3. Compared with his tall, athletic brother, Devon felt ________ on the basketball court.
4. It was ________ twelve o'clock when the lunch bell rang.
5. The lotion is supposed to brighten your ________ so that your skin glows.
6. His performance was ________; there wasn't a single mistake.
7. Sheryl ran without ________ in order to get to school on time.

Writing

Write a Journal Entry Write a journal entry about a time when you discovered something important about yourself. Make the entry come to life by including idioms that you use in everyday conversation.

Literature Online

Selection Resources
For Selection Quizzes, eFlashcards, and Reading-Writing Connection activities, go to glencoe.com and enter QuickPass code GL17527u3.

Before You Read

Yes, It Was My Grandmother and *Good Luck Gold*

Performance Standards

For pages 401–404

ELA6R1g For literary texts, define and explain how tone is conveyed in literature through word choice, punctuation, rhythm, repetition, and rhyme.

Connect to the Poems

Think about your grandparents or other older people you respect and admire. What are they like? How are you like them?

Partner Talk With a partner, talk for a few minutes about one of your grandparents or an older person you admire. Describe how the person looks and acts, or tell a story about the person.

Build Background

When a Chinese baby is one month old, the baby may be the guest of honor at a red egg and ginger party. The baby receives gifts, and the parents announce the baby's given name.

- The guests may receive eggs that are dyed red and some ginger to take home. In Chinese tradition, red symbolizes happiness and good fortune.
- The guests may give the baby "lucky money" or gold jewelry as a sign of good luck and long life.

Set Purposes for Reading

BQ BIG Question

As you read, ask yourself, why are the speakers' grandparents important to them?

Literary Element Tone

Tone is an author's attitude toward a subject. For example, the tone may be witty, serious, or sympathetic. An author reveals tone through the words and images he or she uses to describe a setting, depict a character, or narrate an event. Figurative language, such as metaphors and similes, idioms, or elements in poetry, such as line length, punctuation, rhythm, repetition, and rhyme, may reveal the tone and support the theme.

Identifying the tone helps you know how the author feels about the reader, the subject, or a character.

As you read each poem, ask yourself, which words, images, or other elements reveal the author's attitude toward her subject?

Meet the Authors

Luci Tapahonso

The music, language, and traditions of the Navajo people often shape Luci Tapahonso's poems and stories.

Janet S. Wong

Janet S. Wong often writes about what it was like growing up as the child of immigrants in the United States.

Literature Online

Author Search For more about Luci Tapahonso and Janet S. Wong, go to glencoe.com and enter QuickPass code GL17527u3.

Yes, It Was
My Grandmother

Luci Tapahonso

And So Upon Him She Flew, And She Wasn't Afraid, 2000. Martha Widmann. Acrylic on canvas. Private Collection.

Yes, it was my grandmother
who trained wild horses for pleasure and pay.
People knew of her, saying:
  She knows how to handle them.
  Horses obey that woman.

She worked,
skirts flying, hair tied securely in the wind and dust.
She rode those animals hard and was thrown,
time and time again.
She worked until they were meek
and wanting to please.
  She came home at dusk,
  tired and dusty,
  smelling of sweat and horses.

She couldn't cook,
my father said smiling,
your grandmother hated to cook.
  Oh, Grandmother,
  who freed me from cooking.
  Grandmother, you must have made sure
  I met a man who would not share the kitchen.

  I am small like you and
  do not protect my careless hair
  from wind or rain—it tangles often,
  Grandma, and it is wild and untrained.

Tone What word or words could you use to describe the poem's tone?

BQ BIG Question

What does the speaker's description of her hair suggest about her personality?

Good Luck GOLD

Janet S. Wong

Grandparents, 2002.
Diana Ong.
Computer graphics.

When I was a baby,
one month old,
my grandparents gave me
good luck gold;
a gold ring
so soft it bends,
a golden necklace
hooked at the ends,
a golden bracelet
with coins that say
I will be rich
And happy someday.
I wish that gold
Would work
real soon.
I need my luck
this afternoon.

Tone How does the tone change at the end of the poem?

After You Read

Respond and Think Critically

1. In "Yes, It Was My Grandmother," for what talent is the speaker's grandmother known? **[Recall]**
2. In "Yes, It Was My Grandmother," how are the speaker and her grandmother alike? **[Compare]**
3. In "Good Luck Gold," what is the grandparents' hope for their granddaughter? **[Infer]**
4. In "Good Luck Gold," is the speaker already rich and happy? What clues help you know? **[Interpret]**
5. **Literary Element** **Tone** How is tone revealed in each poem? **[Analyze]**
6. **BQ** **BIG Question** What does each speaker receive from her grandparent(s)? **[Conclude]**

Spelling Link

Doubling the Final Consonant When a word ends with a single consonant following a single vowel, double the consonant before adding *-ing* or *-ed*.

Examples:

sit + ing ⟶ sitting   commit + ed ⟶ committed

run + ing ⟶ running   infer + ed ⟶ inferred

Do not double the final consonant if

- the suffix begins with a consonant
- the accent is not on the last syllable
- the accent moves when the suffix is added
- the word ends in two consonants

If the word ends in *-ll*, drop one *l* before adding the suffix *-ly*.

Practice On a sheet of paper, list these words: *prefer*, *climb*, *nip*, *smell*. Write the word with the *-ing* suffix.

Writing

Write a Scene Identify the main events in one of the poems in this lesson. Rewrite one event as a scene in a story. Keep the same characters and actions that are in the poem. You may want to make the speaker one of the characters. Identify the tone of the poem, and then use words and images to convey the same tone in your scene.

TIP

Comparing
Here are some tips to help you answer question 2. Remember, when you compare, you find similarities.

- Make a list of the grandmother's qualities.
- Make a list of the speaker's qualities.
- Look for the qualities that appear on both of your lists.

Keep track of your ideas about the **BIG Question** in your unit Foldable.

Literature Online

Selection Resources
For Selection Quizzes, eFlashcards, and Reading-Writing Connection activities, go to glencoe.com and enter QuickPass code GL17527u3.

Before You Read

Arachne

Connect to the Myth

Think of an activity that you enjoy doing and can do well. You might choose a sport, a hobby, or a subject in school.

Partner Talk With a partner, talk about the activity. How does it feel to be very good at something? Explain.

Build Background

The word *arachne* (ə rak′ nē) means "spider" in Greek. Many words in the English language come from Greek. For example, spiders are arthropods, animals with jointed legs and segmented bodies. The word *arthropod* comes from the Greek words *arthron*, meaning "joint," and *pod*, meaning "foot." Arachnids are a group of animals that includes spiders, scorpions, ticks, and mites. Fear of spiders is called *arachnophobia*. The story of Arachne explains why spiders are named after her.

Vocabulary

obscure (əb skyoor′) *adj.* not well-known (p. 407).
Few people know about the obscure town of Seashell.

amid (ə mid′) *prep.* in the middle of (p. 408).
Maya found herself amid a crowd of strangers on the dance floor.

mortal (môrt′əl) *adj.* destined to die; human (p. 408).
All things that live are mortal.

obstinacy (ob′ stə nə sē) *n.* state of not giving in to argument, persuasion, or reason (p. 409).
When Tom crossed his arms in obstinacy, we knew that he would not give up easily.

descendants (di sen′ dənts) *n.* people who have a common ancestor (p. 411).
Rob and Tania discovered that they are descendants of a famous explorer.

Meet Olivia E. Coolidge

"A good book should excite, amuse, and interest."
—Olivia E. Coolidge

Bringing the Past to Life As a writer, Olivia E. Coolidge tried to bring the past to life through her carefully researched biographies, histories, and retellings of ancient myths. Coolidge was born in London, England. She taught Greek, Latin, and English in Europe before moving to the United States in 1938.

Literary Works Coolidge wrote more than two dozen books for young people, including *Gandhi, The Statesmanship of Abraham Lincoln,* and *Egyptian Adventures.* "Arachne" was first published in 2001.

Olivia E. Coolidge was born in 1908 and died in 2006.

Literature Online

Author Search For more about Olivia E. Coolidge, go to glencoe.com and enter QuickPass code GL17527u3.

Set Purposes for Reading

BQ BIG Question

As you read, ask yourself, what personality traits does Arachne have?

Literary Element Myth

A **myth** is a traditional story that deals with gods and goddesses, heroes, and supernatural forces. A myth might explain a belief, a custom, or a force of nature.

Myths are important because they tell readers about the beliefs and values of a group of people. Reading myths can help you understand different aspects of the world or of human nature.

As you read, ask yourself, what values does this myth teach?

Reading Strategy Make Generalizations About Plot

A **generalization** is a broad statement that applies to many facts or situations. When you make **generalizations about plot,** you make broad statements based on the events in a story. For example, after reading a myth in which a god solves a problem on Earth, you might generalize that in myths, gods often interfere with life on Earth.

Making generalizations about plot can help you identify the common traits of myths or other types of literature.

To **make generalizations about plot**, think about

- what happens in the myth
- other myths that have similar plots
- what all these plot elements may reveal about myths as a whole

In order to think about the common traits of myths, you may find it helpful to use a graphic organizer like the one below.

Plot elements in this myth: Arachne is very proud.

Similar plot elements in other myths:

Generalizations about myths:

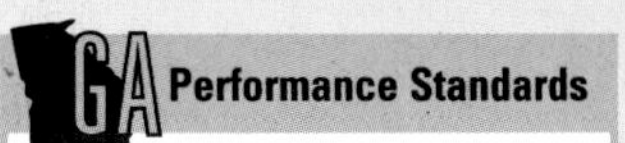

For pages 405–413

ELA6R1j For literary texts, identify and analyze similarities and differences in mythologies from different cultures.

TRY IT

Make Generalizations One day your friend tells you how much he loves his pet dog. On the television news that evening, you watch a story about how a dog saves its owner's life. What generalization do you make about dogs?

ARACHNE

Olivia E. Coolidge

Arachne was a maiden who became famous throughout Greece, though she was neither wellborn nor beautiful and came from no great city. She lived in an **obscure** little village, and her father was a humble dyer of wool. In this he was very skillful, producing many varied shades, while above all he was famous for the clear, bright scarlet which is made from shellfish, and which was the most glorious of all the colors used in ancient Greece. Even more skillful than her father was Arachne. It was her task to spin the fleecy wool into a fine, soft thread and to weave it into cloth on the high, standing loom within the cottage. Arachne was small and pale from much working. Her eyes were light and her hair was a dusty brown, yet she was quick and graceful, and her fingers, roughened as they were, went so fast that it was hard to follow their flickering movements. So soft and even was her thread, so fine her cloth, so gorgeous her embroidery, that soon her products were known all over Greece. No one had ever seen the like of them before.

At last Arachne's fame became so great that people used to come from far and wide to watch her working. Even the graceful nymphs would steal[1] in from stream or forest and peep shyly through the dark doorway, watching in

BQ BIG Question
What is one of Arachne's character traits?

Myth What do people value in the culture from which this myth comes?

1 Here, to ***steal*** is to move secretly so that no one sees you.

Vocabulary

obscure (əb skyoor′) *adj.* not well-known

wonder the white arms of Arachne as she stood at the loom and threw the shuttle[2] from hand to hand between the hanging threads, or drew out the long wool, fine as a hair, from the **distaff** as she sat spinning. "Surely Athene[3] herself must have taught her," people would murmur to one another. "Who else could know the secret of such marvelous skill?"

Arachne was used to being wondered at, and she was immensely proud of the skill that had brought so many to look on her. Praise was all she lived for, and it displeased her greatly that people should think anyone, even a goddess, could teach her anything. Therefore when she heard them murmur, she would stop her work and turn round indignantly to say, "With my own ten fingers I gained this skill, and by hard practice from early morning till night. I never had time to stand looking as you people do while another maiden worked. Nor if I had, would I give Athene credit because the girl was more skillful than I. As for Athene's weaving, how could there be finer cloth or more beautiful embroidery than mine? If Athene herself were to come down and compete with me, she could do no better than I."

One day when Arachne turned round with such words, an old woman answered her, a gray old woman, bent and very poor, who stood leaning on a staff and peering at Arachne **amid** the crowd of onlookers. "Reckless girl," she said, "how dare you claim to be equal to the immortal gods themselves? I am an old woman and have seen much. Take my advice and ask pardon of Athene for your words. Rest content with your fame of being the best spinner and weaver that **mortal** eyes have ever beheld."

"Stupid old woman," said Arachne indignantly, "who gave you a right to speak in this way to me? It is easy to

Visual Vocabulary

A **distaff** is a stick used for spinning, on which wool, flax, cotton, or other fibers are held. The fibers are drawn off the distaff and twisted into thread by hand onto a spindle.

BQ BIG Question

What is Arachne's character flaw?

Make Generalizations About Plot What generalization can you make about conflicts in myths?

---

2 A ***shuttle*** is the part of a loom that moves thread back and forth.

3 ***Athene*** (also spelled *Athena*) is the Greek goddess of wisdom and the arts and crafts. In Roman myths, she is called Minerva.

Vocabulary

amid (ə mid′) *prep.* in the middle of

mortal (môrt′əl) *adj.* destined to die; human

Allegory of Dialectic (also known as *Arachne*), 1575–1577. Oil on canvas, 220 x 150 cm. Sala del Collegio, Palazzo Ducale, Venice.

View the Art If you saw this painting without its title, how would you know that the woman in the painting is Arachne?

see that you were never good for anything in your day, or you would not come here in poverty and rags to gaze at my skill. If Athene resents my words, let her answer them herself. I have challenged her to a contest, but she, of course, will not come. It is easy for the gods to avoid matching their skill with that of men."

Myth Who might this old woman be?

At these words the old woman threw down her staff and stood erect. The wondering onlookers saw her grow tall and fair and stand clad in long robes of dazzling white. They were terribly afraid as they realized that they stood in the presence of Athene. Arachne herself flushed red for a moment, for she had never really believed that the goddess would hear her. Before the group that was gathered there she would not give in; so pressing her pale lips together in **obstinacy** and pride, she led the goddess to one of the great looms and set herself before the other. Without a word both began to thread the long woolen strands that hang from the rollers, and between which the shuttle moves back and forth. Many skeins[4] lay heaped beside them to use, bleached white, and gold, and scarlet, and other shades, varied as the rainbow. Arachne had never thought of giving credit for her success to her

4 ***Skeins*** are continuous strands of yarn or thread coiled in a bundle.

Vocabulary

obstinacy (ob′ stə nə sē) *n.* state of not giving in to argument, persuasion, or reason

The Dispute Between Minerva and Neptune over the Naming of the City of Athens. Rene Antoine Houasse. Chateaux de Versailles et de Trianon, Versailles, France.

father's skill in dyeing, though in actual truth the colors were as remarkable as the cloth itself.

Soon there was no sound in the room but the breathing of the onlookers, the whirring of the shuttles, and the creaking of the wooden frames as each pressed the thread up into place or tightened the pegs by which the whole was held straight. The excited crowd in the doorway began to see that the skill of both in truth was very nearly equal, but that, however the cloth might turn out, the goddess was the quicker of the two. A pattern of many pictures was growing on her loom. There was a border of twined branches of the olive, Athene's favorite tree, while in the middle, figures began to appear. As they looked at the glowing colors, the spectators realized that Athene was weaving into her pattern a last warning to Arachne. The central figure was the goddess herself competing with Poseidon for possession of the city of Athens; but in the four corners were mortals who had tried to strive[5] with gods and pictures of the awful fate that had overtaken them. The goddess ended a little before Arachne and stood

Myth What warning is Athene weaving into her design?

5 ***Strive*** means "to struggle in opposition."

back from her marvelous work to see what the maiden was doing.

Never before had Arachne been matched against anyone whose skill was equal, or even nearly equal to her own. As she stole glances from time to time at Athene and saw the goddess working swiftly, calmly, and always a little faster than herself, she became angry instead of frightened, and an evil thought came into her head. Thus as Athene stepped back a pace to watch Arachne finishing her work, she saw that the maiden had taken for her design a pattern of scenes which showed evil or unworthy actions of the gods, how they had deceived fair maidens, resorted to trickery, and appeared on earth from time to time in the form of poor and humble people. When the goddess saw this insult glowing in bright colors on Arachne's loom, she did not wait while the cloth was judged, but stepped forward, her grey eyes blazing with anger, and tore Arachne's work across. Then she struck Arachne across the face. Arachne stood there a moment, struggling with anger, fear, and pride. "I will not live under this insult," she cried, and seizing a rope from the wall, she made a noose and would have hanged herself.

Make Generalizations About Plot What generalization can you make about who wins conflicts between mortals and gods?

The goddess touched the rope and touched the maiden. "Live on, wicked girl," she said. "Live on and spin, both you and your **descendants**. When men look at you they may remember that it is not wise to strive with Athene." At that the body of Arachne shriveled up, and her legs grew tiny, spindly, and distorted. There before the eyes of the spectators hung a little dusty brown spider on a slender thread.

All spiders descend from Arachne, and as the Greeks watched them spinning their thread wonderfully fine, they remembered the contest with Athene and thought that it was not right for even the best of men to claim equality with the gods.

BQ BIG Question
What does this myth teach about character traits?

Vocabulary

descendants (di sen′ dənts) *adj.* people or animals with a common ancestor

After You Read

Respond and Think Critically

1. What is Arachne's father's profession? **[Recall]**
2. Summarize what happens in the myth. **[Summarize]**
3. What is the reason that Athene first appears as an old woman instead of as a goddess? **[Infer]**
4. What does Arachne's design show? How is her design similar to Athene's? **[Compare]**
5. If Arachne had not insulted Athene with her design, do you think Athene still would have turned Arachne into a spider? Explain your answer. **[Analyze]**
6. BQ **BIG Question** Think about the character traits that lead Arachne to her unfortunate fate. What changes could she have made to avoid her fate? **[Conclude]**

TIP

Comparing
Here are some tips to help you answer question 4. Remember that when you compare, you tell how things are similar.

- Describe Arachne's design.
- Describe Athene's design.
- How are the designs similar?
- How are the purposes of the designs similar?

Keep track of your ideas about the **BIG Question** in your unit Foldable.

Daily Life and Culture

Gods and Myths in Ancient Greece

Mythology played an important role in the lives of the ancient Greeks. They prayed to the gods for protection and prosperity. Every city had at least one official god or goddess to worship.

For example, Athene was the official goddess and protector of Athens.

Myths provided examples of how humans should behave.

These stories were handed down from generation to generation as a means of communicating the values of an earlier culture. Greek sculptors created statues of gods and goddesses, and artists painted mythological scenes on vases, all to preserve their stories.

Group Activity Discuss the following questions with your classmates.

1. Are the characters in "Arachne" typical of characters you might expect to find in a myth? Explain.
2. Which scenes from "Arachne" might have appeared on an ancient Greek vase?

Literary Element Myth

1. A myth often expresses the customs and beliefs of a society. What does the myth of Arachne tell you about what the Greeks thought of spiders?
2. What other myths have you read that explain a natural event?

Review: Oral Tradition

As you learned on page 222, a society's **oral tradition** is the stories, customs, and beliefs passed by word of mouth from one generation to the next. Oral literature was a way of recording the past, glorifying leaders, and teaching morals and traditions to young people.

3. Why might parents have told the myth of Arachne to their children?
4. How does the myth of Arachne express the customs and beliefs of the ancient Greeks?

Reading Strategy Make Generalizations About Plot

Standards Practice  ELA6R1e/ii

5. Like many myths, this story involves a conflict between
   A. a girl and her father.
   B. gods and mortals.
   C. two young school friends.
   D. two brothers.

Vocabulary Practice

Synonyms/Antonyms: Identifying
Identify whether each set of paired words has the same meaning or the opposite meaning. Then write a sentence using each vocabulary word, or draw or find a picture that represents each word.

obscure and unknown
amid and among
mortal and godlike
obstinacy and flexibility
descendants and ancestors

Example:
obscure and unknown = same meaning

Sentence: In Matt's advanced computer-science course, he learned obscure information about how the Internet works.

Academic Vocabulary

Despite warnings, Arachne persisted in **equating** her weaving ability with that of the goddess Athene.

A main theme in this myth addresses the abilities of humans compared to the abilities of gods and goddesses. Using context clues, show your understanding of the word *equating* as used in the sentence above. Check your answer in a dictionary.

LOG ON Literature Online

Selection Resources For Selection Quizzes, eFlashcards, and Reading-Writing Connection activities, go to glencoe.com and enter QuickPass code GL17527u3.

Respond Through Writing

Expository Essay

Analyze Cause and Effect In "Arachne," a stubborn young woman discovers that her skills are no match for an angry goddess. In a short essay, describe how the cause-and-effect relationships in the myth push the plot forward and support the theme.

Understand the Task A **cause** is that which makes something happen. An **effect** is what happens as the result of the cause. They may control the plot and outcome of a story. Analyzing **cause-and-effect relationships** means exploring reasons and examining results.

Prewrite Think of three cause-and-effect relationships in the myth. Then think about how each relationship affects the myth's plot or theme. Keep track of your findings in a chart like the one below.

Effect (Event)	Cause	Effect on Plot or Theme

Draft Before you begin, make an overall plan. For example, you may decide to write an introduction, a paragraph about how cause-and-effect relationships affect plot, a paragraph about how those relationships affect theme, and a conclusion. These sentence frames might help you introduce the body paragraphs of your essay:

Cause-and-effect relationships push the plot forward because ________.

Cause-and-effect relationships support the theme of the myth because ________.

Revise After you write your first draft, read it to determine whether you have supported the main idea of each paragraph with strong examples. Revise as necessary so that your examples support your points.

Edit and Proofread Proofread your paper, correcting any errors in spelling, grammar, and punctuation. See the Word Bank in the side column for words you might use in your expository essay.

GA Performance Standards

For page 414

ELA6W1c Use traditional structures for conveying information (e.g., chronological order, cause and effect, similarity and difference, and posing and answering a question).

Word Bank

Following are some useful words you might want to include in your essay. Check their meanings in a dictionary first to make sure you use them correctly.

acknowledge

capabilities

consequence

impact

precede

Comparing Literature

The Fun They Had and *Why Books Are Dangerous*

BQ BIG Question

As you read these paired selections, think about why books are important to the main characters. How do books help make us who we are?

Literary Element Author's Purpose

The **author's purpose** is his or her intention for writing—to entertain, to inform or explain, to persuade, or even to express emotion. An author often has more than one purpose. You can begin to identify the author's purpose by looking at the author's choice of words and the way in which he or she organizes the writing. As you read, look for clues—such as factual information (to inform), a story (to entertain), or ideas to influence readers (to persuade)—to determine each author's purpose for writing.

Reading Skill Compare and Contrast

Learning to **compare and contrast** two different texts helps you see how the texts are alike or different. You can understand literature better when you compare and contrast the authors' purposes and notice how each author relays a theme through characters, actions, and images. On the following pages, you will compare and contrast the authors' purposes of "The Fun They Had" and "Why Books Are Dangerous." These selections share a subject—books—but their authors deal with that subject quite differently. Use a Venn diagram like the one below to record clues to the authors' purposes as you read the selections.

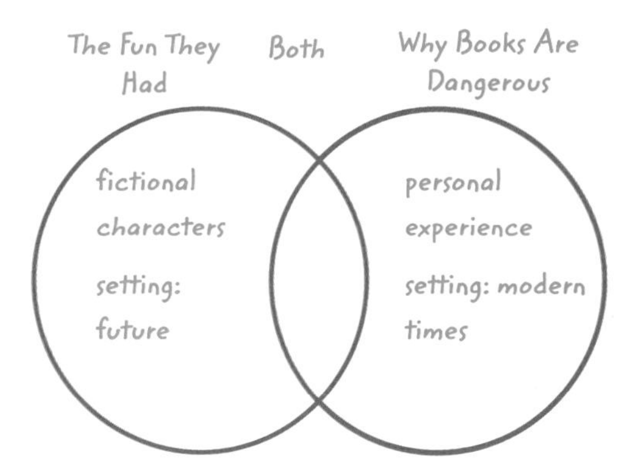

GA Performance Standards

For pages 415–425

ELA6RC2d Evaluate the merits of texts in every subject discipline.

ELA6RC2e Examine the author's purpose in writing.

Meet the Authors

Isaac Asimov

Asimov wrote more than 400 books before he died in 1992.

Neil Gaiman

Neil Gaiman writes comic books, novels, picture books, stories, and screenplays.

Literature Online

Author Search For more about Isaac Asimov and Neil Gaiman, go to glencoe.com and enter QuickPass code GL17527u3.

The Fun They Had

Isaac Asimov

Margie even wrote about it that night in her diary. On the page headed May 17, 2157, she wrote, "Today Tommy found a real book!"

It was a very old book. Margie's grandfather once said that when he was a little boy *his* grandfather told him that there was a time when all stories were printed on paper.

They turned the pages, which were yellow and crinkly, and it was awfully funny to read words that stood still instead of moving the way they were supposed to—on a screen, you know. And then, when they turned back to the page before, it had the same words on it that it had had when they read it the first time.

"Gee," said Tommy, "what a waste. When you're through with the book, you just throw it away, I guess. Our television screen must have had a million books on it and it's good for plenty more. I wouldn't throw *it* away."

Comparing Literature The setting of a story can tell you something about the author's purpose. When does this story take place? How do you know?

"Same with mine," said Margie. She was eleven and hadn't seen as many telebooks as Tommy had. He was thirteen.

She said, "Where did you find it?"

"In my house." He pointed without looking, because he was busy reading. "In the attic."

"What's it about?"

"School."

Margie was scornful. "School? What's there to write about school? I hate school."

Margie always hated school, but now she hated it more than ever. The mechanical teacher had been giving her test after test in geography, and she had been doing worse and worse until her mother had shaken her head sorrowfully and sent for the County Inspector.

He was a round little man with a red face and a whole box of tools with dials and wires. He smiled at Margie and gave her an apple, then took the teacher apart. Margie had hoped he wouldn't know how to put it together again, but he knew how all right, and, after an hour or so, there it was again, large and ugly, with a big screen on which all the lessons were shown and the questions were asked. That wasn't so bad. The part Margie hated most was the slot where she had to put homework and test papers. She always had to write them out in a punch code they made her learn when she was six years old, and the mechanical teacher calculated the mark[1] in no time.

Comparing Literature What purpose does the description of the teacher serve?

The Inspector had smiled after he was finished and patted Margie's head. He said to her mother, "It's not the little girl's fault, Mrs. Jones. I think the geography sector was geared a little too quick. Those things happen sometimes. I've slowed it up to an average ten-year level. Actually, the overall pattern of her progress is quite satisfactory." And he patted Margie's head again.

Comparing Literature Why does the author include this detail?

Margie was disappointed. She had been hoping they would take the teacher away altogether. They had once

1 A ***mark*** is another word for a grade, such as an *A* or a *B*.

taken Tommy's teacher away for nearly a month because the history sector had blanked out completely.

So she said to Tommy, "Why would anyone write about school?"

Tommy looked at her with very superior eyes. "Because it's not our kind of school, stupid. This is the old kind of school that they had hundreds and hundreds of years ago." He added loftily,[2] pronouncing the word carefully, "*Centuries* ago."

Margie was hurt. "Well, I don't know what kind of school they had all that time ago." She read the book over his shoulder for a while, then said, "Anyway, they had a teacher."

"Sure they had a teacher, but it wasn't a *regular* teacher. It was a man."

"A man? How could a man be a teacher?"

"Well, he just told the boys and girls things and gave them homework and asked them questions."

"A man isn't smart enough."

"Sure he is. My father knows as much as my teacher."

"He can't. A man can't know as much as a teacher."

"He knows almost as much, I betcha."

Margie wasn't prepared to dispute[3] that. She said, "I wouldn't want a strange man in my house to teach me."

Tommy screamed with laughter. "You don't know much, Margie. The teachers didn't live in the house. They had a special building and all the kids went there."

"And all the kids learned the same thing?"

"Sure, if they were the same age."

"But my mother says a teacher has to be adjusted to fit the mind of each boy and girl it teaches and that each kid has to be taught differently."

"Just the same, they didn't do it that way then. If you don't like it, you don't have to read the book."

"I didn't say I didn't like it," Margie said quickly. She wanted to read about those funny schools.

Comparing Literature What do you think the author's purpose is for including this conversation?

Comparing Literature Why does the author include this detail?

---

2 ***Loftily*** means "showing more than the necessary pride in oneself."

3 To ***dispute*** is to quarrel or argue about something.

They weren't even half-finished when Margie's mother called, "Margie! School!"

Margie looked up. "Not yet, Mamma."

"Now!" said Mrs. Jones. "And it's probably time for Tommy, too."

Margie said to Tommy, "Can I read the book some more with you after school?"

"Maybe," he said nonchalantly.[4] He walked away whistling, the dusty old book tucked beneath his arm.

Margie went into the schoolroom. It was right next to her bedroom, and the mechanical teacher was on and waiting for her. It was always on at the same time every day except Saturday and Sunday, because her mother said little girls learned better if they learned at regular hours.

Comparing Literature Why is Margie so eager to read more of the book? What do you think the author is suggesting?

4 ***Nonchalantly*** means "with a lack of interest or enthusiasm."

View the Art What feeling do you get from this painting? Is it similar to the feeling you get from reading the story? Explain.

La Nina del Chupetin. Graciela Genoves. Surbaran Galeria, Buenos Aires, Argentina.

Boy and Dog Watching Television. Artist unknown.

The screen was lit up, and it said: "Today's arithmetic lesson is on the addition of proper fractions. Please insert yesterday's homework in the proper slot."

Margie did so with a sigh. She was thinking about the old schools they had when her grandfather's grandfather was a little boy. All the kids from the whole neighborhood came, laughing and shouting in the schoolyard, sitting together in the schoolroom, going home together at the end of the day. They learned the same things, so they could help one another on the homework and talk about it.

And the teachers were people . . .

The mechanical teacher was flashing on the screen: "When we add the fractions ½ and ¼—"

Margie was thinking about how the kids must have loved it in the old days. She was thinking about the fun they had. ❧

Comparing Literature What is the author's reason for ending the story with these words?

Why Books Are Dangerous

Neil Gaiman

When I was a boy, I was almost always carrying a book. It might not have been obvious. Paperbacks were fairly easy to slip into pockets, after all. My father would frisk[1] me for books before family weddings or funerals; otherwise he knew that, while other people were being bored, I'd be sitting comfortably, probably under a table, off in my own world, reading.

Comparing Literature How do you know that books are important to the author?

1 To ***frisk*** someone is to search for something by running one's hands quickly over the person's clothing and through the person's pockets.

Boy Reading. Lina Chesak.

I liked books. I did not yet suspect that books were dangerous. I didn't care what the books were about, as long as they had a story of some kind—spy stories, horror stories, SF[2] or fantasy, histories, adventures, tales. I'd read true-life stories about people who caught spies or captured rare animals for zoos or people who hunted down man-eating tigers. I also was very fond of detectives and the books they came in. These were, I think, looking back on it, all very sensible things for a boy to like, and not the least bit dangerous.

Comparing Literature Does the author really think that books are dangerous?

The headmaster[3] of my school in the south of England, a pipe-smoking, gruff gentleman who was famous for his precise and painful use of the slipper[4] on boys who were sent to him

The Scholar. Norman Rockwell. Saturday Evening Post Cover June 26, 1926.

View the Art This painting shows a student and his teacher. Do you think the artist meant for this picture to be funny? Do you think the picture *is* funny? Explain your answers.

2 ***SF*** is short for "science fiction," which is fiction based on actual or imaginary developments or discoveries in science, often futuristic or fantastic.

3 A ***headmaster*** is the principal or head of a school, especially a private elementary or secondary school.

4 A teacher who is famous for his ***use of the slipper*** is one who is well known for using a slipper or other kind of flexible shoe to spank students.

for misbehaving, once confiscated[5] a book from me. It was called *And to my nephew Albert I leave the island what I won off Fatty Hagen in a poker game,* and it had a photograph of a naked lady on the cover, which was why it was confiscated. This seemed particularly unfair, as in the early 1970s, most books seemed to have naked ladies on the covers, which, at least in the case of *And to my nephew Albert . . .* political comedy, had little or nothing to do with what was going on inside the book. I was interrogated[6] by the headmaster and was given the book back at the end of term, with a warning to watch what I read. He didn't use the slipper, though. Not that time.

Obviously the headmaster understood the dangers of books. He was trying to tell me something. I didn't listen.

Eventually I started to read the dangerous books.

The really dangerous books had titles like *1001 Jolly Interesting Things a Boy Can Do.* You could make dyes from common garden vegetables. It explained it all.

I read the article on making dyes from common garden vegetables, and then I boiled a **beetroot** and soaked a white school shirt in the beet water, and turned it a purply sort of red. I decided that I wouldn't be caught dead wearing it. Then I put it in the washing, and it turned all the shirts and socks and underwear it was washed with a rather startling shade of pink.

I had not learned my lesson. The next thing I found was the toffee[7] recipe.

I learned that if I melted some butter in a saucepan, and then added sugar and golden syrup and a tablespoon of water, and I heated it all together and got it very hot (but didn't burn it), and dripped drops of the boiling liquid into a glass of cold water, when the drops went solid, it was done. Then I'd pour it out onto a greased pie-pan, and let it set hard.

Visual Vocabulary

Beetroot is a vegetable grown for its edible red root.

Comparing Literature Look at the title of the book that the author claims is dangerous. Why do you think the author includes the title of this book in his essay?

Comparing Literature What does the author want you to understand about his personality?

---

5 If someone ***confiscated*** another person's property, he took possession of it by his authority.

6 A person who is ***interrogated*** is asked questions in an orderly and detailed manner.

7 ***Toffee*** is a hard, chewy candy that is made of butter, sugar, and often nuts.

I was so proud. I'd made a golden-clear, buttery toffee. Pure sugar, with a little fat. It tasted amazing. Chewing it was a battle between the toffee and my teeth. Sometimes my teeth would win, sometimes the toffee would prove the victor and pull out a filling, or deal with a loose tooth.

This went on for several months.

I was, I think, in a math lesson. I'd put a fist-sized lump of the toffee into my pocket, where it had melted, slowly, to the shape of my leg. And I had forgotten about it. I also had a handkerchief in the pocket.

"You. Boy," said the teacher. "Gaiman. You're sniveling,[8] boy. Blow your nose."

I said, "Yes, sir," and pulled the handkerchief from the pocket. It came out, and as it did so, a large lump of toffee that was stuck to the handkerchief sailed out across the room and hit the tiled floor.

It shattered when it hit the floor, like glass, into several hundred sharp-edged fragments.[9]

I spent the rest of the lesson on my knees, picking up the sticky-sharp bits of toffee from the floor, while the teacher, convinced that I had done this on purpose to be funny (as if I'd waste a huge lump of toffee on a joke), made sarcastic[10] comments. And, at the end of the lesson, I was sent to the headmaster with a note explaining what I'd done.

The headmaster read the note, puffed on his pipe, then walked slowly to the cupboard at the back of his study and, opening it, produced a large tartan[11] slipper.

That was the day I discovered that books were dangerous.

At least, books that suggested you do something. . . .

Comparing Literature How do you think the author feels about his experience with the book?

Comparing Literature In what way were books "dangerous" for the author? In what ways were books a positive influence in his life?

---

8 Someone who is ***sniveling*** is breathing noisily through the nose or sniffing repeatedly.

9 ***Fragments*** are small pieces that have broken off something.

10 ***Sarcastic*** comments are sharp or cutting remarks that are meant to hurt or make fun of someone.

11 ***Tartan*** refers to a piece of plaid woolen cloth that is woven with one of the patterns of the Scottish Highland clans.

Comparing Literature

BQ BIG Question

Now use the unit Big Question to compare and contrast "The Fun They Had" with "Why Books Are Dangerous." With a group of classmates, discuss questions such as

- What character traits cause Margie and Gaiman to find books so interesting?
- How do books change Margie's and Gaiman's lives?
- How does a love of books make Margie and Gaiman who they are?

Support each answer with evidence from the readings. Talk about the ways each writer develops themes, through characters, images, and actions, that help the writer further his purpose.

Literary Element Author's Purpose

Use the details you wrote in your Venn diagram to think about each author's purpose in "The Fun They Had" and "Why Books Are Dangerous." With a partner, answer the following questions.

1. In what ways are the authors' purposes similar? Think about each author's attitude toward books and school, the events in each selection, and Margie's and Gaiman's views of the world.
2. In what ways are the authors' purposes different in "The Fun They Had" and "Why Books Are Dangerous"? Discuss specific details, feelings, and other ways in which the authors' purposes differ.

Write to Compare

In one or two paragraphs, discuss the authors' purposes in writing "The Fun They Had" and "Why Books Are Dangerous." Focus on these ideas as you write.

- What does the author of each selection do—entertain, inform, persuade, or a combination of these?
- Explain what is similar and what is different about the authors' purposes.
- How did you respond to each selection? Do you think your response is what the author wanted it to be? Explain.

Writing Tip

Paired Conjunctions When you compare, you may want to use paired conjunctions such as *either* and *or,* or *both* and *and.* Remember that each conjunction should be followed by the same part of speech. For example, you might write, "Both *the story* [noun] and *the poem* [noun] deal with love."

Literature Online

Selection Resources
For Selection Quizzes, eFlashcards, and Reading-Writing Connection activities, go to glencoe.com and enter QuickPass code GL17527u3.

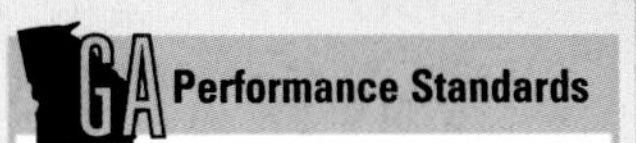

Writing Workshop

Response to Literature

Performance Standards

For pages 426–431

ELA6W2c Demonstrate competence in a variety of genres. Produce a response to literature that advances a judgment that is interpretive, analytic, evaluative, or reflective.

How can you become who you want to be? In this workshop, you will write a response to literature that will help you think about the Unit 3 Big Question: What makes you who you are?

Review the writing prompt, or assignment, below. Then read the Writing Plan. It will tell you what you will do to write your response to literature.

Writing Assignment

A response to literature is an expository essay in which you interpret aspects of a literary selection. Write an interpretation of how one of the poems you have read in this unit addresses the Big Question. The audience, those reading your interpretation, will be your classmates and teacher.

Writing Plan

- Present the thesis, or the main idea, in the introduction of the essay.
- Organize the essay around several clear, insightful ideas.
- Include text evidence from the literary selection to support each idea and to show understanding of the text.
- Use precise and vivid language to help the reader understand the interpretation.
- Conclude by linking back to the thesis of the essay.

Prewrite

Which poem in this unit do you find most interesting? How does this poem address the Big Question?

Gather Ideas

Review the poems in the unit. Ask yourself the following questions and jot down your answers:

- How does each poem address the Big Question?
- Which lines in the poems address the Big Question especially well?

Choose a Poem

Now that you have some ideas, choose a poem to write about. To get started, talk about your poem with a partner.

Partner Talk With a partner, follow these steps:

1. Read your chosen poem aloud.
2. Write some words that describe the poem. Do the words help you think about the poet's overall message? Write a brief thesis statement of how the poem addresses the Big Question using the following sentence frame.

The poem "________" says that ________ make(s) us who we are.

Prewriting Tip

Thesis Statement Remember that a thesis statement expresses an important idea that the writer is trying to convey. That idea can be supported with examples, or evidence.

Get Organized

Use your notes to create a web. Write your thesis statement in the center oval. Then find words or lines from the poem that support the thesis statement and write them in the surrounding ovals.

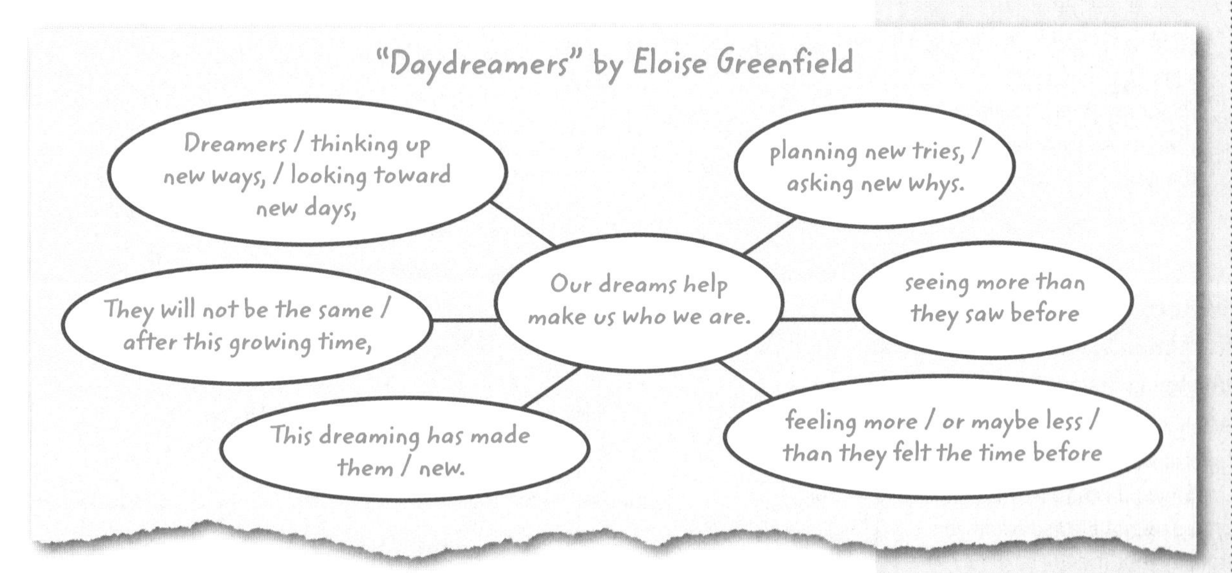
"Daydreamers" by Eloise Greenfield
Dreamers / thinking up new ways, / looking toward new days,
planning new tries, / asking new whys.
Our dreams help make us who we are.
They will not be the same / after this growing time,
seeing more than they saw before
This dreaming has made them / new.
feeling more / or maybe less / than they felt the time before

Now make an outline of your essay. Begin with the strongest evidence that supports your thesis statement.

"Daydreamers" by Eloise Greenfield

Thesis statement: Our dreams help make us who we are.

I. Dreams help us see or feel things differently.
   A. Dreamers / thinking up new ways
   B. seeing more than they saw before
   C. planning new tries / asking new whys

Draft

Now organize your ideas and begin writing.

Get It on Paper

- Review your web, notes, and thesis statement about the poem.
- Begin by writing several sentences connecting the poem to the Big Question. Add your thesis statement.
- For each body paragraph, write a topic sentence that explains how the text evidence relates to the Big Question.
- End your essay by restating your thesis in a different way.
- Don't worry about paragraphs, spelling, grammar, or punctuation.
- Go back and include more evidence if you need to.

LOG ON
Literature Online

Writing and Research
For prewriting, drafting, and revising tools, go to glencoe.com and enter QuickPass code GL17527u3.

Drafting Tip

Transitions To create unity in your essay, use transitional words or phrases such as *in addition, however, after that,* and *more important* to bridge ideas from one paragraph to the next.

TRY IT

Analyzing Cartoons

With a partner, decide what the expression "super duper" means in this cartoon. Would you use that phrase when you talk to your friends or write? What word or phrase would you use instead?

Some elders still speak words from a long-dead language.

Develop Your Draft

1. Present your **thesis statement** in the introduction.

> In her poem "Daydreamers," Eloise Greenfield says that it's your daydreams, or what you wish and hope for while you're awake, that make you who you are.

2. Organize the body of the essay around **clear, insightful ideas.**

> First, she says that daydreaming is easy.

3. Include **examples from the text** that support your main ideas.

> According to Greenfield, as long as you daydream, you're "thinking up new ways" and "asking new whys."

4. Use **precise, vivid language** to help your audience understand your interpretation of the poem.

> Then the thoughts just soar by themselves.

5. Connect your **conclusion** to your thesis.

> The title of Eloise Greenfield's poem says everything you need to know about what helps make you who you are.

Apply Good Writing Traits: Word Choice

Read the sentences below from "Why Books Are Dangerous" by Neil Gaiman. Which words are especially memorable? In what ways do you think the words match the writer's purpose?

> "Gaiman. You're sniveling, boy. Blow your nose."

> It shattered when it hit the floor, like glass, into several hundred sharp-edged fragments.

Use a thesaurus to help choose words that match your purpose.

Analyze a Student Model

Every person is an individual. Everybody—even adults—is always growing and changing. How did you become who you are today? Who will you become tomorrow? In her poem "Daydreamers," Eloise Greenfield says that it's your daydreams, or what you wish and hope for while you're awake, that make you who you are.

The last sentence of the poem makes this message very clear. "This dreaming has made them / new," Greenfield writes. To me, this means that the children in the poem have become what they dreamed of being. Reading the lines of the poem in order explains how this happened.

First, Greenfield says that daydreaming is easy. Daydreamers don't need to do anything special. Just "holding their bodies still / for a time" is all it takes to let the dreams in. Then the thoughts just soar by themselves. According to the poem, as long as you daydream, you're "thinking up new ways" and "asking new whys." That means your thoughts are changing. And if your thoughts change, that means you can change too.

However, the poem says that daydreaming does more than help change you into what you want to become. It also lets daydreamers see "more than they saw before." Greenfield seems to be saying that daydreaming is a way of overcoming time. If you just sit and let the dreams come, you get to see who you were, who you are right now, and who you will become in a whole new way. And that way, magically, you will "have moved / forward."

The title of Eloise Greenfield's poem says everything you need to know about what helps make you who you are. Just sit for a while and do some daydreaming. It couldn't be easier.

Thesis Statement

Help readers focus on the central message by providing a thesis statement in the introduction.

Organization

Organize the essay around well-stated main ideas that support the thesis statement.

Text Evidence

Include words, lines, or ideas from the text that support your main ideas.

Precise, Vivid Language

Choose words that express the specific meaning you intend.

Recall the Thesis

Tie your essay together in the conclusion by reminding readers of your thesis statement.

Revise

Now it's time to revise your draft so your ideas really shine. Revising is what makes good writing great, and great writing takes work!

Peer Review Trade drafts with a partner. Use the chart below to review your partner's draft by answering the questions in the *What to do* column. Talk about your peer review after you have glanced at each other's drafts and have written the answers to the questions. Next, follow the suggestions in the *How to do it* column to revise your draft.

Revising Plan

What to do	How to do it	Example
Did you begin with a clear thesis statement?	State the central message of the essay in the introduction.	In her poem "Daydreamers," Eloise Greenfield ~~talks about what makes~~ ^ says that it's your daydreams that make you who you are.
Is your essay organized around strong main ideas?	Make sure each paragraph has a topic sentence and other sentences add support.	Daydreamers don't need to do anything special. ^Just "holding their bodies still / for a time" is all it takes.
Have you supported your main ideas with evidence?	Include lines from the poem that support and explain your main ideas.	And that way, magically, you will ~~find yourself ahead~~ ^ "have moved / forward."
Have you chosen precise words to explain what you mean?	Think about exactly what you want to say and use precise words.	Greenfield seems to be saying that daydreaming is a way of ~~forgetting about~~ ^ overcoming time.
Does your conclusion link to your thesis statement?	Restate your thesis in different words.	~~In her poem "Daydreamers," Eloise Greenfield says that it's your daydreams that make you who you are.~~ ^ The title of the poem says everything you need to know about what helps make you who you are. Just sit and daydream.

Revising Tip

Circular Ending Restating your thesis in the conclusion reminds readers of your introduction and gives the essay a satisfying completeness.

Edit and Proofread

For your final draft, read your essay one sentence at a time. An editing and proofreading checklist may help you spot errors. Use the proofreading symbols in the chart inside the back cover of this book to mark needed changes. Then make corrections.

Grammar Focus: Quotations from Poetry

When you include lines of a poem in your essay, enclose the words in quotation marks. Insert a slash (/) with a space before and after it between the last word of one line and the first word of the next. Below are problems with citing lines of poetry and their solutions.

Problem: The original quotation is not set apart from the essay's text.

The author says that the children's hands will start to move again.

Solution: Use quotation marks before and after exact words in a line of poetry.

The author says that the children's "hands will start to move again."

Problem: It's not clear where one line of a poem ends and the next begins.

"Scenes passing through their minds make no sound."

Solution: Insert a slash between the lines.

"Scenes passing through their minds / make no sound."

Present

It's almost time to share your writing with others. Write your essay neatly in print or cursive on a separate sheet of paper. If you have access to a computer, type your essay on the computer and check spelling using a word-processing program. Save your document to a disk and print it out.

Grammar Tip

Quotations Double-check to make sure that you have quoted words and lines exactly as they appear in the poem.

Presenting Tip

Background Material
Include a copy of the poem you interpreted on a separate sheet of paper. Cite the author, title, and source of the poem.

Writing and Research For editing and publishing tools, go to glencoe.com and enter QuickPass code GL17527u3.

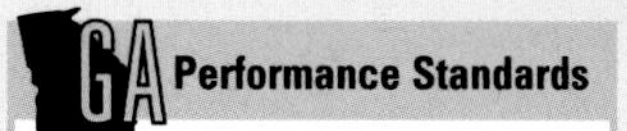

Performance Standards

For page 432

ELA6LSV2b When delivering or responding to presentations, show appropriate changes in delivery.

Speaking, Listening, and Viewing Workshop

Oral Response to Literature

Activity

Connect to Your Writing Deliver an oral response to literature to your classmates. You might want to adapt the response to literature you wrote for the Writing Workshop on pages 426–431. Remember that you focused on the Unit 3 Big Question: What makes you who you are?

Plan Your Presentation

Reread your response to literature and highlight the sections you want to include in your presentation. Just like your written response to literature, your oral response to literature should be organized around several clear, well-supported ideas that help the audience understand your interpretation.

Rehearse Your Presentation

Practice your presentation several times. Try rehearsing in front of a mirror where you can watch your movements and facial expressions. You may use note cards to remind you of your main points and text evidence, but practice your oral response often enough that you won't lose eye contact with your audience.

Deliver Your Presentation

- Speak clearly and precisely.
- Adjust your speaking style to help your audience distinguish between your ideas and quoted material from the text.
- Change the tone, pace, and volume of your speaking to help emphasize important ideas in your interpretation.
- Use gestures to direct the audience's attention to specific points.

Listening to Understand

Take notes as you listen to make sure you understand the oral response. Use the following question frames to learn more about the interpretation from the presenter:

- It seems to me that the tone of this interpretation is __________. Do others agree or disagree?
- Why did you use the gesture __________ to express __________?
- To summarize your interpretation: __________. Is that correct?

Presentation Checklist

Answer the following questions to evaluate your presentation.

- ❑ Did you speak clearly and precisely and with a style that distinguished your ideas from those in the literary text?
- ❑ Did you vary the tone, pace, and volume of your speaking to emphasize important ideas?
- ❑ Did you use gestures to draw attention to specific points?
- ❑ Did you make eye contact with your audience?

Literature Online

Speaking, Listening, and Viewing For project ideas, templates, and presentation tips, go to glencoe.com and enter QuickPass code GL17527u3.

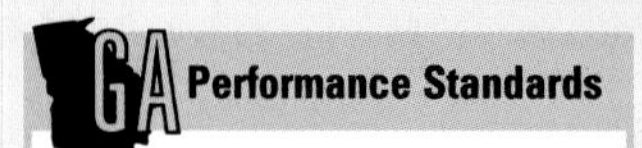

Performance Standards

For page 433

ELA6LSV1a Display appropriate turn-taking behaviors.

Unit Challenge

Answer the Big Question

In Unit 3, you explored the Big Question through reading, writing, speaking, and listening. Now it's time for you to complete one of the Unit Challenges below with your answer to the Big Question.

WHAT Makes You Who You Are?

Use the notes you took in your Unit 3 **Foldable** to complete the Unit Challenge of your choice.

Before you present your Unit Challenge, follow the steps below. Use this first plan if you choose to create a collage about yourself.

On Your Own Activity: Self-Portrait Collage

- ❑ List your hobbies, interests, likes, dislikes, and activities.
- ❑ Gather drawings, photos, or other images that represent you.
- ❑ Put these items on a sheet of heavy paper or poster board. Try different arrangements before you glue things down.
- ❑ Present your collage to the class.

Use this second plan if you choose to see whether your classmates can figure out what makes you who you are.

Group Activity: Play a Game: Who Am I?

- ❑ Form teams of five or six members. Each member will get an index card.
- ❑ On the card, write your likes, dislikes, hobbies and interests, personality traits, and something special about you.
- ❑ Collect the cards and shuffle them, facedown.
- ❑ Have a team member draw a card and read the first entry aloud. Your team will have ten seconds to decide which person that entry describes. Correct guesses are worth five points.
- ❑ If the guess is incorrect, read the second entry and guess again. Each entry after the first is worth one less point.
- ❑ If a team cannot identify the person in five guesses, the team loses two points. The team with the most points wins.

Independent Reading

Fiction

To read more about the Big Question, choose one of these books from your school or library.

Dragon's Gate

by Laurence Yep

Young Otter dreams of leaving China to learn about technology. He joins relatives in the United States, where they help build the Transcontinental Railroad. However, the America that Otter imagined is instead a place of brutal working conditions. Read to find out how Otter struggles to rebuild his dreams.

Holes

by Louis Sachar

Funny, complex, and full of Texas-sized characters, this inventive story will leave you cheering for the underdog, whose name is Stanley Yelnats. Read about Stanley's adventures at Camp Green Lake and about the unlikely friends he makes there.

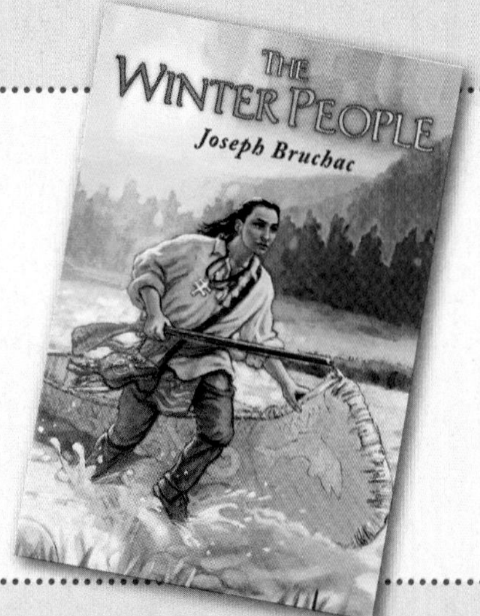

The Winter People

by Joseph Bruchac

When raiders attack fourteen-year-old Saxo's village, he must track them and bring his family back home. This book focuses on family, cultural heritage, courage, and survival.

A Gathering of Days: A New England Girl's Journal, 1830–32

by Joan W. Blos

Thirteen-year-old Catherine records the hardships and joys of pioneer life. When her father remarries, Catherine must cope with changes in her life that are not always welcome to her.

Nonfiction

Carver: A Life in Poems

by Marilyn Nelson

George Washington Carver was born into slavery in 1864, yet he grew up to be a botanist, an inventor, a painter, a musician, and a teacher. The story of how Carver left home to search for an education, eventually earning a master's degree in education, is told in this collection of poems.

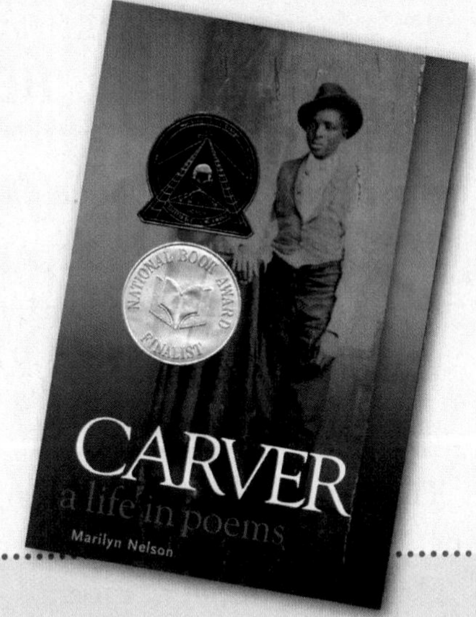

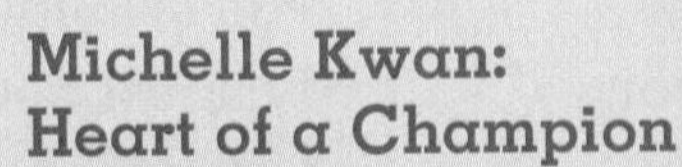

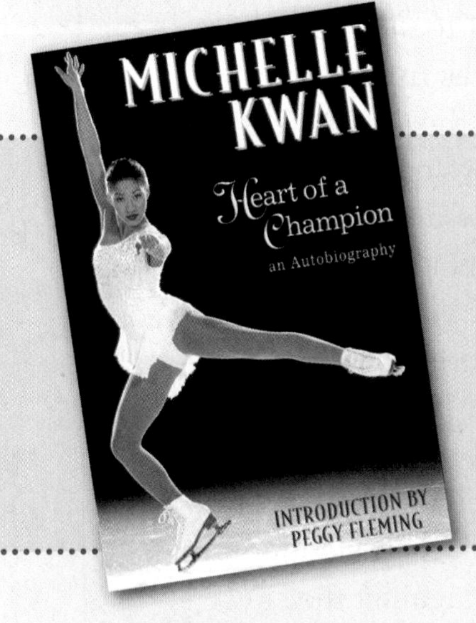

Michelle Kwan: Heart of a Champion

by Michelle Kwan

Ever wondered what it's like to be a figure-skating champion at the age of twelve? If so, check out this firsthand account of Michelle Kwan's triumphs, disasters, and incredible love of skating.

The World According to Dog: Poems and Teen Voices

by Joyce Sidman

This insightful collection of essays and poems explores the bond between teens and the dogs in their lives. The selections offer a look at how dogs accept us, love us, and help make us who we are.

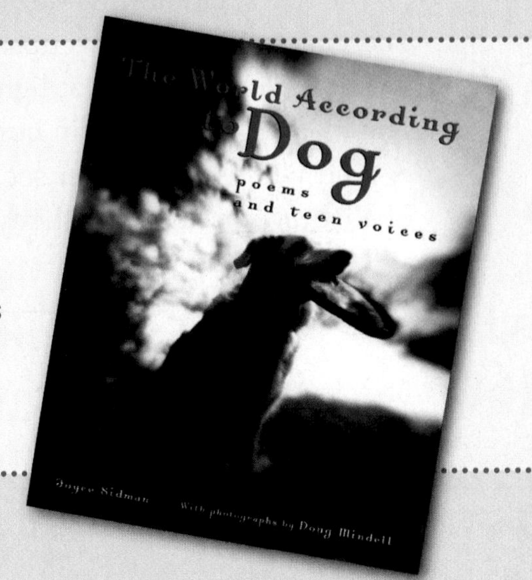

Write a Poem or Story

Write a poem or story based on the book you read. Be sure to build your poem or story from a person or character, an event, or an idea from the book. Ask a classmate to critique your work, and revise your writing based on your classmate's comments.

Assessment

READING

Read the poems and answer the questions. Write your answers on a separate sheet of paper.

"I Remember, I Remember" by Thomas Hood

I remember, I remember,
The house where I was born,
The little window where the sun
Came peeping in at morn;
He never came a wink too soon,
Nor brought too long a day,
But now, I often wish the night
Had borne my breath away.

I remember, I remember,
The roses, red and white;
The violets, and the lily-cups,
Those flowers made of light!
The lilacs where the robin built,
And where my brother set
The laburnum on his birthday—
The tree is living yet!

I remember, I remember,
Where I was used to swing;
And thought the air must rush as fresh
To swallows on the wing:
My spirit flew in feathers then,
That is so heavy now,
And summer pools could hardly cool
The fever on my brow!

I remember, I remember,
The fir trees dark and high;
I used to think their slender tops
Were close against the sky:
It was a childish ignorance,
But now 'tis little joy
To know I'm farther off from Heav'n
Than when I was a boy.

1. In stanza 1, the speaker uses personification to describe
   A. the sun.
   B. the day.
   C. the house.
   D. the window.

2. In which line below are the stressed syllables correctly underlined?
   A. The ros<u>es</u>, red <u>and</u> white
   B. The <u>ro</u>ses, <u>red</u> and <u>white</u>
   C. <u>The</u> roses, <u>red</u> and white
   D. <u>The</u> ros<u>es</u>, red and <u>white</u>

3. What is the meaning of *laburnum* in stanza 2?
   A. a kind of tree
   B. a kind of bird
   C. a kind of flower
   D. a special day

4. The imagery in stanza 3 appeals mainly to the sense of
   A. sight.
   B. smell.
   C. touch.
   D. hearing.

5. In stanza 3, the speaker compares his spirit to a
   A. bird.
   B. pool.
   C. swing.
   D. feather.

6. Which of the following techniques is NOT used to reveal the poet's purpose for writing the poem?
   A. repetition
   B. figurative language
   C. vivid sensory images
   D. unusual spelling and capitalization

Literature Online

Standards Practice For more standards practice, go to glencoe.com and enter QuickPass code GL17527u3.

"Flint" by Christina Rossetti

An emerald is as green as grass;
A ruby red as blood;
A sapphire shines as blue as heaven;
A flint[1] lies in the mud.
A diamond is a brilliant stone,
To catch the world's desire;
An opal holds a fiery spark;
But a flint holds fire.

---

1 **flint:** a stone that produces a spark when struck by steel

7. What idea does the poet emphasize with short lines of one-syllable words?
   A. the qualities of all jewels
   B. the qualities of an opal
   C. the qualities of a sapphire
   D. the qualities of a flint

8. What is the rhyme scheme of "Flint"?
   A. *abba*
   B. *abcb*
   C. *abab*
   D. *aabb*

9. Which line from the poem demonstrates the use of alliteration?
   A. "A ruby red as blood;"
   B. "A flint lies in the mud."
   C. "To catch the world's desire;"
   D. "An opal holds a fiery spark;"

10. What is the MOST reasonable interpretation of the last line of the poem?
    A. Flint can be dangerous.
    B. Flint can only do ordinary things.
    C. Flint has a value not found in other stones.
    D. The ability to do something is less important than actually doing it.

"Between Two Hills" by Carl Sandburg

Between two hills
The old town stands.
The houses loom
And the roofs and trees
And the dusk and the dark,
The damp and the dew
  Are there.

The prayers are said
And the people rest
For sleep is there
And the touch of dreams
  Is over all.

11. Which word would the speaker MOST likely use to describe the town?
    A. dull
    B. exciting
    C. peaceful
    D. frightening

12. An oral reading of this poem would be most effective using which tone?
    A. very soft
    B. calm
    C. frightened
    D. very loud

13. Which pair of words from this poem demonstrates the use of assonance?
    A. dusk, dark
    B. there, touch
    C. old, town
    D. sleep, dreams

14. What is the main purpose of this poem?
    A. to express strong emotions
    B. to inform the reader about small towns
    C. to describe a peaceful scene
    D. to persuade people to behave differently

ENGLISH/LANGUAGE ARTS

Choose the best answer for each question. Write your answers on a separate sheet of paper.

1. Which word or words BEST fill in the blank in the sentence below?

> The peaches are ______________ than the oranges.

A. most sweetest

B. sweetest

C. more sweeter

D. sweeter

2. Which word or words BEST fill in the blank in the sentence below?

> As the bike fell, I ______________ put out an arm to stop it.

A. quick

B. quickly

C. quicklier

D. more quicklier

3. Which sentence below has a compound subject?

A. Most dogs can swim well.

B. Poodles and retrievers are good swimmers.

C. Some dogs can dive and fetch things in the water.

D. Ownership of a dog requires faithful care and discipline.

4. Which sentence below is NOT a complete sentence?

A. Wolves are social animals that live in packs.

B. A wolf pack has from six to ten wolves.

C. Hunts together to bring down large prey such as reindeer.

D. If a pup's mother dies, other adults will care for the pup.

5. In which sentence below does the verb agree with the indefinite pronoun?

A. Everyone is in a cheerful mood.

B. Nobody are having problems.

C. Several of us was having a good time.

D. Everything seem normal.

6. Which word in the sentence below is NOT spelled correctly?

> Trafic at the airport is heavier at midday than at midnight.

A. Trafic

B. heavier

C. midday

D. midnight

WRITING

Read your assigned topic in the box below. Use one piece of paper to jot down your ideas and organize your thoughts. Then neatly write your essay on another sheet of paper.

Expository Writing Topic

Writing Situation

Your school is having a contest to choose a symbol for your school. A symbol is an object used to represent an idea or a quality. For example, a tree may represent strength, or a lion may represent courage. A committee will choose the top three symbols on which the student body will vote.

Directions for Writing

Write an essay in which you suggest a suitable symbol for your school and convince the committee to choose this symbol. Include details and reasons that explain the symbol and help the committee understand your idea.

Writing Checklist

- ☐ Focus on a single topic.
- ☐ Organize your main points in a clear, logical order.
- ☐ Support your ideas or viewpoints with details and examples.
- ☐ Use precise, vivid words.
- ☐ Vary the length and structure of your sentences.
- ☐ Use clear transition words to connect ideas.
- ☐ Correct any errors in spelling, capitalization, punctuation, and usage.

WHAT'S Fair and What's Not?

UNIT FOUR

THE BIG Question

"It's not fair to ask of others what you are not willing to do yourself."

—ELEANOR ROOSEVELT

FOLDABLES® Study Organizer

Throughout Unit 4, you will read, write, and talk about **the BIG Question—"What's Fair and What's Not?"** Use your Unit 4 **Foldable,** shown here, to keep track of your ideas as you read. Turn to the back of this book for instructions on making this **Foldable.**

Explore the BIG Question

WHAT'S Fair and What's Not?

You've seen it happen, or maybe it has happened to you. Someone is treated differently from others. Perhaps a rule doesn't make sense. What do you do when you think something's unfair? Explore how different people feel and react to situations they think are unfair.

Consider these ideas when thinking about what's fair and what's not:

- Seeing Another Side
- Freedom and Equality

What You'll Read

Reading about how people react to situations they find unfair can help you explore this idea for yourself. In this unit, **essays**—short pieces of nonfiction that communicate ideas about a single topic—are excellent sources of information. You will also read short stories, speeches, and other texts that can help you answer the Big Question.

What You'll Write

As you explore the Big Question, you'll write notes in your Unit 4 **Foldable.** Later you'll use these notes to complete two writing assignments related to the Big Question.

1. **Write a Persuasive Essay**
2. **Choose a Unit Challenge**
   - **On Your Own Activity: A Rap or Song**
   - **Group Activity: Television Call-In Show**

What You'll Learn

Literary Elements

style
character
argument
voice
thesis
fable
text structure
mood
foreshadowing

Reading Skills and Strategies

distinguish fact and opinion
draw conclusions about meaning and purpose
recognize author's purpose
analyze figurative language
analyze narrator/point of view
analyze voice
make generalizations about characters
monitor comprehension
make predictions about plot
activate prior knowledge

Explore the BIG Question

TO CAPTAIN JOHN SMITH

Powhatan, Chief of the Powhatan Confederacy

Chief Powhatan in State. Line engraving from John Smith's General History of Virginia, 1624.

In the early 1600s, present-day eastern Virginia was the territory of the Powhatan (pou′ ə tan′) Confederacy, which was made up of several groups of Native Americans. In 1607 a group of English colonists landed and settled along the coast within Powhatan territory. They named their colony Jamestown after their king, James I. Captain John Smith represented the colony in dealings with the Powhatan people and their chief, also called Powhatan. The colonists received

Set a Purpose for Reading

Read this speech to see how Powhatan handles a situation he thinks is unfair.

much help from the Powhatan during their first bitterly cold winters in the New World. However, the colonists claimed lands that the Native Americans considered theirs, and disputes over food and weapons arose. Chief Powhatan made this warning to Captain John Smith.

Jamestown, Virginia, 1609

I am now grown old, and must soon die; and the succession[1] must descend, in order, to my brothers, Opitchapan, Opekankanough, and Catataugh, and then to my two sisters, and their two daughters. I wish their experience was equal to mine; and that your love to us might not be less than ours to you.

Why should you take by force that from us which you can have by love? Why should you destroy us, who have provided you with food? What can you get by war? We can hide our provisions,[2] and fly into the woods; and then you must consequently famish[3] by wronging your friends. What is the cause of your jealousy? You see us unarmed, and willing to supply your wants, if you will come in a friendly manner, and not with swords and guns, as to invade an enemy.

I am not so simple, as not to know it is better to eat good meat, lie well, and sleep quietly with my family; to laugh and be merry with the English; and, being their friend, to have copper, hatchets, and whatever else I want, than to fly from all, to lie cold in the woods, feed upon acorns, roots, and such trash, and to be so hunted, that I cannot rest, eat, or sleep. In such circumstances, my men must watch, and if a twig should but break, all would cry out, "Here comes Captain Smith"; and so, in this miserable manner, to end my miserable life; and,

BQ BIG Question

What is unfair about the situation Powhatan describes?

BQ BIG Question

Why is Powhatan asking Captain Smith to see the conflict from another side?

---

1 ***Succession*** is the order of people in line for a position of leadership. Here, it refers to who will be chief after Powhatan.

2 ***Provisions*** are food supplies.

3 To ***famish*** is to starve.

Captain Smith, this might be soon your fate too, through your rashness and unadvisedness.[4]

I, therefore, exhort[5] you to peaceable councils; and, above all, I insist that the guns and swords, the cause of all our jealousy and uneasiness, be removed and sent away. ❧

4 To act with ***rashness and unadvisedness*** is to act without careful thought or consideration.

5 To ***exhort*** is to urge strongly.

BQ BIG Question

Powhatan gives a warning here. What does he say the reward will be if the English treat his people fairly, and what will the English risk if they do not?

Pocahontas Saving the Life of Captain John Smith, c. 1836–40. John Gadsby Chapman. Oil on canvas. Collection of the New-York Historical Society.

After You Read

Respond and Think Critically

1. Use your own words to explain what Powhatan wants the English to do. **[Summarize]**
2. According to Powhatan, how can both groups benefit if they treat each other fairly? **[Identify]**
3. What does Powhatan mean when he says if his people leave, the English "must consequently famish by wronging [their] friends"? **[Interpret]**
4. Do you think Powhatan makes a convincing argument? Why or why not? Support your opinion with evidence from the text. **[Evaluate]**

Write a Summary Write a one-paragraph summary of the speech. You may want to begin your summary with this topic sentence:

In this speech, Powhatan tells Captain Smith that _________.

Notice that Powhatan's speech is four paragraphs long. The paragraphs tell *who he is, what he wants to know, what he knows,* and *what he wants.* Write one sentence about the first and last paragraphs and two sentences for each middle paragraph.

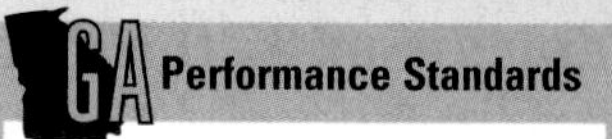

For page 448

ELA6W2d Demonstrate competence in a variety of genres. Produce writing that excludes extraneous and inappropriate information.

Literature Online

Unit Resources For additional skills practice, go to glencoe.com and enter QuickPass code GL17527u4.

Part 1

Seeing Another Side

Opposing Faces. Artist Unknown.

BQ BIG Question What's Fair and What's Not?

In the picture, two people stare at each other face-to-face. How might the picture show the value of seeing both sides of an issue? When has seeing another side given you a new outlook?

Before You Read

Looking for America

Connect to the Essay

Think about a time when it seemed as though one set of rules applied to you and another set of rules applied to others.

Quickwrite Freewrite for a few minutes about the two sets of rules. Was this fair treatment? Is it ever fair to have different rules for different people?

Build Background

The events in Elizabeth Partridge's essay take place during the summer of 1963 in Atlanta, Georgia.

- In the American South at that time, laws kept African Americans segregated, or separated, from whites. These laws were known as Jim Crow laws.
- It was against the law for African Americans and whites to eat at the same restaurants, sit together on buses or trains, or go to school together.
- It was also against the law for African Americans to use bathrooms or drinking fountains labeled "Whites Only." Bathrooms and drinking fountains for African Americans were not always available.

Vocabulary

architect (är′ kə tekt′) *n.* one whose profession is to design, draw plans for, and help create buildings (p. 453).
The architect designed a house made mostly of glass.

beckoned (bek′ənd) *v.* signaled, summoned, or directed by a sign or gesture (p. 455).
Her father beckoned her to come inside and eat dinner.

radiating (rā′ dē āt′ ing) *v.* moving or spreading outward from a center (p. 458).
The warmth from the fire was radiating throughout the room.

discomfort (dis kum′ fərt) *n.* uneasiness; hardship; pain (p. 459).
The discomfort he felt in the hot car was almost unbearable.

buffet (buf′ it) *v.* to strike repeatedly; to knock against (p. 459).
The strong winds buffet the students as they walk to school.

Meet Elizabeth Partridge

"I started figuring out what was well written and what was not that good, because I love it when a story really works, I love the craft of writing."

—Elizabeth Partridge

California Writer Elizabeth Partridge grew up in a large family near San Francisco, California. She traveled with her family as they went camping across the United States every summer.

Literary Works Elizabeth Partridge has written children's books, biographies, and historical fiction, including award-winning nonfiction books about musician Woody Guthrie and photographer Dorothea Lange.

Elizabeth Partridge was born in 1951.

Literature Online

Author Search For more about Elizabeth Partridge, go to glencoe.com and enter QuickPass code GL17527u4.

Set Purposes for Reading

BQ BIG Question

As you read, ask yourself, what does the narrator learn about fairness during her trip?

Literary Element Style

Style is the author's choice and arrangement of words and sentences in a literary work. The author's style reflects the tone and advances the theme of the work.

Paying attention to the author's style can help you understand the author's purpose in writing and attitude toward the subject and audience. Consider the following questions as you read:

- What kind of language does the author use? What figures of speech are included?
- What are the sentence patterns? How important are conversations to the essay?
- How does the author feel about this subject?

As you read, ask yourself, how does the style of the essay reveal the author's attitude toward what she sees during her travels?

Reading Skill Distinguish Fact and Opinion

A **fact** is something that can be proved true. An **opinion** is what someone believes to be true. Research is the basis for facts. Feelings or experiences are the basis for opinions. Opinions cannot be proved.

When you **distinguish fact and opinion,** you decide what can be proved true and what someone believes.

To distinguish fact and opinion, ask yourself,

- Does the author provide a source or supporting evidence?
- Does the information correspond with facts I already know?
- Is the author presenting his or her feelings about the subject?

As you read "Looking for America," record statements of fact and opinion from the selection. You may find it helpful to use a graphic organizer like the one below.

Statement	Fact or opinion?	How Do I know?

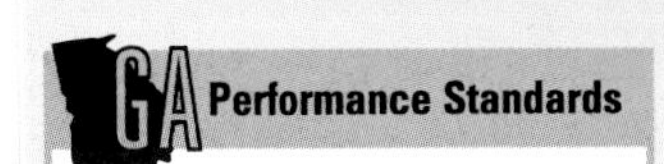

GA Performance Standards

For pages 450–460

ELA6R1g For literary texts, define and explain how tone is conveyed in literature through word choice, sentence structure, punctuation, rhythm, repetition, and rhyme.

TRY IT

Distinguish Fact and Opinion
Your friend just returned from a trip to Beijing, China. She tells you that Beijing is the capital of China. She also says that Beijing is the best place in the world to vacation. Which of her statements is a fact and which is an opinion? How do you know?

Noonlight in Vermont. David Arsenault. Oil on canvas. Private Collection.

Looking for America

Elizabeth Partridge

What I hated most was how people stared at us. I didn't mind so much while we were driving, and I would see people's mouths drop open as we flew by. But I hated it when we pulled into a campground or a gas station. As soon as my father rolled down the window, someone would stick his head in, look us over, and ask, "Where're you folks from?"

"California," my dad would say. They'd nod, like that explained it.

But it didn't, of course. It didn't begin to explain why our family was driving across the country in the summer of 1963, in an old Cadillac limousine painted a bright, metallic gold. The five of us kids didn't sit tidily in a row

Style Is this an unusual way to start an essay? How does it set the tone of the essay?

like regular kids but instead were sprawled on a double bed mattress that my dad had spread across the back. My parents called it "looking for America." I thought it was more like being looked *at* by America.

Distinguish Fact and Opinion Is this a statement of fact or opinion? How do you know?

My dad was a freelance photographer,[1] and to fund our trip he'd arranged to photograph buildings and parks all over the United States. We ranged in age from my seventeen-year-old sister, Joan, to baby Aaron. I was eleven, smack in the middle of the pack, with my brother Josh three years older and my sister Meg two years younger.

We threaded our way through national and state parks, zigzagging toward New York City. In the Southwest we climbed rickety wooden ladders up a cliff into old Pueblo Indian houses; in Yellowstone we were drenched by Old Faithful;[2] in Kansas we rolled out of bed at five A.M. to watch a farmer milk his cows.

Style What details does the author describe in this paragraph? How do they let readers know how she feels about the trip?

"Look at it!" my father would say, throwing his arms out. "Just look at it all." With off-the-cuff comments[3] by my father, and more thoughtful views from my mother, we took in the rhythms and lives of other Americans. "We're lucky to be alive," my father said. "Right now, right here!"

By late August we had made it to New York, camped our way down the Great Smoky Mountains,[4] and were headed for Atlanta, Georgia.

An **architect** my father knew, Mr. McNeeley, had designed his own house in Atlanta. We were invited to

---

1 A ***freelance photographer*** is a photographer who works on his or her own and may have many different employers.

2 The ***Pueblo Indians*** are a group of Native Americans living mainly in New Mexico and Arizona. ***Yellowstone*** is a park in Wyoming, Idaho, and Montana. It is famous for a hot spring known as ***Old Faithful*** that sprays water and steam from the ground.

3 To make an ***off-the-cuff comment*** is to say something without thinking carefully about it.

4 The ***Great Smoky Mountains*** are mountains on the border between North Carolina and Tennessee.

Vocabulary

architect (är′ kə tekt′) *n.* one whose profession is to design, draw plans for, and help create buildings

September 22, 2003: Dowing Street has been attached by Greg Dyke over new laws that will allow an American company to own ITV, 2003. Ben McLaughlin. Oil on panel. Private Collection, Wilson Stephens Fine Art, London.

View the Art What feeling do you think the painter of this scene is trying to convey? Does it relate to how the author views her family's trip to visit the McNeeleys?

stay while my father photographed the house. I was excited—after weeks of smoky fires and pit toilets, we were going to stay in a real house. Maybe they'd even have a TV in their rumpus room[5] and we could spread out on a comfortable couch and watch something like *The Wonderful World of Disney.*

We hit the Deep South just as a hot spell struck. The air was thick and steamy and smelled like mildew. The buzz of cicadas[6] filled my ears.

My mother insisted we stop for the night at a campground outside of Atlanta, so we could clean up. After dinner she handed out towels and shepherded us into the

5 A ***rumpus room*** is a playroom or family room.

6 ***Cicadas*** (si kā′ dəz) are large insects, sometimes called locusts. The male makes a loud, shrill buzzing sound by means of two vibrating plates on its abdomen.

public showers, a squat cement building with huge spiders in the corners and black beetles scuttling across the wet floors. Washing my hair, I discovered a big knotted tangle in the back, but it hurt too much when I tried to brush it out so I just left it. At least my hair was clean.

Late the next morning when we arrived at the McNeeleys', I saw that my mother had been right to tidy us up. Their new house was perfect. Every surface was shiny clean, nothing out of place. Built around a courtyard filled with plants, floor to ceiling glass windows let a dappled[7] green light into every room. Antique Persian rugs[8] covered the smooth cement floors, and modern sculptures made of glass and ceramic perched on back-lit shelves. There wasn't a rumpus room in sight. Mrs. McNeeley wore bright red lipstick and white slacks with a crisp linen blouse. I was painfully aware of the big snarl in my hair.

Mrs. McNeeley showed my sisters and me into a guest room with its own bathroom loaded with huge, fluffy towels and sweet-smelling soap, then left us, saying she needed to speak with the cook about lunch arrangements.

I stood on one foot and stared out into the courtyard. Our mother was right to be concerned: we didn't fit in. "How long do you think we're staying here?" I asked Meg nervously.

At lunchtime my mother **beckoned** me to take the chair next to Aaron. A tall black woman wearing a starched apron came in through a swinging door. She carried a **casserole** with a heavy silver spoon laid across the top.

"Thank you, Annie," said Mrs. McNeeley. I stared at my mother, frozen. What were we supposed to do now? Did we dip the spoon in the casserole and serve ourselves? Did we get served? Annie stood next to my mother, the casserole in her outstretched arms. My mother looked

Visual Vocabulary

A **casserole** is a baked food with many different ingredients inside.

Style Which senses does the author appeal to when she describes the McNeeleys' house?

---

7 Something ***dappled*** is marked with spots or patches of color.

8 ***Antique Persian rugs*** are rugs made in an early period of Iran's history. The rugs are very expensive.

Vocabulary

beckoned (bek′ənd) *v.* signaled, summoned, or directed by a sign or gesture uncomfortable and busied herself with tucking a napkin into the neck of Aaron's shirt. My stomach twisted. Even my mother wasn't sure what to do.

"Please," said Mrs. McNeeley to my mother, "help yourself."

When Annie stood next to me I just looked at her helplessly, afraid I would spill casserole all over my lap from the big silver spoon. She winked at me so quickly I wasn't sure she had, and put a spoonful of casserole on my plate.

After lunch my father started shooting interiors[9] of the house. The rest of us were shepherded to the courtyard. My mother and Mrs. McNeeley sat under a big umbrella, and Annie brought out a pitcher of iced tea and tall glasses full of clinking ice cubes.

Meg and I played hopscotch on the flagstones, while Joan challenged Josh to a game of rummy.[10] Aaron sat and banged on a metal pail. The heat fell down on us, heavy and moist, and the whiny buzz of the cicadas set my teeth on edge. Aaron smashed his hand under the pail and started screaming. Suddenly my head felt like it was exploding with noise and heat and an anxious worry.

I had to get away from my sisters and brothers, away from Mrs. McNeeley sitting stiffly with a tight smile. I slipped inside, crossed the dining room, and bolted through the swinging door, right into the kitchen. Annie stood with her back to me, working at the sink.

Style How does the author use the verbs in this sentence to describe her trip to the kitchen?

"Yes, Ma'am?" she said, turning around. "Oh," she said, surprised to see me. I stood awkwardly, ready to dash out again. Maybe I wasn't allowed in the kitchen. The cook tipped her head toward a small pine table.

"Sit, honey," she said. I tried to ease graciously into the chair but managed to knock my funny bone on the edge of the table and let out a yelp.

"You must be growing," the cook said. "Skinny as all get out, and don't know where your body's at."

I didn't want to tell her I was always banging myself on something. She put two sugar cookies and a tall, cold glass of milk in front of me. As I ate, I watched her wash the

9 If a photographer is ***shooting interiors***, the photographer is taking pictures indoors.

10 ***Flagstones*** are paving stones, and ***rummy*** is a card game for two or more players.

lunch dishes. Steam rose from the sink, and moisture beaded up on her forehead. When she finished she filled a quart-size canning jar with cold water and drank. I was grateful for her quiet company.

When Aaron woke up from his nap we walked to a nearby city park. Though the sun was low, the air still felt like we were walking in a huge oven, with more heat

Style How does the figurative language here add to the mood of the essay?

Confetti Still Life. Lillian Delevoryas. Private Collection.

radiating up from the cement. My mother sat on a bench next to the sandbox and plunked Aaron down in the sand.

I spotted a drinking fountain and ran over, guzzling the water in great big gulps. Meg thumped into my back.

"My turn!" she said. I clung tight to the faucet and jabbed backward at her with my elbows until my stomach was full.

When I stood up, water slid down my neck and under my shirt. Over the fountain was a sign I hadn't noticed: "Whites Only."

"Mom," I yelled back across the playground. "What does 'Whites Only' mean?"

My mother flung her hand out. "Sh. . . ." she said. "Come over here."

I stood next to my mother, who leaned in close. "Negroes aren't allowed to drink from the same fountains as whites in the South, or use the same bathrooms."

I stared at my mother, disbelieving.

"Are those rules?"

"More than rules," she said sadly. "Laws."

I walked all around the playground, but I didn't see any other drinking fountain.

The next morning as my parents were packing the car, I slipped back into the kitchen.

"We're leaving," I said to Annie.

"I know, honey," she said. "You have a good trip now, you hear?"

The breakfast dishes were sitting in the rack drying, carrots and potatoes lay on the counter, next to her half-full jar of water. I wanted to ask Annie what she did when she got thirsty at the park. But it seemed like too big a question. I searched for something I could ask, something that was small and not tangled up.

"Why do you drink from a jar?" I blurted out.

She looked at me, considering. Her eyes were full of a lot of things I couldn't read.

Distinguish Fact and Opinion Is this a statement of fact or opinion? How do you know?

BQ BIG Question
How does this statement reflect the unfairness of the situation?

Vocabulary

radiating (rā′ dē āt′ ing) *v.* moving or spreading outward from a center

"I get mighty thirsty," she finally said. "Those glasses aren't big enough for me."

I didn't understand. She was by the sink all day where she could easily refill her glass.

I heard my father call out, "Let's go!" and I spun out of the kitchen through the swinging door. We drove away from the house of clean rooms and dappled green light and extra-good behavior. Away from the park and kitchen and rules—laws—I didn't understand.

In no time we were out on the highway, my father whistling with the joy of being back on the open road. I leaned over the front seat and asked my mother, "Why did Annie drink out of a jar?"

My mother didn't look at me but spoke softly to her hands resting in her lap. "She probably wasn't allowed to drink from the glasses the family used."

I lay back on the mattress and thought about that. The cook prepared all their food, washing, peeling, chopping, and serving. She set the table, touching every dish. Why couldn't she drink out of their glasses?

My mother must have felt me thinking behind her, because she turned around and said gently, "Some things just don't make sense."

She turned back, **discomfort** settling on her shoulders like an old sorrow. It was all too big, too complicated, even for her.

I still didn't understand. Why would everyone go along with something that didn't make any sense? I rolled down my window and let the hot air **buffet** my face, hoping it would blow away some of the helplessness I felt. ❧

BQ BIG Question

Do you agree with the author's mother? Are there ways to change things that are unfair?

Vocabulary

discomfort (dis kum′ fərt) *n.* uneasiness; hardship; pain

buffet (buf′ it) *v.* to strike repeatedly; to knock against

After You Read

Respond and Think Critically

1. How does Annie help the author at lunch? **[Recall]**
2. Explain why the author is uncomfortable at the McNeeleys' house. **[Summarize]**
3. What question does the author want to ask Annie? Why doesn't she ask this question? **[Infer]**
4. **Literary Element Style** How would you describe the author's style in "Looking for America"? Choose one or two words to describe it, and explain your choice. **[Analyze]**
5. **Reading Skill Distinguish Fact and Opinion** Review the graphic organizer you completed as you read. How does the author use both facts and opinions to tell about segregation? **[Classify]**
6. **BQ BIG Question** At the end of the essay, why does the author feel helpless? What has she learned about fairness? **[Conclude]**

Vocabulary Practice

Match each boldface vocabulary word with a word from the two right columns that has the same or a similar meaning. Two of the words in the right columns will not have matches. Then write a sentence using each vocabulary word or draw or find a picture that represents the word.

1. **architect**	a. signaled	f. spreading
2. **beckoned**	b. beat	g. designer
3. **buffet**	c. bridge	
4. **radiating**	d. pain	
5. **discomfort**	e. dying	

Example sentence: A local architect designed the new mall.

Writing

Write a Letter What is the author's main point in "Looking for America"? Which characters help support the point? Write an informative letter to one of the characters. In the letter, explain how the character's words or actions help support the author's main point. Include supporting details from the essay. Be sure your letter includes a date, a greeting, a closing, and a signature.

TIP

Analyzing
In question 4, to analyze the author's style, think about the language she uses.

- What kind of word choices and sentence structure does she use to describe her experience?
- What examples of figurative language can you find?
- What tone do the words, sentences, and figures of speech create? Is the essay funny? Playful? Dramatic?

Keep track of your ideas about the **BIG Question** in your unit Foldable.

Literature Online

Selection Resources
For Selection Quizzes, eFlashcards, and Reading-Writing Connection activities, go to glencoe.com and enter QuickPass code GL17527u4.

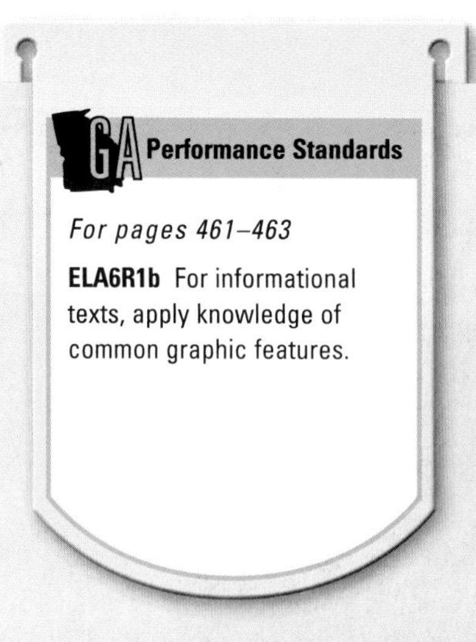

GA Performance Standards

For pages 461–463

ELA6R1b For informational texts, apply knowledge of common graphic features.

TIME

What should students wear to class?

By MELANIE BERTOTTO

At my school in Lemoyne, Pennsylvania, Principal Joseph Gargiulo follows the latest styles. But his interest has nothing to do with a love of fashion. He is just trying to back up Lemoyne Middle School's dress code.

Lemoyne does not let students wear flip-flops and pajama pants. "Pajamas are for sleeping in," says Gargiulo. "School is a student's job. You don't go to your job in pajamas."

Set a Purpose for Reading

Read to understand both sides of the debate about school dress codes.

Preview the Article

1. What does the **title** suggest about school dress codes?
2. What information can you find in the red box, also called a **sidebar**?

Reading Strategy

Recognize Bias

Bias is a tendency to be for or against a certain position. To **recognize bias,** think about the author's purpose and word choices. Also pay attention to whether statements include supporting facts.

Author's purpose	
Important words	
Factual support	

Seventh-grader Leah Hawthorn disagrees. She says that wearing whatever she likes helps her do good work at school. "You worry less about how you look," she says. "So you are more focused on what you're doing in class."

Pennsylvania is one of 28 states that has given school districts[1] the power to decide what students can wear to class. Many who are in charge of education believe that dress codes are good for students. They point to places such as the Long Beach Unified School District in California to prove it. In 1994, that school district became the first public school system to order elementary and middle school students to wear uniforms. Soon after, the school district found that fewer students had been absent and fewer had been put out of school than before.

Some people say that dress codes and uniforms go against the right of freedom of expression. The American Civil Liberties Union (ACLU) has filed lawsuits for parents and students who say that school dress codes are unfair.

1 ***School districts*** are areas containing public schools that are managed together.

Should schools be able to tell students what to wear?

Dorthy Harper was the deputy of the Long Beach Unified School District.

YES! Dress codes can play a major role in helping schools fulfill one of their [main] responsibilities: keeping students safe. Dress codes help schools [set] standards of behavior. This results in safe and orderly classrooms. Most important, dress codes require that all students be held accountable for maintaining a school climate that encourages learning. Schools that successfully adopt[2] dress codes are generally safer, have more positive climates, and have a stronger sense of school pride. That's a lot to gain without having to give up much at all.

2 To ***adopt*** something is to accept it and put it to use.

Allen Lichtenstein is an ACLU lawyer in Nevada.

NO! The Supreme Court has said that students do not leave their constitutional rights at the schoolhouse door. Yet some schools' dress codes restrict students' freedom of expression. Supporters claim that uniforms and dress codes improve discipline[3] and increase student achievement. But there is little evidence to support this. Codes stifle individuality.[4] While no one supports allowing clothing that is dangerous, disruptive, or too revealing, many codes go too far. America has always prided itself on the individual's right to self-expression. That respect should extend to student clothing.

3 Here, ***discipline*** is orderly conduct.

4 ***Individuality*** is the combination of qualities that make one person or thing different from another.

Respond and Think Critically

1. Write a brief summary of the main ideas in this article. For help on writing a summary, see page 170. **[Summarize]**
2. **Text to Self** On which side of the dress code issue are you? What are your reasons for supporting this side over the other? **[Connect]**
3. Why might parents be in favor of, or against, a school dress code? **[Infer]**
4. Look at the two opinions in the sidebar. With whose opinion would most students at your school agree? What evidence best supports that opinion? **[Compare]**
5. **Reading Strategy** **Recognize Bias** In the sidebar, find an example of an unsupported inference or statement.
6. **BQ** **BIG Question** How does seeing both sides of an issue help readers better understand an issue? Whatever side of the dress code debate you are on, write a statement of support for the other side.

Before You Read

Functional Documents

Connect to the Functional Documents

Think about rules you must follow at home or at school.

Partner Talk With a partner, talk about one rule you have in your home or at school. What is the purpose of the rule? What happens if you break it? Do you think the rule is fair?

Build Background

We can't always predict how changes in the world, such as developments in technology, will change the way we live. So we have **surveys,** which are studies that ask for input from people, to help us understand how they think or behave. Other documents, called **policies,** guide our actions. Knowing how to use these documents is an important part of living in modern society.

- **Surveys** collect information from a group of people. When you fill out a survey, you answer questions. You might give your opinion.
- A **policy** is a set of rules. For example, schools have policies for use of equipment. Most policies help you make sure that your actions do not hurt or cause difficulty for anyone else.

Set a Purpose for Reading

Reading Strategy

Draw Conclusions About Meaning and Purpose

A **conclusion** is a general statement about something supported by reasoning and details. When you **draw conclusions about meaning and purpose,** you make a statement about *what* significance the information in the document has and *why* it was written.

You can draw a conclusion about the **meaning** of a document by asking questions that begin with *what.*

- What information is in this document?
- What is the main idea?

You can draw a conclusion about the **purpose** of a document by asking questions that begin with *why.*

- Why did someone write this?
- Why should I read this?

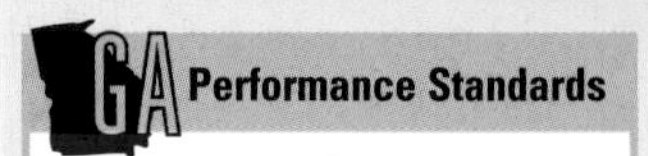

For pages 464–468

ELA6R1b For informational texts, apply knowledge of common graphic features.

Understand Surveys

What kind of information is this survey asking for? Explain when and why someone might want this information.

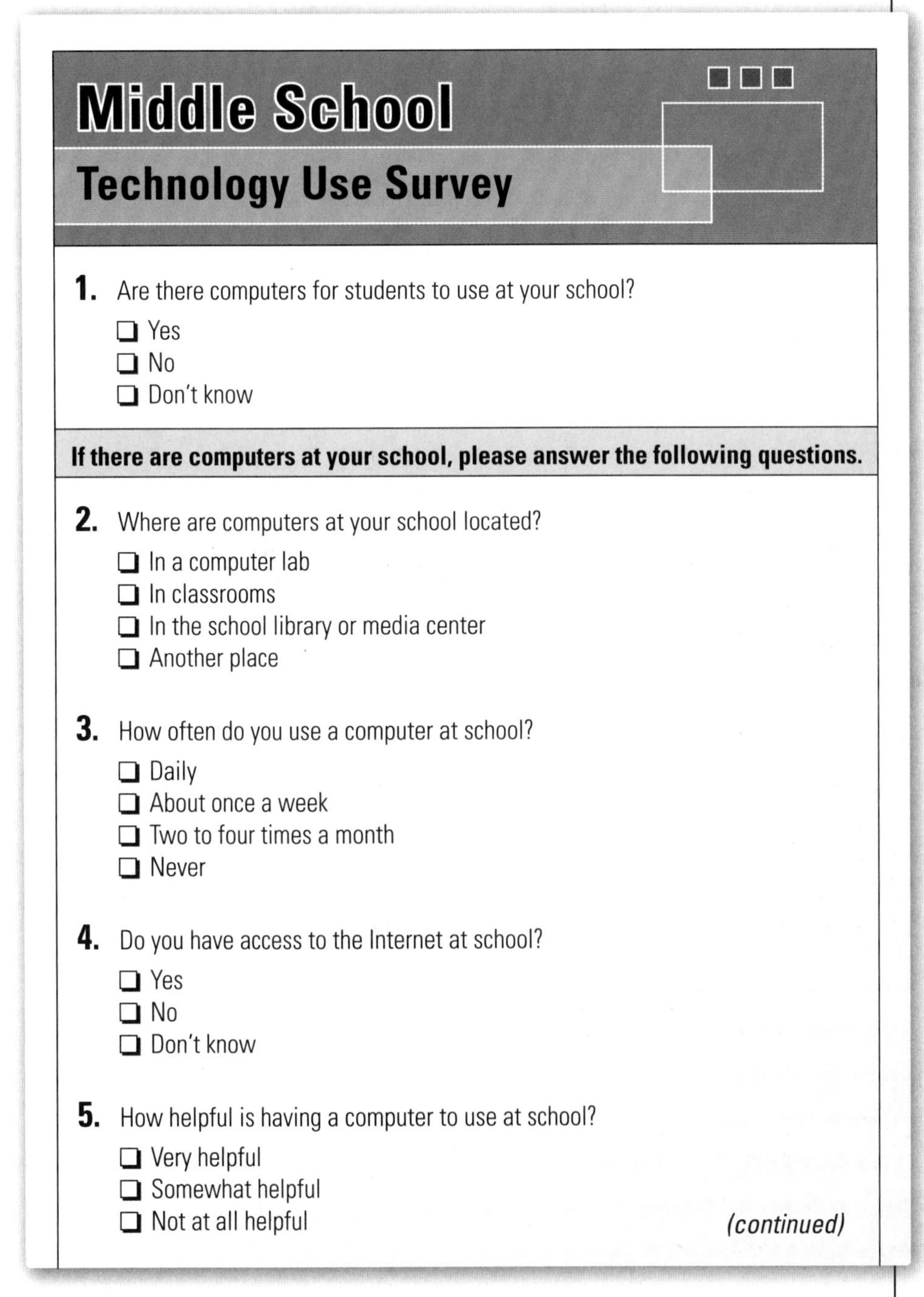

Middle School
Technology Use Survey

1. Are there computers for students to use at your school?

- ❑ Yes
- ❑ No
- ❑ Don't know

If there are computers at your school, please answer the following questions.

2. Where are computers at your school located?

- ❑ In a computer lab
- ❑ In classrooms
- ❑ In the school library or media center
- ❑ Another place

3. How often do you use a computer at school?

- ❑ Daily
- ❑ About once a week
- ❑ Two to four times a month
- ❑ Never

4. Do you have access to the Internet at school?

- ❑ Yes
- ❑ No
- ❑ Don't know

5. How helpful is having a computer to use at school?

- ❑ Very helpful
- ❑ Somewhat helpful
- ❑ Not at all helpful

(continued)

Draw Conclusions About Meaning and Purpose
Read through the questions on this page. Who would complete this survey? Who might want this information? Why might the questions have a multiple-choice format?

6. What do you use a computer for at school? (Check all that apply.)

- ❑ To find out what homework has been assigned
- ❑ To complete homework assignments
- ❑ To practice skills
- ❑ To look up information in online reference works
- ❑ To play educational games
- ❑ To publish a newsletter, newspaper, or online magazine
- ❑ To create art projects
- ❑ Other: ______________________________

7. How often do you use the Internet?

- ❑ Daily
- ❑ About once a week
- ❑ Two to four times a month
- ❑ Never

8. How much do you trust information from the Internet?

- ❑ Completely
- ❑ Quite a lot
- ❑ Just a little
- ❑ Not at all
- ❑ Not sure

9. If you had trouble figuring out how to do something on a computer, which would you most likely do?

- ❑ Look it up in a book or manual.
- ❑ Use the software's help menu.
- ❑ Ask a friend, family member, or teacher for help.
- ❑ Use the telephone to call a help line.
- ❑ Just keep trying until I figured it out.

10. In general, how do you think computer use has affected family and social life?

- ❑ Kids spend more time with family and friends.
- ❑ Kids spend less time with family and friends.
- ❑ It hasn't made much difference.

11. Do you think computer use has led kids to spend more time outdoors, less time outdoors, or hasn't it made much difference?

- ❑ More time outdoors
- ❑ Less time outdoors
- ❑ Hasn't made much difference

Draw Conclusions About Meaning and Purpose

Read the questions on this page of the survey. What kind of information do questions 10 and 11 ask about? Why might someone be interested in this information?

Understand Policies

Think about the purposes of policies. What kinds of rules does this policy contain? Who made these rules? Who must follow them?

Brainwell Middle School

Computer Use Policy

This policy for the use of computer facilities, equipment, and software programs belonging to the Brainwell Middle School applies to all school employees, all students, and any member of the community who uses the school's facilities,[1] equipment, or software. You must agree to these rules or you will be denied computer use at Brainwell Middle School. Any violation of these rules may cause you to lose computer privileges at the school.

1. You may not authorize[2] anyone, except a faculty or staff member, to use your name, password, or files for any reason.
2. You may not use computers for anything other than schoolwork. The use of e-mail, instant messaging, and nonacademic games is not permitted.
3. You may not copy, change, or transfer any software or files provided by the school without permission from the computer supervisor.
4. Remember that it is illegal to copy any software that has a copyright. The use of illegally copied software is considered a criminal offense and is subject to criminal prosecution.
5. You may not tamper with terminals, computers, printers, or other associated equipment.
6. Food, drinks, chewing gum, and candy are prohibited[3] near the school's computer equipment.

Student and Parent Acknowledgment of the Brainwell Middle School Computer Policy

My signature below indicates that I have read and understood the rules, responsibilities, and penalties listed above. I also understand that violation of the rules may result in loss of computer privileges at the school.

Student signature ______________________________

Parent signature ______________________________

Date ______________________________

Draw Conclusions About Meaning and Purpose
Why might a school need these rules? What could happen if there were no rules about school computer use?

---

1 ***Facilities*** are buildings or pieces of equipment that provide ease of use or serve a particular purpose.

2 To ***authorize*** something is to approve it.

3 If something is ***prohibited,*** it is forbidden or not allowed.

After You Read

Respond and Think Critically

Read the questions about the functional documents on pages 465–467 and select the best answer.

Standards Practice  ELA6R1d

1. Someone would most likely use the technology use survey to
   A. track an individual's computer and Internet use.
   B. figure out whether computer use leads to less exercise.
   C. understand how students typically use computers.
   D. check the reliability of information from the Internet.

Standards Practice  ELA6R1d

2. The main purpose of the Middle School Technology Use Survey is to collect information about
   A. high school teachers.
   B. middle school students.
   C. Internet users.
   D. parents.

Standards Practice  ELA6R1d

3. Which of these actions would violate the computer use policy?
   A. typing an essay on a school computer
   B. researching a science project on the Internet
   C. giving a teacher access to your files
   D. chatting online with a school friend

4. If you often use a school computer to look up information in online reference works, to publish a newsletter, and to check out library books, how would you complete question 6 of the Middle School Technology Use Survey?

5. If your friend at Brainwell Middle School wants to use your password to log on to a school computer, how would you explain to your friend that you cannot share your password? To which sentences from the school's computer use policy would you refer?

Writing

Write a Survey A first step to solving problems is to gather information. A survey is a good tool for collecting information.

- Think about a problem at your school or in your community—for example, old playground equipment needs to be replaced or there is dangerous traffic near the school.
- What information do you need to solve this problem? Who could provide this information? Think of questions that would help get the information you want. Use these questions to write a survey.

Literature Online

Selection Resources For Selection Quizzes, eFlashcards, and Reading-Writing Connection activities, go to glencoe.com and enter QuickPass code GL17527u4.

Before You Read

Romulus and Remus

Connect to the Myth

Think about a time when you argued with someone you cared about.

Quickwrite Freewrite for a few minutes about the argument. What was the reason for the quarrel? How did it make you feel? How did the argument end?

Build Background

"Romulus and Remus" is a myth that explains how the city of Rome was built. Centuries ago, Rome was the seat of an empire that stretched over much of Europe. Roman culture influenced many parts of modern life, from legal systems to plumbing to the language we speak.

When the Romans conquered the Greeks, they adopted the stories the Greeks had made up to explain aspects of life. The Romans took the myths back to Italy, but the names of the gods and goddesses were all Greek names. The Romans changed the names in the myths to fit their own culture. Zeus became Jupiter, Ares became Mars, Hermes became Mercury, and so on.

Vocabulary

naked (nā′ kid) *adj.* without clothing or similar covering (p. 471). *A nurse wrapped the naked newborn in a warm blanket.*

ravenous (rav′ ə nəs) *adj.* very eager, as for satisfaction or gratification (p. 473). *His ravenous desire to own every new song by his favorite group resulted in a large collection.*

shunned (shund) *v.* kept away from; avoided (p. 473). *I never understood why Lori shunned our company.*

destiny (des′ tə nē) *n.* what is fated to happen to someone or something; fortune (p. 474). *It was Eric's destiny to be a musician.*

Meet Geraldine McCaughrean

"I took up writing as a child, for the fun of it, to go somewhere else and be someone other than me."

— Geraldine McCaughrean

A Children's Writer Geraldine McCaughrean was born in Enfield, North London, the youngest child of a fireman and a teacher. She received a degree in education but chose to work in a magazine publishing house. Now she works as a children's writer full-time. McCaughrean is the winner of the Carnegie Medal, England's most prestigious children's book award. She and her family live in Berkshire, England.

Literary Works Geraldine McCaughrean has written more than 100 books for both children and adults, including *A Pack of Lies, The Kite Rider,* and *Stop the Train.*

Geraldine McCaughrean was born in 1951.

Literature Online

Author Search For more about Geraldine McCaughrean, go to glencoe.com and enter QuickPass code GL17527u4.

Set Purposes for Reading

BQ BIG Question

As you read, ask yourself, how can seeing things from only one point of view affect an argument?

Literary Element Character

A **character** is a person or creature in a literary work. Characters may change during the story or stay the same. Characters' traits are revealed throughout a story and are often closely tied to the plot. For example, a character who can't keep a secret might accidentally give information to the villain—a conflict. Telling the secret could lead to the climax of the story and the eventual resolution.

Understanding characters can help you make sense of events in a story.

As you read, notice the qualities of Romulus and Remus and how their actions influence the plot and the resolution of the conflict.

Reading Skill Recognize Author's Purpose

When you **recognize author's purpose,** you think about the intended reason for writing. A writer usually writes to explain or inform, to entertain, to persuade, or to express emotion. Sometimes an author has more than one purpose.

Recognizing an author's purpose helps you get more out of your reading.

To recognize author's purpose, ask yourself,

- How is the text organized?
- Who is the intended audience?
- What words does the author choose?

As you read, you may find it helpful to use a graphic organizer like the one below.

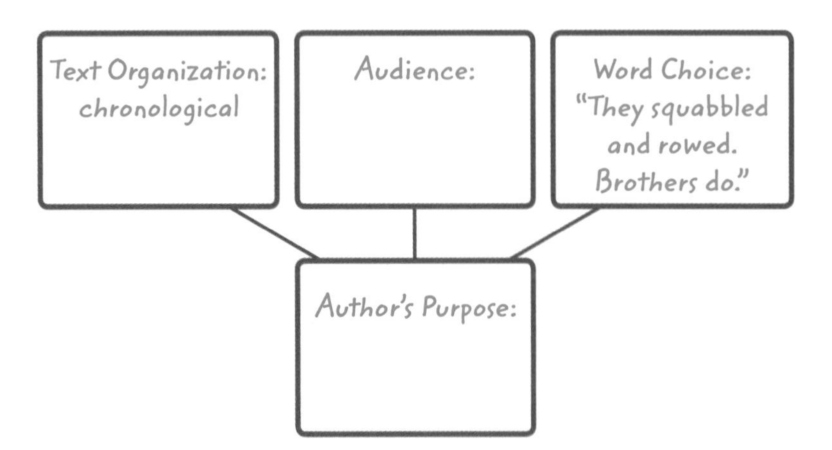

GA Performance Standards

For pages 469–477

ELA6R1e/i. For literary texts, identify and analyze the elements of setting, characterization, plot, and the resolution of the conflict of a story or play: internal/external conflicts.

TRY IT

Recognize Author's Purpose
Your friend writes a letter to the editor of the school paper, giving reasons that are meant to convince the principal to change a dress code. Is your friend trying to entertain, to inform, to persuade, or to express emotion? How do you know?

Romulus AND Remus

retold by
Geraldine McCaughrean

Rhea Silvia, a priestess, and Mars, the god of war, had twin sons. Shortly after the boys' birth, their mother was killed. Their father left the area.

As for the twin boys—Romulus and Remus[1]—they were carried **naked** in a basket to the banks of the Tiber. The servants sent to carry out the task would have tipped them in, midstream. But the Tiber was in flood, and the waters milled by with such terrifying force that they set the basket down on the muddy shore and watched 'til the swollen river swirled the children away toward a watery death.

---

1 ***Romulus*** (rom′ yə ləs), ***Remus*** (rē′ məs)

Vocabulary

naked (nā′ kid) *adj.* without clothing or similar covering

View the Art How does this mosaic make you feel about the relationship between Romulus and Remus and the wolf?

Ah, but weren't Romulus and Remus the sons of Mars, the descendants of Aeneas?[2] Though their tiny pink fists and feet were powerless to save them, they were strong, healthy boys. The cold did not kill them, nor the river spill them, nor **pike** snatch them down to a muddy death. The basket was swept helter-skelter downstream until it snagged[3] on tree roots and spun into a backwater[4] where the wild creatures came to drink. A face loomed over the crying boys—a mask with yellow eyes and a mouth full of

Visual Vocabulary

A **pike** is a large freshwater fish. Pike have many sharp teeth and can be more than four feet long.

2 ***Aeneas*** (i nē′ əs) was a Trojan warrior who was the hero of Virgil's epic poem *The Aeneid.*

3 ***Snagged*** means "caught on something sharp or something that sticks out."

4 A ***backwater*** is an area of water turned or held back by a blockage or an opposing current.

ravenous teeth. The wolf opened wide her grinning jaws, seized on first Romulus, then Remus, and ran with them to her lair. There she dropped them among the soft, tumbling fur of her hungry cubs.

And there she suckled[5] them, letting them drink, as her cubs drank, from her soft, warm underbelly. A woodpecker perched on a branch nearby to keep watch for danger. (If this seems strange beyond belief, you should know that wolf and woodpecker are creatures sacred to Mars.)

A herdsman found them. Out one day hunting the wolves who threatened his livestock, he found two big, squalling baby boys, pink and brawling[6] in a wolf-den, and took them home. Now, the herdsman was no fool: He knew full well who they were—knew that the law had demanded their death. But he and his wife had no children of their own, and neither civic duty[7] nor fear of punishment counted for anything alongside the joy those children brought them.

Perhaps Romulus and Remus drank down the ferocious courage of the she-wolf as they drank her milk. Perhaps they learned courage and endurance from her as she came and went, feeding and fighting for her young. Or perhaps, as sons of Mars, there was already warrior blood in their veins. But Romulus and Remus grew up into brave, quarrelsome boys who never **shunned** a fight and who never lost one, either.

No shepherd life for them! No life in peaceful Latium. Even before their father told them the story of their birth, they were roaring boys, with roaring friends, their sights pinned on glory. They set their hearts on building a new city, a grand city, a city to rival Troy or Carthage or Athens.

Recognize Author's Purpose How is the author organizing ideas? Could all these events really happen?

Character How might these character traits affect the plot?

---

5 ***Suckled*** means "gave milk to."

6 ***Brawling*** is fighting or quarreling noisily and in an unruly way.

7 ***Civic duty*** is something a person is morally or legally obligated to do as a result of being a citizen.

Vocabulary

ravenous (rav′ə nəs) *adj.* very eager, as for satisfaction or gratification

shunned (shund) *v.* kept away from; avoided

"It shall be called Reme," said Remus.

"Rome, you mean," Romulus corrected him. They quarreled about it, naturally; it was their way to squabble and row.[8] Brothers do.

But where was their magnificent city to be built?

"Here," said Romulus, "where the she-wolf suckled us!"

"That's not where she suckled us," said Remus with a scornful snort. "It was over there, near that clump of trees."

"Never!" They squabbled and rowed. Brothers do. The gods looked on with mild amusement.

"Let the gods decide!" said Romulus.

"Yes, we'll watch for a sign," agreed Remus. The gods, too, nodded in agreement, and Jupiter sent a flock of ravens to mark the spot fixed by **Destiny** for the building of the sacred city.

"There! There! Look, three ravens!" cried Remus. "The sacred birds of Jupiter!"

An acorn dropped from the claw of one bird and fell to earth. The brothers, however, were too busy arguing to notice where it fell.

"Seven ravens. There were seven, not three," said Romulus.

"What does it matter? I saw them first. So I choose where Reme is built."

"But I saw more ravens than you!" protested Romulus. "So I shall build in my chosen place. You can do as you like . . . and it will be Rome, not Reme!" They exchanged a string of insults. Brothers do. The gods frowned a little at their squabbling. Time was going to waste.

Obstinate Romulus began to build—where the Tiber snaked between seven hills, where the sunbeams were blade-sharp and golden, and where the stones were mossy massive—heaping the boulders into a wall.

Recognize Author's Purpose How is the repetition of the sentence "Brothers do" related to the author's purpose?

Character How could building the wall add to the conflict?

8 To ***squabble and row*** (skwob′əl, rou) is to argue, especially over something of little importance.

Vocabulary

destiny (des′ tə nē) *n.* what is fated to happen to someone or something; fortune. The word is capitalized here because the author is personifying, or giving human qualities to, the word.

"Call that a wall?" jeered Remus. "I've seen bigger pigsties!" and he jumped over the low walling, his feet dislodging pebbles, his taunts loud and sneering. To and fro he jumped, deriding[9] Romulus's work until all brotherly affection dissolved in Romulus and he hated his brother with a hot loathing.[10] Brothers can. He picked up a boulder. "You do that once more . . ."

BQ BIG Question Why is this a critical shift in the brothers' quarrel?

Remus jumped the wall. A whole section slumped down in a landslide of rocks and pebbles. Romulus lifted the boulder and brought it down on his brother's head. Remus was dead before he even hit the ground. "Thus die all those who ever try to leap the walls of Rome!" Romulus crowed as his young warrior friends ran to the spot and crowded around.

Then Romulus wept, because he had killed his best friend in the world, and all for the sake of a pile of stones.

Character How is this a change in character?

The gods looked on with distaste. How could the destiny of an empire rest on the shoulders of such men?

"It is good," said Mars, dry-eyed, stony-faced. "It is good that blood should water the foundations of Rome."

But Jupiter shook his head. "They were fools to quarrel," he said.

9 ***Deriding*** is mocking or treating with contempt or scorn.

10 ***Loathing*** is extreme disgust.

After You Read

Respond and Think Critically

1. Use your own words to retell the events that lead to the adoption of Romulus and Remus by the herdsman. **[Summarize]**
2. Think about the traits the twins have that cause conflict. What traits do you think are part of a peaceful relationship? **[Connect]**
3. In the myth, what circumstances explain why Romulus and Remus behave the way they do? **[Analyze]**
4. Why do you think the gods do not interfere in the brothers' quarrel? **[Infer]**
5. Is Romulus justified in killing Remus? Why or why not? **[Evaluate]**
6. **BQ** **BIG Question** Romulus and Remus's actions result in tragedy. How could the tragedy have been prevented? Explain. **[Conclude]**

TIP

Inferring
Remember that when you make an inference, you use what you know to make an educated guess.

- What have you read about the Roman gods?
- Think about what you already know about the gods.
- Combine this information to explain the gods' lack of interference.

Keep track of your ideas about the **BIG Question** in your unit Foldable.

Vocabulary Practice

Match each boldface vocabulary word with a word from the right column that has the same meaning. Two of the words in the right column will not have matches. Then write a sentence using each vocabulary word, or draw or find a picture that represents each word.

1. naked	a. fate
2. ravenous	b. angry
3. shunned	c. eager
4. destiny	d. bare
	e. tattered
	f. avoided

Example:
1. naked

Sentence: Jon gasped when the cold water touched his naked feet.

Academic Vocabulary

Romulus and Remus could not **resolve** their differences in a peaceful way. In the preceding sentence, *resolve* means "solve, as in a dispute." Think about a time you were involved in a situation that could not be easily resolved. What was the eventual outcome?

Literature Online

Selection Resources
For Selection Quizzes, eFlashcards, and Reading-Writing Connection activities, go to glencoe.com and enter QuickPass code GL17527u4.

Literary Element Character

Standards Practice 

1. Which words best describe Romulus and Remus?
   A. ravenous and grinning
   B. cheerful but discouraged
   C. powerless and healthy

Review: **Myth**

As you learned on page 406, a **myth** is a traditional story, often involving gods, goddesses, and heroes, that attempts to explain something in nature, a historic event, or a belief or custom.

Standards Practice 

2. You know that this is a myth because
   A. the main characters are twins.
   B. the brothers' father is a god.
   C. the brothers are quarrelsome.
   D. Romulus kills his brother.

Reading Skill Recognize Author's Purpose

Standards Practice 

3. What is the author's main purpose for including the quarrelsome twins as main characters?
   A. to show how destructive unbending attitudes can be
   B. to contrast the twins' personalities
   C. to provide the gods with amusement
   D. to describe how brothers should act

Grammar Link

Parts of Speech A word's **part of speech** is determined by how the word is used in a sentence. Here are seven parts of speech:

A **noun** names a person, place, thing, or idea: A wolf finds the twin boys. A **pronoun** is used in place of a noun: A wolf finds them. A **verb** expresses action or a state of being: The brothers quarrel. They are twins. An **adjective** describes nouns or pronouns: Remus gives a scornful snort. An **adverb** describes verbs, adjectives, or other adverbs. Adverbs often end in *-ly:* The gods are mildly amused. A **preposition** shows the relationship between its object and another word in the sentence: Jupiter sends a flock of ravens. A **conjunction** connects individual words or groups of words: Either Romulus or Remus could have ended the argument calmly.

Practice Look through the myth to find examples of each part of speech. Then label the parts of speech of each underlined word below.

1. Romulus and Remus never knew their parents.
2. As infants, they were suckled by a very fierce wolf.

Speaking and Listening

Performance With a small group, use "Romulus and Remus" to create a play about the mythical founding of Rome. Write a script that includes the necessary characters. Include stage directions. You may want to have one person as a narrator. Rehearse the dialogue, paying attention to your rate, volume, pitch, and tone. Use gestures and eye contact effectively. Group members should provide feedback to one another. Then present your play to the class.

Before You Read

Eulogy on the Dog

Connect to the Speech

Have you ever had or wanted a pet? In what ways might a pet be an ideal friend?

Partner Talk With a partner, share any good experiences you have had with animals. Discuss how animals might sometimes be easier to get along with than people.

Build Background

In 1870 an unusual case called *Burden vs. Hornsby* went to the Missouri Supreme Court. Leonidas Hornsby, a neighbor of Charles Burden, had vowed to shoot any dog he found on his property. Charles Burden's prized hunting dog, Old Drum, wandered onto Hornsby's land one night. After the dog was shot and killed, Burden sued Hornsby in court.

The case went through many trials, but when lawyer George Graham Vest gave this speech to a jury, they decided in Burden's favor. Today a statue of Old Drum stands in front of the courthouse in Warrensburg, Missouri.

A *eulogy* is a formal speech given to praise someone who has died.

Vocabulary

traitors (trā′ tərz) *n.* those who betray a trust (p. 481).
Nick felt that his friends were traitors for telling his secret.

reputation (rep′ yə tā′ shən) *n.* general or public opinion of something or someone (p. 481).
It is important that a leader have a good reputation.

sacrificed (sak′ rə fīst′) *v.* given up, usually for the sake of something else (p. 481).
José sacrificed his free time to help his sister move.

treacherous (trech′ ər əs) *adj.* disloyal (p. 481).
Dana fired her treacherous assistant for stealing her idea.

prosperity (pros per′ ə tē) *n.* state of having success, wealth, or good fortune (p. 481).
Mrs. Chin's family lived in prosperity after she got a raise.

Meet George Graham Vest

First a Lawyer George Graham Vest had many accomplishments, but he is best remembered for a speech about dogs that he gave when he was a lawyer in 1870. Vest's famous tribute to a dog's loyalty is said to have brought the jury to tears, winning the case for the dog's owner.

Senator and Speechmaker For 24 years, George Graham Vest served as a United States senator from Missouri. Vest went on to become one of the leading orators and debaters of his time.

George Graham Vest was born in 1830 and died in 1904.

Literature Online

Author Search For more about George Graham Vest, go to glencoe.com and enter QuickPass code GL17527u4.

Set Purposes for Reading

BQ BIG Question

As you read, ask yourself, how can a speech influence what I think is fair or not fair?

Literary Element Argument

An **argument** is the reason or reasons a writer or a speaker uses to support an opinion. Reasons might appeal to readers' or listeners' emotions, logic, ethics, or sense of authority. In "Eulogy on the Dog," the speaker appeals to both emotion and logic in his argument. Appeals to emotion are meant to make readers or listeners feel a certain way. Appeals to logic are meant to show that the writer's or speaker's opinion makes sense.

Writers of speeches or essays need to make strong arguments to persuade listeners or readers to agree with their opinions. Convincing arguments often contain more than one type of appeal.

As you read, ask yourself, how does the speaker appeal to logic and emotion in his argument?

Reading Skill Analyze Figurative Language

Language that suggests something beyond the exact meaning of the words is called **figurative language.** Two kinds of figurative language are **similes** and **metaphors.** A simile compares two unlike things using the word *like* or *as*—*Her hands were as cold as ice.* A metaphor compares two unlike things without using *like* or *as*—*Her hands were ice cubes.* **Personification** is another type of figurative language. In personification, animals, objects, or ideas are given human characteristics—*The sun smiled down on the meadow.*

Figurative language lets writers express ideas in creative ways. It often includes striking images that make the writing come alive for readers.

To **analyze figurative language,** pay attention to

- unusual comparisons
- strong images
- human traits given to animals or things

As you read, ask yourself, what effect does figurative language have in this speech? You may find it helpful to use a graphic organizer like the one below.

Figurative language	Simile, metaphor, or personification?	Effect

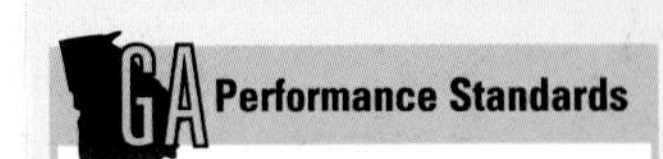

For pages 478–483

ELA6R1h/ii For literary texts, respond to and explain the effects of figurative language.

TRY IT

Analyze Figurative Language Your friend comes in from a rainstorm and says, "I'm a drowned rat!" What kind of figurative language is she using?

Portrait of a Liver and White Pointer. George Garrard. Oil on canvas. Roy Miles Fine Paintings, London.

Eulogy on the Dog

George Graham Vest

Warrensburg, Missouri
September 23, 1870

Gentlemen of the jury:

The best friend a man has in the world may turn against him and become his enemy. His son or daughter that he has reared with loving care may prove ungrateful. Those who are nearest and dearest to us, those whom we trust with our happiness and our good name may become

traitors to their faith. The money that a man has, he may lose. It flies away from him, perhaps when he needs it most. A man's **reputation** may be **sacrificed** in a moment of ill-considered action. The people who are prone to fall on their knees to do us honor when success is with us may be the first to throw the stone of malice when failure settles its cloud upon our heads.

The one absolutely unselfish friend that man can have in this selfish world, the one that never deserts him, the one that never proves ungrateful or **treacherous** is his dog. A man's dog stands by him in **prosperity** and in poverty, in health and in sickness. He will sleep on the cold ground, where the wintry winds blow and the snow drives fiercely, if only he may be near his master's side. He will kiss the hand that has no food to offer; he will lick the wounds and sores that come in encounter with the roughness of the world. He guards the sleep of his pauper[1] master as if he were a prince. When all other friends desert, he remains. When riches take wings, and reputation falls to pieces, he is as constant in his love as the sun in its journey through the heavens.

If fortune drives the master forth an outcast in the world, friendless and homeless, the faithful dog asks no higher privilege than that of accompanying him, to guard him against danger, to fight against his enemies. And when the last scene of all comes, and death takes his master in its embrace and his body is laid away in the cold ground, no matter if all other friends pursue their way, there by the graveside will the noble dog be found, his head between his paws, his eyes sad, but open in alert watchfulness, faithful and true even in death. ❧

Argument What kind of appeal is the speaker using? How do you know?

Analyze Figurative Language Is the dog literally asking his master for the privilege? What type of figurative language is this an example of? Explain why.

BQ BIG Question

How does this speech help you see another side of friendship and fairness?

---

1 A *pauper* is a very poor person.

Vocabulary

traitors (trā′ tərz) *n.* those who betray a trust

reputation (rep′ yə tā′ shən) *n.* general or public opinion of something or someone

sacrificed (sak′ rə fīst′) *v.* given up, usually for the sake of something else

treacherous (trech′ ər əs) *adj.* disloyal

prosperity (pros per′ ə tē) *n.* state of having success, wealth, or good fortune

After You Read

Respond and Think Critically

1. Who is the speaker's audience? **[Recall]**
2. In your own words, state the speaker's main argument. **[Paraphrase]**
3. A eulogy is a speech given in praise of a dead person. Why does Vest feel that a dog deserves a eulogy even though it is not a person? **[Infer]**
4. How does the figurative language that Vest uses help create the feeling that a dog is a person's best friend? Look back at the chart you made for examples. **[Analyze]**
5. Do you find Vest's argument convincing? Why? **[Evaluate]**
6. **BQ BIG Question** Think about what you read in the Build Background and in this speech. Do you think it was fair for someone to shoot Charles Burden's dog for being on Hornsby's property? Explain. **[Conclude]**

TIP

Analyzing
When you analyze, look at separate parts to understand the entire piece. Try these tips to help you answer question 4.

- Skim the selection to find examples of figurative language.
- Think about why Vest made these word choices.
- What effect does the language have?

Keep track of your ideas about the **BIG Question** in your unit Foldable.

Examine Media: Humane Society Advertisement

Appeals to Emotion

Visual advertisements often appeal to emotions to convince people that something will make them happy or deserves their support. Analyze the advertisement to the right.

On Your Own Think about the following questions and write your answers on a separate sheet of paper.

1. How do you think the people who created this advertisement want you to feel when you look at it? Explain.
2. What about this advertisement appeals to your emotions? What else does it appeal to, and how?
3. How could you change this advertisement to make it more effective?

Literary Element **Argument**

Standards Practice  ELA6RC2e

1. Why did George Graham Vest give this speech?
   A. to persuade people to own dogs
   B. to describe how to treat dogs
   C. to entertain a jury
   D. to convince a jury

Review: Text Structure

As you learned on page 47, **text structure** is how a work is organized. This speech is presented using a comparison-and-contrast structure, which can show the similarities and differences between people, things, and ideas.

2. Vest makes many comparisons in his speech. How does the comparison-and-contrast structure help to make his arguments strong? Give two examples of comparisons and two examples of contrasts using a graphic organizer like the one below.

Comparison	Contrast

Reading Skill

Analyze Figurative Language

3. "And when the last scene of all comes, and death takes his master in its embrace . . ."

   Identify an example of figurative language in this sentence. Explain why it is an example of figurative language.

4. What does Vest's use of figurative language add to his speech? Explain.

Vocabulary Practice

Choose the sentence that uses the vocabulary word correctly.

1. **A.** Jessica **sacrificed** her day at the beach to help us.
   B. The mayor **sacrificed** the new town hall by praising it.
2. **A.** The **traitors** gave us apples in exchange for pears.
   B. The **traitors** were put in prison for helping the king's enemies.
3. **A.** Maria has a high **reputation** for her sister's cat.
   B. Brad is careful about what he says, because he wants to keep his good **reputation**.
4. **A.** **Prosperity** is now required for all eighth graders.
   B. In times of **prosperity**, there is plenty of food for all.
5. **A.** Sometimes a person you consider to be your friend turns out to be **treacherous.**
   B. The teacher told Bonita not to be **treacherous** for school again.

Academic Vocabulary

George Graham Vest describes dogs as having a loving and devoted **attitude** toward their masters. Using context clues, describe what *attitude* means in the preceding sentence. Check your answer in a dictionary.

Literature Online

Selection Resources For Selection Quizzes, eFlashcards, and Reading-Writing Connection activities, go to glencoe.com and enter QuickPass code GL17527u4.

Respond Through Writing

Persuasive Essay

Argue a Position George Graham Vest uses appeals to logic and emotion in "Eulogy on the Dog." Think about something in your community you would like to change. For example, you might like to have a recycling program in your neighborhood. Write a persuasive essay using effective appeals.

Understand the Task In addition to appeals to logic and emotion, there are two other types of appeals. An **appeal to ethics** uses people's sense of right and wrong as a reason. An **appeal to authority** gives experts' opinions as a reason. Choose one of these types of appeals to use in your essay.

Prewrite Review "Eulogy on a Dog," paying close attention to Vest's appeals. Then research your topic by talking to people in your community and finding articles and other information about your topic in local newspapers or on the Internet. Using your research, determine your main idea and target audience. Also think about the sequence in which you will present your ideas. Organize your ideas in a chart like the one below. Then make an overall plan for your essay. For example, you may want to write a paragraph for each point you want to present.

Main idea: ______________________

Reasons: 1. ______________________

2. ______________________

3. ______________________

Draft After you figure out your plan, write an opening statement expressing your main idea. This sentence frame might help you: Our community needs ____________, because______________.

Revise After you have written your first draft, read it to a classmate to check that your paragraphs follow a logical order. Revise your text so that your argument is clear and easy to follow.

Edit and Proofread Proofread your paper, correcting any errors in spelling, grammar, and punctuation. Review the Grammar Tip in the side column for information on prepositions.

GA Performance Standards

For page 484

ELA6W2b Produce a multi-paragraph persuasive essay that states a clear position of a proposition or proposal.

Grammar Tip

Prepositions

Prepositions show the relationship of a noun or a pronoun to another word in a sentence. Some prepositions are *about, for, of, on,* and *to.*

Many expressions in persuasive writing use prepositions. Be sure to use them correctly. For example, you feel strongly *about* something, not *on* something.

Correctly using prepositions makes your arguments more convincing because your sentences make sense.

Vocabulary Workshop

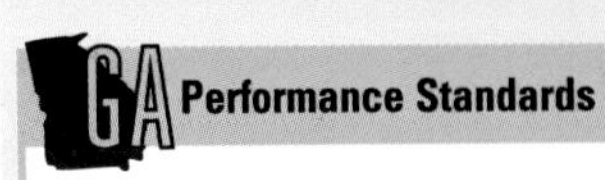

For page 485

ELA6R2a Determine the meaning of unfamiliar words by using word, sentence, and paragraph clues.

Idioms

Connection to Literature

"A man's dog stands by him in prosperity and in poverty, in health and in sickness."

—George Graham Vest, "Eulogy on the Dog"

"Stands by him" is a figure of speech called an **idiom,** which is a phrase that has a different meaning from its literal one. In this statement, the author is not saying that dogs place themselves near their owners every minute of every day, but that dogs will not desert their masters during bad times.

You can often figure out what an unfamiliar idiom means. One way is to think about the actual meanings of the words and use context clues to figure out the meaning of the idiom.

Here are some idioms connected with "Eulogy on the Dog."

Idiom	Meaning
Dogs are not *fair-weather friends.* Dogs stand by you in both good and bad times.	A *fair-weather friend* is someone who is a friend in good times but abandons you in bad times.
People who honor us for our successes may be the first to *throw stones* when we fail.	To *throw stones* is to criticize or say bad things about a person.
When riches *take wing,* a dog still loves its master.	To *take wing* is to leave quickly, to seem to fly away.

TRY IT: Write a short definition or phrase that could be substituted for each underlined idiom.

1. Some people will not lift a finger to help you when you are in need.
2. The absence of the man's beloved dog left a hole in his heart.
3. When he asked his fair-weather friend for help, he was barking up the wrong tree.

Tip

Vocabulary Terms Idioms are phrases that have special meanings, different from their ordinary, literal meanings.

Test-Taking Tip To understand the meaning of an idiom, think about the ordinary meanings of the words. Then use context clues to help you figure out what the words mean in the current context.

Literature Online

Vocabulary For more vocabulary practice, go to glencoe.com and enter QuickPass code GL17527u4.

Before You Read

The Southpaw

Connect to the Story

Has a disagreement ever caused you to lose a friend? How did you feel? Were you able to become friends again?

Quickwrite Freewrite for a few minutes about an argument you had with a friend and how you handled it.

Build Background

A story written in the form of an exchange of letters is called an epistolary (i pis′ tə ler′ ē) story. In "The Southpaw," two friends—a boy and a girl—argue by letter about whether or not girls can play on an all-boys' baseball team.

The following are facts about baseball related to the story:

- *Southpaw* is a term for a left-handed pitcher.
- A batting average indicates how often a batter gets a hit. A batting average higher than .300 is very good.
- Girls were not allowed to play Little League baseball until 1974. This story was first published that year.

Vocabulary

cavities (kav′ ə tēz) *n.* hollow spaces in teeth caused by decay (p. 488). *The dentist found two cavities during my last appointment.*

trophy (trō′ fē) *n.* a small statue gained as a prize or an award for something (p. 490). *The soccer team received a trophy for their victory.*

tonsils (ton′ səlz) *n.* small organs in the throat near the back of the mouth (p. 490). *A doctor may perform surgery to remove infected tonsils.*

sprained (sprānd) *v.* injured by a sudden, severe twist (p. 490). *Daniel slipped on the ice and sprained his ankle.*

unreasonable (un rē′ zə nə bəl) *adj.* not acting according to reason (p. 491). *It is unreasonable to try to run a marathon without training.*

Meet Judith Viorst

Writer and Mother Many of Judith Viorst's works have presented humorous views of her family life. As the mother of three sons, she has often used their worries and concerns as the subjects for her writing. Viorst says, "Four of the books . . . I consciously sat down and wrote because one child or another of mine had a problem. . . . I hoped it might help my boys to laugh at their problems."

Literary Works Viorst has published in various genres, including poems, short stories, novels, and picture books. Her most famous children's book is *Alexander and the Terrible, Horrible, No Good, Very Bad Day.*

Judith Viorst was born in 1931.

Literature Online

Author Search For more about Judith Viorst, go to glencoe.com and enter QuickPass code GL17527u4.

Set Purposes for Reading

BQ BIG Question

As you read, ask yourself, how does communication help two friends solve a problem?

Literary Element Voice

Voice is an author's distinctive style or the particular speech patterns of a character. In "The Southpaw," the author often uses common phrases and idioms to communicate the voices of the characters. Common phrases are phrases you might hear in everyday speech, such as "don't count on it." Idioms are expressions that do not carry a word-for-word meaning, such as "kick a man when he's down."

This selection has two voices—a girl's voice and a boy's voice. Focus on the characters' speech patterns and word choices to understand their personalities and feelings.

As you read, ask yourself, which common phrases and idioms help readers hear the voice of each character? How does each character's voice help set the tone and express the theme of the story?

Reading Skill Analyze Narrator and Point of View

When you **analyze,** you think critically about something. When you **analyze narrator and point of view,** you think critically about the **narrator,** or the person who tells a story. You also think about the **point of view,** or the relationship of the narrator to the story. When the character telling the story is referred to as *I,* the story is being told from the **first-person point of view.**

Analyzing the narrator and point of view can help you understand the narrator's thoughts and feelings. This story is told by two first-person narrators, Janet and Richard.

To analyze narrator and point of view, pay attention to

- what each narrator says and the point of view of each letter
- how each letter reflects that narrator's thoughts and feelings

Then use this information to understand the characters and their particular perspectives in the story. You may find it helpful to record your findings in a graphic organizer like the one below.

Topic	How Richard Feels	How Janet Feels

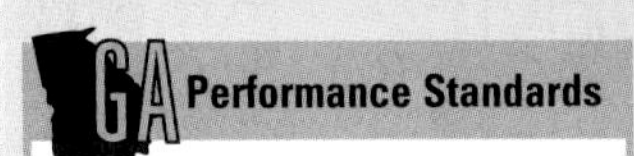

GA Performance Standards

For pages 486–492

ELA6R1b For literary texts, identify and analyze the author's use of dialogue and description.

TRY IT

Analyze You look in your notebook and find two notes addressed to you. Neither note is signed. One note says, "I need you to walk the dog before dinner." The other note says, "Please read Chapter 3 for homework." Who do you think wrote the first note? What is the point of view of this letter? How do you know? Who do you think wrote the second note? Why do you think so?

THE SOUTHPAW

Judith Viorst

Dear Richard,

Don't invite me to your birthday party because I'm not coming. And give back the Disneyland sweatshirt I said you could wear. If I'm not good enough to play on your team, I'm not good enough to be friends with.

Your former friend,

Janet

P.S. I hope when you go to the dentist he finds twenty **cavities**.

Analyze Narrator and Point of View Who is the narrator of this letter? What point of view does the narrator use? How do you know?

Dear Janet,

Here is your stupid Disneyland sweatshirt, if that's how you're going to be. I want my comic books now—finished or not. No girl has ever played on the Mapes Street baseball team, and as long as I'm captain, no girl ever will.

Your former friend,

Richard

P.S. I hope when you go for your checkup you need a tetanus[1] shot.

BQ BIG Question

Do you think this is fair? Why or why not?

Dear Richard,

I'm changing my goldfish's name from Richard to Stanley. Don't count on my vote for class president next year. Just because I'm a member of the ballet club doesn't mean I'm not a terrific ballplayer.

Your former friend,

Janet

P.S. I see you lost your first game, 28–0.

1 ***Tetanus*** is a serious disease that people can get when bacteria enter a wound. A doctor gives a person a tetanus shot to keep the person from getting the disease.

Vocabulary

cavities (kav′ ə tēz) *n.* hollow spaces in teeth caused by decay

Dear Janet,

I'm not saving any more seats for you on the bus. For all I care you can stand the whole way to school. Why don't you forget about baseball and learn something nice like knitting?

Your former friend,
Richard

P.S. Wait until Wednesday.

Dear Richard,

My father said I could call someone to go with us for a ride and hot-fudge sundaes. In case you didn't notice, I didn't call you.

Your former friend,
Janet

P.S. I see you lost your second game, 34–0.

Dear Janet,

Remember when I took the laces out of my blue-and-white sneakers and gave them to you? I want them back.

Your former friend,
Richard

P.S. Wait until Friday.

Dear Richard,

Congratulations on your unbroken record. Eight straight losses, wow! I understand you're the laughingstock[2] of New Jersey.

Your former friend,
Janet

P.S. Why don't you and your team forget about baseball and learn something nice like knitting maybe.

Analyze Narrator and Point of View Who is the narrator? How does this letter reflect the narrator's thoughts and feelings?

Meeting on the Mound, 1994. Gary M. Stretar.

Voice What is Janet's tone? How does it express her feelings?

2 A person is a ***laughingstock*** when people make fun of that person.

Dear Janet,

Here's the silver horseback-riding **trophy** that you gave me. I don't think I want to keep it anymore.

Your former friend,
Richard

P.S. I didn't think you'd be the kind who'd kick a man when he's down.

Dear Richard,

I wasn't kicking exactly. I was kicking back.

Your former friend,
Janet

P.S. In case you were wondering, my batting average is .345.

Dear Janet,

Alfie is having his **tonsils** out tomorrow. We might be able to let you catch next week.

Richard

Dear Richard,

I pitch.

Janet

Dear Janet,

Joel is moving to Kansas and Danny **sprained** his wrist. How about a permanent place in the outfield?

Richard

Dear Richard,

I pitch.

Janet

Voice What do you think this idiom means? Why do you think Richard uses it?

Analyze Narrator and Point of View What pronoun does the narrator use that he has not used before? Why do you think he uses it?

Vocabulary

trophy (trō′ fē) *n.* a small statue gained as a prize or an award for something

tonsils (ton′ səlz) *n.* small organs in the throat near the back of the mouth

sprained (sprānd) *v.* injured by a sudden, severe twist

Dear Janet,

Ronnie caught the chicken pox and Leo broke his toe and Elwood has these stupid violin lessons. I'll give you first base, and that's my final offer.

Richard

Dear Richard,

Susan Reilly plays first base, Marilyn Jackson catches, Ethel Kahn plays center field, I pitch. It's a package deal.[3]

Janet

P.S. Sorry about your 12-game losing streak.

Dear Janet,

Please! Not Marilyn Jackson.

Richard

Dear Richard,

Nobody ever said that I was **unreasonable.** How about Lizzie Martindale instead?

Janet

Dear Janet,

At least could you call your goldfish Richard again?

Your friend,

Richard

BQ BIG Question

Do you think Janet is being fair? Why or why not?

Martha, 1925. Georg Schrimpf. Oil on canvas. Private Collection, ©DACS.

3 A ***package deal*** is an offer that includes several items. Whoever agrees to the deal must take all of the items.

Vocabulary

unreasonable (un rē′ zə nə bəl) *adj.* not acting according to reason

After You Read

Respond and Think Critically

1. What is Janet's disagreement with Richard about? [Recall]
2. When do Richard and Janet start to understand each other? Which note shows the change? [Interpret]
3. Southpaw pitchers are considered valuable because left-handed pitches are often more difficult to hit. Using this information, what do you think the story's title, "The Southpaw," implies? [Infer]
4. **Literary Element** **Voice** Which phrases and idioms in the story do you think best show the voice of each character? Give two examples for each character and explain why you chose them. [Evaluate]
5. **Reading Skill** **Analyze Narrator and Point of View** Refer to the chart you made about the narrators. How does having the story switch between narrators help the plot move along? [Analyze]
6. **BQ** **BIG Question** In the dispute between Janet and Richard, which character do you think is right? Explain. [Conclude]

Vocabulary Practice

Choose the sentence that uses the vocabulary word correctly.

1. A. My throat hurts a lot because my **tonsils** are swollen.
   B. I went to the eye doctor so she could check my **tonsils**.
2. A. I was being **unreasonable** when I took out the trash.
   B. It is **unreasonable** to expect everyone to agree on the issue.
3. A. My friend bought a **trophy** because she won the race.
   B. The winning track team put their **trophy** on display.
4. A. The exercises at gym class will help strengthen my **cavities**.
   B. The dentist congratulated me for having no **cavities**.
5. A. I **sprained** my ankle when I fell while skating.
   B. I **sprained** my eyes from watching too much television.

Writing

Write a Letter Think about a time when you had a disagreement with a friend or felt unfairly excluded from an activity. Write a letter to your friend. Try to persuade your friend to understand your side of the story. Use concrete supporting arguments and evidence and persuasive techniques, such as emotional appeal, in your letter.

TIP

Interpreting
Here are some tips to help you answer question 2. Remember that when you interpret, you use your own understanding to decide what something means.

- Think about what Janet wants.
- Think about what Richard doesn't want.
- Look for where Richard begins to change his mind.
- Think about why Richard changes his mind.

Keep track of your ideas about the **BIG Question** in your unit Foldable.

Literature Online

Selection Resources For Selection Quizzes, eFlashcards, and Reading-Writing Connection activities, go to glencoe.com and enter QuickPass code GL17527u4.

Before You Read

Spiders, from *All I Really Need to Know I Learned in Kindergarten*

Connect to the Essay

Do you get scared when you see a spider? Do you know an adult who does? Have you ever wondered why some people are afraid of something so small?

Partner Talk With a partner, discuss things people fear. Which of these fears seem reasonable? Which seem silly? Why?

Build Background

Did you know that the spider is *not* an insect? It is actually an arachnid (ə rak′ nid), a relative of the insect. The most notable difference is that a spider has eight legs, and an insect has only six. Here are some interesting facts about spiders.

- Spiders are predators that mainly feed on insects. Many insects eat crops, so spiders help control unwanted pests.
- Although many spiders make silk webs to trap their prey, some hunt their prey instead.
- Many spiders kill their prey by injecting poison into it.
- Very few spiders are harmful to people.

Vocabulary

luggage (lug′ ij) *n.* bags, boxes, or suitcases a traveler uses for carrying things (p. 495). *Our luggage was heavy because we packed for a two-week trip.*

frenzied (fren′ zēd) *adj.* in a state of intense emotion or extreme excitement; frantic (p. 496). *The frenzied fans ran across the parking lot to get the quarterback's autograph.*

inhabited (in hab′ it id) *v.* lived in or on (p. 496). *Our apartment is inhabited by four people, two cats, and a turtle.*

catastrophe (kə tas′ trə fē′) *n.* great and sudden disaster or misfortune (p. 498). *A hurricane can be a catastrophe for those who live near the ocean.*

Meet Robert Fulghum

"Share everything. Don't take things that aren't yours. Put things back where you found them. Play fair."

— Robert Fulghum

Best-Selling Author Before becoming an author, Robert Fulghum worked as a ditch-digger, a newspaper carrier, a ranch hand, and a singing cowboy. For more than 20 years, he served as a minister. He also found time to paint, draw, perform in a rock-and-roll band, and write seven books.

Literary Works Fulghum wrote the best-selling book *All I Really Need to Know I Learned in Kindergarten.* The essay "Spiders" comes from this book, which was published in 1986.

Robert Fulghum was born in 1937.

Literature Online

Author Search For more about Robert Fulghum, go to glencoe.com and enter QuickPass code GL17527u4.

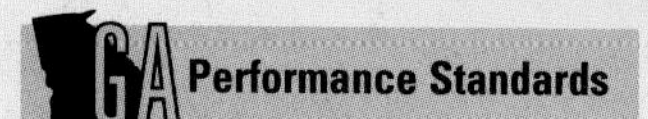

Set Purposes for Reading

BQ BIG Question

As you read, ask yourself, how does the author help readers see his neighbor's situation from another side?

Literary Element Thesis

The **thesis** is the main idea of an essay or other work of nonfiction. A thesis gives focus to an essay. Details in the essay support the thesis. Usually the author directly states the thesis. Sometimes, however, the thesis is implied.

The **thesis** helps you understand what is important to the author. It serves as a clue to the author's purpose for writing.

As you read, ask yourself, what main idea does the author want readers to understand?

Reading Skill Analyze Voice

When you **analyze voice,** you look at the distinctive use of language that conveys the author's personality to readers. In "Spiders," the author uses vivid descriptive language. He also often uses fragments (incomplete sentences), idioms (expressions that have a different meaning than the literal meaning of the words), and word choice. He describes the action in the present tense. These choices all help create a humorous, informal voice.

Analyzing voice can help you understand how the author feels about the subject.

To analyze voice, pay attention to

- word choices, including idioms and fragments
- tone, or the author's attitude toward the subject matter or audience
- mood, or the emotional quality of a literary work

Then think about how voice relates to the subject of the essay. You may find it helpful to use a graphic organizer like the one below.

Fragments	Idioms	Word Choice	Present-tense verbs
Nice lady.	It boggles the mind.	wrapped around a frenzied moving haystack	She turns, sees me

Performance Standards

For pages 493–500

ELA6R1d For literary texts, apply knowledge of the concept that theme refers to the message about life and the world that the author wants us to understand whether implied or stated.

TRY IT

Analyze Voice Your friend is about to play in a piano recital. She tells you that she has butterflies in her stomach. What does this idiom mean? Does she actually have butterfiles inside of her? How does she feel about playing in the recital?

Spiders

from **All I Really Need to Know I Learned in Kindergarten**

Robert Fulghum

This is my neighbor. Nice lady. Coming out her front door, on her way to work and in her "looking good" mode. She's locking the door now and picking up her daily **luggage**: purse, lunch bag, gym bag for aerobics, and the garbage bucket to take out. She turns, sees me, gives me the big, smiling Hello, takes three steps across her front porch. And goes "AAAAAAAAGGGGGGGGHH-HHHHHHH!!!!" (*That's a direct quote.*) At about the level of a fire engine at full cry.

Spider web! She has walked full force into a spider web. And the pressing question, of course: Just where is the spider *now?*

She flings her baggage in all directions. And at the same time does a high-kick, jitterbug[1] sort of dance—like a mating stork in crazed heat. Clutches at her face and hair and goes "AAAAAAAGGGGGGHHHHHHHHH!!!!!" at a new level of intensity. Tries opening the front door

Analyze Voice Why do you think the author starts the essay with sentence fragments?

1 The ***jitterbug*** is a lively dance performed to swing music. It was popular in the 1930s and 1940s.

Vocabulary

luggage (lug′ ij) *n.* bags, boxes, or suitcases a traveler uses for carrying things without unlocking it. Tries again. Breaks key in the lock. Runs around the house headed for the back door. Doppler effect[2] of

"A A A A A G G G H H H H a a g g h . . ."

Now a different view of this scene. Here is the spider. Rather ordinary, medium gray, middle-aged lady spider. She's been up since before dawn working on her web, and all is well. Nice day, no wind, dew point just right to keep things sticky. She's out checking the moorings[3] and thinking about the little gnats she'd like to have for breakfast. Feeling good. Ready for action. All of a sudden all hell breaks loose—earthquake, tornado, volcano. The web is torn loose and is wrapped around a **frenzied** moving haystack, and a huge piece of raw-but-painted meat is making a sound the spider has never heard: "AAAAAAAGGGGGGGHHHHHH!!!!!"

Thesis From what you have read so far, what do you think the thesis of this essay is?

It's too big to wrap up and eat later, and it's moving too much to hold down.

Jump for it? Hang on and hope? Dig in?

Human being. The spider has caught a human being. And the pressing question is, of course: Where is it going and what will it do when it gets there?

The neighbor lady thinks the spider is about the size of a lobster and has big rubber lips and poisonous fangs. The neighbor lady will probably strip to the skin and take a full shower and shampoo just to make sure it's gone—and then put on a whole new outfit to make certain she is not **inhabited**.

The spider? Well, if she survives all this, she will *really* have something to talk about—the one that got away that was THIS BIG. "And you should have seen the JAWS on the thing!"

BQ BIG Question
How do the woman and the spider see the situation differently?

2 The ***Doppler effect*** occurs when sound waves move toward or away from a listener. As the woman moves closer to the author, the Doppler effect causes her scream to sound higher in pitch. As she runs away, the scream sounds lower.

3 ***Moorings*** are lines or chains that secure something in place. In this case, the spider is checking that her web is secure.

Vocabulary

frenzied (fren′ zēd) *adj.* in a state of intense emotion or extreme excitement; frantic

inhabited (in hab′ it id) *v.* lived in or on

Spiders. Amazing creatures. Been around maybe 350 million years, so they can cope with about anything. Lots of them, too—sixty or seventy thousand per suburban acre. Yes. It's the web thing that I envy. Imagine what it would be like if people were equipped like spiders. If we had this little six-nozzled aperture[4] right at the base of our spine and we could make yards of something like glass fiber[5] with it. Wrapping packages would be a cinch!

Home Shopping Mysteries. Dianna Sarto.

View the Art Is this how you picture the woman in the story? Why or why not?

---

4 A ***six-nozzled aperture*** is an opening with six spouts, or channels through which liquid can flow. In this case, the aperture is used for squirting out web material.

5 ***Glass fiber*** is a material made of thin threads of glass. The author is comparing a spider's web to spun glass.

Mountain climbing would never be the same. Think of the Olympic events. And mating and child rearing would take on new dimensions. Well, you take it from there. It boggles the mind. Cleaning up human-sized webs would be a mess, on the other hand.

All this reminds me of a song I know. And you know, too. And your parents and your children, they know. About the itsy-bitsy spider. Went up the waterspout. Down came the rain and washed the spider out. Out came the sun and dried up all the rain. And the itsy-bitsy spider went up the spout again. You probably know the motions, too.

Analyze Voice How do the lyrics from the children's song add to the author's voice?

What's the deal here? Why do we all know that song? Why do we keep passing it on to our kids? Especially when it puts spiders in such a favorable light? Nobody goes "AAAAAAAGGGGGGGHHHHHHHHH!!!!!" when they sing it. Maybe because it puts the life adventure in such clear and simple terms. The small creature is alive and looks for adventure. Here's the **drainpipe**—a long tunnel going up toward some light. The spider doesn't even think about it—just goes. Disaster befalls it—rain, flood, powerful forces. And the spider is knocked down and out beyond where it started. Does the spider say, "To hell with that"? No. Sun comes out—clears things up—dries off the spider. And the small creature goes over to the drainpipe and looks up and thinks it *really* wants to know what is up there. It's a little wiser now—checks the sky first, looks for better toeholds, says a spider prayer, and heads up through mystery toward the light and wherever.

Visual Vocabulary

A **drainpipe** is a tube for emptying water, often from the roof of a building.

Living things have been doing just that for a long, long time. Through every kind of disaster and setback and **catastrophe**. We are survivors. And we teach our kids about that. And maybe spiders tell their kids about it, too, in their spider way.

Thesis Has your idea changed about the thesis of this essay? Why or why not?

So the neighbor lady will survive and be a little wiser coming out the door on her way to work. And the spider, if it lives, will do likewise. And if not, well, there are lots more spiders, and the word gets around. Especially when the word is "AAAAAAAGGGGGGGHHHHHHHHH!!!!"

Vocabulary

catastrophe (kə tas′ trə fē′) *n.* great and sudden disaster or misfortune

After You Read

Respond and Think Critically

1. How does the woman react after walking into the spider web? **[Summarize]**
2. In your own words, restate both the woman's and the spider's "pressing questions." **[Paraphrase]**
3. In what ways do the woman and the spider have trouble understanding each other? **[Compare]**
4. Do you think either the woman or the spider will be wiser in the future? Why or why not? **[Infer]**
5. What wisdom does the author find in the children's song about the itsy-bitsy spider? **[Analyze]**
6. **BQ BIG Question** Did the essay help you see the world from a different perspective? Why or why not? **[Evaluate]**

Vocabulary Practice

Synonyms are words that have the same or almost the same meaning. **Antonyms** are words that have opposite meanings. Identify whether the paired words are synonyms or antonyms. Then use each vocabulary word in a sentence or draw or find a picture that represents the word.

1. **luggage** and baggage
2. **frenzied** and calm
3. **catastrophe** and disaster
4. **inhabited** and empty

Example:
luggage and baggage = synonyms

Sentence: My brother got a set of luggage before he left for college.

Academic Vocabulary

Robert Fulghum's **analysis** of why people pass along the song about the itsy-bitsy spider is that the song "puts the life adventure in such clear and simple terms." In the preceding sentence, *analysis* means "the result of examining carefully and in detail." Do you agree with Fulghum's analysis? What do you think the song can teach people about dealing with setbacks?

TIP

Comparing
Here are some tips to help you answer question 3. Remember that when you compare, you find similarities between two things.

- Recall the description of how the woman views the spider.
- Recall the description of how the spider views the woman.
- Look for the similarities in their mistaken ideas about each other.

Keep track of your ideas about the **BIG Question** in your unit Foldable.

Literature Online

Selection Resources
For Selection Quizzes, eFlashcards, and Reading-Writing Connection activities, go to glencoe.com and enter QuickPass code GL17527u4.

Literary Element Thesis

Standards Practice 

1. Which sentence best expresses the author's attitude toward survival?
   A. Spiders should be admired for their ability to make webs.
   B. The itsy-bitsy spider song is a part of our culture.
   C. The spider is a small creature in search of adventure.
   D. All living things learn to survive in the face of catastrophes.

Review: Tone

As you learned on page 123, **tone** is an author's attitude toward a subject.

Tone is closely related to voice. An author who thinks spiders are scary might choose words such as *fearsome* or *fanged* to create a fearful tone. An author who admires spiders might use words such as *resourceful* or *fascinating* to create a tone of respect and approval.

You can describe an author's tone in the same way you would describe a friend's attitude, such as serious, funny, or angry.

2. List three examples of words or phrases from "Spiders" to show that its tone is lighthearted and humorous.

Reading Skill Analyze Voice

To answer these questions, look back at the chart you created while reading the essay.

3. List five present-tense verbs that the author uses in the essay. Do they make the author's voice more or less formal? Explain.
4. Recall that an idiom is an expression whose meaning is different from its literal meaning. Give two examples of idioms from the essay. Why do you think the author uses them?
5. The author uses fragments to add humor and a conversational tone to the essay. Why do fragments affect the tone in this way?

Grammar Link

Direct Objects You have learned that every sentence has a subject and a predicate. Sometimes the predicate tells who or what received the action of the verb in the predicate.

The spider ***spins*** *a* ***web.***

In the sentence above, *web* receives the action of the verb *spins.* It answers the question *spins what?* In this sentence, the word *web* is called a **direct object.**

- A direct object receives the action of a verb. It answers the question *whom?* or *what?* after an action verb.
- A verb can have more than one direct object.
- Sometimes an action verb does not have a direct object.

The lady screams loudly.

In the sentence above, *loudly* does not answer the question *whom?* or *what?* after the verb *screams.* It is not a direct object.

Grammar Practice Find three sentences in "Spiders" that have direct objects. Then write your own sentence with a direct object. Underline the direct object.

Write with Style

Apply Sentence Structure In this essay, the author describes an ordinary event from an unusual point of view—a spider's. Choose a situation that you have recently witnessed. Then write a paragraph describing it from another point of view. For example, if you saw your brother combing his hair, you could describe it from the point of view of the comb. Use sentence fragments, idioms, and metaphors to create a friendly, informal voice. Also use vivid descriptive language to describe the actions and setting.

Part 2

Freedom and Equality

Students Coming Out of School. Stephen Schildbach.

BQ BIG Question What's Fair and What's Not?

Why might the students in the picture think their school is a free and equal place? What can you do at your school to help other students better understand the meaning of freedom and equality?

Before You Read

The Wolf and the House Dog and *The Donkey and the Lapdog*

Connect to the Fables

Think about a time when you wanted to trade places with someone else—for any reason.

Quickwrite Freewrite for a few minutes about this time. What made you wish for such a change? What do you think would have happened if you had gotten your wish?

Build Background

Aesop's fables are known all over the world. They have been told and retold by countless writers, including the Roman writer Phaedrus, the French poet Jean de La Fontaine, and modern-day American Jerry Pinkney.

The storyteller Aesop may or may not have existed. Some historians say he was born in Africa. Most agree that he was a slave in ancient Greece. Others say he became an advisor to kings. Whether Aesop was real, his name is attached to many fables that people have passed down over the centuries. You probably already know some of these stories, such as "The Tortoise and the Hare."

Vocabulary

sleek (slēk) *adj.* having a healthy, well-groomed, or well-fed appearance; smooth and glossy, as if polished (p. 505). *Carrie looked sleek and well rested after her vacation.*

ease (ēz) *n.* freedom from pain, discomfort, hard work, or worry (p. 507). *Surrounded by servants, the princess lived in ease and luxury.*

toppled (top′ əld) *v.* fell forward, tumbled over (p. 507). *The stack of books toppled with a terrible crash.*

lamented (lə ment′ id) *v.* expressed sorrow aloud; wailed (p. 507). *"I'll never pass math," Steve lamented.*

Meet Jerry Pinkney

"When I'm working on a book . . . satisfaction comes from the actual marks on the paper, and when it sings, it's magic."

—Jerry Pinkney

Award-Winning Illustrator Jerry Pinkney has won many awards as an illustrator, including the Caldecott Honor Book award and the Coretta Scott King Award. He says that good illustrations come from good writing. As a child, Pinkney loved to draw. His mother and teachers recognized his talent and encouraged him to become an artist.

Literary Works Jerry Pinkney has illustrated dozens of picture books.

Jerry Pinkney was born in 1939.

LOG ON **Literature** Online

Author Search For more about Aesop and Jerry Pinkney, go to glencoe.com and enter QuickPass code GL17527u4.

Set Purposes for Reading

BQ BIG Question

As you read, ask yourself, how do the animal characters in these fables define freedom and equality?

GA Performance Standards

For pages 502–509

ELA6R1i For literary texts, compare traditional literature and mythology from different cultures.

Literary Element Fables

A **fable** is a short folktale that teaches a lesson. That lesson is called a **moral**. Characters in fables often are animals that behave like humans but still have animal qualities. For example, a pig might speak like a person but live in a pigsty, not in a house. Fables often use **stereotypes,** or characters that embody certain attitudes and patterns of behavior. A fable about a pig, for example, might teach a lesson about greed.

Fables are important because they teach about right and wrong. They are a simple, entertaining way of passing down wisdom from generation to generation.

As you read, look for the traditional characteristics of fables—morals and animal characters. How do these characteristics help you learn?

Reading Strategy Make Generalizations About Characters

When you **make generalizations,** you develop a broad statement that is supported by details in a work. When you **make generalizations about characters,** you use their words, thoughts, and actions to make a statement about them. For example, a girl in a story might have to stand up to bullies. You could make the generalization that she is brave.

Making generalizations can help you understand the story and the role characters play in affecting the plot, including the conflict and resolution.

To make generalizations about a character, think about

- what the character says, thinks, and does
- what other characters think and say about the character

Then ask yourself whether actions such as the character's actions often lead to similar results. You may find it helpful to use a graphic organizer like the one below.

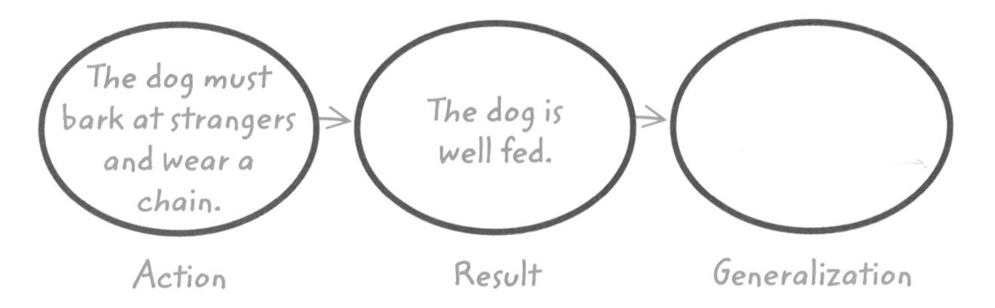

TRY IT

Make Generalizations Your friend doesn't take homework seriously. He says he's too smart to study. Then he scores poorly on a big test. What do you think usually happens to people who don't study?

The Wolf and the House Dog

Aesop, retold by Jerry Pinkney

A wolf who lived in the forest fell on hard times, and could barely catch enough food to keep from starving. Soon her ribs were showing through her coat, and she could hardly sleep at night for hunger.

One day the wolf happened to meet a **sleek**, plump dog from the village. Puzzled, the wolf looked him over and exclaimed, "How is it that you appear to be so well-fed, when game[1] has been so scarce?"

"I never have to hunt for game," boasted the dog. "My master feeds me meat from his own plate, and the servants give me scraps from the kitchen every day. All I have to do is bark at every stranger that comes near and keep watch over the house by night."

The wolf could hardly believe her ears. "If I find a family to take me in," she asked, "will they treat me the same way?"

"No doubt of it!" the dog replied. "Just come along with me and I'll find you a place." Eagerly the wolf trotted beside the dog. But as they left the shadow of the trees, the wolf saw something near the dog's neck flash in the bright sunlight.

"Pardon me, but what is that around your neck?" she asked.

"Oh, nothing," said the dog. "It's just the ring on my collar where they fasten me to the chain."

"Chain!" cried the wolf in horror, stopping in her tracks.

"Of course," said the dog. "They chain us up at night, so we won't run away." The dog looked over his shoulder. "Why did you stop, Wolf? Aren't you coming?"

"Certainly not," said the wolf. "You may go back to your master, if you will. But I'd rather starve to death in the woods than eat one meal with a chain around my neck."

Lean freedom is better than fat slavery.

Fable What clue in the first sentence tells you this is a fable?

Make Generalizations About Characters Why might a wolf be horrified by a dog's chain?

BQ BIG Question

Do you agree with the wolf or with the dog? Why?

---

1 ***Game*** refers to wild animals, birds, or fish that are hunted or caught for food.

Vocabulary

sleek (slēk) *adj.* having a healthy, well-groomed, or well-fed appearance; smooth and glossy, as if polished

The Donkey and the Lapdog

Aesop, retold by Jerry Pinkney

A farmer had a little dog that he kept constantly by his side. The farmer also had a donkey, who lived in a warm stable and got plenty of fresh grain and sweet hay. But the donkey was not satisfied with his lot.[1]

"I slave all day, hauling wood or pulling the cart to market," the donkey grumbled. "And then I'm shut in the stable, while that dog sleeps on the master's lap and eats from his plate!" Perhaps, he thought, if he behaved like the dog, his master would reward him with the same life of **ease**.

That very night, the donkey crept out of the stable and into the house where the farmer sat at supper. "First I'll frisk[2] about and chase my tail, just as the dog does," thought the donkey. And he danced about the room, flinging up his hooves until the table **toppled** over and dishes went flying.

"Now I'll sit on his lap!" said the donkey to himself, and he put his heavy hooves up on the master's chair.

"Help! Save me from this mad beast!" bellowed the terrified farmer. His servants came running and, with shouts and blows, drove the donkey back to the stable.

"I suppose I'm a fine donkey," the donkey **lamented**, "but I'll never be a **lapdog**!"

What's right for one may be wrong for another.

1 Someone's ***lot*** is that person's fate in life—the path, pain, and rewards that the person has by chance.

2 To ***frisk*** is to leap, skip, or move playfully.

Vocabulary

ease (ēz) *n.* freedom from pain, discomfort, hard work, or worry

toppled (top′əld) *v.* fell forward, tumbled over

lamented (lə ment′id) *v.* expressed sorrow aloud; wailed

Fable What traits do donkeys supposedly have? How could those traits affect the plot?

Make Generalizations About Characters From what the donkey says, what generalization can you make?

BQ BIG Question

Is what happens to the donkey fair? Why or why not?

Visual Vocabulary

A **lapdog** is a pet dog, small enough to be held on the lap.

After You Read

Respond and Think Critically

1. What flashes on the dog's neck in the sunlight? **[Identify]**
2. Why does the donkey decide to behave like the lapdog? **[Recall]**
3. The house dog says he is chained up at night so he "won't run away." Why might he run away from such a comfortable life? **[Infer]**
4. What is similar about the lives of the donkey and the lapdog? What is different? What is the reason for the differences? **[Compare and Contrast]**
5. The wolf is willing to die for freedom. Is freedom worth dying for, even when it means a life of hardship? Explain. **[Evaluate]**
6. **BQ** **BIG Question** What lessons about freedom and equality do these two fables teach? **[Conclude]**

TIP

Inferring

Recall that inferring means making a guess based on clues in the text. Here are some tips to help you infer:

- Think about the dog's advantages.
- Think about how the wolf reacts to the dog's chain.
- Now make an educated guess.

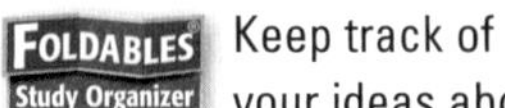

Keep track of your ideas about the **BIG Question** in your unit Foldable.

Examine Media: Movies

As you read, you make generalizations. But one kind of generalization, a **stereotype,** can be hurtful. When you form a stereotype, you assume too much from too little information. For example, you might assume that all smart people wear glasses.

In movies, you use visual and audio features to obtain information. Have you ever seen a movie image of a vicious wolf with bloody fangs? Have you heard a wolf howl, threatening to attack when the hero is alone? In fact, wolves almost never attack people. They are shy around humans. They are social, even playful, with other wolves.

On Your Own Think about the following questions and write your ideas on a separate sheet of paper.

1. Imagine that you encountered a wolf or a donkey, and the only thing you knew about the animal was the stereotype associated with it. What would you do? How might the stereotype hurt you or the animal?
2. Think of a wolf you have seen in a movie. Do you think the animal fits a stereotype? Explain your answer.

Literary Element Fable

Standards Practice  ELA6R1d

1. Which sentence or sentence part from "The Wolf and the House Dog" is an example of a moral?
   A. "I never have to hunt for game," boasted the dog.
   B. Lean freedom is better than fat slavery.
   C. A wolf who lived in the woods fell on hard times, . . .
   D. "They chain us up at night, so we won't run away."

Review: **Theme**

As you learned on page 75, a **theme** is the message about life an author wants to convey. In fables, the theme is often the same as the moral.

2. How would you summarize the moral in each fable?

Reading Strategy Make Generalizations About Characters

3. What personality traits do the wolf and the house dog have? What generalizations can you make about people who have these traits?
4. What personality traits does the donkey have? What generalizations can you make about people who have these traits?
5. Think about what happens to the donkey. Is it reasonable to make the generalization that people who work hard always want to have an easier life? Why or why not?
6. How did making generalizations about the characters help you understand the fables?

Vocabulary Practice

Respond to these questions.

1. Which is more likely to be **sleek**—a wolf in the wild or a cat in a home?
2. Which grade would someone have **lamented**—a failing grade or a passing grade?
3. Which is more likely to be **toppled**—a bookcase or a rug?
4. Who is more likely to live a life of **ease**—a millionaire or a peasant?

Academic Vocabulary

The wolf **rejects** the life of a house dog because it would require her to give up her freedom.

In the preceding sentence, *rejects* means "a refusal to accept." The wolf believes the dog's life would require her to give up too much for too little gain. Think about a time you rejected an offer or an option. Why did you reject it? What led you to believe you should not accept it?

Literature Online

Selection Resources For Selection Quizzes, eFlashcards, and Reading-Writing Connection activities, go to glencoe.com and enter QuickPass code GL17527u4.

Respond Through Writing

Expository Essay

Compare and Contrast Fables "The Wolf and the House Dog" and "The Donkey and the Lapdog" contain lessons about freedom and equality. Write a short essay comparing and contrasting the two fables. Explore the use of animal characters to teach a moral.

Understand the Task When you **compare**, you look for similarities. When you **contrast**, you look for differences. In your essay, you will write about the similarities and differences of the two fables.

Prewrite Make a plan. Consider your purpose, audience, main ideas, and a logical sequence. Think about the way each fable uses animals to demonstrate certain personality traits. Think about the moral that each fable presents. Keep track of similarities and differences in a Venn diagram like the one below.

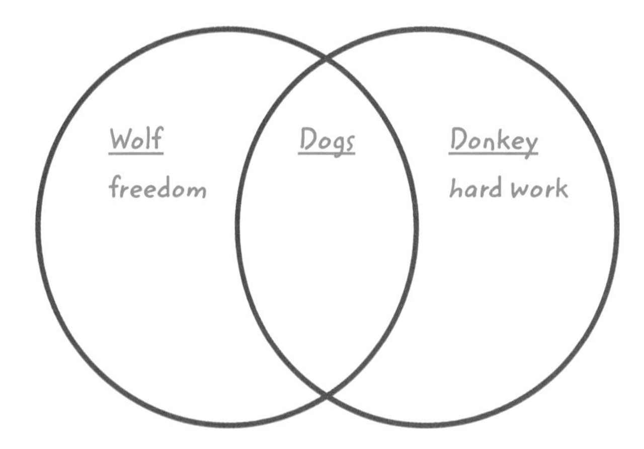

Draft Organize your essay into an introduction, a paragraph about each fable, and a conclusion. Or you may want to write one paragraph about similarities and another paragraph about differences. Write a thesis statement. This sentence frame might help you:

The fables are alike because ______ but different because ______.

Revise After you have written your first draft, read it. Have you organized your essay by comparison and contrast? Have you used text evidence to support your points? Did you use specific language to give a visual image to the reader? Did you write a conclusion?

Edit and Proofread Proofread your paper, combining or deleting sentences to improve clarity. Correct any errors in spelling, grammar, and punctuation.

Performance Standards

For page 510

ELA6W4b Use the writing process to develop, revise, and evaluate writing. Revise manuscripts to improve the organization and consistency of ideas within and between paragraphs.

Grammar Tip

Semicolons

It is often useful to use a **semicolon** to connect independent but related clauses when you compare or contrast. For example:

The house dog is chained; the wolf is free.

You can also join the two thoughts with a semicolon and a conjunctive adverb that shows contrast, such as *however.* For example:

The house dog is chained; however, the wolf is free.

Note that the clause after a semicolon begins with a lowercase letter.

Before You Read

The Shutout

Connect to the Essay

Think about a time when you wanted to join a team, a club, or a group of friends, but you were left out.

QuickWrite Freewrite for a few minutes about the experience. Was it fair, or unfair, to be left out? How did you react?

Build Background

The title "The Shutout" is a pun—a play on words in which a double meaning is given to the same word. In baseball, the word *shutout* means "a game in which one team doesn't score any runs." *Shut out* also means "to exclude" or "to not allow to join or participate."

In this essay, it refers to the time in U.S. history when African American players were kept from joining all-white baseball teams.

Vocabulary

uniquely (ū nēk′ lē) *adv.* distinctively; characteristically (p. 514).
Tourists commented on the world-famous food at this uniquely French-inspired restaurant.

rivaling (rī′ vəl ing) *v.* competing with (p. 514).
Basketball is rivaling football in popularity at our school.

privileged (priv′ ə lijd) *adj.* having or enjoying a right or advantage (p. 517).
The older students feel privileged to eat outside at lunch today.

portrayed (pôr trād′) *v.* set forth a picture of in words; described (p. 518).
The book portrayed the villain as a sly but charming person.

Meet Patricia C. and Fredrick McKissack Jr.

"To me, reading is like breathing; both are essential to life."

—Patricia C. McKissack

A Writing Team The McKissacks are a mother-and-son writing team. Patricia C. McKissack has written many award-winning books, some with her husband, Fredrick McKissack Sr. Fredrick McKissack Jr. began his career as a sportswriter. Now he is a writer and editor of political and feature articles.

Literary Works "The Shutout" is an excerpt from *Black Diamond: The Story of the Negro Baseball Leagues.* Patricia C. McKissack was born in 1944, and Fredrick McKissack Jr. was born in 1965.

Literature Online

Author Search For more about Patricia C. McKissack and Fredrick McKissack Jr., go to glencoe.com and enter QuickPass code GL17527u4.

Set Purposes for Reading

BQ BIG Question

As you read, ask yourself, how has baseball changed over the years, and why was it unfair to shut out certain players from the game?

Literary Element Text Structure

Text structure is a pattern of organization within a piece of writing. One type of structure text is **chronological order.** The purpose of chronological order is to present events in time order.

Understanding chronological order is one way to figure out and recall the writer's ideas. To identify chronological order, look for dates, phrases, or signal words, such as *first, next, then, later,* and *finally.*

As you read, ask yourself, why is chronological order a good way to tell about the history of baseball?

Reading Strategy Monitor Comprehension

When you **monitor comprehension,** you check your understanding as you read.

Monitoring comprehension is important, because no matter what your purposes are for reading, your most important task is to make sure you understand what you have read.

To monitor comprehension,

- carefully reread to clarify what you don't understand
- summarize main thoughts or ideas
- question important ideas and story elements
- predict what will happen next
- evaluate what you have read so far

You may find it helpful to use a graphic organizer like the one below.

History of Baseball

Date	Event
pre-1839	People played stick-and-ball games.

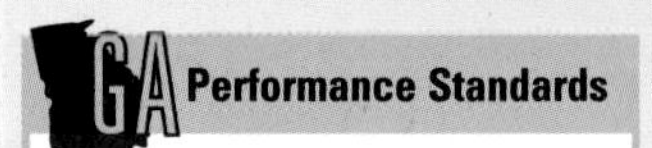

For pages 511–520

ELA6R1c For informational texts, apply knowledge of common organizational structures and patterns.

TRY IT

Monitor Comprehension You are beginning a new chapter in science class. You don't want to highlight or mark up your textbook, so when you don't understand something you read, you write a question on a self-stick note and put it on the page. What else could you do to monitor your comprehension?

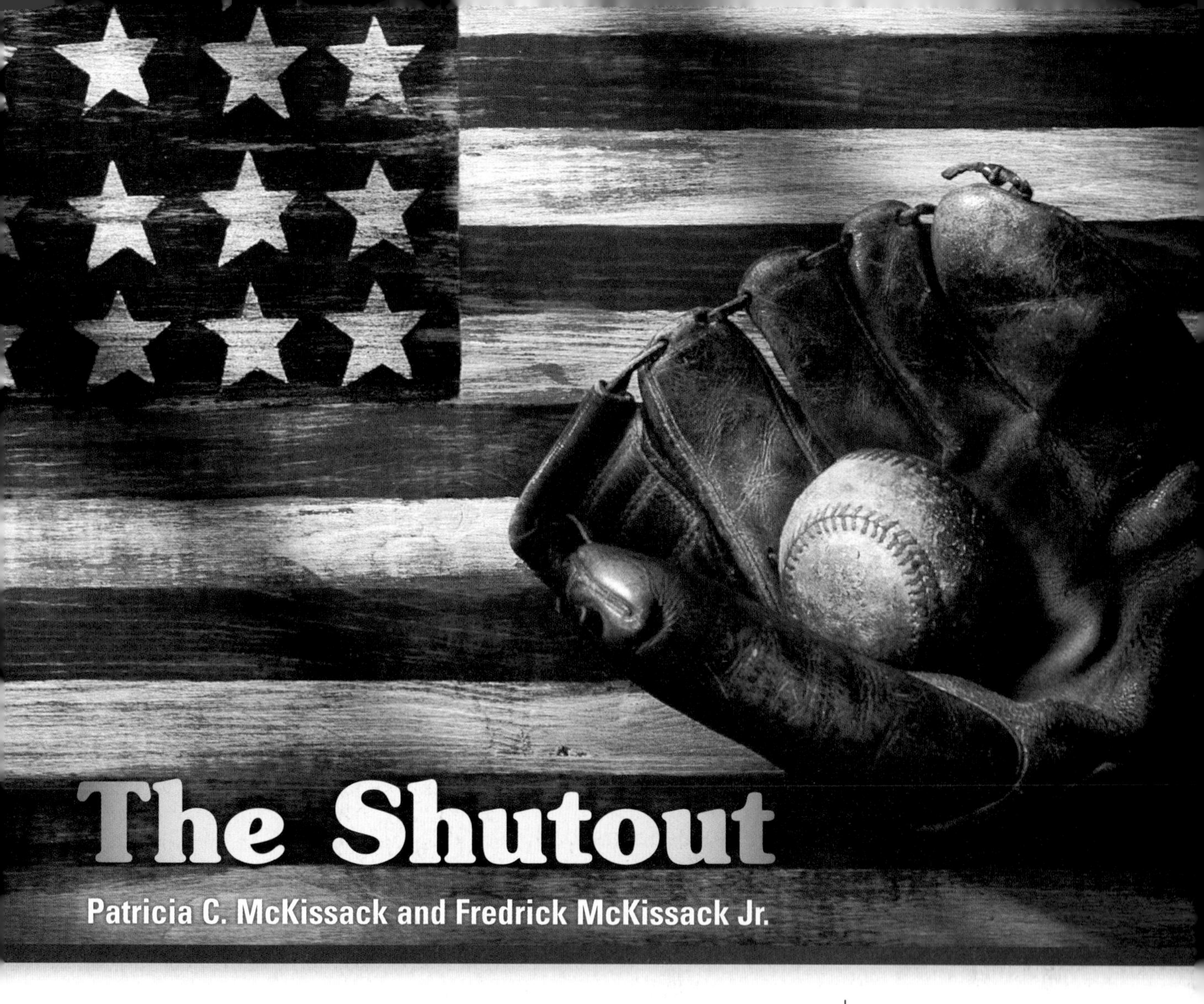

The Shutout

Patricia C. McKissack and Fredrick McKissack Jr.

The history of baseball is difficult to trace because it is embroidered with wonderful anecdotes[1] that are fun but not necessarily supported by fact. There are a lot of myths that persist about baseball—the games, the players, the owners, and the fans—in spite of contemporary research that disproves most of them. For example, the story that West Point cadet[2] Abner Doubleday "invented" baseball in 1839 while at Cooperstown, New York, continues to be widely accepted, even though, according to his diaries, Doubleday never visited Cooperstown.

1 ***Anecdotes*** are short accounts of incidents or events, intended to amuse listeners or to illustrate a point.

2 ***West Point*** is the United States Military Academy, a four-year institution in southeastern New York, which provides college-level instruction and officer training for careers in the U.S. Army. A ***cadet*** is a student at the academy.

A number of records and documents show that people were playing stick-and-ball games long before the 1839 date.

Text Structure What clue is given here to chronological order?

Albigence Waldo, a surgeon with George Washington's troops at Valley Forge,[3] wrote in his diary that soldiers were "batting balls and running bases" in their free time. Samuel Hopkins Adams (1871–1958), an American historical novelist, stated that his grandfather "played baseball on Mr. Mumford's pasture" in the 1820s.

Although baseball is a **uniquely** American sport, it was not invented by a single person. Probably the game evolved[4] from a variety of stick-and-ball games that were played in Europe, Asia, Africa, and the Americas for centuries and brought to the colonies by the most diverse[5] group of people ever to populate a continent. More specifically, some historians believe baseball is an outgrowth of its first cousin, *rounders*, an English game. Robin Carver wrote in his *Book of Sports* (1834) that "an American version of rounders called *goal ball* was **rivaling** cricket[6] in popularity."

It is generally accepted that by 1845, baseball, as it is recognized today, was becoming popular, especially in New York. In that year a group of baseball enthusiasts organized the New York Knickerbocker Club. They tried to standardize the game by establishing guidelines for "proper play."

The Knickerbockers' rules set the playing field—a diamond-shaped infield with four bases (first, second, third, and home) placed ninety feet apart. At that time, the

---

3 ***Valley Forge,*** Pennsylvania, was the site of the 1777–1778 winter quarters of George Washington and the Continental Army during the Revolutionary War.

4 Something that has ***evolved*** has developed slowly.

5 A ***diverse*** group is made up of members from different races or backgrounds.

6 ***Cricket*** is an English ball game played by two sides of eleven players each on a field with two wickets, or sets of stumps, set 66 feet apart. The ball is bowled at the wickets, each of which is defended by a batsman.

Vocabulary

uniquely (ū nēk′ lē) *adv.* distinctively; characteristically

rivaling (rī′ vəl ing) *v.* competing with

Monte Irvin, Willie Mays, and Henry Thompson played in the 1951 World Series for the New York Giants. It was the first time in World Series history that a team had an all African American outfield.

pitching distance was forty-five feet from home base and the "pitch" was thrown underhanded. The three-strikes-out rule, the three-out inning, and the ways in which a player could be called out were also specified. However, the nine-man team and nine-inning game were not established until later. Over the years, the Knickerbockers' basic rules of play haven't changed much.

In 1857–1858, the newly organized National Association of Base Ball Players was formed, and baseball became a business. Twenty-five clubs—mostly from eastern states—formed the Association for the purpose of setting rules and guidelines for club and team competition. The Association defined a professional player as a person who "played for money, place, or emolument (profit)." The Association also authorized an admission fee for one of the first "all-star" games between Brooklyn and New York. Fifteen hundred people paid fifty cents to see that game. Baseball was on its way to becoming the nation's number-one sport.

Monitor Comprehension
What did the National Association of Base Ball Players accomplish? If necessary, reread this paragraph.

A batter for the New York Black Yankees stands at home plate with a Newark Eagles catcher and the umpire waiting for a pitch.

By 1860, the same year South Carolina seceded[7] from the Union, there were about sixty teams in the Association. For obvious reasons none of them were from the South. Baseball's development was slow during the Civil War years, but teams continued to compete, and military records show that, sometimes between battles, Union soldiers chose up teams and played baseball games. It was during this time that records began mentioning African-American players. One war journalist noted that black

Text Structure Although events are still chronological, what new idea does this sentence introduce to the essay?

7 After South Carolina ***seceded*** (si sēd′ ed) from the Union in 1860, ten other states also withdrew and formed the Confederate States of America during the Civil War (1861–1865).

players were "sought after as teammates because of their skill as ball handlers."

Information about the role of African Americans in the early stages of baseball development is slight. Several West African cultures had stick-and-ball and running games, so at least some blacks were familiar with the concept of baseball. Baseball, however, was not a popular southern sport, never equal to boxing, wrestling, footracing, or horse racing among the **privileged** landowners.

Slave owners preferred these individual sports because they could enter their slaves in competitions, watch the event from a safe distance, pocket the winnings, and personally never raise a sweat. There are documents to show that slave masters made a great deal of money from the athletic skills of their slaves.

Free blacks, on the other hand, played on and against integrated[8] teams in large eastern cities and in small midwestern **hamlets**. It is believed that some of the emancipated[9] slaves and runaways who served in the Union Army learned how to play baseball from northern blacks and whites who had been playing together for years.

After the Civil War, returning soldiers helped to inspire a new interest in baseball all over the country. Teams sprung up in northern and Midwestern cities, and naturally African Americans were interested in joining some of these clubs. But the National Association of Base Ball Players had other ideas. They voted in December 1867 not to admit any team for membership that "may be composed of one or more colored persons." Their reasoning was as irrational[10] as the racism that shaped it: "If colored clubs were admitted," the Association stated, "there would be in all probability some division of feeling whereas, by excluding them no injury could result to

Visual Vocabulary

Hamlets are small rural villages.

Text Structure How does the author remind the reader of the chronological order?

Monitor Comprehension Monitor your comprehension by telling who and what the preceding two paragraphs are about. If necessary, reread.

---

8 ***Integrated*** teams were open to both African American and white players.

9 ***Emancipated*** (i man′ sə pāt′ ed) slaves had been freed from slavery.

10 Reasoning that is ***irrational*** is unreasonable or lacking sense.

Vocabulary

privileged (priv′ə lijd) *adj.* having or enjoying a right or advantage anyone . . . and [we wish] to keep out of the convention the discussion of any subjects having a political bearing as this [admission of blacks on the Association teams] undoubtedly would."

So, from the start, organized baseball tried to limit or exclude African-American participation. In the early days a few black ball players managed to play on integrated minor league teams. A few even made it to the majors, but by the turn of the century, black players were shut out of the major leagues until after World War II. That doesn't mean African Americans didn't play the game. They did.

Black people organized their own teams, formed leagues, and competed for championships. The history of the old "Negro Leagues" and the players who barnstormed[11] on black diamonds is one of baseball's most interesting chapters, but the story is a researcher's nightmare. Black baseball was outside the mainstream of the major leagues, so team and player records weren't well kept, and for the most part, the white press ignored black clubs or **portrayed** them as clowns. And for a long time the Baseball Hall of Fame didn't recognize any of the Negro League players. Because of the lack of documentation, many people thought the Negro Leagues' stories were nothing more than myths and yarns, but that is not the case. The history of the Negro Leagues is a patchwork of human drama and comedy, filled with legendary heroes, infamous owners, triple-headers, low pay, and long bus rides home—not unlike the majors. ❧

Monitor Comprehension
Did you slow down, speed up, or maintain the same reading rate as you read the quotation? Explain.

BQ BIG Question
How is this unfair and the opposite of equality?

11 Players who ***barnstormed*** toured rural areas, stopping briefly to take part in baseball games.

Vocabulary

portrayed (pôr trād′) *v.* set forth a picture of in words; described

After You Read

Respond and Think Critically

1. Who created the rules for playing baseball? **[Recall]**
2. What do historians know about the origins of the game of baseball? **[Summarize]**
3. How might you have felt if you were an African American baseball player who was not allowed to play in the major leagues? **[Connect]**
4. What can you infer is the reason the white press portrayed African American players as clowns? **[Infer]**
5. How were the Negro Leagues similar to the major leagues? How were they different? **[Compare and Contrast]**
6. **BQ BIG Question** The National Association of Base Ball Players argued that they were keeping African Americans out of the association so that "no injury could result to anyone." Do you agree with that argument? Explain. **[Evaluate]**

Vocabulary Practice

Respond to these questions.

1. Who would you describe as a **uniquely** talented musician—a world-recognized concert pianist or someone who has been playing piano for two months?
2. Which would be described as **rivaling** for your attention—an empty night sky or a brilliant fireworks display?
3. Whom would you describe as **privileged**—an unemployed person or a wealthy person?
4. How would a king probably be **portrayed** in a movie—as a powerful person or as a powerless person?

Academic Vocabulary

In the early years, a **policy** of the Association of Base Ball Players was to keep African American players from joining its league. Using context clues, try to figure out the meaning of the word *policy* in the preceding sentence. Check your guess in a dictionary.

TIP

Summarizing
Here are some tips to help you summarize. Remember that when you **summarize**, you retell the main ideas or events.

- Skim the selection to identify the main events.
- Retell the events in the order they occurred.
- Use transitional words, such as *first, next, then,* and *finally.*

Keep track of your ideas about the **BIG Question** in your unit Foldable.

Literature Online

Selection Resources
For Selection Quizzes, eFlashcards, and Reading-Writing Connection activities, go to glencoe.com and enter QuickPass code GL17527u4.

Literary Element Text Structure

1. How do dates in the essay help you keep track of information? What phrases help you understand time order?
2. Why is understanding the order of events an important part of understanding the essay?
3. How would the essay be different if the authors had begun with the secession of South Carolina in 1860 and the introduction of African American players to the game? Explain.

Review: Author's Purpose

As you learned on page 163, **author's purpose** is the author's reason for writing. For example, the purpose of a piece of writing may be to entertain, to explain or inform, to persuade, to express emotion, or a combination of these purposes.

Standards Practice  ELA6RC2e

4. Why did the authors write this essay?
   A. to explain that Abner Doubleday was not really the inventor of baseball
   B. to persuade readers that baseball was more fun to play in the 1800s
   C. to inform readers about the entire history of baseball to the present day
   D. to explain the early days in baseball and the role of African Americans in the game

Reading Strategy Monitor Comprehension

5. Why were the years 1845 and 1857–1858 important in the development of baseball?
6. Which parts in the essay demonstrate the determination of African Americans to play baseball despite obstacles? Support your answer.

Grammar Link

An **indirect object** tells *to whom* or *for whom* an action is done.

The New York Knickerbocker Club gave baseball some guidelines for play.

The **direct object** in the sentence above is *guidelines*. The indirect object is *baseball*. *Baseball* answers the question *to whom?* after the action verb *gave*.

An indirect object appears only in a sentence that has a direct object. Two clues will help you find indirect objects.

- The indirect object always comes *before* a direct object.
- You can add *to* or *for* before the indirect object and the sentence will still make sense.

The New York Knickerbocker Club gave (to) baseball some guidelines for play.

Practice

Try finding the indirect and direct object.

The pitcher gave the fan an autograph.

The umpire gave the coach a warning.

Now write your own sentences with indirect objects.

Research and Report

Internet Connection Using search engines and other Internet resources, research the history of another minority group or women in a particular sport. Be sure to use reputable, factual, and current sites. During your research, use a time line to track the order of important events. Use your research and time line to write a report. Paraphrase to convey main ideas and details from your sources. Remember to use signal words, phrases, or dates to indicate time order. Share what you have learned with your classmates.

Media Workshop

Propaganda

No matter how you get the news, you want to get the facts. Sometimes, however, what seems like fact is actually **propaganda.**

Propaganda is used to influence opinions. Writers use propaganda to persuade by using emotional methods instead of presenting accurate facts and details. Such writing may include stereotypes, faulty generalizations, flawed logic, or emotional language.

The goal of propaganda does not always support the common good. Tyrants—leaders who use government for their own purposes—often use propaganda. Sometimes, however, people use propaganda simply to convince someone to buy a product or use a service.

The chart shows how propaganda can appear in the media. What effects do you think propaganda has on people? Why is it important to be aware of propaganda? How does it influence your ideas regarding what is fair and unfair?

Media	Common Types of Propaganda	Beware!
Web sites	**Web sites** may contain propaganda because people can post anything and make it seem factual.	Visit only well-known news sites, such as the official Web site of your local newspaper.
Newspapers, magazines, posters, and other print media	**Print media** may use emotional language, stereotypes, or faulty generalizations to convince you of something. **Advertisements** and **editorials** often rely on propaganda.	Double-check facts with neutral sources, such as reliable news Web sites. Watch out for emotional images or language.
TV and radio	**Talk shows** and **newscasts** may rely on emotional, misleading language and visuals to keep you watching or listening. **Commercials,** like print ads, often rely on propaganda.	Be critical of what you see or hear. Also listen for devices, such as repetition, used by the speaker presenting the information.

GA Performance Standards

For page 521

ELA6LSV2a When responding to visual and oral texts and media, identify persuasive and propaganda techniques used in media and identify false and misleading information.

TRY IT

Analyze Propaganda in Commercials Answer these questions as you watch a TV commercial.

1. What is the product? What company is selling it?
2. Write two statements that the commercial presents as facts.
3. Look up the statements using neutral sources, such as reliable news Web sites. Are the statements true?
4. Does the commercial use emotional language? If so, what does it claim?
5. Write a paragraph about the commercial. Does it use propaganda? How? What is the commercial's purpose?

LOG ON **Literature** Online

Media Literacy For project ideas, templates, and media analysis guides, go to glencoe.com and enter QuickPass code GL17527u4.

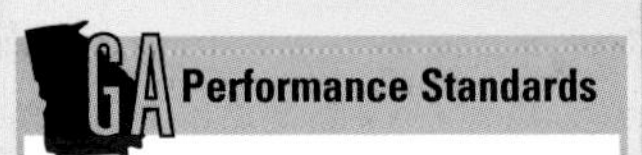

For pages 522–523

ELA6R1c For informational texts, apply knowledge of common organizational structures and patterns.

Genre Focus: Essay

An **essay** is a short piece of nonfiction writing on a single topic. The purpose of an essay is to communicate an idea or opinion. A **formal essay** is serious and impersonal, and its purpose is to instruct or persuade. An **informal essay** entertains while it informs, usually with a light, conversational tone. Essays are generally characterized as personal (informal), expository (formal), or persuasive (formal).

Literary Elements

Many essays, regardless of their type, share the author's thoughts about a subject or an experience. Identifying and using elements common to formal essays helps you obtain and understand information.

Thesis When instructing or persuading, authors may directly state their **thesis,** or main idea, in a logical, highly organized way. Sometimes they may indirectly state the thesis, or imply it. Authors then provide **evidence** or **support** to help make their thesis convincing. Evidence and support may be in the form of **examples, facts,** and **opinions.**

Persuasion and Argument If an author's purpose is to try to convince readers to think or act in a particular way, the author may use **persuasion.** Some authors use logic and specific examples to support what they think. This kind of persuasive writing is called **argument.**

Persuasive Techniques Persuasive techniques are tools that authors use to try to convince readers to see things a certain way. When authors **appeal to logic,** they present facts and reasoning. **Appeals to emotion** can be attempts to scare, entertain, or anger an audience. An **appeal to ethics** tries to engage a reader's sense of right and wrong. An **appeal to authority** uses experts' opinions as support.

Repetition and **parallelism** can also help an author convince the reader. **Parallelism** uses a similar grammatical structure for a series of words. This technique brings unity to an argument. **Repetition** is using the same word or phrase more than once. This technique can help ensure that the main point of an argument is clear and easy to remember.

TRY IT

Using one of the graphic organizers shown on the next page, identify different ways to organize ideas in an essay in this unit.

Characteristics of the Genre

To better understand how an author can organize an essay to create an effect and achieve a desired purpose, look at the examples of graphic organizers below.

Main Idea and Supporting Details Chart from "The Shutout"

Paragraph	Main Idea	Supporting Details
1 and 2	Baseball's history is full of myths.	• supposedly invented in 1839 • similar games played before 1839 • Washington's soldiers played a form of baseball.
3	One person did not invent baseball.	• evolved from many countries • may be related to rounders, an English game

Thesis and Support Chart from "Looking for America"

Thesis: Racial discrimination is wrong.

↓

Examples: Annie can't drink from the fountain at the park. Annie has to drink from a jar instead of a glass.

↓

Facts: Laws at this time required separate drinking fountains and restrooms for African Americans and whites.

↓

Opinions: People follow laws that don't make sense.

Argument and Evidence Chart from "Eulogy on the Dog"

Argument: A dog is your most faithful friend.

Appeals to Logic
- People, wealth, and fame may fail you.
- A dog stands by its master even in the worst of times.

Appeals to Emotion
- A dog loves its master unconditionally.
- A dog is faithful even after its master's death.

Literature Online

Literature and Reading For more selections in this genre, go to glencoe.com and enter Quickpass code GL17527u4.

Before You Read

The Circuit

Connect to the Story

Think about a time when you really wanted something that you didn't get. What kept you from getting what you wanted? How much control did you have over the situation?

Partner Talk With a partner, discuss the difficulties that can keep people from getting what they want.

Build Background

This story about migrant workers takes place during the 1950s in California.

- Migrant workers travel from farm to farm to pick vegetables and fruit by hand.
- They follow the harvest, moving to another farm after each type of crop is harvested.
- Traveling from farm to farm is sometimes called traveling the circuit. Often, migrant workers live in houses provided by the farm owners.

Vocabulary

acquired (ə kwīrd′) *v.* came into possession of (p. 528). *Mr. Watkins acquired books, pans, and a clock at the garage sale.*

drone (drōn) *n.* dull, continuous buzzing or humming sound (p. 529). *I awoke to the drone of a distant lawnmower.*

instinctively (in stingk′tiv lē) *adv.* behaving in a fixed way when moved by something that causes a person to take action (p. 530). *The mother instinctively reached to catch her child as he fell.*

savoring (sā′vər ing) *v.* taking great delight in (p. 531). *Anita is savoring the last days of her summer vacation.*

hesitantly (hez′ət ənt lē) *adv.* reluctantly or unwillingly (p. 532). *The patient hesitantly agreed to have surgery.*

Meet Francisco Jiménez

"I came to realize that learning and knowledge were the only stable things in my life. Whatever I learned in school, that knowledge would stay with me no matter how many times we moved."

—Francisco Jiménez

Young Farm Worker Born in Mexico, Francisco Jiménez came to the United States with his family when he was four years old. At the age of six, he became a farm laborer like others in his family. Jiménez is now a professor of literature at Santa Clara University in California and the author of many books and stories.

Literary Works Jiménez has written numerous books, including the autobiographical book *Breaking Through.*

Francisco Jiménez was born in 1943.

LOG ON  Literature Online

Author Search For more about Francisco Jiménez, go to glencoe.com and enter QuickPass code GL17527u4.

Set Purposes for Reading

BQ BIG Question

As you read, think about the sacrifices migrant farm workers and their families make in order to survive. Ask yourself, what situations does the narrator face that seem unfair?

Literary Element Mood

Mood is the emotional quality or atmosphere of a story. The writer's choice of language, subject matter, setting, and tone in a short story contribute to creating mood. The mood can suggest an emotion, such as fear or joy. It can suggest the quality of a setting, such as gloom.

A story's mood—the feeling or emotion it creates—is important to its overall effect.

As you read, ask yourself, what details in the story help create its mood?

Reading Strategy Make Predictions About Plot

The sequence of events in a story is called the **plot.** When you **make predictions about plot,** you guess what will happen later in the story. You base your predictions on what you have read so far and on your own knowledge and experiences.

Making predictions is one way to think about a story. Asking "What will this character do next?" or "What might happen?" can keep you interested and involved in the outcome of the story.

To make predictions about plot,

- preview the title and any subheads and pictures
- pause as you read to make predictions about what might happen next
- adjust or verify your prediction

To help you make predictions about the plot as you read, you may find it helpful to use a graphic organizer like the one below.

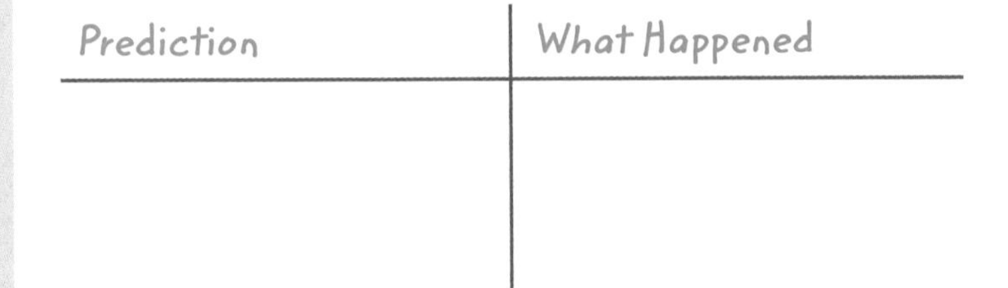

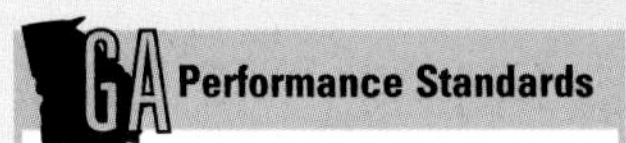

For pages 524–535

ELA6R1g For literary texts, define and explain how tone is conveyed in literature through word choice, sentence structure, punctuation, rhythm, repetition, and rhyme.

TRY IT

Make Predictions You come home from school, drop your backpack on the floor, and kick off your shoes. You eat a bowl of cereal, leaving the open box and the carton of milk on the table. Your mother walks in the door an hour later. What do you predict will happen next?

THE CIRCUIT

Francisco Jiménez

Road. Beatrice Boissegur. Oil on paper. Private Collection.

It was that time of year again. Ito,[1] the strawberry sharecropper,[2] did not smile. It was natural. The peak of the strawberry season was over and the last few days the workers, most of them *braceros*,[3] were not picking as many boxes as they had during the months of June and July.

As the last days of August disappeared, so did the number of braceros. Sunday, only one—the best picker—came to work. I liked him. Sometimes we talked during our half-hour lunch break. That is how I found out he was from Jalisco,[4] the same state in Mexico my family was from. That Sunday was the last time I saw him.

Mood What is the mood of this paragraph? What details help create the mood?

When the sun had tired and sunk behind the mountains, Ito signaled us that it was time to go home. *"Ya esora,"*[5] he yelled in his broken Spanish. Those were the words I waited for twelve hours a day, every day, seven days a week, week after week. And the thought of not hearing them again saddened me.

Make Predictions About Plot Why do you think the narrator will not hear the words again?

---

1 ***Ito*** (ē′ tō)

2 A ***sharecropper*** is a farmer who works land owned by someone else and shares the crop or the money from its sale with the landowner.

3 ***Braceros*** (brä sā′ rōs) are Mexican farm workers.

4 ***Jalisco*** (hə lēs′ kō)

5 ***[Ya esora]*** Ito is trying to say *"Ya es hora"* (yä es o′ rə), which means "It is time."

As we drove home Papa did not say a word. With both hands on the wheel, he stared at the dirt road. My older brother, Roberto, was also silent. He leaned his head back and closed his eyes. Once in a while he cleared from his throat the dust that blew in from outside.

Mood How does the silence of Papa and Roberto affect the mood?

Yes, it was that time of year. When I opened the front door to the shack, I stopped. Everything we owned was neatly packed in cardboard boxes. Suddenly I felt even more the weight of hours, days, weeks, and months of work. I sat down on a box. The thought of having to move to Fresno[6] and knowing what was in store for me there brought tears to my eyes.

That night I could not sleep. I lay in bed thinking about how much I hated this move.

A little before five o'clock in the morning, Papa woke everyone up. A few minutes later, the yelling and screaming of my little brothers and sisters, for whom the move was a great adventure, broke the silence of dawn. Shortly, the barking of the dogs accompanied them.

While we packed the breakfast dishes, Papa went outside to start the "Carcanchita."[7] That was the name Papa gave his old '38 black Plymouth. He bought it in a used-car lot in Santa Rosa in the winter of 1949. Papa was very proud of his little jalopy. He had a right to be proud of it. He spent a lot of time looking at other cars before buying this one. When he finally chose the "Carcanchita," he checked it thoroughly before driving it out of the car lot. He examined every inch of the car. He listened to the motor, tilting his head from side to side like a parrot, trying to detect any noises that spelled car trouble. After being satisfied with the looks and sounds of the car, Papa then insisted on knowing who the original owner was. He never did find out from the car salesman, but he bought the car anyway. Papa figured the original owner must have been an important man because behind the rear seat of the car he found a blue necktie.

---

6 ***Fresno*** is a city in one of California's main farming regions.

7 ***Carcanchita*** (kär′ kən chē′ tə)

Papa parked the car out in front and left the motor running. *"Listo,"*[8] he yelled. Without saying a word, Roberto and I began to carry the boxes out to the car. Roberto carried the two big boxes and I carried the two smaller ones. Papa then threw the mattress on top of the car roof and tied it with ropes to the front and rear bumpers.

Everything was packed except Mama's pot. It was an old large galvanized pot she had picked up at an army surplus store in Santa María the year I was born. The pot had many dents and nicks, and the more dents and nicks it **acquired** the more Mama liked it. *"Mi olla,"*[9] she used to say proudly.

I held the front door open as Mama carefully carried out her pot by both handles, making sure not to spill the cooked beans. When she got to the car, Papa reached out to help her with it. Roberto opened the rear car door and Papa gently placed it on the floor behind the front seat. All of us then climbed in. Papa sighed, wiped the sweat off his forehead with his sleeve, and said wearily: *"Es todo."*[10]

Make Predictions About Plot What can you predict about their trip from the things the family has packed?

As we drove away, I felt a lump in my throat. I turned around and looked at our little shack for the last time.

At sunset we drove into a labor camp near Fresno. Since Papa did not speak English, Mama asked the camp foreman if he needed any more workers. "We don't need no more," said the foreman, scratching his head. "Check with Sullivan down the road. Can't miss him. He lives in a big white house with a fence around it."

When we got there, Mama walked up to the house. She went through a white gate, past a row of rose bushes, up the stairs to the front door. She rang the doorbell. The porch light went on and a tall husky man came out. They exchanged a few words. After the man went in, Mama clasped her hands and hurried back to the car. "We have work! Mr. Sullivan said we can stay there the whole season," she said, gasping and pointing to an old garage near the stables.

Mood How has the mood changed? Why has it changed?

---

8 ***Listo*** (lēs′ tō) means "Ready."

9 Mama's favorite ***olla*** (o′ yä) is a ***galvanized pot,*** which is an iron pot with a thin coat of zinc. She got it at an ***army surplus store,*** which sells goods no longer needed by the U.S. military.

10 ***Es todo*** (es tō dō) means "That's everything."

Vocabulary

acquired (ə kwīrd′) *v.* came into possession of

The garage was worn out by the years. It had no windows. The walls, eaten by termites, strained to support the roof full of holes. The dirt floor, populated by earth worms, looked like a gray road map.

That night, by the light of a **kerosene lamp**, we unpacked and cleaned our new home. Roberto swept away the loose dirt, leaving the hard ground. Papa plugged the holes in the walls with old newspapers and tin can tops. Mama fed my little brothers and sisters. Papa and Roberto then brought in the mattress and placed it on the far corner of the garage. "Mama, you and the little ones sleep on the mattress. Roberto, Panchito, and I will sleep outside under the trees," Papa said.

Early next morning Mr. Sullivan showed us where his crop was, and after breakfast, Papa, Roberto, and I headed for the vineyard to pick.

Around nine o'clock the temperature had risen to almost one hundred degrees.

I was completely soaked in sweat and my mouth felt as if I had been chewing on a handkerchief. I walked over to the end of the row, picked up the jug of water we had brought, and began drinking. "Don't drink too much; you'll get sick," Roberto shouted. No sooner had he said that than I felt sick to my stomach. I dropped to my knees and let the jug roll off my hands. I remained motionless with my eyes glued on the hot sandy ground. All I could hear was the **drone** of insects. Slowly I began to recover. I poured water over my face and neck and watched the dirty water run down my arms to the ground.

I still felt a little dizzy when we took a break to eat lunch. It was past two o'clock and we sat underneath a large walnut tree that was on the side of the road. While we ate, Papa jotted down the number of boxes we had picked. Roberto drew designs on the ground with a stick. Suddenly I noticed Papa's face turn pale as he looked down the road. "Here comes the school bus," he whispered loudly in alarm.

Vocabulary

drone (drōn) *n.* dull, continuous buzzing or humming sound

Visual Vocabulary

A **kerosene lamp** burns **kerosene,** a colorless liquid made from petroleum. When a wick is lighted, the kerosene produces a yellow flame.

Mood How does this detail contribute to the mood?

Trabajadores, 1950.
Castera Bazile.
Oil on canvas, 27 × 19 1/2 in.
Private Collection.

View the Art *Trabajadores* (tra bä ha dō′ rās) means "workers" in Spanish. Do you think it is the beginning or the end of the workers' day?

Instinctively, Roberto and I ran and hid in the vineyards. We did not want to get in trouble for not going to school. The neatly dressed boys about my age got off. They carried books under their arms. After they crossed the street, the bus drove away. Roberto and I came out from hiding and joined Papa. *"Tienen que tener cuidado,"*[11] he warned us. "You have to be careful."

After lunch we went back to work. The sun kept beating down. The buzzing insects, the wet sweat, and the hot dry dust made the afternoon seem to last forever. Finally the mountains around the valley reached out and swallowed the sun. Within an hour it was too dark to continue

Mood How does this image make you feel?

11 ***Tienen que tener cuidado*** (tye′ nen kā tā nār′ kwē dä′ dō)

Vocabulary

instinctively (in stingk′ tiv lē) *adv.* behaving in a fixed way when moved by something that causes a person to take action picking. The vines blanketed the grapes, making it difficult to see the bunches. "*Vámonos,*"[12] said Papa, signaling to us that it was time to quit work. Papa then took out a pencil and began to figure out how much we had earned our first day. He wrote down numbers, crossed some out, wrote down some more. "*Quince,*"[13] he murmured.

When we arrived home, we took a cold shower underneath a water-hose. We then sat down to eat dinner around some wooden crates that served as a table. Mama had cooked a special meal for us. We had rice and tortillas with *carne con chile,*[14] my favorite dish.

The next morning I could hardly move. My body ached all over. I felt little control over my arms and legs. This feeling went on every morning for days until my muscles finally got used to the work.

It was Monday, the first week of November. The grape season was over and I could now go to school. I woke up early that morning and lay in bed, looking at the stars and **savoring** the thought of not going to work and of starting sixth grade for the first time that year. Since I could not sleep, I decided to get up and join Papa and Roberto at breakfast. I sat at the table across from Roberto, but I kept my head down. I did not want to look up and face him. I knew he was sad. He was not going to school today. He was not going tomorrow, or next week, or next month. He would not go until the cotton season was over, and that was sometime in February. I rubbed my hands together and watched the dry, acid stained[15] skin fall to the floor in little rolls.

When Papa and Roberto left for work, I felt relief. I walked to the top of a small grade next to the shack and watched the "Carcanchita" disappear in the distance in a cloud of dust.

Make Predictions About Plot What do you think school will be like for the narrator?

BQ BIG Question

Why does Panchito get to go to school but Roberto does not? How does Panchito feel about the situation?

---

12 ***Vámanos*** (vä′ mə nōs) means "let's go."

13 ***Quince*** (kēn′ sā) means "fifteen."

14 ***Tortillas*** (tôr tē′ yəs) are made from corn or wheat meal and baked on a griddle so that they resemble very flat pancakes. ***Carne con chile*** (kär′ nā kōn chē′ lā) is meat cooked with red peppers and beans.

15 The narrator's hands are ***acid stained*** by grapes. Grapes contain tartaric acid, which can leave a stain on skin and clothing.

Vocabulary

savoring (sa′ vər ing) *v.* taking great delight in

Two hours later, around eight o'clock, I stood by the side of the road waiting for school bus number twenty. When it arrived I climbed in. Everyone was busy either talking or yelling. I sat in an empty seat in the back.

When the bus stopped in front of the school, I felt very nervous. I looked out the bus window and saw boys and girls carrying books under their arms. I put my hands in my pant pockets and walked to the principal's office. When I entered I heard a woman's voice say: "May I help you?" I was startled. I had not heard English for months. For a few seconds I remained speechless. I looked at the lady who waited for an answer. My first instinct was to answer her in Spanish, but I held back. Finally, after struggling for English words, I managed to tell her that I wanted to enroll in the sixth grade. After answering many questions, I was led to the classroom.

Mood How does Panchito feel? Which words hint at how he is feeling?

Mr. Lema, the sixth grade teacher, greeted me and assigned me a desk. He then introduced me to the class. I was so nervous and scared at that moment when everyone's eyes were on me that I wished I were with Papa and Roberto picking cotton. After taking roll, Mr. Lema gave the class the assignment for the first hour. "The first thing we have to do this morning is finish reading the story we began yesterday," he said enthusiastically. He walked up to me, handed me an English book, and asked me to read. "We are on page 125," he said politely. When I heard this, I felt my blood rush to my head; I felt dizzy. "Would you like to read?" he asked **hesitantly**. I opened the book to page 125. My mouth was dry. My eyes began to water. I could not begin. "You can read later," Mr. Lema said understandingly.

For the rest of the reading period I kept getting angrier and angrier with myself. I should have read, I thought to myself.

During recess I went into the restroom and opened my English book to page 125. I began to read in a low voice, pretending I was in class. There were many words I did not know. I closed the book and headed back to the classroom.

Make Predictions About Plot What do you think the narrator will do when he gets back to the classroom?

Vocabulary

hesitantly (hez′ət ənt lē) *adv.* reluctantly or unwillingly

Despedida, 1941. Hector Poleo. Oil on linen, 60 x 50 cm. Private Collection.

View the Art *Despedida* (des pə dē′ də) means "departure" in Spanish. Does the mood of the painting remind you of anything in the story? Explain.

Mr. Lema was sitting at his desk correcting papers. When I entered he looked up at me and smiled. I felt better. I walked up to him and asked if he could help me with the new words. "Gladly," he said.

The rest of the month I spent my lunch hours working on English with Mr. Lema, my best friend at school.

One Friday during lunch hour Mr. Lema asked me to take a walk with him to the music room. "Do you like music?" he asked me as we entered the building.

"Yes, I like *corridos,*"[16] I answered. He then picked up a trumpet, blew on it, and handed it to me. The sound gave me goose bumps. I knew that sound. I had heard it in many *corridos.* "How would you like to learn how to play it?" he asked. He must have read my face because before I could answer, he added: "I'll teach you how to play it during our lunch hours."

That day I could hardly wait to get home to tell Papa and Mama the great news. As I got off the bus, my little brothers and sisters ran up to meet me. They were yelling and screaming. I thought they were happy to see me, but when I opened the door to our shack, I saw that everything we owned was neatly packed in cardboard boxes.

BQ BIG Question

How do you think the narrator feels at the end of the story? Are his feelings justified? Why or why not?

16 ***Corridos*** (kōr rē′ dōs) are songs, especially slow, romantic ones.

After You Read

Respond and Think Critically

1. What does the narrator miss when his family leaves the strawberry farm for Fresno? **[Recall]**
2. What is a day's work like on Mr. Sullivan's farm? **[Summarize]**
3. Why do you think Mr. Lema takes a special interest in Panchito? **[Infer]**
4. How is the ending of the story related to the title? **[Analyze]**
5. The original title of this story was "Cajas de cartón" ("Cardboard Boxes"). Do you prefer the original title or "The Circuit"? Explain. **[Evaluate]**
6. **BQ** **BIG Question** Do you think the story supports the saying "Life isn't fair"? Why or why not? **[Conclude]**

Vocabulary Practice

Respond to these questions.

1. Who would more likely speak **hesitantly**—an angry person or a shy person?
2. How would you feel if you **acquired** a million dollars—excited or unhappy?
3. Which would a person be **savoring**—a headache or an ice cream cone?
4. Which sound might make a person jump **instinctively**—a firecracker or a bird's song?
5. Which is more likely to produce a **drone**—a washing machine or a hammer?

Academic Vocabulary

When the grape season is over, Panchito thinks with **anticipation** about going to school. In the preceding sentence, *anticipation* means "a feeling of excited expectation." Think about a time when you looked forward to something with anticipation. What was it?

TIP

Analyzing
Here are some tips to help you answer question 4.

- Look up the word *circuit* in a dictionary. Think about which of the definitions might fit the events in the story.
- Explain how a circuit is like the way the family lives.
- Consider how the ending of the story reflects the way the family lives.

Keep track of your ideas about the **BIG Question** in your unit Foldable.

Literature Online

Selection Resources
For Selection Quizzes, eFlashcards, and Reading-Writing Connection activities, go to glencoe.com and enter QuickPass code GL17527u4.

Literary Element Mood

1. Describe Mr. Sullivan's garage when the family first arrives. How does this description make you feel?
2. Read the following lines from the story: "After lunch we went back to work. The sun kept beating down. The buzzing insects, the wet sweat, and the hot dry dust made the afternoon seem to last forever." How would you describe the mood? What words create the mood of these lines?
3. Think about the details the author uses to create the mood. How do you think the author wants you to feel about the narrator?

Review: Style

As you learned on page 451, an author's **style** is his or her unique way of putting words and sentences together. **Diction,** an author's choice of words, is an important part of that style. The words the author uses can reveal how the author feels about a subject.

Although "The Circuit" is written in English, the author uses some Spanish words and phrases to show that the characters also speak Spanish. When you read the dialogue or thoughts of the characters, you "hear" their voices differently because of the Spanish words.

4. How does the author's use of Spanish words help you understand Panchito and his family?

Reading Strategy
Make Predictions About Plot

Standards Practice  ELA6R1e/i

5. Based on the events in the story, which sentence is the most logical prediction?
   A. Panchito's family will not move.
   B. Panchito will stay in Mr. Lema's class.
   C. Panchito will not learn to play the trumpet this year.
   D. Panchito's brother Roberto will teach him to play the drums.

Grammar Link

Independent and Dependent Clauses
A **clause** is a group of words that contains a subject and a predicate. An **independent clause** expresses a complete thought. It can stand alone. For example:

> Everything was packed except Mama's pot.

A **dependent clause** has a subject and a predicate, but it cannot stand alone as a sentence. For example:

> As we drove away

A dependent clause depends on an independent clause to form a complete sentence. For example:

> As we drove away, I felt a lump in my throat.

Practice
Look for two sentences in "The Circuit" that have a dependent clause. Write the sentences. Underline the independent clause and circle the dependent clause in each sentence. Then write a sentence of your own that has a dependent clause.

Speaking and Listening

Speech What rights do workers have? Choose a topic from the following questions: Should workers have the right to go on strike? Should workers get health insurance and paid days off when they are sick? Should workers be forced to work under unsafe conditions? Write a persuasive speech supporting your opinion. Organize your main ideas for the greatest impact, using detailed evidence and visual displays effectively. Practice your speech, using pacing, intonation, and expression that will interest your audience. Incorporate gestures and body language that correspond to your words, and establish steady eye contact. Then present your speech to the class.

Visual Perspective

on *The Circuit* by Francisco Jiménez

GA Performance Standards

For pages 536–539

ELA6RC2f Recognize and use the features of disciplinary texts (e.g., charts, graphs, photos, maps, highlighted vocabulary).

from Harvest

by George Ancona

Set a Purpose for Reading

Read to learn more about migrant workers, the subject of the short story "The Circuit."

Build Background

Mexican immigrants have been coming to the United States to find agricultural work for more than 100 years. Many workers depend on this seasonal work for their yearly income.

Reading Skill Analyze Images

To **analyze images,** think about the way the photographs emphasize key points in the text and what messages they convey. Look for important details and determine how they add interest or meaning. As you read, choose an image to analyze. Use a three-column chart like the one below to analyze it.

Description of Image	Meaning of Image	Details That Give Clues to Meaning

These are the farm workers, called *campesinos* in Spanish, who have come to harvest[1] the crops that grow in the rich earth of the Salinas Valley.

Most farmworkers are migrant workers. They travel north from farm to farm to farm harvesting the crops as they ripen. On the East Coast workers flow from Florida north to Maine. A central stream starts in Texas and moves up through the Mid-Western states. In the West the migration begins in southern California and goes north to the state of Washington.

Some workers find places to live in neighborhoods where people will rent them space in their home, their garage, or a trailer parked in the driveway. Farmers rent bunks in barracks near the fields. Workers without money sleep in

1 To ***harvest*** is to gather a crop.

shanties,[2] in caves, or under bridges.

In northern California, vineyards drape the rolling hills. Table grapes must be harvested with great care because they are very delicate. The *campesinos* move up and down the rows with a long wheelbarrow that holds three Styrofoam boxes. Since the grapes ripen at different times, the pickers must search among the leaves to find the ripest grapes. They snip them off with small scissors and carefully place them into boxes. Once the boxes are filled, they take them to a packing shed where another worker cuts off any spoiled or imperfect grapes.

The grapes are then packed into cartons that are stacked onto a pallet.[3] A forklift will lift the pallet onto a truck to take them to market.

Strawberry picking is stoop labor. A picker must work bent over all day. The best time to pick is early in the season when the plants have few leaves and you can see the berries. Later in the season the plants fill out

2 ***Shanties*** are crude, poorly built huts or cabins.

3 Here, a ***pallet*** is a movable platform for storing and transporting goods.

View the Photograph How does this photograph help you understand the expression "stoop labor"?

with leaves and the picker has to search for the hidden berries. A picker picks only the ripe strawberries, and leaves the others to ripen.

Artichokes grow tall. To harvest artichokes a campesino carries a large bag on his back. The men work in clusters, chatting as they walk up and down the rows of plants. With one hand that holds a short knife, a picker reaches for an artichoke, slices it off the plant, and tosses it over his shoulder into the bag. The men wear thick work gloves to protect their hands from the spiny leaves of the artichoke. When a picker's bag is full, he takes it to the waiting truck, where a man lifts the bag off his shoulders and dumps the artichokes.

Raspberries are not as hard to pick because the plants grow to the height of a person. But you still have to be careful because the canes have tiny sharp thorns. Most pickers wear gloves with cut-off fingers. A picker must be able to judge the ripeness of the fruit and pick only the ripe ones, leaving the others to ripen. A field can be harvested two or three times to get all the fruit. Around their waist pickers wear a belt that holds two buckets. When the buckets are full, the picker takes them to a small shed in the middle of the field. There the berries are packed into the plastic containers that are sold in the stores.

At the end of the summer the migrant center has a *fiesta*.[4] A choral group of parents and children sings for the audience as dinner is served. It's a traditional Mexican meal of pozole, a stew of meat, corn, and chili. Then comes chicken with rice, beans, and tortillas.

After the meal two friends play and sing songs from the old country. They are quickly surrounded by families singing the familiar songs. There are many kisses and *abrazos*[5] as the parents carry the sleepy children home.

4 A ***fiesta*** is a party.

5 ***Abrazos*** (ä brä′ sōs) is the Spanish word for "hugs."

Respond and Think Critically

1. Summarize the work of a migrant farmer. For help with writing a summary, see page 170. **[Summarize]**
2. How does the photograph on page 536 help you understand how grapes are harvested? **[Infer]**
3. How do the photographs on pages 537 and 538 help you compare the work of a strawberry picker with the work of an artichoke picker? **[Compare]**
4. **Text to Text** Which details from *Harvest* help you understand the work that Panchito and his family do in "The Circuit"? How is Panchito's life like the lives of the people in the photo essay? **[Connect]**
5. **Reading Skill** **Analyze Images** How do the photographs help you understand the life of a migrant worker? How might migrant workers feel about their jobs?
6. **BQ** **BIG Question** Would you describe the living and working conditions of migrant workers as fair or unfair? Explain your answer. How might their lives be improved?

Before You Read

Persephone

Connect to the Myth

How would you feel if something or someone you loved was taken away from you? What would you do?

Quickwrite Maybe you know someone who lost something important, or perhaps you have lost something yourself. Write about what it feels like to lose someone or something important.

Build Background

"Persephone" is a Greek myth about Demeter (di mē′ tər), the goddess of the harvest, and her daughter, Persephone (pər sef′ ə nē). Other important gods and goddesses in this story include:

- Zeus (zo͞os) is the supreme, or highest, god. He is ruler of the heavens and Earth. He is the brother of Demeter and Hades, and his chief weapon is a thunderbolt.
- Hades (hā′ dēz) is the god who rules the underworld, a place to which the dead go.
- Hermes (hur′ mēz) is the swift messenger of the gods. He is one of Zeus's sons and is usually shown wearing winged sandals and a winged hat or cap.

Vocabulary

deafening (def′ ən ing) *adj.* very loud; earsplitting (p. 542).
The airplane made a deafening noise as it took off.

confirmed (kən furmd′) *v.* established as true (p. 544).
The X-ray confirmed that Doug had broken his arm.

sowing (sō′ ing) *v.* spreading seeds over the ground so that they will grow (p. 544).
A planter is a machine used for sowing corn.

mankind (man′ kīnd′) *n.* all human beings (p. 545).
The scientist's invention will benefit mankind.

compromise (kom′ prə mīz′) *v.* to settle a disagreement by having each side give up something (p. 546).
The brother and sister agreed to compromise by sharing the last piece of cake.

Meet Alice Low

"Painting and ceramics were my first interests. I still sing in a local chorus. Travel stimulates, and many a line has come to me on a tennis court."

—Alice Low

Teacher, Editor, Writer Alice Low is the author of many books, including picture books and a short story collection for young adults. Many of her books for younger readers have humorous plots and colorful characters. She has also written poetry and compiled Greek myths into a collection that can be clearly understood by a young audience. Low is also a writing teacher and an editor.

Literary Works Low's young adult books include *At Jasper's House* and *Kallie's Corner.* "Persephone" comes from *The Macmillan Book of Greek Gods and Heroes.*

Alice Low was born in 1926.

Literature Online

Author Search For more about Alice Low, go to glencoe.com and enter QuickPass code GL17527u4.

Set Purposes for Reading

BQ BIG Question

As you read, ask yourself, how does Demeter deal with an unfair situation?

Literary Element Foreshadowing

Foreshadowing is the use of clues by an author to prepare readers for events that will happen in a story.

Foreshadowing involves readers in a story by creating a feeling of suspense, dread, or eager anticipation. It lets readers predict what will happen and encourages them to read further to find out.

As you read, ask yourself, what clues foreshadow events in the story?

Reading Strategy Activate Prior Knowledge

When you **activate prior knowledge,** you use what you already know to help you understand what you read. For example, think about what you already know about myths from reading "Arachne."

Activating prior knowledge can give meaning to what you read and make and confirm predictions of content, purpose, and organization.

To activate prior knowledge,

- recall what you already know about myths
- recall settings, characters, and lessons in myths you have read
- think about similar settings, characters, or lessons from your own life

You may find it helpful to use a graphic organizer like the one below.

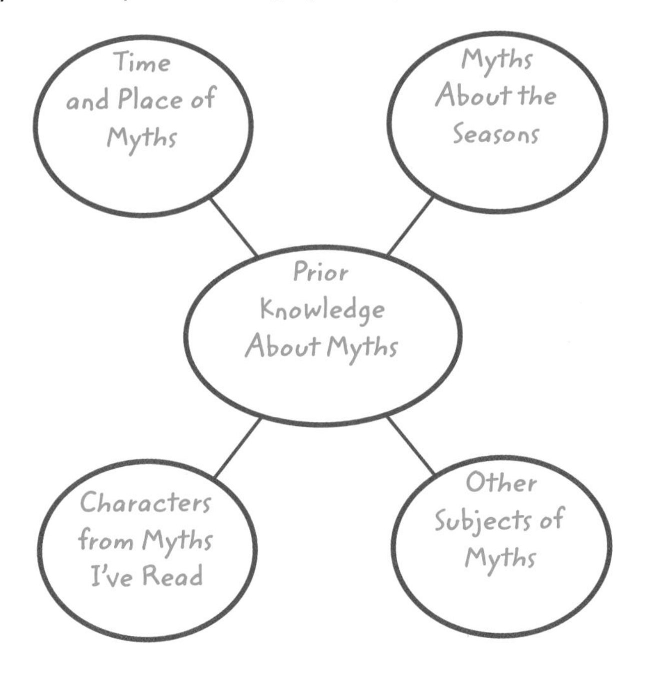

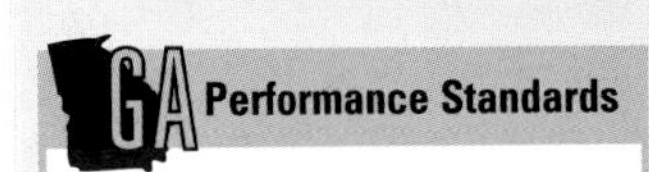

Performance Standards

For pages 540–548

ELA6R1i For literary texts, compare traditional literature and mythology from different cultures.

TRY IT

Activate Prior Knowledge
You're getting ready for school. When you look out the window, you see that it is raining heavily. How will you use prior knowledge as you get dressed?

PERSEPHONE

ALICE LOW

Persephone was a high-spirited, sunny girl who loved springtime and flowers and running outdoors with her friends. She was the daughter of Demeter, goddess of the harvest, and she and her mother spent more time on earth than on Mount Olympus.[1]

One bright day on earth Persephone was picking lilies and violets with her friends. She could not gather enough of them, though her basket was overflowing.

"Persephone, it is time to go home," called her friends.

"Just one minute longer," she called back. "I see the sweetest flower of all—a narcissus, I think. I must have one." She wandered into a far corner of the meadow, and just as she was about to pick the narcissus, she heard a **deafening** noise. Suddenly the earth split open at her feet. Out dashed a golden chariot pulled by black horses and driven by a stern-faced man in black armor.

Persephone dropped her basket and started to run, but the driver grabbed her by the wrist. He pulled her into his chariot, which descended back into the earth as quickly as it had risen. Then the earth closed up after it.

Persephone screamed and wept, but her friends could not hear her. Though they searched for her everywhere, all they found was her basket, with a few crushed flowers lying next to it.

Down into the earth the chariot sped, through dark caverns and underground tunnels, while Persephone cried, "Who are you? Where are you taking me?"

"I am Hades, king of the underworld, and I am taking you there to be my bride."

Activate Prior Knowledge As goddess of the harvest, what natural processes might Demeter control or have power over?

Foreshadowing How has the author built suspense so far?

1 ***Mount Olympus*** is a mountain in northeastern Greece. In Greek mythology, it was regarded as the home of the major gods and goddesses.

Vocabulary

deafening (def′ən ing) *adj.* very loud; earsplitting

Pluto and Proserpine, 1914. Henry Bryson Burroughs. Oil on canvas, 24 × 36 1/4 in. National Academy Museum, NY.

View the Art Pluto and Proserpine are the Latin names for Hades and Persephone. Does this painting include clues that foreshadow what will happen next?

"Take me back to my mother," screamed Persephone. "Take me back."

"Never!" said Hades. "For I have fallen in love with you. Your sunny face and golden hair will light up my dark palace."

The chariot flew over the river Styx[2] where Charon,[3] the boatman, was ferrying ghostly souls across the water. "Now we are at the gate to my kingdom," said Hades, as they landed next to the huge three-headed dog who guarded it.

Persephone shivered, and Hades said, "Oh, that is Cerberus.[4] He guards the gate so that no live mortals enter and no souls of the dead escape. Nobody escapes from the underworld."

Foreshadowing What effect does this strong statement create?

Persephone became speechless. Never escape from this terrible place full of pale, shadowy ghosts, wandering through stony fields full of pale, ghostly flowers!

Beautiful Persephone, who loved sunshine, became Hades' queen and sat on a cold throne in his cold palace. Hades gave her a gold crown and bright jewels, but her heart was like ice and she neither talked nor ate nor drank.

---

2 ***Styx*** (stiks)

3 ***Charon*** (kār′ ən)

4 ***Cerberus*** (sur′ bər əs)

Persephone's mother, Demeter, knew that something terrible had happened to her daughter. She alone had heard Persephone's screams, which had echoed through the mountains and over the sea.

Demeter left Olympus, disguised as an old woman, and wandered the earth for nine days and nine nights, searching for her daughter. She called to the mountains and rivers and sea, "Persephone, where are you? Come back. Come back." But there was never an answer. She did not weep, for goddesses do not cry, but her heart was heavy. She could not eat or drink or rest, so deep was her grief.

Activate Prior Knowledge
How does your own experience help you understand how Demeter feels?

Finally she reached a placed called Eleusis, not far from the spot where Persephone had disappeared. There a prince named Triptolemus[5] recognized her and told her this story: "Over a week ago, my brother was taking care of the royal pigs. He heard a thundering noise, and the earth opened up. Out rushed a chariot, driven by a grim-faced man. He grabbed a beautiful young girl and down into the earth they went. They were swallowed up, along with the pigs."

"That man must have been Hades," cried Demeter. "I fear that he has kidnapped my daughter."

Demeter hurried to the sun, Helios,[6] who sees everything. And the sun **confirmed** Demeter's fears. Demeter cried, "Persephone, my gay lovely daughter, is imprisoned in the underworld, never again to see the light of day or the flowers of spring."

Then Demeter became stony and angry, and she caused the earth to suffer with her. The earth became cold and barren. Trees did not bear fruit, the grass withered and did not grow again, and the cattle died from hunger. A few men succeeded in plowing the hard earth and **sowing** seeds, but no shoots sprouted

Activate Prior Knowledge
From what you know about characters in myths, what do you predict will happen as a result of Demeter's anger?

5 ***Triptolemus*** (trip tol′ ə məs)

6 ***Helios*** (hē′ lē os)

Vocabulary

confirmed (kən furmd′) *v.* established as true

sowing (sō′ ing) *v.* spreading seeds over the ground so that they will grow from them. It was a cruel year for **mankind**. If Demeter continued to withhold her blessings from the earth, people would perish from hunger.

Zeus begged Demeter to let the earth bear fruit again, but Demeter said, "The earth will never be green again. Not unless my daughter returns!"

Then Zeus knew that he must take action to save people from starvation. "I will see that Persephone returns," he told Demeter, "but only on one condition. She must not have eaten any of the food of the dead."

Zeus sent Hermes, messenger of the gods, down to the underworld to ask Hades for Persephone's release. When Persephone saw that Hermes had come to her home, she became lively and smiled and talked for the first time that year.

To her delight, Hades did not protest but said, "Go, my child. Although I love you, I cannot keep you here against Zeus's will. But you must eat a little something before you leave, to give you strength for your journey." Then he gave Persephone several seeds from a red **pomegranate**, which was the fruit eaten by the dead. He knew that if she ate even one, she would have to return to him.

Persephone ate four seeds quickly. Then she climbed into the golden chariot and waved good-by. Hermes drove her to earth, to the temple where Demeter waited, and mother and daughter hugged and laughed and said they would never be parted again. Then Demeter remembered Zeus's warning and said, "I hope you did not eat anything while you were in the underworld."

"I was too sad to eat," said Persephone. "I didn't eat or drink all year."

"Not anything at all?" said Demeter.

"Oh, just a few little pomegranate seeds before I left," said Persephone. "Why do you ask?"

"Because, my dearest," cried Demeter, "if you have eaten any of the food of the dead, you must return to Hades."

Foreshadowing How does this statement build suspense?

Visual Vocabulary

A **pomegranate** (pom′gran′it) is a round, golden-red fruit that contains many small seeds.

Vocabulary

mankind (man′kīnd′) *n.* all human beings

Zeus heard the loud wails of Demeter and her daughter, and he decided to **compromise**. Persephone must spend just four months of each year in the underworld, one for each of the seeds she had eaten. The rest of the year she could be with her mother on earth.

That is why every year, for four months, the earth becomes cold and barren. Persephone is in the dark underworld and Demeter is overcome with grief.

And every year, when Persephone returns to earth, she brings spring with her. The earth is filled with flowers and fruits and grasses. And summer and fall, the seasons of growth and harvest, follow in their natural order. Every year Demeter and the whole earth rejoice that Persephone has returned.

Vocabulary

compromise (kom′ prə mīz′) *v.* to settle a disagreement by having each side give up something

BQ BIG Question

Why does Zeus feel that compromise is necessary?

Activate Prior Knowledge

What natural event does this myth explain?

The Return of Persephone, 1891. Frederic Leighton. Oil on canvas. Leeds Museums and Gallery, UK.

View the Art Which scene from the story does this painting show? How do you know?

After You Read

Respond and Think Critically

1. Why does Hades take Persephone to the underworld? **[Recall]**
2. How does Demeter react to the disappearance of Persephone? How does she finally learn what has happened to her daughter? **[Summarize]**
3. Why do you think the ancient Greeks created a myth to explain the four seasons? **[Interpret]**
4. Who is the hero or heroine of this story? What actions make this character heroic? **[Analyze]**
5. What did the ancient Greeks believe about the power of the gods and goddesses? What was the place of humans in this view of the world? **[Infer]**
6. **BQ** **BIG Question** Hades begins a chain of actions in this myth. Who is treated unjustly? How is compromise used to resolve the problem? **[Evaluate]**

Vocabulary Practice

Respond to these questions.

1. Which would you describe as a **deafening** sound—a crash of thunder or the meow of a cat?
2. Would you think a decision was **confirmed** if everyone voted against it or if everyone voted for it?
3. Who is more likely to be involved in **sowing**—a tailor or a farmer?
4. Who probably needs to **compromise**—two people who disagree or two people who agree?
5. Which beings are part of all **mankind**—children or dogs?

Academic Vocabulary

Demeter, Persephone, and Hades must **submit** to the will of Zeus. In the preceding sentence, *submit* means "give way or surrender to a power or an authority." *Submit* also has other meanings. Example: Eva will **submit** her essay to the teacher. What do you think *submit* means in the preceding sentence? Compare the two meanings.

TIP

Inferring
When you infer, you use clues in the text and your own experiences to draw a conclusion.

- Think about the types of powers the gods and goddesses have. What limits do they have on their powers?
- Recall the role of humans in this story. What hurts or helps the people of ancient Greece?
- Use this information to draw a conclusion about the beliefs of the ancient Greeks.

Keep track of your ideas about the **BIG Question** in your unit Foldable.

Literature Online

Selection Resources
For Selection Quizzes, eFlashcards, and Reading-Writing Connection activities, go to glencoe.com and enter QuickPass code GL17527u4.

Literary Element **Foreshadowing**

1. What does the detail that Persephone loves sunshine and the outdoors foreshadow?
2. What do the details of Demeter's rage and its effects foreshadow?

Review: **Myth**

As you learned on page 406, a **myth** is a traditional story involving goddesses, gods, heroes, and supernatural forces. It attempts to explain a natural phenomenon, a historic event, or the origin of a belief or custom.

3. Most ancient Greeks believed that their myths were true. Why do you think they believed the myth of Persephone?
4. What myths do people believe in today? What myths, if any, do you believe in?

Reading Strategy

Activate Prior Knowledge

5. How did prior knowledge help you better understand the settings in "Persephone"?
6. How did prior knowledge about myths help you understand the actions of the gods and goddesses in "Persephone"? Find two examples of actions that made you recall what you already knew about myths.
7. How did your experiences with the seasons help you to understand this myth?
8. How did you use your own knowledge about or experience with mother-daughter relationships to gain greater understanding or meaning from this myth?

Grammar Link

Capitalization of Sentences It is important to capitalize the first letter of each word at the beginning of a sentence so readers can tell where one sentence ends and the next sentence begins. For example:

The boatman was ferrying ghostly souls.

Practice Read the following sentences. Which words should be capitalized?

The underworld is an eerie place. it is guarded by a three-headed dog. pale, shadowy ghosts wander through stony fields. not even the flowers have color!

Speaking and Listening

Oral Report Think of a time in your life when you had to compromise. Prepare an oral report that tells the story of what happened. Use a graphic organizer like the one below to help you track your ideas. Organize your story clearly around key events. Make sure to explain the outcome, or end result, and tell what you learned.

Practice reading your report aloud fluently with appropriate pacing and intonation. Match your expression and gestures to your purpose—are you trying to be serious or lighthearted? Establish eye contact with your audience and use pictures, drawings, or technology as appropriate during your delivery.

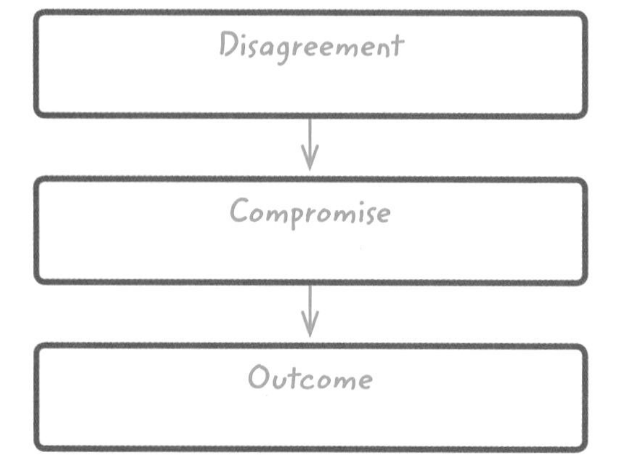

Comparing Literature

The Flying Machine and *All Summer in a Day*

BQ BIG Question

As you read these two short stories, ask yourself, are the flying man in "The Flying Machine" and Margot in "All Summer in a Day" treated fairly by the other characters?

Literary Element Setting

You've learned that the **setting** of a story is the time and place in which the story occurs. Pay attention to how the setting contributes to the mood and how it influences the problem and resolution in each story.

Reading Skill Compare and Contrast

You compare and contrast almost every day. When you compare, you look for similarities. When you contrast, you look for differences. For example, you might want to compare and contrast two football teams before a game. You might think about how the players, the coaches, and the plays they use are alike and how they are different. You could use this information to predict which team is more likely to win.

You can better understand literature when you compare and contrast literary elements, such as setting and characters. On the following pages, you'll compare and contrast the settings of "The Flying Machine" and "All Summer in a Day." Use a comparison chart like the one below to record details about the settings.

	"The Flying Machine"	"All Summer in a Day"
Time and Place		
Effect on the Story		

For pages 549–565

ELA6R1e/i. For literary texts, identify and analyze the elements of setting, characterization, plot, and the resolution of the conflict of a story or play: internal/external conflicts.

Meet Ray Bradbury

Ray Bradbury is best known for his chilling science fiction and fantasy stories. In his writing, he often warns against the dangers of uncontrolled technology. Bradbury's popular novels include *The Martian Chronicles* and *Fahrenheit 451*.

Ray Bradbury was born in 1920.

Literature Online

Author Search For more about Ray Bradbury, go to glencoe.com and enter QuickPass code GL17527u4.

Orchard Around the Great Wall. Chen Jia Qi. Red Lantern Folk Art, Mukashi Collection, Beijing.

THE FLYING MACHINE

Ray Bradbury

In the year A.D. 400, the Emperor Yuan held his throne by the Great Wall of China,[1] and the land was green with rain, readying itself toward the harvest, at peace, the people in his dominion[2] neither too happy nor too sad.

Early on the morning of the first day of the first week of the second month of the new year, the Emperor Yuan was sipping tea and fanning himself against a warm

Comparing Literature List the details of the setting on your comparison chart. How do you think the setting might affect the characters in this story?

1 The ***Great Wall of China*** is a massive wall about thirty feet high and twenty feet wide that took many centuries to construct. It was designed as a defense against Mongol horsemen. Today it extends 3,750 miles.

2 ***Dominion*** refers to the territory or country under the authority of a particular ruler or government.

breeze when a servant ran across the scarlet and blue garden tiles, calling, "Oh, Emperor, Emperor, a miracle!"

"Yes," said the Emperor, "the air *is* sweet this morning."

"No, no, a miracle!" said the servant, bowing quickly.

"And this tea is good in my mouth, surely that is a miracle."

"No, no, Your Excellency."

"Let me guess then—the sun has risen and a new day is upon us. Or the sea is blue. *That* now is the finest of all miracles."

"Excellency, a man is flying!"

"What?" The Emperor stopped his fan.

"I saw him in the air, a man flying with wings. I heard a voice call out of the sky, and when I looked up, there he was, a dragon in the heavens with a man in its mouth, a dragon of paper and bamboo, colored like the sun and the grass."

"It is early," said the Emperor, "and you have just wakened from a dream."

"It is early, but I have seen what I have seen! Come, and you will see it too."

"Sit down with me here," said the Emperor. "Drink some tea. It must be a strange thing, if it is true, to see a man fly. You must have time to think of it, even as I must have time to prepare myself for the sight."

They drank tea.

"Please," said the servant at last, "or he will be gone."

The Emperor rose thoughtfully. "Now you may show me what you have seen."

They walked into a garden, across a meadow of grass, over a small bridge, through a grove of trees, and up a tiny hill.

Comparing Literature
How do these details help you visualize the setting?

"There!" said the servant.

The Emperor looked into the sky.

And in the sky, laughing so high that you could hardly hear him laugh, was a man; and the man was clothed in bright papers and reeds to make wings and a beautiful yellow tail, and he was soaring all about like

How Can One Know, 1984. Hsu Soo Ming.

the largest bird in a universe of birds, like a new dragon in a land of ancient dragons.

The man called down to them from high in the cool winds of morning, "I fly, I fly!"

The servant waved to him. "Yes, yes!"

The Emperor Yuan did not move. Instead he looked at the Great Wall of China now taking shape out of the farthest mist in the green hills, that splendid snake of stones which writhed[3] with majesty across the entire land. That wonderful wall which had protected them for a timeless time from enemy hordes[4] and preserved peace for years without number. He saw the town, nestled to itself by a river and a road and a hill, beginning to waken.

Comparing Literature What is the purpose of the Great Wall of China? Why is it an important part of the setting?

"Tell me," he said to his servant, "has anyone else seen this flying man?"

"I am the only one, Excellency," said the servant, smiling at the sky, waving.

The Emperor watched the heavens another minute and then said, "Call him down to me."

---

3 ***Writhed*** means "moved the body with a twisting or turning motion, as in great pain."

4 ***Hordes*** are large groups or crowds.

"Ho, come down, come down! The Emperor wishes to see you!" called the servant, hands cupped to his shouting mouth.

The Emperor glanced in all directions while the flying man soared down the morning wind. He saw a farmer, early in his fields, watching the sky, and he noted where the farmer stood.

The flying man alit[5] with a rustle of paper and a creak of bamboo reeds. He came proudly to the Emperor, clumsy in his rig, at last bowing before the old man.

"What have you done?" demanded the Emperor.

"I have flown in the sky, Your Excellency," replied the man.

"What *have* you done?" said the Emperor again.

"I have just told you!" cried the flier.

"You have told me nothing at all." The Emperor reached out a thin hand to touch the pretty paper and the birdlike **keel** of the apparatus.[6] It smelled cool, of the wind.

"Is it not beautiful, Excellency?"

"Yes, too beautiful."

"It is the only one in the world!" smiled the man. "And I am the inventor."

"The *only* one in the world?"

"I swear it!"

"Who else knows of this?"

"No one. Not even my wife, who would think me mad with the sun. She thought I was making a kite. I rose in the night and walked to the cliffs far away. And when the morning breezes blew and the sun rose, I gathered my courage, Excellency, and leaped from the cliff. I flew! But my wife does not know of it."

"Well for her, then," said the Emperor. "Come along."

They walked back to the great house. The sun was full in the sky now, and the smell of the grass was refreshing. The Emperor, the servant, and the flier paused within the huge garden.

5 Here, ***alit*** means "landed." It is a past-tense form of *alight.*

6 An ***apparatus*** is something created or invented for a particular purpose.

Comparing Literature
How might the impact of the flying machine be different if the story were set in a different time?

Visual Vocabulary
On a boat or plane, the **keel** is the main piece of timber or steel that runs lengthwise along the bottom and supports the rest of the frame.

The Emperor clapped his hands. "Ho, guards!"

The guards came running.

"Hold this man."

The guards seized the flier.

"Call the executioner,"said the Emperor.

"What's this!" cried the flier, bewildered. "What have I done?" He began to weep, so that the beautiful paper apparatus rustled.

"Here is the man who has made a certain machine," said the Emperor, "and yet asks us what he has created. He does not know himself. It is only necessary that he create, without knowing why he has done so, or what this thing will do."

The executioner came running with a sharp silver ax. He stood with his naked, large-muscled arms ready, his face covered with a serene[7] white mask.

"One moment," said the Emperor. He turned to a nearby table upon which sat a machine that he himself had created. The Emperor took a tiny golden key from his own neck. He fitted this key to the tiny, delicate machine and wound it up. Then he set the machine going.

The machine was a garden of metal and jewels. Set in motion, birds sang in tiny metal trees, wolves walked through miniature forests, and tiny people ran in and out of sun and shadow, fanning themselves with miniature fans, listening to the tiny emerald birds, and standing by impossibly small but tinkling fountains.

"Is *it* not beautiful?" said the Emperor. "If you asked me what I have done here, I could answer you well. I have made birds sing, I have made forests murmur, I have set people to walking in this woodland, enjoying the leaves and shadows and songs. That is what I have done."

"But, oh, Emperor!" pleaded the flier, on his knees, the tears pouring down his face. "I have done a similar thing! I have found beauty. I have flown on the morning wind. I have looked down on all the sleeping houses and gardens. I have smelled the sea and even *seen*

Comparing Literature How does the action here depend on the setting?

---

7 Something that is ***serene*** is calm, peaceful, or undisturbed.

it, beyond the hills, from my high place. And I have soared like a bird; oh, I cannot say how beautiful it is up there, in the sky, with the wind about me, the wind blowing me here like a feather, there like a fan, the way the sky smells in the morning! And how free one feels! *That* is beautiful, Emperor, that is beautiful too!"

"Yes," said the Emperor sadly, "I know it must be true. For I felt my heart move with you in the air and I wondered: What is it like? How does it feel? How do the distant pools look from so high? And how my houses and servants? Like ants? And how the distant towns not yet awake?"

Quang Hsing, Manchu Dynasty. Artist unknown. Metropolitan Museum of Art, NY.

Comparing Literature Why does the author include these details? What do they reveal about the flying man?

"Then spare me!"

"But there are times," said the Emperor, more sadly still, "when one must lose a little beauty if one is to keep what little beauty one already has. I do not fear you, yourself, but I fear another man."

"What man?"

"Some other man who, seeing you, will build a thing of bright papers and bamboo like this. But the other man will have an evil face and an evil heart, and the beauty will be gone. It is this man I fear."

"Why? Why?"

"Who is to say that someday just such a man, in just such an apparatus of paper and reed, might not fly in the sky and drop huge stones upon the Great Wall of China?" said the Emperor.

No one moved or said a word.

"Off with his head," said the Emperor.

The executioner whirled his silver ax.

"Burn the kite and the inventor's body and bury their ashes together," said the Emperor.

The servants retreated to obey.

The Emperor turned to his hand-servant, who had seen the man flying. "Hold your tongue. It was all a dream, a most sorrowful and beautiful dream. And that farmer in the distant field who also saw, tell him it would pay him to consider it only a vision. If ever the word passes around, you and the farmer die within the hour."

"You are merciful, Emperor."

"No, not merciful," said the old man. Beyond the garden wall he saw the guards burning the beautiful machine of paper and reeds that smelled of the morning wind. He saw the dark smoke climb into the sky. "No, only very much bewildered and afraid." He saw the guards digging a tiny pit wherein to bury the ashes. "What is the life of one man against those of a million others? I must take solace[8] from that thought."

Comparing Literature How does this description of the burning of the machine affect the mood of the story? How does it compare with previous descriptions of the setting?

He took the key from its chain about his neck and once more wound up the beautiful miniature garden. He stood looking out across the land at the Great Wall, the peaceful town, the green fields, the rivers and streams. He sighed. The tiny garden whirred its hidden and delicate machinery and set itself in motion; tiny people walked in forests, tiny foxes loped through sun-speckled glades in beautiful shining pelts, and among the tiny trees flew little bits of high song and bright blue and yellow color, flying, flying, flying in that small sky.

Comparing Literature How does this description of the setting help you understand the emperor's decision?

"Oh," said the Emperor, closing his eyes, "look at the birds, look at the birds!" ❧

8 ***Solace*** means "comfort or relief from sorrow."

All Summer in a Day

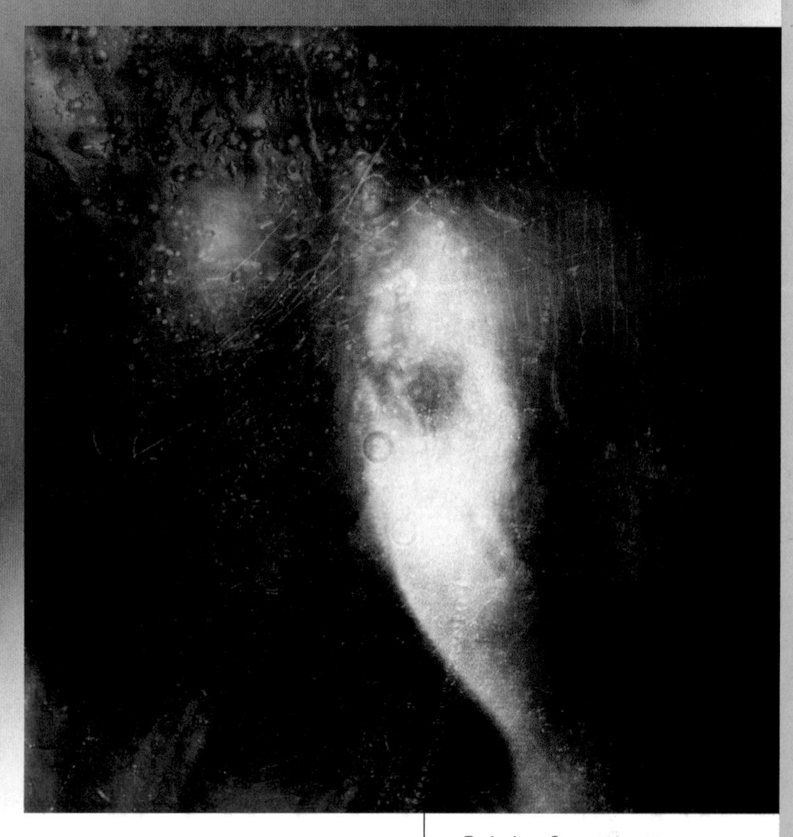

Ray Bradbury

Baby's a Supernova. Scot Frei.

"READY?"

"Ready."

"Now?"

"Soon."

"Do the scientists really know? Will it happen today, will it?"

"Look, look; see for yourself!"

The children pressed to each other like so many roses, so many weeds, intermixed, peering out for a look at the hidden sun.

It rained.

It had been raining for seven years; thousand upon thousands of days compounded and filled from one end to the other with rain, with the drum and gush of water, with the sweet crystal fall of showers and the concussion[1] of storms so heavy they were tidal waves come over the islands. A thousand forests had been crushed under the rain and grown up a thousand times to be crushed again. And this was the way life was forever on the planet Venus, and this was the schoolroom of the children of the rocket men and women who had come to a raining world to set up civilization and live out their lives.

Comparing Literature List the details of the setting on your comparison chart. What is the time and place of the story?

"It's stopping, it's stopping!"

"Yes, yes!"

Margot stood apart from them, from these children who could never remember a time when there wasn't rain and rain and rain. They were all nine years old, and if there had been a day, seven years ago, when the sun came out for an hour and showed its face to the stunned world, they could not recall. Sometimes, at night, she heard them stir, in remembrance, and she knew they were dreaming and remembering gold or a yellow crayon or a coin large enough to buy the world with. She knew they thought they remembered a warmness, like a blushing in the face, in the body, in the arms and legs and trembling hands. But then they always awoke to the tatting drum, the endless shaking down of clear bead necklaces upon the roof, the walk, the gardens, the forests, and their dreams were gone.

Comparing Literature How does the setting affect the children's lives?

All day yesterday they had read in class about the sun. About how like a lemon it was, and how hot. And they had written small stories or essays or poems about it:

I think the sun is a flower,
That blooms for just one hour.

That was Margot's poem, read in a quiet voice in the still classroom while the rain was falling outside.

"Aw, you didn't write that!" protested one of the boys.

"I did," said Margot. "I *did*."

"William!" said the teacher.

But that was yesterday. Now the rain was slackening,[2]

---

1 Here, ***concussion*** refers to a violent shaking or pounding.

2 When the rain was ***slackening***, it was beginning to stop.

Young Woman Under an Arch, 1886. Odilon Redon. ©Christie's Images.

and the children were crushed in the great thick windows.

"Where's teacher?"

"She'll be back."

"She'd better hurry, we'll miss it!"

They turned on themselves, like a feverish wheel, all tumbling spokes.

Margot stood alone. She was a very frail girl who looked as if she had been lost in the rain for years and the rain had washed out the blue from her eyes and the red from her mouth and the yellow from her hair. She was an old photograph dusted from an album, whitened away, and if she spoke at all her voice would be a ghost. Now she stood, separate, staring at the rain and the loud wet world beyond the huge glass.

"What're *you* looking at?" said William.

Margot said nothing.

"Speak when you're spoken to." He gave her a shove. But she did not move; rather she let herself be moved only by him and nothing else.

They edged away from her, they would not look at her. She felt them go away. And this was because she would play no games with them in the echoing tunnels of the underground city. If they tagged her and ran, she stood blinking after them and did not follow.

View the Art Does the person in this painting remind you of Margot? Why or why not?

Comparing Literature
What new information do you learn about Venus? How might this affect the characters?

When the class sang songs about happiness and life and games her lips barely moved. Only when they sang about the sun and the summer did her lips move as she watched the drenched windows.

And then, of course, the biggest crime of all was that she had come here only five years ago from Earth, and she remembered the sun and the way the sun was and the sky was when she was four in Ohio. And they, they had been on Venus all their lives, and they had been only two years old when last the sun came out and had long since forgotten the color and heat of it and the way it really was. But Margot remembered.

Comparing Literature What details do you learn about Earth? How do these details help explain the way the other children feel about Margot?

"It's like a penny," she said once, eyes closed.

"No it's not!" the children cried.

"It's like a fire," she said, "in the stove."

"You're lying, you don't remember!" cried the children.

But she remembered and stood quietly apart from all of them and watched the patterning windows. And once, a month ago, she had refused to shower in the school shower rooms, had clutched her hands to her ears and over her head, screaming the water mustn't touch her head. So after that, dimly, dimly, she sensed it, she was different and they knew her difference and kept away.

There was talk that her father and mother were taking her back to Earth next year; it seemed vital[3] to her that they do so, though it would mean the loss of thousands of dollars to her family. And so, the children hated her for all these reasons of big and little consequence.[4] They hated her pale snow face, her waiting silence, her thinness, and her possible future.

"Get away!" The boy gave her another push. "What're you waiting for?"

Then, for the first time, she turned and looked at him. And what she was waiting for was in her eyes.

"Well, don't wait around here!" cried the boy savagely. "You won't see nothing!"

---

3 Something that is ***vital*** is very important.

4 ***Consequence*** is the effect something has.

Sunrise, 1887. George Inness. Oil on canvas. Brooklyn Museum of Art, NY.

Her lips moved.

"Nothing!" he cried. "It was all a joke, wasn't it?" He turned to the other children. "Nothing's happening today. *Is* it?"

They all blinked at him and then, understanding, laughed and shook their heads. "Nothing, nothing!"

"Oh, but," Margot whispered, her eyes helpless. "But this is the day, the scientists predict, they say, they *know,* the sun . . ."

"All a joke!" said the boy, and seized her roughly. "Hey, everyone, let's put her in a closet before teacher comes!"

"No," said Margot, falling back.

They surged[5] about her, caught her up and bore her, protesting, and then pleading, and then crying, back into a tunnel, a room, a closet, where they slammed and locked the door. They stood looking at the door and saw it tremble from her beating and throwing herself against it. They heard her muffled cries. Then, smiling, they turned and went out and back down the tunnel, just as the teacher arrived.

5 When the children ***surged,*** they pushed or moved forward with a force like a wave.

"Ready, children?" She glanced at her watch.

"Yes!" said everyone.

"Are we all here?"

"Yes!"

The rain slackened still more.

They crowded to the huge door.

The rain stopped.

It was as if, in the midst of a film concerning an avalanche, a tornado, a hurricane, a volcanic eruption, something had, first, gone wrong with the sound apparatus,[6] thus muffling and finally cutting off all noise, all of the blasts and repercussions[7] and thunders, and then, second, ripped the film from the projector and inserted in its place a peaceful tropical slide which did not move or tremor. The world ground to a standstill. The silence was so immense and unbelievable that you felt your ears had been stuffed or you had lost your hearing altogether. The children put their hands to their ears. They stood apart. The door slid back and the smell of the silent, waiting world came in to them.

Comparing Literature What role does sound play in the setting? How does it affect the children?

The sun came out.

It was the color of flaming bronze and it was very large. And the sky around it was a blazing blue tile color. And the jungle burned with sunlight as the children, released from their spell, rushed out, yelling, into the springtime.

Comparing Literature Which details emphasize the change in setting?

"Now, don't go too far," called the teacher after them. "You've only two hours, you know. You wouldn't want to get caught out!"

But they were running and turning their faces up to the sky and feeling the sun on their cheeks like a warm iron; they were taking off their jackets and letting the sun burn their arms.

"Oh, it's better than the sun lamps, isn't it?"

"Much, much better!"

They stopped running and stood in the great jungle

---

6 An ***apparatus*** is something created or invented for a particular purpose.

7 Here, ***repercussions*** are echoes or vibrations.

that covered Venus, that grew and never stopped growing, tumultuously,[8] even as you watched it. It was a nest of **octopi**, clustering up great arms of fleshlike weed, wavering, flowering in this brief spring. It was the color of rubber and ash, this jungle, from the many years without sun. It was the color of stones and white cheeses and ink, and it was the color of the moon.

The children lay out, laughing, on the jungle mattress, and heard it sigh and squeak under them, resilient[9] and alive. They ran among the trees, they slipped and fell, they pushed each other, they played hide-and-seek and tag, but most of all they squinted at the sun until tears ran down their faces, they put their hands up to that yellowness and that amazing blueness and breathed of the fresh, fresh air and listened and listened to the silence which suspended them in a blessed sea of no sound and no motion. They looked at everything and savored everything. Then, wildly, like animals escaped from their caves, they ran and ran in shouting circles. They ran for an hour and did not stop running.

And then—

In the midst of their running one of the girls wailed.

Everyone stopped.

The girl, standing in the open, held out her hand.

"Oh, look, look," she said, trembling.

They came slowly to look at her opened palm.

In the center of it, cupped and huge, was a single raindrop.

She began to cry, looking at it.

They glanced quietly at the sky.

"Oh. Oh."

A few cold drops fell on their noses and their cheeks and their mouths. The sun faded behind a stir of mist. A wind blew cool around them. They turned and started to walk back toward the underground house, their hands at their sides, their smiles vanishing away.

---

8 ***Tumultuously*** means "in a wildly excited or confused way."

9 Something that is ***resilient*** is capable of springing back into position after being bent, stretched, or pressed together.

Visual Vocabulary

Octopi is the plural of *octopus,* which is a sea animal with eight tentacles, or arms.

Comparing Literature Why is this a significant detail? How is the setting affected by it?

A boom of thunder startled them and like leaves before a new hurricane, they tumbled upon each other and ran. Lightning struck ten miles away, five miles away, a mile, a half mile. The sky darkened into midnight in a flash.

They stood in the doorway of the underground for a moment until it was raining hard. Then they closed the door and heard the gigantic sound of the rain falling in tons and avalanches, everywhere and forever.

"Will it be seven more years?"

"Yes. Seven."

Then one of them gave a little cry.

"Margot!"

"What?"

"She's still in the closet where we locked her."

"Margot."

They stood as if someone had driven them, like so many stakes, into the floor. They looked at each other and then looked away. They glanced out at the world that was raining now and raining and raining steadily. They could not meet each other's glances. Their faces were solemn and pale. They looked at their hands and feet, their faces down.

"Margot."

One of the girls said, "Well . . . ?"

No one moved.

"Go on," whispered the girl.

They walked slowly down the hall in the sound of cold rain. They turned through the doorway to the room in the sound of the storm and thunder, lightning on their faces, blue and terrible. They walked over to the closet door slowly and stood by it.

Behind the closet door was only silence.

They unlocked the door, even more slowly, and let Margot out. ❧

Comparing Literature How does silence inside the closet contrast with the weather outside?

Comparing Literature

BQ BIG Question

Now use the unit Big Question to compare and contrast "The Flying Machine" and "All Summer in a Day." With a group of classmates, discuss questions such as

- What makes the flying man and Margot different from the people around them?
- Why do Margot's schoolmates and the emperor act the way they do? How do they feel about their actions during the middle of each story and at the end?
- What lesson does each story teach about fairness?

Support each answer with evidence from the stories.

Literary Element Setting

Use the details you wrote in your comparison chart to think about the settings in "The Flying Machine" and "All Summer in a Day." With a partner, answer the following questions.

1. In what ways are the settings different in "The Flying Machine" and "All Summer in a Day"? Discuss specific details concerning the times, places, moods, or any other ways that the two settings differ.
2. In what ways are the settings similar? For example, think about how the settings influence the choices the characters make or how the settings change within the story. Consider other details from the settings that are similar as well.

Write to Compare

Write a critique that compares and contrasts the effectiveness of the settings in "The Flying Machine" and "All Summer in a Day." Remember to answer questions about the texts such as *How? Why? How well?* You might focus on these ideas as you write.

- Decide what main point the author is making in each story and how the setting influences the plot.
- Tell how the details about the settings affect the feelings and actions of the characters. Consider the emperor, the flying man, Margot, and the other children.
- Include details about the settings that determine whether the characters' choices are fair or unfair.

Writing Tip

Organization Before you begin, think about how you will organize your writing. One way is to discuss all your points about one story first. Then discuss all of your points about the second story. Or you might want to first discuss all the ways that both stories are similar and then discuss all the ways they are different.

Literature Online

Selection Resources
For Selection Quizzes, eFlashcards, and Reading-Writing Connection activities, go to glencoe.com and enter QuickPass code GL17527u4.

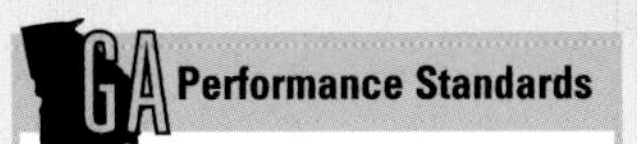

GA Performance Standards

For pages 566–571

ELA6W2f Demonstrate competence in a variety of genres. Produce a multi-paragraph persuasive essay that anticipates and addresses readers' concerns and counter-arguments.

Writing Workshop

Persuasive Essay

In this workshop, you will write a persuasive essay that will help you think about the Unit 4 Big Question: What's fair and what's not?

Review the writing prompt, or assignment, below. Then read the Writing Plan. It will tell you what you will do to write your persuasive essay.

Writing Assignment

Write a persuasive essay about a problem you think is unfair, and persuade your readers to take a specific action. The audience, those reading your essay, will be your classmates and teacher.

Writing Plan

- Present a clear argument in the introduction.
- Organize the relevant evidence for the argument in the most persuasive order.
- Address possible reader concerns and counterarguments.
- Express strong feelings with precise and vivid language.
- Conclude by summarizing the argument and asking readers to take action.

Prewriting Tip

Organization Use your strongest argument to begin or end your persuasive essay.

Prewrite

Think about issues of unfairness presented in the selections in this unit. What solutions are offered to these problems?

Gather Ideas

Write down some problems you feel strongly about. Ask yourself,

- What is unfair about each problem?
- Do I feel strongly about the problems?
- Can I do anything about the problems?

Choose a Topic

Review the list you made. Then choose the problem you care most about. Think about practical and realistic solutions.

Partner Talk Work with a partner to make an idea tree that shows the problem and possible solutions.

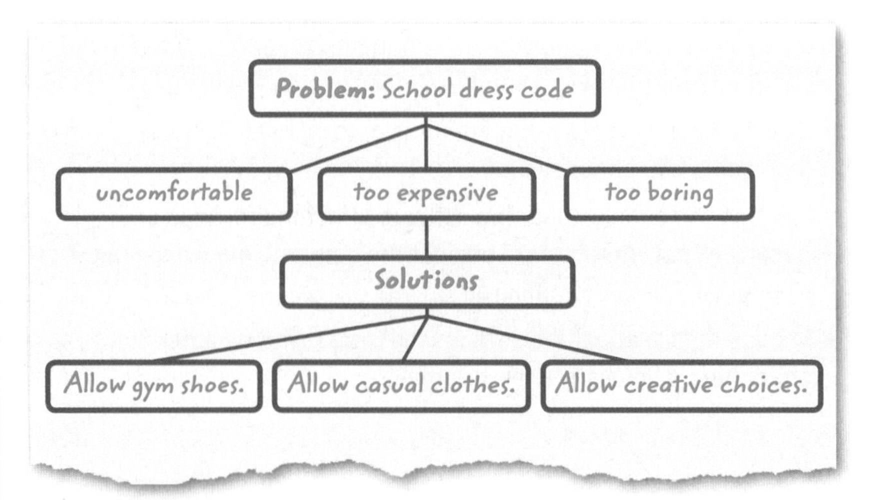

Literature Online

Writing and Research For prewriting, drafting, and revising tools, go to glencoe.com and enter QuickPass code GL17527u4.

Get Organized

Draft a position statement—your argument. Define the problem and tell why it is unfair. Write down pros, or points that support your argument. Then write down cons, or counterarguments. A pro might be "Jeans and gym shoes are more comfortable than dressy clothes." A con might be "Casual clothes encourage students to be too relaxed about studying."

Use your position statement and list of pros and cons to create an outline of your essay.

Draft

Organize your ideas and add more details to your writing. Use the following skills to develop your draft.

Get It on Paper

- Review your outline.
- Open with your position statement, or argument.
- For each body paragraph, write a topic sentence that supports your argument. Add a sentence to support the topic sentence and a sentence to address any counterargument.
- End your essay by summarizing your argument (the points in your topic sentences). Finally, ask your readers to take the specific action required.
- Don't worry about paragraphs, spelling, grammar, or punctuation right now.
- When you're finished, read what you've written. Include more information if you need to.

Develop Your Draft

1. State your **argument** clearly in the introduction.

Our dress code is unfair and needs to be changed.

2. **Organize** your supporting evidence, beginning or ending with your strongest point.

The most important reason the dress code is unfair is that the clothes are uncomfortable and may even be dangerous, such as Dustin's shoes.

Drafting Tip

Appeals Use at least two appeals—to logic, emotion, or authority—to support your argument. Appeals to logic rely on facts and reasoning. Appeals to emotion often include anecdotes. Appeals to authority use the audience's respect for another person who shares the view of the author.

3. Use **counterarguments** to tell why you disagree.

> *Some people might say that blue jeans and gym shoes are just as expensive as dress clothes. That may be true, but they last a long time and are easy to clean.*

4. State your points using **strong, specific words.**

> *The pants itch and the shoes pinch.*

5. End with a **summary of your argument** and a **call to action.**

> *The current dress code makes students uncomfortable, is expensive, and doesn't let us express who we really are. Also, it can be harmful to our health. Write the principal to convince him to make jeans and gym shoes part of the school dress code.*

Apply Good Writing Traits: Voice

Your writer's voice is the words you use and the way you put them together. Your voice reflects your thoughts and personality and makes your writing more interesting to read.

Read the sentences below from "The Circuit" by Francisco Jiménez. What idea is the writer expressing? What does his writing style tell you about his personality?

> I did not want to look up and face him. I knew he was sad. He was not going to school today.

> The sound gave me goose bumps. I knew that sound.

As you draft your essay, read it aloud. Ask yourself, does the reader get to know the real me?

TRY IT

Analyzing Cartoons

With a partner, decide what the boy means when he says, "I've gotta be me." What does his statement have to do with finding your voice?

"I'VE GOTTA BE ME . . . BUT I CAN'T HELP THINKING SOMEONE ELSE WOULD BE MORE QUALIFIED!"

Analyze a Student Model

We missed Dustin Barnes at our class party last Friday. He sprained his ankle during recess and was in the emergency room until midnight. Dustin's street shoes didn't give him enough traction while he was running, and he slipped and fell. If he'd been allowed to wear gym shoes, this wouldn't have happened. Our dress code is unfair and needs to be changed.

The most important reason the dress code is unfair is that the clothes are uncomfortable and may even be dangerous, such as Dustin's shoes. The pants itch and the shoes pinch. According to our principal, the dress code helps students pay attention to their schoolwork rather than to one another's clothes. I disagree because we can't focus on our books when we're miserable.

The second reason the dress code is unfair is that dress clothes are expensive. Many students' families don't have money to spend for clothes that are only worn at school. Some people might say that blue jeans and gym shoes are just as expensive as dress clothes. That may be true, but they last a long time, are easy to clean, and can be worn outside of school too.

Finally, wearing the same clothes as everyone else makes students feel like robots. It's boring to see the same outfits all the time. Students should be allowed to express themselves by choosing their own clothes. School officials who don't think we're able to make that decision need to let us prove we can be responsible in our choices.

The situation is clear. The current dress code makes students uncomfortable, is expensive, and doesn't let us express who we really are. Also, it can be harmful to our health. Write the principal to convince him to make jeans and gym shoes part of the school dress code. Do it now, before another student gets hurt.

Argument

Notice how the writer clearly states a position about the school dress code in the first paragraph.

Organization

Order your points from most to least important—like this writer does—or the other way around.

Counterarguments

Imagine what people who don't agree with you would say and have answers for their counterargument.

Precise and Vivid Language

Use strong, specific words. Comparing students to robots gives the reader a negative picture of people behaving like machines.

Summary and Call to Action

Conclude by summarizing the points of your argument and telling readers exactly what they should do.

Revise

Now it's time to revise your draft so your ideas really shine. Revising is what makes good writing great, and great writing takes work!

Peer Review Trade drafts with a partner. Use the chart below to review your partner's draft by answering the questions in the *What to do* column. Talk about your peer review after you have glanced at each other's drafts and have written the answers to the questions. Next, follow the suggestions in the *How to do it* column to revise your draft.

Revising Plan

What to do	How to do it	Example
Can readers tell right away what the problem is and how you feel about it?	Make sure to state your argument clearly and completely at the beginning of your essay.	Our dress code is unfair,^ and it needs to be changed.
Are your points organized to have the greatest impact on readers?	Use transitional words or phrases to show the order of importance.	The second reason t^~~T~~he dress code is unfair is that dress clothes are expensive.
Have you effectively answered differing points of view?	Prepare reasonable answers in response to counterarguments.	According to our principal, the dress code helps students pay attention to their schoolwork rather than to one another's clothes.^ I disagree, because we can't focus on our books when we're miserable.
Do your words express your ideas vividly and in your own voice?	Read your essay aloud and choose words that reflect your thoughts and personality.	Finally, wearing the same clothes as everyone else makes students feel ~~generic~~^ like robots.
Do readers know your main arguments and what you want people to do?	Summarize your argument and tell readers exactly what action to take.	Write the principal^ to convince him to make jeans and gym shoes part of the school dress code.

Revising Tip

Denotation and Connotation
Some words that have nearly the same dictionary meaning, or denotation, can have different connotations, or the emotional feelings associated with the words. *Boring,* for example, has a stronger and more negative connotation than *dull.* Carefully choose words to express your intended meaning.

Edit and Proofread

For your final draft, read your essay one sentence at a time. Use the proofreading symbols in the chart inside the back cover of this book to mark needed changes. Then make corrections.

Grammar Focus: Parallelism

A good way to emphasize your points and make them memorable is to use parallel structure. Parallel structure is the repeating of words, phrases, or sentences that are similar in meaning and structure. Below are examples of problems with parallelism from the Workshop Model and their solutions.

Problem: The following ideas are similar but are structured differently.

Example A:

The pants itch and our feet will be pinched in the shoes.

Solution: Create similar structures—in this case, subjects followed by present tense verbs.

The pants itch and the shoes pinch.

Example B:

Dress-code clothes are uncomfortable, expensive, and a bore.

Solution: Make sentence parts that are joined by commas parallel. In this case, make all words adjectives.

Dress-code clothes are uncomfortable, expensive, and boring.

Present

It's almost time to share your writing with others. Write your essay neatly in print or cursive on a separate sheet of paper. If you have access to a computer, type your essay, formatting it neatly and acccurately. Check your spelling, grammar, and punctuation. Save your document to a disk and print it out.

Grammar Tip

Parallelism Repeat words, phrases, and sentences with similar grammatical forms in all types of writing to emphasize your ideas and make your thoughts easy to understand.

Presenting Tip

Expert Quotation To set the tone of your essay and add an appeal to authority, find a quotation from a well-known person that relates to your argument. Include it on your title page.

Literature Online

Writing and Research For editing and publishing tools, go to glencoe.com and enter QuickPass code GL17527u4.

Performance Standards

For page 572

ELA6LSV2b When delivering or responding to presentations, show appropriate changes in delivery.

Speaking, Listening, and Viewing Workshop

Persuasive Speech

Activity

Connect to Your Writing Deliver a persuasive speech to your classmates. You might want to adapt the persuasive essay you wrote for the Writing Workshop on pages 566–571. Remember that you focused on the Unit 4 Big Question: What's fair and what's not?

Plan Your Speech

Reread your persuasive essay and highlight the sections you want to include in your speech. Just like your persuasive essay, your speech should present a clear, well-supported argument about a problem and should offer a solution in which the audience can take action.

Rehearse Your Speech

Practice your speech several times. Try rehearsing in front of a mirror where you can watch your movements and facial expressions. You may use note cards to remind you of your main points and persuasive evidence, but practice your speech often enough that you won't lose eye contact with your audience.

Deliver Your Speech

- Speak clearly and precisely.
- Adjust your speaking style for intent and effect, such as varying your cadence or repeating ideas to help your audience distinguish between your arguments and the counterarguments.
- Change the tone, pace, and volume of your speaking to help emphasize important ideas in your speech.
- Use gestures and visual aids to direct the audience's attention to specific points and clarify your arguments.

Listening to Learn

Take notes as you listen to make sure you understand the speech. Use the following question frames to learn more about the speech from the speaker:

- I agree/disagree with your point _________, because _________. Can you offer more evidence for your argument?
- To summarize your speech: _________. Is that correct?

Presentation Checklist

Answer the following questions to evaluate your presentation.

- ❑ Did you speak clearly and precisely and with a style that distinguished your arguments from the counterarguments?
- ❑ Did you vary the tone, pace, and volume of your speaking to emphasize important ideas?
- ❑ Did you use gestures and visual aids to draw attention to specific points?
- ❑ Did you make eye contact with your audience?

Literature Online

Speaking, Listening, and Viewing For project ideas, templates, and presentation tips, go to glencoe.com and enter QuickPass code GL17527u4.

Unit Challenge

Answer the Big Question

In Unit 4, you explored the Big Question through reading, writing, speaking, and listening. Now it's time for you to complete one of the Unit Challenges below with your answer to the Big Question.

WHAT'S Fair and What's Not?

Use the notes in your Unit 4 **Foldable** to complete the Unit Challenge of your choice.

Before you present your Unit Challenge, be sure it meets the requirements below. Use this first plan if you choose to write a rap or song about something you feel is unfair and what you can do about it.

On Your Own Activity: Rap or Song

- ❑ Choose a topic. Ask yourself, what makes this unfair? What effect does it have on me or others? What is the solution?
- ❑ Use the beat, rhyme pattern, or tune of a rap or song you are familiar with. Write your own lyrics.
- ❑ Include lines in your lyrics that will help convince listeners that a problem exists. Then offer solutions.
- ❑ Adjust your rate, volume, pitch, and tone, as well as nonverbal communication, to maintain audience interest when you present your rap or song.

Use this second plan if you choose to write questions and answers for a television-style call-in show that your group will present.

Group Activity: TV Call-In Show

- ❑ Brainstorm a list of questions about unfair situations. Assign parts for the show: host, callers, and "experts."
- ❑ Write a script, including solutions for each unfair situation.
- ❑ Practice reading your script, matching your words with your body language, eye contact, and gestures for best effect.
- ❑ If technology is available, make a video of your call-in show.

GA Performance Standards

For page 573

ELA6LSV1I Employ a group decision-making technique such as brainstorming or a problem-solving sequence (e.g., recognize problem, define problem, identify possible solutions, select optimal solution, implement solution, evaluate solution).

Independent Reading

Fiction

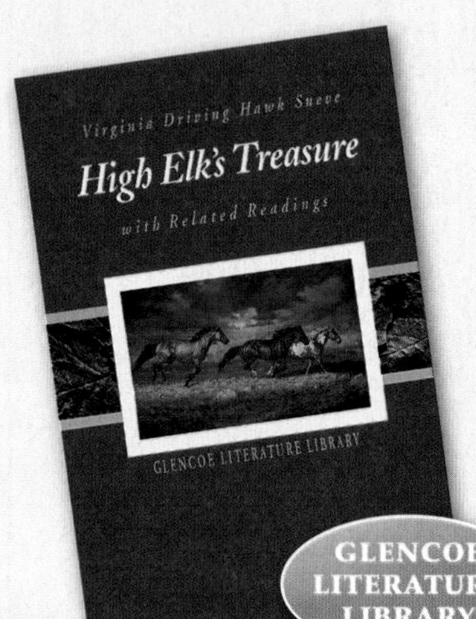

To read more about the Big Question, choose one of these books from your school or local library.

High Elk's Treasure

by Virginia Driving Hawk Sneve

Joe High Elk, a young Lakota, learns the importance of family and cultural heritage in this tale of exploration and adventure. Read to learn about Joe's hunt for historical treasure on the South Dakota reservation where he lives.

The True Confessions of Charlotte Doyle

by Avi

The only passenger aboard an 1832 sailing ship, thirteen-year-old Charlotte must decide whether she will side with a tyrannical captain or a crew ready for mutiny. Dive into this tale of adventure on the high seas!

Lucy's Wish

by Joan Lowery Nixon

Lucy is a ten-year-old orphan on the streets of New York in 1886. She finds hope when the Children's Aid Society sends her to a new home out West. However, her new family is far from perfect.

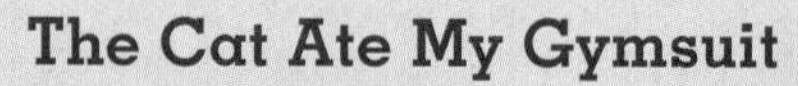

The Cat Ate My Gymsuit

by Paula Danziger

At first, Marcy Lewis just wants to fit in. She is overweight and overlooked—convinced she'll never make friends. Then Marcy stands up for one of her teachers, a woman Marcy admires. Read to find out what Marcy learns about her own convictions.

Nonfiction

Oh, Freedom! Kids Talk About the Civil Rights Movement with the People Who Made It Happen

by Casey King and Linda Barrett Osborne

This collection of oral histories about the civil rights movement includes 31 interviews, all conducted by students. Read these profiles in courage to learn about real people's lives during and after segregation.

When I Was Your Age: Original Stories About Growing Up

edited by Amy Ehrlich

This collection of stories by ten popular writers includes fiction and nonfiction. Read to yourself or read aloud—either way, these short pieces about growing up will give you something to think about.

Words That Built a Nation: A Young Person's Collection of Historic American Documents

by Marilyn Miller

Discover for yourself the Declaration of Independence or the beauty of a Chief Joseph speech. Read this collection of 39 original documents and speeches to learn more about history, language, and the force of big ideas.

Conduct Research

Use the Internet to research the author or topic of the book you read. Create an annotated list of works your classmates might like to read. Explain how each work relates to the book you read and include reasons why the work might be of interest.

Assessment

READING

Read the passages and answer the questions. Write your answers on a separate sheet of paper.

"Noah Webster's Dictionary" by Charles Kuralt

West Hartford, Connecticut. I watched students of West Hartford's Bridlepath School compete in that vanishing standby of American education, the spelling bee. The spelling bee was held in Noah Webster's kitchen. That was a good place for it, because if it hadn't been for Noah Webster, we might never have had spelling bees or even much spelling. Before this Yankee schoolmaster came along, Americans spelled poorly or not at all: George Washington, to cite one atrocious example, spelled pretty much as he pleased. After Noah Webster, Americans spelled the way Noah told them to.

The kids in the spelling bee came from all kinds of backgrounds and from all over the country. That they speak the same language—that a kid from Maine can meet a kid from Oregon and understand him right from the start—that is Noah Webster's gift to us. His little Blue-Backed Speller sold nearly 100 million copies in his lifetime. It wore out printing presses. It was read by nearly every American who could read.

And then, working for twenty-five years, alone and by hand, Noah Webster produced his dictionary—seventy thousand words, including a lot of American words that had never been in a dictionary before: *applesauce, bullfrog, chowder, hickory, skunk.* It was the most valuable piece of scholarship any American ever did.

Noah Webster, from this old house in West Hartford, created American style and American manners. It is not too much to say that he created American education. He was the first teacher of American history, the first influential American newspaper editor.

"What rubbed Mr. Webster's fur the wrong way," West Hartford historian Nelson Burr told me, "was that even after the Revolution, most of America's books and most of America's ideas still came from England. He wanted to put a stop to that. He wanted to create Americanism—not in the sense of jingoistic patriotism, but in the sense of a new literature, a new language."

In the Italy of Noah Webster's day, there were so many dialects that many Italians couldn't talk to one another. The same thing, to a lesser degree, was true in Great Britain. America's common language, with more or less agreed-upon rules for spelling and punctuation, was the work of Noah Webster. He wanted us to be one nation, a new nation, and he showed us how.

1. Which of the following BEST expresses the main idea of the passage?
   A. Spelling correctly is necessary for communication.
   B. American English is very different from British English.
   C. Americans today can spell correctly because of Webster's work.
   D. Webster deserves credit for helping to create an American language.

2. What is the meaning of the word *atrocious* in the first paragraph of this passage?
   A. famous
   B. good
   C. awful
   D. wealthy

3. Which meaning BEST defines the word *Americanism* as used in the fifth paragraph of this passage?
   A. a policy that advances American education through spelling
   B. the patriotic actions of an American citizen in wartime
   C. a person who is born in the United States or becomes an American citizen
   D. the promotion of language, customs, and culture that are uniquely American

4. Which kind of organization does the author use in the last paragraph of this passage?
   A. cause and effect
   B. chronological
   C. compare and contrast
   D. problem and solution

Standards Practice For more standards practice, go to glencoe.com and enter QuickPass code GL17527u4.

"The Lion and the Mouse" by Aesop

There was once a lion, fast asleep, who was awakened by a little mouse running up and down along his back. The lion, snarling, pinned the mouse under his paw and made ready to eat him.

"Oh, wait, king of the beasts!" cried the mouse. "If you release me, I will never forget your kindness. The day may come when you are in need of help from me, and I will certainly provide it."

This idea amused the lion, but the mouse insisted, "You never know; you never know." So the lion lifted his paw and let the mouse go.

Years later, the lion was caught by hunters and tightly bound. He could not even move his head and lay helpless while the hunters went to fetch a wagon in which to carry him away. As he struggled, the little mouse passed by. Seeing the lion's difficulty, he ran up to him and quickly chewed through the ropes that bound the lion, saving him from death.

Little friends may turn out to be great friends.

"The Fox and the Crow" by Aesop

A hungry fox saw a crow fly past with a piece of cheese in his beak. The crow perched on a tree branch to eat the cheese. The fox looked up at the crow and licked his lips. "I am surely clever enough to get that hunk of cheese," thought the fox, who was quite full of himself. "After all, I am a fox!" So he called up to the crow.

"Hello, hello!" said the fox. "How lovely you look today. Your feathers are so shiny, and your eyes are so bright. Looking at you, I feel sure that your voice must be as beautiful as the rest of you. If I could hear just one song, then I could be sure."

The crow, delighted by these words, opened his mouth to produce his best effort at song. Immediately, the cheese fell to the ground from the bird's open beak and was snapped up by the fox.

"That was all I wanted," said the fox. "Thank you for the lovely snack."

Do not trust those who flatter you.

5. Which of the following statements does NOT suggest that these stories are fables?
   A. The stories teach a lesson.
   B. The stories involve a conflict.
   C. The stories are short and clear.
   D. The characters in the stories are animals.

6. Which of the following BEST describes the narrator of these fables?
   A. first-person narrator
   B. second-person narrator
   C. third-person narrator
   D. antagonistic narrator

7. Which of the following statements BEST describes how the fox tricks the crow into dropping the cheese?
   A. He uses evidence and facts.
   B. He uses logical reasons.
   C. He makes an appeal to emotions.
   D. He uses stereotypes.

8. The last sentence of each story, printed in slanted type, states the story's
   A. theme.
   B. climax.
   C. conflict.
   D. resolution.

9. Which sentence below uses the word *bound* with the same meaning as it is used in "The Lion and the Mouse"?
   A. We watched the deer bound away across the meadow.
   B. If you work too quickly, you're bound to make a mistake.
   C. A vine had wrapped around my ankles and bound them.
   D. I wonder how many of those cars are bound for the beach.

10. The lesson of "The Fox and the Crow" would be an appropriate example in a speech about
   A. how people are influenced by others.
   B. how to trap a wild animal with food.
   C. how to identify wild birds and mammals.
   D. how a balanced ecosystem works.

ENGLISH/LANGUAGE ARTS

Choose the best answer for each question. Write your answers on a separate sheet of paper.

1. Which sentence below has a subordinate clause?
   A. Carlos doesn't enjoy car rides.
   B. Carlos gets carsick sometimes in the summer.
   C. He likes going on trips, and he likes watching the scenery.
   D. If the ride is too long, he gets sleepy.

2. In which sentence below is the word *dog* an object of a preposition?
   A. I had to give the dog a bath.
   B. I had scolded the dog when he barked.
   C. I will give this treat to the dog.
   D. After his bath, the dog shook himself.

3. In which sentence below is the word *team* an indirect object?
   A. The team gathered on the field.
   B. The umpire told the team the rules.
   C. The coach spoke seriously to the team.
   D. The team waved to the fans after the game.

4. Which sentence below has a punctuation error?
   A. I was shivering before I got to school today, because I forgot my coat.
   B. Low temperatures and high winds create wind chill; it is a dangerous combination.
   C. Marilyn loves winter sports, but she does not like feeling cold.
   D. If you lose feeling in your hands, you may have frostbite and need medical attention.

5. Which word in the sentence below is an adverb?

On my daily walk, I see a friendly dog that barks loudly and wags its curly tail.

   A. daily
   B. friendly
   C. loudly
   D. curly

WRITING

Read your assigned topic in the box below. Use one piece of paper to jot down your ideas and organize your thoughts. Then neatly write your essay on another sheet of paper.

Expository Writing Topic

Writing Situation

Your school is sponsoring an essay writing contest. The topic is "Why Have School Rules?" The student who writes the best essay on this topic will win a new bike.

Directions for Writing

Write an essay explaining to students at your school why it is necessary for a group, such as students at a school, to have rules. Be sure to include details and examples to support your ideas.

Writing Checklist

- ☐ Focus on a single topic.
- ☐ Organize your main points in a clear, logical order.
- ☐ Support your ideas or viewpoints with details and examples.
- ☐ Use precise, vivid words.
- ☐ Vary the length and structure of your sentences.
- ☐ Use clear transition words to connect ideas.
- ☐ Correct any errors in spelling, capitalization, punctuation, and usage.

WHAT Brings Out the Best in You?

UNIT FIVE

THE BIG Question

> *Always dream and shoot higher than you know how.*
>
> —WILLIAM FAULKNER

FOLDABLES® Study Organizer

Throughout Unit 5, you will read, write, and talk about **the BIG Question—"What Brings Out the Best in You?"** Use your Unit 5 **Foldable,** shown here, to keep track of your ideas as you read. Turn to the back of this book for instructions on making this **Foldable.**

Explore the BIG Question

WHAT Brings Out the Best in You?

Everyone has different challenges in their lives. The way you respond to them shows what type of person you are. For example, you might react bravely, kindly, or patiently. Explore how you respond to different situations and what brings out the best in you.

Think about things that can bring out the best in people, such as

- Using Inner Strength
- Putting Others First

What You'll Read

Reading about what brings out the best in others can help you explore this idea for yourself. In this unit, **biographies** and **autobiographies**—stories of real people's lives—are excellent sources of information. You will also read short stories, poetry, and other texts that can lead you to discover answers to the Big Question.

What You'll Write

As you explore the Big Question, you'll write notes in your Unit 5 **Foldable**. Later you'll use these notes to complete two writing assignments related to the Big Question.

1. **Write a Research Report**
2. **Choose a Unit Challenge**
   - **On Your Own Activity: Your Interview**
   - **Group Activity: Magazine Article**

What You'll Learn

Literary Elements

author's purpose

author's perspective

form

point of view

text features

simile

voice

allusion

Reading Skills and Strategies

analyze tone

analyze cultural context

determine main idea and supporting details

summarize

evaluate description

draw conclusions about author's perspective

Explore the BIG Question

Set a Purpose for Reading

Read this graphic story to find out what brings out the best in a young student named Usagi, who is training to become a samurai. (In Japan in the Middle Ages, a **samurai** was a member of the warrior class. A **sensei** is a teacher or an instructor, usually of Japanese martial arts such as judo or karate.)

BQ BIG Question

What qualities is Sensei trying to teach Usagi?

BQ BIG Question

On what kind of strength is Usagi relying?

BQ BIG Question

Why do you think that Sensei tells Usagi to fetch water?

BQ BIG Question

How can you tell that Usagi does not understand the lesson?

BQ BIG Question

How is the traveler trying to bring out the best in Usagi by calling him "young one"?

BQ **BIG Question**

What does Usagi want to prove?

BQ **BIG Question**

Why does the traveler throw Usagi in the water?

BQ BIG Question

How do the traveler's actions show his inner strength?

YOU HAVEN'T SEEN THE LAST OF ME! I WILL FIND YOU SOME DAY!

YEARS LATER...

BQ BIG Question

Years later, what has Usagi accomplished?

BQ BIG Question

What do you think Usagi will do?

END

BQ BIG Question

What is the most important lesson that Usagi learned? Who or what brings out the best in Usagi?

After You Read

Respond and Think Critically

1. Use your own words to tell how the traveler teaches Usagi a lesson. **[Summarize]**
2. What does Sensei mean when he says, "You focus on the victory but not the battle"? **[Interpret]**
3. Compare the grown-up Usagi with the young student Usagi. **[Compare]**
4. Does Usagi deserve to be a samurai? Explain. **[Evaluate]**

Writing

Reader Response Is it possible that Usagi could have become a better samurai on his own? How responsible were others for bringing out the best in him? How responsible was Usagi for bringing out the best in himself? Write a one-paragraph response telling how you think Usagi became a better samurai. Summarize your ideas, using details from the graphic story to support your response. You may want to begin your paragraph with this sentence:

I think it took some time for Usagi to change because ________.

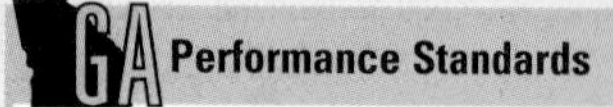

GA Performance Standards

For page 594

ELA6W2b Demonstrate competence in a variety of genres. Produce a response to literature that demonstrates an understanding of the literary work.

Bando Mitsugoro III, 1820. Utagwa Kunisada. Woodblock engraving. Fitzwilliam Museum, University of Cambridge.

LOG ON Literature Online

Unit Resources For additional skills practice, go to glencoe.com and enter QuickPass code GL17527u5.

Part 1

Using Inner Strength

Boy Attacked by Swarm of Insects, 1995. Willie Rodger. Oil on board. Private Collection.

BQ BIG Question What Brings Out the Best in You?

In the painting *Boy Attacked by Swarm of Insects,* the young man faces a challenge and defends himself. Why do his actions show his inner strength? What challenges do you know about that require young people to use their inner strength?

Before You Read

from *Elie Wiesel: Voice from the Holocaust*

Connect to the Biography

Think about a difficult time in your life. It could be a time when you had to deal with a serious problem or face treatment that was unfair or unjust.

Quickwrite Freewrite for a few minutes about the difficult time. What made the problem serious? How did you feel about it? How did you deal with it?

Build Background

Elie Wiesel (e′lē vē zel′) was born in 1928. He spent his childhood in Sighet, Rumania, with his parents and three sisters. In the spring of 1944, Wiesel's life changed forever. Fifteen-year-old Elie and his family were sent to Auschwitz, a death camp in Poland.

- The Nazis were a political party that controlled Germany from 1933 to 1945 under Adolf Hitler.
- The Holocaust was the mass killing of European citizens—mostly Jews—by the Nazis during World War II.
- Approximately six million Jews were killed during the Holocaust.

Vocabulary

distinguished (dis ting′gwisht) *adj.* marked by excellence (p. 598). *The distinguished scientist spoke to the class about her research.*

achievements (ə chēv′məntz) *n.* things completed with great effort or skill (p. 598). *Those who work hard at their studies should be proud of their achievements.*

recognition (rek əg nish′ən) *n.* favorable attention or notice (p. 599). *The volunteers received recognition from the city's mayor.*

tortured (tôr′chərd) *v.* caused to suffer extreme physical or mental pain (p. 600). *After being captured, the soldier was tortured by the enemy.*

Meet Michael A. Schuman

"All I've ever wanted to do since the second grade is write because it's what I do best."

—Michael A. Schuman

Biographer and Travel Writer Michael A. Schuman began his writing career as a sportswriter and travel writer before writing nonfiction—mainly biographies for young adults. He says that writing biographies is exciting because he gets to interview fascinating people. Over the years, he has met politicians, inventors, cartoonists, actors, and famous authors.

Literary Works Schuman has written more than ten biographies. *Elie Wiesel: Voice from the Holocaust* was published in 1994.

Michael A. Schuman was born in 1953.

Literature Online

Author Search For more about Michael A. Schuman, go to glencoe.com and enter QuickPass code GL17527u5.

Set Purposes for Reading

BQ BIG Question

As you read, ask yourself, what qualities does Wiesel call on to turn a horrible experience into something meaningful?

Literary Element Author's Purpose

The **author's purpose** is the author's reason for writing. The purpose may be to entertain, to inform, to persuade, or to express emotion. Sometimes an author will have more than one purpose. In this excerpt from *Elie Wiesel: Voice from the Holocaust,* one purpose is to inform readers about the life of a man of great courage.

Recognizing the author's purpose helps you set your own purpose for reading. When the purpose is to inform, you look for important details, such as facts, as you read. You also consider what the author is trying to teach you.

As you read, ask yourself, how do the facts and personal experiences the author includes help me determine his purpose for writing?

Reading Skill Analyze Tone

Tone is the author's attitude toward a subject. To **analyze tone,** think about the language the author uses to describe the subject. The author might use strong, emotionally charged words to create a humorous, angry, or admiring tone. Or the author might use facts and unemotional descriptions to create a reasonable, unbiased tone.

Analyzing tone can help you better understand the author's message and purpose for writing.

To analyze tone, pay attention to

- details used to describe events
- elements such as word choice, punctuation, sentence structure, and figures of speech
- how word choices reflect the author's feelings and attitudes

As you read, you may find it helpful to use a graphic organizer like the one below.

Words and Details in Text	How They Reveal Author's Attitude

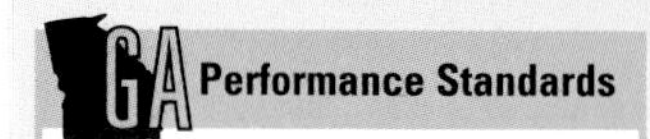

GA **Performance Standards**

For pages 596–603

ELA6RIg Define and explain how tone is conveyed through literature.

ELA6RC2e Examine the author's purpose in writing.

TRY IT

Analyze Tone You receive two letters in the mail. The first is a birthday invitation that says, "Hurray! You're invited to a special party!" The second is a notice that says, "Your library book is overdue. Please return it immediately." What is the tone of the first letter? The second letter?

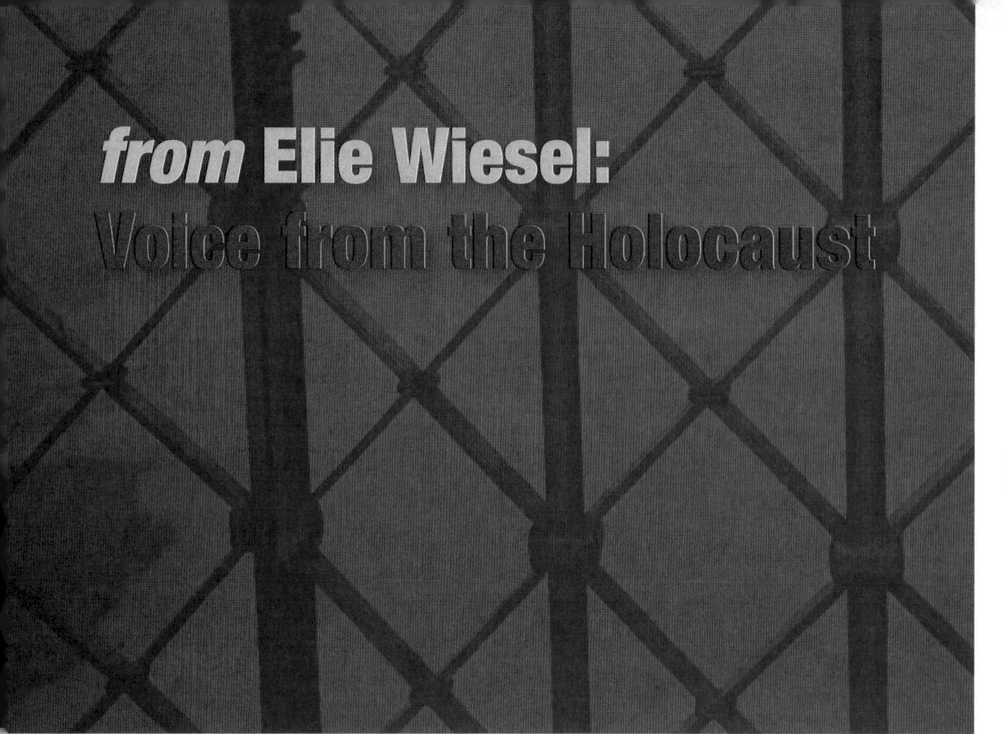

from Elie Wiesel: Voice from the Holocaust

Michael A. Schuman

The people in the audience, all **distinguished** men and women, listened intently to every word spoken by the shy, sad-eyed man standing at the **podium**. Except for the clicking of camera shutters, there was hardly a sound from those gathered in the ceremonial hall at the University of Oslo in Norway. They paid rapt attention to the speaker, who was talking of his experience of both horrors and honors as he accepted the greatest award of his life.

The lecturer was Elie Wiesel and he was receiving the Nobel Peace Prize for 1986. Nobel Prizes pay tribute each year to men and women whose **achievements** have affected citizens all over the world. Nobel Prizes are awarded in the sciences, literature, and economics, but the Nobel Peace Prize could be the most highly regarded of them all. Wiesel was chosen for his work as a writer, teacher, philosopher,[1] and advocate[2] of peace.

Visual Vocabulary A **podium** is a place or structure from which to address a group. The raised platform an orchestra conductor stands on is also called a podium.

Author's Purpose Why do you think the author begins the paragraph with this information?

1 A ***philosopher*** is someone who studies the meaning and purpose of human life.

2 An ***advocate*** is someone who publicly works in support of a cause.

Vocabulary

distinguished (dis ting′ gwisht) *adj.* marked by excellence

achievements (ə chēv′ mәntz) *n.* things completed with great effort or skill

Children and other prisoners liberated by the U.S. Army march from Buchenwald concentration camp in April 1945. The tall youth in the line at left, fourth from the front, is Elie Wiesel.

There was a time in Wiesel's life when it looked as if he would never live to become an adult, let alone win such special **recognition**. Wiesel grew up in a village in Rumania[3] in eastern Europe with his parents and three sisters in the 1930s. In 1939, World War II broke out, and their lives were changed forever.

Analyze Tone What is the tone of this paragraph? What does the tone suggest will happen?

Most young people at age fifteen spend their time attending school, playing sports, or falling in love for the first time. But when Elie was fifteen, he and his family were taken from their home by police serving the German Nazis who had occupied Rumania. Under Adolf Hitler, who had established what was likely the most brutal dictatorship[4] in the twentieth century, the Nazis had embarked on a course of evil that included killing all Jewish people as well as many others they considered inferior to themselves.

3 ***Rumania*** is another way to spell *Romania.*

4 A ***dictatorship*** is a form of government in which a ruler has total control.

Vocabulary

recognition (rek əg nish′ ən) *n.* favorable attention or notice

The Nazis had conquered almost all of Europe and in each of the countries they occupied, they captured Jews who were living peacefully in towns or villages and sent them to concentration camps, confined areas like prisons where they had to work as slaves. Many of the Jews were **tortured** and most were later put to death at separate death camps, which were built specifically for killing Jews and other "undesirables" like Gypsies. In many cases, the death camps were on the grounds of the larger concentration camps.

The Wiesel family was first sent to Auschwitz,[5] a concentration camp in Poland, where Elie's youngest sister and his mother were killed in gas chambers, small rooms filled with poisonous gas. His two older sisters were separated from the family and taken elsewhere. Meanwhile, Elie and his father were transported to a concentration camp in Germany called Buchenwald,[6] where his father died from hunger and disease. It was only after the U.S. Army liberated[7] Buchenwald three months later that Elie, then sixteen, was rescued.

Author's Purpose Why does the author include this information?

As an adult, Wiesel used the memories of his terrifying teenage years to try to ensure that such a catastrophe would never happen again. He did so by writing books and teaching at colleges about his experiences, warning that this type of terror could be repeated if bad dictatorships were not challenged, and advocating fair treatment for all oppressed[8] peoples of the world. A religious man, Wiesel has spent his life urging people to reject bigotry,[9] hatred, and violence.

BQ BIG Question

How has Wiesel turned a terrible experience into something good?

In fact, Wiesel is given credit as one of the first people to use the term *Holocaust* to describe the Nazi mass killings, a word that is accepted by most people as the official label for those murders.

---

5 ***Auschwitz*** (oush′ vits)

6 ***Buchenwald*** (book′ən wôld′)

7 When the U.S. Army ***liberated*** Buchenwald, they freed the prisoners there.

8 People who are ***oppressed*** are treated cruelly and unjustly by a force or an authority.

9 ***Bigotry*** is extreme prejudice or narrow-mindedness.

Vocabulary

tortured (tôr′ chərd) *v.* caused to suffer extreme physical or mental pain

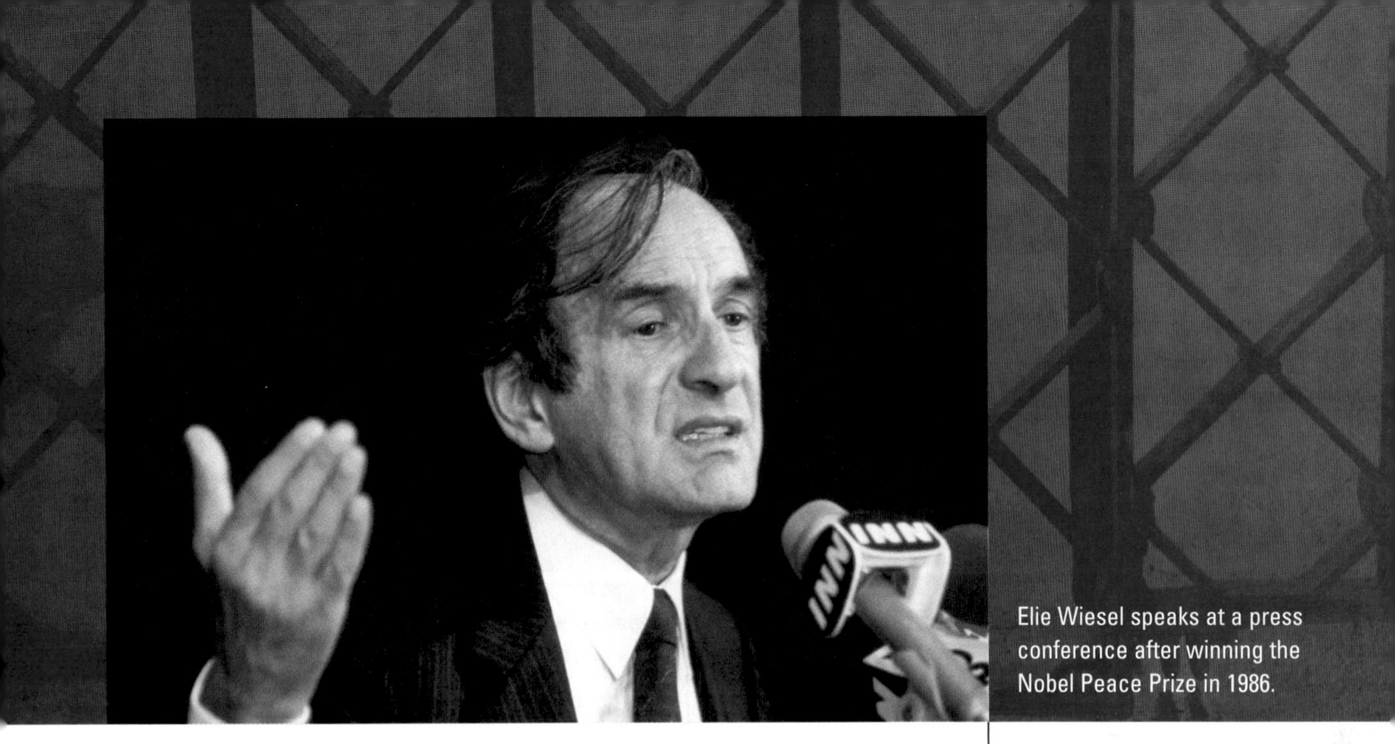

Elie Wiesel speaks at a press conference after winning the Nobel Peace Prize in 1986.

As he gave his acceptance speech in Oslo, Wiesel brought his fourteen-year-old son up to the podium, to demonstrate the fact that despite years of oppression, Jews continued to survive.

There was a bit of irony in the awarding of Wiesel's 1986 prize. Exactly fifty years earlier, the Nobel Peace Prize was given to a German pacifist named Carl von Ossietzky, who had tried to warn the people of his country about the growing strength of the Nazi party and the menace to peace it represented. Many at the time, even those who were moderates, denounced the honoring of Ossietzky with the prize as being an insult to the German government. Wiesel's message about speaking out and challenging evil leaders seemed even more poignant[10] with that anniversary in mind.

At the end of his speech, Wiesel thanked the Norwegians, who responded by applauding in gratitude. As he left the auditorium and walked out into the cold Oslo afternoon, people on the street applauded him too. Smiling, Wiesel turned to his family and friends and hugged them, realizing that his survival had meaning for humankind. ❧

Analyze Tone How does the tone change? How is it a clue to the author's attitude toward Wiesel?

10 Something that is ***poignant*** (poin′ yənt) makes one feel sad or thoughtful.

After You Read

Respond and Think Critically

1. What is the Nobel Peace Prize? To whom is it awarded? Why is it important? **[Recall]**
2. Using your own words, tell what happened to Wiesel and his family during World War II. **[Summarize]**
3. What does it say about the Nazis that they labeled certain groups of people as "undesirable"? **[Interpret]**
4. Why do you think the Peace Prize is valued above all other Nobel awards? **[Analyze]**
5. Why is Wiesel's message of peace still important today? **[Evaluate]**
6. **BQ BIG Question** How did Wiesel's experience during World War II bring out the best in him? How can Wiesel's inner strength serve as an example for others? **[Conclude]**

Vocabulary Practice

Choose the sentence that correctly uses the vocabulary word.

1. **A.** We reached **achievements** about dividing up the project.
   B. His **achievements** include serving as team captain.
2. **A.** The family decided to stay home because of the **recognition** of traveling during the snowstorm.
   B. Julia received **recognition** for her paintings in the art display.
3. **A.** Some war prisoners were **tortured** by their captors.
   B. Miles was **tortured** to discover that he had won the prize.
4. **A.** The **distinguished** professor had received many awards.
   B. Alan was **distinguished** to make it to school on time.

Academic Vocabulary

A religious man, Wiesel has spent his life urging people to **reject** bigotry, hatred, and violence. To become more familiar with the word *reject*, fill out a graphic organizer like the one below.

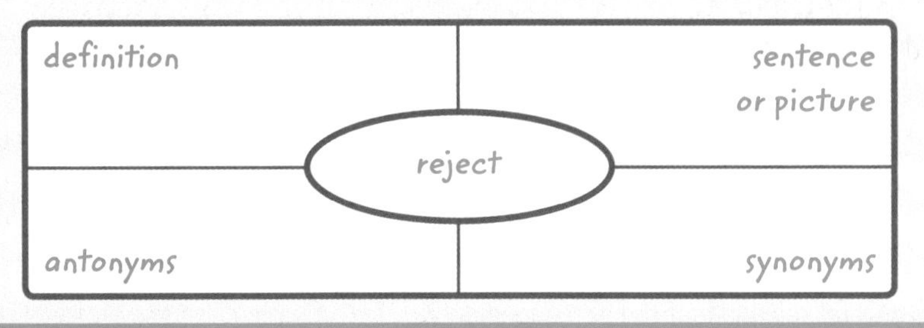

TIP

Evaluating
Remember that when you evaluate, you assess or judge an idea's worth.

- Think about why peace is important to you, your family, and your friends.
- Consider the world today. Are any countries at war? Are any groups oppressed or persecuted?
- Use your own experiences and knowledge of the world to assess the importance of Wiesel's message of peace.

Keep track of your ideas about the **BIG Question** in your unit Foldable.

Literature Online

Selection Resources
For Selection Quizzes, eFlashcards, and Reading-Writing Connection activities, go to glencoe.com and enter QuickPass code GL17527u5.

Literary Element Author's Purpose

Standards Practice  ELA6RC2e

1. Why did the author write this biography?
   - A. to persuade readers to oppose the Nazis
   - B. to describe the Americans' role in World War II
   - C. to inform readers about Elie Wiesel's courageous life
   - D. to explain how to win the Nobel Peace Prize

Review: Narrator

As you learned on page 11, a **narrator** is the person who tells a story. In a biography, the narrator, or author, must interpret the facts of a person's life. The author's opinions and purpose for writing can affect the way the author tells the biography.

2. Think about biographies you have read. What would make you trust or distrust the narrator, or author, of a biography?
3. The author describes the hardships Wiesel endured in concentration camps. Can you trust the author's description of these camps? Why or why not?

Reading Skill Analyze Tone

4. How would you describe the overall tone of this selection? Look at the words below and see whether any of them fit, or choose your own words.

   lighthearted admiring humorous
   serious anxious respectful

5. What is the author's attitude toward Hitler and the Nazis? Find two words or phrases from the selection that reveal the author's attitude toward them.

Grammar Link

Conjunctions A **conjunction** is a word that connects words or groups of words.

Coordinating conjunctions join words or groups of words that are equal in importance. For example:

In 1939 World War II broke out, *and* many lives were changed forever.

Subordinating conjunctions join a dependent clause (a group of words that cannot stand alone) to a main clause (a group of words that can stand alone). For example:

As he gave his acceptance speech in Oslo, Wiesel brought his fourteen-year-old son up to the podium.

Practice
Look for three sentences in the biography that have conjunctions. Then write your own sentences with conjunctions.

Research and Report

Internet Connection Go to the Nobel Foundation's Web site at www.nobelprize.org. Use menus, links, and keyword searches to look up the names of the winners of the Nobel Peace Prize for the last ten years. Record information on a chart like the one below. Then choose one prizewinner and read his or her biography online. Write a brief summary of the prizewinner's life.

Year	Name of Winner	Home Country	Accomplishments

Cultural Perspective

on *Elie Wiesel: Voice from the Holocaust* by Michael A. Schuman

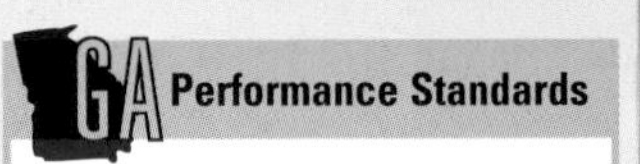

Performance Standards

For pages 604–606

ELA6R1c For literary texts, relate a literary work to historical events of the period.

The Secret Schools

by Susan Goldman Rubin

Sydney Taylor Honor

Set a Purpose for Reading

Read to learn what life was like for Jewish children during World War II at Terezin, a concentration camp in Czechoslovakia.

Build Background

During the Holocaust, an artist and art teacher named Friedl Dicker-Brandeis was sent to the Terezin camp. She was determined to bring art to the children of the camp.

Reading Skill Analyze Historical Context

To analyze the historical context of a literary work, you consider the social, artistic, intellectual, and political forces that influenced the time period. As you read, take notes about the lives of children at Terezin. Use a chart like the one below to record these details.

Children at Terezin	Details

School was not allowed at Terezin. The Nazis[1] only permitted the Jewish children to study music and crafts such as sewing, embroidering,[2] and making pleasant, decorative pictures and greeting cards. So Friedl and the other tutors taught other subjects in secret. During lessons one of the students was posted outside as a lookout. If the ghetto[3] guards or an SS[4] man came along, the lookout gave a signal. Then all the students quickly hid their drawings, exercise books, and pencils and started singing or cleaning the room. Kurt Jiří Kotouč, who lived

1 ***Nazis*** were members of a political party under Adolf Hitler that controlled Germany from 1933 to 1945.

2 ***Embroidering*** is decorating fabric with a design in needlework.

3 A ***ghetto*** was a section of a city where Jews were required to live.

4 The ***SS*** was a Nazi group that ran the concentration camps.

in L417, remembered that classes were "mainly held in the attics, where there was less danger that the SS would suddenly burst in on us."

Since there were no textbooks, the tutors wrote down what they knew about their subjects from memory, and they shared the books they had brought. Children fourteen and older had to work all day, so they studied at night or early in the morning, and on Sunday.

Friedl went from room to crowded room giving lessons to anyone who was interested—even to sick children in the hospital. She was small and lively, and many of the children were taller than she was. Friedl brought paper, paint, and pencils.

Everyone waited eagerly for a turn to work with Friedl, especially the girls in Room 28. "She was cheerful, very gentle and patient," remembered Raja Englanderová-Žákníková. In Room 28 there was only one table, recalled Helga Polláková-Kinsky, so the girls drew in their bunks. Or they "squeezed somewhere and worked on their knees," said Dita Polachová-Kraus. Sometimes they went to Friedl's room.

Through art, Friedl helped the children escape mentally. "She wanted us to get away and go into a nice world," said Helga.

The Seder Supper. Eva Meitnerova. Museum of the Old Jewish Cemetery, Prague.

Girls Dancing in a Meadow. Anita Spitzova. Museum of the Old Jewish Cemetery, Prague.

Some children expressed their fear by writing poems in their free time. Other children couldn't put their feelings into words, so they used a secret code—the secret code of drawing that Friedl understood. Under her guidance they drew pictures showing what they dreaded most: transports.[5]

5 Here, ***transports*** are trains used to carry prisoners from Terezin to death camps.

And to comfort themselves, they drew their dreams. Helga painted a meadow at sunset. In the world of her drawing there was no danger, no threat of transport, and while she was drawing she felt safe and good. From morning till night, in their free time, the children kept drawing. Friedl encouraged the children to talk about their artwork. Discussion helped calm them and restore their hope.

Respond and Think Critically

1. Write a brief summary of the main ideas in this excerpt. For help on writing a summary, see page 170. **[Summarize]**
2. Why do you think the Nazis permitted Jewish children to study only music and crafts such as sewing and making greeting cards? **[Interpret]**
3. What effect did Friedl's visits have on the children? Why? **[Analyze]**
4. **Text to Text** How would you compare the experiences of Elie Wiesel with the children's experiences at Terezin? **[Connect]**
5. **Reading Skill Analyze Historical Context** What made the tutors' refusal to obey the Nazis at Terezin so important?
6. **BQ BIG Question** How do Friedl and the children use inner strength to bring out the best in themselves under terrible circumstances?

Before You Read

Primary Lessons

Connect to the Autobiography

Think about your first day of school. What did you expect to happen? What actually occurred?

Quickwrite Freewrite for a few minutes about your first day of school. How did you feel going to school for the first time? What did you learn? If you cannot remember your first day, choose another memorable school day.

Build Background

"Primary Lessons" takes place in Puerto Rico in the late 1950s. Puerto Rico is a commonwealth of the United States. It is a tropical island in the Caribbean Sea about one thousand miles southeast of Florida.

- Puerto Rico is a little larger than the state of Delaware and has a population of nearly four million people.
- In 1917 Puerto Ricans were granted U.S. citizenship.
- Puerto Rico has two official languages, Spanish and English.

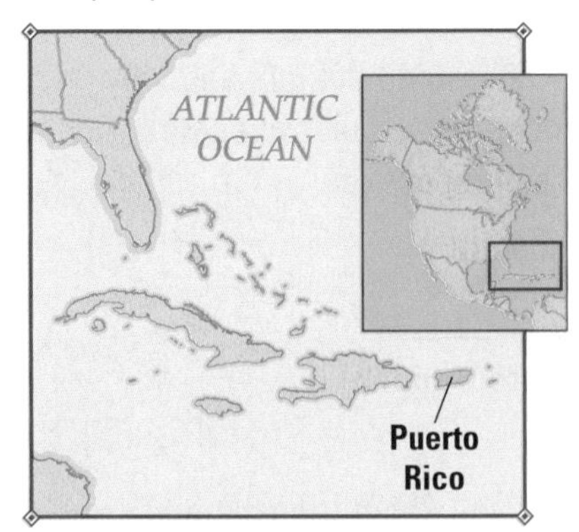

Vocabulary

chaos (kā′ os) *n.* total confusion and disorder (p. 610). *On moving day, our house was in complete chaos.*

defiance (di fī′ əns) *n.* bold resistance to authority (p. 611). *The baker kept his shop open in defiance of the king's order.*

indifference (in dif′ ər əns) *n.* lack of feeling or concern (p. 611). *They were shocked at the queen's indifference to her people.*

relish (rel′ ish) *v.* to enjoy (p. 616). *Alisa and I relish the chance to solve the problem.*

Meet Judith Ortiz Cofer

"The women in my family were wonderful storytellers who infected me at a very early age with the desire to tell stories."

—Judith Ortiz Cofer

Between Two Cultures Born in Puerto Rico, Judith Ortiz Cofer grew up in New Jersey with Spanish-speaking parents. She often writes about things that happened to her when she was a child. Through her writing, she shows readers ways to adapt to new places and new cultures.

Literary Works Cofer has written short stories, essays, novels, and poems. "Primary Lessons" is from *Silent Dancing: A Partial Remembrance of a Puerto Rican Childhood.*

Judith Ortiz Cofer was born in 1952.

Literature Online

Author Search For more about Judith Ortiz Cofer, go to glencoe.com and enter QuickPass code GL17527u5.

Set Purposes for Reading

BQ BIG Question

As you read, ask yourself, what does the author learn from this childhood experience?

Literary Element Author's Perspective

An **author's perspective** is the combination of experiences, values, and ideas that shape the way the author looks at the world. In "Primary Lessons," the author has two perspectives. She describes her childhood and how she felt about it as a child. But she also comments as an adult, with the added perspective of age, education, and experience.

Being aware of the author's perspective helps you understand why the author has chosen to tell a story in a certain way.

As you read, ask yourself, when is the author writing from her childhood perspective? When is she commenting as an adult?

Reading Skill Analyze Cultural Context

The **cultural context** of a work includes the customs, beliefs, attitudes, and relationships that are typical of a given time and place. "Primary Lessons" takes place in Puerto Rico in the 1950s.

Analyzing cultural context helps you understand the plot and why characters act as they do. In an autobiography, cultural context also gives you insight into the author's perspective.

To analyze cultural context, pay attention to

- how the characters live and work
- the dialect or language(s) the characters speak
- what the characters value

Then think about what these details tell you about the time and place. As you read, you may find it helpful to use a graphic organizer like the one below.

Detail	What It Reveals
Everything at school is color-coded.	The school has strict rules.

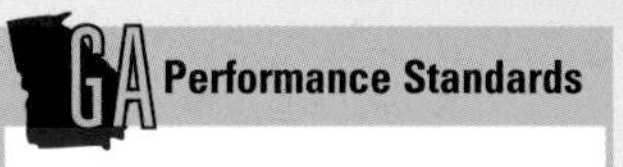

GA Performance Standards

For pages 607–619

ELA6RIe Identify and analyze elements of setting.

ELA6RC2e Examine the author's purpose in writing.

TRY IT

Analyze Cultural Context Look at an old newspaper or magazine photo. What are people wearing? What technology can you see around them? What do these clues tell you about their culture?

Primary LESSONS

Judith Ortiz Cofer

My mother walked me to my first day at school at La Escuela Segundo Ruiz Belvis,[1] named after the Puerto Rican patriot born in our town. I remember yellow cement with green trim. All the classrooms had been painted these colors to identify them as government property. This was true all over the Island.

Everything was color-coded, including the children, who wore uniforms from first through twelfth grade. We were a midget army in white and brown, led by the hand to our battleground. From practically every house in our barrio[2] emerged a crisply ironed uniform inhabited by the wild creatures we had become over a summer of running wild in the sun.

Analyze Cultural Context
What have you learned so far about this particular school in Puerto Rico in the 1950s?

At my grandmother's house where we were staying until my father returned to Brooklyn Yard in New York and sent

---

1 ***La Escuela*** (lä es kwā′ lə) means "school." ***Segundo Ruiz Belvis*** (sā goon′ dō rōō′ ēz bel′ vēz) fought for Puerto Rico's independence from Spain in the 1800s.

2 ***Barrio*** (bä′ rē ō) refers to a Hispanic neighborhood.

Youngsters Trekking to Book Mobile Parked on Road, 1953.

for us, it had been complete **chaos,** with several children to get ready for school. My mother had pulled my hair harder than usual while braiding it, and I had dissolved into a pool of total self-pity. I wanted to stay home with her and *Mamá,* to continue listening to stories in the late afternoon, to drink *café con leche*[3] with them, and to play rough games with my many cousins. I wanted to continue living the dream of summer afternoons in Puerto Rico, and if I could not have that, then I wanted to go back to Paterson, New Jersey, back to where I imagined our apartment waited, peaceful and cool for the three of us to return to our former lives. Our gypsy lifestyle had convinced me, at age six, that one part of life stops and waits for you while you live another for a while—and if you don't like the present, you can always return to the past. Buttoning me into my stiff blouse while I tried to squirm away from her, my mother tried to explain to me that I was a big girl now and should try to understand that, like all the other children my age, I had to go to school.

Author's Perspective Why could this be seen as a childlike perspective on life?

3 ***Café con leche*** (kä′ fā kon lā′ chā) is coffee with milk.

Vocabulary

chaos (kā′ os) *n.* total confusion and disorder

"What about him?" I yelled pointing at my brother who was lounging on the tile floor of our bedroom in his pajamas, playing quietly with a toy car.

"He's too young to go to school, you know that. Now stay still." My mother pinned me between her thighs to button my skirt, as she had learned to do from *Mamá,* from whose grip it was impossible to escape.

"It's not fair, it's not fair. I can't go to school here. I don't speak Spanish." It was my final argument, and it failed miserably because I was shouting my **defiance** in the language I claimed not to speak. Only I knew what I meant by saying in Spanish that I did not speak Spanish. I had spent my early childhood in the U.S. where I lived in a bubble created by my Puerto Rican parents in a home where two cultures and languages became one. I learned to listen to the English from the television with one ear while I heard my mother and father speaking in Spanish with the other. I thought I was an ordinary American kid—like the children on the shows I watched—and that everyone's parents spoke a secret second language at home. When we came to Puerto Rico right before I started first grade, I switched easily to Spanish. It was the language of fun, of summertime games. But school—that was a different matter.

Author's Perspective From the author's childhood perspective, what was her situation like?

I made one last desperate attempt to make my mother see reason: "Father will be very angry. You know that he wants us to speak good English." My mother, of course, ignored me as she dressed my little brother in his playclothes. I could not believe her **indifference** to my father's wishes. She was usually so careful about our safety and the many other areas that he was forever reminding her about in his letters. But I was right, and she knew it.

Our father spoke to us in English as much as possible, and he corrected my pronunciation constantly—not "jes" but "y-es." Y-es, sir. How could she send me to school to

Analyze Cultural Context Why do you think the author's father wants his children to speak proper English?

Vocabulary

defiance (di fī′ əns) *n.* bold resistance to authority

indifference (in dif′ ər əns) *n.* lack of feeling or concern learn Spanish when we would be returning to Paterson in just a few months?

But, of course, what I feared was not language, but loss of freedom. At school there would be no playing, no stories, only lessons. It would not matter if I did not understand a word, and I would not be allowed to make up my own definitions. I would have to learn silence. I would have to keep my wild imagination in check. Feeling locked into my stiffly starched uniform, I only sensed all this. I guess most children can intuit[4] their loss of childhood's freedom on that first day of school. It is separation anxiety[5] too, but mother is just the guardian of the "playground" of our early childhood.

Author's Perspective As a child, what did the author understand about school? What does she know about it now?

The sight of my cousins in similar straits[6] comforted me. We were marched down the hill of our barrio where *Mamá's* robin-egg-blue house stood at the top. I must have glanced back at it with yearning. *Mamá's* house—a place built for children—where anything that could be broken had already been broken by my grandmother's early batch of offspring (they ranged in age from my mother's oldest sisters to my uncle who was six months older than me). Her house had long since been made child-proof. It had been a perfect summer place. And now it was September—the cruelest month for a child.

La Mrs., as all the teachers were called, waited for her class of first-graders at the door of the yellow and green classroom. She too wore a uniform: it was a blue skirt and a white blouse. This teacher wore black high heels with her "standard issue." I remember this detail because when we were all seated in rows she called on one little girl and pointed to the back of the room where there were shelves. She told the girl to bring her a shoebox from the bottom shelf. Then, when the box had been placed in her hands, she did something unusual. She had the little girl kneel at her feet and take the pointy high heels off her feet and

4 When you ***intuit*** (in tōō′ it) something, no one teaches or explains it to you; you just know it.

5 ***Separation anxiety*** is the fear that some people feel when they are separated from their loved ones.

6 Here, ***straits*** means "a troublesome or difficult situation."

replace them with a pair of satin slippers from the shoebox. She told the group that every one of us would have a chance to do this if we behaved in her class. Though confused about the prize, I soon felt caught up in the competition to bring *La Mrs.* her slippers in the morning. Children fought over the privilege.

Our first lesson was English. In Puerto Rico, every child has to take twelve years of English to graduate from school. It is the law. In my parents' schooldays, all subjects were taught in English. The U.S. Department of Education had specified that as U.S. territory, the Island had to be "Americanized," and to accomplish this task, it was necessary for the Spanish language to be replaced in one generation through the teaching of English in all schools. My father began his school day by saluting the flag of the United States and singing "America" and "The Star-Spangled Banner" by rote,[7] without understanding a word of what he was saying. The logic behind this system was that, though the children did not understand the English words, they would remember the rhythms. Even the games the teacher's manuals required them to play became absurd adaptations.[8] "Here We Go Round the Mulberry Bush" became "Here We Go Round the Mango Tree." I have heard about the confusion caused by the use of a primer[9] in which the sounds of animals were featured. The children were forced to accept that a rooster says *cockadoodledoo,* when they knew perfectly well from hearing their own roosters each morning that in Puerto Rico a rooster says *cocorocó.* Even the vocabulary of their pets was changed; there are still family stories circulating about the bewilderment of a first-grader coming home to try to teach his dog to speak in English. The policy of assimilation by immersion[10] failed on the Island. Teachers adhered to it on paper, substituting their own materials

Analyze Cultural Context
What does this description tell you about the Americanization of Puerto Rico?

Author's Perspective
From a child's perspective, why would this be especially confusing?

7 If you do a thing ***by rote,*** you do it without thinking about it, as if you were a machine.

8 ***Absurd*** means "ridiculous." An ***adaptation*** is something that is changed to meet the needs of a certain situation.

9 A ***primer*** (prim′ ər) is a book used to teach children to read.

10 The ***policy of assimilation by immersion*** is the method of teaching English by conducting all schoolwork in English.

for the texts, and no one took their English home. In due time, the program was minimized[11] to the one class in English per day that I encountered when I took my seat in *La Mrs.'s* first-grade class.

Analyze Cultural Context Does this fact surprise you? Why or why not?

Catching us all by surprise, she stood very straight and tall in front of us and began to sing in English: "Pollito—Chicken, Gallina—Hen, Lápiz—Pencil, Y Pluma—Pen."

"Repeat after me, children: Pollito—Chicken," she commanded in her heavily accented English that only I understood, being the only child in the room who had ever been exposed to the language. But I too remained silent. No use making waves, or showing off. Patiently *La Mrs.* sang her song and gestured for us to join in. At some point it must have dawned on the class that this silly routine was likely to go on all day if we did not "repeat after her." It was not her fault that she had to follow the rule in her teacher's manual stating that she must teach English *in* English, and that she must not translate, but must repeat her lesson in English until the children "begin to respond" more or less "unconsciously." This was one of the vestiges of the regimen followed by her predecessors[12] in the last generation. To this day I can recite "Pollito—Chicken" mindlessly, never once pausing to visualize chicks, hens, pencils, or pens.

Author's Perspective Is this statement from the child's or the adult's perspective? How does this perspective make the author's point stronger?

I soon found myself crowned "teacher's pet" without much effort on my part. I was a privileged child in her eyes simply because I lived in "Nueva York," and because my father was in the Navy. His name was an old one in our pueblo, associated with once-upon-a-time landed people and long-gone money. Status is judged by unique standards in a culture where, by definition, everyone is a second-class citizen. Remembrance of past glory is as good as titles and money. Old families living in decrepit old houses rank over factory workers living in modern

11 ***Minimized*** means "cut back." The immersion program was cut back after a while, until only one class each day was all in English.

12 ***Vestiges of the regimen followed by her predecessors:*** In other words, this repetition was one of the last remains of the old "all-English" system that earlier teachers had used.

Puerto Rican school children wearing uniforms, circa 1960.

comfort in cement boxes—all the same. The professions raise a person out of the dreaded "sameness" into a niche of status, so that teachers, nurses, and everyone who went to school for a job were given the honorifics of *El Míster* or *La Mrs.*[13] by the common folks, people who were likely to be making more money in American factories than the poorly paid educators and government workers.

My first impression of the hierarchy[14] began with my teacher's shoe-changing ceremony and the exaggerated respect she received from our parents. *La Mrs.* was always

View the Photograph How is this classroom like the one the author attended in Puerto Rico? How is it different?

13 ***Professions*** are occupations that require special training, such as law, medicine, and education. In Spanish, adding *El* or *La* (which mean "the") to *Mr.* or *Mrs.* is a sign of respect.

14 A ***hierarchy*** (hī′ ər är′ kē) is a ranking of people or things based on certain standards.

right, and adults scrambled to meet her requirements. She wanted all our schoolbooks covered in the brown paper now used for paperbags (used at that time by the grocer to wrap meats and other foods). That first week of school the grocer was swamped with requests for paper which he gave away to the women. That week and the next, he wrapped produce in newspapers. All school projects became family projects. It was considered disrespectful at *Mamá's* house to do homework in privacy. Between the hours when we came home from school and dinner time, the table was shared by all of us working together with the women hovering in the background. The teachers communicated directly with the mothers, and it was a matriarchy[15] of far-reaching power and influence.

Analyze Cultural Context What does this tell you about the importance of schoolwork and family in Puerto Rican culture?

There was a black boy in my first-grade classroom who was also the teacher's pet but for a different reason than I: I did not have to do anything to win her favor; he would do anything to win a smile. He was as black as the cauldron that *Mamá* used for cooking stew and his hair was curled into tight little balls on his head—*pasitas,*[16] like little raisins glued to his skull, my mother had said. There had been some talk at *Mamá's* house about this boy; Lorenzo was his name. I later gathered that he was the grandson of my father's nanny. Lorenzo lived with Teresa, his grandmother, having been left in her care when his mother took off for "Los Nueva Yores" shortly after his birth. And they were poor. Everyone could see that his pants were too big for him—hand-me-downs—and his shoe soles were as thin as paper. Lorenzo seemed unmindful of the giggles he caused when he jumped up to erase the board for *La Mrs.* and his baggy pants rode down to his thin hips as he strained up to get every stray mark. He seemed to **relish** playing the little clown when she asked him to come to the front of the room and sing

15 In a ***matriarchy*** (mā′ trē är′ ke), women have the greatest authority.

16 ***Pasitas*** (pə sē′ təs) means "raisins."

Vocabulary

relish (rel′ish) *v.* to enjoy

his phonetic version of "o-bootifool, forpashios-keeis" leading the class in our incomprehensible[17] tribute to the American flag. He was a bright, loving child, with a talent for song and mimicry[18] that everyone commented on. He should have been chosen to host the PTA show that year instead of me.

At recess one day, I came back to the empty classroom to get something, my cup? My nickel for a drink from the kioskman?[19] I don't remember. But I remember the conversation my teacher was having with another teacher. I remember because it concerned me, and because I memorized it so that I could ask my mother to explain what it meant.

"He is a funny *negrito,* and, like a parrot, he can repeat anything you teach him. But his *mamá* must not have the money to buy him a suit."

"I kept Rafaelito's First Communion suit; I bet Lorenzo could fit in it. It's white with a bow-tie," the other teacher said.

"But, Marisa," laughed my teacher, "in that suit, Lorenzo would look like a fly drowned in a glass of milk."

Both women laughed. They had not seen me crouched at the back of the room, digging into my schoolbag. My name came up then.

"What about the Ortiz girl? They have money."

"I'll talk to her mother today. The superintendent, *El Americano* from San Juan, is coming down for the show.

How about if we have her say her lines in both Spanish and English."

The conversation ends there for me. My mother took me to Mayagüez[20] and bought me a frilly pink dress and two **crinoline petticoats** to wear underneath so that I looked like a pink and white parachute with toothpick legs

Author's Perspective
What does the author suggest about how and why she remembers and interprets events?

Visual Vocabulary
Women and girls used to wear **crinoline petticoats,** stiff underskirts that made dresses or skirts flare out.

17 ***Phonetic*** (fə net′ ik) means "having to do with speech sounds." ***Incomprehensible*** means "difficult or impossible to understand."

18 ***Mimicry*** (mi′ mi krē) is the act of mimicking, or copying, someone.

19 A ***kiosk*** (kē′ osk) is a small structure with one or more open sides, such as a newsstand or bus shelter. A ***kioskman*** is a man who works in a kiosk.

20 ***Mayagüez*** (mī′ ə gwez′) is a city in western Puerto Rico.

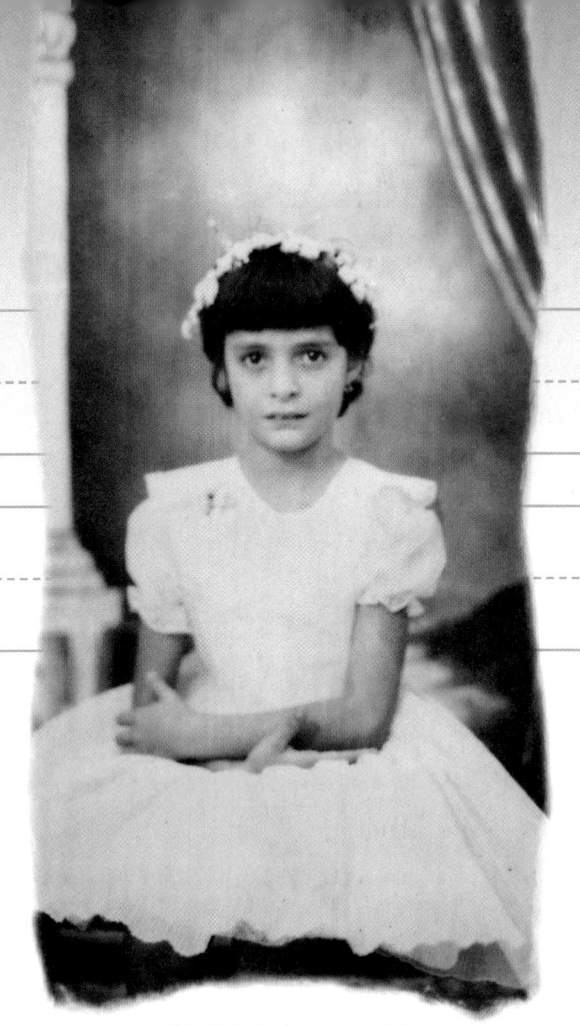

Judith Ortiz Cofer as a child.

sticking out. I learned my lines, "Padres, maestros, Mr. Leonard, bienvenidos[21]/Parents, teachers, Mr. Leonard, welcome . . ." My first public appearance. I took no pleasure in it. The words were formal and empty. I had simply memorized them. My dress pinched me at the neck and arms, and made me itch all over.

I had asked my mother what it meant to be a "mosca en un vaso de leche,"[22] a fly in a glass of milk. She had laughed at the image, explaining that it meant being "different," but it wasn't something I needed to worry about.

BIG Question

Why doesn't this performance bring out the best in the author?

21 ***Padres*** (pä′ drās), ***maestros*** (mīs′ trōs), ***bienvenidos*** (byen′ ve nē′ dōs)

22 ***Mosca en un vaso de leche*** (mäs′ kə en o͞on vā′ sō dā lā′ chā)

After You Read

Respond and Think Critically

1. What reasons does the author give for not wanting to go to school in Puerto Rico? What are her real reasons? [Recall]
2. What kind of person is the author's father? How can you tell? [Infer]
3. Why did the fact that the author had lived in New Jersey cause her to be considered a privileged child in Puerto Rico? [Analyze]
4. **Literary Element** **Author's Perspective** Does the way that the author presents her story help you identify with her? Why or why not? [Evaluate]
5. **Reading Skill** **Analyze Cultural Context** What are some ways in which the culture described in the autobiography differs from your life? What are some ways it is similar? [Compare]
6. **BQ** **BIG Question** Do you think the author's school brought out the best in her? Explain. [Conclude]

TIP

Inferring

Here are some tips to help you make an inference and answer question 2. Recall that **inferring** means making a guess based on clues in the text and what you already know.

- Find all the places in the story where the author mentions her father.
- Pay attention to what he does and what people say about him.
- Think about how these actions make him appear.

Keep track of your ideas about the **BIG Question** in your unit Foldable.

Vocabulary Practice

Identify whether the paired words in each set have the same meaning or opposite meanings. Then write a sentence using each vocabulary word or draw or find a picture that represents the word.

indifference and passion
relish and enjoy
defiance and resistance
chaos and order

Example:

indifference and passion = opposite meaning

Sentence: His indifference toward those suffering after the hurricane surprised me.

Writing

Write a Journal Entry Have you ever felt different from others at school? What was that experience like for you? If you have never felt different, why do you think that is? Describe your thoughts and feelings in a journal entry.

Literature Online

Selection Resources
For Selection Quizzes, eFlashcards, and Reading-Writing Connection activities, go to glencoe.com and enter QuickPass code GL17527u5.

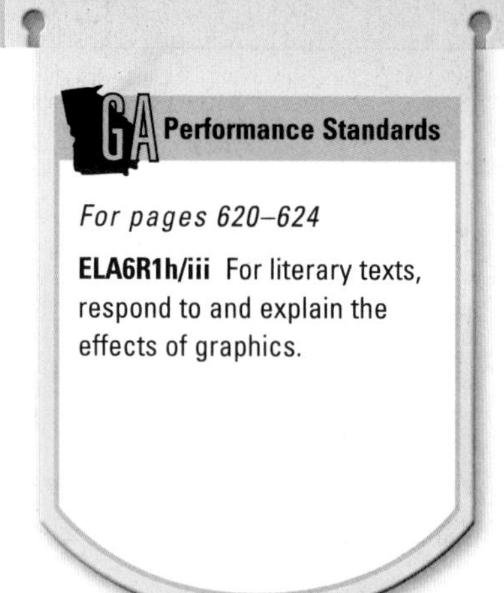

For pages 620–624

ELA6R1h/iii For literary texts, respond to and explain the effects of graphics.

Before You Read

The Sidewalk Racer and *Alone in the Nets*

Connect to the Poems

What activity or game brings out the best in you?

Partner Talk With a partner, discuss this activity or game. Explain what makes it fun for you and how it makes you feel.

Build Background

Skateboarding was probably invented in the 1950s by someone who enjoyed both roller-skating and surfing. Early skateboards had clay wheels. The wheels tended to give a rough ride and to slip easily, throwing the rider off the board.

In the 1970s, plastic wheels came into use. These gripped the ground better than clay wheels, making skateboards easier to control. Riders began wearing helmets and elbow and knee pads to prevent injuries from falls.

Today skateboarding is an international sport in which experts perform stunts in specially designed skateboard parks.

Set Purposes for Reading

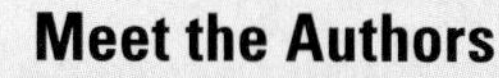

BQ BIG Question

As you read, ask yourself, how does each speaker display inner strength?

Literary Element Form

Poems are made up of lines and groups of lines, called stanzas. Stanzas are like paragraphs in poems. Poetry comes in many forms. Poems with **closed form,** such as sonnets and haiku, have specific rules a poet must follow. Poems with **open form,** or **free verse,** have no fixed pattern of meter, rhyme, line length, or stanza arrangement.

"The Sidewalk Racer" and "Alone in the Nets" are a type of free verse called **concrete poetry.** A concrete poem has words, letters, or symbols that create meaning by what they say and how they look.

As you read, ask yourself how does the meaning of each poem relate to how it looks on the page?

Meet the Authors

Lillian Morrison

Lillian Morrison has written and edited several books of poetry about sports.

Arnold Adoff

Writing a poem is "making music with words and space," says Arnold Adoff.

LOG ON Literature Online

Author Search For more about Lillian Morrison and Arnold Adoff, go to glencoe.com and enter QuickPass code GL17527u5.

The Sidewalk Racer
or On the Skateboard

Lillian Morrison

Skimming
an asphalt° sea
I swerve, I curve, I
sway; I speed to whirring
sound an inch above the
ground; I'm the sailor
and the sail, I'm the
driver and the wheel
I'm the one and only
single engine
human auto
mobile.

Form What shape does this poem take? How does the shape relate to what the poem is about?

BQ BIG Question

How does skateboarding bring out the best in the speaker?

---

2 Roads are paved with ***asphalt***, which is a mixture of a natural substance and gravel, sand, or both.

Alone in the Nets

Arnold Adoff

I
am
alone of course,
in the nets, on this cold and raining afternoon,
and our best defending fullback
is lying on the wet ground out of position.
Half the opposition is pounding
down the field,
and their lead forward° is gliding
so fast, she can just barely keep
the ball in front of her sliding
foot.
Her cleats° are expensive,
and her hair bounces
neatly
like the after
girls in the shampoo commercials.
There is a big grin
on her face.

Form What do you notice about the spacing of the words and lines that describe the lead forward's movement?

---

9 In soccer, a ***forward*** plays closest to the opposing team's goal. The main task of the ***defending fullbacks*** is to stay close to their team's goal and try to prevent the opposing team from getting near it. The speaker is a goalkeeper, who must defend the team's goal, a metal or wooden structure enclosed on three sides by a net.

13 Athletes in some sports wear ***cleats,*** shoes that grip the ground because of pieces of rubber or metal attached to the bottoms.

Now: In This Frozen Moment On This Moving World Through Space

is the right time to ask why am I here just standing
in my frozen place?
Why did I get up on time this morning?
Why did I get up at all?
Why did I listen to the coach and agree to play
this strange position in a r e a l game
in a strange town on this wet and moving world?
Why is it raining?
Why is it raining so h a r d?
Where
are all of our defenders?
Why do all of our players
do all of the falling
down?
Why am I here?

But Frozen Moments Can Unfreeze And I Can Stretch
and reach for the ball flying to the corner of
our
goal.
I can reach and jump
and dive into the s p a c e
between my out
stretched
hands
and the outside poles
of the nets.
My fears evaporate like my sweat in this chilling
breeze,
and I can move with this moving world
and pace my steps
like that old
movie
high
noon sheriff in his just
right
time.
That grinning forward gets her shot away too soon,
and I am there, on my own time, in the air,
to meet the ball,
and fall on it
for the save.
I wave my happy ending wave and get up.
The game goes on.

Form Which word stands out in most of the lines on the top half of this page? Why do you think the poet draws attention to it?

BQ BIG Question
Why does the speaker need to call on her inner strength?

After You Read

Respond and Think Critically

1. Which words in "The Sidewalk Racer" describe the poem's speaker? [Identify]
2. In "The Sidewalk Racer," the speaker refers to "an asphalt sea." What two unlike things does this metaphor compare? How does the metaphor help readers visualize the action in the poem? [Interpret]
3. How is the speaker feeling at the beginning of "Alone in the Nets"? How do you know? [Infer]
4. How does the speaker's attitude in "Alone in the Nets" compare with the speaker's attitude in "The Sidewalk Racer"? [Compare]
5. **Literary Element** **Form** Is open form, or free verse, a good choice for poems about sports? Why? [Evaluate]
6. **BQ** **BIG Question** How can challenges, such as playing a difficult game or learning a difficult skill, bring out the best in people? [Conclude]

Spelling Link

Unstressed Vowels Think about the word *opposition* in "Alone in the Nets." Notice how the vowel sounds in the second syllable. This is an **unstressed vowel.** Dictionaries use the schwa symbol (ə) to indicate this. The unstressed pronunciation can also be spelled using other vowels. Think of a word related to *opposition* in which the vowel in the second syllable is stressed, such as the word *oppose*. When a vowel is stressed it is often spelled as it sounds. This can help you spell the related word with the unstressed vowel.

Unknown Spelling	Related Word	Correct Spelling
opp_sition	opp<u>o</u>se	opp<u>o</u>sition

Practice On a sheet of paper, make a three-column chart like the one above for the words *conf_dent, rel_tive,* and *res_dent.*

Writing

Write a Scene Write a scene that describes how you act and feel while playing a sport or game. Then turn your scene into a concrete poem. How might you arrange the words and lines?

TIP

Interpreting
Here are some tips to help you interpret a metaphor. Remember, a metaphor compares two seemingly unlike things.

- Reread the footnote and think about the qualities of asphalt.
- Think about the qualities of the sea. What words come to mind?
- Which qualities do asphalt and the sea have in common?
- How do these qualities relate to riding a skateboard?

Keep track of your ideas about the **BIG Question** in your unit Foldable.

Literature Online

Selection Resources
For Selection Quizzes, eFlashcards, and Reading-Writing Connection activities, go to glencoe.com and enter QuickPass code GL17527u5.

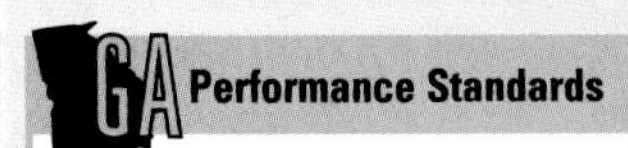

Vocabulary Workshop

Dictionary Skills

Connection to Literature

"'I can't go to school here. I don't speak Spanish.' It was my final argument, and it failed miserably because I was shouting my defiance in the language I claimed not to speak."

—Judith Ortiz Cofer, "Primary Lessons"

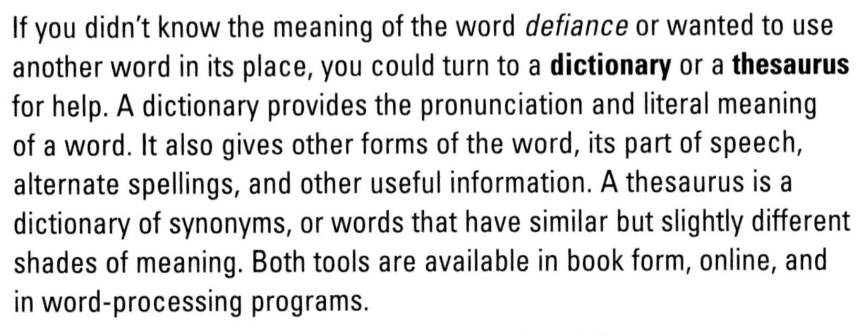

If you didn't know the meaning of the word *defiance* or wanted to use another word in its place, you could turn to a **dictionary** or a **thesaurus** for help. A dictionary provides the pronunciation and literal meaning of a word. It also gives other forms of the word, its part of speech, alternate spellings, and other useful information. A thesaurus is a dictionary of synonyms, or words that have similar but slightly different shades of meaning. Both tools are available in book form, online, and in word-processing programs.

Here are dictionary and thesaurus entries for *defiance.*

Word	Dictionary Entry	Thesaurus Entry
defiance	(di fī′əns) *n.* **1** bold or open resistance to authority or an opposing force. **2** challenge to meet in a fight or contest. **3** to bid defiance to. to defy. **4** in defiance of. in spite of.	*n.* resistance, opposition, disobedience, rebellion

TRY IT: Use the dictionary and thesaurus entries above to help you answer these questions.

1. Which word would best replace *defiance* in the following sentence? *Unhappy with the new rule, workers showed their defiance by walking off the job.*
2. What part of speech is the word *defiance*?
3. Explain the difference in meaning between *resistance* and *rebellion.* Think of each word's connotation, or its suggested or implied meaning.

GA Performance Standards

For page 625

ELA6R2d Understand and acquire new vocabulary. Use reference skills to determine pronunciations, meanings, alternate word choices, and parts of speech of words.

Tip

Vocabulary Terms Dictionary entries give the different meanings of a single word. Thesaurus entries list different words that mean the same or almost the same thing.

Test-Taking Tip When looking at dictionary entries, use the part-of-speech information to help you choose the appropriate meaning of the word.

LOG ON **Literature** Online

Vocabulary For more vocabulary practice, go to glencoe.com and enter QuickPass code GL17527u5.

Before You Read

Satchel Paige

Connect to the Biography

Think about a time when you faced difficulties in order to reach a goal.

Partner Talk With a partner, discuss the difficulties you faced. What kept you working toward your goal? What did you learn about yourself?

Build Background

Baseball, often called "the national pastime," is considered by many to be the national sport of the United States. The game may have come from an English game called rounders, which was played on a diamond-shaped field with four bases. In 1845 a group of amateur players in New York City put together rules for a similar game that became known as baseball.

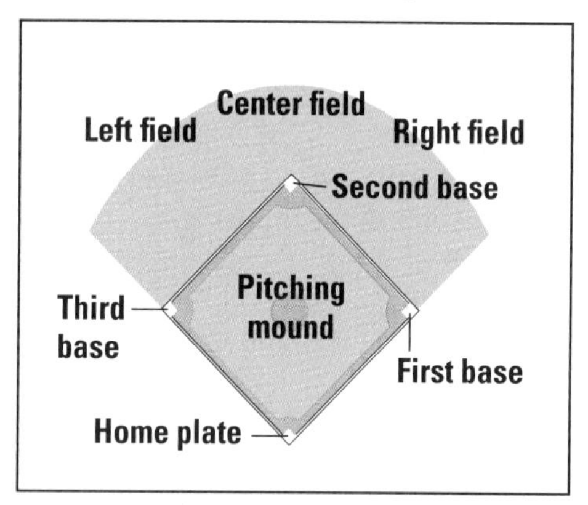

Vocabulary

appreciation (ə prē′ shē ā′ shən) *n.* high regard or gratitude (p. 628). *Sam cooked dinner to show his appreciation for Jody's hard work.*

eventually (i ven′ cho͞o ə lē) *adv.* in the end, finally (p. 628). *After two hours of rain, we eventually admitted that we weren't going to have a ball game.*

prospered (pros′ pərd) *v.* flourished, was successful (p. 630). *Annika's business prospered after she opened her new store.*

leisurely (lē′ zhər lē) *adj.* unhurried, relaxed; free from the demands of work (p. 633). *I love the leisurely days of summer vacation.*

opposing (ə pōz′ ing) *adj.* competing or struggling against (p. 633). *Jorge and I were on opposing sides of the debate.*

Meet Bill Littlefield

"People like to tell their stories to folks inclined to listen, and I'm one of those folks."

—Bill Littlefield

Radio Host, Sportswriter Bill Littlefield writes about sports and also hosts a sports talk show on public radio. His writing shows young readers why it is important to focus on goals and work hard to reach them. One of his books is about athletes who overcame obstacles such as discrimination, poverty, and physical disabilities to achieve greatness. Littlefield is also a professor.

Literary Works Littlefield writes sports essays and books. "Satchel Paige" appeared in the book *Champions: Stories of Ten Remarkable Athletes,* published in 1993.

Bill Littlefield was born in 1948.

Literature Online

Author Search For more about Bill Littlefield, go to glencoe.com and enter QuickPass code GL17527u5.

Set Purposes for Reading

BQ BIG Question

As you read, ask yourself, how does Satchel Paige's inner strength help him through times of great difficulty and injustice?

Literary Element Point of View

Point of view is the relationship of the narrator to the story. A story using **first-person point of view** is told by a character within the story. In a story with a **limited third-person point of view,** the narrator is outside the story. This point of view reveals the thoughts and feelings of only one character. In a story with an **omniscient point of view,** the narrator is also outside the story but can reveal the thoughts and feelings of many characters.

Paying attention to the point of view can help you understand how the narrator's perspective shapes the story.

As you read, ask yourself, who is telling the story?

Reading Skill Determine Main Idea and Supporting Details

When you **determine main idea and supporting details,** you find the most important idea the writer is trying to get across and the details that support it. Sometimes the author directly states the main idea. Sometimes you must figure it out from the details.

Determining the main idea and supporting details helps you understand what the author finds important. It also helps you decide whether or not you agree with the author.

To find the main idea and supporting details, look for

- a general statement about the subject, often stated at the beginning
- facts, examples, incidents, or quotations that illustrate and develop the main idea
- clues that help you figure out an unstated main idea

As you read, you may find it helpful to use a graphic organizer like the one below.

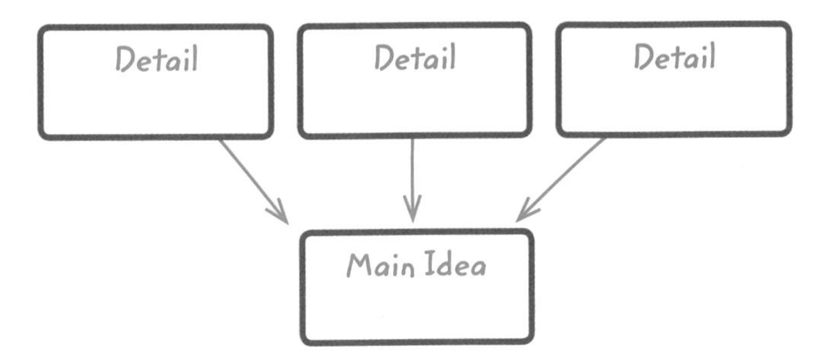

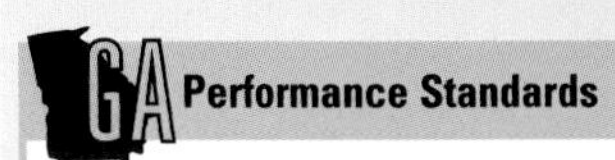

GA Performance Standards

For pages 626–637

ELA6R1d For informational texts, identify and analyze main ideas, supporting ideas, and supporting details.

TRY IT

Determine Main Idea and Supporting Details Basketball tryouts are coming up. Your friend seems distracted. She keeps mentioning professional basketball players. She is late to class because she is perfecting her free throw. What do you think your friend wants to do? What details support this idea?

Satchel Paige

Bill Littlefield

Late in the afternoon of July 9, 1948, Leroy "Satchel" Paige began the long walk from the bullpen to the mound at Cleveland's Municipal Stadium. He didn't hurry. He never hurried. As he said himself, he "kept the juices flowing by jangling gently" as he moved. The crowd roared its **appreciation.** This was the fellow they'd come to see.

When Satchel finally reached the mound, Cleveland manager Lou Boudreau took the ball from starting pitcher Bob Lemon, who would **eventually** be voted into the Hall of Fame but had tired that day, and gave it to Paige. Probably he said something like, "Shut 'em down, Satchel." Whatever he said, Paige had no doubt heard the words a thousand times. Though he was a rookie with the Indians that year, no pitcher in the history of baseball had ever been more thoroughly prepared for a job. He kicked at the rubber, looked in for the sign, and got set to throw. In a moment, twenty-odd years later than it should have happened, Satchel Paige would deliver his first pitch in the big leagues.

Determine Main Idea and Supporting Details What do you think will be the main idea of this selection?

Vocabulary

appreciation (ə prē′ shē ā′ shən) *n.* high regard or gratitude

eventually (i ven′ cho͞o ə lē) *adv.* in the end, finally

The tall, skinny kid named Leroy Paige became Satchel Paige one day at the railroad station in Mobile, Alabama. He was carrying bags for the folks getting on and off the trains, earning all the nickels and dimes he could to help feed his ten brothers and sisters. Eventually it occurred to him that if he slung a pole across his narrow shoulders and hung the bags, or **satchels,** on the ends of the pole, he could carry for more people at once and collect more nickels and dimes. It worked, but it looked a little funny. "You look like some kind of ol' satchel tree," one of his friends told him, and the nickname stuck.

Visual Vocabulary

Satchels are a type of suitcase.

Even in those days, before he was a teenager, Satchel Paige could throw hard and accurately. Years later, Paige swore that when his mother would send him out into the yard to get a chicken for dinner, he would brain the bird[1] with a rock. "I used to kill *flying* birds with rocks, too," he said. "Most people need shotguns to do what I did with rocks."

Determine Main Idea and Supporting Details Why do you think the author included this detail?

It was not a talent that would go unnoticed for long. He was pitching for the semipro[2] Mobile Tigers before he was eighteen . . . or maybe before he was sixteen, or before he was twelve. There is some confusion about exactly when Satchel Paige was born, and Satchel never did much to clarify the matter. But there never has been any confusion about whether he could pitch. His first steady job in baseball was with the Chattanooga Black Lookouts. He was paid fifty dollars a month. In the seasons that followed he would also pitch for the Birmingham Black Barons, the Nashville Elite Giants, the Baltimore Black Sox, the Pittsburgh Crawfords, and the Kansas City Monarchs, among other teams.

Point of View What is the point of view? How do you know?

Satchel Paige and his teammates on the Pittsburgh Crawfords pose as the champions of the Negro National League in 1935.

1 To ***brain the bird*** means "to hit it in the head."

2 The prefix *semi-* means "partly" or "half." A member of a ***semipro*** team is paid to play part-time and may have another, full-time job. A professional player receives a full-time salary.

If those names are not as familiar sounding as those of the New York Yankees, the Los Angeles Dodgers, or the Boston Red Sox, it's because they were all clubs in the Negro leagues, not the major leagues. Today the presence of black baseball players in the big leagues is taken for granted. Hank Aaron is the greatest of the home run hitters,[3] and Rickey Henderson has stolen more bases than any other big leaguer. But before 1947, neither of them would have had the opportunity to do what they have done. Until Brooklyn Dodger general manager Branch Rickey signed Jackie Robinson, black players had no choice but to play for one of the all-black teams, and making that choice, they faced hardships no major-leaguer today could imagine.

Players in the Negro leagues crowded into broken-down cars and bumped over rutted roads to makeshift[4] ball fields with lights so bad that every pitch was a potential weapon. Then they drove all night for an afternoon game three hundred miles away. On good days they played before big, appreciative crowds in parks they'd rented from the major league teams in Chicago, New York, or Pittsburgh. On bad days they learned that the team they were playing for was too broke to finish the season, and they would have to look for a healthier team that could use them, or else find a factory job.

It took talent, hard work, and a sense of humor to survive in the Negro leagues, and Satchel Paige had a lot of all three. But he didn't just survive. He **prospered**.

The first successful Negro Baseball league was started in 1920. The Negro leagues played eleven World Series and created their own All-Star game that became the biggest black sports attraction in the country. This photograph shows players of the Negro Leagues.

Determine Main Idea and Supporting Details What main idea does this detail support?

BQ BIG Question

How can a sense of humor be a source of strength?

---

3 In 2007 Barry Bonds of the San Francisco Giants became the new home-run king with a total of 756 home runs.

4 A road that has been well worn by wheels or travel is ***rutted. Makeshift*** means "a temporary substitute."

Vocabulary

prospered (pros′ pərd) *v.* flourished, was successful

Everybody knows about the fastball, the curve, and the slider. But Satchel threw a "bee" ball, which, he said, "would always *be* where I wanted it to *be*." He featured a trouble ball, which, of course, gave the hitters a lot of trouble. Even the few who could see it couldn't hit it. Sometimes he'd come at them with his hesitation pitch, a delivery so mysterious that the man at the plate would sometimes swing before the ball left Satchel's hand.

Nor was pitching his sole triumph. Early in his career Satchel Paige began building a reputation as a storyteller, a spinner of tall tales as well as shutouts. He particularly liked to recall an occasion upon which he was asked to come on in relief of a pitcher who'd left men on first and third with nobody out. "It was a tight situation," Satchel would say.

We only had a one-run lead, and that was looking mighty slim. But I had an idea. When I left the bench, I stuck a baseball in my pocket, so when the manager gave me the game ball on the mound, I had two. I went into my stretch just like usual. Then I threw one ball to first and the other to third. It was a good pick-off move, you see, and it fooled the batter, too. He swung, even though there was no ball to swing at. Those boys at first and third were both out, of course, and the umpire[5] *called strike three on the batter, so that was it for the inning. It's always good to save your strength when you can.*

Point of View From what point of view is this paragraph told? How do you know?

Major-leaguers today make enough money so that they don't have to work over the winter, but it hasn't always been so. Big-leaguers and Negro-leaguers alike used to make extra money after their regular seasons ended by putting together makeshift teams and playing each other wherever they could draw a paying crowd. This practice was called barnstorming, and Satchel Paige was the world champion at it. For thirty years, from 1929 to 1958, he played baseball summer and winter. When it was too cold to play in the Negro league cities, he played in Cuba, Mexico, and the Dominican Republic. In Venezuela he battled a boa constrictor in the outfield, or so he said, and

Determine Main Idea and Supporting Details Note the contrast in this statement. What do you think will be the main idea of this paragraph?

5 An ***umpire*** is the official in a baseball game. The umpire makes sure the players follow the rules.

in Ciudad Trujillo[6] he dodged the machine-gun fire of fans who'd bet on the losing team.

Throughout the early years of these adventures, the years of Satchel's prime, he often barnstormed against the best white ballplayers of his day. St. Louis Cardinal great Dizzy Dean once told him, "You're a better pitcher than I ever hope to be." Paige beat Bob Feller and struck out Babe Ruth. And when Joe DiMaggio, considered by some the most multi-talented ballplayer ever, beat out an infield hit against Paige in 1936, DiMaggio turned to his teammates and said, "Now I know I can make it with the Yankees. I finally got a hit off of ol' Satch."

Everywhere these confrontations took place, Satchel Paige would hear the same thing: "If only you were white, you'd be a star in the big leagues." The fault, of course, was not with Satchel. The fault and the shame were with major league baseball, which stubbornly, stupidly clung to the same prejudice that characterized many institutions in the United States besides baseball. Prejudice has not yet disappeared from the game. Black players are far less likely than their white counterparts[7] to be hired as managers or general managers. But today's black players can thank Robinson, Paige, and a handful of other pioneers for the opportunities they enjoy.

Point of View How does the narrator feel about the way Satchel Paige was treated?

Though the color line prevented Satchel Paige from pitching in the company his talent and hard work should have earned for him, he was not bitter or defeated. Ignorant white fans would sometimes taunt him, but he kept their insults in perspective. "Some of them would call you names," he said of his early years on the road, "but most of them would cheer you." Years later he worked to shrug off the pain caused by the restaurants that would not serve him, the hotels that would not rent him a room, the fans who would roar for his bee ball but would not acknowledge him on the street the next day. "Fans all holler the same at a ball game," he would say, as if the

BQ BIG Question

How does this statement demonstrate Satchel Paige's inner strength?

---

6 ***Ciudad Trujillo*** (sē′ oo däd′ troo hē′ yō) is the Spanish name for a city in northwestern Venezuela.

7 Here, ***counterparts*** refers to people who hold similar positions.

racists[8] and the racist system had never touched him at all.

When he finally got the chance to become the first black pitcher in the American League at age forty-two (or forty-six, or forty-eight), he made the most of it. On that first day in Cleveland, Satchel Paige did the job he'd never doubted he could do. First he smiled for all the photographers. Then he told the butterflies in his stomach to leave off their flapping around. Then he shut down the St. Louis Browns for two innings before being lifted for a pinch hitter.

Determine Main Idea and Supporting Details What is the most important idea in this paragraph?

And still there were doubters. "Sure," they said to each other the next day when they read the sports section. "The old man could work two innings against the Browns. Who couldn't?"

But Satchel Paige fooled 'em, as he'd been fooling hitters for twenty-five years and more. He won a game in relief six days later, his first major league win. Then on August 3 he started a game against the Washington Senators before 72,000 people. Paige went seven innings and won. In his next two starts he threw shutouts against the Chicago White Sox, and through the waning[9] months of that summer, his only complaint was that he was "a little tired from underwork." The routine on the major league level must have been pretty **leisurely** for a fellow who'd previously pitched four or five times a week.

Satchel Paige finished the 1948 season with six wins and only one loss. He'd allowed the **opposing** teams an average of

Satchel Paige played in his first Major League game on July 9, 1948, at age 42.

8 ***Racists*** believe that differences among races make their own race better than others.

9 Here, ***waning*** means "drawing to a close." In other words, the end of the summer was near.

Vocabulary

leisurely (lē′ zhər lē) *adj.* unhurried, relaxed; free from the demands of work

opposing (ə pōz′ ing) *adj.* competing or struggling against just over two runs a game. Paige was named Rookie of the Year, an honor he might well have achieved twenty years earlier if he'd had the chance. The sports-writers of the day agreed that without Satchel's contribution, the Indians, who won the pennant, would have finished second at best. Many of the writers were dismayed when Satchel appeared for only two-thirds of an inning in the World Series that fall. Paige, too, was disappointed that the manager hadn't chosen to use him more, but he was calm in the face of what others might have considered an insult. The writers told him, "You sure take things good." Satchel smiled and said, "Ain't no other way to take them."

Point of View What does the narrator want you to remember?

Satchel Paige outlasted the rule that said he couldn't play in the big leagues because he was black. Then he made fools of the people who said he couldn't get major league hitters out because he was too old. But his big league numbers over several years—twenty-eight wins and thirty-two saves—don't begin to tell the story of Paige's unparalleled[10] career. Playing for teams that no longer exist in leagues that came and went with the seasons, Satchel Paige pitched in some 2,500 baseball games. Nobody has ever pitched in more. And he had such fun at it. Sometimes he'd accept offers to pitch in two cities on the same day. He'd strike out the side for three innings in one game, then fold his long legs into his car and race down the road toward the next ballpark. If the police could catch him, they would stop him for speeding. But when they recognized him, as often as not they'd escort him to the second game with sirens howling, well aware that there might be a riot in the park if Satchel Paige didn't show up as advertised. Once he'd arrived, he'd instruct his infielders and outfielders to sit down for an inning, then he'd strike out the side again.

Point of View Why don't the numbers tell the whole story? Why is it important that a biographer is telling the story?

For his talent, his energy, and his showmanship, Satchel Paige was the most famous of the Negro league players, but when he got some measure of recognition in the majors, he urged the writers to remember that there had been lots of other great ballplayers in those Negro league

10 If something is ***unparalleled,*** nothing is equal to it or better than it.

games. He named them, and he told their stories. He made their exploits[11] alive and real for generations of fans who'd never have known.

In 1971, the Baseball Hall of Fame in Cooperstown, New York, inducted[12] Satchel Paige. The action was part of the Hall's attempt to remedy baseball's shame, the color line. The idea was to honor Paige and some of the other great Negro league players like Josh Gibson and Cool Papa Bell, however late that honor might come. Satchel Paige could have rejected that gesture. He could have told the baseball establishment that what it was doing was too little, too late. But when the time came for Satchel Paige to speak to the crowd gathered in front of the Hall of Fame to celebrate his triumphs, he told the people, "I am the proudest man on the face of the earth today."

BQ BIG Question
From what you know of Satchel Paige's character, will he reject the gesture? How do you know?

Satchel Paige, whose autobiography was entitled *Maybe I'll Pitch Forever,* died in Kansas City in 1982. He left behind a legend as large as that of anyone who ever played the game, as well as a long list of achievements celebrated in story and song—and in at least one fine poem, by Samuel Allen:

Determine Main Idea and Supporting Details Has the biographer proved this point? If so, what details support it?

To Satch
Sometimes I feel like I will *never* stop
Just go on forever
Till one fine mornin'
I'm gonna reach up and grab me a
 handfulla stars
Swing out my long lean leg
And whip three hot strikes burnin'
 down the heavens
And look over at God and say
How about that!

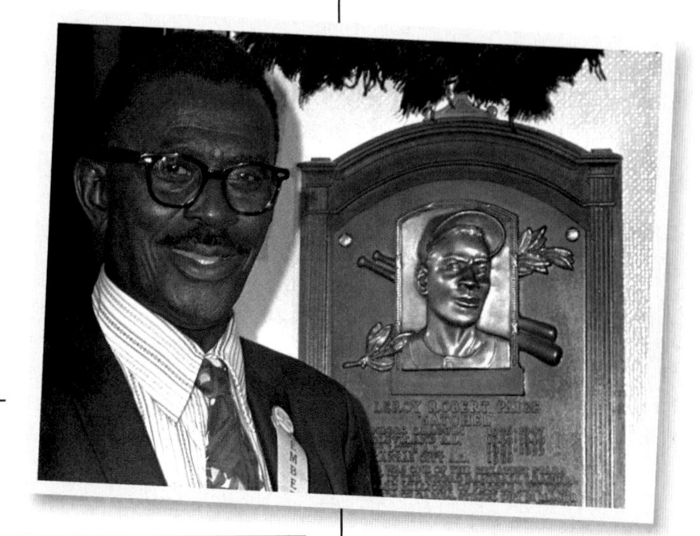

Satchel Paige was the first Negro league star elected to the National Baseball Hall of Fame.

11 ***Exploits*** are brave acts or deeds.

12 To be ***inducted*** is to be admitted or brought into a group. The ***Baseball Hall of Fame*** honors great players, managers, and broadcasters.

After You Read

Respond and Think Critically

1. Why wasn't Satchel Paige allowed to play in the major leagues? **[Recall]**
2. How much did some of the players in the Negro leagues earn per month? What else did they do to make a living? **[Summarize]**
3. Why were the Negro leagues created? **[Infer]**
4. If Satchel Paige were a young baseball player today, how would his life be different? **[Compare]**
5. What kind of person do you think Satchel Paige was? How can you tell? Support your answer with details from the selection. **[Evaluate]**
6. **BQ** **BIG Question** What brought out the best in Satchel Paige? Why do you think he had such inner strength? What can people today learn from his example? **[Conclude]**

TIP

Summarizing
Remember, when you **summarize,** you retell the main ideas or events.

- Skim for main events.
- Retell events in order.
- Use your own words.

FOLDABLES
Study Organizer
Keep track of your ideas about the **BIG Question** in your unit Foldable.

Sport
Monday, July 1
TIME
Message
Just 10 years ago, Duom Deng, David Ayiik, and James Biar were refugees too. During Sudan's civil war, the three boys had seen their parents killed and their villages destroyed. Then they and thousands of other orphaned children walked 1,000 miles

Examine Media

The Language of the Game

Look at this example of newspaper reporting from 1870. Then look at a current newspaper article about a baseball game and compare the two.

> **Base-Ball Match at Elizabeth, N.J.—The Atlantics Give the Resolutes a Lesson—Score, 19 to 0.**
>
> The Atlantic Club of Brooklyn yesterday visited Elizabeth, N.J., to play the Resolute Club of that village, and though the latter Club had recently been strengthened by additions from the Irvington Club, they found the Atlantic nine too strong even to obtain from them a solitary run in a full game of nine innings. This is the most noteworthy triumph the Atlantics have ever achieved, for they have never beaten any club without allowing them to get a run.
>
> *from* The New York Times
> May 14, 1870

On Your Own Write answers to these questions on a separate sheet of paper.

1. What is the same about the two articles?
2. Which has longer sentences and words? Which is easier to read and understand?
3. What has changed about the way we talk about teams? What is the same?

Literary Element Point of View

1. What is the main point of view in this selection? How do you know?
2. Often biographers, looking back at history, write about events that their subjects could not have known at the time. Give two examples from this biography.
3. Sometimes the biographer uses Satchel Paige's own words. How can you tell? How is Paige's voice different from the omniscient narrator's voice?

Review: Theme

As you learned on page 75, the **theme** is the main message that an author wants to convey. The author usually expresses the theme as a general statement.

Standards Practice GA ELA6R1d

4. Which statement best expresses Satchel Paige's attitude toward prejudice?
   - A. If you know your own worth, no one can take it away from you.
   - B. The best defense is a good offense.
   - C. Bullies should be confronted.
   - D. Unjust systems will always be around.

Reading Skill Determine Main Idea and Supporting Details

Standards Practice GA ELA6R1d

5. Read this sentence from the passage.

   Hank Aaron is the greatest of the home run hitters, and Rickey Henderson has stolen more bases than any other big leaguer.

   This sentence supports the main idea that
   - A. African American players are accepted in the major leagues today.
   - B. racial discrimination is still present in baseball.
   - C. some baseball players still prefer to play in the Negro leagues.
   - D. players in the Negro leagues were not paid as much as they deserved.

Vocabulary Practice

Synonyms are words that have the same or nearly the same meaning. **Antonyms** are words that have opposite meanings. Identify whether the paired words in each set are synonyms or antonyms. Then write a sentence using the first word of each pair or draw or find a picture that represents the word.

appreciation and ungratefulness

eventually and immediately

prospered and failed

leisurely and swiftly

opposing and competing

Example: appreciation and ungratefulness = antonyms

Sentence: Some students want to start a teacher-appreciation day.

Academic Vocabulary

Regulations against African American baseball players kept Satchel Paige out of the major leagues for years. To become more familiar with the word *regulations,* fill out a graphic organizer like the one below.

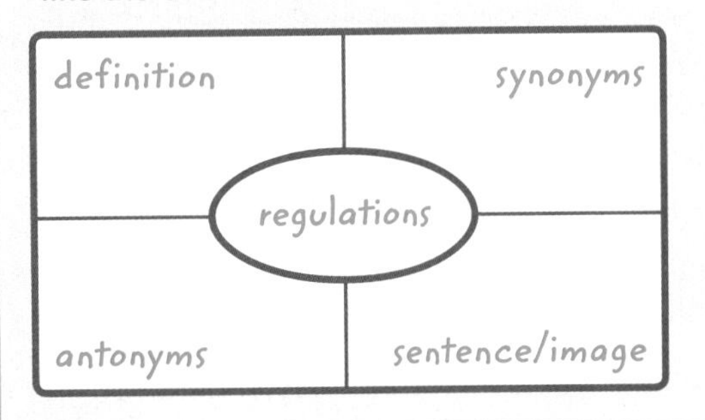

Selection Resources For Selection Quizzes, eFlashcards, and Reading-Writing Connection activities, go to glencoe.com and enter QuickPass code GL17527u5.

Respond Through Writing

Biographical Narrative

Apply Point of View "Satchel Paige" is a **biographical narrative**, which is a biography that reads like a story. It has an **omniscient point of view.** Now it's your turn to write a biographical narrative. Think about a famous athlete or someone with inner strength whom you admire. Write a short biographical narrative describing that person's life and explaining why the person's accomplishments matter.

Understand the Task Recall that a limited third-person narrator or an omniscient narrator is not a character within the story. The narrator uses the pronouns *he*, *she*, and *they*, not *I* and *we*.

Prewrite You may need to do some research before you write. If you are writing about someone you know, interview your subject. Think about what you want to include in your biography. You may want to arrange your research on a time line like the one below.

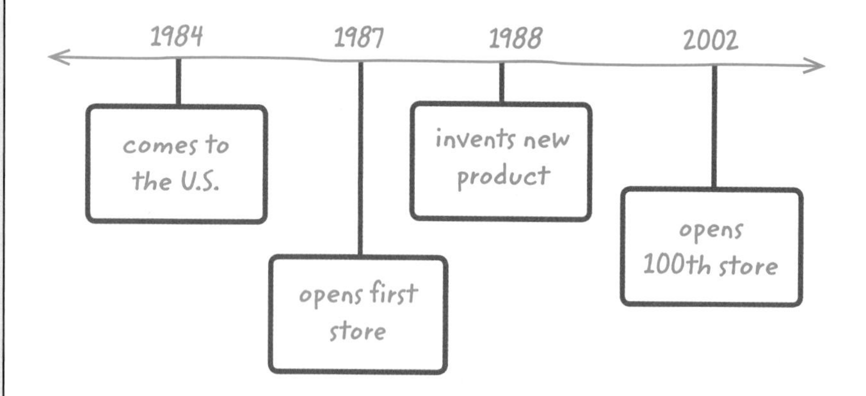

Draft Decide on your point of view. Write your narrative in an engaging style to interest the reader. Develop and organize all five parts of a plot. Write a thesis statement. This sentence frame might help you:

You might not have heard of ______, but [he or she] made a big difference in the life of ______.

Revise Read your draft to determine whether the information follows a logical order. Is your main idea clear and supported? Have you developed the plot, setting, and characters with sensory details? Have you used narrative devices, such as dialogue, to add interest?

Edit and Proofread Proofread your paper, correcting any errors in spelling, grammar, and punctuation. Review the Word Bank in the side column for information on time-order adverbs and phrases.

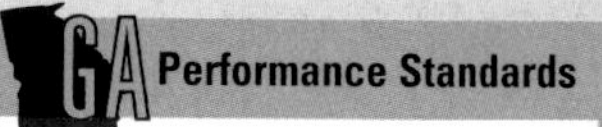

GA Performance Standards

For page 638

ELA6W2a Demonstrate competence in a variety of genres. Produce a narrative that engages readers by establishing and developing a plot, setting, and point of view that are appropriate to the story.

Word Bank

Biographies describe events in the past. Almost all your verbs will be in the past tense. So how can you help readers know what happened when? Following are some useful **time-order adverbs** you might want to include in your biographical narrative.

first

then

next

later

finally

Adverb phrases such as *in 1979, at the same time,* and *later that month* can also help make the order of events clear.

Part 2

Putting Others First

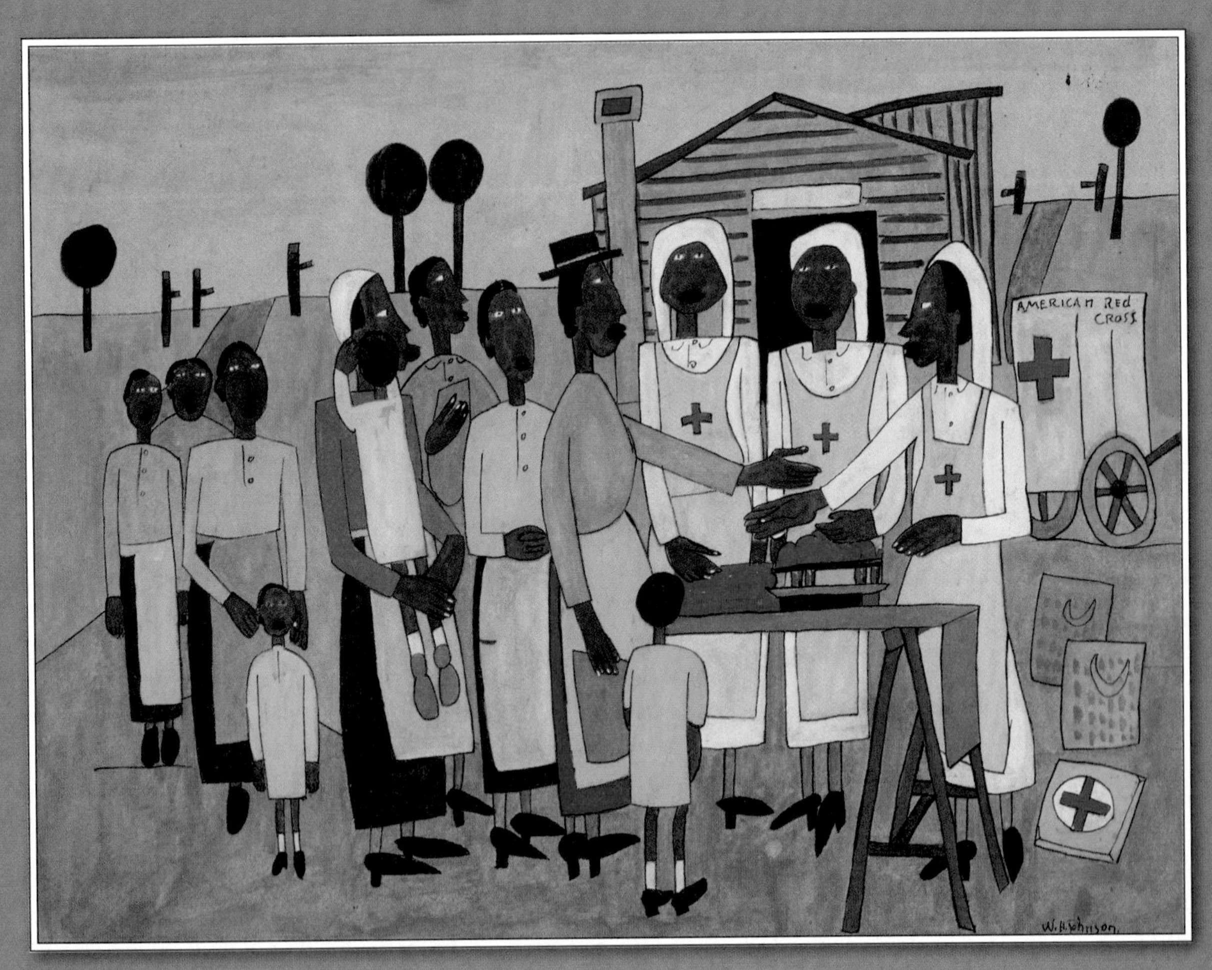

Red Cross Nurses Handing Out Wool for Knitting, c. 1942. William H. Johnson. Smithsonian American Art Museum, Washington, DC. © ARS, NY.

BQ BIG Question What Brings Out the Best in You?

The painting *Red Cross Nurses Handing Out Wool for Knitting* by William H. Johnson honors World War II volunteers. The Red Cross nurses and community workers that are pictured here are going to provide warm clothes for soldiers. How are these people putting other people's needs before their own? What would you like to do that shows you can put others first?

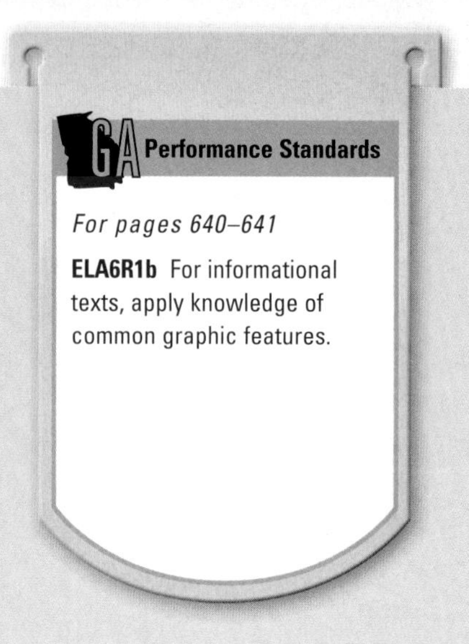

GA Performance Standards
For pages 640–641
ELA6R1b For informational texts, apply knowledge of common graphic features.

Gentleman of the POOL

Mike Blake/Reuters/NewsCom

OLYMPIC WINNER Michael Phelps is all smiles as he shows off one of the six gold medals he won at the 2004 Olympic Games in Athens, Greece.

Michael Phelps didn't beat the Olympic gold medal record at the 2004 Games. But the young swimmer left no doubt. He is a winner in—and out of—the pool.

By ALICE PARK

During the 2004 Olympics in Athens, Greece, the world expected record-breaking success from swimmer Michael Phelps. The 19-year-old American was favored to win the most gold medals ever at a single Olympics. To reach that goal, Phelps would have needed to win 8 gold medals. That number would beat the record held by U.S. swimmer Mark Spitz, who had won 7 gold medals at the 1972 Olympics in Munich, Germany.

Phelps's swimming meets were the most popular events of the first week of the Games. Fans streamed into the Olympic Aquatic Centre. TV ratings hit the roof.[1] Phelps chose to swim in the 200-meter freestyle

1 If the television ratings ***hit the roof,*** a lot of people watched the Olympics on TV.

Set a Purpose for Reading

Read to find out how a top athlete put the needs of others before his own needs.

Preview the Article

1. What does the **title** suggest about Michael Phelps?
2. Read the **deck,** or the text below the title. What details does it provide?

Reading Strategy

Question

Asking **questions** can help you understand what you read. As you read, write your questions in a chart like the one below. Add answers when you finish.

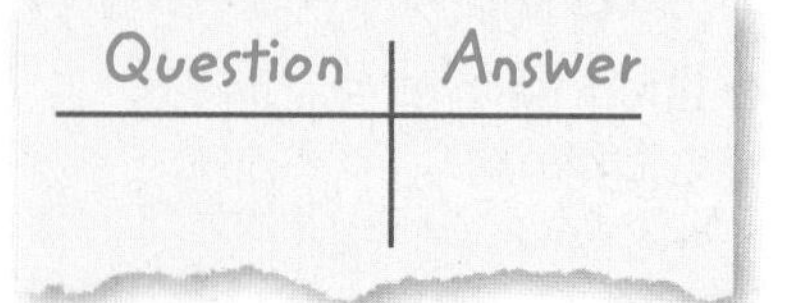

on day three. The teenage swimmer knew he was not favored to win. But that didn't keep him from reaching for a personal goal.

Instead of giving in to doubt and fear, Phelps raced stroke for stroke against Olympic medal winners Ian Thorpe of Australia and Pieter van den Hoogenband of the Netherlands. Phelps came in third place, winning a bronze medal. That third-place win ended the race for the record 8 gold medals that the world had been watching for.

For Phelps, there was more to the Olympics than earning gold medals. The 200-meter bronze medal was proof that he could compete with the world's best—and enjoy it. "Racing the two greatest freestylers of all time in an Olympic final—it's fun," Phelps said after the race. "I had fun out there."

Phelps had gone to Athens as a star attraction. While there, he also became known as a sportsman. After the 200-meter freestyle, the teenage swimmer continued to work toward his goals. But he also cared about the ambitions[2] and feelings of his teammates. Phelps wanted to share the fun of the Games. So he gave up his spot in a medley relay[3] to teammate Ian Crocker. Earlier in the week, Crocker had cost the U.S. team the gold medal in another event. "He wasn't feeling too well [then], and I was willing to give him a chance to step up," says Phelps. "It was the right thing to do."

By the end of the Games in Athens, Phelps had won 8 medals (6 gold medals and 2 bronze). That matched the record for the most medals earned at an Olympics. Building on Phelps's powerful swimming, the U.S. team had achieved its own victory. It swam to a world-record win in the medley relay. Phelps's winning effort had paid off for everyone. The young swimmer was an all-around winner.

---

2 ***Ambitions*** are strong desires to succeed or to achieve something.

3 A ***medley relay*** is a swimming race in which each of the four team members swims his or her part using a different kind of stroke.

Respond and Think Critically

1. Summarize the main ideas in this article. For help on writing a summary, see page 170. **[Summarize]**
2. **Text to Self** What does it mean to put others first? Describe a time when you or someone you know helped another person in this way. **[Connect]**
3. Michael Phelps won a bronze medal. While some might see third place as a failure, why did Phelps say, "I had fun out there"? **[Interpret]**
4. Why might someone who wants to win give this opportunity to a teammate? **[Infer]**
5. **Reading Strategy Question** Look back at the questions and answers you recorded as you read. How did the answers to your questions help you better understand the article?
6. **BQ BIG Question** How did Michael Phelps's participation in the Olympic games in Athens bring out the best in him? How did putting others first help him?

Before You Read

Eleanor Roosevelt

Connect to the Biography

Think of a few ways in which volunteers make a difference in the world. How might you volunteer your time to help people in need?

Partner Talk With a partner, discuss ideas about places in your community where you might be able to volunteer. How could you get involved with helping people in need?

Build Background

Eleanor Roosevelt was a pioneer in many areas. She was the first president's wife to

- speak in front of a national convention,
- write a national newspaper column,
- become a radio commentator, and
- hold regular news conferences.

When Eleanor Roosevelt's husband, President Franklin D. Roosevelt, was paralyzed by polio, she traveled around the United States to act as his eyes and ears and to speak for him.

Vocabulary

drawbacks (drô′ baks′) *n.* shortcomings; disadvantages (p. 647). *Traveling by bicycle is cheap, but it has its drawbacks.*

paralyzed (par′ ə līzd′) *adj.* affected with the loss of motion or sensation in a muscle due to disease of or injury to the nervous system (p. 648). *Polio paralyzed and killed thousands of people every year before there was a vaccine for it.*

slums (slumz) *n.* heavily populated city areas identified by poverty, run-down housing, and wretched living conditions (p. 649). *Slums are "home" to the people who live there.*

depression (di presh′ ən) *n.* a period marked by severely decreasing business activity, rising unemployment, and falling wages (p. 649). *In the United States, the period called the Great Depression lasted from 1929 to 1939.*

effective (i fek′ tiv) *adj.* capable of producing an intended result (p. 653). *The plan was very effective.*

Meet William Jay Jacobs

"America to me is more than just a place of residence. It is a passion."

—William Jay Jacobs

A Passion for History William Jay Jacobs got his passion for American history from his parents, who were immigrants eager to make new lives in the United States. His father came from Hungary, and his mother came from Austria. Jacobs has taught history and education and has written dozens of biographies for young people.

Literary Works Jacobs has written biographies of many famous people, including baseball players, explorers, and presidents.

William Jay Jacobs was born in 1933.

LOG ON Literature Online

Author Search For more about William Jay Jacobs, go to glencoe.com and enter QuickPass code GL17527u5.

Set Purposes for Reading

BQ BIG Question

As you read, ask yourself, how did Eleanor Roosevelt use the advantages and opportunities in her life to help others?

Literary Element Text Features

Some texts include **graphics**—photographs, diagrams, drawings, charts, maps, graphs, and time lines. Graphics present information in a way that makes ideas easy to understand at a glance. Graphics usually have captions that explain what is being shown. Like many biographies and magazine articles, this biography includes a **time line**—a line on which important events and their dates are marked in chronological, or time, order.

Good graphics and good writing go hand in hand to help you understand exactly what an author is trying to say.

As you read, ask yourself, how do the time line and graphics help me understand who Eleanor Roosevelt was and what she accomplished?

Reading Strategy Summarize

When you **summarize,** you briefly retell a selection in your own words. A good summary includes only the selection's main ideas and important details. Main ideas are the major points that a writer or speaker wants you to remember. Important details explain more about the main ideas.

Because it requires that you learn to separate main ideas from details, summarizing a selection helps you understand and remember it clearly.

When you summarize, you should

- create a short version of the original passage using your own words
- present ideas in chronological order, or the order in which they happened
- state only main ideas and important details
- include answers to the questions *Who? What? When? Where? Why?* and *How?*

To help summarize this selection, use a chart like the one below to note important events in Eleanor Roosevelt's life.

Event	When It Happened	Why It Is Important
Within 18 months, Eleanor's mother, her brother, and her father died.	Eleanor was eight.	Her parents' death led to her quiet, lonely childhood.

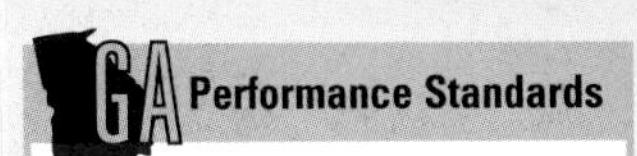

GA Performance Standards

For pages 642–657

ELA6R1b For informational texts, apply knowledge of common graphic features.

ELA6RC2f Recognize and use the features of disciplinary texts.

TRY IT

Summarize Think of an interesting story that you heard recently. You may have heard it from a friend or on the news. Retell the story to another friend, but leave out all of the minor details. Tell only the most important parts of the story.

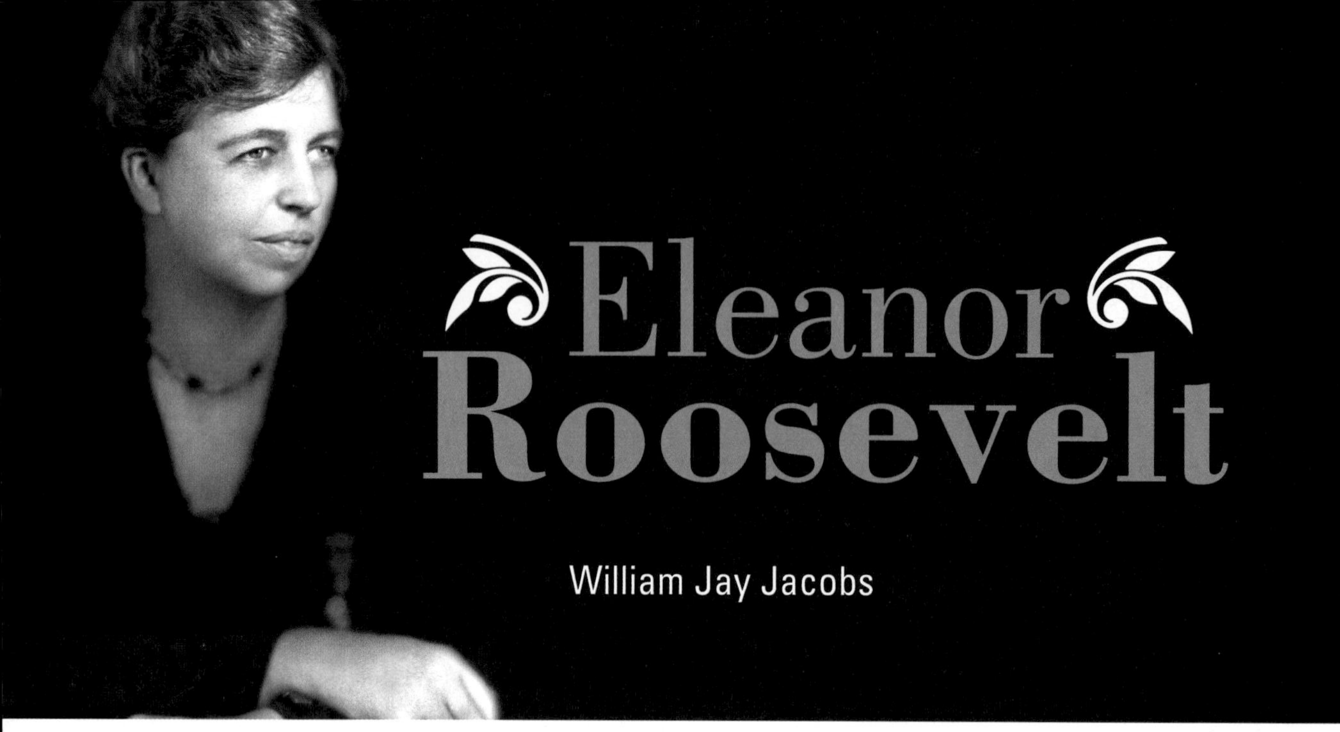

Eleanor Roosevelt

William Jay Jacobs

Eleanor Roosevelt was the wife of President Franklin Delano Roosevelt. But Eleanor was much more than just a president's wife, an echo of her husband's career.

Sad and lonely as a child, Eleanor was called "Granny" by her mother because of her seriousness. People teased her about her looks and called her the "ugly duckling."...

Yet despite all of the disappointments, the bitterness, the misery she experienced, Eleanor Roosevelt refused to give up. Instead she turned her unhappiness and pain to strength. She devoted her life to helping others. Today she is remembered as one of America's greatest women.

BQ BIG Question
What do you think made Eleanor Roosevelt sensitive to the needs of others?

Almost from the day of her birth, October 11, 1884, people noticed that she was an unattractive child. As she grew older, she could not help but notice her mother's extraordinary beauty, as well as the beauty of her aunts and cousins. Eleanor was plain looking, ordinary, even, as some called her, homely. For a time she had to wear a bulky brace on her back to straighten her crooked spine.

When Eleanor was born, her parents had wanted a boy. They were scarcely able to hide their disappointment. Later, with the arrival of two boys, Elliott and Hall, Eleanor watched her mother hold the boys on her lap and lovingly stroke their hair, while for Eleanor there seemed only coolness, distance.

Summarize Briefly state what made Eleanor's childhood so difficult.

Feeling unwanted, Eleanor became shy and withdrawn. She also developed many fears. She was afraid of the dark, afraid of animals, afraid of other children, afraid of being scolded, afraid of strangers, afraid that people would not like her. She was a frightened, lonely little girl.

Text Features What does the photograph of Eleanor as a young girl suggest about her?

Eleanor with her father, Elliott Roosevelt. April 30, 1889.

The one joy in the early years of her life was her father, who always seemed to care for her, love her. He used to dance with her, to pick her up and throw her into the air while she laughed and laughed. He called her "little golden hair" or "darling little Nell."

When Eleanor was eight, her mother, the beautiful Anna, died. Afterward her brother Elliott suddenly caught diphtheria[1] and he, too, died. Eleanor and her baby brother, Hall, were taken to live with their grandmother in Manhattan.[2]

A few months later another tragedy struck. Elliott Roosevelt, Eleanor's father, also died. Within eighteen months Eleanor had lost her mother, a brother, and her dear father.

Few things in life came easily for Eleanor, but the first few years after her father's death proved exceptionally hard. Grandmother Hall's dark and gloomy townhouse had no place for children to play. The family ate meals in silence. Every morning Eleanor and Hall were expected to take cold baths for their health. Eleanor had to work at better posture by walking with her arms behind her back, clamped over a walking stick.

Summarize Briefly restate the events that made it necessary for Eleanor to be in her grandmother's care.

Instead of making new friends, Eleanor often sat alone in her room and read. For many months after her father's death she pretended that he was still alive. She made him the hero of stories she wrote for school. Sometimes, alone and unhappy, she just cried.

1 ***Diphtheria*** is a disease that is caused by bacteria that are easily spread from one person to another. It is identified by fever, the development of a leatherlike tissue that can block the throat, and the body's production of a poison that can harm the heart muscle.

2 ***Manhattan*** is the island that is the financial, business, and cultural center of New York City.

Eleanor as a girl with her horse. She described herself at this age in her autobiography, *This Is My Story:* "I was tall, very thin, and very shy."

Text Features How does the caption support the photo?

Just before Eleanor turned fifteen, Grandmother Hall decided to send her to boarding school in England. The school she chose was Allenswood, a private academy[3] for girls located on the outskirts of London.

It was at Allenswood that Eleanor, still thinking of herself as an "ugly duckling," first dared to believe that one day she might be able to become a swan.

At Allenswood she worked to toughen herself physically. Every day she did exercises in the morning and took a cold shower. Although she did not like competitive team sports, as a matter of self-discipline she tried out for field hockey. Not only did she make the team but, because she played so hard, also won the respect of her teammates.

Eleanor was growing up, and the joy of young womanhood had begun to transform her personality.

In 1902, nearly eighteen years old, she left Allenswood, not returning for her fourth year there. Grandmother Hall insisted that, instead, she must be introduced to society as a debutante—to go to dances and parties and begin to take her place in the social world with other wealthy young women.

BQ BIG Question

How did getting involved in exercise and sports at Allenswood change Eleanor for the better?

3 An ***academy*** is a private school for education after grade school.

Eleanor, as always, did as she was told. She went to all of the parties and dances. But she also began working with poor children at the Rivington Street Settlement House[4] on New York's Lower East Side. She taught the girls gymnastic exercises. She took children to museums and to musical performances. She tried to get the parents interested in politics in order to get better schools and cleaner, safer streets.

Summarize Summarize this paragraph about Eleanor's life as a debutante.

Meanwhile Eleanor's life reached a turning point. She fell in love! The young man was her fifth cousin, Franklin Delano Roosevelt.

Eleanor and Franklin had known each other since childhood. Shortly after her return from Allenswood, they had met by chance on a train. They talked and almost at once realized how much they liked each other.

For a time they met secretly. Then they attended parties together. Franklin—tall, strong, handsome—saw her as a person he could trust. He knew that she would not try to dominate him.

On March 17, 1905, Eleanor and Franklin were married. In May 1906 the couple's first child was born. During the next nine years Eleanor gave birth to five more babies, one of whom died in infancy. Still timid, shy, afraid of making mistakes, she found herself so busy that there was little time to think of her own **drawbacks**.

Franklin and Eleanor Roosevelt with their children, Anna, James, Elliott, Franklin Jr., and John.

Text Features What does the photograph of the Roosevelts and their children emphasize about Eleanor?

4 In the late 1800s, ***settlement house*** was the name given to a city neighborhood institution with a staff of social workers who provided education, recreation, food, and other services for new area residents, usually immigrants.

Vocabulary

drawbacks (drô′baks′) *n.* shortcomings; disadvantages

Meanwhile Franklin's career in politics advanced rapidly. In 1910 he was elected to the New York State Senate. In 1913 President Wilson appointed him Assistant Secretary of the Navy—a powerful position in the national government, which required the Roosevelts to move to Washington, D.C.

In 1917 the United States entered World War I as an active combatant. Like many socially prominent[5] women, Eleanor threw herself into the war effort. Sometimes she worked fifteen and sixteen hours a day. She made sandwiches for soldiers passing through the nation's capital. She knitted sweaters. She used Franklin's influence to get the Red Cross to build a recreation room for soldiers who had been shell-shocked in combat. . . .

In the summer of 1921 disaster struck the Roosevelt family. While on vacation Franklin suddenly fell ill with infantile paralysis—polio—the horrible disease that each year used to kill or cripple thousands of children, and many adults as well. When Franklin became a victim of polio, nobody knew what caused the disease or how to cure it.

Franklin lived, but the lower part of his body remained **paralyzed**. For the rest of his life he never again had the use of his legs. He had to be lifted and carried from place to place. He had to wear heavy steel **braces** from his waist to the heels of his shoes.

His mother, as well as many of his advisers, urged him to give up politics, to live the life of a country gentleman on the Roosevelt estate at Hyde Park, New York. This time, Eleanor, calm and strong, stood up for her ideas. She argued that he should not be treated like a sick person, tucked away in the country, inactive, just waiting for death to come.

Franklin agreed. Slowly he recovered his health. His energy returned. In 1928 he was elected governor of New York. Then, just four years later, he was elected president of the United States.

Visual Vocabulary

Braces are devices used to support or hold in place parts of the body.

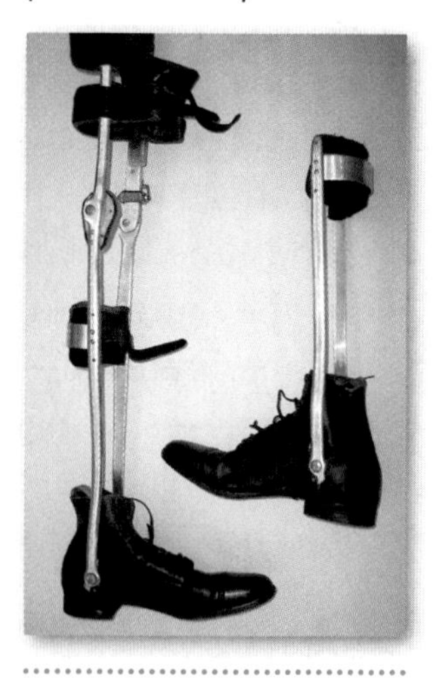

BQ BIG Question

What always seemed to bring out the best in Eleanor?

---

5 A ***prominent*** member of the community is someone who is well known or important.

Vocabulary

paralyzed (par′ə līzd′) *adj.* affected with the loss of motion or sensation in a muscle due to disease of or injury to the nervous system

Meanwhile Eleanor had changed. To keep Franklin in the public eye while he was recovering, she had gotten involved in politics herself. It was, she thought, her "duty." From childhood she had been taught "to do the thing that has to be done, the way it has to be done, when it has to be done."

After becoming interested in the problems of working women, she gave time to the Women's Trade Union League (WTUL). It was through the WTUL that she met a group of remarkable women—women doing exciting work that made a difference in the world. They taught Eleanor about life in the **slums**. They awakened her hopes that something could be done to improve the condition of the poor. She dropped out of the "fashionable" society of her wealthy friends and joined the world of reform—social change.

For hours at a time Eleanor and her reformer friends talked with Franklin. They showed him the need for new laws: laws to get children out of the factories and into schools; laws to cut down the long hours that women worked; laws to get fair wages for all workers.

Summarize Summarize the information about the state of the country when Franklin Roosevelt became president.

By the time that Franklin was sworn in as president, the nation was facing its deepest **depression**. One out of every four Americans was out of work, out of hope. At mealtimes people stood in lines in front of soup kitchens for something to eat. Mrs. Roosevelt herself knew of once-prosperous families who found themselves reduced to eating stale bread from thrift shops or traveling to parts of town where they were not known to beg for money from house to house.

Eleanor and Franklin Roosevelt on election night, 1932.

Vocabulary

slums (slumz) *n.* heavily populated city areas identified by poverty, run-down housing, and wretched living conditions

depression (di presh′ən) *n.* a period marked by severely decreasing business activity, rising unemployment, and falling wages

Eleanor worked in the charity kitchens, ladling out soup. She visited slums. She crisscrossed the country learning about the suffering of coal miners, shipyard workers, migrant[6] farm workers, students, housewives—Americans caught up in the paralysis of the Great Depression. Since Franklin himself remained crippled, she became his eyes and ears, informing him of what the American people were really thinking and feeling. Eleanor also was the president's conscience, personally urging on him some of the most compassionate, forward-looking laws of his presidency.

BQ BIG Question
Why do you think Eleanor was a good choice for this role?

She lectured widely, wrote a regularly syndicated[7] newspaper column, "My Day," and spoke frequently on the radio. She fought for equal pay for women in industry. Like no other First Lady up to that time, she became a link between the president and the American public.

First Lady Eleanor Roosevelt, on the cover of *TIME* magazine, April 17, 1939

Above all she fought against racial and religious prejudice. When Eleanor learned that the DAR (Daughters of the American Revolution) would not allow the great black singer Marian Anderson to perform in their auditorium in Washington, D.C., she resigned from the organization. Then she arranged to have Miss Anderson sing in front of the Lincoln Memorial.

Similarly, when she entered a hall where, as often happened in those days, blacks and whites were seated in separate sections, she made it a point to sit with the blacks.

Text Features How does Eleanor's expression here differ from her expressions in the previous photographs?

6 ***Migrant*** farm workers move each season from one region to another to harvest crops.

7 An article that is ***syndicated*** is sold to several newspapers to be published at the same time.

Her example marked an important step in making the rights of blacks a matter of national priority.[8]

On December 7, 1941, Japanese forces launched a surprise attack on the American naval base at Pearl Harbor, Hawaii. The United States entered World War II, fighting not only against Japan but against the brutal dictators who then controlled Germany and Italy.

Eleanor helped the Red Cross raise money. She gave blood, sold war bonds. But she also did the unexpected. In 1943, for example, she visited barracks and hospitals on islands throughout the South Pacific. When she visited a hospital, she stopped at every bed. To each soldier she said something special, something that a mother might say. Often, after she left, even battle-hardened men had tears in their eyes. Admiral Nimitz, who originally thought such visits would be a nuisance, became one of her strongest admirers. Nobody else, he said, had done so much to help raise the spirits of the men.

By spring 1945 the end of the war in Europe seemed near. Then, on April 12, a phone call brought Eleanor the news that Franklin Roosevelt, who had gone to Warm Springs, Georgia, for a rest, was dead.

With Franklin dead, Eleanor Roosevelt might have dropped out of the public eye, might have been remembered in the history books only as a footnote to the president's program of social reforms. Instead she found new strengths within herself, new ways to live a useful, interesting life—and to help others. Now, moreover, her successes were her own, not the result of being the president's wife.

In December 1945 President Harry S. Truman invited her to be one of the American delegates going to London to begin the work of the United Nations.[9] Eleanor hesitated, but the president insisted. He said that the nation needed her; it was her duty. After that Eleanor agreed.

Summarize Summarize the two paragraphs, beginning with "Above all," about Eleanor's fight against racial and religious prejudice.

BQ BIG Question

Why did Eleanor's presence have such a good effect on those she visited?

---

8 ***A matter of national priority*** is something that deserves to receive the government's chief attention.

9 The ***United Nations,*** which was founded in 1945, is an international organization of independent states that seeks to maintain world peace, works for cooperation among nations, and strengthens respect for treaties and other agreements under international law.

In the beginning some of her fellow delegates[10] from the United States considered her unqualified for the position, but after seeing her in action, they changed their minds.

Mrs. Roosevelt helped draft the United Nations Declaration of Human Rights. The Soviets wanted the declaration to list the duties people owed to their countries. Eleanor insisted that the United Nations should stand for individual freedom—the rights of people to free speech, freedom of religion, and such human needs as health care and education. In December 1948, with the Soviet Union and its allies refusing to vote, the Declaration of Human Rights won approval of the UN General Assembly by a vote of forty-eight to zero.

Summarize Summarize Eleanor's accomplishments following Franklin's death.

10 ***Delegates*** are people who are given the authority to act as representatives of their government.

Eleanor Roosevelt holds a poster of the Universal Declaration of Human Rights. This document was adopted by the United Nations General Assembly on December 10, 1948, in honor of Human Rights Day.

Text Features In what role was Eleanor serving when this photograph was taken?

Even after retiring from her post at the UN, Mrs. Roosevelt continued to travel. In places around the world she dined with presidents and kings. But she also visited tenement slums in Bombay, India; factories in Yugoslavia; farms in Lebanon and Israel.

Everywhere she met people who were eager to greet her. Although as a child she had been brought up to be formal and distant, she had grown to feel at ease with people. They wanted to touch her, to hug her, to kiss her.

Eleanor's doctor had been telling her to slow down, but that was hard for her. She continued to write her newspaper column, "My Day," and to appear on television. She still began working at seven-thirty in the morning and often continued until well past midnight. Not only did she write and speak, she taught special needs children and raised money for health care of the poor.

As author Clare Boothe Luce put it, "Mrs. Roosevelt has done more good deeds on a bigger scale for a longer time than any woman who ever appeared on our public scene. No woman has ever so comforted the distressed or so distressed the comfortable."

Gradually, however, she was forced to withdraw from some of her activities, to spend more time at home.

On November 7, 1962, at the age of seventy-eight, Eleanor died in her sleep. She was buried in the rose garden at Hyde Park, alongside her husband.

Adlai Stevenson, the American ambassador to the United Nations, remembered her as "the First Lady of the World," as the person—male or female—most **effective** in working for the cause of human rights. As Stevenson declared, "She would rather light a candle than curse the darkness."

And perhaps, in sum, that is what the struggle for human rights is all about.

BQ BIG Question Throughout her life, what brought out the best in Eleanor?

Summarize Briefly state the major accomplishments of Eleanor's life that led Adlai Stevenson to make this statement.

Vocabulary

effective (i fek′ tiv) *adj.* capable of producing an intended result

Eleanor Roosevelt's Time *in*

1900

1905 March 17: Eleanor marries Franklin D. Roosevelt in New York.

1910

1912 Eleanor attends her first Democratic Party Convention.[1]

1917 The United States enters World War I.

1920

1920 Congress passes the Nineteenth Amendment,[2] granting women the right to vote.

1926 Eleanor helps purchase Todhunter School, a girls' seminary,[3] where she teaches history and government.

1928 Eleanor is appointed Director of Women's Activities for the Democratic Party; FDR is elected governor of New York.

1930

1933 Frances Perkins becomes Secretary of Labor, the first woman cabinet member in U.S. history.

1 The ***Democratic Party Convention*** is a meeting for people who are members of the Democratic political party.

2 ***Congress*** is the part of the United States government that makes laws. The ***Nineteenth Amendment*** is the nineteenth change made to the United States Constitution since it became the law of the land in 1781.

3 A ***seminary*** is a school or an academy at or beyond high school level, especially a boarding school for young women.

Text Features What happened in 1920? Why does the event make Eleanor Roosevelt's later achievements seem even more remarkable?

1936 FDR runs for and wins reelection. With Eleanor's help, African American Mary McLeod Bethune is appointed director of Negro Affairs in the National Youth Administration (NYA).

1938 Congress passes a law banning child labor.

1941 December 7: The U.S. enters World War II.

1943 Eleanor tours the South Pacific to boost the soldiers' morale.[4]

1945 Eleanor influences the Army Nurse Corps to open its membership to black women; she joins the NAACP[5] board of directors.

April 12: Franklin Delano Roosevelt dies.

September 2: Japan surrenders to the Allies. World War II ends.

1948 Eleanor's leadership leads to passage of the Universal Declaration of Human Rights.

1952 Eleanor resigns from the United Nations.

1954 The *Brown v. Board of Education* decision outlaws segregation in public schools.

1957 Congress passes a law making it a federal crime to prevent an African American from voting.

1961 John F. Kennedy reappoints Eleanor to the United Nations and appoints her as chair of the President's Commission on the Status of Women.

1962 November 7: Eleanor dies at the age of seventy-eight of tuberculosis.[6]

1940 1950 1960 1970

Text Features Look at the photograph for 1961. How did Eleanor Roosevelt influence presidents?

4 ***Morale*** is the attitude or condition of a person or a group with respect to such qualities as courage, confidence, and high spirits.

5 The ***NAACP*** is the National Association for the Advancement of Colored People.

6 ***Tuberculosis*** is a disease that is caused by bacteria, and it can be spread from one person to another. It may affect any part of the body, especially the lungs or joints.

After You Read

Respond and Think Critically

1. What made Eleanor's childhood unhappy? **[Identify]**
2. How did Eleanor's experience at Allenswood change her? **[Recall]**
3. Compare Eleanor's advice to Franklin after he became paralyzed with the advice of his mother and other advisers. Why do you think Eleanor took the position she did? **[Compare]**
4. How do you think the author feels about Eleanor Roosevelt? How can you tell? **[Infer]**
5. Eleanor Roosevelt went through many hard times. What do you notice about the way she faced the challenges in her life? **[Analyze]**
6. **BQ BIG Question** How did Eleanor Roosevelt's work with the United Nations reflect the ideas and values that she promoted in her adult life? **[Conclude]**

TIP

Inferring
When you **infer,** you look at the details in the text and draw conclusions about what you read. To answer question 4, ask yourself,

- On what kinds of details does the author focus? Do the details seem positive or negative?
- What do the details reveal about Eleanor's character?
- Does the author seem sympathetic toward Eleanor?

Keep track of your ideas about the **BIG Question** in your unit Foldable.

Vocabulary Practice

Antonyms are words that have opposite meanings. Match each boldface vocabulary word with a word or phrase from the right column with the opposite meaning. One of the words in the right column will not have a match. Then use each word in a sentence.

1. slums	a. advantages
2. drawbacks	b. in motion
3. paralyzed	c. useless
4. depression	d. countryside
5. effective	e. mistakes
	f. good times

Example:
paralyzed
Sentence: The stray cat was paralyzed with fear.

Academic Vocabulary

During World War I, Eleanor Roosevelt **contributed** to the war effort by working to provide food and clothing for soldiers. In the preceding sentence, *contributed* means "helped with." Think of a large project or effort to which you could contribute. What could you contribute to the project?

Literature Online

Selection Resources
For Selection Quizzes, eFlashcards, and Reading-Writing Connection activities, go to glencoe.com and enter QuickPass code GL17527u5.

Literary Element Text Features

Graphics can deepen your understanding of a text. The **time line** provides additional details about Eleanor Roosevelt's life. Use the time line to answer the following questions.

1. How did Eleanor Roosevelt support women's causes in the 1920s?
2. Look closely at the events that occurred during Franklin D. Roosevelt's presidency. How do you think Eleanor may have influenced her husband?
3. What are some of the advantages of using a time line instead of regular text?

Review: Text Structure

As you learned on page 512, text is often structured in **chronological order.** Chronological order refers to the order in which events take place.

4. When did Franklin D. Roosevelt become ill with polio? Name one important thing that happened *before* he got polio and one important thing that happened *after* he got polio.
5. Did Eleanor Roosevelt become the American delegate to the United Nations before or after Franklin D. Roosevelt died?

Reading Strategy Summarizing

6. Summarize the events in Eleanor Roosevelt's life before she married Franklin D. Roosevelt.
7. Summarize Eleanor Roosevelt's major contributions to society.

Grammar Link

Combine Sentences Too many short sentences can make writing choppy or boring. To make your writing more interesting, combine short sentences that have closely related ideas.

To combine two short sentences, use a coordinating conjunction, such as *and, or, but,* or *so,* between them. Place a comma before the conjunction and change the capital letter at the beginning of the second sentence to a lowercase letter.

> Eleanor was strong. She liked challenges.
>
> Eleanor was strong, and she liked challenges.

Practice In the selection, find two sentences in which a coordinating conjunction was used to combine two short sentences.

Combine each pair of sentences below using *and, or, but,* or *so.*

1. Eleanor wanted to help the poor. She left her wealthy friends to work for social change.
2. Polio left Franklin paralyzed. Eleanor didn't think that he should quit politics.

Speaking and Listening

Speech Think about the ways in which Eleanor Roosevelt changed the role of First Lady. Then write a persuasive speech about what role you think a president's spouse should play in the country's political life and what his or her civic duties should be. Remember to make your speech sound natural. Give it a strong beginning, an informative middle, and a powerful ending. Use persuasive techniques that appeal to listeners' logic, emotions, or ethics. Present your speech to the class.

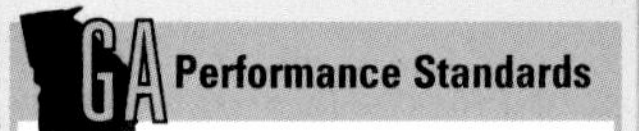

Performance Standards

For pages 658–659

ELA6R1b For informational texts, apply knowledge of common graphic features.

Genre Focus: Biography and Autobiography

A **biography** is the story of a person's life written by someone other than the subject. Most biographies are written about people who have influenced or inspired others. An **autobiography** is the story of a person's life written by that person. Although they are forms of nonfiction, biographies and autobiographies are usually written much like a story.

Diaries, travel journals, memoirs, and anecdotes are shorter forms of biographical and autobiographical writing.

Literary Elements

Facts Biographies and autobiographies are based on facts. Authors must be accurate when stating names, dates, and the like and often need to utilize multiple sources. However, biographies and autobiographies are not just retellings of facts. The author uses the facts to create a plot with a beginning, middle, and end.

Subject In a biography or an autobiography, the main character, or subject, is a real person. Like fiction authors, biographers and autobiographers use direct and indirect characterization to bring their subjects to life.

Setting A biography or an autobiography must accurately show the times and places in which the subject lived or lives, including customs or historical events that affected the subject.

Events Biographies and autobiographies are usually told in chronological (time) order. An author may begin with the subject's childhood and continue forward in time.

Point of View Point of view is the viewpoint from which a story is told. An autobiography is written from the **first-person point of view.** The author is the *I,* or subject of the piece. A biography is told from the point of view of an author. This **third-person point of view** refers to the subject as *he* or *she.*

Theme A theme is a message about life that readers can take from the text. An author may directly state a theme or imply it. Authors choose specific details to convey themes.

Author's Purpose Authors can have different purposes for writing. Some authors might write to explore someone important in history. Other authors might write to describe someone they know. An autobiographer may want to share his or her experiences or life lessons.

TRY IT

Using one of the graphic organizers on the next page, identify the characteristics of a biographical or autobiographical selection in this unit.

Characteristics of the Genre

To better understand the literary elements in biographies and autobiographies, look at the examples in the graphic organizers below.

Characterization Chart for "Satchel Paige"

Detail from the Story	Personality Trait(s) It Reveals	Direct or Indirect Characterization
Narrator praises Paige for "his talent, his energy, and his showmanship."	talent, determination, good presentation	direct (narrator's statement)
Paige doesn't let insults bother him	even temper	indirect (character's words)
Paige supports other African American ballplayers	selflessness	indirect (character's actions)

Story Map for "Primary Lessons"

Subject: Judith Ortiz Cofer

Point of View: first person

Secondary Characters: mother, brother, father, La Mrs., Lorenzo

Setting: Puerto Rico

Conflict: The author must speak Spanish at school, but she doesn't know the language well.

Rising Action

Event 1: The author goes to a new school in Puerto Rico.

Event 2: The author becomes "teacher's pet," along with a boy named Lorenzo.

Climax: The author overhears her teachers say why she was chosen to host the PTA show instead of Lorenzo.

Resolution: The author takes no pleasure in hosting the PTA show.

Before You Read

Ode to Mi Gato

Connect to the Poem

Do you have a pet, or do you wish you had one? Think about some of the responsibilities that go along with caring for a pet as well as the ways a pet can enrich your life.

Partner Talk With a partner, discuss some of the things pet owners must do to care for a pet. Why do you think people agree to take on these responsibilities?

Build Background

An **ode** is a type of **lyric poem,** a poem that expresses strong personal feelings about a subject. Traditionally, an ode is about a dignified or admired subject. It directly addresses the subject and follows a regular pattern of rhyme. But many modern odes do not follow these traditional rules. The poem might not directly address the subject, the lines might not rhyme, and the poem might have a casual or friendly tone. A modern ode can be about something as simple as a sock or a blade of grass.

Set Purposes for Reading

BIG Question

As you read, ask yourself, what qualities does the cat bring out in the poem's speaker?

Literary Element Simile

A **simile** is a figure of speech that uses *like* or *as* to compare two unlike things. "The water was like glass" compares water to glass. Even though water and glass are two very different substances, the simile helps you realize that both are clear and shiny.

Understanding the similes in a poem can help you create a mental picture of what you read. Similes can also give clues about the tone of the poem, or how the narrator feels about the subject. The tone might be serious, funny, or angry. Similes can also point toward the theme of the poem by emphasizing important elements.

Poets often use similes to make unusual comparisons. As you read "Ode to Mi Gato," try to find each simile. Do you notice any unusual comparisons?

GA Performance Standards

For pages 660–663

ELA6R1g For literary texts, define and explain how tone is conveyed in literature through word choice, sentence structure, punctuation, rhythm, repetition, and rhyme.

Meet Gary Soto

The excitement of reading poetry and novels while he was in college helped Gary Soto decide to become a writer. He is the author of short stories, novels, and poetry. Soto is Mexican American, and many of his characters are too. He has written more than 70 books.

Gary Soto was born in 1952.

Literature Online

Author Search For more about Gary Soto, go to glencoe.com and enter QuickPass code GL17527u5.

Ode to Mi Gato

Gary Soto

Cat Lying on Yellow Cushion. Franz Marc. Oil on canvas. Staatliche Galerie Moritzberg, Halle, Germany.

He's white
As spilled milk,
My cat who sleeps
With his belly
Turned toward
The summer sky.
He loves the sun,
Its warmth like a hand.
He loves tuna cans
And milk cartons
With their dribble
Of milk. He loves
Mom when she rattles
The bag of cat food,
The brown nuggets
Raining into his bowl.
And my cat loves
Me, because I saved
Him from a dog,
Because I dressed him
In a hat and a cape
For Halloween,
Because I dangled
A sock of chicken skin

Simile What two things are being compared? How does this simile help you picture the subject of the poem?

Simile How can the sun's warmth be like a hand?

As he stood on his
Hind legs. I love *mi gato,*°
Porque° I found
Him on the fender
Of an abandoned car.
He was a kitten,
With a meow
Like the rusty latch
On a gate. I carried
Him home in the loop
Of my arms.
I poured milk
Into him, let him
Lick chunks of
Cheese from my palms,
And cooked *huevo*°
After *huevo*
Until his purring
Engine kicked in
And he cuddled
Up to my father's slippers.
That was last year.
This spring,
He's excellent at sleeping
And no good
At hunting. At night
All the other cats
In the neighborhood
Can see him slink
Around the corner,
Or jump from the tree
Like a splash of
Milk. We lap up
His love and
He laps up his welcome.

Simile What two things are being compared? How does this simile help you imagine what the cat sounds like?

BQ BIG Question

What does the speaker give the cat? What does the cat give in return?

---

26 In Spanish, ***mi gato*** (mē gä′ tō) means "my cat."

27 ***Porque*** (pôr kā′) is Spanish for "because."

40 ***Huevo*** (wā′ vō) is Spanish for "egg."

After You Read

Respond and Think Critically

1. Name three things the cat loves. **[Recall]**
2. What does the speaker mean when he says, "The brown nuggets / Raining into his bowl"? **[Interpret]**
3. Does the cat really enjoy being dressed in a cape and hat for Halloween? Who do you think really enjoys this activity? **[Infer]**
4. What do you learn about the speaker from the words in his poem? **[Analyze]**
5. **Literary Element** **Simile** Find two similes in the poem that compare the cat to milk. How are they similar? How are they different? **[Compare]**
6. **BQ** **BIG Question** How does caring for the cat bring out the best in the speaker? **[Conclude]**

TIP

Analyzing
When you analyze, you look at separate parts of something to understand the entire piece. To answer question 4, try these tips:

- Think about each of the speaker's actions. What do they reveal about him?
- Notice the words the speaker uses to describe his cat. What can you learn about the speaker from these words?
- Notice the words in italics. Read the footnotes that explain each word. What do they tell you about the speaker?

Spelling Link

Think about the word *underground.* This word is made up of two words: *under* and *ground.* Words that are formed by joining two words together are called **compound words.**

To spell compound words correctly, keep the original spelling of both words.

Examples

home + work = homework

dog + house = doghouse

back + yard = backyard

Practice Use the following words to form three compound words: *news, nail, paper, print, thumb, finger, tack.* Share your words with a partner. Did you form the same three words?

Keep track of your ideas about the **BIG Question** in your unit Foldable.

Writing

Write a Stanza Pick a subject and write one stanza of an ode that praises the subject. Write a traditional ode, in which you directly address the subject and follow a regular rhyming pattern, or write a modern ode that doesn't follow traditional rules. You might write about a pet, or you might select a different topic. Think of at least one simile that would help readers visualize your subject and include it in your poem.

LOG ON **Literature** Online

Selection Resources
For Selection Quizzes, eFlashcards, and Reading-Writing Connection activities, go to glencoe.com and enter QuickPass code GL17527u5.

Before You Read

President Cleveland, Where Are You?

Connect to the Story

Think of a time when you gave something up in order to help someone else.

Quickwrite Freewrite for a few minutes about giving something up to help someone else. Why did you decide to help? How did you feel afterward?

Build Background

This story takes place during the Great Depression in a town called Monument. The Great Depression began in late 1929 and lasted through the 1930s. It was a time of hardship for many people around the world. Banks closed, and so did many other businesses. In the United States, thousands of people lost their homes. Millions of people lost their jobs.

Vocabulary

bonus (bō′ nəs) *n.* something extra (p. 668).
Seeing the baseball game was great, and catching the foul ball was a bonus.

betrayed (bi trād′) *v.* let down; turned against (p. 670).
I felt betrayed when Jacob told my secret to his friends

pouting (pout′ ing) *v.* being sullen or gloomy; sulking (p. 674).
After his team lost, Kevin spent the rest of the day pouting.

dismal (diz′ məl) *adj.* dreary; miserable; cheerless (p. 674).
The heavy rain made it a dismal day.

sympathy (sim′ pə thē) *n.* feeling of pity or compassion for another (p. 677).
When Celia's friend moved away, I expressed my sympathy.

Meet Robert Cormier

"I write for the intelligent reader and this intelligent reader is often twelve or fourteen or sixteen years old."

—Robert Cormier

Young Adult Author Like the main character in the following selection, Robert Cormier was a boy during the 1930s. "The streets were terrible," he remembered. "It was [the] Depression and it was bleak, but home was warm." Cormier grew up in Leominster, Massachusetts, and often used his hometown as a setting for his stories.

Literary Works Cormier wrote many novels for young adults, including *The Chocolate War* and *I Am the Cheese.*

Robert Cormier was born in 1925 and died in 2000.

LOG ON **Literature** Online

Author Search For more about Robert Cormier, go to glencoe.com and enter QuickPass code GL17527u5.

Set Purposes for Reading

BQ BIG Question

As you read, ask yourself, how do the narrator's choices reflect what kind of person he is? How important is his family to him?

Literary Element Voice

In fiction, **voice** refers to the author's or narrator's distinctive use of language. Voice conveys the narrator's personality to the reader. Voice is determined by word choices. These word choices determine the **tone** of the story, or the author's attitude toward the subject matter or audience. Another element of voice is **mood,** the overall emotional quality of a literary work.

Voice can reveal the author's or narrator's attitudes, feelings, or cultural background. Sometimes it hints at what the author or narrator feels but does not say.

As you read, ask yourself, what does the narrator's voice reveal about him? How does it help develop the theme of the story?

Reading Strategy Evaluate Description

When you **evaluate,** you make a judgment or form an opinion. When you **evaluate description,** you make judgments about the strengths and weaknesses of a detailed portrayal of a person, a place, an object, or an event in a story. You should be able to support those judgments with examples from the story.

Good descriptive writing helps readers see, hear, smell, taste, and feel details from a story. It may include **figurative language,** such as **similes** and **metaphors**, that make comparisons between things that seem unrelated.

To evaluate description, ask yourself,

- to which senses does the writing appeal?
- which words are especially vivid? Can I form a picture the scene?
- what comparisons does the author make? Are they new and fresh or have I heard them before?

In evaluating description, you may find it helpful to use a graphic organizer like the one below.

Senses	Strengths	Weaknesses
Sight		
Hearing		
Smell		
Taste		
Touch		

GA Performance Standards

For pages 664–681

ELA6R1g For literary texts, define and explain how tone is conveyed in literature through word choice, sentence structure, punctuation, rhythm, repetition, and rhyme.

TRY IT

Evaluate Description Your friend is on vacation. She sends you a postcard that reads: "Arizona is really HOT! It's like walking through an oven. The Grand Canyon is beautiful. I've never seen this many stars at night." Which details can you imagine clearly? Which parts of the description could be more vivid?

PRESIDENT CLEVELAND, Where Are You?

Robert Cormier

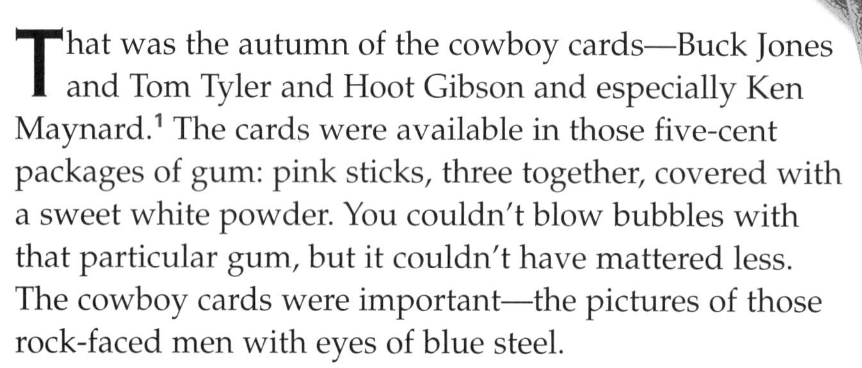

That was the autumn of the cowboy cards—Buck Jones and Tom Tyler and Hoot Gibson and especially Ken Maynard.[1] The cards were available in those five-cent packages of gum: pink sticks, three together, covered with a sweet white powder. You couldn't blow bubbles with that particular gum, but it couldn't have mattered less. The cowboy cards were important—the pictures of those rock-faced men with eyes of blue steel.

On those wind-swept, leaf-tumbling afternoons we gathered after school on the sidewalk in front of Lemire's Drugstore, across from St. Jude's Parochial School,[2] and we swapped and bargained and matched for the cards. Because a Ken Maynard serial[3] was playing at the Globe every Saturday afternoon, he was the most popular cowboy of all, and one of his cards was worth at least ten of any other kind.

Rollie Tremaine had a treasure of thirty or so, and he guarded them jealously. He'd match you for the other cards, but he risked his Ken Maynards only when the other kids threatened to leave him out of the competition altogether.

You could almost hate Rollie Tremaine. In the first place, he was the only son of Auguste Tremaine, who operated

Voice How would you describe the voice of the narrator so far?

---

1 ***Buck Jones, Tom Tyler, Hoot Gibson,*** and ***Ken Maynard*** were all popular stars of cowboy movies in the 1930s.

2 A ***parochial*** (pə rō′ kē əl) ***school*** is run by a church or another religious organization rather than by a city or state government.

3 In the 1930s, moviegoers watched ***serials,*** long stories that were shown in individual episodes.

the Uptown Dry Goods Store, and he did not live in a tenement[4] but in a big white birthday cake of a house on Laurel Street. He was too fat to be effective in the football games between the Frenchtown Tigers and the North Side Knights, and he made us constantly aware of the jingle of coins in his pockets. He was able to stroll into Lemire's and casually select a quarter's worth of cowboy cards while the rest of us watched, aching with envy.

Evaluate Description How does this metaphor help you picture Rollie Tremaine's house?

Once in a while I earned a nickel or dime by running errands or washing windows for blind old Mrs. Belander, or by finding pieces of copper, brass, and other valuable metals at the dump and selling them to the junkman. The coins clutched in my hand, I would race to Lemire's to buy a cowboy card or two, hoping that Ken Maynard would stare boldly out at me as I opened the pack. At one time, before a disastrous matching session with Roger Lussier (my best friend, except where the cards were involved), I owned five Ken Maynards and considered myself a millionaire, of sorts.

Voice What does this tell you about the narrator's personality?

Unemployment. Paul Starrett Sample. Oil on canvas. National Academy Museum, NY.

4 Here, ***tenement*** means "apartment building."

One week I was particularly lucky; I had spent two afternoons washing floors for Mrs. Belander and received a quarter. Because my father had worked a full week at the shop, where a rush order for fancy combs had been received, he allotted my brothers and sisters and me an extra dime along with the usual ten cents for the Saturday-afternoon movie. Setting aside the movie fare, I found myself with a **bonus** of thirty-five cents, and I then planned to put Rollie Tremaine to shame the following Monday afternoon.

Monday was the best day to buy the cards because the candy man stopped at Lemire's every Monday morning to deliver the new assortments. There was nothing more exciting in the world than a fresh batch of card boxes. I rushed home from school that day and hurriedly changed my clothes, eager to set off for the store. As I burst through the doorway, letting the screen door slam behind me, my brother Armand blocked my way.

He was fourteen, three years older than I, and a freshman at Monument High School. He had recently become a stranger to me in many ways—indifferent to such matters as cowboy cards and the Frenchtown Tigers—and he carried himself with a mysterious dignity that was fractured now and then when his voice began shooting off in all directions like some kind of vocal fireworks.

Evaluate Description What two things are being compared? To which of the five senses does the description appeal?

"Wait a minute, Jerry," he said. "I want to talk to you." He motioned me out of earshot of my mother, who was busy supervising the usual after-school skirmish[5] in the kitchen.

I sighed with impatience. In recent months Armand had become a figure of authority, siding with my father and mother occasionally. As the oldest son he sometimes took advantage of his age and experience to issue rules and regulations.

"How much money have you got?" he whispered.

"You in some kind of trouble?" I asked, excitement

5 A ***skirmish*** is a brief or minor conflict.

Vocabulary

bonus (bō′ nəs) *n.* something extra

rising in me as I remembered the blackmail plot of a movie at the Globe a month before.

He shook his head in annoyance. "Look," he said, "it's Pa's birthday tomorrow. I think we ought to chip in and buy him something . . ."

I reached into my pocket and caressed the coins. "Here," I said carefully, pulling out a nickel. "If we all give a nickel we should have enough to buy him something pretty nice."

He regarded me with contempt. "Rita already gave me fifteen cents, and I'm throwing in a quarter. Albert handed over a dime—all that's left of his birthday money. Is that all you can do—a nickel?"

"Aw, come on," I protested. "I haven't got a single Ken Maynard left, and I was going to buy some cards this afternoon."

"Ken Maynard!" he snorted. "Who's more important—him or your father?"

His question was unfair because he knew that there was no possible choice—"my father" had to be the only answer. My father was a huge man who believed in the things of the spirit, although my mother often maintained that the spirits[6] he believed in came in bottles. He had worked at the Monument Comb Shop since the age of fourteen; his booming laugh—or grumble—greeted us each night when he returned from the factory. A steady worker when the shop had enough work, he quickened with gaiety on Friday nights and weekends, a bottle of beer at his elbow, and he was fond of making long speeches about the good things in life. In the middle of the Depression, for instance, he paid cash for a piano, of all things, and insisted that my twin sisters, Yolande and Yvette, take lessons once a week.

I took a dime from my pocket and handed it to Armand.

"Thanks, Jerry," he said. "I hate to take your last cent."

"That's all right," I replied, turning away and consoling myself with the thought that twenty cents was better than nothing at all.

BQ BIG Question
Using what you know about the narrator so far, do you think he will be able to put the interests of others before his own? Why or why not?

Evaluate Description From the description in this paragraph, do you get a vivid impression of the father? Why or why not?

6 Spiritual matters are often called *things of the spirit,* but bottled ***spirits*** are alcoholic beverages.

When I arrived at Lemire's I sensed disaster in the air. Roger Lussier was kicking disconsolately[7] at a tin can in the gutter, and Rollie Tremaine sat sullenly on the steps in front of the store.

"Save your money," Roger said. He had known about my plans to splurge on the cards.

"What's the matter?" I asked.

"There's no more cowboy cards," Rollie Tremaine said. "The company's not making any more."

"They're going to have President cards," Roger said, his face twisting with disgust. He pointed to the store window. "Look!"

A placard in the window announced: "Attention, Boys. Watch for the New Series. Presidents of the United States. Free in Each 5-Cent Package of Caramel Chew."

"President cards?" I asked, dismayed.

I read on: "Collect a Complete Set and Receive an Official Imitation Major League Baseball Glove, Embossed with Lefty Grove's Autograph."[8]

Glove or no glove, who could become excited about Presidents, of all things?

Rollie Tremaine stared at the sign. "Benjamin Harrison, for crying out loud," he said. "Why would I want Benjamin Harrison when I've got twenty-two Ken Maynards?"

I felt the warmth of guilt creep over me. I jingled the coins in my pocket, but the sound was hollow. No more Ken Maynards to buy.

"I'm going to buy a Mr. Goodbar," Rollie Tremaine decided.

I was without appetite, indifferent even to a Baby Ruth, which was my favorite. I thought of how I had **betrayed** Armand and, worst of all, my father.

Evaluate Description What is the author describing here? Do you think the description is effective?

Voice How does the narrator feel about the coins now? How does the narrator's voice contribute to the tone of this statement?

---

7 ***Disconsolately*** means that Roger is so hopelessly unhappy that nothing can help and no one can console him.

8 ***Robert "Lefty" Grove*** (1900–1970) was an outstanding pitcher for the Philadelphia Athletics and the Boston Red Sox between 1925 and 1941. A machine carved his ***embossed*** autograph by making shallow cuts in the glove's leather.

Vocabulary

betrayed (bi trād′) *v.* let down; turned against

Two Boys Seated. Joan Eardley. Oil on canvas, 54 x 75 cm. Private Collection.

"I'll see you after supper," I called over my shoulder to Roger as I hurried away toward home. I took the shortcut behind the church, although it involved leaping over a tall wooden fence, and I zigzagged recklessly through Mr. Thibodeau's garden, trying to outrace my guilt. I pounded up the steps and into the house, only to learn that Armand had already taken Yolande and Yvette uptown to shop for the birthday present.

I pedaled my bike furiously through the streets, ignoring the indignant[9] horns of automobiles as I sliced through the traffic. Finally I saw Armand and my sisters emerge from the Monument Men's Shop. My heart sank when I spied the long, slim package that Armand was holding.

Evaluate Description
Which words in this paragraph and the previous one describe how quickly the narrator is moving? Do you think this description brings the scene to life?

"Did you buy the present yet?" I asked, although I knew it was too late.

"Just now. A blue tie," Armand said. "What's the matter?"

9 If the car horns sound ***indignant***, it is because the drivers are annoyed with the narrator's behavior in traffic.

"Nothing," I replied, my chest hurting.

He looked at me for a long moment. At first his eyes were hard, but then they softened. He smiled at me, almost sadly, and touched my arm. I turned away from him because I felt naked and exposed.

"It's all right," he said gently. "Maybe you've learned something." The words were gentle, but they held a curious dignity, the dignity remaining even when his voice suddenly cracked on the last syllable.

I wondered what was happening to me, because I did not know whether to laugh or cry.

The Messenger. Andrew Gadd. Oil on canvas, 219 x 112 cm. Private Collection.

View the Art Study the expression on the boy's face in this painting. Do you think it expresses how Jerry feels after he meets up with Armand at the Monument Men's Shop?

Voice What does this tell you about the narrator's level of maturity?

Sister Angela was amazed when, a week before Christmas vacation, everybody in the class submitted a history essay worthy of a high mark—in some cases as high as A-minus. (Sister Angela did not believe that anyone in the world ever deserved an A.) She never learned—or at least she never let on that she knew—we all had become experts on the Presidents because of the cards we purchased at Lemire's. Each card contained a picture of a President, and on the reverse side, a summary of his career. We looked at those cards so often that the biographies imprinted themselves on our minds without effort. Even our street-corner conversations were filled with such information as the fact that James Madison was called "The Father of the Constitution," or that John Adams had intended to become a minister.

The President cards were a roaring success and the cowboy cards were quickly forgotten. In the first place we did not receive gum with the cards, but a kind of chewy caramel. The caramel could be tucked into a corner of your mouth, bulging your cheek in much the same manner as wads of tobacco bulged the mouths of baseball stars. In the second place the competition for collecting the cards was fierce and frustrating—fierce because everyone was intent on being the first to send away for a baseball glove and frustrating because although there were only thirty-two Presidents, including Franklin Delano Roosevelt, the variety at Lemire's was at a minimum. When the deliveryman left the boxes of cards at the store each Monday, we often discovered that one entire box was devoted to a single President—two weeks in a row the boxes contained nothing but Abraham Lincoln. One week Roger Lussier and I were the heroes of Frenchtown. We journeyed on our bicycles to the North Side, engaged three boys in a matching bout and returned with five new Presidents, including Chester Alan Arthur, who up to that time had been missing.

Evaluate Description To which senses does this description appeal? What can you imagine about the size and texture of the caramel?

Perhaps to sharpen our desire, the card company sent a sample glove to Mr. Lemire, and it dangled, orange and sleek, in the window. I was half sick with longing, thinking of my old glove at home, which I had inherited from Armand. But Rollie Tremaine's desire for the glove outdistanced my own. He even got Mr. Lemire to agree to give the glove in the window to the first person to get a complete set of cards, so that precious time wouldn't be wasted waiting for the postman.

Voice What does the narrator's choice of words reveal about his attitude toward the glove?

We were delighted at Rollie Tremaine's frustration, especially since he was only a substitute player for the Tigers. Once after spending fifty cents on cards—all of which turned out to be Calvin Coolidge—he threw them to the ground, pulled some dollar bills out of his pocket and said, "The heck with it. I'm going to buy a glove!"

"Not that glove," Roger Lussier said. "Not a glove with Lefty Grove's autograph. Look what it says at the bottom of the sign."

We all looked, although we knew the words by heart: "This Glove Is Not For Sale Anywhere."

Rollie Tremaine scrambled to pick up the cards from the

sidewalk, **pouting** more than ever. After that he was quietly obsessed[10] with the Presidents, hugging the cards close to his chest and refusing to tell us how many more he needed to complete his set.

I too was obsessed with the cards, because they had become things of comfort in a world that had suddenly grown **dismal**. After Christmas a layoff at the shop had thrown my father out of work. He received no paycheck for four weeks, and the only income we had was from Armand's after school job at the Blue and White Grocery Store—a job he lost finally when business dwindled as the layoff continued.

Although we had enough food and clothing—my father's credit had always been good, a matter of pride with him—the inactivity made my father restless and irritable. He did not drink any beer at all, and laughed loudly, but not convincingly, after gulping down a glass of water and saying, "Lent[11] came early this year." The twins fell sick and went to the hospital to have their tonsils removed. My father was confident that he would return to work eventually and pay off his debts, but he seemed to age before our eyes.

When orders again were received at the comb shop and he returned to work, another disaster occurred, although I was the only one aware of it. Armand fell in love.

I discovered his situation by accident, when I happened to pick up a piece of paper that had fallen to the floor in the bedroom he and I shared. I frowned at the paper, puzzled.

"Dear Sally, When I look into your eyes the world stands still . . ."

The letter was snatched from my hands before I finished reading it.

BQ BIG Question
Why do you think it is so important to Rollie to be the first one to have the glove?

Voice Why might the narrator choose the word *disaster* to refer to falling in love? What does it reveal about the narrator?

10 ***Obsessed*** means "concentrating too much on a single emotion or idea."

11 ***Lent*** is the period including the forty weekdays before Easter. During Lent, some Christians show sorrow for their sins by giving up something they enjoy.

Vocabulary

pouting (pout′ ing) *v.* being sullen or gloomy; sulking

dismal (diz′ məl) *adj.* dreary; miserable; cheerless

"What's the big idea, snooping around?" Armand asked, his face crimson. "Can't a guy have any privacy?"

He had never mentioned privacy before. "It was on the floor," I said. "I didn't know it was a letter. Who's Sally?"

He flung himself across the bed. "You tell anybody and I'll muckalize[12] you," he threatened. "Sally Knowlton."

Nobody in Frenchtown had a name like Knowlton.

"A girl from the North Side?" I asked, incredulous.[13]

He rolled over and faced me, anger in his eyes, and a kind of despair too.

"What's the matter with that? Think she's too good for me?" he asked. "I'm warning you, Jerry, if you tell anybody . . ."

"Don't worry," I said. Love had no particular place in my life; it seemed an unnecessary waste of time. And a girl from the North Side was so remote that for all practical purposes she did not exist. But I was curious. "What are you writing her a letter for? Did she leave town, or something?"

"She hasn't left town," he answered. "I wasn't going to send it. I just felt like writing to her."

I was glad that I had never become involved with love—love that brought desperation[14] to your eyes, that caused you to write letters you did not plan to send. Shrugging with indifference, I began to search in the closet for the old baseball glove. I found it on the shelf, under some old sneakers. The webbing was torn and the padding gone. I thought of the sting I would feel when a sharp grounder slapped into the glove, and I winced.

Evaluate Description To which sense does this description appeal? How vivid is this scene to you? Why?

"You tell anybody about me and Sally and I'll—"

"I know. You'll muckalize me."

I did not divulge[15] his secret and often shared his agony, particularly when he sat at the supper table and left my mother's special butterscotch pie untouched. I had never

---

12 ***Muckalize*** is a made-up word. *Muck* is dirty, sticky, slimy mud or anything that is messy and disgusting. The suffix *-ize* means "cause to be or become."

13 To be ***incredulous*** (in krej′ ə ləs) is to be unwilling or unable to believe something.

14 ***Desperation*** means "distress caused by great need or loss of hope."

15 To ***divulge*** a secret is to reveal it or make it known, so that it's no longer a secret.

realized before how terrible love could be. But my compassion[16] was short-lived because I had other things to worry about: report cards due at Eastertime; the loss of income from old Mrs. Belander, who had gone to live with a daughter in Boston; and, of course, the Presidents.

Because a stalemate[17] had been reached, the President cards were the dominant force in our lives—mine, Roger Lussier's and Rollie Tremaine's. For three weeks, as the baseball season approached, each of us had a complete set—complete except for one President, Grover Cleveland. Each time a box of cards arrived at the store we hurriedly bought them (as hurriedly as our funds allowed) and tore off the wrappers, only to be confronted by James Monroe or Martin Van Buren or someone else. But never Grover Cleveland, never the man who had been the twenty-second and the twenty-fourth President of the United States. We argued about Grover Cleveland. Should he be placed between Chester Alan Arthur and Benjamin Harrison as the twenty-second President or did he belong between Benjamin Harrison and William McKinley as the twenty-fourth President? Was the card company playing fair? Roger Lussier brought up a horrifying possibility—did we need two Grover Clevelands to complete the set?

Indignant, we stormed Lemire's and protested to the harassed[18] storeowner, who had long since vowed never to stock a new series. Muttering angrily, he searched his bills and receipts for a list of rules.

The first baseball uniforms were plain and made mostly of wool flannel. The heavy fabric made playing difficult on extremely hot days.

---

16 ***Compassion*** is sympathy for another's suffering, combined with a desire to help.

17 The chess term ***stalemate*** refers to a situation in which no further action is possible.

18 Someone who is ***harassed*** is repeatedly bothered or annoyed by someone else.

"All right," he announced. "Says here you only need one Grover Cleveland to finish the set. Now get out, all of you, unless you've got money to spend."

Outside the store, Rollie Tremaine picked up an empty tobacco tin and scaled it across the street. "Boy," he said. "I'd give five dollars for a Grover Cleveland."

When I returned home I found Armand sitting on the **piazza** steps, his chin in his hands. His mood of dejection[19] mirrored my own, and I sat down beside him. We did not say anything for a while.

"Want to throw the ball around?" I asked.

He sighed, not bothering to answer.

"You sick?" I asked.

He stood up and hitched up his trousers, pulled at his ear and finally told me what the matter was—there was a big dance next week at the high school, the Spring Promenade,[20] and Sally had asked him to be her escort.

I shook my head at the folly of love. "Well, what's so bad about that?"

"How can I take Sally to a fancy dance?" he asked desperately. "I'd have to buy her a **corsage** . . . And my shoes are practically falling apart. Pa's got too many worries now to buy me new shoes or give me money for flowers for a girl."

I nodded in **sympathy**. "Yeah," I said. "Look at me. Baseball time is almost here, and all I've got is that old glove. And no Grover Cleveland card yet . . ."

"Grover Cleveland?" he asked. "They've got some of those up on the North Side. Some kid was telling me there's a store that's got them. He says they're looking for Warren G. Harding."

"Holy Smoke!" I said. "I've got an extra Warren G. Harding!" Pure joy sang in my veins. I ran to my bicycle, swung into the seat—and found that the front tire was flat.

---

19 ***Dejection*** means "sadness; low spirits."

20 A formal dance or ball was once called a ***promenade.*** Today the term is usually shortened to prom.

Vocabulary

sympathy (sim′ pə thē) *n.* feeling of pity or compassion for another

Visual Vocabulary

Here, a **piazza**—also called a veranda—is an open porch, usually roofed, extending along one or more sides of the ground floor of a home.

Visual Vocabulary

A **corsage** (kôr säzh′) is a flower or small bunch of flowers worn by a woman, usually at the shoulder or on the wrist.

Voice What do the narrator's word choices and tone tell you about his emotions?

"I'll help you fix it," Armand said.

Within half an hour I was at the North Side Drugstore, where several boys were matching cards on the sidewalk. Silently but blissfully I shouted: President Grover Cleveland, here I come!

View the Art How does this painting capture the fun of dancing at an event like the Spring Promenade?

The Dance in the Country, c. 1882–3. Pierre Auguste Renoir. Private Collection.

After Armand had left for the dance, all dressed up as if it were Sunday, the small green box containing the corsage under his arm, I sat on the railing of the piazza, letting my feet dangle. The neighborhood was quiet because the Frenchtown Tigers were at Daggett's Field, practicing for the first baseball game of the season.

I thought of Armand and the ridiculous expression on his face when he'd stood before the mirror in the bedroom. I'd avoided looking at his new black shoes. "Love," I muttered.

Spring had arrived in a sudden stampede of apple blossoms and fragrant breezes. Windows had been thrown open and dust mops had banged on the sills all day long as the women busied themselves with housecleaning. I was puzzled by my lethargy.[21] Wasn't spring supposed to make everything bright and gay?

Evaluate Description Do you expect to see a word such as *stampede* in a description of springtime? Why might the narrator use it? What effect does it have?

I turned at the sound of footsteps on the stairs. Roger Lussier greeted me with a sour face.

"I thought you were practicing with the Tigers," I said.

"Rollie Tremaine," he said. "I just couldn't stand him." He slammed his fist against the railing. "Jeez, why did he have to be the one to get a Grover Cleveland? You should see him showing off. He won't let anybody even touch that glove . . ."

---

21 ***Lethargy*** (leth′ ər jē) is a feeling or condition of laziness or drowsiness.

I felt like Benedict Arnold[22] and knew that I had to confess what I had done.

"Roger," I said, "I got a Grover Cleveland card up on the North Side. I sold it to Rollie Tremaine for five dollars."

"Are you crazy?" he asked.

"I needed that five dollars. It was an—an emergency."

"Boy!" he said, looking down at the ground and shaking his head. "What did you have to do a thing like that for?"

I watched him as he turned away and began walking down the stairs.

"Hey, Roger!" I called.

He squinted up at me as if I were a stranger, someone he'd never seen before.

"What?" he asked, his voice flat.

"I had to do it," I said. "Honest."

He didn't answer. He headed toward the fence, searching for the board we had loosened to give us a secret passage.

I thought of my father and Armand and Rollie Tremaine and Grover Cleveland and wished that I could go away someplace far away. But there was no place to go.

Roger found the loose slat in the fence and slipped through. I felt betrayed: weren't you supposed to feel good when you did something fine and noble?

A moment later two hands gripped the top of the fence and Roger's face appeared. "Was it a real emergency?" he yelled.

"A real one!" I called. "Something important!"

His face dropped from sight and his voice reached me across the yard: "All right."

"See you tomorrow!" I yelled.

I swung my legs over the railing again. The gathering dusk began to soften the sharp edges of the fence, the rooftops, the distant church steeple. I sat there a long time, waiting for the good feeling to come.

BQ BIG Question

What was the emergency? Who did the narrator put first? How does he feel about his decision now?

Evaluate Description

To which sense does this description appeal? How does the description reflect the mood, or feeling, of the scene?

22 ***Benedict Arnold*** was an American general who became a traitor to the Colonial cause during the Revolutionary War.

After You Read

Respond and Think Critically

1. What is the setting of the story? **[Identify]**
2. After the cowboy cards, what do the narrator and his friends collect? Why? **[Recall]**
3. Briefly summarize why the Grover Cleveland card is so important to the narrator. **[Summarize]**
4. Why don't the narrator and the other boys like Rollie Tremaine? **[Infer]**
5. As the story ends, why isn't the narrator feeling good about helping Armand? **[Interpret]**
6. **BQ** **BIG Question** What values does the narrator learn from Armand throughout the story? **[Conclude]**

TIP

Interpreting
Here are some tips to help you answer question 5.

- Remember the things the narrator wants most during the story.
- Think about how the narrator and his friends feel about Rollie.
- Consider the narrator's loyalty to his brother and father.

Keep track of your ideas about the **BIG Question** in your unit Foldable.

View the Art

During the 1930s, the United States government hired artists to create different types of public art. The effort was called the Federal Art Project, and it provided work for many artists who had lost their jobs during the Great Depression. Much of the art, such as this woodcut, depicted people at work in their communities.

Group Activity Discuss the following questions with your classmates. Use evidence from the mural to support your answers.

1. In what ways are the men in this artwork similar to your image of the narrator's father? In what ways are they different?
2. What does the artwork tell you about the time period in which the story takes place?
3. Why do you think the artists in the Federal Art Project often chose to depict people at work?

Brick Laying, c. 1935. Adrian Troy.
Woodcut, 6 1/2 x 9 in.
Illinois State Museum Collection.

Literary Element Voice

1. What are some differences between the narrator's voice as he tells the story and the narrator's voice when he speaks dialogue as a character in the story? Why do you think the author might have made these voices different?
2. The narrator often refers to his culture and history, such as the President cards, the serial movies, and his father's loss of a job. What do these references tell you about the narrator and his background?

Review: Conflict

As you learned on page 249, **conflict** is the struggle between opposing forces in a story. An **external conflict** is between a character and some outside force, such as nature, society, or another person. An **internal conflict** exists within the mind of a character torn between opposing goals, ideas, or needs.

3. Is the narrator's main conflict external or internal? Explain.
4. What are the secondary conflicts—the conflicts besides the main conflict—in the story? Is each an internal or external conflict? Explain.

Reading Strategy Evaluate Description

Review your chart showing the strengths and weaknesses of descriptions in the story. Then answer these questions using evidence from the chart.

5. Give an example of a simile or metaphor from the story. How does the comparison strengthen the description?
6. What kinds of sensory details does the author use to describe the father? Do you think these details paint a clear picture of him? Explain.
7. Which description in the story do you think is most effective? Explain.

Vocabulary Practice

Choose the sentence that correctly uses the vocabulary word.

1. A. The cold winds made the hike a long, **dismal** journey.
   B. After cheering so loudly at the game, her voice was **dismal.**
2. A. To keep the secret safe, Alix **betrayed** it to all of her friends.
   B. Steve **betrayed** his family by taking the money from the drawer.
3. A. When Kira didn't get her way, she would sit in the corner **pouting.**
   B. I was tired of her **pouting** me with complaints all day.
4. A. Their worst player was a **bonus** to the team.
   B. Lisa had only expected lunch, so the movie was a nice **bonus.**
5. A. Cass had **sympathy**, so everyone ignored her.
   B. Tim had **sympathy** for Jamal—he'd been in that situation before.

Academic Vocabulary

During the Great Depression, **finances** were tight for many families. To become more familiar with the word *finances*, fill out a graphic organizer like the one below.

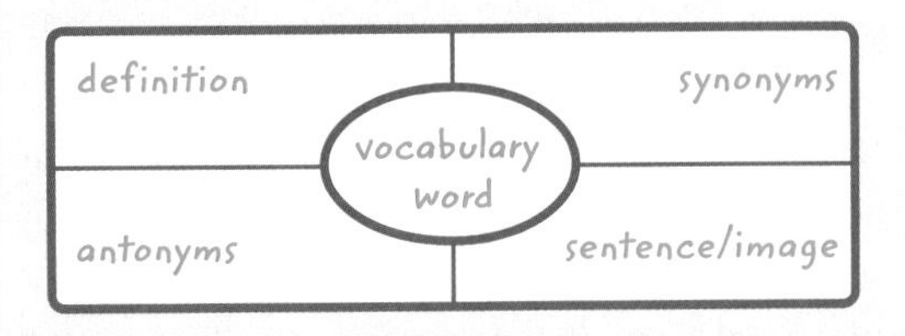

LOG ON Literature Online

Selection Resources For Selection Quizzes, eFlashcards, and Reading-Writing Connection activities, go to glencoe.com and enter QuickPass code GL17527u5.

Respond Through Writing

Autobiographical Narrative

Apply Description of Setting In "President Cleveland, Where Are You?" the narrator learns a humbling lesson. Write an **autobiographical narrative** about an experience in which you made a mistake and later corrected it. In your narrative, use **descriptions** to create a strong setting.

Understand the Task In an **autobiographical narrative,** the author tells a true story about his or her own life. Describe the setting by using sensory details and explore how the setting influences the resolution of the story.

Prewrite Think of a time you made a mistake. Why did you make the mistake? How did you correct it? Find other autobiographical narratives to read or ask friends or family members about life lessons they have learned. Brainstorm sensory details that will help you describe your narrative's setting. Think about creative comparisons that can strengthen your descriptions. Use a web diagram like the one below.

Draft Establish the setting early in your narrative. Use your web diagram to add details. Throughout the narrative, explain how you decided to make your decisions and tell how you felt about them. Have a classmate review your work.

Revise Reread your draft and add details to any descriptions that need to be strengthened. Check the conclusion of your narrative and make sure you reveal what you learned from the experience.

Edit and Proofread Proofread your paper, correcting any errors in spelling, grammar, and punctuation. Review the Grammar Tip in the side column for more information on apostrophes.

Standards Practice

For page 682

ELA6W2c Demonstrate competence in a variety of genres. Produce a narrative that includes sensory details and concrete language to develop plot, setting, and character.

Grammar Tip

Apostrophes

An **apostrophe** can show that a letter or letters have been left out of a word or phrase. This is called a contraction.

cannot ⟶ *can't*

we are ⟶ *we're*

Contractions are most often used in informal writing. They can make dialogue more realistic. Some writers feel that contractions are too casual for formal writing.

Media Workshop

Media Ethics

Media ethics are the rules of professional behavior followed by writers and producers of various kinds of communication. These rules guide writers as they try to do what is right in their work.

Failing to give credit for borrowed work is a form of stealing, a serious offense known as **plagiarism.** Besides being wrong, plagiarism is punishable by law. Those found guilty of plagiarism must pay fines.

Original Article

The weather was perfect on Sunday when the Pine Ridge Scouts gathered to celebrate their successful fundraiser. The scouts raised more than a thousand dollars for the Pine Ridge Animal Shelter, which was in need of funds after tornadoes last summer damaged the roof.

Plagiarized Article

It was a perfect Sunday for the Pine Ridge Scouts, who got together to celebrate a successful fundraiser. The scouts collected over $1,000 for the Pine Ridge Animal Shelter. The Shelter needed funds after last summer's tornadoes damaged the roof.

This chart shows three ways to **avoid plagiarism:** by mentioning the source of your information, by stating an author's idea differently, or by using a different idea.

Original Sentence

But Eleanor was much more than just a president's wife, an echo of her husband's career. ("Eleanor Roosevelt" by William Jay Jacobs)

Plagiarism

Copying the writer's words
Eleanor was much more than just a president's wife, an echo of her husband's career.

Copying most of the writer's words
Eleanor was more than the wife of a president. She wasn't just an echo of her husband's career.

Copying the writer's idea
Eleanor Roosevelt was a great woman, much more than just a shadow of her husband.

Ways to Avoid Plagiarism

Mention the source.
In "Eleanor Roosevelt," William Jay Jacobs says that the First Lady was much more than "an echo of her husband's career."

State the idea differently.
Eleanor Roosevelt was not a typical political wife.

Use a different idea.
Eleanor Roosevelt was a stronger presence than any First Lady before her.

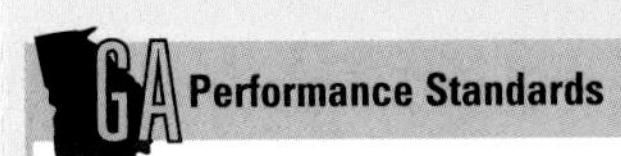

Performance Standards

For page 683

ELA6W3c Use research and technology to support writing. Cite references.

TRY IT

Partner Activity: Identify and Avoid Plagiarism

1. Study the sentences below. Then rewrite the original in three ethical ways.
2. Share your new sentences with a partner.
3. Discuss the challenges of rewriting the original.

Original: Instead of making new friends, Eleanor often sat alone in her room and read. ("Eleanor Roosevelt" by William Jay Jacobs)

Plagiarism: Eleanor often sat in her room by herself and read instead of making new friends.

Literature Online

Media Literacy For project ideas, templates, and media analysis guides, go to glencoe.com and enter QuickPass code GL17527u5.

Before You Read

The Eco-Canoeist

Connect to the Essay

Think of an outdoor place where you enjoy spending time. What makes this place special?

Quickwrite Briefly describe an outdoor place that is special to you. How would you feel if it were dirty or polluted? What could you do to help?

Build Background

Rivers and the land surrounding them are important wildlife habitats, or places where plants and animals live. Pollution can threaten the wildlife and also affect people who use the river's water for drinking or recreation.

- One source of pollution in rivers is waste from factories. Because of laws passed in the 1970s, most factories have changed their processes for eliminating waste.
- Farm materials, such as fertilizer and animal waste, can end up in rivers and lakes.
- Careless people pollute water by pouring used car oil and paint into drains.
- *Urban runoff* is a term for rainwater that flows across human-made surfaces such as roadways and roofs, picking up pollutants from these surfaces. Then this water flows into rivers, lakes, and the ocean.

Vocabulary

weird (wērd) *adj.* strange; unnatural (p. 687). *We decided to investigate the weird sound coming from the shed.*

wreckage (rek′ ij) *n.* remains of anything that has been destroyed (p. 688). *Sometimes wreckage from boats washes up on the beach.*

discarded (dis kärd′ əd) *v.* thrown away (p. 688). *Mia picked up the discarded soda cans in the park.*

dedication (ded′ ə kā′ shən) *n.* faithful agreement or pledge to a person or purpose (p. 689). *Aaron's dedication to running helps keep him physically fit.*

Meet Sy Montgomery

"It's an important time to be writing about the connections we share with our fellow creatures. It's a great time to be alive."

—Sy Montgomery

A Nature Writer
Sy Montgomery has been described as "part Indiana Jones and part Emily Dickinson." While researching her stories, she has been chased by a gorilla in Zaire, bitten by a vampire bat in Costa Rica, and hunted by a tiger in India.

Literary Works Montgomery's award-winning books include *Journey of the Pink Dolphins* and *Search for the Golden Moon Bear.*

Sy Montgomery was born in 1958.

LOG ON  **Literature** Online

Author Search For more about Sy Montgomery, go to glencoe.com and enter QuickPass code GL17527u5.

Set Purposes for Reading

BQ BIG Question

As you read, ask yourself, what makes people want to improve the world around them?

Literary Element Allusion

An **allusion** is a reference to a character, a place, or a situation from history, music, art, or literature. For example, in "The Eco-Canoeist," the author mentions Clark Kent, a character in the Superman comic books and movies. The author doesn't explain who Clark Kent is; she assumes that readers will recognize the name.

Writers can use allusions to advance the theme of a text by making interesting comparisons or describing something familiar in a new way.

As you read, ask yourself, what other allusions does the author use?

Reading Strategy Draw Conclusions About Author's Perspective

An **author's perspective** is the author's way of looking at a subject. Two authors might write about the same subject but have very different perspectives. You can get a good idea about the author's perspective by noticing how the author presents ideas. When you **draw conclusions about the author's perspective,** you figure out more than the author states directly. For example, if an author makes you feel sorry for stray cats, you might draw the conclusion that the author cares about animals.

Drawing conclusions about an author's perspective can help you think about why the author feels a certain way about a topic.

To draw conclusions about author's perspective, pay attention to

- the thesis, or the main idea, of an essay or work of nonfiction
- the words the author chooses to describe the subject
- the author's purpose for writing
- the intended audience for the piece of writing

Then use these clues to explain what the author's perspective is. You may find it helpful to use a graphic organizer like the one below.

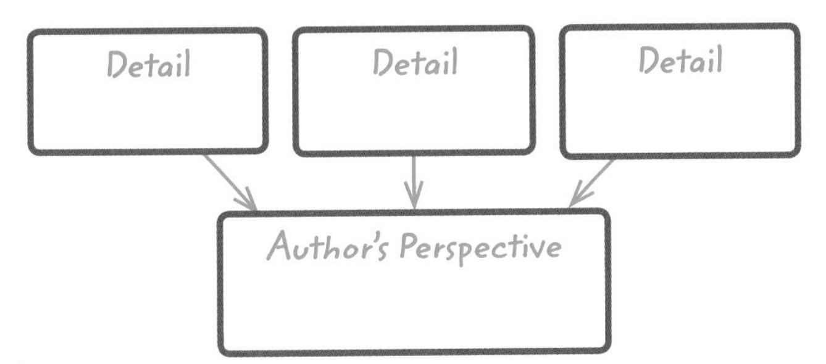

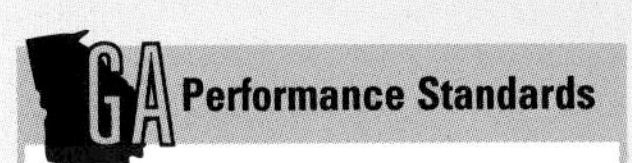

Performance Standards

For pages 684–691

ELA6R1f For literary texts, identify the speaker and recognize the difference between first- and third-person narration.

TRY IT

Draw Conclusions About Author's Perspective Imagine that you read an editorial in your school newspaper arguing for a four-day school week. What might you conclude about the writer and why he or she wants to reduce the number of days students are in school?

The Eco-Canoeist

Sy Montgomery

In the thirteen years Dale Hatch has worked as a ranger at Jay Blanchard Park in Orlando, Florida, he's seen some wonderful and strange things. It's a gem of an urban park,[1] where among the cypress, afternoon calls of barred owls nearly drown out the highway noise. The tea-colored Little Econlohatchee River flows through the park's 412 acres and brings with it herons, wood ducks, otters, egrets, ibis, sandhill cranes, and stinkpot and painted turtles, as well as 484,000 human visitors. You can catch a thirteen-pound largemouth bass here—but the health department warns you to eat fish from the Little Econ only

Draw Conclusions About Author's Perspective
How do you think the author feels about the park? How do you know?

1 An ***urban*** park is in a city.

once a week. There's mercury[2] in the river, though no one is sure where it comes from.

You can find some **weird** stuff in the river, Hatch says: everything from trousers to toilets. The Little Econ drains dozens of housing developments, he says, and after a flood, you can find trash four and five feet up in the trees. But about a decade ago, Hatch and the other rangers noticed something really strange. The trash started disappearing from the water. They would find muddy garbage piling up inside park trash cans. "We couldn't figure out where in the world it was coming from," Hatch says in his Florida drawl.[3] "Somebody was pulling this stuff up out of the river. We didn't know how, but we were sure glad whoever it was was doing it."

For months, as the rangers emptied the trash cans, they wondered who would do such a thing. Then one day, paddling in a canoe piled high with wet garbage was a person Hatch recognized. They'd first met on the park's soccer field some months before. Six feet tall and muscled, the stranger was dressed in **fatigues,** working out beside a maroon van plastered with Marines bumper stickers, practicing martial arts moves with a weapon that looked like nunchakus.[4] At the time, Hatch remembers, he thought, "Uh-oh."

Draw Conclusions About Author's Perspective
Why do you think the author included this quotation?

Visual Vocabulary

Fatigues is the name used for a heavy-duty, two-piece work uniform worn by military people.

2 ***Mercury*** is a poisonous metallic element, used in thermometers. When mercury gets into a water supply, it can have serious effects on the health of wildlife and people.

3 If someone has a ***drawl,*** the person speaks slowly, often drawing out the vowel sounds.

4 ***Nunchakus*** is the name for a weapon, originally from Japan, that consists of two wooden sticks joined at their ends by a short length of rawhide, cord, or chain.

Vocabulary

weird (wērd) *adj.* strange; unnatural

Hatch never suspected that, like Clark Kent, this thirty-four-year-old ex-Marine had an alter ego:[5] the Eco-Canoeist. For more than a decade, few others suspected it either. Unrecognized, unfunded, and usually alone, Steve Nordlinger takes every spare moment, loads his canoe into his van, puts in at waterways around the state, and pursues a goal most people would consider too huge to even try: to clean up, by hand, hundreds of thousands of miles of Florida's rivers, lakes, swamps, canals, and ocean.

It's not just a dirty job but a dangerous one. Sodden river garbage is unwieldy[6]—a truck tire can weigh well over a hundred pounds when it's filled with mud and water, and somehow you have to lift it into your canoe without capsizing.[7] He's hoisted out refrigerators, car parts, boat **wreckage**, picnic tables, doghouses, sofas. But it's the little stuff—the stuff anyone can lift—that arguably does the most harm. Birds choke on fishing line. Turtles die eating Styrofoam.[8] Ordinary rope strangles manatees. Removing brittle, rusty cans and the barbs of **discarded** fishing gear, Steve has cut his own flesh open again and again. But he keeps at it. By his own conservative estimate,[9] he has single-handedly removed 240 tons of trash and fishing line from the state's waterways.

Draw Conclusions About Author's Perspective
Why do you think the author includes this detail?

Hatch recalls his astonishment at the feat. "I could not believe that one person would go out on his own and do something like that—nobody asked him, nobody's paying him, he wasn't even telling us about it so we could praise him," said the ranger. "So we had to catch him accidentally—catch him cleanin' up our river!"

BQ BIG Question
Why do you think Nordlinger would want to remain anonymous?

---

5 An ***alter ego*** is a person who is an extension of oneself, or another self. ***Clark Kent,*** a newspaper reporter, is the alter ego of comic-book hero Superman.

6 Something that is ***sodden*** is soaked through with water. Sodden river garbage becomes so heavy that it is ***unwieldy,*** or difficult to handle, manage, or use.

7 ***Capsizing*** means "overturning."

8 ***Styrofoam*** is a brand name for a lightweight material made of plastic foam. Some drinking cups and packing materials are made from Styrofoam.

9 A ***conservative estimate*** is a cautious or moderate guess.

Vocabulary

wreckage (rek′ ij) *n.* remains of anything that has been destroyed

discarded (dis kärd′ əd) *v.* thrown away

Steve Nordlinger in a canoe full of garbage

View the Photograph
How do this photograph and the one on page 686 help you understand why Steve Nordlinger became the Eco-Canoeist?

Steve seems like a superhero straight out of a comic book. His work has attracted the attention of local press and national radio, the praise of county commissioners, and the **dedication** of so large a group of volunteers that there aren't enough canoes to hold them all—not even with the three new ones that now bring Steve's fleet of canoes to ten, thanks to a small grant recently garnered[10] from Disney.

The Eco-Canoeist is a strange kind of superhero. He's a trained fighter, yet so gentle he scrapes loose and releases the snails anchored inside the tin cans he picks up out of rivers. He's a Mother Teresa of Florida wildlife, dressed in Marines fatigues. He is part Don Quixote[11] and part Superman. But he is also, in important ways, an ordinary person—with an extraordinary will.

Allusion Why do you think the author chose to include this particular allusion?

10 Here, ***garnered*** means "gotten by effort."

11 ***Mother Teresa*** was a nun who spent most of her life in India, caring for the sick and poor. ***Don Quixote*** is a character in a novel by Miguel de Cervantes. Quixote is an idealistic Spanish gentleman who sets off to defend the helpless and defeat the wicked.

Vocabulary

dedication (ded′ ə kā′ shən) *n.* faithful agreement or pledge to a person or purpose

After You Read

Respond and Think Critically

1. What two problems threaten the river in Jay Blanchard Park? **[Identify]**
2. How did Hatch and the rangers find out that someone was removing trash from the river? **[Recall]**
3. What was Hatch's first impression of Steve Nordlinger? How does Hatch change his opinion when he learns more about Nordlinger? **[Infer]**
4. What does Nordlinger's action of scraping loose the snails inside tin cans and then releasing them tell you about him? **[Analyze]**
5. What do you think is the most extraordinary or heroic thing about Nordlinger? Explain. **[Evaluate]**
6. **BQ** **BIG Question** What do you think inspires Nordlinger to clean up Florida's waterways? **[Conclude]**

TIP

Inferring

Here are some tips to help you answer question 3.

- Reread the description of Hatch's first meeting with Nordlinger. Notice what Nordlinger was doing when Hatch saw him for the first time.
- What does Hatch recall thinking when he first saw Nordlinger?
- When does Hatch next see Nordlinger? What does Hatch have to say about him then?

Vocabulary Practice

Choose the sentence that correctly uses the vocabulary word.

1. **A.** The firefighter was rewarded for his **dedication** after risking his life to save a family.
   B. The policeman's **dedication** made him think that the suspect was lying.
2. **A.** I hurried to the library, but it was too **weird** to get there.
   B. Andrew thinks it is **weird** that his sister has a pet spider.
3. **A.** The sidewalk **discarded** the trash everywhere.
   B. Ryan **discarded** the candy wrapper in a trash can.
4. **A.** Lena helped her dad clear away the **wreckage** after the storm.
   B. Mia likes this song, but it sounds like **wreckage** to her brother.

Keep track of your ideas about the **BIG Question** in your unit Foldable.

Academic Vocabulary

Steve Nordlinger works tirelessly to clean up the **environment** in Jay Blanchard Park. In the preceding sentence, *environment* means "the air, water, and soil around a person or place; natural surroundings." Think about what you could do to improve the environment around your school. How could you make a difference?

Literature Online

Selection Resources

For Selection Quizzes, eFlashcards, and Reading-Writing Connection activities, go to glencoe.com and enter QuickPass code GL17527u5.

Literary Element **Allusion**

1. What do the allusions in this essay have in common? How do the allusions give you a more vivid picture of Nordlinger's character?
2. Which allusion do you think makes the most surprising comparison? Explain.

Review: Diction

As you learned on page 395, **diction** is a writer's choice of words. Writers carefully choose their words to convey a particular meaning or effect.

3. Read the following passage: "It's a gem of an urban park, where among the cypress, afternoon calls of barred owls nearly drown out the highway noise. The tea-colored Little Econlohatchee River flows through the park's 412 acres and brings with it herons, wood ducks, otters, egrets, ibis, sandhill cranes, and stinkpot and painted turtles, as well as 484,000 human visitors."

   How does the author's choice of words in this passage create a picture of Jay Blanchard Park?
4. Find another passage in the essay with effective diction and tell what the author accomplishes with her choice of words.

Reading Strategy **Draw Conclusions About Author's Perspective**

Standards Practice  ELA6R1d

5. Why did the author write this article?
   A. She thinks it is important to help the environment.
   B. She thinks that state parks are overcrowded.
   C. She admires soldiers and the service they have given to their country.
   D. She admires Mother Teresa.

Grammar Link

Capitalization of Titles Capitalize the first word, the last word, and any important words in the title of a book, a play, a short story, a poem, a film, a magazine, and a song.

Examples:
Book: Anne of Green Gables
Play: Romeo and Juliet
Short Story: The Gift of the Magi
Poem: Ode to the West Wind
Film: The March of the Penguins
Magazine: Sports Illustrated for Kids
Song: The Star-Spangled Banner

Practice Rewrite the following titles using correct capitalization.

1. the lord of the rings
2. across the universe
3. a wrinkle in time
4. beauty and the beast

Write four correctly capitalized titles of your own.

Research and Report

Visual/Media Presentation Look for examples in the local media of photos or video clips that show people cleaning up litter or helping the environment in some way. Take notes and use word-processing software, if available, to help you organize, format, and present your information. Present your findings to the class. Be sure to give credit to your sources.

Comparing Literature

Going Blind and from *Ray Charles*

BQ BIG Question

"Going Blind" is an excerpt from Ray Charles's autobiography, *Brother Ray.* The other selection is an excerpt from *Ray Charles,* a biography of the musician. As you read, ask yourself, how did Charles's experiences as a child help bring out the best in him?

Literary Element Narrator and Point of View

The **narrator** is the person who tells a story. **Point of view** is the perspective from which a story is told. Recall that an autobiography is a person's account of his or her own life. An autobiography uses the **first-person point of view.** The narrator is the same as the subject of the autobiography and is referred to as *I.* The reader learns the thoughts and feelings of only that person. Because a biography is an account of a person's life written by someone else, a biography uses the **third-person point of view.** The subject of the biography is referred to as *he* or *she*.

As you read each selection, ask yourself, who is telling the story and how does that shape the story?

Reading Skill Compare and Contrast

You often **compare and contrast** things in everyday life. When you compare, you look for similarities. When you contrast, you look for differences. For example, you might compare and contrast two restaurants to help you decide which one to visit. You could compare the type and quality of the food as well as the cost.

Comparing and contrasting narrators and points of view can help you better understand literature. On the following pages, you'll compare and contrast the narrators and points of view in "Going Blind" and the excerpt from *Ray Charles.* Use a chart like the one below to record details about the narrators and points of view.

	Going Blind	Ray Charles
Narrator		
Point of View		

Performance Standards

For pages 692–703

ELA6R1f For literary texts, identify the speaker and recognize the difference between first- and third-person narration.

Meet the Authors

Ray Charles and David Ritz

Ray Charles was a popular musician and composer. David Ritz has helped many people write their autobiographies.

Sharon Bell Mathis

Sharon Bell Mathis was a special education teacher before becoming a writer.

Literature Online

Author Search For more about Ray Charles, David Ritz, and Sharon Bell Mathis, go to glencoe.com and enter QuickPass code GL17527u5.

GOING BLIND

RAY CHARLES AND DAVID RITZ

Going blind. Sounds like a fate worse than death, doesn't it? Seems like something which would get a little kid down, make him afraid, and leave him half-crazy and sad. Well, I'm here to tell you that it didn't happen that way—at least not with me.

That's probably 'cause it took me two years to lose my sight completely. It slipped away gradually. And I suppose that's the reason I was never too frightened.

Images began to blur, and I saw less and less. When I woke up, my little eyes were shut tight as a door, crusted over and so sticky that my eyelids were matted[1] together. Sometimes Mama took a damp cloth and gently mopped around my eyes. After five or ten minutes, I'd slowly start blinking and adjusting to the morning light.

Comparing Literature
What is the point of view in this selection? How do you know?

1 Here, ***matted*** means "formed into a dense mass." Young Ray's eyes were so sticky that he couldn't open them easily.

But soon my horizons grew shorter and shorter. Faraway distances were fading. I was like a guy who stands on top of a mountain and one week sees fifteen miles off, the next week only ten miles, the third week only five. At first, I could still make out large forms, then only colors, then only night from day.

There were only two doctors in Greensville—a Dr. McCloud and a Dr. King. Dr. King was the more expensive of the two, and white folk went to him. Dr. McCloud—who was a white man—took care of everyone. He tried to help me as best he could, treating my eyes with ointments and drops, but there wasn't much he could do.

Finally he suggested that we go to a clinic in Madison, a town close by. So we went. Just Mama and me. We walked into the office of the doctor there and he looked into my eyes and examined me every which way.

"Is there any hope?" Mama asked.

"Well," the doctor answered, his face glum, his head hanging down, "I don't think so. I'm afraid the boy's going blind."

"I understand," Mama said. She was not afraid; she didn't weep or scream for the Lord's mercy. Mama was a strong woman—a smart woman—and she knew what she had to do.

Comparing Literature
What have you learned about the narrator so far?

Mama always wanted me to learn things. Even though she didn't have much education herself, she taught me all she knew—the numbers, the alphabet, the way to spell, how to add and subtract. So when I started going blind, she began looking into schools for me. Remember, I was the only blind person in Greensville; people just didn't know what to do with me.

Comparing Literature
Why do you think the narrator sometimes addresses the reader? What is the effect?

Mama sought out advice. She asked Miss Lad who worked at the post office. She talked to the banker and to Mr. Reams who owned the general store. Soon everyone in town learned about my plight.

Railroad Depot, Greenville (also called Greensville), Florida.

It was the white folks who told Mama about the State School for the Blind in St. Augustine. I think a few of them saw something good in me and cared about making sure that it was nurtured. Maybe they knew I had half a brain; maybe they heard I had some musical talent. I don't know, but Mama was able to get good advice, and I'm certain that many white people were encouraging her to send me to school.

It didn't take her long to decide. I was going to have to go to school and live in St. Augustine.

My own reaction to leaving was a big fat NO. Didn't want to leave Mama and didn't want to leave Mary Jane.[2] That simple. Going blind was one thing; I was getting used to that. But leaving these women was something else. They were all I knew. They were my whole world.

2 ***Mary Jane*** Robinson was a former wife of Ray Charles's father. She helped raise Ray and was like a second mother to him.

Florida School for Blind, Deaf and Dumb, Saint Augustine, Florida.

No matter. Mama told me I was leaving, so I was leaving. End of discussion. I had a couple of months to get used to that idea, and during this last period at home I was treated the same as a normal child. Fact is, I was made to do the same chores I had done when I could see.

Mama was a country woman with a whole lot of common sense. She understood what most of our neighbors didn't—that I shouldn't grow dependent on anyone except myself. "One of these days I ain't gonna be here," she kept hammering inside my head. Meanwhile, she had me scrub floors, chop wood, wash clothes, and play outside like all the other kids. She made sure I could wash and dress myself. And her discipline didn't stop just 'cause I was blind. She wasn't about to let me get away with any foolishness.

So I still had the freedom to fend for myself on the outside. That made me happy. Even though I couldn't see much, I wasn't afraid of running around. I knew every inch of Greensville, and I didn't lose my confidence about finding my way; I went wherever I wanted to.

Comparing Literature
How would this selection be different if it were told from the third-person point of view?

Some of the neighbors gave Mama a hard time. They got on her case when they saw me working out back or helping her in the house.

"He's blind," Mama told them, "but he ain't stupid. He's lost his sight, but he ain't lost his mind."

Mama was looking way down the line.[3]

Blindness didn't break my spirit, but it might have added to my already shy personality. Many kids' games required sight, so I couldn't play with 'em. On the other hand, I had my own circle of friends, and I still raised some hell with the other kids.

I still went over to Mr. Pit's place and climbed up on the piano stool. By then, even at age six, I could fake a little black-bottom blues[4] of my own.

I played around like all kids, getting into more trouble than I should and less than I might. Luckily, Mama held the reins tight, and I was taught to mind my elders. Either that, or my butt would be burning for days.

I wouldn't want you to think I was a model kid.

Comparing Literature
How would you describe the narrator? Is he funny, serious, or angry? How does his attitude affect the tone of the selection?

Look here: Some friend would show up and convince me to follow him down the road, just before dinnertime.

"C'mon, RC, let's go, man."

I was dumb, I was stupid, and even though Mama had instructed me to clean the house, I'd leave anyway. Two hours later I'd come back and Mama'd be burning

---

3 When you look ***down the line,*** you are thinking about the future.

4 ***Black-bottom blues*** is a type of music that gets its name from some poor African American neighborhoods, once referred to as "black bottoms."

mad. She wouldn't whup me right away, though. She had the good sense to realize that you don't hit someone when you're full of rage and anger. No, she'd wait till she was calm—maybe an hour or two later—and then she'd come after me.

But the discipline didn't bother me. I came to expect it. No, I loved my home life, loved my mama, loved Mary Jane, loved the feeling of roaming round the woods with my friends. So when they put me on the train to St. Augustine, I was one unhappy boy.

Comparing Literature How might this part of the story be different if Ray's mother were the narrator?

The idea of leaving Mama and Mary Jane was almost more than I could bear. What did I know 'bout St. Augustine and some strange-sounding school for the blind?

"Mama," I cried, "don't make me go, Mama. I wanna stay with you." But she remained firm.

"You gotta go, son. How else you gonna learn to read and write? I can only take you so far."

I understood that I couldn't go to school in Greensville and learn like normal kids. But at the same time, the thought of getting on a big train and going far, far away—leaving everything and everyone I knew behind—man, that was enough to get me down and keep me down. Remember, I'd never really been outside the country, and here I was going off on my own.

Mama and I had always been very, very tight. It didn't seem possible my life could go on without her. I was just a seven-year-old kid. It didn't seem possible that I had to leave. None of it seemed possible. But let me tell you: It sure enough happened. ❧

from Ray Charles

Sharon Bell Mathis

"Hey, Foots!" a boy yelled. He was on the Black children's side of the wire that ran down the yard of St. Augustine School for the Blind.

"Hey, Foots! Hey, Ray—Ray Charles Robinson![1] Come on and race!"

The barefoot boy, called Foots because he had no shoes, had arrived at the school only a few days before.

Ray stood still and thought for a moment.

He wasn't thinking of his blindness. That didn't matter. It had never stopped him from doing exactly what he wanted.

Ray wanted to run a perfect race. He was thinking of how to win.

Once his mother had held him close.

"You're blind," she said, "not stupid. You lost your sight, not your mind."

Suddenly he knew how to do it. He knew how to win.

Comparing Literature An *omniscient* narrator can tell the reader what the subject of the text is thinking or feeling. Does this story have an omniscient narrator? How do you know?

---

1 ***Ray Charles Robinson*** dropped his last name when he began performing in public to avoid being confused with boxer Sugar Ray Robinson.

A child stood at each end of the wire, pulling it tight. All Ray had to do was grab the wire at the starting point and follow it to the end.

But he didn't grab the wire. His small, seven-year-old fingers felt the wire lightly. If he didn't touch it at all, he could run even faster. But that meant taking a chance of getting too far from the wire and losing the way.

Comparing Literature
You can often figure out how a character is feeling even when the narrator doesn't directly tell you. How do you think Ray feels in this paragraph?

Ray heard the other children running back and forth, racing. The sound was sharp and clear to his ears. He could tell how far away they ran by their voices. Ray figured the wire was about 100 feet long.

He knew how to measure. He had learned by helping his father build and repair things for neighbors. At first he had been able to see. But later, even when he could no longer see, he had still helped.

His mother did not baby him either. She gave him chores to do. One of his chores was to cut wood. He had to use an ax to do it.

One day some women saw the blind boy chopping wood with an ax. They were shocked and angry with his mother. But Ray's mother did not care about them. She cared about her son. She wanted him to do as much as he could without help.

"You running, Foots?"

"Yeah," Ray said. His toes dug into the sandy Florida dirt.

Comparing Literature
How are Ray's thoughts, words, and actions expressed differently in this selection from how they are expressed in "Going Blind"?

"READY, SET, GO!"

Ray started. His hand kept a light touch on the wire. It felt easy.

The running part was easy too. He was used to racing barefoot across dirt yards. He was always speeding across his own yard at home on his way to visit his neighbors.

Ray could hear the children shouting. Faster and faster he ran. He was streaking somewhere in the dark and everything was perfect.

He didn't need to see. Not this time. Not now, not ever. He felt great.

Then sudden pain smashed into him.

WHAM!

They had tricked him. There was no child at the other end of the wire. They had tied it to an iron post.

The hurt was too much. Ray started to cry.

"Little baby!" someone yelled. "Little sissy boy!"

Tears tried hard to get past his eyelids. But Ray squeezed his eyelids tighter.

"Foots is a baby!" the children shouted again and again.

Comparing Literature
How might these sentences be worded if this selection were told from first-person point of view?

Today, the little barefoot boy is a man. He is famous. People don't call him Foots. They call him Ray Charles. The whole world knows him. He is a great musician.

He is still blind, but nobody would dare trick him into hitting an iron post.

Huge crowds of people come to his concerts to see him play the piano and sing. He wears dark glasses and

Comparing Literature
How has the narrator's story changed? What is the narrator's focus here?

rocks back and forth on the piano stool as his body and soul keep time with the beautiful sound of his voice.

The music of Ray Charles is a mix of many styles, including gospel music and jazz. His music has the power of a story. It tells about love and pain and joy and trouble.

You can hear his tears in it.

Sometimes, when people clap and clap and clap, he gets up from the piano and stands, holding his arms out to them. It makes the people feel good.

Sometimes they cry when he sings about trouble.

Ray Charles Robinson, who was born able to see on September 23, 1930, in Albany, Georgia, knows what trouble is. ❧

Comparing Literature

BQ BIG Question

Now use the unit Big Question to compare and contrast "Going Blind" and the excerpt from *Ray Charles.* With a group of classmates, discuss questions such as the following.

- How does each selection present the ways Ray Charles's childhood experiences brought out the best in him?
- Why does Ray's mother make Ray do difficult chores, discipline him, and send him to St. Augustine?
- How does Ray's mother put Ray's best interests before her own?

Support each answer with evidence from the readings.

Literary Element Narrator and Point of View

Use the details you wrote in your comparison chart to think about the narrators and points of view in "Going Blind" and the excerpt from *Ray Charles.* With a partner, answer the following questions.

1. In what ways are the narrators and points of view different? Discuss specific details, writing styles, or any other ways the narrators and points of view differ.
2. In what ways are the narrators and points of view similar? You might think about how each narrator tells the story, how each narrator speaks, or on what thoughts and feelings each narrator focuses.

Write to Compare

In one or two paragraphs, describe how the narrators and points of view affect "Going Blind" and the excerpt from *Ray Charles.* You might focus on these ideas as you write:

- Discuss how each narrator tells the story. How does the narration make you feel? Is the narrator's storytelling exciting, gloomy, or funny?
- Discuss how each selection would be different if it were written from a different person's point of view or if the point of view of the two selections were switched.
- Explain how similarities and differences in the narrators and points of view affect your responses to the two selections.

Writing Tip

Plural Nouns While writing, remember that the plurals of some nouns are not formed simply by adding an *s.* For example, singular nouns that end in a consonant and *y* get an *ies* ending when they become plural (*story/stories*).

LOG ON Literature Online

Selection Resources
For Selection Quizzes, eFlashcards, and Reading-Writing Connection activities, go to glencoe.com and enter QuickPass code GL17527u5.

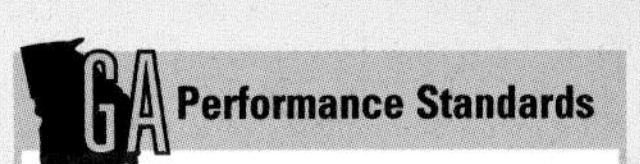

Performance Standards

For pages 704–711

ELA6W3b Use research and technology to support writing. Include research information in different types of products.

Writing Workshop

Research Report

What inner strengths do you possess? In this workshop, you will write a research report that will help you think about the Unit 5 Big Question: What brings out the best in you?

Review the writing prompt, or assignment, below. Then read the Writing Plan. It will tell you what you will do to write your research report.

Writing Assignment

In a research report, you investigate a subject or topic and present information on it, drawing from a variety of reliable, documented sources. Write a research report on a well-known historical or modern-day person whose inner strength helped him or her put others first. The audience, those reading your report, will be your classmates and teacher.

Writing Plan

- Choose a focused subject or topic.
- Draw upon reliable information from multiple sources.
- Incorporate relevant facts and details to support the main idea of the report.
- Organize the report in a logical sequence, concluding with a summary of the main idea.
- Include a list of sources (bibliography) and footnotes.

Prewrite

How did the people you have read about in this unit use their inner strength to help others? Think about the biography of Eleanor Roosevelt, for example. What other historical or modern-day person might be a good subject for your report?

Gather Ideas

Gather information about famous people and their accomplishments. Talk with your friends and family, look through your social studies textbook, and check Web sites and library books. Make a list of the names of people who interest you.

Choose a Topic

Look over the names on your list. From your preliminary research, which person do you admire the most or find most interesting? Choose a person from your list to research.

Plan and Conduct Your Research

Focus your research on a few questions. For example, *What is this person's memorable achievement? How and when did the person achieve it? In what way did this person's inner strength lead to helping others?* Be sure to consult a variety of authoritative sources, such as the *Readers' Guide to Periodical Literature,* magazines, newspapers, encyclopedias, reliable Web sites, or experts, to find the information you need.

Literature Online

Writing and Research
For prewriting, drafting, and revising tools, go to glencoe.com and enter QuickPass code GL17527u5.

Then take notes, using a research chart, or database, to record information such as the following:

- the source number
- author, if mentioned
- name of source
- page number or Web address
- publication details (including the date you used information from a Web site or the copyright or publication date from printed material)
- item of information—indicate if the item is a fact (F) or an opinion (O)

When you take notes in the research chart, do not just copy from your source word for word. Instead, write a summary, which is a shortened version of a longer text, or paraphrase information, which is a restatement of someone's ideas. See Media Literacy at the back of this book for more guidelines on when to give credit to a source.

Prewriting Tip

Taking Notes Put quotation marks around any words you copy directly from a source. Be sure to include complete source information along with the quoted material.

King Sundiata of Mali

Source	Information
1. Koslow, Philip. Mali: Crossroads of Africa. New York: Chelsea, 1995, p. 12.	A griot, or storyteller, named Kouyata says that when Sundiata overcame hardships to serve as the first ruler of Mali, "he was greatly loved." (F)

Evaluate Your Information

In order to evaluate each piece of information in your research chart for its relevance and reliability, ask yourself,

- How important is this information in making my point?
- Is the source reliable?
- Does the information come from a reputable organization or author? Does the author have expert credentials?
- Can I verify the information with another source? Are there factual or grammatical errors that make the source seem questionable?
- Is the writer citing a fact or offering an opinion? Is the source associated with an organization that is biased?
- How current is the information?

Get Organized

Organize your information into an outline. Identify your topic and the overall point you will make. Then list the main points you want to make (I., II., III., and so on). If you have subtopics, you must include at least two under a main idea (A., B., C., and so on). See the Writing Handbook at the back of this book for more guidelines on making an outline.

In your outline, indicate the source number from your research chart that you will use to support each main point.

King Sundiata of Mali overcame hardships to succeed.

I. Background about his life

  A. Son of West African king (source 1)

  B.

Draft

Organize your ideas and add more details to your writing.

Get It on Paper

- Review your research information. Look at your outline.
- Begin with an interesting fact or quotation that draws the reader in. Connect it to a statement that makes your purpose clear.
- For each paragraph in your outline, write a topic sentence that supports your main idea. Then add the information from your research that supports the topic sentence.
- Show readers the source of your information by including a raised footnote number [(1)] at the end of a sentence or quote. The note will appear at the bottom of the page. See the Writing Handbook at the back of this book for more guidelines on how to footnote.
- End your report by summarizing the main idea.
- Don't worry about paragraphs, spelling, grammar, or punctuation right now.
- When you are finished, read what you have written. Include more information if you need to.

Develop Your Draft

1. Provide a focused **subject** for your paper.

> In the beginning of the thirteenth century, a disabled boy was born near the kingdom of Kangba, West Africa. His name was Sundiata Keita, and he overcame his physical challenges to become the first king of Mali.

2. Include information from **multiple authoritative sources.** Give credit for sources in footnotes, numbered consecutively and placed at the end of a sentence or quote. Each footnote number should correspond to a numbered citation at the bottom of the page.

> The legends about Sundiata's life are "the most cherished" of their stories.[2]

3. **Support** your statements with facts, details, and explanations.

> Great obstacles stood in his way, however. Because Sundiata was physically challenged, he was only able to crawl.[4]

4. Present your information logically and conclude with a **summary.**

> The story of Sundiata is a story of inner strength and dedication winning out over misfortune.

5. End with a **list of sources** on the bibliography page. Arrange the sources alphabetically by the author's last name or by the first word of the title if no author's name is given.

> Bibliography
>
> Koslow, Philip. Mali: Crossroads of Africa. New York: Chelsea, 1995.

Drafting Tip

Checklist While writing, check off each piece of information in your research chart as you use it to make sure you haven't missed any important details and that you haven't used the same information more than once.

TRY IT

Analyzing Cartoons

With a partner, discuss how Calvin's mother describes her meeting with his teacher. Why is the cartoon a good example of sentence fluency?

Apply Good Writing Traits: Sentence Fluency

Because a research report conveys a great deal of information, writing with sentence fluency, or a smooth flow from sentence to sentence or from paragraph to paragraph, will help readers understand and enjoy your writing.

Read the sentences below from "Eleanor Roosevelt" by William Jay Jacobs. Are the sentences fluent? Which transitions—words or phrases that connect ideas—act as links from one sentence to another?

> Sad and lonely as a child, Eleanor was called "Granny" by her mother because of her seriousness.
>
> People teased her about her looks and called her the "ugly duckling."
>
> Yet despite all of the disappointments, the bitterness, the misery she experienced, Eleanor Roosevelt refused to give up.
>
> Instead she turned her unhappiness and pain to strength.

As you draft your essay, use transitional words and phrases such as *similarly, then, however, later, most important,* and *as a result* to make the connection between your sentences clear and to help your writing flow.

Analyze a Student Model

In the beginning of the thirteenth century, a disabled boy was born near the kingdom of Kangba, West Africa. His name was Sundiata Keita, and he overcame physical challenges to become the first king of Mali.

Much of what is known about Sundiata comes from West African storytellers, or griots.[1] Like living history books, griots are an important source of information about Africa. The legends about Sundiata's life are "the most cherished" of their stories.[2]

According to the girot Djeli Mamoudou Kouyata, Sundiata was born to a king of the Mandigo people, who live in present-day Mali.[3] At the boy's birth, a prediction was made that he would some day rise to greatness. Great obstacles stood in his way, however.

Because Sundiata was physically challenged, he was only able to crawl.[4] As a result, people teased and made fun of him. He vowed to walk, however, and at seven years old, he took a heavy iron rod and "with trembling legs and a sweaty brow, he proceeded to lift himself up, bending the rod into a bow in the process."[5]

Sundiata went on to become an excellent hunter and warrior and a royal advisor. He later founded the Empire of Mali and served as its first ruler. As Kouyata reported, "he was greatly loved."[6]

The story of Sundiata is a story of inner strength and dedication winning out over misfortune. Insulted as a child, Sundiata became a king known by the highly honored title of "Lord Lion."[7]

[1] Phillip Koslow, Mali: Crossroads of Africa (New York: Chelsea, 1995).

Focused Subject
This interesting fact grabs the reader's attention and makes it clear that the report is about Sundiata.

Sources
Use information from reliable sources to support your ideas. Document the sources in footnotes within the text and at the bottom of the page. Be sure to quote material precisely.

Support
Support the topic sentence of each paragraph with interesting details, facts, or explanations from your research.

Summary
Include a summary of the overall main idea of the report.

Bibliography

Koslow, Philip. Mali: Crossroads of Africa. New York: Chelsea, 1995.

Bibliography
List complete information about your sources in alphabetical order. See the Writing Handbook at the back of this book for more guidelines on making foonotes and bibliographies.

Revise

Now it's time to revise your draft so your ideas really shine. Revising is what makes good writing great, and great writing takes work!

Peer Review Trade drafts with a partner. Use the chart below to review your partner's draft by answering the questions in the *What to do* column. Talk about your peer review after you have glanced at each other's drafts and have written down the answers to the questions. Next, follow the suggestions in the *How to do it* column to revise your draft.

Revising Plan

What to do	How to do it	Example
Can readers tell who your report is about?	State the subject of your report in the first paragraph.	In the beginning of the thirteenth century, a disabled boy was born in West Africa. His name was Sundiata Keita, and he overcame his physical challenges to become the first king of Mali.
Did you use multiple, dependable sources?	Evaluate your sources. Give credit to your sources in footnotes.	As Kouyata reported, "He was greatly loved."[6]
Have you explained and supported your main points?	Add related details to support your statements.	He vowed to walk, however, and at seven years old, he ~~did~~ took a heavy iron rod and "with trembling legs and a sweaty brow, he proceeded to lift himself up, bending the rod into a bow in the process."[5]
Is your research organized sensibly?	Present information in an organized and predictable way.	Sundiata He later founded the Empire of Mali and served as its first ruler. ~~Before that he~~ went on to become an excellent hunter and warrior and a royal advisor.
Will readers be able to locate the sources you used?	Include the author, name of the source, and publisher and date of publication or URL.	Koslow, Philip. Mali: Crossroads of Africa. New York: Chelsea, 1995.

Revising Tip

Documenting Sources Cite sources to give the origin of facts, opinions, or direct quotations, even if you summarize or paraphrase the information. See Media Literacy at the back of this book for help with knowing when to credit a source.

Edit and Proofread

For your final draft, read your research report one sentence at a time. Use the proofreading symbols in the chart inside the back cover of this book to mark needed changes. Then make corrections.

Grammar Focus: Commas in Dates and Place Names

In reporting about a person's life, dates and places are important details. Use commas between days and years and between cities and states, states and countries, and countries and continents or regions. See the Writing Handbook at the back of this book for help with punctuating bibliography and footnote entries. Below are examples of problems with commas from the Workshop Model and their solutions.

Problem: Unfamiliar locations are confusing.

In the beginning of the thirteenth century, a disabled boy was born near the kingdom of Kangba West Africa.

Solution: Add a comma between the kingdom and the region.

In the beginning of the thirteenth century, a disabled boy was born near the kingdom of Kangba, West Africa.

Problem: Commas are missing from the bibliography entry.

Koslow Philip. Mali: Crossroads of Africa. New York: Chelsea 1995.

Solution: Separate the author's last name from the first name with a comma. Put a comma between the publisher and the date of publication.

Koslow, Philip. Mali: Crossroads of Africa. New York: Chelsea, 1995.

Present

It's almost time to share your writing with others. Write your research report neatly in print or cursive on a separate sheet of paper. If you have access to a computer, type your research report on the computer and check spelling. Make sure to use appropriate formatting by applying the proper margins, spacing, and tabs. Save your document to a disk and print it out. Turn in your report to your teacher and share it with the rest of the class.

Grammar Tip

State Names In essays and reports, spell out state names. On envelopes and in charts, use the two-letter abbreviation for a state name. Examples: She was born in Dallas, Texas, in 1978.

Sara Ortiz
548 S. Leland St.
Dallas, TX 75246

Presenting Tip

Visuals To add interest to your research report, include photographs or illustrations of your subject and create a time line of the person's life, like "In Eleanor Roosevelt's Time" on pages 654–655.

Literature Online

Writing and Research For editing and publishing tools, go to glencoe.com and enter QuickPass code GL17527u5.

Performance Standards

For page 712

ELA6LSV2a When delivering or responding to presentations, give oral presentations or dramatic interpretations for various purposes.

Speaking, Listening, and Viewing Workshop

Oral Report

Activity

Connect to Your Writing Deliver an oral report to your classmates. You might want to adapt the research report you wrote for the Writing Workshop on pages 704–711. Remember that you focused on the Unit 5 Big Question: What brings out the best in you?

Plan Your Oral Report

Reread your research report and highlight the sections you want to include in your oral report. Just like your research report, your oral report should present well-researched information on a focused topic.

Rehearse Your Oral Report

Practice your oral report several times. Try rehearsing in front of a mirror where you can watch your movements and facial expressions. You may use note cards to remind you of your main points and information, but practice your oral report often enough that you won't lose eye contact with your audience.

Deliver Your Oral Report

- Speak clearly and precisely.
- Adjust your speaking style to add interest to the information you present.
- Change the tone, pace, and volume of your speaking to help emphasize important information in your oral report.
- Use gestures and visual aids to direct the audience's attention to important points and clarify your information.

Listening to Learn

Take notes as you listen to other oral reports to make sure you understand the topic. Use the following question frames to learn more about the topic from the speaker:

- I found this piece of information the most interesting: ________, because ________. What is the source of that information?
- Why did you choose to focus on this topic?
- To summarize the information in your oral report: ________. Is that correct?

Presentation Checklist

Answer the following questions to evaluate your presentation.

- ❑ Did you speak clearly and precisely—and with a style that helped add interest to the information?
- ❑ Did you vary the tone, pace, and volume of your speaking to emphasize important information?
- ❑ Did you use gestures and visual aids to clarify your information?
- ❑ Did you make eye contact with your audience?

LOG ON **Literature** Online

Speaking, Listening, and Viewing For project ideas, templates, and presentation tips, go to glencoe.com and enter QuickPass code GL17527u5.

Unit Challenge

Answer the Big Question

In Unit 5, you explored the Big Question through reading, writing, speaking, and listening. Now it's time for you to complete one of the Unit Challenges below with your answer to the Big Question.

GA Performance Standards

For pages 713

ELA6W2c Demonstrate competence in a variety of genres. Produce writing that develops a controlling idea that conveys a perspective on the subject.

WHAT Brings Out the Best in You?

Use the notes you took in your Unit 5 **Foldable** to complete the Unit Challenge of your choice.

Before you present your Unit Challenge, be sure it meets the requirements below. Use this first plan if you choose to interview yourself.

On Your Own Activity: Your Interview

- ❑ Write three or four questions that you think an interviewer would ask you about what brings out the best in you.
- ❑ Write answers to your questions.
- ❑ Write a final draft of your interview. Include questions, answers, and details in a logical order. Make sure your sentences are clear. Delete or combine sentences if necessary. Check your final draft for spelling and grammar, and post your interview in the classroom for others to read.

Use this second plan if you choose to work with a group to write an article for a teen magazine.

Group Activity: Magazine Article

- ❑ Brainstorm ideas about something you do well and what brings out your best.
- ❑ Write an article telling others how they can bring out their best in that same area.
- ❑ Write a final draft, making sure to use a logical sequence and clear sentences. Combine your article with other articles from the group to create an issue of your magazine.

Independent Reading

Fiction

To read more about the Big Question, choose one of these books from your school or local library.

Crash

by Jerry Spinelli

Seventh grader Crash Coogan is a bully. He's aggressive, mean, and smug, until an unlikely friendship makes him realize a thing or two about the way he treats others. Read Crash's story to find out what—and who—he comes to care about.

Cezanne Pinto

by Mary Stolz

In this fictional memoir, the main character escapes slavery in Virginia at the age of twelve. He travels to Canada via the Underground Railroad and eventually ends up in Texas. There he becomes a cowboy, finds a home, and begins a family of his own. This complex character's journeys take him both out on the road and deep inside himself.

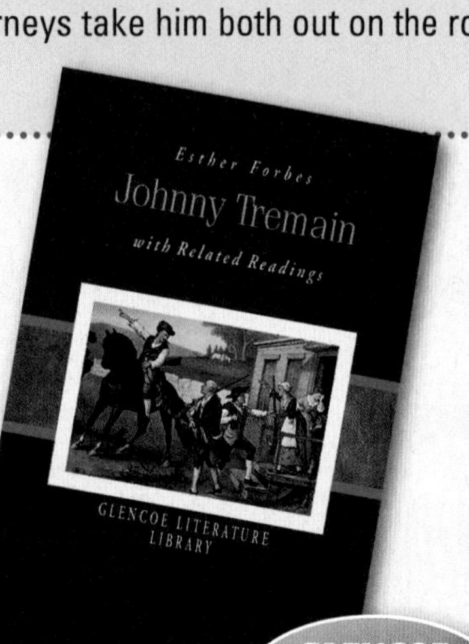

Johnny Tremain

by Esther Forbes

A compelling historical drama, this book chronicles the events leading up to the 1776 signing of the Declaration of Independence. Read this classic story of a boy's journey to adulthood, and let history come to life.

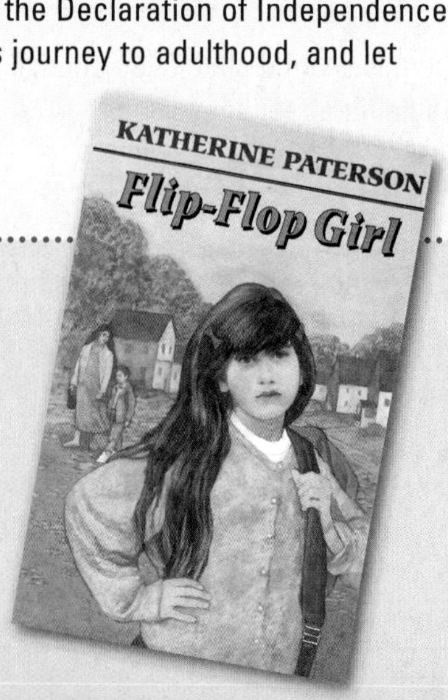

Flip-Flop Girl

by Katherine Paterson

After her father dies, Vinnie and her family move to a small town to live with her grandmother. Things aren't going well when Vinnie makes a new friend at school—someone who is also an outsider. Read to find out how Vinnie's friendship helps her and her family get past their grief.

Nonfiction

Ten Hispanic American Authors

by Christine M. Hill

Read these short profiles to discover the literary influences and childhood experiences that shaped ten important authors, including Sandra Cisneros, Judith Ortiz Cofer, and Gary Soto.

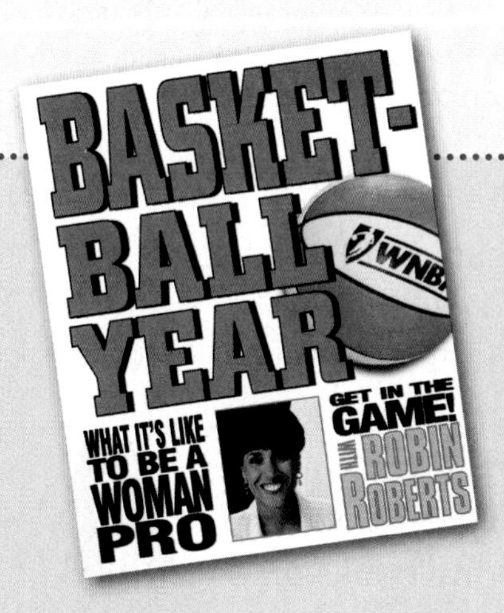

Basketball Year: What It's Like to Be a Woman Pro

by Robin Roberts

Eight players from the Women's National Basketball Association discuss their jobs, their lives, and the elite level at which they compete. Read to learn more about how these amazing athletes have turned their passion into a paycheck—while having a ball.

Ellington Was Not a Street

by Ntozake Shange

Told as an illustrated poem, this account brings to life the language and music of a bygone era. Using biographical sketches of men such as Paul Robeson and Duke Ellington, *Ellington Was Not a Street* depicts an important part of African American history—and some of the great people who made it happen.

Keep a Reader Response Journal

Read one of these books, based on your own interest and/or a recommendation from a friend or a classmate. As you read, make frequent journal entries about what you found interesting, unexpected, challenging, or exciting in the book. Be sure to support your responses with specific examples from the text.

Assessment

READING

Read the passage and answer the questions. Write your answers on a separate sheet of paper.

from **"The Jacket"** by Gary Soto

My clothes have failed me. I remember the green coat that I wore in fifth and sixth grades when you either danced like a champ or pressed yourself against a greasy wall, bitter as a penny toward the happy couples.

When I needed a new jacket and my mother asked what kind I wanted, I described something like bikers wear: black leather and silver studs with enough belts to hold down a small town. We were in the kitchen, steam on the windows from her cooking. She listened so long while stirring dinner that I thought she understood for sure the kind I wanted. The next day when I got home from school, I discovered draped on my bedpost a jacket the color of day-old guacamole. I threw my books on the bed and approached the jacket slowly, as if it were a stranger whose hand I had to shake. I touched the vinyl sleeve, the collar, and peeked at the mustard-colored lining.

From the kitchen my mother yelled that my jacket was in the closet. I closed the door to her voice and pulled at the rack of clothes in the closet, hoping the jacket on the bedpost wasn't for me but my mean brother. No luck. I gave up. From my bed, I stared at the jacket. I wanted to cry because it was so ugly and so big that I knew I'd have to wear it a long time. I was a small kid, thin as a young tree, and it would be years before I'd have a new one. I stared at the jacket, like an enemy, thinking bad things before I took off my old jacket whose sleeves climbed halfway to my elbow.

I put the big jacket on.

I zipped it up and down several times, and rolled the cuffs up so they didn't cover my hands. I put my hands in the pockets and flapped the jacket like a bird's wings. I stood in front of the mirror, full face, then profile, and then looked over my shoulder as if someone had called me.

I sat on the bed, stood against the bed, and combed my hair to see what I would look like doing something natural. I looked ugly. I threw it on my brother's bed and looked at it for a long time before I slipped it on and went out to the backyard, smiling a "thank you" to my mom as I passed her in the kitchen. With my hands in my pockets I kicked a ball against the fence, and then climbed it to sit looking into the alley. I hurled orange peels at the mouth of an open garbage can and when the peels were gone I watched the white puffs of my breath thin to nothing.

I jumped down, hands in my pockets, and in the backyard on my knees I teased my dog, Brownie, by swooping my arms while making bird calls. He jumped at me and missed.

He jumped again and again, until a tooth sunk deep, ripping an L-shaped tear on my left sleeve. I pushed Brownie away to study the tear as I would a cut on my arm. There was no blood, only a few loose pieces of fuzz. Dumb dog, I thought, and pushed him away hard when he tried to bite again. I got up from my knees and went to my bedroom to sit with my jacket on my lap, with the lights out.

That was the first afternoon with my new jacket. The next day I wore it to sixth grade and got a D on a math quiz. During the morning recess Frankie T., the playground terrorist, pushed me to the ground and told me to stay there until recess was over. My best friend, Steve Negrete, ate an apple while looking at me, and the girls turned away to whisper on the monkey bars. The teachers were no help: they looked my way and talked about how foolish I looked in my new jacket. I saw their heads bob with laughter, their hands half-covering their mouths.

Even though it was cold, I took off the jacket during lunch and played kickball in a thin shirt, my arms feeling like Braille from goose bumps. But when I returned to class I slipped the jacket on and shivered until I was warm. I sat on my hands, heating them up, while my teeth chattered like a cup of crooked dice. Finally warm, I slid out of the jacket but a few minutes later put it back on when the fire bell rang. We paraded out into the yard where we, the sixth graders, walked past all the other grades to stand against the back fence.

Everybody saw me. Although they didn't say out loud, "Man, that's ugly," I heard the buzz-buzz of gossip and even laughter that I knew was meant for me.

1. Details about the speaker in this passage show that he lacks
   A. self-control.
   B. intelligence.
   C. imagination.
   D. self-confidence.

2. The main conflict in this narrative can BEST be described as
   A. one character versus another character.
   B. a character versus nature.
   C. a character's internal conflict.
   D. an antagonist versus a protagonist.

3. The dictionary entry for the word guacamole contains this information: (gwä kə mō´lē). Referring to this part of the entry tells you that *guacamole*
   A. means "avocado sauce."
   B. has three syllables.
   C. can be either a noun or an adjective.
   D. is accented on the third syllable.

4. Which of the following is NOT a reason the narrator hates his new jacket?
   A. He doesn't like its size.
   B. He doesn't like its color.
   C. He doesn't like how heavy it is.
   D. He doesn't like what it's made of.

5. Which of the following quotations is the BEST example of hyperbole?
   A. ". . . an L-shaped tear on my left sleeve."
   B. ". . . with enough belts to hold down a small town."
   C. "I was a small kid, thin as a young tree . . ."
   D. ". . . and peeked at the mustard-colored lining."

6. What does the green jacket represent to the narrator?
   A. disloyalty
   B. achievement
   C. embarrassment
   D. physical discomfort

7. Which sentence BEST describes the narrator's character?
   A. He is insecure and fears being unpopular.
   B. He is uncomfortable due to the cold weather.
   C. He is concerned about doing poorly on a quiz.
   D. He does not worry what others think of him.

Standards Practice For more standards practice, go to glencoe.com and enter QuickPass code GL17527u5.

8. Which statement BEST summarizes the message about life that the author is trying to convey?
   A. It is foolish to worry about what other people think.
   B. Parents always know what is best for their children.
   C. A friend who won't stand up for you is no friend at all.
   D. Something others might think is unimportant can have painful effects.

9. The root word of *terrorist* is based on the Latin word *terrere,* meaning "to frighten." Which word below also comes from this root?
   A. terrestrial
   B. terrible
   C. territory
   D. terrace

10. Why does the narrator take off his jacket during lunch?
    A. He does not want it to be damaged while he plays kickball.
    B. He wants the teachers and the girls to notice him.
    C. He believes he looks less foolish with the jacket off.
    D. Frankie T. demands that he remove his jacket.

11. Based on this passage, which one of the following statements is true?
    A. The narrator has no friends.
    B. The narrator's mother does not understand him.
    C. If the jacket is damaged, it will be replaced.
    D. The narrator is small and thin for his age.

12. What is the meaning of the word *natural* in this passage?
    A. not forced or affected
    B. produced by or existing in nature
    C. closely imitating nature
    D. having to do with the study of nature

ENGLISH/LANGUAGE ARTS

Choose the best answer for each question. Write your answers on a separate sheet of paper.

1. Which word BEST fills in the blank in the sentence below?

> My dad thinks that we watch too much television, __________ he has made some new rules.

A. so

B. but

C. or

D. since

2. Which word is NOT spelled correctly in the sentence below?

> Scientists analized the data to determine how many species are endangered.

A. Scientists

B. analized

C. determine

D. species

3. Which group of words in the sentence below is a prepositional phrase?

> Starting tomorrow, our class will be studying about the Civil War.

A. Starting tomorrow

B. our class

C. will be studying

D. about the Civil War

4. The word *before* is a subordinating conjunction in which of the following sentences?

A. I hope you will bring food before noon.

B. I hope you will bring food before I have to leave.

C. I hope you will bring food the way you did before.

D. I had brought the food to them the night before.

WRITING

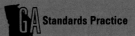

Read your assigned topic in the box below. Use one piece of paper to jot down your ideas and organize your thoughts. Then neatly write your letter on another sheet of paper.

Persuasive Writing Topic

Writing Situation

Your principal wants to make new rules that will reduce the amount of bullying at your school. She has asked students to think of new rules and tell why they think their rules will help.

Directions for Writing

Write a letter to your principal. First, write your new rule in clear, positive terms. Then convince your principal to choose your rule by giving specific reasons why you think the rule will reduce bullying.

Writing Checklist

- ☐ Focus on a single topic.
- ☐ Organize your main points in a clear, logical order.
- ☐ Support your ideas or viewpoints with details and examples.
- ☐ Use precise, vivid words.
- ☐ Vary the length and structure of your sentences.
- ☐ Use clear transition words to connect ideas.
- ☐ Correct any errors in spelling, capitalization, punctuation, and usage.

WHAT Are Worthwhile Goals?

UNIT SIX

THE BIG Question

> *A goal is a dream that has an ending.*
>
> —DUKE ELLINGTON

FOLDABLES® Study Organizer

Throughout Unit 6, you will read, write, and talk about the **BIG Question—"What Are Worthwhile Goals?"** Use your Unit 6 **Foldable,** shown here, to keep track of your ideas as you read. Turn to the back of this book for instructions on making this **Foldable.**

Explore the BIG Question

WHAT Are Worthwhile Goals?

Everyone has dreams. One person's dream might be to create a community garden in the middle of a city. Another person's dream might be to study medicine and help others. Have you ever set goals to achieve a dream? How do you know which goals are worthwhile? Explore how you can identify and set worthwhile goals.

Think about some worthwhile goals:

- Loyalty and Understanding
- Knowledge and Wisdom

What You'll Read

In this unit, you'll focus on reading **drama,** which is a work of literature written to be performed by actors in front of an audience. By reading drama, you share in the characters' discoveries about themselves, the world, and life. Drama and other types of writing in this unit can lead you to discover answers to the Big Question.

What You'll Write

As you explore the Big Question, you'll write notes in your Unit 6 **Foldable.** Later you'll use these notes to complete two writing assignments related to the Big Question.

1. **Write an Expository Essay**
2. **Choose a Unit Challenge**
   - **On Your Own Activity: Bumper Stickers**
   - **Group Activity: Worthwhile Goals Play**

What You'll Learn

Literary Elements

dialogue

conflict

stage directions

act and scene

alliteration and assonance

irony

Reading Skills and Strategies

analyze diction

make generalizations about characters

identify cause-and-effect relationships

paraphrase

interpret author's meaning

Explore the BIG Question

Madam C. J. Walker

Jim Haskins

Madam C. J. Walker was the first American woman to earn a million dollars. There were American women millionaires before her time, but they had inherited their wealth, either from their husbands or from their families. Madam Walker was the first woman to earn her fortune by setting up her own business and proving that women could be financially independent of men. The company she started in the 1900s is still in operation today.

Set a Purpose for Reading

Read this biography to discover the goals Madam C. J. Walker set for herself and how they helped her achieve success.

Madam C. J. Walker was born Sarah Breedlove on December 23, 1867. She grew up in the South under very racist conditions. Her parents, Owen and Minerva Breedlove, had been slaves until President Abraham Lincoln's Emancipation Proclamation and the Union victory in the Civil War had freed the slaves.

After the war, few provisions[1] were made to help former slaves become independent. They did not receive money to help them get started in their new lives. They were uneducated, they had few skills except the ability to grow crops, and many were unaware of what freedom meant. Like the majority of former slaves, the Breedloves remained on the Burney family plantation in Delta, Louisiana. They had little choice but to stay on the same land where they had been slaves, only now they were sharecroppers.[2]

BQ BIG Question

Why would an education be a worthwhile goal for a former slave?

---

1 Here, ***provisions*** (prə vizh′ ənz) are arrangements made for the future.

2 ***Sharecroppers*** are farmers who live and work on someone's land in return for a share of the crops.

The Breedloves sharecropped cotton. Like her brothers and sisters, Sarah was working in the cotton fields by the time she was six. By the time she was eleven, both her parents were dead, and she moved in with her older sister, Louvenia. A few years later, they moved across the river to Vicksburg, Mississippi.

Sarah married a man named McWilliams to get away from her sister's household. At that time, conditions in the South for blacks were actually worse than they had been during slavery. This was the time when Jim Crow laws were passed, segregating[3] southern blacks from whites in nearly every area of life. It was the time when white supremacy groups like the Ku Klux Klan achieved their greatest power, and lynchings[4] of blacks were common.

BQ **BIG Question**

How could this fact have influenced Sarah's goals?

Sarah and her husband lived with the terror of being black as best they could. In 1885 their daughter, Lelia, was born, and her parents dreamed of making a better life for their little girl. Then, when Lelia was two, McWilliams was killed by a lynch mob.[5]

Sarah was a widow at the age of twenty, and the sole support of a two-year-old daughter. She took in laundry to earn a living and was determined to leave the South. With Lelia, she made her way up the Mississippi River and settled in St. Louis, where she worked fourteen hours a day doing other people's laundry. She enrolled Lelia in the St. Louis public schools and was pleased that her daughter would get the education that had been denied to her. But she wanted more for her daughter and for herself.

Not long after they moved to St. Louis, Sarah McWilliams realized that her hair was falling out. She did not know why, but it is likely that the practice of braiding her hair too tightly was part of the cause. At the time, few hair-care products were available for black

---

3 ***Segregating*** means "separating or setting apart."

4 ***Lynchings*** are acts by a mob of putting to death, usually by hanging, without a trial or other due process of law.

5 ***McWilliams . . . mob.*** No documentation actually proves that he died this way.

women. For years she tried every hair-care product available. But nothing worked.

Wonderful Hair Grower was the most popular product made by Madam Walker's company. It was first sold in 1906.

Then one night she had a dream. As she told the story many years later, in her dream "a black man appeared to me and told me what to mix up for my hair. Some of the remedy was grown in Africa, but I sent for it, mixed it, put it on my scalp, and in a few weeks my hair was coming in faster than it had ever fallen out." Sarah never publicly revealed the formula of her mixture.

Sarah's friends remarked on what a full and healthy head of hair she had, and she gave some of her mixture to them. It worked on them, too, so she decided to sell it. She later said that she started her "Hair Grower" business with an investment of $1.50.

She had not been in business long when she received word that a brother who lived in Denver, Colorado, had died, leaving a wife and daughters. Sarah decided to go to Denver to live with her sister-in-law and nieces.

BQ BIG Question
How does this action show Sarah's loyalty to her family?

In Denver, Sarah began to sell her special haircare product and did well. But she realized she needed to advertise to get more customers. Six months after arriving in Denver, she married C. J. Walker, a newspaperman who knew a lot about selling by mail order. With his help, she began to advertise her product, first in black newspapers across the state and later in black newspapers nationwide, and to make more money.

But soon her marriage was in trouble. As Sarah Walker later said of her husband, "I had business disagreements with him, for when we began to make ten dollars a day, he thought that amount was enough and that I should be satisfied. But I was convinced that my hair preparations would fill a longfelt want, and when we found it impossible to agree, due to his narrowness of vision, I embarked in business for myself."

BQ BIG Question
How could understanding what her customers want help Sarah Walker set goals?

In addition to helping her learn about advertising, her marriage gave Sarah Breedlove McWilliams Walker the name she would use for the rest of her life—Madam C. J. Walker. The "Madam" part was an affectation,[6] but Sarah liked the way it sounded. She thought it would be good for her business. By 1906 her business was so good that she was able to stop doing laundry for a living and devote all her time to her hair-care company.

Madam Walker was very proud of being a woman, and she was convinced that she could make it in the business world without the help of men. Almost from the start she determined that her business would be run by women. In 1906 she put her twenty-one-year-old daughter, Lelia, in charge of her growing mail-order business.

Madam Walker realized that the normal outlets for her products—white department stores and pharmacies—were not open to her. These stores would not stock black products because they did not want black customers. In addition to advertising, mostly in black newspapers, Madam Walker had to depend on the institutions in the black communities, the black churches, and the black women's clubs.

BQ BIG Question
How does Madam Walker's knowledge of society at this time affect her goals?

Madam Walker's lectures on hair culture were widely attended. She was an excellent speaker and a commanding woman, nearly six feet tall, who was always beautifully dressed and coiffed.[7] She made a lasting impression wherever she went.

Although she lacked the formal education that most of these women had, Madam Walker never felt ashamed of her shortcomings[8] in that area. She taught herself as much as she could and was not afraid to ask someone to define a word she did not know or explain something she did not understand.

BQ BIG Question
How does this show Madam Walker's wisdom?

---

6 An ***affectation*** (af′ ek tā′ shən) is an artificial way of acting, usually to impress someone.

7 ***Coiffed*** (koift) means "styled," especially hair.

8 ***Shortcomings*** are deficiencies or faults.

Madam Walker also wanted black women to go into business. Why should they toil over hot laundry tubs and clean white people's houses when they could be in business for themselves? Helping other black women also helped the Walker Company, and with this goal in mind Madam Walker recruited[9] and trained scores of women to use and sell Walker products. Many of them set up salons in their own homes. Others traveled door-to-door selling Walker products and demonstrating the Walker System. Madam Walker insisted that her agents sign contracts promising to abide by her strict standards of personal hygiene[10]—long before various states passed similar laws for workers in the cosmetics field. By 1910 the Walker Company had trained around 5,000 black female agents, not just in the United States but in

BQ BIG Question
What makes this a worthwhile goal?

View the Photograph In what ways does this photograph show how these women felt about graduating from beauty school?

9 ***Recruited*** means "hired or obtained the services of."

10 ***Hygiene*** (hī′ jēn) is a term for practices leading to good health.

1939 graduates of the St. Louis Walker Beauty School.

Advertisements like this were placed in newspapers around the country.

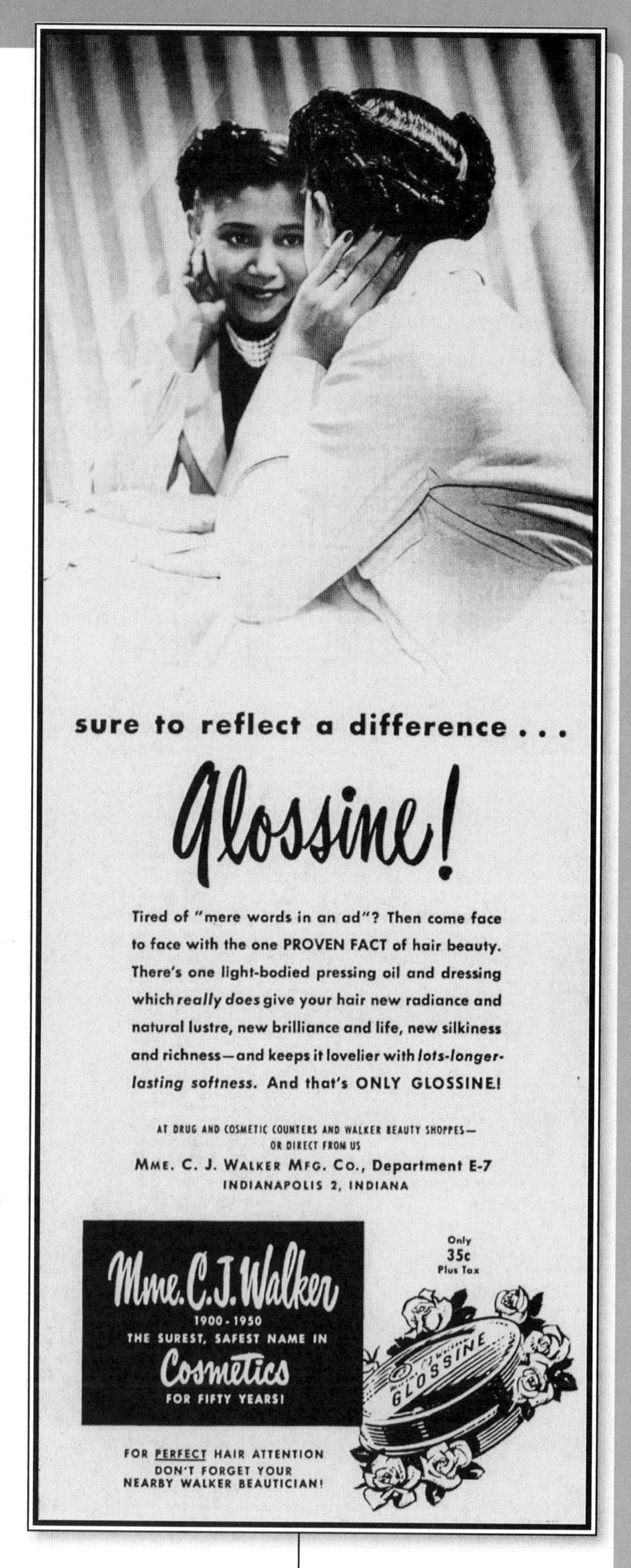

sure to reflect a difference . . .
Glossine!
Tired of "mere words in an ad"? Then come face to face with the one PROVEN FACT of hair beauty. There's one light-bodied pressing oil and dressing which really does give your hair new radiance and natural lustre, new brilliance and life, new silkiness and richness—and keeps it lovelier with lots-longer-lasting softness. And that's ONLY GLOSSINE!
AT DRUG AND COSMETIC COUNTERS AND WALKER BEAUTY SHOPPES—OR DIRECT FROM US
MME. C. J. WALKER MFG. CO., Department E-7
INDIANAPOLIS 2, INDIANA
Mme. C.J. Walker
1900-1950
THE SUREST, SAFEST NAME IN
Cosmetics
FOR FIFTY YEARS!
Only
35c
Plus Tax
GLOSSINE
FOR PERFECT HAIR ATTENTION
DON'T FORGET YOUR
NEARBY WALKER BEAUTICIAN!

England, France, Italy, and the West Indies. The company itself was taking in $1,000 a day, seven days a week.

That same year, Madam Walker's travels took her to Indianapolis, Indiana, a city that impressed her so much that she decided to move her headquarters there.

Madam Walker did not have much of a private life. She spent her time thinking of new ways to increase her business. The friends she had were people who could help her.

By 1917 the years of traveling and overwork began to take their toll on her. She developed high blood pressure, and in 1918 her doctors warned her that she had to slow down. She died quietly of kidney failure resulting from hypertension in May 1919.

In her will, Madam Walker left the bulk of her estate and the business to her daughter, Lelia. But she also provided generously for a variety of educational institutions run by black women. She established a trust fund for an industrial and mission school in West Africa and provided bequests[11] to Negro orphanages, old people's homes, and Negro YWCA branches. In addition, she made bequests to many friends and employees.

Also in her will, Madam Walker insisted that the Madam C. J. Walker Company always be headed by a woman, and her wishes were carried out. Her daughter became president of the company after her death and presided at the dedication of the new company headquarters in Indianapolis in 1927, fulfilling a long-held dream of her mother's.

BQ BIG Question

How did Madam Walker fulfill her dreams?

---

11 ***Bequests*** (bi kwests′) are things handed down or passed on.

In 1917 Madam Walker moved into this mansion in a wealthy suburb of New York and lived there until her death in 1919. The house had more than thirty rooms and was decorated with valuable statues, tapestries, and paintings.

After You Read

Respond and Think Critically

1. Use your own words to tell the major events that describe how Madam C. J. Walker started her own business. **[Summarize]**
2. What obstacles did Madam C. J. Walker have to overcome to be successful? **[Identify]**
3. How do you think the author feels about Madam C. J. Walker? Why do you think he wrote this biography? Use examples to support your opinions. **[Infer]**
4. How do you think Madam C. J. Walker's success influenced other African American women? Explain. **[Evaluate]**

Writing

Reader Response Madam C. J. Walker is famous for being the first American woman who was a self-made millionaire. She succeeded at a time when women and African Americans had far fewer rights than white men. Madam Walker set many goals for herself in order to succeed. Write a paragraph telling which of her goals you think was the most worthwhile. Use specific examples from the text to support your opinion. When you are finished, share your response with the class. You may want to begin your paragraph with this sentence:

Of all of Madam C. J. Walker's goals, I think _______ was the most worthwhile, because _______.

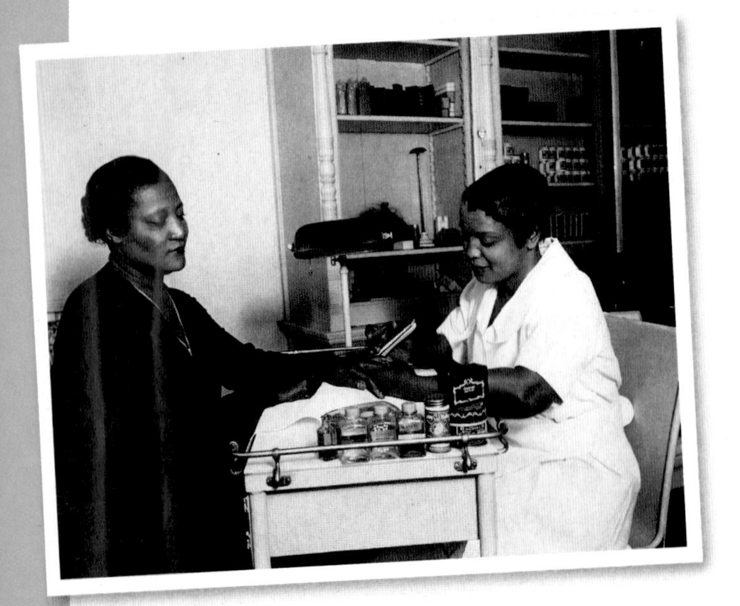

GA Performance Standards

For page 732

ELA6W2c Demonstrate competence in a variety of genres. Produce a response to literature that advances a judgment that is interpretive, analytic, evaluative, or reflective.

LOG ON **Literature** Online

Unit Resources For additional skills practice, go to glencoe.com and enter QuickPass code GL17527u6.

Part 1

Loyalty and Understanding

Juvenile Counsel; Boys on a Doorstep. Henry Lamb. Private Collection.

BQ BIG Question What Are Worthwhile Goals?

In the painting *Juvenile Counsel; Boys on a Doorstep,* three young men share friendly moments together. How do the boys show that they are trying to understand one another? In friendships, how does loyalty grow as understanding develops?

Before You Read

Damon and Pythias

Connect to the Play

Think about friendships you have had. What makes a friendship strong? What do you think is the basis of true friendship?

List Make a list of different traits that are important to friendship. You may want to rank them by order of importance. What does your ranking say about you?

Build Background

More than two thousand years ago, the Roman writer Cicero wrote down an ancient Greek story about two friends, Damon and Pythias. The story is set in the fourth century B.C. in Syracuse, a city on the island of Sicily. Syracuse was a powerful city in the ancient world and was ruled by a tyrant king, Dionysius the Elder. There are many versions of the story of Damon and Pythias. This version was written as a radio play.

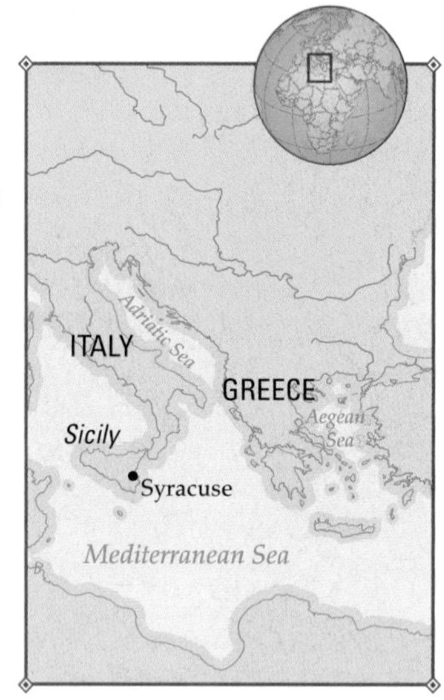

Vocabulary

proclaimed (prə klāmd′) *v.* announced officially; declared publicly (p. 737). *The mayor proclaimed that the town would hold an annual fall parade.*

appointed (ə point′ əd) *v.* named or selected for an office or position (p. 737). *My friends appointed me the treasurer of our club.*

resist (ri zist′) *v.* to act in opposition (p. 737). *The urge to buy new shoes at the sale was hard for Tyra to resist.*

honorable (on′ ər ə bəl) *adj.* characterized by principles of morality and integrity; upright (p. 740). *An honorable player will not intentionally cheat during a game.*

harsh (härsh) *adj.* rough or unpleasant to any of the physical senses (p. 743). *The harsh sound of breaking glass surprised us.*

Meet Fan Kissen

Radio Writer Fan Kissen spent most of her writing career turning folktales and legends into plays for young people. The plays were first performed in a radio series called *Tales from the Four Winds* that ran from 1945 to 1961. Each play included instructions for music and sound effects.

Literary Works Kissen collected and published plays in *The Bag of Fire and Other Tales, The Crowded House and Other Tales,* and *The Straw Ox and Other Tales.*

Fan Kissen was born in 1904 and died in 1978.

Literature Online

Author Search For more about Fan Kissen, go to glencoe.com and enter QuickPass code GL17527u6.

Set Purposes for Reading

BQ BIG Question

As you read, ask yourself, how important is it for a friend to be loyal? Can a person be your friend if he or she is not loyal?

Literary Element Dialogue

Dialogue is conversation between characters in a literary work. A play relies on dialogue to tell a story.

Damon and Pythias was written as a radio play. Its dialogue reveals information about the characters and advances the plot. **Stage directions,** the words in brackets and italics, may describe the setting or tell the actors how to move, look, or say their lines.

As you read, think about what you learn about each character through the dialogue.

Reading Skill Analyze Diction

Diction is an author's choice of words. Skilled writers carefully choose their words to get across a particular meaning or feeling.

Analyzing diction is important because it helps you understand how certain words contribute to the tone or message of the story.

To analyze diction, pay attention to

- the literal meaning, or denotation, of important words. Denotation is the dictionary definition of a word.
- the connotation, or implied meaning, of important words. The connotation of a word causes you to have an emotional response that can be positive, negative, or neutral.
- how the choice of particular words adds to your understanding of the play.

As you read, use a chart like the one below to help you understand the connotation and denotation of particular words.

Word	Denotation—Dictionary Definition	Connotation—Positive, Negative, or Neutral?	Effect of Words on My Understanding
tyrant			

GA Performance Standards

For pages 734–745

ELA6R1b For literary texts, identify and analyze the author's use of dialogue and description.

TRY IT

Analyze Diction You and a friend compare the price of soup at the grocery store. Your friend says that one brand is cheap. You say that it is inexpensive. Which word gives you a more positive feeling? Which gives a negative feeling?

DAMON AND PYTHIAS

Fan Kissen
based on the Greek legend

CAST

Damon
First Robber
First Voice
Pythias
Second Robber
Second Voice
King
Mother
Third Voice
Soldier
Narrator

[*Sound: Iron door opens and shuts. Key in lock.*]
[*Music: Up full and out.*]

NARRATOR. Long, long ago there lived on the island of Sicily two young men named Damon and Pythias. They were known far and wide for the strong friendship each had for the other. Their names have come down to our own times to mean true friendship. You may hear it said of two persons:

FIRST VOICE. Those two? Why, they're like Damon and Pythias!

NARRATOR. The king of that country was a cruel tyrant. He made cruel laws, and he showed no mercy toward anyone who broke his laws. Now, you might very well wonder:

SECOND VOICE. Why didn't the people rebel?

NARRATOR. Well, the people didn't dare rebel because they feared the

---

Analyze Diction What does the author's word choice tell you about the king's character?

king's great and powerful army. No one dared say a word against the king or his laws—except Damon and Pythias speaking against a new law the king had **proclaimed**.

SOLDIER. Ho, there! Who are you that dares to speak so about our king?

PYTHIAS. [*Unafraid.*] I am called Pythias.

SOLDIER. Don't you know it is a crime to speak against the king or his laws? You are under arrest! Come and tell this opinion of yours to the king's face!

[*Music: A few short bars in and out.*]

NARRATOR. When Pythias was brought before the king, he showed no fear. He stood straight and quiet before the throne.

KING. [*Hard, cruel.*] So, Pythias! They tell me you do not approve of the laws I make.

PYTHIAS. I am not alone, your Majesty, in thinking your laws are cruel. But you rule the people with such an iron hand that they dare not complain.

KING. [*Angry.*] But you have the daring to complain for them! Have they **appointed** you their champion?[1]

PYTHIAS. No, your Majesty. I speak for myself alone. I have no wish to make trouble for anyone. But I am not afraid to tell you that the people are suffering under your rule. They want to have a voice in making the laws for themselves. You do not allow them to speak up for themselves.

KING. In other words, you are calling me a tyrant! Well, you shall learn for yourself how a tyrant treats a rebel! Soldier! Throw this man into prison!

SOLDIER. At once, your Majesty! Don't try to **resist**, Pythias!

PYTHIAS. I know better than to try to resist a soldier of the king! And for how long am I to remain in prison, your Majesty, merely for speaking out for the people?

KING. [*Cruel.*] Not for very long, Pythias. Two weeks from today at noon, you shall be put to death in the public square as an example to anyone else who may dare to question my laws or acts. Off to prison with him, soldier!

Dialogue From this question, what impression do you get of the soldier?

Analyze Diction How does the phrase "rule with an iron hand" make you feel?

Vocabulary

proclaimed (prə klāmd′) *v.* announced officially; declared publicly

1 Here, a ***champion*** refers to someone who fights for or speaks for another person.

Dialogue What does this dialogue with Pythias suggest about the relationship between the king and the people?

Vocabulary

appointed (ə point′əd) *v.* named or selected for an office or position

resist (ri zist′) *v.* to act in opposition

[*Music: In briefly and out.*]

NARRATOR. When Damon heard that his friend Pythias had been thrown into prison, and about the severe punishment that was to follow, he was heartbroken. He rushed to the prison and persuaded the guard to let him speak to his friend.

DAMON. Oh, Pythias! How terrible to find you here! I wish I could do something to save you!

PYTHIAS. Nothing can save me, Damon, my dear friend. I am prepared to die. But there is one thought that troubles me greatly.

DAMON. What is it? I will do anything to help you.

PYTHIAS. I'm worried about what will happen to my mother and my sister when I'm gone.

DAMON. I'll take care of them, Pythias, as if they were my own mother and sister.

PYTHIAS. Thank you, Damon. I have money to leave them. But there are other things I must arrange. If only I could go see them before I die! But they live two days' journey from here, you know.

DAMON. I'll go to the king and beg him to give you your freedom for a few days. You'll give your word to return at the end of that time. Everyone in Sicily knows you for a man who has never broken his word.

PYTHIAS. Do you believe for one moment that the king would let me leave this prison, no matter how good my word may have been all my life?

DAMON. I'll tell him that I shall take your place in the prison cell. I'll tell him that if you do not return by the appointed day, he may kill *me* in your place!

PYTHIAS. No, no, Damon! You must not do such a foolish thing! I cannot—I will not—let you do this! Damon! Damon! Don't go! [*To himself.*] Damon, my friend! You may find yourself in a cell beside me!

[*Music: In briefly and out.*]

DAMON. [*Begging.*] Your Majesty! I beg of you! Let Pythias go home for a few days to bid farewell to his mother and sister. He gives his word that he will return at your appointed time. Everyone knows that his word can be trusted.

KING. In ordinary business affairs—perhaps. But he is now a man under sentence of death. To free him even for a few days would strain his honesty—*any* man's honesty—too far. Pythias would never return here!

Analyze Diction What effect does the author's word choice have on the reader?

BQ BIG Question How would you describe Damon and Pythias's friendship?

Analyze Diction What does Damon's style of speaking tell you about him?

The Greek Theatre, Etna. Fernando Gualtieri. Oil on canvas. Private Collection, ©DACS.

I consider him a traitor, but I'm certain he's no fool.

DAMON. Your Majesty! I will take his place in the prison until he comes back. If he does not return, then you may take *my* life in his place.

KING. [*Astonished.*] What did you say, Damon?

DAMON. I'm so certain of Pythias that I am offering to die in his place if he fails to return on time.

KING. I can't believe you mean it!

DAMON. I do mean it, your Majesty.

KING. You make me very curious, Damon, so curious that I'm willing to put you and Pythias to the test. This exchange of prisoners will be made. But Pythias must be back two weeks from today, at noon.

DAMON. Thank you, your Majesty!

KING. The order with my official seal shall go by your own hand,[2] Damon. But I warn you, if your friend does not return on time, you shall surely die in his place! I shall show no mercy.

[*Music: In briefly and out.*]

NARRATOR. Pythias did not like the king's bargain with Damon. He did not like to leave his friend in prison with the chance that he might lose his

BQ BIG Question How is Damon being loyal? How will Pythias need to return this loyalty?

2 In saying the order should go by Damon's ***own hand,*** the king means that Damon should carry the order himself.

life if something went wrong. But at last Damon persuaded him to leave and Pythias set out for his home. More than a week went by. The day set for the death sentence drew near. Pythias did not return. Everyone in the city knew of the condition on which the king had permitted Pythias to go home. Everywhere people met, the talk was sure to turn to the two friends.

FIRST VOICE. Do you suppose Pythias will come back?

SECOND VOICE. Why should he stick his head under the king's ax once he has escaped?

THIRD VOICE. Still would an **honorable** man like Pythias let such a good friend die for him?

FIRST VOICE. There's no telling what a man will do when it's a question of his own life against another's.

SECOND VOICE. But if Pythias doesn't come back before the time is up, he will be killing his friend.

THIRD VOICE. Well, there's still a few days' time. I, for one, am certain that Pythias *will* return in time.

SECOND VOICE. And *I am* just as certain that he will *not*. Friendship is friendship, but a man's own life is something stronger, *I* say!

NARRATOR. Two days before the time was up, the king himself visited Damon in his prison cell.

[*Sound: Iron door unlocked and opened.*]

KING. [*Mocking.*] You see now, Damon, that you were a fool to make this bargain. Your friend has tricked you! He will not come back here to be killed! He has deserted you.

DAMON. [*Calm and firm.*] I have faith in my friend. I know he will return.

KING. [*Mocking.*] We shall see!

[*Sound: Iron door shut and locked.*]

NARRATOR. Meanwhile, when Pythias reached the home of his family, he arranged his business affairs so that his mother and sister would be able to live comfortably for the rest of their years. Then he said a last farewell to them before starting back to the city.

MOTHER. [*In tears.*] Pythias, it will take you two days to get back. Stay another day, I beg you!

PYTHIAS. I dare not stay longer, Mother. Remember, Damon is locked up in my prison cell while I'm gone. Please don't

---

Dialogue What does this sentence make you think about friendship?

Vocabulary

honorable (on′ər ə bəl) *adj.* characterized by principles of morality and integrity; upright

BQ BIG Question What does this statement imply about loyalty and friendship?

Analyze Diction Why do you think the author uses the word *deserted*?

weep for me. My death may help bring better days for all our people.

NARRATOR. So Pythias began his journey in plenty of time. But bad luck struck him on the very first day. At twilight, as he walked along a lonely stretch of woodland, a rough voice called:

FIRST ROBBER. Not so fast there, young man! Stop!

PYTHIAS. [*Startled.*] Oh! What is it? What do you want?

SECOND ROBBER. Your money bags.

PYTHIAS. My money bags? I have only this small bag of coins. I shall need them for some favors, perhaps, before I die.

FIRST ROBBER. What do you mean, before you die? We don't mean to kill you, only take your money.

PYTHIAS. I'll give you my money, only don't delay me any longer. I am to die by the king's order three days from now. If I don't return on time, my friend must die in my place.

FIRST ROBBER. A likely story! What man would be fool enough to go back to prison ready to die?

SECOND ROBBER. And what man would be fool enough to die *for* you?

FIRST ROBBER. We'll take your money, all right. And we'll tie you up while we get away.

Dialogue Why do the robbers ask these questions?

Attic red-figure vase showing a detail from a banquet scene, Greece, late 5th century BC. Pottery. Museo Archeologico Nazionale, Naples, Italy.

PYTHIAS. [*Begging.*] No! No! I must get back to free my friend! [*Fade.*] I must go back!

NARRATOR. But the two robbers took Pythias's money, tied him to a tree, and went off as fast as they could. Pythias struggled to free himself. He cried out for a long time. But no one traveled through that lonesome woodland after dark. The sun had been up for many hours before he finally managed to free himself from the ropes that had tied him to the tree. He lay on the ground, hardly able to breathe.

Roman Censor and Citizens. Jacques Grasset de Saint-Sauveur and L.F. Labrousse.

View the Art Which characters in the play could the people in this painting represent?

[*Music: In briefly and out.*]

NARRATOR. After a while Pythias got to his feet. Weak and dizzy from hunger and thirst and his struggle to free himself, he set off again. Day and night he traveled without stopping, desperately trying to reach the city in time to save Damon's life.

[*Music: Up and out.*]

NARRATOR. On the last day, half an hour before noon, Damon's hands were tied behind his back, and he was taken into the public square. The people muttered angrily as Damon was led in by the jailer. Then the king entered and seated himself on a high platform.

[Sound: Crowd voices in and hold under single voices.]

SOLDIER. *[Loud.]* Long live the king!

FIRST VOICE. *[Low.]* The longer he lives, the more miserable our lives will be!

KING. *[Loud, mocking.]* Well, Damon, your lifetime is nearly up. Where is your good friend Pythias now?

DAMON. *[Firm.]* I have faith in my friend. If he has not returned, I'm certain it is through no fault of his own.

Visual Vocabulary

The **noon mark** is the point on a sundial on which a shadow falls when the sun is at its highest point in the sky.

KING. *[Mocking.]* The sun is almost overhead. The shadow is almost at the **noon mark**. And still your friend has not returned to give back your life!

DAMON. *[Quiet.]* I am ready and happy to die in his place.

KING. *[**Harsh**.]* And you shall, Damon! Jailer, lead the prisoner to the—

[Sound: Crowd voices up to a roar, then under.]

FIRST VOICE. *[Over noise.]* Look! It's Pythias!

SECOND VOICE. *[Over noise.]* Pythias has come back!

PYTHIAS. *[Breathless.]* Let me through! Damon!

DAMON. Pythias!

PYTHIAS. Thank the gods I'm not too late!

DAMON. *[Quiet, sincere.]* I would have died for you gladly, my friend.

CROWD VOICES. *[Loud, demanding.]* Set them free! Set them both free!

KING. *[Loud.]* People of the city! *[Crowd voices out.]* Never in all my life have I seen such faith and friendship, such loyalty between men. There are many among you who call me harsh and cruel. But I cannot kill *any* man who proves such strong and true friendship for another. Damon and Pythias, I set you both free. *[Roar of approval from crowd.]* I am king. I command a great army. I have stores of gold and precious jewels. But I would give all my money and power for one friend like Damon or Pythias.

[Sound: Roar of approval from crowd up briefly and out.]
[Music: Up and out.]

Analyze Diction Why does the author include this phrase that people might have said in ancient times?

Dialogue How is the king feeling now?

Vocabulary

harsh (härsh) *adj.* rough or unpleasant to any of the physical senses

BQ BIG Question How did both Damon and Pythias show faith and loyalty?

After You Read

Respond and Think Critically

1. What crime did Pythias commit? What is his punishment? **[Identify]**
2. What bargain does Damon make with the king? **[Recall]**
3. Why didn't the robbers believe Pythias? **[Summarize]**
4. What is the king's attitude toward Pythias and the people? **[Infer]**
5. In your opinion, if the king had executed Damon or Pythias, would either death help change the laws of the land? Explain. **[Evaluate]**
6. **BQ BIG Question** Was Damon foolish to risk his life on the faithfulness of his friend Pythias? Was Pythias foolish to return to be imprisoned when he was free? Explain your answer. **[Conclude]**

Vocabulary Practice

On a separate sheet of paper, write the vocabulary word that correctly completes each sentence. If none of the words fits the sentence, write *none.*

proclaimed **appointed** **resist** **honorable** **harsh**

1. The audience cheered when the television show host ______ the winners.
2. A swim in the lake was hard to ______ during the record heat.
3. An ______ friend will not spread gossip or rumors.
4. Our teacher ______ three people to design scenery for our class play.
5. They were ______ that so few shoppers showed up for the midnight sale.
6. The ______ sound of screeching brakes alarmed me.
7. We traveled across the ______ state to attend the wedding.

Academic Vocabulary

The reader had to wait until the end of the radio play to learn the **outcome.**

In the preceding sentence, an *outcome* is a result or consequence. Think about a worthwhile goal you have had. What was the outcome in your attempt to achieve the goal?

TIP

Evaluate

When you **evaluate**, you make a judgment about something you are reading. Use these tips to answer question 5.

- Think about the king and his attitude toward his people. What evidence supports the viewpoint that the people like the way he rules?
- Think about Damon and Pythias's friendship and loyalty. What evidence supports the viewpoint that the people would be angry if Damon and Pythias were executed?

Keep track of your ideas about the **BIG Question** in your unit Foldable.

Literature Online

Selection Resources
For Selection Quizzes, eFlashcards, and Reading-Writing Connection activities, go to glencoe.com and enter QuickPass code GL17527u6.

Literary Element **Dialogue**

1. Why does the author have a narrator speak some of the lines in this play? When and how does the narrator participate in dialogue?
2. How does the dialogue help you understand the depth of the friendship between Damon and Pythias?
3. How do the three voices in the radio play help you think about friendship?
4. What kind of stage directions would be unimportant in a radio play? Why?

Review: Plot

As you learned on page 53, the **plot** is the sequence of events in a narrative work, such as a play. The plot centers on a **conflict,** a struggle between opposing forces. The struggle may be against some outside force or an internal conflict. The conflict develops during the **rising action** of the plot. It reaches its greatest point of tension at the **climax.** The conflict gets resolved during the **falling action** and **resolution** of the plot.

5. What is the main conflict of the play? What other conflict occurs in the play?
6. What is the climax of the play? Why do you think this is the climax?

Reading Skill **Analyze Diction**

Standards Practice  ELA6R1g

7. Read this sentence from the play.

   Do you believe for one moment that the king would let me leave this prison, no matter how good my word may have been all my life?

   The author uses *my word* to refer to

   A. the speech patterns Pythias likes to use.
   B. the writings Pythias believes are sacred.
   C. the reputation Pythias has for trustworthiness.
   D. the recommendation Pythias has for changing the king's laws.

Grammar Link

The **subject** is the part of a sentence about which something is being said. The **verb** is the part that tells what the subject is doing.

Subject and verb agreement means the subject and verb agree in person and number.

With a singular subject, you must use the singular form of the verb.

The **king puts** Pythias in prison.

King is a singular subject, so the singular form of the verb, *puts*, is used.

With a plural subject, you must use the plural form of the verb.

Damon and Pythias share a loyal friendship.

Damon and Pythias is the plural subject, so the plural form of the verb, *share*, is used.

Practice

Look for two sentences in *Damon and Pythias* that have a singular subject and three sentences that have a plural subject. Copy each sentence and underline the subject and the verb. Then write four of your own sentences. Two of your sentences should have a singular subject and two should have a plural subject.

Speaking and Listening

Literature Group With a small group, discuss whether the characters, their friendship, and the play are believable. If so, what makes them believable? If not, discuss how you would change the play to make it more believable? Support your ideas with evidence from the play.

Brainstorm a list of situations in which people might offer to make exceptional sacrifices for one another.

Before You Read

The Bracelet

Connect to the Story

Suppose that you have brown hair and a new law states that all brown-haired people must live in an area separated from those with other hair colors. How would you feel if this happened to you? How would you feel if your hair were not brown?

Partner Talk With a partner, discuss your answers to the questions above.

Build Background

During World War II, the United States was at war with Japan. "The Bracelet" is an account of how people of Japanese heritage living in the United States were sent to live in internment (in turn′ mənt) camps, or relocation centers.

- Some U.S. leaders feared that Japanese Americans might spy on or damage military bases.
- In 1942 President Franklin D. Roosevelt gave the U.S. military the authority to take Japanese Americans from their homes and send them to internment camps.
- About 120,000 Japanese Americans were forced to live in internment camps. Two-thirds of them were U.S. citizens.

Vocabulary

aliens (āl′ yənz) *n.* people who are not citizens of the country in which they live (p. 749). *After moving to the United States, most aliens work hard to learn English.*

wilted (wilt′ əd) *adj.* droopy or faded (p. 749). *If you give that wilted plant some water, the leaves will stop drooping.*

register (rej′ is tər) *v.* to enter one's name in a formal record (p. 751). *People who wish to vote must register before the election.*

shabby (shab′ ē) *adj.* faded and dingy from wear or exposure (p. 752). *The library carpet had become thin and shabby after years of use.*

Meet Yoshiko Uchida

"I think it's important for each of us to take pride in our special heritage."

—Yoshiko Uchida

Wrongly Imprisoned Yoshiko Uchida was a college student in California when the United States declared war on Japan in 1941. Her family, along with other Japanese Americans, was sent to live in an internment camp although they had done nothing wrong. This injustice became a theme in Uchida's writing.

Literary Works Uchida was an award-winning writer. She wrote many books for young people, including fiction and collections of Japanese folktales.

Yoshiko Uchida was born in 1921 and died in 1992.

LOG ON Literature Online

Author Search For more about Yoshiko Uchida, go to glencoe.com and enter QuickPass code GL17527u6.

Set Purposes for Reading

BQ BIG Question

As you read, ask yourself, what evidence shows that the Japanese Americans in the story are loyal to the United States?

Literary Element Conflict

Conflict is a struggle between opposing forces in a story. An **external conflict** happens when a character struggles with an outside force, such as another character, the community, or nature. An **internal conflict** happens when a character struggles against something inside, such as feelings of sadness or confusion. Many stories have both internal and external conflicts.

Identifying the main conflict or conflicts in a story helps you focus on the key events.

As you read, ask yourself, how do the characters' responses to conflicts affect the plot and the way the main conflict is resolved?

Reading Skill Make Generalizations About Characters

When you **make a generalization,** you base a broad statement on facts or details. When you **make generalizations about characters,** you use their traits and actions to discover something about them and perhaps about people in general.

Making generalizations about characters can help you understand the ideas the author wants to convey.

To make a generalization about a character, think about

- what the character says, does, thinks, and feels
- how the character handles conflicts
- what other characters say about the character

As you read, you might find it helpful to use a graphic organizer like the one below.

Character	Facts or Details	Generalization
Laurie Madison	Laurie is upset that Ruri is being forced to leave. She gives Ruri a bracelet.	

GA Performance Standards

For pages 746–756

ELA6R1e/i For literary texts, identify and analyze the elements of setting, characterization, plot, and the resolution of the conflict of a story or play: internal/external conflicts.

TRY IT

Make Generalizations About Characters You watch a friend play tennis. After losing a game, she shakes her opponent's hand. At a softball game the next day, she comforts a teammate who has dropped a fly ball. What generalization can you make about your friend's sportsmanship?

Gift Box, 1981. Wayne Thiebaud. Oil on canvas. Private Collection. VAGA, NY.

The Bracelet

Yoshiko Uchida

"Mama, is it time to go?"

I hadn't planned to cry, but the tears came suddenly, and I wiped them away with the back of my hand. I didn't want my older sister to see me crying.

"It's almost time, Ruri," my mother said gently. Her face was filled with a kind of sadness I had never seen before.

I looked around at my empty room. The clothes that Mama always told me to hang up in the closet, the junk piled on my dresser, the old rag doll I could never bear to part with—they were all gone. There was nothing left in my room, and there was nothing left in the rest of the house. The rugs and furniture were gone, the pictures and drapes were down, and the closets and cupboards were empty. The house was like a gift box after the nice thing inside was gone: just a lot of nothingness.

It was almost time to leave our home, but we weren't moving to a nicer house or to a new town. It was April 12, 1942. The United States and Japan were at war, and every Japanese person on the West Coast was being evacuated[1] by the government to a concentration camp.[2] Mama, my sister Keiko, and I were being sent from our home, and out of Berkeley, and eventually out of California.

Conflict What conflict does the narrator face? Is it internal or external?

The doorbell rang, and I ran to answer it before my sister could. I thought maybe by some miracle a messenger from the government might be standing there, tall and proper and buttoned into a uniform, come to tell us it was all a terrible mistake, that we wouldn't have to leave after all. Or maybe the messenger would have a telegram from Papa, who was interned[3] in a prisoner-of-war camp in Montana because he had worked for a Japanese business firm.

The FBI had come to pick up Papa and hundreds of other Japanese community leaders on the very day that Japanese planes had bombed Pearl Harbor.[4] The government thought they were dangerous enemy **aliens**. If it weren't so sad, it would have been funny. Papa could no more be dangerous than the mayor of our city, and he was every bit as loyal to the United States. He had lived here since 1917.

BQ BIG Question

Why does the U.S. government suspect that Papa is not loyal?

When I opened the door, it wasn't a messenger from anywhere. It was my best friend, Laurie Madison, from next door. She was holding a package wrapped up like a birthday present, but she wasn't wearing her party dress, and her face drooped like a **wilted** tulip.

1 When people are ***evacuated*** from a place, they are removed from it.

2 A ***concentration camp*** is a place where political prisoners and prisoners of war are confined.

3 Someone who is ***interned*** is imprisoned or confined.

4 The Japanese bombed the U.S. naval base at ***Pearl Harbor*** in Hawaii on December 7, 1941. This attack brought the United States into World War II.

Vocabulary

aliens (āl′yənz) *n.* people who are not citizens of the country in which they live

wilted (wilt′əd) *adj.* droopy or faded

"Hi," she said. "I came to say goodbye."

She thrust the present at me and told me it was something to take to camp. "It's a bracelet," she said before I could open the package. "Put it on so you won't have to pack it." She knew I didn't have one inch of space left in my suitcase. We had been instructed to take only what we could carry into camp, and Mama had told us that we could each take only two suitcases.

"Then how are we ever going to pack the dishes and blankets and sheets they've told us to bring with us?" Keiko worried.

"I don't really know," Mama said, and she simply began packing those big impossible things into an enormous **duffel bag**—along with umbrellas, boots, a kettle, hot plate, and flashlight.

"Who's going to carry that huge sack?" I asked.

But Mama didn't worry about things like that. "Someone will help us," she said. "Don't worry." So I didn't.

Laurie wanted me to open her package and put on the bracelet before she left. It was a thin gold chain with a heart dangling on it. She helped me put it on, and I told her I'd never take it off, ever.

"Well, goodbye, then," Laurie said awkwardly. "Come home soon."

"I will," I said, although I didn't know if I would ever get back to Berkeley again.

I watched Laurie go down the block, her long blond pigtails bouncing as she walked. I wondered who would be sitting in my desk at Lincoln Junior High now that I was gone. Laurie kept turning and waving, even walking backward for a while, until she got to the corner. I didn't want to watch anymore, and I slammed the door shut.

The next time the doorbell rang, it was Mrs. Simpson, our other neighbor. She was going to drive us to the Congregational Church, which was the Civil Control Station where all the Japanese of Berkeley were supposed to report.

It was time to go. "Come on, Ruri. Get your things," my sister called to me.

Visual Vocabulary

A **duffel bag** is a large bag, usually made of heavy cloth, used for carrying clothes, equipment, or other belongings.

Make Generalizations About Characters From Mama's words and actions so far, what generalization might you make about her?

Conflict What internal conflict is the narrator having?

It was a warm day, but I put on a sweater and my coat so I wouldn't have to carry them, and I picked up my two suitcases. Each one had a tag with my name and our family number on it. Every Japanese family had to **register** and get a number. We were Family Number 13453.

Mama was taking one last look around our house. She was going from room to room, as though she were trying to take a mental picture of the house she had lived in for fifteen years, so she would never forget it.

I saw her take a long last look at the garden that Papa loved. The irises beside the fish pond were just beginning to bloom. If Papa had been home, he would have cut the first iris blossom and brought it inside to Mama. "This one is for you," he would have said. And Mama would have smiled and said, "Thank you, Papa San"[5] and put it in her favorite cut-glass vase.

Make Generalizations About Characters What type of man is Papa? What facts and details support your answer?

5 ***San*** is a term of respect added to Japanese names.

Vocabulary

register (rej′ is tər) *v.* to enter one's name in a formal record

Irises (detail), Edo Period. Ogata Korin. Colour on gilded paper, 150.9 x 338 cm. Nezu Museum, Tokyo, Japan.

But the garden looked **shabby** and forsaken[6] now that Papa was gone and Mama was too busy to take care of it. It looked the way I felt, sort of empty and lonely and abandoned.

When Mrs. Simpson took us to the Civil Control Station, I felt even worse. I was scared, and for a minute I thought I was going to lose my breakfast right in front of everybody. There must have been over a thousand Japanese people gathered at the church. Some were old and some were young. Some were talking and laughing, and some were crying. I guess everybody else was scared too. No one knew exactly what was going to happen to us. We just knew we were being taken to the Tanforan Racetracks,[7] which the army had turned into a camp for the Japanese. There were fourteen other camps like ours along the West Coast.

Make Generalizations About Characters Why would people in this situation feel scared?

What scared me most were the soldiers standing at the doorway of the church hall. They were carrying guns with mounted bayonets.[8] I wondered if they thought we would try to run away and whether they'd shoot us or come after us with their bayonets if we did.

Conflict Why are the soldiers at the Civil Control Station? How does their presence emphasize the story's external conflict?

A long line of buses waited to take us to camp. There were trucks, too, for our baggage. And Mama was right; some men were there to help us load our duffel bag. When it was time to board the buses, I sat with Keiko, and Mama sat behind us. The bus went down Grove Street and passed the small Japanese food store where Mama used to order her bean-curd cakes and pickled radish. The windows were all boarded up, but there was a sign still hanging on the door that read, "We are loyal Americans."

The crazy thing about the whole evacuation was that we were all loyal Americans. Most of us were citizens because we had been born here. But our parents, who had come

---

6 Something that is ***forsaken*** looks and is abandoned.

7 ***Tanforan Racetrack*** was a famous racetrack near San Francisco. It opened in 1899 and burned down in 1964. People came to Tanforan to see horse races and car races.

8 ***Bayonets*** are long knives on the end of rifles.

Vocabulary

shabby (shab′ ē) *adj.* faded and dingy from wear or exposure from Japan, couldn't become citizens because there was a law that prevented any Asian from becoming a citizen. Now everybody with a Japanese face was being shipped off to concentration camps.

"It's stupid," Keiko muttered as we saw the racetrack looming[9] up beside the highway. "If there were any Japanese spies around, they'd have gone back to Japan long ago."

"I'll say," I agreed. My sister was in high school and she ought to know, I thought.

When the bus turned onto Tanforan, there were more and more armed guards at the gate, and I saw barbed wire strung around the entire grounds. I felt as though I were going into a prison, but I hadn't done anything wrong.

We streamed off the buses and poured into a huge room, where doctors looked down our throats and peeled back our eyelids to see if we had any diseases. Then we were given our housing assignments. The man in charge gave Mama a slip of paper. We were in Barrack 16, Apartment 40.

"Mama!" I said. "We're going to live in an apartment!" The only apartment I had ever seen was the one my piano teacher lived in. It was in an enormous building in San Francisco, with an elevator and thick-carpeted hallways. I thought how wonderful it would be to have our own elevator. A house was all right, but an apartment seemed elegant and special.

We walked down the racetrack, looking for Barrack 16. Mr. Noma, a friend of Papa's, helped us carry our bags. I was so busy looking around I slipped and almost fell on the muddy track. Army barracks had been built everywhere, all around the racetrack and even in the center oval.

Mr. Noma pointed beyond the track toward the horse stables. "I think your barrack is out there."

He was right. We came to a long stable that had once housed the horses of Tanforan, and we climbed up the wide ramp. Each stall had a number painted on it, and when we got to 40, Mr. Noma pushed open the door.

---

9 Here, ***looming*** describes something that appears large or threatening.

BQ BIG Question
Why are the Japanese Americans being sent to concentration camps? What evidence shows that most are loyal Americans?

Conflict What is the external conflict in this paragraph? What is the internal conflict?

Our Barrack 7-2-C. Topaz, UT. Yoshiko Uchida.

View the Art Yoshiko Uchida, the author of "The Bracelet," painted this picture while she was living in an internment camp. Which details add to your understanding of the story?

"Well, here it is," he said, "Apartment 40."

The stall was narrow and empty and dark. There were two small windows on each side of the door. Three folded army cots were on the dust-covered floor, and one light-bulb dangled from the ceiling. That was all. This was our apartment, and it still smelled of horses.

Mama looked at my sister and then at me. "It won't be so bad when we fix it up," she began. "I'll ask Mrs. Simpson to send me some material for curtains. I could make some cushions too, and . . . well . . ." She stopped. She couldn't think of anything more to say.

Make Generalizations About Characters What does this statement tell you about Mama's personality?

Mr. Noma said he'd go get some mattresses for us. "I'd better hurry before they're all gone." He rushed off. I think he wanted to leave so that he wouldn't have to see Mama cry. But he needn't have run off, because Mama didn't cry. She just went out to borrow a broom and began sweeping out the dust and dirt. "Will you girls set up the cots?" she asked.

It was only after we'd put up the last cot that I noticed my bracelet was gone. "I've lost Laurie's bracelet!" I screamed. "My bracelet's gone!"

We looked all over the stall and even down the ramp. I wanted to run back down the track and go over every inch of ground we'd walked on, but it was getting dark and Mama wouldn't let me.

I thought of what I'd promised Laurie. I wasn't ever going to take the bracelet off, not even when I went to take a shower. And now I had lost it on my very first day in camp. I wanted to cry.

Conflict Does losing the bracelet present an internal or external conflict? Why?

I kept looking for it all the time we were in Tanforan. I didn't stop looking until the day we were sent to another camp, called Topaz, in the middle of a desert in Utah. And then I gave up.

But Mama told me never mind. She said I didn't need a bracelet to remember Laurie, just as I didn't need anything to remember Papa or our home in Berkeley or all the people and things we loved and had left behind.

"Those are things we can carry in our hearts and take with us no matter where we are sent," she said.

And I guess she was right. I've never forgotten Laurie, even now. ❧

After You Read

Respond and Think Critically

1. How do you think you would feel if your family was forced to move away from home? [Connect]
2. What makes Ruri want to cry the first day she is in her new "apartment" at Tanforan? [Recall]
3. Why do you think the people in the story went to the camps without a fight? [Interpret]
4. **Literary Element** **Conflict** What is the main conflict in the story? Is it internal or external? [Classify]
5. **Reading Skill** **Make Generalizations About Characters** Think about the main characters in the story. How do they react to the difficult situation they are in? How do they treat each other? What generalizations can you make about these characters? Refer to the story and the chart you made to find details to support your answer. [Analyze]
6. **BQ** **BIG Question** Why is the bracelet important to Ruri? What does the author imply by calling the story "The Bracelet"? [Infer]

Vocabulary Practice

Respond to these questions.

1. Where do **aliens** live—in the country where they were born or in a country they moved to?
2. Which of these might help a **wilted** plant—light rain or a hailstorm?
3. Which of these is more likely to be **shabby**—a new pair of boots or an old coat?
4. Who needs to **register** at your school—a new student or a student who graduated years ago?

Writing

Write a Blurb Imagine that you work for a book publisher. You have been asked to write the book-jacket text for a collection of short stories about Japanese Americans. You need to write a blurb about "The Bracelet" that will persuade young people to buy the book and read the story. Think about what drew you into the story and what touched you about the characters. Support your opinions with evidence from the story. Anticipate arguments people may have for not wanting to read such a book and present counterarguments. Convey your thoughts in one paragraph.

TIP

Connecting
Here are some tips to help you connect your experiences with those of a character in a story.

- Reread the passage that relates to the question.
- Note how the character acts and feels.
- Think about a similar experience you have had.
- Think about how you felt and what you did.

Keep track of your ideas about the **BIG Question** in your unit Foldable.

LOG ON **Literature** Online

Selection Resources
For Selection Quizzes, eFlashcards, and Reading-Writing Connection activities, go to glencoe.com and enter QuickPass code GL17527u6.

Cultural Perspective

on *The Bracelet* by Yoshiko Uchida

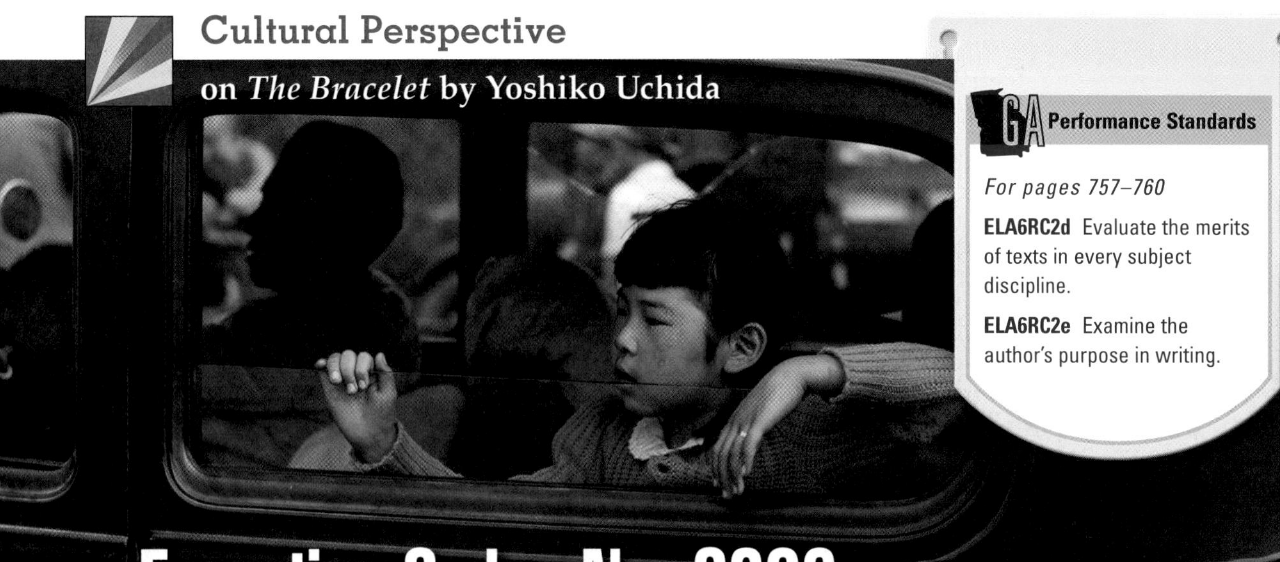

Performance Standards

For pages 757–760

ELA6RC2d Evaluate the merits of texts in every subject discipline.

ELA6RC2e Examine the author's purpose in writing.

Executive Order No. 9066

from I Am an American: *A True Story of Japanese Internment*

by Jerry Stanley

Set a Purpose for Reading

Read to learn how fearful attitudes shaped a presidential decision that changed the lives of many Japanese Americans.

Build Background

After the Japanese attack on Pearl Harbor in 1941, fear caused the U.S. government to send more than 100,000 Japanese Americans to internment camps.

Reading Skill Recognize Author's Purpose

An **author's purpose** is the author's intention for writing. In general, authors write to entertain, to inform, or to persuade. As you read, list details that give clues to the author's purpose. Use a three-column chart like the one below.

Inform	Persuade	Entertain

After Pearl Harbor[1] the Nisei[2] went to great lengths to demonstrate their patriotism. They flooded the streets of San Francisco, Los Angeles, and Seattle in mass demonstrations of loyalty. They waved American flags and recited the pledge[3] of the Japanese American Citizens League. They bought war bonds,[4] donated blood, and ran ads in newspapers denouncing Japan and pledging loyalty to America. In San Francisco, Nisei started a fund-raising

1 ***Pearl Harbor*** was an important U.S. naval base in Hawaii. The Japanese air force bombed Pearl Harbor on December 7, 1941.

2 ***Nisei*** (nē′ sā′) is a name given to the second Japanese immigrant generation; they are children of the Issei generation.

3 A ***pledge*** is a binding promise or agreement.

4 ***War bonds*** are certificates the U.S. government sold to help pay for the war. Although the bonds paid interest, buying them was also a sign of patriotism.

`campaign to buy bombs for attacking Tokyo. In Los Angeles they formed committees to make sure that no person of Japanese ancestry tried to aid Japan. The day after Pearl Harbor the Japanese American Citizens League sent the following telegram to President Roosevelt:

> In this solemn hour we pledge our fullest cooperation to you, Mr. President, and to our country. There can not be any question. . . . We in our hearts know we are Americans, loyal to America.

At first, the demonstrations of loyalty brought pledges of support from government officials, and Japanese internment[5] seemed unlikely. California Congressman Leland Ford said, "These people are American-born. This is their country." United States Attorney General Francis Biddle declared, "At no time will the government engage in wholesale condemnation[6] of any alien group."

It was a series of Japanese victories in the Pacific that started the movement to intern the Japanese. Japan captured Guam on December 13, 1941, Hong Kong on December 24, Manila on January 2, 1942, and Singapore on February 15.

Alarmed at the enemy's swift advance through the Pacific, military officials suggested that Japan might try to invade the west coast of America and that maybe the Issei[7] and Nisei who lived there would aid the invasion. The Western Defense Commander, Lieutenant General John L. DeWitt, who was responsible for the security of the Pacific coast, was influential in spreading the idea that the Japanese might be disloyal. Following the loss of Manila he said, "I have little confidence that the Japanese enemy aliens [Issei] are loyal. I have no confidence in the loyalty of the Nisei whatsoever."

DeWitt's distrust appeared to be confirmed[8] in the Roberts Report, a government investigation of the bombing of Pearl Harbor. Issued at about the time Singapore fell to Japan in February, the report blamed the disaster on lack of military preparedness and on Japanese sabotage[9] in Hawaii. It even suggested that Japanese farmers had planted their crops in the shape of arrows pointing to Pearl Harbor as the target.

Although the charge of Japanese sabotage on Hawaii was totally false, newspaper writers and radio broadcasters began warning of the danger of Japanese sabotage on the west coast. In Los Angeles, radio

5 ***Internment*** refers to being confined or held in one place, especially during a war.

6 ***Condemnation*** is strong disapproval of someone or something.

7 ***Issei*** (ēs′ sā′) is a name given to the first Japanese immigrant generation to come to the United States during the 1880s.

8 Something that is ***confirmed*** is positively declared to be true.

9 ***Sabotage*** is any deliberate interference done by enemy agents in order to hinder a nation's war or defense effort.

View the Photograph How does this scene compare with Yoshiko Uchida's painting on page 754? What features might all internment camps have shared?

commentator John Hughes warned that "Ninety percent or more of American-born Japanese are primarily loyal to Japan." In San Francisco, columnist Henry McLemore wrote, "I am for immediate removal of every Japanese on the West Coast. . . . Herd 'em up, pack 'em off. Let 'em be pinched, hurt and hungry!" Reflecting a tendency to confuse the enemy nation of Japan with American citizens of Japanese ancestry, McLemore thundered, "I hate the Japanese. And that goes for all of them!"

Stunned by the growing hostility, the Nisei tried to appear as un-Japanese as possible. Slowly, sadly, all along the west coast of America, they destroyed what they possessed of their Asian heritage. Japanese books and magazines were burned because of a rumor that FBI agents had found such materials in the homes of Issei arrested on suspicion of sabotage. Priceless diaries, letters, and photographs were burned; porcelain vases, tea sets, and silk tablecloths were buried or dumped on the street.

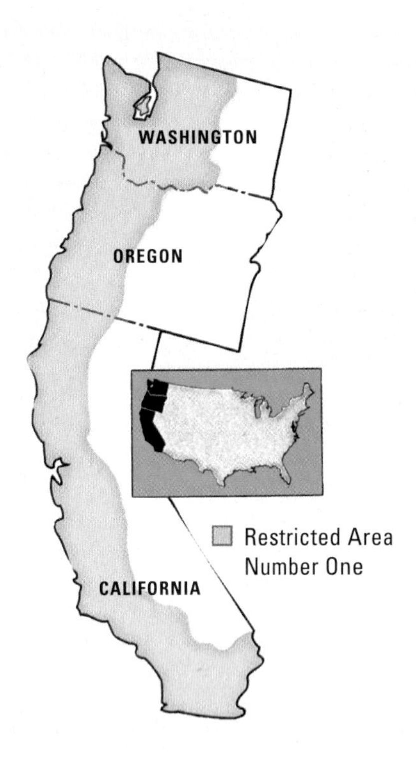

By mid-February the entire coastline of California was designated Restricted Area Number One. DeWitt issued a stern suggestion that the Japanese living in this coastal strip should voluntarily migrate[10] inland. But when some 4,000 tried to move, they were met with hostility. Armed men patrolled the Nevada border to turn them back while main streets in Utah sported signs reading "No Japs Wanted." Because most people in the inland states had never met a person of Japanese ancestry, they decided that if the Japanese were a threat to California then they were also a threat to them.

With no personal knowledge of the Japanese living in America, President Franklin D. Roosevelt yielded to pressure from the California Hotheads,[11] the media, and the military. On February 19, 1942, Roosevelt signed Executive Order No. 9066, which gave the military the authority to remove enemy aliens and anyone else suspected of disloyalty. Although the document never mentioned the Japanese by name, it was understood that the order was meant for them alone.

10 In this instance, to ***migrate*** means to move to a different region.

11 ***Hotheads*** are people who are easily angered.

Respond and Think Critically

1. Write a brief summary of the steps Japanese Americans took to show their loyalty to the United States. For help with writing a summary, see page 170. **[Summarize]**
2. How important was the role of the media in influencing the government to send Japanese Americans to internment camps? **[Analyze]**
3. Was the fear of Japanese Americans justified? **[Evaluate]**
4. **Text to Text** How did President Roosevelt's Executive Order No. 9066 affect the lives of Japanese American families like the one in "The Bracelet"? **[Connect]**
5. **Reading Skill** **Recognize Author's Purpose** What was the author's main purpose in writing this excerpt? Support your answer with examples.
6. **BQ** **BIG Question** How do you know that loyalty to the United States was a worthwhile goal for Japanese Americans during World War II?

Vocabulary Workshop

Word Origins

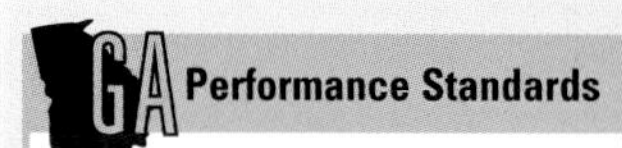

Performance Standards

For page 761

ELA6R2d Understand and acquire new vocabulary. Use reference skills to determine pronunciations, meanings, alternate word choices, and parts of speech.

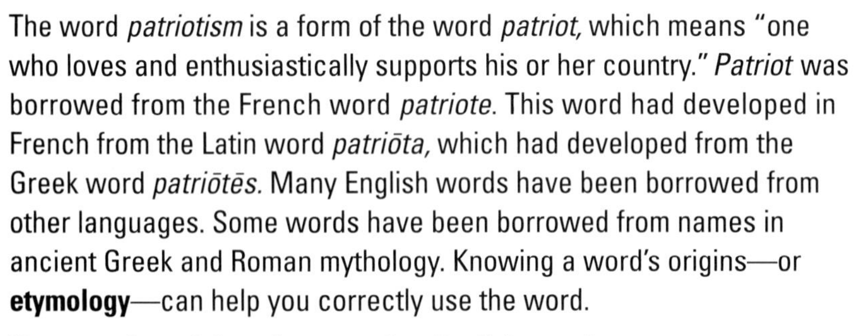

Connection to Literature

"After Pearl Harbor the Nisei went to great lengths to demonstrate their patriotism."

—Jerry Stanley, "Executive Order No. 9066"

The word *patriotism* is a form of the word *patriot,* which means "one who loves and enthusiastically supports his or her country." *Patriot* was borrowed from the French word *patriote.* This word had developed in French from the Latin word *patriōta,* which had developed from the Greek word *patriōtēs.* Many English words have been borrowed from other languages. Some words have been borrowed from names in ancient Greek and Roman mythology. Knowing a word's origins—or **etymology**—can help you correctly use the word.

Here are the origins of some other English words.

Word	Pronunciation/Origin	English Meaning
croissant	(krä sänt′) a French word meaning "crescent"	a crescent-shaped roll
cafeteria	(kaf′ ə tēr′ ē ə) from French *café,* "coffee"	a restaurant in which a customer buys food at a counter
herculean	(hur′ kyə lē′ ən) a word that comes from the name Hercules—a hero in Greek and Roman mythology	requiring great strength or effort, like that shown by Hercules
gesture	(jes′ chər) from Medieval Latin *gestura,* meaning "bearing," from Latin *gestus,* meaning "to perform"	movement of the head, body, or limbs, used to express a thought or feeling or to emphasize what is said

TRY IT: Use the chart above to help you choose the word or phrase that best fits the blank in each sentence. Then read the sentences aloud.

1. Moving so many heavy boxes will be a ______ effort.
2. My mother prefers a ______ over a bagel or doughnut.
3. The officer held up his hand as a signal, or ______, to stop.

Tip

Vocabulary Terms When you look up a word's origin, or etymology, you'll often find it at the end of a dictionary entry within brackets.

Test-Taking Tip Recognizing roots from ancient languages such as Greek *(sphere, auto)* and Latin *(ject, duct)* can help you determine meanings, pronunciations, and spellings in English.

LOG ON **Literature Online**

Vocabulary For more vocabulary practice, go to glencoe.com and enter QuickPass code GL17527u6.

Before You Read

from *Brighton Beach Memoirs*

Connect to the Play

It's not always easy to take a stand—especially when others remain quiet. Think about why it is important to stand up for something you believe in.

Partner Talk With a partner, discuss a situation in which you might have to stand up for something or someone. What would it be like? What are some ways of handling the situation?

Build Background

Brighton Beach Memoirs is a play about a Jewish family living in New York City in 1937. The 1930s were a troubled time in the United States. As a result of the Great Depression, work was scarce. Many people faced hard times.

The main character is a teenager named Eugene Jerome. The Jerome family lives in an area of New York called Brooklyn. Brighton Beach is a Brooklyn neighborhood that borders the Atlantic Ocean.

Vocabulary

temporarily (tem′ pə rer′ ə lē) *adv.* lasting only for a short time; not permanently (p. 764). *All traffic must temporarily use Green Street while the main road is being fixed.*

astounded (əs toun′ ded) *v.* overwhelmed with sudden surprise or amazement (p. 765). *We were astounded to see a bear crossing the empty road.*

principles (prin′ sə pəlz) *n.* rules of personal conduct (p. 767). *The judge is guided by the principles of honesty and fairness.*

worshipped (wur′ shipt) *v.* adored or idolized (p. 767). *Kurt worshipped the soccer player, who had won many championships.*

Meet Neil Simon

"My idea of the ultimate achievement in a comedy is to make a whole audience fall onto the floor, writhing and laughing so hard that some of them pass out."

—Neil Simon

Popular Playwright Neil Simon is one of the most popular playwrights writing today. Most of his plays are comedies that find humor in the everyday problems of ordinary people. Many, such as *Brighton Beach Memoirs,* draw from the working-class New York City neighborhoods in which he grew up.

Literary Works Simon has written dozens of movies, television shows, and plays, including *The Odd Couple.*

Neil Simon was born in 1927.

Literature Online

Author Search For more about Neil Simon, go to glencoe.com and enter QuickPass code GL17527u6.

Set Purposes for Reading

BQ BIG Question

As you read this scene from *Brighton Beach Memoirs,* ask yourself, what do Eugene and his brother, Stan, value?

Literary Element Stage Directions

Stage directions are a playwright's instructions to the actors, the director, and the stage crew. They describe the action, the sets, the costumes, and the lighting. When a play is performed, the actors do not say the stage directions. Instead, the actors *do* the things described in the stage directions. Stage directions are usually italicized and placed in brackets.

Stage directions help you imagine how plays should look and sound when they are performed. Stage directions can also help you understand characters' thoughts and feelings.

As you read, ask yourself, how do the stage directions help me visualize the way a scene should be performed?

Reading Skill Identify Cause-and-Effect Relationships

A **cause** is something that happens that sets something else in motion. An **effect** is the result or outcome. When you **identify cause-and-effect relationships,** you ask yourself, did this happen because of something else? For example, if the marching band practices each day after school, then it will probably perform well at football games.

Identifying cause-and-effect relationships can help you understand why a character is in a certain situation. You may also be able to predict what will happen as a result of the character's actions.

To identify cause-and-effect relationships, ask yourself,

- What caused this action or event?
- What are the possible results of this action?

You may find it helpful to use a graphic organizer like the one below.

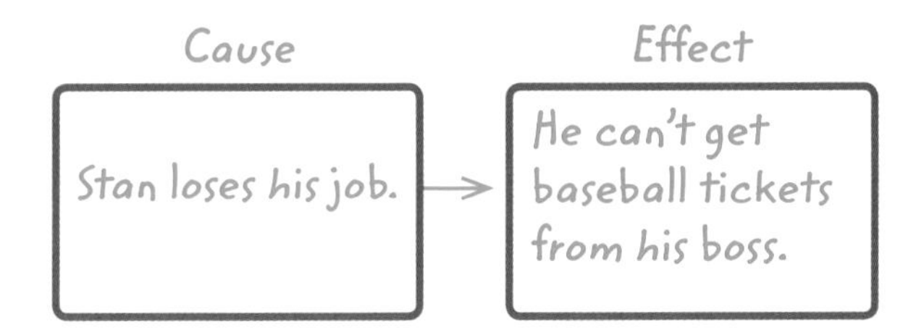

GA Performance Standards

For pages 762–769

ELA6R1b For literary texts, identify and analyze the author's use of dialogue and description.

TRY IT

Identify Cause-and-Effect Relationships A big rainstorm sweeps through your area. Rain falls for most of the night. When you wake up the next morning, the water in a nearby river is running high and fast. What is the cause?

from

Brighton Beach Memoirs

Neil Simon

The cast of the original Broadway production of *Brighton Beach Memoirs*, 1983, starring Matthew Broderick as Eugene.

STAN. [*half whisper*] Hey! Eugie!

EUGENE. Hi, Stan! [*to audience*] My brother, Stan. He's okay. You'll like him. [*to* STAN] What are you doing home so early?

STAN. [*looks around, lowers his voice*] Is Pop home yet?

EUGENE. No . . . Did you ask about the tickets?

STAN. What tickets?

EUGENE. For the Yankee game. You said your boss knew this guy who could get passes. You didn't ask him?

STAN. Me and my boss had other things to talk about. [*He sits on steps, his head down, almost in tears.*] I'm in trouble, Eug. I mean really big trouble.

EUGENE. [*to audience*] This really shocked me. Because Stan is the kind of guy who could talk himself out of *any* kind of trouble. [*to* STAN] What kind of trouble?

STAN. . . . I got fired today!

EUGENE. [*shocked*] Fired? . . . You mean for good?

STAN. You don't get fired **temporarily**. It's permanent. It's a lifetime firing.

EUGENE. Why? What happened?

STAN. It was on account of Andrew. The colored guy who sweeps up. Well, he was cleaning the floor in the

---

Stage Directions How does Eugene speak this line? Does Stan hear him?

Stage Directions What do you learn from Stan's actions?

Vocabulary

temporarily (tem′ pə rer′ ə lē) *adv.* lasting only for a short time; not permanently stock room[1] and he lays his broom against the table to put some junk in the trash can and the broom slips, knocks a can of linseed oil[2] over the table and ruins three brand new hats right out of the box. Nine dollar **Stetsons**. It wasn't his fault. He didn't put the linseed oil there, right?

Visual Vocabulary

Stetsons are felt hats with a broad brim and high crown.

EUGENE. Right.

STAN. So Mr. Stroheim sees the oily hats and he gets crazy. He says to Andrew the hats are going to have to come out of his salary. Twenty-seven dollars. So Andrew starts to cry.

EUGENE. He cried?

STAN. Forty-two years old, he's bawling all over the stock room. I mean, the man hasn't got too much furniture upstairs anyway, but he's real sweet. He brings me coffee, always laughing, telling me jokes. I never understand them but I laugh anyway, make him feel good, you know?

EUGENE. Yeah?

STAN. Anyway, I said to Mr. Stroheim I didn't think that was fair. It wasn't Andrew's fault.

EUGENE. [*astounded*] You said that to him?

STAN. Sure, why not? So Mr. Stroheim says, "You wanna pay for the hats, big mouth?" So I said, "No. I don't want to pay for the hats." So he says, "Then mind your own business, big mouth."

EUGENE. Holy mackerel.

STAN. So Mr. Stroheim looks at me like machine gun bullets are coming out of his eyes. And then he calmly sends Andrew over to the factory to pick up three new hats. Which is usually my job. So guess what Mr. Stroheim tells *me* to do?

EUGENE. What?

STAN. He tells me to sweep up. He says, for this week I'm the cleaning man.

EUGENE. I can't believe it.

STAN. Everybody is watching me now, waiting to see what I'm going to do. [*EUGENE nods in agreement.*] . . . Even Andrew stopped crying and watched.

Identify Cause-and-Effect Relationships What events lead to Mr. Stroheim's becoming angry with Stan?

Identify Cause-and-Effect Relationships Why does Mr. Stroheim make Stan the cleaning man? What do you think will be the effect of this action?

Vocabulary

astounded (əs toun′ ded) *v.* overwhelmed with sudden surprise or amazement

1 A ***stock room*** is a place where people store goods and supplies.

2 ***Linseed oil*** is a liquid made from plant seeds that is used in making paints, inks, and other items.

I felt the dignity of everyone who worked in that store was in my hands . . . so I grit my teeth, and I pick up the broom, and there's this big pile of dirt right in the middle of the floor . . .

EUGENE. Yeah?

STAN. . . . And I sweep it all over Mr. Stroheim's shoes. Andrew had just finished shining them this morning, if you want to talk about irony.

EUGENE. I'm dying. I'm actually dying.

STAN. [*enjoying himself*] You could see everyone in the place is about to bust a gut. Mrs. Mulcahy, the bookkeeper, can hardly keep her false teeth in her mouth. Andrew's eyes are hanging five inches out of their sockets.

EUGENE. This is the greatest story in the history of the world.

STAN. So Mr. Stroheim grabs me and pulls me into his back office, closes the door and pulls down the shades. He gives me this whole story how he was brought up in Germany to respect his superiors.[3] That if he ever — [*in accent*] "did soch a ting like you do, dey would beat me in der cup until dey carried me avay dead."

EUGENE. That's perfect. You got him down perfect.

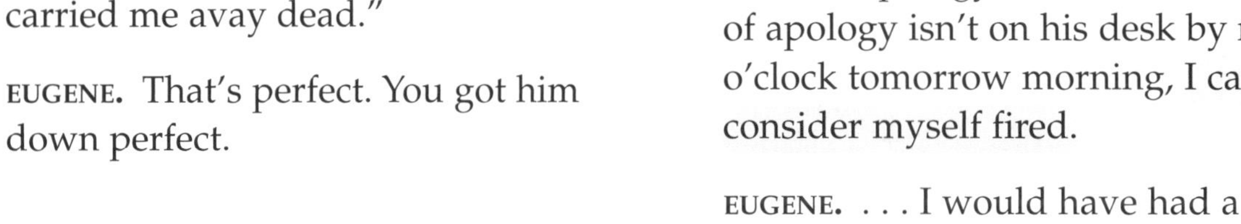

STAN. And I say, "Yeah. But we're not in Germany, old buddy."

EUGENE. You said that to him?

STAN. No. To myself. I didn't want to go too far.

EUGENE. I was wondering.

STAN. Anyway, he says he's always liked me and always thought I was a good boy and that he was going to give me one more chance. He wants a letter of apology. And that if the letter of apology isn't on his desk by nine o'clock tomorrow morning, I can consider myself fired.

EUGENE. . . . I would have had a heart attack . . . What did you say?

---

3 ***Superiors*** are people of higher rank or position.

Stage Directions How might the actor playing Stan make this a funny moment?

Identify Cause-and-Effect Relationships What will happen if Stan writes a letter of apology? What will happen if he doesn't?

STAN. I said I was not going to apologize if Andrew still had to pay for the hats . . . He said that was between him and Andrew . . . and that he expected the letter from me in the morning . . . I said good night, walked out of his office, got my hat and went home . . . ten minutes early.

EUGENE. I'm sweating. I swear to God, I'm sweating all over.

STAN. . . . I don't know why I did it. But I got so mad. It just wasn't fair. I mean, if you give in when you're eighteen and a half, you'll give in for the rest of your life, don't you think?

EUGENE. I suppose so . . . So what's the decision? Are you going to write the letter?

STAN. [*thinks . . .*] . . . No!

EUGENE. Positively?

STAN. Positively. Except I'll have to discuss it with Pop. I know we need the money. But he told me once you always have to do what you think is right in this world and stand up for your **principles.**

EUGENE. And what if he says he thinks you're wrong? That you should write the letter.

STAN. He won't. He's gonna leave it up to me, I know it.

EUGENE. But what if he says, "Write the letter"?

STAN. Well . . . that's something we won't know until after dinner, will we? . . . [*He crosses into the house.*]

EUGENE. [*looks after him, then turns out to audience*] . . . All in all, it was shaping up to be one heck of a dinner. I'll say this though . . . I always had this two way thing about my brother. Either I **worshipped** the ground he walked on . . . or I hated him so much I wanted to kill him . . . I guess you know how I feel about him today.

Stage Directions How might the actor show that his character is thinking?

Vocabulary

principles (prin′ sə pəlz) *n. pl.* rules of personal conduct

---

BQ BIG Question Why does Stan believe his father will allow him to make his own decision? What does this tell you about his father?

Identify Cause-and-Effect Relationships How does Eugene feel about Stan at this moment? What causes him to feel this way?

Vocabulary

worshipped (wur′ shipt) *v.* adored or idolized

After You Read

Respond and Think Critically

1. Although the subject of this scene is serious, the playwright uses humor. What are two humorous moments from the scene? **[Identify]**
2. Use your own words to retell what led to Stan's being fired. **[Summarize]**
3. As Stan describes his confrontation with Mr. Stroheim, he says, "I felt the dignity of everyone who worked in that store was in my hands." What does he mean? How would you feel in his place? **[Interpret]**
4. How do Stan and Eugene feel toward each other? Use examples from the scene to explain their relationship. **[Analyze]**
5. What is Mr. Stroheim's opinion about the way that bosses and workers should treat one another? Where did he learn this? How does Stan feel about this? How do you feel about this? **[Evaluate]**
6. **BQ BIG Question** What principles are important to Stan? How do his principles affect his choices? **[Conclude]**

TIP

Interpreting
Remember that when you interpret, you use your own understanding to decide what something means.

- Find the quotation in the selection.
- Reread what happens before and after the quotation. Think about the meaning of *dignity.*
- In your own words, explain what Stan means. How would you feel if this had happened to you?

Keep track of your ideas about the **BIG Question** in your unit Foldable.

Daily Life and Culture

The Changing Face of Brighton Beach

Brighton Beach, Manhattan Beach, and Coney Island are neigborhoods in Brooklyn, New York. In 1868 Brighton Beach was developed as a beach resort with a grand hotel. In the late 1800s and early 1900s, a flood of working-class immigrants moved to New York City from Europe, hoping for a better life. The immigrants brought with them their own traditional values, especially a strong belief in the importance of family. Many of these families eventually moved into housing projects and huge apartment buildings in Brighton Beach.

Group Activity Discuss the following questions with your classmates.

1. How does the information in this passage help you understand the situation of the Jerome family?
2. How does reading this passage help you understand Stan's choices? How does it help you understand Mr. Stroheim's choices?

Literary Element Stage Directions

Standards Practice  ELA6R1b

1. The stage directions in a play can reveal all of the following except
   A. what the characters say.
   B. the way the characters look.
   C. the way the characters move.
   D. the way the play's sets and costumes look.

Review: Dialogue

As you learned on page 103, **dialogue** is the conversation between characters in a literary work. In a play, the story is told mainly through dialogue. As the characters talk, the dialogue reveals what is happening and conveys what characters are thinking and feeling.

Standards Practice  ELA6R1b

2. The dialogue in this scene from *Brighton Beach Memoirs* does all of the following except
   A. show something about how the characters feel and think.
   B. tell how the sets should look.
   C. tell about action that takes place off stage.
   D. advance the plot by setting up the conflict.

Reading Skill Identify Cause-and-Effect Relationships

3. In this scene, what event sets the action in motion?
4. What is the effect of Stan's sweeping dirt onto Mr. Stroheim's shoes?
5. What is Eugene's reaction to Stan's story? What causes him to react this way?

Vocabulary Practice

Synonyms are words that have the same or nearly the same meaning. **Antonyms** are words that have opposite meanings. Identify whether the word pairs in each set are synonyms or antonyms. Then write a sentence using the first word of each pair or draw or find a picture that represents the word.

temporarily and briefly

astounded and surprised

worshipped and hated

principles and beliefs

Example:

temporarily and briefly = synonyms

Sentence: I was temporarily locked out of my house when I forgot my keys.

Academic Vocabulary

An accident **triggered** a disagreement between Mr. Stroheim and Stan. In the preceding sentence, *triggered* means "began or brought about." Think about what happened in the scene. Then fill in the blank for this statement: The accident that triggered the disagreement was ______.

Literature Online

Selection Resources For Selection Quizzes, eFlashcards, and Reading-Writing Connection activities, go to glencoe.com and enter QuickPass code GL17527u6.

Respond Through Writing

Review

Convince an Audience In this scene from *Brighton Beach Memoirs*, Eugene learns something important about his brother's character. Write a short review that describes the scene's strengths and weaknesses and convinces an audience that the play is worth seeing.

Understand the Task A review should help readers decide whether or not to read—or see—a play. For this review, your audience will be other students your age. Ask yourself, why would other students enjoy reading or seeing this scene? Think about the way vivid, descriptive word choices can make your review more persuasive.

Prewrite Think of at least three strengths or weaknesses of the scene. You might want to consider its theme, characters, humor, or dialogue. Give evidence from the selection that explains each strength or weakness. Keep track of your ideas in a chart like the one below.

Strengths and Weaknesses	Evidence
character (strength)	Stan stands up for someone who has been treated unfairly.

Draft Before you begin drafting, make an overall plan. For example, you may decide to write an introduction, a paragraph about each strength or weakness, and a conclusion. After you figure out your plan, write your thesis statement first. This sentence frame might help you:

> I believe that this scene from *Brighton Beach Memoirs* is _______ because of its _______.

Revise After you have written your first draft, read it to determine whether you have anticipated a reader's counterarguments. A counterargument is a statement that challenges your thesis statement. Make sure that you have chosen the strongest possible evidence to support your positions on the scene's strengths and weaknesses. Be sure to include direct quotations from the play. Also make sure that your ideas are presented clearly and in the most effective order.

Edit and Proofread Proofread your paper, correcting any errors in spelling, grammar, and punctuation. Review the Grammar Tip in the side column for information on end punctuation and the use of ellipses.

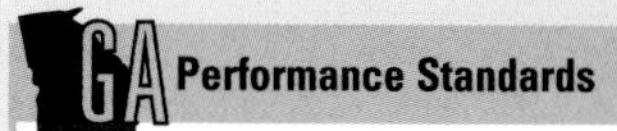

For page 770

ELA6W2a Demonstrate competence in a variety of genres. Produce a response to literature that supports a judgment through references to the text.

Grammar Tip

End Punctuation and Ellipses
When writing a review, you can use periods, question marks, or exclamation points to end your sentences. However, do not use exclamation points often in formal writing.

Some sentences from this scene contain **ellipses** (sets of three periods). Ellipses often show that words have been left out. Here, they show that a character is pausing or his words are trailing off. For example:

Fired? . . . You mean for good?

Quoting a passage that ends with an ellipsis is just like quoting a passage that doesn't end with an ellipsis. Put a comma or period after the ellipsis but inside the quotation marks.

Part 2

Knowledge and Wisdom

Mother and Daughter Looking at Stars Through Telescope. Rob Colvin.

BQ BIG Question What Are Worthwhile Goals?

In the picture, how are the mother and daughter reaching for knowledge and wisdom? What steps have you taken to know more about the world?

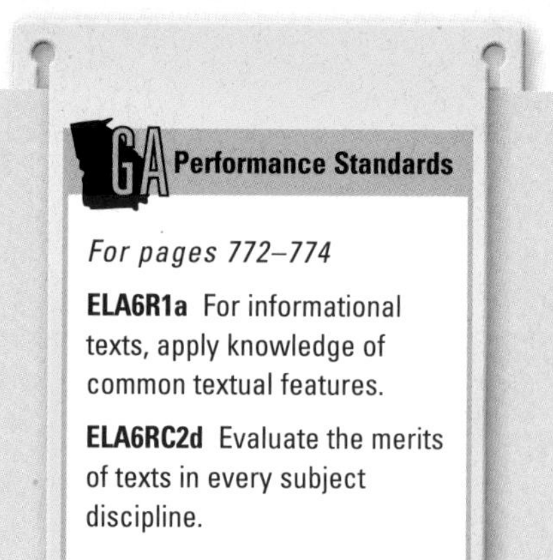

GA Performance Standards
For pages 772–774
ELA6R1a For informational texts, apply knowledge of common textual features.
ELA6RC2d Evaluate the merits of texts in every subject discipline.

Set a Purpose for Reading

As you read, think how you could use your talents to improve some condition in the world.

Preview the Article

1. What does the **title,** also called the headline, suggest about Anthony Shriver's program?
2. Look at the **deck,** which is the information that appears before the first paragraph. What details does the deck provide about the article?

Reading Skill **Distinguish Fact and Opinion** To **distinguish fact from opinion,** think about statements that can be proven and statements based on feelings or views.

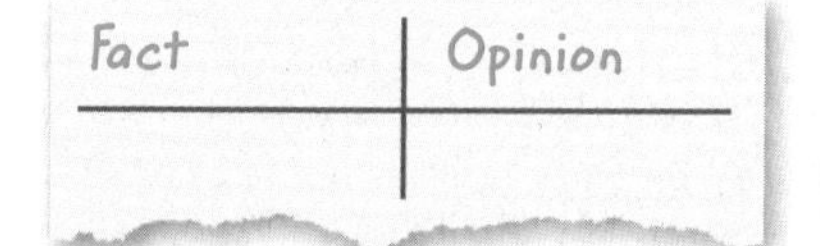

TIME

Best of BUDDIES

Anthony Shriver's program for the mentally disabled encourages people to stop staring and start sharing.

By Kevin Gray and Cindy Dampier

Anthony Kennedy Shriver is thinking about the day in 1994 when he and Jorge Mentado,[1] 39, went shopping together. Shriver and Mentado, who is mentally challenged, are good friends. "You'd think World War III[2] had broken out," says Shriver, with a chuckle. "Jorge is very hard to understand. He had on big boots with the laces untied. In [one shop], he'd say hello to every pretty girl and talk to the salespeople. One woman came in with a little dog, and Jorge started petting it. It was like a movie. People need to see that sort of thing."

1 ***Jorge Mentado*** (hōr′ hā män tä′ dō).

2 ***World War III*** is a name people use for the next global war. World Wars I and II took place in the twentieth century.

Shriver teams up with buddy Jorge Mentado (left).

Stephan Ellison/Corbis Outline

Shriver is founder and president of Best Buddies. The main goal of Best Buddies is to better the lives of people with mental disabilities. The program helps them to make new friends and to find jobs. Another goal "is to make it so people won't stare," says Shriver. "So, when you go downtown or into a church, they're used to having people with mental disabilities in there."

Shriver came up with the idea in 1987 while he was a student at Georgetown University. "I saw a lot of my buddies not doing a whole heck of a lot in the community," he says. "I figured it wouldn't take a huge effort for them to integrate[3] someone into their daily routine." Fifty volunteers came to Shriver's first Best Buddies meeting. He paired them with people from group homes[4] and special schools. After Shriver graduated, interest in the project continued. He received calls from students who wanted to start branches of Best Buddies at other colleges.

"I thought I'd just take a couple of months to get this going at a couple of other colleges. I never stopped," recalls Shriver.

Since then, Best Buddies has grown to include more than 6,500 "buddies." Today, Best Buddies International Inc. has branches in all 50 states and in

3 To ***integrate*** something is to bring together or make something part of a whole.

4 ***Group homes*** give mentally disabled people an opportunity to live away from family.

more than 12 countries. There are even branches in middle schools and high schools and in corporations and churches. Best Buddies Jobs trains the mentally challenged so they can get professional jobs, not just jobs bagging groceries. Shriver believes everyone has a special talent. "It's up to us," he says, "to create opportunities for these individuals to develop and share their skills."

Best Buddies helps people to realize what they have in common, instead of focusing on differences. In schools, students are paired with kids in special education. These friends meet weekly to have lunch, shop, go to an event, or just hang out and talk.

Judy Hales of Miami, whose mentally challenged son David, 12, has a buddy, calls the program a roaring success. "The first time David went out," she says, "our family all said, 'Where's David?' because he never got to go out without one of us." George Zitnay, an expert on mental disabilities, says getting people like David into the community is a great idea. "People with mental disabilities have been isolated[5] for too long," says Zitnay. "Best Buddies addresses the need for valued friendship."

Shriver's hope is that one day Best Buddies will no longer be needed. "Hopefully, people will just start having these friendships naturally," he says. Until then, Best Buddies will continue educating students, employers, and communities about the needs and abilities of people with mental disabilities.

---

5 To be ***isolated*** is to be set or kept away from others.

Respond and Think Critically

1. Write a brief summary of the main ideas in this article. For help on writing a summary, see page 170. **[Summarize]**
2. **Text to Self** What might be some of the difficulties and rewards of befriending someone who is mentally challenged? **[Connect]**
3. Why have people with mental disabilities been isolated for so long? **[Infer]**
4. Does Best Buddies seem like an effective way of integrating people with disabilities into the community? Explain. What other methods might achieve the same goal? **[Evaluate]**
5. **Reading Skill** **Distinguish Fact and Opinion** Look back at your graphic organizer. Does the article contain mostly facts, mostly opinions, or a mix of both? Are the opinions balanced—that is, does the article include opinions from both sides of the issue? Explain.
6. **BQ** **BIG Question** How might helping others help you achieve knowledge? How might it be a source of wisdom?

Before You Read

The Phantom Tollbooth, Act One

Connect to the Play

Think about what it feels like to have nothing to do. How do you keep from getting bored?

List Make a list of your hobbies and interests. Then list topics you would like to learn more about. What, if anything, keeps you from pursuing these goals?

Build Background

The Phantom Tollbooth is based on a book by Norton Juster. As you read, you will come across wordplay and puns.

Wordplay is just what it sounds like—the playful use of words. Wordplay is usually quick, clever, and funny. For example, the Whether Man says, "After all, it's more important to know whether there will be weather than what the weather will be." Wordplay occurs in the repeated sounds of *whether* and *weather.*

A **pun** is a kind of wordplay—a joke involving two meanings of the same word, or two words with the same sound. For example, one character says, "Why not wait for your just desserts?" In this sentence, *desserts* means both "what is deserved" and "sweet food served at the end of a meal."

Vocabulary

guaranteed (gar′ ən tēd′) *v.* made certain; promised (p. 779). *The chef guaranteed a delicious dinner for the guests.*

consideration (kən sid′ ə rā′ shən) *n.* thought or reflection (p. 786). *After careful consideration, Sam decided to volunteer at the retirement center.*

ferocious (fə rō′ shəs) *adj.* fierce and violent (p. 787). *In his dream, Juan was attacked by a ferocious monster.*

assortment (ə sôrt′ mənt) *n.* a collection of different things (p. 789). *Molly found an assortment of crayons, markers, and paints in the art supply box.*

ignorance (ig′ nər əns) *n.* state of lacking in knowledge or education (p. 796). *In his ignorance, Tom broke the rules at his new school.*

Meet Susan Nanus

Writer for Stage and Screen Susan Nanus is an award-winning writer of scripts and adaptations of books for theater, movies, and television. For example, *The Phantom Tollbooth* is a book by Norton Juster. Nanus adapted the story as a play.

Literary Works Nanus has written and co-written many scripts, including *Harvest of Fire,* for which she won an award from the Writers Guild of America in 1997.

Susan Nanus lives in Los Angeles, California.

Literature Online

Author Search For more about Susan Nanus, go to glencoe.com and enter QuickPass code GL17527u6.

Set Purposes for Reading

BQ BIG Question

As you read, ask yourself what happens when a person has no worthwhile goals?

Literary Element Act and Scene

Plays are divided into **acts** and **scenes.** Most plays have two or more acts, but short plays often have only one act. Acts are sometimes further divided into scenes. Scene changes often signal a new setting. When a play is performed, the lights may darken between scenes while the setting is changed.

A playwright uses acts and scenes to divide a play into its most important parts. When you read a play, stage directions at the beginning of a new act and scene can help you understand the setting and learn about characters.

As you read, ask yourself, how do the different scenes help readers understand the organization of Act One?

Reading Strategy Paraphrase

When you **paraphrase,** you put what you read into your own words. Unlike a summary, a paraphrase is usually about the same length as the original passage. When you paraphrase, you might want to look away from the page you are reading. Imagine that you are explaining it to a teacher or friend.

Paraphrasing helps you remember what you have read and tests whether you have understood it. Paraphrasing also helps you organize information and understand the meaning of difficult text.

To paraphrase, you should

- read a passage
- think about the author's meaning
- restate the meaning in your own words

You may find it helpful to use a graphic organizer like the one below.

Line from the Play	My Paraphrase
Funny thing is, time can pass very slowly or very fast, and sometimes even both at once.	Many people are too bored or busy to notice that time has passed.

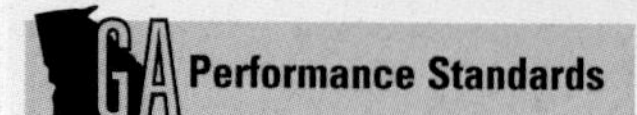

GA Performance Standards

For pages 775–800

ELA6R1e/ii For literary texts, identify and analyze the elements of setting, characterization, plot, and the resolution of the conflict of a story or play.

TRY IT

Paraphrase You are helping your friend with a science project on volcanoes. The dictionary says a volcano is an "opening in the surface of Earth from which molten rock, gases, and rock fragments are expelled." How would you put this into your own words so your friend can understand it?

The Phantom Tollbooth

Susan Nanus
based on the book by Norton Juster

Cast *[in order of appearance]*

The Clock
Milo, a boy
The Whether Man
Six Lethargarians
Tock, the Watchdog (same as The Clock)
Azaz the Unabridged, King of Dictionopolis
The Mathemagician, King of Digitopolis
Princess Sweet Rhyme
Princess Pure Reason
Gatekeeper of Dictionopolis
Three Word Merchants
The Letterman (Fourth Word Merchant)
Spelling Bee
The Humbug
The Duke of Definition
The Minister of Meaning
The Earl of Essence
The Count of Connotation
The Undersecretary of Understanding
A Page

The Sets

MILO'S BEDROOM—with shelves, pennants, pictures on the wall, as well as suggestions of the characters of the Land of Wisdom.

THE ROAD TO THE LAND OF WISDOM—a forest, from which the Whether Man and the Lethargarians emerge.

DICTIONOPOLIS—a marketplace full of open-air stalls as well as little shops. Letters and signs should abound.

Act One

SCENE 1

[The stage is completely dark and silent. Suddenly the sound of someone winding an alarm clock is heard, and after that, the sound of loud ticking is heard.

LIGHTS UP on the CLOCK, a huge alarm clock. The CLOCK reads 4:00. The lighting should make it appear that the CLOCK is suspended in mid-air (if possible). The CLOCK ticks for 30 seconds.]

CLOCK. See that! Half a minute gone by. Seems like a long time when you're waiting for something to happen, doesn't it? Funny thing is, time can pass very slowly or very fast, and sometimes even both at once. The time now? Oh, a little after four, but what that means should depend on you. Too often, we do something simply because time tells us to. Time for school, time for bed, whoops, 12:00, time to be hungry. It can get a little silly, don't you think? Time is important, but it's what you do with it that makes it so. So my advice to you is to use it. Keep your eyes open and your ears perked. Otherwise it will pass before you know it, and you'll certainly have missed something!

Things have a habit of doing that, you know.

Being here one minute and gone the next.
In the twinkling of an eye.
In a jiffy.
In a flash!

I know a girl who yawned and missed a whole summer vacation. And what about that caveman who took a nap one afternoon, and woke up to find himself completely alone. You see, while *he* was sleeping, someone had invented the wheel and everyone had moved to the suburbs.[1] And then of course, there is Milo. *[LIGHTS UP to reveal MILO's Bedroom. The CLOCK appears to be on a shelf in the room of a young boy—a room filled with books, toys, games, maps, papers, pencils, a bed, a desk. There is a dartboard with numbers and the face of the MATHEMAGICIAN, a bedspread made from KING AZAZ's cloak, a kite looking like the SPELLING BEE, a punching bag with the HUMBUG's face, as well as records, a television, a toy car, and a large box that is wrapped and has an envelope taped to the top. The sound of FOOTSTEPS is heard, and then enter MILO dejectedly.[2] He throws*

1 ***Suburbs*** are neighborhoods on the outer edge of a city.

2 When Milo enters ***dejectedly,*** he walks as if he is sad and depressed.

Paraphrase Retell the Clock's advice in your own words.

Act and Scene Where is this scene set? Why do you think the complete setting wasn't shown at the beginning of the scene?

Time is important, but it's what you do with it that makes it so. So my advice to you is to use it.

down his books and coat, flops into a chair, and sighs loudly.] Who never knows what to do with himself—not just sometimes, but always. When he's in school, he wants to be out, and when he's out, he wants to be in. [*During the following speech,* MILO *examines the various toys, tools, and other possessions in the room, trying them out and rejecting them.*] Wherever he is, he wants to be somewhere else—and when he gets there, so what. Everything is too much trouble or a waste of time. Books—he's already read them. Games—boring. T.V.—dumb. So what's left? Another long, boring afternoon. Unless he bothers to notice a very large package that happened to arrive today.

MILO. [*Suddenly notices the package. He drags himself over to it, and disinterestedly reads the label.*] "For Milo, who has plenty of time." Well, that's true. [*Sighs and looks at it.*] No. [*Walks away.*] Well . . . [*Comes back. Rips open envelope and reads.*]

A VOICE. "One genuine turnpike **tollbooth**, easily assembled at home for use by those who have never traveled in lands beyond."

Paraphrase What is Milo's problem?

Visual Vocabulary

A **toll** is a fee drivers pay to use a road or a bridge. Before entering a toll road, a driver must stop at a **tollbooth** and pay a fee.

MILO. Beyond what? [*Continues reading.*]

A VOICE. "This package contains the following items:" [*MILO pulls the items out of the box and sets them up as they are mentioned.*] "One [1] genuine turnpike tollbooth to be erected according to directions. Three [3] precautionary[3] signs to be used in a precautionary fashion. Assorted coins for paying tolls. One [1] map, strictly up to date, showing how to get from here to there. One [1] book of rules and traffic regulations which may not be bent or broken. Warning! Results are not **guaranteed**. If not perfectly satisfied, your wasted time will be refunded."

MILO. [*Skeptically.*[4]] Come off it, who do you think you're kidding? [*Walks around and examines tollbooth.*] What am

3 ***Precautionary*** signs are warning signs.

4 ***Skeptically*** means "doubtfully" or "with suspicion."

Vocabulary

guaranteed (gar′ən tēd′) *v.* made certain; promised

You never know how things are going to get started. But when you're bored, what you need more than anything is a rude awakening.

I supposed to do with this? [*The ticking of the* CLOCK *grows loud and impatient.*] Well . . . what else do I have to do. [MILO *gets into his toy car and drives up to the first sign.*]

VOICE. "HAVE YOUR DESTINATION IN MIND."

MILO. [*Pulls out the map.*] Now, let's see. That's funny. I never heard of any of these places. Well, it doesn't matter anyway. Dictionopolis. That's a weird name. I might as well go there. [*Begins to move, following map. Drives off.*]

CLOCK. See what I mean? You never know how things are going to get started. But when you're bored, what you need more than anything is a rude awakening.

[*The* ALARM *goes off very loudly as the stage darkens. The sound of the alarm is transformed into the honking of a car horn, and is then joined by the blasts, bleeps, roars and growls of heavy highway traffic. When the lights come up,* MILO'S *bedroom is gone and we see a lonely road in the middle of nowhere.*]

BQ BIG Question Does Milo have a destination in mind? Why might this be good advice for Milo?

Act and Scene How do you know that this scene is ending?

Act One

SCENE 2

THE ROAD TO DICTIONOPOLIS.

[ENTER MILO *in his car.*]

MILO. This is weird! I don't recognize any of this scenery at all. [*A* SIGN *is held up before* MILO, *startling him.*] Huh? [*Reads.*] WELCOME TO EXPECTATIONS.[5] INFORMATION, PREDICTIONS AND ADVICE CHEERFULLY OFFERED. PARK HERE AND BLOW HORN. [MILO *blows horn.*]

WHETHER MAN. [*A little man wearing a long coat and carrying an umbrella pops up from behind the sign that he was holding. He speaks very fast and excitedly.*] My, my, my, my, my, welcome, welcome, welcome, welcome to the Land of Expectations, Expectations, Expectations! We don't get many travelers these days; we certainly don't get many travelers. Now what can I do for you? I'm the Whether Man.

MILO. [*Referring to map.*] Uh . . . is this the right road to Dictionopolis?

---

5 ***Expectations*** are things you hope for or look forward to.

WHETHER MAN. Well now, well now, well now, I don't know of any *wrong* road to Dictionopolis, so if this road goes to Dictionopolis at all, it must be the right road, and if it doesn't, it must be the right road to somewhere else, because there are no wrong roads to anywhere. Do you think it will rain?

MILO. I thought you were the Weather Man.

WHETHER MAN. Oh, no, I'm the Whether Man, not the weather man. [*Pulls out a* SIGN *or opens a* FLAP *of his coat, which reads: "*WHETHER.*"*] After all, it's more important to know whether there will be weather than what the weather will be.

MILO. What kind of place is Expectations?

WHETHER MAN. Good question, good question! Expectations is the place you must always go to before you get to where you are going. Of course, some people never go beyond Expectations, but my job is to hurry them along whether they like it or not. Now what else can I do for you? [*Opens his umbrella.*]

MILO. I think I can find my own way.

WHETHER MAN. Splendid, splendid, splendid! Whether or not you find your own way, you're bound to find some way. If you happen to find my way, please return it. I lost it years ago. I imagine by now it must be quite rusty. You did say it was going to rain, didn't you? [*Escorts* MILO *to the car under the open umbrella.*] I'm glad you made your own decision. I do so hate to make up my mind about anything, whether it's good or bad, up or down, rain or shine. Expect everything. I always say, and the unexpected never happens. Goodbye, goodbye, goodbye, good . . . [*A loud* CLAP *of* THUNDER *is heard.*] Oh dear!

[*He looks up at the sky, puts out his hund to feel for rain, and* RUNS AWAY. MILO *watches puzzledly and drives on.*]

MILO. I'd better get out of Expectations, but fast. Talking to a guy like that all day would get me nowhere for sure. [*He tries to speed up, but finds instead that he is moving slower and slower.*] Oh, oh, now what? [*He can barely move. Behind* MILO*, the* LETHARGARIANS[6] *begin to enter from all parts of the stage. They are dressed to blend in with the scenery and carry small pillows that look like rocks. Whenever they fall asleep, they rest on the pillows.*] Now I really am getting nowhere. I hope I didn't take a wrong turn. [*The car stops. He tries to start it. It won't move. He gets out and begins to tinker with it.*] I wonder where I am.

Paraphrase Why do people come to the Land of Expectations?

6 The ***Lethargarians*** get their name from the word *lethargy,* which is a state of being drowsy, sluggish, and without energy.

Paraphrase Paraphrase the Whether Man's words. What do you think of his advice?

In the Doldrums, laughter is frowned upon and smiling is permitted only on alternate Thursdays.

LETHARGARIAN 1. You're. in . . . the . . . Dol . . . drums . . . [*MILO looks around.*]

LETHARGARIAN 2. Yes . . . the . . . Dol . . . drums . . . [*A YAWN is heard.*]

MILO. [*Yelling.*] *WHAT ARE THE DOLDRUMS?*

LETHARGARIAN 3. The Doldrums, my friend, are where nothing ever happens and nothing ever changes. [*Parts of the Scenery stand up or Six People come out of the scenery colored in the same colors of the trees or the road. They move very slowly and as soon as they move, they stop to rest again.*] Allow me to introduce all of us. We are the Lethargarians at your service.

MILO. [*Uncertainly.*] Very pleased to meet you. I think I'm lost. Can you help me?

LETHARGARIAN 4. Don't say think. [*He yawns.*] It's against the law.

LETHARGARIAN 1. No one's allowed to think in the Doldrums. [*He falls asleep.*]

LETHARGARIAN 2. Don't you have a rule book? It's local ordinance[7] 175389-J. [*He falls asleep.*]

MILO. [*Pulls out rule book and reads.*] Ordinance 175389-J: "It shall be unlawful, illegal and unethical to think, think of thinking, surmise, presume, reason, meditate or speculate while in the Doldrums. Anyone breaking this law shall be severely punished." That's a ridiculous law! Everybody thinks.

ALL THE LETHARGARIANS. We don't!

LETHARGARIAN 2. And most of the time, you don't, that's why you're here. You weren't thinking and you weren't paying attention either. People who don't pay attention often get stuck in the Doldrums. Face it, most of the time, you're just like us. [*Falls, snoring, to the ground. MILO laughs.*]

Paraphrase In your own words, how would you describe the Doldrums?

7 An ***ordinance*** is a law.

Paraphrase Why is Milo in the Doldrums?

LETHARGARIAN 5. Stop that at once. Laughing is against the law. Don't you have a rule book? It's local ordinance 574381-W.

MILO. [*Opens rule book and reads.*] "In the Doldrums, laughter is frowned upon and smiling is permitted only on alternate Thursdays." Well, if you can't laugh or think, what can you do?

LETHARGARIAN 6. Anything as long as it's nothing, and everything as long as it isn't anything. There's lots to do. We have a very busy schedule . . .

LETHARGARIAN 1. At 8:00 we get up and then we spend from 8 to 9 daydreaming.

LETHARGARIAN 2. From 9:00 to 9:30 we take our early midmorning nap . . .

LETHARGARIAN 3. From 9:30 to 10:30 we dawdle and delay . . .

LETHARGARIAN 4. From 10:30 to 11:30 we take our late early morning nap . . .

LETHARGARIAN 5 From 11:30 to 12:00 we bide our time and then we eat our lunch.

LETHARGARIAN 6. From 1:00 to 2:00 we linger and loiter[8] . . .

LETHARGARIAN 1. From 2:00 to 2:30 we take our early afternoon nap . . .

LETHARGARIAN 2. From 2:30 to 3:30 we put off for tomorrow what we could have done today . . .

8 To ***loiter*** is to move aimlessly and slowly, or to linger somewhere without a purpose.

LETHARGARIAN 3. From 3:30 to 4:00 we take our early late afternoon nap . . .

LETHARGARIAN 4. From 4:00 to 5:00 we loaf and lounge until dinner . . .

LETHARGARIAN 5. From 6:00 to 7:00 we dilly-dally . . .

LETHARGARIAN 6. From 7:00 to 8:00 we take our early evening nap and then for an hour before we go to bed, we waste time.

LETHARGARIAN 1. [*Yawning.*] You see, it's really quite strenuous[9] doing nothing all day long, and so once a week, we take a holiday and go nowhere.

LETHARGARIAN 5. Which is just where we were going when you came along. Would you care to join us?

MILO. [*Yawning.*] That's where I seem to be going, anyway. [*Stretching.*] Tell me, does everyone here do nothing?

LETHARGARIAN 3. Everyone but the terrible watchdog. He's always sniffing around to see that nobody wastes time. A most unpleasant character.

MILO. The Watchdog?

LETHARGARIAN 6. THE WATCHDOG!

ALL THE LETHARGARIANS. [*Yelling at*

9 ***Strenuous*** activity calls for great effort.

Paraphrase How would you describe the Lethargarians' busy schedule?

once.] RUN! WAKE UP! RUN! HERE HE COMES! THE WATCHDOG! [*They all run off and* ENTER *a large dog with the head, feet, and tail of a dog, and the body of a clock, having the same face as the character* THE CLOCK.]

WATCHDOG. What are you doing here?

MILO. Nothing much. Just killing time. You see . . .

WATCHDOG. KILLING TIME! [*His* ALARM RINGS *in fury.*] It's bad enough wasting time without killing it. What are you doing in the Doldrums, anyway? Don't you have anywhere to go?

MILO. I think I was on my way to Dictionopolis when I got stuck here. Can you help me?

WATCHDOG. Help you! You've got to help yourself. I suppose you know why you got stuck.

MILO. I guess I just wasn't thinking.

WATCHDOG. Precisely. Now you're on your way.

MILO. I am?

WATCHDOG. Of course. Since you got here by not thinking, it seems reasonable that in order to get out, you must *start* thinking. Do you mind if I get in? I love automobile rides. [*He gets in. They wait.*] Well?

Act and Scene How does the mood of this scene change with the entrance of the Watchdog?

Paraphrase The Watchdog and the Clock are played by the same actor. How is the Watchdog's speech similar to that of the Clock?

MILO. All right. I'll try. [*Screws up his face and thinks.*] Are we moving?

WATCHDOG. Not yet. Think harder.

MILO. I'm thinking as hard as I can.

WATCHDOG. Well, think just a little harder than that. Come on, you can do it.

MILO. All right, all right . . . . I'm thinking of all the planets in the solar system, and why water expands when it turns to ice, and all the words that begin with "q," and . . .
[*The wheels begin to move.*] We're moving! We're moving!

WATCHDOG. Keep thinking.

MILO. [*Thinking.*] How a steam engine works and how to bake a pie and the difference between Fahrenheit and Centigrade . . .

WATCHDOG. Dictionopolis, here we come.

MILO. Hey, Watchdog, are you coming along?

TOCK. You can call me Tock, and keep your eyes on the road.

MILO. What kind of place is Dictionopolis, anyway?

TOCK. It's where all the words in the world come from. It used to be a marvelous place, but ever since Rhyme and Reason left, it hasn't been the same.

BQ BIG Question Why must Milo think harder? How does the Watchdog challenge Milo?

MILO. Rhyme and Reason?

TOCK. The two princesses. They used to settle all the arguments between their two brothers who rule over the Land of Wisdom. You see, Azaz is the king of Dictionopolis and the Mathemagician is the king of Digitopolis and they almost never see eye to eye on anything. It was the job of the Princesses Sweet Rhyme and Pure Reason to solve the differences between the two kings, and they always did so well that both sides usually went home feeling very satisfied. But then, one day, the kings had an argument to end all arguments. . . .

[The LIGHTS DIM on TOCK and MILO, and come up on KING AZAZ of Dictionopolis on another part of the stage. AZAZ has a great stomach, a grey beard reaching to his waist, a small crown and a long robe with the letters of the alphabet written all over it.]

AZAZ. Of course, I'll abide by the decision of Rhyme and Reason, though I have no doubt as to what it will be. They will choose *words*, of course. Everyone knows that words are more important than numbers any day of the week.

Everyone knows that words are more important than numbers any day of the week.

[The MATHEMAGICIAN appears opposite AZAZ. The MATHEMAGICIAN wears a long flowing robe covered entirely with complex mathematical equations, and a tall pointed hat. He carries a long staff with a pencil point at one end and a large rubber eraser at the other.]

MATHEMAGICIAN. That's what you think, Azaz. People wouldn't even know what day of the week it is without *numbers*. Haven't you ever looked at a calendar? Face it, Azaz. It's numbers that count.

AZAZ. Don't be ridiculous. [*To audience, as if leading a cheer.*] Let's hear it for WORDS!

MATHEMAGICIAN. [*To audience, in the same manner.*] Cast your vote for NUMBERS!

Act and Scene How many settings have there been in Scene 2 so far?

Paraphrase Explain the pun in this sentence in your own words.

AZAZ. A, B, C's!

MATHEMAGICIAN. 1, 2, 3's!
[*A* FANFARE *is heard.*]

AZAZ AND MATHEMAGICIAN. [*To each other.*] Quiet! Rhyme and Reason are about to announce their decision.

[*RHYME and REASON appear.*]

RHYME. Ladies and gentlemen, letters and numerals, fractions and punctuation marks—may we have your attention, please. After careful **consideration** of the problem set before us by *KING AZAZ* of Dictionopolis [*AZAZ bows.*] and the Mathemagician of Digitopolis [*MATHEMAGICIAN raises his hands in a victory salute.*] we have come to the following conclusion:

REASON. Words and numbers are of equal value, for in the cloak[10] of knowledge, one is the warp and the other is the woof.[11]

RHYME. It is no more important to count the sands than it is to name the stars.

10 A ***cloak*** is a loose outer piece of clothing, with or without sleeves.

11 In weaving, ***warp*** refers to threads running lengthwise in woven fabric. ***Woof*** refers to threads running from side to side and crossing the threads of the warp.

Paraphrase What is Rhyme saying about words and numbers?

Vocabulary

consideration (kən sid′ ə rā′ shən) *n.* thought or reflection

RHYME AND REASON. Therefore, let both kingdoms, Dictionopolis and Digitopolis, live in peace.

[*The sound of* CHEERING *is heard.*]

AZAZ. Boo! is what I say. Boo and Bah and Hiss!

MATHEMAGICIAN. What good are these girls if they can't even settle an argument in anyone's favor? I think I have come to a decision of my own.

AZAZ. So have I.

AZAZ AND MATHEMAGICIAN. [*To the* PRINCESSES.] You are hereby banished[12] from this land to the Castle-in-the-Air. [*To each other.*] And as for you, KEEP OUT OF MY WAY! [*They stalk off in opposite directions.*]

[*During this time, the set has been changed to the Market Square of Dictionopolis.* LIGHTS *come* UP *on the deserted square.*]

TOCK. And ever since then, there has been neither Rhyme nor Reason in this kingdom. Words are misused and numbers are mismanaged. The argument between the two kings has

12 When the princesses are ***banished,*** they are forced to leave the country.

Act and Scene To what setting has the action returned?

It is no more important to count the sands than it is to name the stars.

divided everyone and the real value of both words and numbers has been forgotten. What a waste!

MILO. Why doesn't somebody rescue the Princesses and set everything straight again?

TOCK. That is easier said than done. The Castle-in-the-Air is very far from here, and the one path which leads to it is guarded by **ferocious** demons. But hold on, here we are.

[*A Man appears, carrying a Gate and a small Tollbooth.*]

GATEKEEPER. AHHHHREMMMM! This is Dictionopolis, a happy kingdom, advantageously[13] located in the foothills of Confusion and caressed[14] by gentle breezes from the Sea of Knowledge. Today, by royal proclamation,[15] is Market Day. Have you come to buy or sell?

MILO. I beg your pardon?

GATEKEEPER. Buy or sell, buy or sell. Which is it? You must have come here for a reason.

MILO. Well, I . . .

Vocabulary

ferocious (fə rō′ shəs) *adj.* fierce and violent

13 Dictionopolis is ***advantageously*** located because it is in a good or fortunate place.

14 The breezes ***caressed*** the city with a gentle, loving touch.

15 A royal ***proclamation*** is an announcement from the king.

GATEKEEPER.
Come now, if you don't have a reason, you must at least have an explanation or certainly an excuse.

MILO. [*Meekly.*] Uh . . . no.

GATEKEEPER. [*Shaking his head.*] Very serious. You can't get in without a reason. [*Thoughtfully.*] Wait a minute. Maybe I have an old one you can use. [*Pulls out an old suitcase from the tollbooth and rummages through it.*] No . . . no . . . no . . . this won't do . . . hmmm . . .

MILO. [*To* TOCK.] What's he looking for? [TOCK *shrugs.*]

GATEKEEPER. Ah! This is fine. [*Pulls out a* **Medallion** *on a chain. Engraved in the Medallion is: "*WHY NOT?*"*] Why not. That's a good reason for almost anything . . . a bit used, perhaps, but still quite serviceable. There you are, sir. Now I can truly say: Welcome to Dictionopolis.

Visual Vocabulary

A **medallion** is a large medal, or flat piece of metal with a design. A medallion is often given as an award.

[*He opens the gate and walks off.* CITIZENS *and* MERCHANTS *appear on all levels of the stage, and* MILO *and* TOCK *find themselves in the middle of a noisy marketplace. As some people buy and sell their wares, others hang a large banner which reads:* WELCOME TO THE WORD MARKET.]

MILO. Tock! Look!

MERCHANT 1. Hey-ya, hey-ya, hey-ya, step right up and take your pick. Juicy tempting words for sale. Get your fresh-picked "if's," "and's" and "but's"! Just take a look at these nice ripe "where's" and "when's."

MERCHANT 2. Step right up, step right up, fancy, best-quality words here for sale. Enrich your vocabulary and expand your speech with such elegant items as "quagmire," "flabbergast," or "upholstery."

Act and Scene What is the effect of the arrival of the crowds and merchants in the market?

MERCHANT 3. Words by the bag, buy them over here. Words by the bag for the more talkative customer. A pound of "happy's" at a very reasonable price . . . very useful for "Happy Birthday," "Happy New Year," "happy days," or "happy-go-lucky." Or how about a package of "good's," always handy for "good morning," "good afternoon," "good evening," and "goodbye."

MILO. I can't believe it. Did you ever see so many words?

TOCK. They're fine if you have something to say. [*They come to a Do-It-Yourself bin.*]

MILO. [*To* MERCHANT *4 at the bin.*] Excuse me, but what are these?

MERCHANT 4. These are for people who like to make up their own words. You can pick any **assortment** you like or buy a special box complete with all the letters and a book of instructions. Here, taste an "A." They're very good. [*He pops one into* MILO*'s mouth.*]

MILO. [*Tastes it hesitantly.*] It's sweet! [*He eats it.*]

MERCHANT 4. I knew you'd like it. "A" is one of our best-sellers. All of them aren't that good, you know. The "Z" for instance—very dry and sawdusty. And the "X"? Tastes like a trunkful of stale air. But most of the others aren't bad at all. Here, try the "I."

Vocabulary

assortment (ə sōrt′ mənt) *n.* a collection of different things

MILO. [*Tasting.*] Cool! It tastes icy.

MERCHANT 4. [*To* TOCK.] How about the "C" for you? It's as crunchy as a bone. Most people are just too lazy to make their own words, but take it from me, not only is it more fun, but it's also *de*-lightful, [*Holds up a "D."*] *e*-lating, [*Holds up an "E."*] and extremely *u*seful! [*Holds up a "U."*]

MILO. But isn't it difficult? I'm not very good at making words.

[*The* SPELLING BEE, *a large colorful bee, comes up from behind.*]

SPELLING BEE. Perhaps I can be of some assistance . . . a-s-s-i-s-t-a-n-c-e. [*The Three turn around and see him.*] Don't be alarmed . . . a-l-a-r-m-e-d. I am the Spelling Bee. I can spell anything. Anything. A-n-y-t-h-i-n-g. Try me. Try me.

MILO. [*Backing off,* TOCK *on his guard.*] Can you spell goodbye?

SPELLING BEE. Perhaps you are under the misapprehension[16] . . . m-i-s-a-p-p-r-e-h-e-n-s-i-o-n that I am dangerous. Let me assure you that I am quite peaceful. Now, think of the most difficult word you can, and I'll spell it.

MILO. Uh . . . o.k. [*At this point,* MILO *may turn to the audience and ask them to help him choose a word or he may think of one on his own.*] How about . . . "Curiosity"?

---

16 A ***misapprehension*** is a misunderstanding.

SPELLING BEE. [*Winking.*] Let's see now . . . uh . . . how much time do I have?

MILO. Just ten seconds. Count them off, Tock.

SPELLING BEE. [*As* TOCK *counts.*] Oh dear, oh dear. [*Just at the last moment, quickly.*] C-u-r-i-o-s-i-t-y.

MERCHANT 4. Correct! [ALL *Cheer.*]

MILO. Can you spell anything?

SPELLING BEE. [*Proudly.*] Just about. You see, years ago, I was an ordinary bee minding my own business, smelling flowers all day, occasionally picking up part-time work in people's bonnets. Then one day, I realized that I'd never amount to anything without an education, so I decided that . . .

HUMBUG.[17] [*Coming up in a booming voice.*] BALDERDASH![18] [*He wears a lavish coat, striped pants, checked vest, spats*[19] *and a derby hat*] Let me repeat . . . BALDERDASH! [*Swings his cane and clicks his heels in the air.*] Well, well, what have we here? Isn't someone going to introduce me to the little boy?

SPELLING BEE. [*Disdainfully.*] This is the Humbug. You can't trust a word he says.

17 ***Humbug*** means "foolish or empty talk; nonsense."

18 ***Balderdash*** means "nonsense."

19 Here, ***spats*** are cloth or leather shoe coverings.

Paraphrase What is another way to say "amount to anything"?

HUMBUG. NONSENSE! Everyone can trust a Humbug. As I was saying to the king just the other day . . .

SPELLING BEE. You've never met the king. [*To* MILO.] Don't believe a thing he tells you.

HUMBUG. Bosh, my boy, pure bosh. The Humbugs are an old and noble family, honorable to the core. Why, we fought in the Crusades with Richard the Lionhearted, crossed the Atlantic with Columbus, blazed trails with the pioneers. History is full of Humbugs.

SPELLING BEE. A very pretty speech . . . s-p-e-e-c-h. Now, why don't you go away? I was just advising the lad of the importance of proper spelling.

HUMBUG. BAH! As soon as you learn to spell one word, they ask you to spell another. You can never catch up, so why bother? [*Puts his arm around* MILO.] Take my advice, boy, and forget about it. As my great-great-great-grandfather George Washington Humbug used to say . . .

SPELLING BEE. You, sir, are an imposter i-m-p-o-s-t-e-r who can't even spell his own name!

HUMBUG. What? You dare to doubt my word? The word of a Humbug? The word of a Humbug who has direct access to the ear of a King? And the king shall hear of this, I promise you . . .

Paraphrase Restate the Humbug's opinion. Do you agree with it?

The Humbugs are an old and noble family, honorable to the core. Why, we fought in the Crusades with Richard the Lionhearted, crossed the Atlantic with Columbus, blazed trails with the pioneers. History is full of Humbugs.

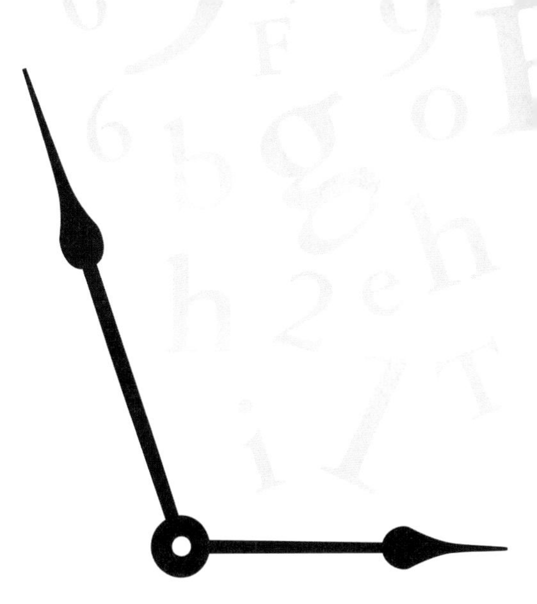

VOICE 1. Did someone call for the king?

VOICE 2. Did you mention the monarch?

VOICE 3. Speak of the sovereign?

VOICE 4. Entreat the Emperor?

VOICE 5. Hail his highness?

[*Five tall, thin gentlemen regally dressed in silks and satins, plumed hats and buckled shoes appear as they speak.*]

MILO. Who are they?

SPELLING BEE. The King's advisors. Or in more formal terms, his cabinet.

MINISTER 1. Greetings!

MINISTER 2. Salutations!

MINISTER 3. Welcome!

MINISTER 4. Good afternoon!

MINISTER 5. Hello!

MILO. Uh . . . Hi.

[*All the* MINISTERS, *from here on called by their numbers, unfold their scrolls and read in order.*]

MINISTER 1. By the order of Azaz the Unabridged . . .[20]

MINISTER 2. King of Dictionopolis . . .

MINISTER 3. Monarch of letters . . .

MINISTER 4. Emperor of phrases, sentences, and miscellaneous[21] figures of speech . . .

MINISTER 5. We offer you the hospitality of our kingdom . . .

MINISTER 1. Country

MINISTER 2. Nation

MINISTER 3. State

MINISTER 4. Commonwealth

MINISTER 5. Realm

---

20 Something that is ***unabridged*** is complete and has not been shortened.

21 ***Miscellaneous*** means "made up of different things."

Nonsense! Fantastic! Ridiculous! Absurd! Bosh!

MINISTER 1. Empire

MINISTER 2. Palatinate

MINISTER 3. Principality.

MILO. Do all those words mean the same thing?

MINISTER 1. Of course.

MINISTER 2. Certainly.

MINISTER 3. Precisely.

MINISTER 4. Exactly.

MINISTER 5. Yes.

MILO. Then why don't you use just one? Wouldn't that make a lot more sense?

MINISTER 1. Nonsense!

MINISTER 2. Ridiculous!

MINISTER 3. Fantastic!

MINISTER 4. Absurd!

MINISTER 5. Bosh!

MINISTER 1. We're not interested in making sense. It's not our job.

MINISTER 2. Besides, one word is as good as another, so why not use them all?

MINISTER 3. Then you don't have to choose which one is right.

MINISTER 4. Besides, if one is right, then ten are ten times as right.

MINISTER 5. Obviously, you don't know who we are. [*Each presents himself and* MILO *acknowledges the introduction.*]

MINISTER 1. The Duke of Definition.

MINISTER 2. The Minister of Meaning.

MINISTER 3. The Earl of Essence.

MINISTER 4. The Count of Connotation.

MINISTER 5. The Undersecretary of Understanding.

ALL FIVE. And we have come to invite you to the Royal Banquet.

Paraphrase Paraphrase these lines, and then describe the way the five ministers talk.

Act and Scene What purpose do the five ministers serve in this scene?

SPELLING BEE. The banquet! That's quite an honor, my boy. A real h-o-n-o-r.

HUMBUG. DON'T BE RIDICULOUS! Everybody goes to the Royal Banquet these days.

SPELLING BEE. [*To the* HUMBUG.] True, everybody does go. But some people are invited and others simply push their way in where they aren't wanted.

HUMBUG. HOW DARE YOU? You buzzing little upstart, I'll show you who's not wanted . . . [*Raises his cane threateningly.*]

SPELLING BEE. You just watch it! I'm warning w-a-r-n-i-n-g you!

[*At that moment, an ear-shattering blast of* TRUMPETS, *entirely off-key, is heard, and a* PAGE *appears.*]

PAGE. King Azaz the Unabridged is about to begin the Royal Banquet. All guests who do not appear promptly at the table will automatically lose their place. [*A huge Table is carried out with* KING AZAZ *sitting in a large chair, carried out at the head of the table.*]

AZAZ. Places. Everyone take your places. [*All the characters, including the* HUMBUG *and the* SPELLING BEE, *who forget their quarrel, rush to take their places at the table.* MILO *and* TOCK *sit near the* KING. AZAZ *looks at* MILO.] And just who is this?

MILO. Your Highness, my name is Milo and this is Tock. Thank you very much for inviting us to your banquet, and I think your palace is beautiful!

MINISTER 1. Exquisite.

MINISTER 2. Lovely.

MINISTER 3. Handsome.

MINISTER 4. Pretty.

MINISTER 5. Charming.

AZAZ. SILENCE! Now tell me, young man, what can you do to entertain us? Sing songs? Tell stories? Juggle plates? Do tumbling tricks? Which is it?

MILO. I can't do any of those things.

AZAZ. What an ordinary little boy. Can't you do anything at all?

MILO. Well . . . I can count to a thousand.

AZAZ. AARGH, numbers! Never mention numbers here. Only use them when we absolutely have to. Now, why don't we change the subject and have some dinner? Since you are the guest of honor, you may pick the menu.

MILO. Me? Well, uh . . . I'm not very hungry. Can we just have a light snack?

AZAZ. A light snack it shall be!

[AZAZ *claps his hands. Waiters rush in with covered trays. When they are uncovered, Shafts of Light pour out. The light may be created through the use of battery-operated flashlights which are secured in the trays and covered with a false bottom. The Guests help themselves.*]

HUMBUG. Not a very substantial[22] meal. Maybe you can suggest something a little more filling.

MILO. Well, in that case, I think we ought to have a square meal . . .

AZAZ. [*Claps his hands.*] A square meal it is! [*Waiters serve trays of Colored Squares of all sizes. People serve themselves.*]

SPELLING BEE. These are awful. [*HUMBUG coughs and all the Guests do not care for the food.*]

AZAZ. [*Claps his hands and the trays are removed.*] Time for speeches. [*To MILO.*] You first.

MILO. [*Hesitantly.*] Your Majesty, ladies and gentlemen, I would like to take this opportunity to say that . . .

AZAZ. That's quite enough. Musn't talk all day.

MILO. But I just started to . . .

AZAZ. NEXT!

HUMBUG. [*Quickly.*] Roast turkey, mashed potatoes, vanilla ice cream.

SPELLING BEE. Hamburgers, corn on the cob, chocolate pudding p-u-d-d-i-n-g. [*Each Guest names two dishes and a dessert.*]

AZAZ. [*The last.*] Pâté de fois gras, soupe à l'oignon, salade endives, fromage et fruits et demi-tasse. [*He claps his hands. Waiters serve each Guest his Words.*] Dig in. [*To MILO.*] Though I can't say I think much of your choice.

MILO. I didn't know I was going to have to eat my words.

AZAZ. Of course, of course, everybody here does. Your speech should have been in better taste.

MINISTER 1. Here, try some somersault. It improves the flavor.

MINISTER 2. Have a rigamarole. [*Offers bread-basket.*]

MINISTER 3. Or a ragamuffin.

MINISTER 4. Perhaps you'd care for a synonym bun.

MINISTER 5. Why not wait for your just desserts?

AZAZ. Ah yes, the dessert. We're having a special treat today . . . freshly made at the half-bakery.

MILO. The half-bakery?

AZAZ. Of course, the half-bakery! Where do you think half-baked ideas

22 A more ***substantial*** meal would be larger and more satisfying.

Paraphrase What does Milo mean by a "square meal"? Explain what makes King Azaz's banquet unique.

Paraphrase What is usually meant when something is said to be "in better taste"? How does this sentence have two meanings?

MILO. I didn't know I was going to have to eat my words.

AZAZ. Of course, of course, everybody here does. Your speech should have been in better taste.

come from? Now, please don't interrupt. By royal command, the pastry chefs have . . .

MILO. What's a half-baked idea?

[*AZAZ gives up the idea of speaking as a cart is wheeled in and the Guests help themselves.*]

HUMBUG. They're very tasty, but they don't always agree with you. Here's a good one. [*HUMBUG hands one to MILO.*]

MILO. [*Reads.*] "The earth is flat."

SPELLING BEE. People swallowed that one for years. [*Picks up one and reads.*] "The moon is made of green cheese." Now, there's a half-baked idea.

[*Everyone chooses one and eats. They include: "It Never Rains But Pours," "Night Air Is Bad Air," "Everything Happens for the Best," "Coffee Stunts Your Growth."*]

AZAZ. And now for a few closing words. Attention! Let me have your attention! [*Everyone leaps up and Exits, except for MILO, TOCK and the HUMBUG.*] Loyal subjects and friends, once again on this gala[23] occasion, we have . . .

MILO. Excuse me, but everybody left.

AZAZ. [*Sadly.*] I was hoping no one would notice. It happens every time.

HUMBUG. They've gone to dinner, and as soon as I finish this last bite, I shall join them.

MILO. That's ridiculous. How can they eat dinner right after a banquet?

AZAZ. SCANDALOUS! We'll put a stop to it at once. From now on, by royal command, everyone must eat dinner before the banquet.

---

23 A ***gala*** occasion is a celebration.

MILO. But that's just as bad.

HUMBUG. Or just as good. Things which are equally bad are also equally good. Try to look at the bright side of things.

MILO. I don't know which side of anything to look at. Everything is so confusing, and all your words only make things worse.

AZAZ. How true. There must be something we can do about it.

HUMBUG. Pass a law.

AZAZ. We have almost as many laws as words.

HUMBUG. Offer a reward. [*AZAZ shakes his head and looks madder at each suggestion.*] Send for help? Drive a bargain? Pull the switch? Lower the boom? Toe the line? [*As AZAZ continues to scowl, the HUMBUG loses confidence and finally gives up.*]

MILO. Maybe you should let Rhyme and Reason return.

AZAZ. How nice that would be. Even if they were a bother at times, things always went so well when they were here. But I'm afraid it can't be done.

HUMBUG. Certainly not. Can't be done.

MILO. Why not?

HUMBUG. [*Now siding with MILO.*] Why not, indeed?

AZAZ. Much too difficult.

HUMBUG. Of course, much too difficult.

MILO. You could, if you really wanted to.

HUMBUG. By all means, if you really wanted to, you could.

AZAZ. [*To HUMBUG.*] How?

MILO. [*Also to HUMBUG.*] Yeah, how?

HUMBUG. Why . . . uh, it's a simple task for a brave boy with a stout heart, a steadfast dog and a serviceable small automobile.

AZAZ. Go on.

HUMBUG. Well, all that he would have to do is cross the dangerous, unknown countryside between here and Digitopolis, where he would have to persuade the Mathemagician to release the Princesses, which we know to be impossible because the Mathemagician will never agree with Azaz about anything. Once achieving that, it's a simple matter of entering the Mountains of **Ignorance** from where no one has ever returned alive, an effortless climb up a two thousand foot

Paraphrase What is another way to say this?

Act and Scene What elements of the plot are contained in Act One, Scene 2?

BQ BIG Question Why is it fitting that the Mountains of Ignorance are such a dangerous place?

Vocabulary

ignorance (ig′ nər əns) *n.* state of lacking in knowledge or education

I don't know which side of anything to look at. Everything is so confusing, and all your words only make things worse.

stairway without railings in a high wind at night to the Castle-in-the-Air. After a pleasant chat with the Princesses, all that remains is a leisurely[24] ride back through those chaotic crags[25] where the frightening fiends[26] have sworn to tear any intruder limb from limb and devour him down to his belt buckle. And finally after doing all that, a triumphal parade! If, of course, there is anything left to parade . . . followed by hot chocolate and cookies for everyone.

AZAZ. I never realized it would be so simple.

MILO. It sounds dangerous to me.

TOCK. And just who is supposed to make that journey?

AZAZ. A very good question. But there is one far more serious problem.

MILO. What's that?

AZAZ. I'm afraid I can't tell you that until you return.

MILO. But wait a minute, I didn't . . .

AZAZ. Dictionopolis will always be grateful to you, my boy, and your dog. [*AZAZ pats TOCK and MILO.*]

TOCK. Now, just one moment, sire . . .

AZAZ. You will face many dangers on your journey, but fear not, for I can give you something for your protection. [*AZAZ gives MILO a box.*] In this box are the letters of the alphabet. With them you can form all the words you will ever need to help you

---

24 A ***leisurely*** ride is relaxed and unhurried.

25 ***Crags*** are steep rocks or cliffs.

26 ***Fiends*** are evil spirits or demons.

In this box are the letters of the alphabet. With them you can form all the words you will ever need to help you overcome the obstacles that may stand in your path.

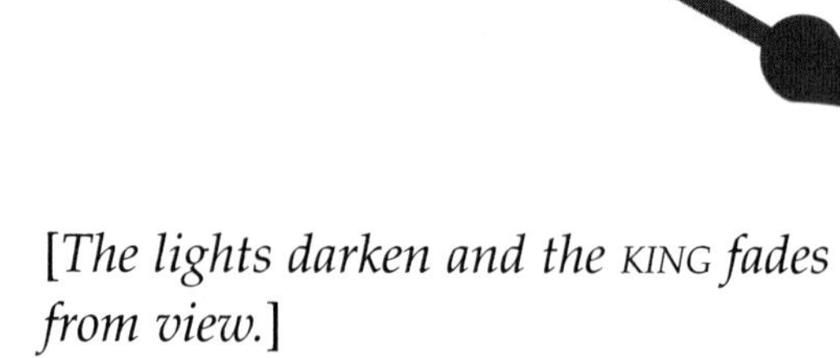

overcome the obstacles[27] that may stand in your path. All you must do is use them well and in the right places.

MILO. [*Miserably.*] Thanks a lot.

AZAZ. You will need a guide, of course, and since he knows the obstacles so well, the Humbug has cheerfully volunteered to accompany you.

HUMBUG. Now, see here . . . !

AZAZ. You will find him dependable, brave, resourceful[28] and loyal.

HUMBUG. [*Flattered.*] Oh, your Majesty.

MILO. I'm sure he'll be a great help. [*They approach the car.*]

TOCK. I hope so. It looks like we're going to need it.

[*The lights darken and the* KING *fades from view.*]

AZAZ. Good luck! Drive carefully! [*The three get into the car and begin to move. Suddenly a thunderously loud* NOISE *is heard. They slow down the car.*]

MILO. What was that?

TOCK. It came from up ahead.

HUMBUG. It's something terrible, I just know it. Oh, no. Something dreadful is going to happen to us. I can feel it in my bones. [*The* NOISE *is repeated. They all look at each other fearfully as the lights fade.*]

END OF ACT ONE

---

27 ***Obstacles*** are things that block the way.

28 Someone who is ***resourceful*** is able to cope with difficult situations.

Paraphrase What gift does Azaz give to Milo? How will it protect him?

Act and Scene What do you predict will happen in Act Two? Where will the action probably take place?

After You Read

Respond and Think Critically

1. How does Milo feel at the beginning of the play? Have you ever felt this way? Why? **[Connect]**
2. List three examples of wordplay or puns from the play. **[Identify]**
3. What places does Milo pass through on the road to Dictionopolis? What characters does he meet? How do these places and characters relate to Milo's life? **[Recall]**
4. What do you think Dictionopolis would be like if the banished characters were allowed to return? **[Infer]**
5. Tock explains that "the real value of both words and numbers has been forgotten." What is the value of words and numbers? Why are they both important parts of knowledge? **[Evaluate]**
6. **BQ** **BIG Question** How do the Whether Man, Tock, the Gatekeeper, and the Humbug challenge Milo? What do these characters teach Milo about having worthwhile goals? **[Conclude]**

TIP

Evaluating
When you evaluate, you make a judgment about the value of something.

- Recall what Dictionopolis is like.
- Consider how the city has forgotten the value of words and numbers.
- Think about the role that words and numbers have in your own life.

Keep track of your ideas about the **BIG Question** in your unit Foldable.

You're the Critic

Two Views of *The Phantom Tollbooth*

Read the two excerpts of literary criticism.

Group Activity Discuss the following questions with classmates. Refer to the quotations and give evidence from Act One of *The Phantom Tollbooth.*

1. Which critic comes closest to explaining how you feel about the play? Explain your opinion.
2. How does *The Phantom Tollbooth* teach readers "to question authority, to question generally"? Explain what this means and give examples from the play.

"Learning to negotiate his way past . . . obstacles, teaches Milo a thing or two about the grownup world. It also gives him powerfully good reasons to arm his mind against dullness, obfuscation and lies, all of which thrive on just the incuriosity of which Milo had been a past master.

"Juster taught his readers to question authority, to question generally, and certainly to leave a kindly mark on the world."—Gregory McNamee

"Juster is endlessly inventive, but the plot is nothing more than a tour that Milo takes across the kingdom. Indeed, Juster hardly hesitates to employ completely artificial plot devices to keep things going . . . And by the nature of the characters' functions, they also serve as little more than embodiments of puns (with the notable exception of Tock, who is great)." —Steven Wu

Literary Element Act and Scene

Standards Practice  ELAR1h/iii

1. What is one reason the playwright has divided Act One into two scenes?
   - A. to keep the mood of the play the same
   - B. to introduce new characters
   - C. to explore a different theme
   - D. to show a different time and place

Review: **Stage Directions**

As you learned on page 763, **stage directions** are the instructions that describe the appearance and actions of characters as well as sets, costumes, and lighting. Stage directions are not spoken aloud when a play is performed.

Standards Practice  ELAR1b

2. All of the following information can be found in the stage directions, except
   - A. changes in lighting and scenery.
   - B. dialogue between characters.
   - C. details about the setting.
   - D. clues about what the characters are feeling.

Reading Strategy Paraphrase

3. Look back at the paraphrase chart you kept while you were reading. Explain how paraphrasing helped you understand the wordplay in *The Phantom Tollbooth.*

4. Paraphrase these sentences, which are spoken by the Clock: "Time is important, but it's what you do with it that makes it so. So my advice to you is to use it. Keep your eyes open and your ears perked. Otherwise it will pass before you know it, and you'll certainly have missed something!"

Vocabulary Practice

Synonyms are words that have the same or nearly the same meaning. Match each boldface vocabulary word with a word from the right column that has the same meaning. Two of the words in the right column will not have matches. Then write a sentence using each vocabulary word or draw or find a picture that represents the word.

1. **guaranteed**	a. reflection
2. **ferocious**	b. honesty
3. **assortment**	c. collection
4. **ignorance**	d. fierce
5. **consideration**	e. knowledge
	f. lack of education
	g. promised

Example:
guaranteed: promised

Sentence: My sister guaranteed that she would get us to the concert on time.

Academic Vocabulary

At the beginning of Scene 1, the stage directions say that "the CLOCK is **suspended** in mid-air." In this sentence, *suspended* means "kept from falling with no apparent support." *Suspended* also has other meanings. For example: At last night's game, play was **suspended** due to rain. What do you think *suspended* means in the preceding sentence?

Literature Online

Selection Resources For Selection Quizzes, eFlashcards, and Reading-Writing Connection activities, go to glencoe.com and enter QuickPass code GL17527u6.

Respond Through Writing

Expository Essay

Analyze Setting In *The Phantom Tollbooth,* Milo receives a tollbooth that allows him to enter a new world. In a short essay, analyze the settings of *The Phantom Tollbooth.* Explain how the settings are related to the plot and characters. In addition, explain how stage directions and dialogue make the settings clear.

Understand the Task Setting is the time and place of a play. In *The Phantom Tollbooth,* the settings present challenges that Milo must face. They also allow the introduction of interesting characters who force Milo to think and act differently.

Prewrite Choose three settings to analyze. Use a chart like the one below to record evidence or supporting details from the play that give a mental picture or necessary information to the intended audience.

Setting	Description	Connection to Plot and Characters
market square of Dictionopolis	The market square is noisy and busy with people buying and selling words.	To pass the Gatekeeper, Milo must give a reason to enter the market.

Draft Before you begin drafting, make an overall plan. For example, you may decide to write an introduction, a paragraph about each setting, and then a conclusion. After you figure out your plan, write your thesis statement. This sentence frame might help you:

In *The Phantom Tollbooth,* the settings of ________,
________, and ________ influence Milo by ________.

Revise After you have written your first draft, read it to determine whether the paragraphs follow a logical order. Rearrange text as necessary so that your ideas are easy to follow.

Edit and Proofread Proofread your paper, correcting any errors in spelling, grammar, and punctuation. Review the Grammar Tip in the side column for information on apostrophes.

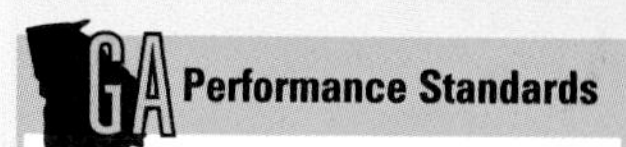

GA Performance Standards

For page 801

ELA6W2c Demonstrate competence in a variety of genres. Produce writing that develops a controlling idea that conveys a perspective on the subject.

Grammar Tip

Apostrophes
Use an **apostrophe** followed by the letter *s* to form the possessive of a singular noun.

At the beginning of the play, a clock is ticking in Milo's bedroom.

To show the possessive form of a plural noun ending in *s,* add an apostrophe after the *s.*

The Lethargarians' busy schedule includes daydreaming, dawdling, and napping.

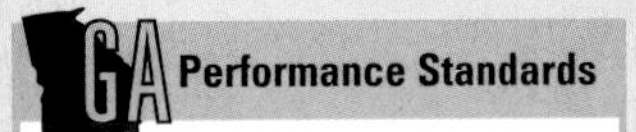

Performance Standards

For pages 802–803

ELA6R1b For literary texts, identify and analyze the author's use of dialogue and description.

Genre Focus: Drama

Drama is a form of entertainment that has a long history. Long ago, people began to act out exciting stories of heroes and their adventures. Throughout the centuries, people have created all kinds of **plays**—stories that are written to be performed in front of an audience. In modern times, authors have written plays to be performed on the radio or on television as well.

Movies and stage, television, and radio plays are examples of drama.

Literary Elements

Plot Like short stories, most dramas have a **plot,** or a sequence of events. The **exposition** introduces the setting, characters, and conflicts, or problems. The **rising action** adds complications to the story's conflicts, leading up to the play's **climax,** which is the point of greatest interest or suspense. The **falling action** is the logical result of the climax, and the **resolution** presents the final outcome.

Character A character is a person or other creature in a literary work. In a drama, actors play the characters. A **dynamic character** changes during the play. A **static character** remains the same throughout the play.

Dialogue The words that characters say are called **dialogue.** A play is a story that is told almost entirely through dialogue. The audience learns about what is happening and what the characters are thinking and feeling through the dialogue. Dialogue reveals the characters' personalities, gives information to the audience, and moves the story forward.

Stage Directions Instructions to guide the way a play is presented are called **stage directions.** The **playwright,** the play's author, writes the stage directions as part of the **script.** Stage directions are often in brackets. They tell the actors what to do, such as when to enter and leave the stage, or how to stand, move, or speak. The stage directions can identify furniture and objects—**props**—to be placed on the stage. Stage directions can call for music, sounds, or lights during the play. When performing a play, the actors do not speak the stage directions. Instead, the actors or others involved with the play do or show what the stage directions indicate.

Act and Scene An **act** is a major division of a play. A play may be divided into several acts. A **scene** is a subdivision of an act. Each scene presents action in one place or one situation. A new scene may require different scenery, lighting, sound, or props to show a new time or place.

TRY IT

Using one of the graphic organizers on the next page, identify the characteristics of a play in this unit.

Characteristics of the Genre

To better understand literary elements in plays, and how playwrights use literary elements to tell a story and achieve their purposes, look at the examples in the graphic organizers below.

Plot Diagram for *Damon and Pythias*

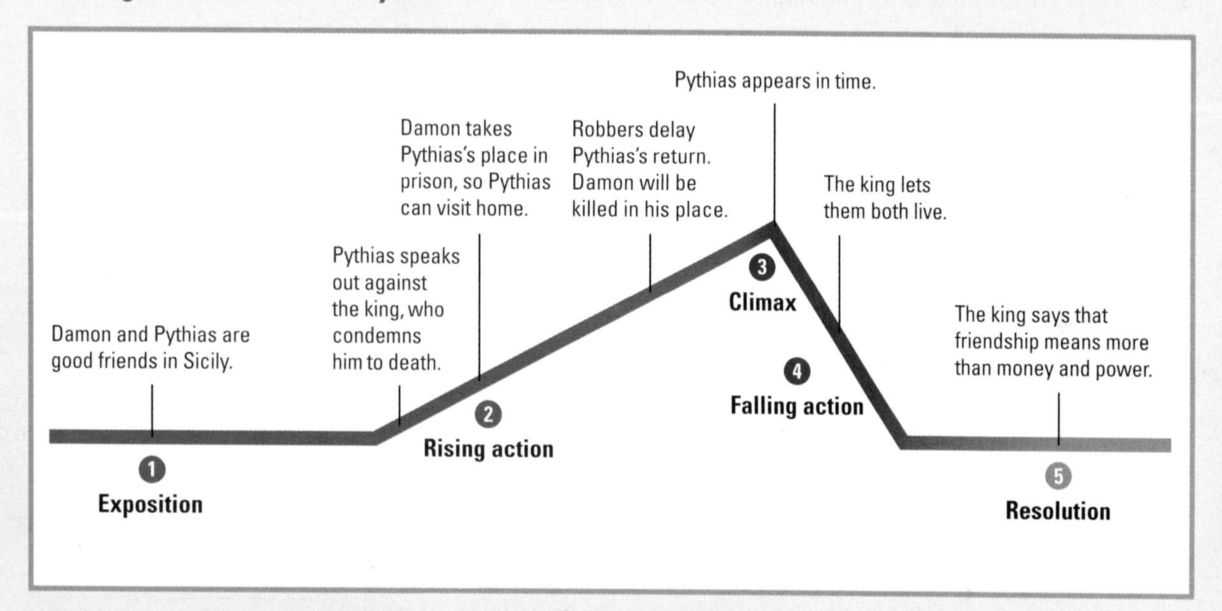

Pythias appears in time.
Damon takes Pythias's place in prison, so Pythias can visit home.
Robbers delay Pythias's return. Damon will be killed in his place.
The king lets them both live.
Pythias speaks out against the king, who condemns him to death.
3 Climax
Damon and Pythias are good friends in Sicily.
The king says that friendship means more than money and power.
4 Falling action
2 Rising action
1 Exposition
5 Resolution

Characterization Chart for Stan from *Brighton Beach Memoirs*

Detail from the Scene	Personality Trait It Reveals	Direct or Indirect Characterization
Eugene says, "He's okay. You'll like him."	likability	indirect (another character's statement)
Stan tells his boss it isn't fair to make Andrew pay for the hats.	fairness; concern for others	indirect (character's statement)
Stan sweeps dirt on his boss's shoes.	boldness; questionable judgment	indirect (character's actions)

LOG ON
Literature Online

Literature and Reading For more selections in this genre, go to glencoe.com and enter QuickPass code GL17527u6.

Before You Read

A Time to Talk and *Silence*

Connect to the Poems

How do you communicate with friends or family members? Think about some ways you share your thoughts and feelings with others.

List Make a list of all the ways you can communicate with your friends or family members. Do all of the ways involve words?

Build Background

Have you ever noticed that it is sometimes hard to figure out a person's emotions in an e-mail compared with talking to him or her face-to-face? That is because much of our communication is *nonverbal*. This means communicating through means other than words. Smiling is an example of nonverbal communication. Gestures, facial expressions, and tone of voice are nonverbal ways we communicate with one another.

Set Purposes for Reading

BQ BIG Question

As you read, ask yourself, how does friendship inspire wisdom in the speaker of each poem?

Literary Element Alliteration and Assonance

Alliteration is the repetition of consonant sounds, usually at the beginning of words. Notice the repetition of the *s* sound and the *m* sound in a line from Lewis Carroll's poem "The Walrus and the Carpenter."

If seven maids with seven mops

Assonance is the repetition of vowel sounds, especially in a line of poetry. For example,

The hot popcorn hopped and popped.

Both **alliteration** and **assonance** affect the sound of a poem and help convey its tone. They can draw attention to certain words or lines, making the poem's meaning clearer. Alliteration and assonance can also make a poem sound more musical.

Read each poem aloud. As you read, listen for places where each poet uses alliteration or assonance.

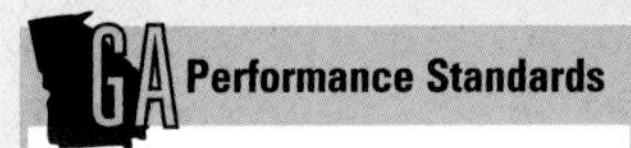

GA Performance Standards

For pages 804–807

ELA6R1h/i For literary texts, respond to and explain the effects of sound.

Meet the Authors

Robert Frost

Robert Frost often wrote about people's relationship to nature. He was born in 1874 and died in 1963.

Paul Laurence Dunbar

Paul Laurence Dunbar was the first African American who made a living from writing. He was born in 1872 and died in 1906.

LOG ON Literature Online

Author Search For more about Robert Frost and Paul Laurence Dunbar, go to glencoe.com and enter QuickPass code GL17527u6.

A Time to Talk

Robert Frost

Field with House, 2006.
Lou Wall.

When a friend calls to me from the road
And slows his horse to a meaning walk,°
I don't stand still and look around
On all the hills I haven't hoed,
And shout from where I am, What is it?
No, not as there is a time to talk.
I thrust my hoe in the mellow° ground,
Blade-end up and five feet tall,
And plod:° I go up to the stone wall
For a friendly visit.

Alliteration and Assonance
What are two examples of alliteration in lines 3 and 4?

BIG Question
What goal is the speaker trying to achieve when a friend calls to him? What does he have the wisdom to realize?

---

2 Here, a ***meaning walk*** is a meaningful or purposeful pace, with the friend slowing down to show that he wishes to talk with the speaker of the poem.

7 Soil that is ***mellow*** is soft and rich in organic material.

9 To ***plod*** is to walk slowly and heavily.

Young Girls on the Beach, c. 1898. Pierre Auguste Renoir. Oil on canvas. Private Collection.

Silence

Paul Laurence Dunbar

'T is better to sit here beside the sea,
   Here on the spray-kissed beach,
In silence, that between such friends as we
   Is full of deepest speech.

Alliteration and Assonance
What are two examples of assonance in the last two lines of the poem?

BQ BIG Question
Why might sitting in silence with a friend be a worthwhile goal?

After You Read

Respond and Think Critically

1. In your own words, retell "A Time to Talk." [Paraphrase]
2. What does the speaker's response to his friend's visit in "A Time to Talk" tell you about the speaker? [Infer]
3. In "Silence," what does the speaker mean when he says that silence is "full of deepest speech"? [Interpret]
4. In "Silence," how are the sea and the beach related? How does the image reflect the relationship of the friends? [Analyze]
5. **Literary Element** **Alliteration and Assonance** In "A Time to Talk," what does the alliteration in the second five lines emphasize? How effective is the poet's use of alliteration in the poem? [Evaluate]
6. **BQ** **BIG Question** How do you think each speaker would answer the question "Is having friends a worthwhile goal?" Explain your answer. [Conclude]

Spelling Link

Forming Plurals Forming plurals can be tricky. For many words, adding *-s* or *-es* forms the plural.

boy → boys solos → solos
box → boxes potato → potatoes

If the word ends in a consonant plus *y*, change *y* to *i* and add *-es*.

baby → babies

For some words, you must change *f* to *v* and add *-es*.

thief → thieves calf → calves

Some plural nouns are the same as the singular noun.

deer → deer

Some plurals do not follow any rules.

woman → women foot → feet

Practice Form plurals of the following singular nouns: *star, echo, bush, hoof, ferry, loaf, man, tooth.* Check your answers in a dictionary to see whether they are correct.

Writing

Write a Stanza Write one stanza of a poem of your own about friendship or something that you have learned about life. Use alliteration and assonance to give your stanza a musical quality.

TIP

Analyzing

Here are some tips to help you answer question 4. Remember, when you **analyze,** you look at separate parts of something to understand the entire piece.

- Visualize the waves washing in and out on a beach.
- Think about the phrase "spray-kissed beach." Why does the poet use the word *kissed* to describe the way the sea moves near the beach?
- How are the sea and the beach like the friends who sit together beside the sea?

Keep track of your ideas about the **BIG Question** in your unit Foldable.

Literature Online

Selection Resources
For Selection Quizzes, eFlashcards, and Reading-Writing Connection activities, go to glencoe.com and enter QuickPass code GL17527u6.

Before You Read

The Golden Touch

Connect to the Myth

Think about a time when you got something you wished for.

Quickwrite Freewrite for a few minutes about getting your wish. Why did you make that particular wish? Was the result what you had expected?

Build Background

In Greek and Roman mythology, gods and goddesses often interact with mortals (humans). A god might seek the affections of a mortal woman or offer advice to a mortal ruler. In fact, the gods behave much like people. They argue, they get angry, and they fall in love. But they also have extraordinary powers.

Bacchus (bak′əs), the Roman god in this story, is called "the merry god" because he is the god of celebration. He is also associated with plentiful harvests. The Greek name for Bacchus is Dionysus (dī′ ə nī′ səs).

Young Man With Fruit (The Sick Young Bacchus), 1591. Michelangelo M. da Caravaggio. Oil on canvas. Galleria Borghese, Rome.

Meet Mary Pope Osborne

"I feel that the years I spent traveling . . . and my interests in philosophy and mythology have all informed and shaped my work."

—Mary Pope Osborne

A Life of Travel "My childhood was spent on different Army posts with my parents, two brothers, and sister," says Mary Pope Osborne. As the daughter of a United States Army colonel, she often moved and traveled with her family. They lived mostly in the southern United States and, for three years, in Austria.

Literary Works Osborne is the author of many works, including *Tales from the Odyssey*, a six-book series that retells the adventures of Odysseus, a hero of Greek mythology.

Osborne was born in 1949.

LOG ON **Literature** Online

Author Search For more about Mary Pope Osborne, go to glencoe.com and enter QuickPass code GL17527u6.

Set Purposes for Reading

BQ BIG Question

As you read, ask yourself, how does King Midas's desire for wealth cause him to choose an unwise goal?

Literary Element Irony

In literature, as in life, things are not always what they seem. **Irony** is a contrast between what is expected and what actually happens. **Situational irony** occurs when the outcome of a situation is the opposite of what might be expected.

Writers may use irony to create humor or surprise. Recognizing irony will help you understand important points the author is making.

As you read, ask yourself, what does King Midas expect and what actually happens?

Reading Strategy Interpret Author's Meaning

To **interpret author's meaning** is to figure out the author's message in a work of literature. You use your own understanding of the world and information the author provides to decide what is the overall point of the events or ideas presented. It is possible for more than one interpretation to be reasonable.

Interpreting meaning gives you a deeper understanding of what you read. Many authors do not directly declare their main ideas. They let the reader do some of the work.

To interpret author's meaning, ask yourself,

- What is the author trying to say?
- What specific details, descriptions, or information from the story back up my thoughts and feelings?
- How have my own experiences and prior knowledge influenced my feelings about this story?

You may find it helpful to use a graphic organizer like the one below.

Situation in Story	My Experience	Possible Interpretation
King Midas wishes that everything he touches would turn to gold.	People place great value on gold.	It may not be good to get everything you wish for.

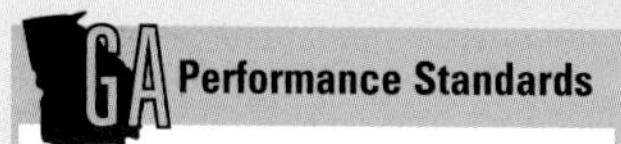

GA Performance Standards

For pages 808–814

ELA6R1j For literary texts, identify and analyze similarities and differences in mythologies from different cultures.

TRY IT

Interpret Author's Meaning A magazine ad says, "Movie stars use *Brilliance* for the whitest smile possible. Are you brilliant?" What is the real message of the advertisement? How do you know?

The Golden Touch

retold by Mary Pope Osborne

Bacchus, the merry god, raised his **goblet.** "To you, King Midas,"[1] he said, "and because you have been so hospitable[2] to me—ask for anything you wish, and I will grant it to you."

"What an idea!" said Midas. "Anything I wish?"

"Indeed, anything," said Bacchus.

"Anything?"

"Yes! Yes!"

"Ah, well," said the king, chuckling. "Of course, there's only one thing: I wish that everything I touch would turn to gold!" Midas looked sideways at Bacchus, for he couldn't believe such a gift could really be his.

"My friend, you already have all the gold you could possibly want," said Bacchus, looking disappointed.

"Oh, no! I don't!" said Midas. "One never has enough gold!"

"Well, if that's what you wish for, I suppose I will have to grant it," said Bacchus.

Visual Vocabulary

A **goblet** is a drinking vessel, usually made of glass, with a base and a stem.

Interpret Author's Meaning

In what way might Bacchus be speaking for the author?

1 ***Midas*** (mī′ dəs)

2 Someone who is ***hospitable*** (hos′ pi tə bəl) offers a friendly and generous welcome to guests or strangers.

Bacchus soon took his leave.[3] As Midas waved good-bye to him, his hand brushed an oak twig hanging from a tree—and the twig turned to gold!

The king screamed with joy, then shouted after Bacchus, "My wish has come true! Thank you! Thank you!"

The god turned and waved, then disappeared down the road.

Midas looked around excitedly. He leaned over and picked a stone up from the ground—and the stone turned into a golden nugget! He kicked the sand—and the sand turned to golden grains!

King Midas threw back his head and shouted, "I'm the richest man in the world!" Then he rushed about his grounds, touching everything. And everything, *everything* turned to gold: ears of corn in his fields! Apples plucked from trees! The pillars of his mansion!

When the king's servants heard him shouting, they rushed to see what was happening. They found their king

King Midas. Arthur Rackham. Pen and ink & watercolor on paper. Private Collection.

Irony What makes Midas's sense of joy ironic?

3 When Bacchus ***took his leave,*** he said good-bye and left.

dancing wildly on his lawn, turning the grass to glittering blades of gold. Everyone laughed and clapped as Midas washed his hands in his fountain and turned the water to a gleaming spray!

Finally, exhausted but overjoyed, King Midas called for his dinner. His servants placed a huge banquet meal before him on his lawn. "Oh, I'm so hungry!" he said as he speared a piece of meat and brought it to his mouth.

King Midas. Artist unknown. Gouache on paper. Private Collection.

But suddenly King Midas realized his wish may not have been as wonderful as he thought—for the moment he bit down on the meat, it, too, turned to gold.

Midas laughed uneasily, then reached for a piece of bread. But as soon as his hands touched the bread, it also became a hard, golden nugget! Weak with dread, Midas reached for his goblet of water. But alas! His lips touched only hard, cold metal. The water had also turned to gold.

Covering his head and moaning, King Midas realized his great wish was going to kill him. He would starve to death or die of thirst!

BQ BIG Question What has King Midas learned about worthwhile goals?

"Bacchus!" he cried, throwing his hands toward heaven. "I've been a greedy fool! Take away your gift! Free me from my golden touch! Help me, Bacchus!"

The sobbing king fell off his chair to his knees. He beat his fists against the ground, turning even the little anthills to gold. His servants grieved for him, but none dared go near him, for they feared he might accidentally turn them to gold, too!

As everyone wailed with sorrow, Bacchus suddenly appeared on the palace lawn. The merry god stood before the sobbing king for a moment, then said, "Rise, Midas."

Irony How are Midas and Bacchus opposites in this description? What is ironic about this contrast?

Stumbling to his feet, King Midas begged Bacchus to forgive him and to take away the curse of the golden touch.

"You were greedy and foolish, my friend," said Bacchus. "But I will forgive you. Now go and wash yourself in the Pactolus River that runs by Sardis, and you'll be cleansed of this desire to have more gold than anyone else!"

King Midas did as Bacchus said. He washed in the Pactolus, leaving behind streams of gold in the river's sands. Then he returned home and happily ate his dinner.

And that is why the sands of the Pactolus River were golden.

Interpret Author's Meaning Is this the real message of the myth? If not, what is the real message?

After You Read

Respond and Think Critically

1. Why does Bacchus offer Midas anything he wants? **[Recall]**
2. Why can't Midas's servants help him? **[Summarize]**
3. What aspects of Midas's wish might be positive? What aspects turn out to be negative? **[Interpret]**
4. **Literary Element** **Irony** What is ironic about Midas's greatest wish? **[Compare]**
5. **Reading Strategy** **Interpret Author's Meaning** Think about what Midas wishes for and what he gets. What might the author be suggesting about human desires? **[Analyze]**
6. **BQ** **BIG Question** What might a wise person have wished for in Midas's place? Explain. **[Conclude]**

TIP

Analyzing
Here are some tips to help you answer question 5. Remember that **analyzing** means looking at the parts to understand the whole.

- Examine the details and events of the story.
- Think about how the parts are related to one another.
- Ask yourself what the story's greater meaning might be. How do the parts of the story support this meaning?

Keep track of your ideas about the **BIG Question** in your unit Foldable.

Spelling Link

Frequently Misspelled Words Frequently misspelled words can cause problems even for experienced writers. Recognizing spelling rules can help you avoid some of these mistakes.

Rules

i* before *e—Place *i* before *e* except after *c* or when both letters are pronounced together as a long *a* sound: **believe, receive, weight.**

Exceptions include *science, weird, either, seize, protein, leisure.*

Silent *e*—If a word ends with a silent *e,* drop the *e* before adding a suffix beginning with a vowel or a *y:* **skat(ing), nois(y).**

Final *y*—When adding a suffix to words ending with a vowel + *y,* keep the *y:* **enjoy(ment), play(ful).** For words ending with a consonant + *y,* change the *y* to *i* unless the suffix begins with *i:* **lazi(ness), happi(ness), fly(ing).**

Practice Find and correct each misspelled word.

ladyes likeing cried nieghbor relieve hoping joyful
triing baker sleigh wisly entirely merrily useing taking

Writing

Write a Summary Write a one-paragraph summary of "The Golden Touch." Remember that when you summarize, you retell a selection's main events and most important details in your own words. A summary should be short and to the point. You may want to reread the selection to identify the main events.

LOG ON Literature Online

Selection Resources
For Selection Quizzes, eFlashcards, and Reading-Writing Connection activities, go to glencoe.com and enter QuickPass code GL17527u6.

Comparing Literature

Zlateh the Goat and *The Boy Who Lived with the Bears*

BQ BIG Question

As you read these paired selections, ask yourself, what do the main characters learn about life?

Literary Element Style

Many elements shape an author's **style**—tone, word choice, sentence length and structure, and literary devices such as figurative language, imagery, and symbols. Style can reveal the author's purpose for writing and the author's attitude toward a subject. As you read each story, notice each author's writing style.

Reading Skill Compare and Contrast

Comparing is thinking about how two things are alike. **Contrasting** is thinking about how two things are different. When you **compare and contrast** two movies with a friend, you might talk about how the action in each movie is alike and how it is different.

Comparing and contrasting can help you understand how authors write. On the following pages, you'll compare and contrast the writing styles in "Zlateh the Goat" and "The Boy Who Lived with the Bears." Use a comparison chart like the one below to record details about the author's style in each story.

	Zlateh the Goat	The Boy Who Lived with the Bears
Word Choice		
Sentence Length/ Structure		
Literary Devices		

GA Performance Standards

For pages 815–831

ELA6R1g For literary texts, define and explain how tone is conveyed in literature through word choice, sentence structure, punctuation, rhythm, repetition, and rhyme.

Meet the Authors

Isaac Bashevis Singer

Singer won the Nobel Prize for literature in 1978.

Joseph Bruchac

Bruchac's writing is inspired by his Native American ancestors.

Literature Online

Author Search For more about Isaac Bashevis Singer and Joseph Bruchac, go to glencoe.com and enter QuickPass code GL17527u6.

Zlateh the Goat

Isaac Bashevis Singer

translated by the author and Elizabeth Shuh

At Hanukkah[1] time the road from the village to the town is usually covered with snow, but this year the winter had been a mild one. Hanukkah had almost come, yet little snow had fallen. The sun shone most of the time. The peasants complained that because of the dry weather there would be a poor harvest of winter grain. New grass sprouted, and the peasants[2] sent their cattle out to pasture.

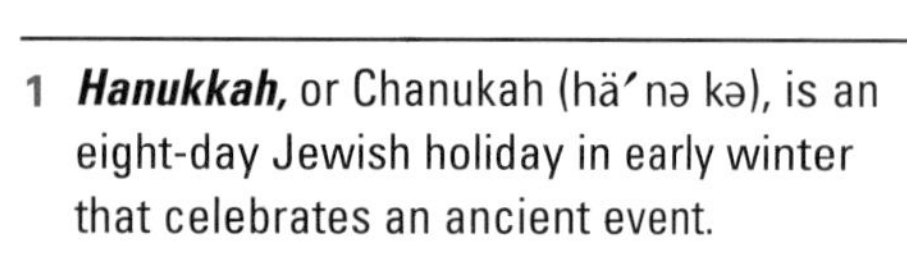

1 ***Hanukkah,*** or Chanukah (hä′ nə kə), is an eight-day Jewish holiday in early winter that celebrates an ancient event.

2 ***Peasants*** were poor farmers.

For Reuven the furrier[3] it was a bad year, and after long hesitation he decided to sell Zlateh the goat. She was old and gave little milk. Feivel the town butcher had offered eight gulden[4] for her. Such a sum would buy Hanukkah candles, potatoes and oil for pancakes, gifts for the children, and other holiday necessaries for the house. Reuven told his oldest boy Aaron to take the goat to town.

Aaron understood what taking the goat to Feivel meant, but had to obey his father. Leah, his mother, wiped the tears from her eyes when she heard the news. Aaron's younger sisters, Anna and Miriam, cried loudly. Aaron put on his quilted jacket and a cap with earmuffs, bound a rope around Zlateh's neck, and took along two slices of bread with cheese to eat on the road. Aaron was supposed to deliver the goat by evening, spend the night at the butcher's, and return the next day with the money.

Comparing Literature What do the descriptive details in this paragraph tell you about Aaron?

While the family said goodbye to the goat, and Aaron placed the rope around her neck, Zlateh stood as patiently and good-naturedly as ever. She licked Reuven's hand. She shook her small white beard. Zlateh trusted human beings. She knew that they always fed her and never did her any harm.

When Aaron brought her out on the road to town, she seemed somewhat astonished. She'd never been led in that direction before. She looked back at him questioningly, as if to say, "Where are you taking me?" But after a while she seemed to come to the conclusion that a goat shouldn't ask questions. Still, the road was different. They passed new fields, pastures, and huts with thatched[5] roofs. Here and there a dog barked and came running after them, but Aaron chased it away with his stick.

Comparing Literature What literary technique is the writer using in this paragraph? As you read, watch for places where the writer uses this technique again.

---

3 A ***furrier*** is someone who makes or sells fur clothing.

4 ***Gulden*** (goold′ən) is the name of gold or silver coins once used in many European countries.

5 A ***thatched*** roof is made of thick grass or straw.

The sun was shining when Aaron left the village. Suddenly the weather changed. A large black cloud with a bluish center appeared in the east and spread itself rapidly over the sky. A cold wind blew in with it. The crows flew low, croaking. At first it looked as if it would rain, but instead it began to hail as in summer. It was early in the day, but it became dark as dusk. After a while the hail turned to snow.

In his twelve years Aaron had seen all kinds of weather, but he had never experienced a snow like this one. It was so dense[6] it shut out the light of the day. In a short time their path was completely covered. The wind became as cold as ice. The road to town was narrow and winding. Aaron no longer knew where he was. He could not see through the snow. The cold soon penetrated[7] his quilted jacket.

At first Zlateh didn't seem to mind the change in weather. She, too, was twelve years old and knew what winter meant. But when her legs sank deeper and deeper into the snow, she began to turn her head and look at Aaron in wonderment. Her mild eyes seemed to ask, "Why are we out in such a storm?" Aaron hoped that a peasant would come along with his cart, but no one passed by.

The snow grew thicker, falling to the ground in large, whirling flakes. Beneath it Aaron's boots touched the softness of a plowed field. He realized that he was no longer on the road. He had gone astray.[8] He could no longer figure out which was east or west, which way was the village, the town. The wind whistled, howled, whirled the snow about in eddies.[9] It looked as if white imps[10] were playing tag on the fields. A white dust rose above the ground. Zlateh stopped. She could walk no

---

6 ***Dense*** snow is closely packed together.

7 ***Penetrated*** means "passed into or through."

8 To go ***astray*** is to go off the right path or route.

9 ***Eddies*** are circling currents of air, water, or snow.

10 Here, ***imps*** are playful, fairylike spirits.

longer. Stubbornly she anchored her cleft hooves[11] in the earth and bleated as if pleading to be taken home. Icicles hung from her white beard, and her horns were glazed with frost.

Aaron did not want to admit the danger, but he knew just the same that if they did not find shelter they would freeze to death. This was no ordinary storm. It was a mighty blizzard. The snowfall had reached his knees. His hands were numb, and he could no longer feel his toes. He choked when he breathed. His nose felt like wood, and he rubbed it with snow. Zlateh's bleating began to sound like crying. Those humans in whom she had so much confidence had dragged her into a trap. Aaron began to pray to God for himself and for the innocent animal.

Comparing Literature What do you notice about the sentences the author uses to describe the blizzard? How does this affect the tone of this paragraph?

Suddenly he made out the shape of a hill. He wondered what it could be. Who had piled snow into such a huge heap? He moved toward it, dragging Zlateh after him. When he came near it, he realized that it was a large haystack which the snow had blanketed.

Aaron realized immediately that they were saved. With great effort he dug his way through the snow. He was a village boy and knew what to do. When he reached the hay, he hollowed out a nest for himself and the goat. No matter how cold it may be outside, in the hay it is always warm. And hay was

11 A ***cleft*** is a space or an opening. Goats, sheep, cattle, and pigs all have ***cleft*** (split) ***hooves.***

food for Zlateh. The moment she smelled it she became contented and began to eat. Outside, the snow continued to fall. It quickly covered the passageway Aaron had dug. But a boy and an animal need to breathe, and there was hardly any air in their hideout. Aaron bored a kind of a window through the hay and snow and carefully kept the passage clear.

Zlateh, having eaten her fill, sat down on her hind legs and seemed to have regained her confidence in man. Aaron ate his two slices of bread and cheese, but after the difficult journey he was still hungry. He looked at Zlateh and noticed her udders were full. He lay down next to her, placing himself so that when he milked her he could squirt the milk into his mouth. It was rich and sweet. Zlateh was not accustomed to being milked that way, but she did not resist. On the contrary, she seemed eager to reward Aaron for bringing her to a shelter whose very walls, floor, and ceiling were made of food.

Comparing Literature How does the author's choice of words make Zlateh seem like a person?

Through the window Aaron could catch a glimpse of the chaos[12] outside. The wind carried before it whole drifts of snow. It was completely dark, and he did not know whether night had already come or whether it was the darkness of the storm. Thank God that in the hay it was not cold. The dried hay, grass, and field flowers exuded[13] the warmth of the summer sun. Zlateh ate frequently; she nibbled from above, below, from the left and right. Her body gave forth an animal warmth, and Aaron cuddled up to her. He had always loved Zlateh, but now she was like a sister. He was alone, cut off from his family, and wanted to talk. He began to talk to Zlateh. "Zlateh, what do you think about what has happened to us?" he asked.

Comparing Literature Which words show Aaron's feelings about Zlateh? What effect do these words have on the reader?

"Maaaa," Zlateh answered.

"If we hadn't found this stack of hay, we would both be frozen stiff by now," Aaron said.

---

12 ***Chaos*** is total confusion.

13 ***Exuded*** means "gave forth."

"Maaaa," was the goat's reply.

"If the snow keeps on falling like this, we may have to stay here for days," Aaron explained.

"Maaaa," Zlateh bleated.

"What does 'maaaa' mean?" Aaron asked. "You'd better speak up clearly."

"Maaaa, maaaa," Zlateh tried.

"Well, let it be 'maaaa' then," Aaron said patiently. "You can't speak, but I know you understand. I need you and you need me. Isn't that right?"

"Maaaa."

Aaron became sleepy. He made a pillow out of some hay, leaned his head on it, and dozed off. Zlateh, too, fell asleep.

When Aaron opened his eyes, he didn't know whether it was morning or night. The snow had blocked up his window. He tried to clear it, but when he had bored through to the length of his arm, he still hadn't reached the outside. Luckily he had his stick with him and was able to break through to the open air. It was still dark outside. The snow continued to fall and the wind wailed, first with one voice and then with many. Sometimes it had the sound of devilish laughter. Zlateh, too, awoke, and when Aaron greeted her, she answered, "Maaaa." Yes, Zlateh's language consisted of only one word, but it meant many things. Now she was saying, "We must accept all that God gives us—heat, cold, hunger, satisfaction, light, and darkness."

Comparing Literature What literary technique does the author use to describe the wind? What is the tone of the description?

Aaron had awakened hungry. He had eaten up his food, but Zlateh had plenty of milk.

For three days Aaron and Zlateh stayed in the haystack. Aaron had always loved Zlateh, but in these three days he loved her more and more. She fed him with her milk and helped him keep warm. She comforted him with her patience. He told her many stories, and she always cocked her ears and listened. When he patted her, she licked his hand and his face. Then she said, "Maaaa," and he knew it meant, I love you, too.

The snow fell for three days, though after the first day it was not as thick and the wind quieted down. Sometimes Aaron felt that there could never have been a summer, that the snow had always fallen, ever since he could remember. He, Aaron, never had a father or mother or sisters. He was a snow child, born of the snow, and so was Zlateh. It was so quiet in the hay that his ears rang in the stillness. Aaron and Zlateh slept all night and a good part of the day. As for Aaron's dreams, they were all about warm weather. He dreamed of green fields, trees covered with blossoms, clear brooks, and singing birds. By the third night the snow had stopped, but Aaron did not dare to find his way home in the darkness. The sky became clear and the moon shone, casting silvery nets on the snow. Aaron dug his way out and looked at the world. It was all white, quiet, dreaming dreams of heavenly splendor. The stars were large and close. The moon swam in the sky as in a sea.

Comparing Literature What figurative language does the author use to show how Aaron feels?

On the morning of the fourth day Aaron heard the ringing of sleigh bells. The haystack was not far from the road. The peasant who drove the sleigh pointed out the way to him—not to the town and Feivel the butcher, but home to the village. Aaron had decided in the haystack that he would never part with Zlateh.

Aaron's family and their neighbors had searched for the boy and the goat but had found no trace of them during the storm. They feared they were lost. Aaron's mother and sisters cried for him; his father remained silent and gloomy. Suddenly one of the neighbors came running to their house with the news that Aaron and Zlateh were coming up the road.

There was great joy in the family. Aaron told them how he had found the stack of hay and how Zlateh had fed him with her milk. Aaron's sisters kissed and hugged Zlateh and gave her a special treat of chopped carrots and potato peels, which Zlateh gobbled up hungrily.

Nobody ever again thought of selling Zlateh, and now that the cold weather had finally set in, the villagers needed the services of Reuven the furrier once more. When Hanukkah came, Aaron's mother was able to fry pancakes every evening, and Zlateh got her portion, too. Even though Zlateh had her own pen, she often came to the kitchen, knocking on the door with her horns to indicate that she was ready to visit, and she was always admitted. In the evening Aaron, Miriam, and Anna played ***dreidel***. Zlateh sat near the stove watching the children and the flickering of the Hanukkah candles.

Once in a while Aaron would ask her, "Zlateh, do you remember the three days we spent together?"

And Zlateh would scratch her neck with a horn, shake her white bearded head, and come out with the single sound which expressed all her thoughts, and all her love.

Visual Vocabulary

Similar to a spinning top, a **dreidel** (drād′ əl) is a toy used in a game played during Hanukkah.

Comparing Literature What is the "single sound"? Why doesn't the author need to state it?

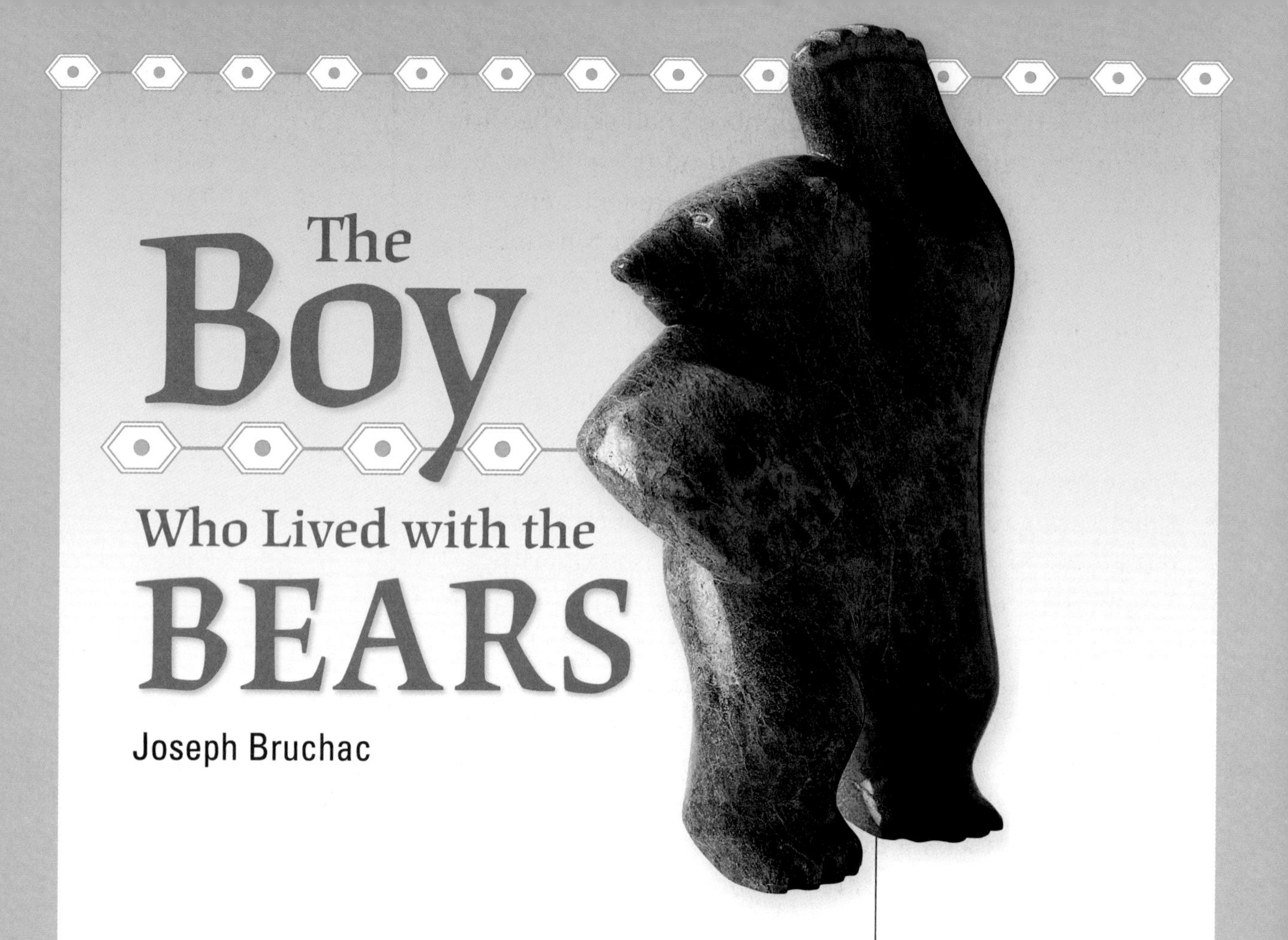

The Boy Who Lived with the BEARS

Joseph Bruchac

Long ago, in a small village of the Haudenosaunee people, there lived a little boy whose parents had died. This boy was living with his uncle, as was the custom in those days, for it was said that no child would ever be without parents.

But this boy's uncle did not have a straight mind. Although it was his duty to take care of his nephew, he resented the fact that he had this boy to care for. Instead of taking care of him, he treated him badly. He dressed him in ragged clothes; he gave him only scraps of food to eat; he never even called the boy by his name. He just would say, "Hey, you, get out of my way!"

Comparing Literature
Writers use descriptive language to develop characters. What does the author mean by saying the uncle does not have "a straight mind"?

Now, this boy had always been taught by his parents to treat elders with respect. So he tried to do everything he could to please his uncle. His uncle was very respected in the village because he was a great hunter. When he and his dog went out, they always brought

back game. One day, the uncle woke up with an idea in his mind. It was a twisted-mind idea, for what the uncle thought was this: "Too long have I been bothered with this troublesome boy. Today, I will get rid of him."

And so he called, "You, come here!" The boy quickly came, because he wanted to please his uncle. The uncle said, "You and I, we're going to go hunting together."

They left the lodge and started for the woods, and that was when the boy noticed something strange. He said, "Uncle, aren't you going to take your dog?" The uncle looked at the boy and said, "Today, you will be my dog."

Then the boy noticed another thing that was strange—they were going toward the north. In the village, when people went hunting, they would go to the east, or the south, or the west, but they would never go to the north, because there, it was said, strange things happened in the forest. Farther and farther the boy and his uncle went, away from any of the trails that people would follow, farther and farther to the north. The boy stayed close behind his uncle.

Finally, they came to a small clearing in the deep forest. On the other side, in the hillside, there was a small cave. The uncle said, "There are animals in there. You are my dog. Crawl in and chase them out." The boy was frightened, but then he thought back to what his parents had always told him: "Do what your elders say. Trust your elders."

So he crawled into the cave, but there was nothing there, no animal at all. As he turned around and began to crawl out, the circle of light that was the mouth of the cave suddenly vanished—the cave mouth had been blocked by a big stone. That was when the boy realized that his uncle meant to leave him there, and he began to cry.

But as his tears came, he remembered the song his

mother had taught him to sing when he needed a friend. Softly, he began to sing:

"Weyanna, weyanna, weyanna, hey.
Weyanna, weyanna, weyanna, hey.
Weyanna, weyanna, weyanna, hey.
Wey, hey yo-o-o, wey hey yo."

Then he stopped, because it seemed as if he could hear soft singing answering him on the other side of that rock. So he sang a little louder:

"Weyanna, weyanna, weyanna, hey.
Weyanna, weyanna, weyanna, hey.
Weyanna, weyanna, weyanna, hey.
Wey, hey yo-o-o, wey hey yo."

Comparing Literature What effect does the song have on your understanding of this folktale?

And from the other side of that rock came back:

"Wey, hey yo-o-o, wey hey yo."

The boy knew now that someone was out there, singing back to him, so he sang louder again. From the other side of the rock the song came back, strongly now. Then, together, the song was sung from both sides of the stone, and it ended together very loudly:

"Wey, hey yo-o-o, wey hey yo."

Comparing Literature Imagine a storyteller telling this folktale aloud to a group of people. How might the listeners participate in the story?

As the song ended, the rock was rolled away, and the boy crawled out into the bright sunlight, blinking his eyes. All around him in the clearing many people were gathered: big people, small people, tall people, skinny people, fat people, people of all shapes and sizes. He blinked his eyes again, and he saw they were not people at all. They were animals, all the animals of the forest: bears, deer, foxes, wolves, beavers, muskrats, and even the small animals—squirrels, woodchucks, chipmunks, moles. All of them were gathered there and all were looking straight at him. He stood up, and all

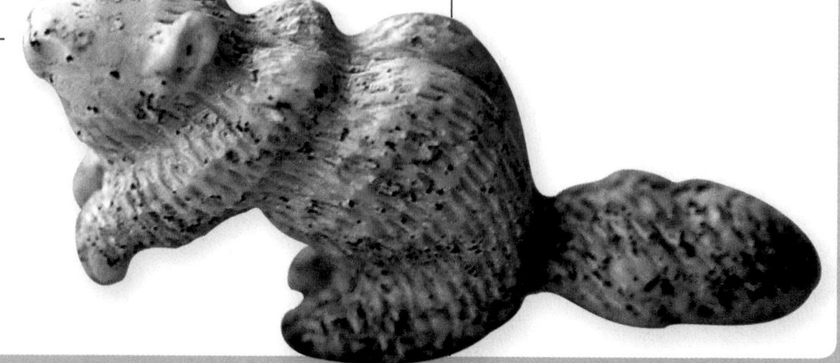

of those animals took one step toward him! The boy did not know what would happen next. And that was when an old grandmother woodchuck shuffled up to him, poked him in the leg, and said, "Grandson, we heard your song. Do you need a friend?"

"Yes," said the boy. "I do need a friend. You've come to help me?"

"Yes," said the old grandmother woodchuck, "but where is your family? Why are you here, trapped in this cave?" The boy shook his head sadly. "My parents died, and only my uncle was left to care for me. But he did not want me. He put me in this cave and left me here to die, so I have no family anywhere in the world."

The old grandmother woodchuck said, "Grandson, we will be your family! Pick any of us, and we will adopt you!" The boy looked around. All the animals were looking at him, but how could he decide?

"My friends," he said, "tell me what your lives are like. Then I can decide which one I will come and live with."

So the animals began to tell him about their lives: The mole told him how he lived in a warm burrow and dug in the earth and ate delicious worms; the beaver described how he swam underwater and lived in a warm lodge and ate tree bark. The boy thanked each animal politely, but said that he did not have the claws to dig like the mole, and that he could not hold his breath and swim underwater like the beaver.

Then the old mother bear came up. "My boy, you would like to be a bear. We take our time going through the forest. We eat the most delicious honey and berries. We sleep in our warm cave. And my two children here will play with you as much as you want." The boy quickly said, "I will be a bear."

And indeed, it was as the old mother bear said. Their lives were very good together. They took their time going through the forest. They ate delicious berries and honey, and the boy grew fat and happy. The bear cubs would wrestle and play with him as much as he wanted. In

Comparing Literature Why do you think the author makes this comment? How might a storyteller's audience react to the comment?

Comparing Literature What literary technique is the author using here? How do you know?

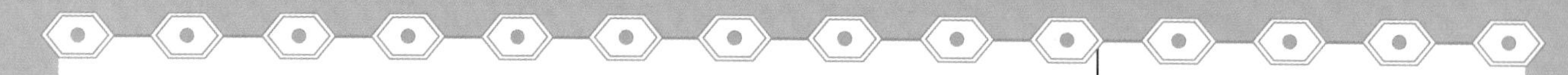

fact, he began to look like a bear himself, because when they wrestled and played, if their claws scratched him, hair would grow there, so that after some time had passed, that boy looked just like a bear, covered with black hair himself.

For two seasons, they lived this way. But then one day, as they were walking through the forest, the old mother bear stopped suddenly and said, "Listen! . . . Listen!"

Well, the boy listened. And before long, he heard the sound of feet walking through the forest, stepping on twigs and brushing past the leaves. The old mother bear began to laugh. "That is the sound of a hunter trying to hunt the bear. But he makes so much noise going through the forest, we call him Heavy Foot. He will never catch a bear!" And so they continued on their way.

Another day came, and again as they walked through the forest, the old mother bear stopped and said, "Listen!" The boy could hear the sound of someone talking to himself, saying, "Ahhh, it is a very good day for hunting. Ah-ha, today I will surely catch a bear! Uh, yes, uh, I will probably catch more than one bear, for I am a great hunter!"

Old mother bear began to laugh. "That's the one who talks to himself while he hunts. We call him Flapping Jaws. He will never catch a bear!"

And so it went on. Each day they listened. They heard the hunter called Bumps into Trees, and the one called Falls in the Lake. None of these hunters was good enough to catch a bear.

Comparing Literature
Native American names are often descriptions of a person's appearance, background, or personality. How do you think the author wants the reader to react to the hunters' names?

But then one day, as they walked along, the old mother bear said, "Stop. Listen!" For a long time, the boy could hear nothing. Then, very, very faintly, he could hear the sound of soft feet, moving through the forest. But it did not sound like two feet. It did not sound like four feet. It sounded like two feet and four feet.

The old mother bear quickly nodded. She said, "This is the one we fear. It is Two Legs and Four Legs. We must RUN!" And she began to run. The boy and the two cubs ran behind her through the forest, but Two Legs and Four Legs were behind them. They ran through the swamps, but Two Legs and Four Legs were getting closer. They ran up the hills, but still Two Legs and Four Legs followed, and now the boy could hear behind them a sound growing louder: *"Wuf, wuf, wuf, wuf, wuf!"* And the boy knew that Two Legs and Four Legs were very close behind.

They came to a clearing where an old tree had fallen. It was hollow. The boy and the two cubs and the old mother bear went into that hollow log to hide.

The boy listened. He heard Two Legs and Four Legs come into the clearing and right up to the log. And then everything became quiet.

"Perhaps they've gone away," the boy thought. But then he began to smell smoke. Smoke was coming into the log! Two Legs had made a fire and was blowing the smoke into the log to make them come out.

It was just at that moment that the boy remembered that he, too, was a Two Legs. He was a person, a human being, and that was a hunter and a dog out there. The boy shouted, "Stop! Don't hurt my family!" And upon these words, the smoke stopped coming into the log.

The boy crawled out, blinking his eyes against the light. There in front of him stood the hunter, and the hunter was his uncle! The uncle stared at the boy. The boy stood up and came closer. The uncle reached out and touched him, and all the hair fell off the boy's body, and he looked like a person again.

"My nephew!" said the uncle. "Is it truly you? Are you alive?"

"Yes, I am, Uncle," said the boy.

"How could this be?" said the uncle. "I went back to the cave, because I realized I had done a twisted-mind thing. But when I got there, the stone had been rolled away. There were the tracks of many animals. I thought they had eaten you."

"No," said the boy. "The bears adopted me. They are my family now, Uncle. You must treat them well."

The uncle nodded. He said, "My nephew, your words are true. Call your family out. I will greet them and I will be their friend." So the boy called, and the old mother bear and the two cubs came out from the log; they came out and sniffed the hunter. He stood there patiently, letting them approach him.

From that day on, the hunter and his nephew were a family, and the bears were part of their family. And ever since then, this story has been told to remind parents and elders always to treat their children well and to show as much love in their hearts as a bear holds in its heart for its children.

That is how the story goes. *Ho? Hey* ❧.

Comparing Literature
Earlier in the folktale, how did the author describe the uncle's mind? How is this description similar to the earlier description?

Comparing Literature

BQ BIG Question

Now use the unit Big Question to compare and contrast "Zlateh the Goat" and "The Boy Who Lived with the Bears." With a group of classmates, discuss questions such as

- What goal does Aaron have when he first sets out on his journey with Zlateh?
- What goal does the uncle have when he takes his nephew into the woods? What goal does the boy have after emerging from the cave into the clearing full of animals?
- How do the characters' goals change by the end of each story? What knowledge and wisdom have the characters gained?

Support each answer with evidence from the readings.

Literary Element Style

Use the details you wrote in your comparison chart to think about the authors' styles in "Zlateh the Goat" and "The Boy Who Lived with the Bears." With a partner, answer the following questions.

1. In what ways are the authors' styles different in "Zlateh the Goat" and "The Boy Who Lived with the Bears"? Discuss word choice, sentence structure and length, and literary devices such as figurative language. Include examples to support your answers.
2. In what ways are the authors' styles similar? Think about how each author tells the story, how each writer mixes humorous and serious moments, or how each describes characters. Include examples from the stories to support your answers.

Write to Compare

In one or two paragraphs, discuss the authors' styles in "Zlateh the Goat" and "The Boy Who Lived with the Bears" and the effect each style has on the reader. You might focus on these ideas as you write:

- Discuss the way each author describes the events in the story. Does the author use descriptive language? Does he use figurative language?
- Consider how each selection would be different if it were written in the style of the other story. Would each story's effect on the reader be the same?
- Think about how the similarities and differences in the writing styles affect your responses to the two stories.

Writing Tip

Paragraphs When writing a longer essay, start a new paragraph when you begin a new topic. Indicate new paragraphs by skipping a line and indenting.

Literature Online

Selection Resources
For Selection Quizzes, eFlashcards, and Reading-Writing Connection activities, go to glencoe.com and enter QuickPass code GL17527u6.

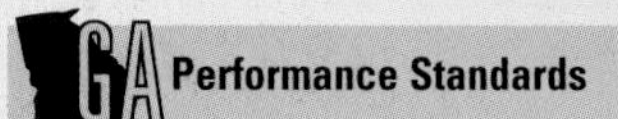

GA Performance Standards

For pages 832–837

ELA6W2c Produce writing that develops a controlling idea that conveys a perspective on the subject.

Writing Workshop

Expository Essay

What do you want to do with your life? Why? In this workshop, you will write an expository essay that will help you think about the Unit 6 Big Question: What are worthwhile goals?

Review the writing prompt, or assignment, below. Then read the Writing Plan. It will tell you what you will do to write your expository essay.

Writing Assignment

An expository essay informs or explains or does both. Write an expository essay informing your readers about one of your lifetime goals. Explain why you chose that goal and how you plan to accomplish it. Also explain the kind of knowledge you need to reach your goal and suggest who might be able to help you reach your goal. The audience—those reading your essay—will be your classmates and teacher.

Writing Plan

- Present the thesis, or the main idea, of the essay in the introduction.
- Organize the essay in an effective and appropriate pattern.
- Include examples to support and clarify ideas.
- Use language techniques to maintain reader interest.
- Conclude by linking back to the thesis of the essay.

Prewrite

Think about the goals of people and characters in this unit. For example, what kinds of goals did Madam C. J. Walker have? How did she reach those goals? Who helped her?

Gather Ideas

Review your journal entries and thumb through newspapers and magazines that interest you. Then spend some quiet time visualizing your future. What goals do you want to pursue? How might you reach them? Who might help you reach them?

Prewriting Tip

Thesis Statement State your thesis directly or simply imply it. At least during the drafting stage, write it down so you can refer to it during the writing processs.

Choose a Goal

Think about the goals you visualized. Choose a goal that seems interesting and within your reach. To get started, talk about your goal with a partner.

Partner Talk With a partner, follow these steps:

1. Explain your goal to a partner.
2. Discuss ways you could reach the goal and who could help you.
3. Write a brief thesis statement explaining why you chose that goal. The following sentence frame may be helpful.

I have a goal of ____________ because ________________.

Get Organized

Create a flowchart showing the steps you will take to reach your goal. Note the reasons for taking each step and who might help you.

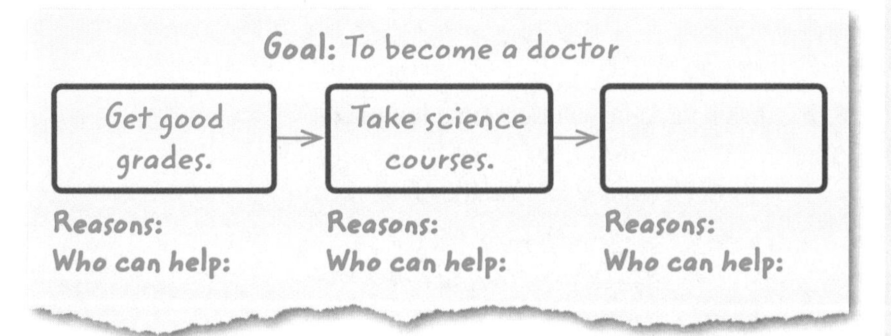

Draft

Organize your ideas and add more details to your writing.

Get It on Paper

- Review your thesis statement about your goal. Look at your flowchart.
- Begin with something to interest your audience, such as an anecdote, that relates to your goal. Connect it to your thesis.
- Write a topic sentence that explains how each step in your flowchart will help you meet your goal. Tell who might help and how.
- End your essay by connecting to your thesis. Summarize your reasons for choosing your goal, make a pledge to follow the steps you outlined, or describe a vision of yourself reaching your goal.
- Don't worry about paragraphs, spelling, grammar, or punctuation right now.
- When you are finished, read what you have written. Include more information if you need to.

Develop Your Draft

1. State your **thesis** in your introduction.

I was so grateful to him that, before I even got out of the hospital, I decided to become a doctor myself.

2. **Organize** your essay into the steps you will take to reach a goal and the reasons for taking them.

I'm already taking the first step—studying hard so I can do well in school.

Writing and Research
For prewriting, drafting, and revising tools, go to glencoe.com and enter QuickPass code GL17527u6.

Drafting Tip

Examples Provide supporting details, such as specific examples, to prove your thesis statement.

3. Include **examples** to support and clarify your ideas.

> Then when I get into high school, I need to take all the science courses I can, especially biology and chemistry.

4. Express your ideas in **interesting language.**

> Finally, like my hero Mother Teresa, I must take care of people throughout my life.

5. Link your **conclusion** to your thesis.

> For now, that's just a dream, but I've already started doing everything I can to make that dream come true.

TRY IT

Analyzing Cartoons

Imagine that the person in the cartoon is a writer. What might the light bulbs represent? What size light bulb would the writer want to catch?

Apply Good Writing Traits: Ideas

The main idea of your essay is the goal you want to achieve. That is what you want your readers to remember the most. Important details explain a lot about the main idea.

Read the sentences below from "Madam C. J. Walker" by Jim Haskins. What main ideas do they express? What details support those ideas?

> She taught herself as much as she could and was not afraid to ask someone to define a word she did not know or explain something she did not understand.

> Madam Walker insisted that her agents sign contracts promising to abide by her strict standards of personal hygiene—long before various states passed similar laws for workers in the cosmetics field.

As you draft your essay, make sure you have included and supported all the ideas you want to express.

Analyze a Student Model

My life's goal became absolutely clear to me when I was seven years old. On the way home from school, I was hit by a car, and my hip and knee were broken in several places. Dr. Steven Moore, a talented surgeon, operated on my leg and gave me hope when I was afraid I'd never walk again. I was so grateful to him that, before I even got out of the hospital, I decided to become a doctor myself.

Reaching that goal is going to take a lot of hard work and dedication. I know that it's important for me to remember my goal and to make decisions that will help me achieve it. I'm already taking the first step—studying hard so I can do well in school. Not only will this give me the basic knowledge I need, but it also will teach me discipline and good study habits. It's not always easy for me to stay focused on my work, so I'm going to ask my teachers and parents to help. They can remind me of my goal and encourage me to study.

Then when I get into high school, I need to take all the science courses I can, especially biology and chemistry. These subjects will give me solid groundwork to build on when I go to college and medical school. Josie's sister, a pre-med major in college, might be able to give me hints on which schools to go to and which courses to take.

Finally, like my hero Mother Teresa, I must take care of people throughout my life. I do what I can to help people in the neighborhood right now. As soon as I'm old enough, I plan to volunteer at the local hospital and the senior center.

Meanwhile, I had a dream the other night. I was at a movie theater and someone started choking on a piece of popcorn. People started screaming, "Is there a doctor in the house?" I jumped from my seat, ran down the aisle, and saved the person's life. For now, that's just a dream, but I've already started doing everything I can to make that dream come true.

Thesis

Relating an anecdote in the introduction can be a good way to present the thesis and interest the reader.

Organization

Include the steps you will take to reach your goal in the order you will take them and give reasons for taking each step. Consider using words such as *first, then, finally,* and so on, to establish that order.

Examples

Use specific examples, such as these particular sciences, to help explain your main ideas.

Interesting Language

Mentioning a famous humanitarian such as Mother Teresa adds interest and explains the writer's desire to help people.

Conclusion

The writer's dream about being a doctor links back to the thesis, reminding readers of the goal and the commitment to reaching it.

Revising Tip

Allusions To help make your language interesting to readers, include allusions, or references to well-known people, places, or events in history or literature.

Revise

Now it's time to revise your draft so your ideas really shine. Revising is what makes good writing great, and great writing takes work!

Peer Review Trade drafts with a partner. Use the chart below to review your partner's draft by answering the questions in the *What to do* column. Talk about your peer review after you have glanced at each other's drafts and have written the answers to the questions. Next, follow the suggestions in the *How to do it* column to revise your draft.

Revising Plan

What to do	How to do it	Example
Did you state your thesis statement in the introduction?	Begin with something to interest your audience, such as an anecdote.	A wonderful doctor operated on my leg. I was so grateful to him ^ that, before I even got out of the hospital, I decided to become a doctor myself.
Is it clear how you plan to reach your goal?	Use time order words to show the sequence of the steps you will take.	Finally, ^ ~~L~~like my hero Mother Teresa, I must take care of people throughout my life.
Have you given enough support to your ideas with specific examples?	Add examples to clarify any questions your audience may have.	^ It's not always easy for me to stay focused on my work, so I'm going to ask my teachers and parents to help.
Have you used interesting language?	Use words that express your ideas clearly and will catch the reader's attention.	These subjects will give me ~~something~~ ^ solid groundwork to build on when I go to college and medical school.
Does your conclusion link to your thesis and provide a satisfying ending?	Refer back to your thesis in the conclusion.	^ Meanwhile, I had a dream the other night. I was at a movie theater and someone started choking on a piece of popcorn.

Edit and Proofread

For your final draft, read your expository essay one sentence at a time. An editing and proofreading checklist may help you spot errors. Use the proofreading symbols in the chart inside the back cover of this book to mark needed changes. Then make corrections.

Grammar Focus: Appositives

One way to include examples to support your main idea is using an appositive, or a word or phrase that follows a noun or pronoun and renames it. An appositive adds new information. If the information is nonessential, put commas around it. Below are examples of problems with appositives from the Workshop Model and their solutions.

Problem: It is not clear which words support the main idea.

Dr. Steven Moore a talented surgeon operated on my leg and gave me hope when I was afraid I'd never walk again.

Solution: Enclose the appositive in commas to show the explanatory information isn't essential to the meaning.

Dr. Steven Moore, a talented surgeon, operated on my leg and gave me hope when I was afraid I'd never walk again.

Problem: Sentences are choppy and do not flow well.

Josie's sister might be able to give me hints on which schools to go to and which courses to take. She is a pre-med major in college.

Solution: Combine the sentences, using an appositive.

Josie's sister, a pre-med major in college, might be able to give me hints on which schools to go to and which courses to take.

Present

It's almost time to share your writing with others. Write your expository essay neatly in print or cursive on a separate sheet of paper. If you have access to a computer, type your essay on the computer, formatting your paper neatly and accurately, and check spelling. Save your document to a disk and print it out.

Grammar Tip

Parentheses with Appositives Use parentheses to enclose explanatory or extra material that interrupts the normal sentence structure. An appositive occasionally may be enclosed in parentheses if it is extremely long.

Presenting Tip

Visuals Make an extra copy of your essay to keep and reflect on later in life—perhaps when you have reached your goal. Create a cover for it and enclose it securely in plastic for safekeeping.

Literature Online

Writing and Research For editing and publishing tools, go to glencoe.com and enter QuickPass code GL17527u6.

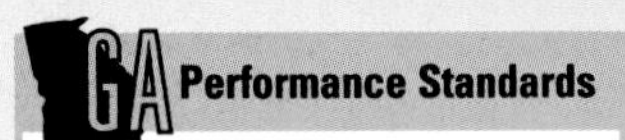

Performance Standards

For page 838

ELA6LSV1b Ask relevant questions.

ELA6LSV1k Clarify, illustrate, or expand on a response.

Speaking, Listening, and Viewing Workshop

Active Listening and Note-Taking

Activity

Working in Groups Working in a group is an opportunity to learn from others. A group discussion gives you an opportunity to share your ideas. It is also a way to listen to others' ideas so you can change or add to your own thoughts. Remember that you focused on the Unit 6 Big Question: What are worthwhile goals? Hold a group discussion about worthwhile goals.

Planning Your Group Discussion

Three to five students is a good size for most small-group tasks. Agree on individual role assignments to give everyone in the group something to do. One student, the group recorder, may take notes. Another may lead the discussion, and another may report the results to the rest of the class. Decide how your group will organize its time.

Being an Active Listener

Active listening involves paying attention to the person speaking, thinking about what is being said, and asking yourself questions about whether you understand and agree with what is being said.

To practice active listening, clear your mind of other thoughts and distractions. Look at the speaker and focus on the words the speaker is saying and how they are being spoken. Pay attention to nonverbal clues such as the speaker's posture, gestures, eye contact, and facial expressions. Determine the speaker's attitude toward the subject by identifying the speaker's tone or mood. Then connect what you hear to your own knowledge and experience. Let your own ideas grow or change as you listen. Be open to different ideas and viewpoints, even if you are reluctant to agree with them at first.

Listening to Learn and Taking Notes

Take notes as you listen. Can you identify the main ideas? Listen for key words or ideas that help you identify the speaker's main points. Use abbreviations and shortened word forms to get your ideas on paper quickly. Jot down questions as they occur to you so you can ask them when the speaker is finished. When it is your turn to talk, address the topic and help the discussion move forward.

Active Listening Checklist

Answer the following questions to evaluate how well you listened.

- ❑ Did you pay attention to the speaker and think about what was said?
- ❑ Did you determine the main ideas?
- ❑ Did you ask questions to help you understand and learn from the discussion?
- ❑ Did you take notes while you were listening?

Literature Online

Speaking, Listening, and Viewing For project ideas, templates, and presentation tips, go to glencoe.com and enter QuickPass code GL17527u6.

Unit Challenge

Answer the Big Question

In Unit 6, you explored the Big Question through reading, writing, speaking, and listening. Now it's time for you to complete one of the Unit Challenges below with your answer to the Big Question.

WHAT Are Worthwhile Goals?

Use the notes you took in your Unit 6 **Foldable** to complete the Unit Challenge of your choice.

Before you present your Unit Challenge, be sure it meets the requirements below. Use this first plan if you choose to create a slogan for a bumper sticker about worthwhile goals.

On Your Own Activity: Bumper Stickers

- ❑ Brainstorm some slogans that encourage people to pursue a worthwhile goal. Recall that slogans are brief phrases or sayings that express an idea.
- ❑ Revise your slogans to make them clear, concise (short), and catchy (memorable and interesting).
- ❑ Design a bumper sticker of your favorite slogan on paper or cardboard and display it.

Use this second plan if you choose to work with a group to write, rehearse, and perform a play about worthwhile goals.

Group Activity: Worthwhile Goals Play

- ❑ Each group will develop a scene for a play based on the Big Question: What are worthwhile goals?
- ❑ Groups will write a script, including details that develop the plot and characters, a conflict, and a resolution. Choose a narrator, actors, set designers, and a director.
- ❑ Draft a final script with stage directions. After rehearsing, give a performance of your scene, holding audience interest with effective rate, volume, pitch, and tone.

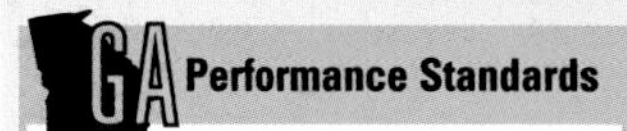

GA Performance Standards

For page 839

ELA6LSV1I Employ a group decision-making technique such as brainstorming or a problem-solving sequence.

Independent Reading

Fiction

To read more about the Big Question, choose one of these books from your school or local library.

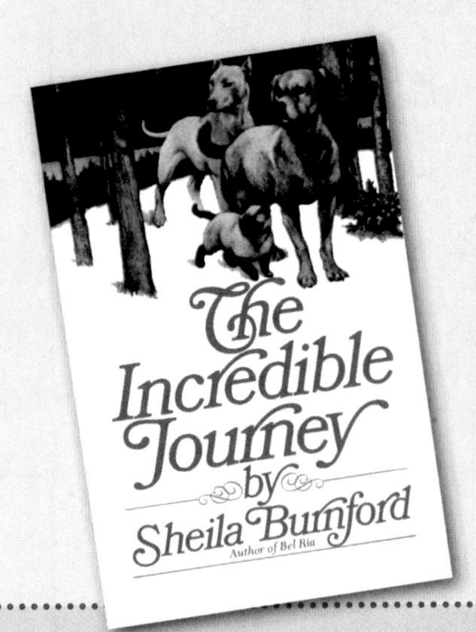

The Incredible Journey

by Sheila Burnford

Two dogs and a cat set out on a 250-mile journey through the Canadian wilderness. Separately they might not survive, but together the three house pets must withstand predators, lack of food, and freezing weather as they attempt to find their way home.

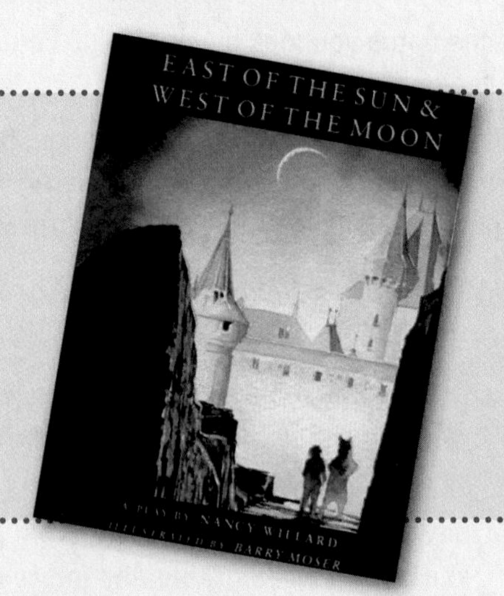

East of the Sun and West of the Moon

by Nancy Willard

This poetic and amusing play, based on a Norwegian folktale, tells the story of a woodcutter's daughter who travels to the ends of the earth to save her prince.

Island of the Blue Dolphins

by Scott O'Dell

A Native American girl, accidentally left behind by her people, must survive on a lonely island. Can she fend off a ferocious pack of wild dogs and Aleutian sea-otter hunters? This is a classic story of courage and self-reliance.

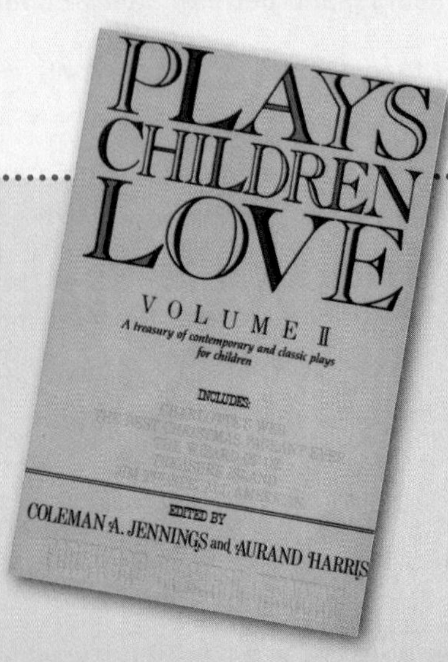

Plays Children Love, Volume II: A Treasury of Contemporary and Classic Plays for Children

edited by Coleman A. Jennings and Aurand Harris

This anthology includes plays based on such classics as *The Wizard of Oz, Treasure Island, Charlotte's Web,* and *The Wind in the Willows.*

Nonfiction

Escape to Freedom: A Play About Young Frederick Douglass

by Ossie Davis

Born enslaved, future statesman Frederick Douglass endured cruelty and injustice before escaping to freedom. This play brings to life the hardships and triumphs that shaped the great orator.

The Invisible Thread

by Yoshiko Uchida

The popular author describes growing up in Berkeley, California, as a Japanese American, including her family's internment in a Nevada concentration camp during World War II. This memoir provides a personal account of a shameful episode in American history.

The Story of Thomas Alva Edison

by Margaret Cousins

Thomas Edison made many mistakes before he invented a successful light bulb. Read to find out how Edison's curiosity about the way things work lasted a lifetime and made the world a brighter place.

Create a Book Cover

Create a book cover for the book you read. Your book cover should be engaging and convey something important about the book without giving too much away. Remember, you want your cover to create interest in reading the book. Ask a classmate who has read the book to critique the cover you created.

Assessment

READING

Read the passage and answer the questions. Write your answers on a separate sheet of paper.

from **You're a Good Man, Charlie Brown** by Clark Gesner

(The following excerpt is from Act One of the play. LINUS *is settled in front of the TV.* LUCY *enters and watches with him for a moment.)*

LUCY. OK, switch channels.

LINUS. Are you kidding? What makes you think you can come right in here and take over?

LUCY *(holding out her hand).* <u>These five fingers individually are nothing. But when I curl them together into a single unit, they become a fighting force terrible to behold.</u>

LINUS. Which channel do you want? *(He looks at his hand.)* Why can't you guys get organized like that?

LUCY. Linus, do you know what I intend? I intend to be a queen. When I grow up, I'm going to be the biggest queen there ever was, and I'll live in this big palace with a big front lawn and have lots of beautiful dresses to wear. And when I go out in my coach, all the people. . .

LINUS. Lucy.

LUCY. . . .all the people will wave, and I will shout at them, and . . .

LINUS. Lucy, I believe "queen" is an inherited title. *(*LUCY *is silent.)* Yes, I'm quite sure. A person can only become a queen by being born into a royal family of the correct <u>lineage</u> so that she can assume the throne after the death of the reigning monarch. I can't think of any possible way that you could ever become a queen. *(*LUCY *is still silent.)* I'm sorry, Lucy, but it's true.

LUCY *(silence, and then).* . . . and in the summertime I will go to my summer palace, and I'll wear my crown in swimming and everything, and all the people will cheer, and I will shout at them . . . *(Her vision pops.)* What do you mean I can't be a queen?

LINUS. It's true.

LUCY. There must be a loophole. This kind of thing always has a loophole. Nobody should be kept from being a queen if she wants to be one. IT'S UNDEMOCRATIC!

LINUS. Good grief.

LUCY. It's usually just a matter of knowing the right people. I'll bet a few pieces of well-placed correspondence and I get to be a queen in no time.

LINUS. I think I'll watch television. *(He returns to the set.)*

LUCY. I know what I'll do. If I can't be a queen, then I'll be very rich. I'll work and work until I'm very, very rich, and then I will buy myself a queendom.

LINUS. Good grief.

LUCY. Yes, I will buy myself a queendom, and then I'll kick out the old queen and take over the whole operation myself. I will be head queen. And when I go out in my coach, all the people will wave, and I will . . . I will . . .

(She has glanced at the TV set and become engrossed. Pretty soon LINUS *turns and looks at her.)*

LINUS. What happened to your queendom?

LUCY. Huh?

LINUS. What happened to your queendom?

LUCY. Oh, that. I've given it up. I've decided to devote my life to cultivating my natural beauty.

(As LINUS *looks at her in disbelief, the scene disappears into blessed darkness . . .)*

1. Based on this passage, what generalization can a reader make about Lucy?
   A. She is bossy.
   B. She is generous.
   C. She is unsure of herself.
   D. She is practical and realistic.

2. What does Lucy mean when she tells Linus that when she curls her fingers *into a single unit, they become a fighting force terrible to behold*?
   A. By using a fist, I could force you to do what I want.
   B. Any group that is willing to fight is a frightening sight.
   C. Let's work together because we'll be stronger that way.
   D. When I put my fingers together, they curl up in a terrible way.

3. Why does Linus agree to change channels on the TV?
   A. He is thoughtful.
   B. He is afraid of Lucy.
   C. He is bored by the other show.
   D. He doesn't care what he watches.

4. In this passage, the word *lineage* contains a suffix with the same meaning as the suffix in which of the following?
   A. orphanage
   B. line-drive
   C. unlined
   D. postage

5. Lucy's response "IT'S UNDEMOCRATIC!" is set in capital letters. The author MOST likely wanted to
   A. emphasize the theme, or main idea, of the play.
   B. emphasize the irony of the words: a royal ruler does not allow democracy.
   C. make sure that Lucy's protest is the loudest part of the play.
   D. make it easier to read the words.

6. Lucy's ideas about a queendom are to a democracy as
   A. a fighting force is to a general.
   B. a loophole is to a lawyer.
   C. a coronation is to an election.
   D. a brother is to a sister.

Standards Practice For more standards practice, go to glencoe.com and enter QuickPass code GL17527u6.

7. What do the stage directions suggest is the reason that Lucy drops her plan to become queen?
   A. She is a deep thinker who likes to solve problems.
   B. She is a sensitive person who is considerate of others.
   C. She is a wise person who uses good judgment.
   D. She is easily distracted and changes her mind often.

8. Which of the following BEST describes the tone of Lucy's lines about the loophole?
   A. an irritated and argumentative tone
   B. a slow and thoughtful tone
   C. a high-pitched and hysterical tone
   D. a calm and queenly tone

9. Which delivery technique would be most useful to the actor who portrays Lucy?
   A. a quiet but commanding voice
   B. a worried expression
   C. nervous pacing
   D. pounding her fist for emphasis

10. Which sentence below uses the word *operation* with the same meaning as it is used in this passage?
    A. My grandmother went to the hospital to have an operation.
    B. Addition is a different mathematical operation than division.
    C. My mom is the boss at her company and runs the operation.
    D. I can't fix the engine because I don't understand its operation.

11. Which of the following BEST explains why Lucy's idea of becoming a queen is humorous?
    A. She lives in the modern-day United States.
    B. Children cannot become kings or queens.
    C. Queens no longer exist anywhere in the world.
    D. Lucy is not a member of a royal family.

12. What does the word *cultivating* mean in this passage?
    A. hiding
    B. ignoring
    C. improving
    D. wishing for

ENGLISH/LANGUAGE ARTS

Choose the best answer for each question. Write your answers on a separate sheet of paper.

1. Which word BEST fills in the blank in the sentence below?

Some ________________ flags look very similar to me.

A. country's

B. countrie's

C. countries'

D. countrys'

2. Which word in the sentence below is NOT spelled correctly?

The pharmacy on the corner is relible and inexpensive, but its hours are limited.

A. pharmacy

B. relible

C. inexpensive

D. limited

3. Which sentence below is written correctly?

A. Kelly and Enmai has finished first.

B. The frogs in that pond is noisy at night.

C. Jim or his brothers are willing to try.

D. Inside that pasture was several big, angry hogs.

4. Which sentence below is a correctly written and punctuated complex sentence?

A. My sister usually gets her way she is forceful and confident.

B. Sometimes siblings argue, but they settle their differences.

C. In looking at the conflict between a brother and sister.

D. When Dad explained the flaw in my plan, I felt foolish.

WRITING

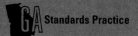

Read your assigned topic in the box below. Use one piece of paper to jot down your ideas and organize your thoughts. Then neatly write your essay on another sheet of paper.

Expository Writing Topic

Writing Situation

People can read plays, or they can be see them performed on a stage. Think about how these two experiences—reading a play and watching a play on a stage—are different.

Directions for Writing

Write an essay explaining to your teacher how reading a play is different from seeing the play performed on stage. Remember to support your ideas with specific details and examples.

Writing Checklist

☐ Focus on a single topic.

☐ Organize your main points in a clear, logical order.

☐ Support your ideas or viewpoints with details and examples.

☐ Use precise, vivid words.

☐ Vary the length and structure of your sentences.

☐ Use clear transition words to connect ideas.

☐ Correct any errors in spelling, capitalization, punctuation, and usage.

Reference Section

Literary Terms Handbook

A

Act A major unit of a drama. A play may be subdivided into several acts. Many modern plays have two or three acts. A short play can be composed of one or more scenes but only one act.

See also Scene.

Alliteration The repetition of consonant sounds, usually at the beginnings of words or syllables. Alliteration gives emphasis to words.
For example,

Over the cobbles he clattered and clashed

Allusion A reference in a work of literature to a well-known character, place, or situation in history, politics, or science or from another work of literature, music, or art.

Analogy A comparison between two things, based on one or more elements that they share. Analogies can help the reader visualize an idea. In informational text, analogies are often used to explain something unfamiliar in terms of something known. For example, a science book might compare the flow of electricity to water moving through a hose. In literature, most analogies are expressed in metaphors or similes.

See also Metaphor, Simile.

Anecdote A brief, entertaining story based on a single interesting or humorous incident or event. Anecdotes are frequently biographical and reveal some aspect of a person's character.

Antagonist A person or force that opposes the protagonist, or central character, in a story or a drama. The reader is generally meant not to sympathize with the antagonist.

See also Conflict, Protagonist.

Anthropomorphism Representing animals as if they had human emotions and intelligence. Fables and fairy tales often contain anthropomorphism.

Aside In a play, a comment made by a character that is heard by the audience but not by the other characters onstage. The speaker turns to one side, or "aside," away from the other characters onstage. Asides are common in older plays—you will find many in Shakespeare's plays—but are infrequent in modern drama.

Assonance The repetition of vowel sounds, especially in a line of poetry.

See also Rhyme, Sound devices.

Author's purpose The intention of the writer. For example, the purpose of a story may be to entertain, to describe, to explain, to persuade, or a combination of these purposes.

Autobiography The story of a person's life written by that person. *Primary Lessons* by Judith Ortiz Cofer is an example of autobiography.

See also Biography, Memoir.

B

Ballad A short musical narrative song or poem. Folk ballads, which usually tell of an exciting or dramatic episode, were passed on by word of mouth for generations before being written down. Literary ballads are written in imitation of folk ballads.

See also Narrative poetry.

Biography The account of a person's life written by someone other than the subject. Biographies can be short or book-length.

See also Autobiography, Memoir.

C

Character A person in a literary work. (If a character is an animal, it displays human traits.) Characters who show varied and sometimes contradictory traits are called **round.** Characters who reveal only one personality trait are called **flat.** A **stereotype** is a flat character of a familiar and often-repeated type. A **dynamic** character changes during the story. A **static** character remains primarily the same throughout the story.

Characterization The methods a writer uses to develop the personality of the character. In **direct characterization,** the writer makes direct statements about a character's personality. In **indirect characterization,** the writer reveals a character's personality through the character's words and actions and through what other characters think and say about the character.

Climax The point of greatest emotional intensity, interest, or suspense in a narrative. Usually the climax comes at the turning point in a story or drama, the point at which the resolution of the conflict becomes clear. The climax in "Wings" occurs when Icarus forgets his father's warning and flies too high.

Comedy A type of drama that is humorous and has a happy ending. A heroic comedy focuses on the exploits of a larger-than-life hero. In American popular culture, comedy can take the form of a scripted performance involving one or more performers—either as a skit that is part of a variety show, as in vaudeville, or as a stand-up monologue.

See also Humor.

Conflict The central struggle between opposing forces in a story or drama. An **external conflict** exists when a character struggles against some outside force, such as nature, society, fate, or another person. An **internal conflict** exists within the mind of a character who is torn between opposing feelings or goals.

See also Antagonist, Plot, Protagonist.

Consonance A pleasing combination of sounds, especially in poetry. Consonance usually refers to the repetition of consonant sounds in stressed syllables.

See also Sound devices.

Couplet Two successive lines of verse that form a unit and usually rhyme.

D

Description Writing that seeks to convey the impression of a setting, a person, an animal, an object, or an event by appealing to the senses. Almost all writing, fiction and nonfiction, contains elements of description.

Details Particular features of things used to make descriptions more accurate and vivid. Authors use details to help readers imagine the characters, scenes, and actions they describe.

Dialect A variation of language spoken by a particular group, often within a particular region. Dialects differ from standard language because they may contain different pronunciations, forms, and meanings.

Dialogue Conversation between characters in a literary work.

See also Monologue.

Drama A story intended to be performed by actors on a stage or before movie or TV cameras. Most dramas before the modern period can be divided into two basic types: tragedy and comedy. The script of a drama includes dialogue (the words the actors speak) and stage directions (descriptions of the action and scenery).

See also Comedy, Tragedy.

E

Elegy A mournful or melancholy poem that honors someone who is dead. Some elegies are written in rhyming couplets that follow a strict metric pattern.

Epic A long narrative poem, written in a dignified style, that celebrates the adventures and achievements of one or more heroic figures of legend, history, or religion.

See also Narrative poetry.

Essay A short piece of nonfiction writing on a single topic. The purpose of the essay is to communicate an idea or opinion. A **formal essay** is serious and impersonal. An **informal essay** entertains while it informs, usually in a light, conversational style.

Exposition The part of the plot of a short story, novel, novella, or play in which the characters, setting, and situation are introduced.

Extended metaphor An implied comparison that continues through an entire poem.

See also Metaphor.

F

Fable A short, simple tale that teaches a moral. The characters in a fable are often animals who speak and act like people. The moral, or lesson, of the fable is usually stated outright.

Falling action In a play or story, the action that follows the climax.

See also Plot.

Fantasy A form of literature that explores unreal worlds of the past, the present, or the future.

Fiction A prose narrative in which situations and characters are invented by the writer. Some aspects of a fictional work may be based on fact or experience. Fiction includes short stories, novellas, and novels.

See also Novel, Novella, Short story.

Figurative language Language used for descriptive effect, often to imply ideas indirectly. Expressions of figurative language are not literally true but express some truth beyond the literal level. Although it appears in all kinds of writing, figurative language is especially prominent in poetry.

See also Analogy, Figure of speech, Metaphor, Personification, Simile, Symbol.

Figure of speech Figurative language of a specific kind, such as **analogy, metaphor, simile,** or **personification.**

First-person narrative *See* Point of view.

Flashback An interruption in a chronological narrative that tells about something that happened before that point in the story or before the story began. A flashback gives readers information that helps explain the main events of the story.

Folklore The traditional beliefs, customs, stories, songs, and dances of the ordinary people (the "folk") of a culture. Folklore is passed on by word of mouth and performance rather than in writing.

See also Folktale, Legend, Myth, Oral tradition.

Folktale A traditional story passed down orally long before being written down. Generally the author of a folktale is anonymous. Folktales include animal stories, trickster stories, fairy tales, myths, legends, and tall tales.

See also Legend, Myth, Oral tradition, Tall tale.

Foreshadowing The use of clues by an author to prepare readers for events that will happen in a story.

Free verse Poetry that has no fixed pattern of meter, rhyme, line length, or stanza arrangement.

See also Rhythm.

G

Genre A literary or artistic category. The main literary genres are prose, poetry, and drama. Each of these is divided into smaller genres. For example, **prose** includes fiction (such as novels, novellas, short stories, and folktales) and nonfiction (such as biography, autobiography, and essays). **Poetry** includes lyric poetry, dramatic poetry, and narrative poetry. **Drama** includes tragedy, comedy, historical drama, melodrama, and farce.

H

Haiku Originally a Japanese form of poetry. A traditional haiku has three lines and seventeen syllables. The first and third lines have five syllables each; the middle line has seven syllables.

Hero A literary work's main character, usually one with admirable qualities. Although the word *hero* is applied only to males in traditional usage (the female form is *heroine*), the term now applies to both sexes.

See also Legend, Myth, Protagonist, Tall tale.

Historical fiction A novel, novella, play, short story, or narrative poem that sets fictional characters against a historical backdrop and contains many details about the period in which it is set.

See also Genre.

Humor The quality of a literary work that makes

the characters and their situations seem funny, amusing, or ludicrous. Humorous writing can be as effective in nonfiction as in fiction.

See also Comedy.

I

Idiom A figure of speech that belongs to a particular language, people, or region and whose meaning cannot be obtained, and might even seem ridiculous, by joining the meanings of the words composing it. You would be using an idiom if you said you *caught* a cold.

Imagery Language that emphasizes sensory impressions to help the reader of a literary work see, hear, feel, smell, and taste the scenes described in the work.

See also Figurative language.

Informational text This type of nonfiction writing conveys facts and information without introducing personal opinion.

Irony A form of expression in which the intended meaning of the words used is the opposite of their literal meaning. **Verbal irony** occurs when a person says one thing and means another—for example, saying "Nice guy!" about someone you dislike. **Situational irony** occurs when the outcome of a situation is the opposite of what was expected.

J

Journal An account of day-to-day events or a record of experiences, ideas, or thoughts. A journal may also be called a diary.

L

Legend A traditional story, based on history or an actual hero, that is passed down orally. A legend is usually exaggerated and gains elements of fantasy over the years. Stories about Daniel Boone and Davy Crockett are American legends.

Limerick A light, humorous poem with a regular metrical scheme and a rhyme scheme of *aabba.*

See also Humor, Rhyme scheme.

Local color The fictional portrayal of a region's features or peculiarities and its inhabitants' distinctive ways of talking and behaving, usually as a way of adding a realistic flavor to a story.

Lyric The words of a song, usually with a regular rhyme scheme.

See also Rhyme scheme.

Lyric poetry Poems, usually short, that express strong personal feelings about a subject or an event.

M

Main idea The most important idea expressed in a paragraph or an essay. It may or may not be directly stated.

Memoir A biographical or autobiographical narrative emphasizing the narrator's personal experience during a period or at an event.

See also Autobiography, Biography.

Metaphor A figure of speech that compares or equates seemingly unlike things. In contrast to a simile, a metaphor implies the comparison instead of stating it directly; hence, there is no use of a connective such as *like* or *as.*

See also Figure of speech, Imagery, Simile.

Meter A regular pattern of stressed and unstressed syllables that gives a line of poetry a predictable rhythm.

See also Rhythm.

Monologue A long speech by a single character in a play or a solo performance.

Mood The emotional quality or atmosphere of a story or poem.

See also Setting.

Myth A traditional story of unknown authorship, often involving goddesses, gods, and heroes, that attempts to explain a natural phenomenon, a historic event, or the origin of a belief or custom.

N

Narration Writing or speech that tells a story. Narration is used in prose fiction and narrative poetry. Narration can also be an important element in biographies, autobiographies, and essays.

Narrative poetry Verse that tells a story.

Narrator The person who tells a story. In some cases the narrator is a character in the story.

See also Point of view.

Nonfiction Factual prose writing. Nonfiction deals with real people and experiences. Among the categories of nonfiction are biographies, autobiographies, and essays.

See also Autobiography, Biography, Essay, Fiction.

Novel A book-length fictional prose narrative. A novel has a greater scope than a short story in its presentation of plot, character, setting, and theme. Because novels are not subject to any limits in their presentation of these elements, they encompass a wide range of narratives.

See also Fiction.

Novella A work of fiction shorter than a novel but longer than a short story. A novella usually has more characters, settings, and events and a more complex plot than a short story.

O

Ode A lyric poem, usually rhymed, often in the form of an address and usually dignified or lofty in subject.

See also Lyric poetry.

Onomatopoeia The use of a word or a phrase that actually imitates or suggests the sound of what it describes.

See also Sound devices.

Oral tradition Stories, knowledge, customs, and beliefs passed by word of mouth from one generation to the next.

See also Folklore, Folktale, Legend, Myth.

P

Parallelism The use of a series of words, phrases, or sentences that have similar grammatical form. Parallelism emphasizes the items that are arranged in the similar structures.

See also Repetition.

Personification A figure of speech in which an animal, object, or idea is given human form or characteristics.

See also Figurative language, Metaphor.

Plot The sequence of events in a story, novel, or play. The plot begins with **exposition,** which introduces the story's characters, setting, and situation. The plot catches the reader's attention with a **narrative hook.** The **rising action** adds complications to the story's conflict, or problem, leading to the **climax,** or point of highest emotional pitch. The **falling action** is the logical result of the climax, and the **resolution** presents the final outcome.

Plot twist An unexpected turn of events in a plot. A surprise ending is an example of a plot twist.

Poetry A form of literary expression that differs from prose in emphasizing the line as the unit of composition. Many other traditional characteristics of poetry—emotional, imaginative language; use of metaphor and simile; division into stanzas; rhyme; regular pattern of stress, or meter—apply to some poems but not to others.

Point of view The relationship of the narrator, or storyteller, to the story. In a story with **first-person point of view,** the story is told by one of the characters, referred to as "I." The reader generally sees everything through that character's eyes. In a story with a **limited third-person point of view,** the narrator reveals the thoughts of only one character, but refers to that character as "he" or "she." In a story with an **omniscient point of view,** the narrator reveals the thoughts of several characters.

Propaganda Speech, writing, or other attempts to influence ideas or opinions, often through the use of stereotypes, faulty generalizations, logical fallacies, and/or emotional language.

Props Theater slang (a shortened form of *properties*) for objects and elements of the scenery of a stage play or movie set.

Prose Writing that is similar to everyday speech and language, as opposed to poetry. Its form is based on sentences and paragraphs without the patterns of rhyme, controlled line length, or meter found in much poetry. Fiction and nonfiction are the major categories of prose. Most modern drama is also written in prose.

See also Drama, Essay, Fiction, Nonfiction.

Protagonist The central character in a story, drama, or dramatic poem. Usually the action revolves around the protagonist, who is involved in the main conflict.

See Antagonist, Conflict.

Pun A humorous play on two or more meanings of the same word or on two words with the same sound. Puns often appear in advertising headlines and slogans—for example, "Our hotel rooms give you suite feelings."

See also Humor.

R

Refrain A line or lines repeated regularly, usually in a poem or song.

Repetition The recurrence of sounds, words, phrases, lines, or stanzas in a speech or piece of writing. Repetition increases the feeling of unity in a work. When a line or stanza is repeated in a poem or song, it is called a refrain.

See also Parallelism, Refrain.

Resolution The part of a plot that concludes the falling action by revealing or suggesting the outcome of the conflict.

Rhyme The repetition of sounds at the ends of words that appear close to each other in a poem. **End rhyme** occurs at the ends of lines. **Internal rhyme** occurs within a single line. Slant rhyme occurs when words include sounds that are similar but not identical. **Slant rhyme** usually involves some variation of **consonance** (the repetition of consonant sounds) or **assonance** (the repetition of vowel sounds).

Rhyme scheme The pattern of rhyme formed by the end rhyme in a poem. Rhyme scheme is designated by the assignment of a different letter of the alphabet to each new rhyme. For example, one common rhyme scheme is *ababcb.*

Rhythm The pattern created by the arrangement of stressed and unstressed syllables, especially in poetry. Rhythm gives poetry a musical quality that helps convey its meaning. Rhythm can be regular (with a predictable pattern or meter) or irregular, as in free verse.

See also Meter.

Rising action The part of a plot that adds complications to the problems in the story and increases reader interest.

See also Falling action, Plot.

S

Scene A subdivision of an act in a play. Each scene takes place in a specific setting and time. An act may have one or more scenes.

See also Act.

Science fiction Fiction dealing with the impact of real science or imaginary superscience on human or alien societies of the past, present, or future. Although science fiction is mainly a product of the twentieth century, nineteenth-century authors such as Mary Shelley, Jules Verne, and Robert Louis Stevenson were pioneers of the genre.

Screenplay The script of a film, usually containing detailed instructions about camera shots and angles in addition to dialogue and stage directions. A screenplay for an original television show is called a teleplay.

See also Drama.

Sensory imagery Language that appeals to a reader's five senses: hearing, sight, touch, taste, and smell.

See also Visual imagery.

Sequence of events The order in which the events in a story take place.

Setting The time and place in which the events of a short story, novel, novella, or play occur. The setting often helps create the atmosphere or mood of the story.

Short story A brief fictional narrative in prose. Elements of the short story include **plot, character, setting, point of view, theme,** and sometimes symbol and irony.

Simile A figure of speech using *like* or *as* to compare seemingly unlike things.

Sonnet A poem containing fourteen lines, usually written in iambic pentameter. Sonnets have strict patterns of rhyme and usually deal with a single theme, idea, or sentiment.

Sound devices Techniques used to create a sense of rhythm or to emphasize particular sounds in writing. For example, sound can be controlled through the use of **onomatopoeia, alliteration, consonance, assonance,** and **rhyme.**

See also Rhythm.

Speaker The voice of a poem—sometimes that of the poet, sometimes that of a fictional person or even a thing. The speaker's words communicate a particular tone or attitude toward the subject of the poem.

Stage directions Instructions written by the dramatist to describe the appearance and actions of characters, as well as sets, costumes, and lighting.

Stanza A group of lines forming a unit in a poem. Stanzas are, in effect, the paragraphs of a poem.

Stereotype A character who is not developed as an individual but as a collection of traits and mannerisms supposedly shared by all members of a group.

Style The author's choice and arrangement of words and sentences in a literary work. Style can reveal an author's purpose in writing and attitude toward his or her subject and audience.

Suspense A feeling of curiosity, uncertainty, or even dread about what is going to happen next. Writers increase the level of suspense in a story by giving readers clues to what may happen.

See also Foreshadowing, Rising action.

Symbol Any object, person, place, or experience that means more than what it is. **Symbolism** is the use of images to represent internal realities.

T

Tall tale A wildly imaginative story, usually passed down orally, about the fantastic adventures or amazing feats of folk heroes in realistic settings.

See also Folklore, Oral tradition.

Teleplay A play written or adapted for television.

Theme The main idea of a story, poem, novel, or play, usually expressed as a general statement. Some works have a **stated theme,** which is expressed directly. More frequently works have an **implied theme,** which is revealed gradually through other elements such as plot, character, setting, point of view, symbol, and irony.

Third-person narrative. *See* Point of view.

Title The name of a literary work.

Tone The attitude of the narrator toward the subject, ideas, theme, or characters. A factual article would most likely have an objective tone, while an editorial on the same topic could be argumentative or satiric.

Tragedy A play in which the main character suffers a downfall. That character often is a person of dignified or heroic stature. The downfall may result from outside forces or from a weakness within the character, which is known as a tragic flaw.

V

Visual imagery Details that appeal to the sense of sight.

Voice An author's distinctive style or the particular speech patterns of a character in a story.

See also Style, Tone.

Reading and Thinking with Foldables®

by Dinah Zike, M.Ed., Creator of Foldables®

As you read the selections in each unit, the following Foldables will help you keep track of your ideas about the Big Questions. Follow these directions to make your Foldable, and then use the directions on the Unit opener for labeling your unit Foldable.

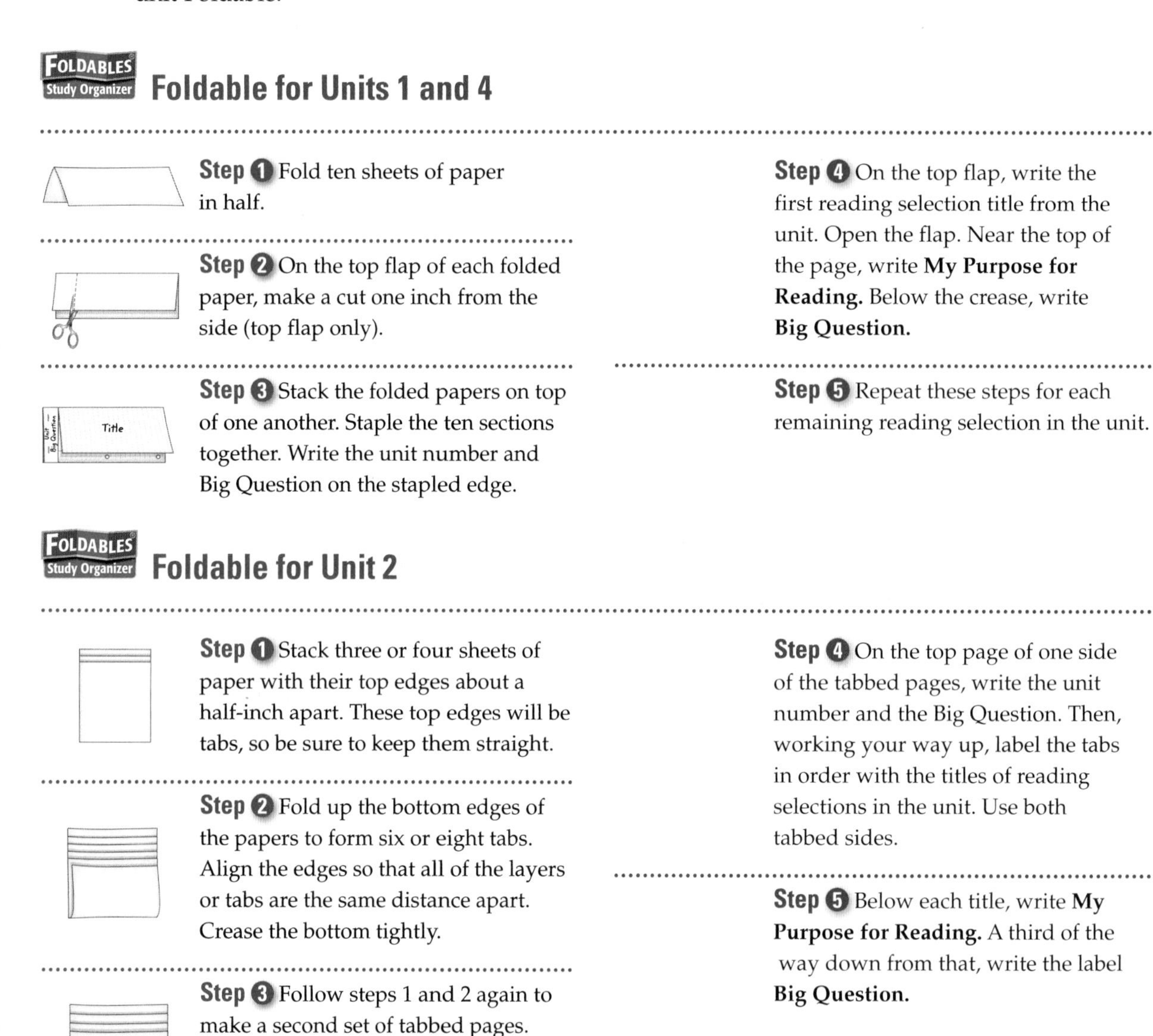

Foldable for Units 1 and 4

Step 1 Fold ten sheets of paper in half.

Step 2 On the top flap of each folded paper, make a cut one inch from the side (top flap only).

Step 3 Stack the folded papers on top of one another. Staple the ten sections together. Write the unit number and Big Question on the stapled edge.

Step 4 On the top flap, write the first reading selection title from the unit. Open the flap. Near the top of the page, write **My Purpose for Reading.** Below the crease, write **Big Question.**

Step 5 Repeat these steps for each remaining reading selection in the unit.

Foldable for Unit 2

Step 1 Stack three or four sheets of paper with their top edges about a half-inch apart. These top edges will be tabs, so be sure to keep them straight.

Step 2 Fold up the bottom edges of the papers to form six or eight tabs. Align the edges so that all of the layers or tabs are the same distance apart. Crease the bottom tightly.

Step 3 Follow steps 1 and 2 again to make a second set of tabbed pages. Then place the two sets of tabbed pages back-to-back and staple them together at the bottom.

Step 4 On the top page of one side of the tabbed pages, write the unit number and the Big Question. Then, working your way up, label the tabs in order with the titles of reading selections in the unit. Use both tabbed sides.

Step 5 Below each title, write **My Purpose for Reading.** A third of the way down from that, write the label **Big Question.**

Foldable for Units 3 and 6

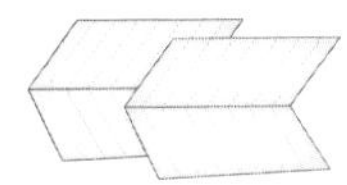

Step 1 Fold six sheets of paper in half and cut the sheets in half along the fold line.

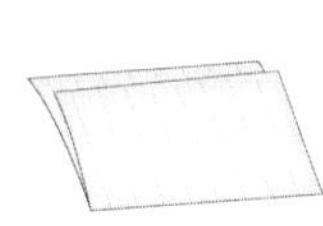

Step 2 Fold each section of paper in half, but fold one side one-half inch shorter than the other side. This will form a tab that is one-half inch long.

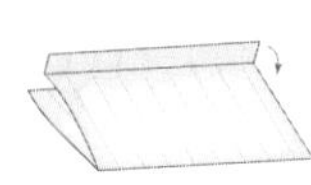

Step 3 Fold each tab over the shorter side and then fold it back the opposite way.

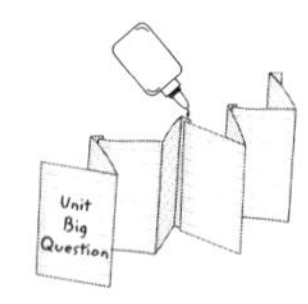

Step 4 Glue the straight edge of one section into the tab valley of another section. Glue all the sections together to form an accordion.

Step 5 On the front cover, write the unit number and the Big Question. Turn the page. Across the top, write a reading selection title. To the left of the crease, write **My Purpose for Reading.** To the right of the crease, write **Big Question.** Repeat until you have all the titles from the unit in your Foldable.

Foldable for Unit 5

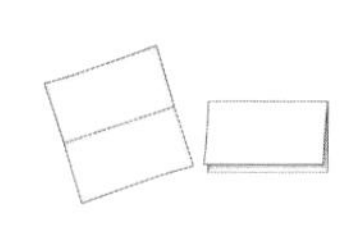

Step 1 Fold a sheet of paper in half so that one side is one inch longer than the other side. Fold the one-inch tab over the short side to form a fold. On the fold, write the Big Question for that unit.

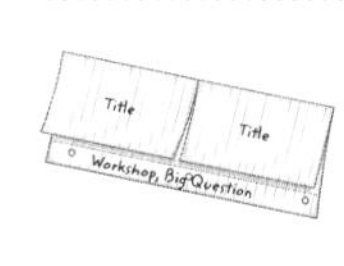

Step 2 Cut the front flap in half toward the top crease to create two flaps. Write the title of a reading selection on each flap.

Step 3 Open the flaps. At the top of each flap, write **My Purpose for Reading.** Below each crease, write **Big Question.**

Step 4 Repeat these steps for each remaining reading selection.

Functional Documents

Business Letter

In the business world, in school, and even at home, there are many standard types of documents that serve specific functions. Understanding these forms of writing will help you to be a better communicator in your everyday life.

The following business letter uses modified block style.

❶ 10 Pullman Lane
Cromwell, CT 06416
January 16, 2009

❷ Mr. Philip Fornaro
Principal
Cromwell School
179 West Maple St.
Cromwell, CT 06416

❸ Dear Mr. Fornaro:

❹ My friends and I in the seventh grade at Brimmer Middle School feel that there is not enough to do in Cromwell during the winter vacation week. Some students can afford to go away for vacation. Many families, however, cannot afford to go away, or the parents have to work.

❺ I would like to suggest that you keep the Brimmer Middle School gym open during the vacation week. If the gym were open, the basketball teams could practice. The fencing club could meet. We could meet our friends there instead of going to the mall.

❻ Thanks for listening to my request. I hope you will think it over.

❼ Sincerely,
Kim Goodwin
Kim Goodwin

❶ In the heading, write your address and the date on separate lines.

❷ In the inside address, write the name and address of the person to whom you are sending the letter.

❸ Use a colon after the greeting.

❹ In your introduction, say who you are and why you are writing.

❺ In the body of your letter, provide details concerning your request.

❻ Conclude by restating your purpose and thanking the person you are writing to.

❼ In the closing, use *Sincerely, Sincerely yours,* or *Yours truly* followed by a comma. Include both your signature and your printed or typed name.

Job Application

When applying for a job, you usually need to fill out a job application. Always read the form carefully before beginning to fill it out. Write neatly and fill out the form completely, providing all information directly and honestly. If a question does not apply to you, indicate that by writing *n/a*, short for "not applicable." Keep in mind that you will have the opportunity to provide additional information in your résumé, in your letter of application, or during the interview process.

Please type or print neatly in blue or black ink.

Name: ______________________ **Today's date:** _____________

Address: ____

Phone #: _______ **Birth date:** ____ **Sex:** ___ **Soc. Sec. #:** _________

****

Job History (List each job held, starting with the most recent job.)

1. Employer: __________________________ Phone #: _________

Dates of employment: ______________________________

Position held: _____________________________________

Duties: ____

2. Employer: __________________________ Phone #: _________

Dates of employment: ______________________________

Position held: _____________________________________

Duties: ____

****

Education (List the most recent level of education completed.)

____

****

Personal References:

1. Name: ____________________________ Phone #: _________

Relationship: ______________________________________

2. Name: ____________________________ Phone #: _________

Relationship: ______________________________________

1. The application provides specific instructions.
2. All of the information requested should be provided in its entirety.
3. The information should be provided neatly and succinctly.
4. Experience should be stated accurately and without embellishment.

Activity

Pick up a job application from a local business or use a copy of the sample application above. Complete the application thoroughly. Fill out the application as if you were actually applying for the job. Be sure to pay close attention to the guidelines mentioned above.

Writing a Memo

A memo, or memorandum, is a brief, efficient way of communicating information to another person or group of people. It begins with a header that provides basic information. A memo does not have a formal closing.

TO: *Brimmer Banner* newspaper staff
FROM: Paul Francis
SUBJECT: Winter issue
DATE: January 18, 2009

Articles for the winter issue of the *Brimmer Banner* are due by February 1. Please see Terry about your assignment as soon as possible! The following articles or features have not yet been assigned:

Cafeteria Mess: Who Is Responsible?
Teacher Profile: Mr. Jinks, Ms. Magee
Sports roundup

Using Electronic Business Correspondence

Imagine that you ordered a game through a company's Web site. When you tried playing the game, you found that it didn't work well. You could send a letter to the company you bought the game from explaining your problem. But it's easier and faster to send an e-mail. Any business that operates on the Internet has a way for customers to reach them—either a hyperlink "button" that will take you to Customer Service, or an e-mail address such as *service@gamecorp.com.*

Here are a few hints for effective business e-mails.

- Your e-mail window includes an area for the subject of your message. Think carefully and make your subject as clear and concise as possible. In a business e-mail, you'll want your recipient to know right away your purpose for writing.
- Reread your message carefully before hitting the Send button. Check your grammar and spelling. Then double-check your spelling by using the spell-checker program on your computer.
- Your e-mail program probably offers options for how to send a message—for example: plain text, rich text, or HTML. If your letter contains some formatting (such as italics or boldface) or special characters (such as a cursive typeface that looks like handwriting), choose rich text or HTML to avoid losing your formatting.

Technical Writing

Technical writing involves the use of very specific vocabulary and a special attention to detail. The purpose of technical writing is to describe a process clearly enough so that the reader can perform the steps and reach the intended goal, such as installing software, connecting a piece of equipment, or programming a device.

Instructions for Connecting DVD Player to HDTV

Your DVD player can be connected to an HDTV using RCA cables or, if available, an HDMI cable.

Connecting with RCA Cables

Step 1: Insert the ends of the red, white, and yellow cables into the jacks labeled "AUDIO/VIDEO OUT." ❶ Be sure to match the color of the cable with the color of the jack.

❷ **Step 2:** Insert the other ends of the RCA cables into the jacks labeled "AUDIO/VIDEO IN" on your HDTV. These are usually located on the side or the back of the television. Again, be sure to match the colors of the cables with the colors of the jacks.

Connecting with HDMI Cable

Step 1: Insert one end of the HDMI cable into the HDMI port located on the back of the DVD player.

Step 2: Insert the other end of the HDMI cable into the HDMI port on your HDTV.

❸ **Note:** Your television may have more than one HDMI port. If so, be sure that you set your television to the correct input when viewing.

❶ Uses specific language to describe the process clearly

❷ Lists each step individually

❸ Brings attention to possible variations the reader may encounter

Activity

Choose a device that you own or have access to, such as an mp3 player or a cell phone. Write brief step-by-step directions on how to perform a specific function on the device, so that someone else can follow your instructions and perform the function successfully.

Research Report Writing

When you write a research report, you explore a topic by gathering factual information from several different resources. Through your research, you develop a point of view or draw a conclusion. This point of view or conclusion becomes the main idea, or thesis, of your report.

Select a Topic

Because a research report usually takes time to prepare and write, your choice of topic is especially important. Follow these guidelines.

- Brainstorm a list of questions about a subject you would like to explore. Choose one that is neither too narrow nor too broad for the length of paper you will write. Use that question as your topic.
- Select a topic that genuinely interests you.
- Be sure you can find information on your topic from several different sources.

Do Research

Start by looking up your topic in an encyclopedia to find general information. Then find specific information in books, magazines, and newspapers, on CD-ROMs and the Internet, and from personal interviews when this seems appropriate. Use the computerized or card catalog in the library to locate books on your topic. Then search for up-to-date information in periodicals (magazines) or newspapers and from electronic sources, such as CD-ROMs or the Internet. If you need help in finding or using any of these resources, ask the librarian.

As you gather information, make sure each source you use relates closely to your topic. Also be sure that your source is reliable. Be extra careful if you are using information from the Internet. If you are not sure about the reliability of a source, consult the librarian or your teacher.

Internet Research

In order to conduct research on the Internet, you will need to use a search engine, a tool that allows you to use keywords to find information on the World Wide Web. There are many different search engines on the Internet, but most of them operate similarly.

First, open a search engine. Somewhere near the top you'll find a white box that you can type into. Next to it will be a button that in most search engines says "Search." Try searching for Web sites about protecting animals in the wild. For keywords, try: "endangered wildlife." The quotation marks tell the search engine to look for the whole phrase rather than for each word by itself. Click on the Search button and the engine will provide you with a list of sites that include the phrase "endangered wildlife." Visit a few of these sites by clicking on the underlined titles.

As you conduct your Internet search, you may want to narrow your search to something more specific, such as "wildlife preserves." Try different keywords to come up with additional sites dealing with your topic. Most search engines also have an advanced search feature, which allows you be even more specific about your search.

Since there is such a huge amount of information on the Internet, you will have to visit many sites and evaluate which ones have the information you need, based on relevance and appropriateness.

Exercise:

Conduct an Internet search using the word "cooking" as a keyword. How many sites do you find? Now do a search to find a recipe for your favorite dessert. Think of exact phrases you could place in quotes to narrow your search.

Make Source Cards

In a research report, you must document the source of your information. To keep track of your sources, write the author, title, publication information, and location of each source on a separate index card. Give each source card a number and write it in the upper right-hand corner. These cards will be useful for preparing a bibliography.

Sample Source Card

❶ Douglas, Marjory Stoneman ❷ 15
❸ **Everglades: River of Grass.**
❹ **Marietta, Georgia: Mockingbird Books, 1986.** ❺

❻ Carrollton Public Library ❼ 654.3 S2

❶ Author
❷ Source number
❸ Title
❹ City of publication/ Publisher
❺ Date of publication
❻ Location of source
❼ Library call number

Take Notes

As you read, you encounter many new facts and ideas. Taking notes will help you keep track of information and focus on the topic. Here are some helpful suggestions:

- Use a new card for each important piece of information. Separate cards will help you to organize your notes.
- At the top of each card, write a key word or phrase that tells you about the information. Also, write the number of the source you used.
- Write only details and ideas that relate to your topic.
- Summarize information in your own words.
- Write down a phrase or a quote only when the words are especially interesting or come from an important source. Enclose all quotes in quotation marks to make clear that the ideas belong to someone else.

This sample note card shows information to include.

Sample Note Card

❶ **Functions of Wetlands** ❷ 15
Besides furnishing a home for a variety of wildlife, the wet, spongy soil of wetlands maintains the level of the water table.
p. 79 ❸

❶ Write a key word or phrase that tells you what the information is about.

❷ Write the source number from your source card.

❸ Write the number of the page or pages on which you found the information.

Develop Your Thesis

As you begin researching and learning about your topic, think about the overall point you want to make. Write one sentence, your *thesis statement*, that says exactly what you plan to report on.

Sample Thesis Statement

Everglades National Park is a beautiful but endangered animal habitat.

Keep your thesis in mind as you continue to do research and think about your topic. The thesis will help you determine what information is important. However, be prepared to change your thesis if the information you find does not support it.

Write an Outline

When you finish taking notes, organize the information in an outline. Write down the main ideas that you want to cover. Write your thesis statement at the beginning of your outline. Then list the supporting details. Follow an outline form like the one below.

❶ Everglades National Park is a beautiful but endangered animal habitat.

- I. Special aspects of the Everglades
  - A. Characteristics of wetlands ❷
  - B. Endangered birds and other animals
- II. Pressures on the Everglades
  - A. Florida agriculture
  - B. Carelessness of visitors
- III. How to protect the Everglades
  - A. Change agricultural practices
  - B. Educate park visitors
    - 1. Mandatory video on safety for individuals and environment ❸
    - 2. Instructional reminders posted throughout the park

❶ The thesis statement identifies your topic and the overall point you will make.

❷ If you have subtopics under a main topic, there must be at least two. They must relate directly to your main topic.

❸ If you wish to divide a subtopic, you must have at least two divisions. Each must relate to the subtopic above it.

Document Your Information

You must document, or credit, the sources of all the information you use in your report. There are two common ways to document information.

Avoiding Plagiarism

Plagiarism is the act of presenting an author's words or ideas as if they were your own. This is not only illegal, it is also unethical. You must credit the source not only for material directly quoted but also for any facts or ideas obtained from the source. See the Media Workshops on Media Ethics (p. 683) for more information.

Footnotes

To document with footnotes, place a number at the end of the information you are documenting. Number your notes consecutively, beginning with number 1. These numbers should be slightly raised and should come after any punctuation. The documentation information itself goes at the bottom of the page, with a matching number.

In-text number for note:

The Declaration of Independence was read in public for the first time on July 6, 1776.[3]

Footnote at bottom of page:

[3] John Smith, <u>The Declaration of Independence</u> (New York: DI, 2001) 221.

Parenthetical Documentation

In this method, you give the source for your information in parentheses at the end of the sentence where the information appears. You do not need to give all the details of the source. Just provide enough information for your readers to identify it. Here are the basic rules to follow.

- Usually it is enough to give the author's last name and the number of the page where you found the information.

  The declaration was first read in public by militia colonel John Nixon (Smith 222).

- If you mention the author's name in the sentence, you do not need to repeat it in the parentheses.

  According to Smith, the reading was greeted with wild applause (224).

- If your source does not identify a particular author, as in a newspaper or encyclopedia article, give the first word or two of the title of the piece.

The anniversary of the reading was commemorated by a parade and fireworks ("Reading Celebrated").

Full information on your sources goes in a list at the end of your paper.

Bibliography or Works Cited

At the end of your paper, list all the sources of information that you used in preparing your report. Arrange them alphabetically by the author's last name (or by the first word in the title if no author is mentioned) as shown below. Title this list *Works Cited.* (Use the term *bibliography* if all your sources are printed media, such as books, magazines, or newspapers.)

Works Cited ❶

❷ Bertram, Jeffrey. "African Bees: Fact or Myth?" *Orlando Sentinel* 18 Aug. 1999: D2.

❸ Gore, Rick. "Neanderthals." National Geographic. January 1996: 2–35. ❽

❹ Gould, Stephen J. The Panda's Thumb. New York: W. W. Norton & Co., 1982.

❺ "Governor Chiles Vetoes Anti-Everglades ❾ Bills–5/13/98." Friends of the Everglades. May 1998. 26 Aug 1998 <http://www. everglades.org/pressrel_may28.htm>.

❻ "Neanderthal man." The Columbia Encyclopedia. 5th Edition. New York: Columbia University Press, 1993.

❼ Pabst, Laura (Curator of Natural History Museum), Interview. March 11, 1998.

❶ Indent all but the first line of each item.

❷ Newspaper article

❸ Magazine article

❹ Book with one author

❺ On-line article

❻ Encyclopedia

❼ Interview

❽ Include page numbers for a magazine article but not for a book, unless the book is a collection of essays by different authors.

❾ Include database (underlined), publication medium (online), computer service, and date of access.

Presenting

For readers to fully appreciate your writing, it is very important that you present it neatly, effectively, and according to the needs of your audience and the purpose of your writing. The following standard is how you should format most of your formal school papers.

Formatting your text

- The standard typeface setting for most school papers is Courier 12 point.
- Double-space your work so that it is easy to read.
- Leave one-inch margins on all sides of every page.
- Include the page number in the upper right-hand corner of each page.
- If you are including charts, graphs, maps, or other visual aids, consider setting them on their own page. This will allow you to show the graphic at a full size that is easy to read.

Exercise:

Look in the library or on the Internet to find style guides for various types of writing, such as short stories or magazine articles. Assess which format is right for your piece of writing and apply it.

Using a Computer for Writing

Using Word Processing Software

A word processor is a digital tool that lets you move your words and ideas around until you find the best way to present them. Each type of word processing software is a bit different, but they all help you plan, draft, revise, edit, and present properly formatted documents.

Menus, Toolbars, and Rulers

Open a word processing document. At the top of your screen, locate the menu bar, one or more toolbars, and a ruler.

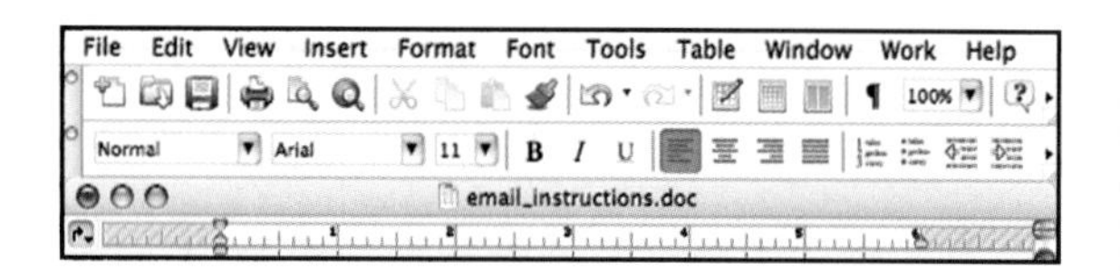

Menu Bar Menus help you perform important processes. The Edit menu, for example, allows you to copy, paste, and find text within your document.

Toolbars There are two basic types of tools. **Function tools** perform some kind of computer function, like printing a document or checking its spelling. **Formatting tools** are used to change the way a document looks—for example, changing its font (typeface) or paragraph style.

Ruler The ruler looks like a measuring stick with little markers at each end. These markers control the margins of your document. Try changing the margins on your document. You can also put tabs on the ruler so that you can use the tab key on your keyboard to send your cursor to those positions.

Exercise:

Use the menu, toolbars, and ruler to properly format your document according to the guidelines on p. R17.

Multimedia Presentations

You can use digital technology, such as a computer with presentation software, to create a multimedia presentation of your work. Adding pictures, video, and sound to your presentation can attract and hold your audience's attention. However, it is important that you understand the rules and laws about using other people's creations in your work. See the Media Workshops on Media Ethics (p. 683) for more information.

Slides

In a multimedia presentation, each screen a viewer sees is called a slide. Generally, a slide consists of text—not too much of it—and an image of some kind. Each slide should be limited to a single idea with a few supporting details. Because you want to get your point across quickly, it's important that you choose your images and words carefully. An Internet search engine can help you find downloadable images to use in your presentation. Most computer images have the file extension "gif" or "jpeg."

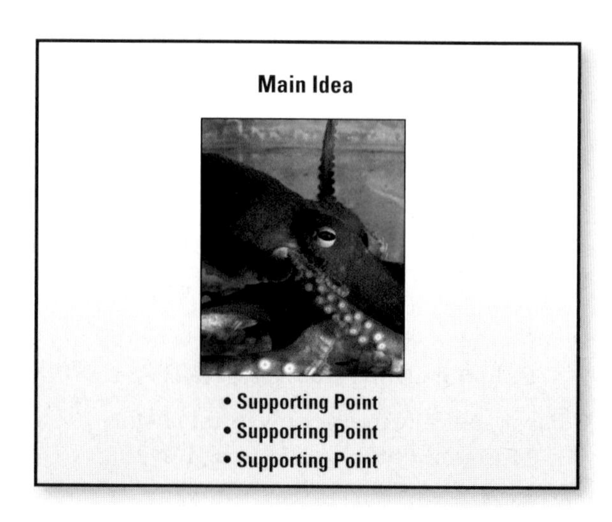

Video

For some types of presentations, adding video can have a big impact. For example, if you're presenting a report on an actor, what better way to illustrate his or her style than with movie clips? You can record video clips from your TV or downloaded them from the Internet. Most movie files have the extensions "avi," "mov," or "mpeg."

You can add your images and video clips to your presentation using the Insert menu in your presentation software. Also, most presentation software has a "wizard" or templates that will help you put together your multimedia presentation.

Exercise:

Working with a partner, choose a movie or television show as the basis for a complete multimedia presentation. Include in your presentation at least six slides with pictures and text and two video clips. Don't forget about media ethics, and be careful not to plagiarize as you choose media for your presentation.

Databases

An electronic database is a software program that allows you to organize, store, and retrieve information. Data is organized into a table of columns and rows. Each single piece of information is called a field.

Once the information is in your database, you can recall it in a number of useful ways. For example, you can arrange an address-book database to show you all the names of people who live in a certain city or zip code.

Exercise:

Create a database of your research materials for a current or upcoming report. Enter fields for authors, titles, types of media, and keywords of what useful information was found in each. Practice organizing the database in different ways. For example, organize your database to show how many magazine articles you used in your research.

Field Columns (Categories)

Record

Name	Address	City	State	Zip
Brown, Katie	12814 South Emerald	Chicago	IL	60601
Hauser, Sam	63 Taylor	Stamford	CT	06904
Marmalard, Greg	1001 Porterhouse	Laredo	TX	78040
O'Hare, Megan	140 Blossom	Shaker Heights	OH	44118
Trumbull, Ellen	302 St. Nicolas	Darien	CT	06820

Field

Language Handbook

Grammar Glossary

This glossary will help you quickly locate information on parts of speech and sentence structure.

A

Absolute phrase. *See* Phrase.

Abstract noun. *See* Noun chart.

Action verb. *See* Verb.

Active voice. *See* Voice.

Adjective A word that modifies a noun or pronoun by limiting its meaning. Adjectives appear in various positions in a sentence. **(The gray cat purred. The cat is gray.)**

Many adjectives have different forms to indicate degree of comparison. **(short, shorter, shortest)**

The positive degree is the simple form of the adjective. **(easy, interesting, good)**

The comparative degree compares two persons, places, things, or ideas. **(easier, more interesting, better)**

The superlative degree compares more than two persons, places, things, or ideas. **(easiest, most interesting, best)**

A predicate adjective follows a linking verb and further identifies or describes the subject. **(The child is happy.)**

A proper adjective is formed from a proper noun and begins with a capital letter. Many proper adjectives are created by adding these suffixes: -an, -ian, -n, -ese, and -ish. **(Chinese, African)**

Adjective clause. *See* Clause chart.

Adverb A word that modifies a verb, an adjective, or another adverb by making its meaning more specific. When modifying a verb, an adverb may appear in various positions in a sentence. **(Cats generally eat less than dogs. Generally, cats eat less than dogs.)** When modifying an adjective or another adverb, an adverb appears directly before the modified word. **(I was quite pleased that they got along so well.)** The word not and the contraction -n't are adverbs. **(Mike wasn't ready for the test today.)** Certain adverbs of time, place, and degree also have a negative meaning. **(He's never ready.)**

Some adverbs have different forms to indicate degree of comparison. **(soon, sooner, soonest)**

The comparative degree compares two actions. **(better, more quickly)**

The superlative degree compares three or more actions. **(fastest, most patiently, least rapidly)**

Adverb clause. *See* Clause chart.

Antecedent. *See* Pronoun.

Appositive A noun or a pronoun that further identifies another noun or pronoun. **(My friend Julie lives next door.)**

Appositive phrase. *See* Phrase.

Article The adjective a, an, or the.

Indefinite articles **(a and an)** refer to one of a general group of persons, places, or things. **(I eat an apple a day.)**

The definite article **(the)** indicates that the noun is a specific person, place, or thing. **(The alarm woke me up.)**

Auxiliary verb. *See* Verb.

B

Base form. *See* Verb tense.

C

Clause A group of words that has a subject and a predicate and that is used as a sentence or part of a sentence. Clauses fall into two categories: main clauses, which are also called independent clauses, and subordinate clauses, which are also called dependent clauses.

Types of Subordinate Clauses			
Clause	**Function**	**Example**	**Begins with . . .**
Adjective clause	Modifies a noun or pronoun	Songs that have a strong beat make me want to dance.	A relative pronoun such as *which, who, whom, whose,* or *that*
Adverb clause	Modifies a verb, an adjective, or an adverb	Whenever Al calls me, he asks to borrow my bike.	A subordinating conjunction such as *after, although, because, if, since, when,* or *where*
Noun clause	Serves as a subject, an object, or a predicate nominative	What Philip did surprised us.	Words such as *how, that, what, whatever, when, where, which, who, whom, whoever, whose,* or *why*

A main clause can stand alone as a sentence. There must be at least one main clause in every sentence. **(The rooster crowed, and the dog barked.)**

A subordinate clause cannot stand alone as a sentence. A subordinate clause needs a main clause to complete its meaning. Many subordinate clauses begin with subordinating conjunctions or relative pronouns. **(When Geri sang her solo, the audience became quiet.)** The chart on this page shows the main types of subordinate clauses.

Collective noun. *See* Noun chart.

Common noun. *See* Noun chart.

Comparative degree. *See* Adjective; Adverb.

Complement A word or phrase that completes the meaning of a verb. The four basic kinds of complements are direct objects, indirect objects, object complements, and subject complements.

A direct object answers the question What? or Whom? after an action verb. **(Kari found a dollar. Larry saw Denise.)**

An indirect object answers the question *to whom, for whom, to what,* or *for what* after an action verb. **(Do me a favor. She gave the child a toy.)**

An object complement answers the question *what* after a direct object. An object complement is a noun, a pronoun, or an adjective that completes the meaning of a direct object by identifying or describing it. **(The director made me the understudy for the role. The little girl called the puppy hers.)**

A subject complement follows a subject and a linking verb. It identifies or describes a subject. The two kinds of subject complements are predicate nominatives and predicate adjectives.

A predicate nominative is a noun or pronoun that follows a linking verb and tells more about the subject. **(The author of "The Raven" is Edgar Allan Poe.)**

A predicate adjective is an adjective that follows a linking verb and gives more information about the subject. **(Ian became angry at the bully.)**

Complex sentence. *See* Sentence.

Compound preposition. *See* Preposition.

Compound sentence. *See* Sentence.

Compound-complex sentence. *See* Sentence.

Conjunction A word that joins single words or groups of words.

A coordinating conjunction **(and, but, or, nor, for, yet, so)** joins words or groups of words that are equal in grammatical importance. **(David and Ruth are twins. I was bored, so I left.)**

Correlative conjunctions **(both . . . and, just as . . . so, not only . . . but also, either . . . or, neither . . . nor, whether . . . or)** work in pairs to join words and groups of words of equal importance. **(Choose either the muffin or the bagel.)**

A subordinating conjunction **(after, although, as if, because, before, if, since, so that, than, though, until, when, while)** joins a dependent idea or clause to a main clause. **(Beth acted as if she felt ill.)**

Conjunctive adverb An adverb used to clarify the relationship between clauses of equal weight in a sentence. Conjunctive adverbs are used to replace and **(also, besides, furthermore, moreover)**; to replace but **(however, nevertheless, still)**; to state a result **(consequently, therefore, so, thus)**; or to state equality **(equally, likewise, similarly)**. **(Ana was determined to get an A; therefore, she studied often.)**

Coordinating conjunction. *See* Conjunction.

Correlative conjunction. *See* Conjunction.

D

Declarative sentence. *See* Sentence.

Definite article. *See* Article.

Demonstrative pronoun. *See* Pronoun.

Direct object. *See* Complement.

E

Emphatic form. *See* Verb tense.

F

Future tense. *See* Verb tense.

G

Gerund A verb form that ends in -ing and is used as a noun. A gerund may function as a subject, the object of a verb, or the object of a preposition. **(Smiling uses fewer muscles than frowning. Marie enjoys walking.)**

Gerund phrase. *See* Phrase.

I

Imperative mood. *See* Mood of verb.

Imperative sentence. *See* Sentence chart.

Indicative mood. *See* Mood of verb.

Indirect object. *See* Complement.

Infinitive A verb form that begins with the word to and functions as a noun, an adjective, or an adverb. **(No one wanted to answer.)** Note: When to precedes a verb, it is not a preposition but instead signals an infinitive.

Infinitive phrase. *See* Phrase.

Intensive pronoun. *See* Pronoun.

Interjection A word or phrase that expresses emotion or exclamation. An interjection has no grammatical connection to other words. Commas follow mild ones; exclamation points follow stronger ones. **(Well, have a good day. Wow!)**

Interrogative pronoun. *See* Pronoun.

Intransitive verb. *See* Verb.

Inverted order In a sentence written in inverted order, the predicate comes before the subject. Some sentences are written in inverted order for variety or special emphasis. **(Up the beanstalk scampered Jack.)** The subject also generally follows the predicate in a sentence that begins with here or there. **(Here was the solution to his problem.)** Questions, or interrogative sentences, are generally written in inverted order. In many questions, an auxiliary verb precedes the subject, and the main verb follows it. **(Has anyone seen Susan?)** Questions that begin with who or what follow normal word order.

Irregular verb. *See* Verb tense.

L

Linking verb. *See* Verb.

M

Main clause. *See* Clause.

Mood of verb A verb expresses one of three moods: indicative, imperative, or subjunctive.

The indicative mood is the most common. It makes a statement or asks a question. **(We are out of bread. Will you buy it?)**

The imperative mood expresses a command or makes a request. **(Stop acting like a child! Please return my sweater.)**

The subjunctive mood is used to express, indirectly, a demand, suggestion, or statement of necessity **(I demand that he stop acting like a child. It's necessary that she buy more bread.)** The subjunctive is also used to state a condition or wish that is contrary to fact. This use of the subjunctive requires the past tense. **(If you were a nice person, you would return my sweater.)**

N

Nominative pronoun. *See* Pronoun.

Noun A word that names a person, a place, a thing, or an idea. The chart on this page shows the main types of nouns.

Noun clause. *See* Clause chart.

Noun of direct address. *See* Noun chart.

Number A noun, pronoun, or verb is singular in number if it refers to one; plural if it refers to more than one.

O

Object. *See* Complement.

P

Participle A verb form that can function as an adjective. Present participles always end in -ing. **(The woman comforted the crying child.)** Many past participles end in -ed. **(We bought the beautifully painted chair.)** However, irregular verbs form their past participles in some other way. **(Cato was Caesar's sworn enemy.)**

Passive voice. *See* Voice.

Past tense. *See* Verb tense.

Perfect tense. *See* Verb tense.

Personal pronoun. *See* Pronoun, Pronoun chart.

Types of Nouns

Noun	Function	Example
Abstract noun	Names an idea, a quality, or a state	independence, energy
Collective noun	Names a group of things or persons	herd, troop, crowd, class
Common noun	Names a general type of person, place, thing, or idea	musician, city, building
Compound noun	Is made up of two or more words	checkerboard, parking lot, mother-in-law
Noun of direct address	Identifies the person or persons being spoken to	Maria, please stand.
Possessive noun	Shows possession, ownership, or the relationship between two nouns	my friend's room, my friend's brother
Proper noun	Names a particular person, place, thing, or idea	Cleopatra, Italy, Christianity

Phrase A group of words that acts in a sentence as a single part of speech.

An absolute phrase consists of a noun or pronoun that is modified by a participle or participial phrase but has no grammatical relation to the complete subject or predicate. **(The vegetables being done, we finally sat down to eat dinner.)**

An appositive phrase is an appositive along with any modifiers. If not essential to the meaning of the sentence, an appositive phrase is set off by commas. **(Jack plans to go to the jazz concert, an important musical event.)**

A gerund phrase includes a gerund plus its complements and modifiers. **(Playing the flute is her hobby.)**

An infinitive phrase contains the infinitive plus its complements and modifiers. **(It is time to leave for school.)**

A participial phrase contains a participle and any modifiers necessary to complete its meaning. **(The woman sitting over there is my grandmother.)**

A prepositional phrase consists of a preposition, its object, and any modifiers of the object. A prepositional phrase can function as an adjective, modifying a noun or a pronoun. **(The dog in the yard is very gentle.)** A prepositional phrase may also function as an adverb when it modifies a verb, an adverb, or an adjective. **(The baby slept on my lap.)**

A verb phrase consists of one or more auxiliary verbs followed by a main verb. **(The job will have been completed by noon tomorrow.)**

Positive degree. *See* Adjective.

Possessive noun. *See* Noun chart.

Predicate The verb or verb phrase and any objects, complements, or modifiers that express the essential thought about the subject of a sentence.

A simple predicate is a verb or verb phrase that tells something about the subject. **(We ran.)**

A complete predicate includes the simple predicate and any words that modify or complete it. **(We solved the problem in a short time.)**

A compound predicate has two or more verbs or verb phrases that are joined by a conjunction and share the same subject. **(We ran to the park and began to play baseball.)**

Predicate adjective. *See* Adjective; Complement.

Predicate nominative. *See* Complement.

Preposition A word that shows the relationship of a noun or pronoun to some other word in the sentence. Prepositions include about, above, across, among, as, behind, below, beyond, but, by, down, during, except, for, from, into, like, near, of, on, outside, over, since, through, to, under, until, with. **(I usually eat breakfast before school.)**

A compound preposition is made up of more than one word. **(according to, ahead of, as to, because of, by means of, in addition to, in spite of, on account of) (We played the game in spite of the snow.)**

Prepositional phrase. *See* Phrase.

Present tense. *See* Verb tense.

Progressive form. *See* Verb tense.

Pronoun A word that takes the place of a noun, a group of words acting as a noun, or another pronoun. The word or group of words that a pronoun refers to is called its antecedent. **(In the following sentence, Mari is the antecedent of she. Mari likes Mexican food, but she doesn't like Italian food.)**

A demonstrative pronoun points out specific persons, places, things, or ideas. **(this, that, these, those)**

An indefinite pronoun refers to persons, places, or things in a more general way than a noun does. **(all, another, any, both, each, either, enough, everything, few, many, most, much, neither, nobody, none, one, other, others, plenty, several, some)**

An intensive pronoun adds emphasis to another noun or pronoun. If an intensive pronoun is omitted, the meaning of the sentence will be the same. **(Rebecca herself decided to look for a part-time job.)**

An interrogative pronoun is used to form questions. **(who? whom? whose? what? which?)**

A personal pronoun refers to a specific person or thing. Personal pronouns have three cases: nominative, possessive, and objective. The case depends upon the function of the pronoun in a sentence. The first chart on this page shows the case forms of personal pronouns.

A reflexive pronoun reflects back to a noun or pronoun used earlier in the sentence, indicating that the same person or thing is involved. **(We told ourselves to be patient.)**

A relative pronoun is used to begin a subordinate clause. **(who, whose, that, what, whom, whoever, whomever, whichever, whatever)**

Proper adjective. *See* Adjective.

Proper noun. *See* Noun chart.

R

Reflexive pronoun. *See* Pronoun.

Relative pronoun. *See* Pronoun.

S

Sentence A group of words expressing a complete thought. Every sentence has a subject and a predicate. Sentences can be classified by function or by structure. The second chart on this page shows the categories by function; the following subentries describe the categories by structure. See also Subject; Predicate; Clause.

Personal Pronouns

Case	Singular Pronouns	Plural Pronouns	Function in Sentence
Nominative	I, you, she, he, it	we, you, they	subject or predicate nominative
Objective	me, you, her, him, it	us, you, them	direct object, indirect object, or object of a preposition
Possessive	my, mine, your, yours, her, hers, his, its	our, ours, your, yours, their, theirs	replacement for the possessive form of a noun

Types of Sentences

Sentence Type	Function	Ends with . . .	Examples
Declarative sentence	Makes a statement	A period	I did not enjoy the movie.
Exclamatory sentence	Expresses strong emotion	An exclamation point	The books are already finished!
Imperative sentence	Expresses a request or a demand	A period or an exclamation point	Please come to the party. Stop!
Interrogative sentence	Asks a question	A question mark	Is the composition due today?

A simple sentence has only one main clause and no subordinate clauses. **(Alan found an old violin.)** A simple sentence may contain a compound subject or a compound predicate or both. **(Alan and Teri found an old violin. Alan found an old violin and tried to play it. Alan and Teri found an old violin and tried to play it.)** The subject and the predicate can be expanded with adjectives, adverbs, prepositional phrases, appositives, and verbal phrases. As long as the sentence has only one main clause, however, it remains a simple sentence. **(Alan, rummaging in the attic, found an old violin.)**

A compound sentence has two or more main clauses. Each main clause has its own subject and predicate, and these main clauses are usually joined by a comma and a coordinating conjunction. **(Cats meow, and dogs bark, but ducks quack.)** Semicolons may also be used to join the main clauses in a compound sentence. **(The helicopter landed; the pilot had saved four passengers.)**

A complex sentence has one main clause and one or more subordinate clauses. **(Since the movie starts at eight, we should leave here by seven-thirty.)**

A compound-complex sentence has two or more main clauses and at least one subordinate clause. **(If we leave any later, we may miss the previews, and I want to see them.)**

Simple predicate. *See* Predicate.

Simple subject. *See* Subject.

Subject The part of a sentence that tells what the sentence is about.

A simple subject is the main noun or pronoun in the subject. **(Babies crawl.)**

A complete subject includes the simple subject and any words that modify it. (The man from New Jersey won the race.) In some sentences, the simple subject and the complete subject are the same. **(Birds fly.)**

A compound subject has two or more simple subjects joined by a conjunction. The subjects share the same verb. **(Firefighters and police officers protect the community.)**

Subjunctive mood. *See* Mood of verb.

Subordinate clause. *See* Clause.

Subordinating conjunction. *See* Conjunction.

Superlative degree. *See* Adjective; Adverb.

T

Tense. *See* Verb tense.

Transitive verb. *See* Verb.

V

Verb A word that expresses action or a state of being. **(cooks, seem, laughed)**

An action verb tells what someone or something does. Action verbs can express either physical or mental action. **(Crystal decided to change the tire herself.)**

A transitive verb is an action verb that is followed by a word or words that answer the question What? or Whom? **(I held the baby.)**

An intransitive verb is an action verb that is not followed by a word that answers the question What? or Whom? **(The baby laughed.)**

A linking verb expresses a state of being by linking the subject of a sentence with a word or an expression that identifies or describes the subject. **(The lemonade tastes sweet. He is our new principal.)** The most commonly used linking verb is be in all its forms **(am, is, are, was, were, will be, been, being)**. Other linking verbs include appear, become, feel, grow, look, remain, seem, sound, smell, stay, taste.

An auxiliary verb, or helping verb, is a verb that accompanies the main verb to form a verb phrase. **(I have been swimming.)** The forms of be and have are the most common auxiliary verbs: **(am, is, are, was, were, being, been; has, have, had, having)**. Other auxiliaries include can, could, do, does, did, may, might, must, shall, should, will, would.

Verbal A verb form that functions in a sentence as a noun, an adjective, or an adverb. The three kinds of verbals are gerunds, infinitives, and participles. See Gerund; Infinitive; Participle.

Verb tense The tense of a verb indicates when the action or state of being occurs. All the verb tenses are formed from the four principal parts of a verb: a base form **(talk)**, a present participle **(talking)**, a simple past form **(talked)**, and a past participle **(talked)**. A regular verb forms its simple past and past participle by adding -ed to the base form. **(climb, climbed)** An irregular verb forms its past and past participle in some other way. **(get, got, gotten)**

In addition to present, past, and future tenses, there are three perfect tenses.

The present perfect tense expresses an action or condition that occurred at some indefinite time in the past. This tense also shows an action or condition that began in the past and continues into the present. **(She has played the piano for four years.)**

The past perfect tense indicates that one past action or condition began and ended before another past action started. **(Andy had finished his homework before I even began mine.)**

The future perfect tense indicates that one future action or condition will begin and end before another future event starts. Use will have or shall have with the past participle of a verb. **(By tomorrow, I will have finished my homework, too.)**

The progressive form of a verb expresses a continuing action with any of the six tenses. To make the progressive forms, use the appropriate tense of the verb be with the present participle of the main verb. **(She is swimming. She has been swimming.)**

The emphatic form adds special force, or emphasis, to the present and past tense of a verb. For the emphatic form, use do, does, or did with the base form. **(Toshi did want that camera.)**

Voice The voice of a verb shows whether the subject performs the action or receives the action of the verb.

A verb is in the active voice if the subject of the sentence performs the action. **(The referee blew the whistle.)**

A verb is in the passive voice if the subject of the sentence receives the action of the verb. **(The whistle was blown by the referee.)**

Troubleshooter

Use the Troubleshooter to recognize and correct common writing errors.

Sentence Fragment

A sentence fragment does not express a complete thought. It may lack a subject or verb or both.

Problem: Fragment that lacks a subject

The lion paced the floor of the cage. Looked hungry. frag

Solution: Add a subject to the fragment to make a complete sentence.

The lion paced the floor of the cage. He looked hungry.

Problem: Fragment that lacks a predicate

I'm painting my room. The walls yellow. frag

Solution: Add a predicate to make the sentence complete.

I'm painting my room. The walls are going to be yellow.

Problem: Fragment that lacks both a subject and a predicate

We walked around the reservoir. Near the parkway. frag

Solution: Combine the fragment with another sentence.

We walked around the reservoir near the parkway.

Tip: When subject and verb are separated by a prepositional phrase, check for agreement by reading the sentence without the prepositional phrase.

Run-on Sentence

A run-on sentence is two or more sentences written incorrectly as one sentence.

Problem: Two main clauses separated only by a comma

Roller coasters make me dizzy, I don't enjoy them. run-on

Solution A: Replace the comma with a period or other end mark. Start the second sentence with a capital letter.

Roller coasters make me dizzy. I don't enjoy them.

Solution B: Replace the comma with a semicolon.

Roller coasters make me dizzy; I don't enjoy them.

Problem: Two main clauses with no punctuation between them

Acid rain is a worldwide problem there are no solutions in sight. run-on

Solution A: Separate the main clauses with a period or other end mark. Begin the second sentence with a capital letter.

Acid rain is a worldwide problem. There are no solutions in sight.

Solution B: Add a comma and a coordinating conjunction between the main clauses.

Acid rain is a worldwide problem, but there are no solutions in sight.

Problem: Two main clauses with no comma before the coordinating conjunction

Our chorus has been practicing all month but we still need another rehearsal. run-on

Solution: Add a comma before the coordinating conjunction.

Our chorus has been practicing all month, but we still need another rehearsal.

Lack of Subject-Verb Agreement

A singular subject calls for a singular form of the verb. A plural subject calls for a plural form of the verb.

Problem: A subject that is separated from the verb by an intervening prepositional phrase

The two policemen at the construction site looks bored. agr

The members of my baby-sitting club is saving money. agr

Solution: Make sure that the verb agrees with the subject of the sentence, not with the object of the preposition. The object of a preposition is never the subject.

The two policemen at the construction site look bored.

The members of my baby-sitting club are saving money.

Tip: When subject and verb are separated by a prepositional phrase, check for agreement by reading the sentence without the prepositional phrase.

Problem: A sentence that begins with **here** or **there**

Here come the last bus to Pelham Heights. agr

There is my aunt and uncle. agr

Solution: In sentences that begin with *here* or *there*, look for the subject after the verb. Make sure that the verb agrees with the subject.

Here comes the last bus to Pelham Heights.

There are my aunt and uncle.

Problem: An indefinite pronoun as the subject

Each of the candidates are qualified. agr

All of the problems on the test was hard. agr

Solution: Some indefinite pronouns are singular; some are plural; and some can be either singular or plural, depending on the noun they refer to. Determine whether the indefinite pronoun is singular or plural, and make sure the verb agrees with it.

Each of the candidates is qualified.

All of the problems on the test were hard.

Problem: A compound subject that is joined by **and**

Fishing tackle and a life jacket was stowed in the boat. agr

Peanut butter and jelly are delicious. agr

Solution A: If the compound subjects refer to different people or things, use a plural verb.

Fishing tackle and a life jacket were stowed in the boat.

Solution B: If the parts of a compound subject name one unit or if they refer to the same person or thing, use a singular verb.

Peanut butter and jelly is delicious.

Problem: A compound subject that is joined by **or** or **nor**

Either my aunt or my parents plans to attend parents' night. agr

Neither onions nor pepper improve the taste of this meatloaf. agr

Solution: Make the verb agree with the subject that is closer to it.

Either my aunt or my parents plan to attend parents' night.

Neither onions nor pepper improves the taste of this meatloaf.

Incorrect Verb Tense or Form

Verbs have different tenses to show when the action takes place.

Problem: An incorrect or missing verb ending

The Parks Department install a new water fountain last week. tense

They have also plant flowers in all the flower beds. tense

Solution: To form the past tense and the past participle, add -ed to a regular verb.

The Parks Department installed a new water fountain last week.

They have also planted flowers in all the flower beds.

Problem: An improperly formed irregular verb

Wendell has standed in line for two hours. tense

I catched the fly ball and throwed it to first base. tense

Solution: Irregular verbs vary in their past and past participle forms. Look up the ones you are not sure of.

Wendell has stood in line for two hours.

I caught the fly ball and threw it to first base.

Problem: Confusion between the past form and the past participle

The cast for The Music Man has began rehearsals. tense

Solution: Use the past participle form of an irregular verb, not its past form, when you use the auxiliary verb *have*.

The cast for The Music Man has begun rehearsals.

Problem: Improper use of the past participle

Our seventh grade drawn a mural for the wall of the cafeteria. tense

Solution: Add the auxiliary verb have to the past participle of an irregular verb to form a complete verb.

Our seventh grade has drawn a mural for the wall of the cafeteria.

Tip: Because irregular verbs vary, it is useful to memorize the verbs that you use most often.

Incorrect Use of Pronouns

The noun that a pronoun refers to is called its antecedent. A pronoun must refer to its **antecedent** clearly. Subject pronouns refer to subjects in a sentence. Object pronouns refer to objects in a sentence.

Problem: A pronoun that could refer to more than one antecedent

Gary and Mike are coming, but he doesn't know the other kids. ant

Solution: Substitute a noun for the pronoun to make your sentence clearer.

Gary and Mike are coming, but Gary doesn't know the other kids.

Problem: Object pronouns as subjects

Him and John were freezing after skating for three hours. pro

Lori and me decided not to audition for the musical. pro

Solution: Use a subject pronoun as the subject part of a sentence.

He and John were freezing after skating for three hours.

Lori and I decided not to audition for the musical.

Problem: Subject pronouns as objects

Ms. Wang asked Reggie and I to enter the science fair. pro

Ms. Wang helped he and I with the project. pro

Solution: Use an object pronoun as the object of a verb or a preposition.

Ms. Wang asked Reggie and me to enter the science fair.

Ms. Wang helped him and me with the project.

Incorrect Use of Adjectives

Some adjectives have irregular forms: comparative forms for comparing two things and superlative forms for comparing more than two things.

Problem: Incorrect use of good, better, best

Their team is more good at softball than ours. adj

They have more better equipment too. adj

Solution: The comparative and superlative forms of good are better and best. Do not use more or most before irregular forms of comparative and superlative adjectives.

Their team is better at softball than ours.

They have better equipment too.

Problem: Incorrect use of bad, worse, worst

The flooding on East Street was the baddest I've seen. adj

Mike's basement was in badder shape than his garage. adj

Solution: The comparative and superlative forms of bad are worse and worst. Do not use more or most or the endings -er or -est with bad.

The flooding on East Street was the worst I've seen.

Mike's basement was in worse shape than his garage.

Problem: Incorrect use of comparative and superlative adjectives

The Appalachian Mountains are more older than the Rockies. adj

Mount Washington is the most highest of the Appalachians. adj

Solution: Do not use both -er and more or -est and most at the same time.

The Appalachian Mountains are older than the Rockies.

Mount Washington is the highest of the Appalachians.

Incorrect Use of Commas

Commas signal a pause between parts of a sentence and help to clarify meaning.

Problem: Missing commas in a series of three or more items

Sergio put mustard catsup and bean sprouts on his hot dog. com

Solution: If there are three or more items in a series, use a comma after each one, including the item preceding the conjunction.

Sergio put mustard, catsup, and bean sprouts on his hot dog.

Problem: Missing commas with direct quotations

"A little cold water" the swim coach said "won't hurt you." com

Solution: The first part of an interrupted quotation ends with a comma followed by quotation marks. The interrupting words are also followed by a comma.

"A little cold water," the swim coach said, "won't hurt you."

Problem: Missing commas with nonessential appositives

My sneakers a new pair are covered with mud. com

Solution: Determine whether the appositive is important to the meaning of the sentence. If it is not essential, set off the appositive with commas.

My sneakers, a new pair, are covered with mud.

Incorrect Use of Apostrophes

An apostrophe shows possession. It can also indicate missing letters in a contraction.

Problem: Singular possessive nouns

A parrots toes are used for gripping. poss

The bus color was bright yellow. poss

Solution: Use an apostrophe and an *s* to form the possessive of a singular noun, even one that ends in *s*.

A parrot's toes are used for gripping.

The bus's color was bright yellow.

Problem: Plural possessive nouns ending in *-s*

The visitors center closes at five o'clock. poss

The guide put several tourists luggage in one compartment. poss

Solution: Use an apostrophe alone to form the possessive of a plural noun that ends in s.

The visitors' center closes at five o'clock.

The guide put several tourists' luggage in one compartment.

Problem: Plural possessive nouns not ending in -s

The peoples applause gave courage to the young gymnast. poss

Solution: Use an apostrophe and an s to form the possessive of a plural noun that does not end in s.

The people's applause gave courage to the young gymnast.

Problem: Possessive personal pronouns

Jenny found the locker that was her's; she waited while her friends found their's. poss

Solution: Do not use apostrophes with possessive personal pronouns.

Jenny found the locker that was hers; she waited while her friends found theirs.

Incorrect Capitalization

Proper nouns, proper adjectives, and the first words of sentences always begin with a capital letter.

Problem: Words referring to ethnic groups, nationalities, and languages

Many canadians in the province of quebec speak french. cap

Solution: Capitalize proper nouns and adjectives that refer to ethnic groups, nationalities, and languages.

Many Canadians in the province of Quebec speak French.

Problem: Words that refer to a family member

Yesterday aunt Doreen asked me to baby-sit. cap

Don't forget to give dad a call. cap

Solution: Capitalize words that are used as part of or in place of a family member's name.

Yesterday Aunt Doreen asked me to baby-sit.

Don't forget to give Dad a call.

Tip: Do not capitalize a word that identifies a family member when it is preceded by a possessive adjective: My father bought a new car.

Problem: The first word of a direct quotation

The judge declared, "the court is now in session." cap

Solution: Capitalize the first word in a direct quotation.

The judge declared, "The court is now in session."

Tip: If you have difficulty with a rule of usage, try rewriting the rule in your own words. Check with your teacher to be sure you understand the rule.

Troublesome Words

This section will help you choose between words and expressions that are often confusing or misused.

accept, except

Accept means "to receive." *Except* means "other than."

Phillip walked proudly to the stage to accept the award.

Everything fits in my suitcase except my sleeping bag.

affect, effect

Affect is a verb meaning "to cause a change in" or "to influence." *Effect* as a verb means "to bring about or accomplish." As a noun, *effect* means "result."

Bad weather will affect our plans for the weekend.

The new medicine effected an improvement in the patient's condition.

The gloomy weather had a bad effect on my mood.

ain't

Ain't is never used in formal speaking or writing unless you are quoting the exact words of a character or a real person. Instead of using *ain't*, say or write *am not, is not, are not;* or use contractions such as *I'm not, she isn't.*

The pizza is not going to arrive for another half hour.

The pizza isn't going to arrive for another half hour.

a lot

The expression *a lot* means "much" or "many" and should always be written as two words. Some authorities discourage its use in formal writing.

A lot of my friends are learning Spanish.

Many of my friends are learning Spanish.

all ready, already

All ready, written as two words, is a phrase that means "completely ready." *Already,* written as one word, is an adverb that means "before" or "by this time."

By the time the fireworks display was all ready, we had already arrived.

all right, alright

The expression *all right* should be written as two words. Some dictionaries do list the single word *alright* but usually not as a preferred spelling.

Tom hurt his ankle, but he will be all right.

all together, altogether

All together means "in a group." *Altogether* means "completely."

The Minutemen stood all together at the end of Lexington Green.

The rebel farmers were not altogether sure that they could fight the British soldiers.

among, between

Use *among* for three or more people, things, or groups. Use *between* for two people, things, or groups.

Mr. Kendall divided the jobs for the car wash among the team members.

Our soccer field lies between the gym and Main Street.

amount, number

Use *amount* with nouns that cannot be counted. Use *number* with nouns that can be counted.

This recipe calls for an unusual amount of pepper.

A record number of students attended last Saturday's book fair.

bad, badly

Bad is an adjective; it modifies a noun. *Badly* is an adverb; it modifies a verb, an adjective, or another adverb.

The badly burnt cookies left a bad smell in the kitchen.

Joseph badly wants to be on the track team.

beside, besides

Beside means "next to." *Besides* means "in addition to."

The zebra is grazing beside a wildebeest.

Besides the zoo, I like to visit the aquarium.

bring, take

Bring means "to carry from a distant place to a closer one." *Take* means "to carry from a nearby place to a more distant one."

Please bring a bag lunch and subway money to school tomorrow.

Don't forget to take your art projects home this afternoon.

can, may

Can implies the ability to do something. *May* implies permission to do something.

You may take a later bus home if you can remember which bus to get on.

Tip: Although *can* is sometimes used in place of *may* in informal speech, a distinction should be made when speaking and writing formally.

choose, chose

Choose means "to select." *Chose*, the past tense of *choose*, means "selected."

Dad helped me choose a birthday card for my grandmother.

Dad chose a card with a funny joke inside.

doesn't, don't

The subject of the contraction *doesn't (does not)* is the third-person singular (*he* or *she*). The subject of the contraction *don't (do not)* is *I, you, we,* or *they.*

Tanya doesn't have any tickets for the concert.

We don't need tickets if we stand in the back row.

farther, further

Farther refers to physical distance. *Further* refers to time or degree.

Our new apartment is farther away from the school.

I will not continue this argument further.

fewer, less

Fewer is used to refer to things or qualities that can be counted. *Less* is used to refer to things or qualities that cannot be counted. In addition, *less* is used with figures that are regarded as single amounts.

Fewer people were waiting in line after lunch.

There is less fat in this kind of peanut butter.

Try to spend less than ten dollars on a present. [The money is treated as a single sum, not as individual dollars.]

good, well

Good is often used as an adjective meaning "pleasing" or "able." *Well* may be used as an adverb of manner telling how ably something is done or as an adjective meaning "in good health."

That is a good haircut.

Marco writes well.

Because Ms. Rodriguez had a headache, she was not well enough to correct our tests.

in, into

In means "inside." *Into* indicates a movement from outside toward the inside.

Refreshments will be sold in the lobby of the auditorium.

The doors opened, and the eager crowd rushed into the auditorium.

it's, its

Use an apostrophe to form the contraction of *it is.* The possessive of the personal pronoun *it* does not take an apostrophe.

It's hard to keep up with computer technology.

The computer industry seems to change its products daily.

lay, lie

Lay means "to place." *Lie* means "to recline."

I will lay my beach towel here on the warm sand.

Help! I don't want to lie next to a hill of red ants!

learn, teach

Learn means "to gain knowledge." *Teach* means "to give knowledge."

I don't learn very quickly.

My uncle is teaching me how to juggle.

leave, let

Leave means "to go away." *Let* means "to allow." With the word *alone,* you may use either *let* or *leave.*

Huang has to leave at eight o'clock.

Mr. Davio lets the band practice in his basement.

Leave me alone. Let me alone.

like, as

Use *like,* a preposition, to introduce a phrase of comparison. Use *as,* a subordinating conjunction, to introduce a subordinate clause. Many authorities believe that *like* should not be used before a clause in formal English.

Andy sometimes acts like a clown.

The detective looked carefully at the empty suitcase as she examined the room.

Tip: *As* can be a preposition in cases like the following: *Jack went to the costume party as a giant pumpkin.*

loose, lose

Loose means "not firmly attached." *Lose* means "to misplace" or "to fail to win."

If you keep wiggling that loose tooth, you might lose it.

raise, rise

Raise means to "cause to move up." *Rise* means "to move upward."

Farmers in this part of Florida raise sugarcane.

The hot air balloon began to rise slowly in the morning sky.

set, sit

Set means "to place" or "to put." *Sit* means "to place oneself in a seated position."

I set the tips of my running shoes against the starting line.

After running the fifty-yard dash, I had to sit down and catch my breath.

than, then

Than introduces the second part of a comparison. *Then* means "at that time" or "after that."

I'd rather go to Disney World in the winter than in the summer.

The park is too crowded and hot then.

their, they're

Their is the possessive form of *they. They're* is the contraction of *they are.*

They're visiting Plymouth Plantation during their vacation.

to, too, two

To means "in the direction of." *Too* means "also" or "to an excessive degree." *Two* is the number after one.

I bought two tickets to the concert.

The music was too loud.

It's my favorite group too.

who, whom

Who is a subject pronoun. *Whom* is an object pronoun.

Who has finished the test already?

Mr. Russo is the man to whom we owe our thanks.

who's, whose

Who's is the contraction of *who is. Whose* is the possessive form of *who.*

Who's going to wake me up in the morning?

The policeman discovered whose car alarm was making so much noise.

Mechanics

This section will help you use correct capitalization, punctuation, and abbreviations in your writing.

Capitalization

Capitalizing Sentences, Quotations, and Salutations

Rule: A capital letter appears at the beginning of a sentence.

Example: *Another gust of wind shook the house.*

Rule: A capital letter marks the beginning of a direct quotation that is a complete sentence.

Example: *Sabrina said, "The lights might go out."*

Rule: When a quoted sentence is interrupted by explanatory words, such as she said, do not begin the second part of the sentence with a capital letter.

Example: *"There's a rainbow," exclaimed Jeffrey, "over the whole beach."*

Rule: When the second part of a quotation is a new sentence, put a period after the explanatory words; begin the new part with a capital letter.

Example: *"Please come inside," Justin said. "Wipe your feet."*

Rule: Do not capitalize an indirect quotation.

Example: *Jo said that the storm was getting worse.*

Rule: Capitalize the first word in the salutation and closing of a letter. Capitalize the title and name of the person addressed.

Example: *Dear Dr. Menino*

Dear Editor

Sincerely

Capitalizing Names and Titles of People

Rule: Capitalize the names of people and the initials that stand for their names.

Example: *Malcolm X; J. F. K.; Robert E. Lee; Queen Elizabeth I*

Rule: Capitalize a title or an abbreviation of a title when it comes before a person's name or when it is used in direct address.

Example: *Dr. Salinas,* "Your patient, Doctor, is waiting."

Rule: Do not capitalize a title that follows or is a substitute for a person's name.

Example: *Marcia Salinas is a good doctor.*
He asked to speak to the doctor.

Rule: Capitalize the names and abbreviations of academic degrees that follow a person's name. Capitalize Jr. and Sr.

Example: *Marcia Salinas, M.D.; Raoul Tobias, Attorney; Donald Bruns Sr.; Ann Lee, Ph.D.*

Rule: Capitalize words that show family relationships when used as titles or as substitutes for a person's name.

Example: *We saw Uncle Carlos.*

She read a book about Mother Teresa.

Rule: Do not capitalize words that show family relationships when they follow a possessive noun or pronoun.

Example: *Your brother will give us a ride.*

I forgot my mother's phone number.

Rule: Always capitalize the pronoun I.

Example: *After I clean my room, I'm going swimming.*

Capitalizing Names of Places
Tip: Do not capitalize articles and prepositions in proper nouns: *the Rock of Gibraltar, the Statue of Liberty.*

Rule: Capitalize the names of cities, counties, states, countries, and continents.

Example: *St. Louis, Missouri; Marin County; Australia; South America*

Rule: Capitalize the names of bodies of water and other geographical features.

Example: *the Great Lakes; Cape Cod; the Dust Bowl*

Rule: Capitalize the names of sections of a country and regions of the world.

Example: *East Asia; New England; the Pacific Rim; the Midwest*

Rule: Capitalize compass points when they refer to a specific section of a country.

Example: *the Northwest; the South*

Rule: Do not capitalize compass points when they indicate direction.

Example: *Canada is north of the United States.*

Rule: Do not capitalize adjectives indicating direction.

Example: *western Utah*

Rule: Capitalize the names of streets and highways.

Example: *Dorchester Avenue; Route 22*

Rule: Capitalize the names of buildings, bridges, monuments, and other structures.

Example: *Chrysler Building; Chesapeake Bay Bridge*

Capitalizing Other Proper Nouns and Adjectives
Rule: Capitalize the names of clubs, organizations, businesses, institutions, and political parties.

Example: *Houston Oilers; the Food and Drug Administration; Boys and Girls Club*

Rule: Capitalize brand names but not the nouns following them.

Example: *Zippo brand energy bar*

Rule: Capitalize the names of days of the week, months, and holidays.

Example: *Saturday; June; Thanksgiving Day*

Rule: Do not capitalize the names of seasons.

Example: *winter; spring; summer; fall*

Rule: Capitalize the first word, the last word, and all important words in the title of a book, play, short story, poem, essay, article, film, television series, song, magazine, newspaper, and chapter of a book.

Example: *Not Without Laughter; World Book Encyclopedia; "Jingle Bells"; Star Wars; Chapter 12*

Rule: Capitalize the names of ethnic groups, nationalities, and languages.

Example: *Latino; Japanese; European; Spanish*

Rule: Capitalize proper adjectives that are formed from the names of ethnic groups and nationalities.

Example: *Shetland pony; Jewish holiday*

Using the Period and Other End Marks

Rule: Use a period at the end of a declarative sentence.

My great-grandfather fought in the Mexican Revolution.

Rule: Use a period at the end of an imperative sentence that does not express strong feeling.

Please set the table.

Rule: Use a question mark at the end of an interrogative sentence.

How did your sneakers get so muddy?

Rule: Use an exclamation point at the end of an exclamatory sentence or a strong imperative.

How exciting the play was!
Watch out!

Using Commas

Rule: Use commas to separate three or more items in a series.

The canary eats bird seed, fruit, and suet.

Rule: Use commas to show a pause after an introductory word and to set off names used in direct address.

Yes, I offered to take care of her canary this weekend.

Please, Stella, can I borrow your nail polish?

Rule: Use a comma after two or more introductory prepositional phrases or when the comma is needed to make the meaning clear. A comma is not needed after a single short prepositional phrase, but it is acceptable to use one.

From the back of the balcony, we had a lousy view of the stage.

After the movie we walked home. (no comma needed)

Rule: Use a comma after an introductory participle and an introductory participial phrase.

Whistling and moaning, the wind shook the little house.

Rule: Use commas to set off words that interrupt the flow of thought in a sentence.

Tomorrow, I think, our projects are due.

Rule: Use a comma after conjunctive adverbs such as however, moreover, furthermore, nevertheless, and therefore.

The skating rink is crowded on Saturday; however, it's the only time I can go.

Rule: Use commas to set off an appositive if it is not essential to the meaning of a sentence.

Ben Wagner, a resident of Pittsfield, won the first round in the golf tournament.

Rule: Use a comma before a conjunction (*and, or, but, nor, so, yet*) that joins main clauses.

We can buy our tickets now, or we can take a chance on buying them just before the show.

Rule: Use a comma after an introductory adverb clause.

Because I stayed up so late, I'm sleepy this morning.

Rule: In most cases, do not use a comma with an adverb clause that comes at the end of a sentence.

The picnic will be canceled unless the weather clears.

Rule: Use a comma or a pair of commas to set off an adjective clause that is not essential to the meaning of a sentence.

Tracy, who just moved here from Florida, has never seen snow before.

Rule: Do not use a comma or pair of commas to set off an essential clause from the rest of the sentence.

Anyone who signs up this month will get a discount.

Rule: Use commas before and after the year when it is used with both the month and the day. If only the month and the year are given, do not use a comma.

On January 2, 1985, my parents moved to Dallas, Texas.

I was born in May 1985.

Rule: Use commas before and after the name of a state or a country when it is used with the name of a city. Do not use a comma after the state if it is used with a ZIP code.

The area code for Concord, New Hampshire, is 603.

Please forward my mail to 6 Madison Lane, Topsham, ME 04086

Rule: Use commas or a pair of commas to set off an abbreviated title or degree following a person's name.

The infirmary was founded by Elizabeth Blackwell, M.D., the first woman in the United States to earn a medical degree.

Rule: Use a comma or commas to set off *too* when *too* means "also."

We, too, bought groceries, from the new online supermarket.

Rule: Use a comma or commas to set off a direct quotation.

"My nose," exclaimed Pinocchio, "is growing longer!"

Rule: Use a comma after the salutation of a friendly letter and after the closing of both a friendly letter and a business letter.

Dear Gary,
Sincerely,
Best regards,

Rule: Use a comma when necessary to prevent misreading of a sentence.

In math, solutions always elude me.

Using Semicolons and Colons

Rule: Use a semicolon to join the parts of a compound sentence when a coordinating conjunction, such as *and, or, nor,* or *but,* is not used.

Don't be late for the dress rehearsal; it begins at 7 o'clock sharp.

Rule: Use a semicolon to join parts of a compound sentence when the main clauses are long and are subdivided by commas. Use a semicolon even if these clauses are already joined by a coordinating conjunction.

In the gray light of early morning, on a remote airstrip in the desert, two pilots prepared to fly on a dangerous mission; but accompanying them were a television camera crew, three newspaper reporters, and a congressman from their home state of Nebraska.

Rule: Use a semicolon to separate main clauses joined by a conjunctive adverb. Be sure to use a comma after the conjunctive adverb.

We've been climbing all morning; therefore, we need a rest.

Rule: Use a colon to introduce a list of items that ends a sentence. Use words such as *these, the following,* or *as follows* to signal that a list is coming.

Remember to bring the following items: a backpack, a bag lunch, sunscreen, and insect repellent.

Rule: Do not use a colon to introduce a list preceded by a verb or preposition.

Remember to bring a backpack, a bag lunch, sunscreen, and insect repellent. (No colon is used after bring.)

Rule: Use a colon to separate the hour and the minutes when you write the time of day.

My Spanish class starts at 9:15.

Rule: Use a colon after the salutation of a business letter.

Dear Dr. Coulombe:
Director of the Personnel Dept.:

Using Quotation Marks and Italics

Rule: Use quotation marks before and after a direct quotation.

"Curiouser and curiouser," said Alice.

Rule: Use quotation marks with both parts of a divided quotation.

"This gymnastics trick," explained Amanda, "took me three months to learn."

Rule: Use a comma or commas to separate a phrase such as *she said* from the quotation itself. Place the comma that precedes the phrase inside the closing quotation marks.

"I will be late," said the cable technician, "for my appointment."

Rule: Place a period that ends a quotation inside the closing quotation marks.

Scott said, "Thanks for letting me borrow your camping tent."

Rule: Place a question mark or an exclamation point inside the quotation marks when it is part of the quotation.

"Why is the door of your snake's cage open?" asked my mother.

Rule: Place a question mark or an exclamation point outside the quotation marks when it is part of the entire sentence.

How I love "The Pit and the Pendulum"!

Rule: Use quotation marks for the title of a short story, essay, poem, song, magazine or newspaper article, or book chapter.

short story: "The Necklace"
poem: "The Fish"
article: "Fifty Things to Make from Bottlecaps"

Rule: Use italics or underlining for the title of a book, play, film, television series, magazine, newspaper, or work of art.

book: *To Kill a Mockingbird*
magazine: *The New Republic*
painting: *Sunflowers*

Rule: Use italics or underlining for the names of ships, trains, airplanes, and spacecraft.

ship: *Mayflower*
airplane: *Air Force One*

Using Apostrophes

Rule: Use an apostrophe and an s ('s) to form the possessive of a singular noun.

my brother's rock collection
Chris's hat

Rule: Use an apostrophe and an s ('s) to form the possessive of a plural noun that does not end in s.

the geese's feathers
the oxen's domestication

Tip: If a thing is owned jointly by two or more individuals, only the last name should show possession: *Mom and Dad's car.* If the ownership is not joint, each name should show possession: *Mom's and Dad's parents are coming for Thanksgiving.*

Rule: Use an apostrophe alone to form the possessive of a plural noun that ends in s.

the animals' habitat
the instruments' sound

Rule: Use an apostrophe and an s ('s) to form the possessive of an indefinite pronoun.

everyone's homework
someone's homework

Rule: Do not use an apostrophe in a possessive pronoun.

The dog knocked over its dish.
Yours is the best entry in the contest.
One of these drawings must be hers.

Rule: Use an apostrophe to replace letters that have been omitted in a contraction.

it + is = it's
can + not = can't
I + have = I've

Rule: Use an apostrophe to form the plural of a letter, a figure, or a word that is used as itself.

Write three 7's.
The word is spelled with two m's.
The sentence contains three and's.

Rule: Use an apostrophe to show missing numbers in a year.

the class of '02

Using Hyphens, Dashes, and Parentheses

Rule: Use a hyphen to show the division of a word at the end of a line. Always divide the word between its syllables.

With the new recycling program, more residents are recycling their trash.

Tip: One-letter divisions (for example, *e-lectric*) are not permissible. Avoid dividing personal names, if possible.

Rule: Use a hyphen in a number written as a compound word.

He sold forty-six ice creams in one hour.

Rule: Use a hyphen in a fraction.

We won the vote by a two-thirds majority.
Two-thirds of the votes have been counted.

Rule: Use a hyphen or hyphens in certain compound nouns.

great-grandmother
merry-go-round

Rule: Hyphenate a compound modifier only when it precedes the word it modifies.

A well-known musician visited our school.
The story was well written.

Rule: Use a hyphen after the prefixes *all-, ex-,* and *self-* when they are joined to any noun or adjective.

all-star
ex-president
self-conscious

Rule: Use a hyphen to separate any prefix from a word that begins with a capital letter.

un-American

mid-January

Rule: Use a dash or dashes to show a sudden break or change in thought or speech.

Daniel—he's kind of a pest—is my youngest cousin.

Rule: Use parentheses to set off words that define or helpfully explain a word in the sentence.

The transverse flute (transverse means "sideways") is a wind instrument.

Abbreviations

Rule: Abbreviate the titles *Mr., Mrs., Ms.,* and *Dr.* before a person's name. Also abbreviate any professional or academic degree that follows a name. The titles *Jr.* and *Sr.* are not preceded by a comma.

Dr. Stanley Livingston (doctor)
Luisa Mendez, M.A. (Master of Arts)
Martin Luther King Jr.

Rule: Use capital letters and no periods with abbreviations that are pronounced letter by letter or as words. Exceptions are *U.S.* and *Washington, D.C.,* which do use periods.

NAACP	**National Association for the Advancement of Colored People**
UFO	**unidentified flying object**
MADD	**Mothers Against Drunk Driving**

Rule: With exact times use A.M. (*ante meridiem,* "before noon") and P.M. (*post meridiem,* "after noon"). For years use B.C. (before Christ) and, sometimes, A.D. (*anno Domini,* "in the year of the Lord," after Christ).

8:15 A.M.	**6:55 P.M.**
5000 B.C.	**A.D. 235**

Rule: Abbreviate days and months only in charts and lists.

School will be closed on
Mon., Sept. 3
Wed., Nov. 11
Thurs., Nov. 27

Rule: In scientific writing abbreviate units of measure. Use periods with English units but not with metric units.

inch(es) in.	**yard(s) yd.**
meter(s) m	**milliliter(s) ml**

Rule: On envelopes only, abbreviate street names and state names. In general text, spell out street names and state names.

Ms. Karen Holmes
347 Grandville St.
Tilton, NH 03276

Karen lives on Grandville Street in Tilton, New Hampshire.

Writing Numbers

Rule: In charts and tables, always write numbers as numerals. Other rules apply to numbers not in charts or tables.

Student Test Scores

Student	Test 1	Test 2	Test 3
Lai, W.	82	89	94
Ostos, A.	78	90	86

Rule: Spell out a number that is expressed in one or two words.

We carried enough supplies for twenty-three days.

Rule: Use a numeral for a number of more than two words.

The tallest mountain in Mexico rises 17,520 feet.

Rule: Spell out a number that begins a sentence, or reword the sentence so that it does not begin with a number.

One hundred forty-three days later the baby elephant was born.

The baby elephant was born 143 days later.

Rule: Write a very large number as a numeral followed by the word *million* or *billion.*

There are 15 million people living in or near Mexico City.

Rule: Related numbers should be written in the same way. If one number must be written as a numeral, use numerals for all the numbers.

There are 365 days in the year, but only 52 weekends.

Rule: Spell out an ordinal number (first, second).

Welcome to our fifteenth annual convention.

Rule: Use words to express the time of day unless you are writing the exact time or using the abbreviation A.M. or P.M.

My guitar lesson is at five o'clock. It ends by 5:45 P.M.

Rule: Use numerals to express dates, house and street numbers, apartment and room numbers, telephone numbers, page numbers, amounts of money of more than two words, and percentages. Write out the word *percent.*

August 5, 1999

9 Davio Dr.

Apartment 9F

24 percent

Spelling

The following rules, examples, and exceptions can help you master the spelling of many words.

Spelling *ie* and *ei*

Put *i* before *e* except when both letters follow *c* or when both letters are pronounced together as an *a* sound.

believe **sieve** **weight**

receive **relieve** **neighborhood**

It is helpful to memorize exceptions to this rule. Exceptions include the following words: *species, science, weird, either, seize, leisure,* and *protein.*

Spelling unstressed vowels

Notice the vowel sound in the second syllable of the word *won-d_r-ful.* This is the unstressed vowel sound; dictionary respellings use the schwa symbol (ə) to indicate it. Because any of several vowels can be used to spell this sound, you might find yourself uncertain about which vowel to use. To spell words with unstressed vowels, try thinking of a related word in which the syllable containing the vowel sound is stressed.

Unknown Spelling	Related Word	Word Spelled Correctly
wond_rful	wonder	wonderful
fort_fications	fortify	fortifications
res_dent	reside	resident

Suffixes and the silent *e*

For most words with silent *e*, keep the *e* when adding a suffix. When you add the suffix *-ly* to a word that ends in *l* plus silent *e*, drop the *-le*. Also drop the silent *e* when you add a suffix beginning with a vowel or a *y*.

wise + ly = wisely

peaceful + ly = peacefully

skate + ing = skating

gentle + ly = gently

There are exceptions to the rule, including the following:

awe + ful = awful

judge + ment = judgment

true + ly = truly

noise + y = noisy

dye + ing = dyeing

mile + age = mileage

Suffixes and the final *y*

When you are adding a suffix to words ending with a vowel + *y*, keep the *y*. For words ending with a consonant + *y*, change the *y* to *i* unless the suffix begins with *i*. To avoid having two *i*'s together, keep the *y*.

enjoy + ment = enjoyment

merry + ment = merriment

display + ed = displayed

lazy + ness = laziness

play + ful = playful

worry + ing = worrying

Note: For some words, there are alternate spellings:

sly + er = slyer or slier

shy + est = shyest or shiest

Adding prefixes

When you add a prefix to a word, do not change the spelling of the word.

un + done = undone

re + schedule = reschedule

il + legible = illegible

semi + sweet = semisweet

Doubling the final consonant

Double the final consonant when a word ends with a single consonant following one vowel and the word is one syllable, or when the last syllable of the word is accented both before and after adding the suffix.

sit + ing = sitting

rub + ing = rubbing

commit + ed = committed

confer + ed = conferred

Do not double the final consonant if the suffix begins with a consonant, if the accent is not on the last syllable, or if the accent moves when the suffix is added.

cancel + ing = canceling

commit + ment = commitment

travel + ed = traveled

defer + ence = deference

Do not double the final consonant if the word ends in two consonants or if the suffix begins with a consonant.

climb + er = climber

nervous + ness = nervousness

import + ance = importance

star + dom = stardom

When adding *-ly* to a word that ends in *ll*, drop one *l*.

hill + ly = hilly **full + ly = fully**

Forming compound words

When forming compound words, keep the original spelling of both words.

home + work = homework

scare + crow = scarecrow

pea + nut = peanut

Forming Plurals

General Rules for Plurals		
If the noun ends in...	**Rule**	**Example**
s, ch, sh, x, or *z*	add *-es*	loss➛losses, latch➛latches, box➛boxes, bush➛bushes, quiz➛quizzes
a consonant + *y*	change *y* to *i* and add *-es*	ferry➛ferries, baby➛babies, worry➛worries
a vowel + *y*	add *-s*	chimney➛chimneys, monkey➛monkeys, toy➛toys
a vowel + *o*	add *-s*	cameo➛cameos, radio➛radios, rodeo➛rodeos
a consonant + *o*	add *-es* but sometimes add *-s*	potato➛potatoes, echo➛echoes photo➛photos, solo➛solos
f or *ff*	add *-s* but sometimes change *f* to *v* and add *-es*	proof➛proofs, bluff➛bluffs sheaf➛sheaves, thief➛thieves, hoof➛hooves
lf	change *f* to *v* and add *-es*	calf➛calves, half➛halves, loaf➛loaves
fe	change *f* to *v* and add *-s*	knife➛knives, life➛lives

Special Rules for Plurals	
Rule	**Example**
To form the plural of most proper names and one-word compound nouns, follow the general rules for plurals.	Jones➛Joneses, Thomas➛Thomases, Hatch➛Hatches
To form the plural of hyphenated compound nouns or compound nouns of more than one word, make the most important word plural.	credit card➛credit cards mother-in-law➛mothers-in-law district attorney➛district attorneys
Some nouns have irregular plural forms and do not follow any rules.	man➛men, foot➛feet, tooth➛teeth
Some nouns have the same singular and plural forms	deer➛deer, species➛species, sheep➛sheep

Speaking, Listening, and Viewing Handbook

A large part of the school day is spent either listening or speaking to others. By becoming a better listener and speaker, you will know more about what is expected of you, and understand more about your audience.

Speaking Effectively

- Speak slowly, clearly, and in a normal tone of voice. Raise your voice a bit, or use gestures to stress important points.
- Pause a few seconds after making an important point.
- Use words that help your audience picture what you're talking about. Visual aids such as pictures, graphs, charts, and maps can also help make your information clear.
- Stay in contact with your audience. Make sure your eyes move from person to person in the group you're addressing.

Speaking informally

Most oral communication is informal. When you speak casually with your friends, family, and neighbors, you use informal speech. Human relationships depend on this form of communication.

- Be courteous. Listen until the other person has finished speaking.
- Speak in a relaxed and spontaneous manner.
- Make eye contact with your listeners.
- Do not monopolize a conversation.
- When telling a story, show enthusiasm.
- When giving an announcement or directions, speak clearly and slowly. Check that your listeners understand the information.

Presenting an oral report

The steps in preparing an oral report are similar to the steps in the writing process. Complete each step carefully and you can be confident of presenting an effective oral report.

Steps in preparing an Oral Report	
Prewriting	• Determine your purpose and audience. • Decide on a topic and narrow it.
Drafting	• Make an outline. • Fill in the supporting details. • Write the report.
Revising and Editing	• Review your draft. • Check the organization of ideas and details. • Reword unclear statements.
Practicing	• Practice the report aloud in front of a family member. • Time the report. • Ask for and accept advice.
Presenting	• Relax in front of your audience. • Make eye contact with your audience. • Speak slowly and clearly.

Practice

Pretend that you have been invited to give an oral report to a group of fifth graders. Your report will tell them what to expect and how to adjust to new conditions when they enter middle school. As you plan your report, keep your purpose and your audience in mind. Include lively descriptions and examples to back up your suggestions and hold your audience's attention. As you practice giving your report, be sure to give attention to your body language as well as your vocal projection. Ask a partner to listen to your report to give you feedback on how to improve your performance. Do the same for your partner after listening to his or her report.

Listening Effectively

Listening to instructions in class

Some of the most important listening in the school day involves listening to instructions. Use the following tips to help you.

- First, make sure you understand what you are listening for. Are you receiving instructions for homework or for a test? What you listen for depends upon the type of instructions being given.
- Think about what you are hearing, and keep your eyes on the speaker. This will help you stay focused on the important points.
- Listen for keywords, or word clues. Examples of word clues are phrases such as above all, most important, or the three basic parts. These clues help you identify important points that you should remember.
- Take notes on what you hear. Write down only the most important parts of the instructions.
- If you don't understand something, ask questions. Then if you're still unsure about the instructions, repeat them aloud to your teacher to receive correction on any key points that you may have missed.

Interpreting nonverbal clues

Understanding nonverbal clues is part of effective listening. Nonverbal clues are everything you notice about a speaker except what the speaker says. As you listen, ask yourself these questions:

- Where and how is the speaker standing?
- Are some words spoken more loudly than others?
- Does the speaker make eye contact?
- Does he or she smile or look angry?
- What message is sent by the speaker's gestures and facial expression?

Practice

Work with a partner to practice listening to instructions. Each of you should find a set of directions for using a simple device–for example, a mechanical tool, a telephone answering machine, or a DVD player. Study the instructions carefully. If you can bring the device to class, ask your partner to try to use it by following your step-by-step instructions. If you cannot have the device in class, ask your partner to explain the directions back to you. Then change roles and listen as your partner gives you a set of directions.

Viewing Effectively

Critical viewing means thinking about what you see while watching a TV program, newscast, film, or video. It requires paying attention to what you hear and see and deciding whether information is true, false, or exaggerated. If the information seems to be true, try to determine whether it is based on a fact or an opinion.

Fact versus opinion

A **fact** is something that can be proved. An opinion is what someone believes is true. **Opinions** are based on feelings and experiences and cannot be proved.

Television commercials, political speeches, and even the evening news contain both facts and opinions. They use emotional words and actions to persuade the viewer to agree with a particular point of view. They may also use faulty reasoning, such as linking an effect with the wrong cause. Think through what is being said. The speaker may seem sincere, but do his or her reasons make sense? Are the reasons based on facts or on unfair generalizations?

Commercials contain both obvious and hidden messages. Just as you need to discover the author's purpose when you read a writer's words, you must be aware of the purpose of nonverbal attempts to persuade you. What does the message sender want, and how is the sender trying to influence you?

For example, a magazine or TV ad picturing a group of happy teenagers playing volleyball on a sunny beach expresses a positive feeling. The advertiser hopes viewers will transfer that positive feeling to the product being advertised—perhaps a soft drink or a brand of beachwear. This technique, called **transfer,** is one of several propaganda techniques regularly used by advertisers to influence consumers.

Following are a few other common techniques.

Testimonial—Famous and admired people recommend or praise a product, a policy, or a course of action even though they probably have no professional knowledge or expertise to back up their opinion.

Bandwagon—People are urged to follow the crowd ("get on the bandwagon") by buying a product, voting for a candidate, or whatever else the advertiser wants them to do.

Glittering generalities—The advertiser uses positive, good-sounding words (for example, *all-American* or *medically proven*) to impress people.

Practice

Think of a television commercial that you have seen often or watch a new one and take notes as you watch it. Then analyze the commercial.

- What is the purpose behind the ad?
- What is expressed in written or spoken words?
- What is expressed nonverbally (in music or sound effects as well as in pictures and actions)?
- What methods does the advertiser use to persuade viewers?
- What questions would you ask the advertiser if you could?
- How effective is the commercial? Why?

Working in Groups

Working in a group is an opportunity to learn from others. Whether you are planning a group project (such as a class trip) or solving a math problem, each person in a group brings specific strengths and interests to the task. When a task is large, such as planting a garden, a group provides the necessary energy and talent to get the job done.

Small groups vary in size according to the nature of the task. Three to five students is a good size for most small-group tasks. Your teacher may assign you to a group, or you may be asked to form your own group. Don't work with your best friend if you are likely to chat too much. Successful groups often have a mix of student abilities and interests.

Individual role assignments give everyone in a group something to do. One student, the group recorder, may take notes. Another may lead the discussion, and another report the results to the rest of the class.

Roles for a Small Group	
Reviewer	Reads or reviews the assignment and makes sure everyone understands it
Recorder 1 (of the process)	Takes notes on the discussion
Recorder 2 (of the results)	Takes notes on the final results
Reporter	Reports results to the rest of the class
Discussion leader	Asks questions to get the discussion going; keeps the group focused
Facilitator	Helps the group resolve disagreements and reach a compromise

For a small group of three or four students, some of these roles can be combined. Your teacher may assign a role to each student in your group. Or you may be asked to choose your own role.

Tips for working in groups

- Review the group assignment and goal. Be sure that everyone in the group understands the assignment.
- Review the amount of time allotted for the task. Decide how your group will organize its time.
- Check that all the group members understand their roles in the group.
- When a question arises, try to solve it as a group before asking a teacher for help.
- Listen to other points of view. Be respectful as you point out mistakes a speaker might have made.
- When it is your turn to talk, address the subject and help the project move forward by building on the ideas of the previous speaker.

Glossary/Glosario

This glossary lists the vocabulary words found in the selections in this book. The definition given is for the word as it is used in the selection; you may wish to consult a dictionary for other meanings of these words. The key below is a guide to the pronunciation symbols used in each entry.

a	at	ō	hope	ng	sing
ā	ape	ô	fork, all	th	thin
ä	father	oo	wood, put	t͟h	this
e	end	o͞o	fool	zh	treasure
ē	me	oi	oil	ə	ago, taken, pencil,
i	it	ou	out		lemon, circus
ī	ice	u	up	′	primary stress
o	hot	ū	use	ˏ	secondary stress

English

A

abandoned (ə ban′dənd) *adj.* deserted, left behind; **p. 167**

absorbs (ab sôrbz′) *v.* takes in and retains energy; **p. 214**

accustomed (ə kus′təmd) *adj.* in the habit of; used to; **p. 78**

achievements (ə chēv′mәntz) *n.* things completed with great effort or skill; **p. 598**

acknowledge (ak nol′ij) *v.* to recognize the authority, validity, or claims of; **p. 79**

acquainted (ə kwān′tid) *adj.* knowing someone, or each other, but not closely; **p. 320**

acquired (ə kwīrd′) *v.* came into possession of **p. 528**

adjoining (ə joi′ning) *adj.* located next to; adjacent; **p. 56**

aliens (āl′yənz) *n.* people who are not citizens of the country in which they live; **p. 749**

ambitious (am bish′əs) *adj.* full of a strong desire to succeed or to achieve something; eager; **p. 33**

Español

A

abandoned/abandonado *adj.* dejado detrás; **p. 167**

absorbs/absorbe *v.* tomar y absorber energía **p. 214**

accustomed/acostumbrado *adj.* con tendencia a; familiarizado con; **p. 78**

achievements/logros *n.* metas alcanzadas con gran esfuerzo o habilidad; **p. 598**

acknowledge/reconocer *v.* admitir la autoridad, validez o aserciones de; **p. 79**

acquainted/conocido *adj.* estar familiarizado con alguien, pero no íntimamente; **p. 320**

acquired/adquirió *v.* logró posesión de; **p. 528**

adjoining/colindante *adj.* localizado al lado de; adyacente; **p. 56**

aliens/extranjeros *n.* personas que no son ciudadanos del país en el que viven; **p. 749**

ambitious/ambicioso *adj.* lleno de un fuerte deseo de tener éxito o lograr algo; ansioso; **p. 33**

amid (ə mid′) *prep.* in the middle of; **p. 408**

application (ap′lə kā′shən) *n.* a putting to use; **p. 104**

appointed (ə point′əd) *v.* named or selected for an office or position; **p. 737**

appreciation (ə prē′shē ā′shən) *n.* high regard or gratitude; **p. 628**

architect (är′kə tekt′) *n.* one whose profession is to design, draw plans for, and help create buildings; **p. 453**

artifacts (är′tə fakts′) *n.* human-made objects used in the daily life of an ancient civilization; **p. 265**

assortment (ə sôrt′mənt) *n.* a collection of different things; **p. 789**

astounded (əs toun′ded) *v.* overwhelmed with sudden surprise or amazement; **p. 765**

authority (ə thôr′ə tē) *n.* a good source of information or advice; **p. 104**

automatically (ô tə mat′ik lē) *adv.* self-regulating; mechanically; **p. 206**

axis (ak′sis) *n.* a straight line passing through an object or body around which the object or body rotates or seems to rotate; **p. 214**

B

barren (bar′ən) *adj.* containing little or no plant life; bare; **p. 130**

beckoned (bek′ənd) *v.* signaled, summoned, or directed by a sign or gesture; **p. 455**

betrayed (bi trād′) *v.* let down; turned against; **p. 670**

blouse (blous) *n.* woman's or girl's shirt; **p. 321**

bonus (bō′nəs) *n.* something extra; **p. 668**

boost (bo͞ost) *n.* something that aids or advances a person or thing; **p. 322**

buffet (buf′it) *v.* to strike repeatedly; to knock against; **p. 459**

C

catastrophe (kə tas′trə fē′) *n.* great and sudden disaster or misfortune; **p. 498**

cavities (kav′ə tēz) *n.* hollow spaces in a tooth caused by decay; **p. 488**

chaos (ka′os) *n.* total confusion and disorder; **p. 610**

civilized (siv′ə līzd) *adj.* advanced beyond that which is primitive or savage; **p. 204**

amid/entre *prep.* en medio de; **p. 408**

application/aplicación *n.* empleo; uso; **p. 104**

appointed/apuntó *v.* nombró o seleccionó para una oficina o puesto; **p. 737**

appreciation/agradecimiento *n.* gran estima o gratitude; **p. 628**

architect/arquitecto *n.* uno cuya profesión es diseñar, construir plans y manejar la construcción de edificios u otras estructuras **p. 453**

artifacts/artefactos *n.* objetos hechos por el hombre, de uso diario en una civilización antigua; **p. 265**

assortment/surtido *n.* colección de cosas distintas; **p. 789**

astounded/pasmado *v.* abrumado con sorpresa o asombro repentino; **p. 765**

authority/autoridad *n.* fuente buena de información o consejo; **p. 104**

automatically/automáticamente *adv.* con regulación propia; mecánicamente; **p. 206**

axis/eje *n.* línea recta, real o imaginaria, que pasa por un objeto o cuerpo y alrededor de la cual dicho objeto parece girar; **p. 214**

B

barren/yermo *adj.* con poca o ninguna vida vegetal; estéril; **p. 130**

beckoned/señaló *v.* llamó, convocó o dirigió por un gesto o una seña; **p. 455**

betrayed/traicionado *v.* decepcionado; que perdió el apoyo; **p. 670**

blouse/blusa *n.* la camisa de una chica o una mujer; **p. 321**

bonus/bono *n.* algo adicional; **p. 668**

boost/estímulo *n.* algo que ayuda o avanza (una persona o cosa); **p. 322**

buffet/abofetear *v.* golpear repetidamente; hacer chocar contra; **p. 459**

C

catastrophe/catástrofe *n.* desastre grande y repentino o mala fortuna; **p. 498**

cavities/caries *n.* espacios vacíos causado por decaimiento; **p. 488**

chaos/caos *n.* confusión y desorden total; **p. 610**

civilized/ civilizado *adj.* avanzado más allá de lo primitivo o salvaje; **p. 204**

coincidence (kō in′si dəns) *n.* the occurrence of unrelated events that appear to be connected; **p. 125**

complexion (kəm plek′shən) *n.* color, texture, and appearance of the skin; **p. 396**

compromise (kom′prə mīz′) *v.* to settle a disagreement by having each side give up something; **p. 546**

confirmed (kən furmd′) *v.* established as true **p. 544**

conscious (kon′shəs) *adj.* deliberate; intentional **p. 50**

consideration (kən sid ə rā′shən) *n.* thought or reflection; **p. 786**

coping (kō′ping) *v.* successfully dealing with something difficult; **p. 328**

criticized (krit′ə sīzd′) *v.* found fault with; **p. 16**

cyclone (sī′klōn) *n.* a violent windstorm in which winds move in a circle, as a tornado; **p. 129**

cylinders (sil′ən dərz) *n.* long, round objects, solid or hollow, with flat ends, such as soup cans; **p. 350**

D

deafening (def′ən ing) *adj.* very loud; earsplitting; **p. 542**

dedication (ded′ə kā′shən) *n.* faithful agreement or pledge to a person or purpose; **p. 689**

defiance ıdi fı¯′əns) *n.* bold resistance to authority; **p. 611**

depression (di presh′ən) *n.* a period marked by severely decreasing business activity, rising unemployment, and falling wages; **p. 649**

dejectedly (di jek′tid lē) *adv.* in a disheartened or depressed way; **p. 255**

descendants (di sen′dənts) *n.* people who have a common ancestor; **p. 411**

desolate (des′ə lit) *adj.* empty of people; deserted; **p. 124**

destiny (des′tə nē) *n.* what is fated to happen to someone or something; fortune; **p. 474**

devised (di vīzd′) *v.* thought out; invented; planned; **p. 364**

disability (dis′ə bil′ə tē) *n.* something that causes a loss or lack of ability; **p. 17**

discarded (dis kärd′əd) *v.* thrown away; **p. 688**

coincidence/coincidencia *n.* ocurrencia de eventos no relacionado que parecen ser conectados; **p. 125**

complexion/cutis *n.* color, textura y apariencia de la tez; **p. 396**

compromise/compromiso *v.* resolver un desacuerdo al obligar que cada lado renuncie algo; **p. 546**

confirmed/confirmó *v.* estableció la verdad de algo; **p. 544**

conscious/consciente *adj.* deliberado; adrede; a propósito; **p. 50**

consideration/consideración *n.* pensamiento o reflexión; **p. 786**

coping/estar contendiendo *v.* tratar exitosamente con algo difícil; **p. 328**

criticized/criticó *v.* señaló una falla; **p. 16**

cyclone/ciclón *n.* tempestad violenta en la que los vientos se mueven en un círculo, como un tornado; **p. 129**

cylinders/cilindros *n.* objetos largos y redondos, sólidos o huecos, con extremos planos, como de latas de sopa; **p. 350**

D

deafening/ensordecedor *adj.* muy fuerte (sonido); que rompe los tímpanos; estridente; **p. 542**

dedication/dedicación *n.* acuerdo o compromiso leal para con una persona o propósito; **p. 689**

defiance/rebeldía *n.* audaz resistencia a la autoridad; **p. 611**

depression/depression *n.* un período denotado por un nivel de actividad comercial en abrupta caída, mayores niveles de desempleo y salaries más bajos; **p. 649**

dejectedly/con desánimo *adv.* de manera deprimida o desalentada; **p. 255**

descendants/descendientes *n.* personas que tienen un antepasado en común; **p. 411**

desolate/desolado *adj.* vacío de personas; abandonado; **p. 124**

destiny/destino *n.* lo que le ocurrirá a una persona o cosa; fortuna; **p. 474**

devised/diseñado *v.* ideado; inventado; planeado; **p. 364**

disability/discapacidad *n.* minusvalidez; **p. 17**

discarded/desechado *v.* botado a la basura; **p. 688**

discomfort (dis kum′fərt) *n.* uneasiness; hardship; pain; **p. 459**

dislodging (dis loj′ing) *v.* moving or forcing out of a place or position; **p. 37**

dismal (diz′məl) *adj.* dreary; miserable; cheerless; **p. 674**

dispute (dis pūt′) *n.* difference of opinion; argument or debate; **p. 77**

distinquished (dis ting′gwisht) *adj.* marked by excellence; **p. 598**

drawbacks (drô′baks′) *n.* shortcomings; disadvantages; **p. 647**

drone (drōn) *n.* dull, continuous buzzing or humming sound; **p. 529**

E

ease (ēz) *n.* freedom from pain, discomfort, hard work, or worry; **p. 507**

eaves (ēvz) *n.* lower edge of a sloping roof projecting beyond the sides of a building; **p. 115**

economic (ek′ə nom′ik) *adj.* relating to money matters; **p. 49**

effective (i fek′tiv) *adj.* producing or capable of producing an intended result; **p. 653**

endured (en doord′) *v.* underwent hardship without giving up; put up with; **p. 55**

enraged (en rājd′) *adj.* greatly angered; **p. 371**

essential (i sen′shəl) *adj.* basic; fundamental; intrinsic; **p. 49**

eternal (i turn′əl) *adj.* existing throughout all time; **p. 205**

eventually (i ven′chōō ə lē) *adv.* in the end; finally; **p. 628**

evidently (ev′ə dənt lē) *adv.* clearly, apparently, obviously; **p. 57**

excavators (eks′kə vā′tərz) *n.* people who uncover something by digging; **p. 40**

exile (eg′zīl) *n.* a person who is forced to leave his or her country or home; **p. 364**

F

factor (fak′tər) *n.* one of several things that brings about a result; **p. 213**

ferocious (fə rō′shəs) *adj.* fierce and violent; **p. 787**

flawless (flô′lis) *adj.* having no mistakes; perfect; **p. 396**

discomfort/incomodidad *n.* inquietud; privación; dolor; **p. 549**

dislodging/estar desalojando *v.* estar quitando o forzando de un lugar o posición; **p. 37**

dismal/sombrío *adj.* deprimente; triste; sin vida; **p. 674**

dispute/disputa *n.* diferencia de opinion; discusión o debate; **p. 77**

distinguished/distinguido *adj.* caracterizado por la excelencia; **p. 598**

drawbacks/inconvenientes *n.* deficiencias; desventajas; **p. 647**

drone/zumbido *n.* sonido contínuo zumbador o susurrante; **p. 529**

E

ease/tranquilidad *n.* libertad de dolor, incomodidad, trabajo duro o preocupación; **p. 507**

eaves/alero *n.* borde inferior de un techo inclinado que se proyecta más allá de los laterales de un edificio; **p. 115**

economic/económico *adj.* relacionado con asuntos de dinero; **p. 49**

effective/efectivo *adj.* que genera o puede generar un resultado pretendido; **p. 653**

endured/soportó *v.* sufrió privación sin rendirse; aguantó; **p. 55**

enraged/enfurecido *adj.* muy enojado; **p. 371**

essential/esencial *adj.* básico; fundamental; intrínsico; **p. 49**

eternal/eterno *adj.* que existe desde el principio de los tiempos; **p. 205**

eventually/finalmente *adv.* al final; por ultimo; **p. 628**

evidently/evidentemente *adv.* claramente, aparentemente, obviamente; **p. 57**

excavators/excavadores *n.* personas que descubren algo desenterrándolo; **p. 40**

exile/exiliado *n.* una persona que se ve forzada a dejar su país u hogar; **p. 364**

F

factor/factor *n.* una de varias cosas que causan un resultado; **p. 213**

ferocious/feroz *adj.* fiero y violento; **p. 787**

flawless/impecable *adj.* sin errores; perfecto **p. 396**

floundering (floun′dər ing) *v.* moving with stumbling motions; struggling awkwardly or clumsily; **p. 63**

forlorn (fôr lôrn′) *adj.* dejected; hopeless; wretched; **p. 183**

formula (fôr′myə lə) *n.* a combination of symbols used in mathematics to state a rule or principle; **p. 350**

frenzied (fren′zēd) *adj.* in a state of intense emotion or extreme excitement; frantic; **p. 496**

G

grudgingly (gruj′ing lē) *adv.* angrily; resentfully; **p. 116**

guaranteed (gar ən tēd′) *v.* made certain; promised; **p. 779**

H

harsh (härsh) *adj.* rough or unpleasant to any of the physical senses; **p. 743**

heed (hēd) *v.* pay careful attention to; **p. 39**

hesitantly (hez′ət ənt lē) *adv.* reluctantly or unwillingly; **p. 532**

historian (his tôr′ē ən) *n.* one who writes a history or about history; **p. 204**

honorable (on′ər ə bəl) *adj.* characterized by principles of morality and integrity; upright; **p. 740**

hospitality (hos′pə tal′ə tē) *n.* the act of being welcoming to guests; **p. 257**

hostile (host′əl) *adj.* not offering a pleasant or sustaining environment; **p. 183**

humidity (hū mid′ə tē) *n.* moisture or dampness, especially of the atmosphere; **p. 212**

I

ignorance (ig′nər əns) *n.* state of lacking in knowledge or education; **p. 796**

immigrant (im′ə grənt) *adj.* coming into a country or region of which one is not a native in order to live there; **p. 104**

inadequate (in ad′ə kwit) *adj.* not good enough; **p. 399**

indifference (in dif′ər əns) *n.* lack of feeling or concern; **p. 611**

floundering/forcejando torpemente *v.* forcejando con movimientos torpes; luchando torpemente; **p. 63**

forlorn/abatido *adj.* desanimado; sin esperanza; miserable; **p. 183**

formula/fórmula *n.* combinación de símbolos usados en las matemáticas para declarar una regla o un principio; **p. 350**

frenzied/frenético *adj.* en estado de emoción intensa o ánimo extremado; desenfrenado; **p. 496**

G

grudgingly/de mala gana *adv.* con enojo; con resentimiento; **p. 116**

guaranteed/garantizó *v.* hizo cierto; prometió; aseguró; **p. 779**

H

harsh/severo *adj.* áspero o incómodo para uno de los sentidos físicos; **p. 743**

heed/hacer caso de *v.* prestar atención cuidadosa a; obedecer; **p. 39**

hesitantly/vacilante *adv.* reaciamente o de mala gana; **p. 532**

historian/historiador *n.* persona que escribe una historia o acerca de la historia; **p. 204**

honorable/honorable *adj.* caracterizado por principios de moralidad e integridad; **p. 740**

hospitality/hospitalidad *n.* acto de darles la bienvenida a los invitados; **p. 257**

hostile/hostil *adj.* carente de un ambiente agradable o sostenedor; **p. 183**

humidity/humedad *n.* medida de cantidad de agua en la atmósfera; **p. 212**

I

ignorance/ignorancia *n.* estado caracterizado por carencia de conocimiento o educación; **p. 796**

immigrant/inmigrante *adj.* describe quien entra en un país o región del que uno no es nativo para residir allí; **p. 104**

inadequate/inadecuado *adj.* no suficientemente bueno; **p. 399**

indifference/indiferencia *n.* falta de sentimientos o preocupaciones; **p. 611**

industrious (in dus′trē əs) *adj.* hardworking; **p. 56**

inhabitants (in hab′ət əntz) *n.* persons or animals that live permanently in a place; **p. 262**

inhabited (in hab′it id) *v.* lived in or on; **p. 496**

inherit (in her′it) *v.* to receive something, such as property or a title, from the former owner at his or her death; **p. 97**

instinctively (in stingk′tiv lē) *adv.* behaving in a fixed way when moved by something that causes a person to take action; **p. 530**

interior (in tēr′ē ər) *n.* inner side, surface, or part; **p. 182**

intricately (in′tri kit lē) *adv.* in a complex way; in an elaborate manner; **p. 265**

intrigued (in trēgd′) *v.* fascinated; made curious; **p. 98**

L

lain (lān) *v.* placed one's body in a flat position on the ground or other surface; **p. 117**

lamented (lə ment′id) *v.* felt or showed deep sorrow or grief; **p. 507**

lavishly (lav′ish lē) *adv.* in a way that provides much more than is needed; **p. 319**

leisurely (lē′zhər lē) *adj.* unhurried, relaxed; free form the demands of work; **p. 633**

luggage (lug′ij) *n.* bags, boxes, or suitcases a traveler uses for carrying things; **p. 495**

M

mankind (man′kīnd′) *n.* all human beings; **p. 545**

manufacturing (man′yə fak′chər ing) *v.* making products, especially on a large scale or with machinery; **p. 351**

meager (mē′gər) *adj.* scarcely enough; insufficient; **p. 368**

meekly (mēk′lē) *adv.* patiently and mildly; gently; **p. 87**

minimum (min′ə məm) *adj.* least possible; lowest; smallest; **p. 13**

monitors (mon′ə tərz) *n.* students with a special duty, such as taking attendance or handing out materials; **p. 349**

mortal (môrt′əl) *adj* destined to die; human; **p. 408**

industrious/industrioso *adj.* laborioso y aplicado; **p. 56**

inhabitants/habitants *n.* personas o animales que viven en forma permanente en un lugar; **p. 262**

inhabited/habitó *v.* ocupó como residencia; **p. 496**

inherit/heredar *v.* recibir algo como, por ejemplo, una propiedad o un título, del propietario anterior al momento de su muerte; **p. 97**

instinctively/instintivamente *adv.* comportándose de manera establecida cuando provocado por algo que causa que uno reaccione; **p. 530**

interior/interior *n.* lado, superficie o aspecto que está en la parte de adentro; **p. 182**

intricately/intrincadamente *adv.* de un modo complejo; de una manera elaborada; **p. 265**

intrigued/intrigado *v.* fascinado; con curiosidad; **p. 98**

L

lain/ acostado *v.* haber colocado el cuerpo en una posición plana sobre la tierra u otra superficie; **p. 117**

lamented/lamentó *v.* sintió o mostró gran pena o tristeza; **p. 507**

lavishly/pródigamente *adv.* de manera que provee mucho más de lo necesario; **p. 319**

leisurely/pausadamente *adj.* sin prisas, relajado; sin las exigencias del trabajo; **p. 633**

luggage/equipaje *n.* bolsas, cajas o maletas usadas por un viajero para llevar cosas; **p. 495**

M

mankind/humanidad *n.* todos los seres humanos; **p. 545**

manufacturing/fabricando *v.* haciendo productos, especialmente en cantidades grandes or con máquinas; **p. 351**

meager/exiguo *adj.* apenas suficiente; insuficiente; **p. 368**

meekly/dócilmente *adv.* paciente y blandamente; suavemente; **p. 87**

minimum/mínimo *adj.* lo menos posible; el más bajo; el más pequeño; **p. 13**

monitors/monitores *n.* estudiantes con un deber especial en la escuela, como averiguar la asistencia o repartir materiales; **p. 349**

mortal/mortal *adj.* destinado a morir; humano; **p. 408**

muster (mus′tər) *v.* to find and gather together; collect or summon; **p. 18**

N

naked (nā′kid) *adj.* without clothing or similar covering; **p. 471**

O

obscure (əb skyoor′) *adj.* not well known; **p. 407**

obstinacy (ob′stə nə sē) *n.* state of not giving in to argument, persuasion, or reason; **p. 409**

opposing (ə pōz′ing) *adj.* competing or struggling against; **p. 633**

ordeals (ôr dēlz′) *n.* experiences that are painful or difficult to endure; **p. 253**

outrages (out′rāj əz) *n.* violent or cruel acts; **p. 104**

P

paralyzed (par′ə līzd′) *adj.* affected with the loss of motion or sensation in a muscle due to disease of, or an injury to, the nervous system; **p. 648**

parched (pärcht) *adj.* dried out or shriveled, usually from heat; **p. 129**

plagued (plāgd) *v.* troubled or annoyed; **p. 84**

plateau (pla tō′) *n.* elevated, fairly flat land area; **p. 268**

political (pə lit′ i kəl) *adj.* relating to government; **p. 98**

pondering (pon′dər ing) *v.* weighing something in the mind; considering or thinking carefully; **p. 35**

portrayed (pôr trād′) *v.* set forth a picture of in words; described; **p. 518**

pouting (pout′ ing) *v.* being sullen or gloomy; sulking; **p. 674**

precede (pri sēd′) *v.* to go or come before or ahead of; **p. 198**

precisely (pri sīs′lē) *adv.* accurately; exactly; **p. 398**

predict (pri dikt′) *v.* to say or guess ahead of time what is going to happen, using observation, experience, or reason; **p. 165**

prevail (pri vāl′) *v.* to be victorious; triumph; **p. 50**

principles (prin′sə pəlz) *n.* rules of personal conduct; **p. 767**

muster/juntar *v.* encontrar y recoger; convocar o reunir; **p. 18**

N

naked/desnudo *adj.* sin vestimenta o protección similar para el cuerpo; **p. 471**

O

obscure/oscuro *adj.* no bien conocido; **p. 407**

obstinacy/obstinación *n.* estado de no rendirse a la argumentación, persuasión o razón; **p. 409**

opposing/enfrentar *adj.* competir o luchar contra algo; **p. 633**

ordeals/pruebas *n.* experiencias que son peligrosas o difíciles de soportar; **p. 253**

outrages/atrocidades *n.* actos violentos o crueles; **p. 104**

P

paralyzed/paralizado *adj.* afectado por la pérdida de la movilidad o de la sensibilidad de un músculo debido a enfermedades o lesiones en el sistema nervioso; **p. 648**

parched/reseco *adj.* secado o encogido, usualmente por el calor; **p. 129**

plagued/acosó *v.* preocupó o fastidió; **p. 84**

plateau/meseta *n.* área de terreno elevada y relativamente plana; **p. 268**

political/politico *adj.* relacionado con el gobierno; **p. 98**

pondering/estar ponderando *v.* reflexionando sobre algo en la mente; considerando o pensando con cuidado; **p. 35**

portrayed/retrató *v.* pintó una escena en palabras; describió; **p. 518**

pouting/afligirse *v.* mostrarse sombrío o triste; estar de mal humor; **p. 674**

precede/preceder *v.* que va o viene antes o delante de; **p. 198**

precisely/precisamente *adv.* correctamente; exactamente; **p. 398**

predict/predecir *v.* decir o adivinar con antelación lo que va a pasar, usando observación, experiencia o razón; **p. 165**

prevail/prevalecer *v.* ser victorioso; triunfar; **p. 50**

principles/principios *n.* reglas de conducta personal; **p. 767**

privileged (priv′ə lijd) *adj.* having or enjoying a right or advantage; **p. 517**

probing (prōb′ ing) *v.* carrying out a thorough investigation or examination; **p. 265**

proclaimed (prə klāmd′) *v.* announced officially; declared publicly; **p. 737**

prominent (prom′ə nənt) *adj.* well known or important; notable; **p. 49**

prospered (pros′ pərd) *v.* flourished; was successful; **p. 630**

prosperity (pros per′ə tē) *n.* state of having success, wealth, or good fortune; **p. 481**

Q

quest (kwest) *n.* search or pursuit made in order to get an object or accomplish a goal; **p. 87**

R

radiating (rā′dē āt′ing) *v.* moving or spreading outward from a center; **p. 458**

ravaged (rav′ijd) *v.* laid waste to; destroyed **p. 84**

ravenous (rav′ ə nəs) *adj.* very eager, as for satisfaction or gratification; **p. 473**

realm (relm) *n.* kingdom; **p. 370**

recognition (rek əg nish′ ən) *n.* favorable attention or notice; **p. 599**

register (rej′is tər) *v.* to enter one's name in a formal record; **p. 751**

reign (rān) *n.* period of rule of a king or queen; **p. 97**

relish (rel′ ish) *v.* to enjoy; **p. 616**

reputation (rep′yə tā′shən) *n.* general or public opinion of something or someone; **p. 481**

resist (ri zist′) *v.* to act in opposition; **p. 737**

rivaling (rī′vəl ing) *v.* competing with; **p. 512**

S

sacrificed (sak′rə fīst′) *v.* given up, usually for the sake of something else; **p. 481**

salary (sal′ə rē) *n.* fixed sum of money regularly paid to a person for a job; **p. 243**

savoring (sā′vər ing) *v.* taking great delight in; **p. 531**

seasonal (sē′zə nəl) *adj.* affected by the seasons; happening at a certain season; **p. 165**

privileged/privilegiado *adj.* tener o gozar de un derecho o ventaja; **p. 517**

probing/sondar *v.* llevar a cabo una investigación o examen completes; **p. 265**

proclaimed/proclamó *v.* anunció oficialmente; declaró públicamente; **p. 737**

prominent/prominente *adj.* bien conocido o importante; notable; **p. 49**

prospered/prosperó *v.* progresó, tuvo éxito; **p. 630**

prosperity/prosperidad *n.* estado de tener éxito, riqueza o buena fortuna; **p. 481**

Q

quest/búsqueda *n.* busca o caza hecha para conseguir un objeto o lograr una meta; **p. 87**

R

radiating/radiante *v.* moviéndose o extendiéndose desde un punto central hacia fuera; **p. 458**

ravaged/asolado *v.* arruinado; destrozado; **p. 84**

ravenous/voraz *adj.* muy ansioso por recibir satisfacción o gratificación; **p. 473**

realm/reino *n.* territorio gobernado por una monarquía; **p. 370**

recognition/reconocimiento *n.* atención o crítica favorable; **p. 599**

register/registrar *v.* inscribir el nombre de una persona en un récord formal; **p. 751**

reign/reinado *n.* período de gobierno de un rey o reina; **p. 97**

relish/deleitarse *v.* disfrutar; **p. 616**

reputation/reputación *n.* opinión general o pública de algo o de alguien; **p. 481**

resist/resistir *v.* actuar en oposición a; **p. 737**

rivaling/rivalizando *v.* compitiendo con; **p. 512**

S

sacrificed/sacrificó *v.* dejó posesión de, usualmente por el beneficio de otra cosa; **p. 481**

salary/salario *n.* cantidad fija de dinero pagado en intérvalos establecidos a una persona por su labor; **p. 243**

savoring/saborear *v.* experimentar gran placer en; **p. 531**

seasonal/estacional *adj.* afectado por las estaciones; ocurre durante una temporada específica; **p. 165**

shabby (shab′ē) *adj.* faded and dingy from wear or exposure; **p. 752**

shrewdest (shro͞od′ist) *adj.* the most clever in practical matters; **p. 252**

shunned (shund) *v.* kept away from; avoided; **p. 473**

sleek (slēk) *adj.* having a healthy, well-groomed, or well-fed appearance; smooth and glossy, as if polished; **p. 505**

slums (slumz) *n.* heavily populated city areas identified by poverty, run-down housing, and wretched living conditions; **p. 649**

soggy (sog′ē) *adj.* filled with water to the point that no more can be absorbed; soaked thoroughly; **p. 164**

sowing (sō′ing) *v.* spreading seeds over the ground so that they will grow; **p. 544**

sprained (sprānd′) *v.* injured by a sudden, severe twist; **p. 490**

squad (skwod) *n.* a small group working for a common purpose; **p. 242**

stadium (stā′dē əm) *n.* a large, usually roofless building surrounding an open area used for sporting events and equipped with many rows of seats; **p. 243**

starvation (star vā′ shən) *n.* act or instance of suffering or dying of hunger; **p. 118**

superintendent (so͞o′prin ten′dənt) *n.* the person who manages and takes care of an apartment building; **p. 349**

sympathy (sim′ pə thē) *n.* feeling of pity or compassion for another; **p. 677**

T

temporarily (tem pə rer′ə lē) *adv.* lasting only for a short time; not permanently; **p. 764**

theory (thē′ər ē) *n.* a guess based on some evidence; **p. 167**

tonsils (ton′səlz) *n.* small organs in the throat near the back of the mouth; **p. 490**

toppled (top′əld) *v.* fell forward, tumbled over; **p. 507**

tortured (tôr′ chərd) *v.* caused to suffer extreme physical or mental pain; **p. 600**

shabby/gastado *adj.* desteñido y sucio por uso o exposición; **p. 752**

shrewdest/el más astuto *adj.* el más listo en asuntos prácticos; **p. 252**

shunned/rechazado *v.* dejado de lado; evitado; **p. 473**

sleek/pulcro/liso *adj.* parecer sano, bien alimentado o acicalado; bruñido y reluciente; **p. 505**

slums/asentamientos precarious *n.* áreas urbanas con gran densidad de población identificadas por: pobreza, viviendas con aspecto de abandono y extremas condiciones de vida; **p. 649**

soggy/empapado *adj.* lleno de agua hasta el punto que no se puede absorber más; saturado completamente; **p. 164**

sowing/sembrando *v.* repartiendo semillas por la tierra para que crezcan; **p. 544**

sprained/torció *v.* se hizo daño por el acto de retorcerse repetina o seriamente; **p. 490**

squad/escuadra *n.* grupo pequeño con un propósito en común; **p. 242**

stadium/estadio *n.* edificio grande, generalmente sin techo, que contiene una zona abierta usada para eventos deportivos y equipada con muchas filas de asientos; **p. 243**

starvation/inanición *n.* acto o momento en el que se sufre o muere de hambre; **p. 118**

superintendent/portero *n.* persona que maneja y es responsible del mantenimiento de un edificio de apartamentos; **p. 349**

sympathy/lástima *n.* sentimiento de pena o compassion por otra persona; **p. 677**

T

temporarily/temporariamente *adv.* que perdura sólo un tiempo breve; no permanentemente **p. 764**

theory/teoría *n.* hipótesis basada en alguna evidencia; **p. 167**

tonsils/amígdalas *n.* órganos pequeños en la garganta acerca de la parte anterior de la boca; **p. 490**

toppled/se tambaleó *v.* se cayó; se vino abajo; **p. 507**

tortured/torturado *v.* obligado a sufrir dolor físico o mental extreme; **p. 600**

traitors (trā′tərz) *n.* those who betray trust; **p. 481**

treacherous (trech′ər əs) *adj.* disloyal; **p. 481**

trophy (trō′fē) *n.* a small statue gained as a prize or an award for something; **p. 490**

tyrant (tī′rənt) *n.* one who uses power or authority in a cruel and unjust manner; **p. 85**

U

uniquely (ū nēk′lē) *adv.* distinctively; characteristically; **p. 512**

unreasonable (un rē′zə nə bəl) *adj.* not using good judgment; **p. 491**

V

vehicles (vē′ə kəlz) *n.* devices designed or used for transporting persons or goods, as an automobile, a sled, or a carriage; **p. 182**

veins (vānz) *n.* vessels that carry blood to the heart from other parts of the body; **p. 398**

vendors (ven′dərz) *n.* people who sell goods **p. 244**

veteran (vet′ər ən) *n.* one who has served in the armed forces; **p. 14**

W

waged (wājd) *v.* carried on or engaged in, such as a war, a battle, or a contest; **p. 99**

wages (wāj′əz) *n.* money paid to a person for work or services, especially on an hourly or daily basis; **p. 244**

weird (wērd) *adj.* strange; unnatural; **p. 687**

wilted (wilt′əd) *adj.* droopy or faded; **p. 749**

worshipped (wur′shipt) *v.* adored or idolized **p. 767**

wreckage (rek′ ij) *n.* remains of anything that has been destroyed; **p. 688**

Y

yearned (yurnd) *v.* felt a strong and deep desire; **p. 76**

traitors/traidores *n.* los que rompen la confianza; **p. 481**

treacherous/traicionero *adj.* desleal; **p. 481**

trophy/trofeo *n.* estátua pequeña recibida como premio o recompensa por algo; **p. 490**

tyrant/tirano *n.* uno que emplea poder o autoridad de manera cruel e injusta; **p. 85**

U

uniquely/únicamente *adv.* distintivamente; característicamente; **p. 512**

unreasonable/irrazonable *adj.* cuando no se evalua bien; **p. 491**

V

vehicles/vehículos *n.* aparatos diseñados o usados para transportar personas o bienes, como un automóvil, trineo o carruaje; **p. 182**

veins/venas *n.* vasos que llevan la sangre del corazón a otras partes del cuerpo; **p. 398**

vendors/vendedores *n.* personas que proveen bienes a cambio de dinero; **p. 244**

veteran/veterano *n.* uno que ha servido en las fuerzas armadas; **p. 14**

W

waged/convocado *v.* llamado a o comprometido con una guerra, batalla o concurso; **p. 99**

wages/sueldo *n.* dinero pagado a una persona por su trabajo o sus servicios, especialmente en cantidades por hora o día; **p. 244**

weird/raro *adj.* extraño; no natural; **p. 687**

wilted/marchitado *adj.* mustio o decaído; **p. 749**

worshipped/veneró *v.* adoró o idealizó; **p. 767**

wreckage/ruinas *n.* restos de algo que ha sido destruido; **p. 688**

Y

yearned/anhelar *v.* sentir un deseo fuerte y profundo; **p. 76**

Academic Word List

To succeed academically in middle school and high school and prepare for college, it is important to know academic vocabulary—special terms used in classroom discussions, assignments, and tests. These words are also used in the workplace and among friends to share information, exchange ideas, make decisions, and build relationships. Research has shown that the words listed below, compiled by Averil Coxhead in 2000, are the ones most commonly used in these ways. You will encounter many of them in the *Glencoe Literature* program. You will also focus on specific terms in connection with particular reading selections.

Note: The lists are ordered by frequency of use from most frequent to least frequent.

List One

analysis
approach
area
assessment
assume
authority
available
benefit
concept
consistent
constitutional
context
contract
create
data
definition
derived
distribution
economic
environment
established
estimate
evidence
export
factors
financial
formula
function
identified
income
indicate
individual
interpretation
involved
issues
labor
legal
legislation
major
method
occur
percent
period
policy
principle
procedure
process
required
research
response
role
section
sector
significant
similar
source
specific
structure
theory
variables

List Two

achieve
acquisition
administration
affect
appropriate
aspects
assistance
categories
chapter
commission
community
complex
computer
conclusion
conduct
consequences
construction
consumer
credit
cultural
design
distinction
elements
equation
evaluation
features
final
focus
impact
injury
institute
investment
items
journal
maintenance
normal
obtained
participation
perceived
positive
potential
previous
primary
purchase
range
region
regulations
relevant
resident
resources
restricted
security
select
site
sought
strategies
survey
text
traditional
transfer

List Three

alternative
circumstances
comments
compensation
components
consent
considerable
constant
constraints
contribution
convention
coordination
core
corporate
corresponding
criteria
deduction
demonstrate
document
dominant
emphasis
ensure
excluded
framework
funds
illustrated
immigration
implies
initial
instance
interaction
justification
layer
link
location

maximum
minorities
negative
outcomes
partnership
philosophy
physical
proportion
published
reaction
registered
reliance
removed
scheme
sequence
sex
shift
specified
sufficient
task
technical
techniques
technology
validity
volume

List Four

access
adequate
annual
apparent
approximated
attitudes
attributed
civil
code
commitment
communication
concentration
conference
contrast
cycle
debate
despite
dimensions
domestic
emerged
error
ethnic
goals
granted
hence
hypothesis
implementation
implications
imposed
integration
internal
investigation
job
label
mechanism
obvious
occupational
option
output
overall
parallel
parameters
phase
predicted
principal
prior
professional
project
promote
regime
resolution
retained
series
statistics
status
stress
subsequent
sum
summary
undertaken

List Five

academic
adjustment
alter
amendment
aware
capacity
challenge
clause
compounds
conflict
consultation
contact
decline
discretion
draft
enable
energy
enforcement
entities
equivalent
evolution
expansion
exposure
external
facilitate
fundamental
generated
generation
image
liberal
license
logic
marginal
medical
mental
modified
monitoring
network
notion
objective
orientation
perspective
precise
prime
psychology
pursue
ratio
rejected
revenue
stability
styles
substitution
sustainable
symbolic
target
transition
trend
version
welfare
whereas

List Six

abstract
accurate
acknowledged
aggregate
allocation
assigned
attached
author
bond
brief
capable
cited
cooperative
discrimination
display
diversity
domain
edition
enhanced
estate
exceed
expert
explicit
federal
fees
flexibility
furthermore
gender
ignored
incentive
incidence
incorporated
index
inhibition
initiatives
input
instructions
intelligence
interval
lecture
migration
minimum
ministry
motivation
neutral
nevertheless
overseas
preceding
presumption
rational
recovery
revealed
scope
subsidiary
tapes
trace
transformation
transport
underlying
utility

List Seven

adaptation
adults
advocate
aid
channel
chemical

classical
comprehensive
comprise
confirmed
contrary
converted
couple
decades
definite
deny
differentiation
disposal
dynamic
eliminate
empirical
equipment
extract
file
finite
foundation
global
grade
guarantee
hierarchical
identical
ideology
inferred
innovation
insert
intervention
isolated
media
mode
paradigm
phenomenon
priority
prohibited
publication
quotation
release
reverse
simulation
solely
somewhat
submitted
successive
survive
thesis
topic
transmission
ultimately
unique
visible
voluntary

List Eight

abandon
accompanied
accumulation
ambiguous
appendix
appreciation
arbitrary
automatically
bias
chart
clarity
conformity
commodity
complement
contemporary
contradiction
crucial
currency
denote
detected
deviation
displacement
dramatic
eventually
exhibit
exploitation
fluctuations
guidelines
highlighted
implicit
induced
inevitably
infrastructure
inspection
intensity
manipulation
minimized
nuclear
offset
paragraph
plus
practitioners
predominantly
prospect
radical
random
reinforced
restore
revision
schedule
tension
termination
theme
thereby
uniform
vehicle
via
virtually
visual
widespread

List Nine

accommodation
analogous
anticipated
assurance
attained
behalf
bulk
ceases
coherence
coincide
commenced
concurrent
confined
controversy
conversely
device
devoted
diminished
distorted
duration
erosion
ethical
format
founded
incompatible
inherent
insights
integral
intermediate
manual
mature
mediation
medium
military
minimal
mutual
norms
overlap
passive
portion
preliminary
protocol
qualitative
refine
relaxed
restraints
revolution
rigid
route
scenario
sphere
subordinate
supplementary
suspended
team
temporary
trigger
unified
violation
vision

List Ten

adjacent
albeit
assembly
collapse
colleagues
compiled
conceived
convinced
depression
encountered
enormous
forthcoming
inclination
integrity
intrinsic
invoked
levy
likewise
nonetheless
notwithstanding
odd
ongoing
panel
persistent
posed
reluctant
so-called
straightforward
undergo
whereby

Index of Skills

Literary Concepts

Reading and Critical Thinking

Vocabulary

Writing

Grammar

Speaking, Listening, and Viewing

Research, Test-Taking, and Study Skills

Interdisciplinary Activities

Index of Authors and Titles

Acknowledgments

Unit 1

"The Fly" from *The Toad Is the Emperor's Uncle* by Mai Vo-Dinh. Copyright © 1970 by Mai Vo-Dinh. Reprinted by permission of the author.

"The Scribe" from *Guests in the Promised Land* by Kristin Hunter. Copyright © 1968 by Kristin E. Lattany. Reprinted by permission of Dystel & Goderich Literary Management.

"Hurricane Heroes": Updated 2005, from *PEOPLE,* October 4, 2004.

"The Dog of Pompeii" by Louis Untermeyer. Reprinted with the permission of Simon & Schuster Adult Publishing Group from *The Fireside Book of Dog Stories,* edited by Jack Goodman. Copyright 1943 by Simon & Schuster Inc. Copyright renewed © 1971 by Simon & Schuster Inc.

"What Exactly Is a Hero?" adapted from *The Hero's Trail: A Guide for a Heroic Life* by Thomas A. Barron, copyright © 2002 by Thomas A. Barron. Used by permission of Philomel Books, A Division of Penguin Young Readers Group, A Member of Penguin Group (USA) Inc., 345 Hudson Street, New York, NY 10014. All rights reserved.

From *Yukon Gold: The Story of the Klondike Gold Rush* by Charlotte Foltz Jones. Copyright © 1999 by Charlotte Foltz Jones. Reprinted by the Estate of Charlotte Foltz Jones.

"All Stories Are Anansi's" from *The Hat-Shaking Dance and Other Ashanti Tales from Ghana* by Harold Courlander with Albert Kofi Prempeh, copyright © 1957, 1985 by Harold Courlander. Reprinted by permission of Michael Courlander.

"Dragon, Dragon" from *Dragon, Dragon and Other Tales* by John Gardner. Copyright © 1975 by Boskydell Artists Ltd. Reprinted by permission of Georges Borchardt, Inc., for the Estate of John Gardner.

"Stray" reprinted with the permission of Atheneum Books for Young Readers, an imprint of Simon & Schuster Children's Publishing Division, from *Every Living Thing* by Cynthia Rylant. Copyright © 1985 Cynthia Rylant.

"Three Queens of Egypt" by Vicky León. *National Geographic Kids,* August 2001. Copyright © 2006 National Geographic Society. Reprinted by permission.

"Pecos Bill" from *American Tall Tales* by Mary Pope Osborne, copyright © 1991 by Mary Pope Osborne. Illustrations copyright © 1991 by Michael McCurdy. Used by permission of Alfred A. Knopf, an imprint of Random House Children's Books, a division of Random House, Inc.

"The Courage That My Mother Had" by Edna St. Vincent Millay, copyright © 1954, 1982 by Norma Millay Ellis. Reprinted with permission of Elizabeth Barnett, Edna St. Vincent Millay Society.

"My Father Is a Simple Man" is reprinted with permission from the publisher of *The Sadness of Days* by Luis Omar Salinas (© 1987 Arte Publico Press—University of Houston).

From *The Gold Cadillac* by Mildred D. Taylor, copyright © 1987 by Mildred D. Taylor, text. Used by permission of Dial Books for Young Readers, A Division of Penguin Young Readers Group, A Member of Penguin Group (USA) Inc., 345 Hudson Street, New York, NY 10014. All rights reserved.

Unit 2

"To Young Readers" by Gwendolyn Brooks. Reprinted by consent of Brooks Permissions.

"Tracking Trash" by Rachel Young. Reprinted by permission of Cricket Magazine Group, Carus Publishing Company, from ASK magazine, November/December 2006, Vol. 5, No. 9, text copyright © 2006 by Carus Publishing Company.

"The Sand Castle" by Alma Luz Villanueva. Reprinted by permission of the author.

"Nobody's Perfect": Updated 2005, from *Sports Illustrated for Kids,* April 1997.

"who knows if the moon's" Copyright 1923, 1925, 1951, 1953 © 1991 by the Trustees for the E. E. Cummings Trust. Copyright © 1976 by George James Firmage, from *Complete Poems: 1904-1962* by E. E. Cummings, edited by George J. Firmage. Used by permission of liveright Publishing Corporation.

"A Strange Discovery," "The Quest for Immortality," and "Inside the Emperor's Tomb" from *The Emperor's Silent Army* by Jane O'Connor, copyright © 2002 by Jane O'Connor. Used by permission of Viking Penguin, A Division of Penguin Young Readers Group, A Member of Penguin Group (USA) Inc., 345 Hudson Street, New York, NY 10014. All rights reserved.

"The End of the World" from *The Sound of Flutes and Other Indian Legends* by Richard Erdoes, illustrated by Paul Goble, copyright © 1976 by Richard Erdoes. Used by permission of Random House Children's Books, a division of Random House, Inc.

"How the Snake Got Poison" from *Mules and Men* by Zora Neale Hurston. Copyright 1935 by Zora Neale Hurston; renewed © 1963 by John C. Hurston and Joel Hurston. Reprinted by permission of HarperCollins Publishers.

Excerpt from *Dust Tracks on a Road* by Zora Neale Hurston. Copyright 1942 by Zora Neale Hurston; renewed © 1970 by John C. Hurston. Reprinted by permission of HarperCollins Publishers.

"Grasses are misty" by Yosa Buson, "Firefly lights" by Kawabata Bōsha, "Red dragonflies" by Yuzuru Miura, and "The sleet falls" by Naitō Jōsō, from *Classic Haiku: A Master's Selection,* selected and translated by Yuzuru Miura. Copyright © 1991 by Charles E. Tuttle Publishing. Reprinted by permission of Tuttle Publishing, a member of the Periplus Publishing Group.

"Ballpark Food" copyright © 2001 by Consumers Union of U.S., Yonkers, NY 10703-1057, a nonprofit organization. Reprinted with permission from Zillions® for educational purposes only. No commercial use or reproduction permitted. www.ConsumerReports.org.

From "Ta-Na-E-Ka" by Mary Whitebird. Published in *Scholastic Voice,* December 13, 1993. Copyright © 1973 by Scholastic Inc. Reprinted by permission.

"He Lion, Bruh Bear, and Bruh Rabbit" from *The People Could Fly: American Black Folktales* by Virginia Hamilton, illustrated by Leo and Diane Dillon, copyright © 1985 by Virginia Hamilton. Illustrations copyright © 1985 by Leo and Diane Dillon. Used by permission of Alfred A. Knopf, an imprint of Random House Children's Books, a division of Random House, Inc.

"The Toad and the Donkey" by Toni Cade Bambara. Reprinted by permission of Karma Bambara.

from "The Everglades Forever?" from *inTIME* vol. 2, copyright 2001. Reprinted by permission.

Excerpt from "La Bamba" from *Baseball in April and Other Stories* by Gary Soto. Copyright © 1990 by Gary Soto. Reproduced by permission of Houghton Mifflin Harcourt Publishing Company. All rights reserved.

Unit 3

"Eleven" from *Woman Hollering Creek.* Copyright © 1991 by Sandra Cisneros. Published by Vintage Books, a division of Random House, Inc. and originally in hardcover by Random House, Inc. Reprinted by permission of Susan Bergholz Literary

Services, New York, NY, and Lamy, NM. All rights reserved.

"My Parents" from *Collected Poems* by Stephen Spender. Copyright © 1934 and renewed 1962 by Stephen Spender. Reprinted by permission of Ed Victor, Ltd.

"Same Song" is reprinted with permission from the publisher of *Borders* by Pat Mora (© 1986 Arte Publico Press—University of Houston).

"Maestro" is reprinted with permission from the publisher of *Borders* by Pat Mora (© 1986 Arte Publico Press—University of Houston).

"The All-American Slurp" by Lensey Namioka, copyright © 1987, from *Visions,* ed. by Donald R. Gallo. Reprinted by permission of Lensey Namioka. All rights reserved by the author.

"Mad" from *Come with Me: Poems for a Journey* by Naomi Shihab Nye. Reprinted by permission of the author.

From an interview with Naomi Shihab Nye by Rachel Barenblat, pifmagazine.com. Reprinted by permission of Naomi Shihab Nye.

"I Dream a World" from *The Collected Poems of Langston Hughes* by Langston Hughes, edited by Arnold Rampersad with David Roessel, Associate Editor, copyright © 1994 by The Estate of Langston Hughes. Used by permission of Alfred A. Knopf, a division of Random House, Inc.

"Life Doesn't Frighten Me," copyright © 1978 by Maya Angelou, from *And Still I Rise* by Maya Angelou. Used by permission of Random House, Inc.

"Geraldine Moore, the Poet" by Toni Cade Bambara. Reprinted by permission of Karma Bambara.

"What I can do I will" and "Fame is a bee" reprinted by permission of the publishers and the Trustees of Amherst College, from *The Poems of Emily Dickinson,* Thomas H. Johnson, ed., Cambridge, Mass: The Belknap Press of Harvard University Press, copyright © 1951, 1955, 1979, 1983 by the President and Fellows of Harvard College.

Wings, by Jane Yolen. Copyright © 1991 by Jane Yolen. First appeared in *Wings,* published by Harcourt Brace. Reprinted by permission of Curtis Brown Ltd.

From *Daydreamers* by Eloise Greenfield, copyright © 1981 by Eloise Greenfield. Used by permission of Dial Books for Young Readers, A Division of Penguin Young Readers Group, A Member of Penguin Group (USA) Inc., 345 Hudson Street, New York, NY 10014. All rights reserved.

"The Gene Scene": Updated 2005, from *TIME for Kids,* May 2001.

"Jimmy Jet and His TV Set" from *Where the Sidewalk Ends* by Shel Silverstein. Copyright © 2004 by Evil Eye Music. Reprinted with permission from the Estate of Shel Silverstein and HarperCollins Children's Books.

"Yes, It Was My Grandmother" by Luci Tapahonso. Reprinted by permission of the author.

"Good Luck Gold" reprinted with the permission of Margaret K. McElderry Books, an imprint of Simon & Schuster Children's Publishing Division, from *Good Luck Gold and Other Poems* by Janet S. Wong. Copyright © 1994 by Janet S. Wong. All rights reserved.

"Arachne" from *Greek Myths* by Olivia E. Coolidge. Copyright 1949 by Olivia E. Coolidge; copyright renewed © 1977 by Olivia E. Coolidge. Reprinted by permission of Houghton Mifflin Company. All rights reserved.

"The Fun They Had" copyright © 1957 by Isaac Asimov, from *Isaac Asimov: The Complete Stories Volume I* by Isaac Asimov. Used by permission of Doubleday, a division of Random House, Inc.

"Why Books are Dangerous" by Neil Gaiman. Reprinted by permission of Writer's House LLC as agent for the author.

Unit 4

"Looking for America" by Elizabeth Partridge, copyright © 2003, from *Open Your Eyes,* ed. by Jill Davies. Reprinted by permission of Elizabeth Partridge. All rights are reserved by the author.

"Dressed for Success?": from *TIME for Kids,* February 4, 2005.

"Romulus and Remus" reprinted with the permission of Margaret K. McElderry Books, an imprint of Simon & Schuster Children's Publishing Division, from *Roman Myths* by Geraldine McCaughrean. Text copyright © 1999 Geraldine McCaughrean

"The Southpaw" by Judith Viorst. Copyright © 1974 by Judith Viorst. From *Free to Be . . . You and Me.* This usage granted by permission. All rights reserved.

"Spiders" from *All I Really Need to Know I Learned in Kindergarten* by Robert L. Fulghum, copyright © 1986, 1988 by Robert L. Fulghum. Used by permission of Villard Books, a division of Random House, Inc.

"The Wolf and the House Dog" and "The Donkey and the Lapdog" from *Aesop's Fables* by Jerry Pinkney. Copyright © 2000 by Jerry Pinkney. Used by permission of Chronicle Books LLC, San Francisco. Visit ChronicleBooks.com.

"The Shutout" from *Black Diamond: The Story of the Negro Baseball Leagues* by Patricia McKissack and Fredrick McKissack, Jr. Copyright © 1994 by Patricia McKissack and Fredrick McKissack, Jr. Reprinted by permission of Scholastic Inc.

"The Circuit" by Francisco Jiménez. Reprinted by permission of the author.

From *Harvest* by George Ancona. Copyright © 2001 by George Ancona. Reprinted by permission of Marshall Cavendish.

"Persephone" reprinted with the permission of Simon & Schuster Books for Young Readers, an imprint of Simon & Schuster Children's Publishing Division, from *The Macmillan Book of Greek Gods and Heroes* by Alive Low. Copyright © 1985 by Macmillan Publishing Company. All rights reserved.

"The Flying Machine" copyright © 1953, renewed 1981 by Ray Bradbury. Reprinted by permission of Don Congdon Associates, Inc.

"All Summer in a Day" copyright © 1954, renewed 1982 by Ray Bradbury. Reprinted by permission of Don Congdon Associates, Inc.

"West Hartford, Connecticut" from *Dateline America* by Charles Kuralt, copyright © 1979 by Harcourt, Inc., reprinted by permission of the publisher. This material may not be reproduced in any form or by any means without the prior written permission of the publisher.

Unit 5

From *Elie Wiesel: Voice from the Holocaust* by Michael A. Schuman. Copyright © 1994 by Michael A. Schuman. Published by Enslow Publishers, Inc., Berkeley Heights, NJ. All rights reserved.

Text copyright © 2000 by Susan Goldman Rubin. All rights reserved. Reprinted from *Fireflies in the Dark: The Story of Friedl Dicker-Brandeis and the Children of Terezin* by permission of Holiday House, Inc.

"Primary Lessons" is reprinted with permission from the publisher of *Silent Dancing* by Judith Ortiz Cofer (© 1990 Arte Publico Press— University of Houston).

"The Sidewalk Racer or On the Skateboard" from *The Sidewalk Racer and Other Poems of Sports and Motion* by Lillian Morrison. Copyright © 1965, 1967, 1968, 1977 by Lillian Morrison. © renewed Lillian Morrison. Reprinted by permission.
"Alone in the Nets" from *Sports Pages* by Arnold Adoff. Text copyright © 1986 by Arnold Adoff. Used by permission of HarperCollins Publishers.
"Satchel Paige" from *Champions* by Bill Littlefield. Copyright © 1993 by Bill Littlefield (Text); Copyright © 1993 by Bernie Fuchs (Illustrations). By permission of Little, Brown & Company.
"Gentleman of the Pool": from *TIME,* August 30, 2004.
"Eleanor Roosevelt" reprinted with the permission of Atheneum Books for Young Readers, an imprint of Simon & Schuster Children's Publishing Division, from *Great Lives, Human Rights* by William Jay Jacobs. Copyright © 1990 by William Jay Jacobs. All rights reserved.
"Ode to Mi Gato" from *Neighborhood Odes: Poems* by Gary Soto. Text copyright © 1992 by Gary Soto. Reproduced by permission of Houghton Mifflin Harcourt Publishing Company. All rights reserved.
"President Cleveland, Where Are You?" copyright © 1965 by Robert Cormier, from *Eight Plus One* by Robert Cormier. Used by permission of Random House Children's Books, a division of Random House, Inc.
From "The Eco-Canoeist" by Sy Montgomery, *Orion Afield* 4, No. 2 (Spring 2000) Copyright © 2000 by Sy Montgomery. Reprinted by permission of the author.
From *Brother Ray: Ray Charles' Own Story* by David Ritz and Ray Charles. Copyright © 1978 by Ray Charles and David Ritz. Reprinted by permission of The Aaron M. Priest Literary Agency, Inc.
From *Ray Charles,* text copyright © 2001, 1973 by Sharon Bell Mathis. Permission arranged with Lee & Low Books Inc., New York, NY 10016.
"The Jacket" from *The Effects of Knut Hamsun on a Fresno Boy: Recollections and Short Essays* by Gary Soto. Copyright © 1983, 2001 by Gary Soto. Reprinted by permission of Persea Books, Inc. (New York) and used with permission of the author and BookStop Literary Agency. All rights reserved.

Unit 6

"Madam C. J. Walker" from *One More River to Cross: The Story of Twelve Black Americans* by Jim Haskins. Copyright © 1992 by James Haskins. Reprinted by permission of Scholastic Inc.
"The Legend of Damon and Pythias" from *The Bag of Fire and Other Plays* by Fan Kissen. Copyright © 1964 by Houghton Mifflin Company, renewed © 1993 by John Kissen Heaslip. Reprinted by permission of Houghton Mifflin Company. All rights reserved.
"The Bracelet" from *Desert Exile* by Yoshiko Uchida. Copyright © 1982 by Yoshiko Uchida. Reprinted by permission of Bancroft Library.
"Executive Order No. 9066" from *I Am an American* by Jerry Stanley, copyright © 1994 by Jerry Stanley. Used by permission of Crown publishers, an imprint of Random House Children's Books, a division of Random House, Inc.
Excerpt from *Brighton Beach Memoirs,* © 1984 by Neil Simon. Professionals and amateurs are hereby warned that *Brighton Beach Memoirs* is fully protected under the Berne Convention and the Universal Copyright Convention and is subject to royalty. All rights, including without limitation professional, amateur, motion picture, television, radio, recitation, lecturing, public reading and foreign translation rights, computer media rights and the rights of reproduction, and electronic storage or retrieval, in whole or in part and in any form, are strictly reserved and none of these rights can be exercised or used without written permission from the copyright owner. Inquiries for stock and amateur performances should be addressed to Samuel French, Inc., 45 West 25th Street, New York, NY 10010. All other inquiries should be addressed to Gary N. DaSilva, 111 N. Sepulveda Blvd., Suite 250, Manhattan Beach, CA 90266-6850.
"Best of Buddies": Updated 2005, from *PEOPLE,* February 27, 1995.
From *The Phantom Tollbooth.* Copyright © 1977 by Susan Nanus and Norton Juster. Reprinted by permission of SLL/Sterling Lord Literistic, Inc.
"The Golden Touch" from *Favorite Greek Myths* retold by Mary Pope Osborne. Copyright © 1989 by Mary Pope Osborne. Reprinted by permission of Scholastic Inc.
"Zlateh the Goat" by Isaac Bashevis Singer. Text copyright © 1966 by Isaac Bashevis Singer. Copyright renewed 1994 by Alma Singer, excerpted from *Zlateh the Goat and Other Stories.* Used by permission of HarperCollins Publishers.
"The Boy Who Lived with the Bears" Copyright © 1995 by Joseph Bruchac. Reprinted by permission of Barbara S. Kouts.
From *You're a Good Man, Charlie Brown* by Clark Gesner, copyright © 1967 by Clark Gesner. Copyright © 1965, 1966, 1967 by Jeremy Music, Inc. Used by permission of Random House, Inc.

Photo Credits

COVER John Newcomb/SuperStock, (bkgd)Farinaz Taghavi/Getty Images; **GA64–1** Dave Nagel/Getty Images; **3** Photospin; **4** Lenard de Selva/CORBIS; **6** akg-images/SuperStock; **7** Photospin; **9** Private Collection, ©Agnew's, London/Bridgeman Art Library; **10** John I. Lattany; **12** Private Collection/Bridgeman Art Library; **15** The Jacob and Gwendolyn Lawrence Foundation/Art Resource, NY; **16** Private Collection, Christie's Images/Bridgeman Art Library; **20** Brand X/PunchStock; **25** Karena Cawthon/Silver Image; **26 27** Ben Baker/Redux; **28** Bettmann/CORBIS; **32** Erich Lessing/Art Resource, NY; **35** (t)Tim Courlas, (b)Stock Montage; **38** Erich Lessing/Art Resource, NY; **40** Bridgeman Art Library/SuperStock; **41** Brand X Pictures; **46** Greg Harring; **48** ImageZoo/SuperStock; **50** Brand X Pictures/SuperStock; **52** Hulton Archive/Getty Images; **54** North Wind Picture Archives; **55** Werner Forman/CORBIS; **58** North Wind Picture Archives; **61** Mary Evans Picture Library; **62** North Wind Picture Archives; **64** Mary Evans Picture Library; **66** Getty Images; **69** Mary Evans Picture Library; **70** North Wind Picture Archives; **71** Bettmann/CORBIS; **73** Private Collection/Bridgeman Art Library; **74** Michael Courlander; **76** Harn Museum of Art Collection, University of Florida. Gift of Rod McGalliard. 1990.14.103; **77** Ian Murphy/Getty Images;

79 The Field Museum, Chicago, IL, Neg #109098c/ photograph by Fleur Hales; **81** Bettmann/CORBIS; **83** Fitzwilliam Museum, University of Cambridge/ Bridgeman Art Library; **88** Art Resource, NY; **90** SuperStock, Inc./SuperStock; **92** Réunion des Musées Nationaux/Art Resource; **95** Art Explostion; **97 98** Kimberly Schamber; **99** (t)Tom Brakefield/ SuperStock, (b)Kimberly Schamber; **100** Kimberly Schamber; **102** Brian Hamill/Hulton Archive/Getty Images; **104–111** From MINOR MIRACLES by Will Eisner. Copyright © 2000 by Will Eisner. Used by permission of W. W. Norton & Company, Inc.; **115** Rommel/Masterfile; **116** Jung Im Jang/Alamy Images; **122** Jessica Hall/AP Images; **124** Nigel Sandor/Illustration Works/CORBIS; **125** Venki Talath/ Illustration Works/Getty Images; **127** ImageZoo/ SuperStock; **129** Getty Images; **131** (l) Images.com/ CORBIS; (r) Bettmann/CORBIS; **135** (t)Library of Congress, (b)Courtesy Karen Harlow-McClintock; **136** GG Kopilak/SuperStock; **137** Stockbyte/ SuperStock; **148** (tr bl)Eclipse Studios, (tl br)The McGraw-Hill Companies; **149** (tr)Eclipse Studios, (l br)The McGraw-Hill Companies; **156–157** Stockybyte/SuperStock; **159** Smithsonian American Art Museum, Washington, DC/Art Resource, NY/ National Museum of American Art/©2007 The Jacob and Gwendolyn Lawrence Foundation, Seattle/Artist Rights Society (ARS), NY; **160** Kactus Foto, Santiago, Chile/SuperStock; **161** Private Collection/Bridgeman Art Library; **162** Getty Images; **164** (t)Rick Rickman, (b)David Hoffman Photo Library/Alamy Images; **165** Rick Rickman; **167** Beth Griffis Johnson; **168** (t)Brand X Pictures, (b)Getty Images; **172 175** Art Explosion; **176** The McGraw-Hill Companies; **178** Leon Canerot; **180** PunchStock; **181** Private Collection/Bridgeman Art Library; **183** Private Collection, ©Gavin Graham Gallery, London/Bridgeman Art Library; **185** Christie's Images/SuperStock; **186** (l) Brand X Pictures, (b) Angelo Cavalli/zefa/CORBIS; **191 193** Keith Locke; **194** Bettmann/CORBIS; **195** Magyar Nemzeti Galeria, Budapest/Bridgeman Art Library; **198** Art Explosion; **200** John Slater/ CORBIS; **202** Steve Vidler/SuperStock; **203** The Art Archive/British Library; **204** Macmillian-McGraw-Hill; **207** Erich Lessing/Art Resource, NY; **208** (l)Danny Lehman/CORBIS, (r)Image Asset Management Ltd./ SuperStock; **210 214** Steve Kaufman/CORBIS; **215** Martin Harvey/CORBIS; **221** Franklin McMahon/ CORBIS; **222** Richard Erdoes; **223** (t)Werner Forman/ Art Resource, NY, (b)Laurie Morton; **224** (t)Werner Forman/Art Resource, NY, (b)Victoria and Albert Museum/Bridgeman Art Library; **227** National Portrait Gallery, Smithsonian Institution/Art Resource, NY; **228** Getty Images; **229** (l)Getty Images, (r)Digital Vision/SuperStock; **232** Nathan Benn/CORBIS; **233** Diana Ong/SuperStock; **234** Private Collection, Photo ©Christie's Images/Bridgeman Art Library; **238** John Bunker/SuperStock; **242** Getty Images; **243** Paul A. Sauders/CORBIS; **244** Getty Images; **244–245** Brand X Pictures; **245** (t)Jason Hosking/ Zefa/CORBIS, (b)Getty Images; **247** Keith Locke; **255** Stockbyte/PunchStock; **262 264** Sissie Brimberg/ National Geographic/Getty Images; **266** Penny Tweedie/CORBIS; **267** age fotostock/SuperStock; **268** Comstock/Alamy Images; **269** Pierre Vauthey/ CORBIS SYGMA; **271** (t)©2008 by arnold adoff. used by permission., (b)Bill Gaskin **272** Private Collection/ Christian Pierre/SuperStock; **273** CORBIS/ SuperStock; **275** Private Collection/Christian Pierre/ SuperStock; **277** PoodlesRock/CORBIS; **278** Powered by Light/Alan Spencer/Alamy Images; **282** Adam @ Home ©1999 by Universal Press Syndicate. Reprinted with permission. All rights reserved; **283** The McGraw-Hill Companies; **288** (tr bl br)Eclipse Studios, (br)The McGraw-Hill Companies; **289** Eclipse Studios; **290** NASA; **296–297** Image Source/SuperStock; **299** Columbus Museum of Art, Ohio; bequest of Frederick W. Schumacher, Cat.#17 accession (57)43.11; **301** Alberto Ruggieri/Images. com; **305** Malcah Zeldis/Art Resource, NY; **306** Howard Coster/Hulton Archive/Getty Images; **307** Private Collection/Bridgeman Art Library; **309** Cheron Bayna; **310** Pam Ingalls/CORBIS; **312** Banque d'Images, ADAGP/Art Resource, NY; **315** University of Washington/Mary Levin; **317** Images.com/CORBIS; **322** JupiterImages/ Comstock; **323 324** Dale Kennington/SuperStock; **327** (t)Pamela Chin Lee/omniphoto.com, (b)Getty Images; **331** Gerardo Somoza/CORBIS; **332** Banque d'Images, ADAGP/Art Resource, NY; **334 335** Ha Lam Photograhy; **337** Walters Art Museum/ Bridgeman Art Library; **338** (t)Library of Congress, (b)Nancy Robinson/AP Images; **339** Images.com/ CORBIS; **341** Elizabeth Barakah Hodges/SuperStock; **346** Bill Gaskins; **348** Diana Ong/SuperStock; **349** Rosebud Pictures/Getty Images; **351** Franklin

McMahon/CORBIS; **353** Diana Ong/SuperStock; **354** Getty Images; **357** Library of Congress; **358** Private Collection/Bridgeman Art Library; **360** Jason Stemple/Newscom.com; **362** (t)Gerrit Greve/CORBIS, (b)Jason Hawkes/Getty Images; **365** Tate Gallery, London/Art Resource, NY; **368** Timothy McCarthy/Art Resource, NY; **370** Private Collection/Bridgeman Art Library; **374** Kurt Scholz/SuperStock; **375** Steve Vidler/SuperStock; **376** Archaeological Museum of Heraklion, Crete /Bridgeman Art Library; **377** Steven M. Cummings; **378** The Grand Design/SuperStock; **383** Hyacinth Manning/SuperStock; **385** Denis Finnin/American Museum of Natural History; **387** Mansell/Time Life Pictures/Getty Images; **388** Michael Ochs Archives/Getty Images; **390 391** Shel Silverstein; **394** Bill Porter; **397** SuperStock, Inc./SuperStock; **398** Patrick Johns/CORBIS; **399** Photo ©Bonhams, London/Bridgeman Art Library; **401** (t)Juliane McRoberts, Courtesy Luci Tapahonso, (b)Anne Lindsay Photography; **402** Martha Widmann/SuperStock; **403** Purestock/SuperStock; **408** Stan Sherer; **409** Cameraphoto/Art Resource, NY; **410** Réunion des Musées Nationaux/Art Resource, NY; **412** (t)Getty Images, (b)Peter Coombs/Alamy Images; **415** (t)Douglas Kirkland/CORBIS, (b)Neville Elder/CORBIS; **416** Getty Images; **419** Zurbaran Galeria/SuperStock; **420** Affordable Illustration Source/Images.com/CORBIS; **421** Lina Chesak/Images.com; **422** Printed by permission by the Norman Rockwell Family Agency. 1926. The Norman Rockwell Family Entities. John Rockwell.; **423** Getty Images; **428** Real Life Adventures ©1997 GarLanco. Reprinted with permission of UNIVERSAL PRESS SYNDICATE. All right reserved.; **434** (tr tl bl)Eclipse Studios, (br)The McGraw-Hill Companies; **435** (tr br)McGraw-Hill Companies, (l)Eclipse Studios; **442–443** Digital Vision/SuperStock; **445** The Granger Collection, New York; **447** ©Collection of the New-York Historical Society/Bridgeman Art Library; **449** Images.com/CORBIS; **450** Courtesy Elizabeth Partridge; **452** Private Collection/Bridgeman Art Library; **454** Private Collection, Wilson Stephens Fine Art, London/Bridgeman Art Library; **455** Alamy Images; **457** Private Collection/Bridgeman Art Library; **461 462** TIME; **463** (l)Courtesy of Long Beach Unified School District, (r)Courtesy of Allen Lichtenstein; **466** Getty Images; **469** Sang Tan/AP Photo; **471** Piotr Adamczyk shapencolour/Alamy Images; **472** (t)Leeds Museums and Art Galleries (City Museum)/Bridgeman Art Library, (b)Reino Hanninen/Alamy Images; **475** Bridgeman-Giraudon/Art Resource, NY; **478** U.S. Senate Historical Office; **480** Roy Miles Fine Paintings/Bridgeman Art Library; **482** (t)Getty Images, (c)Image Ideas, (r)The McGraw-Hill Companies, (b)The Humane Society for Seattle/King County; **486** AP Images; **488** Mark C. Burnett; **489** Gary Stretar; **491** Private Collection, ©DACS/Bridgeman Art Library; **493** Dan Lamont/CORBIS; **495** Dorling Kindersley RF/Getty Images; **497** Dianna Sarto/CORBIS; **498** macana/Alamy Images; **501** Images.com/CORBIS; **504 506** From Aesop's Fables ©2000 by Jerry Pinkney. Used with permission of Chronicle Books LLC, San Francisco. Visit ChronicleBooks.com; **507** Image Source/Getty Images; **508** (t)Getty Images, (c)Image Ideas, (r)The McGraw-Hill Companies, (b)Henrietta Butler/ArenaPAL/Topham/The Image Works; **513** Alamy Images; **515** Bettmann/CORBIS; **516** Lucien Aigner/CORBIS; **517** Bob Krist/CORBIS; **521** The Granger Collection, New York; **524** Courtesy Francisco Jimenez; **526** Private Collection/Bridgeman Art Library; **529** Index Stock Imagery; **530 533** Christie's Images; **536–539** George Ancona; **543** National Academy Museum, NY/Bridgeman Art Library; **545** Shane Wyatt Davis; **546** Leeds Museums and Galleries (City Art Gallery), UK/Bridgeman Art Library; **549** Jean-Claude Amiel/Kipa/CORBIS; **550** The Mukashi Collection/SuperStock; **552** Hsu Soo Ming/SuperStock; **553** Daryl Benson/Masterfile; **555** Metropolitan Museum of Art, NY; **557** Scot Frei/CORBIS; **559** Christie's Images/SuperStock; **561** Brooklyn Museum of Art/CORBIS; **563** CORBIS; **568** Randy Glasbergen; **574 575** Eclipse Studios; **582–583** Bob Krist/CORBIS; **585–593** Usagi Yojimbo TM & ©2005 Stan Sakai; **594** Fitzwilliam Museum, University of Cambridge/Bridgeman Art Library; **595** Private Collection/Bridgeman Art Library; **596** Alexandra D. Schuman; **598** (l)Ira Nowinski/CORBIS, (r)Comstock/SuperStock; **599** Byron H. Rollins/AP Photo, (bkgd)Ira Nowinski/CORBIS; **601** Eric Fougere/VIP Images/CORBIS, (bkgd)Ira Nowinski/CORBIS; **604** Scala/Art Resource, NY, (inset)Courtesy the Sydney Taylor Book Award

Committee, The Association of Jewish Libraries; **605 606** Jewish Museum in Prague; **607** University of Georgia/University of Georgia, Peter Frey; **610** Donald Uhrbrock/Time Life Pictures/ Getty Images; **615** Charles E. Rotkin/CORBIS; **617** Nina Leen/Time Life Pictures/Getty Images; **618** courtesy Judith Ortiz Cofer; **620** (t)Lillian Morrison. Courtesy Marian Reiner Literary Agent, (b) ©2008 by arnold adoff. used by permission.; **621** Getty Images; **622** image 100/SuperStock; **626** WBUR/Mark Ostow; **628** AP Images; **629** (t)PhotoObjects.net/Jupiter Images, (b)National Baseball Hall of Fame Library, Cooperstown, NY; **630** The Granger Collection, New York; **633** Bettmann/CORBIS; **635** AP Images; **636** (t)Getty Images, (c)Image Ideas, (r)The McGraw-Hill Companies; **639** Smithsonian American Art Museum, Washington, DC/Art Resource, NY; **640** Mike Blake/Reuters/NewsCom; **644** Bettmann/ CORBIS; **645** CORBIS; **646** Bettmann/CORBIS; **647** Bachrach/Hulton Archive/Getty Images; **648** Courtesy of the Franklin D. Roosevelt Presidential Library and Museum; **649** The Art Archive/Culver Pictures; **650** Thomas D. Mcavoy/ Time Life Pictures/Getty Images; **652** Topham/The Image Works; **654** Bettmann/CORBIS; **655** CORBIS; **660** Courtesy Gary Soto; **661** SuperStock, Inc./ SuperStock; **664** Courtesy Robert Cormier, photo by Beth Bergman; **666** From the collection of David J. and Janice L. Frent; **667** (l) National Academy Museum, NY/Bridgeman Art Library, (r)From the collection of David J. and Janice L. Frent; **668** From the collection of David J. and Janice L. Frent; **671** Photo ©Bonhams, London/Bridgeman Art Library; **672** Private Collection/Bridgeman Art Library; **673 675** From the collection of David J. and Janice L. Frent; **676** The Art Archive/Culver Pictures; **677** (t)David R. Frazier, (b)David Olds/Getty Images; **678** Private Collection, Photo ©Christie's Images/ Bridgeman Art Library; **680** (t)Getty Images, (b)Collection of the Illinois State Museum, Photography by Gary Andrashko; **684** Photo by Selinda Chiquoine; **686** Maresa Pryor/Animals Animals; **687** RubberBall/Alamy Images; **689** Stephen L. Nordlinger; **692** (t)Reuters/CORBIS, (b)Courtesy Lee and Low Publishing; **693** Frank Driggs Collection/Getty Images; **695 696** Florida Photographic Collection; **699 701 702** ©1973 by George Ford. Permission arranged with Lee & Low Books, Inc.; **708** CALVIN AND HOBBES Watterson. Dist. By UNIVERSAL PRESS SYNDICATE. Reprinted with permission. All rights reserved.; **714** Eclipse Studios; **715** (tr l)Eclipse Studios, (br)The McGraw-Hill Companies; **722–723** Digital Vision/SuperStock; **725-731** A'Lelia Bundles/madamcjwalker.com/ Walker Family Collection; **732** Underwood & Underwood/CORBIS; **733** Private Collection/ Bridgeman Art Library; **739** Private Collection, ©DACS/J.P. Zenobel/Bridgeman Art Library; **741** Museo Archeologico Nazionale, Naples, Italy, Roger-Viollet, Paris/Bridgeman Art Library; **742** Stapleton Collection/CORBIS; **743** The Photolibrary Wales/Alamy Images; **746** Courtesy of The Bancroft Library, University of California, Berkley; **748** Christie's Images/CORBIS; **750** UpperCut Images/Alamy Images; **751** Sakamoto Photo Research Laboratory/CORBIS; **754** Courtesy of The Bancroft Library, University of California, Berkley; **757** Farm Security Administration, Office of War Information Photograph Collection/Library of Congress; **759** CORBIS; **760** Art Explostion; **762** (t)Bettmann/CORBIS, (b)MAPS.com/CORBIS; **764** Martha Swope; **765** Ingram Publishing/ SuperStock; **766 767** Martha Swope; **768** (t)Getty Images, (b)Bettmann/CORBIS; **771** Images.com/ CORBIS; **773** Stephen Ellison/Outline/CORBIS; **779** Bettmann/CORBIS; **788** Jupiter Images/ Ablestock/Alamy Images; **799** Getty Images; **804** E.O. Hoppe/CORBIS; **805** Lou Wall/CORBIS; **806** Private Collection, Photo ©Lefevre Fine Art Ltd., London/Bridgeman Art Library; **808** (t)Jessica Hall/ AP Images, (b)SuperStock, Inc./SuperStock; **810** david hancock/Alamy Images; **811 812** Private Collection/Bridgeman Art Library; **815** (t)Susan Greenwood, (b)Martin Benjamin; **816 819 822** reprinted from Harper-Collins, illustration by Maurice Sendak; **823** Getty Images; **824** Catherine Gehm Photography; **826** Marilyn Angel Wynn/Native Stock; **829** Catherine Gehm Photography; **830** Marilyn Angel Wynn/Native Stock; **834** Images.com/CORBIS; **840** (tl tr br)The McGraw-Hill Companies, (bl)Eclipse Studios; **841** (tr br)Eclipse Studios, (l)The McGraw-Hill Companies; **R18** (l)The McGraw-Hill Companies, (r)CORBIS.